Aesthetics:

A Comprehensive Anthology

Edited by
Steven M. Cahn
and
Aaron Meskin

BLACKWELL PUBLISHING
350 Main Street, Malden, MA 02148-5020, USA
9600 Garsington Road, Oxford OX4 2DQ, UK
550 Swanston Street, Carlton, Victoria 3053, Australia

First published 2008 by Blackwell Publishing Ltd
11 2015

Library of Congress Cataloging-in-Publication Data

Aesthetics : a comprehensive anthology / edited by Steven M. Cahn and Aaron Meskin.
p. cm. — (Blackwell philosophy anthologies ; 27)
Includes bibliographical references and index.
ISBN 978-1-4051-5434-5 (hardcover : alk. paper) — ISBN 978-1-4051-5435-2 (pbk. : alk. paper) 1. Aesthetics. I. Cahn, Steven M. II. Meskin, Aaron.

BH39.A2875 2007
111′.85—dc22

2007018718

A catalogue record for this title is available from the British Library.

Set in 9½/11½pt Minion
by SNP Best-set Typesetter Ltd., Hong Kong
Printed and bound in Singapore
by COS Printers Pte Ltd

The publisher's policy is to use permanent paper from mills that operate a sustainable forestry policy, and which has been manufactured from pulp processed using acid-free and elementary chlorine-free practices. Furthermore, the publisher ensures that the text paper and cover board used have met acceptable environmental accreditation standards.

For further information on
Blackwell Publishing, visit our website:
www.blackwellpublishing.com

Contents

Alternative Table of Contents

The volume provides the opportunity to explore many issues in philosophical aesthetics. The following list of topics and readings may prove helpful to instructors and students. The list is not exhaustive – there are many other themes that recur throughout the selections.

Aesthetic Experience and the Nature of the Aesthetic

Beauty

Creation and Creativity

The Definition of Art

Expression and Emotion in the Arts

Interpretation and Understanding

Knowledge, Truth, and Art

Morality and Politics in Art

Music

The Ontology of Art

Taste, Judgment, and Objectivity

The Visual Arts

Preface and Acknowledgments

We understand the study of aesthetics to be concerned with the arts broadly construed, and with such qualities as beauty and sublimity as found in works of art and in nature. Although the term "aesthetics" goes back only to the eighteenth century, the field has had a long and distinguished history and is currently the scene of far-reaching and provocative exploration. This comprehensive collection offers instructors the opportunity to construct courses in aesthetics combining as wished the classics in the field along with essays in contemporary theory. For those who prefer to approach the subject topically, we have provided an alternative table of contents.

No book of such scope has appeared since the publication nearly forty years ago of *Philosophy of Art and Aesthetics: From Plato to Wittgenstein*, edited by Frank A. Tillman and Steven M. Cahn (Harper & Row, 1969), a work long out of print but one we drew on for inspiration and insight.

We received useful advice on the contents of this volume from many sources. We are especially grateful to Tobyn DeMarco, Matthew Kieran, Peter Kivy, Sheila Lintott, Andrew McGonigal, Daniel Nathan, and Robert Stecker for their detailed comments and suggestions regarding the selection of essays. The advice of anonymous reviewers for Blackwell was also extremely helpful. Special thanks is owed to Susan Feagin for helping out at the last minute with the introduction to the contemporary section. The staff at Blackwell has done a superb job preparing the book for publication. But our greatest debt is to Jeff Dean, editor and aesthetician, who patiently offered guidance and support throughout the production process.

Source Acknowledgments

The editor and publisher gratefully acknowledge the permission granted to reproduce the copyright material in this book:

1. Paul Oskar Kristeller, "The Modern System of the Arts," *Journal of the History of Ideas*, 12 (1978): 496–515, 521–2, 525–6 and 13 (1978): 20–1, 24–9, 32–9, 42. © 1951, 1978. Reprinted by permission of the University of Pennsylvania Press.
2. Plato, "Ion," in *Two Comic Dialogues: Ion and Hippias Major*, trans. Paul Woodruff (Indianapolis, IN, and Cambridge, MA: Hackett Publishing, 1983), pp. 21–35. © 1983 by Hackett Publishing. Reprinted by permission of Hackett Publishing Company, Inc. All rights reserved.
3. Plato, *The Republic*, ed. Andrea Tschemplik, trans. John Llewelyn Davies and David James Vaughn (Lanham, MD: Rowman & Littlefield, 2006), pp. 352–69. © 2006 by Rowman & Littlefield Publishers, Inc. Reprinted by permission of the publisher.
4. Plato, *Symposium*, trans. Alexander Nehamas and Paul Woodruff (Indianapolis, IN, and Cambridge, MA: Hackett Publishing, 1989), pp. 45–60. © 1989 by Hackett Publishing. Reprinted by permission of Hackett Publishing Company, Inc. All rights reserved.
5. Aristotle, *Poetics*, trans. Ingram Bywater (Oxford: Clarendon Press, 1920), pp. 207–31.
6. Plotinus, *Ennead* I, vi, in *Neoplatonic Philosophy: Introductory Readings*, trans. John Dillon and Lloyd P. Gerson (Indianapolis, IN, and Cambridge, MA: Hackett Publishing, 2004), pp. 18–30. © 2004 by Hackett Publishing. Reprinted by permission of Hackett Publishing Company, Inc. All rights reserved.
7. St. Augustine, *St. Augustine's De Musica*, trans. W. F. Jackson Knight (London: The Orthological Institute, 1949), pp. 107–20, 122–4.
8. St. Bonaventure, *De reductione artium ad theologiam*, trans. Sister Emma Therese Healy (St. Bonaventure, NY: The Franciscan Institute, St. Bonaventure College, 1955), sections 1–5, 8–11, 13–18. © 1955 by Sister Emma Therese Healy. Reprinted by permission of The Sisters of St. Joseph of Northwestern Pennsylvania.
9. Third Earl of Shaftesbury, *Characteristics of Men, Manners, Opinions, Times* (1711).
10. Francis Hutcheson, *An Inquiry into the Original of Our Ideas of Beauty and Virtue* (1725).
11. David Hume, *Of the Standard of Taste*, from *Four Dissertations* (1757).
12. Edmund Burke, *A Philosophical Enquiry into the Origin of Our Ideas of the Sublime and Beautiful* (1756).
13. Gotthold Lessing, *Laocoon*, trans. Ellen Frothingham (Latin), William Cullen Bryant (Greek) (New York: Farrar, Straus,

& Giroux, 1957 and 1965), pp. 8, 16–18, 20–1, 58–61, 83–93, 101–3, 105–6, 109–10, 126, 136–9.

14. Immanuel Kant, "Critique of Judgement," in *Critique of Aesthetic Judgement*, trans. J. C. Meredith (Oxford: Clarendon Press, 1978). © 1978. Reprinted by permission of Oxford University Press.
15. Christopher Janaway, "Introduction to Modern Theories," in *The Oxford Companion to Philosophy*, 2nd edition, ed. Ted Honderich (New York and Oxford: Oxford University Press, 2005). © 2005. Reprinted by permission of Oxford University Press.
16. Friedrich Schiller, "Twentieth Letter" and "Twenty-First Letter," in *On the Aesthetic Education of Man: In a Series of Letters*, ed. Elizabeth M. Wilkinson and L. A. Willoughby (Oxford: Clarendon Press, 1985). © 1967 by Oxford University Press.
17. Friedrich Wilhelm Joseph von Schelling, *The Philosophy of Art*, trans. Douglas W. Scott (Minneapolis: University of Minnesota Press, 1989). © 1989 by University of Minnesota Press. Reprinted by permission of the publisher.
18. Georg Wilhelm Friedrich Hegel, *The Philosophy of Fine Art*, trans. F. P. B. Osmaston (London: G. Bell & Sons, 1920).
19. Arthur Schopenhauer, *The World as Will and Representation*, trans. R. B. Haldane and J. Kemp (1883).
20. Eduard Hanslick, *The Beautiful in Music*, trans. Gustav Cohen (1891).
21. Friedrich Nietzsche, *The Birth of Tragedy*, trans. Walter Kaufmann (New York: Random House, 1967), pp. 33–47, 56, 58–62, 73–4. © 1967 by Walter Kaufmann. Used by permission of Random House, Inc.
22. Leo Tolstoy, "What is Art?," in *What is Art and Essays on Art*, ed. Louise and Aylmer Maude (1899).
23. Edward Bullough, "'Psychical Distance' as a Factor in Art and an Aesthetic Principle," *British Journal of Psychology*, 5 (1912).
24. Clive Bell, *Art* (London: Chatto & Windus, 1914). © 1914 by Clive Bell. Reprinted by permission of The Society of Authors as the Literary Representative of the Estate of Clive Bell.
25. Benedetto Croce, "Aesthetics," in *Encyclopaedia Britannica*, 14th edition. (Chicago: Encyclopaedia Britannica, 1938), pp. 263–9. © 1938 by Encyclopaedia Britannica, Inc. Reprinted by permission.
26. R. G. Collingwood, *The Principles of Art* (Oxford: Clarendon Press, 1945), pp. 1–2, 5–6, 109–17, 121–2, 125, 139–40, 308–24. © 1958. Reprinted by permission of Oxford University Press.
27. John Dewey, *Art as Experience*, vol. 10 of *The Collected Works of John Dewey: The Later Works, 1925–1953*, ed. Jo Ann Boydston (Carbondale and Edwardsville: Southern Illinois University Press, 1989), pp. 9–18, 26–34, 42–63. © 1987 by the Board of Trustees, Southern Illinois University. Reproduced by permission of the publisher.
28. Susanne Langer, *Feeling and Form* (New York: Charles Scribner's Sons, 1953), pp. 24–41. © 1953 by Charles Scribner's Sons. Reprinted by permission of Pearson Education, Inc.
29. Walter Benjamin, "The Work of Art in the Age of Mechanical Reproduction," in *Continental Aesthetics: Romanticism to Postmodernism, An Anthology*, ed. Richard Kearney and David Rasmussen (Oxford: Blackwell Publishing, 2001), pp. 166–81. © 1955 by Suhrkamp Verlag, Frankfurt a. M., English translation by Harry Zohn copyright © 1968 and renewed 1996 by Harcourt, Inc., reprinted by permission by Harcourt, Inc., and The Random House Group Ltd.
30. Martin Heidegger, "The Origin of the Work of Art," in *Poetry, Language, Thought* (New York: HarperCollins Publishers, 1971), pp. 17–36, 38–9, 41–6, 48–52, 55–9, 64–6, 69–71, 77–8. © 1971 by Martin Heidegger. Reprinted by permission of HarperCollins Publishers, Inc.
31. Theodor Adorno, *Aesthetic Theory*, ed. Gretel Adorno and Rolf Tiedemann, trans. Robert Hullot-Kentor (Minneapolis: University of Minnesota Press, 1977), pp. 242–53. English translation © 1977 by the Regents of the University of Minnesota. Original German language edition © 1970 by Suhrkamp Verlag. Reprinted by permission of the publisher.

32. Hans-Georg Gadamer, *Truth and Method*, 2nd edition, trans. Joel Weinsheimer and Donald G. Marshall. (London: Continuum International Publishing, 2005). © 2005. Reproduced by kind permission of Continuum International Publishing Group.
33. Susan L. Feagin and Aaron Meskin, "Introduction to Contemporary Aesthetics." New in this volume.
34. Stanley Cavell, "Aesthetic Problems of Modern Philosophy," in *Philosophy in America*, ed. Max Black (Ithaca, NY: Cornell University Press, 1965), pp. 74–97. © 1965. Reprinted by permission of Taylor & Francis Books UK.
35. Morris Weitz, "The Role of Theory in Aesthetics," *Journal of Aesthetics and Art Criticism*, 15/1 (1956): 27–35. © 1956. Reprinted by permission of Blackwell Publishing.
36. Arthur Danto, "The Artworld," *Journal of Philosophy*, 61/19 (1964): 571–84. © 1964 by the *Journal of Philosophy*. Reprinted by permission of the author and the Journal of Philosophy, Inc.
37. George Dickie, "What is Art? An Institutional Analysis," in *Art and the Aesthetic: An Institutional Analysis* (Ithaca, NY: Cornell University Press, 1974), pp. 19–52. © 1974 by George Dickie. Reprinted by permission of the author.
38. Nelson Goodman, "When is Art?," in *Ways of Worldmaking* (Indianapolis, IN: Hackett Publishing, 1978), pp. 57–70. © 1978 by Hackett Publishing. Reprinted by permission of Hackett Publishing Company, Inc. All rights reserved.
39. Noël Carroll, "Identifying Art," in *Philosophy of Art: A Contemporary Introduction* (New York: Routledge, 1999), pp. 249–64. © 1999 by Noël Carroll. Reprinted by permission of Taylor & Francis Books UK.
40. George Dickie, "The Myth of the Aesthetic Attitude," *American Philosophical Quarterly*, 1/1 (1964): 56–65. © 1964 by *American Philosophical Quarterly*. Reprinted by permission of the journal.
41. Richard Wollheim, *Art and Its Objects* (Cambridge: Cambridge University Press, 1980), sections 4–10, 15–16, 18–20, 35–8 (pp. 3–10; 20–4; 26–30; 64–76) © 1980, 1992 by Cambridge University Press. Reprinted by permission of the author and publisher.
42. Jerrold Levinson, "What a Musical Work Is," *Journal of Philosophy*, 77/1 (1980): 5–28. © 1980 by the *Journal of Philosophy*. Reprinted by permission of the author and the Journal of Philosophy, Inc.
43. Frank Sibley, "Aesthetic Concepts," *Philosophical Review*, 68/4 (1959): 421–50. © 1959 by Cornell University Press. All rights reserved. Used by permission of the current publisher, Duke University Press.
44. Mary Mothersill, "The First Thesis," in *Beauty Restored* (Oxford: Oxford University Press, 1986), pp. 100–22. © 1986 by Mary Mothersill.
45. Kendall Walton, "Categories of Art," *Philosophical Review*, 79/3 (1970): 334–67. © 1979 by Cornell University Press. All rights reserved. Used by permission of the current publisher, Duke University Press.
46. Allen Carlson, "Appreciation and the Natural Environment," *Journal of Aesthetics and Art Criticism*, 37/3 (1979): 267–75. © 1979. Reprinted by permission of Blackwell Publishing.
47. W. K. Wimsatt, Jr. and Monroe Beardsley, "The Intentional Fallacy," in *The Verbal Icon: Studies in the Meaning of Poetry*, ed. W. K. Wimsatt, Jr. (Lexington: University of Kentucky Press, 1954), pp. 3–18. © 1954 by University Press of Kentucky. Reprinted by permission of University Press of Kentucky.
48. Alexander Nehamas, "The Postulated Author: Critical Monism as a Regulative Ideal," *Critical Inquiry*, 8/1 (1981): 133–49. © 1981. Reprinted by permission of the author and University of Chicago Press.
49. Noël Carroll, "Art, Intention, and Conversation," in *Intention and Interpretation*, ed. Gary Iseminger (Philadelphia: Temple University Press, 1992), pp. 97–131. © 1992 by Temple University. Used by permission of Temple University Press. All rights reserved.
50. Berys Gaut, "The Ethical Criticism of Art," in *Aesthetics and Ethics: Essays at the Intersection*, ed. Jerrold Levinson (Cambridge: Cambridge University Press, 1998), pp. 182–203. © 1998 by Jerrold Levinson.

Reprinted by permission of Berys Gaut and Cambridge University Press.

51. Guy Sircello, "Expressive Properties of Art," in *Mind and Art: An Essay on the Varieties of Expression*, ed. Guy Sircello (Princeton: Princeton University Press, 1972), pp. 16–46. © 1972, 2000 by Princeton University Press. Reprinted by permission of Princeton University Press.
52. Jenefer Robinson, "Style and Personality in the Literary Work," *Philosophical Review*, 94/2 (1985): 227–47. © 1985 by Cornell University Press. All rights reserved. Used by permission of the current publisher, Duke University Press.
53. Peter Kivy, "Emotions in the Music," in *Introduction to a Philosophy of Music* (Oxford: Oxford University Press, 2002), pp. 31–48. © 2002. Reprinted by permission of Oxford University Press.
54. Kendall Walton, "Fearing Fictions," *Journal of Philosophy*, 75/1 (1978): 5–27. © 1978 by the *Journal of Philosophy*. Reprinted by permission of the author and the Journal of Philosophy, Inc.
55. Mary Devereaux, "Oppressive Texts, Resisting Readers, and the Gendered Spectator: The 'New' Aesthetics," *Journal of Aesthetics and Art Criticism*, 48/4 (1990): 337–47. © 1990. Reprinted by permission of Blackwell Publishing.

Every effort has been made to trace copyright holders and to obtain their permission for the use of copyright material. The publisher apologizes for any errors or omissions in the above list and would be grateful if notified of any corrections that should be incorporated in future reprints or editions of this book.

Part I

Classic Sources

1

Introduction

Paul Oskar Kristeller

Paul Oskar Kristeller (1905–99) was Professor of Philosophy at Columbia University.

I

The fundamental importance of the eighteenth century in the history of aesthetics and of art criticism is generally recognized. To be sure, there has been a great variety of theories and currents within the last two hundred years that cannot be easily brought under one common denominator. Yet all the changes and controversies of the more recent past presuppose certain fundamental notions which go back to that classical century of modern aesthetics. It is known that the very term "Aesthetics" was coined at that time, and, at least in the opinion of some historians, the subject matter itself, the "philosophy of art," was invented in that comparatively recent period and can be applied to earlier phases of Western thought only with reservations. It is also generally agreed that such dominating concepts of modern aesthetics as taste and sentiment, genius, originality and creative imagination did not assume their definite modern meaning before the eighteenth century. Some scholars have rightly noticed that only the eighteenth century produced a type of literature in which the various arts were compared with each other and discussed on the basis of common principles, whereas up to that period treatises on poetics and rhetoric, on painting and architecture, and on music had represented quite distinct branches of writing and were primarily concerned with technical precepts rather than with general ideas. Finally, at least a few scholars have noticed that the term "Art," with a capital A and in its modern sense, and the related term "Fine Arts" (Beaux Arts) originated in all probability in the eighteenth century.

In this paper, I shall take all these facts for granted, and shall concentrate instead on a much simpler and in a sense more fundamental point that is closely related to the problems so far mentioned, but does not seem to have received sufficient attention in its own right. Although the terms "Art," "Fine Arts" or "Beaux Arts" are often identified with the visual arts alone, they are also quite commonly understood in a broader sense. In this broader meaning, the term "Art" comprises above all the five major arts of painting, sculpture, architecture, music and poetry. These five constitute the irreducible nucleus of the modern system of the arts, on which all writers and thinkers seem to agree. On the other hand, certain other arts are sometimes added to the scheme, but with less regularity, depending on the different views and interests of the authors concerned: gardening, engraving and the decorative

Paul Oskar Kristeller, "The Modern System of the Arts," *Journal of the History of Ideas*, 12 (1978): 496–515, 521–2, 525–6 and 13 (1978): 20–1, 24–9, 32–9, 42.

arts, the dance and the theatre, sometimes the opera, and finally eloquence and prose literature.

The basic notion that the five "major arts" constitute an area all by themselves, clearly separated by common characteristics from the crafts, the sciences and other human activities, has been taken for granted by most writers on aesthetics from Kant to the present day. It is freely employed even by those critics of art and literature who profess not to believe in "aesthetics"; and it is accepted as a matter of course by the general public of amateurs who assign to "Art" with a capital A that ever narrowing area of modern life which is not occupied by science, religion, or practical pursuits.

It is my purpose here to show that this system of the five major arts, which underlies all modern aesthetics and is so familiar to us all, is of comparatively recent origin and did not assume definite shape before the eighteenth century, although it has many ingredients which go back to classical, medieval and Renaissance thought. I shall not try to discuss any metaphysical theories of beauty or any particular theories concerning one or more of the arts, let alone their actual history, but only the systematic grouping together of the five major arts. This question does not directly concern any specific changes or achievements in the various arts, but primarily their relations to each other and their place in the general framework of Western culture. Since the subject has been overlooked by most historians of aesthetics and of literary, musical or artistic theories, it is hoped that a brief and quite tentative study may throw light on some of the problems with which modern aesthetics and its historiography have been concerned.

II

The Greek term for Art (τέχνη) and its Latin equivalent (*ars*) do not specifically denote the "fine arts" in the modern sense, but were applied to all kinds of human activities which we would call crafts or sciences. Moreover, whereas modern aesthetics stresses the fact that Art cannot be learned, and thus often becomes involved in the curious endeavor to teach the unteachable, the ancients always understood by Art something that can be taught and learned. Ancient statements about Art and the arts have often been read and understood as if they were meant in the modern sense of the fine arts. This may in some cases have led to fruitful errors, but it does not do justice to the original intention of the ancient writers. When the Greek authors began to oppose Art to Nature, they thought of human activity in general. When Hippocrates contrasts Art with Life, he is thinking of medicine, and when his comparison is repeated by Goethe or Schiller with reference to poetry, this merely shows the long way of change which the term Art had traversed by 1800 from its original meaning. Plato puts art above mere routine because it proceeds by rational principles and rules, and Aristotle, who lists Art among the so-called intellectual virtues, characterizes it as a kind of activity based on knowledge, in a definition whose influence was felt through many centuries. The Stoics also defined Art as a system of cognitions, and it was in this sense that they considered moral virtue as an art of living.

The other central concept of modern aesthetics also, beauty, does not appear in ancient thought or literature with its specific modern connotations. The Greek term καλόν and its Latin equivalent (*pulchrum*) were never neatly or consistently distinguished from the moral good. When Plato discusses beauty in the *Symposium* and the *Phaedrus*, he is speaking not merely of the physical beauty of human persons, but also of beautiful habits of the soul and of beautiful cognitions, whereas he fails completely to mention works of art in this connection. An incidental remark made in the *Phaedrus* and elaborated by Proclus was certainly not meant to express the modern triad of Truth, Goodness and Beauty. When the Stoics in one of their famous statements connected Beauty and Goodness, the context as well as Cicero's Latin rendering suggest that they meant by "Beauty" nothing but moral goodness, and in turn understood by "good" nothing but the useful. Only in later thinkers does the speculation about "beauty" assume an increasingly "aesthetic" significance, but without ever leading to a separate system of aesthetics in the modern sense. Panaetius identifies moral beauty with decorum, a term he borrows from Aristotle's *Rhetoric*, and consequently likes to compare the various arts with each other and with the moral life. His doctrine is known chiefly through Cicero, but it may also have influenced Horace. Plotinus in his famous treatises on beauty is concerned primarily with metaphysical and ethical problems, but he does include in his treatment of sensuous beauty the visible beauty of works of sculpture and architecture, and the audible beauty of music. Likewise, in the speculations on beauty scattered through the works of Augustine there are references to the various arts, yet the doctrine was not primarily designed for an interpretation of the "fine arts." Whether we can speak of aesthetics in the case of Plato, Plotinus or Augustine will depend on our definition of that term, but we should certainly realize that in the theory of beauty a consideration of the arts is quite absent in Plato and secondary in Plotinus and Augustine.

Let us now turn to the individual arts and to the manner in which they were evaluated and grouped by the ancients. Poetry was always most highly respected, and the notion that the poet is inspired by the Muses goes back to Homer and Hesiod. The Latin term (*vates*) also suggests an old link between poetry and religious prophecy, and Plato is hence drawing upon an early notion when in the *Phaedrus* he considers poetry one of the forms of divine madness. However, we should also remember that the same conception of poetry is expressed with a certain irony in the *Ion* and the *Apology*, and that even in the Phaedrus the divine madness of the poet is compared with that of the lover and of the religious prophet. There is no mention of the "fine arts" in this passage, and it was left to the late sophist Callistratus to transfer Plato's concept of inspiration to the art of sculpture.

Among all the "fine arts" it was certainly poetry about which Plato had most to say, especially in the *Republic*, but the treatment given to it is neither systematic nor friendly, but suspiciously similar to the one he gives to rhetoric in some of his other writings. Aristotle, on the other hand, dedicated a whole treatise to the theory of poetry and deals with it in a thoroughly systematic and constructive fashion. The *Poetics* not only contains a great number of specific ideas which exercised a lasting influence upon later criticism; it also established a permanent place for the theory of poetry in the philosophical encyclopaedia of knowledge. The mutual influence of poetry and eloquence had been a permanent feature of ancient literature ever since the time of the Sophists, and the close relationship between these two branches of literature received a theoretical foundation through the proximity of the *Rhetoric* and the *Poetics* in the corpus of Aristotle's works. Moreover, since the order of the writings in the Aristotelian Corpus was interpreted as early as the commentators of late antiquity as a scheme of classification for the philosophical disciplines, the place of the *Rhetoric* and the *Poetics* after the logical writings of the *Organon* established a link between logic, rhetoric and poetics that was emphasized by some of the Arabic commentators, the effects of which were felt down to the Renaissance.

Music also held a high place in ancient thought; yet it should be remembered that the Greek term *μουσική*, which is derived from the Muses, originally comprised much more than we understand by music. Musical education, as we can still see in Plato's *Republic*, included not only music, but also poetry and the dance. Plato and Aristotle, who also employ the term music in the more specific sense familiar to us, do not treat music or the dance as separate arts but rather as elements of certain types of poetry, especially of lyric and dramatic poetry. There is reason to believe that they were thus clinging to an older tradition which was actually disappearing in their own time through the emancipation of instrumental music from poetry. On the other hand, the Pythagorean discovery of the numerical proportions underlying the musical intervals led to a theoretical treatment of music on a mathematical basis, and consequently musical theory entered into an alliance with the mathematical sciences which is already apparent in Plato's *Republic*, and was to last far down into early modern times.

When we consider the visual arts of painting, sculpture and architecture, it appears that their social and intellectual prestige in antiquity was much lower than one might expect from their actual achievements or from occasional enthusiastic remarks which date for the most part from the later centuries. It is true that painting was compared to poetry by Simonides and Plato, by Aristotle and Horace, as it was compared to rhetoric by Cicero, Dionysius of Halicarnassus and other writers. It is also true that architecture was included among the liberal arts by Varro and Vitruvius, and painting by Pliny and Galen, that

Dio Chrysostom compared the art of the sculptor with that of the poet, and that Philostratus and Callistratus wrote enthusiastically about painting and sculpture. Yet the place of painting among the liberal arts was explicitly denied by Seneca and ignored by most other writers, and the statement of Lucian that everybody admires the works of the great sculptors but would not want to be a sculptor oneself, seems to reflect the prevalent view among writers and thinkers. The term δημιουργός, commonly applied to painters and sculptors, reflects their low social standing, which was related to the ancient contempt for manual work. When Plato compares the description of his ideal state to a painting and even calls his world-shaping god a demiurge, he no more enhances the importance of the artist than does Aristotle when he uses the statue as the standard example for a product of human art. When Cicero, probably reflecting Panaetius, speaks of the ideal notions in the mind of the sculptor, and when the Middle Platonists and Plotinus compare the ideas in the mind of God with the concepts of the visual artist they go one step further. Yet no ancient philosopher, as far as I know, wrote a separate systematic treatise on the visual arts or assigned to them a prominent place in his scheme of knowledge.

If we want to find in classical philosophy a link between poetry, music and the fine arts, it is provided primarily by the concept of imitation (μίμησις). Passages have been collected from the writings of Plato and Aristotle from which it appears quite clearly that they considered poetry, music, the dance, painting and sculpture as different forms of imitation. This fact is significant so far as it goes, and it has influenced many later authors, even in the eighteenth century. But aside from the fact that none of the passages has a systematic character or even enumerates all of the "fine arts" together, it should be noted that the scheme excludes architecture, that music and the dance are treated as parts of poetry and not as separate arts, and that on the other hand the individual branches or subdivisions of poetry and of music seem to be put on a par with painting or sculpture. Finally, imitation is anything but a laudatory category, at least for Plato, and wherever Plato and Aristotle treat the "imitative arts" as a distinct group within the larger class of "arts," this group seems to include, besides the "fine arts" in which we are interested, other activities that are less "fine," such as sophistry, or the use of the mirror, of magic tricks, or the imitation of animal voices. Moreover, Aristotle's distinction between the arts of necessity and the arts of pleasure is quite incidental and does not identiy the arts of pleasure with the "fine" or even the imitative arts, and when it is emphasized that he includes music and drawing in his scheme of education in the *Politics*, it should be added that they share this place with grammar (writing) and arithmetic.

The final ancient attempts at a classification of the more important human arts and sciences were made after the time of Plato and Aristotle. They were due partly to the endeavors of rival schools of philosophy and rhetoric to organize secondary or preparatory education into a system of elementary disciplines(τὰ ἐγκύκλια). This system of the co-called "liberal arts" was subject to a number of changes and fluctuations, and its development is not known in all of its earlier phases. Cicero often speaks of the liberal arts and of their mutual connection, though he does not give a precise list of these arts, but we may be sure that he did not think of the "fine arts" as was so often believed in modern times. The definitive scheme of the seven liberal arts is found only in Martianus Capella: grammar, rhetoric, dialectic, arithmetic, geometry, astronomy, and music. Other schemes which are similar but not quite identical are found in many Greek and Latin authors before Capella. Very close to Capella's scheme and probably its source was that of Varro, which included medicine and architecture in addition to Capella's seven arts. Quite similar also is the scheme underlying the work of Sextus Empiricus. It contains only six arts, omitting logic, which is treated as one of the three parts of philosophy. The Greek author, Sextus, was conscious of the difference between the preliminary disciplines and the parts of philosophy, whereas the Latin authors who had no native tradition of philosophical instruction were ready to disregard that distinction. If we compare Capella's scheme of the seven liberal arts with the modern system of the "fine arts," the differences are obvious. Of the fine arts only music, understood as musical theory, appears among the liberal arts. Poetry is not listed among them, yet we know from other sources that it was closely linked with grammar and rhetoric. The visual arts have no place in the scheme, except for occasional attempts at inserting them, of which we have spoken above. On the other hand, the liberal arts include grammar and logic, mathematics and astronomy, that is, disciplines we should classify as sciences.

The same picture is gained from the distribution of the arts among the nine Muses. It should be noted that the number of the Muses was not fixed before a comparatively late period, and that the attempt to assign particular arts to individual Muses is still later and not at all uniform. However, the arts listed in these late schemes are the various branches of poetry and of music, with eloquence, history, the dance, grammar, geometry, and astronomy. In other words, just as in the schemes of the liberal arts, so in the schemes for the Muses poetry and music are grouped with some of the sciences, whereas the visual arts are omitted. Antiquity knew no Muse of painting or of sculpture; they had to be invented by the allegorists of the early modern centuries. And the five fine arts which constitute the modern system were not grouped together in antiquity, but kept quite different company: poetry stays usually with grammar and rhetoric; music is as close to mathematics and astronomy as it is to the dance, and poetry; and the visual arts, excluded from the realm of the Muses and of the liberal arts by most authors, must be satisfied with the modest company of the other manual crafts.

Thus classical antiquity left no systems or elaborate concepts of an aesthetic nature, but merely a number of scattered notions and suggestions that exercised a lasting influence down to modern times but had to be carefully selected, taken out of their context, rearranged, reemphasized and reinterpreted or misinterpreted before they could be utilized as building materials for aesthetic systems. We have to admit the conclusion, distasteful to many historians of aesthetics but grudgingly admitted by most of them, that ancient writers and thinkers, though confronted with excellent works of art and quite susceptible to their charm, were neither able nor eager to detach the aesthetic quality of these works of art from their intellectual, moral, religious and practical function or content, or to use such an aesthetic quality as a standard for grouping the fine arts together or for making them the subject of a comprehensive philosophical interpretation.

III

The early Middle Ages inherited from late antiquity the scheme of the seven liberal arts that served not only for a comprehensive classification of human knowledge but also for the curriculum of the monastic and cathedral schools down to the twelfth century. The subdivision of the seven arts into the Trivium (grammar, rhetoric, dialectic) and Quadrivium (arithmetic, geometry, astronomy and music) seems to have been emphasized since Carolingian times. This classification became inadequate after the growth of learning in the twelfth and thirteenth centuries. The classification schemes of the twelfth century reflect different attempts to combine the traditional system of the liberal arts with the threefold division of philosophy (logic, ethics and physics) known through Isidore, and with the divisions of knowledge made by Aristotle or based on the order of his writings, which then began to become known through Latin translations from the Greek and Arabic. The rise of the universities also established philosophy, medicine, jurisprudence and theology as new and distinct subjects outside the liberal arts, and the latter were again reduced from the status of an encyclopaedia of secular knowledge they had held in the earlier Middle Ages to that of preliminary disciplines they had held originally in late antiquity. On the other hand, Hugo of St. Victor was probably the first to formulate a scheme of seven mechanical arts corresponding to the seven liberal arts, and this scheme influenced many important authors of the subsequent period, such as Vincent of Beauvais and Thomas Aquinas. The seven mechanical arts, like the seven liberal arts earlier, also appeared in artistic representations, and they are worth listing: *lanificium*, *armatura*, *navigatio*, *agricultura*, *venatio*, *medicina*, *theatrica* [fabric making, armament, commerce, agriculture, hunting, medicine, theatrics]. Architecture as well as various branches of sculpture and of painting are listed, along with several other crafts, as subdivisions of *armatura*, and thus occupy a quite subordinate place even among the mechanical arts. Music appears in all these schemes in the company of the mathematical disciplines, whereas poetry, when mentioned, is closely linked to grammar, rhetoric and logic. The fine arts are not grouped together or singled out in any of these schemes, but scattered among various sciences, crafts, and other human activities of a quite disparate nature. Different as are these schemes from each other in detail, they show a persistent general pattern and continued to influence later thought.

If we compare these theoretical systems with the reality of the same period, we find poetry and music among the subjects taught in many schools and universities, whereas the visual arts were confined to the artisans' guilds, in which the painters were sometimes associated with the druggists who prepared their paints, the sculptors with the goldsmiths, and the architects with the masons and carpenters. The treatises also that were written, on poetry and rhetoric, on music, and on some of the arts and crafts, the latter not too numerous, have all a strictly technical and professional character and show no tendency to link any of these arts with the others or with philosophy.

The very concept of "art" retained the same comprehensive meaning it had possessed in antiquity, and the same connotation that it was teachable, And the term *artista* coined in the Middle Ages indicated either the craftsman or the student of the liberal arts. Neither for Dante nor for Aquinas has the term Art the meaning we associate with it, and it has been emphasized or admitted that for Aquinas shoemaking, cooking and juggling, grammar and arithmetic are no less and in no other sense *artes* than painting and sculpture, poetry and music, which latter are never grouped together, not even as imitative arts.

On the other hand, the concept of beauty that is occasionally discussed by Aquinas and somewhat more emphatically by a few other medieval philosophers is not linked with the arts, fine or otherwise, but treated primarily as a metaphysical attribute of God and of his creation, starting from Augustine and from Dionysius the Areopagite. Among the transcendentals or most general attributes of being, *pulchrum* does not appear in thirteenth-century philosophy, although it is considered as a general concept and treated in close connection with *bonum*. The question whether Beauty is one of the transcendentals has become a subject of controversy among Neo-Thomists. This is an interesting sign of their varying attitude toward modern aesthetics, which some of them would like to incorporate in a philosophical system based on Thomist principles. For Aquinas himself, or for other medieval philosophers, the question is meaningless, for even if they had posited *pulchrum* as a transcendental concept, which they did not, its meaning would have been different from the modern notion of artistic beauty in which the Neo-Thomists are interested. Thus it is obvious that there was artistic production as well as artistic appreciation in the Middle Ages, and this could not fail to find occasional expression in literature and philosophy. Yet there is no medieval concept or system of the Fine Arts, and if we want to keep speaking of medieval aesthetics, we must admit that its concept and subject matter are, for better or for worse, quite different from the modern philosophical discipline.

IV

The period of the Renaissance brought about many important changes in the social and cultural position of the various arts and thus prepared the ground for the later development of aesthetic theory. But, contrary to a widespread opinion, the Renaissance did not formulate a system of the fine arts or a comprehensive theory of aesthetics.

Early Italian humanism, which in many respects continued the grammatical and rhetorical traditions of the Middle Ages, not merely provided the old Trivium with a new and more ambitious name (*Studio humanitatis*) but also increased its actual scope, content and significance in the curriculum of the schools and universities and in its own extensive literary production. The *Studia humanitatis* excluded logic, but they added to the traditional grammar and rhetoric not only history, Greek and moral philosophy, but also made poetry, once a sequel of grammar and rhetoric. the most important member of the whole group. It is true that in the fourteenth and fifteenth centuries poetry was understood as the ability to write Latin verse and to interpret the ancient poets, and that the poetry which the humanists defended against some of their theological contemporaries or for which they were crowned by popes and emperors was a quite different thing from what we understand by that name. Yet the name poetry, meaning at first

Latin poetry, received much honor and glamor through the early humanists, and by the sixteenth century vernacular poetry and prose began to share in the prestige of Latin literature. It was the various branches of Latin and vernacular poetry and literature which constituted the main pursuit of the numerous "Academies" founded in Italy during that period and imitated later in the other European countries. The revival of Platonism also helped to spread the notion of the divine madness of the poet, a notion that by the second half of the sixteenth century began to be extended to the visual arts and became one of the ingredients of the modern concept of genius.

[. . .]

The rising social and cultural claims of the visual arts led in the sixteenth century in Italy to an important new development that occurred in the other European countries somewhat later: the three visual arts, painting, sculpture and architecture, were for the first time clearly separated from the crafts with which they had been associated in the preceding period. The term *Arti del disegno*, upon which "Beaux Arts" was probably based, was coined by Vasari, who used it as the guiding concept for his famous collection of biographies. And this change in theory found its institutional expression in 1563 when in Florence, again under the personal influence of Vasari, the painters, sculptors and architects cut their previous connections with the craftsmen's guilds and formed an Academy of Art (*Accademia del Disegno*), the first of its kind that served as a model for later similar institutions in Italy and other countries. The Art Academies followed the pattern of the literary Academies that had been in existence for some time, and they replaced the older workshop tradition with a regular kind of instruction that included such scientific subjects as geometry and anatomy.

The ambition of painting to share in the traditional prestige of literature also accounts for the popularity of a notion that appears prominently for the first time in the treatises on painting of the sixteenth century and was to retain its appeal down to the eighteenth: the parallel between painting and poetry. Its basis was the *Ut pictura poesis* of Horace, as well as the saying of Simonides reported by Plutarch, along with some other passages in Plato, Aristotle and Horace. The history of this notion from the sixteenth to the eighteenth century has been carefully studied, and it has been justly pointed out that the use then made of the comparison exceeded anything done or intended by the ancients. Actually, the meaning of the comparison was reversed, since the ancients had compared poetry with painting when they were writing about poetry, whereas the modern authors more often compared painting with poetry while writing about painting. How seriously the comparison was taken we can see from the fact that Horace's *Ars poetica* was taken as a literary model for some treatises on painting and that many poetical theories and concepts were applied to painting by these authors in a more or less artificial manner. The persistent comparison between poetry and painting went a long way, as did the emancipation of the three visual arts from the crafts, to prepare the ground for the later system of the five fine arts, but it obviously does not yet presuppose or constitute such a system. Even the few treatises written in the late sixteenth and early seventeenth century that dealt with both poetry and painting do not seem to have gone beyond more or less external comparisons into an analysis of common principles.

[. . .]

V

During the seventeenth century the cultural leadership of Europe passed from Italy to France, and many characteristic ideas and tendencies of the Italian Renaissance were continued and transformed by French classicism and the French Enlightenment before they became a part of later European thought and culture. Literary criticism and poetic theory, so prominent in the French classical period, seem to have taken little notice of the other fine arts. [. . .]

Yet the *Siècle de Louis XIV* was not limited in its achievements to poetry and literature. Painting and the other visual arts began to flourish, and with Poussin France produced a painter of European fame. Later in the century Lulli, although of Italian birth, developed a distinctive French style in music, and his great success with the Parisian public went a long way to win for his art the same popularity in France it had long possessed in Italy.

One of the great changes that occurred during the seventeenth century was the rise and emancipation of the natural sciences. By the second half of the century, after the work of Galileo and Descartes had been completed and the Académie des Sciences and the Royal Society had begun their activities, this development could not fail to impress the literati and the general public. It has been rightly observed that the famous *Querelle des Anciens et Modernes*, which stirred many scholars in France and also in England during the last quarter of the century, was due largely to the recent discoveries in the natural sciences. The Moderns, conscious of these achievements, definitely shook off the authority of classical antiquity that had weighed on the Renaissance no less than on the Middle Ages, and went a long ways toward formulating the concept of human progress. Yet this is only one side of the *Querelle*.

The *Querelle* as it went on had two important consequences which have not been sufficiently appreciated. First, the Moderns broadened the literary controversy into a systematic comparison between the achievements of antiquity and of modern times in the various fields of human endeavor, thus developing a classification of knowledge and culture that was in many respects novel, or more specific than previous systems. Secondly, a point by point examination of the claims of the ancients and moderns in the various fields led to the insight that in certain fields, where everything depends on mathematical calculation and the accumulation of knowledge, the progress of the moderns over the ancients can be clearly demonstrated, whereas in certain other fields, which depend on individual talent and on the taste of the critic, the relative merits of the ancients and moderns cannot be so clearly established but may be subject to controversy.

Thus the ground is prepared for the first time for a clear distinction between the arts and the sciences, a distinction absent from ancient, medieval or Renaissance discussions of such subjects even though the same words were used. In other words, the separation between the arts and the sciences in the modern sense presupposes not only the actual progress of the sciences in the seventeenth century but also the reflection upon the reasons why some other human intellectual activities which we now call the Fine Arts did not or could not participate in the same kind of progress. To be sure, the writings of the *Querelle* do not yet attain a complete clarity on these points, and this fact in itself definitely confirms our contention that the separation between the arts and the sciences and the modern system of the fine arts were just in the making at that time. [. . .]

VI

[. . .]

The decisive step toward a system of the fine arts was taken by the Abbé Batteux in his famous and influential treatise, *Les beaux arts réduits à un même principe* (1746). It is true that many elements of his system were derived from previous authors, but at the same time it should not be overlooked that he was the first to set forth a clearcut system of the fine arts in a treatise devoted exclusively to this subject. This alone may account for his claim to originality as well as for the enormous influence he exercised both in France and abroad, especially in Germany. Batteux codified the modern system of the fine arts almost in its final form, whereas all previous authors had merely prepared it. He started from the poetic theories of Aristotle and Horace, as he states in his preface, and tried to extend their principles from poetry and painting to the other arts. In his first chapter, Batteux gives a clear division of the arts. He separates the fine arts which have pleasure for their end from the mechanical arts, and lists the fine arts as follows: music, poetry, painting, sculpture, and the dance. He adds a third group which combines pleasure and usefulness and puts eloquence and architecture in this category. In the central part of his treatise, Batteux tries to show that the "imitation of beautiful nature" is the principle common to all the arts, and he concludes with a discussion of the theatre as a combination of all the other arts. The German critics of the later eighteenth century, and their recent historians, criticized Batteux for his theory of imitation and often failed to recognize that he formulated the system of the arts which they took for granted and for which they were merely trying to find different principles. They also overlooked the fact that the much maligned principle of imitation was the only one a classicist critic such as Batteux could use when he wanted to group the fine arts together with even an appearance of ancient authority. For the "imitative" arts were the only authentic ancient precedent for the "fine arts," and the principle of imitation could be replaced only after the system of the latter had been so firmly established as no longer to need the ancient principle of imitation to link them together. [. . .]

VII

Having followed the French development through the eighteenth century, we must discuss the history of artistic thought in England. The English writers were strongly influenced by the French down to the end of the seventeenth century and later, but during the eighteenth century they made important contributions of their own and in turn influenced continental thought, especially in France and Germany. [. . .] Early in the eighteenth century, Jonathan Richardson was praising painting as a liberal art, and John Dennis in some of his critical treatises on poetics stressed the affinity between poetry, painting and music.

Of greater importance were the writings of Anthony, Earl of Shaftesbury, one of the most influential thinkers of the eighteenth century, not only in England but also on the continent. His interest and taste for literature and the arts are well known, and his writings are full of references to the various arts and to the beauty of their works. The ideal of the *virtuoso* which he embodied and advocated no longer included the sciences, as in the seventeenth century, but had its center in the arts and in the moral life. Since Shaftesbury was the first major philosopher in modern Europe in whose writings the discussion of the arts occupied a prominent place, there is some reason for considering him as the founder of modern aesthetics. Yet Shaftesbury was influenced primarily by Plato and Plotinus, as well as by Cicero, and he consequently did not make a clear distinction between artistic and moral beauty. His moral sense still includes both ethical and aesthetic objects. [. . .]

The philosophical implications of Shaftesbury's doctrine were further developed by a group of Scottish thinkers. Francis Hutcheson, who considered himself Shaftesbury's pupil, modified his doctrine by distinguishing between the moral sense and the sense of beauty. This distinction, which was adopted by Hume and quoted by Diderot, went a long ways to prepare the separation of ethics and aesthetics, although Hutcheson still assigned the taste of poetry to the moral sense. A later philosopher of the Scottish school, Thomas Reid, introduced common sense as a direct criterion of truth, and although he was no doubt influenced by Aristotle's notion of common sense and the Stoic and modern views on "common notions," it has been suggested that his common sense was conceived as a counterpart of Hutcheson's two senses. Thus the psychology of the Scottish school led the way for the doctrine of the three faculties of the soul, which found its final development in Kant and its application in Cousin. [. . .]

VIII

Discussion of the arts does not seem to have occupied many German writers of the seventeenth century, which was on the whole a period of decline. The poet Opitz showed familiarity with the parallel of poetry and painting, but otherwise the Germans did not take part in the development we are trying to describe before the eighteenth century. During the first part of that century interest in literature and literary criticism began to rise, but did not yet lead to a detailed or comparative treatment of the other arts. [. . .]

These critical discussions among poets and literati constitute the general background for the important work of the philosopher Alexander Gottlieb Baumgarten and of his pupil Georg Friedrich Meier. Baumgarten is famous for having coined the term aesthetics, but opinions differ as to whether he must be considered the founder of that discipline or what place he occupies in its history and development. The original meaning of the term aesthetics as coined by Baumgarten, which has been well nigh forgotten by now, is the theory of sensuous knowledge, as a counterpart to logic as a theory of intellectual knowledge. The definitions Baumgarten gives of aesthetics show that he is concerned with the arts and with beauty as one of their main attributes, but he still uses the old term liberal arts, and he considers them as forms of knowledge. The question whether Baumgarten really gave a theory of all the fine arts, or merely a poetics and rhetoric with a new name, has been debated but can be answered easily. In his earlier work, in which he first coined the term aesthetic, Baumgarten was exclusively concerned with poetics and rhetoric, In his later, unfinished work, to which he gave the title *Aesthetica*, Baumgarten states in his introduction that he intends to give a theory of all the arts, and actually makes occasional references to the visual arts and to music. This impression is confirmed by the text of Baumgarten's lectures published only recently, and by the writings of his pupil Meier. On the other hand, it is quite obvious, and was noted by contemporary critics, that Baumgarten and Meier develop their actual theories only in terms of poetry and eloquence and take nearly all their examples from literature. Baumgarten is the founder of aesthetics in so far as he first conceived a general theory of the arts as a separate philosophical discipline with a distinctive and well-defined place in the system of philosophy. He failed to develop his doctrine with reference to the arts other than poetry and eloquence, or even to propose a systematic list and division of these other arts. In this latter respect, he was preceded and surpassed by the French writers, especially by Batteux and the Encyclopaedists, whereas the latter failed to develop a theory of the arts as part of a philosophical system. It was the result of German thought and criticism during the second half of the eighteenth century that the more concrete French conception of the fine arts was utilized in a philosophical theory of aesthetics for which Baumgarten had formulated the general scope and program. [. . .]

The broadening scope of German aesthetics after Baumgarten, which we must now try to trace, was due not only to the influence of Batteux, of the Encyclopaedists, and of other French and English writers but also to the increasing interest taken by writers, philosophers, and the lay public in the visual arts and in music. Winckelmann's studies of classical art are important for the history of our problem for the enthusiasm which he stimulated among his German readers for ancient sculpture and architecture, but not for any opinion he may have expressed on the relation between the visual arts and literature. Lessing's *Laokoon* (1766), too, has a notable importance, not only for its particular theories on matters of poetry and of the visual arts, but also for the very attention given to the latter by one of the most brilliant and most respected German writers of the time. Yet the place of the *Laokoon* in the history of our problem has been misjudged. To say that the *Laokoon* put an end to the age-old tradition of the parallel between painting and poetry that had its ultimate roots in classical antiquity and found its greatest development in the writers of the sixteenth, seventeenth, and early eighteenth century, and thus freed poetry from the emphasis on description, is to give only one side of the picture. It is to forget that the parallel between painting and poetry was one of the most important elements that preceded the formation of the modern system of the fine arts, though it had lost this function as a link between two different arts by the time of Lessing, when the more comprehensive system of the fine arts had been firmly established. In so far as Lessing paid no attention to the broader system of the fine arts, especially to music, his *Laokoon* constituted a detour or a dead end in terms of the development leading to a comprehensive system of the fine arts. It is significant that the *Laokoon* was criticized for this very reason by two prominent contemporary critics, and that Lessing in the posthumous notes for the second part of the work gave some consideration to this criticism, though we have no evidence that he actually planned to extend his analysis to music and to a coherent system of the arts.

The greatest contributions to the history of our problem in the interval between Baumgarten and Kant came from Mendelssohn, Sulzer, and Herder. Mendelssohn, who was well acquainted with French and English writings on the subject, demanded in a famous article that the fine arts (painting, sculpture, music, the dance, and architecture) and belles lettres (poetry and eloquence) should be reduced to some common principle better than imitation, and thus was the first among the Germans to formulate a system of the fine arts. Shortly afterwards, in a book review, he criticized Baumgarten and Meier for not having carried out the program of their new science, aesthetics. They wrote as if they had been thinking exclusively in terms of poetry and literature, whereas aesthetic principles should be formulated in such a way as to apply to the visual arts and to music as well. In his annotations to Lessing's *Laokoon*, published long after his death, Mendelssohn persistently criticizes Lessing for not giving any consideration to music and to the system of the arts as a whole; we have seen how Lessing, in the fragmentary notes for a continuation of the *Laokoon*, tried to meet this criticism; Mendelssohn also formulated a doctrine of the three faculties of the soul corresponding to the three basic realms of goodness, truth and beauty, thus continuing the work of the Scottish philosophers. He did not work out an explicit theory of aesthetics, but under the impact of French and English authors he indicated the direction in which German aesthetics was to develop from Baumgarten to Kant.

What Mendelssohn had merely set forth in a general outline and program, the Swiss thinker Sulzer, who was well versed in French literature but spent the greater part of his life in Northern Germany, was able to develop in a more systematic and elaborate fashion. Sulzer began his literary activity with a few short philosophical articles in which his interest for aesthetics was already apparent, and in which he also leaned toward the conception of an aesthetic faculty of the soul separate from the intellectual and moral faculties, a conception in whose development Mendelssohn and the philosopher Tetens also took their part. Some years later, Sulzer was prompted by the example of Lacombe's little dictionary of the fine arts to compile a similar dictionary in German on a much larger scale. This General Theory of the Fine Arts, which appeared in several editions, has been disparaged on account of its pedantic arrangement, but it is clear, comprehensive and learned, and had a considerable importance in its time. The work covers all the fine arts, not only poetry and eloquence, but also music and the visual arts, and thus represents the first attempt to carry out on a large scale the program formulated by Baumgarten and Mendelssohn. Thanks to its wide diffusion, Sulzer's work went a long way to acquaint the German public with the idea that all the fine arts are related and connected with each other. Sulzer's influence extended also to France, for when the great *Encyclopédie* was published in Switzerland in a second edition, many additions were based on his General Theory, including the article on aesthetics and the section on the Fine Arts.

In the decades after 1760, the interest in the new field of aesthetics spread rapidly in Germany. Courses on aesthetics were offered at a number of universities after the example set by Baumgarten and Meier, and new tracts and textbooks, partly based on these courses, appeared almost every year.

[. . .]

I should like to conclude this survey with Kant, since he was the first major philosopher who included aesthetics and the philosophical theory of the arts as an integral part of his system. Kant's interest in aesthetic problems appears already in his early writing on the beautiful and sublime, which was influenced in its general conception by Burke. He also had occasion to discuss aesthetic problems in several of his courses. Notes based on these courses extant in manuscript have not been published, but have been utilized by a student of Kant's aesthetics. It appears that Kant cited in these lectures many authors he does not mention in his published works, and that he was thoroughly familiar with most of the French, English and German writers on aesthetics, At the time when he published the *Critique of Pure Reason*, he still used the term aesthetics in a sense different from the common one, and explains in an interesting footnote, that he does not follow Baumgarten's terminology since he does not believe in the possibility of a philosophical theory of the arts. In the following years, however, he changed his view, and in his *Critique of Judgment*, which constitutes the third and concluding part of his philosophical system, the larger of its two major divisions is dedicated to aesthetics, whereas the other section deals with teleology. The system of the three *Critiques* as presented in this last volume is based on a threefold division of the faculties of the mind, which adds the faculty of judgment, aesthetic and teleological, to pure and practical reason. Aesthetics, as the philosophical theory of beauty and the arts, acquires equal standing with the theory of truth (metaphysics or epistemology) and the theory of goodness (ethics).

In the tradition of systematic philosophy this was an important innovation, for neither Descartes nor Spinoza nor Leibniz nor any of their ancient or medieval predecessors had found a separate or independent place in their system for the theory of the arts and of beauty, though they had expressed occasional opinions on these subjects. If Kant took this decisive step after some hesitation, he was obviously influenced by the example of Baumgarten and by the rich French, English, and German literature on the arts his century had produced, with which he was well acquainted. In his critique of aesthetic judgment, Kant discusses also the concepts of the sublime and of natural beauty, but his major emphasis is on beauty in the arts, and he discusses many concepts and principles common to all the arts. In section 51 he also gives a division of the fine arts: speaking arts (poetry, eloquence); plastic arts (sculpture, architecture, painting, and gardening); arts of the beautiful play of sentiments (music, and the art of color). This scheme contains a few ephemeral details that were not retained by Kant's successors. However, since Kant aesthetics has occupied a permanent place among the major philosophical disciplines, and the core of the system of the fine arts fixed in the eighteenth century has been generally accepted as a matter of course by most later writers on the subject, except for variations of detail or of explanation.

IX

We shall not attempt to discuss the later history of our problem after Kant, but shall rather draw a few general conclusions from the development so far as we have been able to follow it. The grouping together of the visual arts with poetry and music into the system of the fine arts with which we are familiar did not exist in classical antiquity, in the Middle Ages or in the Renaissance. However, the ancients contributed to the modern system the comparison between poetry and painting and the theory of imitation that established a kind of link between painting and sculpture, poetry and music. The Renaissance brought about the emancipation of the three major visual arts from the crafts, it multiplied the comparisons between the various arts, especially between painting and poetry, and it laid the ground for an amateur interest in the different arts that tended to bring them together from the point of view of the reader, spectator and listener rather than of the artist. The seventeenth century witnessed the emancipation of the natural sciences and thus prepared the way for a clearer separation between the arts and the sciences. Only the early eighteenth century, especially in England and France, produced elaborate treatises written by and for amateurs in which the various fine arts were grouped together, compared with each other and combined in a systematic scheme based on common principles. The second half of the century, especially in Germany, took the additional step of incorporating the comparative and theoretical treatment of the fine arts as a separate discipline into the system of philosophy. The modern system of the fine arts is thus preromantic in its origin, although all romantic as well as later aesthetics takes this system as its necessary basis.

It is not easy to indicate the causes for the genesis of the system in the eighteenth century. The rise of painting and of music since the Renaissance, not so much in their actual achievements as in their prestige and appeal, the rise of literary and art criticism, and above all the rise of an amateur public to which art collections and exhibitions, concerts as well as opera and theatre performances were addressed, must be considered as important factors. The fact that the affinity between the various fine arts is more plausible to the amateur, who feels a comparable kind of enjoyment, than to the artist himself, who is concerned with the peculiar aims and techniques of his art, is obvious in itself and is confirmed by Goethe's reaction. The origin of modern aesthetics in amateur criticism would go a long way to explain why works of art have until recently been analyzed by aestheticians from the point of view of the spectator, reader and listener rather than of the producing artist.

The development we have been trying to understand also provides an interesting object lesson for the historian of philosophy and of ideas in general. We are accustomed to the process by which notions first formulated by great and influential thinkers are gradually diffused among secondary writers and finally become the common property of the general public. Such seems to have been the development of aesthetics from Kant to the present. Its history before Kant is of a very different kind. The basic questions and conceptions underlying modern aesthetics seem to have originated quite apart from the traditions of systematic philosophy or from the writings of important original authors. They had their inconspicuous beginnings in secondary authors, now almost forgotten though influential in their own time, and perhaps in the discussion and conversations of educated laymen reflected in their writings. These notions had a tendency to fluctuate and to grow slowly, but only after they had crystallized into a pattern that seemed generally plausible did they find acceptance among the greater authors and the systematic philosophers. Baumgarten's aesthetics was but a program, and Kant's aesthetics the philosophical elaboration of a body of ideas that had had almost a century of informal and non-philosophical growth. If the absence of the scheme of the fine arts before the eighteenth century and its fluctuations in that century have escaped the attention of most historians, this merely proves how thoroughly and irresistibly plausible the scheme has become to modern thinkers and writers.

Another observation seems to impose itself as a result of our study. The various arts are certainly as old as human civilization, but the manner in which we are accustomed to group them and to assign them a place in our scheme of life and of culture is comparatively recent. This fact is not as strange as may appear on the surface. In the course of history, the various arts change not only their content and style, but also their relations to each other, and their place in the general system of culture, as do religion, philosophy or science. Our familiar system of the five fine arts did not merely originate in the eighteenth century, but it also reflects the particular cultural and social conditions of that time. If we consider other times and places, the status of the various arts, their associations and their subdivisions appear very different. There were important periods in cultural history when the novel, instrumental music, or canvas painting did not exist or have any importance. On the other hand, the sonnet and the epic poem, stained glass and mosaic, fresco painting and book illumination, vase painting and tapestry, bas relief and pottery have all been "major" arts at various times and in a way they no longer are now. Gardening has lost its standing as a fine art since the eighteenth century. On the other hand, the moving picture is a good example of how new techniques may lead to modes of artistic expression for which the aestheticians of the eighteenth and nineteenth century had no place in their systems. The branches of the arts all have their rise and decline, and even their birth and death, and the distinction between "major" arts and their subdivisions is arbitrary and subject to change. There is hardly any ground but critical tradition or philosophical preference for deciding whether engraving is a separate art (as most of the eighteenth-century authors believed) or a subdivision of painting, or whether poetry and prose, dramatic and epic poetry, instrumental and vocal music are separate arts or subdivisions of one major art.

As a result of such changes, both in modern artistic production and in the study of other phases of cultural history, the traditional system of the fine arts begins to show signs of disintegration. Since the latter part of the nineteenth century, painting has moved further away from literature than at any previous time, whereas music has at times moved closer to it, and the crafts have taken great strides to recover their earlier standing as decorative arts. A greater awareness of the different techniques of the various arts has produced dissatisfaction among artists and critics with the conventions of an aesthetic system based on a situation no longer existing, an aesthetics that is trying in vain to hide the fact that its underlying system of the fine arts is hardly more than a postulate and that most of its theories are abstracted from particular arts, usually poetry, and more or less inapplicable to the others. The excesses of aestheticism have led to a healthy reaction which is yet far from universal. The tendency among some contemporary philosophers to consider Art and the aesthetic realm as a pervasive aspect of human experience rather than as the specific domain of the conventional fine arts also goes a long way to weaken the latter notion in its traditional form. All these ideas are still fluid and ill defined, and it is difficult to see how far they will go in modifying or undermining the traditional status of the fine arts and of aesthetics. In any case, these contemporary changes may help to open our eyes to an understanding of the historical origins and limitations of the modern system of the fine arts. Conversely, such historical understanding might help to free us from certain conventional preconceptions and to clarify our ideas on the present status and future prospects of the arts and of aesthetics.

2

Ion

Plato

Plato (ca. 428–347 BCE), the famed Athenian philosopher, wrote a series of dialogues, most of which feature his teacher Socrates (469–399 BCE), who himself wrote nothing but, in conversation, was able to befuddle the most powerful minds of his day.

530 SOCRATES: Ion! Hello. Where have you come
from to visit us this time? From your home in
Ephesus?

ION: No, no, Socrates. From Epidaurus, from the festival of Asclepius.

SOCRATES: Don't tell me the Epidaurians hold a contest for *rhapsodes* in honor of the god?

ION: They certainly do! They do it for every sort of poetry and music.

SOCRATES: Really! Did you enter the contest? And how did it go for you?

b ION: First prize, Socrates! We carried it off.

SOCRATES: That's good to hear. Well, let's see that we win the big games at Athens, next.

ION: We'll do it, Socrates, god willing.

SOCRATES: You know, Ion, many times I've envied you rhapsodes your profession. Physically,
it is always fitting for you in your profession to
be dressed up to look as beautiful as you can; and
at the same time it is necessary for you to be at
work with poets – many fine ones, and with
Homer above all, who's the best poet and the c
most divine – and you have to learn his thought,
not just his verses! Now that is something to envy! I mean, no one would ever get to be a good rhapsode if he didn't understand what is meant by the poet. A rhapsode must come to present the poet's thought to his audience; and he can't do that beautifully unless he knows what the poet means. So this all deserves to be envied.

ION: That's true, Socrates. And that's the part
of my profession that took the most work. I think
I speak more beautifully than anyone else about
Homer; neither Metrodorus of Lampsacus nor d
Stesimbrotus of Thasos nor Glaucon nor anyone
else past or present could offer as many beautiful thoughts about Homer as I can.

SOCRATES: That's good to hear, Ion. Surely you won't begrudge me a demonstration?

ION: Really, Socrates, it's worth hearing how well I've got Homer dressed up. I think I'm worthy to be crowned by the Sons of Homer[1] with a golden crown.

SOCRATES: Really, I shall make time to hear 531
that later. Now I'd just like an answer to this: Are
you so wonderfully clever about Homer alone –
or also about Hesiod and Archilochus?

Plato, "Ion," in *Two Comic Dialogues: Ion and Hippias Major*, trans. Paul Woodruff (Indianapolis, IN, and Cambridge, MA: Hackett Publishing, 1983), pp. 21–35.

Ion: No, no. Only about Homer. That's good enough, I think.

Socrates: Is there any subject on which Homer and Hesiod both say the same things?

Ion: Yes, I think so. A good many.

Socrates: Then, on those subjects, would you explain Homer's verse better and more beautifully than Hesiod's?

b Ion: Just the same Socrates, on those subjects, anyway, where they say the same things.

Socrates: And how about the subjects on which they do not say the same things? Divination, for example. Homer says something about it and so does Hesiod.

Ion: Certainly.

Socrates: Well. Take all the places where those two poets speak of divination, both where they agree and where they don't: who would explain those better and more beautifully, you, or one of the diviners if he's good?

Ion: One of the diviners.

Socrates: Suppose *you* were a diviner: if you were really able to explain the places where the two poets agree, wouldn't you also know how to explain the places where they disagree?

Ion: That's clear.

c Socrates: Then what in the world is it that you're clever about in Homer but not in Hesiod and the other poets? Does Homer speak of any subjects that differ from those of *all* the other poets? Doesn't he mainly go through tales of war, and of how people deal with each other in society – good people and bad, ordinary folks and craftsmen? And of the gods, how *they* deal with each other and with men? And doesn't he recount
d what happens in heaven and in hell, and tell of the births of gods and heroes? Those are the subjects of Homer's poetry-making, aren't they?

Ion: That's true, Socrates.

Socrates: And how about the other poets? Did they write on the same subjects?

Ion: Yes, but Socrates, they didn't do it the way Homer did.

Socrates: How, then? Worse?

Ion: Much worse.

Socrates: And Homer does it better?

Ion: *Really* better.

Socrates: Well now, Ion, dear heart, when a number of people are discussing arithmetic, and one of them speaks best, I suppose *someone* will
e know how to pick out the good speaker.

Ion: Yes.

Socrates: Will it be the same person who can pick out the bad speakers, or someone else?

Ion: The same, of course.

Socrates: And that will he someone who has mastered arithmetic, right?

Ion: Yes.

Socrates: Well. Suppose a number of people are discussing healthy nutrition, and one of them speaks best. Will one person know that the best speaker speaks best, and another that an inferior speaker speaks worse? Or will the same man know both?

Ion: Obviously, the same man.

Socrates: Who is he? What do we call him?

Ion: A doctor.

Socrates: So, to sum it up, this is what we're
saying: when a number of people speak on the 532
same subject, it's always the same person who will know how to pick out good speakers and bad speakers. If he doesn't know how to pick out a bad speaker, he certainly won't know a good speaker – on the same subject, anyway.

Ion: That's so.

Socrates: Then it turns out that the same person is "wonderfully clever" about both speakers.

Ion: Yes.

Socrates: Now *you* claim that Homer and the other poets (including Hesiod and Archilochus) speak on the same subjects, but not equally well. *He's* good, and they're inferior.

Ion: Yes, and it's true.

Socrates: Now if you really do know who's b
speaking well, you'll know that the inferior speakers are speaking worse.

Ion: Apparently so.

Socrates: You're superb! So if we say that Ion is equally clever about Homer and the other poets, we'll make no mistake. Because you agree yourself that the same person will be an adequate judge of all who speak on the same subjects, and that almost all the poets *do* treat the same subjects.

Ion: Then how in the world do you explain
what *I* do, Socrates? When someone discusses c
another poet I pay no attention, and I have no power to contribute anything worthwhile: I simply doze off. But let someone mention Homer and right away I'm wide awake and I'm paying attention and I have plenty to say.

SOCRATES: *That's* not hard to figure out, my friend. Anyone can tell that you are powerless to speak about Homer on the basis of knowledge or mastery. Because if your ability came by mastery, you would be able to speak about all the other poets as well. Look, there is an art of poetry as a whole, isn't there?

ION: Yes.

d SOCRATES: And now take the whole of *any* other subject: won't it have the same discipline throughout? And this goes for every subject that can be mastered. Do you need me to tell you what I mean by this, Ion?

ION: Lord, yes, I do, Socrates. I love to hear you wise men talk.

SOCRATES: I wish that were true, Ion. But
e wise? Surely you are the wise men, you rhapsodes and actors, you and the poets whose work you sing. As for me, I say nothing but the truth, as you'd expect from an ordinary man. I mean, even this question I asked you – look how commonplace and ordinary a matter it is. Anybody could understand what I meant: don't you use the same discipline throughout whenever you master the whole of a subject? Take this for discussion – painting is a subject to be mastered as a whole, isn't it?

ION: Yes.

SOCRATES: And there are many painters, good and bad, and there have been many in the past.

ION: Certainly.

533 SOCRATES: Have you ever known anyone who is clever at showing what's well painted and what's not in the work of Polygnotus, but who's powerless to do that for other painters? Someone who dozes off when the work of other painters is displayed, and is lost, and has nothing to contribute – but when he has to give judgment on Polygnotus or any other painter (so long as it's just *one*), he's wide awake and he's paying attention and he has plenty to say – have you ever known anyone like that?

ION: Good lord no, of course not!

SOCRATES: Well. Take sculpture. Have you
b ever known anyone who is clever at explaining which statues are well made in the case of Daedalus, son of Metion, or Epeius, son of Panopeus, or Theodorus of Samos, or any other *single* sculptor, but who's lost when he's among the products of other sculptors, and he dozes off and has nothing to say?

ION: Good lord no. I haven't.

SOCRATES: And further, it is my opinion, you've never known anyone ever – not in flute-playing, not in cithara-playing, not in singing to the cithara, and not in rhapsodizing – you've never known a man who is clever at explaining c
Olympus or Thamyrus or Orpheus or Phemius, the rhapsode from Ithaca, but who has nothing to contribute about Ion, the rhapsode from Ephesus, and cannot tell when he does his work well and when he doesn't – you've never known a man like that.

ION: I have nothing to say against you on that point, Socrates. But *this* I know about myself: I speak about Homer more beautifully than anybody else and I have lots to say; and everybody says I do it well. But about the other poets I do not. Now see what that means.

SOCRATES: I do see, Ion, and I'm going to d
announce to you what I think that is. As I said earlier, that's not a subject you've mastered – speaking well about Homer; it's a divine power that moves you, as a "Magnetic" stone moves iron rings. (That's what Euripides called it; most people call it "Heraclean.")[2] This stone not only pulls those rings, if they're iron, it also puts power e
in the rings, so that they in turn can do just what the stone does – pull other rings – so that there's sometimes a very long chain of iron pieces and rings hanging from one another. And the power in all of them depends on this stone. In the same way, the Muse makes some people inspired herself, and then through those who are inspired a chain of other enthusiasts is suspended. You know, none of the epic poets, if they're good, are masters of their subject; they are inspired, possessed, and that is how they utter all those beautiful poems. The same goes for lyric poets if 534
they're good: just as the Corybantes are not in their right minds when they dance, lyric poets, too, are not in their right minds when they make those beautiful lyrics, but as soon as they sail into harmony and rhythm they are possessed by Bacchic frenzy. Just as Bacchus worshippers[3] when they are possessed draw honey and milk from rivers, but not when they are in their right minds – the soul of a lyric poet does this too, as they say themselves. For of course poets tell us b
that they gather songs at honey-flowing springs, from glades and gardens of the Muses, and that they bear songs to us as bees carry honey, flying

like bees. And what they say is true. For a poet is
an airy thing, winged and holy, and he is not able
to make poetry until he becomes inspired and
goes out of his mind and his intellect is no longer
in him. As long as a human being has his intellect
in his possession he will always lack the power to
c make poetry or sing prophecy. Therefore because
it's not by mastery that they make poems or say
many lovely things about their subjects (as you
do about Homer) – but because it's by a divine
gift – each poet is able to compose beautifully
only that for which the Muse has aroused him:
one can do dithyrambs, another encomia, one
can do dance songs, another, epics, and yet
another, iambics; and each of them is worthless
for the other types of poetry. You see, it's not
mastery that enables them to speak those verses,
but a divine power, since if they knew how to
speak beautifully on one type of poetry by
mastering the subject, they could do so for all the
d others also. That's why the god takes their intellect
away from them when he uses them as his
servants, as he does prophets and godly diviners,
so that we who hear should know that *they* are
not the ones who speak those verses that are of
such high value, for their intellect is not in them:
the god himself is the one who speaks, and he
gives voice through them to us. The best evidence
for this account is Tynnichus from Chalcis, who
never made a poem anyone would think worth
mentioning, *except* for the praise-song everyone
sings, almost the most beautiful lyric-poem there
e is, and simply, as he says himself, "an invention
of the Muses." In this more than anything, then,
I think, the god is showing us, so that we should
be in no doubt about it, that these beautiful
poems are not human, not even *from* human
beings, but are divine and from gods; that poets
are nothing but representatives of the gods,
535 possessed by whoever possesses them. To show
that, the god deliberately sang the most beautiful
lyric poem through the most worthless poet.
Don't you think I'm right, Ion?

ION: Lord yes, *I* certainly do. Somehow you
touch my soul with your words, Socrates, and
I do think it's by a divine gift that good poets
are able to present these poems to us from the
gods.

SOCRATES: And you rhapsodes in turn present
what the poets say.

ION: That's true too.

SOCRATES: So you turn out to be representatives
of representatives.

ION: Quite right.

SOCRATES: Hold on, Ion; tell me this. Don't b
keep any secrets from *me*. When you recite epic
poetry well and you have the most stunning effect
on your spectators, either when you sing of
Odysseus – how he leapt into the doorway, his
identity now obvious to the suitors, and he poured
out arrows at his feet – or when you sing of Achilles
charging at Hector, or when you sing a pitiful
episode about Andromache or Hecuba or Priam,
are you at that time in your right mind, or do you c
get beside yourself? And doesn't your soul, in its
enthusiasm, believe that it is present at the actions
you describe, whether they're in Ithaca or in Troy
or wherever the epic actually takes place?

ION: What a vivid example you've given me,
Socrates! I won't keep secrets from *you*. Listen,
when *I* tell a sad story, my eyes are full of tears;
and when I tell a story that's frightening or awful,
my hair stands on end with fear and my heart
jumps.

SOCRATES: Well, Ion, should we say this man d
is in his right mind at times like these: when he's
at festivals or celebrations, all dressed up in fancy
clothes, with golden crowns, and he weeps,
though he's lost none of his finery – or when he's
standing among millions of friendly people and
he's frightened, though no one is undressing
him or doing him any harm? Is he in his right
mind then?

ION: Lord no, Socrates. Not at all, to tell the
truth.

SOCRATES: And you know that you have the
same effects on most of your spectators too,
don't you?

ION: I know very well that we do. I look down e
at them every time from up on the rostrum, and
they're crying and looking terrified, and as the
stories are told they are filled with amazement.
You see I must keep my wits and pay close
attention to them: if I start them crying, *I* will
laugh as I take their money, but if *they* laugh, I
shall cry at having lost money.

SOCRATES: And you know that this spectator
is the last of the rings, don't you – the ones that
I said take their power from each other by virtue
of the Heraclean stone [the magnet]? The middle 536
ring is you, the rhapsode or actor, and the first
one is the poet himself. The god pulls people's

souls through all these wherever he wants, looping the power down from one to another. And just as if it hung from that stone, there's an enormous chain of choral dancers and dance teachers and assistant teachers hanging off to the sides of the rings that are suspended from the Muse. One
b poet is attached to one Muse, another to another (we say he is "possessed," and that's near enough, for he is *held*). From these first rings, from the poets, *they* are attached in their turn and inspired, some from one poet, some from another: some from Orpheus, some from Musaeus, and many are possessed and held from Homer. You are one of *them*, Ion, and you are possessed from Homer. And when anyone sings the work of another poet, you're asleep and you're lost about what to say;
c but when any song of that poet is sounded, you are immediately awake, your soul is dancing, and you have plenty to say. You see it's not because you're a master of knowledge about Homer that you can say what you say, but because of a divine gift, because you are possessed. That's how it is with the Corybantes, who have sharp ears only for the specific song that belongs to whatever god possesses them; they have plenty of words and movements to go with *that* song; but they are quite lost if the music is different. That's how it is with you, Ion: when anyone mentions Homer,
d you have plenty to say, but if he mentions the others you are lost; and the explanation of this, for which you ask me – why it is that you have plenty to say about Homer but not about the others – is that it's not mastering the subject, but a divine gift, that makes you a wonderful singer of Homer's praises.

ION: You're a good speaker, Socrates. Still, I would be amazed if you could speak well enough to convince me that I am possessed or crazed when I praise Homer. I don't believe you'd think so if you heard me speaking on Homer.

e SOCRATES: And I really do want to hear you, but not before you answer me this: on which of Homer's subjects do you speak well? I don't suppose you speak well on *all* of them.

ION: I do, Socrates, believe me, on every single one!

SOCRATES: Surely not on those subjects you happen to know nothing about, even if Homer does speak of them.

ION: And these subjects Homer speaks of, but I don't know about – what are they?

SOCRATES: But doesn't Homer speak about 537
professional subjects in many places, and say a great deal? Chariot driving, for example, I'll show you, if I can remember the lines.

ION: No, I'll recite them. I *do* remember.

SOCRATES: Then tell me what Nestor says to his son Antilochus, when he advises him to take care at the turning post in the horse race they held for Patroclus' funeral.

ION: "Lean," he says,

Lean yourself over on the smooth-planed chariot
Just to the left of the pair. Then the horse on the right – b
Goad him, shout him on, easing the reins with your hands.
At the post let your horse on the left stick tight to the turn
So you seem to come right to the edge, with the hub
Of your welded wheel. But escape cropping the stone . . .[4]

SOCRATES: That's enough. Who would know c
better, Ion, whether Homer speaks correctly or not in these particular verses – a doctor or a charioteer?

ION: A charioteer, of course.

SOCRATES: Is that because he is a master of that profession, or for some other reason?

ION: No. It's because he's a master of it.

SOCRATES: Then to each profession a god has granted the ability to know a certain function. I mean, the things navigation teaches us – we won't learn them from medicine as well, will we?

ION: Of course not.

SOCRATES: And the things medicine teaches us we won't learn from architecture.

ION: Of course not. d

SOCRATES: And so it is for every other profession: what we learn by mastering one profession we won't learn by mastering another, right? But first, answer me this. Do you agree that there are different professions – that one is different from another?

ION: Yes.

SOCRATES: And is this how you determine which ones are different? When *I* find that the knowledge [involved in one case] deals with
different subjects from the knowledge [in another e
case], then I claim that one is a different profession from the other. Is that what you do?

ION: Yes.

SOCRATES: I mean if there is some knowledge of the same subjects, then why should we say there are two different professions? – Especially when each of them would allow us to know the same subjects! Take these fingers: I know there are five of them, and you know the same thing about them that I do. Now suppose I asked you whether it's the same profession – arithmetic – that teaches you and me the same things, or whether it's two different ones. Of course you'd say it's the same one.

ION: Yes.

538 SOCRATES: Then tell me now what I was going to ask you earlier. Do you think it's the same way for every profession – the same profession must teach the same subjects, and a different profession, if it *is* different, must teach not the same subjects, but different ones?

ION: That's how I think it is, Socrates.

SOCRATES: Then a person who has not mastered a given profession will not be able to be a good judge of the things which belong to that profession, whether they are things said or things done.

b ION: That's true.

SOCRATES: Then who will know better whether or not Homer speaks beautifully and well in the lines you quoted? You, or a charioteer?

ION: A charioteer.

SOCRATES: That's because you're a rhapsode, of course, and not a charioteer.

ION: Yes.

SOCRATES: And the rhapsode's profession is different from the charioteer's.

ION: Yes.

SOCRATES: If it's different, then its knowledge is of different subjects also.

ION: Yes.

c SOCRATES: Then what about the time Homer tells how Hecamede, Nestor's woman, gave barley-medicine to Machaon to drink? He says something like this –

> *Over wine of Pramnos she grated goat's milk cheese*
> *With a brazen grater. . . . And onion relish for the drink . . .*[5]

Is Homer right or not: would a fine diagnosis here come from a doctor's profession or a rhapsode's?

ION: A doctor's.

SOCRATES: And what about the time Homer says:

> *Leaden she plunged to the floor of the sea like a weight* d
> *That is fixed to a field cow's horn. Given to the hunt*
> *It goes among ravenous fish, carrying death.*[6]

Should we say it's for a fisherman's profession or a rhapsode's to tell whether or not he describes this beautifully and well?

ION: That's obvious, Socrates. It's for a fisherman's.

SOCRATES: All right, look. Suppose you were e
the one asking questions, and you asked me, "Socrates, since you're finding out which passages belong to each of the professions Homer treats – which are the passages that each profession should judge – come tell me this: which are the passages that belong to a diviner and to divination, passages he should be able to judge as to whether they're well or badly composed?" Look how easily I can give you a true answer. Often, in the *Odyssey*, he says things like what Theoclymenus says – the prophet of the sons of Melampus:

> *Are you mad? What evil is this that's upon you? Night* 539
> *Has enshrouded your hands, your faces, and down to your knees.*
> *Wailing spreads like fire, tears wash your cheeks.*
> *Ghosts fill the dooryard, ghosts fill the hall, they rush*
> *To the black gate of hell, they drop below darkness. Sunlight*
> *Has died from a sky run over with evil mist.*[7] b

And often in the *Iliad*, as in the battle at the wall. There he says:

> *There came to them a bird as they hungered to cross over.*
> *An eagle, a high-flier, circled the army's left*
> *With a blood-red serpent carried in its talons, a monster,* c
> *Alive, still breathing, it has not yet forgotten its warlust,*
> *For it struck its captor on the breast, by the neck;*
> *It was writhing back, but the eagle shot it groundwards*

In agony of pain, and dropped it in the midst of the throng,
d *Then itself, with a scream, soared on a breath of the wind.*[8]

I shall say that these passages and those like them belong to a diviner. They are for him to examine and judge.

ION: That's a true answer, Socrates.

SOCRATES: Well, *your* answers are true, too, Ion. Now *you* tell me – just as I picked out for you, from the *Odyssey* and the *Iliad*, passages that
e belong to a diviner and ones that belong to a doctor and ones that belong to a fisherman – in the same way, Ion, since you have more experience with Homer's work than I do, you pick out for me the passages that belong to the rhapsode and to his profession, the passages a rhapsode should be able to examine and to judge better than anyone else.

ION: My answer, Socrates, is "all of them."

SOCRATES: That's not *your* answer, Ion. Not "all of them." Or are you really so forgetful? But no, it would not befit a *rhapsode* to be forgetful.

540 ION: What do you think I'm forgetting?

SOCRATES: Don't you remember you said that a rhapsode's profession is different from a charioteer's?

ION: I remember.

SOCRATES: And didn't you agree that because they are different they will know different subjects?

ION: Yes.

SOCRATES: So a rhapsode's profession, on *your* view, will not know everything, and neither will a rhapsode.

ION: But things like that are exceptions, Socrates.

b SOCRATES: By "things like that" you mean that almost all the subjects of the other professions are exceptions, don't you? But then what sort of thing *will* a rhapsode know, if not everything?

ION: My opinion, anyhow, is that he'll know what it's fitting for a man or a woman to say – or for a slave or a freeman, or for a follower or a leader.

SOCRATES: So – what should a leader say when he's at sea and his ship is hit by a storm – do you mean a rhapsode will know better than a navigator?

ION: No, no. A navigator will know *that*.

SOCRATES: And when he is in charge of a sick c
man, what should a leader say – will a rhapsode know better than a doctor?

ION: Not that, either.

SOCRATES: But he *will* know what a slave should say. Is that what you mean?

ION: Yes.

SOCRATES: For example, what should a slave who's a cowherd say to calm down his cattle when they're going wild – will a rhapsode know what a cowherd does not?

ION: Certainly not.

SOCRATES: And what a woman who spins
yarn should say about working with wool? d

ION: No.

SOCRATES: And what a man should say, if he's a general, to encourage his troops?

ION: Yes! That's the sort of thing a rhapsode will know.

SOCRATES: What? Is a rhapsode's profession the same as a general's?

ION: Well, *I* certainly would know what a general should say.

SOCRATES: Perhaps that's because you're also a general by profession, Ion. I mean, if you were somehow both a horseman and a
cithara-player at the same time, you would e
know good riders from bad. But suppose I asked you: "Which profession teaches you good horse-manship – the one that makes you a horseman, or the one that makes you a cithara-player?"

ION: The horseman, I'd say.

SOCRATES: Then if you also knew good cithara-players from bad, the profession that taught you *that* would be the one which made you a cithara-player, not the one that made you a horseman. Wouldn't you agree?

ION: Yes.

SOCRATES: Now, since you know the business of a general, do you know this by being a general or by being a good rhapsode?

ION: I don't think there's any difference.

SOCRATES: What? Are you saying there's no 541
difference? On your view is there one profession for rhapsodes and generals, or two?

ION: One, I think.

SOCRATES: So anyone who is a good rhapsode turns out to be a good general too.

ION: Certainly, Socrates.

SOCRATES: It also follows that anyone who turns out to be a good general is a good rhapsode too.

ION: No. This time I don't agree.

b SOCRATES: But you do agree to this: anyone who is a good rhapsode is a good general too.

ION: I quite agree.

SOCRATES: And aren't you the best rhapsode in Greece?

ION: By far, Socrates.

SOCRATES: Are you also a general, Ion? Are you the best in Greece?

ION: Certainly, Socrates. That, too, I learned from Homer's poetry.

SOCRATES: Then why in heaven's name, Ion, when you're both the best general *and* the best rhapsode in Greece, do you go around the country
c giving rhapsodies but not commanding troops? Do you think Greece really needs a rhapsode who is crowned with a golden crown? And does not need a general?

ION: Socrates, *my* city is governed and commanded by you [by Athens]; we don't need a general. Besides, neither your city nor Sparta would choose me for a general. You think you're good enough for that yourselves.

SOCRATES: Ion, you're superb. Don't you know Apollodorus of Cyzicus?

ION: What does *he* do?

d SOCRATES: He's a foreigner who has often been chosen by Athens to be their general. And Phanosthenes of Andros and Heraclides of Clazomenae – they're also foreigners; they've demonstrated that they are worth noticing, and Athens appoints them to be generals or other sorts of officials. And do you think that *this* city, that makes such appointments, would not select Ion of Ephesus and honor him, if they
e thought he was worth noticing? Why? Aren't you people from Ephesus Athenians of long standing? And isn't Ephesus a city that is second to none?

But *you*, Ion, you're doing me wrong, if what you say is true that what enables you to praise Homer is knowledge or mastery of a profession. You assured me that you knew many lovely things about Homer, you promised to give a demonstration; but you're cheating me, you're a long way from giving a demonstration. You aren't even willing to tell me what it is that you're so wonderfully clever *about*, though I've been begging you for ages. Really, you're just like Proteus,[9] you twist up and down and take many different shapes, till finally you've escaped me 542
altogether by turning yourself into a general, so as to avoid proving how wonderfully wise you are about Homer.

If you're really a master of your subject, and if, as I said earlier, you're cheating me of the demonstration you promised about Homer, then you're doing me wrong. But if you're not a master of your subject, if you're possessed by a divine gift from Homer, so that you make many lovely speeches about the poet without knowing anything – as *I* said about you – then you're not doing me wrong. So choose, how do you want us to think of you – as a *man* who does wrong, or as someone *divine*?

ION: There's a great difference, Socrates. It's b
much lovelier to be thought divine.

SOCRATES: Then *that* is how we think of you, Ion, the lovelier way: it's as someone divine, and not as master of a profession, that you are a singer of Homer's praises.

Translator's Notes

1 The sons of Homer were a guild of rhapsodes who originally claimed to be descendants of Homer.

2 Natural magnets apparently came from Magnesia and Heracles in Caria in Asia Minor, and were called after those places.

3 Bacchus worshippers apparently danced themselves into a frenzy in which they found streams flowing with honey and milk (Euripides, *Bacchae* 708–11).

4 *Iliad* xxiii.335–40.

5 *Iliad* xi.639–40 with 630.

6 *Iliad* xxiv.80–2.

7 *Odyssey* xx.351–7; line 354 is omitted by Plato.

8 *Iliad* xii.200–7.

9 Proteus was a servant of Posidon. He had the power to take whatever shape he wanted in order to avoid answering questions (*Odyssey* iv.385ff.).

3

The Republic

Plato

Book X

595 Well, I continued, I must say that, while I am led by a variety of considerations to believe that we were unquestionably right in our plans for organizing the city, I am most convinced when I think of our regulations concerning poetry.

What was the nature of them?

They were to the effect that we ought on no account to admit that branch of poetry which is imitative; and now that each of the forms of the soul have been each separately defined, the conviction that such poetry more than anything else
b must not be admitted is to my mind even clearer than it was before.

Explain what you mean.

I am quite sure that you will not denounce me to the tragedians, and the whole company of imitative poets, and therefore I do not mind saying to you, that all imitative poetry would seem to maim the reasoning of those hearers who do not possess an antidote in the knowledge of its real nature.

And what is the point of your remarks?

I must speak my mind, although I confess I am inhibited by a kind of shame and friendship for Homer, which I have had since I was a child.
For of all those beautiful tragic poets he seems c
to have been the first teacher and guide. But it would be wrong to honor a man at the expense of truth, and therefore I must, as I said, speak out.

By all means do so.

Listen then, or rather reply.

Ask your questions.

Can you give me any account of the nature of imitation generally? For I assure you I am at a loss myself to understand what it wants to be.

And so you expect me to understand it?

It would not be extraordinary if you did; for it 596
often happens that shortsighted people see things sooner than the sharp-sighted.

True, but in your presence, if I did make a discovery, I would not be eager to speak. So look for yourself.

Well, is it your wish that we should pursue our usual course in the outset of our investigation? We have, I believe, been in the habit of positing in each instance some one Form, which includes the numerous particular things to which we apply the same name. Do you understand, or not?

I do understand.

Then let us, on the present occasion, take any one of those numerous things that suits your
pleasure. For example, if this instance suits you, b
there are, of course, many couches and many tables.

Certainly.

Plato, *The Republic*, ed. Andrea Tschemplik, trans. John Llewelyn Davies and David James Vaughn (Lanham, MD: Rowman & Littlefield, 2006), pp. 352–69.

But of ideas in connection with these articles, there are, I believe, only two, one the idea of a couch, and one that of a table.

Yes.

Have we not also been accustomed to say that the craftsman of each of these articles is looking at the idea while he is constructing the couches or the tables which we use, or whatever it may be? For, of course, no craftsman constructs the idea itself, because that is impossible.

Certainly it is.

But how will you describe the following craftsman?

c To whom do you allude?

I refer to the one who makes all the things that each of the manual artisans makes.

You are talking of a marvelously clever man.

Wait a little, and you will have better reasons for saying so. Besides being able to make all manufactured articles, the same artisan makes everything that grows out of the ground, and creates all living things, himself among others; and, in addition to this, heaven and earth and the gods and all the heavenly bodies and everything in Hades under the earth is his workmanship.

d What an extraordinarily adept person you are describing.

You are incredulous, are you? Then tell me: Do you think that the existence of such a craftsman is a complete impossibility? Or do you believe that in one way there could, and in another way there could not, be a maker of such a variety of things? Do you not perceive that, in a way, even you yourself could make this multiplicity of things?

And what is this way? he asked.

Far from being difficult, I replied, it is something that can be crafted quickly and in many places. Perhaps the quickest way of all would be
e to take a mirror, and turn it round in every direction. You will not be long in making the sun and the heavenly bodies, nor in making the earth, nor in making yourself, and every other living thing, and all inanimate objects, and plants, and everything that we mentioned just now.

Yes, we can produce so many appearances, but assuredly not truly being things.

Right, and your observation is very much to the point. Now, in my opinion, the painter also belongs to this class of craftsmen. Does he not?

Certainly he does.

But I suppose you will say that all his creations are not true. And yet the painter too, in a way, makes a couch. Or am I wrong?

Yes, the painter too constructs a couch in appearance.

But what of the maker of couches? Did you not 597
say a minute ago, that he did not make the form, which, according to what we have said, is the real couch, but only a particular couch?

Yes, I did say that.

Consequently, if he does not make what really is, must we not say that he does not make what is, but only something like what is, but still unreal? And if anyone were to describe the work of the couch-maker, or of any other artisan, as perfectly real, his account of the matter would be, in all probability, untrue, would it not?

Yes, in the opinion of those who are versed in such discussions as these.

Then let us not be at all surprised at finding that this thing is obscure when contrasted with the truth.

True. b

Should you like us to employ these illustrations in our inquiry into who this imitator is?

If you please, he replied.

Well, here we have three sorts of couches, of which one exists in nature, and this we shall attribute, if I am not mistaken, to the workmanship of god. If not, to whom can we attribute it?

We can attribute it to none other, I think.

The second is made by the carpenter.

Yes.

And the third is the production of the painter. Is it not?

So be it.

Thus we have three forms of couches and three overseers of their manufacture – the painter, the carpenter, and god.

Yes, three.

Now whether it was that god did not choose to c
make more than one couch, or that by necessity he was precluded from making more than one in nature, he has at any rate made only one, which is really in itself a couch. But two, or more than two, such couches have not been created by the god, and never will be.

How so?

Because, if the god had made only two, a single couch would again have made its appearance, whose form would enter into the other two in their turn; and *this* would be that which is a couch, and not the two.

You are right.

d Knowing this, I should suppose, and wishing to be the real maker of the really existing couch, and not a certain indefinite couch-maker, god created a single such couch in nature.

It seems so.

Then are you in favor of our addressing him as the natural maker of this thing or anything else of the sort?

Yes, he replied, it is the just thing to do, seeing that he has made this and everything else by nature.

And what of the carpenter? Is he not the craftsman of the couch?

Yes.

And is the painter the craftsman and maker of this same article?

Certainly not.

Then, by your account, what is he with reference to a couch?

e In my opinion he might most appropriately be styled the imitator of that of which the other two are craftsmen.

Well, then, do you call the creator of that which is twice removed from the natural thing an imitator?

Yes, exactly so.

Hence, since the tragedian is an imitator, we may predicate of him likewise, that he, along with all the other imitators, is twice removed from the king and from truth.

So it would appear.

Then we agree about the imitator. But answer
598 me one question about the painter. Do you
suppose that a painter attempts to imitate the thing itself in nature, or the productions of the craftsman?

The latter, he replied.

As they really are, or as they appear? Define this further.

What do you mean?

I mean this: When you look at a couch sideways, or in front, or from any other position whatever, does it alter its identity at all, or does it continue really the same, though it appears changed? And so of everything else?

The latter is the true account; it appears different, but it is not really changed.

Now this is the point which I wish you to con- b
sider. To which of the two is painting, in every instance, directed? Does it study to imitate the real nature of real objects? Or the apparent nature of appearances? In other words, is it an imitation of a phantasm, or of truth?

Of the former, he replied.

The imitative art, then, is, I conceive, far from the truth; and, apparently, it is enabled to bring about so much, because it only seizes upon an object in a small part of its extent, and that small part is itself only an image. For example, we say the painter will paint us a shoemaker, a carpenter, or any other craftsman, without knowing anything about their trades; and, notwithstanding c
this ignorance on his part, let him be but a good painter, and if he paints a carpenter and displays his picture at a distance, he will deceive children and silly people by making them think that it really is a carpenter.

No doubt he will.

Be that as it may, I will tell you, my friend, what we should bear in mind in all such cases. Whenever a person tells us that he has fallen in with a man who is acquainted with all the crafts, and who sums up in his own person all the
knowledge possessed by other people singly, to a d
degree of accuracy which no one can surpass – we must reply to our informant, that he is a silly fellow, and has, apparently, fallen in with a juggler and mimic, whom he has been deceived into thinking omniscient, because he was himself incapable of discriminating between knowledge and lack of knowledge, and imitation.

That is most true.

And now, I continued, we must proceed to consider the case of tragedy and its leader, Homer, because we are told by some persons that dramatic poets are acquainted not only with all arts, e
but with all things human which bear upon virtue and vice, and also with things divine. For, to write well, a good poet must, they say, possess a knowledge of his subject, or else he could not write at all. Hence we must inquire, whether the poets, whom these people have encountered, are mere
imitators, who have so far imposed upon the 599
spectators, that, when they behold their performances, they fail to perceive that these productions are twice removed from reality, and easily made by a person unacquainted with the truth, because they are phantoms, and not realities – or

whether our informants are to this extent right, that good poets do really know the subjects about which they seem to the multitude to speak well.

Yes, we must by all means investigate the matter.

Well then, do you think, that, if a man could
produce both the original and the image, he
would give himself up seriously to the manufac-
b ture of the images, and make this the object of his
life as the best thing he has?

I do not think so.

On the contrary, if he were truly a knower of the things which he imitates, he would, I imagine, bestow far more industry upon deeds than upon the imitations, and he would endeavor to leave behind him a number of beautiful works, as memorials to himself, and would be more anxious to be praised in song than to be the singer of praise.

I agree with you, said he; for the honor and the benefit are much greater in the one case than in the other.

Now, on ordinary subjects, let us not demand
c an explanation from Homer or any other poet –
asking why, if any of the ancient or modern poets
were adepts in the healing art and not mere imitators of the physician's language, they have not
the credit of having offered any cures like Asclepius, or of having left behind them students of
the physician's art, as Asclepius left his descendants.[1] Nor let us question them concerning the
other arts, which may be dismissed from the
discussion. But concerning those grandest and
most beautiful subjects which Homer undertakes
to treat – such as war, and the conduct of cam-
paigns, and the governance of cities, and the
d education of human beings – it is surely just to
institute an inquiry, and ask the question, thus:
'My dear Homer, if you are not really twice
removed from the truth, with respect to virtue,
but only once removed, and the craftsman of
images, according to our definition of an imitator, and you are able to distinguish between the
pursuits which make men better or worse, in
private and in public, tell us, what city has a better
e constitution thanks to you, as Lacedaemon owes
hers to Lycurgus, and as many cities, great and
small, owe theirs to many other legislators? What
city attributes to you the benefits derived from a
good code of laws? Italy and Sicily recognize
Charondas in this capacity, and we Solon.[2] But
what city recognizes you?' Will he be able to
mention any?

I think not, replied Glaucon; at least we are not told any tale of the kind even by the very poets who claim him as their ancestor.

Well then, does the story go that any war in 600
Homer's time was brought to a happy termina-
tion under his command, or by his advice?

No, not one.

Well, is he said to have been, like Thales the Milesian and Anacharsis the Scythian, the author of a number of ingenious inventions, bearing upon the useful arts or other practical matters, which would convey the impression of his having been a man of wisdom in the active duties of life?[3]

No, certainly nothing of the sort is said of him.

Well then, is it reported of Homer that, though
not a public man, during his lifetime he nevertheless conducted, in private, the education of certain
disciples, who used to delight in his society, and b
handed down to posterity an Homeric way of
living, just as Pythagoras was in an extraordinary
degree beloved personally as a companion, not to
mention that his successors, who to this day call
their mode of living by his name, are considered
to a certain extent outstanding young men?[4]

No, Socrates, nothing of this kind is reported of
him either. Indeed, if the stories about Homer are
true, the education of his friend Creophylus might
possibly be thought even more ridiculous than his
name. For we are told that even Creophylus grossly
neglected Homer during his life-time. c

No doubt that is the story. But do you suppose,
Glaucon, that, if Homer had been really able to
educate men and make them better, from the fact
of being capable not merely of imitating but of
knowing the subjects in question, he could have
failed to attract to his side a multitude of companions, who would have loved and honored
him? For so long as Protagoras of Abdera, and
Prodicus of Ceos, and a host of other persons,[5]
can, as we see, persuade the men of their day by
private intercourse, that they will be incapable d
of managing their own house and city, unless
they oversee their education; and so long as the
wisdom, implied in this, insures to these teachers
an affection so unbounded, that they are almost
carried about on the shoulders of their companions. Is it conceivable that, if Homer and Hesiod

were really capable of improving men in virtue, they should have been allowed by their contemporaries to travel around reciting? Is it not more likely that they would have been hugged more
e closely than gold, and constrained to stay at home with their countrymen? Or else, if this favor were refused, that they would have been escorted in their wanderings, until their disciples had received a satisfactory education?

I believe you are unquestionably right, Socrates.

Then must we not conclude that all writers of poetry, beginning with Homer, imitate phantoms of every subject about which they write, including
601 virtue, and do not grasp the truth? In fact, as we were saying just now, will not the painter, without understanding anything about shoemaking, paint what will be taken for a shoemaker by those who are as ignorant on the subject as himself, and who judge by the colors and shapes?

Yes, certainly he will.

And just in the same way, I think, we shall assert that the poet colors things, using names and phrases, to represent the several professions, of which he only understands enough to be able to imitate them; so that if he writes in meter, rhythm, and harmony, about shoemaking, or about generalship, or about any subject whatever, people who are as ignorant as himself, and who judge merely whether it appears to be well-said,
b look upon his poetry as very excellent. So powerful is the charm which these things naturally possess. For I suppose you know what a poor appearance the works of poets present, when they have been stripped of their musical coloring, and are rehearsed in their proper nakedness. Doubtless you have observed the fact.

Yes, I have, he replied.

Does it not remind one of the withered appearance of the faces of those who in their youth were blooming without being beautiful, whenever their bloom deserted them?

Precisely so.

Now let me ask you to examine the following
c point. According to us, the maker of the image, that is, the imitator, understands only the appearance and not what is. Is it not so?

Yes.

Do not let us leave the matter half explained, but let us examine it satisfactorily.

Proceed.

A painter, by our account, will paint a bit and bridle, will he not?

Yes.

But the bridle and bit will be made by the saddler and the smith, will they not?

Certainly.

Then does the painter understand how the bit and bridle ought to be shaped? Or is it the case, that even the makers, the smith and the saddler, are ignorant on this subject, which is only understood by the rider, who knows how to use the things in question?

That is the true state of the case.

Then may we not assert that all things are in the same predicament?

What do you mean?

May we not assert that each single thing d
involves three particular arts – the province of the first being to use the thing, of the second to make it, of the third to imitate it?

Yes, we may.

Are not virtue, beauty, and correctness of every manufactured article, or living creature, or action, related to nothing else but the use for which each was made or naturally came to be?

True, they are.

Hence the man who makes use of a thing must necessarily be most experienced with it, and must in the course of using it keep the maker informed as to the success or failure of its performances. For example, a flute player, no doubt, informs a
flute maker about the flutes which he employs in e
the exercise of his art, and will direct him how they ought to be made, and the flute maker will submit to his directions.

Of course.

The one has a thorough acquaintance with good and bad flutes, and conveys information, upon which the other relies, and will make them accordingly, is not that the case?

Yes, it is.

Hence, the maker of the instrument will entertain a correct belief with regard to its beauty or badness, by communicating with the person who knows the subject, and by being compelled to listen to his instructions; whereas the user of the
same instrument will possess knowledge on these 602
points.

Exactly so.

But which of the two will the imitator possess? Will he, by actually using the things he describes, know whether his productions are beautiful and right, or not? Or will he entertain correct opinion, on account of being compelled to be with the one who knows and submit to his directions as to the style in which he ought to work?

Neither.

That is to say, the imitator will neither know, nor entertain correct opinions with reference to the beauty or badness of the things which he imitates.

It seems not.

The imitator in his making will be charmingly wise about that which he treats.

Not exactly.

b However, he will go on imitating, notwithstanding his being thoroughly ignorant as to the way in which a thing is good or bad. Apparently he will copy beauty as it appears to the many who do not know.

Yes, what else can he copy?

Then, to all appearance, we are pretty well agreed so far as this, that the imitator knows nothing of importance about the things which he imitates, and that therefore imitation is a kind of play and not a serious business; and that those who cultivate tragic poetry in iambic or in epic verse are without exception in the highest possible degree imitators.

Exactly so.

c Then, in the name of Zeus, I continued, does not this process of imitation deal with something twice removed from the truth? Answer me.

It does.

But how do you describe that part of human nature on which it exercises the power which it possesses?

Explain what part you mean.

I will. Objects of the same size, I believe, appear to us as not being equal, depending on their distance from our eyes.

They do.

And things which look bent under water appear straight when taken out of the water; and the same objects look either concave or convex, owing to mistakes of another kind about colors to which the eye is liable; and clearly there exists
d in the soul a kind of utter confusion of this sort. And it is just this natural condition of ours which is taken advantage of by the art of shadow-painting, as well as by puppetry and the numerous other tricks of the same sort, with every species of witchcraft.

True.

And have not the processes of measuring and counting and weighing made their appearance most agreeably to aid us in dispelling these cases, so that we are not ruled by things as they appear to us greater or smaller, or more or heavier, but by that which has been calculated, or measured, or weighed?

Undoubtedly.

And surely this must be the work of the ratio- e
nal part in the soul.

Yes, certainly it must.

But when this part, after frequent measuring, informs us that one thing is greater or less than, or equal to, another thing, it is contradicted at the same moment by the appearance which the same things present.

Yes.

Did we not assert the impossibility of entertaining, at the same time and with the same part of us, contradictory opinions with reference to the same things?

Yes, and we were right in asserting it.

Then that part of the soul whose opinion runs 603
counter to the measurements cannot be identical with that part which agrees with them.

Certainly not.

But surely that part, which trusts measurement and calculation, must be the best part of the soul.

Doubtless it must.

Hence, that which contradicts this part must be one of the inferior elements of our nature.

Necessarily so.

This was the point which I wished to settle between us, when I said that painting, or to speak generally, the whole art of imitation, is busy about a work which is far removed from truth; and that it associates moreover with that part of
us, which is far removed from prudence, and is b
its mistress and friend for no healthy or true purpose.

Unquestionably.

Thus the art of imitation is the inferior mistress of an inferior friend, and the parent of an inferior progeny.

So it seems.

Does this apply only to the imitation which addresses itself to the eye? Or may we extend it to that which addresses itself to the ear, which I believe we name poetry?

Probably we may.

Well, I proceeded, do not let us rely only on the probable evidence derived from painting, but let us direct further inquiries into that very part
c of the reasoning, with which the imitative art of poetry associates, and let us examine whether it is inferior or serious.

Yes, we ought to do so.

Let us state the case thus. The imitative art, if we are right, imitates men who are engaged in voluntary or involuntary actions, and who, according to the result of their actions, think themselves well off or the reverse; and who, in the midst of all these circumstances, are conscious either of joy or of grief. Is there anything to be added to this?

No, nothing.

Now, in this variety of circumstances, is a
d human being of one mind? Or is he at feud and war with himself in his actions, just as he was at feud and entertained contradictory opinions at the same moment about the same subjects, where his sight was concerned? But I remember, that on this subject we need not come to an agreement now; for we settled all this satisfactorily in the past conversations, in which we admitted that our soul is filled with a myriad of these simultaneous contradictions.

We were right.

Yes, we were, I continued. But there was some-
e thing then omitted, which I think it is now necessary to discuss.

What was that?

We said, I believe, at the time, that a decent man, if he meet with a misfortune, like that of losing a son or anything else that he values most highly, will bear it more easily than other men.

Certainly he will.

But now, let us further examine, whether he will feel no sorrow at all, or whether, this being impossible, he will observe some kind of moderation in grief.

The latter is the truer account.

604 Now let me ask you a question about him. Do you think he will fight against his grief and resist it most, when the eyes of his peers are upon him, or when he is alone by himself in solitude?

He will do so much more, I imagine, when he is observed.

But when he is alone, I think, he will venture to say much, which he would be ashamed to say in the hearing of another person, and he will do much, which he would not like anyone to see him doing.

Just so.

Now that which urges him to resist his grief is
reason and law, is it not? And that which prompts b
him to indulge in the pain is the suffering itself?

True.

But when there are two opposite attractions in a man at the same time in reference to the same thing, he must, as we said, be a double man.

Of course he must.

Is not one part of him prepared to obey the directions of law?

What are they?

The law, I believe, tells him that it is best to keep as quiet as possible in misfortunes, and not to become irritated, because we cannot estimate the amount of good and bad contained in these sorts of things, and at the same time taking it
badly does not help us forwards; and because c
none of the human things is to be valued very earnestly while grief stands in the way of that behavior which we ought to adopt in our troubles without a moment's delay.

To what do you refer?

It is our duty to think over the event that has taken place, and to arrange our affairs to take the way which reason pronounces best, like the player who moves his pieces according to the dice which he has thrown. And, instead of hugging the wounded part, like children after a fall who continue to cry, we ought ever to habituate the soul
to turn with all speed to the task of healing and d
righting the fallen and diseased part, thus putting a stop to lamentation by the aid of medicine.

Certainly that would be the best way to meet what chance brings.

Then the better part of us, we say, consents to be led by such calculation.

Obviously it does.

On the other hand, shall we not maintain, that the part which prompts us to think of, and grieve over, our suffering, and which has an insatiable appetite for lamentations, is irrational and idle, and the friend of cowardice?

Certainly we shall.

This being the case, the irritable character fur- e
nishes a great variety of materials for imitation;

whereas the prudent and calm character is so constantly uniform and unchanging, that it is not easily imitated; and, when imitated, it is not easily understood, especially by a general gathering of all sorts of persons, collected in a theater. For these people witness the imitation of an affection, which, if I am not mistaken, is far from being their own.

605 It is, unquestionably.

Hence it is clear, that the imitative poet has, in the nature of things, nothing to do with any such part of the soul, and that his wisdom is not set on pleasing it, if he intends to gain a good reputation with the many. But his business is with the irritable and changeable character, because it is easily imitated.

That is clear.

Then we shall be justified now in laying hands on him, and taking him as a counterpart to the painter. For he resembles the painter in produc-
b ing things that are inferior when tried by the standard of truth; and he resembles him also in this, that he holds intercourse with a part of the soul which is like himself, and not with the best part. And, this being the case, we shall henceforth be justified in refusing to admit him into a city that is going to be well-governed, because he excites and feeds and strengthens this worthless part of the soul, and thus destroys the rational part – like a person who should strengthen the hands of the wicked members of a city and give over to them supreme power, and at the same time ruin the better sort. In the same way we shall assert that the imitative poet implants a bad constitution in
c the soul of each individual, by gratifying that unthinking part which, instead of distinguishing the greater from the less, regards the same things now as great, and now as small, and manufactures fantastic phantoms that are very widely removed from truth.

Exactly so.

But still, I continued, we have not yet brought forward the heaviest charge in our indictment. For that poetry should be able to damage decent men, except for a few, is, I conceive, most dreadful.

Undoubtedly it is, if it really does that.

Listen, and then judge. The best of us, I believe – while listening to the passages in which Homer or one of the tragedians represents some suffer-
d ing hero, who spins out a long speech in his lamentations, or perhaps some persons engaged in beating their breasts and bemoaning themselves in song – are delighted, as you know, and give ourselves up to be led along, and sympathize with the sufferer, and earnestly praise as a good poet the writer who can bring us as much as possible into such a state.

I know it, of course.

But, on the other hand, whenever sorrow comes home to one of us, you are aware that we pride ourselves upon the opposite conduct – that
is, we glory in being able to endure with calmness, e
because, in our estimation, this behavior is manly, while the other which we praised before is womanish.

I am aware of it, he said.

Then is this praise rightly bestowed? I mean, is it right to feel pleasure and bestow praise, instead of being disgusted, when one sees a man behaving as one would scorn and blush to behave oneself?

No, by Zeus, he replied, this does not seem reasonable.

It does not, said I, if you look at it in another 606
light.

In what light?

If you consider that the part which is forcibly held down when those misfortunes of our own occur, and which has hungered for the privilege of weeping and bewailing itself fully and without holding back, because it is its nature to desire this satisfaction – is the very part that is fed to satiety by the poets, and delights in those descriptions. Meanwhile, that part of us which is naturally the best, from not having been sufficiently trained by reason and by habit, relaxes in its watch over this mournful part, because it is surveying the afflictions of others, and because it is not shameful for
it to praise and pity another man, who professes b
to be good, though his grief is ill-timed. In fact, it looks upon the pleasure to be as much gained, and will not allow itself to be deprived of it by a contempt for the whole poem. For it is given, I think, only to a few to figure out that the conduct of other people must necessarily influence our own, and that it is no easy matter, after feeding the strength of the principle of pity upon the sufferings of others, to keep it under restraint when we suffer ourselves.

That is most true. c

Does not the same reasoning apply also to the laughing part, to jokes which you would yourself be ashamed to make, but which in comic imitation, or even in private life, you will be very well pleased to hear, and will not hate as wicked – acting in this just as you acted in your pity? For on such occasions you give the rein to that element, which, in your own case, you check by reason, when it wants to create laughter, because you dread the reputation of a buffoon; and, thus letting it have its own way, you have often, in your own conduct, been unconsciously seduced into adopting the character of a comic poet.

Very true.

d And in the case of sex and spiritedness, and all desire, pains, and pleasure in the soul, which we hold to accompany all our actions, is it not true that poetic imitation works upon us similar effects? For it waters and cherishes these emotions, which ought to wither with drought, and constitutes them our rulers, when they ought to be our subjects, if we wish to become better and happier instead of worse and more miserable.

I cannot deny it.

e Then, Glaucon, whenever you meet with those who praise Homer, who tell you that he has educated Greece, and that he deserves to be taken up and studied with an eye to the administration and guidance of human affairs, and that a man ought
607 to regulate his whole life by this poet's directions, it will be your duty to greet them affectionately as excellent men doing their best, and to admit that Homer is first and greatest among tragic poets; but you must not forget that, with the single exception of hymns to the gods and panegyrics on the good, no poetry ought to be admitted into a city. For if you determine to admit the highly-seasoned Muse of lyric or epic poetry, pleasure and pain will have sovereign power in your city, instead of law and reason, which is always thought in common to be best.

That is perfectly true.

b Having returned to the subject of poetry, I continued, let this defense serve to show the reasonableness of our former judgment in banishing from our state a pursuit which has the tendencies we have described. For, in doing so, we were yielding to reason. But that poetry may not charge us with being, to a certain extent, harsh and rough, let us address her and say, that there is an ancient quarrel between philosophy and poetry, for those lines.

That yelping bitch, which at its master barks,

and,

Mighty he is in the vain talk of fools,

and, c

The lordly mob of god-wise folks,

and,

Poor are those subtle thinkers,

and a thousand others, are marks of an old antagonism between the two. But nevertheless let us admit, that, if the poetry whose end is to please, and imitation, can give any reasons to show that they ought to exist in a well-ordered city, we for our part will gladly welcome them home again. For we are conscious of being enchanted by such poetry ourselves, though it would not be holy to
betray what seems to us the cause of truth. Am I d
not right in supposing that you, my friend, are enchanted by poetry, especially when you contemplate it under Homer's guidance?

Yes, I am, powerfully.

Then is it not just for poetry to return from exile, when she has made her defense either in lyrical or in some other meter?

Certainly it is.

And I suppose we shall also allow those of her patrons who are lovers of poetry without being poets, to advocate her cause in prose by maintaining that poetry is not only pleasurable, but also beneficial in its bearings upon governments,
and upon human life. And we shall listen e
favorably, for we shall be gainers, I presume, if poetry can be proved to be beneficial as well as pleasurable.

Undoubtedly we shall be gainers.

But if not, why in that case, my dear friend, we must take a lesson from those persons who, after falling in love with someone, deny their passion at any cost, if they think it injurious. For though the love of such poetry which has grown up in us
under the training of our beautiful constitution, 608
will make us cordially desirous that it should appear the best and the truest. Still, so long as it is unable to make good its defense we shall protect ourselves, as we listen, by inwardly repeating, like

a charm, the argument which we have just brought
to a close, and we shall be on our guard against
falling anew into that childish passion, which
most people acknowledge. At any rate, we have
learned that we must not make a serious pursuit
of such poetry, in the belief that it grasps truth.
On the contrary, the listener, apprehending
b danger to the constitution within him, is bound
to be on his guard against it, and to adopt the
opinion which we have expressed on the subject.

I thoroughly agree with you.

Indeed, my dear Glaucon, the choice between becoming a good or a bad man involves a great stake – yes, a greater stake than people suppose. Therefore it is wrong to be heedless of justice and the rest of virtue, under the excitement of honor, or wealth, or power, or even of poetry.

I agree with you, he replied, at the conclusion of our inquiry, and I fancy every one else will do the same.

Translator's Notes

1 Asclepius is the traditional god of medicine or founder of medicine and medical training.

2 Lycurgus was the traditional lawgiver of Sparta (ca. 775 BCE); Charondas (sixth century) of Catana and other Sicilian cities. Solon's constitution for Athens was agreed to in 594 BCE.

3 Thales and Anacharsis were philosophers of the early sixth century BCE.

4 Pythagoras (ca. 582–500 BCE) was a mathematician-philosopher and founder of the Pythagorean school and movement.

5 Protagoras and Prodicus were both fifth-century sophists, traveling teachers around the Greek cities, including Athens.

4

Symposium

Plato

201d SOCRATES: Now I'll let you go. I shall try to go through for you the speech about Love I once heard from a woman of Mantinea, Diotima – a woman who was wise about many things besides this: once she even put off the plague for ten years by telling the Athenians what sacrifices to make. She is the one who taught me the art of love, and I shall go through her speech as best I can on my own, using what Agathon and I have agreed to as a basis.

Following your lead, Agathon, one should first
e describe who Love is and what he is like, and afterwards describe his works – I think it will be easiest for me to proceed the way Diotima did and tell you how she questioned me.

You see, I had told her almost the same things Agathon told me just now: that Love is a great god and that he belongs to beautiful things. And she used the very same arguments against me that I used against Agathon; she showed how, according to my very own speech, Love is neither beautiful nor good.

So I said, "What do you mean, Diotima? Is Love ugly, then, and bad?"

202 But she said, "Watch your tongue! Do you really think that, if a thing is not beautiful, it has to be ugly?"

"I certainly do."

"And if a thing's not wise, it's ignorant? Or haven't you found out yet that there's something in between wisdom and ignorance?"

"What's that?"

"It's judging things correctly without being able to give a reason. Surely you see that this is not the same as knowing – for how could knowledge be unreasoning? And it's not ignorance either – for how could what hits the truth be ignorance? Correct judgment, of course, has this character: it is *in between* understanding and ignorance."

"True," said I, "as you say." b

"Then don't force whatever is not beautiful to be ugly, or whatever is not good to be bad. It's the same with Love: when you agree he is neither good nor beautiful, you need not think he is ugly and bad; he could be something in between," she said.

"Yet everyone agrees he's a great god," I said.

"Only those who don't know?" she said. "Is that how you mean 'everyone'? Or do you include those who do know?"

"Oh, everyone together."

And she laughed. "Socrates, how could those c
who say that he's not a god at all agree that he's a great god?"

"Who says that?" I asked.

"You, for one," she said, "and I for another."

"How can you say this!" I exclaimed.

"That's easy," said she. "Tell me, wouldn't you say that all gods are beautiful and happy? Surely you'd never say a god is not beautiful or happy?"

"Zeus! Not I," I said.

"Well, by calling anyone 'happy,' don't you mean they possess good and beautiful things?"

d "Certainly."

"What about Love? You agreed he needs good and beautiful things, and that's why he desires them – because he needs them."

"I certainly did."

"Then how could he be a god if he has no share in good and beautiful things?"

"There's no way he could, apparently."

"Now do you see? You don't believe Love is a god either!"

"Then, what could Love be?" I asked. "A mortal?"

"Certainly not."

"Then, what is he?"

"He's like what we mentioned before," she said. "He is in between mortal and immortal."

"What do you mean, Diotima?"

e "He's a great spirit, Socrates. Everything spiritual, you see, is in between god and mortal."

"What is their function?" I asked.

"They are messengers who shuttle back and forth between the two, conveying prayer and sacrifice from men to gods, while to men they bring commands from the gods and gifts in return for sacrifices. Being in the middle of the two, they round out the whole and bind fast the all to all.
203 Through them all divination passes, through them the art of priests in sacrifice and ritual, in enchantment, prophecy, and sorcery. Gods do not mix with men; they mingle and converse with us through spirits instead, whether we are awake or asleep. He who is wise in any of these ways is a man of the spirit, but he who is wise in any other way, in a profession or any manual work, is merely a mechanic. These spirits are many and various, then, and one of them is Love."

b "Who are his father and mother?" I asked.

"That's rather a long story," she said. "I'll tell it to you, all the same."

"When Aphrodite was born, the gods held a celebration. Poros, the son of Metis, was there among them.[1] When they had feasted, Penia came begging, as poverty does when there's a party, and stayed by the gates. Now Poros got drunk on nectar (there was no wine yet, you see) and, feeling drowsy, went into the garden of
c Zeus, where he fell asleep. Then Penia schemed up a plan to relieve her lack of resources: she would get a child from Poros. So she lay beside him and got pregnant with Love. That is why Love was born to follow Aphrodite and serve her: because he was conceived on the day of her birth. And that's why he is also by nature a lover of beauty, because Aphrodite herself is especially beautiful.

"As the son of Poros and Penia, his lot in life is set to be like theirs. In the first place, he is always poor, and he's far from being delicate and beautiful (as ordinary people think he is); instead, d
he is tough and shriveled and shoeless and homeless, always lying on the dirt without a bed, sleeping at people's doorsteps and in roadsides under the sky, having his mother's nature, always living with Need. But on his father's side he is a schemer after the beautiful and the good; he is brave, impetuous, and intense, an awesome hunter, always weaving snares, resourceful in his pursuit of intelligence, a lover of wisdom[2] through all his life, a genius with enchantments, potions, and clever pleadings.

"He is by nature neither immortal nor mortal. e
But now he springs to life when he gets his way; now he dies – all in the very same day. Because he is his father's son, however, he keeps coming back to life, but then anything he finds his way to always slips away, and for this reason Love is never completely without resources, nor is he ever rich.

"He is in between wisdom and ignorance 204
as well. In fact, you see, none of the gods loves wisdom or wants to become wise – for they are wise – and no one else who is wise already loves wisdom; on the other hand, no one who is ignorant will love wisdom either or want to become wise. For what's especially difficult about being ignorant is that you are content with yourself, even though you're neither beautiful and good nor intelligent. If you don't think you need anything, of course you won't want what you don't think you need."

"In that case, Diotima, who *are* the people who b
love wisdom, if they are neither wise nor ignorant?"

"That's obvious," she said. "A child could tell you. Those who love wisdom fall in between those two extremes. And Love is one of them, because he is in love with what is beautiful, and wisdom is extremely beautiful. It follows that Love *must* be a lover of wisdom and, as such, is in between being wise and being ignorant. This, too, comes to him from his parentage, from a father who is wise and resourceful and a mother who is not wise and lacks resource.

c "My dear Socrates, that, then, is the nature of the Spirit called Love. Considering what you thought about Love, it's no surprise that you were led into thinking of Love as you did. On the basis of what you say, I conclude that you thought Love was *being loved*, rather than *being a lover*. I think that's why Love struck you as beautiful in every way: because it is what is really beautiful and graceful that deserves to be loved, and this is perfect and highly blessed; but being a lover takes a different form, which I have just described."

So I said, "All right then, my friend. What you
d say about Love is beautiful, but if you're right, what use is Love to human beings?"

"I'll try to teach you that, Socrates, after I finish this. So far I've been explaining the character and the parentage of Love. Now, according to you, he is love for beautiful things. But suppose someone asks us, 'Socrates and Diotima, what is the point of loving beautiful things?'

"It's clearer this way: 'The lover of beautiful things has a desire; what does he desire?'"

"That they become his own," I said.

"But that answer calls for still another question, that is, 'What will this man have, when the beautiful things he wants have become his own?'"

e I said there was no way I could give a ready answer to that question.

Then she said, "Suppose someone changes the question, putting 'good' in place of 'beautiful,' and asks you this: 'Tell me, Socrates, a lover of good things has a desire; what does he desire?'"

"That they become his own," I said.

"And what will he have, when the good things he wants have become his own?"

205 "This time it's easier to come up with the answer," I said. "He'll have happiness."[3]

"That's what makes happy people happy, isn't it – possessing good things. There's no need to ask further, 'What's the point of wanting happiness?' The answer you gave seems to be final."

"True," I said.

"Now this desire for happiness, this kind of love – do you think it is common to all human beings and that everyone wants to have good things forever and ever? What would you say?"

"Just that," I said. "It is common to all."

"Then, Socrates, why don't we say that every- b
one is in love," she asked, "since everyone always loves the same things? Instead, we say some people are in love and others not; why is that?"

"I wonder about that myself," I said.

"It's nothing to wonder about," she said. "It's because we divide out a special kind of love, and we refer to it by the word that means the whole – 'love'; and for the other kinds of love we use other words."

"What do you mean?" I asked.

"Well, you know, for example, that 'poetry' has a very wide range.[4] After all, everything that is responsible for creating something out of nothing c
is a kind of poetry; and so all the creations of every craft and profession are themselves a kind of poetry, and everyone who practices a craft is a poet."

"True."

"Nevertheless," she said, "as you also know, these craftsmen are not called poets. We have other words for them, and out of the whole of poetry we have marked off one part, the part the Muses give us with melody and rhythm, and we refer to this by the word that means the whole. For this alone is called 'poetry,' and those who practice this part of poetry are called poets."

"True." d

"That's also how it is with love. The main point is this: every desire for good things or for happiness is 'the supreme and treacherous love' in everyone. But those who pursue this along any of its many other ways – through making money, or through the love of sports, or through philosophy – we don't say that *these* people are in love, and we don't call them lovers. It's only when people are devoted exclusively to one special kind of love that we use these words that really belong to the whole of it; 'love' and 'in love' and 'lovers.'"

"I am beginning to see your point," I said.

"Now there is a certain story," she said, e
"according to which lovers are those people who seek their other halves. But according to my story, a lover does not seek the half or the whole, unless, my friend, it turns out to be good as well. I say this because people are even willing to cut off their own arms and legs if they think they are diseased. I don't think an individual takes joy in what belongs to him personally unless by 'belonging to me' he means 'good' and by 'belonging

206 to another' he means 'bad.' That's because what everyone loves is really nothing other than the good. Do you disagree?"

"Zeus! Not I," I said.

"Now, then," she said. "Can we simply say that people love the good?"

"Yes," I said.

"But shouldn't we add that, in loving it, they want the good to be theirs?"

"We should."

"And not only that," she said. "They want the good to be theirs forever, don't they?"

"We should add that too."

"In a word, then, love is wanting to possess the good forever."

"That's very true," I said.

b "This, then, is the object of love," she said. "Now, how do lovers pursue it? We'd rightly say that when they are in love they do something with eagerness and zeal. But what is it precisely that they do? Can you say?"

"If I could," I said, "I wouldn't be your student, filled with admiration for your wisdom, and trying to learn these very things."

"Well, I'll tell you," she said. "It is giving birth in beauty,[5] whether in body or in soul."

"It would take divination to figure out what
c you mean. I can't."

"Well, I'll tell you more clearly," she said. "All of us are pregnant, Socrates, both in body and in soul, and, as soon as we come to a certain age, we naturally desire to give birth. Now no one can possibly give birth in anything ugly; only in something beautiful. That's because when a man and a woman come together in order to give birth, this is a godly affair. Pregnancy, reproduction – this is an immortal thing for a mortal
d animal to do, and it cannot occur in anything that is out of harmony, but ugliness is out of harmony with all that is godly. Beauty, however, is in harmony with the divine. Therefore the goddess who presides at childbirth – she's called Moira or Eilithuia – is really Beauty.[6] That's why, whenever pregnant animals or persons draw near to beauty, they become gentle and joyfully disposed and give birth and reproduce; but near ugliness they are foulfaced and draw back in pain; they turn away and shrink back and do not reproduce, and because they hold on to what they carry inside them, the labor is painful. This is the source of
e the great excitement about beauty that comes to anyone who is pregnant and already teeming with life: beauty releases them from their great pain. You see, Socrates," she said, "what Love wants is not beauty, as you think it is."

"Well, what is it, then?"

"Reproduction and birth in beauty."

"Maybe," I said.

"Certainly," she said. "Now, why reproduction? It's because reproduction goes on forever; 207
it is what mortals have in place of immortality. A lover must desire immortality along with the good, if what we agreed earlier was right, that Love wants to possess the good forever. It follows from our argument that Love must desire immortality."

All this she taught me, on those occasions when she spoke on the art of love. And once she asked, "What do you think causes love and desire, Socrates? Don't you see what an awful state a wild animal is in when it wants to reproduce? Footed b
and winged animals alike, all are plagued by the disease of Love. First they are sick for intercourse with each other, then for nurturing their young – for their sake the weakest animals stand ready to do battle against the strongest and even to die for them, and they may be racked with famine in order to feed their young. They would do anything for their sake. Human beings, you'd think, would do this because they understand the reason c
for it; but what causes wild animals to be in such a state of love? Can you say?"

And I said again that I didn't know.

So she said, "How do you think you'll ever master the art of love, if you don't know that?"

"But that's why I came to you, Diotima, as I just said. I knew I needed a teacher. So tell me what causes this, and everything else that belongs to the art of love."

"If you really believe that Love by its nature aims at what we have often agreed it does, then d
don't be surprised at the answer," she said. "For among animals the principle is the same as with us, and mortal nature seeks so far as possible to live forever and be immortal. And this is possible in one way only: by reproduction, because it always leaves behind a new young one in place of the old. Even while each living thing is said to be alive and to be the same – as a person is said to be the same from childhood till he turns into an old man – even then he never consists of the same things, though he is called the same, but he is

e always being renewed and in other respects
passing away, in his hair and flesh and bones and
blood and his entire body. And it's not just in his
body, but in his soul, too, for none of his manners,
customs, opinions, desires, pleasures, pains, or
fears ever remains the same, but some are coming
to be in him while others are passing away. And
what is still far stranger than that is that not only
208 does one branch of knowledge come to be in us
while another passes away and that we are never
the same even in respect of our knowledge, but
that each single piece of knowledge has the same
fate. For what we call *studying* exists because
knowledge is leaving us, because forgetting is the
departure of knowledge, while studying puts back
a fresh memory in place of what went away,
thereby preserving a piece of knowledge, so that
it seems to be the same. And in that way every-
b thing mortal is preserved, not, like the divine, by
always being the same in every way, but because
what is departing and aging leaves behind something new, something such as it had been. By this
device, Socrates," she said, "what is mortal shares
in immortality, whether it is a body or anything
else, while the immortal has another way. So
don't be surprised if everything naturally values
its own offspring, because it is for the sake of
immortality that everything shows this zeal,
which is Love."

c Yet when I heard her speech I was amazed, and
spoke: "Well," said I, "Most wise Diotima, is this
really the way it is?"

And in the manner of a perfect sophist she
said, "Be sure of it, Socrates. Look, if you will, at
how human beings seek honor. You'd be amazed
at their irrationality, if you didn't have in mind
what I spoke about and if you hadn't pondered
the awful state of love they're in, wanting to
become famous and 'to lay up glory immortal
forever,' and how they're ready to brave any
danger for the sake of this, much more than they
are for their children; and they are prepared to
d spend money, suffer through all sorts of ordeals,
and even die for the sake of glory. Do you really
think that Alcestis would have died for Admetus,"
she asked, "or that Achilles would have died after
Patroclus, or that your Codrus would have died
so as to preserve the throne for his sons,[7] if they
hadn't expected the memory of their virtue –
which we still hold in honor – to be immortal?
Far from it," she said. "I believe that anyone will
do anything for the sake of immortal virtue and e
the glorious fame that follows; and the better the
people, the more they will do, for they are all in
love with immortality.

"Now, some people are pregnant in body, and
for this reason turn more to women and pursue
love in that way, providing themselves through
childbirth with immortality and remembrance
and happiness, as they think, for all time to come; 209
while others are pregnant in soul – because there
surely *are* those who are even more pregnant in
their souls than in their bodies, and these are
pregnant with what is fitting for a soul to bear
and bring to birth. And what is fitting? Wisdom
and the rest of virtue, which all poets beget, as
well as all the craftsmen who are said to be creative. But by far the greatest and most beautiful
part of wisdom deals with the proper ordering of
cities and households, and that is called moderation and justice. When someone has been preg- b
nant with these in his soul from early youth,
while he is still a virgin, and, having arrived at the
proper age, desires to beget and give birth, he
too will certainly go about seeking the beauty
in which he would beget; for he will never beget
in anything ugly. Since he is pregnant, then, he is
much more drawn to bodies that are beautiful
than to those that are ugly; and if he also has the
luck to find a soul that is beautiful and noble and
well-formed, he is even more drawn to this com- c
bination; such a man makes him instantly teem
with ideas and arguments about virtue – the
qualities a virtuous man should have and the customary activities in which he should engage; and
so he tries to educate him. In my view, you see,
when he makes contact with someone beautiful
and keeps company with him, he conceives and
gives birth to what he has been carrying inside
him for ages. And whether they are together or
apart, he remembers that beauty. And in common
with him he nurtures the newborn; such people,
therefore, have much more to share than do the
parents of human children, and have a firmer
bond of friendship, because the children in whom
they have a share are more beautiful and more d
immortal. Everyone would rather have such
children than human ones, and would look up to
Homer. Hesiod, and the other good poets with
envy and admiration for the offspring they have
left behind – offspring, which, because they are
immortal themselves, provide their parents with

immortal glory and remembrance. "For example," she said, "those are the sort of children Lycurgus[8] left behind in Sparta as the saviors of Sparta and virtually all of Greece. Among you the honor goes
e to Solon for his creation of your laws. Other men in other places everywhere Greek or barbarian, have brought a host of beautiful deeds into the light and begotten every kind of virtue. Already many shrines have sprung up to honor them for their immortal children, which hasn't happened yet to anyone for human offspring.

210 "Even you, Socrates, could probably come to be initiated into these rites of love. But as for the purpose of these rites when they are done correctly – that is the final and highest mystery, and I don't know if you are capable of it. I myself will tell you," she said, "and I won't stint any effort. And you must try to follow if you can."

"A lover who goes about this matter correctly must begin in his youth to devote himself to beautiful bodies. First, if the leader[9] leads aright, he should love one body and beget beautiful ideas
b there; then he should realize that the beauty of any one body is brother to the beauty of any other and that if he is to pursue beauty of form he'd be very foolish not to think that the beauty of all bodies is one and the same. When he grasps this, he must become a lover of all beautiful bodies, and he must think that this wild gaping after just one body is a small thing and despise it.

"After this he must think that the beauty of people's souls is more valuable than the beauty of
c their bodies, so that if someone is decent in his soul, even though he is scarcely blooming in his body, our lover must be content to love and care for him and to seek to give birth to such ideas as will make young men better. The result is that our lover will be forced to gaze at the beauty of activities and laws and to see that all this is akin to itself, with the result that he will think that the beauty of bodies is a thing of no importance. After customs he must move on to various kinds
d of knowledge. The result is that he will see the beauty of knowledge and be looking mainly not at beauty in a single example – as a servant would who favored the beauty of a little boy or a man or a single custom (being a slave, of course, he's low and small-minded) – but the lover is turned to the great sea of beauty, and, gazing upon this, he gives birth to many gloriously beautiful ideas and theories, in unstinting love of wisdom,[10] until, having grown and been strengthened there, e
he catches sight of such knowledge, and it is the knowledge of such beauty . . .

"Try to pay attention to me," she said, "as best you can. You see, the man who has been thus far guided in matters of Love, who has beheld beautiful things in the right order and correctly, is coming now to the goal of Loving: all of a sudden he will catch sight of something wonderfully beautiful in its nature; that, Socrates, is the reason 211
for all his earlier labors:

"First, it always *is* and neither comes to be nor passes away, neither waxes nor wanes. Second, it is not beautiful this way and ugly that way, nor beautiful at one time and ugly at another, nor beautiful in relation to one thing and ugly in relation to another; nor is it beautiful here but ugly there, as it would be if it were beautiful for some people and ugly for others. Nor will the beautiful appear to him in the guise of a face or hands or anything else that belongs to the body. It will not appear to him as one idea or one kind of knowl- b
edge. It is not anywhere in another thing, as in an animal, or in earth, or in heaven, or in anything else, but itself by itself with itself, it is always one in form; and all the other beautiful things share in that, in such a way that when those others come to be or pass away, this does not become the least bit smaller or greater nor suffer any change. So when someone rises by these stages, through loving boys correctly, and begins to see c
this beauty, he has almost grasped his goal. This is what it is to go aright, or be led by another, into the mystery of Love: one goes always upwards for the sake of this Beauty, starting out from beautiful things and using them like rising stairs: from one body to two and from two to all beautiful bodies, then from beautiful bodies to beautiful customs, and from customs to learning beautiful things, and from these lessons he arrives in the end at this lesson, which is learning of this very Beauty, so that in the end he comes to know d
just what it is to be beautiful.

"And there in life, Socrates, my friend," said the woman from Mantinea, "there if anywhere should a person live his life, beholding that Beauty. If you once see that, it won't occur to you to measure beauty by gold or clothing or beautiful boys and youths – who, if you see them now, strike you out of your senses, and make you, you and many others, eager to be with the boys

you love and look at them forever, if there were
any way to do that, forgetting food and drink,
e everything but looking at them and being with
them. But how would it be, in our view," she
said, "if someone got to see the Beautiful itself,
absolute, pure, unmixed, not polluted by human
flesh or colors or any other great nonsense of
212 mortality, but if he could see the divine Beauty
itself in its one form? Do you think it would
be a poor life for a human being to look there and
to behold it by that which he ought, and to be
with it? Or haven't you remembered," she said,
"that in that life alone, when he looks at Beauty
in the only way that Beauty can be seen – only
then will it become possible for him to give
birth not to images of virtue (because he's in
touch with no images), but to true virtue (because
he is in touch with the true Beauty). The love
of the gods belongs to anyone who has given
b birth to true virtue and nourished it, and if any
human being could become immortal, it would
be he."

Translator's Notes

1 *Poros* means "way," "resource." His mother's name, *Mētis*, means "cunning." *Penia* means "poverty."

2 I.e., a philosopher.

3 *Eudaimonia*: no English word catches the full range of this term, which is used for the whole of well-being and the good, flourishing life.

4 "Poetry" translates *poiēsis*, lit. 'making', which can be used for any kind of production or creation. However, the word *poiētēs*, lit. 'maker', was used mainly for poets – writers of metrical verses that were actually set to music.

5 The preposition is ambiguous between "within" and "in the presence of." Diotima may mean that the lover causes the newborn (which may be an idea) to come to be within a beautiful person; or she may mean that he is stimulated to give birth to it in the presence of a beautiful person.

6 Moira is known mainly as a Fate, but she was also a birth-goddess (*Iliad* xxiv.209), and was identified with the birth-goddess Eilithuia (Pindar, *Olympian Odes* vi.42, *Nemean Odes* vii.1).

7 Codrus was the legendary last king of Athens. He gave his life to satisfy a prophecy that promised victory to Athens and salvation from the invading Dorians if their king was killed by the enemy.

8 Lycurgus was supposed to have been the founder of the oligarchic laws and stern customs of Sparta.

9 The leader: Love.

10 I.e., philosophy.

5

Poetics

Aristotle

Aristotle (384–322 BCE), a student of Plato, had an enormous impact on the development of Western thought, not only in all the branches of philosophy but also in biology, psychology, zoology, meteorology, and astronomy.

1447a 1 Our subject being Poetry, I propose to speak not only of the art in general but also of its species and their respective capacities; of the structure of plot required for a good poem; of the number and nature of the constituent parts of a poem; and likewise of any other matters in the same line of inquiry. Let us follow the natural order and begin with the primary facts.

Epic poetry and Tragedy, as also Comedy, Dithyrambic poetry, and most flute-playing and lyre-playing, are all, viewed as a whole, modes of imitation. But at the same time they differ from one another in three ways, either by a difference of kind in their means, or by differences in the objects, or in the manner of their imitations.

I. Just as colour and form are used as means by some, who (whether by art or constant practice) imitate and portray many things by their aid, and the voice is used by others; so also in the above-mentioned group of arts, the means with them as a whole are rhythm, language, and harmony – used, however, either singly or in certain combinations. A combination of harmony and rhythm alone is the means in flute-playing and lyre-playing, and any other arts there may be of the same description, e.g. imitative piping. 1447b
Rhythm alone, without harmony, is the means in the dancer's imitations; for even he, by the rhythms of his attitudes, may represent men's characters, as well as what they do and suffer. There is further an art which imitates by language alone, without harmony, in prose or in verse, and if in verse, either in some one or in a plurality of metres. This form of imitation is to this day without a name. We have no common name for a mime of Sophron or Xenarchus and a Socratic Conversation; and we should still be without one even if the imitation in the two instances were in trimeters or elegiacs or some other kind of verse – though it is the way with people to take on 'poet' to the name of a metre, and talk of elegiac-poets and epic-poets, thinking that they call them poets not by reason of the imitative nature of their work, but indiscriminately by reason of the metre they write in. Even if a theory of medicine or physical philosophy be put forth in a metrical form, it is usual to describe the writer in this way; Homer and Empedocles, however, have really nothing in common apart from their metre; so that, if the one is to be called a poet, the other should be termed a physicist rather than a poet. We should be in the same position also, if the

Aristotle, *Poetics*, trans. Ingram Bywater (Oxford: Clarendon Press, 1920), pp. 207–31.

imitation in these instances were in all the metres, like the *Centaur* (a rhapsody in a medley of all metres) of Chaeremon; and Chaeremon one has to recognize as a poet. So much, then, as to these arts. There are, lastly, certain other arts, which combine all the means enumerated, rhythm, melody, and verse, e.g. Dithyrambic and Nomic poetry, Tragedy and Comedy; with this difference, however, that the three kinds of means are in some of them employed together, and in others brought in separately, one after the other. These elements of difference in the above arts I term the means of their imitation.

1448a 2 II. The objects the imitator represents are actions, with agents who are necessarily either good men or bad – the diversities of human character being nearly always derivative from this primary distinction, since the line between virtue and vice is one dividing the whole of mankind. It follows, therefore, that the agents represented must be either above our own level of goodness, or beneath it, or just such as we are; in the same way as, with the painters, the personages of Polygnotus are better than we are, those of Pauson worse, and those of Dionysius just like ourselves. It is clear that each of the above-mentioned arts will admit of these differences, and that it will become a separate art by representing objects with this point of difference. Even in dancing, flute-playing, and lyre-playing such diversities are possible; and they are also possible in the nameless art that uses language, prose or verse without harmony, as its means; Homer's personages, for instance, are better than we are; Cleophon's are on our own level; and those of Hegemon of Thasos, the first writer of parodies, and Nicochares, the author of the *Diliad*, are beneath it. The same is true of the Dithyramb and the Nome: the personages may be presented in them with the difference exemplified in the . . . of . . . and Argas, and in the Cyclopses of Timotheus and Philoxenus. This difference it is that distinguishes Tragedy and Comedy also; the one would make its personages worse, and the other better, than the men of the present day.

3 III. A third difference in these arts is in the manner in which each kind of object is represented. Given both the same means and the same kind of object for imitation, one may either (1) speak at one moment in narrative and at another in an assumed character, as Homer does; or (2) one may remain the same throughout, without any such change; or (3) the imitators may represent the whole story dramatically, as though they were actually doing the things described.

As we said at the beginning, therefore, the differences in the imitation of these arts come under three heads, their means, their objects, and their manner.

So that as an imitator Sophocles will be on one side akin to Homer, both portraying good men; and on another to Aristophanes, since both present their personages as acting and doing. This in fact, according to some, is the reason for plays being termed dramas, because in a play the personages act the story. Hence too both Tragedy and Comedy are claimed by the Dorians as their discoveries; Comedy by the Megarians – by those in Greece as having arisen when Megara became a democracy, and by the Sicilian Megarians on the ground that the poet Epicharmus was of their country, and a good deal earlier than Chionides and Magnes; even Tragedy also is claimed by certain of the Peloponnesian Dorians. In support of this claim they point to the words 'comedy' and 'drama'. Their word for the outlying hamlets, they say, is *comae*, whereas Athenians call them *demes* – thus assuming that comedians got the name not from their *comoe* or revels, but from their strolling from hamlet to hamlet, lack of
appreciation keeping them out of the city. Their 1448b
word also for 'to act', they say, is *dran*, whereas Athenians use *prattein*.

So much, then, as to the number and nature of the points of difference in the imitation of these arts.

4 It is clear that the general origin of poetry was due to two causes, each of them part of human nature. Imitation is natural to man from childhood, one of his advantages over the lower animals being this, that he is the most imitative creature in the world, and learns at first by imitation. And it is also natural for all to delight in works of imitation. The truth of this second point is shown by experience: though the objects themselves may be painful to see, we delight to view the most realistic representations of them in art, the forms for example of the lowest animals and of dead bodies. The explanation is to be found in

a further fact: to be learning something is the greatest of pleasures not only to the philosopher but also to the rest of mankind, however small their capacity for it; the reason of the delight in seeing the picture is that one is at the same time learning – gathering the meaning of things, e.g. that the man there is so-and-so; for if one has not seen the thing before, one's pleasure will not be in the picture as an imitation of it, but will be due to the execution or colouring or some similar cause. Imitation, then, being natural to us – as also the sense of harmony and rhythm, the metres being obviously species of rhythms – it was through their original aptitude, and by a series of improvements for the most part gradual on their first efforts, that they created poetry out of their improvisations.

Poetry, however, soon broke up into two kinds according to the differences of character in the individual poets; for the graver among them would represent noble actions, and those of noble personages; and the meaner sort the actions of the ignoble. The latter class produced invectives at first, just as others did hymns and panegyrics. We know of no such poem by any of the pre-Homeric poets, though there were probably many such writers among them; instances, however, may be found from Homer downwards, e.g. his *Margites*, and the similar poems of others, In this poetry of invective its natural fitness brought an iambic metre into use; hence our present term 'iambic', because it was the metre of their 'iambs' or invectives against one another. The result was that the old poets became some of them writers of heroic and others of iambic verse. Homer's position, however, is peculiar: just as he was in the serious style the poet of poets, standing alone not only through the literary excellence, but also through the dramatic character of his imitations, so too he was the first to outline for us the general forms of Comedy by producing not a dramatic invective, but a dramatic picture
1449a of the Ridiculous; his *Margites* in fact stands in the same relation to our comedies as the *Iliad* and *Odyssey* to our tragedies. As soon, however, as Tragedy and Comedy appeared in the field, those naturally drawn to the one line of poetry became writers of comedies instead of iambs, and those naturally drawn to the other, writers of tragedies instead of epics, because these new modes of art were grander and of more esteem than the old.

If it be asked whether Tragedy is now all that it need be in its formative elements, to consider that, and decide it theoretically and in relation to the theatres, is a matter for another inquiry.

It certainly began in improvisations – as did also Comedy; the one originating with the authors of the Dithyramb, the other with those of the phallic songs, which still survive as institutions in many of our cities. And its advance after that was little by little, through their improving on whatever they had before them at each stage. It was in fact only after a long series of changes that the movement of Tragedy stopped on its attaining to its natural form. (1) The number of actors was first increased to two by Aeschylus, who curtailed the business of the Chorus, and made the dialogue, or spoken portion, take the leading part in the play. (2) A third actor and scenery were due to Sophocles. (3) Tragedy acquired also its magnitude. Discarding short stories and a ludicrous diction through its passing out of its satyric stage, it assumed, though only at a late point in its progress, a tone of dignity; and its metre changed then from trochaic to iambic. The reason for their original use of the trochaic tetrameter was that their poetry was satyric and more connected with dancing than it now is. As soon, however, as a spoken part came in, nature herself found the appropriate metre. The iambic, we know, is the most speakable of metres, as is shown by the fact that we very often fall into it in conversation, whereas we rarely talk hexameters, and only when we depart from the speaking tone of voice. (4) Another change was a plurality of episodes or acts. As for the remaining matters, the superadded embellishments and the account of their introduction, these must be taken as said, as it would probably be a long piece of work to go through the details.

5 As for Comedy, it is (as has been observed an imitation of men worse than the average; worse, however, not as regards any and every sort of fault, but only as regards one particular kind, the Ridiculous, which is a species of the Ugly. The Ridiculous may be defined as a mistake or deformity not productive of pain or harm to others; the mask, for instance that excites laughter, is something ugly and distorted without causing pain.

Though the successive changes in Tragedy and their authors are not unknown, we cannot say the

same of Comedy; its early stages passed un-
1449b noticed, because it was not as yet taken up in a serious way. It was only at a late point in its progress that a chorus of comedians was officially granted by the archon; they used to be mere volunteers. It had also already certain definite forms at the time when the record of those termed comic poets begins. Who it was who supplied it with masks, or prologues, or a plurality of actors and the like, has remained unknown. The invented Fable, or Plot, however, originated in Sicily with Epicharmus and Phormis; of Athenian poets Crates was the first to drop the Comedy of invective and frame stories of a general and non-personal nature, in other words, Fables or Plots.

Epic poetry, then, has been seen to agree with Tragedy to this extent, that of being an imitation of serious subjects in a grand kind of verse. It differs from it, however, (1) in that it is in one kind of verse and in narrative form; and (2) in its length – which is due to its action having no fixed limit of time, whereas Tragedy endeavours to keep as far as possible within a single circuit of the sun, or something near that. This, I say, is another point of difference between them, though at first the practice in this respect was just the same in tragedies as in epic poems. They differ also (3) in their constituents, some being common to both and others peculiar to Tragedy – hence a judge of good and bad in Tragedy is a judge of that in epic poetry also. All the parts of an epic are included in Tragedy; but those of Tragedy are not all of them to be found in the Epic.

6 Reserving hexameter poetry and Comedy for consideration hereafter, let us proceed now to the discussion of Tragedy; before doing so, however, we must gather up the definition resulting from what has been said. A tragedy, then, is the imitation of an action that is serious and also, as having magnitude, complete in itself; in language with pleasurable accessories, each kind brought in separately in the parts of the work; in a dramatic, not in a narrative form; with incidents arousing pity and fear, wherewith to accomplish its catharsis of such emotions. Here by 'language with pleasurable accessories' I mean that with rhythm and harmony or song superadded; and by 'the kinds separately' I mean that some portions are worked out with verse only, and others in turn with song.

I. As they act the stories, it follows that in the first place the Spectacle (or stage-appearance of the actors) must be some part of the whole; and in the second Melody and Diction, these two being the means of their imitation. Here by 'Diction' I mean merely this, the composition of the verses; and by 'Melody,' what is too completely understood to require explanation. But further: the subject represented also is an action; and the action involves agents, who must necessarily have their distinctive qualities both of char- 1450a
acter and thought, since it is from these that we ascribe certain qualities to their actions. There are in the natural order of things, therefore, two causes, Thought and Character, of their actions, and consequently of their success or failure in their lives. Now the action (that which was done) is represented in the play by the Fable or Plot. The Fable, in our present sense of the term, is simply this, the combination of the incidents, or things done in the story; whereas Character is what makes us ascribe certain moral qualities to the agents; and Thought is shown in all they say when proving a particular point or, it may be, enunciating a general truth. There are six parts consequently of every tragedy, as a whole (that is) of such or such quality, viz. a Fable or Plot, Characters, Diction, Thought, Spectacle, and Melody; two of them arising from the means, one from the manner, and three from the objects of the dramatic imitation; and there is nothing else besides these six. Of these, its formative elements, then, not a few of the dramatists have made due use, as every play, one may say, admits of Spectacle, Character, Fable, Diction, Melody and Thought.

II. The most important of the six is the combination of the incidents of the story. Tragedy is essentially an imitation not of persons but of action and life, of happiness and misery. All human happiness or misery takes the form of action; the end for which we live is a certain kind of activity, not a quality. Character gives us qualities, but it is in our actions – what we do – that we are happy or the reverse. In a play accordingly they do not act in order to portray the Characters; they include the Characters for the sake of the action. So that it is the action in it, i.e. its Fable or Plot, that is the end and purpose of the tragedy; and the end is everywhere the chief thing. Besides this, a tragedy is impossible without action, but

there may be one without Character. The tragedies of most of the moderns are characterless – a defect common among poets of all kinds, and with its counterpart in painting in Zeuxis as compared with Polygnotus for whereas the latter is strong in character, the work of Zeuxis is devoid of it. And again: one may string together a series of characteristic speeches of the utmost finish as regards Diction and Thought, and yet fail to produce the true tragic effect; but one will have much better success with a tragedy which, however inferior in these respects, has a Plot, a combination of incidents, in it. And again: the most powerful elements of attraction in Tragedy, the Peripeties and Discoveries, are parts of the Plot. A further proof is in the fact that beginners succeed earlier with the Diction and Characters than with the construction of a story; and the
1450b same may be said of nearly all the early dramatists. We maintain, therefore, that the first essential, the life and soul, so to speak, of Tragedy is the Plot and that the Characters come second – compare the parallel in painting where the most beautiful colours laid on without order will not give one the same pleasure as a simple black-and-white sketch of a portrait. We maintain that Tragedy is primarily an imitation of action, and that it is mainly for the sake of the action that it imitates the personal agents. Thus comes the element of Thought, i.e. the power of saying whatever can be said, or what is appropriate to the occasion. This is what, in the speech in Tragedy, falls under the arts of Politics and Rhetoric; for the older poets make their personages discourse like statesmen, and the modern like rhetoricians. One must not confuse it with Character. Character in a play is that which reveals the moral purpose of the agents, i.e. the sort of thing they seek or avoid, where that is not obvious – hence there is no room for Character in a speech on a purely indifferent subject. Thought, on the other hand, is shown in all they say when proving or disproving some particular point, or enunciating some universal proposition. Fourth among the literary elements is the Diction of the personages, i.e., as before explained, the expression of their thoughts in words, which is practically the same thing with verse as with prose. As for the two remaining parts, the Melody is the greatest of the pleasurable accessories of Tragedy. The Spectacle, though an attraction, is the least artistic of all the parts, and has least to do with the art of poetry. The tragic effect is quite possible without a public performance and actors; and besides, the getting-up of the Spectacle is more a matter for the costumier than the poet.

7 Having thus distinguished the parts, let us now consider the proper construction of the Fable or Plot, as that is at once the first and the most important thing in Tragedy. We have laid it down that a tragedy is an imitation of an action that is complete in itself, as a whole of some magnitude; for a whole may be of no magnitude to speak of. Now a whole is that which has beginning, middle, and end. A beginning is that which is not itself necessarily after anything else, and which has naturally something else after it; an end is that which is naturally after something itself, either as its necessary or usual consequent, and with nothing else after it; and a middle, that which is by nature after one thing and has also another after it. A well-constructed Plot, therefore, cannot either begin or end at any point one likes; beginning and end in it must be of the forms just described. Again: to be beautiful, a living creature, and every whole made up of parts, must not only present a certain order in its arrangement of parts, but also be of a certain definite magnitude. Beauty is a matter of size and order, and therefore impossible either (1) in a very minute creature, since our perception becomes indistinct as it approaches instantaneity; or (2) in a creature of vast size – one, say, 1,000
miles long – as in that case, instead of the object 1451a
being seen all at once, the unity and wholeness of it is lost to the beholder. Just in the same way, then, as a beautiful whole made up of parts, or a beautiful living creature, must be of some size, but a size to be taken in by the eye, so a story or Plot must be of some length, but of a length to be taken in by the memory. As for the limit of its length, so far as that is relative to public performances and spectators, it does not fall within the theory of poetry. If they had to perform a hundred tragedies, they would be timed by water-clocks, as they are said to have been at one period. The limit, however, set by the actual nature of the thing is this: the longer the story, consistently with its being comprehensible as a whole, the finer it is by reason of its magnitude. As a rough general formula, 'a length which allows of the

hero passing by a series of probable or necessary stages from misfortune to happiness, or from happiness to misfortune,' may suffice as a limit for the magnitude of the story.

8 The Unity of a Plot does not consist, as some suppose, in its having one man as its subject. An infinity of things befall that one man, some of which it is impossible to reduce to unity; and in like manner there are many actions of one man which cannot be made to form one action. One sees, therefore, the mistake of all the poets who have written a *Heracleid,* a *Theseid,* or similar poems; they suppose that, because Heracles was one man, the story also of Heracles must be one story. Homer, however, evidently understood this point quite well, whether by art or instinct, just in the same way as he excels the rest in every other respect. In writing an *Odyssey,* he did not make the poem cover all that ever befell his hero – it befell him, for instance, to get wounded on Parnassus and also to feign madness at the time of the call to arms, but the two incidents had no necessary or probable connexion with one another – instead of doing that, he took as the subject of the *Odyssey,* as also of the *Iliad,* an action with a Unity of the kind we are describing. The truth is that, just as in the other imitative arts one imitation is always of one thing, so in poetry the story, as an imitation of action, must represent one action, a complete whole, with its several incidents so closely connected that the transposal or withdrawal of any one of them will disjoin and dislocate the whole. For that which makes no perceptible difference by its presence or absence is no real part of the whole.

9 From what we have said it will be seen that
1451b the poet's function is to describe, not the thing that has happened, but a kind of thing that might happen, i.e. what is possible as being probable or necessary. The distinction between historian and poet is not in the one writing prose and the other verse – you might put the work of Herodotus into verse, and it would still be a species of history; it consists really in this, that the one describes the thing that has been, and the other a kind of thing that might be. Hence poetry is something more philosophic and of graver import than history, since its statements are of the nature rather of universals, whereas those of history are singulars. By a universal statement I mean one as to what such or such a kind of man will probably or necessarily say or do – which is the aim of poetry, though it affixes proper names to the characters; by a singular statement, one as to what, say, Alcibiades did or had done to him. In Comedy this has become clear by this time; it is only when their plot is already made up of probable incidents that they give it a basis of proper names, choosing for the purpose any names that may occur to them, instead of writing like the old iambic poets about particular person. In Tragedy, however, they still adhere to the historic names; and for this reason: what convinces is the possible; now whereas we are not yet sure as to the possibility of that which has not happened, that which has happened is manifestly possible, else it would not have come to pass. Nevertheless even in Tragedy there are some plays with but one or two known names in them, the rest being inventions; and there are some without a single known name, e.g. Agathon's *Antheus,* in which both incidents and names are of the poet's invention; and it is no less delightful on that account. So that one must not aim at a rigid adherence to the traditional stories on which tragedies are based. It would be absurd, in fact, to do so, as even the known stories are only known to a few, though they are a delight none the less to all.

It is evident from the above that the poet must be more the poet of his stories or Plots than of his verses, inasmuch as he is a poet by virtue of the imitative element in his work, and it is actions that he imitates. And if he should come to take a subject from actual history, he is none the less a poet for that; since some historic occurrences may very well be in the probable and possible order of things; and it is in that aspect of them that he is their poet.

Of simple Plots and actions the episodic are the worst. I call a Plot episodic when there is neither probability nor necessity in the sequence of its episodes. Actions of this sort bad poets construct through their own fault, and good ones on account of the players. His work being for public performance, a good poet often stretches out a Plot beyond its capabilities, and is thus obliged to twist the sequence of incident.

Tragedy, however, is an imitation not only of 1452a
a complete action, but also of incidents arousing pity and fear. Such incidents have the very

greatest effect on the mind when they occur unexpectedly and at the same time in consequence of one another; there is more of the marvellous in them then than if they happened of themselves or by mere chance. Even matters of chance seem most marvellous if there is an appearance of design as it were in them; as for instance the statue of Mitys at Argos killed the author of Mitys' death by falling down on him when a looker-on at a public spectacle; for incidents like that we think to be not without a meaning. A Plot therefore, of this sort is necessarily finer than others.

10 Plots are either simple or complex, since the actions they represent are naturally of this twofold description. The action, proceeding in the way defined, as one continuous whole, I call simple, when the change in the hero's fortunes takes place without Peripety or Discovery; and complex, when it involves one or the other, or both. These should each of them arise out of the structure of the Plot itself, so as to be the consequence, necessary or probable, of the antecedents. There is a great difference between a thing happening *propter hoc* and *post hoc.*

11 A Peripety is the change of the kind described from one state of things within the play to its opposite, and that too in the way we are saying, in the probable or necessary sequence of events; as it is for instance in *Oedipus:* here the opposite state of things is produced by the Messenger, who, coming to gladden Oedipus and to remove his fears as to his mother, reveals the secret of his birth. And in *Lynceus:* just as he is being led off for execution, with Danaus at his side to put him to death, the incidents preceding this bring it about that he is saved and Danaus put to death. A Discovery is, as the very word implies, a change from ignorance to knowledge, and thus to either love or hate, in the personages marked for good or evil fortune. The finest form of Discovery is one attended by Peripeties, like that which goes with the Discovery in *Oedipus.* There are no doubt other forms of it; what we have said may happen in a way in reference to inanimate things, even things of a very casual kind; and it is also possible to discover whether some one has done
1452b or not done something. But the form most directly connected with the Plot and the action of the piece is the first-mentioned. This, with a Peripety, will arouse either pity or fear – actions of that nature being what Tragedy is assumed to represent; and it will also serve to bring about the happy or unhappy ending. The Discovery, then, being of persons, it may be that of one party only to the other, the latter being already known; or both the parties may have to discover themselves. Iphigenia, for instance, was discovered to Orestes by sending the letter; and another Discovery was required to reveal him to Iphigenia.

Two parts of the Plot, then, Peripety and Discovery, are on matters of this sort. A third part is Suffering; which we may define as an action of a destructive or painful nature, such as murders on the stage, tortures, woundings, and the like. The other two have been already explained.

12 The parts of Tragedy to be treated as formative elements in the whole were mentioned in a previous Chapter. From the point of view, however, of its quantity, i.e. the separate sections into which it is divided, a tragedy has the following parts: Prologue, Episode, Exode, and a choral portion, distinguished into Parode and Stasimon; these two are common to all tragedies. whereas songs from the stage and *Commoe* are only found in some. The Prologue is all that precedes the Parode of the chorus; an Episode all that comes in between two whole choral songs; the Exode all that follows after the last choral song. In the choral portion the Parode is the whole first statement of the chorus; a Stasimon, a song of the chorus without anapaests or trochees; a *Commos,* a lamentation sung by chorus and actor in concert. The parts of Tragedy to be used as formative elements in the whole we have already mentioned; the above are its parts from the point of view of its quantity, or the separate sections into which it is divided.

13 The next points after what we have said above will be these: (1) What is the poet to aim at, and what is he to avoid, in constructing his Plots? and (2) What are the conditions on which the tragic effect depends?

We assume that, for the finest form of Tragedy, the Plot must be not simple but complex; and further, that it must imitate actions arousing fear and pity, since that is the distinctive function of this kind of imitation. It follows, therefore, that

there are three forms of Plot to be avoided. (1) A good man must not be seen passing from happiness to misery, or (2) a bad man from misery to happiness. The first situation is not fear-inspiring or piteous, but simply odious to us. The second is the most untragic that can be; it has no one of the requisites of Tragedy; it does not appeal either to the human feeling in us, or to our pity, or to
1453a our fears. Nor, on the other hand, should (3) an extremely bad man be seen falling from happiness into misery. Such a story may arouse the human feeling in us, but it will not move us to either pity or fear; pity is occasioned by undeserved misfortune, and fear by that of one like ourselves; so that there will be nothing either piteous or fear-inspiring in the situation. There remains, then, the intermediate kind of personage, a man not pre-eminently virtuous and just, whose misfortune, however, is brought upon him not by vice and depravity but by some error of judgement, of the number of those in the enjoyment of great reputation and prosperity; e.g. Oedipus, Thyestes, and the men of note of similar families. The perfect Plot, accordingly, must have a single, and not (as some tell us) a double issue; the change in the hero's fortunes must be not from misery to happiness, but on the contrary from happiness to misery; and the cause of it must lie not in any depravity, but in some great error on his part; the man himself being either such as we have described, or better, not worse, than that. Fact also confirms our theory. Though the poets began by accepting any tragic story that came to hand, in these days the finest tragedies are always on the story of some few houses, on that of Alcmeon, Oedipus, Orestes, Meleager, Thyestes, Telephus, or any others that may have been involved, as either agents or sufferers, in some deed of horror. The theoretically best tragedy, then, has a Plot of this description. The critics, therefore, are wrong who blame Euripides for taking this line in his tragedies, and giving many of them an unhappy ending. It is, as we have said, the right line to take. The best proof is this: on the stage, and in the public performances, such plays, properly worked out, are seen to be the most truly tragic; and Euripides, even if his execution be faulty in every other point, is seen to be nevertheless the most tragic certainly of the dramatists. After this comes the construction of Plot with some rank first, one with a double story (like the *Odyssey*) and an opposite issue for the good and the bad personages. It is ranked as first only through the weakness of the audiences; the poets merely follow their public, writing as its wishes dictate. But the pleasure here is not that of Tragedy. It belongs rather to Comedy, where the bitterest enemies in the piece (e.g. Orestes and Aegisthus) walk off good friends at the end, with no slaying of any one by any one.

14 The tragic fear and pity may be aroused by 1453b
the Spectacle; but they may also be aroused by the very structure and incidents of the play – which is the better way and shows the better poet. The Plot in fact should be so framed that, even without seeing the things take place, he who simply hears the account of them shall be filled with horror and pity at the incidents; which is just the effect that the mere recital of the story in *Oedipus* would have on one. To produce this same effect by means of the Spectacle is less artistic, and requires extraneous aid. Those, however, who make use of the Spectacle to put before us that which is merely monstrous and not productive of fear, are wholly out of touch with Tragedy; not every kind of pleasure should be required of a tragedy, but only its own proper pleasure.

The tragic pleasure is that of pity and fear, and the poet has to produce it by a work of imitation; it is clear, therefore, that the causes should be included in the incidents of his story. Let us see, then, what kinds of incident strike one as horrible, or rather as piteous. In a deed of this description the parties must necessarily be either friends, or enemies, or indifferent to one another. Now when enemy does it on enemy, there is nothing to move us to pity either in his doing or in his meditating the deed, except so far as the actual pain of the sufferer is concerned; and the same is true when the parties are indifferent to one another. Whenever the tragic deed, however, is done within the family – when murder or the like is done or mediated by brother on brother, by son on father, by mother on son, or son on mother – these are the situations the poet should seek after. The traditional stories, accordingly, must be kept as they are, e.g. the murder of Clytaemnestra by Orestes and of Eriphyle by Alcmeon. At the same time even with these there is something left to the poet himself; it is for him to devise the right way of treating them. Let us explain more clearly what we mean by 'the right way'. The deed of horror may be done by the doer knowingly and consciously, as in the old poets, and in Medea's murder of her children in Euripides. Or he may do it, but in ignorance of his relationship, and discover that afterwards, as does the Oedipus in Sophocles. Here the deed is outside the play; but it may be within it, like the act of the Alcmeon in Astydamas, or that of the Telegonus in *Ulysses Wounded.* A third possibility is for one meditating some deadly injury to another, in ignorance of his relationship, to make the discovery in time to draw back. These exhaust the possibilities, since the deed must necessarily be either done or not done, and either knowingly or unknowingly.

The worst situation is when the personage is with full knowledge on the point of doing the deed, and leaves it undone. It is odious and also (through the absence of suffering) untragic;
1454a hence it is that no one is made to act thus except
in some few instances, e.g. Haemon and Creon in *Antigone.* Next after this comes the actual perpetration of the deed mediated. A better situation than that, however, is for the deed to be done in ignorance, and the relationship discovered afterwards, since there is nothing odious in it, and the Discovery will serve to astound us. But the best of all is the last; what we have in *Cresphontes,* for example, where Merope, on the point of slaying her son, recognizes him in time; in *Iphigenia,* where sister and brother are in a like position; and in *Helle,* where the son recognizes his mother, when on the point of giving her up to her enemy.

This will explain why our tragedies are restricted (as we said just now) to such a small number of families. It was accident rather than art that led the poets in quest of subjects to embody this kind of incident in their Plots. They are still obliged, accordingly, to have recourse to the families in which such horrors have occurred.

On the construction of the Plot, and the kind of Plot required for Tragedy, enough has now been said.

15 In the Characters there are four points to aim at. First and foremost, that they shall be good. There will be an element of character in the play, if (as has been observed) what a personage says or does reveals a certain moral purpose; and a good element of character, if the purpose so revealed is good. Such goodness is possible in every type of personage, even in a woman or a slave, though the one is perhaps an inferior, and the other a wholly worthless being. The second point is to make them appropriate. The Character before us may be, say, manly; but it is not appropriate in a female Character to be manly, or clever. The third is to make them like the reality, which is not the same as their being good and appropriate, in our sense of the term. The fourth is to make them consistent and the same throughout; even if inconsistency be part of the man before one for imitation as presenting that form of character, he should still be consistently inconsistent. We have an instance of baseness of character, not required for the story, in the Menelaus in *Orestes;* of the incongruous and unbefitting in the lamentation of Ulysses in *Scylla,* and in the (clever) speech of Melanippe; and of inconsistency in *Iphigenia at Aulis,* where Iphigenia the suppliant is utterly unlike the later Iphigenia. The right thing, however, is in the Characters just as in the incidents of the play to endeavour always after the necessary or the probable; so that whenever such-and-such a personage says or does such-and-such a thing, it shall be the necessary or probable outcome of his character; and whenever this incident follows on that, it shall be
either the necessary or the probable consequence 1454b
of it. From this one sees (to digress for a moment) that the Dénouement also should arise out of the plot itself, and not depend on a stage-artifice, as in *Medea,* or in the story of the (arrested) departure of the Greeks in the *Iliad.* The artifice must be reserved for matters outside the play – for past events beyond human knowledge, or events yet to come, which require to be foretold or announced; since it is the privilege of the Gods to know everything. There should be nothing improbable among the actual incidents. If it be unavoidable, however, it should be outside the tragedy, like the improbability in the *Oedipus* of Sophocles. But to return to the Characters. As Tragedy is an imitation of personages better than the ordinary man, we in our way should follow the example of good portrait-painters, who reproduce the distinctive features of a man, and at the same time, without losing the likeness, make him handsomer than he is. The poet in like

manner, in portraying men quick or slow to anger, or with similar infirmities of character, must know how to represent them as such, and at the same time as good men, as Agathon and Homer have represented Achilles.

All these rules one must keep in mind throughout, and, further, those also for such points of stage-effect as directly depend on the art of the poet, since in these too one may often make mistakes. Enough, however, has been said on the subject in one of our published writings.

16 Discovery in general has been explained already. As for the species of Discovery, the first to be noted is (1) the least artistic form of it, of which the poets make most use through mere lack of invention, Discovery by signs or marks. Of these signs some are congenital, like the 'lance-head which the Earth-born have on them', or 'stars', such as Carcinus brings in his *Thyestes*; others acquired after birth – these latter being either marks on the body, e.g. scars, or external tokens, like necklaces, or (to take another sort of instance) the ark in the Discovery in *Tyro*. Even these, however, admit of two uses, a better and a worse; the scar of Ulysses is an instance; the Discovery of him through it is made in one way by the nurse and in another by the swineherds. A Discovery using signs as a means of assurance is less artistic, as indeed are all such as imply reflection; whereas one bringing them in all of a sudden, as in the *Bath-story*, is of a better order. Next after these are (2) Discoveries made directly by the poet; which are inartistic for that very reason; e.g. Orestes' Discovery of himself in *Iphigenia*: whereas his sister reveals who she is by the letter, Orestes is made to say himself what the poet rather than the story demands. This, therefore, is not far removed from the first-mentioned fault, since he might have presented certain tokens as well. Another instance is the 'shuttle's voice' in the *Tereus* of Sophocles. (3) A third
1455a species is Discovery through memory, from a man's consciousness being awakened by something seen. Thus in *The Cyprioe* of Dicaeogenes, the sight of the picture makes the man burst into tears; and in the *Tale of Alcinous*, hearing the harper Ulysses is reminded of the past and weeps; the Discovery of them being the result. (4) A fourth kind is Discovery through reasoning; e.g. in *The Choephoroe*; 'One like me is here; there is no one like me but Orestes; he, therefore, must be here.' Or that which Polyidus the Sophist suggested for *Iphigenia*; since it was natural for Orestes to reflect: 'My sister was sacrificed, and I am to be sacrificed like her.' Or that in the *Tydeus* of Theodectes: 'I came to find a son, and am to die myself.' Or that in *The Phinidae*: on seeing the place the women inferred their fate, that they were to die there, since they had also been exposed there. (5) There is, too, a composite Discovery arising from bad reasoning on the side of the other party. An instance of it is in Ulysses *the False Messenger*: he said he should know the bow – which he had not seen; but to suppose from that that he would know it again (as though he had once seen it) was bad reasoning. (6) The best of all Discoveries, however, is that arising from the incidents themselves, when the great surprise comes about through a probable incident, like that in the *Oedipus* of Sophocles; and also in *Iphigenia*; for it was not improbable that she should wish to have a letter taken home. These last are the only Discoveries independent of the artifice of signs and necklaces. Next after them come Discoveries through reasoning.

17 At the time when he is constructing his Plots, and engaged on the Diction in which they are worked out, the poet should remember (1) to put the actual scenes as far as possible before his eyes. In this way, seeing everything with the vividness of an eye-witness as it were, he will devise what is appropriate, and be least likely to overlook incongruities. This is shown by what was censured in Carcinus, the return of Amphiaraus from the sanctuary; it would have passed unnoticed, if it had not been actually seen by the audience; but on the stage his play failed, the incongruity of the incident offending the spectators. (2) As far as may be, too, the poet should even act his story with the very gestures of his personages. Given the same natural qualifications, he who feels the emotions to be described will be the most convincing; distress and anger, for instance, are portrayed most truthfully by one who is feeling them at the moment. Hence it is that poetry demands a man with a special gift for it, or else one with a touch of madness in him; the former can easily assume the required mood, and the latter may be actually beside himself with emotion. (3) His story, again, whether already

made or of his own making, he should first sim-
1455b plify and reduce to a universal form, before proceeding to lengthen it out by the insertion of episodes. The following will show how the universal element in *Iphigenia*, for instance, may be viewed: A certain maiden having been offered in sacrifice, and spirited away from her sacrifices into another land, where the custom was to sacrifice all strangers to the Goddess, she was made there the priestess of this rite. Long after that the brother of the priestess happened to come; the fact, however, of the oracle having for a certain reason bidden him go thither, and his object in going, are outside the Plot of the play. On his coming he was arrested, and about to be sacrificed, when he revealed who he was – either as Euripides puts it, or (as suggested by Polyidus) by the not improbable exclamation, 'So I too am doomed to be sacrificed, as my sister was'; and the disclosure led to his salvation. This done, the next thing, after the proper names have been fixed as a basis for the story, is to work in episodes or accessory incidents. One must mind, however, that the episodes are appropriate, like the fit of madness in Orestes, which led to his arrest, and the purifying, which brought about his salvation. In plays, then, the episodes are short; in epic poetry they serve to lengthen out the poem. The argument of the *Odyssey* is not a long one. A certain man has been abroad many years; Poseidon is ever on the watch for him, and he is all alone. Matters at home too have come to this, that his substance is being wasted and his son's death plotted by suitors to his wife. Then he arrives there himself after his grievous sufferings; reveals himself, and falls on his enemies; and the end is his salvation and their death. This being all that is proper to the *Odyssey*, everything else in it is episode.

18 (4) There is a further point to be borne in mind. Every tragedy is in part Complication and in part Dénouement; the incidents before the opening scene, and often certain also of those within the play, forming the Complication; and the rest the Dénouement. By Complication I mean all from the beginning of the story to the
1456a point just before the change in the hero's fortunes; by Dénouement, all from the beginning of the change to the end. In the *Lynceus* of Theodectes, for instance, the Complication includes, together with the presupposed incidents, the seizure of the child and that in turn of the parents; and the Dénouement all from the indictment for the murder to the end. Now it is right, when one speaks of a tragedy as the same or not the same as another, to do so on the ground before all else of their Plot, i.e. as having the same or not the same Complication and Dénouement. Yet there are many dramatists who, after a good Complication, fail in the Dénouement. But it is necessary for both points of construction to be always duly mastered. (5) There are four distinct species of Tragedy – that being the number of the constituents also that have been mentioned: first, the complex Tragedy, which is all Peripety and Discovery; second, the Tragedy of suffering, e.g. the *Ajaxes* and *Ixions*; third, the Tragedy of character, e.g. *The Phthiotides* and *Peleus*. The fourth constituent is that of 'Spectacle', exemplified in *The Phorcides*, in *Prometheus*, and in all plays with the scene laid in the nether world. The poet's aim, then, should be to combine every element of interest, if possible, or else the more important and the major part of them. This is now especially necessary owing to the unfair criticism to which the poet is subjected in these days. Just because there have been poets before him strong in the several species of tragedy, the critics now expect the one man to surpass that which was the strong point of each one of his predecessors. (6) One should also remember what has been said more than once, and not write a tragedy on an epic body of incident (i.e. one with a plurality of stories in it), by attempting to dramatize, for instance, the entire story of the *Iliad*. In the epic owing to its scale every part is treated at proper length; with a drama, however, on the same story the result is very disappointing. This is shown by the fact that all who have dramatized the fall of Illium in its entirety, and not part by part, like Euripides, of the whole of the Niobe story, instead of a portion, like Aeschylus, either fail utterly or have but ill success on the stage; for that and that alone was enough to ruin even a play by Agathon. Yet in their Peripeties, as also in their simple plots, the poets I mean show wonderful skill in aiming at the kind of effect they desire – a tragic situation that arouses the human feeling in one, like the clever villain (e.g. Sisyphus) deceived, or the brave wrongdoer worsted. This is probable, however, only in Agathon's sense, when he speaks

of the probability of even improbabilities coming to pass. (7) The Chorus too should be regarded as one of the actors; it should be an integral part of the whole, and take a share in the action – that which it has in Sophocles, rather than in Euripides. With the later poets, however, the songs in a play of theirs have no more to do with the Plot of that than of any other tragedy. Hence it is that they are now singing intercalary pieces, a practice first introduced by Agathon. And yet what real difference is there between singing such intercalary pieces, and attempting to fit in a speech, or even a whole act, from one play into another?

19 The Plot and Characters having been discussed, it remains to consider the Diction and Thought. As for the Thought, we may assume what is said of it in our Art of Rhetoric, as it belongs more properly to that department of inquiry. The Thought of the personages is shown in everything to be effected by their language – in every effort to prove or disprove, to arouse emotion (pity, fear, anger, and the like), or to
1456b maximize or minimize things. It is clear, also,
that their mental procedure must be on the same lines – their actions likewise, whenever they wish them to arouse pity or horror, or to have a look of importance or probability. The only difference is that with the act the impression has to be made without explanation; whereas with the spoken word it has to be produced by the speaker, and result from his language. What, indeed, would be the good of the speaker, if things appeared in the required light even apart from anything he says? [. . .]

22 The perfection of Diction is for it to be at once clear and not mean. The clearest indeed is that made up of the ordinary words for things, but it is mean, as is shown by the poetry of Cleophon and Sthenelus. On the other hand the Diction becomes distinguished and non-prosaic by the use of unfamiliar terms, i.e. strange words, metaphors, lengthened forms, and everything that deviates from the ordinary modes of speech. – But a whole statement in such terms will be either a riddle or a barbarism, a riddle, if made up of metaphors, a barbarism, if made up of strange words. The very nature indeed of a riddle is this, to describe a fact in an impossible combination of words (which cannot be done with the real names for things, but can be with their metaphorical substitutes); e.g. 'I saw a man glue brass on another with fire', and the like. The corresponding use of strange words results in a barbarism. – A certain admixture, accordingly, of unfamiliar terms is necessary. These, the strange word, the metaphor, the ornamental equivalent, &c., will save the language from seeming mean and prosaic, while the ordinary words in it will
secure the requisite clearness. What helps most, 1458b
however, to render the Diction at once clear and non-prosaic is the use of the lengthened, curtailed, and altered forms of words. Their deviation from the ordinary words will, by making the language unlike that in general use, give it a non-prosaic appearance; and their having much in common with the words in general use will give it the quality of clearness. It is not right, then, to condemn these modes of speech, and ridicule the poet for using them, as some have done; e.g. the elder Euclid, who said it was easy to make poetry if one were to be allowed to lengthen the words in the statement itself as much as one likes. . . . A too apparent use of these licences has certainly a ludicrous effect, but they are not alone in that; the rule of moderation applies to all the constituents of the poetic vocabulary; even with metaphors, strange words, and the rest, the effect will be the same, if one uses them improperly and with a view to provoking laughter. The proper use of them is a very different thing. To realize the difference one should take an epic verse and see how it reads when the normal words are introduced. The same should be done too with the strange word, the metaphor, and the rest; for one has only to put the ordinary words in their place to see the truth of what we are saying. The same iambic, for instance, is found in Aeschylus and Euripides, and as it stands in the former it is a poor line; whereas Euripides, by the change of a single word, the substitution of a strange for what is by usage the ordinary word, has made it seem a fine one. [. . .]

It is a great thing, indeed, to make a proper 1459a
use of these poetical forms, as also of compounds and strange words. But the greatest thing by far is to be a master of metaphor. It is the one thing that cannot be learnt from others; and it is also a sign of genius, since a good metaphor implies an intuitive perception of the similarity in dissimilars.

Of the kinds of words we have enumerated it may be observed that compounds are most in place in the dithyramb, strange words in heroic, and metaphors in iambic poetry. Heroic poetry, indeed, may avail itself of them all. But in iambic verse, which models itself as far as possible on the spoken language, only those kinds of words are in place which are allowable also in an oration, i.e. the ordinary word, the metaphor, and the ornamental equivalent.

Let this, then, suffice as an account of Tragedy, the art imitating by means of action on the stage.

23 As for the poetry which merely narrates, or imitates by means of versified language (without action), it is evident that it has several points in common with Tragedy.

I. The construction of its stories should clearly be like that in a drama; they should be based on a single action, one that is a complete whole in itself, with a beginning, middle, and end, so as to enable the work to produce its own proper pleasure with all the organic unity of a living. Nor should one suppose that there is anything like them in our usual histories. A history has to deal not with one action, but with one period and all that happened in that to one or more persons, however disconnected the several events may have been. Just as two events may take place at the same time, e.g. the sea-fight off Salamis and the battle with the Carthaginians in Sicily, without converging to the same end, so too of two consecutive events one may sometimes come after the other with no one end as their common issue. Nevertheless most of our epic poets, one may say, ignore the distinction.

Herein, then, to repeat what we have said before, we have a further proof of Homer's marvellous superiority to the rest. He did not attempt to deal even with the Trojan war in its entirety, though it was a whole with a definite beginning and end – through a feeling apparently that it was too long a story to be taken in in one view, or if not that, too complicated from the variety of incident in it. As it is, he has singled out one section of the whole; many of the other incidents, however, he brings in as episodes, using the Catalogue of the Ships, for instance, and other episodes to relieve the uniformity of his narrative. [. . .]

24 II. Besides this, Epic poetry must divide 1459b
into the same species as Tragedy; it must be either simple or complex, a story of character or one of suffering. Its parts, too, with the exception of Song and Spectacle, must be the same, as it requires Peripeties, Discoveries, and scenes of suffering just like Tragedy. Lastly, the Thought and Diction in it must be good in their way. All these elements appear in Homer first; and he has made due use of them. His two poems are each examples of construction, the *Iliad* simple and a story of suffering, the *Odyssey* complex (there is Discovery throughout it) and a story of character. And they are more than this, since in Diction and Thought too they surpass all other poems.

There is, however, a difference in the Epic as compared with Tragedy, (1) in its length, and (2) in its metre. (1) As to its length, the limit already suggested will suffice: it must be possible for the beginning and end of the work to be taken in in one view – a condition which will be fulfilled if the poem be shorter than the old epics, and about as long as the series of tragedies offered for one hearing. For the extension of its length epic poetry has a special advantage, of which it makes large use. In a play one cannot represent an action with a number of parts going on simultaneously; one is limited to the part on the stage and connected with the actors. Whereas in epic poetry the narrative form makes it possible for one to describe a number of simultaneous incidents; and these, if germane to the subject, increase the body of the poem. This then is a gain to the Epic, tending to give it grandeur, and also variety of interest and room for episodes of diverse kinds. Uniformity of incident by the satiety it soon creates is apt to ruin tragedies on the stage. (2) As for its metre, the heroic has been assigned it from experience; were any one to attempt a narrative poem in some one, or in several, of the other metres, the incongruity of the thing would be apparent. The heroic in fact is the gravest and weightiest of metres – which is what makes it more tolerant than the rest of strange words and metaphors, that also being a point in which the narrative form of poetry goes beyond all others. The iambic and trochaic, on the other hand, are
metres of movement, the one representing that 1460a
of life and action, the other that of the dance. Still more unnatural would it appear, if one were to write an epic in a medley of metres, as

Chaeremon did. Hence it is that no one has ever written a long story in any but heroic verse; nature herself, as we have said, teaches us to select the metre appropriate to such a story.

Homer, admirable as he is in every other respect, is especially so in this, that he alone among epic poets is not unaware of the part to be played by the poet himself in the poem. The poet should say very little *in propria persona*, as he is no imitator when doing that. Whereas the other poets are perpetually coming forward in person, and say but little, and that only here and there, as imitators, Homer after a brief preface brings in forthwith a man, a woman, or some other Character – no one of them characterless, but each with distinctive characteristics.

The marvellous is certainly required in Tragedy. The Epic, however, affords more opening for the improbable, the chief factor in the marvellous, because in it the agents are not visibly before one. The scene of the pursuit of Hector would be ridiculous on the stage – the Greeks halting instead of pursuing him, and Achilles shaking his head to stop them; but in the poem the absurdity is overlooked. The marvellous, however, is a cause of pleasure, as is shown by the fact that we all tell a story with additions, in the belief that we are doing our hearers a pleasure.

Homer more than any other has taught the rest of us the art of framing lies in the right way. I mean the use of paralogism. Whenever, if A is or happens, a consequent, B, is or happens, men's notion is that, if the B is, the A also is – but that is a false conclusion. Accordingly, if A is untrue, but there is something else, B, that on the assumption of its truth follows as its consequent, the right thing then is to add on the B. Just because we know the truth of the consequent, we are in our minds led on to the erroneous inference of the truth of the antecedent. Here is an instance, from the *Bath-story* in the *Odyssey*.

A likely impossibility is always preferable to an unconvincing possibility. The story should never be made up of improbable incidents; there should he nothing of the sort in it. If, however, such incidents are unavoidable, they should he outside the piece, like the hero's ignorance in *Oedipus* of the circumstances of Laius' death; not within it, like the report of the Pythian games in *Electra*, or the man's having come to Mysia from Tegea without uttering a word on the way, in *The Mysians*. So that it is ridiculous to say that one's Plot would have been spoilt without them, since it is fundamentally wrong to make up such Plots. If the poet has taken such a Plot, however, and one sees that he might have put it in a more probable form, he is guilty of absurdity as well as a fault of art. Even in the *Odyssey* the improbabilities in the setting-ashore of Ulysses would be
clearly intolerable in the hands of an inferior 1460b
poet. As it is, the poet conceals them, his other excellences veiling their absurdity. Elaborate Diction, however, is required only in places where there is no action, and no Character or Thought to be revealed. Where there is Character or Thought, on the other hand, an over-ornate Diction tends to obscure them.

25 As regards Problems and their Solutions, one may see the number and nature of the assumptions on which they proceed by viewing the matter in the following way. (1) The poet being an imitator just like the painter or other maker of likenesses, he must necessarily in all instances represent things in one or other of three aspects, either as they were or are, or as they are said or thought to be or to have been, or as they ought to be. (2) All this he does in language, with an admixture, it may be, of strange words and metaphors, as also of the various modified forms of words, since the use of these is conceded in poetry. (3) It is to be remembered, too, that there is not the same kind of correctness in poetry as in politics, or indeed any other art. There is, however, within the limits of poetry itself a possibility of two kinds of error, the one directly, the other only accidentally connected with the art. If the poet meant to describe the thing correctly, and failed through lack of power of expression, his art itself is at fault. But if it was through his having meant to describe it in some incorrect way (e.g. to make the horse in movement have both right legs thrown forward) that the technical error (one in a matter of, say, medicine or some other special science), or impossibilities of whatever kind they may be, have got into his description, his error in that case is not in the essentials of the poetic art. These, therefore, must be the premisses of the Solutions in answer to criticisms involved in the Problems.

I. As to the criticisms relating to the poet's art itself. Any impossibilities there may be in his descriptions of things are faults. But from another point of view they are justifiable, if they serve the end of poetry itself – if (to assume what we have said of that end) they make the effect of either that very portion of the work or some other portion more astounding. The Pursuit of Hector is an instance in point. If, however, the poetic end might have been as well or better attained without sacrifice of technical correctness in such matters, the impossibility is not to be justified, since the description should be, if it can, entirely free from error. One may ask, too, whether the error is in a matter directly or only accidentally connected with the poetic art; since it is a lesser error in an artist not to know, for instance, that the hind has no horns, than to produce an unrecognizable picture of one.

II. If the poet's description be criticized as not true to fact, one may urge perhaps that the object ought to be as described – an answer like that of Sophocles, who said that he drew men as they ought to be, and Euripides as they were. If the description, however, be neither true nor of the thing as it ought to be, the answer must be then, that it is in accordance with opinion. The tales about Gods, for instance, may be as wrong as
1461a Xenophanes thinks, neither true nor the better
thing to say; but they are certainly in accordance with opinion. Of other statements in poetry one may perhaps say, not that they are better than the truth, but that the fact was so at the time; e.g. the description of the arms: 'their spears stood upright, butt-end upon the ground'; for that was the usual way of fixing them then, as it is still with the Illyrians. As for the question whether something said or done in a poem is morally right or not, in dealing with that one should consider not only the intrinsic quality of the actual word or deed, but also the person who says or does it, the person to whom he says or does it, the time, the means, and the motive of the agent – whether he does it to attain a greater good, or to avoid a greater evil. [. . .]

26 The question may be raised whether the epic or the tragic is the higher form of imitation. It may be argued that, if the less vulgar is the higher, and the less vulgar is always that which addresses the better public, an art addressing any and every one is of a very vulgar order. It is a belief that their public cannot see the meaning, unless they add something themselves, that causes the perpetual movements of the performers – bad flute-players, for instance, rolling about, if quoit-throwing is to be represented, and pulling at the conductor, if Scylla is the subject of the piece. Tragedy, then, is said to be an art of this order – to be in fact just what the later actors were in the eyes of their
predecessors; for Mynniscus used to call Callip- 1462a
pides 'the ape', because he thought he so over-acted his parts; and a similar view was taken of Pindarus also. All Tragedy, however, is said to stand to the Epic as the newer to the older school of actors. The one, accordingly, is said to address a cultivated audience, which does not need the accompaniment of gesture; the other, an uncultivated one. If, therefore, Tragedy is a vulgar art, it must clearly be lower than the Epic.

The answer to this is twofold. In the first place, one may urge (1) that the censure does not touch the art of the dramatic poet, but only that of his interpreter; for it is quite possible to overdo the gesturing even in an epic recital, as did Sosistratus, and in a singing contest, as did Mnasitheus of Opus. (2) That one should not condemn all movement, unless one means to condemn even the dance, but only that of ignoble people – which is the point of the criticism passed on Callippides and in the present day on others, that their women are not like gentlewomen. (3) That Tragedy may produce its effect even without movement or action in just the same way as Epic poetry; for from the mere reading of a play its quality may be seen. So that, if it be superior in all other respects, this element of inferiority is no necessary part of it.

In the second place, one must remember (1) that Tragedy has everything that the Epic has (even the epic metre being admissible), together with a not inconsiderable addition in the shape of the Music (a very real factor in the pleasure of the drama) and the Spectacle. (2) That its reality of presentation is felt in the play as read, as well as in the play as acted. (3) That the tragic imitation requires less space for the attainment of its 1462b
end; which is a great advantage, since the more concentrated effect is more pleasurable than one with a large admixture of time to dilute it – consider the *Oedipus* of Sophocles, for instance, and the effect of expanding it into the number of lines of the *Iliad*. (4) That there is less unity in the imitation of the epic poets, as is proved by the

fact that any one work of theirs supplies matter for several tragedies; the result being that, if they take what is really a single story, it seems curt when briefly told, and thin and waterish when on the scale of length usual with their verse. In saying that there is less unity in an epic, I mean an epic made up of a plurality of actions, in the same way as the *Iliad* and *Odyssey* have many such parts, each one of them in itself of some magnitude; yet the structure of the two Homeric poems is as perfect as can be, and the action in them is as nearly as possible one action. If, then, Tragedy is superior in these respects, and also, besides these, in its poetic effect (since the two forms of poetry should give us, not any or every pleasure, but the very special kind we have mentioned), it is clear that, as attaining the poetic effect better than the Epic, it will be the higher form of art.

So much for Tragedy and Epic poetry – for these two arts in general and their species; the number and nature of their constituent parts; the causes of success and failure in them; the Objections of the critics, and the Solutions in answer to them.

6

Ennead I, vi

Plotinus

Plotinus (ca. 205–70), the founder of Neoplatonism, was born in Egypt and lived in Rome, where he started a school of philosophy.

§1. Beauty is found for the most part in what is seen, but it is also found in sounds, when these are composed into words, and in all the arts generally.[1] For songs and rhythms are also beautiful. And beauty is also found by those who turn away from sense-perception towards the higher region; that is, practices,[2] actions, habits, and types of knowledge are beautiful, to say nothing of the beauty of the virtues. If there is some beauty prior to these, this discussion will show it.

What, then, is it that has made us imagine bodies to be beautiful and our sense of hearing incline to sounds, finding them beautiful? And as for the things that depend directly on the soul, how are all of these beautiful? Is it because all of them are beautiful by one and the same beauty, or is it that there is one sort of beauty in the body and another in other things? And what, then, are these sorts of beauty, or what is this beauty?

For some things, such as bodies, are not beautiful owing to what they are in themselves, but rather by participation, whereas some things are beautiful in themselves, such as the nature that virtue is. This is so because bodies themselves sometimes appear beautiful and sometimes do not since the body and the beauty are distinct. What is it, then, that is present in the bodies [that makes them beautiful]? It is this that we must examine first. What is it, then, that moves the eyes of spectators and turns them[3] towards it and draws them on and makes them rejoice at the sight? By finding this and using it as a stepping-stone, we might also be in a position to see the rest.

Practically everyone claims that proportion of parts in relation to each other and to the whole added to fine coloration makes something beautiful to see. And, generally, in regard to the objects of sight and all other things, their beauty consists in their proportion or measure. For those who hold this view, no simple thing will be beautiful; necessarily, beauty will exist only in the composite. The whole will be beautiful for them, while each of the parts will not have its own beauty but will be a contributing factor in making the whole beautiful. But it should be the case that if the whole is beautiful, the parts are also beautiful. For beauty is not made up out of ugly things; all of its parts are beautiful.

For these people, the beauty of colors, for example, and the light of the sun, since they are simple, do not have proportion and so will be

Plotinus, *Ennead* I, vi, in *Neoplatonic Philosophy: Introductory Readings*, trans. John Dillon and Lloyd P. Gerson (Indianapolis, IN, and Cambridge, MA: Hackett Publishing, 2004), pp. 18–30.

excluded from being beautiful. But, then, how is gold beautiful? And how about lightning in the night and the stars, which are beautiful to see? And as for the beauty of sounds, the simple ones will be eliminated for the same reason, although it is frequently the case that in the beauty of a whole [composition], each sound is itself beautiful. Further, when a face sometimes appears beautiful and sometimes not, though the proportion remains the same, would we not have to say that beauty is other than the proportion and that the proportion is beautiful because of something other than itself?

If they pass on to beautiful practices and expressions and attribute their beauty to proportion, what does it mean to say that there is proportion in beautiful practices or laws or studies or types of knowledge? For how could theories be proportional to each other? If it is because they are in harmony, it is also the case that there is agreement and harmony among bad theories. For example, to say that "self-control is stupidity" and "justice is silly nobility" is to say two things that are harmonious, or in concord, or agree with each other.

And then every type of virtue is a beauty in the soul and a beauty that is truer than the previous ones. But how are these proportioned? It is not as magnitudes or numbers[4] that they are proportioned. And since there are several parts of the soul, what is the formula for the combination or the mixture of the parts or of the theories? And what would be the beauty of intellect taking it in isolation?[5]

§2. Taking up the matter again, let us say what, then, is the primary beauty in bodies. There is, of course, something that is perceived at first glance, and the soul speaks about it as it does about that with which it is familiar, and takes it in as something that it recognizes and, in a way, it finds itself in concord with it. But when it encounters the ugly, it holds back and rejects it and recoils from it as something with which it is not in harmony and as something that is alien to it. We say, then, that the soul, having the nature it does and turned in the direction of the greater essence in the realm of true reality, when it sees something to which it has an affinity or something that is a trace of that to which it has an affinity, is both delighted and thrilled and returns to itself and recalls itself and what belongs to itself.

What likeness is there, then, between the things here in relation to the things that are beautiful in the intelligible world? For if there is a likeness, then we assume that there are like things. How, then, are things here and there both beautiful? We say that these are beautiful by participation in Form. For everything that is shapeless but is by nature capable of receiving shape or form is, having no share in an expressed principle or form, ugly and stands outside of divine reason. This is complete ugliness.

But something is also ugly if it has not been mastered by shape and an expressed principle owing to the fact that its matter has not allowed itself to be shaped completely according to form. The form, then, approaches [the matter] and orders that which is to be a single composite from many parts, and guides it into being a completed unity and makes it one by the parts' acceptance of this; and since the form is one, that which is shaped had to be one, to the extent possible for that which is composed of many parts.

Beauty is, then, situated over that which is shaped at the moment when, the parts having been arranged into one whole, it gives itself to the parts and to the wholes. Whenever beauty takes hold of something that is one and uniform in its parts, it gives the same thing to the whole. It is, in a way, like art, that sometimes gives beauty to a whole house along with its parts and sometimes like some nature that gives beauty to a single stone. Thus, a body comes to be beautiful by its association with an expressed principle coming from the divine [Forms].

§3. The power [in the soul][6] corresponding to beauty recognizes it, and there is nothing more authoritative in judging its own concerns, especially when the rest of the soul judges along with it. Perhaps the rest of the soul also expresses itself by bringing into concord the beautiful object with the form inside itself, using that for judgment like a ruler used to judge the straightness of something.

But how does the beauty in the body harmonize with that which is prior to body? How can the architect, harmonizing the external house with the form of the house internal to him, claim that the former is beautiful? In fact, it is because the external house is, apart from the stones, the inner form divided by the external mass of matter. Being in fact undivided, it appears divided into many parts. Then, whenever sense-perception sees the form in the bodies binding together and mastering the contrary nature, which is shapeless – that is, whenever it sees an overarching shape on top of other shapes – it gathers together as one that which was in many places and brings it back and collects it into the soul's interior as something without parts and at that moment gives it to the interior [judging power of the soul] as something having the harmony and concord that is dear to it. This is just as when a good man sees in the fresh face of a youth a trace of the virtue that is in harmony with the truth that is inside himself.

The simple beauty of a color resides in shape and in the mastery of the darkness in matter by the presence of incorporeal light and of an expressed principle and a form. This is the reason why fire itself, among all the other bodies, is beautiful: it has the role of form in relation to the other elements, highest in position, finest of the other bodies, being as close as possible to the incorporeal, and alone is not receptive of the other [elements], though the others receive it. For it heats them, but is itself not cooled, and is primarily colored, whereas the others get the form of color from it. So it shines and glows as if it were form. That [color] which fades in a fire's light, unable to master [the matter], is no longer beautiful, since it does not partake of the whole form of the color. As for the imperceptible harmonies in sounds that make the perceptible ones, they make the soul grasp them so as to have comprehension of beauty in the same way, showing the same thing in another way.

It is logical that perceptible harmonies be measured by numbers, though not by every formula but only by one that serves in the production of form for the purpose of mastering. And so regarding perceptible beauties, which are reflections and shadows that come to matter as if they were making a dash there to beautify it and thrill us when they appear, enough said.

§4. Regarding the more elevated beauties that sense-perception is not fated to see, soul sees them and speaks about them without the instruments of sense-perception, but it has to ascend to contemplate them, leaving sense-perception down below. But just as in the case of the beauties perceived by the senses, it is not possible to speak about them to those who have not seen them or to those who have never grasped them for what they are, for example, those who have been blind since birth; in the same way, it is not possible to speak about the beauty of practices to those who have not accepted their beauty nor that of types of knowledge and other such things. Nor can one speak about the "splendor" of virtue to those who have not even imagined for themselves the beauty of the visage of justice and self-control, "not even the evening nor the morning star are so beautiful."

But such a sight must be reserved for those who see it with that in the soul by which it sees such things, and seeing it are delighted and shocked and overwhelmed much more than in the previous cases, since we are now speaking of those who have already got hold of true beauties. For these are the emotions one should experience in regard to that which is [truly] beautiful: astonishment, and a sweet shock, and longing, and erotic thrill, and a feeling of being overwhelmed with pleasure. It is possible to have these emotions, and practically all souls do have them in regard to all the unseen beauties, so to say, but in particular those souls who are more enamored of these. It is the same with regard to the [beautiful] bodies that all can see, though not everyone is "stung" equally by their beauty. Those who are stung especially are those who are called "lovers."

§5. We should next ask those who are enamored of the beauties not available to the senses: "What is it you experience in regard to the practices said to be beautiful and to beautiful ways of being in the world and to self-controlled characters and, generally, to the products of virtue and dispositions, I mean the beauty of souls?" And "When you see your own 'interior beauty,' what do you feel?" And "Can you describe the frenzied and excited state you are in and your longing to be with your [true] selves, when extricating yourselves from your bodies?" For this is how those who are truly enamored feel.

But what is it that makes them feel this way? It is not shapes or colors or some magnitude, but rather they feel this way about soul, it being itself "without color" and having self-control that is also without color and the rest of the "splendor" of virtues. You feel this way whenever you see in yourselves or someone else greatness of soul or a just character or sheer self-control or the awe-inspiring visage of courage or dignity and reserve circling around a calm and untroubled disposition with divine intellect shining on them all.

So, we love and are attracted to these qualities, but what do we mean when we say that they are beautiful? For they are real and appear to us so, and no one who has ever seen them says anything else but that they are really real. What does "really real" mean? In fact, it means that they are beautiful things. But the argument still needs to show why real things have made the soul that of which they are enamored. What is that striking thing shining on all the virtues like a light?

Would you like to consider the opposites, the ugly things that come to be in the soul, and contrast them with the beauties? For perhaps a consideration of what ugliness is and why it appears as such would contribute to our achieving what we are seeking. Well, then, let there be an ugly soul, one that is unrestrained and unjust, filled with all manner of appetites and every type of dread, mired in fear owing to cowardice and envy owing to pettiness, thinking that everything it can think of is mortal and base, deformed in every way, a lover of impure pleasures, that is, one who lives a life in which bodily pleasures are measured by their vileness.

Shall we not say, therefore, that this very vileness supervenes on his soul just as would a beauty added to it, which both harmed it and made it impure, "mixed with much evil" no longer having a life or perceptions that are pure, but rather living a murky life by an evil adulteration that includes much death in it, no longer seeing what a soul should see, no longer even being allowed to remain in itself owing to its always being dragged to the exterior and downward into darkness?

This is what I regard as an impure soul, dragged in every direction by its chains towards whatever it happens to perceive with its senses, with much of what belongs to the body adulterating it, deeply implicating itself with the material element and, taking that element into itself owing to that adulteration that only makes it worse, it exchanges the form it has for another. It is as if someone fell into mud or slime and the beauty he had is no longer evident, whereas what is seen is what he wiped on himself from the mud or slime. But the ugliness that has been added to him has come from an alien source, and his job, if he is again to be beautiful, is to wash it off and to be clean[7] as he was before.

So we would be speaking correctly in saying that the soul becomes ugly by a mixture or adulteration and by an inclination in the direction of the body and matter. And this is ugliness for a soul: not being pure or uncorrupted like gold, but filled up with the earthly which, were someone to remove that from it, would just be gold and would be beautiful, isolated from other things and being just what it is itself. In the same way, the soul – being isolated from appetites, which it acquires because of that body with which it associates too much – when it is separated from other affections and is purified of what it has that is bodily, remains just what it is when it has put aside all the ugliness that comes from that other nature.

§6. For it is the case, as the ancient doctrine has it, that self-control and courage and, indeed, every virtue is a purification and is wisdom itself. For this reason, the mysteries correctly offer the enigmatic saying that one who has not been purified will lie in Hades in slime, because one who is not pure likes slime owing to his wickedness. They are like pigs that, with unclean bodies, like such things.

What would true self-control be, besides not having anything to do with the pleasures of the body and fleeing them as impure, as not belonging to one who is pure? And what is courage but the absence of fear of death? But death is the separation of the soul from the body. And this is not feared by one who loves to be isolated.[8] And greatness of soul is contempt for the things here below. And wisdom is the process of thought consisting in a turning away from the things below, leading the soul to the things above.

The soul, then, when it is purified, becomes a form, and an expressed principle, and entirely incorporeal and intellectual and wholly divine, which is the source of beauty and of all things that have an affinity to it. Soul then, being borne up to Intellect, becomes even more beautiful. And Intellect and the things that come from Intellect are soul's beauty, since they belong to it, that is, they are not alien to it, because it is then really soul alone.[9] For this reason, it is correctly said that goodness and being beautiful for the soul consist in "being assimilated to god" because it is there that beauty is found as well as the rest of the destiny of real beings. Or rather, true being is beauty personified[10] and ugliness is the other nature, primary evil itself, so that for god, "good," and "beautiful" are the same, or rather goodness and beauty are the same.[11]

In a similar way, then, we should seek out what is beautiful and good and ugly and evil. And first we should posit Beauty, which is the Good from which Intellect comes, which is identical with the Form of Beauty. And soul is beautiful by Intellect. Other things are beautiful as soon as they are shaped by soul, including the beauties in actions and in practices. And the bodies that are said to be beautiful are so as soon as soul makes them so. Since it is divine and, in a way, a part of beauty, it makes all that it grasps and masters beautiful insofar as it is possible for them to partake in beauty.

§7. We must, then, ascend to the Good, which every soul desires. If someone then has seen it, he knows what I mean when I say how beautiful it is. For it is desired as good, and the desire is for this, though the attainment of it is for those who ascend upward and revert to it and who divest themselves of the garments they put on when they descended. It is just like those who ascend to the sacred religious rites where there are acts of purification and the removal of the cloaks they had worn before they went inside naked. One proceeds in the ascent, passing by all that is alien to the god until one sees by oneself alone that which is itself alone uncorrupted, simple and pure, that upon which everything depends[12] and towards which one looks and is and lives and thinks.[13] For it is the cause of life and intellect and being. And then if someone see this, what pangs of love will he feel, what longings and, wanting to be united with it, how would he <not> be overcome with pleasure?

For though it is possible for one who has not yet seen it to desire it as good, for one who has seen it, there is amazement and delight in beauty, and he is filled with pleasure and he undergoes a painless shock, loving with true love and piercing longing. And he laughs at other loves and is disdainful of the things he previously regarded as beautiful. It is like the experience of those who have happened upon apparitions of gods or daemons after which they can no longer look at the beauty of other bodies in the same way.

What, then, should we think if someone sees pure beauty itself by itself, not contaminated by flesh or bodies, not on the earth or in heaven, in order that it may remain pure? For all these things are added on and have been mixed in and are not primary, rather, they come from that [the Good]. If, then, one sees that which orchestrates everything, remaining by itself while it gives everything, though it does not receive anything into itself, if he remains in sight of this and enjoys it by making himself like it, what other beauty would he need? For this, since it is itself supremely beautiful and the primary beauty, makes its lovers beautiful and lovable.

And with the Good as the prize, the greatest and "ultimate battle is set before souls," in which battle our entire effort is directed to not being deprived of the most worthy vision. And the one who attains this is "blessed," since he is seeing a blessed sight, whereas the one who does not is without luck. It is not the one who does not attain beautiful colors or bodies or power or ruling positions or a kingship who is without luck, but the one who does not attain this and this alone. For the sake of this he ought to cede the attainment of kingship and ruling positions over the whole earth, sea, and heaven, if by abandoning these things and ignoring them he could revert to the Good and see it.

§8. How, then, can we do this? What technique should we employ? How can one see the "inconceivable beauty" as it remains within the sacred temple, not venturing outside, lest the uninitiated should see it? Let he who is able go and follow inside leaving outside the sight of his eyes, not allowing himself to turn back to the splendor of the bodies he previously saw. When he does see beautiful bodies, he should not run after them, but realizing that they are images and traces and shadows, he should flee them in the direction of that of which these are images. For if someone runs towards the image, wanting to grasp it as something true like one wanting to grasp a beautiful reflection in water (as some story has it, in a riddling way, I think) and falls into the water and disappears, in the same way, the one holding on to beautiful bodies and not letting them go plunges down, not with his body but with his soul, into the depths, where there is no joy for intellect and where he stays, blind in Hades. spending time with shadows everywhere he turns.

Someone would be better advised to say "Let us flee to our beloved fatherland." But what is this flight, and how is it accomplished? Let us set sail in the way Homer, in a riddling way, I think, tells us Odysseus did from the sorceress Circe or from Calypso. Odysseus was not satisfied to remain there, even though he had visual pleasures and passed his time with sensual beauty. Our fatherland, from where we have come, and our father are both in the intelligible world.

What is our course, and what is our means of flight? We should not rely on our feet to get us there, for our feet just take us everywhere on earth, one place after another. Nor should you saddle up a horse or prepare some sea-going vessel. You should put aside all such things and stop looking; just shut your eyes, and change your way of looking, and wake up. Everyone has this ability, but few use it.

§9. What, then, is that inner way of looking? Having just awakened, the soul is not yet able to look at the bright objects before it. The soul must first be accustomed to look at beautiful practices, then beautiful works – not those works that the arts produce, but those that men who are called "good" produce – then to look at the soul of those who produce these beautiful works.

How, then, can you see the kind of beauty that a good soul has? Go back into yourself and look. If you do not yet see yourself as beautiful, then be like a sculptor, making a statue that is supposed to be beautiful, who removes a part here and polishes a part there so that he makes the latter smooth and the former just right until he has given the statue a beautiful face. In the same way, you should remove superfluities and straighten things that are crooked, work on the things that are dark, making them bright, and not stop "working on your statue" until the divine splendor of virtue shines in you, until you see "self-control enthroned on the holy seat."

If you have become this and have seen it and find yourself in a purified state, you have no impediment to becoming one in this way nor do you have something else mixed in with yourself, but you are entirely yourself, true light alone, neither measured by magnitude nor reduced by a circumscribing shape nor expanded indefinitely in magnitude but being unmeasured everywhere, as something greater than every measure and better than every quantity. If you see that you have become this, at that moment you have become sight, and you can be confident about yourself, and you have at this moment ascended here, no longer in need of someone to show you. Just open your eyes and see, for this alone is the eye that sees the great beauty.

But if the eye approaches that sight bleary with evils and not having been purified or weak and, owing to cowardice, is not able to see all the bright objects, it does not see them even if someone else shows it that they are present and able to be seen. For the one who sees has an affinity to that which is seen, and he must make himself like it if he is to attain the sight. For no eye has ever seen the sun without becoming sunlike, nor could a soul ever see beauty without becoming beautiful. You must become wholly godlike and wholly beautiful if you intend to see god and beauty.

For first, the soul will come in its ascent to Intellect, and in the intelligible world it will see all the beautiful Forms and will declare that these Ideas are what beauty is.[14] For all things are beautiful, owing to these by the products of Intellect, that is, by essence.[15] But we say that that which "transcends" Intellect is the Idea of the Good, a nature that holds beauty in front of itself. So roughly speaking, the Good is the primary beauty. But if one distinguishes the intelligibles apart, one will say that the "place" of the Forms is intelligible beauty, whereas the Good transcends that and is the "source and principle" of beauty. Otherwise, one will place the Good and the primary beauty in the same thing. In any case, beauty is in the intelligible world.

Translator's Notes

1 Literally, in all that is governed by the Muses, including poetry, literature, music, and dance. Later, these also included philosophy, astronomy, and intellectual practices generally.
2 Moral practices that lead to the acquisition of virtues are meant here.
3 The word [. . .] indicates a reorienting of the soul in the direction of the One, away from other objects of desire.
4 Magnitude and number are the two species of quantity. Hence Plotinus is implying that if beauty is a type of proportion, it is not a proportion of quantities.
5 That is, intellect which is distinct from the soul.
6 Plotinus here means the "calculative" or "rational" part of the entire soul.

7 The word [. . .] indicates both physical cleanliness and moral or spiritual purity.

8 That is, from whatever is alien to him.

9 That is, when soul rises to Intellect, it realizes its true self.

10 Plotinus is using the term here to refer to the One, or the Good, the source of all intelligible beauty or goodness. So in a way, since the One is beyond all intelligible reality, the essence of beauty is beyond beauty.

11 That is, for Intellect, but also for the One or the Good itself.

12 It is only when one strips off in oneself all that is other than intellect and uses the "eye" of intellect alone that one sees one's dependence on the One.

13 To say that one "is and lives and thinks" in *relation* to the Good or the One is to indicate that these activities depend on the One.

14 The words here, "Forms" [. . .] and "Ideas" [. . .] are used by Plotinus synonymously.

15 Here, the Forms are treated as the products of Intellect, though Intellect is, in actuality, not prior to the Forms.

7

De Musica

St. Augustine

St. Augustine (354–430), who served as Bishop of Hippo in North Africa, was a highly influential Christian philosopher.

Book VI

x. 29 We must not hate what is below us, but rather with God's help put it in its right place, setting in right order what is below us, ourselves, and what is above us, and not being offended by the lower, but delighting only in the higher. "The soul is weighed in the balance by what delights her". Delight or enjoyment sets the soul in her ordered place. "Where your treasure is, there will your heart be also" (Matth. 6[21]). Where the delight is, there is the treasure; where the heart is, there is the blessedness or misery. The higher things are those in which equality resides, supreme, unshaken, unchangeable, eternal; where there is no time, because no mutability; whence, in imitation of eternity, times in our world are made, ordered, and modified, as long as the circling sky continually returns to its place of starting, recalling thither the heavenly bodies too, with the days, months, years, periods of five years, and other cycles of time which are marked by the stars, according to the laws of equality, unity, and order. So earthly things are subject to heavenly things, seeming to associate the cycles of their own durations in rhythmic succession with the song of the great whole.

In this array there are many things which to xi. 30
us appear out of order and confused, because we have been attached to their order, their station in existence, according to our own limited merits, not knowing the glorious plan which Divine Providence has in operation concerning us. It is as if some one were put to stand like a statue in a corner of a fine, large house, and found that, being a part of it himself, he could not perceive the beauty of the structure. A soldier on the battlefield cannot see the dispositions of the whole army. If syllables in a poem had life and perception for just as long as their sounds lasted, the rhythmicality and beauty of the whole intricately inwoven work could not give them pleasure. They could not review and approve the whole poem, which is built of their own transient selves. God made sinful man ugly; but it was not an ugly act to make him so. Man became ugly by his own wish. He lost the whole, which, in obedience to God's laws, he once possessed, and was given his place in part of it, since he is unwilling to practise the law, and therefore is governed by the law instead. Lawful acts are just, and just acts are not essentially ugly. Even in our bad deeds there are good works of God. Man, as man, is good. Adultery is bad. But from adultery,

St. Augustine, *St. Augustine's De Musica*, trans. W. F. Jackson Knight (London: The Orthological Institute, 1949), pp. 107–20, 122–4.

a bad act of man, is born a man, a good act of God.

xi. 31 To return, those rhythms excel by virtue of the beauty of reason, which, if we were cut off from them altogether when we incline towards the body, would cease to govern the Progressive Rhythm perceptible to sense, and to create perceptible beauties of temporal durations by bodily movement. [. . .] It is the same psyche which receives all these impulses, which are in fact its own, multiplying them in some sense within itself, and making them capable of being remembered. This particular power of the psyche is called memory, and it is an instrument of great assistance in the busy activities of human life.

xi. 32 Whatever things are retained by memory from movements of the psyche performed in response to the body's affects are called in Greek phantasies. [. . .] To treat these phantasies as things ascertained and understood is to live the life of mere opinion, the life that is set at the very point where error has entry. For such phantasies, moving within the psyche, a seething welter at the mercy of diverse and contradictory blasts from the wind of attention, come into mutual contact and from one another procreate new movements within the psyche, which are no longer things delivered by impressions from the senses, resulting from impacts delivered by bodily affects and retained afterwards by the psyche, but are now rather the images of images to which the conventional name of phantasms has been given. I think differently about my father whom I have seen and about my grandfather whom I have never seen. My thought of my father comes from memory, but my thought of my grandfather comes from mental movements arising out of other mental movements which are contained in memory. Their origin is hard to discover and to explain. I think that, if I had never seen any human bodies, I could not imagine them. Whatever I make out of anything which I have seen, I make by means of memory. There is a difference between finding a phantasy in memory and making a phantasm from memory. The power of the psyche can do all of this. But it is the greatest error to mistake even true phantasms for ascertained facts; though there is in both these classes of being something which we can without absurdity say that we know, that is, either something which we have perceived, or else something of which we can form a mental image. I am not rash to assert that I had a father and a grandfather, but it would be utter insanity if I ventured to say that they were the very men whom my mind holds, either in phantasy or in a phantasm. There are people who follow their phantasms in headlong haste; and indeed we can say that the universal cause of false opinion is the mistake of regarding phantasies or phantasms as true facts ascertained by sense-perception. We should, of course, resist them; we must not accommodate to them our mental activity, wrongly thinking that, just because there is an element of thought in them, therefore it is by our understanding that we apprehend them.

But, if rhythm of this sort, occurring in a soul, xi. 33
abandoned to temporal things, has a beauty within the limitations of its own kind, even though it is only transiently that it stimulates that soul, why would Divine Providence regard this kind of beauty with jealous disapproval? This kind of beauty is formed out of our penal mortality, which, by a law of God, a law most just, we have fully deserved. But he has not so forsaken us that we cannot be recalled from carnal delight, and quickly retrace our way, for His pity stretches out its hand. Carnal delight powerfully fixes in the memory all that it derives from our treacherous senses. This intimacy between our souls and the flesh, the result of carnal affection, is called the flesh in the Divine Scriptures. The flesh wrestles with the mental part of us, and so the Apostle could say, "With the mind I myself serve the law of God; but with the flesh the law of sin" (Rom. 7[25]). But when the mental part of us is uplifted to attachment to spiritual things, the impulse of this intimacy is broken; it is gradually suppressed, and then extinguished. It was stronger when we followed it; when we bridle it, it still has some strength, but it is now weaker. If we with firm steps draw back from every lascivious thought, in which there must always be a reduction of the soul's full existence, our delight in the Rhythm of Reason is restored, and our whole life is turned to God, not now receiving pleasure from the body, but giving to it a rhythm of health. This result happens because the outer man is consumed away, and the man himself is transformed into something finer.

But memory gathers not only the carnal xii. 34
movements of the mind that constitute the rhythm of which we have just spoken, but also

spiritual movements, which we have now shortly to treat. Being simple, they have need of fewer words: but they have the utmost need of undisturbed mental activity. That equality which we failed to find, fixed and enduring, in perceptible rhythm, but which we recognized as shadowed in it while it passed us by, would nowhere have been an object of our mind's aspiration, if somewhere it had not become known to our mind. But it cannot have been somewhere in the world of space and time. Spatial things expand, temporal things pass. Where then can it have been? Not in bodily forms, which can never be called truly equal to one another if they are fairly weighed by free judgment, nor in intervals of time, in which we never know whether something is longer or shorter in duration than something else, the inequality being unobserved by our perception. Where then is that equality at which we must be looking, if we are so led to desire equality in bodily things and their movements, and yet dare not trust them, then we consider them with care? Presumably it is in the place which is higher and finer than any bodily things, but whether that is in the soul, or above it, is obscure.

xii. 35 Our rhythmic or metric art, which is used by makers of verses, comprises certain rhythmical measurements according to which they make the verses. The measurements, that is, the rhythm, remain when the verses stop or pass. The verse or rhythm which passes is really manufactured by the rhythm which remains. The art is an active conformation of the mind of the artist. This conformation is not in the mind of any man who is unskilled, or who has forgotten the art. Now one who has forgotten a rhythm can be reminded of it by questions asked of him. The rhythm returns to his memory, but obviously not from the questioner. The man who had forgotten makes movements within the sphere of his own mental activity in response to something, and hence the forgotten thing may be restored. Can he even be reminded of the quantities of syllables, which vary in their temporal duration according to the decree of the ancients? For if these quantities had been stable, securely fixed by nature or doctrine, modern scholars would not have been committing the errors in quantity which they do commit. We cannot say that everything forgotten can be recalled to memory by questions; we could not be made by questions to remember a dinner eaten a year ago, nor could questions recall to memory detailed quantities of syllables. The *I* of *Italia*, Italy, was made short ⌣ in the past by the wish of some individual men. Now it is long –, *Ī*, *Ītalia,* made long by the wish of others. This is convention. But no one, past, present, or future, can by his wish make 1 + 2 anything but 3, or prevent 2 from being twice 1. If one who has never learnt rhythm, that is, not one who has learnt and then forgotten it, is thoroughly questioned about it, and answers are elicited from him, then, just as arithmetical answers about 1 and 2 and the rest can be elicited by questions, so too the learner may learn the art of rhythm, except the quantities of syllables, which depend on authority. The questioner does not impart anything, but the learner acts within himself in such a way as to understand what is asked, and answers. Through this mental movement rhythm is imprinted on his faculty of mental activity, and he achieves the active conformation, which is called art.

This rhythm is immutable and eternal, with xii. 36
no inequality possible in it. Therefore it must come from God. The learner who is questioned moves inwardly to God to understand immutable truth; and unless he retains in memory the same movement which once he made, the learner cannot be recalled to an apprehension of that same immutable truth without external help.

Presumably the learner had abandoned xiii. 37
thoughts of that truth, and needed to be recalled by memory, because he was intent on something else. What distracted him from thoughts of the supreme, immutable equality, must have been either equal in value, or higher, or lower. Obviously it must have been lower. The soul admits that immutable equality exists, but also that it is itself lower than it, because it looks sometimes at this equality and sometimes at something else. Set on various objects, the soul performs a variety of temporal rhythms, with no existence in the realm of eternal and immutable things. This active conformation by which the soul first understands what are eternal things, then realizes that temporal things are inferior to them even when they are in itself, and finally knows that the higher is more to be sought than the lower, is wisdom.

The soul has, then, the power to know eternal xiii. 38
things as things to which it should cling fast, but

it has not at the same time the power to do so. To find the reason, we must observe what we notice most attentively, and for what we show great care, for that is what we love much. We love the beautiful; True, some love ugly things, the "lovers of putrefaction", in Greek. But what matters is how much more beautiful are the things which most people like. Clearly no one loves what disgusts the perception, that is, sheer repulsiveness. Beautiful things please by proportion, and here as we have shown equality is not found only in sounds for the ear and in bodily movements, but also in visible forms, in which hitherto equality has been identified with beauty even more customarily than in sounds. Nothing can be proportionate or rhythmic without equality, with pairs of equivalent members responding to each other. All that is single must have some central place, so that equality may be preserved in the intervals extending to the central individual part from either side. Visible light has the presidency over all colours, colour of course being a source of delight in bodily forms. And in all light and all colours we aspire to something which is in harmony with our eyes. We turn away from too bright a light, and dislike looking at what is too dark, just as we shrink from too loud a sound and do not like a whisper. Nothing here depends on intervals of time, but everything on the actual sound which is here the very light of the rhythm, the sound to which silence is the contrary, just as darkness is the contrary to light. In all this we act according to our nature's capacity, seeking according to agreeability or rejecting according to disagreeability, though we perceive that what is disagreeable to us is often agreeable to the other animals; and we are in fact here too rejoicing in what is really a code of equality, discovering that, in ways remote from our usual thinking, equivalences have yet been furnished to match on another. In smell, taste, and touch this may equally be observed, and could easily be explored, but it would take too long to unravel the secret in detail. Every perceptible thing which pleases us, pleases us by equality or similitude. Where there is equality or similitude, there is rhythmicality, for nothing is so equal or so similar to anything as one is to one.

xiii. 39 All this, as we have discovered, is not passively sustained by the soul from physical bodies, but actively performed by the soul in physical bodies. Love of active performance, in reaction to the affects of its own body, diverts the soul from contemplation of eternal things, and care for the pleasure of perception calls its attention away. [. . .]

The general love of activity, which diverts us xiii. 40
from truth, starts from pride, the vice which made the soul prefer to imitate God rather than to serve God. Rightly it is written in the Holy Books, "The beginning of a man's pride is to revolt from God", and "The beginning of all sin is pride". [. . .] The soul by itself is nothing, or it would not have been mutable, and suffered default from its own essence. The whole quality of the soul's existence is from God, and therefore, while it remains within its own order of being, it is enlivened in mental activity and in self-consciousness by God's presence. Such goodness the soul has deeply within it. To become distended with pride is to move towards the external and to become empty within, that is, to exist less and less fully. To move away to what is outside is to sacrifice what is deeply inside, and to put God far away, by a distance not of space but of mental conditions.

Such a soul's appetite is to have other souls xiii. 41
subjected to it, not the souls of animals, which is allowed by Divine law, but rational souls, the souls that are its relatives and friends and partners under the same law. The soul has conceived the desire to behave concerning them with pride, regarding this behaviour concerning them as so much more excellent than behaviour concerning physical bodies as every soul is better than every body. But only God can act upon rational souls directly and not through the body. Yet it so transpires through our condition of sinfulness that souls are permitted to act concerning other souls, moving them by signals conveyed by the physical body of either of the souls involved, either with natural gestures, as facial expression or a nod, or by conventional indications such as words. We give orders and apply persuasion, and carry out all other actions by which souls act concerning or with other souls, by means of signs. Now it follows from the code by which we live that whatever, in pride, desires to excel all else rules not even its own parts and its own body without difficulty and pain, partly because of stupidity within itself and partly because it is depressed by the weight of mortal members. By these rhythmical

movements, by means of which souls behave in response to one another, they are diverted, through aspiration to honours and tributes of praise, from any deep understanding of that other truth, the truth that is pure and unsullied. It is only from God that a soul can win true honour. He can render it blessed, living in His presence in unseen life of righteousness and piety.

xiii. 42 Accordingly, the movements extruded by a soul in concern with what clings to itself, and in concern with other souls subject to it, are like Progressive Rhythm, for the soul is acting as if upon its own body. The movements which it extrudes, in its desire to gather souls into its flock, or to subject them to itself, are counted among Occursive Rhythm. For the soul is acting virtually in the realm of the senses, straining, to compel something, which is fetched to it from outside, to become one with itself, or alternatively, if it cannot become one with itself, to repel it. Memory now gathers both kinds of movement, and renders them recordable, that is, capable of being recollected, as the phantasies and phantasms of past actions, in a seething welter. Involved with this is something which can be called a "Weighing Rhythm", whose task is to discern which activities prove convenient to the active soul and which inconvenient. This rhythm we should not be sorry to call "Perceptive Rhythm", for it consists of the perceptible indications by means of which souls behave in response to other souls. When a soul is involved with all these serious distractions, it is scarcely surprising if it is diverted from the contemplation of truth, only possible for it in so far as it has respite from them. It is not allowed to remain in the truth, because it has not won final victory over them. That is why the soul has not inherently and simultaneously both the power to know on what it should take its stand and also the power to do so.

xiv. 43 After thus considering, as well as we could, how the soul is tainted with defilement and weighted by its load, it remains for us to see that action is commanded of the soul by Divine authority, so that through such action it may be purged and unburdened, and may then fly back to peace, and may enter into the joy of its Lord. But of course the Holy Scriptures, with the authority that is theirs, are all the time telling us to love God, our Lord, from our whole heart, our whole soul, and our whole mind, and our neighbour, as ourself. So there is scarcely much for us to say. If we were to refer all the movements of human action and all the rhythms, which we have examined, to this great end, without doubt we shall be cleansed. Yet on the other hand the difficulty of practical obedience is as great as the time taken to hear the command is short.

xiv. 44 It is easy to love colours, musical sounds, cakes, roses and the body's soft, smooth surface. In all of them the soul is in quest of nothing except equality and similitude, and even when it reflects with some thoughtfulness it scarcely detects, amid such dark shadows, the trace of it. If so, it must indeed be easy to love God. For when the soul thinks of Him, as well as it can with the wounds and the stains impeding its thoughts, even so it cannot believe that in Him there is anything unequal, or unlike Himself, or divided by space, or varied in time. Our soul delights in the construction of tall houses, and indulgence in the efforts involved in such operations. Here, if it is the proportion which is the source of pleasure, and I find nothing else that can be, all the equality and similitude discernible would be derided by the arguments of true and methodical reason. Why, then, does our soul slip from the truest citadel of equality, and then, with the mere débris which it drags from it, erect terrestial structures instead? The reason is not the promise of Him who knows not to deceive, "For my yoke is easy" (Matth, 11^{30}). Indeed, the love of this world is far more laborious. In this world the soul looks for permanence and eternity, but never finds them, because only the lowest kind of beauty can be achieved by such transience, and whatever there is in this world which in any decree copies permanenece, is transmitted through our soul by God; for an appearance, which is changeable only in time, is precedent to an appearance which is changeable both in time and in space. The Lord has taught the soul of men what they should not love. "Love not the world. . . . For all that is in the world, the lust of the flesh, and lust of the eyes, and the pride of life <is not of the Father, but is of the world>" (I John 2^{15-16}).

xiv. 45 Now consider what kind of man he is, who finds a better method with which to meet these occurrences. A man who relates, not to mere pleasure, but to the preservation of his bodily self all such rhythms whose source is in the body and in the responses to the affects of the body, and who brings into use, the residue from such rhythms retained in the memory, and others operating from other souls in the vicinity, or extruded in order to attach to the soul those other souls, or their residue retained in memory, not for its own proud ambition to excel, but for the advantage of those other souls themselves; and who employs that other rhythm, which presides, with an examiner's control, over such rhythms of either kind which subsist in the transience of perception, not for the purpose of satisfying an unjustifiable and harmful curiosity, but only for essential proof or disproof – such a man, surely, performs every rhythm without being entrapped in their entanglements. His choice is that bodily health should not be obstructed, and he refers every action to the advantage of his neighbour, whom by the bond of nature he must love as himself. He would obviously be a great man and a great gentleman.

xiv. 46 Rhythm which does not attain the level of reason is devoid of beauty; and any love of the lower beauty defiles the soul. The soul loves not only equality but order also. It has lost its true order. But it still resides in the order of things where, and how, truest order requires it to reside. There is a difference between possessing order, and being possessed by order. The soul possesses order by itself, loving all that is higher than itself, that is, in fact, God, and also the souls that are its companions, loving them as itself. By virtue of this love it orders, that is, sets in right order, all that is lower than itself, without becoming defiled. What defiles the soul is not evil, for even the body, though it is very low in the scale, is a creature of God, and is only scorned when it is compared with the dignity of the soul. Gold is defiled even by the purest silver, if it is alloyed with it. We must not deny to rhythm which is concerned with our penal mortality its inclusion within the works of the Divine fabrication, for such rhythm is within its own kind beautiful. But we must not love such rhythm as if it could make us blessed. We must treat it as we would a plank amid the waves of the sea, not casting it away as a burden, but not embracing it and clinging to it as if we imagined it firmly fixed. We must use such rhythm well, so that eventually we may dispense with it. For love of our neighbour, a love as strong as, according to the command, it must be, is the surest step towards an ability to cling to God; indeed, we should not only be possessed by the order which He imposes, but also possess our own order sure.

Even on the evidence of Perceptive Rhythm, xiv. 47
the soul is proved to like order. Why else is the first foot a pyrrhic ⏑ ⏑, the second an iamb ⏑ –, the third a trochee – ⏑, and so on? It may be said that this is not a matter of intuitive perception, but of reason. Yet Perceptive Rhythm has at least the credit for the equivalence by which eight long syllables occupy the same duration as sixteen short syllables; though it prefers a mixture of long and short syllables together. Reason, in fact, judges perception. Proceleumatics ⏑ ⏑ ⏑ ⏑ are reported by perception as equal to spondees – –. Here reson finds only a potentiality of order. Long syllables are only long by comparison with short syllables, and short syllables short by comparison with long syllables. Iambic ⏑ – verse, however, slowly pronounced, is always in ratio 1 : 2, and remains iambic ⏑ –. But purely pyrrhic ⏑ ⏑ verse, pronounced slowly enough, becomes spondaic – –, not, of course, according to any rule of grammar, but according to the requirement of music. Dactyls – ⏑ ⏑ and anapaests ⏑ ⏑ – remain dactyls and anapaests, on account of the comparison between long and short syllables which is always present, however long the duration in pronunciation may be. Again, at the ends and beginnings of sequences of feet, half-feet are added according to different laws, all needing to have the same ictus as the contiguous feet, and the final half-foot requiring to have sometimes two short syllables in place of one long syllable. Throughout sense-perception applies its modifications. Now here quantitative equality will not account for everything, for either choice might have been made without loss of equality. Decisions are enforced by the bond of right order. It would take too long to display here the rest of the evidence for this, which is provided by durations of time. So too perception, in dealing with visible forms, rejects some of them, for example a figure bending over too far or standing on its head, and so on, when there is no loss of equality, but there is some fault of order. In all that we perceive and in all that we make, we gradually get used to what at first we rejected. It is by order that we weave our pleasure into one. We only like what has a beginning harmoniously woven on to the middle

part, and a middle part harmoniously woven on to the end.

xiv. 48 Therefore we must not place our joys in carnal pleasure, nor in honour and tributes of praise, nor in our thought for anything extrinsic to our body; for we have God within us, and there all that we love is fixed and changeless. Temporal things are with us, but we are not ourselves involved in them, and we feel no pain in being parted from all that is outside our bodies. Even our bodies themselves can be taken from us without pain, or at least without much pain, and restored where, by the death of their old nature, they may be formed anew. The concentration of the soul, fixed on some part of the body, becomes readily involved in transactions in which is no peace, and in a devotion to some private operation in neglect of universal law, though even such an operation can never be quite estranged from the totality ruled by God. Thus even he who does not love the laws is still subjected to them.

xv. 49 Now if we normally think with closest attention about immaterial, changeless things, and if it happens that, at the time, we are performing temporal rhythm in one of the kinds of bodily movement which are ordinary and quite easy, such as walking or singing, we may never notice the rhythm, though it depends on our own activity, and so, too, if we are occupied in our own vain phantasms, again we perform the rhythm, but do not notice it. Now how much more, and how much more constantly, when this "corruptible must put on incorruption, and this mortal must put on immortality" (I Cor. 15[53]), that is, when God has revived our mortal bodies, as the Apostle says, "by his Spirit that dwelleth in" us (Rom. 8[11]), how much more, concentrated on the One God, and on truth seen perspicuous, or, as we are told, "face to face", shall we perceive, with joy, the rhythm by which we actuate our bodies with no unpeacefulness? For we can hardly be expected to believe that the soul, which can derive joy from the things which are good through its own self only, cannot derive joy from the things from which its own goodness comes.

[. . .]

xvii. 56 God has arranged that even a sinful and sorrowful soul can be moved by rhythm and can rightly perform it, even down to the lowest corruption of the flesh. So degraded, rhythm becomes less and less beautiful, but it must always have some beauty. God is jealous of no beauty due to the soul's damnation, regression, or persistence. Number, the base of rhythm, begins from unity. It has beauty by equality and by similitude, and it has interconnection by order. All nature requires order. It seeks to be like itself, and it possesses its own safety and its own order, in spaces or in times or in bodily form, by methods of balance. We have to admit that in number and rhythm all, without exception and without limit, starting from the single origin of unity, is complete and secure, in a structure of equality and similitude and wealth of goodness, cohering from unity onwards in most intimate affection.

Deus creator omnium has a pleasant rhythm xvii. 57
for the ear, but the soul loves the sequence far more for the health and truth in it. We must not believe the dull wits, to use no harsher term, of those who say that nothing can come from nothing, for God Almighty is said to have by His act disproved it. A craftsman operates rationally with rhythm in his art, using Perceptive Rhythm in the artistic tradition, and, besides that, Progressive Rhythm, with which he makes bodily movements, according to intervals of time, or visible forms in wood, rhythmic with intervals of space. If so, surely nature, in obedience to God, can in the ultimate beginning make the wood used by the craftsman, and make it from nothing. Of course it can. The numerical or rhythmic structure of a tree is spatial, and it must be preceded by a numerical or rhythmic structure which is temporal. All growing things in the vegetable world grow by temporal dimensions, and it is from some deeply abstruse numerical system in them that they put forth their reproductive power. Such, perhaps even more truly such, is the growth of physical bodies in the animal world, where the disposition of limbs and all else is based on rhythmic intervals and equality. Every tiny particle must be distended beyond the size of an indivisible point. They are all made from elements, and the elements themselves must be made from nothing. It cannot be supposed that they contain anything of less worth or lowlier than earth. But even earth has its equality of parts, and its length, breadth, and height. In it there is a regular progression, which may be Latinized as "corrationality", from point through length to breadth and height. All is due to the

supreme eternal presidency of numerical rhythm, similitude, equality, and order. If this presidency of mathematical structure is taken from earth, nothing remains. Clearly God in the beginning made earth out of nothing at all.

xvii. 58 The specific appearance of earth, which distinguishes it from the other elements, shows a kind of unity in so far as so base an element is capable of it. No part of it is unlike the whole of it. This element occupies the lowest place, which is entirely suited to its well-being, so harmoniously are its parts interconnected. The nature of water is spread all over earth. Water is a unity, all the more beautiful and transparent on account of a yet greater similitude of its parts, on guard over its order and its security. Air has still greater unity and internal regularity than water. Finally the sky, where the totality of visible things ends, is the highest of all the elements, and has the greatest well-being. Anything which the ministry of carnal perception can count, and anything contained in it, cannot be furnished with, or possess, any numerical rhythm in space which can be estimated, unless previously a numerical rhythm in time has preceded in silent movement. Before even that, there comes vital movement, agile with temporal intervals, and it modifies what it finds, serving the Lord of All Things. Its numerical structure is undistributed into intervals of time; the durations are supplied by potentiality; here, beyond even the rational and intellectual rhythm of blessed and saintly souls, here is the very Law of God, by which a leaf falls not, and for which the very hairs of our head are numbered; and, no nature intervening, they transmit them to the law of earth, and the law below.

8

On the Reduction of the Arts to Theology

St. Bonaventure

St. Bonaventure (ca. 1217–74), an Italian philosopher and theologian, sought to reconcile the thought of Aristotle with that of St. Augustine, while maintaining that the culmination of wisdom is found in contemplation of God.

1. *Every best gift and every perfect gift is from above, coming down from the Father of Lights*, James in the first chapter of his Epistle. These words of Sacred Scripture not only reveal the source of all illumination but they likewise point out the generous flow of manifold rays which issue from the Fount of light. Notwithstanding the fact that every illumination of knowledge is within, still, we can with propriety distinguish what we may call the *external* light, or the light of mechanical skill; the *lower* light, or the light of sense perception; the *inner* light, or the light of philosophical knowledge; and the *higher* light, or the light of grace and of Sacred Scripture. The first light illumines the consideration of the *arts and crafts*; the second, in regard to *natural form*; the third, in regard to *intellectual truth*; the fourth and last, in regard to *saving truth.*

St. Bonaventure, *De reductione artium ad theologiam*, trans. Sister Emma Therese Healy (St. Bonaventure, NY: The Franciscan Institute, St. Bonaventure College, 1955), sections 1–5, 8–11, 13–18.

2. The first light, then since it enlightens the mind for an appreciation of the *arts and crafts*, which are, as it were, exterior to man and intended to supply the needs of the body, is called the light *of mechanical skill.* Being, in a certain sense, servile and of a lower nature than philosophical knowledge, this light can rightly be termed *external.* It has seven divisions corresponding to the seven mechanical arts enumerated by Hugh in his *Disdascalion*, namely, weaving, armor-making, agriculture, hunting, navigation, medicine, and the dramatic art. That the above mentioned arts *suffice* for all the needs of mankind is shown in the following way: every mechanical art is intended for man's *consolation* or his *comfort*; its purpose, therefore, is to banish either *sorrow* or *want*; it either *benefits* or *delights*, according to the words of Horace

> Either to serve or to please is the wish of the poets.

And again:

> He hath gained universal applause who hath combined the profitable with the pleasing.

If its aim is to afford *consolation* and amusement, it is *dramatic art*, or the art of exhibiting plays, which embraces every form of entertainment, be it song, music drama, or pantomime. If, however, it is intended for the *comfort* or betterment of the exterior man, it can accomplish its purpose by providing either *covering* or *food*, or by *serving as an aid in the acquisition of either*. In the matter of *covering*, if it provides a soft and light material, it is weaving; if, a strong and hard material, it is *armor-making* or metal-working, an art which extends to every tool or implement fashioned of iron or of any metal whatsoever, of stone, or of wood.

In the matter of food, mechanical skill may benefit in two ways, for we derive our sustenance from *vegetables* and from *flesh meats*. If it supplies us with *vegetables*, it is *farming*; if it provides us with *flesh meats*, it is *hunting*. Or, again, as regards *food*, mechanical skill has a twofold advantage: either it aids in the *production* and multiplication of crops, in which case it is agriculture, or in various ways of *preparing* food under which aspect it is hunting, an art which extends to every conceivable way of preparing foods, drinks, and delicacies – a task with which bakers, cooks, and innkeepers are concerned. The term "hunting" (*venatio*), however, is derived from one single aspect of the trade, undoubtedly, on account of the excellent nature of game and the popularity of the chase at court.

Furthermore, as an aid in the *acquisition of each of these necessities*, the mechanical arts contribute to the welfare of man in two ways: either by *supplying a want*, and in this case it is *navigation*, which includes all commerce of articles of covering or of food; or by *removing impediments* and ills of the body, under which aspect it is *medicine*, whether it is concerned with the preparation of drugs, potions, or ointments, with the healing of wounds or with the amputation of members, in which latter case it is called surgery. Dramatic art, on the other hand, is in a class by itself. Considered in this light, the classification of the mechanical arts seems adequate.

3. The second light, which enables us to discern *natural forms*, is the light of *sense perception*. Rightly is it called the *lower* light because sense perception begins with a material object and takes place by the aid of corporeal light. It has five divisions corresponding to the five senses. In his third book on Genesis, St. Augustine in the following way bases the *adequacy* of the senses on the nature of the light present in the elements: if the light or brightness, which makes possible the discernment of things corporeal, exists in a *high degree of its own property* and in a certain purity, it is the sense of *sight*; *commingled with the air*, it is *hearing*; *with vapor*, it is smell; *with a fluid* of the body, it is *taste*; *with a solid earthy substance*, it is *touch*. Now the sensitive life of the body partakes of the nature of light for which reason it thrives in the nerves which are naturally unobstructed and capable of transmitting impressions, and in these five sense it possesses more or less vigor according to the greater or less soundness of the nerves. Therefore, since there are in the world five simple substances, namely, the four elements and the fifth essence, man has for the perception of all these corporeal forms five senses well adapted to these substances, because, on account of the well-defined nature of each sense, apprehension can take place only when there is a certain conformity and rapport between the faculty and the object. There is another way of determining the adequacy of the senses, but St. Augustine sanctions this method and it seems reasonable since corresponding elements on the part of the faculty, the medium, and the object lend joint support to the proof.

4. The third light which guides man in the investigation of *intelligible truths* is the light of *philosophical knowledge*. It is called *inner* because it inquires into inner and hidden causes through principles of knowledge and natural truth, which are inherent in man. It is a threefold light diffusing itself over the three divisions of philosophy: *rational, natural, and moral*, a classification which seems suitable, since there is truth of *speech*, truth of *things*, and truth of *morals*. *Rational* philosophy considers the truth of *speech*; *natural* philosophy, the truth of *things*; and *moral* philosophy, the truth of *conduct*. Or considering it in a different light: just as we believe that the principle of the efficient, the formal or exemplary, and the final cause exists in the Most High God, since "He is the Cause of being the Principle of knowledge, and the Pattern of human life," so do we believe that it is contained in the illumination of philosophy which enlightens the mind to discern the *causes of being* in which case it is physics; or to understand *principles of reasoning* in which case

it is *logic*; or to learn the *right way of living* in which case it is *moral* or practical philosophy. Considering it under its third aspect: the light of philosophical knowledge illumines the intellect itself and this enlightenment may be threefold: if it governs the *motive*, it is *moral* philosophy; if it sways the *reason*, it is *natural* philosophy; if it directs the *interpretation*, it is *discursive* philosophy. As a result, man is enlightened as regards the truth of life, the truth of knowledge, and the truth of doctrine.

And since one may, through the medium of *speech*, give expression to his thoughts with a threefold purpose in view: namely, to communicate his ideas, to propose something for belief, or to arouse love or hatred, for this reason, *discursive* or rational philosophy has three subdivisions: *grammar*, *logic*, and *rhetoric*. Of these sciences the first aims to express; the second, to teach; the third, to persuade. The first considers the mind as *apprehending*; the second as *judging*; the third, as *motivating*, and since the mind apprehends by means of *correct* speech, with good reason does this triple science consider these three qualities in speech.

Again, since our intellect must be guided in its judgment by fixed principles, these principles, likewise, must be considered under three aspects: when they pertain to *matter*, they are termed *formal causes*; when they pertain to the *mind*, they are termed *intellectual causes*; and when they pertain to *Divine Wisdom*, they are called *ideal causes*; Natural philosophy, therefore, is subdivided into *physics properly so-called*, into *mathematics*, and *metaphysics*. Physics, accordingly treats of the knowledge of all entities, which leads back to one ultimate Principle from which they proceeded according to ideal causes, that is, to God since He is the *Beginning*, the *End*, and the *Exemplar*. Concerning these ideal causes, however, there has been some controversy among metaphysicists.

Finally, since there are three standards of ethical principles, namely, those governing the *individual*, the *family*, and the *state*, so are there three corresponding divisions of moral philosophy; namely, *ethical*, *economic*, and *political*, the content of each being clearly indicated by its name.

5. Now the fourth light, which illumines the mind for the understanding of *saving truth*, is the light of *Sacred Scripture*. This light is called *higher* because it leads to things above by the manifestation of truths which are beyond reason and also because it is not acquired by human research, but comes down by inspiration from the "*Father of lights*." Although in its literal sense, it is *one*, still, in its spiritual and mystical sense, it is *threefold*, for in all the books of Sacred Scripture, in addition to the *literal* meaning which the words clearly express, there is implied a threefold *spiritual* meaning: namely, the *allegorical*, by which we are taught what to believe concerning the Divinity and humanity; the *moral* by which we are taught how to live; and the *anogogical* by which we are taught how to keep close to God. Hence all of Sacred Scripture teaches these three truths: namely, the eternal generation and Incarnation of Christ, the pattern of human life, and the union of the soul with God. The first regards *faith*; the second, *morals*; the third, the *purpose of both*. To the study of the first, the doctors should devote themselves; on that of the second, the preachers should concentrate; and to the attainment of the third, the contemplatives should aspire. . . .

8. Let us see, therefore, how the other illuminations of knowledge are to be reduced to the light of Sacred Scripture. First of all, let us consider the illumination of *sense* perception, which is concerned exclusively with the cognition of sensible objects, a process in which three phases are to be considered: namely, the *medium* of perception, the *exercise* of perception, and the *delight* of perception. If we consider the *medium* of perception, we shall see therein the Word begotten from all eternity and made man in time. Indeed, a sensible object can make an impression upon a cognitive faculty only through the medium of a likeness which proceeds from the object as an offspring from its parent, and in every sensation, this likeness must be present either generically, specifically, or symbolically. That likeness, however, results in actual sensation only if it is brought into contact with the organ and the faculty, and once that contact is established, there results a new percept, an expressed image by means of which the mind reverts to the object. And even though the object is not always present to the senses, still, the fact remains that perception in its finished form begets an image. In like manner, know that from the mind of the Most High, Who is knowable by the interior senses of the mind,

from all eternity there emanated a Likeness, an Image, and an Offspring; and afterwards, when "the fullness of time had come" he was united to a mind and body and assumed the form of man which He had never been before, and through Him all our minds, which bear the likeness of the Father through faith in our hearts, are brought back to God.

9. To be sure, if we consider the *exercise* of sense perception, we shall see therein the pattern of human life, for each sense applies itself to its own object, shrinks from what may harm it, and does not appropriate the object of any other sense. In like manner, the *spiritual sense* operates in an orderly way, for while applied to its proper object, it opposes *negligence*; while refraining from what is harmful, it combats *concupiscence*; and while respecting the rights of other, it acts in opposition to *pride*. Of a truth, every irregularity springs from negligence, from concupiscence, or from pride. Surely, then, he who lives a prudent, temperate, and submissive life leads a well-ordered life, for thereby he avoids negligence in his duties, concupiscence in his appetites, and pride in his excellence.

10. Furthermore, if we consider the *delight*, we shall see therein the union of the soul with God. Indeed, every sense seeks its proper sensible with longing, finds it with delight, and seeks it again without ceasing, because "the eye is not filled with seeing, neither is the ear filled with hearing." In the same way, our spiritual senses must seek longingly, find joyfully, and seek again without ceasing the beautiful, the harmonious, the fragrant, the sweet, or the delightful to the touch. Behold how the divine Wisdom lies hidden in sense perception and how wonderful is the contemplation of the five spiritual senses in the light of their conformity to the senses of the body.

11. By the same process of reasoning is Divine Wisdom to be found in the illumination of the mechanical arts, the sole purpose of which is the *production of works of art*. In this illumination we can see the *eternal generation and Incarnation of the Word, the pattern of human life, and the union of the soul with God*. And this is true if we consider the *skill of the artist, the quality of the effect produced*, and the *utility of the advantage to be derived therefrom*.

If we consider the *production*, we shall see that the work of art proceeds from the artificer according to a model existing in his mind; this pattern or model the artificer studies carefully before he produces and then he produces as he has predetermined. The artificer, moreover, produces an exterior work bearing the closest possible resemblance to the interior model, and if it were in his power to produce an effect which would know and love him, this he would assuredly do; and if that creature could know its maker, it would be by means of a likeness according to which it came from the hands of the artificer; and if the eyes of the understanding were so darkened that the creature could not be elevated to things above, in order to bring it to a knowledge of its maker, it would be necessary for the likeness according to which the effect was produced to lower itself even to that nature which the creature could grasp and know. In like manner, understand that no creature has proceeded from the Most High Creator except through the Eternal Word, "in Whom He ordered all things," and by which Word He produced creatures bearing not only the nature of His *vestige* but also of His *image* so that through knowledge and love, they might be united to Him. And since by sin the rational creature had dimmed the eye of contemplation, it was most fitting that the Eternal and invisible should become visible and take flesh that He might lead us back to the Father and, indeed, this is what is related in the fourteenth chapter of St. John: "No man cometh to the Father but by Me"; and in the eleventh chapter of St. Matthew: "Neither knoweth any man the Father save the Son, and he to whomsoever the Son will reveal Him." For that reason, then, it is said, "The Word was made flesh." Therefore, considering the illumination of mechanical skill as regards the production of the work, we shall see therein the Word begotten and made incarnate, that is, the Divinity and the Humanity and the integrity of all faith.

13. If we consider the *effect*, we shall see therein the *pattern of human life*, for every artificer, indeed, aims to produce a work that is beautiful, useful, and enduring, and only when it possesses these three qualities is the work highly valued and acceptable. Corresponding to the above-mentioned qualities, in the pattern of life there must be found three elements: "knowledge, will, and unaltering and persevering toil." *Knowledge* renders the work beautiful; the *will* renders it useful; *perseverance* renders it lasting. The first

resides in the rational, the second in the concupiscible, and the third in the irascible appetite.

14. If we consider the *advantage*, we shall find the union of the soul with God, for every artificer who fashions a work does so that he may derive *praise*, *benefit*, or *delight* therefrom – a threefold purpose which corresponds to the three formal objects of the appetites: namely, a *noble* good, a *useful* good, and an *agreeable* good. It was for this same threefold reason that God made the soul rational, namely, that of its own accord, it might *praise* Him, *serve* Him, *find delight* in Him, and be at rest; and this takes place through charity. "He that abidith in it, abideth in God and God in him"; in such a way that there is found therein a kind of wondrous union and from that union comes a wondrous delight, for in the Book of Proverbs it is written, "My delights were to be with the children of men." Behold how the illumination of mechanical knowledge is the path to the illumination of Sacred Scripture. There is nothing therein which does not bespeak true wisdom and for this reason Sacred Scripture quite rightly makes frequent use of such similitudes.

15. In the same way is Divine Wisdom to be found in the illumination of *rational philosophy*, the main purpose of which is concerned with *speech*. Here are to be considered three elements corresponding to the threefold consideration of speech itself: namely, as regards the *person speaking*, the *delivery* of the speech, and its final purpose or its effect upon the *hearer*.

16. Considering speech in the light of the *speaker*, we see that all speech is the expression of a *mental concept*. That inner concept is the word of the mind and its offspring which is known to the person conceiving it, but that it may become known to the hearer, it assumes the nature of the voice and clothed in that form, the intelligible word becomes sensible and is heard without; it is received into the ear of the person listening and, still, it does not depart from the mind of the person uttering it. Practically the same procedure is seen in the begatting of the Eternal Word, because the Father conceived Him, begatting Him from all eternity, as it is written in the eighth chapter of the Book of Proverbs. "The depths were not as yet, and I was already conceived." But that He might be known by man who is endowed with senses, He assumed the nature of flesh, and "the Word was made flesh and dwelt amongst us," and yet He remained "in the bosom of His Father."

17. Considering speech in the light of its *delivery*, we shall use therein the *pattern of human life*, for three essential qualities work together for the perfection of speech: namely, *propriety*, *truth*, and *ornament*. Corresponding to these three qualities, every act of ours should be characterized by *measure*, *form*, and *order* so that it may be *restrained* by propriety in its outward accomplishment, *rendered beautiful* by purity of affection, *regulated* and adorned by uprightness of intention. For then truly, does one live a correct and well-ordered life which his intention is upright, his affection pure, and his deeds unassuming.

18. Considering speech in the light of its *purpose*, we find that it aims to *express*, to *instruct*, and to *persuade*; but it never *expresses* except by means of a likeness; it never *teaches* except by means of a clear light; and it never *persuades* except by power, and it is evident that these effects are accomplished only by means of an inherent likeness, light, and power intrinsically united to the soul. Therefore, St. Augustine concludes that he alone is a true teacher who can imprint a likeness, shed light, and grant power to the heart of his hearer. Hence it is that "He that teaches within hearts has His throne in heaven." Now, as perfection of speech requires the union of power, light, and a likeness within the soul, so, too, for the instruction of the soul in the knowledge of God by interior conversation with Him, there is required a union with Him who is "the brightness of glory and the figure of His substance, upholding all things by the word of His power." Hence we see how wondrous is this contemplation by which St. Augustine in his many writings leads soul to Divine Wisdom.

9

Characteristics of Men, Manners, Opinions, Times

Third Earl of Shaftesbury

The third Earl of Shaftesbury (1671–1713) was an English philosopher who maintained the disinterestedness of aesthetic judgments and found in nature both beauty and sublimity.

The Moralists

Part III, Section II

Methinks, said he, Philocles (changing to a familiar voice), we had better leave these unsociable places whither our fancy has transported us, and return to ourselves here again in our more conversable woods and temperate climates. Here no fierce heats nor colds annoy us, no precipices nor cataracts amaze us. Nor need we here be afraid of our own voices whilst we hear the notes of such a cheerful choir, and find the echoes rather agreeable and inviting us to talk.

I confess, said I, those foreign nymphs (if there were any belonging to those miraculous woods) were much too awful beauties to please me. I found our familiar home-nymphs a great deal more to my humour. Yet for all this, I cannot help being concerned for your breaking off just when we were got half the world over, and wanted only to take America in our way home. Indeed, as for Europe, I could excuse your making any great tour there, because of the little variety it would afford us. Besides that, it would be hard to see it in any view without meeting still that politic face of affairs which would too much disturb us in our philosophical flights. But for the western tract, I cannot imagine why you should neglect such noble subjects as are there, unless perhaps the gold and silver, to which I find you such a bitter enemy, frighted you from a mother-soil so full of it. If these countries had been as bare of those metals as old Sparta, we might have heard more perhaps of the Perus and Mexicos than of all Asia and Africa. We might have had creatures, plants, woods, mountains, rivers, beyond any of those we have passed. How sorry am I to lose the noble Amazon! How sorry——

Here, as I would have proceeded, I saw so significant a smile on Theocles's face that it stopped me, out of curiosity, to ask him his thought.

Nothing, said he; nothing but this very subject itself. Go on – I see you'll finish it for me. The spirit of this sort of prophecy has seized you. And Philocles, the cold indifferent Philocles, is become a pursuer of the same mysterious beauty.

'Tis true, said I, Theocles, I own it. Your genius, the genius of the place, and the Great

Third Earl of Shaftesbury, *Characteristics of Men, Manners, Opinions, Times* (1711).

Genius have at last prevailed. I shall no longer resist the passion growing in me for things of a natural kind, where neither art nor the conceit or caprice of man has spoiled their genuine order by breaking in upon that primitive state. Even the rude rocks, the mossy caverns, the irregular unwrought grottos and broken falls of waters, with all the horrid graces of the wilderness itself, as representing Nature more, will be the more engaging, and appear with a magnificence beyond the formal mockery of princely gardens. . . . But tell me, I entreat you, how comes it that, excepting a few philosophers of your sort, the only people who are enamoured in this way, and seek the woods, the rivers, or seashores, are your poor vulgar lovers?

Say not this, replied he, of lovers only. For is it not the same with poets, and all those other students in nature and the arts which copy after her? In short, is not this the real case of all who are lovers either of the Muses or the Graces?

However, said I, all those who are deep in this romantic way are looked upon, you know, as a people either plainly out of their wits, or overrun with melancholy and enthusiasm. We always endeavour to recall them from these solitary places. And I must own that often when I have found my fancy run this way, I have checked myself, not knowing what it was possessed me, when I was passionately struck with objects of this kind.

No wonder, replied he, if we are at a loss when we pursue the shadow for the substance. For if we may trust to what our reasoning has taught us, whatever in Nature is beautiful or charming is only the faint shadow of that first beauty. So that every real love depending on the mind, and being only the contemplation of beauty either as it really is in itself or as it appears imperfectly in the objects which strike the sense, how can the rational mind rest here, or be satisfied with the absurd enjoyment which reaches the sense alone?

From this time forward then, said I, I shall no more have reason to fear those beauties which strike a sort of melancholy, like the places we have named, or like these solemn groves. No more shall I avoid the moving accents of soft music, or fly from the enchanting features of the fairest human face.

If you are already, replied he, such a proficient in this new love that you are sure never to admire the representative beauty except for the sake of the original, nor aim at other enjoyment than of the rational kind, you may then be confident. I am so, and presume accordingly to answer for myself. However, I should not be ill satisfied if you explained yourself a little better as to this mistake of mine you seem to fear. Would it be any help to tell you, "That the absurdity lay in seeking the enjoyment elsewhere than in the subject loved"? The matter, I must confess, is still mysterious. Imagine then, good Philocles, if being taken with the beauty of the ocean, which you see yonder at a distance, it should come into your head to seek how to command it, and, like some mighty admiral, ride master of the sea, would not the fancy be a little absurd?

Absurd enough, in conscience. The next thing I should do, 'tis likely, upon this frenzy, would be to hire some bark and go in nuptial ceremony, Venetian-like, to wed the gulf, which I might call perhaps as properly my own.

Let who will call it theirs, replied Theocles, you will own the enjoyment of this kind to be very different from that which should naturally follow from the contemplation of the ocean's beauty. The bridegroom-Doge, who in his stately Bucentaur floats on the bosom of his Thetis, has less possession than the poor shepherd, who from a hanging rock or point of some high promontory, stretched at his case, forgets his feeding flocks, while he admires her beauty. But to come nearer home, and make the question still more familiar. Suppose (my Philocles) that, viewing such a tract of country as this delicious vale we see beneath us, you should, for the enjoyment of the prospect, require the property or possession of the land.

The covetous fancy, replied I, would be as absurd altogether as that other ambitious one.

O Philocles! said he, may I bring this yet a little nearer, and will you follow me once more? Suppose that, being charmed as you seem to be with the beauty of those trees under whose shade we rest, you should long for nothing so much as to taste some delicious fruit of theirs; and having obtained of Nature some certain relish by which these acorns or berries of the wood became as palatable as the figs or peaches of the garden, you should afterwards, as oft as you revisited these groves, seek hence the enjoyment of them by satiating yourself in these new delights.

The fancy of this kind, replied I, would be sordidly luxurious, and as absurd, in my opinion, as either of the former.

Can you not then, on this occasion, said he, call to mind some other forms of a fair kind among us, where the admiration of beauty is apt to lead to as irregular a consequence?

I feared, said I, indeed, where this would end, and was apprehensive you would force me at last to think of certain powerful forms in human kind which draw after them a set of eager desires, wishes, and hopes; no way suitable, I must confess, to your rational and refined contemplation of beauty. The proportions of this living architecture, as wonderful as they are, inspire nothing of a studious or contemplative kind. The more they are viewed, the further they are from satisfying by mere view. Let that which satisfies be ever so disproportionable an effect, or ever so foreign to its cause, censure it as you please; you must allow, however, that it is natural. So that you, Theocles, for aught I see, are become the accuser of Nature by condemning a natural enjoyment.

Far be it from us both, said he, to condemn a joy which is from Nature. But when we spoke of the enjoyment of these woods and prospects, we understood by it a far different kind from that of the inferior creatures, who, rifling in these places, find here their choicest food. Yet we too live by tasteful food, and feel those other joys of sense in common with them. But 'twas not here (my Philocles) that we had agreed to place our good, nor consequently our enjoyment. We who were rational, and had minds, methought, should place it rather in those minds which were indeed abused, and cheated of their real good, when drawn to seek absurdly the enjoyment of it in the objects of sense, and not in those objects they might properly call their own, in which kind, as I remember, we comprehended all which was truly fair, generous, or good.

So that beauty, said I, and good with you, Theocles, I perceive, are still one and the same.

'Tis so, said he. And thus are we returned again to the subject of our yesterday's morning conversation. Whether I have made good my promise to you in showing the true good, I know not. But so, doubtless, I should have done with good success had I been able in my poetic ecstasies, or by any other efforts, to have led you into some deep view of Nature and the sovereign genius. We then had proved the force of divine beauty, and formed in ourselves an object capable and worthy of real enjoyment.

O Theocles! said I, well do I remember now the terms in which you engaged me that morning when you bespoke my love of this mysterious beauty. You have indeed made good your part of the condition, and may now claim me for a proselyte. If there be any seeming extravagance in the case I must comfort myself the best I can, and consider that all sound love and admiration is enthusiasm: "The transports of poets, the sublime of orators, the rapture of musicians, the high strains of the virtuosi – all mere enthusiasm! Even learning itself, the love of arts and curiosities, the spirit of travellers and adventurers, gallantry, war, heroism – all, all enthusiasm!" 'Tis enough; I am content to be this new enthusiast in a way unknown to me before.

And I, replied Theocles, am content you should call this love of ours enthusiasm, allowing it the privilege of its fellow-passions. For is there a fair and plausible enthusiasm, a reasonable ecstasy and transport allowed to other subjects, such as architecture, painting, music; and shall it be exploded here? Are there senses by which all those other graces and perfections are perceived, and none by which this higher perfection and grace is comprehended? Is it so preposterous to bring that enthusiasm hither, and transfer it from those secondary and scanty objects to this original and comprehensive one? Observe how the case stands in all those other subjects of art or science. What difficulty to be in any degree knowing! How long ere a true taste is gained! How many things shocking, how many offensive at first, which afterwards are known and acknowledged the highest beauties! For 'tis not instantly we acquire the sense by which these beauties are discoverable. Labour and pains are required, and time to cultivate a natural genius ever so apt or forward. But who is there once thinks of cultivating this soil, or of improving any sense or faculty which Nature may have given of this kind? And is it a wonder we should be dull then, as we are, confounded and at a loss in these affairs, blind as to this higher scene, these nobler representations? Which way should we come to understand better? which way be knowing in these beauties? Is study, science, or learning necessary to understand all beauties else? And for the sovereign beauty, is there no skill or science required? In painting there are shades and masterly strokes which the vulgar understand not, but find fault with; in architecture there is the rustic; in music the chromatic kind, and skilful mixture of dissonancies: and is there nothing which answers to this in the whole?

I must confess, said I, I have hitherto been one of those vulgar who could never relish the shades, the rustic, or the dissonancies you talk of. I have never dreamt of such masterpieces in Nature. 'Twas my way to censure freely on the first view. But I perceive I am now obliged to go far in the pursuit of beauty, which lies very absconded and deep; and if so, I am well assured that my enjoyments hitherto have been very shallow. I have dwelt, it seems, all this while upon the surface, and enjoyed only a kind of slight superficial beauties, having never gone in search of beauty itself, but of what I fancied such. Like the rest of the unthinking world, I took for granted that what I liked was beautiful, and what I rejoiced in was my good. I never scrupled loving what I fancied, and aiming only at the enjoyment of what I loved; I never troubled myself with examining what the subjects were, nor ever hesitated about their choice.

Begin then, said he, and choose. See what the subjects are, and which you would prefer, which honour with your admiration, love, and esteem. For by these again you will be honoured in your turn. Such, Philocles, as is the worth of these companions, such will your worth be found. As there is emptiness or fulness here, so will there be in your enjoyment. See therefore where fulness is, and where emptiness. See in what subject resides the chief excellence, where beauty reigns, where 'tis entire, perfect, absolute; where broken, imperfect, short. View these terrestrial beauties and whatever has the appearance of excellence and is able to attract. See that which either really is, or stands as in the room of fair, beautiful, and good. "A mass of metal, a tract of land, a number of slaves, a pile of stones, a human body of certain lineaments and proportions." Is this the highest of the kind? Is beauty founded then in body only, and not in action, life, or operation? [. . .]

Hold! hold! said I, good Theocles, you take this in too high a key above my reach. If you would have me accompany you, pray lower this strain a little, and talk in a more familiar way.

Thus then, said he (smiling), whatever passion you may have for other beauties, I know, good Philocles, you are no such admirer of wealth in any kind as to allow much beauty to it, especially in a rude heap or mass. But in medals, coins, embossed work, statues, and well-fabricated pieces, of whatever sort, you can discover beauty and admire the kind. True, said I, but not for the metal's sake. 'Tis not then the metal or matter which is beautiful with you? No. But the art? Certainly. The art then is the beauty? Right. And the art is that which beautifies? The same. So that the beautifying, not the beautified, is the really beautiful? It seems so. For that which is beautified, is beautiful only by the accession of something beautifying, and by the recess or withdrawing of the same, it ceases to be beautiful? Be it. In respect of bodies therefore, beauty comes and goes? So we see. Nor is the body itself any cause either of its coming or staying? None. So that there is no principle of beauty in body? None at all. For body can no way be the cause of beauty to itself? No way. Nor govern nor regulate itself? Nor yet this. Nor mean nor intend itself? Nor this neither. Must not that, therefore, which means and intends for it, regulates and orders it, be the principle of beauty to it? Of necessity. And what must that be? Mind, I suppose, for what can it be else?

Here then, said he, is all I would have explained to you before. "That the beautiful, the fair, the comely, were never in the matter, but in the art and design; never in body itself, but in the form or forming power." Does not the beautiful form confess this, and speak the beauty of the design whenever it strikes you? What is it but the design which strikes? What is it you admire but mind, or the effect of mind? 'Tis mind alone which forms. All which is void of mind is horrid, and matter formless is deformity itself.

Of all forms then, said I, those (according to your scheme) are the most amiable, and in the first order of beauty, which have a power of making other forms themselves. From whence methinks they may be styled the forming forms. So far I can easily concur with you, and gladly give the advantage to the human form, above those other beauties of man's formation. The palaces, equipages and estates shall never in my account be brought in competition with the original living forms of flesh and blood. And for the other, the dead forms of Nature, the metals and stones, however precious and dazzling, I am resolved to resist their splendour, and make abject things of them, even in their highest pride, when they pretend to set off human beauty, and are officiously brought in aid of the fair.

Do you not see then, replied Theocles, that you have established three degrees or orders of beauty? As how? Why first, the dead forms, as you properly have called them, which bear a fashion, and are formed, whether by man or Nature, but have no forming power, no action, or intelligence. Right. Next, and as the second kind, the forms which form, that is, which have intelligence, action, and operation. Right still. Here therefore is double beauty. For here is both the form (the effect of mind) and mind itself. The first kind low and despicable in respect of this other, from whence the dead form receives its lustre and force of beauty. For what is a mere body, though a human one, and ever so exactly fashioned, if inward form be wanting, and the mind be monstrous or imperfect, as in an idiot or savage? This too I can apprehend, said I, but where is the third order?

Have patience, replied he, and see first whether you have discovered the whole force of this second beauty. How else should you understand the force of love, or have the power of enjoyment? Tell me, I beseech you, when first you named these the forming forms, did you think of no other productions of theirs besides the dead kinds, such as the palaces, the coins, the brazen or the marble figures of men? Or did you think of something nearer life?

I could easily, said I, have added, that these forms of ours had a virtue of producing other living forms like themselves. But this virtue of theirs, I thought, was from another form above them, and could not properly be called their virtue or art, if in reality there was a superior art or something artist-like, which guided their hand, and made tools of them in this specious work.

Happily thought, said he; you have prevented a censure which I hardly imagined you could escape. And here you have unawares discovered that third order of beauty, which forms not only such as we call mere forms but even the forms which form. For we ourselves are notable architects in matter, and can show lifeless bodies brought into form, and fashioned by our own hands, but that which fashions even minds themselves, contains in itself all the beauties fashioned by those minds, and is consequently the principle, source, and fountain of all beauty.

It seems so.

Therefore whatever beauty appears in our second order of forms, or whatever is derived or produced from thence, all this is eminently, principally, and originally in this last order of supreme and sovereign beauty.

True.

Thus architecture, music, and all which is of human invention, resolves itself into this last order.

Right, said I; and thus all the enthusiasms of other kinds resolve themselves into ours. The fashionable kinds borrow from us, and are nothing without us. We have undoubtedly the honour of being originals.

Now therefore say again, replied Theocles: whether are those fabrics of architecture, sculpture, and the rest of that sort the greatest beauties which man forms, or are there greater and better? None which I know, replied I. Think, think again, said he; and setting aside those productions which just now you excepted against, as masterpieces of another hand; think what there are which more immediately proceed from us, and may more truly be termed our issue. I am barren, said I, for this time; you must be plainer yet, in helping me to conceive. How can I help you? replied he. Would you have me be conscious for you, of that which is immediately your own, and is solely in and from yourself? You mean my sentiments, said I. Certainly, replied he, and together with your sentiments, your resolutions, principles, determinations, actions; whatsoever is handsome and noble in the kind; whatever flows from your good understanding, sense, knowledge, and will; whatever is engendered in your heart (good Philocles!) or derives itself from your parent-mind, which, unlike to other parents, is never spent or exhausted, but gains strength and vigour by producing. So you, my friend, have proved it, by many a work, not suffering that fertile part to remain idle and unactive. Hence those good parts, which from a natural genius you have raised by due improvement. And here, as I cannot but admire the pregnant genius and parent-beauty, so am I satisfied of the offspring, that it is and will be ever beautiful.

I took the compliment, and wished (I told him) the case were really as he imagined, that I might justly merit his esteem and love. My study therefore should be to grow beautiful, in his way of beauty, and from this time forward I would do all I could to propagate that lovely race of mental children, happily sprung from such a high enjoyment and from a union with what was fairest and best. But 'tis you, Theocles, continued I, must help my labouring mind, and be as it were the midwife to those conceptions; which else, I fear, will prove abortive.

You do well, replied he, to give me the midwife's part only; for the mind conceiving of itself, can only be, as you say, assisted in the birth. Its pregnancy is from its nature. Nor could it ever have been thus impregnated by any other mind than that which formed it at the beginning; and which, as we have already proved, is original to all mental as well as other beauty.

Do you maintain then, said I, that these mental children, the notions and principles of fair, just, and honest, with the rest of these ideas, are innate?

Anatomists, said he, tell us that the eggs, which are principles in body, are innate, being formed already in the foetus before the birth. But when it is, whether before, or at, or after the birth, or at what time after, that either these or other principles, organs of sensation, or sensations themselves, are first formed in us, is a matter, doubtless, of curious speculation, but of no great importance. The question is, whether the principles spoken of are from art or Nature? If from Nature purely, 'tis no matter for the time; nor would I contend with you though you should deny life itself to be innate, as imagining it followed rather than preceded the moment of birth. But this I am certain of, that life and the sensations which accompany life, come when they will, are from mere Nature, and nothing else. Therefore if you dislike the word innate, let us change it, if you will, for instinct, and call instinct that which Nature teaches, exclusive of art, culture, or discipline.

Content, said I.

Leaving then, replied he, those admirable speculations to the virtuosi, the anatomists, and school divines, we may safely aver, with all their consents, that the several organs, particularly those of generation, are formed by Nature. Whether is there also from Nature, think you, any instinct for the after use of them? or whether must learning and experience imprint this use? 'Tis imprinted, said I, enough in conscience. The impression or instinct is so strong in the case, that 'twould be absurdity not to think it natural, as well in our own species as in other creatures, amongst whom (as you have already taught me) not only the mere engendering of the young, but the various and almost infinite means and methods of providing for them, are all foreknown. For thus much we may indeed discern in the preparatory labours and arts of these wild creatures, which demonstrate their anticipating fancies, pre-conceptions, or pre-sensations, if I may use a word you taught me yesterday.

I allow your expression, said Theocles, and will endeavour to show you that the same preconceptions, of a higher degree, have place in human kind. Do so, said I, I entreat you; for so far am I from finding in myself these preconceptions of fair and beautiful, in your sense, that methinks, till now of late, I have hardly known of anything like them in Nature. How then, said he, would yon have known that outward fair and beautiful of human kind, if such an object (a fair fleshly one) in all its beauty had for the first time appeared to you, by yourself, this morning, in these groves? Or do you think perhaps you should have been unmoved, and have found no difference between this form and any other, if first you had not been instructed?

I have hardly any right, replied I, to plead this last opinion, after what I have owned just before.

Well then, said he, that I may appear to take no advantage against you, I quit the dazzling form which carries such a force of complicated beauties, and I am contented to consider separately each of those simple beauties, which taken all together create this wonderful effect. For you will allow, without doubt, that in respect of bodies, whatever is commonly said of the unexpressible, the unintelligible, the I-know-not-what of beauty, there can lie no mystery here, but what plainly belongs either to figure, colour, motion or sound. Omitting therefore the three latter, and their dependent charms, let us view the charm in what is simplest of all, mere figure. Nor need we go so high as sculpture, architecture, or the designs of those who from this study of beauty have raised such delightful arts. 'Tis enough if we consider the simplest of figures, as either a round ball, a cube, or dye. Why is even an infant pleased with the first view of these proportions? Why is the sphere or globe, the cylinder and obelisk preferred; and the irregular figures, in respect of these, rejected and despised?

I am ready, replied I, to own there is in certain figures a natural beauty, which the eye finds as soon as the object is presented to it.

Is there then, said he, a natural beauty of figures? and is there not as natural a one of actions? No sooner the eye opens upon figures, the ear to sounds, than straight the beautiful results and grace and harmony are known and acknowledged. No sooner are actions viewed, no sooner the human affections and passions discerned (and they are most of them as soon discerned as felt) than straight an inward eye distinguishes, and sees the fair and shapely, the amiable and admirable, apart from the deformed, the foul, the odious, or the despicable. How is it possible therefore not to own "that as these distinctions have their foundation in Nature, the discernment itself is natural, and from Nature alone"?

If this, I told him, were as he represented it, there could never, I thought, be any disagreement among men concerning actions and behaviour, as which was base, which worthy; which handsome, and which deformed. But now we found perpetual variance among mankind, whose differences were chiefly founded on this disagreement in opinion; "The one affirming, the other denying that this, or that, was fit or decent."

Even by this, then, replied he, it appears there is fitness and decency in actions; since the fit and decent is in this controversy ever pre-supposed. And whilst men are at odds about the subjects, the thing itself is universally agreed. For neither is there agreement in judgments about other beauties. 'Tis controverted "which is the finest pile, the loveliest shape or face": but without controversy 'tis allowed "there is a beauty of each kind." This no one goes about to teach: nor is it learnt by any, but confessed by all. All own the standard, rule, and measure: but in applying it to things disorder arises, ignorance prevails, interest and passion breed disturbance. Nor can it otherwise happen in the affairs of life, whilst that which interests and engages men as good, is thought different from that which they admire and praise as honest. But with us, Philocles, 'tis better settled, since for our parts we have already decreed "that beauty and good are still the same."

I remember, said I, what you forced me to acknowledge more than once before. And now, good Theocles, that I am become so willing a disciple, I want not so much Ito be convinced, methinks, as to he confirmed and strengthened. And I hope this last work may prove your easiest task.

Not unless you help in it yourself, replied Theocles, for this is necessary as well as becoming. It had been indeed shameful for you to have yielded without making good resistance. To help oneself to be convinced is to prevent reason, and bespeak error and delusion. But upon fair conviction to give our heart up to the evident side, and reinforce the impression, this is to help reason heartily. And thus we may be said honestly to persuade ourselves. Show me then how I may best persuade myself.

Have courage, said he, Philocles (raising his voice), be not offended that I say, have courage! 'Tis cowardice alone betrays us. For whence can false shame be, except from cowardice? To be ashamed of what one is sure can never be shameful, must needs be from the want of resolution. We seek the right and wrong in things; we examine what is honourable, what shameful; and having at last determined, we dare not stand to our own judgment, and are ashamed to own there is really a shameful and an honourable. "Hear me" (says one who pretends to value Philocles, and be valued by him), "there can be no such thing as real valuableness or worth; nothing in itself estimable or amiable, odious or shameful. All is opinion. 'Tis opinion which makes beauty, and unmakes it. The graceful or ungraceful in things, the decorum arid its contrary, the amiable and unamiable, vice, virtue, honour, shame, all this is founded in opinion only. Opinion is the law and measure. Nor has opinion any rule besides mere chance, which varies it, as custom varies; and makes now this, now that, to be thought worthy, according to the reign of fashion and the ascendant power of education." What shall we say to such a one? How represent to him his absurdity and extravagance?

Will he desist the sooner? Or shall we ask, what shame, of one who acknowledges no shameful? Yet he derides, and cries, ridiculous! By what right? what title? For thus, if I were Philocles, would I defend myself: "Am I ridiculous? As how? What is ridiculous? Everything? or nothing?" Ridiculous indeed! But something, then, something there is ridiculous; and the notion, it seems, is right, "of a shameful and ridiculous in things."

How then shall we apply the notion? For this being wrong applied, cannot itself but be ridiculous. Or will he who cries shame refuse to acknowledge any in his turn? Does he not blush, nor seem discountenanced on any occasion? If he does, the case is very distinct from that of mere grief or fear. The disorder he feels is from a sense of what is shameful and odious in itself, not of what is hurtful or dangerous in its consequences. For the greatest danger in the world can never breed shame; nor can the opinion of all the world compel us to it, where our own opinion is not a party. We may be afraid of appearing impudent, and may therefore feign a modesty. But we can never really blush for anything beside what we think truly shameful, and what we should still blush for were we ever so secure as to our interest, and out of the reach of all inconvenience which could happen to us from the thing we were ashamed of.

Thus, continued he, should I be able by anticipation to defend myself, and looking narrowly into men's lives, and that which influenced them on all occasions. I should have testimony enough to make me say within myself, "Let who will be my adversary in this opinion, I shall find him some way or other prepossessed with that of which he would endeavour to dispossess me." Has he gratitude or resentment, pride or shame? Whichever way it be, he acknowledges a sense of just and unjust, worthy and mean. If he be grateful or expects gratitude. I ask "why? and on what account?" If he be angry, if he indulges revenge, I ask "how? and in what case? Revenged of what? of a stone, or madman?" Who is so mad? "But for what? For a chance hurt? an accident against thought or intention?" Who is so unjust? Therefore there is just and unjust; and belonging to it a natural presumption or anticipation on which the resentment or anger is founded. For what else should make the wickedest of mankind often prefer the interest of their revenge to all other interests, and even to life itself, except only a sense of wrong natural to all men, and a desire to prosecute that wrong at any rate? Not for their own sakes, since they sacrifice their very being to it, but out of hatred to the imagined wrong and from a certain love of justice, which even in unjust men is by this example shown to be beyond the love of life itself.

Thus as to pride, I ask, "why proud? why conceited? and of what? Does any one who has pride think meanly or indifferently of himself?" No; but honourably. And how this, if there be no real honour or dignity pre-supposed? For self-valuation supposes self-worth; and in a person conscious of real worth, is either no pride, or a just and noble one. In the same manner self-contempt supposes a self-meanness or defectiveness; and may be either a just modesty or unjust humility. But this is certain, that whoever is proud must be proud of something. And we know that men of thorough pride will be proud even in the meanest circumstances, and when there is no visible subject for them to be proud of. But they descry a merit in themselves which others cannot: and 'tis this merit they admire. No matter whether it be really in them, as they imagine, it is a worth still, an honour or merit which they admire, and would do, wherever they saw it, in any subject besides. For then it is, then only, that they are humbled, "when they see in a more eminent degree in others what they respect and admire so much in themselves." And thus as long as I find men either angry or revengeful, proud or ashamed, I am safe. For they conceive an honourable and dishonourable, a foul and fair, as well as I. No matter where they place it, or how they are mistaken in it, this hinders not my being satisfied "that the thing is, and is universally acknowledged; that it is of nature's impression, naturally conceived, and by no art or counter-nature to be eradicated or destroyed."

And now, what say you, Philocles (continued he), to this defence I have been making for you? 'Tis grounded, as you see, on the supposition of your being deeply engaged in this philosophical cause. But perhaps you have yet many difficulties to get over, ere you can so far take part with beauty as to make this to be your good.

I have no difficulty so great, said I, as not to be easily removed. My inclinations lead me strongly this way, for I am ready enough to yield there is no real good beside the enjoyment of beauty. And I am as ready, replied Theocles, to yield there is no real enjoyment of beauty beside what is good. Excellent! but upon reflection I fear I am little beholden to you for your concession. As how? Because should I offer to contend for any enjoyment of beauty out of your mental way, you would, I doubt, call such enjoyment of mine absurd, as you did once before. Undoubtedly I should. For what is it should enjoy or be capable of enjoyment, except mind? or shall we say, body enjoys? By the help of sense, perhaps, not otherwise. Is beauty, then, the object of sense? Say how? Which way? For otherwise the help of sense is nothing in the case; and if body be of itself incapable, and sense no help to it to apprehend or enjoy beauty, there remains only the mind which is capable either to apprehend or to enjoy.

True, said I, but show me, then, "Why beauty may not be the object of the sense?" Show me first, I entreat you, "Why, where, or in what you fancy it may be so?" Is it not beauty which first excites the sense, and feeds it afterwards in the passion we call love? Say in the same manner, "That it is beauty first excites the sense, and feeds it afterwards in the passion we call hunger." . . . You will not say it. The thought, I perceive, displeases you. As great as the pleasure is of good eating, you disdain to apply the notion of beauty to the good dishes which create it. You would hardly have applauded the preposterous fancy of some luxurious Romans of old, who could relish a fricassee the better for hearing it was composed of birds which wore a beautiful feather or had sung deliciously. Instead of being incited by such a historical account of meats, you would be apt, I believe, to have less appetite the more you searched their origin, and descended into the kitchen science, to learn the several forms and changes they had undergone ere they were served at this elegant voluptuous table. But though the kitchen forms be ever so disgraceful, you will allow that the materials of the kitchen, such, for instance, as the garden furnishes, are really fair and beautiful in their kind. Nor will you deny beauty to the wild field, or to these flowers which grow around us on this verdant couch. And yet, as lovely as are these forms of Nature, the shining grass or silvered moss, the flowery thyme, wild rose or honeysuckle; 'tis not their beauty allures the neighbouring herds, delights the browsing fawn or kid, and spreads the joy we see amidst the feeding flocks; 'tis not the form rejoices, but that which is beneath the form; 'tis savouriness attracts, hunger impels, and thirst better allayed by the clear brook than the thick puddle, makes the fair nymph to be preferred, whose form is otherwise slighted. For never can the form be of real force where it is uncontemplated, unjudged of, unexamined, and stands only as the accidental note or token of what appeases provoked sense, and satisfies the brutish part. Are you persuaded of this, good Philocles? or, rather than not give brutes the advantage of enjoyment, will you allow them also a mind and rational part?

Not so, I told him.

If brutes, therefore, said he, be incapable of knowing and enjoying beauty, as being brutes, and having sense only (the brutish part) for their own share, it follows "that neither can man by the same sense or brutish part conceive or enjoy beauty; but all the beauty and good he enjoys is in a nobler way, and by the help of what is noblest, his mind and reason." Here lies his dignity and highest interest, here his capacity toward good and happiness. His ability or incompetency, his power of enjoyment or his impotence, is founded in this alone'. As this is sound, fair, noble, worthy, so are its subjects, acts and employments. For as the riotous mind, captive to sense, can never enter in competition, or contend for beauty with the virtuous mind of reason's culture; so neither can the objects which allure the former compare with those which attract and charm the latter. And when each gratifies itself in the enjoyment and possession of its object, how evidently fairer are the acts which join the latter pair, and give a soul the enjoyment of what is generous and good? This at least. Philocles, you will surely allow, that when you place a joy elsewhere than in the mind, the enjoyment itself will be no beautiful subject, nor of any graceful or agreeable appearance. But when you think how friendship is enjoyed, how honour, gratitude, candour, benignity, and all internal beauty; how all the social pleasures, society itself, and all which constitutes the worth and happiness of mankind; you will here surely allow beauty in the act, and think it worthy to be viewed and passed in review often by the glad mind, happily conscious of the generous part, and of its own advancement and growth in beauty.

Thus, Philocles (continued he, after a short pause), thus have I presumed to treat of beauty before so great a judge, and such a skilful admirer as yourself. For, taking rise from Nature's beauty, which transported me, I gladly ventured further in the chase, and have accompanied you in search of beauty, as it relates to us, and makes our highest good in its sincere and natural enjoyment. And if we have not idly spent our hours, nor ranged in vain through these deserted regions, it should appear from our strict search that there is nothing so divine as beauty, which belonging not to body, nor having any principle or existence except in mind and reason, is alone discovered and acquired by this diviner part, when it inspects itself, the only object worthy of itself. For whatever is void of mind, is void and darkness to the mind's eye. This languishes and grows dim whenever detained on foreign subjects, but thrives and attains its natural vigour when employed in contemplation of what is like itself. 'Tis thus the improving mind, slightly surveying other objects, and passing over bodies and the common forms (where only a shadow of beauty rests), ambitiously presses onward to its source, and views the original of form and order in that which is intelligent. And thus, O Philocles, may we improve and become artists in the kind; learning "to know ourselves, and what that is, which by improving, we may be sure to advance our worth and real self-interest." For neither is this knowledge acquired by contemplation of bodies, or the outward forms, the view of pageantries, the study of estates and honours; nor is he to be esteemed that self-improving artist who makes a fortune out of these, but he (he only) is the wise and able man, who with a slight regard to these things, applies himself to cultivate another soil, builds in a different matter from that of stone or marble; and having righter models in his eye, becomes in truth the architect of his own life and fortune, by laying within himself the lasting and sure foundations of order, peace, and concord. [. . .] But now 'tis time to think of returning home. The morning is far spent. Come! let us away and leave these uncommon subjects, till we retire again to these remote and unfrequented places.

At these words Theocles, mending his pace, and going down the hill, left me at a good distance, till he heard me calling earnestly after him. Having joined him once again, I begged he would stay a little longer, or if he were resolved so soon to leave both the woods and that philosophy which he confined to them, that he would let me, however, part with them more gradually, and leave the best impression on me he could against my next return. For as much convinced as I was, and as great a convert to his doctrine, my danger still, I owned to him, was very great. and I foresaw that when the charm of these places and his company was ceased, I should be apt to relapse and weakly yield to that too powerful charm, the world. Tell me, continued I, how is it possible to hold out against it and withstand the general opinion of mankind, who have so different a notion of that which we call good? Say truth now, Theocles, can anything be more odd or dissonant from the common voice of the world than what we have determined in this matter?

Whom shall we follow, then? replied he. Whose judgment or opinion shall we take concerning what is good, what contrary? If all or any part of mankind are consonant with themselves, and can agree in this, I am content to leave philosophy and follow them. If otherwise, why should we not adhere to what we have chosen?

10

An Inquiry into the Original of Our Ideas of Beauty and Virtue

Francis Hutcheson

Francis Hutcheson (1694–1746), a British philosopher who held a professorship at the University of Glasgow, argued that just as we have a moral sense, so we have a sense of beauty.

The Preface

There is no part of philosophy of more importance than a just knowledge of human nature and its various powers and dispositions. Our late inquiries have been very much employed about our understanding and the several methods of obtaining truth. We generally acknowledge that the importance of any truth is nothing else than its moment or its efficacy to make men happy or to give them the greatest and most lasting pleasure; and wisdom denotes only a capacity of pursuing this end by the best means. It must surely then be of the greatest importance to have distinct conceptions of this end itself, as well as of the means necessary to obtain it, so that we may find out which are the greatest and most lasting pleasures and, thus, not employ our reason, after all our laborious improvements of it, in trifling pursuits. Indeed, it is to be feared that without this inquiry most of our studies will be of very little use to us, for they seem to have scarcely any other tendency than to lead us into speculative knowledge itself. Nor are we distinctly told how it is that knowledge, or truth, is pleasant to us.

This consideration put the author of the following papers upon inquiring into the various pleasures which human nature is capable of receiving. We shall generally find in our modern philosophic writings nothing further on this head than some bare division of them into sensible, and rational, and some trite commonplace arguments to prove the latter more valuable than the former. Our sensible pleasures are slightly passed over and explained only by some instances in tastes, smells, sounds, or such like, which men of any tolerable reflection generally look upon as very trifling satisfactions. Our rational pleasures have had much the same kind of treatment. We are seldom taught any other notion of rational pleasure than that which we have upon reflecting on our possession, or claim to those objects, which may be occasions of pleasure. Such objects we call advantageous. But advantage, or interest, cannot be distinctly conceived, till we know what those pleasures are which advantageous objects are apt to excite, and what senses or powers of perception we have with respect to such objects.

Francis Hutcheson, *An Inquiry into the Original of Our Ideas of Beauty and Virtue* (1725).

We may perhaps find such an inquiry of more importance in morals, to prove what we call the reality of virtue, or that it is the surest happiness of the agent, than one would at first imagine.

In reflecting upon our external senses, we plainly see that our perceptions of pleasure, or pain, do not depend directly on our will. Objects do not please us, according as we incline they should. The presence of some objects necessarily pleases us, and the presence of others necessarily displeases us. Nor by our will, do we procure pleasure or avoid pain except by procuring the former kinds of objects and avoiding the latter. By the very frame of our nature, the one is made the occasion of delight, and the other of dissatisfaction.

The same observation will hold in all our other pleasures and pains. For there are many other sorts of objects which please, or displease, us as necessarily as material objects do when they operate upon our organs of sense. There is scarcely any object which our minds are employed about which is not thus constituted the necessary occasion of some pleasure or pain. Thus we find ourselves pleased with a regular form, a piece of architecture or painting, a composition of notes, a theorem, an action, an affection, a character. And we are conscious that this pleasure necessarily arises from the contemplation of the idea, which is then present in our minds with all its circumstances, even though some of these ideas have nothing of what we call sensible perception in them. And in those which have, the pleasure arises from some uniformity, order, arrangement, or imitation, not from the simple ideas of color, sound, or mode of extension separately considered.

These determinations to be pleased with any forms, or ideas which occur to our observation, are what the author chooses to call senses distinguishing them from the powers which commonly go by that name by calling our power of perceiving the beauty of regularity, order, harmony an internal sense. And the determination to be pleased with the contemplation of those affections, actions, or characters of rational agents which we call virtuous is what he marks by the name of a moral sense.

His principal design is to show "That human nature was not left quite indifferent in the affair of virtue, to form to itself observations concerning the advantage, or disadvantage of actions, and accordingly to regulate its conduct." The weakness of our reason, and the avocations arising from the infirmity and necessities of our nature, are so great that very few men could ever have formed those long deductions of reason which show some actions to be in the whole advantageous to the agent, and their contraries pernicious. The author of nature has much better furnished us for a life of virtuous conduct than our moralists seem to imagine by almost as quick and powerful instructions as we have for the preservation of our bodies. He has made virtue a lovely form, to excite our pursuit of it, and has given us strong affections to be springs of each virtuous action.

This moral sense of beauty in actions and affections may appear strange at first view. Some of our moralists themselves are offended at it in my Lord Shaftesbury, so accustomed are they to deduce every approbation, or aversion, from rational views of interest (except it be merely in the simple ideas of the external senses) and have such a horror at innate ideas, which they imagine this borders upon. But this moral sense has no relation to innate ideas, as will appear in the second treatise. Our gentlemen of good taste can tell us of a great many senses, tastes, and relishes for beauty, harmony, imitation in painting and poetry. And may not we find too in mankind a relish for a beauty in characters, in manners? I doubt we have made philosophy, as well as religion, by our foolish management of it, so austere and ungainly a form that a gentleman cannot easily bring himself to like it, and those who are strangers to it can scarcely bear to hear our description of it. So much is it changed from what was once the delight of the finest gentlemen among the ancients and their recreation after the hurry of public affairs!

In the first treatise, the author has perhaps in some instances gone too far in supposing a greater agreement of mankind in their sense of beauty than experience will confirm, but all he is solicitous about is to show "That there is some sense of beauty natural to men; that we find as great an agreement of men in their relishes of forms, as in their external senses which all agree to be natural; and that pleasure or pain, delight or aversion, are naturally joined to their perceptions." If the reader is convinced of such determinations of the mind to be pleased with forms, proportions, resemblances, and theorems, it will be no difficult matter to apprehend another superior sense, natural also to men, determining them to be pleased with actions, characters, and affections. This is the moral sense, which makes the subject of the second treatise.

The proper occasions of perception by the external senses occur to us as soon as we come into the world, whence perhaps we easily look upon these senses to be natural, but the objects of the superior senses of beauty and virtue generally do not. It is probably some little time before children reflect, or at least let us know that they reflect, upon proportion and similitude, upon affections, characters, and tempers, or come to know the external actions which are evidences of them. Hence we imagine that their sense of beauty, and their moral sentiments of actions, must be entirely owing to instruction and education, whereas it is as easy to conceive how a character or a temper, as soon as it is observed, may be constituted by nature the necessary occasion of pleasure or an object of approbation, as a taste or a sound, though it be sometime before these objects present themselves to our observation.

Sect. I Concerning some Powers of Perception, Distinct from What Is Generally Understood by Sensation

To make the following observations understood, it may be necessary to introduce some definitions and observations, either universally acknowledged or sufficiently proved by many writers both ancient and modern, concerning our perceptions called sensations and the actions of the mind consequent upon them.

1. Those ideas which are raised in the mind upon the presence of external objects, and their acting upon our bodies, are called sensations. We find that the mind in such cases is passive and has not power directly to prevent the perception or idea or to vary it at its reception, as long as we continue our bodies in a state fit to be acted upon by the external object.

2. When two perceptions are entirely different from each other, or agree in nothing but the general idea of sensation, we call the powers of receiving those different perceptions different senses. Thus seeing and hearing denote the different powers of receiving the ideas of colors and sounds. And, although colors have vast differences among themselves, as also have sounds, there is a great agreement among the most opposite colors than between any color and a sound; hence, we call all colors perceptions of the same sense. All the several senses seem to have their distinct organs, except feeling, which is in some degree diffused over the whole body.

3. The mind has a power of compounding ideas which were received separately, of comparing their objects by means of the ideas, and of observing their relations and each of the simple ideas which might perhaps have been impressed jointly in the sensation. This last operation we commonly call abstraction.

4. The ideas of substances are compounded of the various simple ideas jointly impressed when they presented themselves to our senses. We define substances only by enumerating these sensible ideas. And such definitions may raise an idea clear enough of the substance in the mind of one who never immediately perceived the substance, provided he has separately received by his senses all the simple ideas which are in the composition of the complex one of the substance defined. But if there be any simple ideas which he has not received, or if he lacks any of the senses necessary for the perception of them, no definition can raise any simple idea which has not been before perceived by the senses.

5. Hence it follows "That, when instruction, education, or prejudice of any kind raise any desire or aversion toward an object, this desire or aversion must be founded upon an opinion of some perfection or of some deficiency in those qualities for perception of which we have the proper senses." Thus if beauty be desired by one who has not the sense of sight, the desire must be raised by some apprehended regularity of figure, sweetness of voice, smoothness, softness, or some other quality perceivable by the other senses without relation to the ideas of color.

6. Many of our sensitive perceptions are pleasant, and many are painful, immediately, without any knowledge of the cause of this pleasure or pain, or the means by which the objects excite it or are the occasions of it, or our seeing to what further advantage or detriment the use of such objects might tend. And the most accurate

knowledge of these things would vary neither the pleasure nor pain of the perception, however it might give a rational pleasure distinct from the sensible or might raise a distinct joy, from a prospect of further advantage in the object, or aversion, from an apprehension of evil.

7. The simple ideas raised in different persons by the same object are probably in some way different, when they disagree in their approbation or dislike, and in the same person, when his fancy at one time differs from what it was at another. This will appear from reflecting on those objects to which we have now an aversion though they were formerly agreeable. And we shall generally find that there is some accidental conjunction of a disagreeable idea which always recurs with the object, as in those wines to which men acquire an aversion after they have taken them in an emetic preparation. In this case we are conscious that the idea is altered from what it was when that wine was agreeable by the conjunction of the ideas of loathing and sickness of stomach. The like change of idea may be insensibly made by the change of our bodies as we advance in years, or when we are accustomed to any object which may occasion an indifference toward meats we were fond of in our childhood, and may make some objects cease to raise the disagreeable ideas which they excited upon our first use of them. Many of our simple perceptions are disagreeable only through the too great intenseness of the quality. Thus moderate light is agreeable, very strong light may be painful; moderate bitter may be pleasant, a higher degree may be offensive. A change in our organs will necessarily occasion a change in the intenseness of the perception at least and sometimes will even occasion a quite contrary perception. Thus a warm hand shall feel that water cold which a cold hand shall feel warm.

We shall not find it perhaps so easy to account for the diversity of fancy in more complex ideas of objects wherein we regard many ideas of different senses at once, as in some perceptions of those called primary qualities and some secondary, as explained by Mr. Locke – for instance, in the different fancies about architecture, gardening, dress. Of architecture and gardening, we shall offer something in Sect. VI; as to dress, we may generally account for the diversity of fancies from a like conjunction of ideas. Thus, if, either from anything in nature or from the opinion of our country or acquaintance, the fancying of glaring colors be looked upon as evidence of levity or of any other evil quality of mind, or if any color or fashion be commonly used by rustics or by men of any disagreeable profession, employment, or temper, these additional ideas may recur constantly with that of the color or fashion and cause a constant dislike to them in those who join the additional ideas, even though the color or form is in no way disagreeable to themselves and actually does please others who ascribe no such ideas to them. But there seems to be no ground for believing such a diversity in human minds, that is, that the same simple idea or perception should give pleasure to one and pain to another, or to the same person at different times, though this is not to say that it seems a contradiction or that the same simple idea should do so.

8. The only pleasure of sense which our philosophers seem to consider is that which accompanies the simple ideas of sensation. But there are vastly greater pleasures in those complex ideas of objects which obtain the names of beautiful, regular, harmonious. Thus everyone acknowledges he is more delighted with a fine face or a just picture than with the view of any one color, were it as strong and lively as possible, and more pleased with a prospect of the sun arising among settled clouds and coloring their edges than with a starry hemisphere, a fine landscape, a regular building than with a clear blue sky, a smooth sea, or a large open plain, not diversified by woods, hills, waters, buildings, and yet even these latter appearances are not quite simple. So, in music, the pleasure of fine composition is incomparably greater than that of any one note, however sweet, full, or swelling.

9. Let it be observed that, in the following papers, the word beauty is taken for the idea raised in us and a sense of beauty for our power of receiving this idea. Harmony also denotes our pleasant ideas arising from composition of sounds, a good ear (as it is generally taken) being the power of perceiving this pleasure. In the following sections, an attempt is made to discover "what is the immediate occasion of these pleasant ideas, or what real quality in the objects ordinarily excites them."

10. It is of no consequence whether we call these ideas of beauty and harmony perceptions of the external senses of seeing and hearing, or not. I should rather choose to call our power of perceiving these ideas an internal sense, were it only for the convenience of distinguishing them from other sensations of seeing and hearing which men may have without perception of beauty and harmony. It is plain from experience that many men have, in the common meaning, the senses of seeing and hearing perfect enough; they perceive all the simple ideas separately and have their pleasure. They distinguish them from each other, such as one color from another, either as quite different or as the stronger or fainter of the same color when they are placed beside each other, although they may often confound their names when they occur apart from each other, as some do the names of green and blue. They can tell, in separate notes, the higher, lower, sharper, or flatter when separately sounded. In figures, they discern the length, breadth, width of each line, surface, angle and may be as capable of hearing and seeing at great distances as any men whatsoever. And yet, perhaps, they shall find no pleasure in musical compositions, in painting, architecture, natural landscape or, perhaps, but a very weak one in comparison with what others enjoy from the same objects. This greater capacity of receiving such pleasant ideas we commonly call a fine genius or taste. In music we seem universally to acknowledge something like a distinct sense from the external one of hearing and call it a good ear. And we should probably acknowledge the like distinction in other objects, had we the distinct names to denote these powers of perception.

11. There will appear another reason, perhaps afterwards, for calling this power of perceiving the ideas of beauty an internal sense, for it is from this, that in some other affairs where our external senses are not much concerned, we discern a sort of beauty very like, in many respects, to that observed in sensible objects and accompanied with like pleasure. Such is that beauty perceived in theorems or universal truths, in general causes, and in some extensive principles of action.

12. Let everyone here consider how different we must suppose the perception to be with which a poet is transported upon the prospect of any of those objects of natural beauty which ravish us even in his description, from that cold lifeless conception which we image in a dull critic, or one of the virtuosos, without what we call a fine taste. This latter class of men may have greater perfection in that knowledge which is derived from external sensation. They can tell all the specific differences of trees, herbs, minerals, metals; they know the form of every leaf, stalk, root, flower, and seed of all the species about which the poet is often very ignorant. And yet the poet shall have a vastly more delightful perception of the whole – and not only the poet, but any man of a fine taste. Our external senses may, by measuring, teach us all the proportions of architecture to the tenth of an inch and the situation of every muscle in the human body, and a good memory may retain these. And yet there is still something further necessary, not only to make a man a complete master in architecture, painting, or statuary, but even a tolerable judge in these works, or capable of receiving the highest pleasure in contemplating them. Since then there are such different powers of perception where what are commonly called the external senses are the same, since the most accurate knowledge of what the external senses discover often does not give the pleasure of beauty or harmony which yet one of a good taste will enjoy at once without much knowledge. We may justly use another name for these higher, and more delightful, perceptions of beauty and harmony and call the power of receiving such impressions an internal sense. The difference of the perceptions seems sufficient to vindicate the use of a different name, especially when we are told in what meaning the word is applied.

13. This superior power of perception is justly called a sense, because of its affinity to the other senses in that the pleasure neither arises from any knowledge of principles, proportions, causes, or of the usefulness of the object, but strikes us at first with the idea of beauty, nor does the most accurate knowledge increase this pleasure of beauty, however it may add a distinct rational pleasure from prospects of advantage, or from the increase of knowledge.

14. And, further, the ideas of beauty and harmony, like other sensible ideas, are necessarily

pleasant to us, as well as immediately so; neither can any resolution of our own, nor any prospect of advantage or disadvantage, vary the beauty or deformity of an object, for, as in the external sensations, no view of interest will make an object grateful, and no view of detriment, distinct from immediate pain in the perception, will make it disagreeable to the sense. So propose the whole world as a reward, or threaten the greatest evil, to make us approve a deformed object or disapprove a beautiful one; dissimulation may be procured by rewards or threatenings, or we may in external conduct abstain from any pursuit of the beautiful and pursue the deformed. But our sentiments of the forms and our perceptions would continue invariably the same.

15. Hence it plainly appears "that some objects are immediately the occasions of this pleasure of beauty, that we have senses fitted for perceiving it, and that it is distinct from that joy which arises from self-love upon prospect of advantage." Do not we often see convenience and use neglected to obtain beauty, without any other prospect of advantage in the beautiful form than the suggesting the pleasant ideas of beauty? Now this shows us that, however we may pursue beautiful objects from self-love, with a view to obtain the pleasures of beauty, as in architecture, gardening, and many other affairs, there must be a sense of beauty antecedent to prospects even of this advantage, without which sense these objects would not be thus advantageous or excite in us this pleasure which constitutes them advantageous. Our sense of beauty from objects by which they are constituted good to us is very distinct from our desire of them when they are thus constituted. Our desire of beauty may be counterbalanced by rewards or threats, but never our sense of it, even as fear of death, or love of life, may make us choose and desire a bitter portion, or neglect those meats which the sense of taste would recommend as pleasant. And yet no prospect of advantage, or fear of evil, can make that potion agreeable to the sense, or meat disagreeable to it, which was not so antecedently to this prospect. Just in the same manner as to the sense of beauty and harmony is it that the pursuit of such objects is frequently neglected, from prospects of advantage, aversion to labor, or any other motive of self-love, which does not prove that we have no sense of beauty, but only that our desire of it may be counterbalanced by a stronger desire. So gold outweighing silver is never adduced as a proof that the latter is void of gravity.

16. Had we no such sense of beauty and harmony, houses, gardens, dress, equipage might have been recommended to us as convenient, fruitful, warm, easy, but never as beautiful. And in faces I see nothing which could please us but liveliness of color and smoothness of surface. And yet nothing is more certain than the fact that all these objects are recommended under quite different views on many occasions and that no custom, education, or example could ever give us perceptions distinct from those of the senses which we had the use of before, or recommend objects under another conception than our being grateful to have them. But the influence of custom, education, and example upon the sense of beauty shall be treated below.

17. Beauty is either original or comparative, or, if any like the terms better, absolute, or relative. Only let it be observed that by absolute or original beauty is not meant any quality supposed to be in the object which should of itself be beautiful without relation to any mind which perceives it, for beauty, like other names of sensible ideas, properly denotes the perception of some mind; so cold, hot, sweet, and bitter denote in our minds sensations to which perhaps there is no resemblance in the objects which excite these ideas in us, however we generally imagine that there is something in the object just like our perception. The ideas of beauty and harmony being excited upon our perception of some primary quality, and having relation to figure and time, may indeed have a nearer resemblance to objects than these sensations, which seem not so much any pictures of objects, as modifications of the perceiving mind. And yet were there no mind with a sense of beauty to contemplate objects, I see not how they could be called beautiful. We therefore by absolute beauty understand only that beauty, which we perceive in objects without comparison to anything external, of which the object is supposed an imitation or picture, such as that beauty perceived from the works of nature, artificial forms, figures, or theorems. Comparative or relative beauty is that which we perceive in objects commonly considered as imitations or resemblances of something else. These two kinds of beauty are the subject of the three following sections.

Sect. II Of Original or Absolute Beauty

1. Since it is certain that we have ideas of beauty and harmony, let us examine what quality in objects excites these ideas or is the occasion of them. And let it be here observed that our inquiry is only about the qualities which are beautiful to men, or about the foundation of their sense of beauty, for, as was above hinted, beauty has always relation to the sense of some mind, and when we afterwards show how generally the objects which occur to us are beautiful, we mean that such objects are agreeable to the sense of men. As there are not a few objects which seem no way beautiful to men, so we see a variety of other animals who seem delighted with them; they may have senses otherwise constituted than those of men and may have the ideas of beauty excited by objects of a quite different form. We see animals fitted for every place, and what to men appears rude and shapeless, or loathsome, may be to them a paradise.

2. That we may more distinctly discover the general foundation or occasion of the ideas of beauty among men, it will be necessary to consider it first in its simpler kinds, such as occurs to us in regular figures. And we may perhaps find that the same foundation extends to all the more complex species of it.

3. The figures which excite in us the ideas of beauty seem to be those in which there is uniformity amidst variety. There are many conceptions of objects which are agreeable upon other accounts, such as grandeur, novelty, sanctity, and some others, which shall be mentioned hereafter. But what we call beautiful in objects, to speak in the mathematical style, seems to be in a compound ratio of uniformity and variety. Thus where the uniformity of bodies is equal, the beauty is as the variety, and where the variety is equal, the beauty is as the uniformity. This will be plain from examples.

First, the variety increases the beauty in equal uniformity. The beauty of an equilateral triangle is less than that of the square, which is less than that of a pentagon, and this again is surpassed by the hexagon. When indeed the number of sides is much increased, the proportion of them to the radius or to the diameter of the figure, or of the circle to which regular polygons have an obvious relation, is so much lost to our observation that the beauty does not always increase with the number of sides, and the want of parallelism in the sides of heptagons and other figures of odd numbers may also diminish their beauty. So, in solids, the eicosihedron surpasses the dodecahedron and thus the octahedron, which is still more beautiful than the cube, and this again surpasses the regular pyramid. The obvious ground of this is greater variety with equal uniformity.

The greater uniformity increases the beauty amidst equal variety in these instances: An equilateral triangle, or even an isosceles, surpasses the scalenum; a square surpasses the rhombus or lozenge, and this again the rhomboid, which is still more beautiful than the trapezium or any figure with irregular curved sides. So the regular solids vastly surpass all other solids of equal number of plain surfaces. And the same is observable not only in the five perfectly regular solids but in all those which have any considerable uniformity, such as cylinders, prisms, pyramids, and obelisks, which please every eye more than any rude figures, where there is no unity or resemblance among the parts.

Instances of the compound ratio we have in comparing circles or spheres with ellipses or spheroids and in comparing the compound solids, the exoctahedron, and eicosidodecahedron with the perfectly regular ones of which they are compounded are not very eccentric. And we shall find that the want of that most perfect uniformity observable in the latter is compensated by the greater variety in the others, so that the beauty is nearly equal.

4. These observations would probably hold true for the most part and might be confirmed by the judgment of children in the simpler figures, where the variety is not too great for their comprehension. And however uncertain some of the particular aforesaid instances may seem, it is perpetually to be observed that children are fond of all regular figures in their little diversions, even though they be no more convenient or useful to them than the figures of our common pebbles. We see how early they discover a taste or sense of beauty in desiring to see buildings, regular gardens, or even representations of them in pictures of any kind.

5. It is the same foundation which we have for our sense of beauty in the works of nature. In every part of the world which we call beautiful,

there is a vast uniformity amidst an almost infinite variety. Many parts of the universe seem not at all designed for the use of man; in fact, it is but a very small spot with which we have any acquaintance. The figures and motions of the great bodies are not obvious to our senses but are found out by reasoning and reflection upon many long observations. And yet as far as we can by sense discover or by reasoning enlarge our knowledge and extend our imagination, we generally find their structure, order, and motion agreeable to our sense of beauty. Every particular object in nature does not indeed appear beautiful to us, but there is a vast profusion of beauty over most of the objects which occur either to our senses or reasonings upon observation. That is, not to mention the apparent situation of the heavenly bodies in the circumference of a great sphere, which is wholly occasioned by the imperfection of our sight in discerning distances, the forms of all the great bodies in the universe are nearly spherical, the orbits of their revolutions generally elliptical and without great eccentricity, in those which continually occur to our observation. Now these are figures of great uniformity and therefore pleasing to us.

Further, to pass by the less obvious uniformity in the proportion of their quantities of matter, distances, and times of revolving to each other, what can exhibit a greater instance of uniformity amidst variety than the constant tenor of revolutions in nearly equal times of each planet around its axis and the central fire or sun through all the ages of which we have any records and in nearly the same orbit and, by which, after certain periods, all the same appearances are again renewed? The alternate successions of light and shade, or day and night, are constantly pursuing each other around each planet with an agreeable and regular diversity in the times they possess the several hemispheres in the summer, harvest, winter, and spring, and the various phases, aspects, and situations of the planets to each other, their conjunctions, and their oppositions in which they suddenly darken each other with their conic shades in eclipses are repeated to us at their fixed periods with invariable constancy. These are the beauties which charm the astronomer and make his tedious calculations pleasant.

6. Again, as to the dry part of the surface of our globe, a great part of which is covered with a very pleasant inoffensive color, how beautifully is it diversified with various degrees of light and shade according to the different situations of the parts of its surface, in mountains, valleys, hills, and open plains which are variously inclined toward the great luminary!

7. If we descend to the more minute works of nature, what vast uniformity there is among all the species of plants and vegetables in the manner of their growth and propagation! What exact resemblance there is among all the plants of the same species whose numbers surpass our imagination! And this uniformity is not only observable in the form in gross; rather, in this it is not so very exact in all instances but in the structure of their minutest parts, which no eye unassisted with glasses can discern. In the almost infinite multitude of leaves, fruit, seed, or flowers of any one species, we often see an exact uniformity in the structure and situation of the smallest fibers. This is the beauty which charms an ingenious botanist. [. . .]

14. But in all these instances of beauty let it be observed that the pleasure is communicated to those who never reflected on this general foundation and that all here alleged is this, "That the pleasant sensation arises only from objects in which there is uniformity amidst variety." We may have the sensation without knowing what is the occasion of it, as a man's taste may suggest ideas of sweets, acids, and bitters, though he be ignorant of the forms of the small bodies or their motions which excite these perceptions in him.

Sect. III Of the Beauty of Theorems

1. The beauty of theorems, or universal truths demonstrated, deserves a distinct consideration, being of a nature pretty different from the former kinds of beauty, and yet there is none in which we shall see such an amazing variety with uniformity. Hence what arises is a very great pleasure distinct from prospects of any further advantage.

2. In one theorem, for example, we may find included, with the most exact agreement, not an infinite multitude of particular truths, but often an infinity of infinities, so that, although the necessity of forming abstract ideas and universal theorems arises perhaps from the limitation of

our minds which cannot admit an infinite multitude of singular ideas or judgments at once, this power gives us an evidence of the largeness of the human capacity above our imagination. Thus, for instance, the forty-seventh proposition of the first book of Euclid's *Elements* contains an infinite multitude of truths concerning the infinite possible sizes of right-angled triangles as you make the area greater or less, and in each of these sizes you may find an infinite multitude of dissimilar triangles as you vary the proportion of the base to the perpendicular, all which infinities of infinites agree in the general theorem. In algebraic and fluxional calculations, we shall still find a greater variety of particular truths included in general theorems, not only in general equations applicable to all kinds of quantity, but in more particular investigations of areas and tangents, in which one manner of operation shall discover theorems applicable to infinite orders or species of curves, to the infinite sizes of each species, and to the infinite points of the infinite individuals of each size.

3. That we may the better discern this agreement, or unity of an infinity of objects, in the general theorem to be the foundation of the beauty or pleasure attending their discovery, let us compare our satisfaction in such discoveries with the uneasy state of mind in which we are when we can only measure lines or surfaces by a scale or are making experiments which we can reduce to no general canon but only heaping up a multitude of particular incoherent observations. Now each of these trials discovers a new truth, but with no pleasure or beauty, notwithstanding the variety, till we can discover some sort of unity or reduce them to some general canon.

4. Again, let us take a metaphysical axiom such as this that every whole is greater that its part, and we shall find no beauty in the contemplation, for, though this proposition contains many infinities of particular truths, the unity is inconsiderable, since they all agree only in a vague undetermined conception of whole and part and in an indefinite excess of the former above the latter, which is sometimes great and sometimes small. So, should we hear that the cylinder is greater than the inscribed sphere, and this again greater than the cone of the same altitude and diameter with the base, we shall find no pleasure in this knowledge of a general relation of greater and less without any precise difference or proportion. But, when we see the universal exact agreement of all possible sizes of such systems of solids that they preserve to each other the constant ratio of 3, 2, 1, how beautiful is the theorem, and how are we ravished with its first discovery!

We may likewise observe that easy or obvious propositions, even where the unity is sufficiently distinct and determinate, do not please us so much as those which being less obvious give us some surprise in the discovery. Thus we find little pleasure in discovering that a line bisecting the vertical angle of an isosceles triangle bisects the base, or the reverse, or, that equilateral triangles are equiangular. These truths we almost know intuitively without demonstration. They are like common goods or those which men have long possessed which do not give such sensible joys as much smaller new additions may give us. But let none hence imagine that the sole pleasure of theorems is from surprise, for the same novelty of a single experiment does not please us much. And we ought not to conclude from the greater pleasure accompanying a new or unexpected advantage that surprise or novelty is the only pleasure of life, or the only ground of delight in truth.

5. There is another beauty in propositions which cannot be omitted, namely, when one theorem contains a vast multitude of corollaries easily deducible from it. Thus that theorem which gives us the equation of a curve, whence perhaps most of its properties may be deduced, does in some way please and satisfy our mind above any other proposition. Such a theorem also is the thirty-fifth of the first book of Euclid, from which the whole art of measuring right-lined areas is deduced by resolution into triangles which are the halves of so many parallelograms, and these are each respectively equal to so many rectangles of the base into the perpendicular altitude. The forty-seventh, of the first book is another of like beauty, and so are many others.

In the search of nature there is like beauty in the knowledge of some great principles or universal forces from which innumerable effects do flow. Such is gravitation in Sir Isaac Newton's scheme; such also is the knowledge of the original of rights, perfect and imperfect and external, alienable and unalienable, with their manner of translations, from whence the greatest part of moral duties may be deduced in the various relations of human life. [. . .]

8. As to the works of art, were we to run through the various artificial contrivances or structures, we should constantly find the foundation of the beauty which appears in them to be some kind of uniformity or unity of proportion among the parts, and of each part to the whole. As there is a vast diversity of proportions possible, and different kinds of uniformity, so there is room enough for that diversity of fancies observable in architecture, gardening, and such like arts in different nations. They all may have uniformity, though the parts in one may differ from those in another. The Chinese or Persian buildings are not like the Grecian and Roman, and yet the former has its uniformity of the various parts to each other and to the whole, as well as the latter.

Sect. IV Of Relative or Comparative Beauty

1. If the preceding thoughts concerning the foundation of absolute beauty be just, we may easily understand wherein relative beauty consists. All beauty is relative to the sense of some mind perceiving it, but what we call relative is that which is apprehended in any object commonly considered as an imitation of some original. And this beauty is founded on a conformity or a kind of unity between the original and the copy. The original may be either some object in nature or some established idea, for, if there be any known ideas as a standard and rules to fix this image or idea by, we may make a beautiful imitation. Thus a sculptor, painter, or poet may please us with a Hercules, if his piece retains that grandeur and those marks of strength and courage which we imagine in that hero.

And farther, to obtain comparative beauty alone, it is not necessary that there be any beauty in the original. The imitation of absolute beauty may indeed in the whole make a more lovely piece, so that an exact imitation shall still be beautiful, though the original were entirely void of it. Thus the deformities of old age, or the rudest rocks or mountains in a landscape, in a picture, if well represented, shall have abundant beauty, though perhaps not so great as if the original were absolutely beautiful and as well represented.

2. The same observation holds true in the descriptions of the poets either of natural objects or persons, and this relative beauty is what they should principally endeavor to obtain as the peculiar beauty of their works. By the Moratæ Fabulæ we are not to understand virtuous manners in a moral sense, but a just representation of manners or characters as they are in nature, and the fact that the actions and sentiments must be suited to the characters of the persons to whom they are ascribed in epic and dramatic poetry. Perhaps very good reasons may be suggested from the nature of our passions to prove that a poet should not draw his characters perfectly virtuous; these characters indeed abstractly considered might give more pleasure and have more beauty than the imperfect ones which occur in life with a mixture of good and evil. But it may suffice at present to suggest against this choice in that we have more lively ideas of imperfect men with all their passions than we do of morally perfect heroes, such as those that really never occur to our observation and of which consequently we cannot judge exactly as to their agreement with the copy. And, further, through consciousness of our own state, we are more nearly touched and affected by the imperfect characters, since in them we see represented in the persons of others the contrasts of inclinations and the struggles between the passions of self-love and those of honor and virtue which we often feel in our own breasts. This is the perfection of beauty for which Homer is justly admired, as well as for the variety of his characters.

3. Many other beauties of poetry may be reduced under this class of relative beauty. The probability is absolutely necessary to make us imagine resemblance, since it is by resemblance that the similitudes, metaphors, and allegories are made beautiful, whether the subject or the thing compared to it have beauty or not; the beauty indeed is greater when both have some original beauty or dignity as well as resemblance. And this is the foundation of the rule of studying decency in metaphors and similes as well as likeness. The measures and cadence are instances of harmony and come under the heading of absolute beauty.

4. We may here observe a strange proneness in our minds to make perpetual comparisons of all things which occur to our observation, even those which would seem very remote. There are certain resemblances in the motions of all animals upon like passions which easily found a comparison, but this does not serve to entertain our fancy. Inanimate objects often have positions that resemble those of the human body in various circumstances, and these airs or gestures of the body are indications of certain dispositions in the mind, so that our very passions and affections as well as other circumstances obtain a resemblance to natural inanimate objects. Thus a tempest at sea is often an emblem of wrath; a plant or tree drooping under the rain is an emblem of a person in sorrow; a poppy bending its stalk, or a flower withering when cut by the plow, resembles the death of a blooming hero; an aged oak in the mountains shall represent an old empire; a flame seizing a wood shall represent a war. In short, everything in nature, by our strange inclination to resemblance, shall be brought to represent other things, even the most remote, especially the passions and circumstances of human nature in which we are more nearly concerned. And to confirm this, and furnish instances of it, one need only look into Homer or Virgil. A fruitful fancy would find in a grove, or a wood, an emblem for every character in a commonwealth and every turn of temper or station in *life*. [. . .]

Sect. VI Of the Universality of the Sense of Beauty among Men

1. We insinuated before "that all beauty has a relation to some perceiving power," and consequently that, since we know not how great a variety of senses there may be among animals, there is no form in nature concerning which we can pronounce "that it has no beauty," for it may still please some perceiving power. But our inquiry is confined to men, and before we examine the universality of this sense of beauty, or their agreement in approving uniformity, it may be proper to consider "whether, as the other senses which give us pleasure do also give us pain, so this sense of beauty does make some objects disagreeable to us, and the occasion of pain."

That many objects give no pleasure to our sense is obvious – many are certainly void of beauty. But then there is no form which seems necessarily disagreeable of itself when we dread no other evil from it and compare it with nothing better of the kind. Many objects are naturally displeasing and distasteful to our external senses just as others are pleasing and agreeable, as smells, tastes, and some separate sounds. But, as to our sense of beauty, no composition of objects which give not unpleasant simple ideas seems positively unpleasant or painful of itself had we never observed anything better of the kind. Deformity is only the absence of beauty, or deficiency in the beauty expected in any species. Thus bad music pleases rustics who never heard any better, and the finest ear is not offended by the tuning of instruments if it is not too tedious and when no harmony is expected, whereas a much smaller dissonance shall offend amidst the performance when harmony is expected. A rude heap of stones is no way offensive to one who shall be displeased with irregularity in architecture when beauty was expected. And had there been a species of that form which we call now ugly or deformed, and had we never seen or expected greater beauty, we should have received no disgust from it, even though the pleasure would not have been so great in this form as in those we now admire. Our sense of beauty seems designed to give us positive pleasure but not positive pain or disgust that is any greater than what arises from disappointment.

2. There are indeed many faces which at first view are apt to raise dislike, but this is generally not from any positive deformity which of itself is positively displeasing; rather, it is from want of expected beauty or much more from some natural indications of morally bad dispositions which we all acquire a faculty of discerning in countenances, airs, and gestures. That this is not occasioned by any form positively disgusting will appear from this if, upon long acquaintance, we are sure of finding sweetness of temper, humanity, and cheerfulness, and, even though the bodily form continues, it shall give us no disgust or displeasure, whereas, if anything was naturally disagreeable, or the occasion of pain, or positive distaste, it would always continue so, even though the aversion we might have toward it were counterbalanced by other considerations. There are horrors raised by some objects which

are only the effect of fear for ourselves or compassion toward others, when either reason or some foolish association of ideas makes us appehend danger and not the effect of anything in the form of itself, for we find that most of those objects which excite horror at first, such as ravenous beasts, a tempestuous sea, a craggy precipice, a dark shady valley, may become the occasions of pleasure when experience or reason has removed the fear.

3. We shall see hereafter "that associations of ideas make objects pleasant, and delightful, which are not naturally apt to give any such pleasures, and that, in the same way, the casual conjunctions of ideas may give a disgust where there is nothing disagreeable in the form itself." And this is the occasion of many fantastic aversions to figures of some animals and to some other forms. Thus swine, serpents of all kinds, and some insects really beautiful enough are beheld with aversion by many people who have got some accidental ideas associated to them. And, for distastes of this kind, no other account can be given.

4. But, as to the universal agreement of mankind in their sense of beauty from uniformity amidst variety, we must consult experience. And, as we allow all men reason, since all men are capable of understanding simple arguments, though few are capable of complex demonstrations, so in this case it must be sufficient to prove this sense of beauty universal, "if all men are better pleased with uniformity in the simpler instances than the contrary, even when there is no advantage observed attending it and, likewise, if all men, according as their capacity enlarges, so as to receive and compare more complex ideas, have a greater delight in uniformity and are pleased with its more complex kinds, both original and relative."

Now let us consider if ever any person was void of this sense in the simpler instances. Few trials have been made in the simplest instances of harmony, because as soon as we find an ear incapable of relishing complex compositions, such as our tunes are, no further pains are employed about such. But, in figures, did ever any man make choice of a trapezium or any irregular curve for the ichnography or plan of his house without necessity or some great motive of convenience, or to make the opposite walls not parallel or unequal in height? Were ever trapeziums, irregular polygons, or curves chosen for the forms of doors or windows, though these figures might have answered the uses as well and would have often saved a great part of the time, labor, and expense to workmen which is now employed in suiting the stones and timber to the regular forms? Among all the fantastic modes of dress, none was ever quite void of uniformity, if it were only the resemblance of two sides of the same robe and in some general aptitude to the human form. The representational painting had always relative beauty by its resemblance to other objects, and often those objects were originally beautiful. But never were any so extravagant as to affect such figures as are made by the casual spilling of liquid colors. Who was ever pleased with an inequality of heights in windows of the same range or dissimilar shapes of them, with unequal legs or arms, eyes or cheeks in a mistress? It must however be acknowledged "That interest may often counterbalance our sense of beauty in this affair as well as in others, and superior good qualities may make us overlook such imperfections."

5. Further, it may perhaps appear "That regularity and uniformity are so copiously diffused through the universe, and we are so readily determined to pursue this as the foundation of beauty in works of art, that there is scarcely anything ever fancied as beautiful where there is not really something of this uniformity and regularity." We are indeed often mistaken in imagining that there is the greatest possible beauty, where it is but very imperfect, but still it is some degree of beauty which pleases, even though there may be higher degrees which we do not observe, and our sense acts with full regularity when we are pleased, even though we are kept by a false prejudice from pursuing objects which would please us more.

A Goth, for instance, is mistaken, when from education he imagines the architecture of his country to be the most perfect. And a conjunction of some hostile ideas may make him adverse to Roman buildings and study to demolish them, as some of our reformers did papal buildings, not being able to separate the ideas of the superstitious worship from the forms of the buildings where it was practiced. And yet it is still real beauty which pleases the Goth, founded upon uniformity amidst variety. For the Gothic pillars are uniform to each other, not only in their sections, which are lozenge formed, but also in their heights and ornaments. Their arches are not one uniform curve, yet they are segments of similar curves and generally equal in the same ranges. Indian buildings have some kind of uniformity, and many of the Eastern nations, though they differ much from us, have great regularity in their manner as did the Romans in theirs. Our Indian screens, which wonderfully supply the regular imaginations of our ladies with ideas of deformity in which nature is very churlish and sparing, do indeed lack all the beauty arising from proportion of parts and conformity to nature; yet they cannot divest themselves of all beauty and uniformity in the separate parts. And this diversification of the human body into various contortions may give some wild pleasure from variety, since some uniformity to the human shape is still retained.

6. There is one sort of beauty which might perhaps have been better mentioned before but will not be impertinent here, because the taste or relish of it is universal in all nations and with the young as well as the old, and that is the beauty of history. Everyone knows how dull a study it is to read over a collection of newspapers which shall perhaps relate all the same events with history: The superior pleasure then of history must arise, like that of poetry, from manners just as when we see a character well drawn wherein we find the secret causes of a great diversity of seemingly inconsistent actions, or an interest of state laid open, or an artful view nicely unfolded, the execution of which influences very different and opposite actions as the circumstances may alter. Now this reduces the whole to a unity of design at least. And this may be observed in the very fables which entertain children; otherwise, we cannot make them relish them.

7. What has been said will probably be assented to, if we always remember in our inquiries into the universality of the sense of beauty, "That there may be real beauty where there is not the greatest, and that there are an infinity of different forms which may all have some unity and yet differ from each other," so that men may have different fancies of beauty, but uniformity will be the universal foundation of our approbation of any form whatsoever as beautiful. And we shall find that it is so in the architecture, gardening, dress, equipage, and furniture of houses, even among the most uncultivated nations, where uniformity still pleases, without any other advantage than the pleasure of the contemplation of it.

8. On this subject, we should consider how, in like cases, we form very different judgments concerning the internal and external senses. Nothing is more ordinary among those who, after Mr. Locke, have shaken off the groundless opinions about innate ideas then allege "That all our relish for beauty and order is either from prospect of advantage, custom, or education," for no other reason but for the variety of fancies in the world. And from this they conclude "That our fancies do not arise from any natural power of perception or sense." Yet all allow that our external senses are natural and that the pleasures or pains of their sensations, however they may be increased or diminished by custom or education and counterbalanced by interest, really precede custom, habit, education, or prospect of interest. Now it is certain "That there is at least as great a variety of fancies about their objects, as the objects of beauty." But, in fact, it is much more difficult, and perhaps impossible, to bring the fancies or relishes of the external senses to any general foundation at all, or to find any rule for the agreeable or disagreeable, though we all allow "that these are natural powers of perception."

9. The reason for this different judgment can be no other than our having distinct names for the external senses and none, or very few, for the internal and, by this are led, as in many other cases, to look upon the former as more fixed, real, and natural than the latter. The sense of harmony has got its name, a good ear, and we are generally brought to acknowledge that this is a natural power of perception or a sense in some way distinct from hearing. Now it is certain "That there is, as necessary, a perception of beauty upon the presence of regular objects, just as there is of harmony upon hearing certain sounds."

10. But let it be observed here once and for all "That an internal sense no more presupposes an innate idea, or principle of knowledge, than the external." Both are natural powers of perception or determinations of the mind to receive necessarily certain ideas from the presence of objects. The internal sense is a passive power of receiving ideas of beauty from all objects in which there is uniformity amidst variety. And there seems to be nothing more difficult in this matter

than that the mind should be always determined to receive the idea of sweet when particles of such a form enter the pores of the tongue, or to have the idea of sound upon any quick undulation of the air. The one seems to have as little connection with its idea as the other. And the same power could with equal ease constitute the former's occasion of ideas as the latter.

11. The association of ideas hinted at above is one great cause of the apparent diversity of fancies in the sense of beauty as well as in the external senses, and it often makes men have an aversion to objects of beauty and a liking to others lacking it but under different conceptions than those of beauty or deformity. And here it may not be improper to give some instances of some of these associations. The beauty of trees, their cool shades, and their aptness to conceal from observation have made groves and woods the usual retreat to those who love solitude, especially to the religious, the pensive, the melancholy, and the amorous. And do not we find that we have so joined the ideas of these dispositions of mind with those external objects that they always recur to us along with them? The cunning of the heathen priests might make such obscure places the scene of the fictitious appearances of their deities, and hence we ascribe ideas of something divine to them. We know the like effect in the ideas of our churches from the perpetual use of them only in religious exercises. The faint light in Gothic buildings has had the same association of a very foreign idea, which our poet shows in his epithet,

A dim religious light.

In like manner it is known that often all the circumstances of actions, or places, or dresses of persons, or voice or song, which have occurred at any time together when we were strongly affected by any passion will be so connected that any one of these will make all the rest recur. And this is often the occasion both of great pleasure and pain, delight and aversion to many objects, which of themselves might have been perfectly indifferent to us. But these approbations, or distastes, are remote from the ideas of beauty, being plainly different ideas.

12. There is also another charm to various persons in music, which is distinct from the harmony and is occasioned by its raising of agreeable passions. The human voice is obviously varied by all the stronger passions. And, when our ear discerns any resemblance between the air of a tune, whether sung or played upon an instrument, in its time, or modulation, or any other circumstance, and the sound of the human voice in any passion, we shall be touched by it in a very sensible manner and have melancholy, joy, gravity, or thoughtfulness excited in us by a sort of sympathy or contagion. The same connection is observable between the very air of a tune and the words expressing any passion which we have heard it fitted to, so that they shall both recur to us together, though but one of them affects our senses.

Now in such a diversity of pleasing or displeasing ideas which may he joined with forms of bodies, or tunes, when men are of such different dispositions and prone to such a variety of passions, it is no wonder "that they should often disagree in their fancies of objects, even though their sense of beauty and harmony were perfectly uniform," because many other ideas may either please or displease, according to persons' tempers and past circumstances. We know how agreeable a very wild country may be to any person who has spent the cheerful days of his youth in it, and how disagreeable very beautiful places may be if they were the scenes of his misery. And this may help us in many cases to account for the diversities of fancy without denying the uniformity of our internal sense of beauty.

13. Grandeur and novelty are two ideas that differ from beauty but that often recommend objects to us. The reason for this is foreign to the present subject.

Sect. VII Of the Power of Custom, Education, and Example as to Our Internal Senses

1. Custom, education, and example are so often alleged in this affair as the occasion of our relish for beautiful objects, and for our approbation of, or delight in, a certain conduct in life, in a moral sense, that it is necessary to examine these three particularly to make it appear "that there is a natural power of perception or sense of beauty in objects that precedes all custom, education, or example."

2. Custom, as distinct from the other two, operates in this manner. As to actions, it only enables the mind or body more easily to perform those actions which have been frequently repeated. It neither leads us to apprehend them under any other view than those under which we were capable of apprehending them at first, nor does it give us any new power of perception about them. We are naturally capable of sentiments of fear and dread of any powerful presence, and so custom may connect the ideas of religious horror to certain buildings. But custom could never have made a being naturally incapable of fear receive such ideas. So, had we no other power of perceiving or forming ideas of actions but as they were advantageous or disadvantageous, custom could only have made us more ready at perceiving the advantage or disadvantage of actions. But this is not to our present purpose.

As to our approbation of, or delight in, external objects, when the blood or spirits of which anatomists talk are roused, quickened, or fermented as they call it, in any agreeable manner by medicine or nutriment, or any glands frequently stimulated to secretion, it is certain that, to preserve the body's ease, we shall delight in objects of taste which in and of themselves are not immediately pleasant to it if they promote that agreeable state to which the body had been accustomed. Further, custom will so alter the state of the body that what at first raised uneasy sensations will cease to do so, or perhaps raise another agreeable idea of the same sense. But custom can never give us any idea of a sense different from those we had prior to it; it will never make those who have no sight approve objects as colored, or those who have no taste approve meats as delicious, however they might approve them as strengthening or exhilarating. When our glands and the parts about them were void of feeling, did we perceive no pleasure from certain brisker motions in the blood? Custom could never make stimulating or intoxicating fluids or medicines agreeable when they were not so to the taste. So, by like reasoning, had we no natural sense of beauty from uniformity, custom could never have made us imagine any beauty in objects; that is, if we had had no ear, custom could never have given us the pleasures of harmony. When we have these natural senses antecedently, custom may make us capable of extending our views further and of receiving more complex ideas of beauty in bodies, or harmony in sounds, by increasing our attention and quickness of perception. But however custom may increase our power of receiving or comparing complex ideas, it seems rather to weaken than to strengthen the ideas of beauty or the impressions of pleasure from regular objects; otherwise, how is it possible that any person could go into the open air on a sunny day, or clear evening, without the most extravagant raptures such as those Milton ascribes to our ancestor after his first creation? For such raptures any person should certainly fall into, when first viewing that kind of scene.

Custom in like manner may make it easier for any person to discern the use of a complex machine and approve it as advantageous, but he would never have imagined it beautiful had he no natural sense of beauty. Custom may make us quicker in apprehending the truth of complex theorems, but, although we all find the pleasure or beauty of theorems as strong at first as ever, custom makes us more capable of retaining and comparing complex ideas so as to discern more complicated uniformity which escapes the observation of novices in any art. However, all this presupposes a natural sense of beauty in uniformity, for, had there been nothing in forms which was constituted as the necessary occasion of pleasure to our senses, no repetition of indifferent ideas as to pleasure or pain, beauty or deformity, could ever have made them grow pleasing or displeasing.

3. The effect of education is this: that thereby we receive many speculative opinions, which are sometimes true and sometimes false, and are often led to believe that objects may be naturally apt to give pleasure or pain to our external senses, but which in reality have no such qualities. And further, by education, there are some strong associations of ideas without any reason, by mere accident sometimes, as well as by design, which it is very hard for us ever after to break asunder. Thus aversions are raised to darkness, and to many kinds of meat, and to certain innocent actions. Approbations without ground are raised in like manner. But in all these instances education never makes us apprehend any qualities in objects for which we do not naturally have senses capable of perceiving. We know what sickness of the stomach is and may without ground believe

that very healthful meats will raise this, and, by our sight and smell, we receive disagreeable ideas of the food of swine, and their sties, and perhaps cannot prevent the recurrence of these ideas at table. But never were men naturally blindly prejudiced against objects, as of a disagreeable color, or in favor of others, as of a beautiful color; they perhaps hear men disparage one color and may imagine this color to be some quite different sensible quality of the other senses, but that is all. And, in the same way, a man naturally void of taste could by no education receive the ideas of taste or be prejudiced in favor of meats as delicious. So, had we no natural sense of beauty and harmony, we could never be prejudiced in favor of objects or sounds as being beautiful or harmonious. Education may make an unattentive Goth imagine that his countrymen have attained the perfection of architecture and an aversion to his enemies, the Romans, may have created some disagreeable ideas about Roman buildings, even causing them to be demolished, but he would never have formed these prejudices had he been void of a sense of beauty. Did blind men debate ever whether purple or scarlet were the finer color? Or could any education prejudice them in favor of either as colors?

Thus education and custom may influence our internal senses, where they already exist, by enlarging the capacity of our minds to retain and compare the parts of complex compositions, and then, if the finest objects are presented to us, we grow conscious of a pleasure far superior to what common performances excite. But all this presupposes that our sense of beauty is natural. Instruction in anatomy and observation of nature and those airs of the countenance and attitudes of body which accompany any sentiment, action, or passion may enable us to know where there is a just imitation. But why should an exact imitation please upon observation, if we did not naturally have a sense of beauty in it, any more than observing the situation of fifty or a hundred pebbles thrown at random? And, should we observe them ever so often, we should never dream of their growing beautiful.

11

Of the Standard of Taste

David Hume

The Scotsman David Hume (1711–76) was an essayist, historian, and one of the most influential of all philosophers.

The great variety of Taste, as well as of opinion, which prevails in the world, is too obvious not to have fallen under every one's observation. Men of the most confined knowledge are able to remark a difference of taste in the narrow circle of their acquaintance, even where the persons have been educated under the same government, and have early imbibed the same prejudices. But those, who can enlarge their view to contemplate distant nations and remote ages, are still more surprized at the great inconsistence and contrariety. We are apt to call *barbarous* whatever departs widely from our own taste and apprehension: But soon find the epithet of reproach retorted on us. And the highest arrogance and self-conceit is at last startled, on observing an equal assurance on all sides, and scruples, amidst such a contest of sentiment, to pronounce positively in its own favour.

As this variety of taste is obvious to the most careless enquirer; so will it be found, on examination, to be still greater in reality than in appearance. The sentiments of men often differ with regard to beauty and deformity of all kinds, even while their general discourse is the same. There are certain terms in every language, which import blame, and others praise; and all men, who use the same tongue, must agree in their application of them. Every voice is united in applauding elegance, propriety, simplicity, spirit in writing; and in blaming fustian, affectation, coldness, and a false brilliancy: But when critics come to particulars, this seeming unanimity vanishes; and it is found, that they had affixed a very different meaning to their expressions. In all matters of opinion and science, the case is opposite: The difference among men is there oftener found to lie in generals than in particulars; and to be less in reality than in appearance. An explanation of the terms commonly ends the controversy; and the disputants are surprized to find, that they had been quarrelling, while at bottom they agreed in their judgment.

Those who found morality on sentiment, more than on reason, are inclined to comprehend ethics under the former observation, and to maintain, that, in all questions, which regard conduct and manners, the difference among men is really greater than at first sight it appears. It is indeed obvious, that writers of all nations and all ages concur in applauding justice, humanity, magnanimity, prudence, veracity; and in blaming the opposite qualities. Even poets and other authors, whose compositions are chiefly calculated to please the imagination, are yet found, from Homer down to Fenelon, to inculcate the same moral precepts, and to bestow their applause and blame on the same virtues and vices. This great unanimity is usually ascribed to the influence of

David Hume, *Of the Standard of Taste*, from *Four Dissertations* (1757).

plain reason; which, in all these cases, maintains similar sentiments in all men, and prevents those controversies, to which the abstract sciences are so much exposed. So far as the unanimity is real, this account may be admitted as satisfactory: But we must also allow that some part of the seeming harmony in morals may be accounted for from the very nature of language. The word *virtue*, with its equivalent in every tongue, implies praise; as that of *vice* does blame: And no one, without the most obvious and grossest impropriety, could affix reproach to a term, which in general acceptation is understood in a good sense; or bestow applause, where the idiom requires disapprobation. Homer's general precepts, where he delivers any such, will never be controverted; but it is obvious, that, when he draws particular pictures of manners, and represents heroism in Achilles and prudence in Ulysses, he intermixes a much greater degree of ferocity in the former, and of cunning and fraud in the latter, than Fenelon would admit of. The sage Ulysses in the Greek poet seems to delight in lies and fictions, and often employs them without any necessity or even advantage: But his more scrupulous son, in the French epic writer, exposes himself to the most imminent perils, rather than depart from the most exact line of truth and veracity.

The admirers and followers of the Alcoran insist on the excellent moral precepts interspersed throughout that wild and absurd performance. But it is to be supposed, that the Arabic words, which correspond to the English, equity, justice, temperance, meekness, charity, were such as, from the constant use of that tongue, must always be taken in a good sense; and it would have argued the greatest ignorance, not of morals, but of language, to have mentioned them with any epithets, besides those of applause and approbation. But would we know, whether the pretended prophet had really attained a just sentiment of morals? Let us attend to his narration; and we shall soon find, that he bestows praise on such instances of treachery, inhumanity, cruelty, revenge, bigotry, as are utterly incompatible with civilized society. No steady rule of right seems there to be attended to; and every action is blamed or praised, so far only as it is beneficial or hurtful to the true believers.

The merit of delivering true general precepts in ethics is indeed very small. Whoever recommends any moral virtues, really does no more than is implied in the terms themselves. That people, who invented the word *charity*, and used it in a good sense, inculcated more clearly and much more efficaciously, the precept, *be charitable*, than any pretended legislator or prophet, who should insert such a *maxim* in his writings. Of all expressions, those, which, together with their other meaning, imply a degree either of blame or approbation, are the least liable to be perverted or mistaken.

It is natural for us to seek a *Standard of Taste*; a rule, by which the various sentiments of men may be reconciled; at least, a decision, afforded, confirming one sentiment, and condemning another.

There is a species of philosophy, which cuts off all hopes of success in such an attempt, and represents the impossibility of ever attaining any standard of taste. The difference, it is said, is very wide between judgment and sentiment. All sentiment is right; because sentiment has a reference to nothing beyond itself, and is always real, wherever a man is conscious of it. But all determinations of the understanding are not right; because they have a reference to something beyond themselves, to wit, real matter of fact; and are not always conformable to that standard. Among a thousand different opinions which different men may entertain of the same subject, there is one, and but one, that is just and true; and the only difficulty is to fix and ascertain it. On the contrary, a thousand different sentiments, excited by the same object, are all right: Because no sentiment represents what is really in the object. It only marks a certain conformity or relation between the object and the organs or faculties of the mind; and if that conformity did not really exist, the sentiment could never possibly have being. Beauty is no quality in things themselves: It exists merely in the mind which contemplates them; and each mind perceives a different beauty. One person may even perceive deformity, where another is sensible of beauty; and every individual ought to acquiesce in his own sentiment, without pretending to regulate those of others. To seek the real beauty, or real deformity, is as fruitless an enquiry, as to pretend to ascertain the real sweet or real bitter. According to the disposition of the organs, the same object may be both sweet and bitter; and the proverb has justly determined it to be fruitless to dispute concerning tastes. It is very natural, and even quite necessary, to extend this axiom to mental, as well as bodily taste; and thus common sense, which is so often at variance with philosophy, especially with the sceptical kind, is found, in one instance at least, to agree in pronouncing the same decision.

But though this axiom, by passing into a proverb, seems to have attained the sanction of common sense; there is certainly a species of common sense which opposes it, at least serves to modify and restrain it. Whoever would assert an equality of genius and elegance between Ogilby and Milton, or Bunyan and Addison, would be thought to defend no less an extravagance, than if he had maintained a mole-hill to be as high as Teneriffe, or a pond as extensive as the ocean. Though there may be found persons, who give the preference to the former authors; no one pays attention to such a taste; and we pronounce without scruple the sentiment of these pretended critics to be absurd and ridiculous. The principle of the natural equality of tastes is then totally forgot, and while we admit it on some occasions, where the objects seem near an equality, it appears an extravagant paradox, or rather a palpable absurdity, where objects so disproportioned are compared together.

It is evident that none of the rules of composition are fixed by reasonings *a priori*, or can be esteemed abstract conclusions of the understanding, from comparing those habitudes and relations of ideas, which are eternal and immutable. Their foundation is the same with that of all the practical sciences, experience; nor are they any thing but general observations, concerning what has been universally found to please in all countries and in all ages. Many of the beauties of poetry and even of eloquence are founded on falsehood and fiction, on hyperboles, metaphors, and an abuse or perversion of terms from their natural meaning. To check the sallies of the imagination, and to reduce every expression to geometrical truth and exactness, would be the most contrary to the laws of criticism; because it would produce a work, which, by universal experience, has been found the most insipid and disagreeable. But though poetry can never submit to exact truth, it must be confined by rules of art, discovered to the author either by genius or observation. If some negligent or irregular writers have pleased, they have not pleased by their transgressions of rule or order, but in spite of these transgressions: They have possessed other beauties, which were conformable to just criticism; and the force of these beauties has been able to overpower censure, and give the mind a satisfaction superior to the disgust arising from the blemishes. Ariosto pleases; but not by his monstrous and improbable fictions, by his bizarre mixture of the serious and comic styles, by the want of coherence in his stories, or by the continual interruptions of his narration. He charms by the force and clearness of his expression, by the readiness and variety of his inventions, and by his natural pictures of the passions, especially those of the gay and amorous kind: And however his faults may diminish our satisfaction, they are not able entirely to destroy it. Did our pleasure really arise from those parts of his poem, which we denominate faults, this would be no objection to criticism in general: It would only be an objection to those particular rules of criticism, which would establish such circumstances to be faults, and would represent them as universally blameable. If they are found to please, they cannot be faults; let the pleasure, which they produce, be ever so unexpected and unaccountable.

But though all the general rules of art are founded only on experience and on the observation of the common sentiments of human nature, we must not imagine, that, on every occasion, the feelings of men will be conformable to these rules. Those finer emotions of the mind are of a very tender and delicate nature, and require the concurrence of many favourable circumstances to make them play with facility and exactness, according to their general and established principles. The least exterior hindrance to such small springs, or the least internal disorder, disturbs their motion, and confounds the operation of the whole machine. When we would make an experiment of this nature, and would try the force of any beauty or deformity, we must choose with care a proper time and place, and bring the fancy to a suitable situation and disposition. A perfect serenity of mind, a recollection of thought, a due attention to the object; if any of these circumstances be wanting, our experiment will be fallacious, and we shall be unable to judge of the catholic and universal beauty. The relation, which nature has placed between the form and the sentiment, will at least be more obscure; and it will require greater accuracy to trace and discern it. We shall be able to ascertain its influence not so much from the operation of each particular beauty, as from the durable admiration, which attends those works, that have survived all the caprices of mode and fashion, all the mistakes of ignorance and envy.

The same Homer, who pleased at Athens and Rome two thousand years ago, is still admired at Paris and at London. All the changes of climate, government, religion, and language, have not been able to obscure his glory. Authority or prejudice may give a temporary vogue to a bad poet or orator; but his reputation will never be durable or general. When his compositions are examined by posterity or by foreigners, the enchantment is dissipated, and his faults appear in their true colours. On the contrary, a real genius, the longer his works endure, and the more wide they are spread, the more sincere is the admiration which he meets with. Envy and jealousy have too much place in a narrow circle; and even familiar acquaintance with his person may diminish the applause due to his performances: But when these obstructions are removed, the beauties, which are naturally fitted to excite agreeable sentiments, immediately display their energy; and while the world endures, they maintain their authority over the minds of men.

It appears then, that, amidst all the variety and caprice of taste, there are certain general principles of approbation or blame, whose influence a careful eye may trace in all operations of the mind. Some particular forms or qualities, from the original structure of the internal fabric, are calculated to please, and others to displease; and if they fail of their effect in any particular instance, it is from some apparent defect or imperfection in the organ. A man in a fever would not insist on his palate as able to decide concerning flavours; nor would one, affected with the jaundice, pretend to give a verdict with regard to colours. In each creature, there is a sound and a defective state; and the former alone can be supposed to afford us a true standard of taste and sentiment. If, in the sound state of the organ, there be an entire or a considerable uniformity of sentiment among men, we may thence derive an idea of the perfect beauty; in like manner as the appearance of objects in day-light, to the eye of a man in health, is denominated their true and real colour, even while colour is allowed to be merely a phantasm of the senses.

Many and frequent are the defects in the internal organs, which prevent or weaken the influence of those general principles, on which depends our sentiment of beauty or deformity. Though some objects, by the structure of the mind, be naturally calculated to give pleasure, it is not to be expected, that in every individual the pleasure will be equally felt. Particular incidents and situations occur, which either throw a false light on the objects, or hinder the true from conveying to the imagination the proper sentiment and perception.

One obvious cause, why many feel not the proper sentiment of beauty, is the want of that *delicacy* of imagination, which is requisite to convey a sensibility of those finer emotions. This delicacy every one pretends to: Every one talks of it; and would reduce every kind of taste or sentiment to its standard. But as our intention in this essay is to mingle some light of the understanding with the feelings of sentiment, it will be proper to give a more accurate definition of delicacy, than has hitherto been attempted. And not to draw our philosophy from too profound a source, we shall have recourse to a noted story in Don Quixote.

It is with good reason, says Sancho to the squire with the great nose, that I pretend to have a judgment in wine: This is a quality hereditary in our family. Two of my kinsmen were once called to give their opinion of a hogshead, which was supposed to be excellent, being old and of a good vintage. One of them tastes it; considers it; and after mature reflection pronounces the wine to be good, were it not for a small taste of leather, which he perceived in it. The other, after using the same precautions, gives also his verdict in favour of the wine; but with the reserve of a taste of iron, which he could easily distinguish. You cannot imagine how much they were both ridiculed for their judgment. But who laughed in the end? On emptying the hogshead, there was found at the bottom, an old key with a leathern thong tied to it.

The great resemblance between mental and bodily taste will easily teach us to apply this story. Though it be certain, that beauty and deformity, more than sweet and bitter, are not qualities in objects, but belong entirely to the sentiment, internal or external; it must be allowed, that there are certain qualities in objects, which are fitted by nature to produce those particular feelings. Now as these qualities may be found in a small degree, or may be mixed and confounded with each other, it often happens, that the taste is not affected with such minute qualities, or is not able to distinguish all the particular flavours, amidst the disorder, in which they are presented. Where the organs are so fine, as to allow nothing to escape them; and at the same time so exact as to perceive every ingredient in the composition: This we call delicacy of taste, whether we employ these terms in the literal or metaphorical sense. Here then the general rules of beauty are of use; being drawn from established models, and from the observation of what pleases or displeases, when presented singly and in a high degree: And if the same qualities, in a continued composition and in a smaller degree, affect not the organs with a sensible delight or uneasiness, we exclude the person from all pretensions to this delicacy. To produce these general rules or avowed patterns of composition is like finding the key with the leathern thong; which justified the verdict of Sancho's kinsmen, and confounded those pretended judges who had condemned them. Though the hogshead had never been emptied, the taste of the one was still equally delicate, and that of the other equally dull and languid: But it would have been more difficult to have proved the superiority of the former, to the conviction of every by-stander. In like manner, though the beauties of writing had never been methodized, or reduced to general principles; though no excellent models had ever been acknowledged; the different degrees of taste would still have subsisted, and the judgment of one man been preferable to that of another; but it would not have been so easy to silence the bad critic, who might always insist upon his particular sentiment, and refuse to submit to his antagonist. But when we show him an avowed principle of art; when we illustrate this principle by examples, whose operation, from his own particular taste, he acknowledges to be conformable to the principle; when we prove, that the same principle may be applied to the present case, where he did not perceive or feel its influence: He must conclude, upon the whole, that the fault lies in himself, and that he wants the delicacy, which is requisite to make him sensible of every beauty and every blemish, in any composition or discourse.

It is acknowledged to be the perfection of every sense or faculty, to perceive with exactness its most minute objects, and allow nothing to escape its notice and observation. The smaller the objects are, which become sensible to the eye, the finer is that organ, and the more elaborate its make and composition. A good palate is not tried by strong flavours; but by a mixture of small ingredients, where we are still sensible of each part, notwithstanding its minuteness and its confusion with the rest. In like manner, a quick and acute perception of beauty and deformity must be the perfection of our mental taste; nor can a man be satisfied with himself while he suspects, that any excellence or blemish in a discourse has passed him unobserved. In this case, the perfection of the man, and the perfection of the sense or feeling, are found to be united. A very delicate palate, on many occasions, may be a great inconvenience both to a man himself and to his friends: But a delicate taste of wit or beauty must always be a desirable quality; because it is the source of all the finest and most innocent enjoyments, of which human nature is susceptible. In this decision the sentiments of all mankind are agreed. Wherever you can ascertain a delicacy of taste, it is sure to meet with approbation; and the best way of ascertaining it is to appeal to those models and principles, which have been established by the uniform consent and experience of nations and ages.

But though there be naturally a wide difference in point of delicacy between one person and another, nothing tends further to encrease and improve this talent, than *practice* in a particular art, and the frequent survey or contemplation of a particular species of beauty. When objects of any kind are first presented to the eye or imagination, the sentiment, which attends them, is obscure and confused; and the mind is, in a great measure, incapable of pronouncing concerning their merits or defects. The taste cannot perceive the several excellences of the performance; much less distinguish the particular character of each excellency, and ascertain its quality and degree. If it pronounce the whole in general to be beautiful or deformed, it is the utmost that can be expected; and even this judgment, a person, so unpractised, will be apt to deliver with great hesitation and reserve. But allow him to acquire experience in those objects, his feeling becomes more exact and nice: He not only perceives the beauties and defects of each part, but marks the distinguishing species of each quality, and assigns it suitable praise or blame. A clear and distinct sentiment attends him through the whole survey of the objects; and he discerns that very degree and kind of approbation or displeasure, which each part is naturally fitted to produce. The mist dissipates, which seemed formerly to hang over the object: The organ acquires greater perfection in its operations; and can pronounce, without danger of mistake, concerning the merits of every performance. In a word, the same address and dexterity, which practice gives to the execution of any work, is also acquired by the same means, in the judging of it.

So advantageous is practice to the discernment of beauty, that, before we can give judgment on any work of importance, it will even be requisite, that that very individual performance be more than once perused by us, and be surveyed in different lights with attention and deliberation. There is a flutter or hurry of thought which attends the first perusal of any piece, and which confounds the genuine sentiment of beauty. The relation of the parts is not discerned: The true characters of style are little distinguished: The several perfections and defects seem wrapped up in a species of confusion, and present themselves indistinctly to the imagination. Not to mention, that there is a species of beauty, which, as it is florid and superficial, pleases at first; but being found incompatible with a just expression either of reason or passion, soon palls upon the taste, and is then rejected with disdain, at least rated at a much lower value.

It is impossible to continue in the practice of contemplating any order of beauty, without being frequently obliged to form *comparisons* between the several species and degrees of excellence, and estimating their proportion to each other. A man, who has had no opportunity of comparing the different kinds of beauty, is indeed totally unqualified to pronounce an opinion with regard to any object presented to him. By comparison alone we fix the epithets of praise or blame, and learn how to assign the due degree of each. The coarsest daubing contains a certain lustre of colours and exactness of imitation, which are so far beauties, and would affect the mind of a peasant or Indian with the highest admiration. The most vulgar ballads are not entirely destitute of harmony or nature; and none but a person, familiarized to superior beauties, would pronounce their numbers harsh, or narration uninteresting. A great inferiority of beauty gives pain to a person conversant in the highest excellence of the kind, and is for that reason pronounced a deformity: As the most finished object, with which we are acquainted, is naturally supposed to have reached the pinnacle of perfection, and to be entitled to the highest applause. One accustomed to see, and examine, and weigh the several performances, admired in different ages and nations, can only rate the merits of a work exhibited to his view, and assign its proper rank among the productions of genius.

But to enable a critic the more fully to execute this undertaking, he must preserve his mind free from all *prejudice*, and allow nothing to enter into his consideration, but the very object which is submitted to his examination. We may observe, that every work of art, in order to produce its due effect on the mind, must be surveyed in a certain point of view, and cannot be fully relished by persons, whose situation, real or imaginary, is not conformable to that which is required by the performance. An orator addresses himself to a particular audience, and must have a regard to their particular genius, interests, opinions, passions, and prejudices; otherwise he hopes in vain to govern their resolutions, and inflame their affections. Should they even have entertained some prepossessions against him, however unreasonable, he must not overlook this disadvantage; but, before he enters upon the subject, must endeavour to conciliate their affection, and acquire their good graces. A critic of a different age or nation, who should peruse this discourse, must have all these circumstances in his eye, and must place himself in the same situation as the audience, in order to form a true judgment of the oration. In like manner, when any work is addressed to the public, though I should have a friendship or enmity with the author, I must depart from this situation; and considering myself as a man in general, forget, if possible, my individual being and my peculiar circumstances. A person influenced by prejudice, complies not with this condition; but obstinately maintains his natural position, without placing himself in that point of view, which the performance supposes. If the work be addressed to persons of a different age or nation, he makes no allowance for their peculiar views and prejudices; but, full of the manners of his own age and country, rashly condemns what seemed admirable in the eyes of those for whom alone the discourse was calculated. If the work be executed for the public, he never sufficiently enlarges his comprehension, or forgets his interest as a friend or enemy, as a rival or commentator. By this means, his sentiments are perverted; nor have the same beauties and blemishes the same influence upon him, as if he had imposed a proper violence on his imagination, and had forgotten himself for a moment. So far his taste evidently departs from the true standard; and of consequence loses all credit and authority.

It is well known, that in all questions, submitted to the understanding, prejudice is destructive of sound judgment, and perverts all operations of the intellectual faculties: It is no less contrary to good taste; nor has it less influence to corrupt our sentiment of beauty. It belongs to *good sense* to check its influence in both cases; and in this respect, as well as in many others, reason, if not an essential part of taste, is at least requisite to the operations of this latter faculty. In all the nobler productions of genius, there is a mutual relation and correspondence of parts; nor can either the beauties or blemishes be perceived by him, whose thought is not capacious enough to comprehend all those parts, and compare them with each other, in order to perceive the consistence and uniformity of the whole. Every work of art has also a certain end or purpose, for which it is calculated; and is to be deemed more or less perfect, as it is more or less fitted to attain this end. The object of eloquence is to persuade, of history to instruct, of poetry to please by means of the passions and the imagination. These ends we must carry constantly in our view, when we peruse any performance; and we must be able to judge how far the means employed are adapted to their respective purposes. Besides, every kind of composition, even the most poetical, is nothing but a chain of propositions and reasonings; not always, indeed, the justest and most exact, but still plausible and specious, however disguised by the colouring of the imagination. The persons introduced in tragedy and epic poetry, must be represented as reasoning, and thinking, and concluding, and acting, suitably to their character and circumstances; and without judgment, as well as taste and invention, a poet can never hope to succeed in so delicate an undertaking. Not to mention, that the same excellence of faculties which contributes to the improvement of reason, the same clearness of conception, the same exactness of distinction, the same vivacity of apprehension, are essential to the operations of true taste, and are its infallible concomitants. It seldom, or never happens, that a man of sense, who has experience in any art, cannot judge of its beauty; and it is no less rare to meet with a man who has a just taste without a sound understanding.

Thus, though the principles of taste be universal, and, nearly, if not entirely the same in all men; yet few are qualified to give judgment on any work of art, or establish their own sentiment as the standard of beauty. The organs of internal sensation are seldom so perfect as to allow the general principles their full play, and produce a feeling correspondent to those principles. They either labour under some defect, or are vitiated by some disorder; and by that means, excite a sentiment, which may be pronounced erroneous. When the critic has no delicacy, he judges without any distinction, and is only affected by the grosser and more palpable qualities of the object: The finer touches pass unnoticed and disregarded. Where he is not aided by practice, his verdict is attended with confusion and hesitation. Where no comparison has been employed, the most frivolous beauties, such as rather merit the name of defects, are the object of his admiration. Where he lies under the influence of prejudice, all his natural sentiments are perverted. Where good sense is wanting, he is not qualified to discern the beauties of design and reasoning, which are the highest and most excellent. Under some or other of these imperfections, the generality of men labour; and hence a true judge in the finer arts is observed, even during the most polished ages, to be so rare a character: Strong sense, united to delicate sentiment, improved by practice, perfected by comparison, and cleared of all prejudice, can alone entitle critics to this valuable character; and the joint verdict of such, wherever they are to be found, is the true standard of taste and beauty.

But where are such critics to be found? By what marks are they to be known? How distinguish them from pretenders? These questions are embarrassing; and seem to throw us back into the same uncertainty, from which, during the course of this essay, we have endeavoured to extricate ourselves.

But if we consider the matter aright, these are questions of fact, not of sentiment. Whether any particular person be endowed with good sense and a delicate imagination, free from prejudice, may often be the subject of dispute, and be liable to great discussion and enquiry: But that such a character is valuable and estimable will be agreed in by all mankind. Where these doubts occur, men can do no more than in other disputable questions, which are submitted to the understanding: They must produce the best arguments, that their invention suggests to them; they must acknowledge a true and decisive standard to exist somewhere, to wit, real existence and matter of fact; and they must have indulgence to such as differ from them in their appeals to this standard. It is sufficient for our present purpose, if we have proved, that the taste of all individuals is not upon an equal footing, and that some men in general, however difficult to be particularly pitched upon, will be acknowledged by universal sentiment to have a preference above others.

But in reality the difficulty of finding, even in particulars, the standard of taste, is not so great as it is represented. Though in speculation, we may readily avow a certain criterion in science and deny it in sentiment, the matter is found in practice to be much more hard to ascertain in the former case than in the latter. Theories of abstract philosophy, systems of profound theology, have prevailed during one age: In a successive period, these have been universally exploded: Their absurdity has been detected: Other theories and systems have supplied their place, which again gave place to their successors: And nothing has been experienced more liable to the revolutions of chance and fashion than these pretended decisions of science. The case is not the same with the beauties of eloquence and poetry. Just expressions of passion and nature are sure, after a little time, to gain public applause, which they maintain for ever. Aristotle, and Plato, and Epicurus, and Descartes, may successively yield to each other: But Terence and Virgil maintain an universal, undisputed empire over the minds of men. The abstract philosophy of Cicero has lost its credit: The vehemence of his oratory is still the object of our admiration.

Though men of delicate taste be rare, they are easily to be distinguished in society, by the soundness of their understanding and the superiority of their faculties above the rest of mankind. The ascendant, which they acquire, gives a prevalence to that lively approbation, with which they receive any productions of genius, and renders it generally predominant. Many men, when left to themselves, have but a faint and dubious perception of beauty, who yet are capable of relishing any fine stroke, which is pointed out to them. Every convert to the admiration of the real poet or orator is the cause of some new conversion. And though prejudices may prevail for a time, they never unite in celebrating any rival to the true genius, but yield at last to the force of nature and just sentiment. Thus, though a civilized nation may easily be mistaken in the choice of their admired philosopher, they never have been found long to err, in their affection for a favorite epic or tragic author.

But notwithstanding all our endeavours to fix a standard of taste, and reconcile the discordant apprehensions of men, there still remain two sources of variation, which are not sufficient indeed to confound all the boundaries of beauty and deformity, but will often serve to produce a difference in the degrees of our approbation or blame. The one is the different humours of particular men; the other, the particular manners and opinions of our age and country. The general principles of taste are uniform in human nature: Where men vary in their judgments, some defect or perversion in the faculties may commonly be remarked; proceeding either from prejudice, from want of practice, or want of delicacy; and there is just reason for approving one taste, and condemning another. But where there is such a diversity in the internal frame or external situation as is entirely blameless on both sides, and leaves no room to give one the preference above the other; in that case a certain degree of diversity in judgment is unavoidable, and we seek in vain for a standard, by which we can reconcile the contrary sentiments.

A young man, whose passions are warm, will be more sensibly touched with amorous and tender images, than a man more advanced in years, who takes pleasure in wise, philosophical reflections concerning the conduct of life and moderation of the passions. At twenty, Ovid may be the favourite author; Horace at forty; and perhaps Tacitus at fifty. Vainly would we, in such cases, endeavour to enter into the sentiments of others, and divest ourselves of those propensities, which are natural to us. We choose our favourite author as we do our friend, from a conformity of humour and disposition. Mirth or passion, sentiment or reflection; whichever of these most predominates in our temper, it gives us a peculiar sympathy with the writer who resembles us.

One person is more pleased with the sublime; another with the tender; a third with raillery. One has a strong sensibility to blemishes, and is extremely studious of correctness: Another has a more lively feeling of beauties, and pardons twenty absurdities and defects for one elevated or pathetic stroke. The ear of this man is entirely turned towards conciseness and energy; that man is delighted with a copious, rich, and harmonious expression. Simplicity is affected by one; ornament by another. Comedy, tragedy, satire, odes, have each its partizans, who prefer that particular species of writing to all others. It is plainly an error in a critic, to confine his approbation to one species or style of writing, and condemn all the rest. But it is almost impossible not to feel a predilection for that which suits our particular turn and disposition. Such preferences are innocent and unavoidable, and can never reasonably be the object of dispute, because there is no standard, by which they can be decided.

For a like reason, we are more pleased, in the course of our reading, with pictures and characters, that resemble objects which are found in our own age or country, than with those which describe a different set of customs. It is not without some effort, that we reconcile ourselves to the simplicity of ancient manners, and behold princesses carrying water from the spring, and kings and heroes dressing their own victuals. We may allow in general, that the representation of such manners is no fault in the author, nor deformity in the piece; but we are not so sensibly touched with them. For this reason, comedy is not easily transferred from one age or nation to another. A Frenchman or Englishman is not pleased with the Andria of Terence, or Clitia of Machiavel; where the fine lady, upon whom all the play turns, never once appears to the spectators, but is always kept behind the scenes, suitably to the reserved humour of the ancient Greeks and modern Italians. A man of learning and reflection can make allowance for these peculiarities of manners; but a common audience can never divest themselves so far of their usual ideas and sentiments, as to relish pictures which in no wise resemble them.

But here there occurs a reflection, which may, perhaps, be useful in examining the celebrated controversy concerning ancient and modern learning; where we often find the one side excusing any seeming absurdity in the ancients from the manners of the age, and the other refusing to admit this excuse, or at least, admitting it only as an apology for the author, not for the performance. In my opinion, the proper boundaries in this subject have seldom been fixed between the contending parties. Where any innocent peculiarities of manners are represented, such as those above mentioned, they ought certainly to be admitted; and a man, who is shocked with them, gives an evident proof of false delicacy and refinement. The poet's *monument more durable than brass*, must fall to the ground like common brick or clay, were men to make no allowance for the continual revolutions of manners and customs, and would admit of nothing but what was suitable to the prevailing fashion. Must we throw aside the pictures of our ancestors, because of their ruffs and fardingales? But where the ideas of morality and decency alter from one age to another, and where vicious manners are described, without being marked with the proper characters of blame and disapprobation; this must be allowed to disfigure the poem, and to be a real deformity. I cannot, nor is it proper I should, enter into such sentiments; and however I may excuse the poet, on account of the manners of his age, I never can relish the composition. The want of humanity and of decency, so conspicuous in the characters drawn by several of the ancient poets, even sometimes by Homer and the Greek tragedians, diminishes considerably the merit of their noble performances, and gives modern authors an advantage over them. We are not interested in the fortunes and sentiments of such rough heroes: We are displeased to find the limits of vice and virtue so much confounded: And whatever indulgence we may give to the writer on account of his prejudices, we cannot prevail on ourselves to enter into his sentiments, or bear an affection to characters, which we plainly discover to be blameable.

The case is not the same with moral principles, as with speculative opinions of any kind. These are in continual flux and revolution. The son embraces a different system from the father. Nay, there scarcely is any man, who can boast of great constancy and uniformity in this particular. Whatever speculative errors may be found in the polite writings of any age or country, they detract but little from the value of those compositions. There needs but a certain turn of thought or imagination to make us enter into all the opinions, which then prevailed, and relish the sentiments or conclusions derived from them. But a very violent effort is requisite to change our judgment of manners, and excite sentiments of approbation or blame, love or hatred, different from those to which the mind from long custom has been familiarized. And where a man is confident of the rectitude of that moral standard, by which he judges, he is justly jealous of it, and will not pervert the sentiments of his heart for a moment, in complaisance to any writer whatsoever.

Of all speculative errors, those, which regard religion, are the most excusable in compositions of genius; nor is it ever permitted to judge of the civility or wisdom of any people, or even of single persons, by the grossness or refinement of their theological principles. The same good sense, that directs men in the ordinary occurrences of life, is not hearkened to in religious matters, which are supposed to be placed altogether above the cognizance of human reason. On this account, all the absurdities of the pagan system of theology must be overlooked by every critic, who would pretend to form a just notion of ancient poetry; and our posterity, in their turn, must have the same indulgence to their forefathers. No religious principles can ever be imputed as a fault to any poet, while they remain merely principles, and take not such strong possession of his heart, as to lay him under the imputation of *bigotry* or *superstition*. Where that happens, they confound the sentiments of morality, and alter the natural boundaries of vice and virtue. They are therefore eternal blemishes, according to the principle above mentioned; nor are the prejudices and false opinions of the age sufficient to justify them.

It is essential to the Roman catholic religion to inspire a violent hatred of every other worship, and to represent all pagans, mahometans, and heretics as the objects of divine wrath and vengeance. Such sentiments, though they are in reality very blameable, are considered as virtues by the zealots of that communion, and are represented in their tragedies and epic poems as a kind of divine heroism. This bigotry has disfigured two very fine tragedies of the French theatre. Polieucte and Athalia; where an intemperate zeal for particular modes of worship is set off with all the pomp imaginable, and forms the predominant character of the heroes. 'What is this,' says the sublime Joad to Josabet, finding her in discourse with Mathan, the priest of Baal, 'Does the daughter of David speak to this traitor? Are you not afraid, lest the earth should open and pour forth flames to devour you both? Or lest these holy walls should fall and crush you together? What is his purpose? Why comes that enemy of God hither to poison the air, which we breathe, with his horrid presence?' Such sentiments are received with great applause on the theatre of Paris; but at London the spectators would be full as much pleased to hear Achilles tell Agamemnon, that he was a dog in his forehead, and a deer in his heart, or Jupiter threaten Juno with a sound drubbing, if she will not be quiet.

Religious principles are also a blemish in any polite composition, when they rise up to superstition, and intrude themselves into every sentiment, however remote from any connection with religion. It is no excuse for the poet, that the customs of his country had burthened life with so many religious ceremonies and observances, that no part of it was exempt from that yoke. It must for ever be ridiculous in Petrarch to compare his mistress Laura, to Jesus Christ. Nor is it less ridiculous in that agreeable libertine, Boccace, very seriously to give thanks to God Almighty and the ladies, for their assistance in defending him against his enemies.

12

A Philosophical Enquiry into the Origin of Our Ideas of the Sublime and Beautiful

Edmund Burke

Sir Edmund Burke (1729–97) was an Irish political writer and statesman who early in his career wrote a work on art that marked a transition from the classical emphasis on intellectual clarity to the romantic stress on the imaginative power of the infinite.

Part One

Section II
Pain and pleasure

It seems then necessary towards moving the passions of people advanced in life to any considerable degree, that the objects designed for that purpose, besides their being in some measure new, should be capable of exciting pain or pleasure from other causes. Pain and pleasure are simple ideas, incapable of definition. People are not liable to be mistaken in their feelings, but they are very frequently wrong in the names they give them, and in their reasonings about them. Many are of opinion, that pain arises necessarily from the removal of some pleasure; as they think pleasure does from the ceasing or diminution of some pain. For my part I am rather inclined to imagine, that pain and pleasure in their most simple and natural manner of affecting, are each of a positive nature, and by no means necessarily dependent on each other for their existence. The human mind is often, and I think it is for the most part, in a state neither of pain nor pleasure, which I call a state of indifference. When I am carried from this state into a state of actual pleasure, it does not appear necessary that I should pass through the medium of any sort of pain. If in such a state of indifference, or ease, or tranquillity, or call it what you please, you were to be suddenly entertained with a concert of music; or suppose some object of a fine shape, and bright lively colours to be presented before you; or imagine your smell is gratified with the fragrance of a rose; or if without any previous thirst you were to drink of some pleasant kind of wine; or to taste of some sweetmeat without being hungry; in all the several senses, of hearing, smelling, and tasting, you undoubtedly find a pleasure; yet if I

Edmund Burke, *A Philosophical Enquiry into the Origin of Our Ideas of the Sublime and Beautiful* (1756).

enquire into the state of your mind previous to these gratifications, you will hardly tell me that they found you in any kind of pain; or having satisfied these several senses with their several pleasures, will you say that any pain has succeeded, though the pleasure is absolutely over? Suppose on the other hand, a man in the same state of indifference, to receive a violent blow, or to drink of some bitter potion, or to have his ears wounded with some harsh and grating sound; here is no removal of pleasure; and yet here is felt, in every sense which is affected, a pain very distinguishable. It may be said perhaps, that the pain in these cases had its rise from the removal of the pleasure which the man enjoyed before, though that pleasure was of so low a degree as to be perceived only by the removal. But this seems to me a subtilty, that is not discoverable in nature. For if, previous to the pain, I do not feel any actual pleasure, I have no reason to judge that any such thing exists; since pleasure is only pleasure as it is felt. The same may be said of pain, and with equal reason. I can never persuade myself that pleasure and pain are mere relations, which can only exist as they are contrasted: but I think I can discern clearly that there are positive pains and pleasures, which do not at all depend upon each other. Nothing is more certain to my own feelings than this. There is nothing which I can distinguish in my mind with more clearness than the three states, of indifference, of pleasure, and of pain. [. . .]

Section VI
Of the passions which belong to self-preservation

Most of the ideas which are capable of making a powerful impression on the mind, whether simply of Pain or Pleasure, or of the modifications of those, may be reduced very nearly to these two heads, *self-preservation* and *society*; to the ends of one or the other of which all our passions are calculated to answer. The passions which concern self-preservation, turn mostly on *pain* or *danger*. The ideas of *pain*, *sickness*, and *death*, fill the mind with strong emotions of horror; but *life* and *health*, though they put us in a capacity of being affected with pleasure, they make no such impression by the simple enjoyment. The passions therefore which are conversant about the preservation of the individual, turn chiefly on *pain* and *danger*, and they are the most powerful of all the passions.

Section VII
Of the sublime

Whatever is fitted in any sort to excite the ideas of pain, and danger, that is to say, whatever is in any sort terrible, or is conversant about terrible objects, or operates in a manner analogous to terror, is a source of the *sublime*; that is, it is productive of the strongest emotion which the mind is capable of feeling. I say the strongest emotion, because I am satisfied the ideas of pain are much more powerful than those which enter on the part of pleasure. Without all doubt, the torments which we may be made to suffer, are much greater in their effect on the body and mind, than any pleasures which the most learned voluptuary could suggest, or than the liveliest imagination, and the most sound and exquisitely sensible body could enjoy. Nay I am in great doubt, whether any man could be found who would earn a life of the most perfect satisfaction, at the price of ending it in the torments, which justice inflicted in a few hours on the late unfortunate regicide in France. But as pain is stronger in its operation than pleasure, so death is in general a much more affecting idea than pain; because there are very few pains, however exquisite, which are not preferred to death; nay, what generally makes pain itself, if I may say so, more painful, is, that it is considered as an emissary of this king of terrors. When danger or pain press too nearly, they are incapable of giving any delight, and are simply terrible; but at certain distances, and with certain modifications, they may be, and they are delightful, as we every day experience. The cause of this I shall endeavour to investigate hereafter.

Section XII
Sympathy, imitation, and ambition

Under this denomination of society, the passions are of a complicated kind, and branch out into a variety of forms agreeable to that variety of ends they are to serve in the great chain of society. The three principal links in this chain are *sympathy*, *imitation*, and *ambition*.

Section XIII
Sympathy

It is by the first of these passions that we enter into the concerns of others; that we are moved as they are moved, and are never suffered to be indifferent spectators of almost any thing which men can do or suffer. For sympathy must be considered as a sort of substitution, by which we are put into the place of another man, and affected in many respects as he is affected; so that this passion may either partake of the nature of those which regard self-preservation, and turning upon pain may be a source of the sublime; or it may turn upon ideas of pleasure; and then, whatever has been said of the social affections, whether they regard society in general, or only some particular modes of it, may be applicable here. It is by this principle chiefly that poetry, painting, and other affecting arts, transfuse their passions from one breast to another, and are often capable of grafting a delight on wretchedness, misery, and death itself. It is a common observation, that objects which in the reality would shock, are in tragical, and such like representations, the source of a very high species of pleasure. This taken as a fact, has been the cause of much reasoning. The satisfaction has been commonly attributed, first, to the comfort we receive in considering that so melancholy a story is no more than a fiction; and next, to the contemplation of our own freedom from the evils which we see represented. I am afraid it is a practice much too common in inquiries of this nature, to attribute the cause of feelings which merely arise from the mechanical structure of our bodies, or from the natural frame and constitution of our minds, to certain conclusions of the reasoning faculty on the objects presented to us; for I should imagine, that the influence of reason in producing our passions is nothing near so extensive as it is commonly believed.

Section XIV
The effects of sympathy in the distresses of others

To examine this point concerning the effect of tragedy in a proper manner, we must previously consider, how we are affected by the feelings of our fellow creatures in circumstances of real distress. I am convinced we have a degree of delight, and that no small one, in the real misfortunes and pains of others; for let the affection be what it will in appearance, if it does not make us shun such objects, if on the contrary it induces us to approach them, if it makes us dwell upon them, in this case I conceive we must have a delight or pleasure of some species or other in contemplating objects of this kind. Do we not read the authentic histories of scenes of this nature with as much pleasure as romances or poems, where the incidents are fictitious? The prosperity of no empire, nor the grandeur of no king, can so agreeably affect in the reading, as the ruin of the state of Macedon, and the distress of its unhappy prince. Such a catastrophe touches us in history as much as the destruction of Troy does in fable. Our delight in cases of this kind, is very greatly heightened, if the sufferer be some excellent person who sinks under an unworthy fortune. Scipio and Cato are both virtuous characters; but we are more deeply affected by the violent death of the one, and the ruin of the great cause he adhered to, than with the deserved triumphs and uninterrupted prosperity of the other; for terror is a passion which always produces delight when it does not press too close, and pity is a passion accompanied with pleasure, because it arises from love and social affection. Whenever we are formed by nature to any active purpose, the passion which animates us to it, is attended with delight, or a pleasure of some kind, let the subject matter be what it will; and as our Creator has designed we should be united by the bond of sympathy, he has strengthened that bond by a proportionable delight; and there most where our sympathy is most wanted, in the distresses of others. If this passion was simply painful, we would shun with the greatest care all persons and places that could excite such a passion; as, some who are so far gone in indolence as not to endure any strong impression actually do. But the case is widely different with the greater part of mankind; there is no spectacle we so eagerly pursue, as that of some uncommon and grievous calamity; so that whether the misfortune is before our eyes, or whether they are turned back to it in history, it always touches with delight. This is not an unmixed delight, but blended with no small uneasiness. The delight we have in such things, hinders us from shunning scenes of misery; and the pain we feel prompts us to relieve ourselves in relieving those who suffer; and all this antecedent to any reasoning, by an instinct that works us to its own purposes, without our concurrence.

Section XV
Of the effects of tragedy

It is thus in real calamities. In imitated distresses the only difference is the pleasure resulting from the effects of imitation; for it is never so perfect, but we can perceive it is an imitation, and on that principle are somewhat pleased with it. And indeed in some cases we derive as much or more pleasure from that source than from the thing itself. But then I imagine we shall be much mistaken if we attribute any considerable part of our satisfaction in tragedy to a consideration that tragedy is a deceit, and its representations no realities. The nearer it approaches the reality, and the further it removes us from all idea of fiction, the more perfect is its power. But be its power of what kind it will, it never approaches to what it represents. Choose a day on which to represent the most sublime and affecting tragedy we have; appoint the most favourite actors; spare no cost upon the scenes and decorations; unite the greatest efforts of poetry, painting and music; and when you have collected your audience, just at the moment when their minds are erect with expectation, let it be reported that a state criminal of high rank is on the point of being executed in the adjoining square; in a moment the emptiness of the theatre would demonstrate the comparative weakness of the imitative arts, and proclaim the triumph of the real sympathy. I believe that this notion of our having a simple pain in the reality, yet a delight in the representation, arises from hence, that we do not sufficiently distinguish what we would by no means choose to do, from what we should be eager enough to see if it was once done. We delight in seeing things, which so far from doing, our heartiest wishes would be to see redressed. This noble capital, the pride of England and of Europe, I believe no man is so strangely wicked as to desire to see destroyed by a conflagration or an earthquake, though he should be removed himself to the greatest distance from the danger. But suppose such a fatal accident have happened, what numbers from all parts would croud to behold the ruins, and amongst them many who would have been content never to have seen London in its glory? Nor is it either in real or fictitious distresses, our immunity from them which produces our delight; in my own mind I can discover nothing like it. I apprehend that this mistake is owing to a sort of sophism, by which we are frequently imposed upon; it arises from our not distinguishing between what is indeed a necessary condition to our doing or suffering any thing in general, and what is the *cause* of some particular act. If a man kills me with a sword, it is a necessary condition to this that we should have been both of us alive before the fact; and yet it would be absurd to say, that our being both living creatures was the cause of his crime and of my death. So it is certain, that it is absolutely necessary my life should be out of any imminent hazard before I can take a delight in the sufferings of others, real or imaginary, or indeed in any thing else from any cause whatsoever. But then it is a sophism to argue from thence, that this immunity is the cause of my delight either on these or on any occasions. No one can distinguish such a cause of satisfaction in his own mind I believe; nay when we do not suffer any very acute pain, nor are exposed to any imminent danger of our lives, we can feel for others, whilst we suffer ourselves; and often then most when we are softened by affliction; we see with pity even distresses which we would accept in the place of our own.

Part Two

Section V
Power

Besides these things which *directly* suggest the idea of danger, and those which produce a similar effect from a mechanical cause, I know of nothing sublime which is not some modification of power. And this branch rises as naturally as the other two branches, from terror, the common stock of every thing that is sublime. The idea of power at first view, seems of the class of these indifferent ones, which may equally belong to pain or to pleasure. But in reality, the affection arising from the idea of vast power, is extremely remote from that neutral character. For first, we must remember, that the idea of pain, in its highest degree, is much stronger than the highest degree of pleasure; and that it preserves the same superiority through all the subordinate gradations. From hence it is, that where the chances for equal degrees of suffering or enjoyment are in any sort equal, the idea of the suffering must always be prevalent. And indeed the ideas of pain, and above all of death, are so very affecting, that whilst we remain in the presence of whatever is supposed to have the power of inflicting either, it is impossible to be perfectly free from terror. Again, we know by experience, that for the enjoyment of pleasure, no great efforts of power are at all necessary; nay we know, that such efforts would go a great way towards destroying our satisfaction: for pleasure must be stolen, and not forced upon us; pleasure follows the will; and therefore we are generally affected with it by many things of a force greatly inferior to our own. But pain is always inflicted by a power in some way superior, because we never submit to pain willingly. So that strength, violence, pain and terror, are ideas that rush in upon the mind together. Look at a man, or any other animal of prodigious strength, and what is your idea before reflection? Is it that this strength will be subservient to you, to your ease, to your pleasure, to your interest in any sense? No; the emotion you feel is, lest this enormous strength should be employed to the purposes of rapine and destruction. That power derives all its sublimity from the terror with which it is generally accompanied, will appear evidently from its effect in the very few cases, in which it may be possible to strip a considerable degree of strength of its ability to hurt. When you do this, you spoil it of every thing sublime, and it immediately becomes contemptible. An ox is a creature of vast strength; but he is an innocent creature, extremely serviceable, and not at all dangerous; for which reason the idea of an ox is by no means grand. A bull is strong too; but his strength is of another kind; often very destructive, seldom (at least amongst us) of any use in our business; the idea of a bull is therefore great, and it has frequently a place in sublime descriptions, and elevating comparison. Let us look at another strong animal in the two distinct lights in which we may consider him. The horse in the light of an useful beast, fit for the plough, the road, the draft, in every social useful light the horse has nothing of the sublime; but is it thus that we are affected with him, *whose neck is cloathed with thunder, the glory of whose nostrils is terrible, who swalloweth the ground with fierceness and rage, neither believeth that it is the sound of the trumpet?* In this description the useful character of the horse entirely disappears, and the terrible and sublime blaze out together. We have continually about us animals of a strength that is considerable, but not pernicious. Amongst these we never look for the sublime: it comes upon us in the gloomy forest, and in the howling wilderness, in the form of the lion, the tiger, the panther, or rhinoceros. Whenever strength is only useful, and employed for our benefit or our pleasure, then it is never sublime; for nothing can act agreeably to us, that does not act in conformity to our will; but to act agreeably to our will, it must be subject to us; and therefore can never be the cause of a grand and commanding conception. The description of the wild ass, in Job, is worked up into no small sublimity, merely by insisting on his freedom, and his setting mankind at defiance; otherwise the description of such an animal could have had nothing noble in it. *Who hath loosed* (says he) *the bands of the wild ass? whose house I have made the wilderness, and the barren land his dwellings. He scorneth the multitude of the city, neither regardeth he the voice of the driver. The range of the mountains is his pasture.* The magnificent description of the unicorn and of leviathan in the same book, is full of the same heightening circumstances. *Will the unicorn be willing to serve thee? canst thou bind the unicorn with his band in the furrow? wilt thou trust him because his strength is great? – Canst thou draw out leviathan with an hook? will he make a covenant with thee? wilt thou take him for a servant for ever? shall not one be cast down even at the sight of him?* In short, wheresoever we find strength, and in what light soever we look upon power, we shall all along observe the sublime the concomitant of terror, and contempt the attendant on a strength that is subservient and innoxious. [. . .]

In the scripture, wherever God is represented as appearing or speaking, every thing terrible in nature is called up to heighten the awe and solemnity of the divine presence. The psalms, and the prophetical books, are crouded with instances of this kind. *The earth shook* (says the psalmist) *the heavens also dropped at the presence of the Lord.* And what is remarkable, the painting preserves the same character, not only when he is supposed descending to take vengeance upon the wicked, but even when he exerts the like plenitude of power in acts of beneficence to mankind. *Tremble, thou earth! at the presence of the Lord; at the presence of the God of Jacob; which turned the rock into standing water, the flint into a fountain of waters.* It were endless to enumerate all the passages both in the sacred and profane writers, which establish the general sentiment of mankind, concerning the inseparable union of a sacred and reverential awe, with our ideas of the divinity. [. . .] Thus we have traced power through its several gradations unto the highest of all, where our imagination is finally lost; and we find terror quite throughout the progress, its inseparable companion, and growing along with it, as far as we can possibly trace them. Now as power is undoubtedly a capital source of the sublime, this will point out evidently from whence its energy is derived, and to what class of ideas we ought to unite it.

Section VII
Vastness

Greatness of dimension, is a powerful cause of the sublime. This is too evident, and the observation too common, to need any illustration; it is not so common, to consider in what ways greatness of dimension, vastness of extent, or quantity, has the most striking effect. For certainly, there are ways, and modes, wherein the same quantity of extension shall produce greater effects than it is found to do in others. Extension is either in length, height, or depth. Of these the length strikes least; an hundred yards of even ground will never work such an effect as a tower an hundred yards high, or a rock or mountain of that altitude. I am apt to imagine likewise, that height is less grand than depth; and that we are more struck at looking down from a precipice, than at looking up at an object of equal height, but of that I am not very positive. A perpendicular has more force in forming the sublime, than an inclined plane; and the effects of a rugged and broken surface seem stronger than where it is smooth and polished. It would carry us out of our way to enter in this place into the cause of these appearances; but certain it is they afford a large and fruitful field of speculation. [. . .]

Section VIII
Infinity

Another source of the sublime, is *infinity*; if it does not rather belong to the last. Infinity has a tendency to fill the mind with that sort of delightful horror, which is the most genuine effect, and truest test of the sublime. There are scarce any things which can become the objects of our senses that are really, and in their own nature infinite. But the eye not being able to perceive the bounds of many things, they seem to be infinite, and they produce the same effects as if they were really so. We are deceived in the like manner, if the parts of some large object are so continued to any indefinite number, that the imagination meets no check which may hinder its extending them at pleasure. [. . .]

Section XII
Difficulty

Another source of greatness is *Difficulty*. When any work seems to have required immense force and labour to effect it, the idea is grand. Stonehenge, neither for disposition nor ornament, has any thing admirable; but those huge rude masses of stone, set on end, and piled each on other, turn the mind on the immense force necessary for such a work. Nay the rudeness of the work increases this cause of grandeur, as it excludes the idea of art, and contrivance; for dexterity produces another sort of effect which is different enough from this.

Section XIII
Magnificence

Magnificence is likewise a source of the sublime. A great profusion of things which are splendid or valuable in themselves, is *magnificent*. The starry heaven, though it occurs so very frequently to our view, never fails to excite an idea of grandeur. This cannot be owing to any thing in the stars themselves, separately considered. The number is certainly the cause. The apparent disorder augments the grandeur, for the appearance of care is highly contrary to our ideas of magnificence. Besides, the stars lye in such apparent confusion, as makes it impossible on ordinary occasions to reckon them. This gives them the advantage of a sort of infinity. In works of art, this kind of grandeur, which consists in multitude, is to be very cautiously admitted; because, a profusion of excellent things is not to be attained, or with too much difficulty; and, because in many cases this splendid confusion would destroy all use, which should be attended to in most of the works of art with the greatest care; besides it is to be considered, that unless you can produce an appearance of infinity by your disorder, you will have disorder only without magnificence. There are, however, a sort of fireworks, and some other things, that in this way succeed well, and are truly grand. There are also many descriptions in the poets and orators which owe their sublimity to a richness and profusion of images, in which the mind is so dazzled as to make it impossible to attend to that exact coherence and agreement of the allusions, which we should require on every other occasion. [. . .]

Part Three

Section XII
The real cause of beauty

Having endeavoured to show what beauty is not, it remains that we should examine, at least with equal attention, in what it really consists. Beauty is a thing much too affecting not to depend upon some positive qualities. And, since it is no creature of our reason, since it strikes us without any reference to use, and even where no use at all can be discerned, since the order and method of nature is generally very different from our measures and proportions, we must conclude that beauty is, for the greater part, some quality in bodies, acting mechanically upon the human mind by the intervention of the senses. We ought therefore to consider attentively in what manner those sensible qualities are disposed, in such things as by experience we find beautiful, or which excite in us the passion of love, or some correspondent affection.

Section XIII
Beautiful objects small

The most obvious point that presents itself to us in examining any object, is its extent or quantity. [. . .] A great beautiful thing, is a manner of expression scarcely ever used; but that of a great ugly thing, is very common. There is a wide difference between admiration and love. The sublime, which is the cause of the former, always dwells on great objects, and terrible; the latter on small ones, and pleasing; we submit to what we admire, but we love what submits to us; in one case we are forced, in the other we are flattered into compliance. In short, the ideas of the sublime and the beautiful stand on foundations so different, that it is hard, I had almost said impossible, to think of reconciling them in the same subject, without considerably lessening the effect of the one or the other upon the passions. So that attending to their quantity, beautiful objects are comparatively small.

Section XIV
Smoothness

The next property constantly observable in such objects is *Smoothness*. A quality so essential to beauty, that I do not now recollect any thing beautiful that is not smooth. In trees and flowers, smooth leaves are beautiful; smooth slopes of earth in gardens; smooth streams in the landscape; smooth coats of birds and beasts in animal beauties; in fine women, smooth skins; and in several sorts of ornamental furniture, smooth and polished surfaces. A very considerable part of the effect of beauty is owing to this quality; indeed the most considerable. For take any beautiful object, and give it a broken and rugged surface, and however well formed it may be in other respects, it pleases no longer. Whereas let it want ever so many of the other constituents, if it wants not this, it becomes more pleasing than almost all the others without it. This seems to me so evident, that I am a good deal surprised, that none who have handled the subject have made any mention of the quality of smoothness in the enumeration of those that go to the forming of beauty. For indeed any ruggedness, any sudden projection, any sharp angle, is in the highest degree contrary to that idea.

Section XV
Gradual variation

But as perfectly beautiful bodies are not composed of angular parts, so their parts never continue long in the same right line. They vary their direction every moment, and they change under the eye by a deviation continually carrying on, but for whose beginning or end you will find it difficult to ascertain a point. The view of a beautiful bird will illustrate this observation. Here we see the head increasing insensibly to the middle, from whence it lessens gradually until it mixes with the neck; the neck loses itself in a larger swell, which continues to the middle of the body, when the whole decreases again to the tail; the tail takes a new direction; but it soon varies its new course; it blends again with the other parts; and the line is perpetually changing, above, below, upon every side. In this description I have before me the idea of a dove; it agrees very well with most of the conditions of beauty. It is smooth and downy; its parts are (to use that expression) melted into one another; you are presented with no sudden protuberance through the whole, and yet the whole is continually changing. [. . .]

Section XVI
Delicacy

An air of robustness and strength is very prejudicial to beauty. An appearance of *delicacy*, and even of fragility, is almost essential to it. Whoever examines the vegetable or animal creation, will find this observation to be founded in nature, It is not the oak, the ash, or the elm, or any of the robust trees of the forest, which we consider as beautiful; they are awful and majestic; they inspire a sort of reverence. It is the delicate myrtle, it is the orange, it is the almond, it is the jessamine, it is the vine, which we look on as vegetable beauties. It is the flowery species, so remarkable for its weakness and momentary duration, that gives us the liveliest idea of beauty, and elegance. [. . .]

Section XVII
Beauty in colour

As to the colours usually found in beautiful bodies; it may be somewhat difficult to ascertain them, because in the several parts of nature, there is an infinite variety. However, even in this variety, we may mark out something on which to settle. First, the colours of beautiful bodies must not be dusky or muddy, but clean and fair. Secondly, they must not be of the strongest kind. Those which seem most appropriated to beauty, are the milder of every sort; light greens; soft blues; weak whites; pink reds; and violets. Thirdly, if the colours be strong and vivid, they are always diversified, and the object is never of one strong colour; there are almost always such a number of them (as in variegated flowers) that the strength and glare of each is considerably abated. [. . .]

Section XXVII
The sublime and beautiful compared

On closing this general view of beauty, it naturally occurs, that we should compare it with the sublime; and in this comparison there appears a remarkable contrast. For sublime objects are vast in their dimensions, beautiful ones comparatively small; beauty should be smooth, and polished; the great, rugged and negligent; beauty should shun the right line, yet deviate from it insensibly; the great in many cases loves the right line, and when it deviates, it often makes a strong deviation; beauty should not be obscure; the great ought to be dark and gloomy; beauty should be light and delicate; the great ought to be solid, and even massive. They are indeed ideas of a very different nature, one being founded on pain, the other on pleasure; and however they may vary afterwards from the direct nature of their causes, yet these causes keep up an eternal distinction between them, a distinction never to be forgotten by any whose business it is to affect the passions. In the infinite variety of natural combinations we must expect to find the qualities of things the most remote imaginable from each other united in the same object. We must expect also to find combinations of the same kind in the works of art. But when we consider the power of an object upon our passions, we must know that when any thing is intended to affect the mind by the force of some predominant property, the affection produced is like to be the more uniform and perfect, if all the other properties or qualities of the object be of the same nature, and tending to the same design as the principal;

> If black, and white blend, soften, and unite,
> A thousand ways, are there no black and white?

If the qualities of the sublime and beautiful are sometimes found united, does this prove, that they are the same, does it prove, that they are any way allied, does it prove even that they are not opposite and contradictory? Black and white may soften, may blend, but they are not therefore the same. Nor when they are so softened and blended with each other, or with different colours, is the power of black as black, or of white as white, so strong as when each stands uniform and distinguished.

Part Four

Section V
How the sublime is produced

Having considered terror as producing an unnatural tension and certain violent emotions of the nerves; it easily follows, from what we have just said, that whatever is fitted to produce such a tension, must be productive of a passion similar to terror, and consequently must be a source of the sublime, though it should have no idea of danger connected with it. So that little remains towards showing the cause of the sublime, but to show that the instances we have given of it in the second part, relate to such things, as are fitted by nature to produce this sort of tension, either by the primary operation of the mind or the body. With regard to such things as affect by the associated idea of danger, there can be no doubt but that they produce terror, and act by some modification of that passion; and that terror, when sufficiently violent, raises the emotions of the body just mentioned, can as little be doubted. But if the sublime is built on terror, or some passion like it, which has pain for its object; it is previously proper to enquire how any species of delight can be derived from a cause so apparently contrary to it. I say, delight, because, as I have often remarked, it is very evidently different in its cause, and in its own nature, from actual and positive pleasure.

Section VI
How pain can be a cause of delight

Providence has so ordered it, that a state of rest and inaction, however it may flatter our indolence, should be productive of many inconveniences; that it should generate such disorders, as may force us to have recourse to some labour, as a thing absolutely requisite to make us pass our lives with tolerable satisfaction; for the nature of rest is to suffer all the parts of our bodies to fall into a relaxation, that not only disables the members from performing their functions, but takes away the vigorous tone of fibre which is requisite for carrying on the natural and necessary secretions. At the same time, that in this languid inactive state, the nerves are more liable to the most horrid convulsions, than when they are sufficiently braced and strengthened. Melancholy, dejection, despair, and often self-murder, is the consequence of the gloomy view we take of things in this relaxed state of body. The best remedy for all these evils is exercise or labour; and labour is a surmounting of difficulties, an exertion of the contracting power of the muscles; and as such resembles pain, which consists in tension or contraction, in every thing but degree. Labour is not only requisite to preserve the coarser organs in a state fit for their functions, but it is equally necessary to these finer and more delicate organs, on which, and by which, the imagination, and perhaps the other mental powers act. Since it is probable, that not only the inferior parts of the soul, as the passions are called, but the understanding itself makes use of some fine corporeal instruments in its operation; though what they are, and where they are, may be somewhat hard to settle: but that it does make use of such, appears from hence; that a long exercise of the mental powers induce a remarkable lassitude of the whole body; and on the other hand, that great bodily labour, or pain, weakens, and sometimes actually destroys the mental faculties. Now, as a due exercise is essential to the coarse muscular parts of the constitution, and that without this rousing they would become languid, and diseased, the very same rule holds with regard to those finer parts we have mentioned; to have them in proper order, they must be shaken and worked to a proper degree.

13

Laocoon

Gotthold Lessing

Gotthold Lessing (1729–81) was a German philosopher, dramatist, and critic, whose emphasis on the free expression of passion paved the way toward romanticism.

II

Be it truth or fable that Love made the first attempt in the imitative arts, thus much is certain: that she never tired of guiding the hand of the great masters of antiquity. For although painting, as the art which reproduces objects upon flat surfaces, is now practised in the broadest sense of that definition, yet the wise Greek set much narrower bounds to it. He confined it strictly to the imitation of beauty. The Greek artist represented nothing that was not beautiful. Even the vulgarly beautiful, the beauty of inferior types, he copied only incidentally for practice or recreation. The perfection of the subject must charm in his work. He was too great to require the beholders to be satisfied with the mere barren pleasure arising from a successful likeness or from consideration of the artist's skill. Nothing in his art was dearer to him or seemed to him more noble than the ends of art. [. . .]

Gotthold Lessing, *Laocoon*, trans. Ellen Frothingham (Latin), William Cullen Bryant (Greek) (New York: Farrar, Straus, & Giroux, 1957 and 1965), pp. 8, 16–18, 20–1, 58–61, 83–93, 101–3, 105–6, 109–10, 126, 136–9.

III

[. . .] [T]he realm of art has in modern times been greatly enlarged. Its imitations are allowed to extend over all visible nature, of which beauty constitutes but a small part. Truth and expression are taken as its first law. As nature always sacrifices beauty to higher ends, so should the artist subordinate it to his general purpose, and not pursue it further than truth and expression allow. Enough that truth and expression convert what is unsightly in nature into a beauty of art.

Allowing this idea to pass unchallenged at present for whatever it is worth, are there not other independent considerations which should set bounds to expression, and prevent the artist from choosing for his imitation the culminating point of any action?

The single moment of time to which art must confine itself, will lead us, I think, to such considerations. Since the artist can use but a single moment of ever-changing nature, and the painter must further confine his study of this one moment to a single point of view, while their works are made not simply to be looked at, but to be contemplated long and often, evidently the most fruitful moment and the most fruitful aspect of that moment must be chosen. Now that only is fruitful which allows free play to the imagination. The more we see the more we must be able to imagine; and the more we imagine, the more we must think we see. But no moment in the whole course of an action is so disadvantageous in this respect as that of its culmination. There is nothing beyond, and to present the uttermost to the eye is to bind the wings of Fancy, and compel her, since she cannot soar beyond the impression made on the senses, to employ herself with feebler images, shunning as her limit the visible fulness already expressed. When, for instance, Laocoon sighs, imagination can hear him cry; but if he cry, imagination can neither mount a step higher, nor fall a step lower, without seeing him in a more endurable, and therefore less interesting, condition. We hear him merely groaning, or we see him already dead.

Again, since this single moment receives from art an unchanging duration, it should express nothing essentially transitory. All phenomena, whose nature it is suddenly to break out and as suddenly to disappear, which can remain as they are but for a moment; all such phenomena, whether agreeable or otherwise, acquire through the perpetuity conferred upon them by art such an unnatural appearance, that the impression they produce becomes weaker with every fresh observation, till the whole subject at last wearies or disgusts us. La Mettrie, who had himself painted and engraved as a second Democritus, laughs only the first time we look at him. Looked at again, the philosopher becomes a buffoon, and his laugh a grimace. So it is with a cry. Pain, which is so violent as to extort a scream, either soon abates or it must destroy the sufferer. Again, if a man of firmness and endurance cry, he does not do so unceasingly, and only this apparent continuity in art makes the cry degenerate into womanish weakness or childish impatience. This, at least, the sculptor of the Laocoon had to guard against, even had a cry not been an offence against beauty, and were suffering without beauty a legitimate subject of art. [. . .]

IV

A review of the reasons here alleged for the moderation observed by the sculptor of The Laocoon in the expression of bodily pain, shows them to lie wholly in the peculiar object of his art and its necessary limitations. Scarce one of them would be applicable to poetry.

Without inquiring here how far the poet can succeed in describing physical beauty, so much at least is clear, that since the whole infinite realm of perfection lies open for his imitation, this visible covering under which perfection becomes beauty will be one of his least significant means of interesting us in his characters. Indeed, he often neglects it altogether, feeling sure that if his hero has gained our favor, his nobler qualities will either so engross us that we shall not think of his body, or have so won us that, if we think of it, we shall naturally attribute to him a beautiful, or, at least, no unsightly one. Least of all will he have reference to the eye in every detail not especially addressed to the sense of sight. When Virgil's Laocoon screams, who stops to think that a scream necessitates an open mouth, and that an open mouth is ugly? Enough that "clamores horrendos ad sidera tollit" is fine to the ear, no matter what its effect on the eye. Whoever requires a beautiful picture has missed the whole intention of the poet.

Further, nothing obliges the poet to concentrate his picture into a single moment. He can take up every action, if he will, from its origin, and carry it through all possible changes to its issue. Every change, which would require from the painter a separate picture, costs him but a single touch; a touch, perhaps, which, taken by itself, might offend the imagination, but which, anticipated, as it has been, by what preceded, and softened and atoned for by what follows, loses its individual effect in the admirable result of the whole. Thus were it really unbecoming in a man to cry out in the extremity of bodily pain, how can this momentary weakness lower in our estimation a character whose virtues have previously won our regard? Virgil's Laocoon cries; but this screaming Laocoon is the same we know and love as the most far-seeing of patriots and the tenderest of fathers. We do not attribute the cry to his character, but solely to his intolerable sufferings. We hear in it only those, nor could they have been made sensible to us in any other way.

Who blames the poet, then? Rather must we acknowledge that he was right in introducing the cry, as the sculptor was in omitting it. [. . .]

VIII

[. . .] The gods and other spiritual beings represented by the artist are not precisely the same as those introduced by the poet. To the artist they are personified abstractions which must always be characterized in the same way, or we fail to recognize them. In poetry, on the contrary, they are real beings, acting and working, and possessing, besides their general character, qualities and passions which may upon occasion take precedence. Venus is to the sculptor simply love. He must therefore endow her with all the modest beauty, all the tender charms, which, as delighting us in the beloved object, go to make up our abstract idea of love. The least departure from this ideal prevents our recognizing her image. Beauty distinguished more by majesty than modesty is no longer Venus but Juno. Charms commanding and manly rather than tender, give us, instead of a Venus, a Minerva. A Venus all wrath, a Venus urged by revenge and rage, is to the sculptor a contradiction in terms. For love, as love, never is angry, never avenges itself. To the poet, Venus is love also, but she is the goddess of love, who has her own individuality outside of this one characteristic, and can therefore be actuated by aversion as well as affection. What wonder, then, that in poetry she blazes into anger and rage, especially under the provocation of insulted love?

The artist, indeed, like the poet, may, in works composed of several figures, introduce Venus or any other deity, not simply by her one characteristic, but as a living, acting being. But the actions, if not the direct results of her character, must not be at variance with it. Venus delivering to her son the armor of the gods is a subject equally suitable to artist and poet. For here she can be endowed with all the grace and beauty befitting the goddess of love. Such treatment will be of advantage as helping us the more easily to recognize her. But when Venus, intent on revenging herself on her contemners, the men of Lemnos, wild, in colossal shape, with cheeks inflamed and dishevelled hair, seizes the torch, and, wrapping a black robe about her, flies downward on the storm-cloud, – that is no moment for the painter, because he has no means of making us recognize her. The poet alone has the privilege of availing himself of it. He can unite it so closely with some other moment when the goddess is the true Venus, that we do not in the fury forget the goddess of love. Flaccus does this, –

> Gracious the goddess is not emulous to appear, nor does she bind her hair with the burnished gold, letting her starry tresses float about her. Wild she is and huge, her cheeks suffused with spots; most like to the Stygian virgins with crackling torch and black mantle.

And Statius also, –

> Leaving ancient Paphos and the hundred altars, not like her former self in countenance or the fashion of her hair, she is said to have loosened the nuptial girdle and have sent away her doves. Some report that in the dead of night, bearing other fires and mightier arms, she had hasted with the Tartarean sisters to bed-chambers, and filled the secret places of homes with twining snakes, and all thresholds with cruel fear.

Or, we may say, the poet alone possesses the art of so combining negative with positive traits as to unite two appearances in one. No longer now the tender Venus, her hair no more confined with golden clasps, no azure draperies floating about her, without her girdle, armed with other flames and larger arrows, the goddess hastens downward, attended by furies of like aspect with herself. Must the poet abstain from the use of this device because artists are debarred from it? If painting claim to be the sister of poetry, let the younger at least not be jealous of the elder, nor seek to deprive her of ornaments unbecoming to herself.

XIII

If Homer's works were completely destroyed, and nothing remained of the Iliad and Odyssey but this series of pictures proposed by Caylus, should we from these – even supposing them to be executed by the best masters – form the same idea that we now have of the poet's descriptive talent alone, setting aside all his other qualities as a poet?

Let us take the first piece that comes to hand, – the picture of the plague. What do we see on the canvas? Dead bodies, the flame of funeral pyres, the dying busied with the dead, the angry god upon a cloud discharging his arrows. The profuse wealth of the picture becomes poverty in the poet. Should we attempt to restore the text of Homer from this picture, what can we make him say? "Thereupon the wrath of Apollo was kindled, and he shot his arrows among the Grecian army. Many Greeks died, and their bodies were burned." Now let us turn to Homer himself:

> Down he came,
> Down from the summit of the Olympian
> mount,
> Wrathful in heart; his shoulders bore the bow
> And hollow quiver; there the arrows rang
> Upon the shoulders of the angry god,
> As on he moved. He came as comes the night,
> And, seated from the ships aloof, sent forth
> An arrow; terrible was heard the clang
> Of that resplendent bow. At first he smote
> The mules and the swift dogs, and then on
> man
> He turned the deadly arrow. All around
> Glared evermore the frequent funeral piles.[1]

The poet here is as far beyond the painter, as life is better than a picture. Wrathful, with bow and quiver, Apollo descends from the Olympian towers. I not only see him, but hear him. At every step the arrows rattle on the shoulders of the angry god. He enters among the host like the night. Now he seats himself over against the ships, and, with a terrible clang of the silver bow, sends his first shaft against the mules and dogs. Next he turns his poisoned darts upon the warriors themselves, and unceasing blaze on every side of corpse-laden pyres. It is impossible to translate into any other language the musical painting heard in the poet's words. Equally impossible would it be to infer it from the canvas. Yet this is the least of the advantages possessed by the poetical picture. Its chief superiority is that it leads us through a whole gallery of pictures up to the point depicted by the artist.

But the plague is perhaps not a favorable subject for a picture. Take the council of the gods, which is more particularly addressed to the eye. An open palace of gold, groups of the fairest and most majestic forms, goblet in hand, served by eternal youth in the person of Hebe. What architecture! what masses of light and shade! what contrasts! what variety of expression! Where shall I begin, where cease, to feast my eyes? If the painter thus enchant me, how much more will the poet! I open the book and find myself deceived. I read four good, plain lines, which might very appropriately be written under the painting. They contain material for a picture, but are in themselves none.

> Meantime the immortal gods with Jupiter
> Upon his golden pavement sat and held
> A council. Hebe, honored of them all,
> Ministered nectar, and from cups of gold
> They pledged each other, looking down on
> Troy.[2]

Apollonius, or a more indifferent poet still, would not have said it worse. Here Homer is as far behind the artist as, in the former instance, he surpassed him.

Yet, except in these four lines, Caylus finds no single picture in the whole fourth book of the Iliad. "Rich as this book is," he says, "in its manifold exhortations to battle, in the abundance of its conspicuous and contrasting characters, in the skill with which the masses to be set in motion are brought before us, it is yet entirely unavailable for painting." "Rich as it otherwise is," he might have added, "in what are called poetic pictures." For surely in this fourth book we find as many such pictures, and as perfect, as in any of the whole poem. Where is there a more detailed, a more striking picture than that of Pandarus breaking the truce at the instigation of Minerva, and discharging his arrow at Menelaus? than that of the advance of the Grecian army? or of the mutual attack? or of the deed of Ulysses, whereby he avenges the death of his friend Leucus?

What must we conclude, except that not a few of the finest pictures in Homer are no pictures for the artist? that the artist can extract pictures from him where he himself has none? that such of his as the artist can use would be poor indeed did they show us no more than we see on the canvas? what, in short, but a negative answer to my question? Painted pictures drawn from the poems of Homer, however numerous and however admirable they may be, can give us no idea of the descriptive talent of the poet.

XIV

If it, then, be true that a poem not in itself picturesque may yet be rich in subjects for an artist, while another in a high degree picturesque may yield him nothing, this puts an end to the theory of Count Caylus, that the test of a poem is its availability for the artist, and that a poet's rank should depend upon the number of pictures he supplies to the painter.

Far be it from us to give this theory even the sanction of our silence. Milton would be the first to fall an innocent victim. Indeed, the contemptuous judgment which Caylus passes upon the English poet would seem to be the result not so much of national taste as of this assumed rule. Milton resembles Homer, he says, in little excepting loss of sight. Milton, it is true, can fill no picture galleries. But if, so long as I retained my bodily eye, its sphere must be the measure of my inward vision, then I should esteem its loss a gain, as freeing me from such limitations.

The fact that "Paradise Lost" furnishes few subjects for a painter no more prevents it from being the greatest epic since Homer, than the story of the passion of Christ becomes a poem, because you can hardly insert the head of a pin in any part of the narrative without touching some passage which has employed a crowd of the greatest artists. The evangelists state their facts with the dryest possible simplicity, and the painter uses their various details while the narrators themselves manifested not the smallest spark of genius for the picturesque. There are picturesque and unpicturesque facts, and the historian may relate the most picturesque without picturesqueness, as the poet can make a picture of those least adapted to the painter's use.

To regard the matter otherwise is to allow ourselves to be misled by the double meaning of a word. A picture in poetry is not necessarily one which can be transferred to canvas. But every touch, or every combination of touches, by means of which the poet brings his subject so vividly before us that we are more conscious of the subject than of his words, is picturesque, and makes what we call a picture; that is, it produces that degree of illusion which a painted picture is peculiarly qualified to excite, and which we in fact most frequently and naturally experience in the contemplation of the painted canvas.

XV

Experience shows that the poet can produce this degree of illusion by the representation of other than visible objects. He therefore has at his command whole classes of subjects which elude the artist. Dryden's "Ode on Cecilia's Day" is full of musical pictures, but gives no employment to the brush. But I will not lose myself in examples of this kind, for they after all teach us little more than that colors are not tones, and ears not eyes.

I will confine myself to pictures of visible objects, available alike to poet and painter. What is the reason that many poetical pictures of this class are unsuitable for the painter, while many painted pictures lose their chief effect in the hands of the poet?

Examples may help us. I revert to the picture of Pandarus in the fourth book of the Iliad, as one of the most detailed and graphic in all Homer. From the seizing of the bow to the flight of the arrow every incident is painted; and each one follows its predecessor so closely, and yet is so distinct from it, that a person who knew nothing of the use of a bow could learn it from this picture alone. Pandarus brings forth his bow, attaches the string, opens the quiver, selects a well-feathered arrow never before used, adjusts the notch of the arrow to the string, and draws back both string and arrow; the string approaches his breast, the iron point of the arrow nears the bow, the great arched bow springs back with a mighty twang, the cord rings, and away leaps the eager arrow speeding towards the mark.

Caylus cannot have overlooked this admirable picture. What, then, did he find which made him judge it no fitting subject for an artist? And what in the council and carousal of the gods made that seem more adapted to his purpose? The subjects are visible in one case as in the other, and what more does the painter need for his canvas?

The difficulty must be this. Although both themes, as representing visible objects, are equally adapted to painting, there is this essential difference between them: one is a visible progressive action, the various parts of which follow one another in time; the other is a visible stationary action, the development of whose various parts takes place in space. Since painting, because its signs or means of imitation can be combined only in space, must relinquish all representations of time, therefore progressive actions, as such, cannot come within its range. It must content itself with actions in space; in other words, with mere bodies, whose attitude lets us infer their action. Poetry, on the contrary –

XVI

But I will try to prove my conclusions by starting from first principles.

I argue thus. If it be true that painting employs wholly different signs or means of imitation from poetry, – the one using forms and colors in space, the other articulate sounds in time, – and if signs must unquestionably stand in convenient relation with the thing signified, then signs arranged side by side can represent only objects existing side by side, or whose parts so exist, while consecutive signs can express only objects which succeed each other, or whose parts succeed each other, in time.

Objects which exist side by side, or whose parts so exist, are called bodies. Consequently bodies with their visible properties are the peculiar subjects of painting.

Objects which succeed each other, or whose parts succeed each other in time, are actions. Consequently actions are the peculiar subjects of poetry.

All bodies, however, exist not only in space, but also in time. They continue, and, at any moment of their continuance, may assume a different appearance and stand in different relations. Every one of these momentary appearances and groupings was the result of a preceding, may become the cause of a following, and is therefore the centre of a present, action. Consequently painting can imitate actions also, but only as they are suggested through forms.

Actions, on the other hand, cannot exist independently, but must always be joined to certain agents. In so far as those agents are bodies or are regarded as such, poetry describes also bodies, but only indirectly through actions.

Painting, in its coexistent compositions, can use but a single moment of an action, and must therefore choose the most pregnant one, the one most suggestive of what has gone before and what is to follow.

Poetry, in its progressive imitations, can use but a single attribute of bodies, and must choose that one which gives the most vivid picture of the body as exercised in this particular action.

Hence the rule for the employment of a single descriptive epithet, and the cause of the rare occurrence of descriptions of physical objects.

I should place less confidence in this dry chain of conclusions, did I not find them fully confirmed by Homer, or, rather, had they not been first suggested to me by Homer's method. These principles alone furnish a key to the noble style of the Greek, and enable us to pass just judgment on the opposite method of many modern poets who insist upon emulating the artist in a point where they must of necessity remain inferior to him.

I find that Homer paints nothing but progressive actions. All bodies, all separate objects, are painted only as they take part in such actions, and generally with a single touch. No wonder, then, that artists find in Homer's pictures little or nothing to their purpose, and that their only harvest is where the narration brings together in a space favorable to art a number of beautiful shapes in graceful attitudes, however little the poet himself may have painted shapes, attitudes, or space. If we study one by one the whole series of pictures proposed by Caylus, we shall in every case find proof of the justness of these conclusions. [. . .]

XVII

But, it may be urged, the signs employed in poetry not only follow each other, but are also arbitrary; and, as arbitrary signs, they are certainly capable of expressing things as they exist in space. Homer himself furnishes examples of this. We have but to call to mind his shield of Achilles to have an instance of how circumstantially and yet poetically a single object can be described according to its coexistent parts.

I will proceed to answer this double objection. I call it double, because a just conclusion must hold, though unsupported by examples, and on the other hand the example of Homer has great weight with me, even when I am unable to justify it by rules.

It is true that since the signs of speech are arbitrary, the parts of a body can by their means be made to follow each other as readily as in nature they exist side by side. But this is a property of the signs of language in general, not of those peculiar to poetry. The prose writer is satisfied with being intelligible, and making his representations plain and clear. But this is not enough for the poet. He desires to present us with images so vivid, that we fancy we have the things themselves before us, and cease for the moment to be conscious of his words, the instruments with which he effects his purpose. That was the point made in the definition given above of a poetical picture. But the poet must always paint; and now let us see in how far bodies, considered in relation to their parts lying together in space, are fit subjects for this painting.

How do we obtain a clear idea of a thing in space? First we observe its separate parts, then the union of these parts, and finally the whole. Our senses perform these various operations with such amazing rapidity as to make them seem but one. This rapidity is absolutely essential to our obtaining an idea of the whole, which is nothing more than the result of the conception of the parts and of their connection with each other. Suppose now that the poet should lead us in proper order from one part of the object to the other; suppose he should succeed in making the connection of these parts perfectly clear to us; how much time will he have consumed?

The details, which the eye takes in at a glance, he enumerates slowly one by one, and it often happens that, by the time he has brought us to the last, we have forgotten the first. Yet from these details we are to form a picture. When we look at an object the various parts are always present to the eye. It can run over them again and again. The ear, however, loses the details it has heard, unless memory retain them. And if they be so retained, what pains and effort it costs to recall their impressions in the proper order and with even the moderate degree of rapidity necessary to the obtaining of a tolerable idea of the whole. [...]

Once more, then, I do not deny that language has the power of describing a corporeal whole according to its parts. It certainly has, because its signs, although consecutive, are nevertheless arbitrary. But I deny that this power exists in language as the instrument of poetry. For illusion, which is the special aim of poetry, is not produced by these verbal descriptions of objects, nor can it ever be so produced. The coexistence of the body comes into collision with the sequence of the words, and although while the former is getting resolved into the latter, the dismemberment of the whole into its parts is a help to us, yet the reunion of these parts into a whole is made extremely difficult, and not infrequently impossible. [...]

XVIII

And shall Homer nevertheless have fallen into those barren descriptions of material objects?

Let us hope that only a few such passages can be cited. And even those few, I venture to assert, will be found really to confirm the rule, to which they appear to form an exception.

The rule is this, that succession in time is the province of the poet, coexistence in space that of the artist.

To bring together into one and the same picture two points of time necessarily remote, as Mazzuoli does the rape of the Sabine women and the reconciliation effected by them between their husbands and relations; or as Titian does, representing in one piece the whole story of the Prodigal Son, – his dissolute life, his misery, and repentance, – is an encroachment of the painter on the domain of the poet, which good taste can never sanction.

To try to present a complete picture to the reader by enumerating in succession several parts or things which in nature the eye necessarily takes in at a glance, is an encroachment of the poet on the domain of the painter, involving a great effort of the imagination to very little purpose.

Painting and poetry should be like two just and friendly neighbors, neither of whom indeed is allowed to take unseemly liberties in the heart of the other's domain, but who exercise mutual forbearance on the borders, and effect a peaceful settlement for all the petty encroachments which circumstances may compel either to make in haste on the rights of the other. [...]

XX

To return, then, to my road, if a saunterer can be said to have a road.

What I have been saying of bodily objects in general applies with even more force to those which are beautiful.

Physical beauty results from the harmonious action of various parts which can be taken in at a glance. It therefore requires that these parts should lie near together; and, since things whose parts lie near together are the proper subjects of painting, this art and this alone can imitate physical beauty.

The poet, who must necessarily detail in succession the elements of beauty, should therefore desist entirely from the description of physical beauty as such. He must feel that these elements arranged in a series cannot possibly produce the same effect as in juxtaposition; that the concentrating glance which we try to cast back over them immediately after their enumeration, gives us no harmonious picture; and that to conceive the effect of certain eyes, a certain mouth and nose taken together, unless we can recall a similar combination of such parts in nature or art, surpasses the power of human imagination. [. . .]

XXI

But are we not robbing poetry of too much by taking from her all pictures of physical beauty?

Who seeks to take them from her? We are only warning her against trying to arrive at them by a particular road, where she will blindly grope her way in the footsteps of a sister art without ever reaching the goal. We are not closing against her other roads whereon art can follow only with her eyes.

Homer himself, who so persistently refrains from all detailed descriptions of physical beauty, that we barely learn, from a passing mention, that Helen had white arms[3] and beautiful hair,[4] even he manages nevertheless to give us an idea of her beauty, which far surpasses any thing that art could do. Recall the passage where Helen enters the assembly of the Trojan elders. The venerable men see her coming, and one says to the others: –

> Small blame is theirs if both the Trojan
> knights
> And brazen-mailed Achaians have endured
> So long so many evils for the sake
> Of that one woman. She is wholly like
> In feature to the deathless goddesses.[5]

What can give a more vivid idea of her beauty than that cold-blooded age should deem it well worth the war which had cost so much blood and so many tears?

What Homer could not describe in its details, he shows us by its effect. Paint us, ye poets, the delight, the attraction, the love, the enchantment of beauty, and you have painted beauty itself. [. . .]

Yet another way in which poetry surpasses art in the description of physical beauty, is by turning beauty into charm. Charm is beauty in motion, and therefore less adapted to the painter than the poet. The painter can suggest motion, but his figures are really destitute of it.

Charm therefore in a picture becomes grimace, while in poetry it remains what it is, a transitory beauty, which we would fain see repeated. It comes and goes, and since we can recall a motion more vividly and easily than mere forms and colors, charm must affect us more strongly than beauty under the same conditions. [. . .] Here we have, therefore, a fresh illustration of what was urged above, that the poet, even when speaking of a painting or statue, is not bound to confine his description within the limits of art.

Translator's Notes

1 *Iliad* i.44–53.
2 *Iliad* iv.1–4.
3 *Iliad* iii.121.
4 Ibid. 319.
5 Ibid. 156–8.

14

Critique of Judgement

Immanuel Kant

Immanuel Kant (1724–1804), who lived his entire life in the Prussian town of Königsberg, is a preeminent figure in the history of philosophy, having made groundbreaking contributions in virtually every area of the subject.

Part I
Critique of Aesthetic Judgement

First Section
Analytic of Aesthetic Judgement

First Book
Analytic of the Beautiful

First Moment of the Judgement of Taste:[1] Moment of Quality

I
The judgement of taste is aesthetic

If we wish to discern whether anything is beautiful or not, we do not refer the representation of it to the Object by means of understanding with a view to cognition, but by means of the imagination (acting perhaps in conjunction with understanding) we refer the representation to the Subject and its feeling of pleasure or displeasure. The judgement of taste, therefore, is not a cognitive judgement, and so not logical, but is aesthetic – which means that it is one whose determining ground *cannot be other than subjective*. Every reference of representations is capable of being objective, even that of sensations (in which case it signifies the real in an empirical representation). The one exception to this is the feeling of pleasure or displeasure. This denotes nothing in the object, but is a feeling which the Subject has of itself and of the manner in which it is affected by the representation.

To apprehend a regular and appropriate building with one's cognitive faculties, be the mode of representation clear or confused, is quite a different thing from being conscious of this representation with an accompanying sensation of delight. Here the representation is referred wholly to the Subject, and what is more to its feeling of life – under the name of feeling of pleasure or displeasure – and this forms the basis of a quite separate faculty of discriminating and estimating, that contributes nothing to knowledge. All it does is to compare the given

Immanuel Kant, "Critique of Judgement," in *Critique of Aesthetic Judgement*, trans. J. C. Meredith (Oxford: Clarendon Press, 1978).

representation in the Subject with the entire faculty of representations of which the mind is conscious in the feeling of its state. Given representations in a judgement may be empirical, and so aesthetic; but the judgement which is pronounced by their means is logical, provided it refers them to the Object. Conversely, be the given representations even rational, but referred in a judgement solely to the Subject (to its feeling), they are always to that extent aesthetic.

II
The delight which determines the judgement of taste is independent of all interest

The delight which we connect with the representation of the real existence of an object is called interest. Such a delight, therefore, always involves a reference to the faculty of desire, either as its determining ground, or else as necessarily implicated with its determining ground. Now, where the question is whether something is beautiful, we do not want to know, whether we, or any one else, are, or even could be, concerned in the real existence of the thing, but rather what estimate we form of it on mere contemplation (intuition or reflection). If any one asks me whether I consider that the palace I see before me is beautiful, I may, perhaps, reply that I do not care for things of that sort that are merely made to he gaped at. [. . .]

All this may be admitted and approved; only it is not the point now at issue. All one wants to know is whether the mere representation of the object is to my liking, no matter how indifferent I may be to the real existence of the object of this representation. It is quite plain that in order to say that the object is *beautiful*, and to show that I have taste, everything turns on the meaning which I can give to this representation, and not on any factor which makes me dependent on the real existence of the object. Every one must allow that a judgement on the beautiful which is tinged with the slightest interest, is very partial and not a pure judgement of taste. One must not be in the least prepossessed in favour of the real existence of the thing, but must preserve complete indifference in this respect, in order to play the part of judge in matters of taste.

This proposition, which is of the utmost importance, cannot be better explained than by contrasting the pure disinterested delight which appears in the judgement of taste with that allied to an interest – especially if we can also assure ourselves that there are no other kinds of interest beyond those presently to be mentioned.

III
Delight in the agreeable is coupled with interest

That is agreeable *which the senses find pleasing in sensation.* This at once affords a convenient opportunity for condemning and directing particular attention to a prevalent confusion of the double meaning of which the word 'sensation' is capable. All delight (as is said or thought) is itself sensation (of a pleasure). Consequently everything that pleases, and for the very reason that it pleases, is agreeable – and according to its different degrees, or its relations to other agreeable sensations, is attractive, charming, delicious, enjoyable, &c. But if this is conceded, then impressions of sense, which determine inclination, or principles of reason, which determine the will, or mere contemplated forms of intuition, which determine judgement, are all on a par in everything relevant to their effect upon the feeling of pleasure, for this would be agreeableness in the sensation of one's state; and since, in the last resort, all the elaborate work of our faculties must issue in and unite in the practical as its goal, we could credit our faculties with no other appreciation of things and the worth of things, than that consisting in the gratification which they promise. How this is attained is in the end immaterial; and, as the choice of the means is here the only thing that can make a difference, men might indeed blame one another for folly or imprudence, but never for baseness or wickedness; for they are all, each according to his own way of looking at things, pursuing one goal, which for each is the gratification in question.

When a modification of the feeling of pleasure or displeasure is termed sensation, this expression is given quite a different meaning to that which it bears when I call the representation of a thing (through sense as a receptivity pertaining to the faculty of knowledge) sensation. For in the latter case the representation is referred to the Object, but in the former it is referred solely to the Subject and is not available for any cognition, not even for that by which the Subject *cognizes* itself.

Now in the above definition the word sensation is used to denote an objective representation of sense; and, to avoid continually running the risk of misinterpretation, we shall call that which must always remain purely subjective, and is absolutely incapable of forming a representation of an object, by the familiar name of feeling. The green colour of the meadows belongs to *objective* sensation, as the perception of an object of sense; but its agreeableness to *subjective* sensation, by which no object is represented: i.e. to feeling, through which the object is regarded as an Object of delight (which involves no cognition of the object).

Now, that a judgement on an object by which its agreeableness is affirmed, expresses an interest in it, is evident from the fact that through sensation it provokes a desire for similar objects, consequently the delight presupposes, not the simple judgement about it, but the bearing its real existence has upon my state so far as affected by such an Object. Hence we do not merely say of the agreeable that it *pleases,* but that it *gratifies.* I do not accord it a simple approval, but inclination is aroused by it, and where agreeableness is of the liveliest type a judgement on the character of the Object is so entirely out of place, that those who are always intent only on enjoyment (for that is the word used to denote intensity of gratification) would fain dispense with all judgement.

IV
Delight in the good is coupled with interest

That is *good* which by means of reason commends itself by its mere concept. We call that *good for something* (useful) which only pleases as a means; but that which pleases on its own account we call *good in itself.* In both cases the concept of an end is implied, and consequently the relation of reason to (at least possible) willing, and thus a delight in the *existence* of an Object or action, i.e. some interest or other.

To deem something good, I must always know what sort of a thing the object is intended to be, i.e. I must have a concept of it. That is not necessary to enable me to see beauty in a thing. Flowers, free patterns, lines aimlessly intertwining – technically termed foliage, – have no signification, depend upon no definite concept, and yet please. Delight in the beautiful must depend upon the reflection on an object precursory to some (not definitely determined) concept. It is thus also differentiated from the agreeable, which rests entirely upon sensation.

In many cases, no doubt, the agreeable and the good seem convertible terms. Thus it is commonly said that all (especially lasting) gratification is of itself good; which is almost equivalent to saying that to be permanently agreeable and to be good are identical. But it is readily apparent that this is merely a vicious confusion of words, for the concepts appropriate to these expressions are far from interchangeable. The agreeable, which, as such, represents the object solely in relation to sense, must in the first instance be brought under principles of reason through the concept of an end, to be, as an object of will, called good. But that the reference to delight is wholly different where what gratifies is at the same time called *good,* is evident from the fact that with the good the question always is whether it is mediately or immediately good, i.e. useful or good in itself; whereas with the agreeable this point can never arise, since the word always means what pleases immediately – and it is just the same with what I call beautiful. [. . .]

V
Comparison of the three specifically different kinds of delight

Both the Agreeable and the Good involve a reference to the faculty of desire, and are thus attended, the former with a delight pathologically conditioned (by stimuli), the latter with a pure practical delight. Such delight is determined not merely by the representation of the object, but also by the represented bond of connexion between the Subject and the real existence of the object. It is not merely the object, but also its real existence, that pleases. On the other hand the judgement of taste is simply *contemplative,* i.e. it is a judgement which is indifferent as to the existence of an object, and only decides how its character stands with the feeling of pleasure and displeasure. But not even is this contemplation itself directed to concepts; for the judgement of taste is not a cognitive judgement (neither a theoretical one nor a practical), and hence, also, is not *grounded* on concepts, nor yet *intentionally directed* to them.

The agreeable, the beautiful, and the good thus denote three different relations of representations to the feeling of pleasure and displeasure, as a feeling in respect of which we distinguish different objects or modes of representation. Also, the corresponding expressions which indicate our satisfaction in them are different. The *agreeable* is what GRATIFIES a man; the *beautiful* what simply PLEASES him; the *good* what is ESTEEMED (*approved*), i.e. that on which he sets an objective worth. Agreeableness is a significant factor even with irrational animals; beauty has purport and significance only for human beings, i.e. for beings at once animal and rational (but not merely for them as rational – intelligent beings – but only for them as at once animal and rational); whereas the good is good for every rational being in general; – a proposition which can only receive its complete justification and explanation in the sequel. Of all these three kinds of delight, that of taste in the beautiful may be said to be the one and only disinterested and *free* delight; for, what it, no interest, whether of sense or reason, extorts approval. And so we may say that delight, in the three cases mentioned, is related to *inclination*, to *favour*, or to *respect*. For FAVOUR is the only free liking. An object of inclination, and one which a law of reason imposes upon our desire, leaves us no freedom to turn anything into an object of pleasure. All interest presupposes a want, or calls one forth; and, being a ground determining approval, deprives the judgement on the object freedom. [. . .]

Definition of the beautiful derived from the first moment

Taste is the faculty of estimating an object or a mode of representation by means of a delight or aversion *apart from any interest*. The object of such a delight is called *beautiful*. [. . .]

VI
The beautiful is that which, apart from concepts, is represented as the object of a universal delight

This definition of the beautiful is deducible from the foregoing definition of it as an object of delight apart from any interest. For where any one is conscious that his delight in an object is with him independent of interest, it is inevitable that he should look on the object as one containing a ground of delight for all men. For, since the delight is not based on any inclination of the Subject (or on any other deliberate interest), but the Subject feels himself completely *free* in respect of the liking which he accords to the object, he can find as reason for his delight no personal conditions to which his own subjective self might alone be party. Hence he must regard it as resting on what he may also presuppose in every other person; and therefore he must believe that he has reason for demanding a similar delight from everyone. Accordingly he will speak of the beautiful as if beauty were a quality of the object and the judgement logical (forming a cognition of the Object by concepts of it); although it is only aesthetic, and contains merely a reference of the representation of the object to the Subject; – because it still bears this resemblance to the logical judgement, that it may be presupposed to be valid for all men. But this universality cannot spring from concepts. For from concepts there is no transition to the feeling of pleasure or displeasure (save in the case of pure practical laws, which, however, carry an interest with them; and such an interest does not attach to the pure judgement of taste). The result is that the judgement of taste, with its attendant consciousness of detachment from all interest, must involve a claim to validity for all men, and must do so apart from universality attached to Objects, i.e. there must be coupled with it a claim to subjective universality.

VII
Comparison of the beautiful with the agreeable and the good by means of the above characteristic

As regards the *agreeable* every one concedes that his judgement, which he bases on a private feeling, and in which he declares that an object pleases him, is restricted merely to himself personally. Thus he does not take it amiss if, when he says that Canary-wine is agreeable, another corrects the expression and reminds him that he ought to say: It is agreeable *to me*. This applies not only to the taste of the tongue, the palate, and the throat, but to what may with any one be agreeable to eye or ear. A violet colour is to one soft and lovely: to another dull and faded. [. . .]

With the agreeable, therefore, the axiom holds good: *Every one has his own taste* (that of sense).

The beautiful stands on quite a different footing. It would, on the contrary, be ridiculous if any one who plumed himself on his taste were to think of justifying himself by saying: This object (the building we see, the dress that person has on, the concert we hear, the poem submitted to our criticism) is beautiful *for me*. For if it merely pleases *him*, he must not call it *beautiful*. Many things may for him possess charm and agreeableness – no one cares about that; but when he puts a thing on a pedestal and calls it beautiful, he demands the same delight from others. He judges not merely for himself, but for all men, and then speaks of beauty as if it were a property of things. Thus he says the *thing* is beautiful; and it is not as if he counted on others agreeing in his judgement of liking owing to his having found them in such agreement on a number of occasions, but he *demands* this agreement of them. He blames them if they judge differently, and denies them taste, which he still requires of them as something they ought to have; and to this extent it is not open to men to say: Every one has his own taste. This would be equivalent to saying that there is no such thing at all as taste, i.e. no aesthetic judgement capable of making a rightful claim upon the assent of all men.

Yet even in the case of the agreeable we find that the estimates men form do betray a prevalent agreement among them, which leads to our crediting some with taste and denying it to others, and that, too, not as an organic sense but as a critical faculty in respect of the agreeable generally. So of one who knows how to entertain his guests with pleasures (of enjoyment through all the senses) in such a way that one and all are pleased, we say that he has taste. But the universality here is only understood in a comparative sense; and the rules that apply are, like all empirical rules, *general* only, not *universal*, – the latter being what the judgement of taste upon the beautiful deals or claims to deal in. It is a judgement in respect of sociability so far as resting on empirical rules. In respect of the good it is true that judgements also rightly assert a claim to validity for every one; but the good is only represented as an Object of universal delight *by means of a concept*, which is the case neither with the agreeable nor the beautiful.

VIII
In a judgement of taste the universality of delight is only represented as subjective

[. . .] First of all we have here to note that a universality which does not rest upon concepts of the Object (even though these are only empirical) is in no way logical, but aesthetic, i.e. does not involve any objective quantity of the judgement, but only one that is subjective. For this universality I use the expression *general validity*, which denotes the validity of the reference of a representation, not to the cognitive faculties, but to the feeling of pleasure or displeasure for every Subject. (The same expression, however, may also be employed for the logical quantity of the judgement, provided we add *objective* universal validity, to distinguish it from the merely subjective validity which is always aesthetic.)

Now a judgement that has *objective universal validity* has always got the subjective also, i.e. if the judgement is valid for everything which is contained under a given concept, it is valid also for all who represent an object by means of this concept. But from a *subjective universal validity*, i.e. the aesthetic, that does not rest on any concept, no conclusion can be drawn to the logical; because judgements of that kind have no bearing upon the Object. But for this very reason the aesthetic universality attributed to a judgement must also be of a special kind, seeing that it does not join the predicate of beauty to the concept of the *Object* taken in its entire logical sphere, and yet does extend this predicate over the whole sphere of *judging Subjects*.

In their logical quantity all judgements of taste are *singular* judgements. For, since I must present the object immediately to my feeling of pleasure or displeasure, and that, too, without the aid of concepts, such judgements cannot have the quantity of judgements with objective general validity. Yet by taking the singular representation of the Object of the judgement of taste, and by comparison converting it into a concept according to the conditions determining that judgement, we can arrive at a logically universal judgement. For instance, by a judgement of taste I describe the rose at which I am looking as beautiful. The judgement, on the other hand, resulting from the comparison of a number of singular representations: Roses in general are beautiful, is no longer pronounced as a purely aesthetic judgement, but as a logical judgement founded on one that is aesthetic. Now the judgement, 'The rose is agreeable' (to smell) is also, no doubt, an aesthetic and singular judgement, but then it is not one of taste but of sense. For it has this point of difference from a judgement of taste, that the latter imports an *aesthetic quantity* of universality, i.e. of validity for every one which is not to be met with in a judgement upon the agreeable. It is only judgements upon the good which, while also determining the delight in an object, possess logical and not mere aesthetic universality; for it is as involving a cognition of the Object that they are valid of it, and on that account valid for every one.

In forming an estimate of Objects merely from concepts, all representation of beauty goes by the board. There can, therefore, be no rule according to which any one is to be compelled to recognize anything as beautiful. Whether a dress, a house, or a flower is beautiful is a matter upon which one declines to allow one's judgement to be swayed by any reasons or principles. We want to get a look at the Object with our own eyes, just as if our delight depended on sensation. And yet, if upon so doing, we call the object beautiful, we believe ourselves to be speaking with a universal voice, and lay claim to the concurrence of every one, whereas no private sensation would be decisive except for the observer alone and *his* liking.

Here, now, we may perceive that nothing is postulated in the judgement of taste but such a *universal voice* in respect of delight that is not mediated by concepts; consequently, only the *possibility* of an aesthetic judgement capable of being at the same time deemed valid for every one. The judgement of taste itself does not *postulate* the agreement of every one (for it is only competent for a logically universal judgement to do this, in that it is able to bring forward reasons); it only *imputes* this agreement to every one, as an instance of the rule in respect of which it looks for confirmation, not from concepts, but from the concurrence of others. The universal voice is, therefore, only an idea – resting upon grounds the investigation of which is here postponed. [...]

IX
Investigation of the question of the relative priority in a judgement of taste of the feeling of pleasure and the estimating of the object

The solution of this problem is the key to the Critique of taste, and so is worthy of all attention.

Were the pleasure in a given object to be the antecedent, and were the universal communicability of this pleasure to be all that the judgement of taste is meant to allow to the representation of the object, such a sequence would be selfcontradictory. For a pleasure of that kind would be nothing but the feeling of mere agreeableness to the senses, and so, from its very nature, would possess no more than private validity, seeing that it would be immediately dependent on the representation through which the object *is given*.

Hence it is the universal capacity for being communicated incident to the mental state in the given representation which, as the subjective condition of the judgement of taste, must be fundamental, with the pleasure in the object as its consequent. Nothing, however, is capable of being universally communicated but cognition and representation so far as appurtenant to cognition. For it is only as thus appurtenant that the representation is objective, and it is this alone that gives it a universal point of reference with which the power of representation of every one is obliged to harmonize. If, then, the determining ground of the judgement as to this universal communicability of the representation is to be merely subjective, that is to say, is to be conceived independently of any concept of the object, it can be nothing else than the mental state that presents itself in the mutual relation of the powers of representation so far as they refer a given representation *to cognition in general.*

The cognitive powers brought into play by this representation are here engaged in a free play, since no definite concept restricts them to a particular rule of cognition. Hence the mental state in this representation must be one of a feeling of the free play of the powers of representation in a given representation for a cognition in general. Now a representation, whereby an object is given, involves, in order that it may become a source of cognition at all, *imagination* for bringing together the manifold of intuition, and *understanding* for the unity of the concept uniting the representations. This state of *free play* of the cognitive faculties attending a representation by which an object is given must admit of universal communication: because cognition, as a definition of the Object with which given representations (in any Subject whatever) are to accord, is the one and only representation which is valid for every one.

As the subjective universal communicability of the mode of representation in a judgement of taste is to subsist apart from the presupposition of any definite concept, it can be nothing else than the mental state present in the free play of imagination and understanding (so far as these are in mutual accord, as is requisite for *cognition in general*): for we are conscious that this subjective relation suitable for a cognition in general must be just as valid for every one, and consequently as universally communicable, as is any determinate cognition, which always rests upon that relation as its subjective condition.

Now this purely subjective (aesthetic) estimating of the object, or of the representation through which it is given, is antecedent to the pleasure in it, and is the basis of this pleasure in the harmony of the cognitive faculties. Again, the above-described universality of the subjective conditions of estimating objects forms the sole foundation of this universal subjective validity of the delight which we connect with the representation of the object that we call beautiful.

That an ability to communicate one's mental state, even though it be only in respect of our cognitive faculties, is attended with a pleasure, is a fact which might easily be demonstrated from the natural propensity of mankind to social life, i.e. empirically and psychologically. But what we have here in view calls for something more than this. In a judgement of taste the pleasure felt by us is exacted from every one else as necessary, just as if, when we call something beautiful, beauty was to be regarded as a quality of the object forming part of its inherent determination according to concepts; although beauty is for itself, apart from any reference to the feeling of the Subject, nothing. But the discussion of this question must be reserved until we have answered the further one of whether, and how, aesthetic judgements are possible *a priori*.

At present we are exercised with the lesser question of the way in which we become conscious, in a judgement of taste, of a reciprocal subjective common accord of the powers of cognition. Is it aesthetically by sensation and our mere internal sense? Or is it intellectually by consciousness of our intentional activity in bringing these powers into play?

Now if the given representation occasioning the judgement of taste were a concept which united understanding and imagination in the estimate of the object so as to give a cognition of the Object, the consciousness of this relation would be intellectual (as in the objective schematism of judgement dealt with in the Critique). But, then, in that case the judgement would not be laid down with respect to pleasure and displeasure, and so would not be a judgement of taste. But, now, the judgement of taste determines the Object, independently of concepts, in respect of delight and of the predicate of beauty. There is, therefore, no other way for the subjective unity of the relation in question to make itself known than by sensation. The quickening of both faculties (imagination and understanding) to an indefinite, but yet, thanks to the given representation, harmonious activity, such as belongs to cognition generally, is the sensation whose universal communicability is postulated by the judgement of taste. An objective relation can, of course, only be thought, yet in so far as, in respect of its conditions, it is subjective, it may be felt in its effect upon the mind, and, in the case of a relation (like that of the powers of representation to a faculty of cognition generally) which does not rest on any concept, no other consciousness of it is possible beyond that through sensation of its effect upon the mind – an effect consisting in the more facile play of both mental powers (imagination and understanding) as quickened by their mutual accord. A representation which is singular and independent of comparison with other representations, and, being such, yet accords with the conditions of the universality that is the general concern of understanding, is one that brings the cognitive faculties into that proportionate accord which we require for all cognition and which we therefore deem valid for every one who is so constituted as to judge by means of understanding and sense conjointly (i.e. for every man).

Definition of the beautiful drawn from the second moment

The *beautiful* is that which, apart from a concept, pleases universally. [. . .]

X
Finality in general

Let us define the meaning of 'an end' in transcendental terms (i.e. without presupposing anything empirical, such as the feeling of pleasure). An end is the object of a concept so far as this concept is regarded as the cause of the object (the real ground of its possibility); and the causality of a *concept* in respect of its *Object* is finality (*forma finalis*). Where, then, not the cognition of an object merely, but the object itself (its form or real existence) as an effect, is thought to be possible only through a concept of it, there we imagine an end. The representation of the effect is here the determining ground of its cause and takes the lead of it. The consciousness of the causality of a representation in respect of the state of the Subject as one tending *to preserve a continuance* of that state, may here be said to denote in a general way what is called pleasure; whereas displeasure is that representation which contains the ground for converting the state of the representations into their opposite (for hindering or removing them).

The faculty of desire, so far as determinable only through concepts, i.e. so as to act in conformity with the representation of an end, would be the will. But an Object, or state of mind, or even an action may, although its possibility does not necessarily presuppose the representation of an end, be called final simply on account of its possibility being only explicable and intelligible for us by virtue of an assumption on our part of a fundamental causality according to ends, i.e. a will that would have so ordained it according to a certain represented rule. Finality, therefore, may exist apart from an end, in so far as we do not locate the causes of this form in a will, but yet are able to render the explanation of its possibility intelligible to ourselves only by deriving it from a will. Now we are not always obliged to look with the eye of reason into what we observe (i.e. to consider it in its possibility). So we may at least observe a finality of form, and trace it in objects – though by reflection only – without resting it on an end (as the material of the *nexus finalis*).

XI
The sole foundation of the judgement of taste is the form of finality of an object (or mode of representing it)

Whenever an end is regarded as a source of delight it always imports an interest as determining ground of the judgement on the object of pleasure. Hence the judgement of taste cannot rest on any subjective end as its ground. But neither can any representation of an objective end, i.e. of the possibility of the object itself on principles of final connexion, determine the judgement of taste, and, consequently, neither can any concept of the good. For the judgement of taste is an aesthetic and not a cognitive judgement, and so does not deal with any *concept* of the nature or of the internal or external possibility, by this or that cause, of the object, but simply with the relative bearing of the representative powers so far as determined by a representation.

Now this relation, present when an object is characterized as beautiful, is coupled with the feeling of pleasure. This pleasure is by the judgement of taste pronounced valid for every one; hence an agreeableness attending the representation is just as incapable of containing the determining ground of the judgement as the representation of the perfection of the object or the concept of the good. We are thus left with the subjective finality in the representation of an object, exclusive of any end (objective or subjective) – consequently the bare form of finality in the representation whereby an object is *given* to us, so far as we are conscious of it – as that which is alone capable of constituting the delight which, apart from any concept, we estimate as universally communicable, and so of forming the determining ground of the judgement of taste. [. . .]

XIII
The pure judgement of taste is independent of charm and emotion

Every interest vitiates the judgement of taste and robs it of its impartiality. This is especially so where instead of, like the interest of reason, making finality take the lead of the feeling of pleasure, it grounds it upon this feeling – which is what always happen in aesthetic judgements upon anything so far as it gratifies or pains. Hence judgements so influenced can either lay no claim at all to a universally valid delight, or else must abate their claim in proportion as sensations of the kind in question enter into the determining grounds of taste. Taste that requires an added element of *charm* and *emotion* for its delight, not to speak of adopting this as the measure of its approval, has not yet emerged from barbarism.

And yet charms are frequently not alone ranked with beauty (which ought properly to be a question merely of the form) as supplementary to the aesthetic universal delight, but they have been accredited as intrinsic beauties, and consequently the matter of delight passed off for the form. This is a misconception which, like many others that have still an underlying element of truth, may be removed by a careful definition of these concepts.

A judgement of taste which is uninfluenced by charm or emotion, (though these may be associated with the delight in the beautiful,) and whose determining ground, therefore, is simply finality of form, is a *pure judgement of taste.*

XIV
Exemplification

Aesthetic, just like theoretical (logical) judgements, are divisible into empirical and pure. The first are those by which agreeableness or disagreeableness, the second those by which beauty, is predicated of an object or its mode of representation. The former are judgements of sense (material aesthetic judgements), the latter (as formal) alone judgements of taste proper.

A judgement of taste, therefore, is only pure so far as its determining ground is tainted with no merely empirical delight. But such a taint is always present where charm or emotion have a share in the judgement by which something is to be described as beautiful.

Here now there is a recrudescence of a number of specious pleas that go the length of putting forward the case that charm is not merely a necessary ingredient of beauty, but is even of itself sufficient to merit the name of beautiful. A mere colour, such as the green of a plot of grass, or a mere tone (as distinguished from sound or noise), like that of violin, is described by most people as in itself beautiful, notwithstanding the fact that both seem to depend merely on the matter of the representations – in other words, simply on sensation, which only entitles them to be called agreeable. But it will at the same time be observed that sensations of colour as well as of tone are only entitled to be immediately regarded as beautiful where, in either case, they are *pure.* This is a determination which at once goes to their form, and it is the only one which these representations possess that admits with certainty of being universally communicated. For it is not to be assumed that even the quality of the sensations agrees in all Subjects, and we can hardly take it for granted that the agreeableness of a colour, or of the tone of a musical instrument, which we judge to be preferable to that of another, is given a like preference in the estimate of every one. [. . .]

But the purity of a simple mode of sensation means that its uniformity is not disturbed or broken by any foreign sensation. It belongs merely to the form; for abstraction may there be made from the quality of the mode of such sensation (what colour or tone, if any, it represents). For this reason all simple colours are regarded as beautiful so far as pure. Composite colours have not this advantage, because, not being simple, there is no standard for estimating whether they should be called pure or impure.

But as for the beauty ascribed to the object on account of its form, and the supposition that it is capable of being enhanced by charm, this is a common error and one very prejudicial to genuine, uncorrupted, sincere taste. Nevertheless charms may be added to beauty to lend to the mind, beyond a bare delight, an adventitious interest in the representation of the object, and thus to advocate taste and its cultivation. This applies especially where taste is as yet crude and untrained. But they are positively subversive of the judgement of taste, if allowed to obtrude themselves as grounds of estimating beauty. For so far are they from contributing to beauty, that it is only where taste is still weak and untrained, that, like aliens, they are admitted as a favour, and only on terms that they do not violate that beautiful form.

In painting, sculpture, and in fact in all the formative arts, in architecture and horticulture, so far as fine arts, the *design* is what is essential. Here it is not what gratifies in sensation but merely what pleases by its form, that is the fundamental prerequisite for taste. The colours which give brilliancy to the sketch are part of the charm. They may no doubt, in their own way, enliven the object for sensation, but make it really worth looking at and beautiful they cannot. Indeed, more often than not the requirements of the beautiful form restrict them to a very narrow compass, and, even where charm is admitted, it is only this form that gives them a place of honour.

All form of objects of sense (both of external and also, mediately, of internal sense) is either *figure* or *play*. In the latter case it is either play of figures (in space: mimic and dance), or mere play of sensations (in time). The *charm* of colours, or of the agreeable tones of instruments, may be added: but the *design* in the former and the *composition* in the latter constitute the proper object of the pure judgement of taste. To say that the purity alike of colours and of tones, or their variety and contrast, seem to contribute to beauty, is by no means to imply that, because in themselves agreeable, they therefore yield an addition to the delight in the form and one on a par with it. The real meaning rather is that they make this form more clearly, definitely, and completely intuitable, and besides stimulate the representation by their charm, as they excite and sustain the attention directed to the object itself.

XV
The judgement of taste is entirely independent of the concept of perfection

Objective finality can only be cognized by means of a reference of the manifold to a definite end, and hence only through a concept. This alone makes it clear that the beautiful, which is estimated on the ground of a mere formal finality, i.e. a finality apart from an end, is wholly independent of the representation of the good. For the latter presupposes an objective finality, i.e. the reference of the object to a definite end.

Objective finality is either external, i.e. the *utility*, or internal, i.e. the *perfection*, of the object. That the delight in an object on account of which we call it beautiful is incapable of resting on the representation of its utility, is abundantly evident from the two preceding articles; for in that case, it would not be an immediate delight in the object, which latter is the essential condition of the judgement upon beauty. But in an objective, internal finality, i.e. perfection, we have what is more akin to the predicate of beauty, and so this has been held even by philosophers of reputation to be convertible with beauty, though subject to the qualification: *where it is thought in a confused way*. [. . .]

For estimating objective finality we always require the concept of an end, and, where such finality has to be, not an external one (utility), but an internal one, the concept of an internal end containing the ground of the internal possibility of the object. Now an end is in general that, the *concept* of which may he regarded as the ground of the possibility of the object itself. So in order to represent an objective finality in a thing we must first have a concept of *what sort of a thing it is to be*. The agreement of the manifold in a thing with this concept (which supplies the rule of its synthesis) is the *qualitative perfection* of the thing. *Quantitative* perfection is entirely distinct from this. It consists in the completeness of anything after its kind, and is a mere concept of quantity (of totality). In its case the question of *what the thing is to be* is regarded as definitely disposed of, and we only ask whether it is possessed of *all* the requisites that go to make it such. What is formal in the representation of a thing, i.e. the agreement of its manifold with a unity (i.e. irrespective of what it is to be) does not, of itself, afford us any cognition whatsoever of objective finality. For since abstraction is made from this unity as *end* (what the thing is to be) nothing is left but the subjective finality of the representations in the mind of the Subject intuiting. This gives a certain finality of the representative state of the Subject, in which the Subject feels itself quite at home in its effort to grasp a given form in the imagination, but no perfection of any

Object, the latter not being here thought through any concept. For instance, if in a forest I light upon a plot of grass, round which trees stand in a circle, and if I do not then form any representation of an end, as that it is meant to be used, say, for country dances, then not the least hint of a concept of perfection is given by the mere form. To suppose a formal *objective* finality that is yet devoid of an end, i.e. the mere form of a *perfection* (apart from any matter or *concept* of that to which the agreement relates, even though there was the mere general idea of a conformity to law) is a veritable contradiction.

Now the judgement of taste is an aesthetic judgement, i.e. one resting on subjective grounds. No concept can be its determining ground, and hence not one of a definite end. Beauty, therefore, as a formal subjective finality, involves no thought whatsoever of a perfection of the object, as a would-be formal finality which yet, for all that, is objective: and the distinction between the concepts of the beautiful and the good, which represents both as differing only in their logical form, the first being merely a confused, the second a clearly defined, concept of perfection, while otherwise alike in content and origin, all goes for nothing: for then there would be no *specific* difference between them, but the judgement of taste would be just as much a cognitive judgement as one by which something is described as good – just as the man in the street, when he says that deceit is wrong, bases his judgement on confused, but the philosopher on clear grounds, while both appeal in reality to identical principles of reason. [. . .]

XVI
A judgement of taste by which an object is described as beautiful under the condition of a definite concept is not pure

There are two kinds of beauty: free beauty (*pulchritudo vaga*), or beauty which is merely dependent (*pulchritudo adhaerens*). The first presupposes no concept of what the object should be; the second does presuppose such a concept and, with it, an answering perfection of the object. Those of the first kind are said to be (self-subsisting) beauties of this thing or that thing; the other kind of beauty, being attached to a concept (conditioned beauty), is ascribed to Objects which come under the concept of a particular end.

Flowers are free beauties of nature. Hardly any one but a botanist knows the true nature of a flower, and even he, while recognizing in the flower the reproductive organ of the plant, pays no attention to this natural end when using his taste to judge of its beauty. Hence no perfection of any kind – no internal finality, as something to which the arrangement of the manifold is related – underlies this judgement. Many birds (the parrot, the humming-bird, the bird of paradise), and a number of crustacea, are self-subsisting beauties which are not appurtenant to any object defined with respect to its end, but please freely and on their own account. So designs *à la grecque*, foliage for framework or on wall-papers, &c., have no intrinsic meaning; they represent nothing – no Object under a definite concept – and are free beauties. We may also rank in the same class what in music are called fantasias (without a theme), and, indeed, all music that is not set to words.

In the estimate of a free beauty (according to mere form) we have the pure judgement of taste. No concept is here presupposed of any end for which the manifold should serve the given Object, and which the latter, therefore, should represent – an incumbrance which would only restrict the freedom of the imagination that, as it were, is at play in the contemplation of the outward form.

But the beauty of man (including under this head that of a man, woman, or child), the beauty of a horse, or of a building, . . . presupposes a concept of the end that defines what the thing has to be, and consequently a concept of its perfection; and is therefore merely appendant beauty. Now, just as it is a clog on the purity of the judgement of taste to have the agreeable (of sensation) joined with beauty to which properly only the form is relevant, so to combine the good with beauty, (the good, namely, of the manifold to the thing itself according to its end), mars its purity. [. . .]

Taste, it is true, stands to gain by this combination of intellectual delight with the aesthetic. For it becomes fixed, and, while not universal, it enables rules to be prescribed for it in respect of certain definite final Objects. But these rules are then not rules of taste, but merely rules for establishing a union of taste with reason, i.e. of the beautiful with the good – rules by which the former becomes available as an intentional instrument in respect of the latter, for the purpose of bringing that temper of the mind which is self-sustaining and of subjective universal validity to the support and maintenance of that mode of thought which, while possessing objective universal validity, can only be preserved by a resolute effort. But, strictly speaking, perfection neither gains by beauty, nor beauty by perfection. The truth is rather this, when we compare the representation through which an object is given to us with the Object (in respect of what it is meant to be) by means of a concept, we cannot help reviewing it also in respect of the sensation in the Subject. Hence there results a gain to the *entire faculty* of our representative power when harmony prevails between both states of mind. [. . .]

XVII
The ideal of beauty

There can be no objective rule of taste by which what is beautiful may be defined by means of concepts. For every judgement from that source is aesthetic, i.e. its determining ground is the feeling of the Subject, and not any concept of an Object. It is only throwing away labour to look for a principle of taste that affords a universal criterion of the beautiful by definite concepts; because what is sought is a thing impossible and inherently contradictory. But in the universal communicability of the sensation (of delight or aversion) – a communicability, too, that exists apart from any concept – in the accord, so far as possible, of all ages and nations as to this feeling in the representation of certain objects, we have the empirical criterion, weak indeed and scarce sufficient to raise a presumption, of the derivation of a taste, thus confirmed by examples, from grounds deep-seated and shared alike by all men, underlying their agreement in estimating the forms under which objects are given to them.

For this reason some products of taste are looked on as *exemplary* – not meaning thereby that by imitating others taste may be acquired. For taste must be an original faculty; whereas one who imitates a model, while showing skill commensurate with his success, only displays taste as himself a critic of this model. Hence it follows that the highest model, the archetype of taste, is a mere idea, which each person must beget in his own consciousness, and according to which he must form his estimate of everything that is an Object of taste, or that is an example of critical taste, and even of universal taste itself. Properly speaking, an *idea* signifies a concept of reason, and an *ideal* the representation of an individual existence as adequate to an idea. Hence this archetype of taste – which rests, indeed, upon reason's indeterminate idea of a maximum, but is not, however, capable of being represented by means of concepts, but only in an individual presentation – may more appropriately be called the ideal of the beautiful. While not having this ideal in our possession, we still strive to beget it within us. But it is bound to be merely an ideal of the imagination, seeing that it rests, not upon concepts, but upon the presentation – the faculty of presentation being the imagination. – Now, how do we arrive at such an ideal of beauty? Is it *a priori* or empirically? Further, what species of the beautiful admits of an ideal?

First of all, we do well to observe that the beauty for which an ideal has to be sought cannot be a beauty that is *free and at large*, but must be one *fixed* by a concept of objective finality. Hence it cannot belong to the Object of an altogether pure judgement of taste, but must attach to one that is partly intellectual. In other words, where an ideal is to have place among the grounds upon which any estimate is formed, then beneath grounds of that kind there must lie some idea of reason according to determinate concepts, by which the end underlying the internal possibility of the object is determined *a priori*. An ideal of beautiful flowers, of a beautiful suite of furniture, or of a beautiful view, is unthinkable. But, it may also be impossible to represent an ideal of a beauty dependent on definite ends, e.g. a beautiful residence, a beautiful tree, a beautiful garden, &c., presumably because their ends are not sufficiently defined and fixed by their concept, with the result that their finality is nearly as free as with beauty that is quite *at large*. Only what has in itself the end of its real existence – only *man* that is able himself to determine his ends by reason, or, where he has to derive them from external perception, can still compare them with essential and universal ends, and then further pronounce aesthetically upon their accord with such ends, only he, among all objects in the world, admits, therefore, of an ideal of *beauty*, just as humanity in his person, as intelligence, alone admits of the ideal of *perfection*. [. . .]

But the *ideal* of the beautiful . . . is only to be sought in the *human figure*. Here the ideal consists in the expression of the *moral*, apart from which the object would not please at once universally and positively (not merely negatively in a presentation academically correct). The visible expression of moral ideas that govern men inwardly can, of course, only be drawn from experience; but their combination with all that our reason connects with the morally good in the idea of the highest finality – benevolence, purity, strength, or equanimity, &c. – may be made, as it were, visible in bodily manifestation (as effect of what is internal), and this embodiment involves a union of pure ideas of reason and great imaginative power, in one who would even form an estimate of it, not to speak of being the author of its presentation. The correctness of such an ideal of beauty is evidenced by its not permitting any sensuous charm to mingle with the delight in its Object, in which it still allows us to take a great interest. This fact in turn shows that an estimate formed according to such a standard can never be purely aesthetic, and that one formed according to an ideal of beauty cannot be a simple judgement of taste.

Definition of the beautiful derived from this third moment

Beauty is the form of *finality* in an object, so far as perceived in it *apart from the representation of an end*. [. . .]

XVIII
Nature of the modality in a judgement of taste

I may assert in the case of every representation that the synthesis of a pleasure with the representation (as a Cognition) is at least *possible*. Of what I call *agreeable* I assert that it *actually* causes pleasure in me. But what we have in mind in the case of the *beautiful* is a *necessary* reference on its part to delight. However, this necessity is of a special kind. It is not a theoretical objective necessity – such as would let us cognize *a priori* that every one *will feel* this delight in the object that is called beautiful by me. Nor yet is it a practical necessity, in which case, thanks to concepts of a pure rational will in which free agents are supplied with a rule, this delight is the necessary consequence of an objective law, and simply means that one ought absolutely (without ulterior object) to act in a certain way. Rather, being such a necessity as is thought in an aesthetic judgement, it can only be termed *exemplary*. In other words it is a necessity of the assent of *all* to a judgement regarded as exemplifying a universal rule incapable of formulation. Since an aesthetic judgement is not an objective or cognitive judgement, this necessity is not derivable from definite concepts, and so is not apodictic. Much less is it inferable from universality of experience (of a thorough-going agreement of judgements about the beauty of a certain object). For, apart from the fact that experience would hardly furnish evidences sufficiently numerous for this purpose, empirical judgements do not afford any foundation for a concept of the necessity of these judgements.

XIX
The subjective necessity attributed to a judgement of taste is conditioned

The judgement of taste exacts agreement from every one; and a person who describes something as beautiful insists that every one *ought* to give the object in question his approval and follow suit in describing it as beautiful. The *ought* in aesthetic judgement, therefore, despite an accordance with all the requisite data for passing judgement, is still only pronounced conditionally. We are suitors for agreements from every one else, because we are fortified with a ground common to all. Further, we would be able to count on this agreement, provided we were always assured of the correct subsumption of the case under that ground as the rule of approval.

XX
The condition of the necessity advanced by a judgement of taste is the idea of a common sense

Were judgements of taste (like cognitive judgements) in possession of a definite objective principle, then one who in his judgement followed such a principle would claim unconditioned necessity for it. Again, were they devoid of any principle, as are those of the mere taste of sense, then no thought of any necessity on their part would enter one's head. Therefore they must have a subjective principle, and one which determines what pleases or displeases, by means of feeling only and not through concepts, but yet with universal validity. Such a principle, however, could only be regarded as a *common sense*. This differs essentially from common understanding, which is also sometimes called common sense (*sensus communis*): for the judgement of the latter is not one by feeling, but always one by concepts, though usually only in the shape of obscurely represented principles.

The judgement of taste, therefore, depends on our presupposing the existence of a common sense. (But this is not to be taken to mean some external sense, but the effect arising from the free play of our powers of cognition.) Only under the presupposition, I repeat, of such a common sense, are we able to lay down a judgement of taste. [. . .]

XXII
The necessity of the universal assent that is thought in a judgement of taste, is a subjective necessity which, under the presupposition of a common sense, is represented as objective

In all judgements by which we describe anything as beautiful we tolerate no one else being of a different opinion, and in taking up this position we do not rest our judgement upon concepts, but only on our feeling. Accordingly we introduce this fundamental feeling not as a private feeling, but as a public sense. Now, for this purpose, experience cannot be made the ground of this common sense, for the latter is invoked to justify judgements containing an 'ought.' The assertion is not that every one *will* fall in with our judgement, but rather that every one *ought* to agree with it. Here I put forward my judgement of taste as an example of the judgement of common sense, and attribute to it on that account *exemplary* validity. Hence common sense is a mere ideal norm. With this as presupposition, a judgement that accords with it, as well as the delight in an Object expressed in that judgement, is rightly converted into a rule for every one. For the principle, while it is only subjective, being yet assumed as subjectively universal (a necessary idea for every one), could, in what concerns the consensus of different judging Subjects, demand universal assent like an objective principle, provided we were assured of our subsumption under it being correct.

This indeterminate norm of a common sense is, as a matter of fact, presupposed by us; as is shown by our presuming to lay down judgements of taste. But does such a common sense in fact exist as a constitutive principle of the possibility of experience, or is it formed for us as a regulative principle by a still higher principle of reason, that for higher ends first seeks to beget in us a common sense? Is taste, in other words, a natural and original faculty, or is it only the idea of one that is artificial and to be acquired by us, so that a judgement of taste, with its demand for universal assent, is but a requirement of reason for generating such a *consensus*, and does the 'ought,' i.e. the objective necessity of the coincidence of the feeling of all with the particular feeling of each, only betoken the possibility of arriving at some sort of unanimity in these matters, and the judgement of taste only adduce an example of the application of this principle? These are questions which as yet we are neither willing nor in a position to investigate. For the present we have only to resolve the faculty of taste into its elements, and to unite these ultimately in the idea of a common sense.

Definition of the beautiful drawn from the fourth moment
The beautiful is that which, apart from a concept, is cognized as object of a *necessary* delight.

General Remark on the First Section of the Analytic

The result to be extracted from the foregoing analysis is in effect this: that everything runs up into the concept of taste as a critical faculty by which an object is estimated in reference to the *free conformity to law* of the imagination. If, now, imagination must in the judgement of taste be regarded in its freedom, then, to begin with, it is not taken as reproductive, as in its subjection to the laws of association, but as productive and exerting an activity of its own (as originator of arbitrary forms of possible intuitions). And although in the apprehension of a given object of sense it is tied down to a definite form of this Object and, to that extent, does not enjoy free play, (as it does in poetry,) still it is easy to conceive that the object may supply ready-made to the imagination just such a form of the arrangement of the manifold, as the imagination, if it were left to itself, would freely project in harmony with the general *conformity to law of the understanding.* But that the *imagination* should be both *free* and of *itself conformable to law,* i.e. carry autonomy with it, is a contradiction. The understanding alone gives the law. Where, however, the imagination is compelled to follow a course laid down by a definite law, then what the form of the product is to be is determined by concepts; but, in that case, as already shown, the delight is not delight in the beautiful, but in the good, (in perfection, though it be no more than formal perfection), and the judgement is not one due to taste. Hence it is only a conformity to law without a law, and a subjective harmonizing of the imagination and the understanding without an objective one – which latter would mean that the representation was referred to a definite concept of the object – that can consist with the free conformity to law of the understanding (which has also been called finality apart from an end) and with the specific character of a judgement of taste.

Now geometrically regular figures, a circle, a square, a cube, and the like, are commonly brought forward by critics of taste as the most simple and unquestionable examples of beauty. And yet the very reason why they are called regular, is because the only way of representing them is by looking on them as mere presentations of a determinate concept by which the figure has its rule (according to which alone it is possible) prescribed for it. One or other of these two views must, therefore, be wrong: either the verdict of the critics that attributes beauty to such figures, or else our own, which makes finality apart from any concept necessary for beauty.

One would scarce think it necessary for a man to have taste to take more delight in a circle than in a scrawled outline, in an equilateral and equiangular quadrilateral than in one that is all lob-sided, and, as it were, deformed. The requirements of common understanding ensure such a preference without the least demand upon taste. Where some purpose is perceived, as, for instance, that of forming an estimate of the area of a plot of land, or rendering intelligible the relation of divided parts to one another and to the whole, then regular figures, and those of the simplest kind, are needed; and the delight does not rest immediately upon the way the figure strikes the eye, but upon its serviceability for all manner of possible purposes. A room with the walls making oblique angles, a plot laid out in a garden in a similar way, even any violation of symmetry, as well in the figure of animals (e.g. being one-eyed) as in that of buildings, or of flower-beds, is displeasing because of its perversity of form, not alone in a practical way in respect of some definite use to which the thing may be put, but for an estimate that looks to all manner of possible purposes. With the judgement of taste the case is different. For, when it is pure, it combines delight or aversion immediately with the bare *comtemplation* of the object irrespective of its use or of any end.

The regularity that conduces to the concept of an object is, in fact, the indispensable condition (*conditio sine qua non*) of grasping the object as a single representation and giving to the manifold its determinate form. This determination is an end in respect of knowledge; and in this connexion it is invariably coupled with delight (such as attends the accomplishment of any, even problematical, purpose). Here, however, we have merely the value set upon the solution that satisfies the problem, and not a free and indeterminately final entertainment of the mental powers with what is called beautiful. In the latter case understanding is at the service of imagination, in the former this relation is reversed.

With a thing that owes its possibility to a purpose, a building, or even an animal, its regularity, which consists in symmetry, must express the unity of the intuition accompanying the concept of its end, and belongs with it to cognition. But where all that is intended is the maintenance of a free play of the powers of representation (subject, however, to the condition that there is to be nothing for understanding to take exception to), in ornamental gardens, in the decoration of rooms, in all kinds of furniture that shows good taste, &c., regularity in the shape of constraint is to be avoided as far as possible. Thus English taste in gardens, and fantastic taste in furniture, push the freedom of imagination to the verge of what is grotesque – the idea being that in this divorce from all constraint of rules the precise instance is being afforded where taste can exhibit its perfection in projects of the imagination to the fullest extent.

All stiff regularity (such as borders on mathematical regularity) is inherently repugnant to taste, in that the contemplation of it affords us no lasting entertainment. Indeed, where it has neither cognition nor some definite practical end expressly in view, we get heartily tired of it. On the other hand, anything that gives the imagination scope for unstudied and final play is always fresh to us. We do not grow to hate the very sight of it. [. . .]

XXXIV
An objective principle of taste is not possible

A principle of taste would mean a fundamental premiss under the condition of which one might subsume the concept of an object, and then, by a syllogism, draw the inference that it is beautiful. That, however, is absolutely impossible. For I must feel the pleasure immediately in the representation of the object, and I cannot be talked into it by any grounds of proof. Thus although critics, as Hume says, are able to reason more plausibly than cooks, they must still share the same fate. For the determining ground of their judgement they are not able to look to the force of demonstrations, but only to the reflection of the Subject upon his own state (of pleasure or displeasure), to the exclusion of precepts and rules.

There is, however, a matter upon which it is competent for critics to exercise their subtlety, and upon which they ought to do so, so long as it tends to the rectification and extension of our judgements of taste. But that matter is not one of exhibiting the determining ground of aesthetic judgements of this kind in a universally applicable formula – which is impossible. Rather is it the investigation of the faculties of cognition and their function in these judgements, and the illustration, by the analysis of examples, of their mutual subjective finality, the form of which in a given representation has been shown above to constitute the beauty of their object. Hence with regard to the representation whereby an Object is given, the Critique of Taste itself is only subjective; viz. it is the art or science of reducing the mutual relation of the understanding and the imagination in the given representation (without reference to antecedent sensation or concept), consequently their accordance or discordance, to rules, and of determining them with regard to their conditions. It is *art* if it only illustrates this by examples; it is *science* if it deduces the possibility of such an estimate from the nature of these faculties as faculties of knowledge in general. It is only with the latter, as Transcendental Critique, that we have here any concern. Its proper scope is the development and justification of the subjective principle of taste, as an *a priori* principle of judgement. As an art, Critique merely looks to the physiological (here psychological), and, consequently, empirical rules, according to which in actual fact taste proceeds, (passing by the question of their possibility,) and seeks to apply them in estimating its objects. The latter Critique criticizes the products of fine art, just as the former does the faculty of estimating them. [. . .]

XL
Taste as a kind of sensus communis

The name of sense is often given to judgement where what attracts attention is not so much its reflective act as merely its result. So we speak of a sense of truth, of a sense of propriety, or of justice, &c. And yet, of course, we know, or at least ought well enough to know, that a sense cannot be the true abode of these concepts, not to speak of its being competent, even in the slightest degree, to pronounce universal rules. On the contrary, we recognize that a representation of this kind, be it of truth, propriety, beauty, or justice, could never enter our thoughts were we not able to raise ourselves above the level of the senses to that of higher faculties of cognition. *Common human understanding* which, as mere sound (not yet cultivated) understanding, is looked upon as the least we can expect from any one claiming the name of man, has therefore the doubtful honour of having the name of common sense (*sensus communis*) bestowed upon it; and bestowed, too, in an acceptation of the word *common* (not merely in our own language, where it actually has a double meaning, but also in many others, which makes it amount to what is *vulgar* – what is everywhere to be met with – a quality which by no means confers credit or distinction upon its possessor).

However, by the name *sensus communis* is to be understood the idea of a *public* sense, i.e. a critical faculty which in its reflective act takes account (*a priori*) of the mode of representation of every one else, in order, *as it were*, to weigh its judgement with the collective reason of mankind, and thereby avoid the illusion arising from subjective and personal conditions which could readily be taken for objective, an illusion that would exert a prejudicial influence upon its judgement. This is accomplished by weighing the judgement, not so much with actual, as rather with the merely possible, judgements of others, and by putting ourselves in the position of every one else, as the result of a mere abstraction from the limitations which contingently affect our own estimate. This, in turn, is effected by so far as possible letting go the element of matter, i.e. sensation, in our general state of representative activity, and confining attention to the formal peculiarities of our representation or general state of representative activity. Now it may seem that this operation of reflection is too artificial to be attributed to the faculty which we call *common* sense. But this is an appearance due only to its expression in abstract formulae. In itself nothing is more natural than to abstract from charm and emotion where one is looking for a judgement intended to serve as a universal rule. [. . .]

Taste is, therefore, the faculty of forming an *a priori* estimate of the communicability of the feelings that, without the mediation of a concept, are connected with a given representation.

Supposing, now, that we could assume that the mere universal communicability of our feeling must of itself carry with it an interest for us (an assumption, however, which we are not entitled to draw as a conclusion from the character of a merely reflective judgement), we should then be in a position to explain how the feeling in the judgement of taste comes to be exacted from every one as a sort of duty. [. . .]

XLII
The intellectual interest in the beautiful

It has been with the best intentions that those who love to see in the ultimate end of humanity, namely the morally good, the goal of all activities to which men are impelled by the inner bent of their nature, have regarded it as a mark of a good moral character to take an interest in the beautiful generally. But they have, not without reason, been contradicted by others who appeal to the fact of experience, that *virtuosi* in matters of taste, being not alone often, but one might say as a general rule, vain, capricious, and addicted to injurious passions, could perhaps more rarely than others lay claim to any pre-eminent attachment to moral principles. And so it would seem, not only that the feeling for the beautiful is specifically different from the moral feeling (which as a matter of fact is the case), but also that the interest which we may combine with it, will hardly consort with the moral, and certainly not on grounds of inner affinity.

Now I willingly admit that the interest in the *beautiful of art* (including under this heading the artificial use of natural beauties for personal adornment, and so from vanity) gives no evidence at all of a habit of mind attached to the morally good, or even inclined that way. But, on the other hand, I do maintain that to take an *immediate interest* in the beauty of *nature* (not merely to have taste in estimating it) is always a mark of a good soul; and that, where this interest is habitual, it is at least indicative of a temper of mind favourable to the moral feeling that it should readily associate itself with the *contemplation of nature*. It must, however, be borne in mind that I mean to refer strictly to the beautiful *forms* of nature, and to put to one side the *charms* which she is wont so lavishly to combine with them; because, though the interest in these is no doubt immediate, it is nevertheless empirical.

One who alone (and without any intention of communicating his observations to others) regards the beautiful form of a wild flower, a bird, an insect, or the like, out of admiration and love of them, and being loath to let them escape him in nature, even at the risk of some misadventure to himself – so far from there being any prospect of advantage to him – such a one takes an immediate, and in fact intellectual, interest in the beauty of nature. This means that he is not alone pleased with nature's product in respect of its form, but is also pleased at its existence, and is so without any charm of sense having a share in the matter, or without his associating with it any end whatsoever.

In this connexion, however, it is of note that were we to play a trick on our lover of the beautiful, and plant in the ground artificial flowers (which can he made so as to look just like natural ones), and perch artfully carved birds on the branches of trees, and he were to find out how he had been taken in, the immediate interest which these things previously had for him would at once vanish – though, perhaps, a different interest might intervene in its stead, that, namely, of vanity in decorating his room with them for the eyes of others. The fact is that our intuition and reflection must have as their concomitant the thought that the beauty in question is nature's handiwork; and this is the sole basis of the immediate interest that is taken in it. Failing this we are either left with a bare judgement of taste void of all interest whatever, or else only with one that is combined with an interest that is mediate, involving, namely, a reference to society; which latter affords no reliable indication of morally good habits of thought.

The superiority which natural beauty has over that of art, even where it is excelled by the latter in point of form, in yet being alone able to awaken an immediate interest, accords with the refined and well-grounded habits of thought of all men who have cultivated their moral feeling. If a man with taste enough to judge of works of fine art with the greatest correctness and refinement readily quits the room in which he meets with those beauties that minister to vanity or, at least, social joys, and betakes himself to the beautiful in nature, so that he may there find as it were a feast for his soul in a train of thought which he can never completely evolve, we will then regard this his choice even with veneration, and give him credit for a beautiful soul, to which no connoisseur or art collector can lay claim on the score of the interest which his objects have for him. – Here, now, are two kinds of Objects which in the judgement of mere taste could scarcely contend with one another for a superiority. What then, is the distinction that makes us hold them in such different esteem?

We have a faculty of judgement which is merely aesthetic – a faculty of judging of forms without the aid of concepts, and of finding, in the mere estimate of them, a delight that we at the same time make into a rule for every one, without this judgement being founded on an interest, or yet producing one. – On the other hand we have also a faculty of intellectual judgement for the mere forms of practical maxims, (so far as they are of themselves qualified for universal legislation,) – a faculty of determining an *a priori* delight, which we make into a law for every one, without our judgement being founded on any interest, *though here it produces one.* The pleasure or displeasure in the former judgement is called that of taste; the latter is called that of the moral feeling.

But, now, reason is further interested in ideas (for which in our moral feeling it brings about an immediate interest,) having also objective reality. That is to say, it is of interest to reason that nature should at least show a trace or give a hint that it contains in itself some ground or other for assuming a uniform accordance of its products with our wholly disinterested delight (a delight which we cognize *a priori* as a law for every one without being able to ground it upon proofs). That being so, reason must take an interest in every manifestation on the part of nature of some such accordance. Hence the mind cannot reflect on the beauty of *nature* without at the same time finding its interest engaged. But this interest is akin to the moral. One, then, who takes such an interest in the beautiful in nature can only do so in so far as he has previously set his interest deep in the foundations of the morally good. On these grounds we have reason for presuming the presence of at least the germ of a good moral disposition in the case of a man to whom the beauty of nature is a matter of immediate interest. [. . .]

XLIII
Art in general

(1.) *Art* is distinguished from *nature* as making (*facere*) is from acting or operating in general (*agere*), and the product or the result of the former is distinguished from that of the latter as *work* (*opus*) from operation (*effectus*).

By right it is only production through freedom, i.e. through an act of will that places reason at the basis of its action, that should be termed art. For, although we are pleased to call what bees produce (their regularly constructed cells) a work of art, we only do so on the strength of an analogy with art; that is to say, as soon as we call to mind that no rational deliberation forms the basis of their labour, we say at once that it is a product of their nature (of instinct), and it is only to their Creator that we ascribe it as art.

If, as sometimes happens, in a search through a bog, we light on a piece of hewn wood, we do not say it is a product of nature but of art. Its producing cause had an end in view to which the object owes its form. Apart from such cases, we recognize an art in everything formed in such a way that its actuality must have been preceded by a representation of the thing in its cause (as even in the case of the bees), although the effect could not have been *thought* by the cause. But where anything is called absolutely a work of art, to distinguish it from a natural product, then some work of man is always understood.

(2.) *Art*, as human skill, is distinguished also from *science* (as *ability* from *knowledge*), as a practical from a theoretical faculty, as technic from theory (as the art of surveying from geometry). For this reason, also, what one *can* do the moment one only *knows* what is to be done, hence without anything more than sufficient knowledge of the desired result, is not called art. To art that alone belongs for which the possession of the most complete knowledge does not involve one's having then and there the skill to do it. [. . .]

(3.) *Art* is further distinguished from *handicraft*. The first is called *free*, the other may be called *industrial art*. We look on the former as something which could only prove final (be a success) as play, i.e. an occupation which is agreeable on its own account; but on the second as labour, i.e. a business, which on its own account is disagreeable (drudgery), and is only attractive by means of what it results in (e.g. the pay), and which is consequently capable of being a compulsory imposition. . . . It is not amiss, however, to remind the reader of this: that in all free arts something of a compulsory character is still required, or, as it is called, a *mechanism*, without which the *soul*, which in art must be *free*, and which alone gives life to the work, would be bodyless and evanescent (e.g. in the poetic art there must be correctness and wealth of language, likewise prosody and metre). For not a few leaders of a newer school believe that the best way to promote a free art is to sweep away all restraint, and convert it from labour into mere play.

XLIV
Fine art

There is no science of the beautiful, but only a Critique. Nor, again, is there an elegant (*schöne*) science, but only a fine (*schöne*) art. . . . What has given rise to the current expression *elegant sciences* is, doubtless, no more than this, that common observation has, quite accurately, noted the fact that for fine art, in the fulness of its perfection, a large store of science is required. [. . .]

Where art, merely seeking to actualize a possible object to the *cognition* of which it is adequate, does whatever acts are required for that purpose, then it is *mechanical*. But should the feeling of pleasure be what it has immediately in view it is then termed *aesthetic* art. As such it may be either *agreeable* or *fine* art. The description 'agreeable art' applies where the end of the art is that the pleasure should accompany the representations considered as mere *sensations*, the description 'fine art' where it is to accompany them considered as *modes of cognition*.

Agreeable arts are those which have mere enjoyment for their object. Such are all the charms that can gratify a dinner party: entertaining narrative, the art of starting the whole table in unrestrained and sprightly conversation, or with jest and laughter inducing a certain air of gaiety.

Fine art, on the other hand, is a mode of representation which is intrinsically final, and which, although devoid of an end, has the effect of advancing the culture of the mental powers in the interests of social communication.

The universal communicability of a pleasure involves in its very concept that the pleasure is not one of enjoyment arising out of mere sensation, but must be one of reflection. Hence aesthetic art, as art which is beautiful, is one having for its standard the reflective judgement and not organic sensation.

XLV
Fine art is an art so far as it has at the same time the appearance of being nature

A product of fine art must be recognized to be art and not nature. Nevertheless the finality in its form must appear just as free from the constraint of arbitrary rules as if it were a product of mere nature. Upon this feeling of freedom in the play of our cognitive faculties – which play has at the same time to be final – rests that pleasure which alone is universally communicable without being based on concepts. Nature proved beautiful when it wore the appearance of art; and art can only be termed beautiful, where we are conscious of its being art, while yet it has the appearance of nature.

For, whether we are dealing with beauty of nature or beauty of art, we may make the universal statement: *that is beautiful which pleases in the mere estimate of it* (not in sensation or by means of a concept). Now art has always got a definite intention of producing something. Were this 'something,' however, to be mere sensation (something merely subjective), intended to be accompanied with pleasure, then such product would, in our estimation of it, only please through the agency of the feeling of the senses. On the other hand, were the intention one directed to the production of a definite object, then, supposing this were attained by art, the object would only please by means of a concept. But in both cases the art would please, not in *the mere estimate of it*, i.e. not as fine art, but rather as mechanical art.

Hence the finality in the product of fine art, intentional though it be, must not have the appearance of being intentional; i.e. fine art must be clothed *with the aspect* of nature, although we recognize it to be art. But the way in which a product of art seems like nature, is by the presence of perfect *exactness* in the agreement with rules prescribing how alone the product can be what it is intended to be, but with an absence of *laboured effect*, (without academic form betraying itself,) i.e. without a trace appearing of the artist having always had the rule present to him and of its having fettered his mental powers.

XLVI
Fine art is the art of genius

Genius is the talent (natural endowment) which gives the rule to art. Since talent, as an innate productive faculty of the artist, belongs itself to nature, we may put it this way: *Genius* is the innate mental aptitude (*ingenium*) *through which* nature gives the rule to art.

Whatever may be the merits of this definition, and whether it is merely arbitrary, or whether it is adequate or not to the concept usually associated with the word *genius* (a point which the following sections have to clear up), it may still be shown at the outset that, according to this acceptation of the word, fine arts must necessarily be regarded as arts of *genius.*

For every art presupposes rules which are laid down as the foundation which first enables a product, if it is to be called one of art, to be represented as possible. The concept of fine art, however, does not permit of the judgement upon the beauty of its product being derived from any rule that has a *concept* for its determining ground, and that depends, consequently, on a concept of the way in which the product is possible. Consequently fine art cannot of its own self excogitate the rule according to which it is to effectuate its product. But since, for all that, a product can never be called art unless there is a preceding rule, it follows that nature in the individual (and by virtue of the harmony of his faculties) must give the rule to art, i.e. fine art is only possible as a product of genius.

From this it may be seen that genius (1) is a *talent* for producing that for which no definite rule can be given: and not an aptitude in the way of cleverness for what can be learned according to some rule; and that consequently *originality* must be its primary property. (2) Since there may also be original nonsense, its products must at the same time be models, i.e. be *exemplary*; and, consequently, though not themselves derived from imitation, they must serve that purpose for others, i.e. as a standard or rule of estimating. (3) It cannot indicate scientifically how it brings about its product, but rather gives the rule as *nature.* Hence, where an author owes a product to his genius, he does not himself know how the *ideas* for it have entered into his head, nor has he it in his power to invent the like at pleasure, or methodically, and communicate the same to others in such precepts as would put them in a position to produce similar products. . . . (4) Nature prescribes the rule through genius not to science but to art, and this also only in so far as it is to be fine art.

XLVII
Elucidation and confirmation of the above explanation of genius

Every one is agreed on the point of the complete opposition between genius and the *spirit of imitation*. Now since learning is nothing but imitation, the greatest ability, or aptness as an pupil (capacity), it still, as such, not equivalent to genius. Even though a man weaves his own thoughts or fancies, instead of merely taking in what others have thought, and even though he go so far as to bring fresh gains to art and science, this does not afford a valid reason for calling such a man of *brains*, and often great brains, a *genius*, in contradistinction to one who goes by the name of *shallow-pate*, because he can never do more than merely learn and follow a lead. For what is accomplished in this way is something that *could* have been learned. Hence it all lies in the natural path of investigation and reflection according to rules, and so is not specifically distinguishable from what may be acquired as the result of industry backed up by imitation. So all that *Newton* has set forth in his immortal work on the Principles of Natural Philosophy may well be learned, however great a mind it took to find it all out, but we cannot learn to write in a true poetic vein, no matter how complete all the precepts of the poetic art may be, or however excellent its models. The reason is that all the steps that Newton had to take from the first elements of geometry to his greatest and most profound discoveries were such as he could make intuitively evident and plain to follow, not only for himself but for every one else. On the other hand no *Homer or Wieland* can show how his ideas, so rich at once in fancy and in thought, enter and assemble themselves in his brain, for the good reason that he does not himself know, and so cannot teach others. In matters of science, therefore, the greatest inventor differs only in degree from the most laborious imitator and apprentice, whereas he differs specifically from one endowed by nature for fine art. No disparagement, however, of those great men, to whom the human race is so deeply indebted, is involved in this comparison of them with those who on the score of their talent for fine art are the elect of nature. The talent for science is formed for the continued advances of greater perfection in knowledge, with all its dependent practical advantages, as also for imparting the same to others. Hence scientists can boast a ground of considerable superiority over those who merit the honour of being called geniuses, since genius reaches a point at which art must make a halt, as there is a limit imposed upon it which it cannot transcend. This limit has in all probability been long since attained. In addition, such skill cannot be communicated, but requires to be bestowed directly from the hand of nature upon each individual, and so with him it dies, awaiting the day when nature once again endows another in the same way – one who needs no more than an example to set the talent of which he is conscious at work on similar lines. [. . .]

XLVIII
The relation of genius to taste

For *estimating* beautiful objects, as such, what is required is *taste*; but for fine art, i.e. the *production* of such objects, one needs *genius*.

If we consider genius as the talent for fine art (which the proper signification of the word imports), and if we would analyse it from this point of view into the faculties which must concur to constitute such a talent, it is imperative at the outset accurately to determine the difference between beauty of nature, which it only requires taste to estimate, and beauty of art, which requires genius for its possibility (a possibility to which regard must also be paid in estimating such an object).

A beauty of nature is a *beautiful thing*; beauty of art is a *beautiful representation* of a thing.

To enable me to estimate a beauty of nature, as such, I do not need to be previously possessed of a concept of what sort of a thing the object is intended to be, i.e. I am not obliged to know its material finality (the end), but, rather, in forming an estimate of it apart from any knowledge of the end, the mere form pleases on its own account. If, however, the object is presented as a product of art, and is as such to be declared beautiful, then, seeing that art always presupposes an end in the cause (and its causality), a concept of what the thing is intended to be must first of all be laid at its basis. And, since the agreement of the manifold in a thing with an inner character belonging to it as its end constitutes the perfection of the thing, it follows that in estimating beauty of art the perfection of the thing must be also taken into account – a matter which in estimating a beauty of nature, as beautiful, is quite irrelevant. – It is true that in forming an estimate, especially of animate objects of nature, e.g. of a man or a horse, objective finality is also commonly taken into account with a view to judgement upon their beauty; but then the judgement also ceases to be purely aesthetic, i.e. a mere judgement of taste. Nature is no longer estimated as it appears like art, but rather in so far as it actually *is* art, though superhuman art; and the teleological judgement serves as basis and condition of the aesthetic, and one which the latter must regard. In such a case, where one says, for example, 'that is a beautiful woman,' what one in fact thinks is only this, that in her form nature excellently portrays the ends present in the female figure. For one has to extend one's view beyond the mere form to a concept, to enable the object to be thought in such manner by means of an aesthetic judgement logically conditioned.

Where fine art evidences its superiority is in the beautiful descriptions it gives of things that in nature would be ugly or displeasing. The Furies, diseases, devastations of war, and the like, can (as evils) be very beautifully described, nay even represented in pictures. One kind of ugliness alone is incapable of being represented conformably to nature without destroying all aesthetic delight, and consequently artistic beauty, namely, that which excites *disgust*. For, as in this strange sensation, which depends purely on the imagination, the object is represented as insisting, as it were, upon our enjoying it, while we still set our face against it, the artificial representation of the object is no longer distinguishable from the nature of the object itself in our sensation, and so it cannot possibly be regarded as beautiful. The art of sculpture, again, since in its products art is almost confused with nature, has excluded from its creations the direct representation of ugly objects, and, instead, only sanctions, for example, the representation of death (in a beautiful genius), or of the warlike spirit (in Mars), by means of an allegory, or attributes which wear a pleasant guise, and so only indirectly, through an interpretation on the part of reason, and not for the pure aesthetic judgement.

So much for the beautiful representation of an object, which is properly only the form of the presentation of a concept, and the means by which the latter is universally communicated. To give this form, however, to the product of fine art, taste merely is required. By this the artist, having practised and corrected his taste by a variety of examples from nature or art, controls his work and, after many, and often laborious, attempts to satisfy taste, finds the form which commends itself to him. Hence this form is not, as it were, a matter of inspiration, or of a free swing of the mental powers, but rather of a slow and even painful process of improvement, directed to making the form adequate to his thought without prejudice to the freedom in the play of those powers.

Taste is, however, merely a critical, not a productive faculty; and what conforms to it is not, merely on that account, a work of fine art. It may belong to useful and mechanical art, or even to science, as a product following definite rules which are capable of being learned and which must be closely followed. But the pleasing form imparted to the work is only the vehicle of communication and a mode, as it were, of execution, in respect of which one remains to a certain extent free, notwithstanding being otherwise tied down to a definite end. So we demand that table appointments, or even a moral dissertation, and, indeed, a sermon, must bear this form of fine art, yet without its appearing *studied*. But one would not call them on this account works of fine art. A poem, a musical composition, a picture-gallery, and so forth, would, however, be placed under this head; and so in a would-be work of fine art we may frequently recognize genius without taste, and in another taste without genius.

XLIX
The faculties of the mind which constitute genius

Of certain products which are expected, partly at least, to stand on the footing of fine art, we say they are *soul*less; and this, although we find nothing to censure in them as far as taste goes. A poem may be very pretty and elegant, but is soulless. A narrative has precision and method, but is soulless. . . . Now what do we here mean by 'soul'?

'*Soul*' (*Geist*) in an aesthetical sense, signifies the animating principle in the mind. But that whereby this principle animates the psychic substance (*Seele*) – the material which it employs for that purpose – is that which sets the mental powers into a swing that is final, i.e. into a play which is self-maintaining and which strengthens those powers for such activity.

Now my proposition is that this principle is nothing else than the faculty of presenting *aesthetic ideas.* But, by an aesthetic idea I mean that representation of the imagination which induces much thought, yet without the possibility of any definite thought whatever, i.e. *concept*, being adequate to it, and which language, consequently, can never get quite on level terms with or render completely intelligible. – It is easily seen, that an aesthetic idea is the counterpart (pendant) of a *rational idea*, which, conversely, is a concept, to which no *intuition* (representation of the imagination) can be adequate.

The imagination (as a productive faculty of cognition) is a powerful agent for creating, as it were, a second nature out of the material supplied to it by actual nature. It affords us entertainment where experience proves too commonplace; and we even use it to remodel experience, always following, no doubt, laws that are based on analogy, but still also following principles which have a higher seat in reason (and which are every whit as natural to us as those followed by the understanding in laying hold of empirical nature). By this means we get a sense of our freedom from the law of association (which attaches to the empirical employment of the imagination), with the result that the material can be borrowed by us from nature in accordance with the law, but be worked up by us into something else – namely, what surpasses nature.

Such representations of the imagination may be termed *ideas.* This is partly because they at least strain after something lying out beyond the confines of experience, and so seek to approximate to a presentation of rational concepts (i.e. intellectual ideas), thus giving to these concepts the semblance of an objective reality. But, on the other hand, there is this most important reason, that no concept can be wholly adequate to them as internal intuitions. The poet essays the task of interpreting to sense the rational ideas of invisible beings, the kingdom of the blessed, hell, eternity, creation, &c. Or, again, as to things of which examples occur in experience, e.g. death, envy, and all vices, as also love, fame, and the like, transgressing the limits of experience he attempts with the aid of an imagination which emulates the display of reason in its attainment of a maximum to body them forth to sense with a completeness of which nature affords no parallel; and it is in fact precisely in the poetic art that the faculty of aesthetic ideas can show itself to full advantage. This faculty, however, regarded solely on its own account, is properly no more than a talent (of the imagination).

If, now, we attach to a concept a representation of the imagination belonging to its presentation, but inducing solely on its own account such a wealth of thought as would never admit of comprehension in a definite concept, and, as a consequence, giving aesthetically an unbounded expansion to the concept itself, then the imagination here displays a creative activity, and it puts the faculty of intellectual ideas (reason) into motion – a motion, at the instance of a representation, towards an extension of thought, that, while germane, no doubt, to the concept of the object, exceeds what can be laid hold of in that representation or clearly expressed.

Those forms which do not constitute the presentation of a given concept itself, but which, as secondary representations of the imagination, express the derivatives connected with it, and its kinship with other concepts, are called (aesthetic) *attributes* of an object, the concept of which, as an idea of reason, cannot be adequately presented. In this way Jupiter's eagle, with the lightning in its claws, is an attribute of the mighty kind of heaven, and the peacock of its stately queen. They do not, like *logical attributes*, represent what lies in our concepts of the sublimity and majesty of creation, but rather something else – something that gives the imagination an incentive to spread its flight over a whole host of kindred representations that provoke more thought than admits of expression in a concept determined by words. They furnish an *aesthetic idea*, which serves the above rational idea as a substitute for logical presentation, but with the proper function, however, of animating the mind by opening out for it a prospect into a field of kindred representations stretching beyond its ken. But it is not alone in the arts of painting or sculpture, where the name of attribute is customarily employed, that fine art acts in this way; poetry and rhetoric also derive the soul that animates their works wholly from the aesthetic attributes of the objects – attributes which go hand in hand with the logical, and give the imagination an impetus to bring more thought into play in the matter, though in an undeveloped manner, than allows of being brought within the embrace of a concept, or, therefore, of being definitely formulated in language. [. . .]

On the other hand, even an intellectual concept may serve, conversely, as attribute for a representation of sense, and so animate the latter with the idea of the supersensible; but only by the aesthetic factor subjectively attaching to the consciousness of the supersensible being employed for the purpose. So, for example, a certain poet says in his description of a beautiful morning: 'The sun arose, as out of virtue rises peace.' The consciousness of virtue, even where we put ourselves only in thought in the position of a virtuous man, diffuses in the mind a multitude of sublime and tranquillizing feelings, and gives a boundless outlook into a happy future, such as no expression within the compass of a definite concept completely attains.

In a word, the aesthetic idea is a representation of the imagination, annexed to a given concept, with which, in the free employment of imagination, such a multiplicity of partial representations are bound up, that no expression indicating a definite concept can be found for it – one which on that account allows a concept to be supplemented in thought by much that is indefinable in words, and the feeling of which quickens the cognitive faculties, and with language, as a mere thing of the letter, binds up the spirit (soul) also. [. . .]

If, after this analysis, we cast a glance back upon the above definition of what is called *genius*, we find: *First*, that it is a talent for art – not one for science, in which clearly known rules must take the lead and determine the procedure. *Secondly*, being a talent in the line of art, it presupposes a definite concept of the product – as its end. Hence it presupposes understanding, but, in addition, a representation, indefinite though it be, of the material, i.e. of the intuition, required for the presentation of that concept, and so a relation of the imagination to the understanding. *Thirdly*, it displays itself, not so much in the working out of the projected end in the presentation of a definite *concept*, as rather in the portrayal, or expression of *aesthetic ideas* containing a wealth of material for effecting that intention. Consequently the imagination is represented by it in its freedom from all guidance of rules, but still as final for the presentation of the given concept. *Fourthly*, and lastly, the unsought and undesigned subjective finality in the free harmonizing of the imagination with the understanding's conformity to law presupposes a proportion and accord between these faculties such as cannot be brought about by any observance of rules, whether of science or mechanical imitation, but can only be produced by the nature of the individual.

Genius, according to these presuppositions, is the exemplary originality of the natural endowments of an individual in the *free* employment of his cognitive faculties. On this showing, the product of a genius (in respect of so much in this product as is attributable to genius, and not to possible learning or academic instruction,) is an example, not for imitation (for that would mean the loss of the element of genius, and just the very soul of the work), but to be followed by another genius – one whom it arouses to a sense of his own originality in putting freedom from the constraint of rules so into force in his art, that for art itself a new rule is won – which is what shows a talent to be exemplary. Yet, since the genius is one of nature's elect – a type that must be regarded as but a rare phenomenon – for other clever minds his example gives rise to a school, that is to say a methodical instruction according to rules, collected, so far as the circumstances admit, from such products of genius and their peculiarities. And, to that extent, fine art is for such persons a matter of imitation, for which nature, through the medium of a genius, gave the rules. [. . .]

LI
The division of the fine arts

Beauty (whether it be of nature or of art) may in general be termed the *expression* of aesthetic ideas. But the proviso must be added that with beauty of art this idea must be excited through the medium of a concept of the Object, whereas with beauty of nature the bare reflection upon a given intuition, apart from any concept of what the object is intended to be, is sufficient for awakening and communicating the idea of which that Object is regarded as the *expression*.

Accordingly, if we wish to make a division of the fine arts, we can choose for that purpose, tentatively at least, no more convenient principle than the analogy which art bears to the mode of expression of which men avail themselves in speech, with a view to communicating themselves to one another as completely as possible, i.e. not merely in respect of their concepts but in respect of their sensations also. – Such expression consists in *word*, *gesture*, and *tone* (articulation, gesticulation, and modulation). It is the combination of these three modes of expression which alone constitutes a complete communication of the speaker. For thought, intuition, and sensation are in this way conveyed to others simultaneously and in conjunction.

Hence there are only three kinds of fine art: the art of *speech*, *formative* art, and art of the *play of sensations* (as external sense impressions). This division might also be arranged as a dichotomy, so that fine art would be divided into that of the expression of thoughts or intuitions, the latter being subdivided according to the distinction between the form and the matter (sensation). It would, however, in that case appear too abstract, and less in line with popular conceptions.

(1) The arts of SPEECH are *rhetoric* and *poetry*. *Rhetoric* is the art of transacting a serious business of the understanding as if it were a free play of the imagination; *poetry* that of conducting a free play of the imagination as if it were a serious business of the understanding.

Thus the *orator* announces a serious business, and for the purpose of entertaining his audience conducts it as if it were a mere *play* with ideas. The *poet* promises merely an entertaining *play* with ideas, and yet for the understanding there enures as much as if the promotion of its business had been his one intention. [. . .]

The orator, therefore, gives something which he does not promise, viz. an entertaining play of the imagination. On the other hand, there is something in which he fails to come up to his promise, and a thing, too, which is his avowed business, namely, the engagement of the understanding to some end. The poet's promise, on the contrary, is a modest one, and a mere play with ideas is all he holds out to us, but he accomplishes something worthy of being made a serious business, namely, the using of play to provide food for the understanding, and the giving of life to its concepts by means of the imagination. Hence the orator in reality performs less than he promises, the poet more.

(2) The FORMATIVE arts, or those for the expression of ideas in *sensuous intuition* (not by means of representations of mere imagination that are excited by words) are arts either of *sensuous truth* or of *sensuous semblance*. The first is called *plastic* art, the second *painting*. Both use figures in space for the expression of ideas: the former makes figures discernible to two senses, sight and touch (though, so far as the latter sense is concerned, without regard to beauty), the latter makes them so to the former sense alone. The aesthetic idea (archetype, original) is the fundamental basis of both in the imagination; but the figure which constitutes its expression (the ectype, the copy) is given either in its bodily extension (the way the object itself exists) or else in accordance with the picture which it forms of itself in the eye (according to its appearance when projected on a flat surface). Or, whatever the archetype is, either the reference to an actual end or only the semblance of one may be imposed upon reflection as its condition.

To *plastic* art, as the first kind of formative fine art, belong *sculpture* and *architecture*. The first is that which presents concepts of things corporeally, as they *might exist in nature* (though as fine art it directs its attention to aesthetic finality). The *second* is the art of presenting concepts of things which are possible *only through art*, and the determining ground of whose form is not nature but an arbitrary end – and of presenting them both with a view to this purpose and yet, at the same time, with aesthetic finality. In architecture the chief point is a certain *use* of the artistic object to which, as the condition, the aesthetic ideas are limited. In sculpture the mere *expression* of aesthetic ideas is the main intention. Thus statues of men, gods, animals, &c., belong to sculpture; but temples, splendid buildings for public concourse, or even dwelling-houses, triumphal arches, columns, mausoleums, &c., erected as monuments, belong to architecture, and in fact all household furniture (the work of cabinet-makers, and so forth – things meant to be used) may be added to the list, on the ground that adaptation of the product to a particular use is the essential element in a *work of architecture*. On the other hand, a mere *piece of sculpture*, made simply to be looked at, and intended to please on its own account, is, as a corporeal presentation, a mere imitation of nature, though one in which regard is paid to aesthetic ideas, and in which, therefore, *sensuous truth* should not go the length of losing the appearance of being an art and a product of the elective will.

Painting, as the second kind of formative art, which presents the *sensuous semblance* in artful combination with ideas, I would divide into that of the beautiful *portrayal of nature*, and that of the beautiful *arrangement* of its *products*. The first is *painting proper*, the second *landscape gardening*. For the first gives only the semblance of bodily extension; whereas the second, giving this, no doubt, according to its truth, gives only the semblance of utility and employment for ends other than the play of the imagination in the contemplation of its forms. The latter consists in no more than decking out the ground with the same manifold variety (grasses, flowers, shrubs, and trees, and even water, hills, and dales) as that with which nature presents it to our view, only arranged differently and in obedience to certain ideas. . . . The justification, however, of bringing formative art (by analogy) under a common head with gesture in a speech, lies in the fact that through these figures the soul of the artist furnishes a bodily expression for the substance and character of his thought, and makes the thing itself speak, as it were, in mimic language – a very common play of our fancy, that attributes to lifeless things a soul suitable to their form, and that uses them as its mouthpiece.

(3) The art of the BEAUTIFUL PLAY OF SENSATIONS, (sensations that arise from external stimulation,) which is a play of sensations that has nevertheless to permit of universal communication, can only be concerned with the proportion of the different degrees of tension in the sense to which the sensation belongs, i.e. with its tone. In this comprehensive sense of the word it may be divided into the artificial play of sensations of hearing and of sight, consequently into *music* and the *art of colour*. – It is of note that these two senses, over and above such susceptibility for impressions as is required to obtain concepts of external objects by means of these impressions, also admit of a peculiar associated sensation of which we cannot well determine whether it is based on sense or reflection; and that this sensibility may at times be wanting, although the sense, in other respects, and in what concerns its employment for the cognition of objects, is by no means deficient but particularly keen. [. . .]

LXIV
The distinctive character of things considered as physical ends

A thing is possible only as an end where the causality to which it owes its origin must not be sought in the mechanism of nature, but in a cause whose capacity of acting is determined by conceptions. What is required in order that we may perceive that a thing is only possible in this way is that its form is not possible on purely natural laws – that is to say, such laws as we may cognize by means of unaided understanding applied to objects of sense – but that, on the contrary, even to know it empirically in respect of its cause and effect presupposes conceptions of reason. Here we have, as far as any empirical laws of nature go, a *contingency* of the form of the thing in relation to reason. Now reason in every case insists on cognizing the necessity of the form of a natural product, even where it only desires to perceive the conditions involved in its production. In the given form above mentioned, however, it cannot get this necessity. Hence the contingency is itself a ground for making us look upon the origin of the thing as if, just because of that contingency, it could only be possible through reason. But the causality, so construed, becomes the faculty of acting according to ends – that is to say, a will; and the Object, which is represented as only deriving its possibility from such a will, will be represented as possible only as an end.

Suppose a person was in a country that seemed to him uninhabited and was to see a geometrical figure, say a regular hexagon, traced on the sand. As he reflected, and tried to get a conception of the figure, his reason would make him conscious, though perhaps obscurely, that in the production of this conception there was unity of principle. His reason would then forbid him to consider the sand, the neighbouring sea, the winds, or even animals with their footprints, as causes familiar to him, or any other irrational cause, as the ground of the possibility of such a form. For the contingency of coincidence with a conception like this, which is only possible in reason, would appear to him so infinitely great that there might just as well be no law of nature at all in the case. Hence it would seem that the cause of the production of such an effect could not be contained in the mere mechanical operation of nature, but that, on the contrary, a conception of such an Object, as a conception that only reason can give and compare the Object with, must likewise be what alone contains that causality. On these grounds it would appear to him that this effect was one that might without reservation be regarded as an end, though not as a natural end. In other words he would regard it as a product of *art – vestigium hominis video*.

But where a thing is recognized to be a product of nature, then something more is required – unless, perhaps, our very estimate involves a contradiction – if, despite its being such a product, we are yet to estimate it as an end, and, consequently, as a *physical end*. As a provisional statement I would say that a thing exists as a physical end *if it is* (though in a double sense) *both cause and effect of itself*. For this involves a kind of causality that we cannot associate with the mere conception of a nature unless we make that nature rest on an underlying end, but which can then, though incomprehensible, be thought without contradiction. Before analysing the component factors of this idea of a physical end, let us first illustrate its meaning by an example.

A tree produces, in the first place, another tree, according to a familiar law of nature. But the tree which it produces is of the same genus. Hence, in its *genus*, it produces itself. In the genus, now as effect, now as cause, continually generated from itself and likewise generating itself, it preserves itself generically.

Secondly, a tree produces itself even as an *individual*. It is true that we only call this kind of effect growth; but growth is here to be understood in a sense that makes it entirely different from any increase according to mechanical laws, and renders it equivalent, though under another name, to generation. The plant first prepares the matter that it assimilates and bestows upon it a specifically distinctive quality which the mechanism of nature outside it cannot supply, and it develops itself by means of a material which, in its composite character, is its own product. For, although in respect of the constituents that it derives from nature outside, it must be regarded as only an educt, yet in the separation and recombination of this raw material we find an original capacity of selection and construction on the part of natural beings of this kind such as infinitely outdistances all the efforts of art, when the latter attempts to reconstitute those products of the vegetable kingdom out of the elements which it obtains through their analysis, or else out of the material which nature supplies for their nourishment.

Thirdly, a part of a tree also generates itself in such a way that the preservation of one part is reciprocally dependent on the preservation of the other parts. [. . .]

LXV
Things considered as physical ends are organisms

Where a thing is a product of nature and yet, so regarded, has to be cognized as possible only as a physical end, it must, from its character as set out in the preceding section, stand to itself reciprocally in the relation of cause and effect. This is, however, a somewhat inexact and indeterminate expression that needs derivation from a definite conception.

In so far as the causal connexion is thought merely by means of understanding it is a nexus constituting a series, namely of causes and effects, that is invariably progressive. The things that as effects presuppose others as their causes cannot themselves in turn be also causes of the latter. This causal connexion is termed that of efficient causes (*nexus effectivus*). On the other hand, however, we are also able to think a causal connexion according to a rational concept, that of ends, which, if regarded as a series, would involve regressive as well as progressive dependency. It would be one in which the thing that for the moment is designated effect deserves none the less, if we take the series regressively, to be called the cause of the thing of which it was said to be the effect. In the domain of practical matters, namely in art, we readily find examples of a nexus of this kind. Thus a house is certainly the cause of the money that is received as rent, but yet, conversely, the representation of this possible income was the cause of the building of the house. A causal nexus of this kind is termed that of final causes (*nexus finalis*). The former might, perhaps, more appropriately be called the nexus of real, and the latter the nexus of ideal causes, because with this use of terms it would be understood at once that there cannot be more than these two kinds of causality.

Now the *first* requisite of a thing, considered as a physical end, is that its parts, both as to their existence and form, are only possible by their relation to the whole. For the thing is itself an end, and is, therefore, comprehended under a conception or an idea that must determine *a priori* all that is to be contained in it. But so far as the possibility of a thing is only thought in this way, it is simply a work of art. It is the product, in other words, of an intelligent cause, distinct from the matter, or parts, of the thing, and of one whose causality, in bringing together and combining the parts, is determined by its idea of a whole made possible through that idea, and consequently, not by external nature.

But if a thing is a product of nature, and in this character is notwithstanding to contain intrinsically and in its inner possibility a relation to ends, in other words, is to be possible only as a physical end and independently of the causality of the conceptions of external rational agents, then this *second* requisite is involved, namely, that the parts of the thing combine of themselves into the unity of a whole by being reciprocally cause and effect of their form. For this is the only way in which it is possible that the idea of the whole may conversely, or reciprocally, determine in its turn the form and combination of all the parts, not as cause – for that would make it an art-product – but as the epistemological basis upon which the systematic unity of the form and combination of all the manifold contained in the given matter becomes cognizable for the person estimating it.

What we require, therefore, in the case of a body which in its intrinsic nature and inner possibility has to be estimated as a physical end, is as follows. Its parts must in their collective unity reciprocally produce one another alike as to form and combination, and thus by their own causality produce a whole, the conception of which, conversely, – in a being possessing the causality according to conceptions that is adequate for such a product – could in turn be the cause of the whole according to a principle, so that, consequently, the nexus of *efficient causes* might be no less estimated as an *operation brought about by final* causes.

In such a natural product as this every part is thought as *owing* its presence to the *agency* of all the remaining parts, and also as existing *for the sake of the others* and of the whole, that is as an instrument, or organ. But this is not enough – for it might be an instrument of art, and thus have no more than its general possibility referred to an end. On the contrary the part must be an organ *producing* the other parts – each consequently, reciprocally producing the others. No instrument of art can answer to this description, but only the instrument of that nature from whose resources the materials of every instrument are drawn – even the materials for instruments of art. Only under these conditions and upon these terms can such a product be an *organized* and *self-organized being*, and, as such, be called a *physical end*.

In a watch one part is the instrument by which the movement of the others is effected, but one wheel is not the efficient cause of the production of the other. One part is certainly present for the sake of another, but it does not owe its presence to the agency of that other. For this reason, also, the producing cause of the watch and its form is not contained in the nature of this material, but lies outside the watch in a being that can act according to ideas of a whole which its causality makes possible. Hence one wheel in the watch does not produce the other, and, still less, does one watch produce other watches, by utilizing, or organizing, foreign material; hence it does not of itself replace parts of which it has been deprived, nor, if these are absent in the original construction, does it make good the deficiency by the subvention of the rest; nor does it, so to speak, repair its own causal disorders. But these are all things which we are justified in expecting from organized nature. – An organized being is, therefore, not a mere machine. For a machine has solely *motive power*, whereas an organized being possesses inherent *formative* power, and such, moreover, as it can impart to material devoid of it – material which it organizes. This, therefore, is a selfpropagating formative power, which cannot be explained by the capacity of movement alone, that is to say, by mechanism.

We do not say half enough of nature and her capacity in organized products when we speak of this capacity as being the *analogue of art*. For what is here present to our minds is an artist – a rational being – working from without. But nature, on the contrary, organizes itself, and does so in each species of its organized products – following a single pattern, certainly, as to general features, but nevertheless admitting deviations calculated to secure self-preservation under particular circumstances. We might perhaps come nearer to the description of this impenetrable property if we were to call it an *analogue of life*. But then either we should have to endow matter as mere matter with a property (hylozoism) that contradicts its essential nature; or else we should have to associate with it a foreign principle *standing in community* with it (a soul). But, if such a product is to be a natural product, then we have to adopt one or other of two courses in order to bring in a soul. Either we must presuppose organized matter as the instrument of such a soul, which makes organized matter no whit more intelligible, or else we must make the soul the artificer of this structure, in which case we must withdraw the product from (corporal) nature. Strictly speaking, therefore, the organization of nature has nothing analogous to any causality known to us. Natural beauty may justly be termed the analogue of art, for it is only ascribed to the objects in respect of reflection upon the *external* intuition of them and, therefore, only on account of their superficial form. But *intrinsic natural perfection*, as possessed by things that are only possible as *physical ends*, and that are therefore called organisms, is unthinkable and inexplicable on any analogy to any known physical, or natural, agency, not even excepting – since we ourselves are part of nature in the widest sense – the suggestion of any strictly apt analogy to human art.

The concept of a thing as intrinsically a physical end is, therefore, not a constitutive conception either of understanding or of reason, but yet it may be used by reflective judgement as a regulative conception for guiding our investigation of objects of this kind by a remote analogy with our own causality according to ends generally, and as a basis of reflection upon their supreme source. But in the latter connexion it cannot be used to promote our knowledge either of nature or of such original source of those objects, but must on the contrary be confined to the service of just the same practical faculty of reason in analogy with which we considered the cause of the finality in question.

Organisms are, therefore, the only beings in nature that, considered in their separate existence and apart from any relation to other things, cannot be thought possible except as ends of nature. It is they, then, that first afford objective reality to the conception of an *end* that is an end *of nature* and not a practical end. Thus they supply natural science with the basis for a teleology, or, in other words, a mode of estimating its Objects on a special principle that it would otherwise be absolutely unjustifiable to introduce into that science – seeing that we are quite unable to perceive *a priori* the possibility of such a kind of causality.

LXVI
The principle on which the intrinsic finality in organisms is estimated

This principle, the statement of which serves to define what is meant by organisms, is as follows: *an organized natural product is one in which every part is reciprocally both end and means*. In such a product nothing is in vain, without an end, or to be ascribed to a blind mechanism of nature.

It is true that the occasion for adopting this principle must be derived from experience – from such experience, namely, as is methodically arranged and is called observation. But owing to the universality and necessity which that principle predicates of such finality, it cannot rest merely on empirical grounds, but must have some underlying *a priori* principle. This principle, however, may be one that is merely regulative, and it may be that the ends in question only reside in the idea of the person forming the estimate and not in any efficient cause whatever. Hence the above named principle may be called a *maxim* for estimating the intrinsic finality of organisms.

It is common knowledge that scientists who dissect plants and animals, seeking to investigate their structure and to see into the reasons why and the end for which they are provided with such and such parts, why the parts have such and such a position and interconnexion, and why the internal form is precisely what it is, adopt the above maxim as absolutely necessary. So they say that nothing in such forms of life is in *vain*, and they put the maxim on the same footing of validity as the fundamental principle of all natural science, that *nothing* happens *by chance*. They are, in fact, quite as unable to free themselves from this teleological principle as from that of general physical science. For just as the abandonment of the latter would leave them without any experience at all, so the abandonment of the former would leave them with no clue to assist their observation of a type of natural things that have once come to be thought under the conception of physical ends.

Indeed this conception leads reason into an order of things entirely different from that of a mere mechanism of nature, which *mere mechanism* no longer proves adequate in this domain. An idea has to underlie the possibility of the natural product. But this idea is an absolute unity of the representation, whereas the material is a plurality of things that of itself can afford no definite unity of composition. Hence, if that unity of the idea is actually to serve as the *a priori* determining ground of a natural law of the causality of such a form of the composite, the end of nature must be made to extend to *everything* contained in its product. For if once we lift such an effect out of the sphere of the blind mechanism of nature and relate it *as a whole* to a supersensible ground of determination, we must then estimate it out and out on this principle. We have no reason for assuming the form of such a thing to be still partly dependent on blind mechanism, for with such confusion of heterogeneous principles every reliable rule for estimating things would disappear.

It is no doubt the case that in an animal body, for example, many parts might be explained as accretions on simple mechanical laws (as skin, bone, hair). Yet the cause that accumulates the appropriate material, modifies and fashions it, and deposits it in its proper place, must always be estimated teleologically. Hence, everything in the body must be regarded as organized, and everything, also, in a certain relation to the thing is itself in turn an organ.

Note

1 The definition of taste here relied upon is that it is the faculty of estimating the beautiful. But the discovery of what is required for calling an object beautiful must be reserved for the analysis of judgements of taste. In my search for the moments to which attention is paid by this judgement in its reflection, I have followed the guidance of the logical functions of judging (for a judgement of taste always involves a reference to understanding). I have brought the moment of quality first under review, because this is what the aesthetic judgement on the beautiful looks to in the first instance.

Part II
Modern Theories

15

Introduction

Christopher Janaway

Christopher Janaway is Professor of Philosophy at the University of Southampton.

Immediately after Kant's *Critique of Judgement* (1790) – commonly regarded as the single most influential work in the field – aesthetics entered one of its most fertile periods. For Friedrich Schiller (1759–1805) art has an exalted role in human life because of its freedom from constraints of moral duty and physical need. Human beings have two essential drives, the material and the formal, and these are united in a 'play drive', manifest in art which in its freedom succeeds in uniting form and matter. An emphasis on freedom, autonomy, spontaneity, runs through the main movements of the day: early romanticism and German idealism. Art was seen as the prime arena for human self-expression and as important in the quest for a problematic union with nature and with society. In the early philosophical work of F. W. J. von Schelling (1775–1854) art is seen as uniquely unifying the conscious productivity of mind and the unconscious productivity of nature. But the most substantial and enduring contribution to aesthetics from this period of German idealism was the work of G. W. F. Hegel, principally in his *Lectures on Aesthetics* delivered in the 1820s. Art has a cognitive value for Hegel: it does what religion and ultimately philosophy do more perfectly, that is allow humans to attain self-understanding as freely self-determining conscious beings. Art's distinctive manner of achieving this is via the making of sensuous material objects. Hegel is much concerned with beauty, though unlike Kant he excludes from consideration the beauty of nature, because for him philosophy studies the development of the human mind or reason through history. Hegel's pronouncement that his topic is 'the beauty of art' fixes in place the confluence of interests that defined but also bedevilled philosophical aesthetics long afterwards.

For Hegel beauty in art is conceived neither in terms of mere form nor principally in terms of its giving pleasure: rather it is 'sensuous appearance of the idea', a manifestation of truth through some experienceable medium. Hegel not only gives a thorough systematic account of architecture, sculpture, painting, music and poetry, but provides a unified history of the development of the arts, embracing a wide range of epochs and cultures (including non-Western ones). This historical approach has been vastly influential on the practice of art history and criticism, and indeed on the practice of the arts to this day. Hegel divided the history of art into a pre-classical 'symbolic' phase, then the classical phase of the ancient Greeks, which he regarded as superior because of its attainment of unity between content

Christopher Janaway, "Introduction to Modern Theories," in *The Oxford Companion to Philosophy*, 2nd edition, ed. Ted Hondreich (New York and Oxford: Oxford University Press, 2005).

and sensory medium, and a third phase of romanticism which embraced medieval Christian art and the art of modernity. Art had already declined in the modern period, and must end, according to Hegel, superseded by religion and philosophy.

Two further German philosophers of the nineteenth century produced original aesthetic theories of lasting interest: Schopenhauer and Nietzsche. In *The World as Will and Representation* (1818) Schopenhauer developed one of the earliest 'aesthetic attitude' theories. Aesthetic experience is for him a suspension of the will, allowing the subject to enter a higher state of consciousness, freed from desire or interest towards the object of contemplation, and free of the suffering that attends willing. This state of peaceful elevation is of peculiar value to Schopenhauer because of his philosophical pessimism, the view that human individuals must strive and suffer without attaining any lasting or redeeming goals. Aesthetic experience is a temporary relief from the misery of an existence we would prefer not to have if we understood it properly. But Schopenhauer also attaches to the aesthetic state a supreme cognitive value, in that by freeing ourselves of will we free ourselves of subjective forms and achieve a purer knowledge, which he says is of Ideas, conceived in a Platonic manner. Art – treated here in a resolutely a historical manner – is of special value because through the work of a genius, who can suspend individual willing and merely perceive, we are enabled to experience reality more objectively. Schopenhauer gives accounts of the distinctive value of the different art forms. Of special note is his view that music is unique among the arts in dispensing with representation of Platonic Ideas and rather copying directly the movements of the will, of which, according to his metaphysics, the whole of reality consists.

In his early period Nietzsche was influenced by Schopenhauer, but he took seriously the more Hegelian emphasis on the historical development of the arts, imbued his theory with scholarship of the ancient world, and sought to promote the recent oeuvre of Richard Wagner as a model art form. The result of this mixture was Nietzsche's first book *The Birth of Tragedy* (1872). Nietzsche's central opposition here is between two Greek deities, Apollo and Dionysus, who have complex symbolic significance. Apollo is associated with sun, light, appearance, and clarity, Dionysus with trance, abandon, and ritual dance. Nietzsche takes them to symbolize natural forces or drives whose key-words are *dream* and *intoxication*. We have drives to immerse ourselves in an alternative world of appearance and beauty, and to lose our sense of self in a drunken transport or trance in which we become conscious of an identity with nature as a whole. The plastic arts and music respectively answer to these drives in their purest forms. But Nietzsche's central claim is that in tragic drama of the classical age in Athens these two creative drives became fused so as to create the perfect art form. Tragedy represents the individual in image, but uses the music and dance of the chorus to provide an identification with a greater unity, a viewpoint from which the suffering and destruction of the individual can be witnessed with fulfilment and joy. Nietzsche pronounces that 'it is only as an aesthetic phenomenon that existence and the world are eternally justified', in part because of a pessimism similar to Schopenhauer's: life itself is brief, painful and ultimately without point, so that only when transfigured by art is it something we can celebrate.

Nietzsche's narrative concludes with the claim that philosophy brought about the death of tragedy through the figure of Socrates, who held an optimistic view of human happiness and devalued anything for which there was not a rational explanation. Nietzsche's unorthodox book, which he himself more or less disowned in later years, was influential in revealing the expressive and irrational in Greek culture. More recently it has attained great resonance in postmodern critiques of traditional philosophy and its treatment of the arts. The later Nietzsche was preoccupied with a critique of post-Christian culture, including its morality, metaphysics and conception of truth. He produced no other systematic work in aesthetics, but regarded artistic creativity, with its licence to form fictions that disregard truth but affirm life, as paradigmatic of autonomous agency and value formation, so that in a sense his moral psychology and theory of value are at the same time contributions to the philosophy of art.

German philosophy continued its tradition of aesthetic theorizing into the twentieth century, where it emerged variously in the form of phenomenology, hermeneutics and Marxism. A unique body of work arising out of phenomenology is that of Martin Heidegger, whose 1936 essay 'The Origin of the Work of Art' is his most studied work in the philosophy of art. Heidegger was influenced by Hegel and Nietzsche, and by his reading of the poet Hölderlin. A preoccupation with art as revelatory of truth and frequent reference to Greek paradigms show continuity with Hegel, but Heidegger invents a quite new way of describing the work of art and what it does. It is for him a fundamental mistake characteristic of modernity to regard the work of art as a thing present in the world; rather, for Heidegger a work of art 'opens up a world' and is a 'happening of truth'. The being of things in our experience is 'unconcealed' by an art work: for example, a Van Gogh painting of peasant shoes allegedly 'lets us know what shoes are in truth'. Heidegger makes rich, quasi-poetic use of the concepts 'world' and 'earth', to convey that which opens itself to us in our lived experience of using 'equipment', and the firm but concealed basis on which human lives are lived. Art is a uniquely revelatory form of *poeisis* or 'bringing forth', for Heidegger, and fundamentally challenges traditional ontology and the technological conceptions of things that he criticizes in modernity. Hans-Georg Gadamer, a pupil of Heidegger, is the principal exponent of the tradition of hermeneutics, or theory of interpretation, in the German tradition. His *Truth and Method* (1960) seeks a conception of 'experience of truth' which is absent from traditional Kantian conceptions of aesthetic experience, and which sees the experience of art works as transformatory of our own self-understanding.

The most discussed writers in Marxist theoretical aesthetics are Walter Benjamin, whose essay 'The Work of Art in the Age of Mechanical Reproduction' (1936) is especially widely read, and Theodor Adorno, whose later work is woven from many influences apart from Marxism, including Kant, Hegel, Nietzsche, twentieth-century music – in which he was expert and on which he wrote sophisticated criticism – and aesthetic modernism more generally. Adorno analysed art works as commodities within Western capitalism, but also saw art as having the potential for an autonomy which enabled 'truth content' and a critical standpoint towards society. In his *Aesthetic Theory* (published posthumously in 1970) he adopts a complex dialectical approach, multiplying pairs of opposed concepts to describe art works from many perspectives.

In the English-speaking world the late nineteenth and early twentieth century saw the prevalence of aestheticism and formalism. Formalism in the visual arts was championed by Clive Bell, who in his book *Art* (1914) wrote that art was united by its having 'significant form', or 'a combination of lines and colours that moves me aesthetically'. In the case of music, formalism had found an earlier proponent in the work of Eduard Hanslick, whose influential book *On the Musically Beautiful* (1854) argued that music cannot express or represent emotions and consisted merely of the movement of tonal forms. Aestheticism arose out of specific artistic preoccupations in Victorian Britain, and is sloganized as the 'art for art's sake' movement, with Oscar Wilde one of its notable proponents. In 1912 Edward Bullough published an influential essay entitled '"Psychical Distance" as a Factor in Art and an Aesthetic Principle', in which he characterized the aesthetic attitude, using the central notion of distance, somewhat akin to the notion of disinterestedness that is traced back to Kant. These theories mirrored modernist developments in the various art forms, and reflected a tendency to secure autonomy for art by linking it with a conception of pure aesthetic experience. Such aesthetic theories had their opponents, most notably perhaps Leo Tolstoy in *What is Art?* (1898) and the American pragmatist John Dewey in *Art as Experience* (1934). Tolstoy rejected much of the celebrated art of his day because it did not fulfil his preferred criterion of communicating moral feeling between human beings. Dewey also accentuated the role of communication and opposed the notion of the single detached subject of aesthetic experience. In a highly developed though recently rather neglected theory, he sought a more comprehensive conception of art, opposing the separation of art from the rest of human experience, and viewing art – conceived more broadly than the traditional fine arts – as an activity productive of consummatory experience.

In *The Principles of Art* (1938) R. G. Collingwood, influenced by the Italian aesthetician Benedetto Croce with whom he is often linked, presents the view that 'art proper' is the expression of emotion. Some activities that are called art Collingwood relegates to the categories of amusement and 'magic', the latter being the arousal of emotions with social usefulness such as solidarity and religious allegiance, while amusement is the arousal of emotions for the sake simply of enjoying them. Collingwood opposes the conception of art as a craft or technique of arousing emotions by making representations, and regards representation as inessential to art. Expressing an emotion is quite distinct from arousing it; expression involves the authentic realization, through an artistic medium, of the emotion that one is feeling, and independently of this there can be no adequate characterization of what the expressed emotion is. Another original approach to the issue of emotion in art was made by the American philosopher Susanne Langer, who in *Philosophy in a New Key* (1942) and *Feeling and Form* (1953) conceived art as 'the creation of forms symbolic of human feeling'. For Langer, art does not express the artist's state of mind, but symbolizes feelings, using what she describes as 'non-discursive' or 'presentational' symbols.

16

Letter of an Aesthetic Education of Man

Friedrich Schiller

Friedrich Schiller (1759–1805) was a German dramatist, poet, and philosopher who stressed the importance of the aesthetic impulse and strongly influenced the development of German romanticism.

Twentieth Letter

1. That freedom cannot be affected by anything whatsoever follows from our very notion of freedom. But that freedom is itself an effect of Nature (this work taken in its widest sense) and not the work of Man, that it can, therefore, also be furthered or thwarted by natural means, follows no less inevitably [...] It arises only when man is a complete being, when both his fundamental drives [for form and matter] are fully developed; it will, therefore, be lacking as long as he is incomplete, as long as one of the two drives is excluded, and it should be capable of being restored by anything which gives him back his completeness.

2. Now we can, in fact, in the species as a whole as well as in the individual human being, point to a moment in which man is not yet complete, and in which one of his two drives is exclusively active within him. We know that he begins by being nothing but life, in order to end by becoming form; that he is an Individual before he is a Person, and that he proceeds from limitation to infinity. The sensuous drive, therefore, comes into operation earlier than the rational, because sensation precedes consciousness, and it is this priority of the sensuous drive which provides the clue to the whole history of human freedom.

3. For there is, after all, a moment in which the life-impulse, just because the form-impulse is not yet running counter to it, operates as nature and as necessity; a moment in which the life of sense is a power because man has not yet begun to be a human being; for in the human being proper there cannot exist any power other than the will. But in the state of reflection into which he is now to pass, it will be precisely the opposite: Reason is to be a power, and a logical or moral necessity to take the place of that physical necessity. Hence sensation as a power must first be destroyed before law can be enthroned as such. It is, therefore, not simply a matter of something beginning which was not there before; something which was there must first cease to be. Man cannot pass directly from feeling to thought; he must first take one step backwards, since only

Friedrich Schiller, "Twentieth Letter" and "Twenty-First Letter," in *On the Aesthetic Education of Man: In a Series of Letters*, ed. Elizabeth M. Wilkinson and L. A. Willoughby (Oxford: Clarendon Press, 1985).

through one determination being annulled again can a contrary determination take its place. In order to exchange passivity for autonomy, a passive determination for an active one, man must therefore be momentarily free of all determination whatsoever, and pass through a state of pure determinability. He must consequently, in a certain sense, return to that negative state of complete absence of determination in which he found himself before anything at all had made an impression upon his senses. But that former condition was completely devoid of content; and now it is a question of combining such sheer absence of determination, and an equally unlimited determinability, with the greatest possible content, since directly from this condition something positive is to result. The determination he has received through sensation must therefore be preserved, because there must be no loss of reality; but at the same time it must, inasmuch as it is limitation, be annulled, since an unlimited determinability is to come into existence. The problem is, therefore, at one and the same time to destroy and to maintain the determination of the condition – and this is possible in one way only: by confronting it with another determination. The scales of the balance stand level when they are empty; but they also stand level when they contain equal weights.

4. Our psyche passes, then, from sensation to thought *via* a middle disposition in which sense and reason are both active at the same time. Precisely for this reason, however, they cancel each other out as determining forces, and bring about a negation by means of an opposition. This middle disposition, in which the psyche is subject neither to physical nor to moral constraint, and yet is active in both these ways, pre-eminently deserves to be called a free disposition; and if we are to call the condition of sensuous determination the physical, and the condition of rational determination the logical or moral, then we call this condition of real and active determinability the aesthetic. [(For readers not altogether familiar with the precise meaning of this word, which is so much abused through ignorance, the following may serve as an explanation. Every thing which is capable of phenomenal manifestation may be thought of under four different aspects. A thing can relate directly to our sensual condition (to our being and well-being): that is its physical character. Or it can relate to our intellect, and afford us knowledge: that is its logical character. Or it can relate to our will, and be considered as an object of choice for a rational being: that is its moral character. Or, finally, it can relate to the totality of our various functions without being a definite object for any single one of them: that is its aesthetic character. A man can please us through his readiness to oblige; he can, through his discourse, give us food for thought; he can, through his character, fill us with respect; but finally he can also, independently of all this, and without our taking into consideration in judging him any law or any purpose, please us simply as we contemplate him and by the sheer manner of his being. Under this last-named quality of being we are judging him aesthetically. Thus there is an education to health, an education to understanding, an education to morality, an education to taste and beauty. This last has as its aim the development of the whole complex of our sensual and spiritual powers in the greatest possible harmony. Because, however, misled by false notions of taste and confirmed still further in this error by false reasoning, people are inclined to include in the notion of the aesthetic the notion of the arbitrary too, I add here the superfluous comment (despite the fact that these Letters on Aesthetic Education are concerned with virtually nothing else but the refutation of that very error) that our psyche in the aesthetic state does indeed act freely, is in the highest degree free from all compulsion, but is in no wise free from laws; and that this aesthetic freedom is distinguishable from logical necessity in thinking, or moral necessity in willing, only by the fact that the laws according to which the psyche then behaves do not become apparent as such, and since they encounter no resistance, never appear as a constraint.)]

Twenty-First Letter

1. There is, as I observed at the beginning of the last Letter, a twofold condition of determinability and a twofold condition of determination. I can now clarify this statement.

2. The psyche may be said to be determinable simply because it is not determined at all; but it is also determinable inasmuch as it is determined in a way which does not exclude anything, i.e., when the determination it undergoes is of a

kind which does not involve limitation. The former is mere indetermination (it is without limits, because it is without reality); the latter is aesthetic determinability (it has no limits, because it embraces all reality).

3. And the psyche may be said to be determined inasmuch as it is limited at all; but it is also determined inasmuch as it limits itself, by virtue of its own absolute power. It finds itself in the first of these two states whenever it feels; in the second, whenever it thinks. What thought is in respect of determination, therefore, the aesthetic disposition is in respect of determinability; the former is limitation by virtue of the infinite force within it, the latter is negation by virtue of the infinite abundance within it. Even as sensation and thought have one single point of contact – viz., that in both states the psyche is determined, and man is something, either individual or person, to the exclusion of all else – but in all other respects are poles apart: so, in like manner, aesthetic determinability has one single point of contact with mere indetermination – viz., that both exclude any determinate mode of existence – while in all other respects they are to each other as nothing is to everything, hence, utterly and entirely different. If therefore, the latter – indetermination through sheer absence of determination – was thought of as an empty infinity, then aesthetic freedom of determination, which is its counterpart in reality, must be regarded as an infinity filled with content: an idea which accords completely with the results of the foregoing inquiry.

4. In the aesthetic state, then, man is Nought, if we are thinking of any particular result rather than of the totality of his powers, and considering the absence in him of any specific determination. Hence we must allow that those people are entirely right who declare beauty, and the mood it induces in us, to be completely indifferent and unfruitful as regards either knowledge or character. They are entirely right; for beauty produces no particular result whatsoever, neither for the understanding nor for the will. It accomplishes no particular purpose, neither intellectual nor moral; it discovers no individual truth, helps us to perform no individual duty and is, in short, as unfitted to provide a firm basis for character as to enlighten the understanding. By means of aesthetic culture, therefore, the personal worth of a man, or his dignity, inasmuch as this can depend solely upon himself, remains completely indeterminate; and nothing more is achieved by it than that he is henceforth enabled by the grace of Nature to make of himself what he will – that the freedom to be what he ought to be is completely restored to him.

5. But precisely thereby something Infinite is achieved. For as soon as we recall that it was precisely of this freedom that he was deprived by the one-sided constraint of nature in the field of sensation and by the exclusive authority of reason in the realm of thought, then we are bound to consider the power which is restored to him in the aesthetic mode as the highest of all bounties, as the gift of humanity itself. True, he possesses this humanity *in potentia* before every determinate condition into which he can conceivably enter. But he loses it in practice with every determinate condition into which he does enter. And if he is to pass into a condition of an opposite nature, this humanity must be restored to him each time anew through the life of the aesthetic. (Admittedly the rapidity with which certain types pass from sensation to thought or decision scarcely – if indeed at all – allows them to become aware of the aesthetic mode through which they must in that time necessarily pass. Such natures cannot for any length of time tolerate the state of indetermination, but press impatiently for some result which in the state of aesthetic limitlessness they cannot find. In others, by contrast, who find enjoyment more in the feeling of total capacity than in any single action, the aesthetic state tends to spread itself over a much wider area. Much as the former dread emptiness, just as little are the latter capable of tolerating limitation. I need scarcely say that the former are born for detail and subordinate occupations, the latter, provided they combine this capacity with a sense of reality, destined for wholeness and for great roles.)

6. It is, then, not just poetic licence but philosophical truth when we call beauty our second creatress. For although it only offers us the possibility of becoming human beings, and for the rest leaves it to our own free will to decide how far we wish to make this a reality, it does in this resemble our first creatress, Nature, which likewise conferred upon us nothing more than the power of becoming human, leaving the use and practice of that power to our own free will and decision.

17

Philosophy of Art

Friedrich Wilhelm Joseph von Schelling

Friedrich Wilhelm Joseph von Schelling (1775–1854), the leading philosopher of German romanticism, maintained that art is the highest manifestation of intelligence.

Introduction

The methodical study or science of art can first of all mean the historical construction of art. In this sense it requires as its necessary external condition the direct evaluation of extant monuments and examples. Since such evaluation is generally possible with regard to literary works, such science in this regard, as philology, is expressly included among the objects of academic discussion. In spite of this, nothing is taught less often at universities than philology in this sense, though this cannot surprise us, since philology is just as much an art as is poesy, and the philologist no less than the poet must be born, not made.

The idea of a historical construction of the works of the formative arts is even rarer in universities, since it is robbed of any direct observation of such works. Even where such lectures are attempted for the sake of honor and with the support of a rich library, they automatically restrict themselves to merely scholarly knowledge of art history.

Friedrich Wilhelm Joseph von Schelling, *The Philosophy of Art*, trans. Douglas W. Scott (Minneapolis: University of Minnesota Press, 1989).

Since universities are not art schools, the science of art in a practical or technical sense can be taught there with even less justification.

Thus only the completely speculative science is left, one not directed toward the cultivation of the empirical intuition of art, but rather of its intellectual intuition. Yet just this constitutes the prerequisite for a philosophical construction of art, one against which significant doubts can be raised from the side of both philosophy and art.

In the first place, should the philosopher, whose intellectual intuition should be directed only toward that particular truth that is concealed to sensual eyes, unattainable and accessible only to the spirit itself – should that philosopher concern himself with the science of art? For the latter intends only the production of beautiful appearances, and either shows merely the deceiving, reflected images of the same or is totally sensual. This is how the majority of people understand art, viewing it as sensual stimulation, as recreation, as relaxation for a spirit fatigued by more serious matters and as a pleasant stimulant, one with the advantage of occurring through a more delicate medium. For the judgment of the philosopher, however, who in addition must view it as an effect of sensual impulse or desire, it thereby acquires the even more objectionable imprint of corruption and civilization. According to this view, only through absolute condemnation might philosophy distinguish itself from the flaccid sensuality art tolerates in this respect.

I am speaking of a more sacred art, one that in the words of antiquity is a tool of the gods, a proclaimer of divine mysteries, the unveiler of the ideas; I am speaking of that unborn beauty whose undesecrated radiance only dwells in and illuminates purer souls, and whose form is just as concealed and inaccessible to the sensual eye as is the truth corresponding to it. Nothing of that which a baser sensibility calls art can concern the philosopher. For him it is a necessary phenomenon emanating directly from the absolute, and only to the extent it can be presented and proved as such does it possess reality for him.

But did not even the divine Plato condemn imitative art in his *Republic*, and ban poets from his state of reason not only as useless members but as pernicious as well, and can any authority be more persuasive for the incompatibility of poesy and philosophy than this judgment of the king of philosophers?

It is essential that we recognize the particular standpoint from which Plato speaks this judgment on poets. If any philosopher observed the careful distinction between points of view, he did, and as is the case everywhere, without such differentiation it would be impossible, especially here, to comprehend all the ramifications of his meaning or to unite the contradictions in his works concerning the same topic. We must first resolve to understand the higher philosophy, and that of Plato in particular, as the decisive opposing factor within Greek culture with respect not only to the sensual concepts of religion but also to the objective and thoroughly real forms of the state. An answer to the question of whether in a completely ideal and, in a sense, inner state such as the Platonic one there might be other ways of speaking about poesy, and whether that restriction he imposes might not be a necessary one – this answer would lead us too far astray here. That particular opposition of all public institutions against philosophy necessarily had to elicit a similar opposition of the latter toward the former, and Plato is neither the earliest nor the only example of this. From Pythagoras onward, and even further back, down to Plato, philosophy perceived itself as an exotic plant in Greek soil, and this feeling expressed itself among other places in the universal impulse leading those initiated into higher teachings – either through the wisdom of earlier philosophers on through the mysteries – back to the birthplace of the ideas, namely, the Orient.

Yet aside from this merely historical, not philosophical, opposition, an opposition philosophers readily admit, what is Plato's rejection of the poetic arts – compared particularly with what he says in other works in praise of enthusiastic poesy – other than a polemic against poetic realism, a foreboding of that later inclination of the spirit in general and of poesy in particular? That judgment could be applied least of all to Christian poesy, which on the whole just as decisively displays the character of the infinite as the poesy of antiquity as a whole displays that of the finite. We owe it to the experience of subsequent ages that we can determine the limits of the latter more exactly than could Plato, who was not acquainted with its opposite. For just that reason we are able to elevate ourselves to a more comprehensive understanding and construction of poesy than he. That which he saw as the objectionable element in the poesy of his age we refer to only as its beautiful limitations, and we see it as the fulfillment of what Plato foresaw but did not experience. The Christian religion, and with it a sensibility directed toward the intellectual and ideal – a sensibility that in the poesy of antiquity could find neither its full satisfaction nor even the means for portrayal – created its own poesy and art in which such sensibility could find satisfaction. This creates the conditions for a complete and totally objective view of art, including that of antiquity.

This shows clearly that the construction of that art is a worthy object not only of the philosopher as such but of the Christian philosopher in particular, who should make it his concern to measure and present the universe of that art.

Viewing things from the other side, we must ask whether the philosopher for his own part is suited to penetrate the essence of art and to portray it with truth.

Who can, I already hear being asked, speak worthily of that divine principle driving the artist, and of that spiritual breath animating his works, other than he who is himself possessed by this sacred flame? Can one really attempt to subject to construction that which is just as incomprehensible in its origin as it is miraculous in its effects? Can one claim to subsume and to determine according to laws that whose essence is precisely to recognize no law other than itself? Or cannot genius be comprehended by concepts just as little as it can be created through methodical principles? Who dares to claim actual insights into that which is obviously the most free and absolute element in the entire universe? Or to claim an expansion of his own mental horizon beyond the ultimate boundaries in order to establish yet newer boundaries there?

Such could speak a certain enthusiasm that had comprehended art only in its effects, and which was genuinely acquainted neither with art itself nor with the position given to philosophy in the universe. Even assuming that art is not comprehensible from any higher perspective, that law of the universe which decrees that everything encompassed by it have its prototype of reflex in something else is so pervasive and so omnipotent, and the form of the universal juxtaposition of the real and the ideal is so absolute, that even at the ultimate boundaries of the infinite and the finite, where the contradictions of phenomenal appearance disappear into the purest absoluteness, the same relationship asserts its rights and recurs in the final potence. This is the relationship between philosophy and art.

The ultimate, albeit completely absolute, and perfect informing into unity of the real and the ideal is itself related to philosophy as the real to the ideal. In the latter the final contradiction of knowledge resolves itself into pure identity, and nonetheless it too, in its antithesis to art, always remains only ideal. Hence, both encounter one another on the final pinnacle, and precisely by virtue of that common absoluteness are for one another both prototype and reflex. This is the reason no sensibility can penetrate scientifically more deeply into the interior of art than that of philosophy; indeed, this is why the philosopher possesses better vision within the essence of art than does the artist himself. Insofar as the ideal is always a higher reflex of the real, the philosopher necessarily possesses an even higher ideal reflex of that which in the artist is real. This indicates not only in a larger sense that art can become the object of knowledge in philosophy, but more specifically that outside of philosophy and other than through philosophy, nothing can be known about art in an absolute fashion.

Since in the artist the same principle is objective that in the philosopher reflects itself subjectively, he thus does not relate to that principle subjectively or consciously – though he, too, could become conscious of it through a higher reflex. He is not, however, conscious of it in the quality of being an artist. As such he is driven by that principle and for just that reason does not himself possess it. When he does achieve the standpoint of the ideal reflex with regards to that principle, he thereby elevates himself as an artist to a higher potence, yet as an artist still always relates to it *objectively*. The subjective element within him passes over again to the objective element, just as in the philosopher the objective element is constantly taken up into the subjective one. For this reason philosophy, notwithstanding its inner identity with art, is nonetheless always and necessarily science, that is, ideal, whereas art is always and necessarily art, that is, real.

Hence, the way in which the philosopher is thus able to pursue art even into its secret primal source and into the first workshop of its production is incomprehensible only from the purely objective standpoint, or from that of a philosophy that does not achieve the same heights within the ideal as does art within the real. The particular rules that genius is able to cast off are only those that a merely mechanical understanding may prescribe. Genius is autonomous, yet it escapes only external determination by laws, not determination by its own laws, since it is only genius insofar as it actually constitutes the highest law-governed qualities. Yet it is precisely this absolute legislation that philosophy recognizes in it. It is not only itself autonomous but also penetrates through to the principle of all autonomy. Thus in all ages it has been evident that the true artists are self-contained, simple, great, and necessary in their own fashion, just as is nature. That enthusiasm that sees in them nothing but genius unfettered by rules itself emerges first only through reflection, which recognizes only the negative side of genius. It is a derivative enthusiasm, not that which inspires the artist and which in its godlike freedom is simultaneously the purest and highest necessity.

Yet even if the philosopher is best suited for presenting the unfathomable quality of art, and for recognizing the absolute within it, will he be just as skilled at comprehending that which really is comprehensible within it and in determining it according to laws? I mean the technical side of art: will philosophy be able to lower itself to the empirical sphere of execution and of the medium itself and the conditions for execution?

Philosophy, which concerns itself only with ideas, must present only the general laws of phenomenal appearance as regards the empirical side of art, and must present these only in the form of ideas, for the forms of art are the essential forms of things as they are in the archetypes. Hence, to the extent that these can be comprehended universally and from the perspective of the universe in and for itself, their presentation is a necessary part of the philosophy of art, not, however, to the extent that they encompass rules for the execution and the practice of art. Philosophy of art in the larger sense is the presentation of the absolute world in the form of art. Only theory concerns itself directly with the particular or with a goal, and only according to theory can a project be executed empirically. In contrast, philosophy is totally unconditioned and without external purpose. Even if one were to object that the technical side of art is that whereby it acquires the appearance of truth, the concern for which might then fall to the philosopher, this truth is nonetheless merely empirical. That which the philosopher must recognize and present in it is of a higher sort, and is one and the same with absolute beauty: the truth of the ideas.

The situation of contradiction and dissension, even concerning the primary concepts, in which artistic judgment must necessarily find itself in an age that wishes to reopen the exhausted sources of art, makes it doubly desirable that the absolute view of art be carried through in a methodical, scientific fashion also as regards the forms in which art expresses itself, from the first principles onward. As long as this has not been done, a limited, one-sided, and capricious view will persist both in judgment and in demands, alongside what is already base and vulgar in and of itself.

The construction of art in each of its specific forms all the way into the concrete leads of itself to the determination of art through temporal conditions, and thus passes over into historical construction. One can doubt neither the possibility of such a construction nor its expansion to include the entire history of art; that is, such doubt is removed when the pervasive dualism of the universe in the antithesis between ancient and modern art has been presented in this area as well and has been thoroughly validated partly through the organ of poesy itself, partly through criticism. Since construction as such is the suspension of antitheses, and since those that obtain regarding art through its temporal dependency must, like time itself, be nonessential and merely formal, then scientific construction will consist in the presentation of the common unity from which these features have emanated, and thus will elevate itself above them to a more comprehensive viewpoint.

Such a construction of art can by no means be compared with anything that has existed up to the present under the name of aesthetics, theory of the fine arts and sciences, or any other designation. In the most general principles of the first founder of that designation there still inhered at least the trace of the idea of the beautiful as that archetypal element appearing in the concrete and reflected world. Since then this designation has acquired an ever more definite dependency on the moral and useful, just as in psychological theories certain phenomena have been explained away more or less like ghost stories or similar superstitions, until Kantian formalism, following upon all this, bore a new and higher view, though also a host of artistically empty doctrines of art.

The seeds of a genuine methodical presentation or science of art that excellent spirits have sown since then have not yet structured themselves into a scientific whole – something they do, however, lead us to expect. The philosophy of art is a necessary goal of the philosopher, who in art views the inner essence of his own discipline as if in a magic and symbolic mirror. As a science it is important to him in and for itself, just as is, for example, the philosophy of nature, as the construction of the most remarkable of all products and phenomenal appearances, or as the construction of a world as self-enclosed and as perfect as nature itself. Through such philosophy the inspired natural scientist learns to recognize symbolically or emblematically the true archetypes of forms in works of art, archetypes he finds expressed only in a confused fashion in nature: through such works of art themselves he learns to recognize symbolically the way sensual things emerge from those archetypes.

The inner bond uniting art and religion – the total impossibility on the one hand of giving the former any other poetic world than within and through religion, and the impossibility on the other hand of bringing the latter to any true objective manifestation other than through art – makes the scientific knowledge of art in this respect a necessity for the genuinely religious person.

Finally, it is shameful for anyone either directly or indirectly involved in state government to have neither receptivity for art nor any true knowledge of it. Just as nothing is more honorable for princes and those in power than to value and appreciate the arts, to respect artistic works, and to elicit them through encouragement, nothing, in contrast, is more grievous and disgraceful than for those who have the means to promote art to its highest fruition to squander such means on tastelessness, barbarianism, or ingratiating baseness. Even if not everyone can comprehend that art is a necessary and integral part of a state constitution conceived according to ideas, at least antiquity should remind us of this fact, for the universal festivals of antiquity, its immortalizing monuments and plays, as well as all the actions of public life were merely the different branches of *one* universal, objective, and living work of art.

During the following lectures, I would like for you constantly to keep in mind their purely scientific intentions. Just as in the case of all other scientific or methodical investigations, so also is the science of art interesting *in itself* and without any external purpose. So many unimportant objects attract the attention of our desire for knowledge and even the attention of scientific investigation – how utterly peculiar if art itself were not able to do so, this *one* object that almost by itself encompasses the loftiest objects of our admiration.

That person is still lagging far behind for whom art has not yet appeared just as unified, organic, and in all its parts necessary a whole as does nature. If we feel perpetually moved to view the inner essence of nature and to discover that fertile source that generates so many great phenomena with eternal consistency of form and regularity, how much more must it interest us to penetrate the organism of art, which generates the highest unity and regularity and reveals to us far more directly than does nature the miracles of our own spirit? If we are interested in tracing as far as possible the structure, inner disposition, relationships, and intricacies of a plant or of an organic being in general, how much more alluring must it be for us to recognize the same intricacies and relationships in the much more highly organized and complex growths that we call works of art?

Most people have the same experience with art as Molière's Monsieur Jourdain had with prose: he was astonished to find he had spoken prose his whole life without even knowing it. Very few people realize that even the language in which they express themselves is the most perfect work of art. How many people have stood before a theater without asking themselves even once just how many conditions are necessary to ensure even a relatively successful theatrical production? How many have enjoyed the noble effect of beautiful architecture without ever being tempted to retrace the source of the harmony therein that addresses them? How many have been affected by a poem or by a sublime dramatic piece, have been moved by it, enchanted, or stirred without ever looking to see by what means the artist has succeeded in dominating their disposition, cleansing their soul, and exciting their innermost being – without ever thinking of transforming this completely passive and to that extent rather lowly pleasure into the much more sublime pleasure of active perception and reconstruction of the work of art by the understanding!

We consider crude and uncultured any person who does not *everywhere* allow art to flow over and affect him. It is, however, while perhaps not to the same degree, nonetheless in the same spirit just as crude if the merely sensual feelings, responses, and pleasure elicited by works of art are taken to be the effects of art as such.

All effects of art are merely effects of nature for the person who has not attained a perception of art that is free, that is, one that is both passive and active, both swept away and reflective. Such a person behaves merely as a creature of nature and has never really experienced and appreciated art as art. What moves him are perhaps individual moments of beauty, while in the true work of art there is no individualized beauty; only the whole is beautiful. The person who has not yet elevated himself to the idea of the *whole* is totally incapable of evaluating a work of art. Yet in spite of this indifference, the majority of those who consider themselves cultured are most prone to display their judgment in matters of art and to play the connoisseur; rarely is a negative judgment more painful for them than the accusation that they have no taste at all. Those who sense a weakness in their own judgment would rather withhold judgment entirely – regardless of how decisively a work of art affects them or how original their view of it may well be – than expose that weakness. Others, those who are less modest, make fools of themselves with their judgment or annoy those who do understand. It is therefore an integral part of one's general social education – since there is in any case no realm of study that is more social than that of art – to acquire a methodical and well-founded knowledge of art, to cultivate the ability to comprehend the *idea* or the whole as well as the mutual relationships between the various parts and between those parts and the whole. Yet this is possible only through *science*, and specifically through philosophy. The more strictly one construes the idea both of art and of the work of art, the more strictly can one provide a corrective both for the laxity of judgement and for those thoughtless attempts made in art or poesy usually undertaken without any idea of what art actually is.

In what follows I want to indicate briefly just how necessary precisely this kind of strictly methodical view of art is for the cultivation of the intellectual intuition of a work of art as well as for the cultivation of artistic judgement itself.

Very often, particularly nowadays, one finds that even artists themselves disagree in their judgement; indeed they often hold completely opposite opinions in matters of art. This phenomenon can be easily explained. In periods in which art flourishes, the necessity of the generally dominant spirit of the time, fortunate circumstances, and what one might call the springtime of the age generate more or less a common, fundamental agreement among the great masters. As the history of art shows, this causes the great works of art to arise and mature virtually on one another's heels, almost simultaneously, as if animated by a common breath of life beneath a common sun: Albrecht Dürer simultaneous with Raphael, Cervantes and Calderón simultaneous with Shakespeare. When such a fortunate age of pure production has passed, reflection enters, and with it an element of estrangement. What was earlier living spirit is now transmitted theory.

The inclination of the artists of antiquity proceeded from the center out toward the periphery. Later artists take the externally extracted form and seek to imitate it, retaining the shadow without the body. Each forms his own particular point of view regarding art and employs it to evaluate even existing art. Those who notice the emptiness of form without content preach the return to substantiality by means of imitation of nature. Those who cannot elevate themselves above that empty and vacant external extraction of form preach the ideal, the imitation of what has already been formed. None, however, returns to the true primal sources of art from which form and substance issue together as one. This is more or less the present situation of art and of artistic judgment. As multifarious as art is within itself, so also are the various viewpoints of artistic evaluation multifarious and full of nuances. None of the disputants understands the others. The one judges according to the standard of truth, the other according to that of beauty; yet neither knows what truth or beauty is. With few exceptions, one can learn very little about the essence of art from those who actually practice art in such an age, since as a rule they have no guide concerning the actual idea of art and of beauty. Precisely this dominant disagreement even among those who practice art is a compelling reason for seeking the true idea and principles of art itself by means of science.

A serious study of art based on ideas is even more necessary in this age of literary peasant wars, wars conducted against all that is sublime, great, or ideal, indeed against beauty itself in poesy and art, an age in which the frivolous, the sensually provocative, or nobly base are the idols to which the greatest reverence is paid.

Only philosophy can reopen the primal sources of art for reflection, sources that for the most part no longer nourish production. Only through philosophy can we hope to attain a true science of art. Philosophy cannot lend meaning to art; only a god can do that. It cannot bestow artistic sensibility on someone to whom nature has already denied such sensibility.

Philosophy can, however, express immutably in ideas that which true artistic sensibility actually intuits in the concrete work of art, and can disclose those factors determining genuine artistic judgement.

I think it is appropriate that I also indicate which *specific* factors have prompted me not only to study this science but also to give these lectures.

Above all I request that you not confuse this science of art with anything previously presented under this or any other title as aesthetics or as a theory of the fine arts and sciences. There does not yet exist anywhere a scientific and philosophical doctrine of art. At most only fragments of such a doctrine exist, and even these are little understood and can be comprehended only within the context of the whole.

All pre-Kantian doctrines of art in Germany were merely children of Baumgarten's *Aesthetica*, since the latter was the first to employ the term aesthetics. It suffices merely to point out that this aesthetics was in its own turn an offspring of Wolffian philosophy. In the period immediately preceding Kant, a period in which shallow popularity and philosophical empiricism held sway, various well-known theories of the fine arts and sciences were proposed, theories whose foundations were the psychological principles of the English and the French. One tried to explain beauty using empirical psychology, and in general treated the miracles of art the same way one treated ghost stories and other superstitions: by enlightening us and explaining them away. We still encounter fragments of this empiricism even in later writings, writings that at least in part have been conceived according to a much more sophisticated point of view.

Other aesthetics are virtual recipes or cookbooks in which the recipe for a tragedy reads approximately as follows: a great deal of fright, but not too much; as much sympathy as possible, and tears without end.

Kant's *Critique of Judgment* experienced the same fate as his other writings. From the Kantians themselves one could naturally expect the most extreme tastelessness, just as one could expect complete sterility of spirit in their philosophy. A multitude of people learned the *Critique of Judgment* by heart and then presented it both from the lectern and in writing as aesthetics.

After Kant a few excellent minds provided us with some admirable points of departure for the idea of a genuine philosophical science of art and even with various contributions to such a science. No one, however, has yet brought forth a scientifically constructed whole or even the *absolute* principles themselves, principles that would be universally valid and presented in a consistent, strict form. Furthermore, many of these people have not yet rigorously separated empiricism from philosophy, a separation absolutely necessary for true scientific investigation.

The system of the philosophy of art that I intend to present here will thus differentiate itself fundamentally from the previous systems, and will do so as regards both form and content; I will retrace even the principles themselves further back than has hitherto been the case. The method by which, if I am not mistaken, my philosophy of nature has been able to unravel the intricately entwined web of nature to a certain extent and to order the chaos of its phenomena – this same method will guide us through the even more labyrinthine entwinements of the world of art and will illuminate anew the objects of that world.

I can be less sure of satisfying my own demands regarding the *historical* side of art, a side that as I will explain later, is an essential element of any construction. I recognize too well how difficult it is in this most infinite of all areas to acquire even the most general knowledge of each part, not to speak of acquiring the most pointed and specific knowledge about all of those parts. The only thing I can claim for myself is that I have long been engaged in serious study of both ancient and contemporary works of poesy, and that I have made it my most earnest business to acquire some acquaintance and views regarding works of the plastic arts. I have spent time with actual practicing artists, and must admit that I have in part become acquainted only with their own disagreement and lack of understanding of the matter at hand; yet I have also spent time with those who besides having been successful in their artistic endeavors have also considered their art philosophically. From all these I have acquired at least a part of the historical background I consider necessary for my present purpose.

For those already acquainted with my system of philosophy, the philosophy of art will be merely the repetition of that same philosophy in the highest potence. For those not yet acquainted with it, its method as I employ it in the present context will be perhaps even more obvious and clear.

The construction will encompass not merely generalities, but will also extend to those individuals who represent an entire genre. I will construe both them and the world of their poesy. For now I will mention only Homer, Dante, and Shakespeare. In the discussion of the formative or plastic arts the personalities of the greatest masters will be discussed in a general sense. In the discussion of poesy and poetic genres I will even progress as far as a characterization of individual works of the most preeminent poets, for example, Shakespeare, Cervantes, and Goethe, so as to provide the contemporary view of those poets that is as yet still lacking.

In general philosophy we are fortunate to view the stern countenance of truth in and for itself. In the particular sphere of philosophy circumscribing the philosophy of art we attain to an intuition of eternal beauty and of the archetypes of all that is beautiful.

Philosophy is the basis of everything, encompasses everything, and extends its constructions to all potences and objects of knowledge. Only through it does one have access to the highest. By means of the doctrine of art an even smaller circle is formed within philosophy itself, one in which we view more immediately the eternal in a visible form, as it were. Hence, the doctrine of art, properly understood, is in complete agreement with philosophy.

A hint at what the philosophy of art actually is has in part already been suggested in our discussion. It is necessary, however, that I now explain myself more specifically in this regard. I will pose the question in the most general terms: *how is the philosophy of art possible?* (Proof of possibility as regards science is also proof of its reality.)

Anyone can see that the concept of a philosophy of art combines antithetical elements. Art is real and objective, philosophy ideal and subjective. We might thus define in advance the task of the philosophy of art as *the presentation in the ideal medium of the real element inherent in art.* Of course, the question is then precisely what it means to present *something real in the ideal*; before we know this, we have not yet sufficiently clarified our concept of the philosophy of art. Hence, we must address the investigation on an even deeper level. Since presentation within an ideal medium in general = construction, and hence also the philosophy of art should = construction of art, this investigation will of necessity simultaneously have to penetrate more deeply into the nature of construction itself. [. . .]

In the philosophy of art I accordingly intend to construe first of all not art *as* art, as this *particular*, but rather *the universe in the form of art*, and the philosophy of art is *the science of the All in the form or potence of art.* Not until we have taken this step do we elevate ourselves regarding this science to the level of an absolute science of art.

The assertion that the philosophy of art is the presentation of the universe in the form of art does not yet, however, give us any complete idea of this science; we must specify more closely the *mode* of construction necessary for a philosophy of art.

An object of construction and thereby of philosophy is essentially only that which is capable as a particular of taking up the infinite into itself. Therefore, art, in order to be the object of philosophy, must as such either genuinely represent the infinite within itself as the particular, or must be capable of doing so. Not only does this actually take place as regards art, but it also stands as a representation of the infinite on the same level with philosophy; just as philosophy presents the absolute in the *archetype* so also does art present the absolute in a *reflex* or *reflected image.*

Since art exactly corresponds to philosophy and is merely the latter's complete objective reflex, it must also proceed through all the potences within the real as does philosophy in the ideal. This one fact suffices to remove all doubt regarding the necessary method of our science.

Philosophy does not present real things, but rather only their archetypes; the same holds true for art. The same archetypes that according to philosophy are merely reproduced imperfectly by these (the real things) are those that become objective in art itself – as archetypes and accordingly in their perfection. They thus represent the intellectual world in the reflected world. As examples we might take *music*, which is nothing other than the primal rhythm of nature and of the universe itself, which by means of this art breaks through into the world of representation. The complete forms generated by the *plastic* arts are the objectively portrayed archetypes of organic nature itself. The Homeric epic is identity itself as this identity lies at the base of history within the absolute. Every painting discloses the intellectual world.

Given these assertions, in the philosophy of art we will have all those problems to solve regarding art that we also must solve in general philosophy regarding the universe.

(1) In the philosophy of art, no principle other than that of the infinite can serve as our point of departure; hence, we must present the infinite as the unconditioned principle of art. Just as for philosophy in general the absolute is the archetype of truth, so also for art is it the archetype of *beauty*. We must therefore show that truth and beauty are merely two different ways of viewing the one absolute.

(2) The second question, both as regards philosophy as such as well as the philosophy of art, will be just how this principle, a principle that is in and for itself absolutely one and simple, can pass over into multiplicity and differentiation, and thus how individual beautiful things can issue from universal and absolute beauty. Philosophy answers this question with the doctrine of the ideas or archetypes. The absolute is absolutely one; viewed absolutely in particular forms, however, such that the absolute is thereby not suspended, this one = idea. The same holds true for art. It, too, views or intuits primal beauty only in ideas as particular forms, each of which, however, is divine and absolute for itself. Whereas philosophy intuits these ideas as they are *in themselves,* art intuits them *objectively*. The *ideas,* to the extent that they are intuited objectively, are therefore the substance and as it were the universal and absolute material of art from which all particular works of art emerge as mature entities. These *real* or *objective,* living and existing ideas are the gods. The universal symbolism or universal *representation* of the *ideas* as real is thus given in mythology, and the solution to the second aforementioned task consists in the construction of mythology. Indeed, the gods of any mythology are nothing other than the ideas of philosophy intuited objectively or concretely.

This still does not answer the question of how a *real,* individual work of art comes to be. Just as the absolute or unreal is always characterized by the condition of identity, so also is the real always characterized by the nonidentity of the universal and the particular, by disjunction, such that either the particular or universal predominates. An antithesis thus arises here, one between plastic or formative art on the one hand, and verbal art on the other. Formative and verbal art = the real and ideal series of philosophy. The former is characterized by that unity in which the infinite is taken up into the finite, and the construction of this series corresponds to the *philosophy of nature*. The latter is characterized by the other unity, the one in which the finite is formed into the infinite, and the construction of this series corresponds to *idealism* in the general system of philosophy. I will call the first unity the real unity, the second the ideal unity; that which encompasses both I will call indifference.

If we now concentrate on each of these unities individually, then, since each is absolute for itself, the same unities must recur in each; hence, the real unity, the ideal unity, and that in which both are one must all recur in the real unity itself. The same holds true for the ideal unity.

A particular form of art corresponds to each of these forms to the extent that they are encompassed within the real or ideal unity. *Music* corresponds to the real form within the real series. *Paining* corresponds to the ideal form within the real series. The *plastic arts* correspond to that form within the real series that represents the confluence of the previous two unities.

The same holds true as regards the ideal unity, which in its own turn encompasses within itself the three forms of lyric, epic, and dramatic poetry. Lyric poetry = the informing of the infinite into the finite = the particular. The epic = the representation (subsumption) of the finite within the infinite = the universal. Drama = the synthesis of the universal and the particular. Hence, the entire world of art is to be construed according to these basic forms both in its real and ideal manifestation.

By tracing art in each of its particular forms all the way into the concrete, we also arrive at a determination of art within the conditions of time. Just as art is inherently eternal and necessary, so also is there no fortuitousness in its temporal manifestation, but rather only absolute necessity. In this respect, too, it is the object of possible knowledge, and the elements of this construction are given in the antitheses manifested in art in its temporal appearance. Any antitheses posited as regards art in its temporal dependence, however, are, as is time itself, necessarily nonessential and merely formal antitheses; hence, they are completely different from those *real antitheses* grounded in the essence or in the idea of art itself. This universal, formal antithesis extending through all branches of art is that of *ancient* and *modern* art.

It would be an essential weakness of our construction if we were to neglect the consideration of this antithesis in our discussion of each individual form of art. Since, however, we consider this antithesis to be a merely formal one, its construction necessarily consists in negation or suspension. By considering this antithesis, we will simultaneously present the *historical* dimension of art; only by this means can we hope to bring our construction in the larger sense to its final completion.

According to my entire understanding here, art is itself an emanation of the absolute. The history of art will show us most revealingly its immediate connections to the conditions of the universe and thereby to that absolute identity in which art is preordained. Only in the history of art does the essential and inner unity of all works of art reveal itself, a unity showing that all poetry is of the same spirit, a spirit that even in the antitheses of ancient and modern art is merely showing us two different faces.

18

The Philosophy of Fine Art

Georg Wilhelm Friedrich Hegel

Georg Wilhelm Friedrich Hegel (1770–1831), who became Professor of Philosophy in Berlin, where he wrote voluminously, attracted a multitude of students and played a dominant role in the development of post-Kantian thought.

V

1. After the above introductory observations we may now pass on to the consideration of our subject itself. We are, however, still within the introduction; and being so I do not propose to attempt anything more than indicate by way of sketch the main outlines of the general course of the scientific inquiry which is to follow it. Inasmuch, however, as we have referred to art as issuing from the absolute Idea itself, and, indeed, have assigned as its end the sensuous presentation of the Absolute itself, it will be incumbent on us to conduct this survey of the entire field in such a way, as at least to disclose generally, how the particular parts originate in the notional concept of the beauty of art. We must therefore attempt to awaken some idea of this notion in its broadest significance.

It has already been stated that the content of art is the Idea, and the form of its display the configuration of the sensuous or plastic image. It is further the function of art to mediate these two aspects under the reconciled mode of free totality. The *first* determinant implied by this is the demand that the content, which has to secure artistic representation, shall disclose an essential capacity for such display. If this is not so all that we possess is a defective combination. A content that, independently, is ill adapted to plastic form and external presentment is compelled to accept this form, or a matter that is of itself prosaic in its character is driven to make the best it can of a mode of presentation which is antagonistic to its nature.

The *second* requirement, which is deducible from the first, is the demand that the content of art should be nothing essentially abstract. This does not mean, however, that it should be merely concrete in the sense that the sensuous object is such in its contrast to all that is spiritual and the content of thought, regarding these as the essentially simple and abstract. Everything that possesses truth for Spirit, no less than as part of Nature, is essentially concrete, and, despite its universality, possesses both ideality and particularity essentially within it. When we state, for example, of God that he is simple One, the

Georg Wilhelm Friedrich Hegel, *The Philosophy of Fine Art*, trans. F. P. B. Osmaston (London: G. Bell & Sons, 1920).

Supreme Being as such, we have thereby merely given utterance to a lifeless abstraction of the irrational understanding. Such a God, as He is thus not conceived in His concrete truth, can supply no content for art, least of all plastic art. Consequently neither the Jews nor the Turks have been able to represent their God, who is not even an abstraction of the understanding in the above sense, under the positive mode in which Christians have represented Him. For in Christianity God is conceived in His Truth, and as such essentially concrete, as personality, as the subjective focus of conscious life, or, more accurately defined, as Spirit. And what He is as Spirit is made explicit to the religious apprehension as a trinity of persons, which at the same time are, in their independence, regarded as One. Here is essentiality, universality, and particularity, no less than their reconciled unity, and it is only a unity such as this which gives us the concrete. And inasmuch as a content, in order to unveil truth at all, must be of this concrete character, art makes the demand for a like concreteness, and, for this reason, that a purely abstract universal does not in itself possess the property to proceed to particularity and external manifestation, and to unity with itself therein.

If, then, a sensuous form and configuration is to be correspondent with a true and therefore concrete content, such must in the third place likewise be as clearly individual, entirely concrete and a self-enclosed unity. This character of concreteness, predictable of both aspects of art, the content no less than the representation, is just the point in which both coalesce and fall in with one another. The natural form of the human body is, for example, such a sensuous concrete capable of displaying Spirit in its essential concreteness and of adapting itself wholly to such a presentment. For which reason we must quit ourselves of the idea that it is a matter of mere accident that an actual phenomenon of the objective world is accepted as the mode in which to embody such a form coalescent with truth. Art does not lay hold of this form either because it is simply there or because there is no other. The concrete content itself implies the presence of external and actual, we may even add the sensuous appearance. But to make this possible this sensuous concrete, which is essentially impressed with a content that is open to mind, is also essentially addressed to the inward conscious life, and the external mode of its configuration, whereby it is visible to perception and the world of idea, has for its aim the being there exclusively for the soul and mind of man. This is the sole reason that content and artistic conformation are dovetailed one into the other. The *purely* sensuous concrete, that is external Nature as such, does not exclusively originate in such an end. The variously coloured plumage of birds is resplendent unseen; the notes of this song are unheard. The Cereus, which only blossoms for a night, withers away without any admiration from another in the wilderness of the southern forests; and these forests, receptacles themselves of the most beautiful and luxuriant vegetation, with the richest and most aromatic perfumes, perish and collapse in like manner unenjoyed. The work of art has no such naive and independent being. It is essentially a question, an address to the responding soul of man, an appeal to affections and intelligence.

Although the endowment by art of sensuous shape is not in this respect accidental, yet on the other hand it is not the highest mode of grasping the spiritually concrete. Thought is a higher mode of presentment than that of the sensuous concrete. Though abstract in a relative sense; yet it must not be one-sided, but concrete thinking, in order to be true and rational. The extent to which a definite content possesses for its appropriate form sensuous artistic representation, or essentially requires, in virtue of its nature, a higher and more spiritual embodiment is a question of difference exemplified at once if we compare the Greek gods with God as conceived under Christian ideas. The Greek god is not abstract, but individual, and is in close association with the natural human form. The Christian God is also, no doubt, a concrete personality, but under the mode of pure spiritual actuality, who is cognized as Spirit and in Spirit. His medium of determinate existence is therefore essentially knowledge of the mind and not external natural shape, by means of which His representation can only be imperfect, and not in the entire depths of His idea or notional concept.

Inasmuch, however, as it is the function of art to represent the Idea to immediate vision in sensuous shape and not in the form of thought and pure spirituality in the strict sense, and inasmuch as the value and intrinsic worth of this presentment consists in the correspondence and unity of the two aspects, that is the Idea and its sensuous shape, the supreme level and excellence of art and the reality, which is truly consonant with its notion, will depend upon the degree of intimacy and union with which idea and configuration appear together in elaborated fusion. The higher truth consequently is spiritual content which has received the shape adequate to the conception of its essence; and this it is which supplies the principle of division for the philosophy of art. For before the mind can attain to the true notion of its absolute essence, it is constrained to traverse a series of stages rooted in this very notional concept; and to this course of stages which it unfolds to itself, corresponds a coalescent series, immediately related therewith, of the plastic types of art, under the configuration whereof mind as art-spirit presents to itself the consciousness of itself.

This evolution within the art-spirit has further itself two sides in virtue of its intrinsic nature. *First*, that is to say, the development is itself a spiritual and universal one; in other words there are the definite and comprehensive views of the world in their series of gradations which give artistic embodiment to the specific but widely embracing consciousness of Nature, man, and God. *Secondly*, this ideal or *universal* art-development has to provide for itself immediate existence and sensuous configuration, and the definite modes of this art-actualization in the sensuous medium are themselves a totality of necessary distinctions in the realm of art – that is to say, they are the *particular types* of art. No doubt the types of artistic configuration on the one hand are, in respect to their spirituality, of a general character, and not restricted to any one material, and the sensuous existence is similarly itself of varied multiplicity of medium. Inasmuch, however, as this material potentially possesses, precisely as the mind or spirit does, the Idea for its inward soul or significance, it follows that a definite sensuous involves with itself a closer relation and secret bond of association with the spiritual distinctions and specific types of artistic embodiment.

Relatively to these points of view our philosophy will be divided into three fundamental parts.

First, we have a *general* part. It has for its content and object the universal Idea of fine art, conceived here as the Ideal, together with the more elaborated relation under which it is placed respectively to Nature and human artistic production.

Secondly, we have evolved from the notional concept of the beauty of art a *particular* part, in so far as the essential distinctions, which this idea contains in itself, are unfolded in a graduated series of *particular* modes of configuration.

Thirdly, there results a *final* part which has to consider the particularized content of fine art itself. It consists in the advance of art to the sensuous realization of its shapes and its consummation in a system of the several arts and their genera and species.

2. In respect to the first and second of these divisions it is important to recollect, in order to make all that follows intelligible, that the Idea, viewed as the beautiful in art, is not the Idea in the strict sense, that is as a metaphysical Logic apprehends it as the Absolute. It is rather the Idea as carried into concrete form in the direction of express realization, and as having entered into immediate and adequate unity with such reality. For the *Idea as such*, although it is both potentially and explicitly true, is only truth in its universality and not as yet presented in objective embodiment. The Idea as fine art, however, is the Idea with the more specific property of being essentially individual reality, in other words, an individual configuration of reality whose express function it is to make manifest the Idea – in its appearance. This amounts to the demand that the Idea and its formative configuration as concrete realization must be brought together under a mode of complete adequacy. The Idea as so conceived, a reality, that is to say, moulded in conformity with the notional concept of the Idea, is the Ideal. The problem of such consonancy might, in the first instance, be understood in the wholly formal sense that the Idea might be any idea so long as the actual shape, it matters not what the shape might be, represented this particular Idea and no other. In that case, however, the required truth of the Ideal is a fact simply interchangeable with mere correctness, a correctness which consists in the expression of any significance in a manner adapted to it, provided that its meaning is thereby directly discoverable in the form. The Ideal, however, is not to be thus understood. According to the standard or test of its own nature any content whatever can receive

adequate presentation, but it does not necessarily thereby possess a claim to be the fine art of the Ideal. Nay, more, in comparison with ideal beauty the presentation will even appear defective. And in this connection we may once for all observe – though actual proof is reserved to a later stage – that the defects of a work of art are not invariably to be attributed to defects of executive skill. *Defectiveness of form* arises also from *defectiveness of content*. The Chinese, Hindoos, and Egyptians, for example, in their artistic images, sculptured deities and idols, never passed beyond a formless condition, or a definition of shape that was vicious and false, and were unable to master true beauty. And this was so for the reason that their mythological conceptions, the content and thought of their works of art, were still essentially indeterminate, or only determinate in a false sense, did not, in fact, attain to a content which was absolute in itself. Viewed in this sense the excellence of works of art is so much the greater in the degree that their content and thought is ideal and profound. And in affirming this we have not merely in our mind the degree of executive mastery displayed in the grasp and imitation of natural form as we find it in the objective world. For in certain stages of the artistic consciousness and its reproductive effects the desertion and distortion of the conformations of Nature is not so much due to unintentional technical inexperience or lack of ability, as it is to deliberate alteration, which originates in the mental content itself, and is demanded by the same. From this point of view there is therefore imperfect art, which, both in technical and other respects, may be quite consummate in its *own specific sphere*, yet if tested with the true notion of art and the Ideal can only appear as defective. Only in the highest art are the Idea and the artistic presentation truly consonant with one another in the sense that the objective embodiment of the Idea is in itself essentially and as realized the true configuration, because the content of the Idea thus expressed is itself in truth the genuine content. It is appertinent to this, as already noted, that the Idea must be defined in and through itself as concrete totality, thereby essentially possessing in itself the principle and standard of its particularization and definition as thus manifested objectively. For example, the Christian imagination will only be able to represent God in human form and with man's means of spiritual expression, because it is herein that God Himself is fully known in Himself as mind or Spirit. Determinacy is, as it were, the bridge to phenomenal presence. Where this determinacy is not totality derived from the Idea itself, where the Idea is not conceived as that which is self-definitive and self-differentiating, it remains abstract and possesses its definition, and with it the principle for the particular mode of embodiment adapted to itself not within itself but as something outside it. And owing to this the Idea is also still abstract and the configuration it assumes is not as yet posited by itself. The Idea, however, which is essentially concrete, carries the principle of its manifestation in itself, and is thereby the means of its own free manifestation. Thus it is only the truly concrete Idea that is able to evoke the true embodiment, and this appropriate coalescence of both is the Ideal.

3. But inasmuch as in this way the Idea is concrete unity, this unity can only enter the artistic consciousness by the expansion and further mediation of the particular aspects of the Idea; and it is through this evolution that the beauty of art receives a *totality of particular stages and forms*. Therefore, after we have considered fine art in its essence and on its own account, we must see how the beautiful in its entirety breaks up into its particular determinations. This gives, as our second part, the *doctrine of the types of art*. The origin of these types is to be found in the varied ways under which the Idea is conceived as the content of art; it is by this means that a distinction in the mode of form under which it manifests itself is conditioned. These types are therefore simply the different modes of relation which obtain between the Idea and its configuration relations which emanate from the Idea itself, and thereby present us with the general basis of division for this sphere. For the principle of division must always be found in the notional concept, the particularization and division of which it is.

We have here to consider *three* relations of the Idea to its external process of configuration.

(*a*) *First*, the origin of artistic creation proceeds from the Idea when, being itself still involved in defective definition and obscurity, or in vicious and untrue determinacy, it becomes embodied in the shapes of art. As indeterminate it does not as yet possess in itself that individuality which the Ideal demands. Its abstract character and one-sidedness leaves its objective presentment still defective and contingent. Consequently this first type of art is rather a mere search after plastic configuration than a power of genuine representation. The Idea has not as yet found the formative principle within itself, and therefore still continues to be the mere effort and strain to find it. We may in general terms describe this form as the *symbolic* type of art. The abstract Idea possesses in it its external shape outside itself in the purely material substance of Nature, from which the shaping process proceeds, and to which in its expression it is entirely yoked. Natural objects are thus in the first instance left just as they are, while, at the same time the substantive Idea is imposed upon them as their significance, so that their function is henceforth to express the same, and they claim to be interpreted, as though the Idea itself was present in them. A rationale of this is to be found in the fact that the external objects of reality do essentially possess an aspect in which they are qualified to express a universal import. But as a completely adequate coalescence is not yet possible, all that can be the outcome of such a relation is an *abstract attribute*, as when a lion is understood to symbolize strength.

On the other hand this abstractness of the relation makes present to consciousness no less markedly how the Idea stands relatively to natural phenomena as an alien; and albeit it expatiates in all these shapes, having no other means of expression among all that is real, and seeks after itself in their unrest and defects of genuine proportion, yet for all that it finds them inadequate to meet its needs. It consequently exaggerates natural shapes and the phenomena of Nature in every degree of indefinite and limitless extension; it flounders about in them like a drunkard, and seethes and ferments, doing violence to their truth with the distorted growth of unnatural shapes, and strives vainly by the contrast, hugeness, and splendour of the forms accepted to exalt the phenomena to the plane of the Idea. For the Idea is here still more or less indeterminate, and unadaptable, while the objects of Nature are wholly definite in their shape.

Hence, on account of the incompatibility of the two sides of ideality and objective form to one another, the relation of the Idea to the other becomes a *negative* one. The former, being in its nature ideal, is unsatisfied with such an embodiment, and posits itself as its inward or ideally universal substance under a relation of *sublimity* over and above all this inadequate superfluity of natural form. In virtue of this sublimity the natural phenomena, of course, and the human form and event are accepted and left simply as they are, but at the same time, recognized as unequal to their significance, which is exalted far above all earthly content.

These features constitute in general terms the character of the primitive artistic pantheism of the East, which, on the one hand, charges the meanest objects with the significance of the absolute Idea, or, on the other, compels natural form, by doing violence to its structure, to express its world-ideas. And, in consequence, it becomes bizarre, grotesque, and deficient in taste, or turns the infinite but abstract freedom of the substantive Idea contemptuously against all phenomenal existence as alike nugatory and evanescent. By such means the significance cannot be completely presented in the expression, and despite all straining and endeavour the final inadequacy of plastic configuration to Idea remains insuperable. Such may be accepted as the first type of art – symbolic art with its yearning, its fermentation, its mystery, and sublimity.

(*b*) In the *second* type of art, which we propose to call "Classical," the twofold defect of symbolic art is annulled. Now the symbolic configuration is imperfect, because, first, the Idea here only enters into consciousness in *abstract* determinacy or indeterminateness: and, secondly, by reason of the fact that the coalescence of import with embodiment can only throughout remain defective, and in its turn also wholly abstract. The classical art-type solves both these difficulties. It is, in fact, the free and adequate embodiment of the Idea in the shape which, according to its notional concept, is uniquely appropriate to the Idea itself. The Idea is consequently able to unite in free and completely assonant concord with it. For this reason the classical type of art is the first to present us with the creation and vision of the complete Ideal, and to establish the same as realized fact.

The conformability, however, of notion and reality in the classical type ought not to be taken in the purely *formal* sense of the coalescence of a content with its external form, any more than this was possible in the case of the Ideal. Otherwise every copy from Nature, and every kind of portrait, every landscape, flower, scene, and so forth, which form the aim of the presentment, would at once become classical in virtue of the fact of the agreement it offers between such content and form. In classical art, on the contrary, the characteristic feature of the content consists in this, that it is itself concrete Idea, and as such the concrete spiritual; for it is only that which pertains to Spirit which is veritable ideality. To secure such a content we must find out that in Nature which on its own account is that which is essentially and explicitly appropriate to the spiritual. It must be the *original* notion itself, which has invented the form for concrete spirituality, and now the *subjective* notion – in the present case the spirit of art – has merely *discovered* it, and made it, as an existence possessed of natural shape, concordant with free and individual spirituality. Such a configuration, which the Idea essentially possesses as spiritual, and indeed as individually determinate spirituality, when it must perforce appear as a temporal phenomenon, is the *human form.* Personification and anthropomorphism have frequently been abused as a degradation of the spiritual. But art, in so far as its function is to bring to vision the spiritual in sensuous guise, must advance to such anthropomorphism, inasmuch as Spirit is only adequately presented to perception in its bodily presence. The transmigration of souls in this respect an abstract conception, and physiology ought to make it one of its fundamental principles, that life has necessarily, in the course of its evolution, to proceed to the human form, for the reason that it is alone the visible phenomenon adequate to the expression of intelligence.

The human bodily form, then, is employed in the classical type of art not as purely sensuous existence, but exclusively as the existence and natural shape appropriate to mind. It has therefore to be relieved of all the defective excrescences which adhere to it in its purely physical aspect, and from the contingent finiteness of its phenomenal appearance. The external shape must in this way be purified in order to express in itself the content adequate for such a purpose; and, furthermore, along with this, that the coalescence of import and embodiment may be complete, the spirituality which constitutes the content must be of such a character that it is completely able to express itself in the natural form of man, without projecting beyond the limits of such expression within the sensuous and purely physical sphere of existence. Under such a condition Spirit is at the same time defined as particular, the spirit or mind of man, not as simply absolute and eternal. In this latter case it is only capable of asserting and expressing itself as intellectual being.

Out of this latter distinction arises, in its turn, the defect which brings about the dissolution of the classical type of art, and makes the demand for a third and higher form, namely the *romantic* type.

(*c*) The romantic type of art annuls the completed union of the Idea and its reality, and occurs, if on a higher plane, to the difference and opposition of both sides, which remained unovercome in symbolic art. The classical type of art no doubt attained the highest excellence of which the sensuous embodiment of art is capable. The defect, such as it is, is due to the defect which obtains in art itself throughout, the limitations of its entire province, that is to say. The limitation consists in this, that art in general and, agreeably to its fundamental idea, accepts for its object Spirit, the notion of which is infinite concrete universality, under the guise of sensuously concrete form. In the classical type it sets up the perfected coalescence of spiritual and sensuous existence as adequate conformation of both. As a matter of fact, however, in this fusion mind itself is not represented agreeably to its *true notional concept.* Mind is the infinite subjectivity of the Idea, which as absolute inwardness, is not capable of freely expanding in its entire independence, so long as it remains within the mould of the bodily shape, fused therein as in the existence wholly congenial to it.

To escape from such a condition the romantic type of art once more cancels that inseparable unity of the classical type, by securing a content which passes beyond the classical stage and its mode of expression. This content, if we may recall familiar ideas – is coincident with what Christianity affirms to be true of God as Spirit, in contrast to the Greek faith in gods which forms the essential and most fitting content of classical art. In Greek art the concrete ideal substance is potentially, but not as fully realized, the unity of the human and divine nature; a unity which for the very reason that it is purely *immediate* and not wholly explicit, is manifested without defect under an immediate and *sensuous* mode. The Greek god is the object of naive intuition and sensuous imagination. His shape is therefore the bodily form of man. The sphere of his power and his being is individual and individually limited; and in his opposition to the individual person is an essence and a power with whom the inward life of soul is merely potentially in unity, but does not itself possess this unity as inward subjective knowledge. The higher stage is the *knowledge* of this *implied* unity, which in its latency the classical art-type receives as its content and is able to perfectly represent in bodily shape. This elevation of mere potentiality into self-conscious knowledge constitutes an enormous difference. It is nothing less than the infinite difference which, for example, separates man generally from the animal creation. Man is animal; but even in his animal functions he is not restricted within the potential sphere as the animal is, but becomes conscious of them, learns to understand them, and raises them – as, for instance, the process of digestion – into self-conscious science. By this means man dissolves the boundaries of his merely potential immediacy; in virtue of the very fact that he knows himself to be animal he ceases to be merely animal, and as mind is endowed with self-knowledge.

If, then, in this way the unity of the human and divine nature, which in the previous stage was potential, is raised out of this immediate into a self-conscious unit, it follows that the genuine medium for the reality of this content is no longer the sensuous and immediate existence of what is spiritual, that is, the physical body of man, but the *self-aware* inner life of *soul itself*. Now it is Christianity – for the reason that it presents to mind God as *Spirit*, and not as particular individual spirit, but as absolute in spirit and in truth – which steps back from the sensuousness of imagination into the inward life of reason, and makes *this* rather than *bodily* form the medium and determinate existence of its content. So also, the unity of the human and divine nature is a conscious unity exclusively capable of realization by means of *spiritual* knowledge, and in *Spirit*. The new content secured thereby is consequently not indefeasibly bound up with the sensuous presentation, as the mode completely adequate, but is rather delivered from this immediate existence, which has to be hypostatized as a negative factor, overcome and reflected back into the spiritual unity. In this way romantic art must be regarded as art transcending itself, albeit within the boundary of its own province, and in the form of art itself.

We may therefore briefly summarize our conclusion that in this third stage the object of art consists in the free and concrete presence of spiritual activity, whose vocation it is to appear as such a presence or activity for the inner world of conscious intelligence. In consonance with such an object art cannot merely work for sensuous perception. It must deliver itself to the inward life, which coalesces with its object simply as though this were none other than itself, in other words, to the intimacy of soul, to the heart, the emotional life, which as the medium of Spirit itself essentially strives after freedom, and seeks and possesses its reconciliation only in the inner chamber of spirit. It is this inward or ideal world which constitutes the content of the romantic sphere: it will therefore necessarily discover its representation as such inner idea or feeling, and in the show or appearance of the same. The world of the soul and intelligence celebrates its triumph over the external world, and, actually in the medium of that outer world, makes that victory to appear, by reason of which the sensuous appearance sinks into worthlessness.

On the other hand, this type of art, like every other, needs an external vehicle of expression. As already stated, the spiritual content has here withdrawn from the external world and its immediate unity into its own world. The sensuous externality of form is consequently accepted and represented, as in the symbolic type, as unessential and transient; furthermore the subjective finite spirit and volition is treated in a similar way; a treatment which even includes the idiosyncrasies or caprice of individuals, character, action, or the particular features of incident and plot. The aspect of external existence is committed to contingency and handed over to the adventurous action of imagination, whose caprice is just as able to reflect the facts given *as* they are, as it can change the shapes of the external world into a medley of its own invention and distort them to mere caricature. For this external element has no longer its notion and significance in its own essential province, as in classical art. It is now discovered in the emotional realm, and this is manifested in the medium of that realm itself rather than in the external and *its* form of reality, and is able to secure or to recover again the condition of reconciliation with itself in every accident, in all the chance circumstance that falls into independent shape, in all misfortune and sorrow, nay, in crime itself.

Hence it comes about that the characteristics of symbolic art, its indifference, incompatibility and severance of Idea from configurative expression, are here reproduced once more, if with essential difference. And this difference consists in the fact that in romantic art the Idea, whose defectiveness, in the case of the symbol, brought with it the defect of external form, has to display itself as Spirit and in the medium of soul-life as essentially self-complete. And it is to complete fundamentally this higher perfection that it withdraws itself from the external element. It can, in short, seek and consummate its true reality and manifestation nowhere but in its own domain.

This we may take to be in general terms the character of the symbolic, romantic types of art, which in fact constitute the three relations of the Idea to its embodiment in the realm of human art. They consist in the aspiration after, the attainment and transcendency of the Ideal, viewed as the true concrete notion of beauty.

4. In contrast to these two previous divisions of our subject the *third* part presupposes the notional concept of the Ideal, and the universal art-types. It in other words consists in their realization through specific sensuous media. We have consequently no longer to deal with the inner or ideal evolution of the beauty of art in conformity with its widest and most fundamental determinations. What we have now before us to consider is how these ideal determinants pass into actual existence, how they are distinguishable in their external aspect, and how they give an independent and a realized shape to every element implied in the evolution of this Idea of beauty as *a work of art*, and not merely as a *universal type*. Now it is the peculiar differences immanent in the Idea of beauty which are carried over by it into external existence. For this reason in this third fundamental division these general art-types must themselves supply the basic principle for the articulation and definition of the *particular arts*. Or, to put the same thing another way, the several species of art possess in themselves the same essential differences, which we have already become acquainted with as the universal art-types. *External* objectivity, however, to which these types are subjected in a sensuous and consequently *specific* material, necessitates the differentiation of these types into diverse and independent modes of realization, in other words, those of particular arts. Each general type discovers its determinate character in one determinate external material or medium, in which its adequate presentation is secured under the manner it prescribes. But, from another point of view, these types of art, inasmuch as their definition is none the less consistent with the fact of the *universality* of their typical import, break through the boundaries of their *specific* realization in some definite art-species, and achieve an existence in other arts no less, although their position in such is of subordinate importance. For this reason, albeit the particular arts belong specifically to one of these general art-types respectively, the *adequate* external embodiment whereof they severally constitute, yet this does not prevent them, each after its own mode of external configuration, from representing the totality of these art-types. To summarize, then, in this third principal division we are dealing with the beauty of art, as it unveils itself in a world of realized beauty by means of the arts and their creations. The content of this world is the beautiful, and the true beautiful, as we have seen, is spiritual being in concrete form, the Ideal; or apprehended with still more intimacy it is the absolute mind and truth itself. This region of divine truth artistically presented to sensuous vision and emotion forms the centre of the entire world of art. It is the independent, free and divine Image, which has completely appropriated the externality of form and medium, and now wears them simply as the means of its self-manifestation. Inasmuch, however, as the beautiful is unfolded here as *objective* reality, and in this process is differentiated into particular aspects and phases, this centre posits its extremes, as realized in their peculiar actuality, in antithetical relation to itself. Thus one of these extremes consists of an objectivity as yet devoid of mind, which we may call the natural environment of God. Here the external element, when it receives form, remains as it was, and does not possess its spiritual aim and content in itself, but in another. The other extreme is the divine as inward,

something known, as the manifold particularized *subjective* existence of Deity. It is the truth as operative and vital in sense, soul, and intelligence of particular persons, which does not persist as poured forth into its mould of external shape, but returns into the inward life of individuals. The Divine is under such a mode at once distinguishable from its pure manifestation as Godhead, and passes itself thereby into the variety of particularization which belongs to every kind of particular subjective knowledge, feeling, perception, and emotion. In the analogous province of religion with which art, at its highest elevation, is immediately connected, we conceive the same distinction as follows. First, we imagine the natural life on Earth in its finitude as standing on one side; but then, secondly, the human consciousness accepts God for its object, in which the distinction between objectivity and subjectivity falls away; then, finally, we advance from God as such to the devotion of the *community*, that is to God as He is alive and present in the subjective consciousness. These three fundamental modifications present themselves in the world of art in independent evolution.

(*a*) The *first* of the particular arts with which, according to their fundamental principle, we have to start is architecture considered as a fine art. Its function consists in so elaborating the external material of inorganic Nature that the same becomes intimately connected with Spirit as an artistic and external environment. Its medium is matter itself as an external object, a heavy mass that is subject to mechanical laws; and its forms persist as the forms of inorganic Nature coordinated with the relations of the abstract understanding such as symmetry and so forth. In this material and in these forms the Ideal is incapable of realization as concrete spirituality, and the reality thus presented remains confronting the Idea as an external fabric with which it enters into no fusion, or has only entered so far as to establish an abstract relation. And it is in consequence of this that the fundamental type of the art of building is that of *symbolism*. Architecture is in fact the first pioneer on the highway toward the adequate realization of Godhead. In this service it is put to severe labour with objective nature, that it may disengage it by its effort from the confused growth of finitude and the distortions of contingency. By this means it levels a space for the God, informs His external environment, and builds Him His temple, as a fit place for the concentration of Spirit, and its direction to the absolute objects of intelligent life. It raises an enclosure for the congregation of those assembled, as a defence against the threatening of the tempest, against rain, the hurricane, and savage animals. It in short reveals the will thus to assemble, and although under an external relation, yet in agreement with the principles of art. A significance such as this it can to a greater or less extent import into its material and its forms, in proportion as the determinate content of its fabric, which is the object of its operations and effort, is more or less significant, is more concrete or more abstract, more profound in penetrating its own essential depth, or more obscure and superficial. Indeed architecture may in this respect proceed so far in the execution of such a purpose as to create an adequate artistic existence for such an ideal content in its very forms and material. In doing so, however, it has already passed beyond its peculiar province and is diverted into the stage immediately above it of sculpture. For the boundary of sculpture lies precisely in this that it retains the spiritual as an inward being which persists in direct contrast to the external embodiment of architecture. It can consequently merely point to that which is absorbed in soul-life as to something external to itself.

(*b*) Nevertheless, as above explained, the external and inorganic world purified by architecture, it is coordinated under symmetrical laws, and made cognate with mind, and as a result the temple of God, the house of his community, stands before us. Into this temple, in the *second* place, the God himself enters in the lightning-flash of individuality which smites its way into the inert mass, permeating the same with its presence. In other words the infinite and no longer purely symmetrical form belonging to intelligence brings as it were to a focus and informs the shape in which it is most at home. This is the task of *sculpture*. In so far as in it the inward life of Spirit, to which the art of architecture can merely point away to, makes its dwelling within the sensuous shape and its external material, and to the extent that these two sides come into plastic communion with one another in such a manner that neither is predominant, sculpture receives as its fundamental type the *classical* art-form.

For this reason the sensuous element on its own account admits of no expression here which is not affected by spiritual affinities, just as, conversely, sculpture can reproduce with completeness no spiritual content which does not maintain throughout adequate presentation to perception in bodily form. What sculpture, in short, has to do is to make the presence of Spirit stand before us in its bodily shape and in immediate union therewith at rest and in blessedness; and this form has to be made vital by means of the content of spiritual individuality. The external sensuous material is consequently no longer elaborated either in conformity with its mechanical quality alone, as a mass of weight, nor in shapes of the inorganic world simply, nor in entire indifference to colour, etc. It is carried into the ideal forms of the human figure, and, we may add, in the completeness of all three spatial dimensions. In other words and relatively to such a process we must maintain for sculpture that in it the inward or ideal content of Spirit are first revealed in their eternal repose and essential self-stability. To such repose and unity with itself there can only correspond that external shape which itself persists in such unity and repose. And this condition is satisfied by configuration viewed in its *abstract spatiality*. The spirit which sculpture represents is that which is essentially sound, not broken up in the play of chance conceits and passions; and for this reason its external form also is not dissolved in the manifold variety of appearance, but exhibits itself under this one presentment only as the abstraction of space in the totality of its dimensions.

Assuming, then, that the art of architecture has executed its temple and the hand of sculpture has placed therein the image of the god, we have in the *third* place to assume the *community* of the faithful as confronting the god thus presented to vision in the wide chambers of his dwelling-place Now this community is the spiritual reflection into its own world of that sensuous presence, the subjective and inward animating life of soul, in its union with which, both for the artistic content and the external material which manifests it, the determining principle may be identified with particularization in varied shapes and qualities, individualization and the life of soul which they imply. The downright and solid fact of unity the god possesses in sculpture breaks up into the multiplicity of a world of particular souls, whose union is no longer sensuous but wholly ideal.

Here for the first time God Himself is revealed as veritably Spirit – viz., the Spirit revealed in His community. Here at last He is seen apprehended as this moving to-and-fro, as this alternation between His own essential unity and His realization in the knowledge of individual persons and that separation which it involves, as also in the universal spiritual being and union of the many. In such a community God is disengaged from the abstraction of His unfolded self-seclusion and self-identity, no less than from the immediate absorption in bodily shape, in which He is presented by sculpture. He is, in a word, lifted into the actual sphere of spiritual existence and knowledge, into the reflected appearance, whose manifestation is essentially inward and the life of heart and soul. Thereby the higher content is now the nature of Spirit, and that in its ultimate or absolute shape. But at the same time the separation to which we have alluded displays this as *particular* spiritual being, a specific emotional life. Moreover, for the reason that the main thing here is not the untroubled repose of the God in himself, but his manifestation simply, the Being which is *for another*, self-revealment in fact, it follows that, on the plane we have now reached, all the varied content of human subjectivity in its vital movement and activity, whether viewed as passion, action, or event, or more generally the wide realm of human feeling, volition and its discontinuance, become one and all for their own sake objects of artistic representation.

Agreeably with such a content the sensuous element of art has likewise to show itself potentially adapted to such particularization and the display of such an inward content of heart and mind. Media of this description are supplied by colour, musical tones, and finally in sound as mere sign for ideal perceptions and conceptions; and we further obtain the means of realizing with the use of such media a content of this kind in the arts of painting, music, and poetry. Throughout this sphere the sensuous medium is found to be essentially disparate in itself and throughout posited as ideal. In this way it responds in the highest degree to the fundamentally spiritual content of art, and the coalescence of spiritual significance and sensuous material attains a more intimate union than was possible either in architecture or sculpture. At the same time such a union is necessarily more near to soul-life, leaning exclusively to the subjective side of human experience; one which, in so far as form and content are thus constrained to particularization and to posit their result as ideal, can only be actually effected at the expense of the objective universality of the content as also of the fusion with the immediately sensuous medium.

The arts, then, which are lifted into a higher strain of ideality, abandoning as they do the symbolism of architecture and the classical Ideal of sculpture, accept their predominant type from the *romantic* art-form; and these are the arts most fitted to express its mode of configuration. They are, however, a totality of arts, because the romantic type is itself essentially the most concrete.

(*c*) The articulation of this *third sphere* of the particular arts may be fixed as follows:

(α) The *first* art which comes next to sculpture is that of painting. It avails itself for a medium of its content and the plastic configuration of the same of visibility as such, to the extent that it is differentiated in its own nature, in other words is defined in the continuity of colour. No doubt the material of architecture and sculpture is likewise both visible and coloured. It is, however, not, as in painting, visibility in its pure nature, not the essentially simple light, which by its differentiating of itself in its opposition to darkness, and in association with that darkness; gives rise to colour. This quality of visibility made essentially ideal and treated as such no longer either requires, as in architecture, the abstractly mechanical qualities of mass as appropriate to materials of weight, nor, as is the case with sculpture, the complete dimensuration of spatial condition, even when concentrated into organic forms. The visibility and the making apparent, which belong to painting, possess differences of quality under a more ideal mode – that is, in the specific varieties of colour – which liberates art from the objective totality, of spatial condition, by being limited to a plane surface.

On the other hand the content also attains the widest compass of particularity. Whatever can find a place in the human heart, as emotion, idea, and purpose, whatever it is capable of actually shaping – all such diversity may form part of the varied presentations of painting. The entire world of particular existence, from the most exalted embodiment of mind to the most insignificant natural fact, finds a place here. For it is possible even for finite Nature, in its particular scenes and phenomena, to form part of such artistic display, provided only that we have some reference to conscious life which makes it akin to human thought and emotion.

(β) The *second* art which continues the further realization of the romantic type and forms as distinct contrast to painting is that of *music*. Its medium, albeit still sensuous, yet proceeds into still profounder subjectivity and particularization. We have here, too, the deliberate treatment of the sensuous medium as ideal, and it consists in the negation and idealization into the isolated unity of a single point, the indifferent external collocation of space, whose complete appearance is retained by painting and deliberately feigned in its completeness. This isolated point, viewed as this process of negation, is an essentially concrete and active process of cancellation within the determinate substance of the material medium, viewed, that is, as motion and vibration of the material object within itself and in its relation to itself. Such an inchoate ideality of matter, which no longer appears under the form of space, but as temporal idealty, is sound or tone. We have here the sensuous set down as negated, and its abstract visibility converted into audibility. In other words sound liberates the ideal content from its fetters in the material substance. This earliest secured inwardness of matter and impregnation of it with soul-life supplies the medium for the intimacy and soul of Spirit – itself as yet indefinite – permitting, as it does, the echo and reverberation of man's emotional world through its entire range of feelings and passions. In this way music forms the centre of the romantic arts, just as sculpture represents the midway point of arrest between architecture and the arts of the romantic subjectivity. Thus, too, it forms the point of transition between the abstract, spatial sensuousness of painting and the abstract spirituality of poetry. Music carries within itself, like architecture, and in contrast to the emotional world simply and its inward self-seclusion, a relation of quantity conformable to the principles of the understanding and their modes of co-ordinated configuration.

(γ) We must look for our *third* and most spiritual type of artistic presentation among the romantic arts in that of *poetry*. The supreme characteristic of poetry consists in the power with which it brings into vassalage of the mind and its conceptions the sensuous element from which music and painting began to liberate art. For sound, the only remaining external material retained by poetry, is in it no longer the feeling of the sonorous itself, but is a mere sign without independent significance. And it is, moreover, a sign of idea which has become essentially concrete, and not merely of indefinite feeling and its subtle modes and gradations. And this is how sound develops into the Word, as essentially articulate voice, whose intention it is to indicate ideas and thoughts. The purely negative moment to which music advanced now asserts itself as the wholly concrete point, the point which is mind itself, the self-conscious individual, which produces from itself the infinite expansion of its ideas and unites the same with the temporal condition of sound. Yet this sensuous element, which was still in music immediately united to emotion, is in poetry separated from the content of consciousness. Mind, in short, here determines this content for its own sake and apart from all else into the content of idea; to express such idea it no doubt avails itself of sound, but employs it merely as a sign without independent worth or substance. Thus viewed, the sound here may be just as well reproduced by the mere letter, for the audible, like the visible, is here reduced to a mere indication of mind. For this reason, the true medium of poetical representation is the poetical imagination and the intellectual presentation itself; and inasmuch as this element is common to all types of art it follows that poetry is a common thread through them all, and is developed independently in each. Poetry is, in short, the universal art of the mind, which has become essentially free, and which is not fettered in its realization to an externally sensuous material, but which is creatively active in the space and time belonging to the inner world of ideas and emotion. Yet it is precisely in this its highest phase, that art terminates, by transcending itself; it is just here that it deserts the medium of a harmonious presentation of mind in sensuous shape and passes from the poetry of imaginative idea into the prose of thought.

Such we may accept as the articulate totality of the particular arts; they are the external art of architecture, the objective art of sculpture and the subjective arts of painting, music, and poetry. Many other classifications than these have been attempted, for a work of art presents such a wealth of aspects, that it is quite possible, as has frequently been the case, to make first one and then another the basis of division. For instance, you may take the sensuous medium simply. Architecture may then be viewed as a kind of crystallization; sculpture, as the organic configuration of material in its sensuous and spatial totality; painting as the coloured surface and line, while in music, space, as such, passes over into the point or moment of time replete with content in itself, until we come finally to poetry, where the external medium is wholly suppressed into insignificance. Or, again, these differences have been viewed with reference to their purely abstract conditions of space and time. Such abstract divisions of works of art may, as their medium also may be consequentially traced in their characteristic features. They cannot, however, be worked out as the final and fundamental principle, because such aspects themselves derive their origins from a higher principle, and must therefore fall into subordination thereto.

This higher principle we have discovered in the types of art – symbolic, classical, and romantic – which are the universal stages or phases of the Idea of beauty itself.

Their relation to the individual arts in their concrete manifestation as embodiment is of a kind that these arts constitute the real and positive existence of these general art-types. For *symbolic* art attains its most adequate realization and most pertinent application in *architecture*, in which it expatiates in the full import of its notion, and is not as yet depreciated, as it were, into the merely inorganic nature dealt with by some other art. The *classical* type of art finds its unfettered realization, on the other hand, in sculpture, treating architecture merely as the enclosure which surrounds it, and being unable to elaborate painting and music into the wholly adequate forms of its content. Finally, the *romantic* art-type is supreme in the products of painting and music, and likewise in poetical composition, as their preeminent and unconditionally adequate modes of expression. Poetry is, however, conformable to all types of the beautiful, and its embrace reaches them all for the reason that the poetic imagination is its own proper medium, and imagination is essential to every creation of beauty, whatever its type may be.

To sum up, then, what the particular arts realize in particular works of art, are according to their fundamental conception, simply the universal types which constitute the self-unfolding Idea of beauty. It is as the external realization of this Idea that the wide Pantheon of art is being raised; and the architect and builder thereof is the spirit of beauty as it gradually comes to self-cognition, and to complete which the history of the world will require its evolution of centuries.

19

The World as Will and Representation

Arthur Schopenhauer

Arthur Schopenhauer (1788–1860) was a German philosopher who maintained that the essence of the world is will, that each individual is identical with that will, that the will is without purpose, and that our lives of blind willing are doomed to misery, but that temporary relief can be found in the contemplation of art.

Book III

§ 30.

In the first book the world was shown to be mere *representation*, object for a subject. In the second book, we considered it from its other side, and found that this is *will*, which proved to be simply what this world is besides being representation. In accordance with this knowledge, we called the world as representation, both as a whole and in its parts, the *objectivity of the will*, which accordingly means the will become object, i.e., representation. Now we recall further that such objectification of the will had many but definite grades, at which, with gradually increasing distinctness and completeness, the inner nature of the will appeared in the representation, in other words, presented itself as object. In these grades we recognized the Platonic Ideas once more, namely in so far as such grades are just the definite species, or the original unchanging forms and properties of all natural bodies, whether organic or inorganic, as well as the universal forces that reveal themselves according to natural laws. Therefore these Ideas as a whole present themselves in innumerable individuals and in isolated details, and are related to them as the archetype is to its copies. The plurality of such individuals can be conceived only through time and space, their arising and passing away through causality. In all these forms we recognize only the different aspects of the principle of sufficient reason that is the ultimate principle of all finiteness, of all individuation, and the universal form of the representation as it comes to the knowledge of the individual as such. On the other hand, the Idea does not enter into that principle; hence neither plurality nor change belongs to it. While the individuals in which it expresses itself are innumerable and are incessantly coming into existence and passing away, it remains unchanged as one and the same, and the principle of sufficient reason has no meaning for it. But now, as this principle is the form under which all knowledge of the subject comes, in so far as the subject knows as an *individual*, the Ideas will also lie quite outside the sphere of its knowledge as such.

Arthur Schopenhauer, *The World as Will and Representation*, trans. R. B. Haldane and J. Kemp (1883).

Therefore, if the Ideas are to become object of knowledge, this can happen only by abolishing individuality in the knowing subject. [. . .]

§ 31.

First of all, however, the following very essential remark. I hope that in the preceding book I have succeeded in producing the conviction that what in the Kantian philosophy is called the *thing-in-itself*, and appears therein as so significant but obscure and paradoxical a doctrine, is, if reached by the entirely different path we have taken, nothing but the *will* in the sphere of this concept, widened and defined in the way I have stated. It appears obscure and paradoxical in Kant especially through the way in which he introduced it, namely by inference from what is grounded to what is the ground, and it was considered to be a stumbling-block, in fact the weak side of his philosophy. Further, I hope that, after what has been said, there will be no hesitation in recognizing again in the definite grades of the objectification of that will, which forms the in-itself of the world, what Plato called the *eternal Ideas* or unchangeable forms. [. . .]

§ 33.

Now since as individuals we have no other knowledge than that which is subject to the principle of sufficient reason, this form, however, excluding knowledge of the Ideas, it is certain that, if it is possible for us to raise ourselves from knowledge of particular things to that of the Ideas, this can happen only by a change taking place in the subject. Such a change is analogous and corresponds to that great change of the whole nature of the object, and by virtue of it the subject, in so far as it knows an Idea, is no longer individual. [. . .]

[K]nowledge in general itself belongs to the objectification of the will at its higher grades. Sensibility, nerves, brain, just like other parts of the organic being, are only an expression of the will at this grade of its objectivity; hence the representation that arises through them is also destined to serve the will as a means [. . .] for the attainment of its now complicated [. . .] ends, for the maintenance of a being with many different needs. Thus, originally and by its nature, knowledge is completely the servant of the will, and, like the immediate object which, by the application of the law of causality, becomes the starting-point of knowledge, is only objectified will. And so all knowledge which follows the principle of sufficient reason remains in a nearer or remoter relation to the will. For the individual finds his body as an object among objects, to all of which it has many different relations and connexions according to the principle of sufficient reason. Hence a consideration of these always leads back, by a shorter or longer path, to his body, and thus to his will. As it is the principle of sufficient reason that places the objects in this relation to the body and so to the will, the sole endeavour of knowledge, serving this will, will be to get to know concerning objects just those relations that are laid down by the principle of sufficient reason, and thus to follow their many different connexions in space, time, and causality. For only through these is the object *interesting* to the individual, in other words, has it a relation to the will. Therefore, knowledge that serves the will really knows nothing more about objects than their relations, knows the objects only in so far as they exist at such a time, in such a place, in such and such circumstances, from such and such causes, and in such and such effects – in a word, as particular things. If all these relations were eliminated, the objects also would have disappeared for knowledge, just because it did not recognize in them anything else. We must also not conceal the fact that what the sciences consider in things is also essentially nothing more than all this, namely their relations, the connexions of time and space, the causes of natural changes, the comparison of forms, the motives of events, and thus merely relations. What distinguishes science from ordinary knowledge is merely its form, the systematic, the facilitating of knowledge by summarizing everything particular in the universal by means of the subordination of concepts, and the completeness of knowledge thus attained. All relation has itself only a relative existence; for example, all being in time is also a non-being, for time is just that by which opposite determinations can belong to the same thing. Therefore every phenomenon in time again is not, for what separates its beginning from its end is simply time, essentially an evanescent, unstable, and relative thing, here called duration. But time is the most universal form of all objects of this knowledge that is in the service of the will, and is the prototype of the remaining forms of such knowledge.

Now as a rule, knowledge remains subordinate to the service of the will, as indeed it came into being for this service; in fact, it sprang from the will, so to speak, as the head from the trunk. With the animals, this subjection of knowledge to the will can never be eliminated. With human beings, such elimination appears only as an exception as will shortly be considered in more detail. [. . .]

§ 34.

As we have said, the transition that is possible, but to be regarded only as an exception, from the common knowledge of particular things to knowledge of the Idea takes place suddenly, since knowledge tears itself free from the service of the will precisely by the subject's ceasing to be merely individual, and being now a pure will-less subject of knowledge. Such a subject of knowledge no longer follows relations in accordance with the principle of sufficient reason; on the contrary, it rests in fixed contemplation of the object presented to it out of its connexion with any other, and rises into this. [. . .]

Raised up by the power of the mind, we relinquish the ordinary way of considering things, and cease to follow under the guidance of the forms of the principle of sufficient reason merely their relations to one another, whose final goal is always the relation to our own will. Thus we no longer consider the where, the when, the why, and the whither in things, but simply and solely the *what.* Further, we do not let abstract thought, the concepts of reason, take possession of our consciousness, but, instead of all this, devote the whole power of our mind to perception, sink ourselves completely therein, and let our whole consciousness be filled by the calm contemplation of the natural object actually present, whether it be a landscape, a tree, a rock, a crag, a building, or anything else. We *lose* ourselves entirely in this object, to use a pregnant expression; in other words, we forget our individuality, our will, and continue to exist only as pure subject, as clear mirror of the object, so that it is as though the object alone existed without anyone to perceive it, and thus we are no longer able to separate the perceiver from the perception, but the two have become one, since the entire consciousness is filled and occupied by a single image of perception. If, therefore, the object has to such an extent passed out of all relation to something outside it, and the subject has passed out of all relation to the will, what is thus known is no longer the individual thing as such, but the *Idea*, the eternal form, the immediate objectivity of the will at this grade. Thus at the same time, the person who is involved in this perception is no longer an individual, for in such perception the individual has lost himself; he is *pure* will-less, painless, timeless *subject of knowledge.* [. . .] Now in such contemplation, the particular thing at one stroke becomes the *Idea* of its species, and the perceiving individual becomes the *pure subject of knowing.* The individual, as such knows only particular things; the pure subject of knowledge knows only Ideas. For the individual is the subject of knowledge in its relation to a definite particular phenomenon of will and in subjection thereto. This particular phenomenon of will is, as such, subordinate to the principle of sufficient reason in all its forms; therefore all knowledge which relates itself to this, also follows the principle of sufficient reason, and no other knowledge than this is fit to be of any use to the will; it always has only relations to the object. The knowing individual as such and the particular thing known by him are always in a particular place, at a particular time, and are links in the chain of causes and effects. The pure subject of knowledge and its correlative, the Idea, have passed out of all these forms of the principle of sufficient reason. Time, place, the individual that knows, and the individual that is known, have no meaning for them. First of all, a knowing individual raises himself in the manner described to the pure subject of knowing, and at the same time raises the contemplated object to the Idea; the *world as representation* then stands out whole and pure, and the complete objectification of the will takes place, for only the Idea is the *adequate objectivity* of the will. In itself, the Idea includes object and subject in like manner, for these are its sole form. In it, however, both are of entirely equal weight; and as the object also is here nothing but the representation of the subject, so the subject, by passing entirely into the perceived object, has also become that object itself, since the entire consciousness is nothing more than its most distinct image. This consciousness really constitutes the whole *world as representation*, since we picture to ourselves the whole of the Ideas, or grades of the will's objectivity, passing through it successively. The particular things of all particular times and spaces are nothing but the Ideas multiplied through the principle of sufficient reason (the form of knowledge of the individuals as such), and thus obscured in their pure objectivity. When the Idea appears, subject and object can no longer be distinguished in it, because the Idea, the adequate objectivity of the will, the real world as representation, arises only when subject and object reciprocally fill and penetrate each other completely. In just the same way the knowing and the known individual, as things-in-themselves, are likewise not different. For if we look entirely away from that true *world as representation*, there is nothing left but the *world as will*. The will is the "in-itself" of the Idea that completely objectifies it; it is also the "in-itself" of the particular thing and of the individual that knows it, and these two objectify it incompletely. As will, outside the representation and all its forms, it is one and the same in the contemplated object and in the individual who soars aloft in this contemplation, who becomes conscious of himself as pure subject. Therefore in themselves these two are not different; for in themselves they are the will that here knows itself. Plurality and difference exist only as the way in which this knowledge comes to the will, that is to say, only in the phenomenon, by virtue of its form, the principle of sufficient reason. [. . .]

§ 35.

In order to reach a deeper insight into the nature of the world, it is absolutely necessary for us to learn to distinguish the will as thing-in-itself from its adequate objectivity, and then to distinguish the different grades at which this objectivity appears more distinctly and fully, i.e., the Ideas themselves, from the mere phenomenon of the Ideas in the forms of the principle of sufficient reason, the restricted method of knowledge of individuals. We shall then agree with Plato, when he attributes actual being to the Ideas alone, and only an apparent, dreamlike existence to the things in space and time, to this world that is real for the individual. We shall then see how one and the same Idea reveals itself in so many phenomena, and presents its nature to knowing individuals only piecemeal, one side after another. Then we shall also distinguish the Idea itself from the way in which its phenomenon comes into the observation of the individual, and shall recognize the former as essential, and the latter as inessential. We intend to consider this by way of example on the smallest scale, and then on the largest. When clouds move, the figures they form are not essential, but indifferent to them. But that as elastic vapour they are pressed together, driven off, spread out, and torn apart by the force of the wind, this is their nature, this is the essence of the forces that are objectified in them, this is the Idea. The figures in each case are only for the individual observer. To the brook which rolls downwards over the stones, the eddies, waves, and foam-forms exhibited by it are indifferent and inessential; but that it follows gravity, and behaves as an inelastic, perfectly mobile, formless, and transparent fluid, this is its essential nature, this, *if known through perception*, is the Idea. Those foam-forms exist only for us so long as we know as individuals. The ice on the window-pane is formed into crystals according to the laws of crystallization, which reveal the essence of the natural force here appearing, which exhibit the Idea. But the trees and flowers formed by the ice on the window-pane are inessential, and exist only for us. What appears in clouds, brook, and crystal is the feeblest echo of that will which appears more completely in the plant, still more completely in the animal, and most completely in man. But only the *essential* in all these grades of the will's objectification constitutes the *Idea*; on the other hand, its unfolding or development, because drawn apart in the forms of the principle of sufficient reason into a multiplicity of many-sided phenomena, is inessential to the Idea; it lies merely in the individual's mode of cognition, and has reality only for that individual. [. . .]

In the many different forms and aspects of human life, and in the interminable change of events, he will consider only the Idea as the abiding and essential, in which the will-to-live has its most perfect objectivity, and which shows its different sides in the qualities, passions, errors, and excellences of the human race, in selfishness, hatred, love, fear, boldness, frivolity, stupidity, slyness, wit, genius, and so on. All of these, running and congealing together into a thousand different forms and shapes (individuals), continually produce the history of the great and the small worlds, where in itself it is immaterial whether they are set in motion by nuts or by crowns. [. . .]

§ 36.

History follows the thread of events; it is pragmatic in so far as it deduces them according to the law of motivation, a law that determines the appearing will where that will is illuminated by knowledge. At the lower grades of its objectivity, where it still acts without knowledge, natural science as etiology considers the laws of the changes of its phenomena, and as morphology considers what is permanent in them. This almost endless theme is facilitated by the aid of concepts that comprehend the general, in order to deduce from it the particular. Finally, mathematics considers the mere forms, that is, time and space, in which the Ideas appear drawn apart into plurality for the knowledge of the subject as individual. All these, the common name of which is science, therefore follow the principle of sufficient reason in its different forms, and their theme remains the phenomenon, its laws, connexion, and the relations resulting from these. But now, what kind of knowledge is it that considers what continues to exist outside and independently of all relations, but which alone is really essential to the world, the true content of its phenomena, that which is subject to no change, and is therefore known with equal truth for all time, in a word, the *Ideas* that are the immediate and adequate objectivity of the thing-in-itself, of the will? It is *art*, the work of genius. It repeats the eternal Ideas apprehended through pure contemplation, the essential and abiding element in all the phenomena of the world. According to the material in which it repeats, it is sculpture, painting, poetry, or music. Its only source is knowledge of the Ideas; its sole aim is communication of this knowledge. Whilst science, following the restless and unstable stream of the fourfold forms of reasons or grounds and consequents, is with every end it attains again and again directed farther, and can never find an ultimate goal or complete satisfaction, any more than by running we can reach the point where the clouds touch the horizon; art, on the contrary, is everywhere at its goal. For it plucks the object of its contemplation from the stream of the world's course, and holds it isolated before it. This particular thing, which in that stream was an infinitesimal part, becomes for art a representative of the whole, an equivalent of the infinitely many in space and time. It therefore pauses at this particular thing; it stops the wheel of time; for it the relations vanish; its object is only the essential, the Idea. We can therefore define it accurately as *the way of considering things independently of the principle of sufficient reason*, in contrast to the way of considering them which proceeds in exact accordance with this principle, and is the way of science and experience. This latter method of consideration can be compared to an endless line running horizontally, and the former to a vertical line cutting the horizontal at any point. The method of consideration that follows the principle of sufficient reason is the rational method, and it alone is valid and useful in practical life and in science. The method of consideration that looks away from the content of this principle is the method of genius, which is valid and useful in art alone. The first is Aristotle's method; the second is, on the whole, Plato's. [. . .] Only through the pure contemplation described above, which becomes absorbed entirely in the object, are the Ideas comprehended; and the nature of *genius* consists precisely in the preeminent ability for such contemplation. Now as this demands a complete forgetting of our own person and of its relations and connexions, the *gift of genius* is nothing but the most complete *objectivity*, i.e., the objective tendency of the mind, as opposed to the subjective directed to our own person, i.e., to the will. Accordingly, genius is the capacity to remain in a state of pure perception, to lose oneself in perception, to remove from the service of the will the knowledge which originally existed only for this service. In other words, genius is the ability to leave entirely out of sight our own interest, our willing, and our aims, and consequently to discard entirely our own personality for a time, in order to remain *pure knowing subject*, the clear eye of the world; and this not merely for moments, but with the necessary continuity and conscious thought to enable us to repeat by deliberate art what has been apprehended, and "what in wavering apparition gleams fix in its place with thoughts that stand for ever!" For genius to appear in an individual, it is as if a measure of the power of knowledge must have fallen to his lot far exceeding that required for the service of an individual will; and this superfluity of knowledge having become free, now becomes the subject purified of will, the clear mirror of the inner nature of the world. This explains the animation, amounting to disquietude, in men of genius, since the present can seldom satisfy them, because it does not fill their consciousness. This gives them that restless zealous nature, that constant search for new objects worthy of contemplation, and also that longing, hardly ever satisfied, for men of like nature and stature to whom they may open their hearts. The common mortal, on the other hand, entirely filled and satisfied by the common present, is absorbed in it, and, finding everywhere his like, has that special ease and comfort in daily life which are denied to the man of genius. Imagination has been rightly recognized as an essential element of genius; indeed, it has sometimes been regarded as identical with genius, but this is not correct. The objects of genius as such are the eternal Ideas, the persistent, essential forms of the world and of all its phenomena; but knowledge of the Idea is necessarily knowledge through perception, and is not abstract. Thus the knowledge of the genius would be restricted to the Ideas of objects actually present to his own person, and would be dependent on the concatenation of circumstances that brought them to him, did not imagination extend his horizon far beyond the reality of his personal experience, and enable him to construct all the rest out of the little that has come into his own actual apperception, and thus to let almost all the possible scenes of life pass by within himself. Moreover, the actual objects are almost always only very imperfect copies of the Idea that manifests itself in them. Therefore the man of genius requires imagination, in order to see in things not what nature has actually formed, but what she endeavoured to form, yet did not bring about, because of the conflict of her forms with one another. [. . .] Thus imagination extends the mental horizon of the genius beyond the objects that actually present themselves to his person, as regards both quality and quantity. For this reason, unusual strength of imagination is a companion, indeed a condition, of genius. But the converse is not the case, for strength of imagination is not evidence of genius; on the contrary, even men with little or no touch of genius may have much imagination. For we can consider an actual object in two opposite ways, purely objectively, the way of genius grasping the Idea of the object, or in the common way, merely in its relations to other objects according to the principle of sufficient reason, and in its relations to our own will. In a similar manner, we can also perceive an imaginary object in these two ways. Considered in the first way, it is a means to knowledge of the Idea, the communication of which is the work of art. In the second case, the imaginary object is used to build castles in the air, congenial to selfishness and to one's own whim, which for the moment delude and delight; thus only the relations of the phantasms so connected are really ever known. The man who indulges in this game is a dreamer; he will easily mingle with reality the pictures that delight his solitude, and will thus become unfit for real life. Perhaps he will write down the delusions of his imagination, and these will give us the ordinary novels of all kinds which entertain those like him and the public at large, since the readers fancy themselves in the position of the hero, and then find the description very "nice."

As we have said, the common, ordinary man, that manufactured article of nature which she daily produces in thousands, is not capable, at any rate continuously, of a consideration of things wholly disinterested in every sense, such as is contemplation proper. He can direct his attention to things only in so far as they have some relation to his will, although that relation may be only very indirect. As in this reference that always demands only knowledge of the relations, the abstract concept of the thing is sufficient and often even more appropriate, the ordinary man does not linger long over the mere perception, does not fix his eye on an object for long, but, in everything that presents itself to him, quickly looks merely for the concept under which it is to be brought, just as the lazy man looks for a chair, which then no longer interests him. [. . .] On the other hand, the man of genius, whose power of knowledge is, through its excess, withdrawn for a part of his time from the service of his will, dwells on the consideration of life itself, strives to grasp the Idea of each thing, not its relations to other things. In doing this, he frequently neglects a consideration of his own path in life, and therefore often pursues this with insufficient skill.

Whereas to the ordinary man his faculty of knowledge is a lamp that lights his path, to the man of genius it is the sun that reveals the world. This great difference in their way of looking at life soon becomes visible even in the outward appearance of them both. The glance of the man in whom genius lives and works readily distinguishes him; it is both vivid and firm and bears the character of thoughtfulness, of contemplation. We can see this in the portraits of the few men of genius which nature has produced here and there among countless millions. On the other hand, the real opposite of contemplation, namely spying or prying, can be readily seen in the glance of others, if indeed it is not dull and vacant, as is often the case. Consequently a face's "expression of genius" consists in the fact that a decided predominance of knowing over willing is visible in it, and hence that there is manifested in it a knowledge without any relation to a will, in other words, a *pure knowing*. On the other hand, in the case of faces that follow the rule, the expression of the will predominates, and we see that knowledge comes into activity only on the impulse of the will, and so is directed only to motives.

As the knowledge of the genius, or knowledge of the Idea, is that which does not follow the principle of sufficient reason, so, on the other hand, the knowledge that does follow this principle gives us prudence and rationality in life, and brings about the sciences. Thus individuals of genius will be affected with the defects entailed in the neglect of the latter kind of knowledge. Here, however, a limitation must be observed, that what I shall state in this regard concerns them only in so far as, and while, they are actually engaged with the kind of knowledge peculiar to the genius. Now this is by no means the case at every moment of their lives, for the great though spontaneous exertion required for the will-free comprehension of the Ideas necessarily relaxes again, and there are long intervals during which men of genius stand in very much the same position as ordinary persons, both as regards merits and defects. On this account, the action of genius has always been regarded as an inspiration, as indeed the name itself indicates, as the action of a superhuman being different from the individual himself, which takes possession of him only periodically. The disinclination of men of genius to direct their attention to the content of the principle of sufficient reason will show itself first in regard to the ground of being, as a disinclination for mathematics. The consideration of mathematics proceeds on the most universal forms of the phenomenon, space and time, which are themselves only modes or aspects of the principle of sufficient reason; and it is therefore the very opposite of that consideration that seeks only the content of the phenomenon, namely the Idea expressing itself in the phenomenon apart from all relations. Moreover, the logical procedure of mathematics will be repugnant to genius, for it obscures real insight and does not satisfy it; it presents a mere concatenation of conclusions according to the principle of the ground of knowing. Of all the mental powers, it makes the greatest claim on memory, so that one may have before oneself all the earlier propositions to which reference is made. Experience has also confirmed that men of great artistic genius have no aptitude for mathematics; no man was ever very distinguished in both at the same time. Alfieri relates that he was never able to understand even the fourth proposition of Euclid. Goethe was reproached enough with his want of mathematical knowledge by the ignorant opponents of his colour theory. Here, where it was naturally not a question of calculation and measurement according to hypothetical data, but one of direct knowledge by understanding cause and effect, this reproach was so utterly absurd and out of place, that they revealed their total lack of judgement just as much by such a reproach as by the rest of their Midas-utterances. The fact that even today, nearly half a century after the appearance of Goethe's colour theory, the Newtonian fallacies still remain in undisturbed possession of the professorial chair even in Germany, and that people continue to talk quite seriously about the seven homogeneous rays of light and their differing refrangibility, will one day be numbered among the great intellectual peculiarities of mankind in general, and of the Germans in particular. From the same above-mentioned cause may be explained the equally well-known fact that, conversely, distinguished mathematicians have little susceptibility to works of fine art. [. . .] Further, as keen comprehension of relations according to the laws of causality and motivation really constitutes prudence or sagacity, whereas the knowledge of genius is not directed to relations, a prudent man will not be a genius insofar as and while he is prudent, and a genius will not be prudent insofar as and while he is a genius. Finally, knowledge of perception generally, in the province of which the Idea entirely lies, is directly opposed to rational or abstract knowledge which is guided by the principle of the ground of knowing. It is also well known that we seldom find great genius united with preeminent reasonableness; on the contrary, men of genius are often subject to violent emotions and irrational passions. But the cause of this is not weakness of the faculty of reason, but partly unusual energy of that whole phenomenon of will, the individual genius. This phenomenon manifests itself through vehemence of all his acts of will. The cause is also partly a preponderance of knowledge from perception through the senses and the understanding over abstract knowledge, in other words, a decided tendency to the perceptive. In such men the extremely energetic impression of the perceptive outshines the colourless concepts so much that conduct is no longer guided by the latter, but by the former, and on this very account becomes irrational. Accordingly, the impression of the present moment on them is very strong, and carries them away into thoughtless actions, into emotion and passion. Moreover, since their knowledge has generally been withdrawn in part from the service of the will, they will not in conversation think so much of the person with whom they are speaking as of the thing they are speaking about, which is vividly present in their minds. Therefore they will judge or narrate too objectively for their own interests; they will not conceal what it would be more prudent to keep concealed, and so on. Finally, they are inclined to soliloquize, and in general may exhibit several weaknesses that actually are closely akin to madness. It is often remarked that genius and madness have a side where they touch and even pass over into each other, and even poetic inspiration has been called a kind of madness. [. . .] I must mention having found, in frequent visits to lunatic asylums, individual subjects endowed with unmistakably great gifts. Their genius appeared distinctly through their madness which had completely gained the upper hand. Now this cannot be ascribed to chance, for on the one hand the number of mad persons is relatively very small, while on the other a man of genius is a phenomenon rare beyond all ordinary estimation, and appearing in nature only as the greatest exception. We may be convinced of this from the mere fact that we can compare the number of the really great men of genius produced by the whole of civilized Europe in ancient and modern times, with the two hundred and fifty millions who are always living in Europe and renew themselves every thirty years. Among men of genius, however, can be reckoned only those who have furnished works that have retained through all time an enduring value for mankind. Indeed, I will not refrain from mentioning that I have known some men of decided, though not remarkable, mental superiority who at the same time betrayed a slight touch of insanity. Accordingly, it might appear that every advance of the intellect beyond the usual amount as an abnormality, already disposes to madness. [. . .]

§ 37.

Now according to our explanation, genius consists in the ability to know, independently of the principle of sufficient reason, not individual things which have their existence only in the relation, but the Ideas of such things, and in the ability to be, in face of these, the correlative of the Idea, and hence no longer individual, but pure subject of knowing. Yet this ability must be inherent in all men in a lesser and different degree, as otherwise they would be just as incapable of enjoying works of art as of producing them. Generally they would have no susceptibility at all to the beautiful and to the sublime; indeed, these words could have no meaning for them. We must therefore assume as existing in all men that power of recognizing in things their Ideas, of divesting themselves for a moment of their personality, unless indeed there are some who are not capable of any aesthetic pleasure at all. The man of genius excels them only in the far higher degree and more continuous duration of this kind of knowledge. These enable him to retain that thoughtful contemplation necessary for him to repeat what is thus known in a voluntary and international work, such repetition being the work of art. Through this he communicates to others the Idea he has grasped. Therefore this Idea remains unchanged and the same, and hence aesthetic pleasure is essentially one and the same, whether it be called forth by a work of art, or directly by the contemplation of nature and of life. The work of art is merely a means of facilitating that knowledge in which this pleasure consists. That the Idea comes to us more easily from the work of art than directly from nature and from reality, arises solely from the fact that the artist, who knew only the Idea and not reality, clearly repeated in his work only the Idea, separated it out from reality, and omitted all disturbing contingencies. The artist lets us peer into the world through his eyes. That he has these eyes, that he knows the essential in things which lies outside all relations, is the gift of genius and is inborn; but that he is able to lend us this gift, to let us see with his eyes, is acquired, and is the technical side of art. Therefore, after the account I have given in the foregoing remarks of the inner essence of the aesthetic way of knowing in its most general outline, the following more detailed philosophical consideration of the beautiful and the sublime will explain both simultaneously, in nature and in art, without separating them further. We shall first consider what takes place in a man when he is affected by the beautiful and the sublime. Whether he draws this emotion directly from nature, from life, or partakes of it only through the medium of art, makes no essential difference, but only an outward one.

§ 38.

In the aesthetic method of consideration we found *two inseparable constituent parts*: namely, knowledge of the object not as individual thing, but as Platonic *Idea*, in other words, as persistent form of this whole species of things; and the self-consciousness of the knower, not as individual, but as *pure, will-less subject of knowledge*. The condition under which the two constituent parts appear always united was the abandonment of the method of knowledge that is bound to the principle of sufficient reason, a knowledge that, on the contrary, is the only appropriate kind for serving the will and also for science. Moreover, we shall see that the *pleasure* produced by contemplation of the beautiful arises from those two constituent parts, sometimes more from the one than from the other, according to what the object of aesthetic contemplation may be.

All *willing* springs from lack, from deficiency, and thus from suffering. Fulfilment brings this to an end; yet for one wish that is fulfilled there remain at least ten that are denied. Further, desiring lasts a long time, demands and requests go on to infinity; fulfilment is short and meted out sparingly. But even the final satisfaction itself is only apparent; the wish fulfilled at once makes way for a new one; the former is a known delusion, the latter a delusion not as yet known. No attained object of willing can give a satisfaction that lasts and no longer declines; but it is always like the alms thrown to a beggar, which reprieves him today so that his misery may be prolonged till tomorrow. Therefore, so long as our consciousness is filled by our will, so long as we are given up to the throng of desires with its constant hopes and fears, so long as we are the subject of willing, we never obtain lasting happiness or peace. Essentially, it is all the same whether we pursue or flee, fear harm or aspire to enjoyment; care for the constantly demanding will, no matter in what form, continually fills and moves consciousness; but without peace and calm, true well-being is absolutely impossible. [. . .]

When, however, an external cause or inward disposition suddenly raises us out of the endless stream of willing, and snatches knowledge from the thraldom of the will, the attention is now no longer directed to the motives of willing, but comprehends things free from their relation to the will. Thus it considers things without interest, without subjectivity, purely objectively; it is entirely given up to them in so far as they are merely representations, and not motives. Then all at once the peace, always sought but always escaping us on that first path of willing, comes to us of its own accord, and all is well with us. [. . .]

But this is just the state that I described above as necessary for knowledge of the Idea, as pure contemplation, absorption in perception, being lost in the object, forgetting all individuality, abolishing the kind of knowledge which follows the principle of sufficient reason, and comprehends only relations. It is the state where, simultaneously and inseparably, the perceived individual thing is raised to the Idea of its species, and the knowing individual to the pure subject of will-less knowing, and now the two, as such, no longer stand in the stream of time and of all other relations. It is then all the same whether we see the setting sun from a prison or from a palace.

Inward disposition, predominance of knowing over willing, can bring about this state in any environment. This is shown by those admirable Dutchmen who directed such purely objective perception to the most insignificant objects, and set up a lasting monument of their objectivity and spiritual peace in paintings of *still life*. The aesthetic beholder does not contemplate this without emotion, for it graphically describes to him the calm, tranquil, will-free frame of mind of the artist which was necessary for contemplating such insignificant things so objectively, considering them so attentively, and repeating this perception with such thought. Since the picture invites the beholder to participate in this state, his emotion is often enhanced by the contrast between it and his own restless state of mind, disturbed by vehement willing, in which he happens to be. In the same spirit landscape painters, especially Ruysdael, have often painted extremely insignificant landscape objects, and have thus produced the same effect even more delightfully.

So much is achieved simply and solely by the inner force of an artistic disposition; but that purely objective frame of mind is facilitated and favoured from without by accommodating objects, by the abundance of natural beauty that invites contemplation, and even presses itself on us. Whenever it presents itself to our gaze all at once, it almost always succeeds in snatching us, although only for a few moments, from subjectivity, from the thraldom of the will, and transferring us into the state of pure knowledge. This is why the man tormented by passions, want, or care, is so suddenly revived, cheered, and comforted by a single, free glance into nature. The storm of passions, the pressure of desire and fear, and all the miseries of willing are then at once calmed and appeased in a marvellous way. For at the moment when, torn from the will, we have given ourselves up to pure, will-less knowing, we have stepped into another world, so to speak, where everything that moves our will, and thus violently agitates us, no longer exists. This liberation of knowledge lifts us as wholly and completely above all this as do sleep and dreams. Happiness and unhappiness have vanished; we are no longer the individual; that is forgotten; we are only pure subject of knowledge. We are only that *one* eye of the world which looks out from all knowing creatures, but which in man alone can be wholly free from serving the will. In this way, all difference of individuality disappears so completely that it is all the same whether the perceiving eye belongs to a mighty monarch or to a stricken beggar; for beyond that boundary neither happiness nor misery is taken with us. There always lies so near to us a realm in which we have escaped entirely from all our affliction; but who has the strength to remain in it for long? As soon as any relation to our will, to our person, even of those objects of pure contemplation, again enters consciousness, the magic is at an end. We fall back into knowledge governed by the principle of sufficient reason; we now no longer know the Idea, but the individual thing, the link of a chain to which we also belong, and we are again abandoned to all our woe. Most men are almost always at this standpoint, because they entirely lack objectivity, i.e., genius. Therefore they do not like to be alone with nature; they need company, or at any rate a book, for their knowledge remains subject to the will. Therefore in objects they seek only some relation to their will, and with everything that has not such a relation there sounds within them, as it were like a ground-bass, the constant, inconsolable lament, "It is of no use to me." Thus in solitude even the most beautiful surroundings have for them a desolate, dark, strange, and hostile appearance.

Finally, it is also that blessedness of will-less perception which spreads so wonderful a charm over the past and the distant, and by a self-deception presents them to us in so flattering a light. For by our conjuring up in our minds days long past spent in a distant place, it is only the objects recalled by our imagination, not the subject of will, that carried around its incurable sorrows with it just as much then as it does now. But these are forgotten, because since then they have frequently made way for others. Now in what is remembered, objective perception is just as effective as it would be in what is present, if we allowed it to have influence over us, if, free from will, we surrendered ourselves to it. Hence it happens that, especially when we are more than usually disturbed by some want, the sudden recollection of past and distant scenes flits across our minds like a lost paradise. The imagination recalls merely what was objective, not what was individually subjective, and we imagine that that something objective stood before us then just as pure and undisturbed by any relation to the will as its image now stands in the imagination; but the relation of objects to our will caused us just as much affliction then as it does now. We can withdraw from all suffering just as well through present as through distant objects, whenever we raise ourselves to a purely objective contemplation of them, and are thus able to produce the illusion that only those objects are present, not we ourselves. Then, as pure subject of knowing, delivered from the miserable self, we become entirely one with those objects, and foreign as our want is to them, it is at such moments just as foreign to us. Then the world as representation alone remains; the world as will has disappeared.

In all these remarks, I have sought to make clear the nature and extent of the share which the subjective condition has in aesthetic pleasure, namely the deliverance of knowledge from the service of the will, the forgetting of oneself as individual, and the enhancement of consciousness to the pure, will-less, timeless subject of knowing that is independent of all relations. With this subjective side of aesthetic contemplation there always appears at the same time as necessary correlative its objective side, the intuitive apprehension of the Platonic Idea. But before we turn to a closer consideration of this and to the achievements of art in reference to it, it is better to stop for a while at the subjective side of aesthetic pleasure, in order to complete our consideration of this by discussing the impression of the *sublime*, which depends solely on it, and arises through a modification of it. After this, our investigation of aesthetic pleasure will be completed by a consideration of its objective side. [. . .]

§ 39.

[. . .] Now so long as it is this accommodation of nature, the significance and distinctness of its forms, from which the Ideas individualized in them readily speak to us; so long as it is this which moves us from knowledge of mere relations serving the will into aesthetic contemplation, and thus raises us to the will-free subject of knowing, so long is it merely the *beautiful* that affects us, and the feeling of beauty that is excited. But these very objects, whose significant forms invite us to a pure contemplation of them, may have a hostile relation to the human will in general, as manifested in its objectivity, the human body. They may be opposed to it; they may threaten it by their might that eliminates all resistance, or their immeasurable greatness may reduce it to nought. Nevertheless, the beholder may not direct his attention to this relation to his will which is so pressing and hostile, but, although he perceives and acknowledges it, he may consciously turn away from it, forcibly tear himself from his will and its relations, and, giving himself up entirely to knowledge, may quietly contemplate, as pure, will-less subject of knowing, those very objects so terrible to the will. He may comprehend only their Idea that is foreign to all relation, gladly linger over its contemplation, and consequently be elevated precisely in this way above himself, his person, his willing, and all willing. In that case, he is then filled with the feeling of the *sublime*; he is in the state of exaltation, and therefore the object that causes such a state is called *sublime*. Thus what distinguishes the feeling of the sublime from that of the beautiful is that, with the beautiful, pure knowledge has gained the upper hand without a struggle, since the beauty of the object, in other words that quality of it which facilitates knowledge of its Idea, has removed from consciousness, without resistance and hence imperceptibly, the will and knowledge of relations that slavishly serve this will. What is then left is pure subject of knowing, and not even a recollection of the will remains. On the other hand, with the sublime, that state of pure knowing is obtained first of all by a conscious and violent tearing away from the relations of the same object to the will which are recognized as unfavourable, by a free exaltation, accompanied by consciousness, beyond the will and the knowledge related to it. This exaltation must not only be won with consciousness, but also be maintained, and it is therefore accompanied by a constant recollection of the will, yet not of a single individual willing, such as fear or desire, but of human willing in general, in so far as it is expressed universally through its objectivity, the human body. If a single, real act of will were to enter consciousness through actual personal affliction and danger from the object, the individual will, thus actually affected, would at once gain the upper hand. The peace of contemplation would become impossible, the impression of the sublime would be lost, because it had yielded to anxiety, in which the effort of the individual to save himself supplanted every other thought. A few examples will contribute a great deal to making clear this theory of the aesthetically sublime, and removing any doubt about it. At the same time they will show the difference in the degrees of this feeling of the sublime. For in the main it is identical with the feeling of the beautiful, with pure will-less knowing, and with the knowledge, which necessarily appears therewith, of the Ideas out of all relation that is determined by the principle of sufficient reason. The feeling of the sublime is distinguished from that of the beautiful only by the addition, namely the exaltation beyond the known hostile relation of the contemplated object to the will in general. Thus there result several degrees of the sublime, in fact transitions from the beautiful to the sublime, according as this addition is strong, clamorous, urgent, and near, or only feeble, remote, and merely suggested. [. . .]

[. . .] But above all else, the beautiful in architecture is enhanced by the favour of light, and through it even the most insignificant thing becomes a beautiful object. Now if in the depth of winter, when the whole of nature is frozen and stiff, we see the rays of the setting sun reflected by masses of stone, where they illuminate without warming, and are thus favourable only to the purest kind of knowledge, not to the will, then contemplation of the beautiful effect of light on these masses moves us into the state of pure knowing, as all beauty does. Yet here, through the faint recollection of the lack of warmth from those rays, in other words, of the absence of the principle of life, a certain transcending of the interest of the will is required. There is a slight challenge to abide in pure knowledge, to turn away from all willing, and precisely in this way we have a transition from the feeling of the beautiful to that of the sublime. It is the faintest trace of the sublime in the beautiful, and beauty itself appears here only in a slight degree. [. . .]

The following environment can cause this in an even higher degree. Nature in turbulent and tempestuous motion; semi-darkness through threatening black thunder-clouds; immense, bare, overhanging cliffs shutting out the view by their interlacing; rushing, foaming masses of water; complete desert; the wail of the wind sweeping through the ravines. Our dependence, our struggle with hostile nature, our will that is broken in this, now appear clearly before our eyes. Yet as long as personal affliction does not gain the upper hand, but we remain in aesthetic contemplation, the pure subject of knowing gazes through this struggle of nature, through this picture of the broken will, and comprehends calmly, unshaken and unconcerned, the Ideas in those very objects that are threatening and terrible to the will. In this contrast is to be found the feeling of the sublime.

But the impression becomes even stronger, when we have before our eyes the struggle of the agitated forces of nature on a large scale, when in these surroundings the roaring of a falling stream deprives us of the possibility of hearing our own voices. Or when we are abroad in the storm of tempestuous seas; mountainous waves rise and fall, are dashed violently against steep cliffs, and shoot their spray high into the air. The storm howls, the sea roars, the lightning flashes from black clouds, and thunder-claps drown the noise of storm and sea. Then in the unmoved beholder of this scene the twofold nature of his consciousness reaches the highest distinctness. Simultaneously, he feels himself as individual, as the feeble phenomenon of will, which the slightest touch of these forces can annihilate, helpless against powerful nature, dependent, abandoned to chance, a vanishing nothing in face of stupendous forces; and he also feels himself as the eternal, serene subject of knowing, who as the condition of every object is the supporter of this whole world, the fearful struggle of nature being only his mental picture or representation; he himself is free from, and foreign to, all willing and all needs, in the quiet comprehension of the Ideas. This is the full impression of the sublime. Here it is caused by the sight of a power beyond all comparison superior to the individual, and threatening him with annihilation.

The impression of the sublime can arise in quite a different way by our imagining a mere magnitude in space and time, whose immensity reduces the individual to nought. By retaining Kant's terms and his correct division, we can call the first kind the dynamically sublime, and the second the mathematically sublime, although we differ from him entirely in the explanation of the inner nature of that impression, and can concede no share in this either to moral reflections or to hypostases from scholastic philosophy. [. . .]

Our explanation of the sublime can indeed be extended to cover the ethical, namely what is described as the sublime character. Such a character springs from the fact that the will is not excited here by objects certainly well calculated to excite it, but that knowledge retains the upper hand. Such a character will accordingly consider men in a purely objective way, and not according to the relations they might have to his will. For example, he will observe their faults, and even their hatred and injustice to himself, without being thereby stirred to hatred on his own part. He will contemplate their happiness without feeling envy, recognize their good qualities without desiring closer association with them, perceive the beauty of women without hankering after them. His personal happiness or unhappiness will not violently affect him. [. . .]

§ 40.

Since opposites throw light on each other, it may here be in place to remark that the real opposite of the sublime is something that is not at first sight recognized as such, namely the *charming or attractive*. By this I understand that which excites the will by directly presenting to it satisfaction, fulfilment. [. . .] [T]he charming or attractive draws the beholder down from pure contemplation, demanded by every apprehension of the beautiful, since it necessarily stirs his will by objects that directly appeal to it. Thus the beholder no longer remains pure subject of knowing, but becomes the needy and dependent subject of willing. That every beautiful thing of a cheering nature is usually called charming or attractive is due to a concept too widely comprehended through want of correct discrimination, and I must put it entirely on one side, and even object to it. But in the sense already stated and explained, I find in the province of art only two species of the charming, and both are unworthy of it. The one species, a very low one, is found in the still life painting of the Dutch, when they err by depicting edible objects. By their deceptive appearance these necessarily excite the appetite, and this is just a stimulation of the will which puts an end to any aesthetic contemplation of the object. Painted fruit, however, is, admissible, for it exhibits itself as a further development of the flower, and as a beautiful product of nature through form and colour, without our being positively forced to think of its edibility. But unfortunately we often find, depicted with deceptive naturalness, prepared and served-up dishes, oysters, herrings, crabs, bread and butter, beer, wine, and so on, all of which is wholly objectionable. In historical painting and in sculpture the charming consists in nude figures, the position, semi-drapery, and whole treatment of which are calculated to excite lustful feeling in the beholder. Purely aesthetic contemplation is at once abolished, and the purpose of art thus defeated. This mistake is wholly in keeping with what was just censured when speaking of the Dutch. In the case of all beauty and complete nakedness of form, the ancients are almost always free from this fault, since the artist himself created them with a purely objective spirit filled with ideal beauty, not in the spirit of subjective, base sensuality. The charming, therefore, is everywhere to be avoided in art.

There is also a negatively charming, even more objectionable than the positively charming just discussed, and that is the disgusting or offensive. Just like the charming in the proper sense, it rouses the will of the beholder, and therefore disturbs purely aesthetic contemplation. But it is a violent non-willing, a repugnance, that it excites; it rouses the will by holding before it objects that are abhorrent. It has therefore always been recognized as absolutely inadmissible in art, where even the ugly can be tolerated in its proper place so long as it is not disgusting, as we shall see later.

§ 41.

The course of our remarks has made it necessary to insert here a discussion of the sublime, when the treatment of the beautiful has been only half completed, merely from one side, the subjective. For it is only a special modification of this subjective side which distinguishes the sublime from the beautiful. [. . .] In the object the two are not essentially different, for in every case the object of aesthetic contemplation is not the individual thing, but the Idea in it striving for revelation, in other words, the adequate objectivity of the will at a definite grade. [. . .]

By calling an object *beautiful*, we thereby assert that it is an object of our aesthetic contemplation, and this implies two different things. On the one hand, the sight of the thing makes us *objective*, that is to say, in contemplating it we are no longer conscious of ourselves as individuals, but as pure, will-less subjects of knowing. On the other hand, we recognize in the object not the individual thing, but an Idea; and this can happen only in so far as our contemplation of the object is not given up to the principle of sufficient reason, does not follow the relation of the object to something outside it (which is ultimately always connected with relations to our own willing), but rests on the object itself. For the Idea and the pure subject of knowing always appear simultaneously in consciousness as necessary correlatives, and with this appearance all distinction of time at once vanishes, as both are wholly foreign to the principle of sufficient reason in all its forms. Both lie outside the relations laid down by this principle. [. . .] Therefore if, for example, I contemplate a tree aesthetically, i.e., with artistic eyes, and thus recognize not it but its Idea, it is immediately of no importance whether it is this tree or its ancestor that flourished a thousand years ago, and whether the contemplator is this individual, or any other living anywhere and at any time. The particular thing and the knowing individual are abolished with the principle of sufficient reason, and nothing remains but the Idea and the pure subject of knowing, which together constitute the adequate objectivity of the will at this grade. And the Idea is released not only from time but also from space; for the Idea is not really this spatial form which floats before me, but its expression, its pure significance, its innermost being, disclosing itself and appealing to me; and it can be wholly the same, in spite of great difference in the spatial relations of the form.

Now since, on the one hand, every existing thing can be observed purely objectively and outside all relation, and, on the other, the will appears in everything at some grade of its objectivity, and this thing is accordingly the expression of an Idea, everything is also *beautiful*. That even the most insignificant thing admits of purely objective and will-less contemplation and thus proves itself to be beautiful, is testified by the still life paintings of the Dutch, already mentioned in this connexion in para. 38. But one thing is more beautiful than another because it facilitates this purely objective contemplation, goes out to meet it, and, so to speak, even compels it, and then we call the thing very beautiful. This is the case partly because, as individual thing, it expresses purely the Idea of its species through the very distinct, clearly defined, and thoroughly significant relation of its parts. It also completely reveals that Idea through the completeness, united in it, of all the manifestations possible to its species, so that it greatly facilitates for the beholder the transition from the individual thing to the Idea, and thus also the state of pure contemplation. Sometimes that eminent quality of special beauty in an object is to be found in the fact that the Idea itself, appealing to us from the object, is a high grade of the will's objectivity, and is therefore most significant and suggestive. For this reason, man is more beautiful than all other objects, and the revelation of his inner nature is the highest aim of art. Human form and human expression are the most important object of plastic art, just as human conduct is the most important object of poetry. Yet each thing has its own characteristic beauty, not only everything organic that manifests itself in the unity of an individuality, but also everything inorganic and formless, and even every manufactured article. For all these reveal the Ideas through which the will objectifies itself at the lowest grades; they sound, as it were, the deepest, lingering bass-notes of nature. Gravity, rigidity, fluidity, light, and so on, are the Ideas that express themselves in rocks, buildings, and masses of water. Landscape-gardening and architecture can do no more than help them to unfold their qualities distinctly, perfectly, and comprehensively. They give them the opportunity to express themselves clearly, and in this way invite and facilitate aesthetic contemplation. On the other hand, this is achieved in a slight degree, or not at all, by inferior buildings and localities neglected by nature or spoiled by art. Yet these universal basic Ideas of nature do not entirely disappear even from them. Here too they address themselves to the observer who looks for them, and even bad buildings and the like are still capable of being aesthetically contemplated; the Ideas of the most universal properties of their material are still recognizable in them. The artificial form given to them, however, is a means not of facilitating, but rather of hindering, aesthetic contemplation. Manufactured articles also help the expression of Ideas, though here it is not the Idea of the manufactured articles that speaks from them, but the Idea of the material to which this artificial form has been given. [. . .] Consequently, from our point of view, we cannot agree with Plato when he asserts (*Republic*, X [596 ff.] [. . .] that table and chair express the Ideas of table and chair, but we say that they express the Ideas already expressed in their mere material as such. However, according to Aristotle (*Metaphysics*, xii, chap. 3), Plato himself would have allowed Ideas only of natural beings and entities [. . .] and in chapter 5 it is said that, according to the Platonists, there are no Ideas of house and ring. [. . .] We may take this opportunity to mention yet another point in which our theory of Ideas differs widely from that of Plato. Thus he teaches (*Republic*, X [601] [. . .]) that the object which art aims at expressing, the prototype of painting and poetry, is not the Idea, but the individual thing. The whole of our discussion so far maintains the very opposite, and Plato's opinion is the less likely to lead us astray, as it is the source of one of the greatest and best known errors of that great man, namely of his disdain and rejection of art, especially of poetry. His false judgement of this is directly associated with the passage quoted.

§ 42.

I return to our discussion of the aesthetic impression. Knowledge of the beautiful always supposes, simultaneously and inseparably, a purely knowing subject and a known Idea as object. But yet the source of aesthetic enjoyment will lie sometimes rather in the apprehension of the known Idea, sometimes rather in the bliss and peace of mind of pure knowledge free from all willing, and thus from all individuality and the pain that results therefrom. And in fact, this predominance of the one or the other constituent element of aesthetic enjoyment will depend on whether the intuitively grasped Idea is a higher or a lower grade of the will's objectivity. Thus with aesthetic contemplation (in real life or through the medium of art) of natural beauty in the inorganic and vegetable kingdoms and of the works of architecture, the enjoyment of pure, will-less knowing will predominate, because the Ideas here apprehended are only low grades of the will's objectivity, and therefore are not phenomena of deep significance and suggestive content. On the other hand, if animals and human beings are the object of aesthetic contemplation or presentation, the enjoyment will consist rather in the objective apprehension of these Ideas that are the most distinct revelations of the will. For these exhibit the greatest variety of forms, a wealth and deep significance of phenomena; they reveal to us most completely the essence of the will, whether in its violence, its terribleness, its satisfaction, or its being broken (this last in tragic situations), finally even in its change or self-surrender, which is the particular theme of Christian painting. Historical painting and the drama generally have as object the Idea of the will enlightened by full knowledge. We will now go over the arts one by one, and in this way the theory of the beautiful that we put forward will gain in completeness and distinctness.

§ 43.

[. . .] Now if we consider *architecture* merely as a fine art and apart from its provision for useful purposes, in which it serves the will and not pure knowledge, and thus is no longer art in our sense, we can assign it no purpose other than that of bringing to clearer perceptiveness some of those Ideas that are the lowest grades of the will's objectivity. Such Ideas are gravity, cohesion, rigidity, hardness, those universal qualities of stone, those first, simplest, and dullest visibilities of the will, the fundamental bass-notes of nature; and along with these, light, which is in many respects their opposite. Even at this low stage of the will's objectivity, we see its inner nature revealing itself in discord; for, properly speaking, the conflict between gravity and rigidity is the sole aesthetic material of architecture; its problem is to make this conflict appear with perfect distinctness in many different ways. It solves this problem by depriving these indestructible forces of the shortest path to their satisfaction, and keeping them in suspense through a circuitous path; the conflict is thus prolonged, and the inexhaustible efforts of the two forces become visible in many different ways. The whole mass of the building, if left to its original tendency, would exhibit a mere heap or lump, bound to the earth as firmly as possible, to which gravity, the form in which the will here appears, presses incessantly, whereas rigidity, also objectivity of the will, resists. But this very tendency, this effort, is thwarted in its immediate satisfaction by architecture, and only an indirect satisfaction by roundabout ways is granted to it. The joists and beams, for example, can press the earth only by means of the column; the arch must support itself, and only through the medium of the pillars can it satisfy its tendency towards the earth, and so on. By just these enforced digressions, by these very hindrances, those forces inherent in the crude mass of stone unfold themselves in the most distinct and varied manner; and the purely aesthetic purpose of architecture can go no farther. Therefore the beauty of a building is certainly to be found in the evident and obvious suitability of every part, not to the outward arbitrary purpose of man (to this extent the work belongs to practical architecture), but directly to the stability of the whole. The position, size, and form of every part must have so necessary a relation to this stability that if it were possible to remove some part, the whole would inevitably collapse. For only by each part bearing as much as it conveniently can, and each being supported exactly where it ought to be and to exactly the necessary extent, does this play of opposition, this conflict between rigidity and gravity, that constitutes the life of the stone and the manifestations of its will, unfold itself in the most complete visibility. These lowest grades of the will's objectivity distinctly reveal themselves. In just the same way, the form of each part must be determined not arbitrarily, but by its purpose and its relation to the whole. The column is the simplest form of support, determined merely by the purpose or intention. The twisted column is tasteless; the four-cornered pillar is in fact less simple than the round column, though it happens to be more easily made. Also the forms of frieze, joist, arch, vault, dome are determined entirely by their immediate purpose, and are self-explanatory therefrom. Ornamental work on capitals, etc., belongs to sculpture and not to architecture, and is merely tolerated as an additional embellishment, which might be dispensed with. From what has been said, it is absolutely necessary for an understanding and aesthetic enjoyment of a work of architecture to have direct knowledge through perception of its matter as regards its weight, rigidity, and cohesion. Our pleasure in such a work would suddenly be greatly diminished by the disclosure that the building material was pumice-stone, for then it would strike us as a kind of sham building. We should be affected in almost the same way if we were told that it was only of wood, when we had assumed it to be stone, just because this alters and shifts the relation between rigidity and gravity, and thus the significance and necessity of all the parts; for those natural forces reveal themselves much more feebly in a wooden building. Therefore, no architectural work as fine art can really be made of timber, however many forms this may assume; this can be explained simply and solely by our theory. [. . .]

Now architectural works have a quite special relation to light; in full sunshine with the blue sky as a background they gain a twofold beauty; and by moonlight again they reveal quite a different effect. Therefore when a fine work of architecture is erected, special consideration is always given to the effects of light and to the climate. The reason for all this is to be found principally in the fact that only a bright, strong illumination makes all the parts and their relations clearly visible. Moreover, I am of the opinion that architecture is destined to reveal not only gravity and rigidity, but at the same time the nature of light, which is their very opposite. The light is intercepted, impeded, and reflected by the large, opaque, sharply contoured and variously formed masses of stone, and thus unfolds its nature and qualities in the purest and clearest way, to the great delight of the beholder; for light is the most agreeable of things as the condition and objective correlative of the most perfect kind of knowledge through perception.

Now since the Ideas, brought to clear perception by architecture, are the lowest grades of the will's objectivity, and since, in consequence, the objective significance of what architecture reveals to us is relatively small, the aesthetic pleasure of looking at a fine and favourably illuminated building will lie not so much in the apprehension of the Idea as in the subjective correlative thereof which accompanies this apprehension. Hence this pleasure will consist preeminently in the fact that, at the sight of this building, the beholder is emancipated from the kind of knowledge possessed by the individual, which serves the will and follows the principle of sufficient reason, and is raised to that of the pure, will-free subject of knowing. Thus it will consist in pure contemplation itself, freed from all the suffering of will and of individuality. In this respect, the opposite of architecture, and the other extreme in the series of fine arts, is the drama, which brings to knowledge the most significant of all the Ideas; hence in the aesthetic enjoyment of it the objective side is predominant throughout.

Architecture is distinguished from the plastic arts and poetry by the fact that it gives us not a copy, but the thing itself. Unlike those arts, it does not repeat the known Idea, whereby the artist lends his eyes to the beholder. But in it the artist simply presents the object to the beholder, and makes the apprehension of the Idea easy for him by bringing the actual individual object to a clear and complete expression its nature. [. . .]

§ 44.

[. . .] The landscape-beauty of a spot depends for the most part on the multiplicity of the natural objects found together in it, and on the fact that they are clearly separated, appear distinctly, and yet exhibit themselves in fitting association and succession. It is these two conditions that are assisted by artistic horticulture; yet this art is not nearly such a master of its material as architecture is of its, and so its effect is limited. The beauty displayed by it belongs almost entirely to nature; the art itself does little for it. On the other hand, this art can also do very little against the inclemency of nature, and where nature works not for but against it, its achievements are insignificant.

Therefore, in so far as the plant world, which offers itself to aesthetic enjoyment everywhere without the medium of art, is an object of art, it belongs principally to landscape-painting, and in the province of this is to be found along with it all the rest of nature-devoid-of-knowledge. In paintings of still life and of mere architecture, ruins, church interiors, and so on, the subjective side of aesthetic pleasure is predominant, in other words, our delight does not reside mainly in the immediate apprehension of the manifested Ideas, but rather in the subjective correlative of this apprehension, in pure will-less knowing. For since the painter lets us see the things through his eyes, we here obtain at the same time a sympathetic and reflected feeling of the profound spiritual peace and the complete silence of the will, which were necessary for plunging knowledge so deeply into those inanimate objects, and for comprehending them with such affection, in other words with such a degree of objectivity. Now the effect of landscape-painting proper is on the whole also of this kind; but because the Ideas manifested, as higher grades of the will's objectivity, are more significant and suggestive, the objective side of aesthetic pleasure comes more to the front, and balances the subjective. Pure knowing as such is no longer entirely the main thing, but the known Idea, the world as representation at an important grade of the will's objectification, operates with equal force.

But an even much higher grade is revealed by animal painting and animal sculpture. Of the latter we have important antique remains, for example, the horses in Venice, on Monte Cavallo, in the Elgin Marbles, also in Florence in bronze and marble; in the same place the ancient wild boar, the howling wolves; also the lions in the Venice Arsenal; in the Vatican there is a whole hall almost filled with ancient animals and other objects. In these presentations the objective side of aesthetic pleasure obtains a decided predominance over the subjective. The peace of the subject who knows these Ideas, who has silenced his own will, is present, as indeed it is in any aesthetic contemplation, but its effect is not felt, for we are occupied with the restlessness and impetuosity of the depicted will. It is that willing, which also constitutes our own inner nature, that here appears before us in forms and figures. In these the phenomenon of will is not, as in us, controlled and tempered by thoughtfulness, but is exhibited in stronger traits and with a distinctness verging on the grotesque and monstrous. On the other hand, this phenomenon manifests itself without dissimulation, naïvely and openly, freely and evidently, and precisely on this rests our interest in animals. The characteristic of the species already appeared in the presentation of plants, yet it showed itself only in the forms; here it becomes much more significant, and expresses itself not only in the form, but in the action, position, and deportment, though always only as the character of the species, not of the individual. This knowledge of the Ideas at higher grades, which we receive in painting through the agency of another person, can also be directly shared by us through the purely contemplative perception of plants, and by the observation of animals, and indeed of the latter in their free, natural, and easy state. The objective contemplation of their many different and marvellous forms, and of their actions and behaviour, is an instructive lesson from the great book of nature; it is the deciphering of the true *signatura rerum*. We see in it the manifold grades and modes of manifestation of the will that is one and the same in all beings and everywhere wills the same thing. This will objectifies itself as life, as existence, in such endless succession and variety, in such different forms, all of which are accommodations to the various external conditions, and can be compared to many variations on the same theme. [. . .]

§ 45.

Finally, the great problem of historical painting and of sculpture is to present, immediately and for perception, the Idea in which the will reaches the highest degree of its objectification. The objective side of pleasure in the beautiful is here wholly predominant, and the subjective is now in the background. Further, it is to he observed that at the next grade below this, in other words, in animal painting, the characteristic is wholly one with the beautiful; the most characteristic lion, wolf, horse, sheep, or ox is always the most beautiful. The reason for this is that animals have only the character of the species, not an individual character. But in the manifestation of man the character of the species is separated from the character of the individual. The former is now called beauty (wholly in the objective sense), but the latter retains the name of character or expression, and the new difficulty arises of completely presenting both at the same time in the same individual.

Human beauty is an objective expression that denotes the will's most complete objectification at the highest grade at which this is knowable, namely the Idea of man in general, completely and fully expressed in the perceived form. But however much the objective side of the beautiful appears here, the subjective still always remains its constant companion. No object transports us so rapidly into purely aesthetic contemplation as the most beautiful human countenance and form, at the sight of which we are instantly seized by an inexpressible satisfaction and lifted above ourselves and all that torments us. This is possible only because of the fact that this most distinct and purest perceptibility of the will raises us most easily and rapidly into the state of pure knowing in which our personality, our willing with its constant pain, disappears, as long as the purely aesthetic pleasure lasts. Therefore, Goethe says that "Whoever beholds human beauty cannot be infected with evil; he feels in harmony with himself and the world." Now, that nature succeeds in producing a beautiful human form must be explained by saying that the will at this highest grade objectifies itself in an individual, and thus, through fortunate circumstances and by its own power, completely overcomes all the obstacles and opposition presented to it by phenomena of the lower grades. Such are the forces of nature from which the will must always wrest and win back the matter that belongs to them all. Further, the phenomenon of the will at the higher grades always has multiplicity in its form. The tree is only a systematic aggregate of innumerably repeated sprouting fibres. This combination increases more and more the higher we go, and the human body is a highly complex system of quite different parts, each of which has its *vita propria*, a life subordinate to the whole, yet characteristic. That all these parts are precisely and appropriately subordinated to the whole and coordinated with one another; that they conspire harmoniously to the presentation of the whole, and there is nothing excessive or stunted; all these are the rare conditions, the result of which is beauty, the completely impressed character of the species. Thus nature: but how is it with art? It is imagined that this is done by imitating nature. But how is the artist to recognize the perfect work to be imitated, and how is he to discover it from among the failures, unless he anticipates the beautiful *prior to experience?* Moreover, has nature ever produced a human being perfectly beautiful in all his parts? It has been supposed that the artist must gather the beautiful parts separately distributed among many human beings, and construct a beautiful whole from them; an absurd and meaningless opinion. Once again, it is asked, how is he to know that just these forms and not others are beautiful? We also see how far the old German painters arrived at beauty by imitating nature. Let us consider their nude figures. No knowledge of the beautiful is at all possible purely *a posteriori* and from mere experience. It is always, at least partly, *a priori*, though of quite a different kind from the forms of the principle of sufficient reason, of which we are *a priori* conscious. These concern the universal form of the phenomenon as such, as it establishes the possibility of knowledge in general, the universal *how* of appearance without exception, and from this knowledge proceed mathematics and pure natural science. On the other hand, that other kind of knowledge *a priori*, which makes it possible to present the beautiful, concerns the content of phenomena instead of the form, the *what* of the appearance instead of the *how*. We all recognize human beauty when we see it, but in the genuine artist this takes place with such clearness that he shows it as he has never seen it, and in his presentation he surpasses nature. Now this is possible only because *we ourselves* are the will, whose adequate objectification at its highest grade is here to be judged and discovered. In fact, only in this way have we an anticipation of what nature (which is in fact just the will constituting our own inner being) endeavours to present. In the true genius this anticipation is accompanied by a high degree of thoughtful intelligence, so that, by recognizing in the individual thing its *Idea*, he, so to speak, *understands nature's half-spoken words*. He expresses clearly what she merely stammers. He impresses on the hard marble the beauty of the form which nature failed to achieve in a thousand attempts, and he places it before her, exclaiming as it were, "This is what you desired to say!" And from the man who knows comes the echoing reply, "Yes, that is it!" Only in this way was the Greek genius able to discover the prototype of the human form, and to set it up as the canon for the school of sculpture. Only by virtue of such an anticipation also is it possible for all of us to recognize the beautiful where nature has actually succeeded in the particular case. This anticipation is the *Ideal*; it is the *Idea* in so far as it is known *a priori*, or at any rate half-known; and it becomes practical for art by accommodating and supplementing as such what is given *a posteriori* through nature. The possibility of such anticipation of the beautiful *a priori* in the artist, as well as of its recognition *a posteriori* by the connoisseur, is to be found in the fact that artist and connoisseur are themselves the "in-itself" of nature, the will objectifying itself. [. . .]

Human beauty was declared above to be the most complete objectification of the will at the highest grade of its knowability. It expresses itself through the form, and this resides in space alone, and has no necessary connexion with time, as movement for example has. To this extent we can say that the adequate objectification of the will through a merely spatial phenomenon is beauty, in the objective sense. The plant is nothing but such a merely spatial phenomenon of the will; for no movement, and consequently no relation to time (apart from its development), belong to the expression of its nature. Its mere form expresses and openly displays its whole inner being. Animal and man, however, still need for the complete revelation of the will appearing in them a series of actions, and thus that phenomenon in them obtains a direct relation to time. [. . .] As the merely spatial phenomenon of the will can objectify that will perfectly or imperfectly at each definite grade – and it is just this that constitutes beauty or ugliness – so also can the temporal objectification of the will, i.e., the action, and indeed the direct action, and hence the movement, correspond purely and perfectly to the will which objectifies itself in it, without foreign admixture, without superfluity, without deficiency, expressing only the exact act of will determined in each case; or the converse of all this may occur. In the first case, the movement occurs with *grace*; in the second, without it. Thus as beauty is the adequate and suitable manifestation of the will in general, through its merely spatial phenomenon, so *grace* is the adequate manifestation of the will through its temporal phenomenon, in other words, the perfectly correct and appropriate expression of each act of will through the movement and position that objectifies it. As movement and position presuppose the body, Winckelmann's expression is very true and to the point when he says: "Grace is the peculiar relation of the acting person to the action." (*Werke*, Vol. I [. . .]) It follows automatically that beauty can be attributed to plants, but not grace, unless in a figurative sense; to animals and human beings, both beauty and grace. In accordance with what has been said, grace consists in every movement being performed and every position taken up in the easiest, most appropriate, and most convenient way, and consequently in being the purely adequate expression of its intention or of the act of will, without any superfluity that shows itself as unsuitable meaningless bustle or absurd posture; without any deficiency that shows itself as wooden stiffness. Grace presupposes a correct proportion in all the limbs, a symmetrical, harmonious structure of the body, as only by means of these are perfect ease and evident appropriateness in all postures and movements possible. Therefore grace is never without a certain degree of beauty of the body. The two, complete and united, are the most distinct phenomenon of the will at the highest grade of its objectification.

As mentioned above, it is one of the distinguishing features of mankind that therein the character of the species and that of the individual are separated so that [. . .] each person exhibits to a certain extent an Idea that is wholly characteristic of him. Therefore the arts, aiming at a presentation of the Idea of mankind, have as their problem both beauty as the character of the species, and the character of the individual, which is called *character par excellence.* Again, they have this only in so far as this character is to be regarded not as something accidental and quite peculiar to the man as a single individual, but as a side of the Idea of mankind, specially appearing in this particular individual; and thus the presentation of this individual serves to reveal this Idea. Therefore the character, although individual as such, must be comprehended and expressed ideally in other words, with emphasis on its significance in regard to the idea of mankind in general (to the objectifying of which it contributes in its own way). Moreover, the presentation is a portrait, a repetition of the individual as such, with all his accidental qualities. And as Winckelmann says, even the portrait should be the ideal of the individual. [. . .]

In sculpture beauty and grace remain the principal matter. The real character of the mind, appearing in emotion, passion, alternations of knowing and willing, which can be depicted only by the expression of the face and countenance, is preeminently the province of *painting.* For although eyes and colour, lying outside the sphere of sculpture, contribute a great deal to beauty, they are far more essential for the character. Further, beauty unfolds itself more completely to contemplation from several points of view, on the other hand, the expression, the character, can be completely apprehended from a single viewpoint. [. . .]

§ 49.

The truth which lies at the foundation of all the remarks we have so far made on art is that the object of art, the depiction of which is the aim of the artist, and the knowledge of which must consequently precede his work as its germ and source, is an *Idea* in Plato's sense, and absolutely nothing else; not the particular thing, the object of common apprehension, and not the concept, the object of rational thought and of science. Although Idea and concept have something in common, in that both as unities represent a plurality of actual things, the great difference between the two will have become sufficiently clear and evident from what was said in the first book about the concept, and what has been said in the present book about the Idea. I certainly do not mean to assert that Plato grasped this difference clearly; indeed many of his examples of Ideas and his discussions of them are applicable only to concepts. However, we leave this aside, and go our way, glad whenever we come across traces of a great and noble mind, yet pursuing not his footsteps, but our own aim. The *concept* is abstract, discursive, wholly undetermined within its sphere, determined only by its limits, attainable and intelligible only to him who has the faculty of reason, communicable by words without further assistance, entirely exhausted by its definition. The *Idea*, on the other hand, definable perhaps as the adequate representative of the concept, is absolutely perceptive, and, although representing an infinite number of individual things, is yet thoroughly definite. It is never known by the individual as such, but only by him who has raised himself above all willing and all individuality to the pure subject of knowing. [. . .]

The *Idea* is the unity that has fallen into plurality by virtue of the temporal and spatial form of our intuitive apprehension. The *concept*, on the other hand, is the unity once more produced out of plurality by means of abstraction through our faculty of reason; the latter can be described as *unitas post rem*, and the former as *unitas ante rem*. Finally, we can express the distinction between concept and Idea figuratively, by saying that the *concept* is like a dead receptacle in which whatever has been put actually lies side by side, but from which no more can be taken out [. . .] than has been put in [. . .] The *Idea*, on the other hand, develops in him who has grasped it representations that are new as regards the concept of the same name; it is like a living organism, developing itself and endowed with generative force, which brings forth that which was not previously put into it.

Now it follows from all that has been said that the concept, useful as it is in life, serviceable, necessary, and productive as it is in science, is eternally barren and unproductive in art. The apprehended Idea, on the contrary, is the true and only source of every genuine work of art. In its powerful originality it is drawn only from life itself, from nature, from the world, and only by the genuine genius, or by him whose momentary inspiration reaches the point of genius. Genuine works bearing immortal life arise only from such immediate apprehension. Just because the Idea is and remains perceptive, the artist is not conscious *in abstract* of the intention and aim of his work. Not a concept but an Idea is present in his mind; hence he cannot give an account of his actions. He works, as people say, from mere feeling and unconsciously, indeed instinctively. On the other hand, imitators, mannerists, *imitatores, servum pecus*, in art start from the concept. They note what pleases and affects in genuine works, make this clear to themselves, fix it in the concept, and hence in the abstract, and then imitate it, openly or in disguise, with skill and intention. [. . .]

§ 51.

If with the foregoing observations on art in general we turn from the plastic and pictorial arts to *poetry*, we shall have no doubt that its aim is also to reveal the Ideas, the grades of the will's objectification, and to communicate them to the hearer with that distinctness and vividness in which they were apprehended by the poetical mind. Ideas are essentially perceptive; therefore, if in poetry only abstract concepts are directly communicated by words, yet it is obviously the intention to let the hearer perceive the Ideas of life in the representatives of these concepts; and this can take place only by the assistance of his own imagination. But in order to set this imagination in motion in accordance with the end in view, the abstract concepts that are the direct material of poetry, as of the driest prose, must be so arranged that their spheres intersect one another, so that none can continue in its abstract universality, but instead of it a perceptive representative appears before the imagination, and this is then modified further and further by the words of the poet according to his intention. [. . .] For the Idea can be known only through perception, but knowledge of the Idea is the aim of all art. The skill of a master in poetry as in chemistry enables one always to obtain the precise precipitate that was intended. The many epithets in poetry serve this purpose, and through them the universality of every concept is restricted more and more till perceptibility is reached. To almost every noun Homer adds an adjective, the concept of which cuts, and at once considerably diminishes, the sphere of the first concept, whereby it is brought so very much nearer to perception. [. . .]

Revelation of that Idea which is the highest grade of the will's objectivity, namely the presentation of man in the connected series of his efforts and actions, is thus the great subject of poetry. It is true that experience and history teach us to know man, yet more often *men* rather than *man*; in other words, they give us empirical notes about the behaviour of men towards one another. From these we obtain rules for our own conduct rather than a deep insight into the inner nature of man. This latter, however, is by no means ruled out; yet, whenever the inner nature of mankind itself is disclosed to us in history or in our own experience, we have apprehended this experience poetically, and the historian has apprehended history with artistic eyes, in other words, according to the Idea, not to the phenomenon; according to its inner nature, not to the relations. Our own experience is the indispensable condition for understanding poetry as well as history, for it is, so to speak, the dictionary of the language spoken by both. But history is related to poetry as portrait-painting to historical painting; the former gives us the true in the individual, the latter the true in the universal; the former has the truth of the phenomenon and can verify it therefrom; the latter has the truth of the Idea, to be found in no particular phenomenon, yet speaking from them all. The poet from deliberate choice presents us with significant characters in significant situations; the historian takes both as they come. In fact, he has to regard and select the events and persons not according to their inner genuine significance expressing the Idea, but according to the outward, apparent, and relatively important significance in reference to the connexion and to the consequences. [. . .] The poet, however, apprehends the Idea, the inner being of mankind outside all relation and all time, the adequate objectivity of the thing-in-itself at its highest grade. Even in that method of treatment necessary to the historian, the inner nature, the significance of phenomena, the kernel of all those shells, can never be entirely lost, and can still be found and recognized by the person who looks for it. Yet that which is significant in itself, not in the relation, namely the real unfolding of the Idea, is found to be far more accurate and clear in poetry than in history; therefore, paradoxical as it may sound, far more real, genuine, inner truth is to be attributed to poetry than to history. [. . .]

Tragedy is to be regarded, and is recognized, as the summit of poetic art, both as regards the greatness of the effect and the difficulty of the achievement. For the whole of our discussion, it is very significant and worth noting that the purpose of this highest poetical achievement is the description of the terrible side of life. The unspeakable pain, the wretchedness and misery of mankind, the triumph of wickedness, the scornful mastery of chance, and the irretrievable fall of the just and the innocent are all here presented to us; and here is to be found a significant hint as to the nature of the world and of existence. It is the antagonism of the will with itself which is here most completely unfolded at the highest grade of its objectivity, and which comes into fearful prominence. It becomes visible in the suffering of mankind which is produced partly by chance and error; and these stand forth as the rulers of the world, personified as fate through their insidiousness which appears almost like purpose and intention. In part it proceeds from mankind itself through the self-mortifying efforts of will on the part of individuals, through the wickedness and perversity of most. It is one and the same will, living and appearing in them all, whose phenomena fight with one another and tear one another to pieces. In one individual it appears powerfully, in another more feebly. Here and there it reaches thoughtfulness and is softened more or less by the light of knowledge, until at last in the individual case this knowledge is purified and enhanced by suffering itself. It then reaches the point where the phenomenon, the veil of Maya, no longer deceives it. It sees through the form of the phenomenon, the *principium individuationis*; the egoism resting on this expires with it. The *motives* that were previously so powerful now lose their force, and instead of them, the complete knowledge of the real nature of the world, acting as a *quieter* of the will, produces resignation, the giving up not merely of life, but of the whole will-to-live itself. Thus we see in tragedy the noblest men, after a long conflict and suffering, finally renounce for ever all the pleasures of life and the aims till then pursued so keenly, or cheerfully and willingly give up life itself. Thus the steadfast prince of Calderón, Gretchen in *Faust,* Hamlet whom his friend Horatio would gladly follow, but who enjoins him to remain for a while in this harsh world and to breathe in pain in order to throw light on Hamlet's fate and clear his memory; also the *Maid of Orleans*, the *Bride of Messina*. They all die purified by suffering, in other words after the will-to-live has already expired in them. In Voltaire's *Mohammed* this is actually expressed in the concluding words addressed to Mohammed by the dying Palmira: "The world is for tyrants: live!" On the other hand, the demand for so-called poetic justice rests on an entire misconception of the nature of tragedy, indeed of the nature of the world. It boldly appears in all its dullness in the criticisms that Dr. Samuel Johnson made of individual plays of Shakespeare, since he very naïvely laments the complete disregard of it; and this disregard certainly exists, for what wrong have the Ophelias, the Desdemonas, and the Cordelias done? But only a dull, insipid, optimistic, Protestant-rationalistic, or really Jewish view of the world will make the demand for poetic justice, and find its own satisfaction in that of the demand. The true sense of the tragedy is the deeper insight that what the hero atones for is not his own particular sins, but original sin, in other words, the guilt of existence itself [. . .]

§ 52.

[. . .] After this, we find that there is yet another fine art that remains excluded, and was bound to be excluded, from our consideration, for in the systematic connexion of our discussion there was no fitting place for it; this art is *music.* It stands quite apart from all the others. In it we do not recognize the copy, the repetition, of any Idea of the inner nature of the world. Yet it is such a great and exceedingly fine art, its effect on man's innermost nature is so powerful, and it is so completely and profoundly understood by him in his innermost being as an entirely universal language, whose distinctness surpasses even that of the world of perception itself, that in it we certainly have to look for more than that *exercitium arithmeticae occultum nescientis se numerare animi* which Leibniz took it to be. Yet he was quite right, in so far as he considered only its immediate and outward significance, its exterior. But if it were nothing more, the satisfaction afforded by it would inevitably be similar to that which we feel when a sum in arithmetic comes out right, and could not be that profound pleasure with which we see the deepest recesses of our nature find expression. Therefore, from our standpoint, where the aesthetic effect is the thing we have in mind, we must attribute to music a far more serious and profound significance that refers to the innermost being of the world and of our own self. In this regard the numerical ratios into which it can be resolved are related not as the thing signified, but only as the sign. That in some sense music must be related to the world as the depiction to the thing depicted, as the copy to the original, we can infer from the analogy with the remaining arts, to all of which this character is peculiar; from their effect on us, it can be inferred that of music is on the whole of the same nature, only stronger, more rapid, more necessary and infallible. Further, its imitative reference to the world must be very profound, infinitely true, and really striking, since it is instantly understood by everyone, and presents a certain infallibility by the fact that its form can be reduced to quite definite rules expressible in numbers, from which it cannot possibly depart without entirely ceasing to be music. Yet the point of comparison between music and the world, the regard in which it stands to the world in the relation of a copy or a repetition, is very obscure. Men have practised music at all times without being able to give an account of this; content to understand it immediately, they renounce any abstract conception of this direct understanding itself.

I have devoted my mind entirely to the impression of music in its many different forms; and then I have returned again to reflection and to the train of my thought expounded in the present work, and have arrived at an explanation of the inner essence of music, and the nature of its imitative relation to the world, necessarily to be presupposed from analogy. This explanation is quite sufficient for me, and satisfactory for my investigation, and will be just as illuminating also to the man who has followed me thus far, and has agreed with my view of the world. I recognize, however, that it is essentially impossible to demonstrate this explanation, for it assumes and establishes a relation of music as a representation to that which of its essence can never be representation, and claims to regard music as the copy of an original that can itself never be directly represented. Therefore, I can do no more than state [. . .] this explanation of the wonderful art of tones which is sufficient for me. I must leave the acceptance or denial of my view to the effect that both music and the whole thought communicated in this work have on each reader. [. . .]

The (Platonic) Ideas are the adequate objectification of the will. To stimulate the knowledge of these by depicting individual things (for works of art are themselves always such) is the aim of all the other arts (and is possible with a corresponding change in the knowing subject). Hence all of them objectify the will only indirectly, in other words, by means of the Ideas. As our world is nothing but the phenomenon or appearance of the Ideas in plurality through entrance into the *principium individuationis* (the form of knowledge possible to the individual as such), music, since it passes over the Ideas, is also quite independent of the phenomenal world, positively ignores it, and, to a certain extent, could still exist even if there were no world at all, which cannot be said of the other arts. Thus music is as *immediate* an objectification and copy of the whole *will* as the world itself is, indeed as the Ideas are, the multiplied phenomenon of which constitutes the world of individual things. Therefore music is by no means like the other arts, namely a copy of the

Ideas, but a *copy of the will itself*, the objectivity of which is the Ideas. For this reason the effect of music is so very much more powerful and penetrating than is that of the other arts, for these others speak only of the shadow, but music of the essence. However, as it is the same will that objectifies itself both in the Ideas and in music, though in quite a different way in each, there must be, not indeed an absolutely direct likeness, but yet a parallel, an analogy, between music and the Ideas. The phenomenon of which in plurality and in incompleteness is the visible world. [. . .]

[. . .] The composer reveals the innermost nature of the world, and expresses the profoundest wisdom in a language that his reasoning faculty does not understand, just as a magnetic somnambulist gives information about things of which she has no conception when she is awake. Therefore in the composer, more than in any other artist, the man is entirely separate and distinct from the artist. [. . .]

The inexpressible depth of all music, by virtue of which it floats past us as a paradise quite familiar and yet eternally remote, and is so easy to understand and yet so inexplicable, is due to the fact that it reproduces all the emotions of our innermost being, but entirely without reality and remote from its pain. In the same way, the seriousness essential to it and wholly excluding the ludicrous from its direct and peculiar province is to be explained from the fact that its object is not the representation, in regard to which deception and ridiculousness alone are possible, but that this object is directly the will; and this is essentially the most serious of all things, as being that on which all depends. How full of meaning and significance the language of music is we see from the repetition signs, as well as from the *Da capo* which would be intolerable in the case of works composed in the language of words. In music, however, they are very appropriate and beneficial; for to comprehend it fully, we must hear it twice.

In the whole of this discussion on music I have been trying to make it clear that music expresses in an exceedingly universal language, in a homogeneous material, that is, in mere tones, and with the greatest distinctness and truth, the inner being, the in-itself, of the world, which we think of under the concept of will, according to its most distinct manifestation. Further, according to my view and contention, philosophy is nothing but a complete and accurate repetition and expression of the inner nature of the world in very general concepts, for only in these is it possible to obtain a view of that entire inner nature which is everywhere adequate and applicable. Thus whoever has followed me and has entered into my way of thinking will not find it so very paradoxical when I say that, supposing we succeeded in giving a perfectly accurate and complete explanation of music which goes into detail, and thus a detailed repetition in concepts of what it expresses, this would also be at once a sufficient repetition and explanation of the world in concepts, or one wholly corresponding thereto, and hence the true philosophy. [. . .] This purely knowable side of the world and its repetition in any art is the element of the artist. He is captivated by a consideration of the spectacle of the will's objectification. He sticks to this, and does not get tired of contemplating it, and of repeating it in his descriptions. Meanwhile, he himself bears the cost of producing that play; in other words, he himself is the will objectifying itself and remaining in constant suffering. That pure, true, and profound knowledge of the inner nature of the world now becomes for him an end in itself; at it he stops. Therefore it does not become for him a quieter of the will [. . .]; it does not deliver him from life for ever, but only for a few moments. For him it is not the way out of life, but only an occasional consolation in it, until his power, enhanced by this contemplation, finally becomes tired of the spectacle, and seizes the serious side of things.

20

The Beautiful in Music

Eduard Hanslick

Eduard Hanslick (1825–1904) was an influential Austrian music critic, who defended the self-sufficiency of music.

Has Music any subject? This has been a burning question ever since people began to reflect upon music. It has been answered both in the affirmative and in the negative. Many prominent men, almost exclusively *philosophers*, among whom we may mention Rousseau, Kant, Hegel, Herbart, Kahlert, &c., hold that music has no subject. The numerous physiologists who endorse this view include such eminent thinkers as Lotze and Helmholtz, whose opinions, strengthened as they are by musical knowledge, carry great weight and authority. Those who contend that music *has a subject* are numerically far stronger: among them are the trained *musicians* of the literary profession, and their convictions are shared by the bulk of the public.

It may seem almost a matter for surprise that just those who are familiar with the technical side of music should be unwilling to concede the untenableness of a doctrine which is at variance with those very technical principles, and which thinkers on abstract subjects might perhaps be pardoned for propounding. The reason is, that many of these musical authors are more anxious to save the so-called honour of their art than to ascertain the truth. They attack the doctrine that music has no subject, not as one opinion against another, but as heresy against dogma. The contrary view appears to them in the light of a degrading error and a form of crude and heinous materialism. "What! the art that charms and elevates us; to which so many noble minds have devoted a whole lifetime; which is the vehicle of the most sublime thoughts; *that* art to be cursed with unmeaningness, to be mere food for the senses, mere empty sound!" Hackneyed exclamations of this description which, though made up of several disconnected propositions, are generally uttered in one breath, neither prove nor disprove anything. The question is not a point of honour, not a party-badge, but simply the discovery of truth; and in order to attain this object, it is of the first importance to be clear regarding the points which are under debate.

It is the indiscriminate use of the terms, *contents, subject, matter*, which has been, and still is, responsible for all this ambiguity; the same meaning being expressed by different terms, or the same term associated with different meanings. "*Contents*," in the true and original sense, is that which a thing *contains*, what it holds within. The *notes* of which a piece of music is composed, and which are the parts that go to make up the whole, are the contents in this sense. The circumstance that nobody will accept this definition as a satisfactory solution, but that it is dismissed as a truism, is due to the word "contents" (subject) being usually confounded with the word "object."

Eduard Hanslick, *The Beautiful in Music*, trans. Gustav Cohen (1891).

An enquiry into the "contents" of musical compositions raises in such people's minds the conception of an "*object*" (subject-matter; topic), which latter, being the idea, the ideal element, they represent to themselves as almost antithetical to the "material part," the musical notes. Music has, indeed, no contents as thus understood; no *subject* in the sense that the subject to be treated is something extraneous to the musical notes. Kahlert is right in emphatically maintaining that music, unlike painting, admits of no "description in words" (Aesth. 380), though his subsequent assumption that a description in words may, at times, "compensate for the want of aesthetic enjoyment," is false. It may be the means, however, of clearly perceiving the real bearing of the question. The query "what" is the subject of the music, must necessarily be answerable in words, if music really has a "*subject*," because an "indefinite subject" upon which everyone puts a different construction, which can only be felt and not translated into words, is not a subject as we have defined it.

Music consists of successions and forms of sound, and these alone constitute the subject. They again remind us of architecture and dancing which likewise aim at beauty in form and motion, and are also devoid of a definite subject. Now, whatever be the effect of a piece of music on the individual mind, and howsoever it be interpreted, it has no *subject* beyond the combinations of notes we hear, for music does not only speak *by means of sounds*, it speaks nothing but *sound*.

Krüger – the opponent of Hegel and Kahlert – who is probably the most learned advocate of the doctrine that music has a "subject" – contends that this art presents but a different side of the subject which other arts, such as painting, represent. "All plastic figures," he says (Beiträge, 131), "are in a state of quiescence; they do not exhibit present, but past action, or the state of things at a given moment. The painting, therefore, does not show Apollo vanquishing, but it represents the victor, the furious warrior," &c. Music, on the other hand, "supplies to those plastic and quiescent forms the motive force, the active principle, the inner waves of motion; and whereas in the former instance we knew the true, but inert subject, to be anger, love, &c., we here know the true and active subject to be loving, rushing, heaving, storming, fuming." The latter portion is only partly true, for though music may be said to "rush, heave, and storm," it can neither "love" nor be "angry." These sentiments we ourselves import into the music, and we must here refer our readers to the second chapter of this book. Krüger then proceeds to compare the definiteness of the *painter's subject* with the *musical subject*, and remarks: "The *painter* represents Orestes, pursued by the Furies: his outward appearance, his eyes, mouth, forehead, and posture, give us the impression of flight, gloom, and despair; at his heels the spirits of divine vengeance, whose imperious and sublimely terrible commands he cannot evade, but who likewise present unchanging outlines, features, and attitudes. The *composer* does not exhibit fleeing Orestes in fixed lines, but from a point of view from which the painter cannot portray him: he puts into his music the tremor and shuddering of his soul, his inmost feelings at war, urging his flight," &c. This, in our opinion, is entirely false; the composer is unable to represent Orestes either in one way or another; in fact, *he cannot represent him at all.*

The objection that sculpture and painting are also unable to represent to us a given historical personage, and that we could not know the figure to be *this very* individual, but for our previous knowledge of certain historical facts, does not hold good. True, the figure does not proclaim itself to be Orestes; the man who has gone through such or such experiences, and whose existence is bound up with certain biographic incidents; none but the *poet* can represent that, since he alone can narrate the events; but the painting "Orestes" unequivocally shows us a youth with noble features, in Greek attire, his looks and attitude betokening fear and mental anguish; and it shows us this youth pursued and tormented by the awe-inspiring goddesses of vengeance. All this is clear and indubitable; a visible narrative – no matter whether the youth be called Orestes or otherwise. Only the antecedent causes – namely, that the youth has committed matricide, &c., cannot be expressed. Now, what can music give us in point of definiteness as a counterpart to the visible subject of the painter – apart from the historical element? Chords of a diminished seventh, themes in minor keys, a rolling bass, &c. – musical forms, in brief, which might signify a woman just as well as a youth; one pursued by myrmidons instead of furies; somebody tortured by jealousy or by bodily pain; one bent on revenge – in short, anything we can think of, if we must needs imagine a subject for the composition.

It seems almost superfluous to expressly recall the proposition, already established by us, that whenever the subject and the descriptive power of music are under debate, *instrumental music* alone can be taken into account. Nobody is likely to disregard this so far as to instance Orestes in Gluck's "Iphigenia," for this "Orestes" is not the *composer's* creation. The words of the poet, the appearance and gestures of the actor, the costume and the painter's decorations produce the complete Orestes. The composer's contribution – the melody – is possibly the most *beautiful* part of all, but it happens to be just that factor which has nothing whatever to do with the real Orestes.

Lessing has shown with admirable perspicuity what the poet and what the sculptor or painter may make of the story of Laocoon. The poet by the aid of speech gives us the historical, individually-defined Laocoon; the painter and sculptor shows us the terrible serpents, crushing in their coils an old man and two boys (of determinate age and appearance, dressed after a particular fashion, &c.), who by their looks, attitudes, and gestures express the agonies of approaching death. Of the *composer* Lessing says nothing, and this was only to be expected, since there is nothing in "Laocoon" which could be turned into music.

We have already alluded to the intimate connection between the question of *subject* in musical compositions and the relation of music to the *beauties of Nature.* The composer looks in vain for models such as those which render the subjects of other art-products both definite and recognisable, and an art for which Nature can provide no aesthetic model must, properly speaking, be incorporeal. A prototype of its mode of manifestation is nowhere to be met with, and it can, therefore, not be included in the range of living experiences. It does not reproduce an already known and classified subject, and for this reason it has no subject that can be taken hold of by the intellect, as the latter can be exercised only on definite conceptions.

The term *subject* (substance) can, properly speaking, be applied to an art-product only, if we regard it as the correlative of *form.* The terms "form" and "substance" supplement each other, and one cannot be thought of except in relation to the other. Wherever the "form" appears mentally inseparable from the "substance," there can be no question of an independent "substance" (subject). Now, in music, substance and form, the subject and its working out, the image and the realised conception are mysteriously blended in one undecomposable whole. This complete fusion of substance and form is exclusively characteristic of music, and presents a sharp contrast to poetry, painting, and sculpture, inasmuch as these arts are capable of representing the same idea and the same event in different forms. The story of William Tell supplied to Florian the subject for a historical novel, to Schiller the subject for a play, while Goethe began to treat it as an epic poem. The substance is everywhere the same, equally resolvable into prose, and capable of being narrated; always clearly recognisable, and yet the form differs in each case. Aphrodite emerging from the sea is the subject of innumerable paintings and statues, the various forms of which it is, nevertheless, impossible to confuse. In music, no distinction can be made between substance and form, as it has no form independently of the substance. Let us look at this more closely.

In all compositions the independent, aesthetically undecomposable subject of a musical conception is the *theme,* and by the theme, the musical microcosm, we should always be able to test the alleged subject underlying the music as such. Let us examine the leading theme of some composition, say that of Beethoven's Symphony in B flat major. What is its subject (substance)? What its form? Where does the latter commence and the former end? That its subject does not consist of a determinate feeling, we think we have conclusively proved, and this truth becomes only the more evident when tested by this or by any other concrete example. What then is to be called its *subject*? The groups of sounds? Undoubtedly; but they have a form already. And what is the *form*? The groups of sounds again; but here they are a *replete* form. Every practical attempt at resolving a theme into subject and form ends in arbitrariness and contradiction. Take, for instance, a theme repeated by another instrument or in the higher octave. Is the subject changed thereby or the form? If, as is generally the case, the latter is said to be changed, then all that remains as the *subject* of the theme would simply be the series of intervals, the skeleton frame for the musical notation as the score presents them to the eye. But this is not *musical* definiteness, it is an abstract notion. It may be likened to a pavilion with stained window panes, through which the same environment appears, now red, now blue, and now yellow. The environment itself changes neither in *substance* nor in *form*, but merely in *colour*. This property of exhibiting the same forms in countless hues, from the most glaring contrasts down to the finest distinction of shade, is quite peculiar to music and is one of the most fertile and powerful causes of its effectiveness.

A theme originally composed for the piano and subsequently arranged for the orchestra acquires thereby a *new form* but not a *form for the first time*, the formal element being part and parcel of the primary conception. The assertion that a theme by the process of instrumentation changes its subject while retaining its form is even less tenable, as such a theory involves still greater contradictions, the listener being obliged to affirm, that though he recognises it to be the same subject "it somehow sounds like a different one."

It is true that in looking at a composition in the aggregate and more particularly at musical works of great length, we are in the habit of speaking of form and subject; in such a case, however, these terms are not understood in their primitive and logical sense, but in a specifically *musical* one, What we call the "form" of a Symphony, an Overture, a Sonata, an Aria, a Chorus, &c., is the architectonic combination of the units and groups of units of which a composition is made up; or more definitely speaking, the symmetry of their successions, their contrasts, repetitions, and general working out. But thus understood the subject is identical with the *themes* with which this architectonic structure is built up. Subject is here, therefore, no longer construed in the sense of an "object," but as the subject in a purely musical sense. The words "sub-stance" and "form" in respect of entire compositions are used in an aesthetic, and not in a strictly logical sense. If we wish to apply them to music in the latter sense, we must do so, not in relation to the composition in the aggregate, as a whole consisting of parts, but in relation to its ultimate and aesthetically undecomposable idea. This ultimate idea is the *theme* or *themes*, and in the latter substance and form are indissolubly connected. We cannot acquaint anybody with the "subject" of a theme, *except by playing it*. The subject of a composition can, therefore, not be understood as an object derived from an external source, but as something intrinsically musical; in other words, as the concrete group of sounds in a piece of music. Now, as a composition must comply with the formal laws of beauty, it cannot run on arbitrarily and at random, but must develop gradually with intelligible and organic definiteness, as buds develop into rich blossoms.

Here we have the *principal theme*; the true topic or subject of the entire composition. Everything it contains, though originated by the unfettered imagination, is nevertheless the natural outcome and effect of the theme which determines and forms, regulates and pervades its every part. We may compare it to a self-evident truth which we accept for a moment as satisfactory, but which our mind would fain see tested and developed, and in the musical working out this development takes place analogously to the logical train of reasoning in an argument. The theme, not unlike the chief hero in a novel, is brought by the composer into the most varied states and surrounding conditions, and is made to pass through ever-changing phases and moods – everything, no matter what contrasts it may present, is conceived and formed in relation to the theme.

The epithet *without a subject*, might possibly be applied to the freest form of extemporising, during which the performer indulges in chords, arpeggios, and rosalias, by way of a rest, rather than as a creative effort, and which does not end in the production of a definite and connected whole. Such extempore playing has no individuality of its own, by which one might recognise or distinguish it, and it would be quite correct to say that it has no subject (in the wider sense of the term), because it has no theme.

Thus the theme or the themes are the real subject of a piece of music.

In aesthetic and critical reviews far too little importance is attached to the *leading theme* of a composition; it alone reveals at once the mind which conceived the work. Every musician, on hearing the first few opening bars of Beethoven's Overture to "Leonore" or Mendelssohn's Overture to "The Hebrides," though he may be totally unaware of the subsequent development of the theme, must recognise at once the treasure that lies before him; whereas the music of a theme from Donizetti's "Fausta" Overture or Verdi's Overture to "Louisa Miller" will, without the need of further examination, convince us that the music is fit only for low music halls. German theorists and executants prize the musical working-out far more than the inherent merits of the theme. But whatever is not contained in the theme (be it overtly or in disguise) is incapable of organic growth, and if the present time is barren of orchestral works of the Beethoven type it is, perhaps, due not so much to an imperfect knowledge of the working out, as to the want of symphonic power and fertility of the *themes.*

On enquiring into the *subject* of music we should, above all, beware of using the term "subject" in a eulogistic sense. From the fact that music has no extrinsic subject (object) it does not follow that it is without any *intrinsic merit.* It is clear that those who, with the zeal of partisanship, contend that music has a "subject," really mean "intellectual merit." We can only ask our readers to revert to our remarks in the third chapter of this book. Music is to be played, but it is not to be played with. Thoughts and feelings pervade with vital energy the musical organism, the embodiment of beauty and symmetry, and though they are not identical with the *organism itself* nor yet *visible*, they are, as it were, its breath of life. The composer *thinks* and *works*; but he thinks and works in *sound*, away from the realities of the external world. We deliberately repeat this commonplace, for even those who admit it in principle, deny and violate it when carried to its logical conclusions. They conceive the act of composing as a translation into sound of a given subject, whereas the sounds themselves are the untranslatable and original tongue. If the composer is obliged to think in sounds, it follows as a matter of course that music has no subject external to itself, for of a subject in this sense we ought to be able to think in *words.*

Though, when examining into the *subject* of music, we rigorously excluded compositions written for given sets of words as being inconsistent with the conception of music pure and simple, yet the masterpieces of vocal music are indispensable for the formation of an accurate judgment respecting the *intrinsic worth* of music. From the simple song to the complex opera and the time-honoured practice of using music for the celebration of religious services, music has never ceased to accompany the most tender and profound affections of the human mind and has thus been the indirect means of glorifying them.

Apart from the existence of an *intrinsic merit*, there is a second corollary which we wish to emphasize. Though music possesses beauty of form without any extrinsic subject, this does not deprive it of the quality of *individuality.* The act of inventing a certain theme, and the mode of working it out, are always so unique and specific as to defy their inclusion in a wider generality. These processes are distinctly and unequivocally *individual* in nature. A theme of Mozart or Beethoven rests on as firm and independent a foundation as a poem by Goethe, an epigram by Lessing, a statue by Thorwaldsen, or a painting by Overbeck. The independent musical thoughts (themes) possess the identity of a quotation and the distinctness of a painting; they are individual, personal, eternal.

Unable, as we were, to endorse Hegel's opinion respecting the want of intellectual merit in music, it seems to us a still more glaring error on his part to assert that the sole function of music is the expressing of an "inner non-individuality." Even from Hegel's musical point of view, which, while overlooking the inherently form-giving and objective activity of the composer, conceives music as the free manifestation of purely *subjective states*, its want of individuality follows by no means, since the subjectively-producing mind is essentially individual.

How the individuality shows itself in the choice and working out of the various musical elements, we have already pointed out in the third chapter. The *stigma* that music has no subject is, therefore, quite unmerited. Music has a subject – *i.e.*, a musical subject, which is no less a vital spark of the divine fire than the beautiful of any other art. Yet, only by steadfastly denying the existence of any other "subject" in music, is it possible to save its "true subject." The indefinite emotions which at best underlie the other kind of subject, do not explain its spiritual force. The latter can only be attributed to the definite beauty of musical form, as the result of the untrammeled working of the human mind on material susceptible of intellectual manipulation.

21

The Birth of Tragedy

Friedrich Nietzsche

Friedrich Nietzsche (1844–1900) was an influential German philosopher who explored the sources of artistic creation.

I

We shall have gained much for the science of aesthetics, once we perceive not merely by logical inference, but with the immediate certainty of vision, that the continuous development of art is bound up with the *Apollinian* and *Dionysian* duality – just as procreation depends on the duality of the sexes, involving perpetual strife with only periodically intervening reconciliations. The terms Dionysian and Appollinian we borrow from the Greeks, who disclose to the discerning mind the profound mysteries of their view of art, not, to be sure, in concepts, but in the intensely clear figures of their gods. Through Apollo and Dionysus, the two art deities of the Greeks, we come to recognize that in the Greek world there existed a tremendous opposition, in origin and aims, between the Apollinian art of sculpture, and the nonimagistic, Dionysian art of music. These two different tendencies run parallel to each other, for the most part openly at variance; and they continually incite each other to new and more powerful births, which perpetuate an antagonism, only superficially reconciled by the common term "art"; till eventually, by a metaphysical miracle of the Hellenic "will," they appear coupled with each other, and through this coupling ultimately generate an equally Dionysian and Appollinian form of art – Attic tragedy.

In order to grasp these two tendencies, let us first conceive of them as the separate art words of *dreams* and *intoxication*. These physiological phenomena present a contrast analogous to that existing between the Apollinian and the Dionysian. It was in dreams, says Lucretius, that the glorious divine figures first appeared to the souls of men; in dreams the great shaper beheld the splendid bodies of superhuman beings; and the Hellenic poet, if questioned about the mysteries of poetic inspiration, would likewise have suggested dreams and he might have given an explanation like that of Hans Sachs in the *Meistersinger*:

> The poet's task is this, my friend,
> to read his dreams and comprehend.
> The truest human fancy seems
> to be revealed to us in dreams:
> all poems and versification
> are but true dreams' interpretation.

The beautiful illusion of the dream worlds, in the creation of which every man is truly an artist, is the prerequisite of all plastic art, and, as we shall

Friedrich Nietzsche, *The Birth of Tragedy*, trans. Walter Kaufmann (New York: Random House, 1967), pp. 33–47, 56, 58–62, 73–4.

see, of an important part of poetry also. In our dreams we delight in the immediate understanding of figures; all forms speak to us; there is nothing unimportant or superfluous. But even when this dream reality it most intense, we still have, glimmering through it, the sensation that it is *mere appearance*: at least this my experience, and for its frequency – indeed, normality – I could adduce many proofs, including the saying of the poets. Philosophical men even have a presentiment that the reality in which we live and have our being is also mere appearance, and that another, quite different reality lies beneath it. Schopenhauer actually indicates as the criterion of philosophical ability the occasional ability to view men and things as mere phantoms or dream images. Thus the aesthetically sensitive man stands in the same relation to the reality of dreams as the philosopher does to the reality of existence; he is a close and willing observer, for these images afford him an interpretation of life, and by reflecting on these processes he trains himself for life. It is not only the agreeable and friendly images that he experiences as something universally intelligible: the serious, the troubled, the sad, the gloomy, the sudden restraints, the tricks of accident, anxious expectations, in short, the whole divine comedy of life, including the inferno, also pass before him, not like mere shadows on a wall – for he lives and suffers with these scenes – and yet not without that fleeting sensation of illusion. And perhaps many will, like myself, recall how amid the dangers and terrors of dreams they have occasionally said to themselves in self-encouragement, and not without success: "It is a dream! I will dream on!" I have likewise heard of people who were able to continue one and the same dream for three and even more successive nights – facts which indicate clearly how our innermost being, our common ground, experiences dreams with profound delight and a joyous necessity.

This joyous necessity of the dream experience has been embodied by the Greeks in their Apollo: Apollo, the god of all plastic energies, is at the same time the soothsaying god. He, who (as the etymology of the name indicates) is the "shining one," the deity of light, is also ruler over the beautiful illusion of the inner world of fantasy. The higher truth, the perfection of these states in contrast to the incompletely intelligible everyday world, this deep consciousness of nature, healing and helping in sleep and dreams, is at the same time the symbolical analogue of the soothsaying faculty and of the arts generally, which make life possible and worth living. But we must also include in our image of Apollo that delicate boundary which the dream image must not overstep lest it have a pathological effect (in which case mere appearance would deceive us as if it were crude reality). We must keep in mind that measured restraint, that freedom from the wilder emotions, that calm of the sculptor god. His eye must be "sunlike," as befits his origin; even when it is angry and distempered it is still hallowed by beautiful illusion. And so, in one sense, we might apply to Apollo the words of Schopenhauer when he speaks of the man wrapped in the veil of *māyā* (*Welt als Wille und Vorstellung*, I, p. 416): "Just as in a stormy sea that, unbounded in all directions, raises and drops mountainous wayes, howling, a sailor sits in a boat and trusts in his frail bark: so in the midst of a world of torments the individual human being sits quietly, supported by and trusting in the *principium individuationis*." In fact, we might say of Apollo that in him the unshaken faith in this *principium* and the calm repose of the man wrapped up in it receive their most sublime expression; and we might call Apollo himself the glorious divine image of the *principium individuationis*, through whose gestures and eyes all the joy and wisdom of "illusion," together with its beauty, speak to us.

In the same work Schopenhauer has depicted for us the tremendous *terror* which seizes man when he is suddenly dumbfounded by the cognitive form of phenomena because the principle of sufficient reason, in some one of its manifestations, seems to suffer an exception. If we add to this terror the blissful ecstasy that wells from the innermost depths of man, indeed of nature, at this collapse of the *principium individuationis*, we steal a glimpse into the nature of the *Dionysian*, which is brought home to us most intimately by the analogy of intoxication. Either under the influence of the narcotic draught, of which the songs of all primitive men and peoples speak, or with the potent coming of spring that penetrates all nature with joy, these Dionysian emotions awake, and as they grow in intensity everything subjective vanishes into complete self-forgetfulness. In the German Middle Ages, too, singing and dancing crowds, ever increasing in number, whirled themselves from place to place under this same Dionysian impulse. In these dancers of St. John and St. Vitus, we rediscover the Bacchic choruses of the Greeks, with their prehistory in Asia Minor, as far back as Babylon and the orgiastic Sacaea. There are some who, from obtuseness or lack of experience, turn away from such phenomena as from "folk-diseases," with contempt or pity born of the consciousness of their own "healthy-mindedness." But of course such poor wretches have no idea how corpselike and ghostly their so-called "healthy-mindedness" looks when the glowing life of the Dionysian revelers roars past them.

Under the charm of the Dionysian not only is the union between man and man reaffirmed, but nature which has become alienated, hostile, or subjugated, celebrates once more her reconciliation with her lost son, man. Freely, earth proffers her gifts, and peacefully the beasts of prey of the rocks and desert approach. The chariot of Dionysus is covered with flowers and garlands; panthers and tigers walk under its yoke. Transform Beethoven's "Hymn to Joy" into a painting; let your imagination conceive the multitudes bowing to the dust, awestruck – then you will approach the Dionysian. Now the slave is a free man; now all the rigid, hostile barriers that necessity, caprice, or "impudent convention" have fixed between man and man are broken. Now, with the gospel of universal harmony, each one feels himself not only united, reconciled, and fused with his neighbor, but as one with him, as if the veil of *māyā* had been torn aside and were now merely fluttering in tatters before the mysterious primordial unity. In song and in dance man expresses himself as a member of a higher community; he has forgotten how to walk and speak and is on the way toward flying into the air, dancing. His very gestures express enchantment. Just as the animals now talk, and the earth yields milk and honey, supernatural sounds emanate from him, too: he feels himself a god, he himself now walks about enchanted, in ecstasy, like the gods he saw walking in his dreams. He is no longer an artist, he has become a work of art: in these paroxysms of intoxication the artistic power of all nature reveals itself to the highest gratification of the primordial unity. The noblest clay, the most costly marble, man, is here kneaded and cut, and to the sound of the chisel strokes of the Dionysian world-artist rings out the cry of the Eleusinian mysteries: "Do you prostrate yourselves, millions? Do you sense your Maker, world?"

II

Thus far we have considered the Apollinian and its opposite, the Dionysian, as artistic energies which burst forth from nature herself, *without the mediation of the human artist* – energies in which nature's art impulses are satisfied in the most immediate and direct way – first in the image world of dreams, whose completeness is not dependent upon the intellectual attitude or the artistic culture of any single being; and then as intoxicated reality, which likewise does not heed the single unit, but even seeks to destroy the individual and redeem him by a mystic feeling of oneness. With reference to these immediate art-states of nature, every artist is an "imitator," that is to say, either an Apollinian artist in dreams, or a Dionysian artist in ecstasies, or finally – as for example in Greek tragedy – at once artist in both dreams and ecstasies; so we mar perhaps picture him sinking down in his Dionysian intoxication and mystical self-abnegation, alone and apart from the singing revelers, and we may imagine how, through Apollinian dream-inspiration, his own state, i.e., his oneness with the inmost ground of the world, is revealed to him in a *symbolical dream image*.

So much for these general premises and contrasts. Let us now approach the *Greeks* in order to learn how highly these *art impulses of nature* were developed in them. Thus we shall be in a position to understand and appreciate more deeply that relation of the Greek artist to his archetypes which is, according to the Aristotelian expression, "the imitation of nature." In spite of all the dream literature and the numerous dream anecdotes of the Greeks, we can speak of their *dreams* only conjecturally, though with reasonable assurance. If we consider the incredibly precise and unerring plastic power of their eyes, together with their vivid, frank delight in colors, we can hardly refrain from assuming even for their dreams (to the shame of all those born later) a certain logic of line and contour, colors and groups, a certain pictorial sequence reminding us of their finest bas-reliefs whose perfection would certainly justify us, if a comparison were possible, in designating the dreaming Greeks as Homers and Homer as a dreaming Greek – in a deeper sense than that in which modern man, speaking of his dreams, ventures to compare himself with Shakespeare.

On the other hand, we need not conjecture regarding the immense gap which separates the *Dionysian Greek* from the Dionysian barbarian. From all quarters of the ancient world – to say nothing here of the modern – from Rome to Babylon, we can point to the existence of Dionysian festivals, types which bear, at best, the same relation to the Greek festivals which the bearded satyr, who borrowed his name and attributes from the goat, bears to Dionysus himself. In nearly every case these festivals centered in extravagant sexual licentiousness, whose waves overwhelmed all family life and its venerable traditions; the most savage natural instincts were unleashed, including even that horrible mixture of sensuality and cruelty which has always seemed to me to be the real "witches' brew." For some time, however, the Greeks were apparently perfectly insulated and guarded against the feverish excitements of these festivals, though knowledge of them must have come to Greece on all the routes of land and sea; for the figure of Apollo, rising full of pride, held out the Gorgon's head to this grotesquely uncouth Dionysian power – and really could not have countered any more dangerous force. It is in Doric art that this majestically rejecting attitude of Apollo is immortalized. The opposition between Apollo and Dionysus became more hazardous and even impossible, when similar impulses finally burst forth from the deepest roots of the Hellenic nature and made a path for themselves: the Delphic god, by a seasonably effected reconciliation, now contented himself with taking the destructive weapons from the hands of his powerful antagonist. This reconciliation is the most important moment in the history of the Greek cult: wherever we turn we note the revolutions resulting from this event. The two antagonists were reconciled; the boundary lines to be observed henceforth by each were sharply defined, and there was to be a periodical exchange of gifts of esteem. At bottom, however, the chasm was not bridged over. But if we observe how, under the pressure of this treaty of peace, the Dionysian power revealed itself, we shall now recognize in the Dionysian orgies of the Greeks, as compared with the Babylonian Sacaea with their reversion of man to the tiger and the ape, the significance of festivals of world redemption and days of transfiguration. It is with them that nature for the first time attains her artistic jubilee; it is with them that the destruction of the *principium individuationis* for the first time becomes an artistic phenomenon. The horrible "witches' brew" of sensuality and cruelty becomes ineffective; only the curious blending and duality in the emotions of the Dionysian revelers remind us – as medicines remind us of deadly poisons – of the phenomenon that pain begets joy, that ecstasy may wring sounds of agony from us. At the very climax of joy there sounds a cry of horror or a yearning lamentation for an irretrievable loss. In these Greek festivals, nature seems to reveal a sentimental trait; it is as if she were heaving a sigh at her dismemberment into individuals. The song and pantomime of such dually-minded revelers was something new and unheard-of in the Homeric-Greek world; and the Dionysian *music* in particular excited awe and terror. If music, as it would seem, had been known previously as an Apollinian art, it was so, strictly speaking, only as the wave beat of rhythm, whose formative power was developed for the representation of Apollinian states. The music of Apollo was Doric architectonics in tones, but in tones that were merely suggestive, such as those of the cithara. The very element which forms the essence of Dionysian music (and hence of music in general) is carefully excluded as un-Apollinian – namely, the emotional power of the tone, the uniform flow of the melody, and the utterly incomparable world of harmony. In the Dionysian dithyramb man is incited to the greatest exaltation of all his symbolic faculties; something never before experienced struggles for utterance – the annihilation of the viel of *māyā*, oneness as the soul of the race and of nature itself. The essence of nature is now to be expressed symbolically; we need a new world of symbols; and the entire symbolism of the body is called into play, not the mere symbolism of the lips, face, and speech but the whole pantomine of dancing, forcing every member into rhythmic movement, Then the other symbolic powers suddenly press forward, particularly those of music, in rhythmics, dynamics, and harmony. To grasp this collective release of all the symbolic powers, man must have already attained that height of self-abnegation which seeks to express itself symbolically through all these powers – and so the dithyrambic votary of Dionysus is understood only by his peers. With what astonishment must the Apollinian Greek have beheld him! With an astonishment that was all the greater the more it was mingled with the shuddering suspicion that all this was actually not so very alien to him after all, in fact, that it was only his Apollinian consciousness which, like a veil, hid this Dionysian world from his vision.

III

To understand this, it becomes necessary to level the artistic structure of the *Apollinian culture*, as it were, stone by stone, till the foundations on which it rests become visible. First of all we see the glorious *Olympian* figures of the gods, standing on the gables of this structure. Their deeds, pictured in brilliant reliefs, adorn its friezes. We must not be misled by the fact that Apollo stands side by side with the others as an individual deity, without any claim to priority of rank. For the same impulse that embodied itself in Apollo gave birth to this entire Olympian world, and in this sense Apollo is its father. What terrific need was it that could produce such an illustrious company of Olympian beings?

Whoever approaches these Olympians with another religion in his heart, searching among them for moral elevation, even for sanctity, for disincarnate spirituality, for charity and benevolence, will soon be forced to turn his hack on them, discouraged and disappointed. For there is nothing here that suggests asceticism, spirituality, or duty. We hear nothing but the accents of an exuberant, triumphant life in which all things, whether good or evil, are deified. And so the spectator may stand quite bewildered before this fantastic excess of life, asking himself by virtue of what magic potion these high-spirited men could have found life so enjoyable that, wherever they turned, their eyes beheld the smile of Helen, the ideal picture of their own existence, "floating in sweet sensuality." But to this spectator, who has already turned his back, we must say: "Do not go away, but stay and hear what Greek folk wisdom has to say of this very life, which with such inexplicable gaiety unfolds itself before your eyes. "There is an ancient story that King Midas hunted in the forest a long time for the wise Silenus, the companion of Dionysus, without capturing him. When Silenus at last fell into his hands, the king asked what was the best and most desirable of all things for man. Fixed and immovable, the demigod said not a word, till at last, urged by the king, he gave a shrill laugh and broke out into these words: 'Oh, wretched ephemeral race, children of chance and misery, why do you compel me to tell you what it would be most expedient for you not to hear? What is best of all is utterly beyond your reach: not to be born, not to *be*, to be *nothing*. But the second best for you is – to die soon.'"

How is the world of the Olympian gods related to this folk wisdom? Even as the rapturous vision of the tortured martyr to his suffering.

Now it is as if the Olympian magic mountain had opened before us and revealed its roots to us. The Greek knew and felt the terror and horror of existence. That he might endure this terror at all, he had to interpose between himself and life the radiant dream-birth of the Olympians. That overwhelming dismay in the face of the titanic powers of nature, the Moira enthroned inexorably over all knowledge, the vulture of the great lover of mankind, Prometheus, the terrible fate of the wise Oedipus, the family curse of the Atridae which drove Orestes to matricide: in short, that entire philosophy of the sylvan god, with its mythical exemplars, which caused the downfall of the melancholy Etruscans – all this was again and again overcome by the Greeks with the aid of the Olympian *middle world* of art; or at any rate it was veiled and withdrawn from sight. It was in order to be able to live that the Greeks had to create these gods from a most profound need. Perhaps we may picture the process to ourselves somewhat as follows: out of the original Titanic divine order of terror, the Olympian divine order of joy gradually evolved through the Apollinian impulse toward beauty, just as roses burst from thorny bushes. How else could this people, so sensitive, so vehement in its desires, so singularly capable of *suffering*, have endured existence, if it had not been revealed to them in their gods, surrounded with a higher glory? The same impulse which calls art into being, as the complement and consummation of existence, seducing one to a continuation of life, was also the cause of the Olympian world which the Hellenic "will" made use of as a transfiguring mirror. Thus do the gods justify the life of man: they themselves live it – the only satisfactory theodicy! Existence under the bright sunshine of such gods is regarded as desirable in itself, and the real pain of Homeric men is caused by parting from it, especially by early parting: so that now, reversing the wisdom of Silenus, we might say of the Greeks that "to die soon is worst of all for them, the next worst – to die at all." Once heard, it will ring out again; do not forget the lament of the short-lived Achilles, mourning the leaflike change and vicissitudes of the race of men and the decline of the heroic age. It is not unworthy of the greatest hero to long for a continuation of life, even though he live as a day laborer. At the Apollinian stage of development, the "will" longs so vehemently for this existence, the Homeric man feels himself so completely at one with it, that lamentation itself becomes a song of praise.

Here we should note that this harmony which is contemplated with such longing by modern man, in fact, this oneness of man with nature (for which Schiller introduced the technical term "naïve"), is by no means a simple condition that comes into being naturally and as if inevitably. It is not a condition that, like a terrestrial paradise, *must* necessarily be found at the gate of every culture. Only a romantic age could believe this, an age which conceived of the artist in terms of Rousseau's *Emile* and imagined that in Homer it had found such an artist Emile, reared at the bosom of nature. Where we encounter the "naïve" in art, we should recognize the highest effect of Apollinian culture – which always must first overthrow an empire of Titans and slay monsters, and which must have triumphed over an abysmal and terrifying view of the world and the keenest susceptibility to suffering through recourse to the most forceful and pleasurable illusions. But how rarely is the naïve attained – that consummate immersion in the beauty of mere appearance! How unutterably sublime is *Homer* therefore, who, as an individual being, bears the same relation to this Apollinian folk culture as the individual dream artist does to the dream faculty of the people and of nature in general. The Homeric "naïveté" can be understood only as the complete victory of Apollinian illusion: this is one of those illusions which nature so frequently employs to achieve her own ends. The true goal is veiled by a phantasm: and while we stretch out our hands for the latter, nature attains the former by means of our illusion. In the Greeks the "will" wished to contemplate itself in the transfiguration of genius and the world of art; in order to glorify themselves, its creatures had to feel themselves worthy of glory; they had to behold themselves again in a higher sphere, without this perfect world of contemplation acting as a command or a reproach. This is the sphere of beauty, in which they saw their mirror images, the Olympians. With this mirroring of beauty the Hellenic will combated its artistically correlative talent for suffering and for the wisdom of suffering – and, as a monument of its victory, we have Homer, the naïve artist.

IV

Now the dream analogy may throw some light on the naïve artist. Let us imagine the dreamer: in the midst of the illusion of the dream world and without disturbing it, he calls out to himself: "It is a dream, I will dream on." What must we infer? That he experiences a deep inner joy in dream contemplation; on the other hand, to be at all able to dream with this inner joy in contemplation, he must have completely lost sight of the waking reality and its ominous obtrusiveness. Guided by the dream-reading Apollo, we may interpret all these phenomena in roughly this way. Though it is certain that of the two halves of our existence, the waking and the dreaming states, the former appeals to us as infinitely preferable, more important, excellent, and worthy of being lived, indeed, as that which alone is lived – yet in relation to that mysterious ground of our being of which we are the phenomena, I should, paradoxical as it may seem, maintain the very opposite estimate of the value of dreams. For the more clearly I perceive in nature those omnipotent art impulses, and in them an ardent longing for illusion, for redemption through illusion, the more I feel myself impelled to the metaphysical assumption that the truly existent primal unity, eternally suffering and contradictory, also needs the rapturous vision, the pleasurable illusion, for its continuous redemption. And we, completely wrapped up in this illusion and composed of it, are compelled to consider this illusion as the truly nonexistent – i.e., as a perpetual becoming in time, space, and causality – in other words, as empirical reality. If, for the moment, we do not consider the question of our own "reality," if we conceive of our empirical existence, and of that of the world in general, as a continuously manifested representation of the primal unity, we shall then have to look upon the dream as a *mere appearance of mere appearance*, hence as a still higher appeasement of the primordial desire for mere appearance. And that is why the innermost heart of nature feels that ineffable joy in the naïve artist and the naïve work of art, which is likewise only "mere appearance of mere appearance." In a symbolic painting, *Raphael*, himself one of these immortal "naïve" ones, has represented for us this demotion of appearance to the level of mere appearance, the primitive process of the naïve artist and of Apollinian culture. In his *Transfiguration*, the lower half of the picture, with the possessed boy, the despairing bearers, the bewildered, terrified disciples, shows us the reflection of suffering, primal and eternal, the sole ground of the world: the "mere appearance" here is the reflection of eternal contradiction, the father of things. From this mere appearance arises, like ambrosial vapor, a new visionary world of mere appearances, invisible to those wrapped in the first appearance – a radiant floating in purest bliss, a serene contemplation beaming from wide-open eyes. Here we have presented, in the most sublime artistic symbolism, that Apollinian world of beauty and its substratum, the terrible wisdom of Silenus; and intuitively we comprehend their necessary interdependence. Apollo, however, again appears to us the apotheosis of the *principium individuationis*, in which alone is consummated the perpetually attained goal of the primal unity, its redemption through mere appearance. With his sublime gestures, he shows us how necessary is the entire world of suffering, that by means of it the individual may be impelled to realize the redeeming vision, and then, sunk in contemplation of it, sit quietly in his tossing bark, amid the waves.

If we conceive of it all as imperative and mandatory, this apotheosis of individuation knows but one law – the individual, i.e., the delimiting of the boundaries of the individual, *measure* in the Hellenic sense. Apollo, as ethical deity, exacts measure of his disciples, and, to be able to maintain it, he requires self-knowledge. And so, side by side with the aesthetic necessity for beauty, there occur the demands "know theyself" and "nothing in excess"; consequently overweening pride and excess are regarded as the truly hostile demons of the non-Apollinian sphere, hence as characteristics of the pre-Apollinian age – that of the Titans; and of the extra-Apollinian world – that of the barbarians. Because of his titanic love for man, Prometheus must be torn to pieces by vultures; because of his excessive wisdom, which could solve the riddle of the Sphinx, Oedipus must be plunged into a bewildering vortex of crime. Thus did the Delphic god interpret the Greek past.

The effects wrought by the *Dionysian* also seemed "titanic" and "barbaric" to the Apollinian Greek; while at the same time he could not conceal from himself that he, too, was inwardly related to these overthrown Titans and heroes. Indeed, he had to recognize even more than this: despite all its beauty and moderation, his entire existence rested on a hidden substratum of suffering and of knowledge, revealed to him by the Dionysian. And behold: Apollo could not live without Dionysus! The "titanic" and the "barbaric" were in the last analysis as necessary as the Apollinian.

And now let us imagine how into this world, built on mere appearance and moderation and artificially dammed up, there penetrated, in tones ever more bewitching and alluring, the ecstatic sound of the Dionysian festival; how in these strains all of nature's *excess* in pleasure, grief, and knowledge became audible, even in piercing shrieks; and let us ask ourselves what the psalmodizing artist of Apollo, with his phantom harpsound, could mean in the face of this demonic folk-song! The muses of the arts of "illusion" paled before an art that, in its intoxication, spoke the truth. The wisdom of Silenus cried "Woe! woe!" to the serene Olympians. The individual, with all his restraint and proportion, succumbed to the self-oblivion of the Dionysian states, forgetting the precepts of Apollo. *Excess* revealed itself as truth. Contradiction, the bliss born of pain, spoke out from the very heart of nature. And so, wherever the Dionysian prevailed, the

Apollinian was checked and destroyed. But, on the other hand, it is equally certain that, wherever the first Dionysian onslaught was successfully withstood, the authority and majesty of the Delphic god exhibited itself as more rigid and menacing than ever. For to me the *Doric* state and Doric art are explicable only as a permanent military encampment of the Apollinian. Only incessant resistance to the titanic-barbaric nature of the Dionysian could account for the long survival of an art so defiantly prim and so encompassed with bulwarks, a training so warlike and rigorous, and a political structure so cruel and relentless.

Up to this point we have simply enlarged upon the observation made at the beginning of this essay: that the Dionysian and the Apollinian, in new births ever following and mutually augmenting one another, controlled the Hellenic genius; that out of the age of "bronze," with its wars of the Titans and its rigorous folk philosophy, the Homeric world developed under the sway of the Apollinian impulse to beauty; that this "naïve" splendor was again overwhelmed by the influx of the Dionysian; and that against this new power the Apollinian rose to the austere majesty of Doric art and the Doric view of the world. If amid the strife to these two hostile principles, the older Hellenic history thus falls into four great periods of art, we are now impelled to inquire after the final goal of these developments and processes, lest perchance we should regard the last-attained period, the period of Doric art, as the climax and aim of these artistic impulses. And here the sublime and celebrated art of *Attic tragedy* and the dramatic dithyramb presents itself as the common goal of both these tendencies whose mysterious union, after many and long precursory struggles, found glorious consummation in this child – at once Antigone and Cassandra.

VII

We must now avail ourselves of all the principles of art considered so far, in order to find our way through the labyrinth, as we must call it, of *the origin of Greek tragedy*. I do not think I am unreasonable in saying that the problem of this origin has as yet not even been seriously posed, to say nothing of solved, however often the ragged tatters of ancient tradition have been sewn together in various combinations and torn apart again. This tradition tells us quite unequivocally *that tragedy arose from the tragic chorus*, and was originally only chorus and nothing but chorus. Hence we consider it our duty to look into the heart of this tragic chorus as the real proto-drama, without resting satisfied with such arty clichés as that the chorus is the "ideal spectator" or that it represents the people in contrast to the aristocratic region of the scene. [. . .]

It is indeed an "ideal" domain, as Schiller correctly perceived, in which the Greek satyr chorus, the chorus of primitive tragedy, was wont to dwell. It is a domain raised high above the actual paths of mortals. For this chorus the Greek built up the scaffolding of a fictitious *natural state* and on it placed fictitious *natural beings*. On this foundation tragedy developed and so, of course, it could dispense from the beginning with a painstaking portrayal of reality. Yet it is no arbitrary world placed by whim between heaven and earth; rather it is a world with the same reality and credibility that Olympus with its inhabitants possessed for the believing Hellene. The satyr, as the Dionysian chorist, lives in a religiously acknowledged reality under the sanction of myth and cult. That tragedy should begin with him, that he should be the voice of the Dionysian wisdom of tragedy, is just as strange a phenomenon for us as the general derivation of tragedy from the chorus.

Perhaps we shall have a point of departure for our inquiry if I put forward the proposition that the satyr, the fictitious natural being, bears the same relation to the man of culture that Dionysian music bears to civilization. Concerning the latter, Richard Wagner says that it is nullified by music just as lamplight is nullified by the light of day. Similarly, I believe, the Greek man of culture felt himself nullified in the presence of the satyric chorus; and this is the most immediate effect of the Dionysian tragedy, that the state and society and, quite generally, the gulfs between man and man give way to an overwhelming feeling of unity leading back to the very heart of nature. The metaphysical comfort – with which, I am suggesting even now, every true tragedy leaves us – that life is at the bottom of things, despite all the changes of appearances, indestructibly powerful and pleasurable – this comfort appears in incarnate clarity in the chorus of satyrs, a chorus of natural beings who live ineradicably, as it were, behind all civilization and remain eternally the same, despite the changes of generations and of the history of nations.

With this chorus the profound Hellene, uniquely susceptible to the tenderest and deepest suffering, comforts himself, having looked boldly right into the terrible destructiveness of so-called world history as well as the cruelty of nature, and being in danger of longing for a Buddhistic negation of the will. Art saves him, and through art – life.

For the rapture of the Dionysian state with its annihilation of the ordinary bounds and limits of existence contains, while it lasts, a *lethargic* element in which all personal experiences of the past become immersed. This chasm of oblivion separates the worlds of everyday reality and of Dionysian reality. But as soon as this everyday reality re-enters consciousness, it is experienced as such, with nausea: an ascetic, will-negating mood is the fruit of these states. In this sense the Dionysian man resembles Hamlet: both have once looked truly into the essence of things, they have *gained knowledge*, and nausea inhibits action; for their action could not change anything in the eternal nature of things; they feel it to be ridiculous or humiliating that they should be asked to set right a world that is out of joint. Knowledge kills action; action requires the veils of illusion: that is the doctrine of Hamlet, not that cheap wisdom of Jack the Dreamer who reflects too much and, as it were, from an excess of possibilities does not get around to action. Not reflection, no – true knowledge, an insight into the horrible truth, outweighs any motive for action, both in Hamlet and in the Dionysian man. Now no comfort avails any more; longing transcends a world after death, even the gods; existence is negated along with its glittering reflection in the gods or in an immortal beyond. Conscious of the truth he has once seen, man now sees everywhere only the horror or absurdity of existence; now he understands what is symbolic in Ophelia's fate; now he understands the wisdom of the sylvan god, Silenus: he is nauseated.

Here, when the danger to his will is greatest, *art* approaches as a saving sorceress, expert at healing. She alone knows how to turn these nauseous thoughts about the horror or absurdity of existence into notions with which one can live: these are the *sublime* as the artistic taming of the horrible, and the *comic* as the artistic discharge of the nausea of absurdity. The satyr chorus of the dithyramb is the saving deed of Greek art; faced with the intermediary world of these Dionysian companions, the feelings described here exhausted themselves.

VIII

The satyr, like the idyllic shepherd of more recent times, is the offspring of a longing for the primitive and the natural; but how firmly and fearlessly the Greek embraced the man of the woods, and how timorously and mawkishly modern man dallied with the flattering image of a sentimental, flute-playing, tender shepherd! Nature, as yet unchanged by knowledge, with the bolts of culture still unbroken – that is what the Greek saw in his satyr who nevertheless was not a mere ape. On the contrary, the satyr was the archetype of man, the embodiment of his highest and most intense emotions, the ecstatic reveler enraptured by the proximity of his god, the sympathetic companion in whom the suffering of the god is repeated, one who proclaims wisdom from the very heart of nature, a symbol of the sexual omnipotence of nature which the Greeks used to contemplate with reverent wonder. The satyr was something sublime and divine: thus he had to appear to the painfully broken vision of Dionysian man. The contrived shepherd in his dress-ups would have offended him: on the unconcealed and vigorously magnificent characters of nature, his eye rested with sublime satisfaction; here the true human being was disclosed, the bearded satyr jubilating to his god. Confronted with him, the man of culture shriveled into a mendacious caricature. Schiller is right about these origins of tragic art, too: the chorus is a living wall against the assaults of reality because it – the satyr chorus – represents existence more truthfully, really, and completely than the man of culture does who ordinarily considers himself as the only reality. The sphere of poetry does not lie outside the world as a fantastic impossibility spawned by a poet's brain: it desires to be just the opposite, the unvarnished expression of the truth, and must precisely for that reason discard the mendacious finery of that alleged reality of the man of culture.

The contrast between this real truth of nature and the lie of culture that poses as if it were the only reality is similar to that between the eternal core of things, the thing-in-itself, and the whole world of appearances: just as tragedy, with its metaphysical comfort, points to the eternal life of this core of existence which abides through the perpetual destruction of appearances, the symbolism of the satyr chorus proclaims this primordial relationship between the thing-in-itself and appearance. The idyllic shepherd of modern man is merely a counterfeit of the sum of cultural illusions that arc allegedly nature; the Dionysian Greek wants truth and nature in their most forceful form – and sees himself changed, as by magic, into a satyr. [. . .]

Such magic transformation is the presupposition of all dramatic art. In this magic transformation the Dionysian reveler sees himself as a satyr, *and as a satyr, in turn, he sees the god*, which means that in his metamorphosis he beholds another vision outside himself, as the Apollinian complement of his own state. With this new vision the drama is complete.

In the light of this insight we must understand Greek tragedy as the Dionysian chorus which ever anew discharges itself in an Apollinian world of images. Thus the choral parts with which tragedy is interlaced are, as it were, the womb that gave birth to the whole of the so-called dialogue, that is, the entire world of the stage, the real drama. In several successive discharges this primal ground of tragedy radiates this vision of the drama which is by all means a dream apparition and to that extent epic in nature; but on the other hand, being the objectification of a Dionysian state, it represents not Apollinian redemption through mere appearance but, on the contrary, the shattering of the individual and his fusion with primal being. Thus the drama is the Dionysian embodiment of Dionysian insights and effects and thereby separated, as by a tremendous chasm, from the epic. [. . .]

X

The tradition is undisputed that Greek tragedy in its earliest form had for its sole theme the sufferings of Dionysus and that for a long time the only stage hero was Dionysus himself. But it may be claimed with equal confidence that until Euripides, Dionysus never ceased to be the tragic hero; that all the celebrated figures of the Greek stage – Prometheus, Oedipus, etc. – are mere masks of this original hero, Dionysus. That behind all these masks there is a deity, that is one essential reason for the typical "ideality" of these famous figures which has caused so much astonishment. Somebody, I do not know who, has claimed that all individuals, taken as individuals, are comic and hence untragic – from which it would follow that the Greeks simply *could* not suffer individuals on the tragic stage. In fact, this is what they seem to have felt; and the Platonic distinction and evaluation of the "idea" and the "idol," the mere image, is very deeply rooted in the Hellenic character. Using Plato's terms we should have to speak of the tragic figures of the Hellenic stage somewhat as follows: the one truly real Dionysus appears in a variety of forms, in the mask of a fighting hero, and entangled, as it were, in the net of the individual will. The god who appears talks and acts so as to resemble an erring, striving, suffering individual. That he *appears* at all with such epic precision and clarity is the work of the dream-interpreter, Apollo, who through this symbolic appearance interprets to the chorus its Dionysian state. In truth, however, the hero is the suffering Dionysus of the Mysteries, the god experiencing in himself the agonies of individuation, of whom wonderful myths tell that as a boy he was torn to pieces by the Titans and now is worshiped in this state as Zagreus. Thus it is intimated that this dismemberment, the properly Dionysian *suffering*, is like a transformation into air, water, earth, and fire, that we are therefore to regard the state of individuation as the origin and primal cause of all suffering, as something objectionable in itself. From the smile of this Dionysus sprang the Olympian gods, from his tears sprang man. In this existence as a dismembered god, Dionysus possesses the dual nature of a cruel, barbarized demon and a mild, gentle ruler. But the hope of the epopts looked toward a rebirth of Dionysus, which we must now dimly conceive as the end of individuation. It was for this coming third Dionysus that the epopts' roaring hymns of joy resounded. And it is this hope alone that casts a gleam of joy upon the features of a world torn asunder and shattered into individuals; this is symbolized in the myth of Demeter, sunk in eternal sorrow, who *rejoices* again for the first time when told that she may *once more* give birth to Dionysus. This view of things already provides us with all the elements of a profound and pessimistic view of the world, together with the *mystery doctrine of tragedy*: the fundamental knowledge of the oneness of everything existent, the conception of individuation as the primal cause of evil, and of art as the joyous hope that the spell of individuation may be broken in augury of a restored oneness.

We have already suggested that the Homeric epos is the poem of Olympian culture, in which this culture has sung its own song of victory over the terrors of the war of the Titans. Under the predominating influence of tragic poetry, these Homeric myths are now born anew; and this metempsychosis reveals that in the meantime the Olympian culture also has been conquered by a still more profound view of the world. The defiant Titan Prometheus has announced to his Olympian tormentor that some day the greatest danger will menace his rule, unless Zeus should enter into an alliance with him in time. In Aeschylus we recognize how the terrified Zeus, fearful of his end, allies himself with the Titan. Thus the former age of the Titans is once more recovered from Tartarus and brought to the light. The philosophy of wild and naked nature beholds with the frank, undissembling gaze of truth the myths of the Homeric world as they dance past: they turn pale, they tremble under the piercing glance of this goddess – till the powerful fist of the Dionysian artist forces them into the service of the new deity. Dionysian truth takes over the entire domain of myth as the symbolism of *its* knowledge which it makes known partly in the public cult of tragedy and partly in the secret celebrations of dramatic mysteries, but always in the old mythical garb.

22

What is Art?

Leo Tolstoy

Leo Tolstoy (1828–1910), the famed Russian novelist who wrote *War and Peace* and *Anna Karenina*, considered art a medium for communicating feelings.

What, then, is this conception of beauty so stubbornly held to by people of our circle and day as furnishing a definition of art?

In the subjective aspect, we call beauty that which supplies us with a particular kind of pleasure.

In the objective aspect, we call beauty something absolutely perfect, and we acknowledge it to be so only because we receive, from the manifestation of this absolute perfection, a certain kind of pleasure; so this objective definition is nothing but the subjective conception differently expressed. In reality both conceptions of beauty amount to one and the same thing – namely, the reception by us of a certain kind of pleasure; i.e., we call "beauty" that which pleases us without evoking in us desire.

Such being the position of affairs, it would seem only natural that the science of art should decline to content itself with a definition of art based on beauty (i.e., on that which pleases), and seek a general definition which should apply to all artistic productions, and by reference to which we might decide whether a certain article belonged to the realm of art or not. But no such definition is supplied, as the reader may see from those summaries of the aesthetic theories which I have given, and as he may discover even more clearly from the original aesthetic works if he will be at the pains to read them. All attempts to define absolute beauty in itself – whether as an imitation of nature, or as suitability to its object, or as a correspondence of parts, or as symmetry, or as harmony, or as unity in variety, etc. – either define nothing at all or define only some traits of some artistic productions and are far from including all that everybody has always held, and still holds, to be art.

There is no objective definition of beauty. The existing definitions (both the metaphysical and the experimental) amount only to one and the same subjective definition, which (strange as it seems to say so) is that art is that which makes beauty manifest, and beauty is that which pleases (without exciting desire). Many aestheticians have felt the insufficiency and instability of such a definition, and, in order to give it a firm basis, have asked themselves why a thing pleases. And they have converted the discussion on beauty into a question concerning taste, as did Hutcheson, Voltaire, Diderot, and others. But all attempts to define what taste is must lead to nothing, as the reader may see both from the history of aesthetics and experimentally. There is and can be no explanation of why one thing pleases one man and displeases another, or vice versa. So that the

Leo Tolstoy, "What is Art?," in *What is Art and Essays on Art*, ed. Louise and Aylmer Maude (1899).

whole existing science of aesthetics fails to do what we might expect from it, being a mental activity calling itself a science; namely, it does not define the qualities and laws of art or of the beautiful (if that be the content of art), or the nature of taste (if taste decides the question of art and its merit), and then, on the basis of such definitions, acknowledge as art those productions which correspond to these laws and reject those which do not come under them. But this science of aesthetics consists in first acknowledging a certain set of productions to be art (because they please us), and then framing such a theory of art that all those productions which please a certain circle of people should fit into it. There exists an art canon according to which certain productions favored by our circle are acknowledged as being art – Phidias, Sophocles, Homer, Titian, Raphael, Bach, Beethoven, Dante, Shakespeare, Goethe, and others – and the aesthetic laws must be such as to embrace all these productions. In aesthetic literature you will incessantly meet with opinions on the merit and importance of art, founded not on any certain laws by which this or that is held to be good or bad, but merely on the consideration whether this art tallies with the art canon we have drawn up.

The other day I was reading a far from ill-written book by Folgeldt. Discussing the demand for morality in works of art, the author plainly says that we must not demand morality in art. And in proof of this he advances the fact that if we admit such a demand, Shakespeare's *Romeo and Juliet* and Goethe's *Wilhelm Meister* would not fit into the definition of good art; but since both these books are included in our canon of art, he concludes that the demand is unjust. And therefore it is necessary to find a definition of art which shall fit the works; and instead of a demand for morality, Folgeldt postulates as the basis of art a demand for the important (*das Bedeutungsvolle*).

All the existing aesthetic standards are built on this plan. Instead of giving a definition of true art and then deciding what is and what is not good art by judging whether a work conforms or does not conform to the definition, a certain class of works which for some reason please a certain circle of people is accepted as being art, and a definition of art is then devised to cover all these productions. I recently came upon a remarkable instance of this method in a very good German work, *The History of Art in the Nineteenth Century*, by Muther. Describing the pre-Raphaelites, the Decadents and the Symbolists (who are already included in the canon of art), he not only does not venture to blame their tendency, but earnestly endeavors to widen his standard so that it may include them all, they appearing to him to represent a legitimate reaction from the excesses of realism. No matter what insanities appear in art, when once they find acceptance among the upper classes of our society a theory is quickly invented to explain and sanction them, just as if there had never been periods in history when certain special circles of people recognized and approved false, deformed, and insensate art which subsequently left no trace and has been utterly forgottern. And to what lengths the insanity and deformity of art may go, especially when, as in our days, it knows that it is considered infallible, may be seen by what is being done in the art of our circle today.

So the theory of art founded on beauty, expounded by aesthetics, and in dim outline professed by the public, is nothing but the setting up as good of that which has pleased and pleases us, i.e., pleases a certain class of people.

In order to define any human activity it is necessary to understand its sense and importance. And in order to do that it is primarily necessary to examine that activity in itself, in its dependence on its causes and in connection with its effects, and not merely in relation to the pleasure we can get from it.

If we say that the aim of any activity is merely our pleasure, and define it solely by that pleasure, our definition will evidently be a false one. But this is precisely what has occurred in the efforts to define art. Now, if we consider the food question it will not occur to anyone to affirm that the importance of food consists in the pleasure we receive when eating it. Everyone understands that the satisfaction of our taste cannot serve as a basis for our definition of the merits of food, and that we have therefore no right to presuppose that the dinners with cayenne pepper, Limburg cheese, alcohol, etc., to which we are accustomed and which please us, form the very best human food.

And in the same way, beauty, or that which pleases us, can in no sense serve as the basis for the definition of art; nor can a series of objects which afford us pleasure serve as the model of what art should be.

To see the aim and purpose of art in the pleasure we get from it is like assuming (as is done by people of the lowest moral development, e.g., by savages) that the purpose and aim of food is the pleasure derived when consuming it.

Just as people who conceive the aim and purpose of food to be pleasure cannot recognize the real meaning of eating, so people who consider the aim of art to be pleasure cannot realize its true meaning and purpose because they attribute to an activity the meaning of which lies in its connection with other phenomena of life, the false and exceptional aim of pleasure. People come to understand that the meaning of eating lies in the nourishment of the body only when they cease to consider that the object of that activity is pleasure. And it is the same with regard to art. People will come to understand the meaning of art only when they cease to consider that the aim of that activity is beauty, i.e., pleasure. The acknowledgment of beauty (i.e., of a certain kind of pleasure received from art) as being the aim of art not only fails to assist us in finding a definition of what art is, but, on the contrary, by transferring the question into a region quite foreign to art (into metaphysical, psychological, physiological, and even historical discussions as to why such a production pleases one person, and such another displeases or pleases someone else), it renders such definition impossible. And since discussions as to why one man likes pears and another prefers meat do not help toward finding a definition of what is essential in nourishment, so the solution of questions of taste in art (to which the discussions on art involuntarily come) not only does not help to make clear in what this particular human activity which we call art really consists, but renders such elucidation quite impossible until we rid ourselves of a conception which justifies every kind of art at the cost of confusing the whole matter.

To the question, what is this art to which is offered up the labor of millions, the very lives of men, and even morality itself? we have extracted replies from the existing aesthetics, which all amount to this: that the aim of art is beauty, that beauty is recognized by the enjoyment it gives, and that artistic enjoyment is a good and important thing because it *is* enjoyment. In a word, enjoyment is good because it is enjoyment. Thus what is considered the definition of art is no definition at all, but only a shuffle to justify existing art. Therefore, however strange it may seem to say so, in spite of the mountains of books written about art no exact definition of art has been constructed. And the reason for this is that the conception of art has been based on the conception of beauty. [. . .]

What is art – if we put aside the conception of beauty, which confuses the whole matter? The latest and most comprehensible definitions of art, apart from the conception of beauty, are the following: (1) Art is an activity arising even in the animal kingdom, *a*, springing from sexual desire and the propensity to play (Schiller, Darwin, Spencer), and *b*, accompanied by a pleasurable excitement of the nervous system (Grant Allen). This is the physiological-evolutionary definition. (2) Art is the external manifestation by means of lines, colors, movements, sounds, or words, of emotions felt by man (Véron). This is the experimental definition. According to the very latest definition, (3) Art is "the production of some permanent object or passing action, which is fitted, not only to supply an active enjoyment to the producer, but to convey a pleasurable impression to a number of spectators or listeners, quite apart from any personal advantage to be derived from it" (Sully).

Notwithstanding the superiority of these definitions to the metaphysical definitions which depended on the conception of beauty, they are yet far from exact. The first, the physiological-evolutionary definition (1*a*), is inexact because, instead of speaking about the artistic activity itself, which is the real matter in hand, it treats of the derivation of art. The modification of it (1*b*), based on the physiological effects on the human organism, is inexact because within the limits of such definition many other human activities can be included, as has occurred in the neo-aesthetic theories, which reckon as art the preparation of handsome clothes, pleasant scents, and even victuals.

The experimental definition (2), which makes art consist in the expression of emotions, is inexact because a man may express his emotions by means of lines, colors, sounds, or words, and yet may not act on others by such expression, and then the manifestation of his emotions is not art.

The third definition (that of Sully) is inexact because in the production of objects or actions affording pleasure to the producer and a pleasant emotion to the spectators or hearers, apart from personal advantage, may be included the showing of conjuring tricks or gymnastic exercises and other activities which are not art. And further, many things, the production of which does not afford pleasure to the producer and the sensation received from which is unpleasant, such as gloomy, heartrending scenes in a poetic description or a play, may nevertheless be undoubted works of art.

The inaccuracy of all these definitions arises from the fact that in them all (as also in the metaphysical definitions) the object considered is the pleasure art may give, and not the purpose it may serve in the life of man and of humanity.

In order correctly to define art, it is necessary, first of all, to cease to consider it as a means to pleasure and to consider it as one of the conditions of human life. Viewing it in this way we cannot fail to observe that art is one of the means of intercourse between man and man.

Every work of art causes the receiver to enter into a certain kind of relationship both with him who produced, or is producing, the art, and with all those who, simultaneously, previously, or subsequently, receive the same artistic impression.

Speech, transmitting the thoughts and experiences of men, serves as a means of union among them, and art acts in a similar manner. The peculiarity of this latter means of intercourse, distinguishing if from intercourse by means of words, consists in this, that whereas by words a man transmits his thoughts to another, by means of art he transmits his feelings.

The activity of art is based on the fact that a man, receiving through his sense of hearing or sight another man's expression of feeling, is capable of experiencing the emotion which moved the man who expressed it. To take the simplest example: one man laughs, and another who hears becomes merry; or a man weeps, and another who hears feels sorrow. A man is excited or irritated, and another man seeing him comes to a similar state of mind. By his movements or by the sounds of his voice, a man expresses courage and determination or sadness and calmness, and this state of mind passes on to others. A man suffers, expressing his sufferings by groans and spasms, and this suffering transmits itself to other people; a man expresses his feeling of admiration, devotion, fear, respect, or love to certain objects, persons, or phenomena, and others are infected by the same feelings of admiration, devotion, fear, respect, or love to the same objects, persons, and phenomena.

And it is upon this capacity of man to receive another man's expression of feeling and experience those feelings himself, that the activity of art is based.

If a man infects another or others directly, immediately, by his appearance or by the sounds he gives vent to at the very time he experiences the feeling; if he causes another man to yawn when he himself cannot help yawning, or to laugh or cry when he himself is obliged to laugh or cry, or to suffer when he himself is suffering – that does not amount to art.

Art begins when one person, with the object of joining another or others to himself in one and the same feeling, expresses that feeling by certain external indications. To take the simplest example: a boy, having experienced, let us say, fear on encountering a wolf, relates that encounter; and, in order to evoke in others the feeling he has experienced, describes himself, his condition before the encounter, the surroundings, the wood, his own lightheartedness, and then the wolf's appearance, its movements, the distance between himself and the wolf, etc. All this, if only the boy, when telling the story, again experiences the feelings he had lived through and infects the hearers and compels them to feel what the narrator had experienced, is art. If even the boy had not seen a wolf but had frequently been afraid of one, and if, wishing to evoke in others the fear he had felt, he invented an encounter with a wolf and recounted it so as to make his hearers share the feelings he experienced when he feared the wolf, that also would be art. And just in the same way it is art if a man, having experienced either the fear of suffering or the attraction of enjoyment (whether in reality or in imagination), expresses these feelings on canvas or in marble so that others are infected by them. And it is also art if a man feels or imagines to himself feelings of delight, gladness, sorrow, despair, courage, or despondency and the transition from one to another of these feelings, and expresses these feelings by sounds so that the hearers are infected by them and experience them as they were experienced by the composer.

The feelings with which the artist infects others may be most various – very strong or very weak, very important or very insignificant, very bad or very good: feelings of love for one's own country, self-devotion and submission to fate or to God expressed in a drama, raptures of lovers described in a novel, feelings of voluptuousness expressed in a picture, courage expressed in a triumphal march, merriment evoked by a dance, humor evoked by a funny story, the feeling of quietness transmitted by an evening landscape or by a lullaby, or the feeling of admiration evoked by a beautiful arabesque – it is all art.

If only the spectators or auditors are infected by the feelings which the author has felt, it is art.

To evoke in oneself a feeling one has once experienced, and having evoked it in oneself, then, by means of movements, lines, colors, sounds, or forms expressed in words, so to transmit that feeling that others may experience the same feeling – this is the activity of art.

Art is a human activity consisting in this, that one man consciously, by means of certain external signs, hands on to others feelings he has lived through, and that other people are infected by these feelings and also experience them.

Art is not, as the metaphysicians say, the manifestation of some mysterious Idea of beauty or God; it is not, as the aesthetical physiologists say, a game in which man lets off his excess of stored-up energy; it is not the expression of man's emotions by external signs; it is not the production of pleasing objects; and, above all, it is not pleasure; but it is a means of union among men, joining them together in the same feelings, and indispensable for the life and progress toward well-being of individuals and of humanity.

As, thanks to man's capacity to express thoughts by words, every man may know all that has been done for him in the realms of thought by all humanity before his day, and can in the present, thanks to this capacity to understand the thoughts of others, become a sharer in their activity and can himself hand on to his contemporaries and descendants the thoughts he has assimilated from others, as well as those which have arisen within himself; so, thanks to man's capacity to be infected with the feelings of others by means of art, all that is being lived through by his contemporaries is accessible to him, as well as the feelings experienced by men thousands of years ago, and he has also the possibility of transmitting his own feelings to others.

If people lacked this capacity to receive the thoughts conceived by the men who preceded them and to pass on to others their own thoughts, men would be like wild beasts, or like Kaspar Hauser.[1]

And if men lacked this other capacity of being infected by art, people might be almost more savage still, and, above all, more separated from, and more hostile to, one another.

And therefore the activity of art is a most important one, as important as the activity of speech itself and as generally diffused.

We are accustomed to understand art to be only what we hear and see in theaters, concerts, and exhibitions, together with buildings, statues, poems, novels. . . . But all this is but the smallest part of the art by which we communicate with each other in life. All human life is filled with works of art of every kind – from cradlesong, jest, mimicry, the ornamentation of houses, dress, and utensils, up to church services, buildings, monuments, and triumphal processions. It is all artistic activity. So that by art, in the limited sense of the word, we do not mean all human activity transmitting feelings, but only that part which we for some reason select from it and to which we attach special importance.

This special importance has always been given by all men to that part of this activity which transmits feelings flowing from their religious perception, and this small part of art they have specifically called art, attaching to it the full meaning of the word.

That was how men of old – Socrates, Plato, and Aristotle – looked on art. Thus did the Hebrew prophets and the ancient Christians regard art; thus it was, and still is, understood by the Mohammedans, and thus it still is understood by religious folk among our own peasantry.

Some teachers of mankind – as Plato in his *Republic* and people such as the primitive Christians, the strict Mohammedans, and the Buddhists – have gone so far as to repudiate all art.

People viewing art in this way (in contradiction to the prevalent view of today which regards any art as good if only it affords pleasure) considered, and consider, that art (as contrasted with speech, which need not be listened to) is so highly dangerous in its power to infect people against their wills that mankind will lose far less by banishing all art than by tolerating each and every art.

Evidently such people were wrong in repudiating all art, for they denied that which cannot be denied – one of the indispensable means of communication, without which mankind could not exist. But not less wrong are the people of civilized European society of our class and day in favoring any art if it but serves beauty, i.e., gives people pleasure.

Formerly people feared lest among the works of art there might chance to be some causing corruption, and they prohibited art altogether. Now they only fear lest they should be deprived of any enjoyment art can afford, and patronize any art. And I think the last error is much grosser than the first and that its consequences are far more harmful. [. . .]

But how could it happen that that very art, which in ancient times was merely tolerated (if tolerated at all), should have come in our times to be invariably considered a good thing if only it affords pleasure?

It has resulted from the following causes. The estimation of the value of art (i.e., of the feelings it transmits) depends on men's perception of the meaning of life, depends on what they consider to be the good and the evil of life. And what is good and what is evil is defined by what are termed religions.

Humanity unceasingly moves forward from a lower, more partial and obscure understanding of life to one more general and more lucid. And in this, as in every movement, there are leaders – those who have understood the meaning of life more clearly than others – and of these advanced men there is always one who has in his words and by his life expressed this meaning more clearly, accessibly, and strongly than others. This man's expression of the meaning of life, together with those superstitions, traditions, and ceremonies which usually form themselves round the memory of such a man, is what is called a religion. Religions are the exponents of the highest comprehension of life accessible to the best and foremost men at a given time in a given society – a comprehension toward which, inevitably and irresistibly, all the rest of that society must advance. And therefore only religions have always served, and still serve, as bases for the valuation of human sentiments. If feelings bring men nearer the ideal their religion indicates, if they are in harmony with it and do not contradict it, they are good; if they estrange men from it and oppose it, they are bad.

If the religion places the meaning of life in worshiping one God and fulfilling what is regarded as His will, as was the case among the Jews, then the feelings flowing from love to that God and to His law successfully transmitted through the art of poetry by the prophets, by the psalms, or by the epic of the book of Genesis, is good, high art. All opposing that, as for instance the transmission of feelings of devotion to strange gods or of feelings incompatible with the law of God, would be considered bad art. Or if, as was the case among the Greeks, the religion places the meaning of life in earthly happiness, in beauty and in strength, then art successfully transmitting the joy and energy of life would be considered good art, but art which transmitted feelings of effeminacy or despondency would be bad art. If the meaning of life is seen in the well-being of one's nation or in honoring one's ancestors and continuing the mode of life led by them, as was the case among the Romans and the Chinese respectively, then art transmitting feelings of joy at sacrificing one's personal well-being for the common weal, or at exalting one's ancestors and maintaining their traditions, would be considered good art, but art expressing feelings contrary to this would be regarded as bad. If the meaning of life is seen in freeing oneself from the yoke of animalism, as is the case among the Buddhists, then art successfully transmitting feelings that elevate the soul and humble the flesh will be good art, and all that transmits feelings strengthening the bodily passions will be bad art.

In every age and in every human society there exists a religious sense, common to that whole society, of what is good and what is bad, and it is this religious conception that decides the value of the feelings transmitted by art. And therefore, among all nations art which transmitted feelings considered to be good by this general religious sense was recognized as being good and was encouraged, but art which transmitted feelings considered to be bad by this general religious conception was recognized as being bad, and was rejected. [. . .]

Art, in our society, has been so perverted that not only has bad art come to be considered good, but even the very perception of what art really is has been lost. In order to be able to speak about the art of our society, it is, therefore, first of all necessary to distinguish art from counterfeit art.

There is one indubitable indication distinguishing real art from its counterfeit, namely, the infectiousness of art. If a man, without exercising effort and without altering his standpoint on reading, hearing, or seeing another man's work, experiences a mental condition which unites him with that man and with other people who also partake of that work of art, then the object evoking that condition is a work of art. And however poetical, realistic, effectful, or interesting a work may be, it is not a work of art if it does not evoke that feeling (quite distinct from all other feelings) of joy and of spiritual union with another (the author) and with others (those who are also infected by it).

It is true that this indication is an *internal* one, and that there are people who have forgotten what the action of real art is, who expect something else from art (in our society the great majority are in this state), and that therefore such people may mistake for this aesthetic feeling the feeling of diversion and a certain excitement which they receive from counterfeits of art. But though it is impossible to undeceive these people, just as it is impossible to convince a man suffering from "Daltonism" that green is not red, yet, for all that, this indication remains perfectly definite to those whose feeling for art is neither perverted nor atrophied, and it clearly distinguishes the feeling produced by art from all other feelings.

The chief peculiarity of this feeling is that the receiver of a true artistic impression is so united to the artist that he feels as if the work were his own and not someone else's – as if what it expresses were just what he had long been wishing to express. A real work of art destroys, in the consciousness of the receiver, the separation between himself and the artist – not that alone, but also between himself and all whose minds receive this work of art. In this freeing of our personality from its separation and isolation, in this uniting of it with others, lies the chief characteristic and the great attractive force of art.

If a man is infected by the author's condition of soul, if he feels this emotion and this union with others, then the object which has effected this is art; but if there be no such infection, if there be not this union with the author and with others who are moved by the same work – then it is not art. And not only is infection a sure sign of art, but the degree of infectiousness is also the sole measure of excellence in art.

The stronger the infection, the better is the art as art, speaking now apart from its subject matter, i.e., not considering the quality of the feelings it transmits.

And the degree of the infectiousness of art depends on three conditions:

1. On the greater or lesser individuality of the feeling transmitted;
2. on the greater or lesser clearness with which the feeling is transmitted;
3. on the sincerity of the artist, i.e., on the greater or lesser force with which the artist himself feels the emotion he transmits.

The more individual the feeling transmitted the more strongly does it act on the receiver; the more individual the state of soul into which he is transferred, the more pleasure does the receiver obtain, and therefore the more readily and strongly does he join in it.

The clearness of expression assists infection because the receiver, who mingles in consciousness with the author, is the better satisfied the more clearly the feeling is transmitted, which, as it seems to him, he has long known and felt, and for which he has only now found expression.

But most of all is the degree of infectiousness of art increased by the degree of sincerity in the artist. As soon as the spectator, hearer, or reader feels that the artist is infected by his own production, and writes, sings, or plays for himself, and not merely to act on others, this mental condition of the artist infects the receiver; and contrariwise, as soon as the spectator, reader, or hearer feels that the author is not writing, singing, or playing for his own satisfaction – does not himself feel what he wishes to express – but is doing it for him, the receiver, a resistance immediately springs up, and the most individual and the newest feelings and the cleverest technique not only fail to produce any infection but actually repel.

I have mentioned three conditions of contagiousness in art, but they may be all summed up into one, the last, sincerity, i.e., that the artist should be impelled by an inner need to express his feeling. That condition includes the first; for if the artist is sincere he will express the feeling as he experienced it. And as each man is different from everyone else, his feeling will be individual for everyone else; and the more individual it is – the more the artist has drawn it from the depths of his nature – the more sympathetic and sincere will it be. And this same sincerity will impel the artist to find a clear expression of the feeling which he wishes to transmit.

Therefore this third condition – sincerity – is the most important of the three. It is always complied with in peasant art, and this explains why such art always acts so powerfully; but it is a condition almost entirely absent from our upper-class art, which is continually produced by artists actuated by personal aims of covetousness or vanity.

Such are the three conditions which divide art from its counterfeits, and which also decide the quality of every work of art apart from its subject matter.

The absence of any one of these conditions excludes a work from the category of art and relegates it to that of art's counterfeits. If the work does not transmit the artist's peculiarity of feeling and is therefore not individual, if it is unintelligibly expressed, or if it has not proceeded from the author's inner need for expression – it is not a work of art. If all these conditions are present, even in the smallest degree, then the work, even if a weak one, is yet a work of art.

The presence in various degrees of these three conditions – individuality, clearness, and sincerity – decides the merit of a work of art as art, apart from subject matter. All works of art take rank of merit according to the degree in which they fulfill the first, the second, and the third of these conditions. In one the individuality of the feeling transmitted may predominate; in another, clearness of expression; in a third, sincerity; while a fourth may have sincerity and individuality but be deficient in clearness; a fifth, individuality and clearness but less sincerity; and so forth, in all possible degrees and combinations.

Thus is art divided from that which is not art, and thus is the quality of art as art decided, independently of its subject matter, i.e., apart from whether the feelings it transmits are good or bad.

But how are we to define good and bad art with reference to its subject matter? [. . .]

Art, like speech, is a means of communication, and therefore of progress, i.e., of the movement of humanity forward toward perfection. Speech renders accessible to men of the latest generations all the knowledge discovered by the experience and reflection, both of preceding generations and of the best and foremost men of their own times; art renders accessible to men of the latest generations all the feelings experienced by their predecessors, and those also which are being felt by their best and foremost contemporaries. And as the evolution of knowledge proceeds by truer and more necessary knowledge, dislodging and replacing what is mistaken and unnecessary, so the evolution of feeling proceeds through art – feelings less kind and less needful for the well-being of mankind are replaced by others kinder and more needful for that end. That is the purpose of art. And, speaking now of its subject matter, the more art fulfills that purpose the better the art, and the less it fulfills it, the worse the art.

And the appraisement of feelings (i.e., the acknowledgment of these or those feelings as being more or less good, more or less necessary for the well-being of mankind) is made by the religious perception of the age.

In every period of history, and in every human society, there exists an understanding of the meaning of life which represents the highest level to which men of that society have attained, an understanding defining the highest good at which that society aims. And this understanding is the religious perception of the given time and society. And this religious perception is always clearly expressed by some advanced men, and more or less vividly perceived by all the members of the society. Such a religious perception and its corresponding expression exists always in every society. If it appears to us that in our society there is no religious perception, this is not because there really is none, but only because we do not want to see it. And we often wish not to see it because it exposes the fact that our life is inconsistent with that religious perception.

Religious perception in a society is like the direction of a flowing river. If the river flows at all, it must have a direction. If a society lives, there must be a religious perception indicating the direction in which, more or less consciously, all its members tend.

And so there always has been, and there is, a religious perception in every society. And it is by the standard of this religious perception that the feelings transmitted by art have always been estimated. Only on the basis of this religious perception of their age have men always chosen from the endlessly varied spheres of art that art which transmitted feelings making religious perception operative in actual life. And such art has always been highly valued and encouraged, while art transmitting feelings already outlived, flowing from the antiquated religious perceptions of a former age, has always been condemned and despised. All the rest of art, transmitting those most diverse feelings by means of which people commune together, was not condemned, and was tolerated, if only it did not transmit feelings contrary to religious perception. Thus, for instance, among the Greeks art transmitting the feeling of beauty, strength, and courage (Hesiod, Homer, Phidias) was chosen, approved, and encouraged, while art transmitting feelings of rude sensuality, despondency, and effeminacy was condemned and despised. Among the Jews, art transmitting feelings of devotion and submission to the God of the Hebrews and to His will (the epic of Genesis, the prophets, the Psalms) was chosen and encouraged, while art transmitting feelings of idolatry (the golden calf) was condemned and despised. All the rest of art – stories, songs, dances, ornamentation of houses, of utensils, and of clothes – which was not contrary to religious perception was neither distinguished nor discussed. Thus, in regard to its subject matter, has art been appraised always and everywhere, and thus it should be appraised; for this attitude toward art proceeds from the fundamental characteristics of human nature, and those characteristics do not change.

I know that according to an opinion current in our times religion is a superstition which humanity has outgrown, and that it is therefore assumed that no such thing exists as a religious perception, common to us all, by which art, in our time, can be evaluated. I know that this is the opinion current in the pseudo-cultured circles of today. People who do not acknowledge Christianity in its true meaning because it undermines all their social privileges, and who, therefore, invent all kinds of philosophic and aesthetic theories to hide from themselves the meaninglessness and wrongness of their lives, cannot think otherwise. These people intentionally, or sometimes unintentionally, confusing the conception of a religious cult with the conception of religious perception think that by denying the cult they get rid of religious perception. But even the very attacks on religion and the attempts to establish a life-conception contrary to the religious perception of our times most clearly demonstrate the existence of a religious perception condemning the lives that are not in harmony with it.

If humanity progresses, i.e., moves forward, there must inevitably be a guide to the direction of that movement. And religions have always furnished that guide. All history shows that the progress of humanity is accomplished not otherwise than under the guidance of religion. But if the race cannot progress without the guidance of religion – and progress is always going on, and consequently also in our own times – then there must be a religion of our times. So that, whether it pleases or displeases the so-called cultured people of today, they must admit the existence of religion – not of a religious cult, Catholic, Protestant, or another, but of a religious perception – which, even in our times, is the guide always present where there is any progress. And if a religious perception exists among us, then our art should be appraised on the basis of that religious perception; and, as has always and everywhere been the case, art transmitting feelings flowing from the religious perception of our time should be chosen from all the indifferent art, should be acknowledged, highly esteemed, and encouraged, while art running counter to that perception should be condemned and despised, and all the remaining indifferent art should neither be distinguished nor encouraged.

The religious perception of our time, in its widest and most practical application, is the consciousness that our well-being, both material and spiritual, individual and collective, temporal and eternal, lies in the growth of brotherhood among all men – in their loving harmony with one another. This perception is not only expressed by

Christ and all the best men of past ages, it is not only repeated in the most varied forms and from most diverse sides by the best men of our own times, but it already serves as a clue to all the complex labor of humanity, consisting as this labor does, on the one hand, in the destruction of physical and moral obstacles to the union of men, and, on the other hand, in establishing the principles common to all men which can and should unite them into one universal brotherhood. And it is on the basis of this perception that we should appraise all the phenomena of our life, and, among the rest, our art also; choosing from all its realms whatever transmits feelings flowing from this religious perception, highly prizing and encouraging such art, rejecting whatever is contrary to this perception, and not attributing to the rest of art an importance not properly pertaining to it.

The chief mistake made by people of the upper classes of the time of the so-called Renaissance – a mistake which we still perpetuate – was not that they ceased to value and to attach importance to religious art (people of that period could not attach importance to it, because, like our own upper classes, they could not believe in what the majority considered to be religion), but their mistake was that they set up in place of religious art, which was lacking, an insignificant art which aimed only at giving pleasure, i.e., they began to choose, to value, and to encourage in place of religious art something which in any case did not deserve such esteem and encouragement.

One of the Fathers of the Church said that the great evil is not that men do not know God, but that they have set up, instead of God, that which is not God. So also with art. The great misfortune of the people of the upper classes of our time is not so much that they are without a religious art as such; instead of a supreme religious art, chosen from all the rest as being specially important and valuable, they have chosen a most insignificant and, usually, harmful art which aims at pleasing certain people and which, therefore, if only by its exclusive nature, stands in contradiction to that Christian principle of universal union which forms the religious perception of our time. Instead of religious art, an empty and often vicious art is set up, and this hides from men's notice the need of that true religious art which should be present in order to improve life.

It is true that art which satisfies the demands of the religious perception of our time is quite unlike former art, but, notwithstanding this dissimilarity, to a man who does not intentionally hide the truth from himself, it is very clear and definite what does form the religious art of our age. In former times, when the highest religious perception united only some people (who, even if they formed a large society, were yet but one society surrounded by others – Jews, or Athenian, or Roman citizens), the feelings transmitted by the art of that time flowed from a desire for the might, greatness, glory, and prosperity of that society, and the heroes of art might be people who contributed to that prosperity by strength, by craft, by fraud, or by cruelty (Ulysses, Jacob, David, Samson, Hercules, and all the heroes). But the religious perception of our times does not select any one society of men; on the contrary, it demands the union of all – absolutely of all people without exception – and above every other virtue it sets brotherly love to all men. And therefore, the feelings transmitted by the art of our time not only cannot coincide with the feelings transmitted by former art, but must run counter to them.

Translator's Note

1 "The foundling of Nuremburg," found in the market place of that town on May 26, 1828, apparently some sixteen years old. He spoke little and was almost totally ignorant even of common objects. He subsequently explained that he had been brought up in confinement underground and visited by only one man, whom he seldom saw.

23

"Psychical Distance" as a Factor in Art and an Aesthetic Principle

Edward Bullough

Edward Bullough (1880–1934), a Professor of Italian Literature at Cambridge University, stressed the importance of disinterestedness in the appreciation of a work of art.

I

1. The conception of 'Distance' suggests, in connexion with Art, certain trains of thought by no means devoid of interest or of speculative importance. Perhaps the most obvious suggestion is that of *actual spatial* distance, i.e. the distance of a work of Art from the spectator, or that of *represented spatial* distance, i.e. the distance represented within the work. Less obvious, more metaphorical, is the meaning of *temporal* distance. The first was noticed already by Aristotle in his *Poetics*; the second has played a great part in the history of painting in the form of perspective; the distinction between these two kinds of distance assumes special importance theoretically in the differentiation between sculpture in the round, and relief-sculpture. Temporal distance, remoteness from us in point of time, though often a cause of misconceptions, has been declared to be a factor of considerable weight in our appreciation.

Edward Bullough, "'Psychical Distance' as a Factor in Art and an Aesthetic Principle," *British Journal of Psychology*, 5 (1912).

It is not, however, in any of these meanings that 'Distance' is put forward here, though it will be clear in the course of this essay that the above mentioned kinds of distance are rather special forms of the conception of Distance as advocated here, and derive whatever *aesthetic* qualities they may possess from Distance in its *general* connotation. This general connotation is 'Psychical Distance.'

A short illustration will explain what is meant by 'Psychical Distance.' Imagine a fog at sea: for most people it is an experience of acute unpleasantness. Apart from the physical annoyance and remoter forms of discomfort such as delays, it is apt to produce feelings of peculiar anxiety, fears of invisible dangers, strains of watching and listening for distant and unlocalised signals. The listless movements of the ship and her warning calls soon tell upon the nerves of the passengers; and that special, expectant, tacit anxiety and nervousness, always associated with this experience, make a fog the dreaded terror of the sea (all the more terrifying because of its very silence and gentleness) for the expert seafarer no less than for the ignorant landsman.

Nevertheless, a fog at sea can be a source of intense relish and enjoyment. Abstract from the experience of the sea fog, for the moment, its danger and practical unpleasantness, just as every one in the enjoyment of a mountain-climb disregards its physical labour and its danger (though, it is not denied, that these may incidentally enter into the enjoyment and enhance it); direct the attention to the features 'objectively' constituting the phenomenon – the veil surrounding you with an opaqueness as of transparent milk, blurring the outline of things and distorting their shapes into weird grotesqueness; observe the carrying-power of the air, producing the impression as if you could touch some far-off siren by merely putting out your hand and letting it lose itself behind that white wall; note the curious creamy smoothness of the water, hypocritically denying as it were any suggestion of danger; and, above all, the strange solitude and remoteness from the world, as it can be found only on the highest mountain tops: and the experience may acquire, in its uncanny mingling of repose and terror, a flavour of such concentrated poignancy and delight as to contrast sharply with the blind and distempered anxiety of its other aspects. This contrast, often emerging with startling suddenness, is like a momentary switching on of some new current, or the passing ray of a brighter light, illuminating the outlook upon perhaps the most ordinary and familiar objects – an impression which we experience sometimes in instants of direst extremity, when our practical interest snaps like a wire from sheer over-tension, and we watch the consummation of some impending catastrophe with the marvelling unconcern of a mere spectator.

It is a difference of outlook, due – if such a metaphor is permissible – to the insertion of Distance. This Distance appears to lie between our own self and its affections, using the latter term in its broadest sense as anything which affects our being, bodily or spiritually, e.g. as sensation, perception, emotional state or idea. Usually, though not always, it amounts to the same thing to say that the Distance lies between our own self and such objects as are the sources or vehicles of such affections.

Thus, in the fog, the transformation by Distance is produced in the first instance by putting the phenomenon, so to speak, out of gear with our practical, actual self; by allowing it to stand outside the context of our personal needs and ends – in short, by looking at it 'objectively,' as it has often been called, by permitting only such reactions on our part as emphasise the 'objective' features of the experience, and by interpreting even our 'subjective' affections not as modes of *our* being but rather as characteristics of the phenomenon.

The working of Distance is, accordingly, not simple, but highly complex. It has a *negative,* inhibitory aspect – the cutting-out of the practical sides of things and of our practical attitude to them – and a *positive* side – the elaboration of the experience on the new basis created by the inhibitory action of Distance.

2. Consequently, this distanced view of things is not, and cannot be, our normal outlook. As a rule, experiences constantly turn the same side towards us, namely, that which has the strongest practical force of appeal. We are not ordinarily aware of those aspects of things which do not touch us immediately and practically, nor are we generally conscious of impressions apart from our own self which is impressed. The sudden view of things from their reverse, usually unnoticed, side, comes upon us as a revelation, and such revelations are precisely those of Art. In this most general sense, Distance is a factor in all Art.

3. It is, for this very reason, also an aesthetic principle. The aesthetic contemplation and the aesthetic outlook have often been described as 'objective.' We speak of 'objective' artists as Shakespeare or Velasquez, of 'objective' works or art forms as Homer's *Iliad* or the drama. It is a term constantly occurring in discussions and criticisms, though its sense, if pressed at all, becomes very questionable. For certain forms of Art, such as lyrical poetry, are said to be 'subjective'; Shelley, for example, would usually be considered a 'subjective' writer. On the other hand, no work of Art can be genuinely 'objective' in the sense in which this term might be applied to a work on history or to a scientific treatise; nor can it be 'subjective' in the ordinary acceptance of that term, as a personal feeling, a direct statement of a wish or belief, or a cry of passion is subjective. 'Objectivity' and 'subjectivity' are a pair of opposites which in their mutual exclusiveness when applied to Art soon lead to confusion.

Nor are they the only pair of opposites. Art has with equal vigour been declared alternately 'idealistic' and 'realistic,' 'sensual' and 'spiritual,' 'individualistic' and 'typical.' Between the defence of either terms of such antitheses most aesthetic theories have vacillated. It is one of the contentions of this essay that such opposites find their synthesis in the more fundamental conception of Distance.

Distance further provides the much needed criterion of the beautiful as distinct from the merely agreeable.

Again, it marks one of the most important steps in the process of artistic creation and serves as a distinguishing feature of what is commonly so loosely described as the 'artistic temperament.'

Finally, it may claim to be considered as one of the essential characteristics of the 'aesthetic consciousness,' – if I may describe by this term that special mental attitude towards, and outlook upon, experience, which finds its most pregnant expression in the various forms of Art.

II

Distance, as I said before, is obtained by separating the object and its appeal from one's own self, by putting it out of gear with practical needs and ends. Thereby the 'contemplation' of the object becomes alone possible. But it does not mean that the relation between the self and the object is broken to the extent of becoming 'impersonal.' Of the alternatives 'personal' and 'impersonal' the latter surely comes nearer to the truth; but here, as elsewhere, we meet the difficulty of having to express certain facts in terms coined for entirely different uses. To do so usually results in paradoxes, which are nowhere more inevitable than in discussions upon Art. 'Personal' and 'impersonal,' 'subjective' and 'objective' are such terms, devised for purposes other than aesthetic speculation, and becoming loose and ambiguous as soon as applied outside the sphere of their special meanings. In giving preference therefore to the term 'impersonal' to describe the relation between the spectator and a work of Art, it is to be noticed that it is not impersonal in the sense in which we speak of the 'impersonal' character of Science, for instance. In order to obtain 'objectively valid' results, the scientist excludes the 'personal factor,' i.e. his personal wishes as to the validity of his results, his predilection for any particular system to be proved or disproved by his research. It goes without saying that all experiments and investigations are undertaken out of a personal interest in the science, for the ultimate support of a definite assumption, and involve personal hopes of success; but this does not affect the 'dispassionate' attitude of the investigator, under pain of being accused of 'manufacturing his evidence.'

1. Distance does not imply an impersonal, purely intellectually interested relation of such a kind. On the contrary, it describes a *personal* relation, often highly emotionally coloured, but *of a peculiar character.* Its peculiarity lies in that the personal character of the relation has been, so to speak, filtered. It has been cleared of the practical, concrete nature of its appeal, without, however, thereby losing its original constitution. One of the best-known examples is to be found in our attitude towards the events and characters of the drama: they appeal to us like persons and incidents of normal experience, except that that side of their appeal, which would usually affect us in a directly personal manner, is held in abeyance. This difference, so well known as to be almost trivial, is generally explained by reference to the knowledge that the characters and situations are 'unreal,' imaginary. In this sense Witasek,[1] operating with Meinong's theory of *Annahmen,* has described the emotions involved in witnessing a drama as *Scheingefühle,* a term which has so frequently been misunderstood in discussions of his theories. But, as a matter of fact, the 'assumption' upon which the imaginative emotional reaction is based is not necessarily the condition, but often the consequence, of Distance; that is to say, the converse of the reason usually stated would then be true: viz, that Distance, by changing our relation to the characters, renders them seemingly fictitious, not that the fictitiousness of the characters alters our feelings toward them. It is, of course, to be granted that the actual and admitted unreality of the dramatic action reinforces the effect of Distance. But surely the proverbial unsophisticated yokel whose chivalrous interference in the play on behalf of the hapless heroine can only be prevented by impressing upon him that 'they are only pretending,' is not the ideal type of theatrical audience. The proof of the seeming paradox that it is Distance which primarily gives to dramatic action the appearance of unreality and not *vice versâ,* is the observation that the same filtration of our sentiments and the same seeming 'unreality' of *actual* men and things

occur, when at times, by a sudden change of inward perspective, we are overcome by the feeling that "all the world's a stage."

2. This personal, but 'distanced' relation (as I will venture to call this nameless character of our view) directs attention to a strange fact which appears to be one of the fundamental paradoxes of Art: it is what I propose to call 'the antinomy of Distance.'

It will be readily admitted that a work of Art has the more chance of appealing to us the better it finds us prepared for its particular kind of appeal. Indeed, without some degree of predisposition on our part, it must necessarily remain incomprehensible, and to that extent unappreciated. The success and intensity of its appeal would seem, therefore, to stand in direct proportion to the completeness with which it corresponds with our intellectual and emotional peculiarities and the idiosyncracies of our experience. The absence of such a concordance between the characters of a work and of the spectator is, of course, the most general explanation for differences of 'tastes.'

At the same time, such a principle of concordance requires a qualification, which leads at once to the antinomy of Distance.

Suppose a man, who believes that he has cause to be jealous about his wife, witnesses a performance of 'Othello.' He will the more perfectly appreciate the situation, conduct and character of Othello, the more exactly the feelings and experiences of Othello coincide with his own – at least he *ought* to on the above principle of concordance. In point of fact, he will probably do anything but appreciate the play. In reality, the concordance will merely render him acutely conscious of his own jealousy; by a sudden reversal of perspective he will no longer see Othello apparently betrayed by Desdemona, but himself in an analogous situation with his own wife. The reversal of perspective is the consequence of the loss of Distance.

If this be taken as a typical case, it follows that the qualification required is that the coincidence should be as complete as is compatible with maintaining Distance. The jealous spectator of 'Othello' will indeed appreciate and enter into the play the more keenly, the greater the resemblance with his own experience – *provided* that he succeeds in keeping the Distance between the action of the play and his personal feelings: a very difficult performance in the circumstances. It is on account of the same difficulty that the expert and the professional critic make a bad audience, since their expertness and critical professionalism are *practical* activities, involving their concrete personality and constantly endangering their Distance. [It is, by the way, one of the reasons why Criticism is an art, for it requires the constant interchange from the practical to the distanced attitude and *vice versâ*, which is characteristic of artists.]

The same qualification applies to the artist. He will prove artistically most effective in the formulation of an intensely *personal* experience, but he can formulate it artistically only on condition of a detachment from the experience *quâ personal.* Hence the statement of so many artists that artistic formulation was to them a kind of catharsis, a means of ridding themselves of feelings and ideas the acuteness of which they felt almost as a kind of obsession. Hence, on the other hand, the failure of the average man to convey to others at all adequately the impression of an overwhelming joy or sorrow. His personal implication in the event renders it impossible for him to formulate and present it in such a way as to make others, like himself, feel all the meaning and fulness which it possesses for him.

What is therefore, both in appreciation and production, most desirable is the *utmost decrease of Distance without its disappearance.*

3. Closely related, in fact a presupposition to the 'antinomy,' is the *variability of Distance.* Herein especially lies the advantage of Distance compared with such terms as 'objectivity' and 'detachment.' Neither of them implies a *personal* relation – indeed both actually preclude it; and the mere inflexibility and exclusiveness of their opposites render their application generally meaningless.

Distance, on the contrary, admits naturally of degrees, and differs not only according to the nature of the *object,* which may impose a greater or smaller degree of Distance, but varies also according to the *individual's capacity* for maintaining a greater or lesser degree. And here one may remark that not only do *persons differ from each other* in their habitual measure of Distance, but that the *same individual differs* in his ability to maintain it in the face of different objects and of different arts.

There exist, therefore, two different sets of conditions affecting the degree of Distance in any given case: those offered by the object and those realised by the subject. In their interplay they afford one of the most extensive explanations for varieties of aesthetic experience, since loss of Distance, whether due to the one or the other, means loss of aesthetic appreciation.

In short, Distance may be said to *be variable both according to the distancing-power of the individual, and according to the character of the object.*

There are two ways of losing Distance: either to 'under-distance' or to over-distance.' 'Under-distancing' is the commonest failing of the *subject,* an excess of Distance is a frequent failing of *Art,* especially in the past. Historically it looks almost as if Art had attempted to meet the deficiency of Distance on the part of the subject and had overshot the mark in this endeavour. It will be seen later that this is actually true, for it appears that over-distanced Art is specially designed for a class of appreciation which has difficulty to rise spontaneously to any degree of Distance. The consequence of a loss of Distance through one or other cause is familiar: the verdict in the case of under-distancing is that the work is 'crudely naturalistic,' 'harrowing,' 'repulsive in its realism.' An excess of Distance produces the impression of improbability, artificiality, emptiness or absurdity.

The individual tends, as I just stated, to under-distance rather than to lose Distance by over-distancing. *Theoretically* there is no limit to the decrease of Distance. In theory, therefore, not only the usual subjects of Art, but even the most personal affections, whether ideas, percepts or emotions, can be sufficiently distanced to be aesthetically appreciable. Especially artists are gifted in this direction to a remarkable extent. The average individual, on the contrary, very rapidly reaches his limit of decreasing Distance, his 'Distance-limit,' i.e. that point at which Distance is lost and appreciation either disappears or changes its character.

In the *practice,* therefore, of the average person, a limit does exist which marks the minimum at which his appreciation can maintain itself in the aesthetic field, and this average minimum lies considerably higher than the Distance-limit of the artist. It is practically impossible to fix this average limit, in the absence of data, and on account of the wide fluctuations from person to person to which this limit is subject. But it is safe to infer that, in art practice, explicit references to organic affections, to the material existence of the body, especially to sexual matters, lie normally below the Distance-limit, and can be touched upon by Art only with special precautions. Allusions to social institutions of any degree of personal importance – in particular, allusions implying any doubt as to their validity – the questioning of some generally recognised ethical sanctions, references to topical subjects occupying public attention at the moment, and such like, are all dangerously near the average limit and may at any time fall below it, arousing, instead of aesthetic appreciation, concrete hostility or mere amusement.

This difference in the Distance-limit between artists and the public has been the source of much misunderstanding and injustice. Many an artist has seen his work condemned, and himself ostracized for the sake of so-called 'immoralities' which to him were *bonâ fide* aesthetic objects. His power of distancing, nay, the necessity of distancing feelings, sensations, situations which for the average person are too intimately bound up with his concrete existence to be regarded in that light, have often quite unjustly earned for him accusations of cynicism, sensualism, morbidness or frivolity. The same misconception has arisen over many 'problem plays' and 'problem novels' in which the public have persisted in seeing nothing but a supposed 'problem' of the moment, whereas the author may have been – and often has demonstrably been – able to distance the subject-matter sufficiently to rise above its practical problematic import and to regard it simply as a dramatically and humanly interesting situation.

The variability of Distance in respect to Art, disregarding for the moment the subjective complication, appears both as a general feature in Art, and in the differences between the special arts.

It has been an old problem why the 'arts of the eye and of the ear' should have reached the practically exclusive predominance over arts of other senses. Attempts to raise 'culinary art' to the level of a Fine Art have failed in spite of all propaganda, as completely as the creation of scent or liqueur 'symphonies.' There is little doubt that, apart from other excellent reasons[2] of a partly psycho-physical, partly technical nature, the actual, *spatial distance* separating objects of sight and hearing from the subject has contributed strongly to the development of this monopoly. In a similar manner *temporal remoteness* produces Distance, and objects removed from us in point of time are *ipso facto* distanced to an extent which was impossible for their contemporaries. Many pictures, plays and poems had, as a matter of fact, rather an expositary or illustrating significance – as for instance much ecclesiastical Art – or the force of a direct practical appeal – as the invectives of many satires or comedies – which seem to us nowadays irreconcilable with their aesthetic claims. Such works have consequently profited greatly by lapse of time and have reached the level of Art only with the help of temporal distance, while others, on the contrary, often for the same reason have suffered a loss of Distance, through *over*-distancing.

Special mention must be made of a group of artistic conceptions which present excessive Distance in their form of appeal rather than in their actual presentation – a point illustrating the necessity of distinguishing between distancing an object and distancing the appeal of which it is the source. I mean here what is often rather loosely termed 'idealistic Art,' that is, Art springing from abstract conceptions, expressing allegorical meanings, or illustrating general truths. Generalisations and abstractions suffer under this disadvantage that they have too much general applicability to invite a personal interest in them, and too little individual concreteness to prevent them applying to us in all their force. They appeal to everybody and therefore to none. An axiom of Euclid belongs to nobody, just because it compels everyone's assent; general conceptions like Patriotism, Friendship, Love, Hope, Life, Death, concern as much Dick, Tom and Harry as myself, and I therefore either feel unable to get into any kind of personal relation to them or, if I do so, they become at once, emphatically or concretely, *my* Patriotism, *my* Friendship, *my* Love, *my* Hope, *my* Life and Death. By mere force of generalisation, a general truth or a universal ideal is so far distanced from myself that I fail to realise it concretely at all, or, when I do so, I can realise it only as part of my *practical actual being*, i.e. it falls below the Distance-limit altogether. 'Idealistic Art' suffers consequently under the peculiar difficulty that its excess of Distance turns generally into an *under*-distanced appeal – all the more easily, as it is the usual failing of the subject to *under*-rather than to *over*-distance.

The different special arts show at the present time very marked variations in the degree of Distance which they usually impose or require for their appreciation. Unfortunately here again the absence of data makes itself felt and indicates the necessity of conducting observations, possibly experiments, so as to place these suggestions upon a securer basis. In one single art, viz, the *theatre*, a small amount of information is available, from an unexpected source, namely the proceedings of the censorship committee,[3] which on closer examination might be made to yield evidence of interest to the psychologist. In fact, the whole censorship problem, as far as it does not turn upon purely economic questions, may be said to hinge upon Distance; if every member of the public could be trusted to keep it, there would be no sense whatever in the existence of a censor of plays. There is, of course, no doubt that, speaking generally, theatrical performances *eo ipso* run a special risk of a loss of Distance owing to the material presentment[4] of its subject-matter. The physical presence of living human beings as vehicles of dramatic art is a difficulty which no art has to face in the same way. A similar, in many ways even greater, risk confronts *dancing*: though attracting perhaps a less widely spread human interest, its animal spirits are frequently quite unrelieved by any glimmer of spirituality and consequently form a proportionately stronger lure to under-distancing. In the higher forms of dancing technical execution of the most wearing kind makes up a great deal for its intrinsic tendency towards a loss of Distance, and as a popular performance, at least in southern Europe, it has retained much of its ancient artistic glamour, producing a peculiarly subtle balancing of Distance between the pure delight of bodily movement and high technical accomplishment. In passing, it is interesting to observe (as bearing upon the development of Distance), that this art, once as much a fine art as music and considered by the Greeks as a particularly valuable educational exercise, should – except in sporadic cases – have fallen so low from the pedestal it once occupied. Next to the theatre and dancing stands *sculpture*. Though not using a *living* bodily medium, yet the human form in its full spatial materiality constitutes a similar threat to Distance. Our northern habits of dress and ignorance of the human body have enormously increased the difficulty of distancing Sculpture, in part through the gross misconceptions to which it is exposed, in part owing to a complete lack of standards of bodily perfection, and an inability to realise the distinction between sculptural form and bodily shape, which is the only but fundamental point distinguishing a statue from a cast taken from life. In *painting* it is apparently the form of its presentment and the usual reduction in scale which would explain why this art can venture to approach more closely than sculpture to the normal Distance-limit. As this matter will be discussed later in a special connexion this simple reference may suffice here. *Music* and *architecture* have a curious position. These two most abstract of all arts show a remarkable fluctuation in their Distances. Certain kinds of music, especially 'pure' music, or 'classical' or 'heavy' music, appear for many people over-distanced; light, 'catchy' tunes, on the contrary, easily reach that degree of decreasing Distance below which they cease to be Art and become a pure amusement. In spite of its strange abstractness which to many philosophers has made it comparable to architecture and mathematics, music possesses a sensuous, frequently sensual, character: the undoubted physiological and muscular stimulus of its melodies and harmonies, no less than its rhythmic aspects, would seem to account for the occasional disappearance of Distance. To this might be added its strong tendency, especially in unmusical people, to stimulate trains of thought quite disconnected with itself, following channels of subjective inclinations, – day-dreams of a more or less directly personal character. *Architecture* requires almost uniformly a very great Distance; that is to say, the majority of persons derive no aesthetic appreciation from architecture as such, apart from the incidental impression of its decorative features and its associations. The causes are numerous, but prominent among them are the confusion of building with architecture and the predominance of utilitarian purposes, which overshadow the architectural claims upon the attention.

4. That all art requires a Distance-limit beyond which, and a Distance within which only, aesthetic appreciation becomes possible, is the *psychological formulation of a general characteristic of Art*, viz, its *anti-realistic nature*. Though seemingly paradoxical, this applies as much to 'naturalistic' as to 'idealistic' Art. The difference commonly expressed by these epithets is at bottom merely the difference in the degree of Distance; and this produces, so far as 'naturalism' and 'idealism' in Art are not meaningless labels, the usual result that what appears obnoxiously 'naturalistic' to one person, may be 'idealistic' to another. To say that Art is anti-realistic simply insists upon the fact that Art is not nature, never pretends to be nature and strongly resists any confusion with nature. It emphasizes the *art*-character of Art: 'artistic' is synonymous with 'anti-realistic'; it explains even sometimes a very marked degree of artificiality.

"Art is an imitation of nature," was the current art-conception in the 18th century. It is the fundamental axiom of the standard-work of that time upon aesthetic theory by the Abbé Du Bos, *Réflexions critiques sur la poésie et la peinture*, 1719; the idea received strong support from the literal acceptance of Aristotle's theory of *μιμησις* and produced echoes everywhere, in Lessing's *Laocoon* no less than in Burke's famous statement that "all Art is great as it deceives." Though it may be assumed that since the time of Kant and of the Romanticists this notion has died out, it still lives in unsophisticated minds. Even when formally denied, it persists, for instance, in the belief that "Art idealises nature," which means after all only that Art copies nature with certain improvements and revisions. Artists themselves are unfortunately often responsible for the spreading of this conception. Whistler indeed said that to produce Art by imitating nature would be like trying to produce music by sitting upon the piano, but the selective, idealising imitation of nature finds merely another support in such a saying. Naturalism, pleinairism, impressionism, – even the guileless enthusiasm of the artist for the works of nature, her wealth of suggestion, her delicacy of workmanship, for the steadfastness of her guidance, only produce upon the public the impression that Art is, after all, an imitation of nature. Then how can it be anti-realistic? The antithesis, Art *versus* nature, seems to break down. Yet if it does, what is the sense of Art?

Here the conception of Distance comes to the rescue. The solution of the dilemma lies in the 'antinomy of Distance' with its demand: utmost decrease of Distance without its disappearance. The simple observation that Art is the more effective, the more it falls into line with our predispositions which are inevitably moulded on general experience and nature, has always been the original motive for 'naturalism.' 'Naturalism,' 'impressionism' is no new thing; it is only a new name for an innate leaning of Art, from the time of the Chaldeans and Egyptians down to the present day. Even the Apollo of Tenea apparently struck his contemporaries as so startlingly 'naturalistic' that the subsequent legend attributed a superhuman genius to his creator. A constantly closer approach to nature, a perpetual refining of the limit of Distance, yet without overstepping the dividing line of art and nature, has always been the inborn bent of art. To deny this dividing line has occasionally been the failing of naturalism. But no theory of naturalism is complete which does not at the same time allow for the intrinsic idealism of Art: for both are merely degrees in that wide range lying beyond the Distance-limit. To imitate nature so as to trick the spectator into the deception that it is nature which he beholds, is to forsake Art, its anti-realism, its distanced spirituality, and to fall below the limit into sham, sensationalism or platitude.

But what, in the theory of antinomy of Distance requires explanation is the existence of an *idealistic, highly distanced* Art. There are numerous reasons to account for it; indeed in so complex a phenomenon as Art, *single* causes can be pronounced almost *a priori* to be false. Foremost among such causes which have contributed to the formation of an idealistic Art appears to stand the subordination of Art to some extraneous purpose of an impressive, exceptional character. Such a subordination has consisted – at various epochs of Art history – in the use to which Art was put to subserve commemorative, hieratic, generally religious, royal or patriotic functions. The object to be commemorated had to stand out from among other still existing objects or persons; the thing or the being to be worshipped had to be distinguished as markedly as possible from profaner objects of reverence and had to be invested with an air of sanctity by a removal from its ordinary context of occurrence. Nothing could have assisted more powerfully the introduction of a high Distance than this attempt to differentiate objects of common experience in order to fit them for their exalted position. Curious, unusual things of nature met this tendency half-way and easily assumed divine rank; but others had to be distanced by an exaggeration of their size, by extraordinary attributes, by strange combinations of human and animal forms, by special insistence upon particular characteristics, or by the careful removal of all noticeably individualistic and concrete features. Nothing could be more striking than the contrast, for example, in Egyptian Art between the monumental, the works, and of the remarkable interpenetration of Art with the most ordinary routine of life, in order to realise the scarcely perceptible dividing line between the sphere of Art and the realm of practical existence. In a sense, the assertion that idealistic Art marks periods of a generally low and narrowly restricted culture is the converse to the oft-repeated statement that the flowering periods of Art coincide with epochs of decadence: for this so-called decadence represents indeed in certain respects a process of disintegration, politically, racially, often nationally, but a disruption necessary to the formation of larger social units and to the breakdown of outgrown national restrictions. For this very reason it has usually also been the sign of the growth of personal independence and of an expansion of individual culture.

To proceed to some more special points illustrating the distanced and therefore anti-realistic character of art, – both in subject-matter and in the form of presentation Art has always safeguarded its distanced view. Fanciful, even phantastic, subjects have from time immemorial been the accredited material of Art, No doubt things, as well as our view of them, have changed in the course of time: *Polyphemus* and the *Lotus-Eaters* for the Greeks, the *Venusberg* or the *Magnetic Mountain* for the Middle Ages were less incredible, more realistic than to us. But *Peter Pan* or *L'Oiseau Bleu* still appeal at the present day in spite of the prevailing note of realism of our time. 'Probability' and 'improbability' in Art are not to be measured by their correspondence (or lack of it) with actual experience. To do so had involved the theories of the 15th to the 18th centuries in endless contradictions. It is rather a matter of *consistency* of Distance. The note of realism, set by a work as a whole, determines *intrinsically* the greater or smaller degree of fancy which it permits; and consequently we feel the loss of Peter Pan's shadow to be infinitely more probable than some trifling improbability which shocks our sense of proportion in a naturalistic work. No doubt also, fairy-tales, fairy-plays, stories of strange adventures were primarily invented to satisfy the craving of curiosity, the desire for the marvellous, the shudder of the unwonted and the longing for imaginary experiences. But by their mere eccentricity in regard to the normal facts of experience they cannot have failed to arouse a strong feeling of Distance.

Again, certain conventional subjects taken from mythical and legendary traditions, at first closely connected with the concrete, practical, life of a devout public, have gradually, by the mere force of convention as much as by their inherent anti-realism, acquired Distance for us to-day. Our view of Greek mythological sculpture, of early Christian saints and martyrs must be considerably distanced, compared with that of the Greek and medieval worshipper. It is in part the result of lapse of time, but in part also a real change of attitude. Already the outlook of the Imperial Roman had altered, and Pausanias shows a curious dualism of standpoint, declaring the Athene Lemnia to be the supreme achievement of Phidias's genius, and gazing awe-struck upon the roughly hewn tree-trunk representing some primitive Apollo. Our understanding of Greek tragedy suffers admittedly under our inability to revert to the point of view for which it was originally written. Even the tragedies of Racine demand an imaginative effort to put ourselves back into the courtly atmosphere of red-heeled, powdered ceremony. Provided the Distance is not too wide, the result of its intervention has everywhere been to enhance the *art*-character of such works and to lower their original ethical and social force of appeal. Thus in the central dome of the Church (Sta. Maria dei Miracoli) at Saronno are depicted the heavenly hosts in ascending tiers, crowned by the benevolent figure of the Divine Father, bending from the window of heaven to bestow His blessing upon the assembled community. The mere realism of foreshortening and of the boldest vertical perspective may well have made the naïve Christian of the 16th century conscious of the Divine Presence – but for us it has become a work of Art.

The unusual, exceptional, has found its especial home in tragedy. It has always – except in highly distanced tragedy – been a popular objection to it that 'there is enough sadness in life without going to the theatre for it.' Already Aristotle appears to have met with this view among his contemporaries clamouring for 'happy endings.' Yet tragedy is not sad; if it were, there would indeed be little sense in its existence. For the tragic is just in so far different from the merely sad, as it is distanced; and it is largely the exceptional which produces the Distance of tragedy: exceptional situations, exceptional characters, exceptional destinies and conduct. Not of course, characters merely cranky, eccentric, pathological. The exceptional element in tragic figures – that which makes them so utterly different from characters we meet with in ordinary experience – is a consistency of direction, a fervour of ideality, a persistence and driving-force which is far above the capacities of average men. The tragic of tragedy would, transposed into ordinary life, in nine cases out of ten, end in drama, in comedy, even in farce, for lack of steadfastness, for fear of conventions, for the dread of 'scenes,' for a hundred-and-one petty faithlessnesses towards a belief or an ideal: even if for none of these, it would end in a compromise simply because man forgets and time heals.[5] Again, the sympathy, which aches with the sadness of tragedy is another such confusion, the under-distancing of tragedy's appeal. Tragedy trembles always on the knife-edge of a *personal* reaction, and sympathy which finds relief in tears tends almost always towards a loss of Distance. Such a loss naturally renders tragedy unpleasant to a degree: it becomes sad, dismal, harrowing, depressing. But real tragedy (melodrama has a very strong tendency to speculate upon sympathy), truly appreciated, is not sad. "The pity of it – oh, the pity of it," that essence of all genuine tragedy is not the pity of mild, regretful sympathy. It is a chaos of tearless, bitter bewilderment, of upsurging revolt and rapturous awe before the ruthless and inscrutable fate; it is the homage to the great and exceptional in the man who in a last effort of spiritual tension can rise to confront blind, crowning Necessity even in his crushing defeat.

As I explained earlier, the form of presentation sometimes endangers the maintenance of Distance, but it more frequently acts as a considerable support. Thus the bodily vehicle of *drama* is the chief factor of risk to Distance. But, as if to counterbalance a confusion with nature, other features of stage-presentation exercise an opposite influence. Such are the general theatrical *milieu*, the shape and arrangement of the stage, the artificial lighting, the costumes, *mise-en-scène* and make-up, even the language, especially verse. Modern reforms of staging, aiming primarily at the removal of artistic incongruities between excessive decoration and the living figures of the actors and at the production of a more homogeneous stage-picture, inevitably work also towards a greater emphasis and homogeneity of Distance. The history of staging and dramaturgy is closely bound up with the evolution of Distance, and its fluctuations lie at the bottom not only of the greater part of all the talk and writing about 'dramatic probability' and the Aristotelian 'unities,' but also of 'theatrical illusion.' In *sculpture,* one distancing factor of presentment is its lack of colour. The aesthetic, or rather inaesthetic effect of realistic colouring, is in no way touched by the controversial question of its use historically; its attempted resuscitation, such as by Klinger, seems only to confirm its disadvantages. The distancing use even of pedestals, although originally no doubt serving other purposes, is evident to anyone who has experienced the oppressively crowded sensation of moving in a room among life-sized statues placed directly upon the floor. The circumstance that the space of statuary is the same space as ours (in distinction to relief sculpture or painting, for instance) renders a distancing by pedestals, i.e. a removal from our spatial context, imperative.[6] Probably the framing of *pictures* might be shown to serve a similar purpose – though paintings have intrinsically a much greater Distance – because neither their space (perspective and imaginary space) nor their lighting coincides with our (actual) space or light, and the usual reduction in scale of the represented objects prevents a feeling of undue proximity. Besides, painting always retains to some extent a *two*-dimensional character, and this character supplies *eo ipso* a Distance. Nevertheless, life-size pictures, especially if they possess strong relief, and their light happens to coincide with the actual lighting, can occasionally produce the impression of actual presence which is a far from pleasant, though fortunately only a passing, illusion. For decorative purposes, in pictorial renderings of vistas, garden-perspectives and architectural extensions, the removal of Distance has often been consciously striven after, whether with aesthetically satisfactory results is much disputed.

A general help towards Distance (and therewith an anti-realistic feature) is to be found in the 'unification of presentment'[7] of all art-objects. By unification of presentment are meant such qualities as symmetry, opposition, proportion, balance, rhythmical distribution of parts, light-arrangements, in fact all so-called 'formal' features, 'composition' in the widest sense. Unquestionably, Distance is not the only, nor even the principal function of composition; it serves to render our grasp of the presentation easier and to increase its intelligibility. It may even in itself constitute the principal aesthetic feature of the object, as in linear complexes or patterns, partly also in architectural designs. Yet, its distancing effect can hardly be underrated. For, every kind of visibly intentional arrangement or unification must, by the mere fact of its presence, enforce Distance, by distinguishing the object from the confused, disjointed and scattered forms of actual experience. This function can be gauged in a typical form in cases where composition produces an exceptionally marked impression of artificiality (not in the bad sense of that term, but in the sense in which all art is artificial); and it is a natural corollary to the differences of Distance in different arts and of different subjects, that the arts and subjects vary in the degree of artificiality which they can bear. It is this sense of artificial finish which is the source of so much of that elaborate charm of Byzantine work, of Mohammedan decoration, of the hieratic stiffness of so many primitive madonnas and saints. In general the emphasis of composition and technical finish increases with the Distance of the subject-matter: heroic conceptions lend themselves better to verse than to prose; monumental statues require a more general treatment, more elaboration of setting and artificiality of pose than impressionistic statuettes like those of Troubetzkoi; an ecclesiastic subject is painted with a degree of symmetrical arrangement which would be ridiculous in a Dutch interior, and a naturalistic drama carefully avoids the tableau impression characteristic of a mystery play. In a similar manner the variations of Distance in the arts go hand in hand with a visibly greater predominance of composition and 'formal' elements, reaching a climax in architecture and music. It is again a matter of 'consistency of Distance.' At the same time, while from the point of view of the artist this is undoubtedly the case, from the point of view of the public the emphasis of composition and technical finish appears frequently to relieve the impression of highly distanced subjects by *diminishing the Distance of the whole.* The spectator has a tendency to see in composition and finish merely evidence of the artist's 'cleverness,' of his mastery over his material. Manual dexterity is an enviable thing to possess in everyone's experience, and naturally appeals to the public *practically,* thereby putting it into a directly personal relation to things which intrinsically have very little personal appeal for it. It is true that this function of composition is hardly an aesthetic one: for the admiration of mere technical cleverness is not an artistic enjoyment, but by a fortunate chance it has saved from oblivion and entire loss, among much rubbish, also much genuine Art, which otherwise would have completely lost contact with our life.

5. This discussion, necessarily sketchy and incomplete, may have helped to illustrate the sense in which, I suggested, Distance appears as a fundamental principle to which such antitheses as idealism and realism are reducible. The difference between 'idealistic' and 'realistic' Art is not a clear-cut dividing-line between the art-practices described by these terms, but is a difference of degree in the Distance-limit which they presuppose on the part both of the artist and of the public. A similar reconciliation seems to me possible between the opposite 'sensual' and 'spiritual,' 'individual' and 'typical.' That the appeal of Art is sensuous, even sensual, must be taken as an indisputable fact. Puritanism will never be persuaded, and rightly so, that this is not the case. The sensuousness of Art is a natural implication of the 'antinomy of Distance,' and will appear again in another connexion. The point of importance here is that the whole sensual side of Art is purified, spiritualised, 'filtered' as I expressed it earlier, by Distance. The most sensual appeal becomes the translucent veil of an underlying spirituality, once the grossly personal and practical elements have been removed from it. And – a matter of special emphasis here – this *spiritual aspect of the appeal is the more penetrating, the more personal and direct its sensual appeal would have been* BUT FOR THE PRESENCE OF DISTANCE. For the artist, to trust in this delicate transmutation is a natural act of faith which the Puritan hesitates to venture upon: which of the two, one asks, is the greater idealist?

6. The same argument applies to the contradictory epithets 'individual' and 'typical.' A discussion in support of the fundamental individualism of Art lies outside the scope of this essay. Every artist has taken it for granted. Besides it is rather in the sense of 'concrete' or 'individualised,' that it is usually opposed to 'typical.' On the other hand, 'typical,' in the sense of 'abstract,' is as diametrically opposed to the whole nature of Art, as individualism is characteristic of it. It is in the sense of 'generalised' as a 'general human element' that it is claimed as a necessary ingredient in Art. This antithesis is again one which naturally and without mutual sacrifice finds room within the conception of Distance. Historically the 'typical' has had the effect of counteracting *under*-distancing as much as the 'individual' has opposed *over*-distancing. Naturally the two ingredients have constantly varied in the history of Art; they represent, in fact, two sets of conditions to which Art has invariably been subject: the personal and the social factors. It is Distance which on one side prevents the emptying of Art of its concreteness and the development of the typical into abstractness; which, on the other, suppresses the directly personal element of its individualism; thus reducing the antitheses to the peaceful interplay of these two factors. It is just this interplay which constitutes the "antinomy of Distance.'

III

It remains to indicate the value of Distance as *an aesthetic principle*: as criterion in some of the standing problems of Aesthetics; as representing a phase of artistic creation; and as a characteristic feature of the 'aesthetic consciousness.'

1. The axiom of 'hedonistic Aesthetics' is that beauty is pleasure. Unfortunately for hedonism the formula is not reversible: not all pleasure is beauty. Hence the necessity of some

limiting criterion to separate the beautiful within the 'pleasure-field' from the merely agreeable. This relation of the beautiful to the agreeable is the ever recurring crux of all hedonistic Aesthetics, as the problem of this relation becomes inevitable when once the hedonistic basis is granted. It has provoked a number of widely different solutions, some manifestly wrong, and all as little satisfactory as the whole hedonistic groundwork upon which they rest: the shareableness of beauty as opposed to the 'monopoly' of the agreeable (Bain),[8] the passivity of beauty-pleasure (Grant Allen),[9] or most recently, the 'relative permanence of beauty-pleasure in revival' (H. R. Marshall).[10]

Distance offers a distinction which is as simple in its operation as it is fundamental in its importance: *the agreeable is a non-distanced pleasure.* Beauty in the widest sense of aesthetic value is impossible without the insertion of Distance. The agreeable stands in precisely the same relation to the beautiful (in its narrower sense) as the sad stands to the tragic, as indicated earlier. Translating the above formula, one may say, that the agreeable is felt as an affection of our concrete, practical self; the centre of gravity of an agreeable experience lies in the self which experiences the agreeable. The aesthetic experience, on the contrary, has its centre of gravity in itself or in the object mediating it, not in the self which has been distanced out of the field of the inner vision of the experiencer: "not the fruit of experience, but experience itself, is the end." It is for this reason that to be asked in the midst of an intense aesthetic impression "whether one likes it," is like a somnambulist being called by name: it is a recall to one's concrete self, an awakening of practical consciousness which throws the whole aesthetic mechanism out of gear. One might almost venture upon the paradox that the more intense the aesthetic absorption, the less one "likes," consciously, the experience. The failure to realise this fact, so fully borne out by all genuine artistic experience, is the fundamental error of hedonistic Aesthetics.

The problem of the relation of the beautiful and the agreeable has taken more definite shape in the question of the aesthetic value of the so-called 'lower senses' (comprising sensations of taste and temperature, muscular and tactile, and organic sensations). Sight and hearing have always been the 'aesthetic senses' *par excellence.* Scent has been admitted to the status of an aesthetic sense by some, excluded by others. The ground for the rejection of the lower senses has always been that they mediate only agreeable sensations, but are incapable of conveying aesthetic experiences. Though true normally, this rigid distinction is theoretically unfair to the senses, and in practice often false. It is undoubtedly very difficult to reach an aesthetic appreciation through the lower senses, because the materialness of their action, their proximity and bodily connexion are great obstacles to their distancing. The aroma of coffee may be a kind of foretaste, taste etherialised, but still a taste. The sweetness of scent of a rose is usually felt more as a bodily caress than as an aesthetic experience. Yet poets have not hesitated to call the scents of flowers their "souls." Shelley has transformed the scent to an imperceptible sound.[11] We call such conceptions 'poetical': they mark the transition from the merely agreeable to the beautiful by means of Distance.

M. Guyau, in a well-known passage,[12] has described the same transformation of a taste. Even muscular sensations may present aesthetic possibilities, in the free exercise of bodily movement, the swing of a runner, in the ease and certainty of the trained gymnast; nay, such diffuse organic sensations as the buoyancy of well-being, and the elasticity of bodily energy, can, in privileged moments, be aesthetically enjoyed. That they admit of no material fixation, such as objects of sight and hearing do, and for that reason form no part of Art in the narrower sense; that they exist as aesthetic objects only for the moment and for the single being that enjoys them, is no argument against their aesthetic character. Mere material existence and permanence is no aesthetic criterion.

This is all the more true, as even among the experience of lasting things, such as are generally accounted to yield aesthetic impressions, the merely agreeable occurs as frequently as the beautiful.

To begin with the relatively simple case of colour-appreciation. Most people imagine that because they are not colour-blind, physically or spiritually, and prefer to live in a coloured world rather than in an engraving, they possess an aesthetic appreciation of colour as such. This is the sort of fallacy which hedonistic art-theories produce, and the lack of an exchange of views on the subject only fosters. Everybody believes that he enjoys colour – and for that matter other things – just like anyone else. Yet rather the contrary is the case. By far the greater number, when asked why they like a colour, will answer, that they like it, because it strikes them as warm or cold, stimulating or soothing, heavy or light. They constitute a definite type of colour-appreciation and form about sixty per cent of all persons. The remainder assumes, for the greater part, a different attitude. Colours do not appeal to them as effects (largely organic) upon themselves. Their appreciation attributes to colours a kind of personality: colours are energetic, lively, serious, pensive, melancholic, affectionate, subtle, reserved, stealthy, treacherous, brutal, etc. These characters are not mere imaginings, left to the whim of the individual, romancing whatever he pleases into the colours, nor are they the work simply of accidental associations. They follow, on the contrary, definite rules in their applications; they are, in fact, the same organic effects as those of the former type, but transformed into, or interpreted as, attributes of the colour, instead of as affections of one's own self. In short, they are the result of the distancing of the organic effects: they form an aesthetic appreciation of colour, instead of a merely agreeable experience like those of the former kind.[13]

A similar parallelism of the agreeable and the beautiful (in the widest sense of aesthetic value) occurs also within the sphere of recognised art-forms. I select for special notice *comedy* and *melodrama* (though the same observation can be made in painting, architecture and notably in music), firstly as counterparts to tragedy, discussed earlier, secondly, because both represent admitted art-forms, in spite of their at least partially, inadequate claims to the distinction, and lastly because all these types, tragedy, comedy and melodrama, are usually grouped together as 'arts of the theatre' no less than as forms of 'literature.'

From the point of view of the present discussion, the case of *comedy* is particularly involved. What we mean by comedy as a class of theatrical entertainment covers several different kinds,[14] which actually merge into each other and present historically a continuity which allows of no sharp lines of demarcation (a difficulty, by the way, which besets all distinctions of literary or artistic *species*, as opposed to artistic *genera*). The second difficulty is that the 'laughable' includes much more than the comic of comedy. It may enter, in all its varieties of the ridiculous, silly, naïve, brilliant, especially as the humorous, into comedy as ingredients, but the comic is not coextensive with the laughable as a whole.

The fact to be noted here is, that the different types of comedy, as well as the different kinds of the laughable, presuppose different degrees of Distance. Their tendency is to have none at all. Both to laugh and to weep are direct expressions of a throughly practical nature, indicating almost always a concrete personal affection. Indeed, given suitable circumstances and adequate distancing-power, both can be distanced, but only with great difficulty; nor is it possible to decide which of the two offers the greater difficulty. The balance seems almost to incline in favour of tears as the easier of the two, and this would accord with the acknowledged difficulty of producing a really good comedy, or of maintaining a consistent aesthetic attitude in face of a comic situation. Certainly the tendency to *under*-distance is more felt in comedy even than in tragedy; most types of the former presenting a *non-distanced*, practical and personal appeal, which precisely implies that their enjoyment is generally hedonic, not aesthetic. In its lower forms comedy consequently is a mere amusement and falls as little under the heading of Art as pamphleteering would be considered as *belles-lettres*, or a burglary as a dramatic performance. It may be spiritualised, polished and refined to the sharpness of a dagger-point or the subtlety of foil-play, but there still clings to it an atmosphere of amusement pure and simple, sometimes of a rude, often of a cruel kind. This, together with the admitted preference of comedy for generalised types rather than for individualised figures, suggests the conclusion that its point of view is the survival of an attitude which the higher forms of Art have outgrown. It is noteworthy that this tendency decreases with every step towards high comedy, character-comedy and drama, with the growing spiritualisation of the comic elements and the first appearance of Distance. Historically the development has been slow and halting. There is no doubt that the 17th century considered the *Misanthrope* as amusing. We are nowadays less harsh and less socially intolerant and *Alceste* appears to us no longer as frankly ridiculous. The supreme achievement of comedy is unquestionably that 'distanced ridicule' which we call *humour*. The self-contradiction of smiling at what we love, displays, in the light vein, that same perfect and subtle balance of the 'antinomy of Distance' which the truly tragic shows in the serious mood. The tragic and the humorous are the genuine aesthetic opposites; the tragic and the comic are contradictory in the matter of Distance, as aesthetic and hedonic objects respectively.

A similar hedonic opposition in the other direction is to be found between tragedy and *melodrama*. Whereas comedy tends to *under*distance, melodrama suffers from *over*distancing. For a cultivated audience its overcharged idealism, the crude opposition of vice and virtue, the exaggeration of its underlined moral, its innocence of *nuance*, and its sentimentality with violin-accompaniment are sufficient cause to stamp it as inferior Art. But perhaps its excessive distance is the least Distance obtainable by the public for which it is designed, and may be a great help to an unsophisticated audience in distancing the characters and events. For it is more than probable that we make a mistake in assuming an analogy between a cultivated audience at a serious drama, and a melodramatic audience. It is very likely that the lover of melodrama does not present that subtle balance of mind towards a play, implied in the 'antinomy of Distance.' His attitude is rather either that of a matter-of-fact adult or of a child: i.e. he is either in a frankly personal relation to the events of the play and would like to cudgel the villain who illtreats the innocent heroine, and rejoices loudly in his final defeat – just as he would in real life – or, he is completely lost in the excessive distance imposed by the work and watches naïvely the wonders he sees, as a child listens enchantedly to a fairy-tale. In neither case is his attitude aesthetic; in the one the object is *under-*, in the other *over*distanced; in the former he confuses it with the reality he *knows* (or thinks he knows) to exist, in the other with a reality whose existence he does *not know, but accepts*. Neither bears the twofold character of the aesthetic state in which *we know* a thing *not* to exist, but *accept its existence*. From the point of view of moral advantage – in the absence of any aesthetic advantage – the former attitude might seem preferable. But even this may be doubted; for if he believes what he sees in a great spectacular melodrama, every marble-lined hall of the most ordinary London hotel that he passes after the play must appear to him as a veritable Hell, and every man or woman in evening-dress as the devil incarnate. On either supposition, the moral effect must be deplorable in the extreme, and the melodrama is generally a much more fitting object of the censor's attention than any usually censored play. For in the one case the brutalising effect of the obtrusively visible wickedness cannot possibly be outweighed by any retaliatory poetic justice, which must seem to him singularly lacking in real life; in the other, the effect is purely negative and narcotic; in both his perspective of real life is hopelessly outfocussed and distorted.

2. The importance of Distance in artistic creation has already been briefly alluded to in connexion with the 'antinomy of Distance.'

Distancing might, indeed, well be considered as the especial and primary function of what is called the 'creative act' in artistic production: distancing is the *formal* aspect of creation in Art. The view that the artist 'copies nature' has already been dismissed. Since the 'imitation-of-nature' theory was officially discarded at the beginning of the 19th century, its place in popular fancy has been taken by the conception of the 'self-expression of the artist,' supported by the whole force of the Romantic Movement in Europe. Though true as a crude statement of the subjective origin of an artistic conception, though in many ways preferable to its predecessor and valuable as a corollary of such theories as that of the 'organic growth' of a work of Art, it is apt to lead to confusions and to one-sided inferences, to be found even in such deliberate and expert accounts of artistic production as that of Benedetto Croce.[15] For, to start with, the 'self-expression' of an artist is not such as the 'self-expression' of a letter-writer or a public speaker: it is not the *direct* expression of the concrete personality of the artist; it is not even an *indirect* expression of his concrete personality, in the sense in which, for instance, Hamlet's 'self-expression' might be supposed to be the indirect reflexion of Shakespeare's ideas. Such a denial, it might be argued, runs counter to the observation that in the works of a literary artist, for example, are to be found echoes and mirrorings of his times and of his personal experiences and convictions. But it is to be noted that to find these *is* in fact impossible, unless you previously know what reflexions to look for. Even in the relatively most direct transference from personal experience to their expression, viz. in lyrical poetry, such a connexion cannot he established backwards, though it is easy enough to prove it forwards: i.e. given the knowledge of the experiences, there is no difficulty in tracing their echoes, but it is impossible to infer biographical data of any detail or concrete value from an author's works alone. Otherwise Shakespeare's *Sonnets* would not have proved as refractory to biographical research as they have done, and endless blunders in literary history would never have been committed. What proves so impossible in literature, which after all offers an exceptionally adequate medium to 'self-expression,' is *a fortiori* out of question in other arts, in which there is not even an equivalence between the personal experiences and the material in which they are supposed to be formulated. The fundamental two-fold error of the 'self-expression' theory is to speak of 'expression' in the sense of 'intentional communication,' and to identify straightway the artist and the man. An intentional communication is as far almost from the mind of the true artist as it would be from that of the ordinary respectable citizen to walk about naked in the streets, and the idea has repeatedly been indignantly repudiated by artists. The second confusion is as misleading in its theoretical consequences, as it is mischievous and often exceedingly painful to the 'man' as well as to the 'artist.' The numberless instances in history of the astonishing difference, often the marked contrast between the *man* and his *work* is one of the most disconcerting riddles of Art, and should serve as a manifest warning against the popular illusion of finding the 'artist's mind' in his productions.[16]

Apart from the complication of technical necessities, of conventional art-forms, of the requirements of unification and composition, all impeding the direct transference of an actual mental content into its artistic formulation, there is the interpolation of Distance which stands between the artist's conception and the man's. For the 'artist' himself is already distanced from the concrete, historical personality, who ate and drank and slept and did the ordinary business of life. No doubt here also are *degrees* of Distance, and the 'antinomy' applies to this case too. Some figures in literature and other arts are unquestionably self-portraits; but even self-portraits are not, and cannot be, the direct and faithful cast taken from the living soul. In short, so far from being 'self-expression,' *artistic production is the indirect formulation of a distanced mental content.*

I give a short illustration of this fact. A well-known dramatist described to me the process of production as taking place in his case in some such way as follows:

The starting-point of his production is what he described as an 'emotional idea,' i.e. some more or less general conception carrying with it a strong emotional tone. This idea may be suggested by an actual experience; anyhow the idea itself *is* an actual experience, i.e. it occurs within the range of his normal, practical being. Gradually it condenses itself into a situation made up of the interplay of certain characters, which may be of partly objective, partly imaginative descent. Then ensues what he described as a "life and death struggle" between the idea and the characters for existence: if the idea gains the upper hand, the conception of the whole is doomed. In the successful issue, on the contrary, the idea is, to use his phrase, "sucked up" by the characters as a sponge sucks up water, until no trace of the idea is left outside the characters. It is a process, which, he assured me, he is quite powerless to direct or even to influence. It is further of interest to notice that during this period the idea undergoes sometimes profound, often wholesale changes. Once the stage of complete fusion of the idea with the characters is reached, the conscious elaboration of the play can proceed. What follows after this, is of no further interest in this connexion.

This account tallies closely with the procedure which numerous dramatists are known to have followed. It forms a definite type. There are other types, equally well supported by evidence, which proceed along much less definite lines of a semi-logical development, but rather show sudden flash-like illuminations and much more subconscious growth.

The point to notice is the "life and death struggle" between the idea and the characters. As

I first remarked, the idea is the '*man's*,' it is the reflexion of the dramatist's concrete and practical self. Yet this is precisely the part which must "*die*." The paradox of just the germpart of the whole being doomed, particularly impressed my informant as a kind of life-tragedy. The 'characters' on the other hand belong to the imaginary world, to the 'artist's.' Though they may be partially suggested by actuality, their full-grown development is divorced from it. This process of the 'idea' being "sucked up" by the characters and being destroyed by it, is a phase of artistic production technically known as the 'objectivation' of the conception. In it the 'man' dies and the 'artist' comes to life, and with him the work of Art. It is a change of death and birth in which there is no overlapping of the lives of parent and child. The result is the distanced finished production. As elsewhere, the distancing means the separation of personal affections, whether idea or complex experience, from the concrete personality of the experiencer, its filtering by the extrusion of its personal aspects, the throwing out of gear of its personal potency and significance.

The same transformation through distance is to be noticed in *acting*. Here, even more than in the other arts, a lingering bias in favour of the 'imitation of nature' theory has stood in the way of a correct interpretation of the facts. Yet acting supplies in this and other respects exceptionally valuable information, owing to its medium of expression and the overlapping – at least in part – of the process of producing with the finished production, which elsewhere are separated in point of time. It illustrates, as no other art can, the cleavage between the concrete, normal person and the distanced personality. [The acting here referred to is, of course, not that style which consists in 'walking on.' What is meant here is 'creative' acting, which in its turn must be distinguished from 'reproductive' acting – two different types traceable through the greater part of theatrical history, which in their highest development are often outwardly indistinguishable, but nevertheless retain traces of differences, characteristic of their procedures and psychical mechanism.] This cleavage between the two streams or layers of consciousness is so obvious that it has led to increasing speculation from the time when acting first attracted intelligent interest, since the middle of the 18th century. From the time of Diderot's *Paradoxe sur le Comédien* (itself only the last of a series of French studies) down to Mr. William Archer's *Masks or Faces* (1888) and the controversy between Coquelin and Salvini (in the nineties), theory has been at pains to grapple with this phenomenon. Explanations have differed widely, going from the one extreme of an identification of the acting and the normal personality to the other of a separation so wide as to be theoretically inconceivable and contradicted by experience. It is necessary to offer some conception which will account for the differences as well as for the indirect connexion between the two forms of being, and which is applicable not merely to acting, but to other kinds of art as well. Distance, it is here contended, meets the requirement even in its subtlest shades. To show this in detail lies outside the scope of this essay, and forms rather the task of a special treatment of the psychology of acting.

3. In the interest of those who may be familiar with the developments of aesthetic theories of late years, I should like to add that Distance has a special bearing upon many points raised by them. It is essential to the occurrence and working of 'empathy' (*Einfühlung*), and I mentioned earlier its connexion with Witasek's theory of *Scheingefühle* which forms part of his view on 'empathy.' The distinction between sympathy and 'empathy' as formulated by Lipps[17] is a matter of the relative degree of Distance. Volkelt's[18] suggestion of regarding the ordinary apprehension of expression (say of a person's face) as the first rudimentary stage of *Einfühlung*, leading subsequently to the lowering of our consciousness of reality ("*Herabsetzung des Wirklichkeitsgefühls*"), can similarly be formulated in terms of Distance. K. Lange's[19] account of aesthetic experience in the form of 'illusion as conscious self-deception' appears to me a wrong formulation of the facts expressed by Distance. Lange's 'illusion' theory seems to me, among other things,[20] to be based upon a false opposition between Art and reality (nature) as the subject-matter of the former, whereas Distance does not imply any comparison between them in the act of experiencing and removes altogether the centre of gravity of the formula from the opposition.]

4. In this way Distance represents in aesthetic appreciation as well as in artistic

production a quality inherent in the impersonal, yet *so* intensely personal, relation which the human being entertains with Art, either as mere beholder or as producing artist.

It is Distance which makes the aesthetic object 'an end in itself.' It is that which raises Art beyond the narrow sphere of individual interest and imparts to it that 'postulating' character which the idealistic philosophy of the 19th century regarded as a metaphysical necessity. It renders questions of origin, of influences, or of purposes almost as meaningless as those of marketable value, of pleasure, even of moral importance, since it lifts the work of Art out of the realm of practical systems and ends.

In particular, it is Distance, which supplies one of the special criteria of aesthetic values as distinct from practical (utilitarian), scientific, or social (ethical) values. All these are concrete values, either *directly* personal as utilitarian, or *indirectly* remotely personal, as moral values. To speak, therefore, of the 'pleasure value' of Art, and to introduce hedonism into aesthetic speculation, is even more irrelevant than to speak of moral hedonism in Ethics. Aesthetic hedonism is a compromise. It is the attempt to reconcile for public use utilitarian ends with aesthetic values. Hedonism, as a practical, personal appeal has no place in the distanced appeal of Art. Moral hedonism is even more to the point than aesthetic hedonism, since ethical values, *quâ* social values, lie on the line of prolongation of utilitarian ends, sublimating indeed the *directly* personal object into the realm of socially or universally valuable ends, often demanding the sacrifice of individual happiness, but losing neither its *practical* nor even its *remotely personal* character.

In so far, Distance becomes one of the distinguishing features of the 'aesthetic consciousness,' of that special mentality or outlook upon experience and life, which, as I said at the outset, leads in its most pregnant and most fully developed form, both appreciatively and productively, to Art.

Notes

1 H. Witasek, 'Zur psychologischen Analyse der aesthetischen Einfühlung,' *Ztsch. für Psychol. u. Physiol. der Sinnesorg.* 1901, xxv. 1 ff.; *Grundzüge der Aesthetik*, Leipzig, 1904.

2 J. Volkelt, 'Die Bedeutung der niederen Empfindungen für die aesthetische Einfühlung,' *Ztsch. für Psychol. u. Physiol. der Sinnesorg.* xxxii. 15, 16; *System der Aesthetik*, 1905, i. 260 ff.

3 Report from the Joint Select Committee of the House of Lords and the House of Commons on the Stage Plays (Censorship), 1909.

4 I shall use the term 'presentment' to denote the manner of presenting, in distinction to 'presentation' as that which is presented.

5 The famous 'unity of time,' so senseless as a 'canon,' is all the same often an indispensable condition of tragedy. For in many a tragedy the catastrophe would be even intrinsically impossible, if fatality did not overtake the hero with that rush which gives no time to forget and none to heal. It is in cases such as these that criticism has often blamed the work for 'improbability' – the old confusion between Art and nature – forgetting that the death of the hero is the convention of the art-form, as much as grouping in a picture is such a convention and that probability is not the correspondence with average experience, but consistency of Distance.

6 An instance which might be adduced to disprove this point only shows its correctness on closer inspection: for it was on purpose and with the intention of removing Distance, that Rodin originally intended his *citoyens de Calais* to be placed, without pedestals, upon the market-place of that town.

7 See note 2.

8 Bain, *The Emotions and the Will*, 2nd ed. 1850.

9 G. Allen, *Physiological Aesthetics*, 1897.

10 H. R. Marshall, *Pain, Pleasure and Aesthetics*, 1894; *Aesthetic Principles*, 1895.

11 Cf. "The Sensitive Plant."

12 M. Guyau, *Problèmes de l'Esthétique contemporaline*, Paris, 1847, 4me ed. Livre i. chap. vi.

13 Cf. E. Bullough, 'The Perceptive Problem in the Aesthetic Appreciation of Single Colours,' [*British Journal of Psychology*], 1908, ii. 406ff.

14 Comedy embraces *satirical comedy*, i.e. dramatic invectives of all degrees of personal directness, from the attack on actually existing persons (such as is prohibited by the censorship, but has flourished everywhere) to skits upon existing professions, customs, evils, or society; secondly, *farce*, rarely unmixed with satire, but occasionally *pure* nonsense and horseplay; thirdly, *comedy proper*, a sublimation of farce into the pure comedy of general human situation, or genuine character-comedy, changing easily into the fourth class, the type of play described on the Continent as *drama* (in the narrower sense), i.e. a play involving serious situations, sometimes with tragic

prospects, but having an happy, if often unexpected, ending.

15 Benedetto Croce, *Aesthetic*, translated by Douglas Ainslie, Macmillan, 1909.

16 Some well-known examples of this difference are, for instance: Mozart, Beethoven, Watteau, Murillo, Molière, Schiller, Verlasne, Zola.

17 Th. Lipps, *Aesthetik*, Hamburg and Leipzig, 1903, I.; 'Aesthetische Einfühlung,' *Ztsch. für Psychol. u. Physiol. der Sinnesorg.* XXII. 415 ff.

18 J. Volkelt, *System der Aesthetik*, 1905, I. 217 ff. and 488 ff.

19 K. Lange, *Des Wesen der Kunst*, 1901, 2 vols.

20 J. Segal, 'Die bewusste Selbsttäuschung als Kern des aesthetischen Geniessens,' *Arch. f. d. ges. Psychol.* VI. 254 ff.

24

Art

Clive Bell

Clive Bell (1881–1964) was a highly influential critic of art and literature, who belonged to the celebrated Bloomsbury group, which included his sister-in-law, Virginia Woolf.

It is improbable that more nonsense has been written about aesthetics than about anything else: the literature of the subject is not large enough for that. It is certain, however, that about no subject with which I am acquainted has so little been said that is at all to the purpose. The explanation is discoverable. He who would elaborate a plausible theory of aesthetics must possess two qualities – artistic sensibility and a turn for clear thinking. Without sensibility a man can have no aesthetic experience, and, obviously, theories not based on broad and deep aesthetic experience are worthless. Only those for whom art is a constant source of passionate emotion can possess the data from which profitable theories may be deduced; but to deduce profitable theories even from accurate data involves a certain amount of brain-work, and, unfortunately, robust intellects and delicate sensibilities are not inseparable. As often as not, the hardest thinkers have had no aesthetic experience whatever. I have a friend blessed with an intellect as keen as a drill, who, though he takes an interest in aesthetics, has never during a life of almost forty years been guilty of an aesthetic emotion. So, having no faculty for distinguishing a work of art from a handsaw, he is apt to rear up a pyramid of irrefragable argument on the hypothesis that a handsaw is a work of art. This defect robs his perspicuous and subtle reasoning of much of its value; for it has ever been a maxim that faultless logic can win but little credit for conclusions that are based on premises notoriously false. Every cloud, however, has its silver lining, and this insensibility, though unlucky in that it makes my friend incapable of choosing a sound basis for his argument, mercifully blinds him to the absurdity of his conclusions while leaving him in full enjoyment of his masterly dialectic. People who set out from the hypothesis that Sir Edwin Landseer was the finest painter that ever lived will feel no uneasiness about an aesthetic which proves that Giotto was the worst. So, my friend, when he arrives very logically at the conclusion that a work of art should be small or round or smooth, or that to appreciate fully a picture you should pace smartly before it or set it spinning like a top, cannot guess why I ask him whether he has lately been to Cambridge, a place he sometimes visits.

On the other hand, people who respond immediately and surely to works of art, though, in my judgment, more enviable than men of

Clive Bell, *Art* (London: Chatto & Windus, 1914).

massive intellect but slight sensibility, are often quite as incapable of talking sense about aesthetics. Their heads are not always very clear. They possess the data on which any system must be based; but, generally, they want the power that draws correct inferences from true data. Having received aesthetic emotions from works of art, they are in a position to seek out the quality common to all that have moved them, but, in fact, they do nothing of the sort. I do not blame them. Why should they bother to examine their feelings when for them to feel is enough? Why should they stop to think when they are not very good at thinking? Why should they hunt for a common quality in all objects that move them in a particular way when they can linger over the many delicious and peculiar charms of each as it comes? So, if they write criticism and call it aesthetics, if they imagine that they are talking about Art when they are talking about particular works of art or even about the technique of painting, if, loving particular works they find tedious the consideration of art in general, perhaps they have chosen the better part. If they are not curious about the nature of their emotion, nor about the quality common to all objects that provoke it, they have my sympathy, and, as what they say is often charming and suggestive, my admiration too. Only let no one suppose that what they write and talk is aesthetics; it is criticism, or just "shop."

The starting-point for all systems of aesthetics must be the personal experience of a peculiar emotion. The objects that provoke this emotion we call works of art. All sensitive people agree that there is a peculiar emotion provoked by works of art. I do not mean, of course, that all works provoke the same emotion. On the contrary, every work produces a different emotion. But all these emotions are recognisably the same in kind; so far, at any rate, the best opinion is on my side. That there is a particular kind of emotion provoked by works of visual art, and that this emotion is provoked by every kind of visual art, by pictures, sculptures, buildings, pots, carvings, textiles, &c., &c., is not disputed, I think, by anyone capable of feeling it. This emotion is called the aesthetic emotion; and if we can discover some quality common and peculiar to all the objects that provoke it, we shall have solved what I take to be the central problem of aesthetics. We shall have discovered the essential quality in a work of art, the quality that distinguishes works of art from all other classes of objects.

For either all works of visual art have some common quality, or when we speak of "works of art" we gibber. Everyone speaks of "art," making a mental classification by which he distinguishes the class "works of art" from all other classes. What is the justification of this classification? What is the quality common and peculiar to all members of this class? Whatever it be, no doubt it is often found in company with other qualities; but they are adventitious – it is essential. There must be some one quality without which a work of art cannot exist; possessing which, in the least degree, no work is altogether worthless. What is this quality? What quality is shared by all objects that provoke our aesthetic emotions? What quality is common to Sta. Sophia and the windows at Chartres, Mexican sculpture, a Persian bowl, Chinese carpets, Giotto's frescoes at Padua, and the masterpieces of Poussin, Piero della Francesca, and Cézanne? Only one answer seems possible – significant form. In each, lines and colours combined in a particular way, certain forms and relations of forms, stir our aesthetic emotions. These relations and combinations of lines and colours, these aesthetically moving forms, I call "Significant Form"; and "Significant Form" is the one quality common to all works of visual art.

At this point it may be objected that I am making aesthetics a purely subjective business, since my only data are personal experiences of a particular emotion. It will be said that the objects that provoke this emotion vary with each individual, and that therefore a system of aesthetics can have no objective validity. It must be replied that any system of aesthetics which pretends to be based on some objective truth is so palpably ridiculous as not to be worth discussing. We have no other means of recognising a work of art than our feeling for it. The objects that provoke aesthetic emotion vary with each individual. Aesthetic judgments are, as the saying goes, matters of taste; and about tastes, as everyone is proud to admit, there is no disputing. A good critic may be able to make me see in a picture that had left me cold things that I had overlooked, till at last, receiving the aesthetic emotion, I recognise it as a work of art. To be continually pointing out those parts, the sum, or rather the combination, of which unite to produce significant form, is the function of criticism. But it is useless for a critic to tell me that something is a work of art; he must make me feel it for myself. This he can do only by making me see; he must get at my emotions through my eyes. Unless he can make me see something that moves me, he cannot force my emotions. I have no right to consider anything a work of art to which I cannot react emotionally; and I have no right to look for the essential quality in anything that I have not *felt* to be a work of art. The critic can affect my aesthetic theories only by affecting my aesthetic experience. All systems of aesthetics must be based on personal experience – that is to say, they must be subjective.

Yet, though all aesthetic theories must be based on aesthetic judgments, and ultimately all aesthetic judgments must be matters of personal taste, it would be rash to assert that no theory of aesthetics can have general validity. For, though A, B, C, D are the works that move me, and A, D, E, F the works that move you, it may well be that *x* is the only quality believed by either of us to be common to all the works in his list. We may all agree about aesthetics, and yet differ about particular works of art. We may differ as to the presence or absence of the quality *x*. My immediate object will be to show that significant form is the only quality common and peculiar to all the works of visual art that move me; and I will ask those whose aesthetic experience does not tally with mine to see whether this quality is not also, in their judgment, common to all works that move them, and whether they can discover any other quality of which the same can be said.

Also at this point a query arises, irrelevant indeed, but hardly to be suppressed: "Why are we so profoundly moved by forms related in a particular way?" The question is extremely interesting, but irrelevant to aesthetics. In pure aesthetics we have only to consider our emotion and its object: for the purposes of aesthetics we have no right, neither is there any necessity, to pry behind the object into the state of mind of him who made it. Later, I shall attempt to answer the question; for by so doing I may be able to develop my theory of the relation of art to life. I shall not, however, be under the delusion that I am rounding off my theory of aesthetics. For a discussion of aesthetics, it need be agreed only that forms arranged and combined according to certain unknown and mysterious laws do move us in a particular way, and that it is the business of an artist so to combine and arrange them that they shall move us. These moving combinations and arrangements I have called, for the sake of convenience and for a reason that will appear later, "Significant Form."

A third interruption has to be met.

"Are you forgetting about colour?" someone inquires. Certainly not; my term "significant form" included combinations of lines and of colours. The distinction between form and colour is an unreal one; you cannot conceive a colourless line or a colourless space; neither can you conceive a formless relation of colours. In a black and white drawing the spaces are all white and all are bounded by black lines; in most oil paintings the spaces are multi-coloured and so are the boundaries; you cannot imagine a boundary line without any content, or a content without a boundary line, Therefore, when I speak of significant form, I mean a combination of lines and colours (counting white and black as colours) that moves me aesthetically.

Some people may be surprised at my not having called this "beauty." Of course, to those who define beauty as "combinations of lines and colours that provoke aesthetic emotion," I willingly concede the right of substituting their word for mine. But most of us, however strict we may be, are apt to apply the epithet "beautiful" to objects that do not provoke that peculiar emotion produced by works of art. Everyone, I suspect, has called a butterfly or a flower beautiful. Does anyone feel the same kind of emotion for a butterfly or a flower that he feels for a cathedral or a picture? Surely, it is not what I call an aesthetic emotion that most of us feel, generally, for natural beauty. I shall suggest, later, that some people may, occasionally, see in nature what we see in art, and feel for her an aesthetic emotion; but I am satisfied that, as a rule, most people feel a very different kind of emotion for birds and flowers and the wings of butterflies from that which they feel for pictures, pots, temples and statues. Why these beautiful things do not move us as works of art move is another, and not an aesthetic, question. For our immediate purpose we have to discover only what quality is common to objects that do move us as works of art. In the last part of this chapter, when I try to answer the question – "Why are we so profoundly moved by some combinations of lines and colours?" I shall hope to offer an acceptable explanation of why we are less profoundly moved by others.

Since we call a quality that does not raise the characteristic aesthetic emotion "Beauty," it would be misleading to call by the same name the quality that does. To make "beauty" the object of the aesthetic emotion, we must give to the word an over-strict and unfamiliar definition. Everyone sometimes uses "beauty" in an unaesthetic sense; most people habitually do so. To everyone, except perhaps here and there an occasional aesthete, the commonest sense of the word is unaesthetic. Of its grosser abuse, patent in our chatter about "beautiful huntin'" and "beautiful shootin'," I need not take account; it would be open to the precious to reply that they never do so abuse it. Besides, here there is no danger of confusion between the aesthetic and the non-aesthetic use; but when we speak of a beautiful woman there is. When an ordinary man speaks of a beautiful woman he certainly does not mean only that she moves him aesthetically; but when an artist calls a withered old hag beautiful he may sometimes mean what he means when he calls a battered torso beautiful. The ordinary man, if he be also a man of taste, will call the battered torso beautiful, but he will not call a withered hag beautiful because, in the matter of women, it is not to the aesthetic quality that the hag may possess, but to some other quality that he assigns the epithet. Indeed, most of us never dream of going for aesthetic emotions to human beings, from whom we ask something very different. This "something," when we find it in a young woman, we are apt to call "beauty." We live in a nice age. With the man-in-the-street "beautiful" is more often than not synonymous with "desirable"; the word does not necessarily connote any aesthetic reaction whatever, and I am tempted to believe that in the minds of many the sexual flavour of the word is stronger than the aesthetic. I have noticed a consistency in those to whom the most beautiful thing in the world is a beautiful woman, and the next most beautiful thing a picture of one. The confusion between aesthetic and sensual beauty is not in their case so great as might be supposed. Perhaps there is none; for perhaps they have never had an aesthetic emotion to confuse with their other emotions. The art that they call "beautiful" is generally closely related to the women. A beautiful picture is a photograph of a pretty girl; beautiful music, the music that provokes emotions similar to those provoked by young ladies in musical farces; and beautiful poetry, the poetry that recalls the same emotions felt, twenty years earlier, for the rector's daughter. Clearly the word "beauty" is used to connote the objects of quite distinguishable emotions, and that is a reason for not employing a term which would land me inevitably in confusions and misunderstandings with my readers.

On the other hand, with those who judge it more exact to call these combinations and arrangements of form that provoke our aesthetic emotions, not "significant form," but "significant relations of form," and then try to make the best of two worlds, the aesthetic and the metaphysical, by calling these relations "rhythm," I have no quarrel whatever. Having made it clear that by "significant form" I mean arrangements and combinations that move us in a particular way, I willingly join hands with those who prefer to give a different name to the same thing.

The hypothesis that significant form is the essential quality in a work of art has at least one merit denied to many more famous and more striking – it does help to explain things. We are all familiar with pictures that interest us and excite our admiration, but do not move us as works of art. To this class belongs what I call "Descriptive Painting" – that is, painting in which forms are used not as objects of emotion, but as means of suggesting emotion or conveying information. Portraits of psychological and historical value, topographical works, pictures that tell stories and suggest situations, illustrations of all sorts, belong to this class. That we all recognise the distinction is clear, for who has not said that such and such a drawing was excellent as illustration, but as a work of art worthless? Of course many descriptive pictures possess, amongst other qualities, formal significance, and are therefore works of art: but many more do not. They interest us; they may move us too in a hundred different ways, but they do not move us aesthetically. According to my hypothesis they are not works of art. They leave untouched our aesthetic emotions because it is not their forms but the ideas or information suggested or conveyed by their forms that affect us.

Few pictures are better known or liked than Frith's "Paddington Station"; certainly I should be the last to grudge it its popularity. Many a weary forty minutes have I whiled away disentangling its fascinating incidents and forging for each an imaginary past and an improbable future. But certain though it is that Frith's masterpiece, or engravings of it, have provided thousands with half-hours of curious and fanciful pleasure, it is not less certain that no one has experienced before it one half-second of aesthetic rapture – and this although the picture contains several pretty passages of colour, and is by no means badly painted. "Paddington Station" is not a work of art; it is an interesting and amusing document. In it line and colour are used to recount anecdotes, suggest ideas, and indicate the manners and customs of an age: they are not used to provoke aesthetic emotion. Forms and the relations of forms were for Frith not objects of emotion, but means of suggesting emotion and conveying ideas.

The ideas and information conveyed by "Paddington Station" are so amusing and so well presented that the picture has considerable value and is well worth preserving. But, with the perfection of photographic processes and of the cinematograph, pictures of this sort are becoming otiose. Who doubts that one of those *Daily Mirror* photographers in collaboration with a *Daily Mail* reporter can tell us far more about "London day by day" than any Royal Academician? For an account of manners and fashions we shall go, in future, to photographs, supported by a little bright journalism, rather than to descriptive painting. Had the imperial academicians of Nero, instead of manufacturing incredibly loathsome imitations of the antique, recorded in fresco and mosaic the manners and fashions of their day, their stuff, though artistic rubbish, would now be an historical gold-mine. If only they had been Friths instead of being Alma Tademas! But photography has made impossible any such transmutation of modern rubbish. Therefore it must be confessed that pictures in the Frith tradition are grown superfluous; they merely waste the hours of able men who might be more profitably employed in works of a wider beneficence. Still, they are not unpleasant, which is more than can be said for that kind of descriptive painting of which "The Doctor" is the most flagrant example. Of course "The Doctor" is not a work of art. In it form is not used as an object of emotion, but as a means of suggesting emotions. This alone suffices to make it nugatory; it is worse than nugatory because the emotion it suggests is false. What it suggests is not pity and admiration but a sense of complacency in our own pitifulness and generosity. It is sentimental. Art is above morals, or, rather, all art is moral because, as I hope to show presently, works of art are immediate means to good. Once we have judged a thing a work of art, we have judged it ethically of the first importance and put it beyond the reach of the moralist. But descriptive pictures which are not works of art, and, therefore, are not necessarily means to good states of mind, are proper objects of the ethical philosopher's attention. Not being a work of art, "The Doctor" has none of the immense ethical value possessed by all objects that provoke aesthetic ecstasy; and the state of mind to which it is a means, as illustration, appears to me undesirable.

The works of those enterprising young men, the Italian Futurists, are notable examples of descriptive painting. Like the Royal Academicians, they use form, not to provoke aesthetic emotions, but to convey information and ideas. Indeed, the published theories of the Futurists prove that their pictures ought to have nothing whatever to do with art. Their social and political theories are respectable, but I would suggest to young Italian painters that it is possible to become a Futurist in thought and action and yet remain an artist, if one has the luck to be born one. To associate art with politics is always a mistake. Futurist pictures are descriptive because they aim at presenting in line and colour the chaos of the mind at a particular moment; their forms are not intended to promote aesthetic emotion but to convey information. These forms, by the way, whatever may be the nature of the ideas they suggest, are themselves anything but revolutionary. In such Futurist pictures as I have seen – perhaps I should except some by Severini – the drawing, whenever it becomes representative as it frequently does, is found to be in that soft and common convention brought into fashion by Besnard some thirty years ago, and much affected by Beaux-Art students ever since. As works of art, the Futurist pictures are negligible; but they are not to be judged as works of art. A good Futurist picture would succeed as a good piece of psychology succeeds; it would reveal, through line and colour, the complexities of an interesting state of mind. If Futurist pictures seem to fail, we must seek an explanation, not in a lack of artistic qualities that they never were intended to possess, but rather in the minds the states of which they are intended to reveal.

Most people who care much about art find that of the work that moves them most the greater part is what scholars call "Primitive." Of course there are bad primitives. For instance, I remember going, full of enthusiasm, to see one of the earliest Romanesque churches in Poitiers (Notre-Dame-la-Grande), and finding it as ill-proportioned, over-decorated, coarse, fat and heavy as any better class building by one of those highly civilised architects who flourished a thousand years earlier or eight hundred later. But such exceptions are rare. As a rule primitive art is good – and here again my hypothesis is helpful – for, as a rule, it is also free from descriptive qualities. In primitive art you will find no accurate representation; you will find only significant form. Yet no other art moves us so profoundly. Whether we consider Sumerian sculpture or pre-dynastic Egyptian art, or archaic Greek, or the Wei and T'ang masterpieces, or those early Japanese works of which I had the luck to see a few superb examples (especially two wooden Bodhisattvas) at the Shepherd's Bush Exhibition in 1910, or whether, coming nearer home, we consider the primitive Byzantine art of the sixth century and its primitive developments amongst the Western barbarians, or, turning far afield, we consider that mysterious and majestic art that flourished in Central and South America before the coming of the white men, in every case we observe three common characteristics – absence of representation, absence of technical swagger, sublimely impressive form. Nor is it hard to discover the connection between these three. Formal significance loses itself in preoccupation with exact representation and ostentatious cunning.

Naturally, it is said that if there is little representation and less saltimbancery in primitive art, that is because the primitives were unable to catch a likeness or cut intellectual capers. The contention is beside the point. There is truth in it, no doubt, though, were I a critic whose reputation depended on a power of impressing the public with a semblance of knowledge, I should be more cautious about urging it than such people generally are. For to suppose that the Byzantine masters wanted skill, or could not have created an illusion had they wished to do so, seems to imply ignorance of the amazingly dexterous realism of the notoriously bad works of that age. Very often, I fear, the misrepresentation of the primitives must be attributed to what the critics call, "wilful distortion." Be that as it may, the point is that, either from want of skill or want of will, primitives neither create illusions, nor make display of extravagant accomplishment, but concentrate their energies on the one thing needful – the creation of form. Thus have they created the finest works of art that we possess.

Let no one imagine that representation is bad in itself; a realistic form may be as significant, in its place as part of the design, as an abstract. But if a representative form has value, it is as form, not as representation. The representative element in a work of art may or may not be harmful; always it is irrelevant. For, to appreciate a work of art we need bring with us nothing from life, no knowledge of its ideas and affairs, no familiarity with its emotions. Art transports us from the world of man's activity to a world of aesthetic exaltation. For a moment we are shut off from human interests; our anticipations and memories are arrested; we are lifted above the stream of life. The pure mathematician rapt in his studies knows a state of mind which I take to be similar, if not identical. He feels an emotion for his speculations which arises from no perceived relation between them and the lives of men, but springs, inhuman or super-human, from the heart of an abstract science. I wonder, sometimes, whether the appreciators of art and of mathematical solutions are not even more closely allied. Before we feel an aesthetic emotion for a combination of forms, do we not perceive intellectually the rightness and necessity of the combination? If we do, it would explain the fact that passing rapidly through a room we recognise a picture to be good, although we cannot say that it has provoked much emotion. We seem to have recognised intellectually the rightness of its forms without staying to fix our attention, and collect, as it were, their emotional significance. If this were so, it would be permissible to inquire whether it was the forms themselves or our perception of their rightness and necessity that caused aesthetic emotion. But I do not think I need linger to discuss the matter here. I have been inquiring why certain combinations of forms move us; I should not have travelled by other roads had I enquired, instead, why certain combinations are perceived to be right and necessary, and why our perception of their rightness and necessity is moving. What I have to say is this: the rapt philosopher, and he who contemplates a work of art, inhabit a world with an intense and peculiar significance of its own; that significance is unrelated to the significance of life. In this world the emotions of life find no place. It is a world with emotions of its own.

To appreciate a work of art we need bring with us nothing but a sense of form and colour and a knowledge of three-dimensional space. That bit of knowledge, I admit, is essential to the appreciation of many great works, since many of the most moving forms ever created are in three dimensions. To see a cube or a rhomboid as a flat pattern is to lower its significance, and a sense of three-dimensional space is essential to the full appreciation of most architectural forms. Pictures which would be insignificant if we saw them as flat patterns are profoundly moving because, in fact, we see them as related planes. If the representation of three-dimensional space is to be called "representation," then I agree that there is one kind of representation which is not irrelevant. Also, I agree that along with our feeling for line and colour we must bring with us our knowledge of space if we are to make the most of every kind of form. Nevertheless, there are magnificent designs to an appreciation of which this knowledge is not necessary: so, though it is not irrelevant to the appreciation of some works of art it is not essential to the appreciation of all. What we must say is that the representation of three-dimensional space is neither irrelevant nor essential to all art, and that every other sort of representation is irrelevant.

That there is an irrelevant representative or descriptive element in many great works of art is not in the least surprising. Why it is not surprising I shall try to show elsewhere. Representation is not of necessity baneful, and highly realistic forms may be extremely significant. Very often, however, representation is a sign of weakness in an artist. A painter too feeble to create forms that provoke more than a little aesthetic emotion will try to eke that little out by suggesting the emotions of life. To evoke the emotions of life he must use representation. Thus a man will paint an execution, and, fearing to miss with his first barrel of significant form, will try to hit with his second by raising an emotion of fear or pity. But if in the artist an inclination to play upon the emotions of life is often the sign of a flickering inspiration, in the spectator a tendency to seek, behind form, the emotions of life is a sign of defective sensibility always. It means that his aesthetic emotions are weak or, at any rate, imperfect. Before a work of art people who feel little or no emotion for pure form find themselves at a loss. They are deaf men at a concert. They know that they are in the presence of something great, but they lack the power of apprehending it. They know that they ought to feel for it a tremendous emotion, but it happens that the particular kind of emotion it can raise is one that they can feel hardly or not at all. And so they read into the forms of the work those facts and ideas for which they are capable of feeling emotion, and feel for them the emotions that they can feel – the ordinary emotions of life. When confronted by a picture, instinctively they refer back its forms to the world from which they came. They treat created form as though it were imitated form, a picture as though it were a photograph. Instead of going out on the stream of art into a new world of aesthetic experience, they turn a sharp corner and come straight home to the world of human interests. For them the significance of a work of art depends on what they bring to it; no new thing is added to their lives, only the old material is stirred. A good work of visual art carries a person who is capable of appreciating it out of life into ecstasy: to use art as a means to the emotions of life is to use a telescope for reading the news. You will notice that people who cannot feel pure aesthetic emotions remember pictures by their subjects; whereas people who can, as often as not, have no idea what the subject of a picture is. They have never noticed the representative element, and so when they discuss pictures they talk about the shapes of forms and the relations and quantities of colours. Often they can tell by the quality of a single line whether or no a man is a good artist. They are concerned only with lines and colours, their relations and quantities and qualities; but from these they win an emotion more profound and far more sublime than any that can be given by the description of facts and ideas.

This last sentence has a very confident ring – over-confident, some may think. Perhaps I shall be able to justify it, and make my meaning clearer too, if I give an account of my own feelings about music. I am not really musical. I do not understand music well. I find musical form exceedingly difficult to apprehend, and I am sure that the profounder subtleties of harmony and rhythm more often than not escape me. The form of a musical composition must be simple indeed if I am to grasp it honestly. My opinion about music is not worth having. Yet, sometimes, at a concert, though my appreciation of the music is limited and humble, it is pure. Sometimes, though I have poor understanding, I have a clean palate. Consequently, when I am feeling bright and clear and intent, at the beginning of a concert for instance, when something that I can grasp is being played, I get from music that pure aesthetic emotion that I get from visual art. It is less intense, and the rapture is evanescent; I understand music too ill for music to transport me far into the world of pure aesthetic ecstasy. But at moments I do appreciate music as pure musical form, as sounds combined according to the laws of a mysterious necessity, as pure art with a tremendous significance of its own and no relation whatever to the significance of life; and in those moments I lose myself in that infinitely sublime state of mind to which pure visual form transports me. How inferior is my normal state of mind at a concert. Tired or perplexed, I let slip my sense of form, my aesthetic emotion collapses, and I begin weaving into the harmonies, that I cannot grasp, the ideas of life. Incapable of feeling the austere emotions of art, I begin to read into the musical forms human emotions of terror and mystery, love and hate, and spend the minutes, pleasantly enough, in a world of turbid and inferior feeling. At such times, were the grossest pieces of onomatopoeic representation – the song of a bird, the galloping of horses, the cries of children, or the laughing of demons – to be introduced into the symphony, I should not be offended. Very likely I should be pleased; they would afford new points of departure for new trains of romantic feeling or heroic thought. I know very well what has happened. I have been using art as a means to the emotions of life and reading into it the ideas of life. I have been cutting blocks with a razor. I have tumbled from the superb peaks of aesthetic exaltation to the snug foothills of warm humanity. It is a jolly country. No one need be ashamed of enjoying himself there. Only no one who has ever been on the heights can help feeling a little crestfallen in the cosy valleys. And let no one imagine, because he has made merry in the warm tilth and quaint nooks of romance, that he can even guess at the austere and thrilling raptures of those who have climbed the cold, white peaks of art.

About music most people are as willing to be humble as I am. If they cannot grasp musical form and win from it a pure aesthetic emotion, they confess that they understand music imperfectly or not at all. They recognise quite clearly that there is a difference between the feeling of the musician for pure music and that of the cheerful concert-goer for what music suggests. The latter enjoys his own emotions, as he has every right to do, and recognises their inferiority. Unfortunately, people are apt to be less modest about their powers of appreciating visual art. Everyone is inclined to believe that out of pictures, at any rate, he can get all that there is to be got; everyone is ready to cry "humbug" and "impostor" at those who say that more can be had. The good faith of people who feel pure aesthetic emotions is called in question by those who have never felt anything of the sort. It is the prevalence of the representative element, I suppose, that makes the man in the street so sure that he knows a good picture when he sees one. For I have noticed that in matters of architecture, pottery, textiles, &c., ignorance and ineptitude are more willing to defer to the opinions of those who have been blest with peculiar sensibility. It is a pity that cultivated and intelligent men and women cannot be induced to believe that a great gift of aesthetic appreciation is at least as rare in visual as in musical art. A comparison of my own experience in both has enabled me to discriminate very clearly between pure and impure appreciation. Is it too much to ask that others should be as honest about their feelings for pictures as I have been about mine for music? For I am certain that most of those who visit galleries do feel very much what I feel at concerts. They have their moments of pure ecstasy; but the moments are short and unsure. Soon they fall back into the world of human interests and feel emotions, good no doubt, but inferior. I do not dream of saying that what they get from art is bad or nugatory; I say that they do not get the best that art can give.

I do not say that they cannot understand art; rather I say that they cannot understand the state of mind of those who understand it best. I do not say that art means nothing or little to them; I say they miss its full significance. I do not suggest for one moment that their appreciation of art is a thing to be ashamed of; the majority of the charming and intelligent people with whom I am acquainted appreciate visual art impurely; and, by the way, the appreciation of almost all great writers has been impure. But provided that there be some fraction of pure aesthetic emotion, even a mixed and minor appreciation of art is, I am sure, one of the most valuable things in the world – so valuable, indeed, that in my giddier moments I have been tempted to believe that art might prove the world's salvation.

Yet, though the echoes and shadows of art enrich the life of the plains, her spirit dwells on the mountains. To him who woos, but woos impurely, she returns enriched what is brought. Like the sun, she warms the good seed in good soil and causes it to bring forth good fruit. But only to the perfect lover does she give a new strange gift – a gift beyond all price. Imperfect lovers bring to art and take away the ideas and emotions of their own age and civilisation. In twelfth-century Europe a man might have been greatly moved by a Romanesque church and found nothing in a T'ang picture. To a man of a later age, Greek sculpture meant much and Mexican nothing, for only to the former could he bring a crowd of associated ideas to be the objects of familiar emotions. But the perfect lover, he who can feel the profound significance of form, is raised above the accidents of time and place. To him the problems of archaeology, history, and hagiography are impertinent. If the forms of a work are significant its provenance is irrelevant. Before the grandeur of those Sumerian figures in the Louvre he is carried on the same flood of emotion to the same aesthetic ecstasy as, more than four thousand years ago, the Chaldean lover was carried. It is the mark of great art that its appeal is universal and eternal. Significant form stands charged with the power to provoke aesthetic emotion in anyone capable of feeling it. The ideas of men go buzz and die like gnats; men change their institutions and their customs as they change their coats; the intellectual triumphs of one age are the follies of another; only great art remains stable and unobscure. Great art remains stable and unobscure because the feelings that it awakens are independent of time and place, because its kingdom is not of this world. To those who have and hold a sense of the significance of form what does it matter whether the forms that move them were created in Paris the day before yesterday or in Babylon fifty centuries ago? The forms of art are inexhaustible; but all lead by the same road of aesthetic emotion to the same world of aesthetic ecstasy.

25

Aesthetics

Benedetto Croce

Benedetto Croce (1866–1952) was an Italian philosopher and historian who viewed all art as an expression of emotion that generates understanding.

If we examine a poem in order to determine what it is that makes us feel it to be a poem, we at once find two constant and necessary elements: a complex of *images*, and a *feeling* that animates them. Let us, for instance, recall a passage learnt at school: Virgil's lines (Aeneid, iii, 294, sqq.), in which Aeneas describes how on hearing that in the country to whose shores he had come the Trojan Helenus was reigning, with Andromache, now his wife, he was overcome with amazement and a great desire to see this surviving son of Priam and to hear of his strange adventures. Andromache, whom he meets outside the walls of the city, by the waters of a river renamed Simois, celebrating funeral rites before a cenotaph of green turf and two altars to Hector and Astyanax; her astonishment on seeing him, her hesitation, the halting words in which she questions him, uncertain whether he is a man or a ghost; Aeneas's no less agitated replies and interrogations, and the pain and confusion with which she recalls the past – how she lived through scenes of blood and shame, how she was assigned by lot as slave and concubine to Pyrrhus, abandoned by him and united to Helenus, another of his slaves, how Pyrrhus fell by the hand of Orestes and Helenus became a free man and a king; the entry of Aeneas and his men into the city, and their reception by the son of Priam in this little Troy, this mimic Pergamon with its new Xanthus, and its Scaean Gate whose threshold Aeneas greets with a kiss – all these details, and others here omitted, are images of persons, things, attitudes, gestures, sayings, joy and sorrow; mere images, not history or historical criticism, for which they are neither given nor taken. But through them all there runs a feeling, a feeling which is our own no less than the poet's, a human feeling of bitter memories, of shuddering horror, of melancholy, of homesickness, of tenderness, of a kind of childish *pietas* that could prompt this vain revival of things perished, these playthings fashioned by a religious devotion, the *parva Troia*, the *Pergama simulata magnis*, the *arentem Xanthi cognomine rivum*: something inexpressible in logical terms, which only poetry can express in full. Moreover, these two elements may appear as two in a first abstract analysis, but they cannot be regarded as two distinct threads, however intertwined; for, in effect, the feeling is altogether converted into images, into this complex of images, and is thus a feeling that is contemplated and therefore resolved and transcended. Hence poetry must be called neither feeling, nor image, nor yet the sum

Benedetto Croce, "Aesthetics," in *Encyclopaedia Britannica*, 14th edition. (Chicago: Encyclopaedia Britannica, 1938), pp. 263–9.

of the two, but "contemplation of feeling" or "lyrical intuition" or (which is the same thing) "pure intuition" – pure, that is, of all historical and critical reference to the reality or unreality of the images of which it is woven, and apprehending the pure throb of life in its ideality. Doubtless, other things may be found in poetry besides these two elements or moments and the synthesis of the two; but these other things are either present as extraneous elements in a compound (reflections, exhortations, polemics, allegories, etc.), or else they are just these image-feelings themselves taken in abstraction from their context as so much material, restored to the condition in which it was before the act of poetic creation. In the former case, they are non-poetic elements merely interpolated into or attached to the poem; in the latter, they are divested of poetry, rendered unpoetical by a reader either unpoetical or not at the moment poetical, who has dispelled the poetry, either because he cannot live in its ideal realm, or for the legitimate ends of historical enquiry or other practical purposes which involve the degradation – or rather, the conversion – of the poem into a document or an instrument.

ARTISTIC QUALITIES. – What has been said of "poetry" applies to all the other "arts" commonly enumerated; painting, sculpture, architecture, music. Whenever the artistic quality of any product of the mind is discussed, the dilemma must be faced, that either it is a lyrical intuition, or it is something else, something just as respectable, but not art. If painting (as some theorists have maintained) were the imitation or reproduction of a given object, it would be, not art, but something mechanical and practical; if the task of the painter (as other theorists have held) were to combine lines and lights and colours with ingenious novelty of invention and effect, he would be, not an artist, but an inventor; if music consisted in similar combinations of notes, the paradox of Leibniz and Father Kircher would come true, and a man could write music without being a musician; or alternatively we should have to fear (as Proudhon did for poetry and John Stuart Mill for music) that the possible combinations of words or notes would one day be exhausted, and poetry or music would disappear. As in poetry, so in these others acts, it is notorious that foreign elements sometimes intrude themselves; foreign either *a parte objecti* or *a parte subjecti*, foreign either in fact or from the point of view of an inartistic spectator or listener. Thus the critics of these arts advise the artist to exclude, or at least not to rely upon, what they call the "literary" elements in painting, sculpture and music, just as the critic of poetry advises the writer to look for "poetry" and not be led astray by mere literature. The reader who understands poetry goes straight to this poetic heart and feels its beat upon his own; where this beat is silent, he denies that poetry is present, whatever and however many other things may take its place, united in the work, and however valuable they may be for skill and wisdom, nobility of intellect, quickness of wit and pleasantness of effect. The reader who does not understand poetry loses his way in pursuit of these other things. He is wrong not because he admires them, but because he thinks he is admiring poetry.

OTHER FORMS OF ACTIVITY AS DISTINCT FROM ART. – By defining art as lyrical or pure intuition we have implicitly distinguished it from all other forms of mental production. If such distinctions are made explicit, we obtain the following negations:

1. *Art is not philosophy*, because philosophy is the logical thinking of the universal categories of being, and art is the unreflective intuition of being. Hence, while philosophy transcends the image and uses it for its own purposes, art lives in it as in a kingdom. It is said that art cannot behave in an irrational manner and cannot ignore logic; and certainly it is neither irrational nor illogical; but its own rationality, its own logic, is a quite different thing from the dialectical logic of the concept, and it was in order to indicate this peculiar and unique character that the name "logic of sense" or "aesthetic" was invented. The not uncommon assertion that art has a logical character, involves either an equivocation between conceptual logic and aesthetic logic, or a symbolic expression of the latter in terms of the former.

2. *Art is not history*, because history implies the critical distinction between reality and unreality; the reality of the passing moment and the reality of a fancied world: the reality of fact and the reality of desire. For art, these distinctions are as yet unmade; it lives, as we have said, upon

pure images. The historical existence of Helenus, Andromache and Aeneas makes no difference to the poetical quality of Virgil's poem. Here, too, an objection has been raised: namely that art is not wholly indifferent to historical criteria, because it obeys the laws of "verisimilitude"; but, here again, "verisimilitude" is only a rather clumsy metaphor for the mutual coherence of images, which without this internal coherence would fail to produce their effect as images, like Horace's *delphinus in silvis* and *aper in fluctibus.*

3. *Art is not natural science,* because natural science is historical fact classified and so made abstract; nor is it *mathematical science,* because mathematics performs operations with abstractions and does not contemplate. The analogy sometimes drawn between mathematical and poetical creation is based on merely external and generic resemblances; and the alleged necessity of a mathematical or geometrical basis for the arts is only another metaphor, a symbolic expression of the constructive, cohesive and unifying force of the poetic mind building itself a body of images.

4. *Art is not the play of fancy,* because the play of fancy passes from image to image, in search of variety, rest or diversion, seeking to amuse itself with the likenesses of things that give pleasure or have an emotional and pathetic interest; whereas in art the fancy is so dominated by the single problem of converting chaotic feeling into clear intuition, that we recognize the propriety of ceasing to call it fancy and calling it imagination, poetic imagination or creative imagination. Fancy as such is as far removed from poetry as are the works of Mrs. Radcliffe or Dumas *père.*

5. *Art is not feeling in its immediacy.* – Andromache, on seeing Aeneas, becomes *amens, diriguit visu in medio, labitur, longo vix tempore fatur,* and when she speaks *longos cietbat incassum fletus;* but the poet does not lose his wits or grow stiff as he gazes; he does not totter or weep or cry; he expresses himself in harmonious verses, having made these various perturbations the object of which he sings. Feelings in their immediacy are "expressed" for if they were not, if they were not also sensible and bodily facts ("psycho-physical phenomena," as the positivists used to call them) they would not be concrete things, and so they would be nothing at all. Andromache expressed herself in the way described above. But "expression" in this sense, even when accompanied by consciousness, is a mere metaphor from "mental" or "aesthetic expression" which alone really expresses, that is, gives to feeling a theoretical form and converts it into words, song and outward shape. This distinction between contemplated feeling or poetry, and feeling enacted or endured, is the source of the power, ascribed to art, of "liberating us from the passions" and "calming" us (the power of *catharsis*), and of the consequent condemnation, from an aesthetic point of view, of works of art, or parts of them, in which immediate feeling has a place or finds a vent. Hence, too, arises another characteristic of poetic expression – really synonymous with the last – namely its "infinity" as opposed to the "finitude" of immediate feeling or passion; or, as it is also called, the "universal" or "cosmic" character of poetry. Feeling, not crushed but contemplated by the work of poetry, is seen to diffuse itself in widening circles over all the realm of the soul, which is the realm of the universe, echoing and re-echoing endlessly: joy and sorrow, pleasure and pain, energy and lassitude, earnestness and frivolity, and so forth, are linked to each other and lead to each other through infinite shades and gradations; so that the feeling, while preserving its individual physiognomy and its original dominating motive, is not exhausted by or restricted to this original character. A comic image, if it is poetically comic, carries with it something that is not comic, as in the case of Don Quixote or Falstaff; and the image of something terrible is never, in poetry, without an atoning element of loftiness, goodness and love.

6. *Art is not instruction or oratory:* it is not circumscribed and limited by service to any practical purpose whatever, whether this be the inculcation of a particular philosophical, historical or scientific truth, or the advocacy of a particular way of feeling and the action corresponding to it. Oratory at once robs expression of its "infinity" and independence, and, by making it the means to an end, dissolves it in this end. Hence arises what Schiller called the "non-determining" character of art, as opposed to the "determining" character of oratory; and hence the justifiable suspicion of "political poetry" – political poetry being, proverbially, bad poetry.

7. As art is not to be confused with the form of practical action most akin to it, namely instruction and oratory, so *a fortiori,* it must not be

confused with other forms directed to the production of certain effects, whether these consist in pleasure, enjoyment and utility, or in goodness and righteousness. We must exclude from art not only meretricious works, but also those inspired by a desire for goodness, as equally, though differently, inartistic and repugnant to lovers of poetry. Flaubert's remark that indecent books lacked *vérité*, is parallel to Voltaire's gibe that certain "poésies sacrées" were really "sacrées, car personne n'y touche."

ART IN ITS RELATIONS. – The "negations" here made explicit are obviously, from another point of view, "relations"; for the various distinct forms of mental activity cannot be conceived as separate each from the rest and acting in self-supporting isolation. This is not the place to set forth a complete system of the forms or categories of the mind in their order and their dialectic; confining ourselves to art, we must be content to say that the category of art, like every other category, mutually presupposes and is presupposed by all the rest: it is conditioned by them all and conditions them all. How could the aesthetic synthesis, which is poetry, arise, were it not preceded by a state of mental commotion? *Si vis me flere, dolendum est*, and so forth. And what is this state of mind which we have called feeling, but the whole mind, with its past thoughts, volitions and actions, now thinking and desiring and suffering and rejoicing, travailing within itself? Poetry is like a ray of sunlight shining upon this darkness, lending it its own light and making visible the hidden forms of things. Hence it cannot be produced by an empty and dull mind; hence those artists who embrace the creed of pure art or art for art's sake, and close their hearts to the troubles of life and the cares of thought, are found to be wholly unproductive, or at most rise to the imitation of others or to an impressionism devoid of concentration. Hence the basis of all poetry is human personality, and, since human personality finds its completion in morality, the basis of all poetry is the moral consciousness. Of course this does not mean that the artist must be a profound thinker or an acute critic; nor that he must be a pattern of virtue or a hero; but he must have a share in the world of thought and action which will enable him, either in his own person or by sympathy with others, to live the whole drama of human life. He may sin, lose the purity of his heart, and expose himself, as a practical agent, to blame; but he must have a keen sense of purity and impurity, righteousness and sin, good and evil. He may not be endowed with great practical courage; he may even betray signs of timidity and cowardice; but he must feel the dignity of courage. Many artistic inspirations are due, not to what the artist, as a man, is in practice, but to what he is not, and feels that he ought to be admiring and enjoying the qualities he lacks when he sees them in others. Many, perhaps the finest, pages of heroic and warlike poetry are by men who never had the nerve or the skill to handle a weapon. On the other hand, we are not maintaining that the possession of a moral personality is enough to make a poet or an artist. To be a *vir bonus* does not make a man even an orator, unless he is also *dicendi peritus*. The *sine qua non* of poetry is poetry, that form of theoretical synthesis which we have defined above; the spark of poetical genius without which all the rest is mere fuel, not burning because no fire is at hand to light it. But the figure of the pure poet, the pure artist, the votary of pure Beauty, aloof from contact with humanity, is no real figure but a caricature.

That poetry not only presupposes the other forms of human mental activity but is presupposed by them, is proved by the fact that without the poetic imagination which gives contemplative form to the workings of feeling, intuitive expression to obscure impressions, and thus becomes representations and works, whether spoken or sung or painted or otherwise uttered, logical thought could not arise. Logical thought is not language, but it never exists without language, and it uses the language which poetry has created; by means of concepts, it discerns and dominates the representations of poetry, and it could not dominate them unless they, its future subjects, had first an existence of their own. Further, without the discerning and criticizing activity of thought, action would be impossible; and if action, then good action, the moral consciousness, duty. Every man, however much he may seem to be all logical thinker, critic, scientist, or all absorbed in practical interests or devoted to duty, cherishes at the bottom of his heart his own private store of imagination and poetry; even Faust's pedantic *famulus*, Wagner, confessed that he often had his "grillenhafte Stunden." Had this element been altogether denied him, he would not have been a man, and therefore not even a thinking or acting being. This extreme case is an absurdity; but in proportion as this private store is scanty, we find a certain superficiality and aridity in thought, and a certain coldness in action.

THE SCIENCE OF ART, OR AESTHETICS, AND ITS PHILOSOPHICAL CHARACTER. – The concept of art expounded above is in a sense the ordinary concept, which appears with greater or less clarity in all statements about art, and is constantly appealed to, explicitly or implicitly, as the fixed point round which all discussions on the subject gravitate: and this, not only nowadays, but at all times, as could be shown by the collection and interpretation of things said by writers, poets, artists, laymen and even the common people. But it is desirable to dispel the illusion that this concept exists as an innate idea, and to replace this by the truth, that it operates as an *a priori* concept. Now an *a priori* concept does not exist by itself, but only in the individual products which it generates. Just as the *a priori* reality called Art, Poetry or Beauty does not exist in a transcendent region where it can be perceived and admired in itself, but only in the innumerable works of poetry, of art and of beauty which it has formed and continues to form, so the logical *a priori* concept of art exists nowhere but in the particular judgments which it has formed and continues to form, the refutations which it has effected and continues to effect, the demonstrations it makes, the theories it constructs, the problems and groups of problems, which it solves and has solved. The definitions and distinctions and negations and relations expounded above have each its own history, and have been progressively worked out in the course of centuries, and in them we now possess the fruits of this complex and unremitting toil. Aesthetic, or the science of art, has not therefore the task (attributed to it by certain scholastic conceptions) of defining art once for all and deducing from this conception its various doctrines, so as to cover the whole field of aesthetic science; it is only the perpetual systematization, always renewed and always growing, of the problems arising from time to time out of reflection upon art, and is identical with the solutions of the difficulties and the criticisms of the errors which act as stimulus and material to the unceasing progress of thought. This being so, no exposition of aesthetic (especially a summary exposition such as can alone be given here) can claim to deal exhaustively with the innumerable problems which have arisen and may arise in the course of the history of aesthetics; it can only mention and discuss the chief, and among these, by preference, those which still make themselves felt and resist solution in ordinary educated thought; adding an implied "et cetera," so that the reader may pursue the subject according to the criteria set before him, either by going again over old discussions, or by entering into those of to-day, which change and multiply and assume new shapes almost daily. Another warning must not be omitted: namely that aesthetics, though a special philosophical science, having as its principle a special and distinct category of the mind, can never, just because it is philosophical, be detached from the main body of philosophy; for its problems are concerned with the relations between art and the other mental forms, and therefore imply both difference and identity: Aesthetics is really the whole of philosophy, but with special emphasis on that side of it which concerns art. Many have demanded or imagined or desired a self-contained aesthetics, devoid of any general philosophical implications, and consistent with more than one, or with any, philosophy; but the project is impossible of execution because self-contradictory. Even those who promise to expound a naturalistic, inductive, physical, physiological or psychological aesthetics – in a word, a non-philosophical aesthetics – when they pass from promise to performance surreptitiously introduce a general positivistic, naturalistic or even materialistic philosophy. And anyone who thinks that the philosophical ideas of positivism, naturalism and materialism are false and out of date, will find it an easy matter to refute he aesthetic or pseudo-aesthetic doctrines which mutually support them and are supported by them, and will not regard their problems as problems still awaiting solution or worthy of discussion – or, at least, protracted discussion. For instance, the downfall of psychological associationism (or the substitution of mechanism for *a priori* synthesis) implies the downfall not only of logical associationism but of aesthetics also, with its association of "content" and "form," or of two "representations," which (unlike Campanella's *tactus intrinsecus*, effected *cum magna suavitate*) was a *contactus extrinsecus* whose terms were no sooner united than they *discedebant*. The collapse of biological and evolutionary explanations of logical and ethical values implies the same collapse in the case of aesthetic value. The proved inability of empirical methods to yield knowledge of reality, which in fact they can only classify and reduce to types, involves the impossibility of an aesthetics arrived at by collecting aesthetic facts in classes and discovering their laws by induction.

INTUITION AND EXPRESSION. – One of the first problems to arise, when the work of art is defined as "lyrical image," concerns the relation of "intuition" to "expression" and the manner of the transition from the one to the other. At bottom this is the same problem which arises in other parts of philosophy: the problem of inner and outer, of mind and matter, of soul and body, and, in ethics, of intention and will, will and action, and so forth. Thus stated, the problem *is* insoluble; for once we have divided the inner from the outer, body from mind, will from action, or intuition from expression, there is no way of passing from one to the other or of reuniting them, unless we appeal for their reunion to a third term, variously represented as God or the Unknowable. Dualism leads necessarily either to transcendence or to agnosticism. But when a problem is found to be insoluble in the terms in which it is stated the only course open is to criticize these terms themselves, to inquire how they have been arrived at, and whether their genesis was logically sound. In this case, such inquiry leads to the conclusion that the terms depend not upon a philosophical principle, but upon an empirical and naturalistic classification, which has created two groups of facts called internal and external respectively (as if internal facts were not also external, and as if an external fact could exist without being also internal), or souls and bodies, or images and expressions; and everyone knows that it is hopeless to try to find a dialectical unity between terms that have been distinguished not philosophically or formally but only empirically and materially. The soul is only a soul in so far as it is a body; the will is only a will in so far as it moves arms and legs, or is action; intuition is only intuition in so far as it is, in that very act, expression. An image that does not express, that is not speech, song, drawing, painting, sculpture or architecture – speech at least murmured to oneself, song at least echoing within one's own breast, line and colour seen in imagination and colouring with its own tint the whole soul and organism – is an image that does not exist. We may assert its existence, but we cannot support our assertion; for the only thing we could adduce in support of it would be the fact that the image was embodied or expressed. This profound philosophical doctrine, the *identity of intuition and expression* is, moreover, a principle of ordinary common sense, which laughs at people who claim to have thoughts they cannot express or to have imagined a great picture which they cannot paint. *Rem tene, verba sequentur*; if there are no *verba*, there is no *res*. This identity, which applies to every sphere of the mind, has in the sphere of art a clearness and self-evidence lacking, perhaps, elsewhere. In the creation of a work of poetry, we are present, as it were, at the mystery of the creation of the world; hence the value of the contribution made by aesthetics to philosophy as a whole, or the conception of the One that is All. Aesthetics, by denying in the life of art an abstract spiritualism and the resulting dualism, prepares the way and leads the mind towards idealism or absolute spiritualism.

EXPRESSION AND COMMUNICATION. – Objections to the identity of intuition and expression generally arise from psychological illusions which lead us to believe that we possess at any given moment a profusion of concrete and lively images, when in fact we only possess signs and names for them; or else from faulty analysis of cases like that of the artist who is believed to express mere fragments of a world of images that exists in his mind in its entirety, whereas he really has in his mind only these fragments, together with – not the supposed complete world, but at most an aspiration or obscure working towards it, towards a greater and richer image which may take shape or may not. But these objections also arise from a confusion between *expression* and *communication*, the latter being really distinct from the image and its expression. Communication is the fixation of the intuition-expression upon an object metaphorically called material or physical; in reality, even here we are concerned not with material or physical things but with a mental process. The proof that the so-called physical object is unreal, and its resolution into terms of mind, is primarily of interest for our general philosophical conceptions, and only indirectly for the elucidation of aesthetic questions; hence for brevity's sake we may let the metaphor or symbol stand and speak of matter or nature. It is clear that the poem is complete as soon as the poet has expressed it in words which he repeats to himself. When he comes to repeat them aloud, for others to hear, or looks for someone to learn them by heart and repeat them to others as in *a schola cantorum*, or sets them down in writing or in printing, he has entered upon a new stage, not aesthetic but practical, whose social and cultural importance need not, of course, be insisted upon. So with the painter; he paints on his panel or canvas, but he could not paint unless at every stage in his work, from the original blur or sketch to the finishing touches, the intuited image, the line and colour painted in his imagination, preceded the brush-stroke. Indeed, when the brush-stroke outruns the image, it is cancelled and replaced by the artist's correction of his own work. The exact line that divides expression from communication is difficult to draw in the concrete case, for in the concrete case the two processes generally alternate rapidly and appear to mingle, but it is clear in idea, and it must be firmly grasped. Through overlooking it, or blurring it through insufficient attention, arise the confusions between *art* and *technique*. Technique is not an intrinsic element of art but has to do precisely with the concept of communication. In general it is a cognition or complex of cognitions disposed and directed to the furtherance of practical action; and, in the case of art, of the practical action which makes objects and instruments for the recording and communicating of works of art; *e.g.*, cognitions concerning the preparation of panels, canvases or walls to be painted, pigments, varnishes, ways of obtaining good pronunciation and declamation and so forth. Technical treatises are not aesthetic treatises, nor yet parts or chapters of them. Provided, that is, that the ideas are rigorously conceived and the words used accurately in relation to them it would not be worth while to pick a quarrel over the use of the word "technique" as a synonym for the artistic work itself, regarded as "inner technique" or the formation of intuition-expressions. The confusion between art and technique is especially beloved by impotent artists, who hope to obtain from practical things and practical devices and inventions the help which their strength does not enable them to give themselves.

ARTISTIC OBJECTS: THE THEORY OF THE SPECIAL ARTS, AND THE BEAUTY OF NATURE. – The work of communicating and conserving artistic images, with the help of technique, produces the material objects metaphorically called "*artistic objects*" or "*works of art*": pictures, sculptures and buildings, and, in a more complicated manner, literary and musical writings, and, in our own times, gramophones and records which make it possible to reproduce voices and sounds. But neither these voices and sounds nor the symbols of writing, sculpture and architecture, are works of art; works of art exist only in the minds that create or re-create them. To remove the appearance of paradox from the truth that beautiful objects, beautiful things, do not exist, it may be opportune to recall the analogous case of economic science, which knows perfectly well that in the sphere of economics there are no naturally or physically *useful* things, but only demand and labour, from which physical things acquire, metaphorically, this epithet. A student of economics who wished to deduce the economic value of things from their physical qualities would be perpetrating a gross *ignoratio elenchi*.

Yet this same *ignoratio elenchi* has been, and still is, committed in aesthetic, by the theory of special *arts*, and the limits or peculiar aesthetic character of each. The divisions between the arts are merely technical or physical, according as the artistic objects consist of physical sounds, notes, coloured objects, carved or modelled objects, or constructed objects having no apparent correspondence with natural bodies (poetry, music, painting, sculpture, architecture, etc.). To ask what is the artistic character of each of these arts, what it can and cannot do, what kinds of images can be expressed in sounds, what in notes, what in colours, what in lines, and so forth, is like asking in economics what things are entitled by their physical qualities to have a value and what are not, and what relative values they are entitled to have; whereas it is clear that physical qualities do not enter into the question, and anything may be desired or demanded or valued more than another, or more than anything else at all, according to circumstances and needs. Even Lessing found himself slipping down the slope leading to this truth, and was forced to such strange conclusions as that actions belonged to poetry and bodies to sculpture; even Richard Wagner attempted to find a place in the list for a comprehensive art, namely Opera, including in itself by a process of aggregation the powers of all the arts. A reader with any artistic sense finds in a single solitary line from a poet at once musical and picturesque qualities, sculpturesque strength and architectural structure; and the same with a picture, which is never a mere thing of the eyes but an affair of the whole soul, and exists in the soul not only as colour but as sound and speech. But when we try to grasp these musical or picturesque or other qualities, they elude us and turn into each other, and melt into a unity, however we may be accustomed to distinguish them by different names; a practical proof that art is one and cannot be divided into arts. One, and infinitely varied; not according to the technical conceptions of the several arts, but according to the infinite variety of artistic personalities and their states of mind.

With this relation (and confusion) between artistic creations and instruments of communication or *objets d'art* must be connected the problem of *natural beauty*. We shall not discuss the question, raised by certain aestheticians, whether there are in nature other poets, other artistic beings, beside man; a question which ought to be answered in the affirmative not only out of respect for the song-birds, but, still more, out of respect for the idealistic conception of the world as life and spirituality throughout; even if (as the fairy-tale goes) we have lost the magic herb which when we put it in our mouth, gives us the power of understanding the language of animals and plants. The phrase *natural beauty* properly refers to persons, things and places whose effect is comparable to that of poetry, painting, sculpture and the other arts. There is no difficulty in allowing the existence of such "natural *objets d'art*," for the process of poetic communication may take place by means of objects naturally given as well as by means of objects artificially produced. The lover's imagination creates a woman beautiful to him, and personifies her in Laura; the pilgrim's imagination creates the charming or sublime landscape, and embodies it in the scene of a lake or a mountain; and these creations of theirs are sometimes shared by more or less wide social circles, thus becoming the "professional beauties" admired by everyone and the famous "views" before which all experience a more or less sincere rapture. No doubt, these creations are mortal; ridicule sometimes kills them, satiety may bring neglect, fashion may replace them by others; and – unlike works of art – they do not admit of authentic interpretation. The bay of Naples, seen from the height of one of the most beautiful Neapolitan villas, was after some time described by the Russian lady who owned the villa as *une cuvette bleue*, whose blue encircled by green so wearied her that she sold the villa. But even the *cuvette bleue* was a legitimate poetical creation.

LITERARY KINDS AND AESTHETIC CATEGORIES. – Effects at once greater and more detrimental upon the criticism and historical study of art and literature have been produced by a theory of similar but slightly different origin, the theory of *literacy and artistic kinds*. This, like the foregoing, is based on a classification in itself justifiable and useful. The foregoing is based on a technical or physical classification of artistic objects; this is based on a classification according to the feelings which form their content or motive, into *tragic*, *comic*, *lyrical*, *heroic*, *erotic*, *idyllic*, *romantic* and so on, with divisions and subdivisions. It is useful in practice to distribute an artist's works, for purposes of publication, into these classes, putting lyrics in one volume, dramas in another, poems in a third and romances in a fourth; and it is convenient, in fact, indispensable, to refer to works and groups of works by these names in speaking and writing of them. But here again we must deny and pronounce illegitimate the transition from these classificatory concepts to the poetic laws of composition and aesthetic criteria of judgment, as when people try to decide that a tragedy must have a subject of a certain kind, characters of a certain kind, a plot of a certain kind and a certain length; and, when confronted by a work, instead of looking for and appraising its own poetry, ask whether it is a tragedy or a poem, and whether it obeys the "laws" of one or other "kind." The literary criticism of the 19th century owed its great progress largely to its abandonment of the criteria of kinds, in which the criticism of the Renaissance and the French classicists had always been entangled, as may be seen from the discussions arising out of the poems of Dante, Ariosto and Tasso, Guarini's *Pastor fido*, Corneille's *Cid*, and Lope de Vega's *comedias*. Artists have profited by this liberation less than critics; for anyone with artistic genius bursts the fetters of such servitude, or even makes them the instruments of his power; and the artist with little or no genius turns his very freedom into a new slavery.

It has been thought that the divisions of kinds could be saved by giving them a philosophical significance; or at any rate one such division, that of lyric, epic and dramatic, regarded as the three moments of a process of objectification passing from the lyric, the outpouring of the ego, to the epic, in which the ego detaches its feeling from itself by narrating it, and thence to the drama, in which it allows this feeling to create of itself its own mouthpieces, the *dramatis personae*. But the lyric is not a pouring-forth; it is not a cry or a lament; it is an objectification in which the ego sees itself on the stage, narrates itself, and dramatizes itself; and this lyrical spirit forms the poetry both of epic and of drama, which are therefore distinguished from the lyric only by external signs. A work which is altogether poetry, like *Macbeth* or *Antony and Cleopatra*, is substantially a lyric in which the various tones and successive verses are represented by characters and scenes.

In the old aesthetics, and even to-day in those which perpetuate the type, an important place is given to the so-called categories of beauty: the *sublime*, the *tragic*, the *comic*, the *graceful*, the *humorous* and so forth, which German philosophers not only claimed to treat as philosophical concepts, whereas they are really mere psychological and empirical concepts, but developed by means of that dialectic which belongs only to pure or speculative concepts, philosophical categories. Thus they arranged them in an imaginary progress culminating now in the Beautiful, now in the Tragic, now in the Humorous. Taking these concepts at their face value, we may observe their substantial correspondence with the concepts of the literary and artistic kinds; and this is the source from which, as excerpts from manuals of literature, they have found their way into philosophy. As psychological and empirical concepts, they do not belong to aesthetics; and as a whole, in their common quality, they refer merely to the world of feelings, empirically grouped and classified, which forms the permanent matter of artistic intuition.

RHETORIC, GRAMMAR AND PHILOSOPHY OF LANGUAGE. – Every error has in it an element of truth, and arises from an arbitrary combination of things which in themselves are legitimate. This principle may be confirmed by an examination of other erroneous doctrines which have been prominent in the past and are still to a less degree prominent to-day. It is perfectly legitimate, in teaching people to write, to make use of distinctions like that between simple style, ornate style and metaphorical style and its forms, and to point out that here the pupil ought to express himself literally and there metaphorically, or that here the metaphor used is incoherent or drawn out to excessive length, and that here the figure of "preterition," there "hypotyposis" or "irony," would have been suitable. But when people lose sight of the merely practical and didactic origin of these distinctions and construct a philosophical theory of form as divisible into simple form and ornate form, logical form and affective form, and so forth, they are introducing elements of rhetoric into aesthetics and vitiating the true concept of expression. For expression is never logical, but always affective, that is, lyrical and imaginative; and hence it is never metaphorical but always "proper"; it is never simple in the sense of lacking elaboration, or ornate in the sense of being loaded with extraneous elements; it is always adorned with itself, *simplex munditiis*. Even logical thought or science, so far as it is expressed, becomes feeling and imagination, which is why a philosophical or historical or scientific book can be not only true but beautiful, and must always be judged not only logically but also aesthetically. Thus we sometimes say that a book is a failure as theory, or criticism, or historical truth, but a success as a work of art, in view of the feeling animating it and expressed in it. As for the element of truth which is obscurely at work in this distinction between logical form and metaphorical form, dialectic and rhetoric, we may detect in it the need of a science of aesthetics side by side with that of logic; but it was a mistake to try to distinguish the two sciences within the sphere of expression which belongs to one of them alone.

Another element in education, namely the teaching of languages, has no less legitimately, ever since ancient times, classified expressions into periods, propositions and words, and words into various species, and each species according to the variations and combinations of roots and suffixes, syllables and letters; and hence have arisen alphabets, grammars and vocabularies, just as in another way for poetry has arisen a science of prosody, and for music and the figurative and architectural arts there have arisen musical and pictorial grammars and so forth. But here, too, the ancients did not succeed in avoiding an illegitimate transition *ab intellectu ad rem*, from abstractions to reality, from the empirical to the philosophical, such as we have already observed elsewhere; and this involved thinking of speech as an aggregation of words, and words as aggregations of syllables or of roots and suffixes; whereas the *prius* is speech itself, a continuum, resembling an organism, and words and syllables and roots are a *posterius*, an anatomical preparation, the product of the abstracting intellect, not the original or real fact. If grammar, like the rhetoric in the case above considered, is transplanted into aesthetic, the result is a distinction between expression and the means of expression, which is a mere reduplication; for the means of expression are just expression itself, broken into pieces by grammarians. This error, combined with the error of distinguishing between simple and ornate form, has prevented people from seeing that the philosophy of language is not a philosophical grammar, but is wholly devoid of grammatical elements. It does not raise grammatical classifications to a philosophical level; it ignores them, and, when they get in its way, destroys them. The philosophy of language, in a word, is identical with the philosophy of poetry and art, the science of intuition-expression, aesthetics; which embraces language in its whole extension, passing beyond the limits of phonetic and syllabic language, and in its unimpaired reality as living and completely significant expression.

CLASSICAL AND ROMANTIC. – The problems reviewed above belong to the past – a past extending through centuries – rather than to the present; of their mis-stated questions and misconceived solutions there now remain mere relics and superstitions which affect academic treatises more than they do the consciousness and culture of ordinary people. But it is necessary to watch carefully for new shoots from the old stock, which still appear from time to time, in order to cut them down. Such is, in our own time, the theory of styles applied to the history of art (Wölfflin and others) and extended to the history of poetry (Strick and others), a new irruption of rhetorical abstractions into the judgment and history of works of art. But the chief problem of our time, to be overcome by aesthetics, is connected with the crisis in art and in judgments upon art produced by the romantic period. Not that this crisis was not foreshadowed by precedents and parallels in earlier history, like Alexandrian art and that of the late Roman period, and in modern times the Baroque art and poetry which followed upon that of the Renaissance. The crisis of the romantic period, together with sources and characteristics peculiar to itself, had a magnitude all of its own. It asserted an antithesis between *naïve* and *sentimental* poetry, *classical* and *romantic* art, and thus denied the unity of art and asserted a duality of two fundamentally different arts, of which it took the side of the second, as that appropriate to the modern age, by upholding the primary importance in art of feeling, passion and fancy. In part this was a justifiable reaction against the rationalistic literature of classicism in the French manner, now satirical, now frivolous, weak in feeling and imagination and deficient in a deep poetic sense; but in part, *romanticism* was a rebellion not against *classicism* but against the classical as such: against the idea of the serenity and infinity of the artistic image, against catharsis and in favour of a turbid emotionalism that could not and would not undergo purification. This was very well understood by Goethe, the poet both of passion and of serenity, and therefore, because he was a poet, a classical poet; who opposed romantic poetry as "hospital poetry." Later, it was thought that the disease had run its course and that romanticism was a thing of the past; but though some of its contents and some of its forms were dead, its soul was not: its soul consisting in this tendency on the part of art towards an immediate expression of passions and impressions. Hence it changed its name but went on living and working. It called itself "realism," "verism," "symbolism," "artistic style," "impressionism," "sensualism," "imagism," "decadentism," and nowadays, in its extreme forms, "expressionism" and "futurism." The very conception of art is attacked by these doctrines, which tend to replace it by the conception of one or other kind of non-art; and the statement that they are fighting against art is confirmed by the hatred of the extremists of this movement for museums and libraries and all the art of the past – that is, for the idea of art which on the whole corresponds with art as it has been historically realized. The connection of this movement, in its latest modern form, with industralism and the psychology produced and fostered by industrialism is obvious. What art is contrasted with is practical life as lived to-day; and art, for this movement, is not the expression of life and hence the transcending of life in the contemplation of the infinite and universal, but the cries and gesticulations and broken colours of life itself. The real poets and artists, on the other hand, rare at any time, naturally continue, nowadays as always, to work according to the old and only idea of what art is, expressing their feelings in harmonious forms; and the real connoisseurs (rarer, these also, than people think) continue to judge their work according to this same idea. In spite of this, the tendency to destroy the idea of art is a characteristic of our age; and this tendency is based on the *proton pseudos* which confuses mental or aesthetic expression with natural or practical expression – the expression which passes confusedly from sensation to sensation and is a mere effect of sensation, with the expression which art elaborates, as it builds, draws, colours or models, and which is its beautiful creation. The problem for aesthetics to-day is the reassertion and defence of the classical as against romanticism: the synthetic, formal theoretical element which is the *proprium* of art, as against the affective element which it is the business of art to resolve into itself, but which to-day has turned against it and threatens to displace it. Against the inexhaustible fertility of creative mind, the gates of hell shall not prevail; but the hostility which endeavours to make them prevail is disturbing, even if only in an incidental manner, the artistic taste, the artistic life and consequently the intellectual and moral life of to-day.

THE CRITICISM AND HISTORY OF ART AND LITERATURE. – Another group of questions raised in works on aesthetics, though not unsuitable to such works, properly belongs to logic and the theory of historical thought. These concern the aesthetic judgment and the history of poetry and the arts. By showing that the aesthetic activity (or art) is one of the forms of mind, a value, a category, or whatever we choose to call it, and not (as philosophers of various schools have thought) an empirical concept referable to certain orders of utilitarian or mixed facts, by establishing the *autonomy of aesthetic value*, aesthetics has also shown that it is the predicate of a special judgment, the *aesthetic judgment*, and the subject-matter of history, of a special history, the history of poetry and the arts, *artistic and literary history*.

The questions that have been raised concerning the aesthetic judgment and artistic and literary history are making allowance for the peculiar character of art, identical with the methodological questions that arise in every field of historical study. It has been asked whether the aesthetic judgment is *absolute* or *relative*; but every historical judgment (and the aesthetic judgment affirming the reality and quality of aesthetic facts is an historical judgment) is always both absolute and relative at once: absolute, in so far as the category involved in the construction possesses universal truth; relative, in so far as the object constructed by that category is historically conditioned: hence in the historical judgment the category is individualized and the individual becomes absolute. Those who in the past have denied the absoluteness of the aesthetic judgment (sensationalistic, hedonistic or utilitarian aestheticians) denied in effect the quality, reality and autonomy of art. It has been asked whether a knowledge of the history of the time – the whole history of the time in question – is necessary for the aesthetic judgment of the art of that time; it certainly is, because, as we know, poetic creation presupposes all the rest of the mind which it is converting into lyrical imagery, and the one aesthetic creation presupposes all the other creations (passions, feelings, customs, etc.) of the given historical moment. Hence may be seen the error both of those who advocate a merely historical judgment upon art (historical critics) and of those who advocate a merely aesthetic (aesthetic critics). The former would find in art all the rest of history (social conditions, biography of the artist, etc.), but would omit that part which is proper to art; the latter would judge the work of art in abstraction from history, depriving it of its real meaning and giving it an imaginary meaning or testing it by arbitrary standards. Lastly, there has appeared a kind of scepticism or pessimism as to the possibility of understanding the art of the past; a scepticism or pessimism which in that case ought to extend to every part of history (history of thought, politics, religion and morality), and refutes itself by a *reductio ad absurdum*, since what we call contemporary art and history really belong to the past as much as those of more distant ages, and must, like them, be re-created in the present, in the mind that feels them and the intellect that understands them. There are artistic works and periods that remain to us unintelligible; but this only means that we are not now in a position to enter again into their life and to understand them, and the same is true of the ideas and customs and actions of many peoples and ages. Humanity, like the individual, remembers some things and forgets many others; but it may yet, in the course of its mental development, reach a point where its memory of them revives.

A final question concerns the form proper to artistic and literary history, which, in the form that arose in the romantic period, and still prevails to-day, expounds the history of works of art as a function of the concepts and social needs of its various periods, regarding them as aesthetic expressions of these things and connecting them closely with civil history. This tends to obscure and almost to render invisible the peculiar character of the individual work of art, the character which makes it impossible to confuse one work of art with any other, and results in treating them as documents of social life. In practice no doubt this method is tempered by what may be called the "individualizing" method, which emphasizes the individual character of the works; but the mixture has the defects of all eclecticism. To escape this, there is nothing to do but consistently to develop individualizing history, and to treat works of art not in relation to social history but as each a world in itself, into which from time to time the whole of history is concentrated, transfigured and imaginatively transcended in the individuality of the poetic work, which is a creation, not a reflection, a monument, not a document. Dante is not simply a document of the middle ages, nor Shakespeare of the English Renaissance; as such, they have many equals or superiors among bad poets and non-poets. It has been objected that this method imposed on artistic and literary history the form of a series of disconnected essays or monographs; but, obviously, the connection is provided by human history as a whole, of which the personalities of poets constitute a part, and a somewhat conspicuous part (Shakespearian poetry is an event no less important than the Reformation or the French Revolution), and, precisely because they are a part of it, they ought not to be submerged and lost in it, that is, in its other parts, but ought to retain their proper proportions and their original character.

26

The Principles of Art

R. G. Collingwood

Robin George Collingwood (1889–1943), an Englishman who was a Professor of Philosophy at the University of Oxford as well as a noted historian of Rome, developed provocative views on the nature of art that drew on the work of Benedetto Croce.

Introduction

1. The two conditions of an aesthetic theory

The business of this book is to answer the question: What is art?

A question of this kind has to be answered in two stages. First, we must make sure that the key word (in this case 'art') is a word which we know how to apply where it ought to be applied and refuse where it ought to be refused. It would not be much use beginning to argue about the correct definition of a general term whose instances we could not recognize when we saw them. Our first business, then, is to bring ourselves into a position in which we can say with confidence 'this and this and this are art; that and that and that are not art'. [...]

Secondly, we must proceed to a definition of the term 'art'. This comes second, and not first, because no one can even try to define a term until he has settled in his own mind a definite usage of it: no one can define a term in common use until he has satisfied himself that his personal usage of it harmonizes with the common usage. Definition necessarily means defining one thing in terms of something else; therefore, in order to define any given thing, one must have in one's head not only a clear idea of the thing to be defined, but an equally clear idea of all the other things by reference to which one defines it. People often go wrong over this. They think that in order to construct a definition or (what is the same thing) a 'theory' of something, it is enough to have a clear idea of that one thing. That is absurd. Having a clear idea of the thing enables them to recognize it when they see it, just as having a clear idea of a certain house enables them to recognize it when they are there; but defining the thing is like explaining where the house is or pointing out its position on the map; you must know its relations to other things as well, and if your ideas of these other things are vague, your definition will be worthless. [...]

R. G. Collingwood, *The Principles of Art* (Oxford: Clarendon Press, 1945), pp. 1–2, 5–6, 109–17, 121–2, 125, 139–40, 308–24.

4. History of the word 'art'

In order to clear up the ambiguities attaching to the word 'art', we must look to its history. The aesthetic sense of the word, the sense which here concerns us, is very recent in origin. *Ars* in ancient Latin, like τέχνη [technē] in Greek, means something quite different. It means a craft or specialized form of skill, like carpentry or smithying or surgery. The Greeks and Romans had no conception of what we call art as something different from craft; what we call art they regarded merely as a group of crafts, such as the craft of poetry (ποιητικη τέχνη, *ars poetica*), which they conceived, sometimes no doubt with misgivings, as in principle just like carpentry and the rest, and differing from any one of these only in the sort of way in which any one of them differs from any other.

It is difficult for us to realize this fact, and still more so to realize its implications. If people have no word for a certain kind of thing, it is because they are not aware of it as a distinct kind. Admiring as we do the art of the ancient Greeks, we naturally suppose that they admired it in the same kind of spirit as ourselves. But we admire it as a kind of art, where the word 'art' carries with it all the subtle and elaborate implications of the modern European aesthetic consciousness. We can be perfectly certain that the Greeks did not admire it in any such way. They approached it from a different point of view. What this was, we can perhaps discover by reading what people like Plato wrote about it; but not without great pains, because the first thing every modern reader does, when he reads what Plato has to say about poetry, is to assume that Plato is describing an aesthetic experience similar to our own. The second thing he does is to lose his temper because Plato describes it so badly. With most readers there is no third stage.

Ars in medieval Latin, like 'art' in the early modern English which borrowed both word and sense, meant any special form of book-learning, such as grammar or logic, magic or astrology. That is still its meaning in the time of Shakespeare: 'lie there, my art', says Prospero, putting off his magic gown. But the Renaissance, first in Italy and then elsewhere, re-established the old meaning; and the Renaissance artists, like those of the ancient world, did actually think of themselves as craftsmen. It was not until the seventeenth century that the problems and conceptions of aesthetic began to be disentangled from those of technic or the philosophy of craft. In the late eighteenth century the disentanglement had gone so far as to establish a distinction between the fine arts and the useful arts; where 'fine' arts meant, not delicate or highly skilled arts, but 'beautiful' arts (*les beaux arts, le belle arti, die schöne Kunst*). In the nineteenth century this phrase, abbreviated by leaving out the epithet and generalized by substituting the singular for the distributive plural, became 'art'. [. . .]

VI. Art Proper: (1) As Expression

2. Expressing emotion and arousing emotion

Our first question is this. Since the artist proper has something to do with emotion, and what he does with it is not to arouse it, what is it that he does? It will be remembered that the kind of answer we expect to this question is an answer derived from what we all know and all habitually say; nothing original or recondite, but something entirely commonplace.

Nothing could be more entirely commonplace than to say he expresses them. The idea is familiar to every artist, and to every one else who has any acquaintance with the arts. To state it is not to state a philosophical theory or definition of art; it is to state a fact or supposed fact about which, when we have sufficiently identified it, we shall have later to theorize philosophically. For the present it does not matter whether the fact that is alleged, when it is said that the artist expresses emotion, is really a fact or only supposed to be one. Whichever it is, we have to identify it, that is, to decide what it is that people are saying when they use the phrase. Later on, we shall have to see whether it will fit into a coherent theory.

They are referring to a situation, real or supposed, of a definite kind. When a man is said to express emotion, what is being said about him comes to this. At first, he is conscious of having an emotion, but not conscious of what this emotion is. All he is conscious of is a perturbation or excitement, which he feels going on within him, but of whose nature he is ignorant. While in this state, all he can say about his emotion is:

'I feel . . . I don't know what I feel.' From this helpless and oppressed condition he extricates himself by doing something which we call expressing himself. This is an activity which has something to do with the thing we call language: he expresses himself by speaking. It has also something to do with consciousness: the emotion expressed is an emotion of whose nature the person who feels it is no longer unconscious. It has also something to do with the way in which he feels the emotion. As unexpressed, he feels it in what we have called a helpless and oppressed way; as expressed, he feels it in a way from which this sense of oppression has vanished. His mind is somehow lightened and eased.

This lightening of emotions which is somehow connected with the expression of them has a certain resemblance to the 'catharsis' by which emotions are earthed through being discharged into a make-believe situation; but the two things are not the same. Suppose the emotion is one of anger. If it is effectively earthed, for example by fancying oneself kicking some one down stairs, it is thereafter no longer present in the mind as anger at all: we have worked it off and are rid of it. If it is expressed, for example by putting it into hot and bitter words, it does not disappear from the mind; we remain angry; but instead of the sense of oppression which accompanies an emotion of anger not yet recognized as such, we have that sense of alleviation which comes when we are conscious of our own emotion as anger, instead of being conscious of it only as an unidentified perturbation. This is what we refer to when we say that it 'does us good' to express our emotions.

The expression of an emotion by speech may be addressed to some one; but if so it is not done with the intention of arousing a like emotion in him. If there is any effect which we wish to produce in the hearer, it is only the effect which we call making him understand how we feel. But, as we have already seen, this is just the effect which expressing our emotions has on ourselves. It makes us, as well as the people to whom we talk, understand how we feel. A person arousing emotion sets out to affect his audience in a way in which he himself is not necessarily affected. He and his audience stand in quite different relations to the act, very much as physician and patient stand in quite different relations towards a drug administered by the one and taken by the other. A person expressing emotion, on the contrary, is treating himself and his audience in the same kind of way; he is making his emotions clear to his audience, and that is what he is doing to himself.

It follows from this that the expression of emotion, simply as expression, is not addressed to any particular audience. It is addressed primarily to the speaker himself, and secondarily to any one who can understand. Here again, the speaker's attitude towards his audience is quite unlike that of a person desiring to arouse in his audience a certain emotion. If that is what he wishes to do, he must know the audience he is addressing. He must know what type of stimulus will produce the desired kind of reaction in people of that particular sort; and he must adapt his language to his audience in the sense of making sure that it contains stimuli appropriate to their peculiarities. If what he wishes to do is to express his emotions intelligibly, he has to express them in such a way as to be intelligible to himself; his audience is then in the position of persons who overhear him doing this. Thus the stimulus-and-reaction terminology has no applicability to the situation.

The means-and-end, or technique, terminology too is inapplicable. Until a man has expressed his emotion, he does not yet know what emotion it is. The act of expressing it is therefore an exploration of his own emotions. He is trying to find out what these emotions are. There is certainly here a directed process: an effort, that is, directed upon a certain end; but the end is not something foreseen and preconceived, to which appropriate means can be thought out in the light of our knowledge of its special character, Expression is an activity of which there can be no technique.

3. *Expression and individualization*

Expressing an emotion is not the same thing as describing it. To say 'I am angry' is to describe one's emotion, not to express it. The words in which it is expressed need not contain any reference to anger as such at all. Indeed, so far as they simply and solely express it, they cannot contain any such reference. [. . .]

The reason why description, so far from helping expression, actually damages it, is that description generalizes. To describe a thing is to call it a thing of such and such a kind: to bring it under a conception, to classify it. Expression, on the contrary, individualizes. The anger which I feel here and now, with a certain person, for a certain cause, is no doubt an instance of anger, and in describing it as anger one is telling truth about it; but it is much more than mere anger: it is a peculiar anger, not quite like any anger that I ever felt before, and probably not quite like any anger I shall ever feel again. To become fully conscious of it means becoming conscious of it not merely as an instance of anger, but as this quite peculiar anger. Expressing it, we saw, has something to do with becoming conscious of it; therefore, if being fully conscious of it means being conscious of all its peculiarities, fully expressing it means expressing all its peculiarities. The poet, therefore, in proportion as he understands his business, gets as far away as possible from merely labelling his emotions as instances of this or that general kind, and takes enormous pains to individualize them by expressing them in terms which reveal their difference from any other emotion of the same sort.

This is a point in which art proper, as the expression of emotion, differs sharply and obviously from any craft whose aim it is to arouse emotion. The end which a craft sets out to realize is always conceived in general terms, never individualized. However accurately defined it may be, it is always defined as the production of a thing having characteristics that could be shared by other things. A joiner, making a table out of these pieces of wood and no others, makes it to measurements and specifications which, even if actually shared by no other table, might in principle be shared by other tables. A physician treating a patient for a certain complaint is trying to produce in him a condition which might be, and probably has been, often produced in others, namely, the condition of recovering from that complaint. So an 'artist' setting out to produce a certain emotion in his audience is setting out to produce not an individual emotion, but an emotion of a certain kind. It follows that the means appropriate to its production will be not individual means but means of a certain kind: that is to say, means which are always in principle replaceable by other similar means. As every good craftsman insists, there is always a 'right way' of performing any operation. A 'way' of acting is a general pattern to which various individual actions may conform. In order that the 'work of art' should produce its intended psychological effect, therefore, whether this effect be magical or merely amusing, what is necessary is that it should satisfy certain conditions, possess certain characteristics: in other words be, not this work and no other, but a work of this kind and of no other. [. . .]

Art proper, as expression of emotion, has nothing to do with all this. The artist proper is a person who, grappling with the problem of expressing a certain emotion, says, 'I want to get this clear.' It is no use to him to get something else clear, however like it this other thing may be. Nothing will serve as a substitute. He does not want a thing of a certain kind, he wants a certain thing. This is why the kind of person who takes his literature as psychology, saying 'How admirably this writer depicts the feelings of women, or bus-drivers, or homosexuals . . .', necessarily misunderstands every real work of art with which he comes into contact, and takes for good art, with infallible precision, what is not art at all.

4. *Selection and aesthetic emotion*

It has sometimes been asked whether emotions can be divided into those suitable for expression by artists and those unsuitable. If by art one means art proper, and identifies this with expression, the only possible answer is that there can be no such distinction. Whatever is expressible is expressible. There may be ulterior motives in special cases which make it desirable to express some emotions and not others; but only if by 'express' one means express publicly, that is, allow people to overhear one expressing oneself. This is because one cannot possibly decide that a certain emotion is one which for some reason it would be undesirable to express thus publicly, unless one first becomes conscious of it; and doing this, as we saw, is somehow bound up with expressing it. If art means the expression of emotion, the artist as such must be absolutely candid; his speech must be absolutely free. This is not a precept, it is a statement. It does not mean that the artist ought to be candid, it means that he is an artist only in so far as he is candid. Any kind of selection, any decision to express this emotion and not that, is inartistic not in the sense that it damages the perfect sincerity which distinguishes good art from bad, but in the sense that it represents a further process of a non-artistic kind, carried out when the work of expression proper is already complete. For until that work is complete one does not know what emotions one feels; and is therefore not in a position to pick and choose, and give one of them preferential treatment.

From these considerations a certain corollary follows about the division of art into distinct arts. Two such divisions are current: one according to the medium in which the artist works, into painting, poetry, music, and the like; the other according to the kind of emotion he expresses, into tragic, comic, and so forth. We are concerned with the second. If the difference between tragedy and comedy is a difference between the emotions they express, it is not a difference that can be present to the artist's mind when he is beginning his work; if it were, he would know what emotion he was going to express before he had expressed it. No artist, therefore, so far as he is an artist proper, can set out to write a comedy, a tragedy, an elegy, or the like. [. . .]

The same considerations provide an answer to the question whether there is such a thing as a specific 'aesthetic emotion'. If it is said that there is such an emotion independently of its expression in art, and that the business of artists is to express it, we must answer that such a view is nonsense. It implies, first, that artists have emotions of various kinds, among which is this peculiar aesthetic emotion; secondly, that they select this aesthetic emotion for expression. If the first proposition were true, the second would have to be false. If artists only find out what their emotions are in the course of finding out how to express them, they cannot begin the work of expression by deciding what emotion to express.

In a different sense, however, it is true that there is a specific aesthetic emotion. As we have seen, an unexpressed emotion is accompanied by a feeling of oppression; when it is expressed and thus comes into consciousness the same emotion is accompanied by a new feeling of alleviation or easement, the sense that this oppression is removed. It resembles the feeling of relief that comes when a burdensome intellectual or moral problem has been solved. We may call it, if we like, the specific feeling of having successfully expressed ourselves; and there is no reason why it should not be called a specific aesthetic emotion. But it is not a specific kind of emotion pre-existing to the expression of it, and having the peculiarity that when it comes to be expressed it is expressed artistically. It is an emotional colouring which attends the expression of any emotion whatever. [. . .]

7. *Expressing emotion and betraying emotion*

Finally, the expressing of emotion must not be confused with what may be called the betraying of it, that is, exhibiting symptoms of it. When it is said that the artist in the proper sense of that word is a person who expresses his emotions, this does not mean that if he is afraid he turns pale and stammers; if he is angry he turns red and bellows; and so forth. These things are no doubt called expressions; but just as we distinguish proper and improper senses of the word 'art', so we must distinguish proper and improper senses of the word 'expression', and in the context of a discussion about art this sense of expression is an improper sense. The characteristic mark of expression proper is lucidity or intelligibility; a person who expresses something thereby becomes conscious of what it is that he is expressing, and enables others to become conscious of it in himself and in them. Turning pale and stammering is a natural accompaniment of fear, but a person who in addition to being afraid also turns pale and stammers does not thereby become conscious of the precise quality of his emotion. About that he is as much in the dark as he would be if (were that possible) he could feel fear without also exhibiting these symptoms of it.

Confusion between these two senses of the word 'expression' may easily lead to false critical estimates, and so to false aesthetic theory. It is sometimes thought a merit in an actress that when she is acting a pathetic scene she can work herself up to such an extent as to weep real tears. There may be some ground for that opinion if acting is not an art but a craft, and if the actress's object in that scene is to produce grief in her audience; and even then the conclusion would follow only if it were true that grief cannot be produced in the audience unless symptoms of grief are exhibited by the performer. And no doubt this is how most people think of the actor's work. But if his business is not amusement but art, the object at which he is aiming is not to produce a preconceived emotional effect on his audience but by means of a system of expressions, or language, composed partly of speech and partly of gesture, to explore his own emotions: to discover emotions in himself of which he was unaware, and, by permitting the audience to witness the discovery, enable them to make a similar discovery about themselves. In that case it is not her ability to weep real tears that would mark out a good actress; it is her ability to make it clear to herself and her audience what the tears are about.

This applies to every kind of art. The artist never rants. [. . .]

VII. Art Proper: (2) As Imagination

1. *The problem defined*

The next question in the programme laid down at the beginning of the preceding chapter was put in this way: What is a work of art, granted that there is something in art proper (not only in art falsely so called) to which that name is applied, and that, since art is not craft, this thing is not an artifact? It is something made by the artist, but not made by transforming a given raw material, nor by carrying out a preconceived plan, nor by way of realizing the means to a preconceived end. What is this kind of making? [. . .]

5. *The work of art as imaginary object*

If the making of a tune is an instance of imaginative creation, a tune is an imaginary thing. And the same applies to a poem or a painting or any other work of art. This seems paradoxical; we are apt to think that a tune is not an imaginary thing but a real thing, a real collection of noises; that a painting is a real piece of canvas covered with real colours; and so on. I hope to show, if the reader will have patience, that there is no paradox here; that both these propositions express what we do as a matter of fact say about works of art; and that they do not contradict one another, because they are concerned with different things.

When, speaking of a work of art (tune, picture, &c.), we mean by art a specific craft, intended as a stimulus for producing specific emotional effects in an audience, we certainly mean to designate by the term 'work of art' something that we should call real. The artist as magician or purveyor of amusement is necessarily a craftsman making real things, and making them out of some material according to some plan. His works are as real as the works of an engineer, and for the same reason.

But it does not at all follow that the same is true of an artist proper. His business is not to produce an emotional effect in an audience, but, for example, to make a tune. This tune is already complete and perfect when it exists merely as a tune in his head, that is, an imaginary tune. Next, he may arrange for the tune to be played before an audience. Now there comes into existence a real tune, a collection of noises. But which of these two things is the work of art? Which of them is the music? The answer is implied in what we have already said: the music, the work of art, is not the collection of noises, it is the tune in the composer's head. The noises made by the performers, and heard by the audience, are not the music at all; they are only means by which the audience, if they listen intelligently (not otherwise), can reconstruct for themselves the imaginary tune that existed in the composer's head.

This is not a paradox. It is not something *παρα λοξαν*, contrary to what we ordinarily believe and express in our ordinary speech. We all know perfectly well, and remind each other often enough, that a person who hears the noises the instruments make is not thereby possessing himself of the music. Perhaps no one can do that unless he does hear the noises; but there is something else which he must do as well. Our ordinary word for this other thing is listening; and the listening which we have to do when we hear the noises made by musicians is in a way rather like the thinking we have to do when we hear the noises made, for example, by a person lecturing on a scientific subject. We hear the sound of his voice; but what he is doing is not simply to make noises, but to develop a scientific thesis. The noises are meant to assist us in achieving what he assumes to be our purpose in coming to hear him lecture, that is, thinking this same scientific thesis for ourselves. The lecture, therefore, is not a collection of noises made by the lecturer with his organs of speech; it is a collection of scientific thoughts related to those noises in such a way that a person who not only hears but thinks as well becomes able to think thought by means of speech, if we like; but if we do, we must think of communication not as an 'imparting' of thought by the speaker to the hearer, the speaker somehow planting his thought in the hearer's receptive mind, but as a 'reproduction' of the speaker's thought by the hearer, in virtue of his own active thinking. [. . .]

XIV. The Artist and the Community

4. The audience as understander

What is meant by saying that the painter 'records' in his picture the experience which he had in painting it? With this question we come to the subject of the audience, for the audience consists of anybody and everybody to whom such records are significant.

It means that the picture, when seen by some one else or by the painter himself subsequently, produces in him (we need not ask how) sensuous-emotional or psychical experiences which, when raised from impressions to ideas by the activity of the spectator's consciousness, are transmuted into a total imaginative experience identical with that of the painter. This experience of the spectator's does not repeat the comparatively poor experience of a person who merely looks at the subject; it repeats the richer and more highly organized experience of a person who has not only looked at it but has painted it as well.

That is why, as so many people have observed, we 'see more in' a really good picture of a given subject than we do in the subject itself. That is why, too, many people prefer what is called 'nature' or 'real life' to the finest pictures, because they prefer not to be shown so much, in order to keep their apprehensions at a lower and more manageable level, where they can embroider what they see with likes and dislikes, fancies and emotions of their own, not intrinsically connected with the subject. A great portrait painter, in the time it takes him to paint a sitter, intensely active in absorbing impressions and converting them into an imaginative vision of the man, may easily see through the mask that is good enough to deceive a less active and less pertinacious observer, and detect in a mouth or an eye or the turn of a head things that have long been concealed. There is nothing mysterious about this insight. Every one judges men by the impressions he gets of them and his power of becoming aware of these impressions; and the artist is a man whose life's work consists in doing that. The wonder is rather that so few artists do it revealingly. That is perhaps because people do not want it done, and artists fall in with their desire for what is called a good likeness, a picture that reveals nothing new, but only recalls what they have already felt in the sitter's presence.

How is any one to know that the imaginative experience which the spectator, by the work of his consciousness, makes out of the sensations he receives from a painting 'repeats', or is 'identical' with, the experience which the artist had in painting it? That question has already been raised about language in general [. . .] and answered by saying that there is no possibility of an absolute assurance; the only assurance we can have 'is an empirical and relative assurance, becoming progressively stronger as conversation proceeds, and based on the fact that neither party seems to the other to be talking nonsense'. The same answer holds good here. We can never absolutely know that the imaginative experience we obtain from a work of art is identical with that of the artist. In proportion as the artist is a great one, we can be pretty certain that we have only caught his meaning partially and imperfectly. But the same applies to any case in which we hear what a man says or read what he writes. And a partial and imperfect understanding is not the same thing as a complete failure to understand.

For example, a man reading the first canto of the *Inferno* may have no idea what Dante meant by the three beasts. Are they deadly sins, or are they potentates, or what are they? he may ask. In that perplexity, however, he has not completely lost contact with his author. There is still a great deal in the canto which he can understand, that is to say, transmute from impression into idea by the work of his consciousness; and all this, he can be fairly confident, he grasps as Dante meant it. And even the three beasts, though he does not understand them completely (something remains obstinately a mere untransmuted impression) he understands in part; he sees that they are something the poet dreads, and he imaginatively experiences the dread, though he does not know what it is that is dreaded.

Or take (since Dante may be ruled out as allegorical and therefore unfair) an example from modern poetry. I do not know how many readers of Mr. Eliot's poem *Sweeney among the Nightingales* have the least idea what precisely the situation is which the poet is depicting. I have never heard or read any expression of such an idea. Sweeney has dropped asleep in a restaurant, vaguely puzzled by the fact that the Convent of the Sacred Heart, next door, has reminded him of something, he cannot tell what. A wounded Heart, and waiting husbandless women. As he snores all through the second verse a prostitute in a long cloak comes and sits on his knees, and at that moment he dreams the answer. It is Agamemnon's cry – 'O, I am wounded mortally to the heart' – wounded to death at his homecoming by the false wife he had left behind. He wakes, stretching and laughing (tilting the girl off his knee), as he realizes that in the queer working of his mind the hooded husbandless nuns and the cloaked husbandless girl, waiting there like a spider for her prey, are both Klytaemnestra, the faithless wife who threw her cloak (the 'net of death') round her lord and stabbed him.

I quote this case because I had known and enjoyed the poem for years before I saw that this was what it was all about; and nevertheless I understood enough to value it highly. And I am willing to believe that the distinguished critic who thinks that the 'liquid siftings' of the nightingales were not their excrement, but their songs, values it highly too, and not everywhere so unintelligently as that sample would suggest.

The imaginative experience contained in a work of art is not a closed whole. There is no sense in putting the dilemma that a man either understands it (that is, has made that entire experience his own) or does not. Understanding it is always a complex business, consisting of many phases, each complete in itself but each leading on to the next. A determined and intelligent audience will penetrate into this complex far enough, if the work of art is a good one, to get something of value; but it need not on that account think it has extracted 'the' meaning of the work, for there is no such thing. The doctrine of a plurality of meanings, expounded for the case of holy scripture by St. Thomas Aquinas, is in principle perfectly sound: as he states it, the only trouble is that it does not go far enough. In some shape or other, it is true of all language.

5. *The audience as collaborator*

The audience as understander, attempting an exact reconstruction in its own mind of the artist's imaginative experience, is engaged on an endless quest. It can carry out this reconstruction only in part. This looks as if the artist were a kind of transcendent genius whose meaning is always too profound for his audience of humbler mortals to grasp in a more than fragmentary way. And an artist inclined to give himself airs will no doubt interpret the situation like that. But another interpretation is possible. The artist may take his audience's limitations into account when composing his work; in which case they will appear to him not as limitations on the extent to which his work will prove comprehensible, but as conditions determining the subject-matter or meaning of the work itself. In so far as the artist feels himself at one with his audience, this will involve no condescension on his part; it will mean that he takes it as his business to express not his own private emotions, irrespectively of whether any one else feels them or not, but the emotions he shares with his audience. Instead of conceiving himself as a mystagogue, leading his audience as far as it can follow along the dark and difficult paths of his own mind, he will conceive himself as his audience's spokesman, saying for it the things it wants to say but cannot say unaided. Instead of setting up for the great man who (as Hegel said) imposes upon the world the task of understanding him, he will be a humbler person, imposing upon himself the task of understanding his world, and thus enabling it to understand itself.

In this case his relation to his audience will no longer be a mere by-product of his aesthetic experience, as it still was in the situation described in the preceding section; it will be an integral part of that experience itself. If what he is trying to do is to express emotions that are not his own merely, but his audience's as well, his success in doing this will be tested by his audience's reception of what he has to say. What he says will be something that his audience says through his mouth; and his satisfaction in having expressed what he feels will be at the same time, in so far as he communicates this expression to them, their satisfaction in having expressed what they feel. There will thus be something more than mere communication from artist to audience, there will be collaboration between audience and artist.

We have inherited a long tradition, beginning in the late eighteenth century with the cult of 'genius', and lasting all through the nineteenth, which is inimical to this second alternative. But I have already said that this tradition is dying away. Artists are less inclined to give themselves airs than they used to be; and there are many indications that they are more willing than they were, even a generation ago, to regard their audiences as collaborators. It is perhaps no longer foolish to hope that this way of conceiving the relation between artist and audience may be worth discussing.

There are grounds for thinking that this idea of the relation is the right one. [. . .] [W]e must look at the facts; and we shall find that, whatever airs they may give themselves, artists have always been in the habit of treating the public as collaborators. On a technical theory of art, this is, in a sense, comprehensible. If the artist is trying to arouse certain emotions in his audience, a refusal on the part of the audience to develop these emotions proves that the artist has failed. But this is one of the many points in which the technical theory does not so much miss the truth as misrepresent it. An artist need not be a slave to the technical theory, in order to feel that his audience's approbation is relevant to the question whether he has done his work well or ill. There have been painters who would not exhibit, poets who would not publish, musicians who would not have their works performed; but those who have made this great refusal, so far as one knows them, have not been of the highest quality. There has been a lack of genuineness about their work, corresponding to this strain of secretiveness in their character, which is inconsistent with good art. The man who feels that he has something to say is not only willing to say it in public: he craves to say it in public, and feels that until it has been thus said it has not been said at all. The public is always, no doubt, a circumscribed one: it may consist only of a few friends, and at most it includes only people who can buy or borrow a book or get hold of a theatre ticket; but every artist knows that publication of some kind is a necessity to him.

Every artist knows, too, that the reception he gets from his public is not a matter of indifference to him. He may train himself to take rebuffs with a stiff lip, and go on working in spite of bad sales and hostile reviews. He must so train himself, if he is to do his best work; because with the best will in the world (quite apart from venality in reviewers and frivolity in readers) no one enjoys having his unconscious emotions dragged into the light of consciousness, and consequently there is often a strongly painful element in a genuine aesthetic experience, and a strong temptation to reject it. But the reason why the artist finds it so hard to train himself in this way is because these rebuffs wound him not in his personal vanity, but in his judgement as to the soundness of the work he has done.

Here we come to the point. One might suppose that the artist by himself is in his own eyes a sufficient judge of his work's value. If he is satisfied with it, why should he mind what others think? But things do not work like that. The artist, like any one else who comes before an audience, must put a bold face on it; he must do the best he can, and pretend that he knows it is good. But probably no artist has ever been so conceited as to be wholly taken in by his own pretence. Unless he sees his own proclamation, 'This is good', echoed on the faces of his audience – 'Yes, that is good' – he wonders whether he was speaking the truth or not. He thought he had enjoyed and recorded a genuine aesthetic experience, but has he? Was he suffering from a corruption of consciousness? Has his audience judged him better than he judged himself?

These are facts which no artist, I think, will deny, unless in that feverish way in which we all deny what we know to be true and will not accept. If they are facts, they prove that, in spite of all disclaimers, artists do look upon their audiences as collaborators with themselves in the attempt to answer the question: is this a genuine work of art or not? But this is the thin edge of a wedge. Once the audience's collaboration is admitted thus far, it must be admitted farther.

The artist's business is to express emotions; and the only emotions he can express are those which he feels, namely, his own. No one can judge whether he has expressed them except some one who feels them. If they are his own and no one else's, there is no one except himself who can judge whether he has expressed them or not. If he attaches any importance to the judgement of his audience, it can only be because he thinks that the emotions he has tried to express are emotions not peculiar to himself, but shared by his audience, and that the expression of them he has achieved (if indeed he has achieved it) is as valid for the audience as it is for himself. In other words, he undertakes his artistic labour not as a personal effort on his own private behalf, but as a public labour on behalf of the community to which he belongs. Whatever statement of emotion he utters is prefaced by the implicit rubric, not 'I feel', but 'we feel'. And it is not strictly even a labour undertaken by himself on behalf of the community. It is a labour in which he invites the community to participate; for their function as audience is not passively to accept his work, but to do it over again for themselves. If he invites them to do this, it is because he has reason to think they will accept his invitation, that is, because he thinks he is inviting them to do what they already want to do.

In so far as the artist feels all this (and an artist who did not feel it would not feel the craving to publish his work, or take seriously the public's opinion of it), he feels it not only after his work is completed, but from its inception and throughout its composition. The audience is perpetually present to him as a factor in his artistic labour; not as an anti-aesthetic factor, corrupting the sincerity of his work by considerations of reputation and reward, but as an aesthetic factor, defining what the problem is which as an artist he is trying to solve – what emotions he is to express – and what constitutes a solution of it. The audience which the artist thus feels as collaborating with himself may be a large one or a small one, but it is never absent.

6. *Aesthetic individualism*

The understanding of the audience's function as collaborator is a matter of importance for the future both of aesthetic theory and of art itself. The obstacle to understanding it is a traditional individualistic psychology through which, as through distorting glasses, we are in the habit of looking at artistic work. We think of the artist as a self-contained personality, sole author of everything he does: of the emotions he expresses as his personal emotions, and of his expression of them as his personal expression. We even forget what it is that he thus expresses, and speak of his work as 'self-expression', persuading ourselves that what makes a poem great is the fact that it 'expresses a great personality', whereas, if self-expression is the order of the day, whatever value we set on such a poem is due to its expressing not the poet – what is Shakespeare to us, or we to Shakespeare? – but ourselves.

It would be tedious to enumerate the tangles of misunderstanding which this nonsense about self-expression has generated. To take one such only: it has set us off looking for 'the man Shakespeare' in his poems, and trying to reconstruct his life and opinions from them, as if that were possible, or as if, were it possible, it would help us to appreciate his work. It has degraded criticism to the level of personal gossip, and confused art with exhibitionism. What I prefer to attempt is not a tale of misdeeds, but a refutation.

In principle, this refutation is simple. Individualism conceives a man as if he were God, a self-contained and self-sufficient creative power whose only task is to be himself and to exhibit his nature in whatever works are appropriate to it. But a man, in his art as in everything else, is a finite being. Everything that he does is done in relation to others like himself. As artist, he is a speaker; but a man speaks as he has been taught; he speaks the tongue in which he was born. The musician did not invent his scale or his instruments; even if he invents a new scale or a new instrument he is only modifying what he learnt from others. The painter did not invent the idea of painting pictures or the pigments and brushes with which he paints them. Even the most precocious poet hears and reads poetry before he writes it. Moreover, just as every artist stands in relation to other artists from whom he has acquired his art, so he stands in relation to some audience to whom he addresses it. The child learning his mother tongue, as we have seen, learns simultaneously to be a speaker and to be a listener; he listens to others speaking, and speaks to others listening. It is the same with artists. They become poets or painters or musicians not by some process of development from within, as they grow beards; but by living in a society where these languages are current. Like other speakers, they speak to those who understand.

The aesthetic activity is the activity of speaking. Speech is speech only so far as it is both spoken and heard. A man may, no doubt, speak to himself and be his own hearer; but what he says to himself is in principle capable of being said to any one sharing his language. As a finite being, man becomes aware of himself as a person only so far as he finds himself standing in relation to others of whom he simultaneously becomes aware as persons. And there is no point in his life at which a man has finished becoming aware of himself as a person. That awareness is constantly being reinforced, developed, applied in new ways. On every such occasion the old appeal must be made: he must find others whom he can recognize as persons in this new fashion, or he cannot as a finite being assure himself that this new phase of personality is genuinely in his possession. If he has a new thought, he must explain it to others, in order that, finding them able to understand it, he may be sure it is a good one. If he has a new emotion, he must express it to others, in order that, finding them able to share it, he may be sure his consciousness of it is not corrupt.

This is not inconsistent with the doctrine, stated elsewhere in this book, that the aesthetic experience or aesthetic activity is one which goes on in the artist's mind. The experience of being listened to is an experience which goes on in the mind of the speaker, although in order to [assure] its existence a listener is necessary, so that the activity is a collaboration. Mutual love is a collaborative activity; but the experience of this activity in the mind of each lover taken singly is a different experience from that of loving and being spurned.

A final refutation of aesthetic individualism will, therefore, turn on analysis of the relation between the artist and his audience, developing the view stated in the last section that this is a case of collaboration. But I propose to lead up to this by way of two other arguments. I shall try to show that the individualistic theory of artistic creation is false (1) as regards the relation between a given artist and those fellow artists who in terms of the individualistic theory are said to 'influence' him; (2) as regards his relation with those who are said to 'perform his works'; and (3) as regards his relation with the persons known as his 'audience'. In each case, I shall maintain, the relation is really collaborative.

7. Collaboration between artists

Individualism would have it that the work of a genuine artist is altogether 'original', that is to say, purely his own work and not in any way that of other artists. The emotions expressed must be simply and solely his own, and so must his way of expressing them. It is a shock to persons labouring under this prejudice when they find that Shakespeare's plays, and notably *Hamlet*, that happy hunting-ground of self-expressionists, are merely adaptations of plays by other writers, scraps of Holinshed, Lives by Plutarch, or excerpts from the *Gesta Romanorum*; that Handel copied out into his own works whole movements by Arne; that the Scherzo of Beethoven's C minor Symphony begins by reproducing the Finale of Mozart's G Minor, differently barred; or that Turner was in the habit of lifting his composition from the works of Claude Lorrain. Shakespeare or Handel or Beethoven or Turner would have thought it odd that anybody should be shocked. All artists have modelled their style upon that of others, used subjects that others have used, and treated them as others have treated them already. A work of art so constructed is a work of collaboration. It is partly by the man whose name it bears, partly by those from whom he has borrowed. What we call the works of Shakespeare, for example, proceed in this way not simply and solely from the individual mind of the man William Shakespeare of Stratford (or, for that matter, the man Francis Bacon of Verulam) but partly from Kyd, partly from Marlowe, and so forth.

The individualistic theory of authorship would lead to the most absurd conclusions. If we regard the *Iliad* as a fine poem, the question whether it was written by one man or by many is automatically, for us, settled. If we regard Chartres cathedral as a work of art, we must contradict the architects who tell us that one spire was built in the twelfth century and the other in the sixteenth, and convince ourselves that it was all built at once. Or again: English prose of the early seventeenth century may be admired when it is original; but not the Authorized Version, for that is a translation, and a translation, because no one man is solely responsible for it, cannot be a work of art. I am very willing to allow with Descartes that 'often there is less perfection in works put together out of several parts, and made by the hands of different masters, than in those at which one only has worked'; but not to replace his 'often' by 'always'. I am very willing to recognize that, under the reign of nineteenth-century individualism, good artists have seldom been willing to translate, because they have gone chasing after 'originality'; but not to deny the name of poetry to Catullus's rendering of Sappho merely because I happen to know it for a translation.

If we look candidly at the history of art, or even the little of it that we happen to know, we shall see that collaboration between artists has always been the rule. I refer especially to that kind of collaboration in which one artist grafts his own work upon that of another, or (if you wish to be abusive) plagiarizes another's for incorporation in his own. A new code of artistic morality grew up in the nineteenth century, according to which plagiarism was a crime. I will not ask how much that had to do, whether as cause or as effect, with the artistic barrenness and mediocrity of the age (though it is obvious, I think, that a man who can be annoyed with another for stealing his ideas must be pretty poor in ideas, as well as much less concerned for the intrinsic value of what ideas he has than for his own reputation); I will only say that this fooling about personal property must cease. Let painters and writers and musicians steal with both hands whatever they can use, wherever they can find it. And if any one objects to having his own precious ideas borrowed by others, the remedy is easy. He can keep them to himself by not publishing; and the public will probably have cause to thank him.

8. *Collaboration between author and performer*

Certain kinds of artist, notably the dramatist and the musician, compose for performance. Individualism would maintain that their works, however 'influenced', as the phrase goes, by those of other artists, issue from the writer's pen complete and finished; they are plays by Shakespeare and symphonies by Beethoven, and these men are great artists, who have written on their own responsibility a text which, as the work of a great artist, imposes on the theatre and the orchestra a duty to perform it exactly as it stands.

But the book of a play or the score of a symphony, however cumbered with stage-directions, expression-marks, metronome figures, and so forth, cannot possibly indicate in every detail how the work is to be performed. Tell the performer that he must perform the thing exactly as it is written, and he knows you are talking nonsense, He knows that however much he tries to obey you there are still countless points he must decide for himself. And the author, if he is qualified to write a play or a symphony, knows it too, and reckons on it. He demands of his performers a spirit of constructive and intelligent co-operation. He recognizes that what he is putting on paper is not a play or a symphony, or even complete directions for performing one, but only a rough outline of such directions, where the performers, with the help, no doubt, of producer and conductor, are not only permitted but required to fill in the details. Every performer is co-author of the work he performs.

This is obvious enough, but in our tradition of the last hundred years and more we have been constantly shutting our eyes to it. Authors and performers have found themselves driven into a state of mutual suspicion and hostility. Performers have been told that they must not claim the status of collaborators, and must accept the sacred text just as they find it; authors have tried to guard against any danger of collaboration from performers by making their book or their text fool-proof. The result has been not to stop performers from collaborating (that is impossible), but to breed up a generation of performers who are not qualified to collaborate boldly and competently. When Mozart leaves it to his soloist to improvise the cadenza of a concerto, he is in effect insisting that the soloist shall be more than a mere executant; he is to be something of a composer, and therefore trained to collaborate intelligently. Authors who try to produce a fool-proof text are choosing fools as their collaborators.

9. *The artist and his audience*

The individualism of the artist, broken down by collaboration with his fellow artists and still further by collaboration with his performers, where he has them, is not yet wholly vanquished.

There still remains the most difficult and important problem of all, namely, that of his relation to his audience. We have seen in § 6 that this, too, must in theory be a case of collaboration; but it is one thing to argue the point in theory, and quite another to show it at work in practice. In order to do this, I will begin with the case where the artist is a collaborative unit consisting of author and performers, as in the theatre, and consider how, as a matter of empirical fact, this unit is related to the audience.

If one wants to answer this question for oneself, the best way to proceed is to attend the dress rehearsal of a play. In the rehearsal of any given passage, scenery, lighting, and dresses may all be exactly as they are at a public performance; the actors may move and speak exactly as they will 'on the night'; there may be few interruptions for criticism by the producer; and yet the spectator will realize that everything is different. The company are going through the motions of acting a play, and yet no play is being acted. This is not because there have been interruptions, breaking the thread of the performance. A work of art is very tolerant of interruption. The intervals between acts at a play do not break the thread, they rest the audience. Nobody ever read the *Iliad* or the *Commedia* at a sitting, but many people know what they are like. What happens at the dress rehearsal is something quite different from interruption. It can be described by saying that every line, every gesture, falls dead in the empty house. The company is not acting a play at all; it is performing certain actions which will become a play when there is an audience present to act as a sounding-board. It becomes clear, then, that the aesthetic activity which is the play is not an activity on the part of the author and the company together, which this unit can perform in the audience's absence. It is an activity in which the audience is a partner.

Any one, probably, can learn this by watching a dress rehearsal; but the principle does not apply to the theatre alone. It applies to rehearsals by a choir or orchestra, or to a skilled and successful public speaker rehearsing a speech. A careful study of such things will convince any one who is open to conviction that the position of the audience is very far from being that of a licensed eavesdropper, overhearing something that would be complete without him. Performers know it already. They know that their audience is not passively receptive of what they give it, but is determining by its reception of them how their performance is to be carried on. A person accustomed to extempore speaking, for example, knows that if once he can make contact with his audience it will somehow tell him what he is to say, so that he finds himself saying things he had never thought of before. These are the things which, on that particular subject, he and nobody else ought to be saying to that audience and no other. People to whom this is not a familiar experience are, of course, common; but they have no business to speak in public.

It is a weakness of printed literature that this reciprocity between writer and reader is difficult to maintain. The printing-press separates the writer from his audience and fosters cross-purposes between them. The organization of the literary profession and the 'technique' of good writing, as that is understood among ourselves, consist to a great extent of methods for mitigating this evil; but the evil is only mitigated and not removed. It is intensified by every new mechanization of art. The reason why gramophone music is so unsatisfactory to any one accustomed to real music is not because the mechanical reproduction of the sounds is bad – that could be easily compensated by the hearer's imagination – but because the performers and the audience are out of touch. The audience is not collaborating, it is only overhearing. The same thing happens in the cinema, where collaboration as between author and producer is intense, but as between this unit and the audience non-existent. Performances on the wireless have the same defect. The consequence is that the gramophone, the cinema, and the wireless are perfectly serviceable as vehicles of amusement or of propaganda, for here the audience's function is merely receptive and not concreative; but as vehicles of art they are subject to all the defects of the printing-press in an aggravated form. 'Why', one hears it asked, 'should not the modern popular entertainment of the cinema, like the Renaissance popular entertainment of the theatre, produce a new form of great art?' The answer is simple. In the Renaissance theatre collaboration between author and actors on the one hand, and audience on the other, was a lively reality. In the cinema it is impossible.

The conclusion of this chapter may be summarized briefly. The work of artistic creation is not a work performed in any exclusive or complete fashion in the mind of the person whom we call the artist. That idea is a delusion bred of individualistic psychology, together with a false view of the relation not so much between body and mind as between experience at the psychical level and experience at the level of thought. The aesthetic activity is an activity of thought in the form of consciousness, converting into imagination an experience which, apart from being so converted, is sensuous. This activity is a corporate activity belonging not to any one human being but to a community. It is performed not only by the man whom we individualistically call the artist, but partly by all the other artists of whom we speak as 'influencing' him, where we really mean collaborating with him. It is performed not only by this corporate body of artists, but (in the case of the arts of performance) by executants, who are not merely acting under the artist's orders, but are collaborating with him to produce the finished work. And even now the activity of artistic creation is not complete; for that, there must be an audience, whose function is therefore not a merely receptive one, but collaborative too. The artist (although under the spell of individualistic prejudices he may try to deny it) stands thus in collaborative relations with an entire community; not an ideal community of all human beings as such, but the actual community of fellow artists from whom he borrows, executants whom he employs, and audience to whom he speaks. By recognizing these relations and counting upon them in his work, he strengthens and enriches that work itself; by denying them he impoverishes it.

27

Art as Experience

John Dewey

John Dewey (1859–1952), the foremost American philosopher of the first half of the twentieth century, made contributions to virtually every area of philosophical inquiry.

1. The Live Creature

By one of the ironic perversities that often attend the course of affairs, the existence of the works of art upon which formation of an esthetic theory depends has become an obstruction to theory about them. For one reason, these works are products that exist externally and physically. In common conception, the work of art is often identified with the building, book, painting, or statue in its existence apart from human experience. Since the actual work of art is what the product does with and in experience, the result is not favorable to understanding. In addition, the very perfection of some of these products, the prestige they possess because of a long history of unquestioned admiration, creates conventions that get in the way of fresh insight. When an art product once attains classic status, it somehow becomes isolated from the human conditions under which it was brought into being and from the human consequences it engenders in actual life-experience.

When artistic objects are separated from both conditions of origin and operation in experience, a wall is built around them that renders almost opaque their general significance, with which esthetic theory deals. Art is remitted to a separate realm, where it is cut off from that association with the materials and aims of every other form of human effort, undergoing, and achievement. A primary task is thus imposed upon one who undertakes to write upon the philosophy of the fine arts. This task is to restore continuity between the refined and intensified forms of experience that are works of art and the everyday events, doings, and sufferings that are universally recognized to constitute experience. Mountain peaks do not float unsupported; they do not even just rest upon the earth. They *are* the earth in one of its manifest operations. It is the business of those who are concerned with the theory of the earth, geographers and geologists, to make this fact evident in its various implications. The theorist who would deal philosophically with fine art has a like task to accomplish.

If one is willing to grant this position, even if only by way of temporary experiment, he will see that there follows a conclusion at first sight surprising. In order to understand the meaning of

John Dewey, *Art as Experience*, vol. 10 of *The Collected Works of John Dewey: The Later Works, 1925–1953*, ed. Jo Ann Boydston (Carbondale and Edwardsville: Southern Illinois University Press, 1989), pp. 9–18, 26–34, 42–63.

artistic products, we have to forget them for a time, to turn aside from them and have recourse to the ordinary forces and conditions of experience that we do not usually regard as esthetic. We must arrive at the theory of art by means of a detour. For theory is concerned with understanding, insight, not without exclamations of admiration, and stimulation of that emotional outburst often called appreciation. It is quite possible to enjoy flowers in their colored form and delicate fragrance without knowing anything about plants theoretically. But if one sets out to *understand* the flowering of plants, he is committed to finding out something about the interactions of soil, air, water and sunlight that condition the growth of plants.

By common consent, the Parthenon is a great work of art. Yet it has esthetic standing only as the work becomes an experience for a human being. And, if one is to go beyond personal enjoyment into the formation of a theory about that large republic of art of which the building is one member, one has to be willing at some point in his reflections to turn from it to the bustling, arguing, acutely sensitive Athenian citizens, with civic sense identified with a civic religion, of whose experience the temple was an expression, and who built it not as a work of art but as a civic commemoration. The turning to them is as human beings who had needs that were a demand for the building and that were carried to fulfillment in it; it is not an examination such as might be carried on by a sociologist in search for material relevant to his purpose. The one who sets out to theorize about the esthetic experience embodied in the Parthenon must realize in thought what the people into whose lives it entered had in common, as creators and as those who were satisfied with it, with people in our own homes and on our own streets.

In order to *understand* the esthetic in its ultimate and approved forms, one must begin with it in the raw; in the events and scenes that hold the attentive eye and ear of man, arousing his interest and affording him enjoyment as he looks and listens: the sights that hold the crowd – the fire-engine rushing by; the machines excavating enormous holes in the earth; the human-fly climbing the steeple-side; the men perched high in air on girders, throwing and catching red-hot bolts. The sources of art in human experience will be learned by him who sees how the tense grace of the ball-player infects the onlooking crowd; who notes the delight of the housewife in tending her plants, and the intent interest of her goodman in tending the patch of green in front of the house; the zest of the spectator in poking the wood burning on the hearth and in watching the darting flames and crumbling coals. These people, if questioned as to the reason for their actions, would doubtless return reasonable answers. The man who poked the sticks of burning wood would say he did it to make the fire burn better; but he is none the less fascinated by the colorful drama of change enacted before his eyes and imaginatively partakes in it. He does not remain a cold spectator. What Coleridge said of the reader of poetry is true in its way of all who are happily absorbed in their activities of mind and body: "The reader should be carried forward, not merely or chiefly by the mechanical impulse of curiosity, not by a restless desire to arrive at the final solution, but by the pleasurable activity of the journey itself."

The intelligent mechanic engaged in his job, interested in doing well and finding satisfaction in his handiwork, caring for his materials and tools with genuine affection, is artistically engaged. The difference between such a worker and the inept and careless bungler is as great in the shop as it is in the studio. Oftentimes the product may not appeal to the esthetic sense of those who use the product. The fault, however, is oftentimes not so much with the worker as with the conditions of the market for which his product is designed. Were conditions and opportunities different, things as significant to the eye as those produced by earlier craftsmen would be made.

So extensive and subtly pervasive are the ideas that set Art upon a remote pedestal, that many a person would be repelled rather than pleased if told that he enjoyed his casual recreations, in part at least, because of their esthetic quality. The arts which today have most vitality for the average person are things he does not take to be arts: for instance, the movie, jazzed music, the comic strip, and, too frequently, newspaper accounts of love-nests, murders, and exploits of bandits. For, when what he knows as art is relegated to the museum and gallery, the unconquerable impulse towards experiences enjoyable in themselves finds such outlet as the daily environment provides. Many a person who protests against the museum conception of art, still shares the fallacy from which that conception springs. For the popular notion comes from a separation of art from the objects and scenes of ordinary experience that many theorists and critics pride themselves upon holding and even elaborating. The times when select and distinguished objects are closely connected with the products of usual vocations are the times when appreciation of the former is most rife and most keen. When, because of their remoteness, the objects acknowledged by the cultivated to be works of fine art seem anemic to the mass of people, esthetic hunger is likely to seek the cheap and the vulgar.

The factors that have glorified fine art by setting it upon a far-off pedestal did not arise within the realm of art nor is their influence confined to the arts. For many persons an aura of mingled awe and unreality encompasses the "spiritual" and the "ideal" while "matter" has become by contrast a term of depreciation, something to be explained away or apologized for. The forces at work are those that have removed religion as well as fine art from the scope of the common or community life. These forces have historically produced so many of the dislocations and divisions of modern life and thought that art could not escape their influence. We do not have to travel to the ends of the earth nor return many millennia in time to find peoples for whom everything that intensifies the sense of immediate living is an object of intense admiration. Bodily scarification, waving feathers, gaudy robes, shining ornaments of gold and silver, of emerald and jade, formed the contents of esthetic arts, and, presumably, without the vulgarity of class exhibitionism that attends their analogues today. Domestic utensils, furnishings of tent and house, rugs, mats, jars, pots, bows, spears, were wrought with such delighted care that today we hunt them out and give them places of honor in our art museums. Yet in their own time and place, such things were enhancements of the processes of everyday life. Instead of being elevated to a niche apart, they belonged to display of prowess, the manifestation of group and clan membership, worship of gods, feasting and fasting, fighting, hunting, and all the rhythmic crises that punctuate the stream of living.

Dancing and pantomime, the sources of the art of the theater, flourished as part of religious rites and celebrations. Musical art abounded in the fingering of the stretched string, the beating of the taut skin, the blowing with reeds. Even in the caves, human habitations were adorned with colored pictures that kept alive to the senses experiences with the animals that were so closely bound with the lives of humans. Structures that housed their gods and the instrumentalities that facilitated commerce with the higher powers were wrought with especial fineness. But the arts of the drama, music, painting, and architecture thus exemplified had no peculiar connection with theaters, galleries, museums. They were part of the significant life of an organized community.

The collective life that was manifested in war, worship, the forum, knew no division between what was characteristic of these places and operations, and the arts that brought color, grace, and dignity, into them. Painting and sculpture were organically one with architecture, as that was one with the social purpose that buildings served. Music and song were intimate parts of the rites and ceremonies in which the meaning of group life was consummated. Drama was a vital reenactment of the legends and history of group life. Not even in Athens can such arts be torn loose from this setting in direct experience and yet retain their significant character. Athletic sports, as well as drama, celebrated and enforced traditions of race and group, instructing the people, commemorating glories, and strengthening their civic pride.

Under such conditions, it is not surprising that the Athenian Greeks, when they came to reflect upon art, formed the idea that it is an act of reproduction, or imitation. There are many objections to this conception. But the vogue of the theory is testimony to the close connection of the fine arts with daily life; the idea would not have occurred to any one had art been remote from the interests of life. For the doctrine did not signify that art was a literal copying of objects, but that it reflected the emotions and ideas that are associated with the chief institutions of social life. Plato felt this connection so strongly that it led him to his idea of the necessity of censorship of poets, dramatists, and musicians. Perhaps he exaggerated when he said that a change from the Doric to the Lydian mode in music would be the sure precursor of civic degeneration. But no contemporary would have doubted that music was an integral part of the ethos and the institutions of the community. The idea of "art for art's sake" would not have been even understood.

There must then be historic reasons for the rise of the compartmental conception of fine art. Our present museums and galleries to which works of fine art are removed and stored illustrate some of the causes that have operated to segregate art instead of finding it an attendant of temple, forum, and other forms of associated life. An instructive history of modern art could be written in terms of the formation of the distinctively modern institutions of museum and exhibition gallery. I may point to a few outstanding facts. Most European museums are, among other things, memorials of the rise of nationalism and imperialism. Every capital must have its own museum of painting, sculpture, etc., devoted in part to exhibiting the greatness of its artistic past, and, in other part, to exhibiting the loot gathered by its monarchs in conquest of other nations; for instance, the accumulations of the spoils of Napoleon that are in the Louvre. They testify to the connection between the modern segregation of art and nationalism and militarism. Doubtless this connection has served at times a useful purpose, as in the case of Japan, who, when she was in the process of westernization, saved much of her art treasures by nationalizing the temples that contained them.

The growth of capitalism has been a powerful influence in the development of the museum as the proper home for works of art, and in the promotion of the idea that they are apart from the common life. The *nouveaux riches*, who are an important by-product of the capitalist system, have felt especially bound to surround themselves with works of fine art which, being rare, are also costly. Generally speaking, the typical collector is the typical capitalist. For evidence of good standing in the realm of higher culture, he amasses paintings, statuary, and artistic *bijoux*, as his stocks and bonds certify to his standing in the economic world.

Not merely individuals, but communities and nations, put their cultural good taste in evidence by building opera houses, galleries, and museums. These show that a community is not wholly absorbed in material wealth, because it is willing to spend its gains in patronage of art. It erects these buildings and collects their contents as it now builds a cathedral. These things reflect and establish superior cultural status, while their segregation from the common life reflects the fact that they are not part of a native and spontaneous culture. They are a kind of counterpart of a holier-than-thou attitude, exhibited not toward persons as such but toward the interests and occupations that absorb most of the community's time and energy.

Modern industry and commerce have an international scope. The contents of galleries and museums testify to the growth of economic cosmopolitanism. The mobility of trade and of populations, due to the economic system, has weakened or destroyed the connection between works of art and the *genius loci* of which they were once the natural expression. As works of art have lost their indigenous status, they have acquired a new one – that of being specimens of fine art and nothing else. Moreover, works of art are now produced, like other articles, for sale in the market. Economic patronage by wealthy and powerful individuals has at many times played a part in the encouragement of artistic production. Probably many a savage tribe had its Maecenas. But now even that much of intimate social connection is lost in the impersonality of a world market. Objects that were in the past valid and significant because of their place in the life of a community now function in isolation from the conditions of their origin. By that fact they are also set apart from common experience, and serve as insignia of taste and certificates of special culture.

Because of changes in industrial conditions the artist has been pushed to one side from the main streams of active interest. Industry has been mechanized and an artist cannot work mechanically for mass production. He is less integrated than formerly in the normal flow of social services. A peculiar esthetic "individualism" results. Artists find it incumbent upon them to betake themselves to their work as an isolated means of "self-expression." In order not to cater to the trend of economic forces, they often feel obliged to exaggerate their separateness to the point of eccentricity. Consequently artistic products take on to a still greater degree the air of something independent and esoteric.

Put the action of all such forces together, and the conditions that create the gulf which exists generally between producer and consumer in modern society operate to create also a chasm between ordinary and esthetic experience. Finally we have, as the record of this chasm, accepted as if it were normal, the philosophies of art that locate it in a region inhabited by no other creature, and that emphasize beyond all reason the merely contemplative character of the esthetic. Confusion of values enters in to accentuate the separation. Adventitious matters, like the pleasure of collecting, of exhibiting, of ownership and display, simulate esthetic values. Criticism is affected. There is much applause for the wonders of appreciation and the glories of the transcendent beauty of art indulged in without much regard to capacity for esthetic perception in the concrete.

My purpose, however, is not to engage in an economic interpretation of the history of the arts, much less to argue that economic conditions are either invariably or directly relevant to perception and enjoyment, or even to interpretation of individual works of art. It is to indicate that *theories* which isolate art and its appreciation by placing them in a realm of their own, disconnected from other modes of experiencing, are not inherent in the subject-matter but arise because of specifiable extraneous conditions. Embedded as they are in institutions and in habits of life, these conditions operate effectively because they work so unconsciously. Then the theorist assumes they are embedded in the nature of things. Nevertheless, the influence of these conditions is not confined to theory. As I have already indicated, it deeply affects the practice of living, driving away esthetic perceptions that are necessary ingredients of happiness, or reducing them to the level of compensating transient pleasurable excitations.

Even to readers who are adversely inclined to what has been said, the implications of the statements that have been made may be useful in defining the nature of the problem: that of recovering the continuity of esthetic experience with normal processes of living. The understanding of art and of its role in civilization is not furthered by setting out with eulogies of it nor by occupying ourselves exclusively at the outset with great works of art recognized as such. The comprehension which theory essays will be arrived at by a detour; by going back to experience of the common or mill run of things to discover the esthetic quality such experience possesses. Theory can start with and from acknowledged works of art only when the esthetic is already compartmentalized, or only when works of art are set in a niche apart instead of being celebrations, recognized as such, of the things of ordinary experience. Even a crude experience, if authentically an experience, is more fit to give a clue to the intrinsic nature of esthetic experience than is an object already set apart from any other mode of experience. Following this clue we can discover how the work of art develops and accentuates what is characteristically valuable in things of everyday enjoyment. The art product will then be seen to issue from the latter, when the full meaning of ordinary experience is expressed, as dyes come out of coal tar products when they receive special treatment.

Many theories about art already exist. If there is justification for proposing yet another philosophy of the esthetic, it must be found in a new mode of approach. Combinations and permutations among existing theories can easily be brought forth by those so inclined. But, to my mind, the trouble with existing theories is that they start from a ready-made compartmentalization, or from a conception of art that "spiritualizes" it out of connection with the objects of concrete experience. The alternative, however, to such spiritualization is not a degrading and Philistinish materialization of works of fine art, but a conception that discloses the way in which these works idealize qualities found in common experience. Were works of art placed in a directly human context in popular esteem, they would have a much wider appeal than they can have when pigeon-hole theories of art win general acceptance.

A conception of fine art that sets out from its connection with discovered qualities of ordinary experience will be able to indicate the factors and forces that favor the normal development of common human activities into matters of artistic value. It will also be able to point out those conditions that arrest its normal growth. Writers on esthetic theory often raise the question of whether esthetic philosophy can aid in cultivation of esthetic appreciation. The question is a branch of the general theory of criticism, which, it seems to me, fails to accomplish its full office if it does not indicate what to look for and what to find in concrete esthetic objects. But, in any case, it is safe to say that a philosophy of art is sterilized unless it makes us aware of the function of art in relation to other modes of experience, and unless it indicates why this function is so inadequately realized, and unless it suggests the conditions under which the office would be successfully performed.

The comparison of the emergence of works of art out of ordinary experiences to the refining of raw materials into valuable products may seem to some unworthy, if not an actual attempt to reduce works of art to the status of articles manufactured for commercial purposes. The point, however, is that no amount of ecstatic eulogy of finished works can of itself assist the understanding or the generation of such works. Flowers can be enjoyed without knowing about the interactions of soil, air, moisture, and seeds of which they are the result. But they cannot be *understood* without taking just these interactions into account – and theory is a matter of understanding. Theory is concerned with discovering the nature of the production of works of art and of their enjoyment in perception. How is it that the everyday making of things grows into that form of making which is genuinely artistic? How is it that our everyday enjoyment of scenes and situations develops into the peculiar satisfaction that attends the experience which is emphatically esthetic? These are the questions theory must answer. The answers cannot be found, unless we are willing to find the germs and roots in matters of experience that we do not currently regard as esthetic. Having discovered these active seeds, we may follow the course of their growth into the highest forms of finished and refined art. [. . .]

2. The Live Creature and "Ethereal Things"[1]

Why is the attempt to connect the higher and ideal things of experience with basic vital roots so often regarded as betrayal of their nature and denial of their value? Why is there repulsion when the high achievements of fine art are brought into connection with common life, the life that we share with all living creatures? Why is life thought of as an affair of low appetite, or at its best a thing of gross sensation, and ready to sink from its best to the level of lust and harsh cruelty? A complete answer to the question would involve the writing of a history of morals that would set forth the conditions that have brought about contempt for the body, fear of the senses, and the opposition of flesh to spirit.

One aspect of this history is so relevant to our problem that it must receive at least passing notice. The institutional life of mankind is marked by disorganization. This disorder is often disguised by the fact that it takes the form of static division into classes, and this static separation is accepted as the very essence of order as long as it is so fixed and so accepted as not to generate open conflict. Life is compartmentalized and the institutionalized compartments are classified as high and as low; their values as profane and spiritual, as material and ideal. Interests are related to one another externally and mechanically, through a system of checks and balances. Since religion, morals, politics, business has each its own compartment, within which it is fitting each should remain, art, too, must have its peculiar and private realm. Compartmentalization of occupations and interests brings about separation of that mode of activity commonly called "practice" from insight, of imagination from executive doing, of significant purpose from work, of emotion from thought and doing. Each of these has, too, its own place in which it must abide. Those who write the anatomy of experience then suppose that these divisions inhere in the very constitution of human nature.

Of much of our experience as it is actually lived under present economic and legal institutional conditions, it is only too true that these separations hold. Only occasionally in the lives of many are the senses fraught with the sentiment that comes from deep realization of intrinsic meanings. We undergo sensations as mechanical stimuli or as irritated stimulations, without having a sense of the reality that is in them and behind them: in much of our experience our different senses do not unite to tell a common and enlarged story. We see without feeling; we hear, but only a second-hand report, second hand because not reenforced by vision. We touch, but the contact remains tangential because it does not fuse with qualities of senses that go below the surface. We use the senses to arouse passion but not to fulfill the interest of insight, not because that interest is not potentially present in the exercise of sense but because we yield to conditions of living that force sense to remain an excitation on the surface. Prestige goes to those who use their minds without participation of the body and who act vicariously through control of the bodies and labor of others.

Under such conditions, sense and flesh get a bad name. The moralist, however, has a truer sense of the intimate connections of sense with the rest of our being than has the professional psychologist and philosopher, although his sense of these connections takes a direction that reverses the potential facts of our living in relation to the environment. Psychologist and philosopher have in recent times been so obsessed with the problem of knowledge that they have treated "sensations" as mere elements of knowledge. The moralist knows that sense is allied with emotion, impulse and appetition. So he denounces the lust of the eye as part of the surrender of spirit to flesh. He identifies the sensuous with the sensual and the sensual with the lewd. His moral theory is askew, but at least he is aware that the eye is not an imperfect telescope designed for intellectual reception of material to bring about knowledge of distant objects.

"Sense" covers a wide range of contents: the sensory, the sensational, the sensitive, the sensible, and the sentimental, along with the sensuous. It includes almost everything from bare physical and emotional shock to sense itself – that is, the meaning of things present in immediate experience. Each term refers to some real phase and aspect of the life of an organic creature as life occurs through sense organs. But sense, as meaning so directly embodied in experience as to be its own illuminated meaning, is the only signification that expresses the function of sense organs when they are carried to full realization. The senses are the organs through which the live creature participates directly in the ongoings of the world about him. In this participation the varied wonder and splendor of this world are made actual for him in the qualities he experiences. This material cannot be opposed to action, for motor apparatus and "will" itself are the means by which this participation is carried on and directed. It cannot be opposed to "intellect," for mind is the means by which participation is rendered fruitful through sense; by which meanings and values are extracted, retained, and put to further service in the intercourse of the live creature with his surroundings.

Experience is the result, the sign, and the reward of that interaction of organism and environment which, when it is carried to the full, is a transformation of interaction into participation and communication. Since sense-organs with their connected motor apparatus are the means of this participation, any and every derogation of them, whether practical or theoretical, is at once effect and cause of a narrowed and dulled life-experience. Oppositions of mind and body, soul and matter, spirit and flesh all have their origin, fundamentally, in fear of what life may bring forth. They are marks of contraction and withdrawal. Full recognition, therefore, of the continuity of the organs, needs and basic impulses of the human creature with his animal forbears, implies no necessary reduction of man to the level of the brutes. On the contrary, it makes possible the drawing of a ground-plan of human experience upon which is erected the superstructure of man's marvelous and distinguishing experience. What is distinctive in man makes it possible for him to sink below the level of the beasts. It also makes it possible for him to carry to new and unprecedented heights that unity of sense and impulse, of brain and eye and ear, that is exemplified in animal life, saturating it with the conscious meanings derived from communication and deliberate expression.

Man excels in complexity and minuteness of differentiations. This very fact constitutes the necessity for many more comprehensive and exact relationships among the constituents of his being. Important as are the distinctions and relations thus made possible, the story does not end here. There are more opportunities for resistance and tension, more drafts upon experimentation and invention, and therefore more novelty in action, greater range and depth of insight and increase of poignancy in feeling. As an organism increases in complexity, the rhythms of struggle and consummation in its relation to its environment are varied and prolonged, and they come to include within themselves an endless variety of sub-rhythms. The designs of living are widened and enriched. Fulfillment is more massive and more subtly shaded.

Space thus becomes something more than a void in which to roam about, dotted here and there with dangerous things and things that satisfy the appetite. It becomes a comprehensive and enclosed scene within which are ordered the multiplicity of doings and undergoings in which man engages. Time ceases to be either the endless and uniform flow or the succession of instantaneous points which some philosophers have asserted it to be. It, too, is the organized and organizing medium of the rhythmic ebb and flow of expectant impulse, forward and retracted movement, resistance and suspense, with fulfillment and consummation. It is an ordering of growth and maturations – as James said, we learn to skate in summer after having commenced in winter. Time as organization in change is growth, and growth signifies that a varied series of change enters upon intervals of pause and rest; of completions that become the initial points of new processes of development. Like the soil, mind is fertilized while it lies fallow, until a new burst of bloom ensues.

When a flash of lightning illumines a dark landscape, there is a momentary recognition of objects. But the recognition is not itself a mere point in time. It is the focal culmination of long, slow processes of maturation. It is the manifestation of the continuity of an ordered temporal experience in a sudden discrete instant of climax. It is as meaningless in isolation as would be the drama of Hamlet were it confined to a single line or word with no context. But the phrase "the rest is silence" is infinitely pregnant as the conclusion of a drama enacted through development in time; so may be the momentary perception of a natural scene. Form, as it is present in the fine arts, is the art of making clear what is involved in the organization of space and time prefigured in every course of a developing life-experience.

Moments and places, despite physical limitation and narrow localization, are charged with accumulations of long-gathering energy. A return to a scene of childhood that was left long years before floods the spot with a release of pent-up memories and hopes. To meet in a strange country one who is a casual acquaintance at home may arouse a satisfaction so acute as to bring a thrill. Mere recognitions occur only when we are occupied with something else than the object or person recognized. It marks either an interruption or else an intent to use what is recognized as a means for something else. To see, to perceive, is more than to recognize. It does not identify something present in terms of a past disconnected from it. The past is carried into the present so as to expand and deepen the content of the latter. There is illustrated the translation of bare continuity of external time into the vital order and organization of experience. Identification nods and passes on. Or it defines a passing moment in isolation, it marks a dead spot in experience that is merely filled in. The extent to which the process of living in any day or hour is reduced to labeling situations, events, and objects as "so-and-so" in mere succession marks the cessation of a life that is a conscious experience. Continuities realized in an individual, discrete, form are the essence of the latter.

Art is thus prefigured in the very processes of living. A bird builds its nest and a beaver its dam when internal organic pressures cooperate with external materials so that the former are fulfilled and the latter are transformed in a satisfying culmination. We may hesitate to apply the word "art," since we doubt the presence of directive intent. But all deliberation, all conscious intent, grows out of things once performed organically through the interplay of natural energies. Were it not so, art would be built on quaking sands, nay, on unstable air. The distinguishing contribution of man is consciousness of the relations found in nature. Through consciousness, he converts the relations of cause and effect that are found in nature into relations of means and consequence. Rather, consciousness itself is the inception of such a transformation. What was mere shock becomes an invitation; resistance becomes something to be used in changing existing arrangements of matter; smooth facilities become agencies for executing an idea. In these operations, an organic stimulation becomes the bearer of meanings, and motor responses are changed into instruments of expression and communication; no longer are they mere means of locomotion and direct reaction. Meanwhile, the organic substratum remains as the quickening and deep foundation. Apart from relations of cause and effect in nature, conception and invention could not be. Apart from the relation of processes of rhythmic conflict and fulfillment in animal life, experience would be without design and pattern. Apart from organs inherited from animal ancestry, idea and purpose would be without a mechanism of realization. The primeval arts of nature and animal life are so much the material, and, in gross outline, so much the model for the intentional achievements of man, that the theologically minded have imputed conscious intent to the structure of nature – as man, sharing many activities with the ape, is wont to think of the latter as imitating his own performances.

The existence of art is the concrete proof of what has just been stated abstractly. It is proof that man uses the materials and energies of nature with intent to expand his own life, and that he does so in accord with the structure of his organism – brain, sense-organs, and muscular system. Art is the living and concrete proof that man is capable of restoring consciously, and thus on the plane of meaning, the union of sense, need, impulse and action characteristic of the live creature. The intervention of consciousness adds regulation, power of selection, and redisposition. Thus it varies the arts in ways without end. But its intervention also leads in time to the *idea* of art as a conscious idea – the greatest intellectual achievement in the history of humanity.

The variety and perfection of the arts in Greece led thinkers to frame a generalized conception of art and to project the ideal of an art of organization of human activities as such – the art of politics and morals as conceived by Socrates and Plato. The ideas of design, plan, order, pattern, purpose emerged in distinction from and relation to the materials employed in their realization. The conception of man as the being that uses art became at once the ground of the distinction of man from the rest of nature and of the bond that ties him to nature. When the conception of art as the distinguishing trait of man was made explicit, there was assurance that, short of complete relapse of humanity below even savagery, the possibility of invention of new arts would remain, along with use of old arts, as the guiding ideal of mankind. Although recognition of the fact still halts, because of traditions established before the power of art was adequately recognized, science itself is but a central art auxiliary to the generation and utilization of other arts.[2]

It is customary, and from some points of view necessary, to make a distinction between fine art and useful or technological art. But the point of view from which it is necessary is one that is extrinsic to the work of art itself. The customary distinction is based simply on acceptance of certain existing social conditions. I suppose the fetiches of the Negro sculptor were taken to be useful in the highest degree to his tribal group, more so even than spears and clothing. But now they are fine art, serving in the twentieth century to inspire renovations in arts that had grown conventional. But they are fine art only because the anonymous artist lived and experienced so fully during the process of production. An angler may eat his catch without thereby losing the esthetic satisfaction he experienced in casting and playing. It is this degree of completeness of living in the experience of making and of perceiving that makes the difference between what is fine or esthetic in art and what is not. Whether the thing made is put to use, as are bowls, rugs, garments, weapons, is, *intrinsically* speaking, a matter of indifference. That many, perhaps most, of the articles and utensils made at present for use are not genuinely esthetic happens, unfortunately, to be true. But it is true for reasons that are foreign to the relation of the "beautiful" and "useful" as such. Wherever conditions are such as to prevent the act of production from being an experience in which the whole creature is alive and in which he possesses his living through enjoyment, the product will lack something of being esthetic. No matter how useful it is for special and limited ends, it will not be useful in the ultimate degree – that of contributing directly and liberally to an expanding and enriched life. The story of the severance and final sharp opposition of the useful and the fine is the history of that industrial development through which so much of production has become a form of postponed living and so much of consumption a superimposed enjoyment of the fruits of the labor of others. [...]

3. Having an Experience

Experience occurs continuously, because the interaction of live creature and environing conditions is involved in the very process of living. Under conditions of resistance and conflict, aspects and elements of the self and the world that are implicated in this interaction qualify experience with emotions and ideas so that conscious intent emerges. Oftentimes, however, the experience had is inchoate. Things are experienced but not in such a way that they are composed into *an* experience. There is distraction and dispersion; what we observe and what we think, what we desire and what we get, are at odds with each other. We put our hands to the plow and turn back; we start and then we stop, not because the experience has reached the end for the sake of which it was initiated but because of extraneous interruptions or of inner lethargy.

In contrast with such experience, we have *an* experience when the material experienced runs its course to fulfillment. Then and then only is it integrated within and demarcated in the general stream of experience from other experiences. A piece of work is finished in a way that is satisfactory; a problem receives its solution; a game is played through; a situation, whether that of eating a meal, playing a game of chess, carrying on a conversation, writing a book, or taking part in a political campaign, is so rounded out that its close is a consummation and not a cessation. Such an experience is a whole and carries with it its own individualizing quality and self-sufficiency. It is *an* experience.

Philosophers, even empirical philosophers, have spoken for the most part of experience at large. Idiomatic speech, however, refers to experiences each of which is singular, having its own beginning and end. For life is no uniform uninterrupted march or flow. It is a thing of histories, each with its own plot, its own inception and movement toward its close, each having its own particular rhythmic movement; each with its own unrepeated quality pervading it throughout. A flight of stairs, mechanical as it is, proceeds by individualized steps, not by undifferentiated progression, and an inclined plane is at least marked off from other things by abrupt discreteness.

Experience in this vital sense is defined by those situations and episodes that we spontaneously refer to as being "real experiences"; those things of which we say in recalling them, "that *was* an experience." It may have been something of tremendous importance – a quarrel with one who was once an intimate, a catastrophe finally averted by a hair's breadth. Or it may have been something that in comparison was slight – and which perhaps because of its very slightness illustrates all the better what it is to be an experience. There is that meal in a Paris restaurant of which one says "that *was* an experience." It stands out as an enduring memorial of what food may be. Then there is that storm one went through in crossing the Atlantic – the storm that seemed in its fury, as it was experienced, to sum up in itself all that a storm can he, complete in itself, standing out because marked out from what went before and what came after.

In such experiences, every successive part flows freely, without seam and without unfilled blanks, into what ensues. At the same time there is no sacrifice of the self-identity of the parts. A river, as distinct from a pond, flows. But its flow gives a definiteness and interest to its successive portions greater than exist in the homogenous portions of a pond. In an experience, flow is from something to something. As one part leads into another and as one part carries on what went before, each gains distinctness in itself. The enduring whole is diversified by successive phases that are emphases of its varied colors.

Because of continuous merging, there are no holes, mechanical junctions, and dead centres when we have *an* experience. There are pauses, places of rest, but they punctuate and define the quality of movement. They sum up what has been undergone and prevent its dissipation and idle evaporation. Continued acceleration is breathless and prevents parts from gaining distinction. In a work of art, different acts, episodes, occurrences melt and fuse into unity, and yet do not disappear and lose their own character as they do so – just as in a genial conversation there is a continuous interchange and blending, and yet each speaker not only retains his own character but manifests it more clearly than is his wont.

An experience has a unity that gives it its name, *that* meal, that storm, that rupture of friendship. The existence of this unity is constituted by a single *quality* that pervades the entire experience in spite of the variation of its constituent parts. This unity is neither emotional, practical, nor intellectual, for these terms name distinctions that reflection can make within it. In discourse *about* an experience, we must make use of these adjectives of interpretation. In going over an experience in mind *after* its occurrence, we may find that one property rather than another was sufficiently dominant so that it characterizes the experience as a whole. There are absorbing inquiries and speculations which a scientific man and philosopher will recall as "experiences" in the emphatic sense. In final import they are intellectual. But in their actual occurrence they were emotional as well; they were purposive and volitional. Yet the experience was not a sum of these different characters; they were lost in it as distinctive traits. No thinker can ply his occupation save as he is lured and rewarded by total integral experiences that are intrinsically worth while. Without them he would never know what it is really to think and would be completely at a loss in distinguishing real thought from the spurious article. Thinking goes on in trains of ideas, but the ideas form a train only because they are much more than what an analytic psychology calls ideas. They are phases, emotionally and practically distinguished, of a developing underlying quality; they are its moving variations, not separate and independent like Locke's and Hume's so-called ideas and impressions, but are subtle shadings of a pervading and developing hue.

We say of an experience of thinking that we reach or draw a conclusion. Theoretical formulation of the process is often made in such terms as to conceal effectually the similarity of "conclusion" to the consummating phase of every developing integral experience. These formulations apparently take their cue from the separate propositions that are premisses and the proposition that is the conclusion as they appear on the printed page. The impression is derived that there are first two independent and ready-made entities that are then manipulated so as to give rise to a third. In fact, in an experience of thinking, premisses emerge only as a conclusion becomes manifest. The experience, like that of watching a storm reach its height and gradually subside, is one of continuous movement of subject-matters. Like the ocean in the storm, there are a series of waves; suggestions reaching out and being broken in a clash, or being carried onwards by a cooperative wave. If a conclusion is reached, it is that of a movement of anticipation and cumulation, one that finally comes to completion. A "conclusion" is no separate and independent thing; it is the consummation of a movement.

Hence *an* experience of thinking has its own esthetic quality. It differs from those experiences that are acknowledged to he esthetic, but only in its materials. The material of the fine arts consists of qualities; that of experience having intellectual conclusion are signs or symbols having no intrinsic quality of their own, but standing for things that may in another experience be qualitatively experienced. The difference is enormous. It is one reason why the strictly intellectual art will never be popular as music is popular. Nevertheless, the experience itself has a satisfying emotional quality because it possesses internal integration and fulfillment reached through ordered and organized movement. This artistic structure may be immediately felt. In so far, it is esthetic. What is even more important is that not only is this quality a significant motive in undertaking intellectual inquiry and in keeping it honest, but that no intellectual activity is an integral event (is *an* experience), unless it is rounded out with this quality. Without it, thinking is inconclusive. In short, esthetic cannot be sharply marked off from intellectual experience since the latter must bear an esthetic stamp to be itself complete.

The same statement holds good of a course of action that is dominantly practical, that is, one that consists of overt doings. It is possible to be efficient in action and yet not have a conscious experience. The activity is too automatic to permit of a sense of what it is about and where it is going. It comes to an end but not to a close or consummation in consciousness. Obstacles are overcome by shrewd skill, but they do not feed experience. There are also those who are wavering in action, uncertain, and inconclusive like the shades in classic literature. Between the poles of aimlessness and mechanical efficiency, there lie those courses of action in which through successive deeds there runs a sense of growing meaning conserved and accumulating toward an end that is felt as accomplishment of a process. Successful politicians and generals who turn statesmen like Caesar and Napoleon have something of the showman about them. This of itself is not art, but it is, I think, a sign that interest is not exclusively, perhaps not mainly, held by the result taken by itself (as it is in the case of mere efficiency), but by it as the outcome of a process. There is interest in completing an experience. The experience may be one that is harmful to the world and its consummation undesirable. But it has esthetic quality.

The Greek identification of good conduct with conduct having proportion, grace, and harmony, the *kalon-agathon*, is a more obvious example of distinctive esthetic quality in moral action. One great defect in what passes as morality is its anesthetic quality. Instead of exemplifying wholehearted action, it takes the form of grudging piecemeal concessions to the demands of duty. But illustrations may only obscure the fact that any practical activity will, provided that it is integrated and moves by its own urge to fulfillment, have esthetic quality.

A generalized illustration may be had if we imagine a stone, which is rolling down hill, to have an experience. The activity is surely sufficiently "practical." The stone starts from somewhere, and moves, as consistently as conditions permit, toward a place and state where it will be at rest – toward an end. Let us add, by imagination, to these external facts, the ideas that it looks forward with desire to the final outcome; that it is interested in the things it meets on its way, conditions that accelerate and retard its movement with respect to their bearing on the end; that it acts and feels toward them according to the hindering or helping function it attributes to them; and that the final coming to rest is related to all that went before as the culmination of a continuous movement. Then the stone would have an experience, and one with esthetic quality.

If we turn from this imaginary case to our own experience, we shall find much of it is nearer to what happens to the actual stone than it is to anything that fulfills the conditions fancy just laid down. For in much of our experience we are not concerned with the connection of one incident with what went before and what comes after. There is no interest that controls attentive rejection or selection of what shall be organized into the developing experience. Things happen, but they are neither definitely included nor decisively excluded; we drift. We yield according to external pressure, or evade and compromise. There are beginnings and cessations, but no genuine initiations and concludings. One thing replaces another, but does not absorb it and carry it on. There is experience, but so slack and discursive that it is not *an* experience. Needless to say, such experiences are anesthetic.

Thus the non-esthetic lies within two limits. At one pole is the loose succession that does not begin at any particular place and that ends – in the sense of ceasing – at no particular place. At the other pole is arrest, constriction, proceeding from parts having only a mechanical connection with one another. There exists so much of one and the other of these two kinds of experience that unconsciously they come to be taken as norms of all experience. Then, when the esthetic appears, it so sharply contrasts with the picture that has been formed of experience, that it is impossible to combine its special qualities with the features of the picture and the esthetic is given an outside place and status. The account that has been given of experience dominantly intellectual and practical is intended to show that there is no such contrast involved in having an experience; that, on the contrary, no experience of whatever sort is a unity unless it has esthetic quality.

The enemies of the esthetic are neither the practical nor the intellectual. They are the humdrum; slackness of loose ends; submission to convention in practice and intellectual procedure. Rigid abstinence, coerced submission, rightness on one side and dissipation, incoherence and aimless indulgence on the other, are deviations in opposite directions from the unity of an experience. Some such considerations perhaps induced Aristotle to invoke the "mean proportional" as the proper designation of what is distinctive of both virtue and the esthetic. He was formally correct. "Mean" and "proportion" are, however, not self-explanatory, nor to be taken over in a prior mathematical sense, but are properties belonging to an experience that has a developing movement toward its own consummation.

I have emphasized the fact that every integral experience moves toward a close, an ending, since it ceases only when the energies active in it have done their proper work. This closure of a circuit of energy is the opposite of arrest, of *stasis*. Maturation and fixation are polar opposites. Struggle and conflict may be themselves enjoyed, although they are painful, when they are experienced as means of developing an experience;

members in that they carry it forward, not just because they are there. There is, as will appear later, an element of undergoing, of suffering in its large sense, in every experience. Otherwise there would be no taking in of what preceded. For "taking in" in any vital experience is something more than placing something on the top of consciousness over what was previously known. It involves reconstruction which may be painful. Whether the necessary undergoing phase is by itself pleasurable or painful is a matter of particular conditions. It is indifferent to the total esthetic quality, save that there are few intense esthetic experiences that are wholly gleeful. They are certainly not to be characterized as amusing, and as they bear down upon us they involve a suffering that is none the less consistent with, indeed a part of, the complete perception that is enjoyed.

I have spoken of the esthetic quality that rounds out an experience into completeness and unity as emotional. The reference may cause difficulty. We are given to thinking of emotions as things as simple and compact as are the words by which we name them. Joy, sorrow, hope, fear, anger, curiosity, are treated as if each in itself were a sort of entity that enters full-made upon the scene, an entity that may last a long time or a short time, but whose duration, whose growth and career, is irrelevant to its nature. In fact emotions are qualities, when they are significant, of a complex experience that moves and changes. I say, when they are *significant*, for otherwise they are but the outbreaks and eruptions of a disturbed infant. All emotions are qualifications of a drama and they change as the drama develops. Persons are sometimes said to fall in love at first sight. But what they fall into is not a thing of that instant. What would love be were it compressed into a moment in which there is no room for cherishing and for solicitude? The intimate nature of emotion is manifested in the experience of one watching a play on the stage or reading a novel. It attends the development of a plot; and a plot requires a stage, a space, wherein to develop and time in which to unfold. Experience is emotional but there are no separate things called emotions in it.

By the same token, emotions are attached to events and objects in their movement. They are not, save in pathological instances, private. And even an "objectless" emotion demands something beyond itself to which to attach itself, and thus it soon generates a delusion in lack of something real. Emotion belongs of a certainty to the self. But it belongs to the self that is concerned in the movement of events toward an issue that is desired or disliked. We jump instantaneously when we are scared, as we blush on the instant when we are ashamed. But fright and shamed modesty are not in this case emotional states. Of themselves they are but automatic reflexes. In order to become emotional they must become parts of an inclusive and enduring situation that involves concern for objects and their issues. The jump of fright becomes emotional fear when there is found or thought to exist a threatening object that must be dealt with or escaped from. The blush becomes the emotion of shame when a person connects, in thought, an action he has performed with an unfavorable reaction to himself of some other person.

Physical things from far ends of the earth are physically transported and physically caused to act and react upon one another in the construction of a new object. The miracle of mind is that something similar takes place in experience without physical transport and assembling. Emotion is the moving and cementing force. It selects what is congruous and dyes what is selected with its color, thereby giving qualitative unity to materials externally disparate and dissimilar. It thus provides unity in and through the varied parts of an experience. When the unity is of the sort already described, the experience has esthetic character even though it is not, dominantly, an esthetic experience.

Two men meet; one is the applicant for a position, while the other has the disposition of the matter in his hands. The interview may be mechanical, consisting of set questions, the replies to which perfunctorily settle the matter. There is no experience in which the two men meet, nothing that is not a repetition, by way of acceptance or dismissal, of something which has happened a score of times. The situation is disposed of as if it were an exercise in bookkeeping. But an interplay may take place in which a new experience develops. Where should we look for an account of such an experience? Not to ledger-entries nor yet to a treatise on economics or sociology or personnel-psychology, but to drama or fiction. Its nature and import can he expressed only by art, because there is a unity of experience that can be expressed only as an experience. The *experience* is of material fraught with suspense and moving toward its own consummation through a connected series of varied incidents. The primary emotions on the part of the applicant may be at the beginning hope or despair, and elation or disappointment at the close. These emotions qualify the experience as a unity. But as the interview proceeds, secondary emotions are evolved as variations of the primary underlying one. It is even possible for each attitude and gesture, each sentence, almost every word, to produce more than a fluctuation in the intensity of the basic emotion; to produce, that is, a change of shade and tint in its quality. The employer sees by means of his own emotional reactions the character of the one applying. He projects him imaginatively into the work to be done and judges his fitness by the way in which the elements of the scene assemble and either clash or fit together. The presence and behavior of the applicant either harmonize with his own attitudes and desires or they conflict and jar. Such factors as these, inherently esthetic in quality, are the forces that carry the varied elements of the interview to a decisive issue. They enter into the settlement of every situation, whatever its dominant nature, in which there are uncertainty and suspense.

There are, therefore, common patterns in various experiences, no matter how unlike they are to one another in the details of their subject matter. There are conditions to be met without which an experience cannot come to be. The outline of the common pattern is set by the fact that every experience is the result of interaction between a live creature and some aspect of the world in which he lives. A man does something; he lifts, let us say, a stone. In consequence he undergoes, suffers, something: the weight, strain, texture of the surface of the thing lifted. The properties thus undergone determine further doing. The stone is too heavy or too angular, not solid enough; or else the properties undergone show it is fit for the use for which it is intended. The process continues until a mutual adaptation of the self and the object emerges and that particular experience comes to a close. What is true of this simple instance is true, as to form, of every experience. The creature operating may be a thinker in his study and the environment with which he interacts may consist of ideas instead of a stone. But interaction of the two constitutes the total experience that is had, and the close which completes it is the institution of a felt harmony.

An experience has pattern and structure, because it is not just doing and undergoing in alternation, but consists of them in relationship. To put one's hand in the fire that consumes it is not necessarily to have an experience. The action and its consequence must be joined in perception. This relationship is what gives meaning; to grasp it is the objective of all intelligence. The scope and content of the relations measure the significant content of an experience. A child's experience may be intense, but, because of lack of background from past experience, relations between undergoing and doing are slightly grasped, and the experience does not have great depth or breadth. No one ever arrives at such maturity that he perceives all the connections that are involved. There was once written (by Mr. Hinton) a romance called "The Unlearner." It portrayed the whole endless duration of life after death as a living over of the incidents that happened in a short life on earth, in continued discovery of the relationships involved among them.

Experience is limited by all the causes which interfere with perception of the relations between undergoing and doing. There may be interference because of excess on the side of doing or of excess on the side of receptivity, of undergoing. Unbalance on either side blurs the perception of relations and leaves the experience partial and distorted, with scant or false meaning. Zeal for doing, lust for action, leaves many a person, especially in this hurried and impatient human environment in which we live, with experience of an almost incredible paucity, all on the surface. No one experience has a chance to complete itself because something else is entered upon so speedily. What is called experience becomes so dispersed and miscellaneous as hardly to deserve the name. Resistance is treated as an obstruction to be beaten down, not as an invitation to reflection. An individual comes to seek, unconsciously even more than by deliberate choice, situations in which he can do the most things in the shortest time.

Experiences are also cut short from maturing by excess of receptivity. What is prized is then the mere undergoing of this and that, irrespective of perception of any meaning. The crowding together of as many impressions as possible is thought to be "life," even though no one of them is more than a flitting and a sipping. The sentimentalist and the day-dreamer may have more fancies and impressions pass through their consciousness than has the man who is animated by lust for action. But his experience is equally distorted, because nothing takes root in mind when there is no balance between doing and receiving. Some decisive action is needed in order to establish contact with the realities of the world and in order that impressions may be so related to facts that their value is tested and organized.

Because perception of relationship between what is done and what is undergone constitutes the work of intelligence, and because the artist is controlled in the process of his work by his grasp of the connection between what he has already done and what he is to do next, the idea that the artist does not think as intently and penetratingly as a scientific inquirer is absurd. A painter must consciously undergo the effect of his every brush stroke or he will not be aware of what he is doing and where his work is going. Moreover, he has to see each particular connection of doing and undergoing in relation to the whole that he desires to produce. To apprehend such relations is to think, and is one of the most exacting modes of thought. The difference between the pictures of different painters is due quite as much to differences of capacity to carry on this thought as it is to differences of sensitivity to bare color and to differences in dexterity of execution. As respects the basic quality of pictures, difference depends, indeed, more upon the quality of intelligence brought to bear upon perception of relations than upon anything else – though of course intelligence cannot be separated from direct sensitivity and is connected, though in a more external manner, with skill.

Any idea that ignores the necessary role of intelligence in production of works of art is based upon identification of thinking with use of one special kind of material, verbal signs and words. To think effectively in terms of relations of qualities is as severe a demand upon thought as to think in terms of symbols, verbal and mathematical. Indeed, since words are easily manipulated in mechanical ways, the production of a work of genuine art probably demands more intelligence than does most of the so-called thinking that goes on among those who pride themselves on being "intellectuals."

I have tried to show in these chapters that the esthetic is no intruder in experience from without, whether by way of idle luxury or transcendent ideality, but that it is the clarified and intensified development of traits that belong to every normally complete experience. This fact I take to be the only secure basis upon which esthetic theory can build. It remains to suggest some of the implications of the underlying fact.

We have no word in the English language that unambiguously includes what is signified by the two worlds "artistic" and "esthetic." Since "artistic" refers primarily to the act of production and "esthetic" to that of perception and enjoyment, the absence of a term designating the two processes taken together is unfortunate. Sometimes, the effect is to separate the two from each other, to regard art as something superimposed upon esthetic material, or, upon the other side, to an assumption that, since art is a process of creation, perception and enjoyment of it have nothing in common with the creative act. In any case, there is a certain verbal awkwardness in that we are compelled sometimes to use the term "esthetic" to cover the entire field and sometimes to limit it to the receiving perceptual aspect of the whole operation. I refer to these obvious facts as preliminary to an attempt to show how the conception of conscious experience as a perceived relation between doing and undergoing enables us to understand the connection that art as production and perception and appreciation as enjoyment sustain to each other.

Art denotes a process of doing or making. This is as true of fine as of technological art. Art involves molding of clay, chipping of marble, casting of bronze, laying on of pigments, construction of buildings, singing of songs, playing of instruments, enacting roles on the stage, going through rhythmic movements in the dance. Every art does something with some physical material, the body or something outside the body, with or without the use of intervening tools, and with a view to production of something visible, audible, or tangible. So marked is the active or "doing" phase of art, that the dictionaries usually define it in terms of skilled action, ability in execution. The *Oxford Dictionary* illustrates by a quotation from John Stuart Mill: "Art is an endeavour after perfection in execution" while Matthew Arnold calls it "pure and flawless workmanship."

The word "esthetic" refers, as we have already noted, to experience as appreciative, perceiving, and enjoying. It denotes the consumer's rather than the producer's standpoint. It is Gusto, taste; and, as with cooking, overt skillful action is on the side of the cook who prepares, while taste is on the side of the consumer, as in gardening there is a distinction between the gardener who plants and tills and the householder who enjoys the finished product.

These very illustrations, however, as well as the relation that exists in having an experience between doing and undergoing, indicate that the distinction between esthetic and artistic cannot be pressed so far as to become a separation. Perfection in execution cannot be measured or defined in terms of execution; it implies those who perceive and enjoy the product that is executed. The cook prepares food for the consumer and the measure of the value of what is prepared is found in consumption. Mere perfection in execution, judged in its own terms in isolation, can probably be attained better by a machine than by human art. By itself, it is at most technique, and there are great artists who are not in the first ranks as technicians (witness Cézanne), just as there are great performers on the piano who are not great esthetically, and as Sargent is not a great painter.

Craftsmanship to be artistic in the final sense must be "loving"; it must care deeply for the subject matter upon which skill is exercised. A sculptor comes to mind whose busts are marvelously exact. It might be difficult to tell in the presence of a photograph of one of them and of a photograph of the original which was of the person himself. For virtuosity they are remarkable. But one doubts whether the maker of the busts had an experience of his own that he was concerned to have those share who look at his products. To be truly artistic, a work must also be esthetic – that is, framed for enjoyed receptive perception. Constant observation is, of course, necessary for the maker while he is producing. But if his perception is not also esthetic in nature, it is a colorless and cold recognition of what has been done, used as a stimulus to the next step in a process that is essentially mechanical.

In short, art, in its form, unites the very same relation of doing and undergoing, outgoing and incoming energy, that makes an experience to be an experience. Because of elimination of all that does not contribute to mutual organization of the factors of both action and reception into one another, and because of selection of just the aspects and traits that contribute to their interpenetration of each other, the product is a work of esthetic art. Man whittles, carves, sings, dances, gestures, molds, draws and paints. The doing or making is artistic when the perceived result is of such a nature that *its* qualities *as perceived* have controlled the question of production. The act of producing that is directed by intent to produce something that is enjoyed in the immediate experience of perceiving has qualities that a spontaneous or uncontrolled activity does not have. The artist embodies in himself the attitude of the perceiver while he works.

Suppose, for the sake of illustration, that a finely wrought object, one whose texture and proportions are highly pleasing in perception, has been believed to be a product of some primitive people. Then there is discovered evidence that proves it to be an accidental natural product. As an external thing, it is now precisely what it was before. Yet at once it ceases to be a work of art and becomes a natural "curiosity." It now belongs in a museum of natural history, not in a museum of art. And the extraordinary thing is that the difference that is thus made is not one of just intellectual classification. A difference is made in appreciative perception and in a direct way. The esthetic experience – in its limited sense – is thus seen to be inherently connected with the experience of making.

The sensory satisfaction of eye and ear, when esthetic, is so because it does not stand by itself but is linked to the activity of which it is the consequence. Even the pleasures of the palate are different in quality to an epicure than in one who merely "likes" his food as he eats it. The difference is not of mere intensity. The epicure is conscious of much more than the taste of the food. Rather, there enter into the taste, as directly experienced, qualities that depend upon reference to its source and its manner of production in connection with criteria of excellence. As production must absorb into itself qualities of the product as perceived and be regulated by them, so, on the other side, seeing, hearing, tasting, become esthetic when relation to a distinct manner of activity qualifies what is perceived.

There is an element of passion in all esthetic perception. Yet when we are overwhelmed by passion, as in extreme rage, fear, jealousy, the experience is definitely non-esthetic. There is no relationship felt to the qualities of the activity that has generated the passion. Consequently, the material of the experience lacks elements of balance and proportion. For these can be present only when, as in the conduct that has grace or dignity, the act is controlled by an exquisite sense of the relations which the act sustains – its fitness to the occasion and to the situation.

The process of art in production is related to the esthetic in perception organically – as the Lord God in creation surveyed his work and found it good. Until the artist is satisfied in perception with what he is doing, he continues shaping and reshaping. The making comes to an end when its result is experienced as good – and that experience comes not by mere intellectual and outside judgment but in direct perception. An artist, in comparison with his fellows, is one who is not only especially gifted in powers of execution but in unusual sensitivity to the qualities of things. This sensitivity also directs his doings and makings.

As we manipulate, we touch and feel; as we look, we see; as we listen, we hear. The hand moves with etching needle or with brush. The eye attends and reports the consequence of what is done. Because of this intimate connection, subsequent doing is cumulative and not a matter of caprice nor yet of routine. In an emphatic artistic-esthetic experience, the relation is so close that it controls simultaneously both the doing and the perception. Such vital intimacy of connection cannot be had if only hand and eye are engaged. When they do not, both of them, act as organs of the whole being, there is but a mechanical sequence of sense and movement, as in walking that is automatic. Hand and eye, when the experience is esthetic, are but instruments through which the entire live creature, moved and active throughout, operates. Hence the expression is emotional and guided by purpose.

Because of the relation between what is done and what is undergone, there is an immediate sense of things in perception as belonging together or as jarring; as reenforcing or as interfering. The consequences of the act of making as reported in sense show whether what is done carries forward the idea being executed or marks a deviation and break. In as far as the development of an experience is *controlled* through reference to these immediately felt relations of order and fulfillment, that experience becomes dominantly esthetic in nature. The urge to action becomes an urge to that kind of action which will result in an object satisfying in direct perception. The potter shapes his clay to make a bowl useful for holding grain; but he makes it in a way so regulated by the series of perceptions that sum up the serial acts of making, that the bowl is marked by enduring grace and charm. The general situation remains the same in painting a picture or molding a bust. Moreover, at each stage there is anticipation of what is to come. This anticipation is the connecting link between the next doing and its outcome for sense. What is done and what is undergone are thus reciprocally, cumulatively, and continuously instrumental to each other.

The doing may be energetic, and the undergoing may be acute and intense. But unless they are related to each other to form a whole in perception, the thing done is not fully esthetic. The making for example may be a display of technical virtuosity, and the undergoing a gush of sentiment or a revery. If the artist does not perfect a new vision in his process of doing, he acts mechanically and repeats some old model fixed like a blue print in his mind. An incredible amount of observation and of the kind of intelligence that is exercised in perception of qualitative relations characterizes creative work in art. The relations must be noted not only with respect to one another, two by two, but in connection with the whole under construction; they are exercised in imagination as well as in observation. Irrelevancies arise that are tempting distractions; digressions suggest themselves in the guise of enrichments. There are occasions when the grasp of the dominant idea grows faint, and then the artist is moved unconsciously to fill in until his thought grows strong again. The real work of an artist is to build up an experience that is coherent in perception while moving with constant change in its development.

When an author puts on paper ideas that are already clearly conceived and consistently ordered, the real work has been previously done. Or, he may depend upon the greater perceptibility induced by the activity and its sensible report to direct his completion of the work. The mere act of transcription is esthetically irrelevant save as it enters integrally into the formation of an experience moving to completeness. Even the composition conceived in the head and, therefore, physically private, is public in its significant content, since it is conceived with reference to execution in a product that is perceptible and hence belongs to the common world. Otherwise it would be an aberration or a passing dream. The urge to express through painting the perceived qualities of a landscape is continuous with demand for pencil or brush. Without external embodiment, an experience remains incomplete; physiologically and functionally, sense organs are motor organs and are connected, by means of distribution of energies in the human body and not merely anatomically, with other motor organs. It is no linguistic accident that "building," "construction," "work," designate both a process and its finished product. Without the meaning of the verb that of the noun remains blank.

Writer, composer of music, sculptor, or painter can retrace, during the process of production, what they have previously done. When it is not satisfactory in the undergoing or perceptual phase of experience, they can to some degree start afresh. This retracting is not readily accomplished in the case of architecture – which is perhaps one reason why there are so many ugly buildings. Architects are obliged to complete their idea before its translation into a complete object of perception takes place. Inability to build up simultaneously the idea and its objective embodiment imposes a handicap. Nevertheless, they too are obliged to think out their ideas in terms of the medium of embodiment and the object of ultimate perception unless they work mechanically and by rote. Probably the esthetic quality of medieval cathedrals is due in some measure to the fact that their constructions were not so much controlled by plans and specifications made in advance as is now the case. Plans grew as the building grew. But even a Minerva-like product, if it is artistic, presupposes a prior period of gestation in which doings and perceptions projected in imagination interact and mutually modify one another. Every work of art follows the plan of, and pattern of, a complete experience, rendering it more intensely and concentratedly felt.

It is not so easy in the case of the perceiver and appreciator to understand the intimate union of doing and undergoing as it is in the case of the maker. We are given to supposing that the former merely takes in what is there in finished form, instead of realizing that this taking in involves activities that are comparable to those of the creator. But receptivity is not passivity. It, too, is a process consisting of a series of responsive acts that accumulate toward objective fulfillment. Otherwise, there is not perception but recognition. The difference between the two is immense. Recognition is perception arrested before it has a chance to develop freely. In recognition there is a beginning of an act of perception. But this beginning is not allowed to serve the development of a full perception of the thing recognized. It is arrested at the point where it will serve some *other* purpose, as we recognize a man on the street in order to greet or to avoid him, not so as to see him for the sake of seeing what is there.

In recognition we fall back, as upon a stereotype, upon some previously formed scheme. Some detail or arrangement of details serves as cue for bare identification. It suffices in recognition to apply this bare outline as a stencil to the present object. Sometimes in contact with a human being we are struck with traits, perhaps of only physical characteristics, of which we were not previously aware. We realize that we never knew the person before; we had not seen him in any pregnant sense. We now begin to study and to "take in." Perception replaces bare recognition. There is an act of reconstructive doing, and consciousness becomes fresh and alive. *This* act of seeing involves the cooperation of motor elements even though they remain implicit and do not become overt, as well as cooperation of all funded ideas that may serve to complete the new picture that is forming. Recognition is too easy to arouse vivid consciousness. There is not enough resistance between new and old to secure consciousness of the experience that is had. Even a dog that barks and wags his tail joyously on seeing his master return is more fully alive in his reception of his friend than is a human being who is content with mere recognition.

Bare recognition is satisfied when a proper tag or label is attached, "proper" signifying one that serves a purpose outside the act of recognition – as a salesman identifies wares by a sample. It involves no stir of the organism, no inner commotion. But an act of perception proceeds by waves that extend serially throughout the entire organism. There is, therefore, no such thing in perception as seeing or hearing *plus* emotion. The perceived object or scene is emotionally pervaded throughout. When an aroused emotion does not permeate the material that is perceived or thought of, it is either preliminary or pathological.

The esthetic or undergoing phase of experience is receptive. It involves surrender. But adequate yielding of the self is possible only through a controlled activity that may well be intense. In much of our intercourse with our surroundings we withdraw; sometimes from fear, if only of expending unduly our store of energy; sometimes from preoccupation with other matters, as in the case of recognition. Perception is an act of the going-out of energy in order to receive, not a withholding of energy. To steep ourselves in a subject-matter we have first to plunge into it. When we are only passive to a scene, it overwhelms us and, for lack of answering activity, we do not perceive that which bears us down, We must summon energy and pitch it at a responsive key in order to *take* in.

Every one knows that it requires apprenticeship to see through a microscope or telescope, and to see a landscape as the geologist sees it. The idea that esthetic perception is an affair for odd moments is one reason for the backwardness of the arts among us. The eye and the visual apparatus may be intact; the object may be physically there, the cathedral of Notre Dame, or Rembrandt's portrait of Hendrickje Stoffels. In some bald sense, the latter may be "seen." They may be looked at, possibly recognized, and have their correct names attached. But for lack of continuous interaction between the total organism and the objects, they are not perceived, certainly not esthetically. A crowd of visitors steered through a picture-gallery by a guide, with attention called here and there to some high point, does not perceive; only by accident is there even interest in seeing a picture for the sake of subject matter vividly realized.

For to perceive, a beholder must *create* his own experience. And his creation must include relations comparable to those which the original producer underwent. They are not the same in any literal sense. But with the perceiver, as with the artist, there must be an ordering of the elements of the whole that is in form, although not in details, the same as the process of organization the creator of the work consciously experienced. Without an act of recreation the object is not perceived as a work of art. The artist selected, simplified, clarified, abridged and condensed according to his interest. The beholder must go through these operations according to his point of view and interest. In both, an act of abstraction, that is of extraction of what is significant, takes place. In both, there is comprehension in its literal signification – that is, a gathering together of details and particulars physically scattered into an experienced whole. There is work done on the part of the percipient as there is on the part of the artist. The one who is too lazy, idle, or indurated in convention to perform this work will not see or hear. His "appreciation" will be a mixture of scraps of learning with conformity to norms of conventional admiration and with a confused, even if genuine, emotional excitation.

The considerations that have been presented imply both the community and the unlikeness, because of specific emphasis, of *an* experience, in its pregnant sense, and esthetic experience. The former has esthetic quality; otherwise its materials would not be rounded out into a single coherent experience. It is not possible to divide in a vital experience the practical, emotional, and intellectual from one another and to set the properties of one over against the characteristics of the others. The emotional phase binds parts together into a single whole; "intellectual" simply names the fact that the experience has meaning;

"practical" indicates that the organism is interacting with events and objects which surround it. The most elaborate philosophic or scientific inquiry and the most ambitious industrial or political enterprise has, when its different ingredients constitute an integral experience, esthetic quality. For then its varied parts are linked to one another, and do not merely succeed one another. And the parts through their experienced linkage move toward a consummation and close, not merely to cessation in time. This consummation, moreover, does not wait in consciousness for the whole undertaking to be finished. It is anticipated throughout and is recurrently savored with special intensity.

Nevertheless, the experiences in question are dominantly intellectual or practical, rather than *distinctively* esthetic, because of the interest and purpose that initiate and control them. In an intellectual experience, the conclusion has value on its own account. It can be extracted as a formula or as a "truth," and can be used in its independent entirety as factor and guide in other inquiries. In a work of art there is no such single self-sufficient deposit. The end, the terminus, is significant not by itself but as the integration of the parts. It has no other existence. A drama or novel is not the final sentence, even if the characters are disposed of as living happily ever after. In a distinctively esthetic experience, characteristics that are subdued in other experiences are dominant; those that are subordinate are controlling – namely, the characteristics in virtue of which the experience is an integrated complete experience on its own account.

In every integral experience there is form because there is dynamic organization. I call the organization dynamic because it takes time to complete it, because it is a growth. There is inception, development, fulfillment. Material is ingested and digested through interaction with that vital organization of the results of prior experience that constitutes the mind of the worker. Incubation goes on until what is conceived is brought forth and is rendered perceptible as part of the common world. An esthetic experience can be crowded into a moment only in the sense that a climax of prior long enduring processes may arrive in an outstanding movement which so sweeps everything else into it that all else is forgotten. That which distinguishes an experience as esthetic is conversion of resistance and tensions, of excitations that in themselves are temptations to diversion, into a movement toward an inclusive and fulfilling close.

Experiencing like breathing is a rhythm of intakings and outgivings. Their succession is punctuated and made a rhythm by the existence of intervals, periods in which one phase is ceasing and the other is inchoate and preparing. William James aptly compared the course of a conscious experience to the alternate flights and perchings of a bird. The flights and perchings are intimately connected with one another; they are not so many unrelated lightings succeeded by a number of equally unrelated hoppings. Each resting place in experience is an undergoing in which is absorbed and taken home the consequences of prior doing, and, unless the doing is that of utter caprice or sheer routine, each doing carries in itself meaning that has been extracted and conserved. As with the advance of an army, all gains from what has been already effected are periodically consolidated, and always with a view to what is to be done next. If we move too rapidly, we get away from the base of supplies – of accrued meanings – and the experience is flustered, thin, and confused. If we dawdle too long after having extracted a net value, experience perishes of inanition.

The *form* of the whole is therefore present in every member. Fulfilling, consummating, are continuous functions, not mere ends, located at one place only. An engraver, painter, or writer is in process of completing at every stage of his work. He must at each point retain and sum up what has gone before as a whole and with reference to a whole to come. Otherwise there is no consistency and no security in his successive acts. The series of doings in the rhythm of experience give variety and movement; they save the work from monotony and useless repetitions. The undergoings are the corresponding elements in the rhythm, and they supply unity; they save the work from the aimlessness of a mere succession of excitations. An object is peculiarly and dominantly esthetic, yielding the enjoyment characteristic of esthetic perception, when the factors that determine anything which can be called *an* experience are lifted high above the threshold of perception and are made manifest for their own sake.

Notes

1 The sun, the Moon, the Earth and its contents, are material to form greater things, that is, ethereal things – greater things than the Creator himself made. – JOHN KEATS.

2 I have developed this point in *Experience and Nature*, in Chapter Nine, on Experience, Nature and Art. As far as the present point is concerned, the conclusion is contained in the statement that "art, the mode of activity that is charged with meanings capable of immediately enjoyed possession, is the complete culmination of nature, and that science is properly a handmaiden that conducts natural events to this happy issue." (p. 358.) [*Later Works* 1:269.]

28

Feeling and Form

Susanne Langer

Susanne Langer (1895–1985), who was Professor of Philosophy at Connecticut College, developed an influential view of the symbolic nature of art.

In the book to which the present one is a sequel there is a chapter entitled "On Significance in Music." The theory of significance there developed is a special theory, which does not pretend to any further application than the one made of it in that original realm, namely music. Yet, the more one reflects on the significance of art generally, the more the music theory appears as a lead. And the hypothesis certainly suggests itself that the oft-asserted fundamental unity of the arts lies not so much in parallels between their respective elements or analogies among their techniques, as in the singleness of their characteristic import, the meaning of "significance" with respect to any and each of them. "Significant Form" (which really has significance) is the essence of every art; it is what we mean by calling anything "artistic."

If the proposed lead will not betray us, we have here a principle of analysis that may be applied within each separate art gender in explaining its peculiar choice and use of materials; a criterion of what is or is not relevant in judging works of art in any realm; a direct exhibition of the unity of all the arts (without necessitating a resort to "origins" in fragmentary, doubtful history, and still more questionable prehistory); and the making of a truly general theory of art as such, wherein the several arts may be distinguished as well as connected, and almost any philosophical problems they present – problems of their relative values, their special powers or limitations, their social function, their connection with dream and fantasy or with actuality, etc., etc. – may be tackled with some hope of decision. The proper way to construct a general theory is by generalization of a special one; and I believe the analysis of musical significance in *Philosophy in a New Key* is capable of such generalization, and of furnishing a valid theory of significance for the whole Parnassus.

The study of musical significance grew out of a prior philosophical reflection on the meaning of the very popular term "expression." In the literature of aesthetics this word holds a prominent place; or rather, it holds prominent places, for it is employed in more than one sense and consequently changes its meaning from one book to another, and sometimes even from passage to passage in a single work. Sometimes writers who are actually in close agreement use it in incompatible ways, and literally contradict each other's statements, yet actually do not become aware of this fact, because each will read the word as the other intended it, not as he really used it where it happens to occur. Thus Roger Fry tried to

Susanne Langer, *Feeling and Form* (New York: Charles Scribner's Sons, 1953), pp. 24–41. © 1953 by Charles Scribner's Sons. Reprinted by permission of Pearson Education, Inc.

elucidate Clive Bell's famous but cryptic phrase, "Significant Form," by identifying it with Flaubert's "expression of the Idea"; and Bell probably subscribes fully to Fry's exegesis, as far as it goes (which, as Fry remarks, is unfortunately not very far, since the "Idea" is the next hurdle). Yet Bell himself, trying to explain his meaning, says: "It is useless to go to a picture gallery in search of expression; you must go in search of Significant Form." Of course Bell is thinking here of "expression" in an entirely different sense. Perhaps he means that you should not look for the artist's *self*-expression, i.e., for a record of his emotions. Yet this reading is doubtful, for elsewhere in the same book he says: "It seems to me possible, though by no means certain, that created form moves us so profoundly because it expresses the emotion of its creator." Now, is the emotion of the creator the "Idea" in Flaubert's sense, or is it not? Or does the same work have, perhaps, two different expressive functions? And what about the kind we must *not* look for in a picture gallery?

We may, of course, look for any kind of expression we like, and there is even a fair chance that, whatever it be, we shall find it. A work of art is often a spontaneous expression of feeling, i.e., a symptom of the artist's state of mind. If it represents human beings it is probably also a rendering of some sort of facial expression which suggests the feelings those beings are supposed to have. Moreover, it may be said to "express," in another sense, the life of the society from which it stems, namely to *indicate* customs, dress, behavior, and to reflect confusion or decorum, violence or peace. And besides all these things it is sure to express the unconscious wishes and nightmares of its author. All these things may be found in museums and galleries if we choose to note them.

But they may also be found in wastebaskets and in the margins of schoolbooks. This does not mean that someone has discarded a work of art, or produced one when he was bored with long division. It merely means that all drawings, utterances, gestures, or personal records of any sort express feelings, beliefs, social conditions, and interesting neuroses; "expression" in any of these senses is not peculiar to art, and consequently is not what makes for artistic values.

Artistic significance, or "expression of the Idea," is "expression" in still a different sense and, indeed, a radically different one. In all the contexts mentioned above, the art work or other object functioned as a *sign* that pointed to some matter of fact – how someone felt, what he believed, when and where he lived, or what bedeviled his dreams. But *expression of an idea*, even in ordinary usage, where the "idea" has no capital *I*, does not refer to the signific function, i.e. the indication of a fact by some natural symptom or invented signal. It usually refers to the prime purpose of language, which is discourse, the presentation of mere ideas. When we say that something is well expressed, we do not necessarily believe the expressed idea to refer to our present situation, or even to be true, but only to be given clearly and objectively for contemplation. Such "expression" is the function of symbols: articulation and presentation of *concepts*. Herein symbols differ radically from signals.[1] A signal is comprehended if it serves to make us notice the object or situation it bespeaks. A symbol is understood when we conceive the idea it presents.

The logical difference between signals and symbols is sufficiently explained, I think, in *Philosophy in a New Key* to require no repetition here, although much more could be said about it than that rather general little treatise undertook to say. Here, as there, I shall go on to a consequent of the logical studies, a theory of significance that points the contrast between the functions of art and of discourse, respectively; but this time with reference to all the arts, not only the non-verbal and essentially non-representative art of music.

The theory of music, however, is our point of departure, wherefore it may be briefly recapitulated here as it finally stood in the earlier book:

The tonal structures we call "music" bear a close logical similarity to the forms of human feeling – forms of growth and of attenuation, flowing and stowing, conflict and resolution, speed, arrest, terrific excitement, calm, or subtle activation and dreamy lapses – not joy and sorrow perhaps, but the poignancy of either and both – the greatness and brevity and eternal passing of everything vitally felt. Such is the pattern, or logical form, of sentience; and the pattern of music is that same form worked out in pure, measured sound and silence. Music is a tonal analogue of emotive life.

Such formal analogy, or congruence of logical structures, is the prime requisite for the relation between a symbol and whatever it is to mean. The symbol and the object symbolized must have some common logical form.

But purely on the basis of formal analogy, there would be no telling which of two congruent structures was the symbol and which the meaning, since the relation of congruence, or formal likeness, is symmetrical, i.e. it works both ways. (If John looks so much like James that you can't tell him from James, then you can't tell James from John. either.) There must be a motive for choosing, as between two entities or two systems, one to be the symbol of the other. Usually the decisive reason is that one is easier to perceive and handle than the other. Now sounds are much easier to produce, combine, perceive, and identify, than feelings. Forms of sentience occur only in the course of nature, but musical forms may be invented and intoned at will. Their general pattern may be reincarnated again and again by repeated performance. The effect is actually never quite the same even though the physical repetition may be exact, as in recorded music, because the exact degree of one's familiarity with a passage affects the experience of it, and this factor can never be made permanent. Yet within a fairly wide range such variations are, happily, unimportant. To some musical forms even much less subtle changes are not really disturbing, for instance certain differences of instrumentation and even, within limits, of pitch or tempo. To others, they are fatal. But in the main, sound is a negotiable medium, capable of voluntary composition and repetition, whereas feeling is not; this trait recommends tonal structures for symbolic purposes.

Furthermore, a symbol is used to articulate ideas of something we wish to think about, and until we have a fairly adequate symbolism we cannot think about it. So *interest* always plays a major part in making one thing, or realm of things, the meaning of something else, the symbol or system of symbols.

Sound, as a sheer sensory factor in experience, may be soothing or exciting, pleasing or torturing; but so are the factors of taste, smell, and touch. Selecting and exploiting such somatic influences is self-indulgence, a very different thing from art. An enlightened society usually has some means, public or private, to support its artists, because their work is regarded as a spiritual triumph and a claim to greatness for the whole tribe. But mere epicures would hardly achieve such fame. Even chefs, perfumers, and upholsterers, who produce the means of sensory pleasure for others, are not rated as the torch-bearers of culture and inspired creators. Only their own advertisements bestow such titles on them. If music, patterned sound, had no other office than to stimulate and soothe our nerves, pleasing our ears as well-combined foods please our palates, it might be highly popular, but never culturally important. Its historic development would be too trivial a subject to engage many people in its lifelong study, though a few desperate PhD theses might be wrung from its anecdotal past under the rubric of "social history." And music conservatories would be properly rated exactly like cooking schools.

Our interest in music arises from its intimate relation to the all-important life of feeling, whatever that relation may be. After much debate on current theories, the conclusion reached in *Philosophy in a New Key* is that the function of music is not stimulation of feeling, but expression of it; and furthermore, not the symptomatic expression of feelings that beset the composer but a symbolic expression of the forms of sentience as he understands them. It bespeaks his imagination of feelings rather than his own emotional state, and expresses what he *knows about* the so-called "inner life"; and this may exceed his personal case, because music is a symbolic form to him through which he may learn as well as utter ideas of human sensibility.

There are many difficulties involved in the assumption that music is a symbol, because we are so deeply impressed with the paragon of symbolic form, namely language, that we naturally carry its characteristics over into our conceptions and expectations of any other mode. Yet music is not a kind of language. Its significance is really something different from what is traditionally and properly called "meaning." Perhaps the logicians and positivistic philosophers who have objected to the term "implicit meaning," on the ground that "meaning" properly so-called is always explicable, definable, and translatable, are prompted by a perfectly rational desire to keep so difficult a term free from any further entanglements and sources of confusion; and if this can be done without barring the concept itself which I have designated as "implicit meaning," it certainly seems the part of wisdom to accept their strictures.

Probably the readiest way to understand the precise nature of musical symbolization is to consider the characteristics of language and then, by comparison and contrast, note the different structure of music, and the consequent differences and similarities between the respective functions of those two logical forms. Because the prime purpose of language is discourse, the conceptual framework that has developed under its influence is known as "discursive reason." Usually, when one speaks of "reason" at all one tacitly assumes its discursive pattern. But in a broader sense any appreciation of form, any awareness of patterns in experience, is "reason" and discourse with all its refinements (e.g. mathematical symbolism, which is an extension of language) is only one possible pattern. For practical communication, scientific knowledge, and philosophical thought it is the only instrument we have. But on just that account there are whole domains of experience that philosophers deem "ineffable." If those domains appear to anyone the most important, that person is naturally inclined to condemn philosophy and science as barren and false. To such an evaluation one is entitled; not, however, to the claim of a better way to philosophical truth through instinct, intuition, feeling, or what have you. Intuition is the basic process of all understanding, just as operative in discursive thought as in clear sense perception and immediate judgment; there will be more to say about that presently. But it is no substitute for discursive logic in the making of any theory, contingent or transcendental.

The difference between discursive and non-discursive logical forms, the respective advantages and limitations, and their consequent symbolic use have already been discussed in the previous book, but because the theory there developed of music as a symbolic form is our starting point here for a whole philosophy of art, the underlying semantic principles should perhaps be explicitly recalled first.

In language, which is the most amazing symbolic system humanity has invented, separate words are assigned to separately conceived items of experience on a basis of simple, one-to-one correlation. A word that is not composite (made of two or more independently meaningful vocables, such as "omni-potent," "com-posite") may be assigned to mean any object *taken as one*. We may even, by fiat, take a word like "omnipotent," and regarding it as one, assign it a connotation that is not composite, for instance by naming a race horse "Omnipotent." Thus Praisegod Barbon ("Barebones") was an indivisible being although his name is a composite word. He had a brother called "If-Christ-had-not-come-into-the-world-thou-wouldst-have-been-damned." The simple correlation between a name and its bearer held here between a whole sentence taken as one word and an object to which it was arbitrarily assigned. Any symbol that names something is "taken as one"; so is the object. A "crowd" is a lot of people, but *taken as a lot*, i.e. as one crowd.

So long as we correlate symbols and concepts in this simple fashion we are free to pair them as we like. A word or mark used arbitrarily to denote or connote something may be called an associative symbol, for its meaning depends entirely on association. As soon, however, as words taken to denote different things are used in combination, something is expressed by the way they are combined. The whole complex is a symbol, because the combination of words brings their connotations irresistibly together in a complex, too, and this complex of ideas is analogous to the word-complex. To anyone who knows the meanings of all the constituent words in the name of Praisegod's brother, the name is likely to sound absurd, because it is a sentence. The concepts associated with the words form a complex concept, the parts of which are related in a pattern analogous to the word-pattern. Word-meanings and grammatical forms, or rules for word-using, may be freely assigned; but once they are accepted, propositions emerge automatically as the meanings of sentences. One may say that the elements of propositions are *named* by words, but propositions themselves are *articulated* by sentences.

A complex symbol such as a sentence, or a map (whose outlines correspond formally to the vastly greater outlines of a country), or a graph (analogous, perhaps, to invisible conditions, the rise and fall of prices, the progress of an epidemic) is an *articulate form*. Its characteristic symbolic function is what I call *logical expression*.

It expresses relations; and it may "mean" – connote or denote – any complex of elements that is of the same articulate form as the symbol, the form which the symbol "expresses."

Music, like language, is an articulate form. Its parts not only fuse together to yield a greater entity, but in so doing they maintain some degree of separate existence, and the sensuous character of each element is affected by its function in the complex whole. This means that the greater entity we call a composition is not merely produced by mixture, like a new color made by mixing paints, but is *articulated*, i.e. its internal structure is given to our perception.

Why, then, is it not a *language* of feeling, as it has often been called? Because its elements are not words – independent associative symbols with a reference fixed by convention. Only as an articulate form is it found to fit anything; and since there is no meaning assigned to any of its parts, it lacks one of the basic characteristics of language – fixed association, and therewith a single, unequivocal reference. We are always free to fill its subtle articulate forms with any meaning that fits them; that is, it may convey an idea of anything conceivable in its logical image. So, although we do receive it as a significant form, and comprehend the processes of life and sentience through its audible, dynamic pattern, it is not a language, because it has no vocabulary.

Perhaps, in the same spirit of strict nomenclature, one really should not refer to its content as "meaning," either. Just as music is only loosely and inexactly called a language, so its symbolic function is only loosely called meaning, because the factor of conventional reference is missing from it. In *Philosophy in a New Key* music was called an "unconsummated" symbol.[2] But meaning, in the usual sense recognized in semantics, includes the condition of conventional reference, or consummation of the symbolic relationship. Music has *import* and this import is the pattern of sentience – the pattern of life itself, as it is felt and directly known. Let us therefore call the significance of music its "vital import" instead of "meaning," using "vital" not as a vague laudatory term, but as a qualifying adjective restricting the relevance of "import" to the dynamism of subjective experience.

So much, then, for the theory of music; music is "significant form," and its significance is that of a symbol, a highly articulated sensuous object, which by virtue of its dynamic structure can express the forms of vital experience which language is peculiarly unfit to convey. Feeling, life, motion and emotion constitute its import.

Here, in rough outline, is the special theory of music which may, I believe, be generalized to yield a theory of art as such. The basic concept is the articulate but non-discursive form having import without conventional reference, and therefore presenting itself not as a symbol in the ordinary sense, but as a "significant form," in which the factor of significance is not logically discriminated, but is felt as a quality rather than recognized as a function. If this basic concept be applicable to all products of what we call "the arts," i.e. if all works of art may be regarded as significant forms in exactly the same sense as musical works, then all the essential propositions in the theory of music may be extended to the other arts, for they all define or elucidate the nature of the symbol and its import.

That crucial generalization is already given by sheer circumstance: for the very term "significant form" was originally introduced in connection with other arts than music, in the development of another special theory; all that has so far been written about it was supposed to apply primarily, if not solely, to visual arts. Clive Bell, who coined the phrase, is an art critic, and (by his own testimony) not a musician. His own introduction of the term is given in the following words:

"Every one speaks of 'art,' making a mental classification by which he distinguishes the class 'works of art' from all other classes. What is the justification of this classification? . . . There must be some one quality without which a work of art cannot exist; possessing which, in the least degree, no work is altogether worthless. What is this quality? What quality is shared by all objects that provoke our aesthetic emotions? What quality is common to Santa Sophia and the Windows at Chartres, Mexican sculpture, a Persian bowl, Chinese carpets, Giotto's frescoes at Padua, and the masterpieces of Poussin, Piero della Francesca, and Cézanne? Only one answer seems possible – significant form. In each, lines and colours combined in a particular way, certain forms and relations of forms, stir our aesthetic emotions. These relations and combinations of lines and colours, these aesthetically moving forms, I call

'Significant Form'; and 'Significant Form' is the one quality common to all works of visual art."[3]

Bell is convinced that the business of aesthetics is to contemplate the aesthetic emotion and its object, the work of art, and that the reason why certain objects move us as they do lies beyond the confines of aesthetics.[4] If that were so, there would be little of interest to contemplate. It seems to me that the *reason* for our immediate recognition of "significant form" is the heart of the aesthetical problem; and Bell himself has given several hints of a solution, although his perfectly justified dread of heuristic theories of art kept him from following out his own observations. But, in the light of the music theory that culminates in the concept of "significant form," perhaps the hints in his art theory are enough.

"Before we feel an aesthetic emotion for a combination of forms," he says (only to withdraw hastily, even before the end of the paragraph, from any philosophical commitment) "do we not perceive intellectually the rightness and necessity of the combination? If we do, it would explain the fact that passing rapidly through a room we recognize a picture to be good, although we cannot say that it has provoked much emotion. We seem to have recognized intellectually the rightness of its forms without staying to fix our attention, and collect, as it were, their emotional significance. If this were so, it would be permissible to inquire whether it was the forms themselves or our perception of their rightness and necessity that caused aesthetic emotion."[5]

Certainly "rightness and necessity" are properties with philosophical implications, and the perception of them a more telling incident than an inexplicable emotion. To recognize that something is right and necessary is a rational act, no matter how spontaneous and immediate the recognition may be; it points to an intellectual principle in artistic judgment, and a rational basis for the feeling Bell calls "the aesthetic emotion." This emotion is, I think, a result of artistic perception, as he suggested in the passage quoted above; it is a personal reaction to the discovery of "rightness and necessity" in the sensuous forms that evoke it. Whenever we experience it we are in the presence of Art, i.e. of "significant form." He himself has identified it as the same experience in art appreciation and in pure musical hearing, although he says he has rarely achieved it musically. But if it is common to visual and tonal arts, and if indeed it bespeaks the artistic value of its object, it offers another point of support for the theory that significant form is the essence of all art.

That, however, is about all that it offers. Bell's assertion that every theory of art must begin with the contemplation of "the aesthetic emotion," and that, indeed, nothing else is really the business of aesthetics,[6] seems to me entirely wrong. To dwell on one's state of mind in the presence of a work does not further one's understanding of the work and its value. The question of what gives one the emotion is exactly the question of what makes the object artistic; and that, to my mind, is where philosophical art theory begins.

The same criticism applies to all theories that begin with an analysis of the "aesthetic attitude": they do not get beyond it. Schopenhauer, who is chiefly responsible for the notion of a completely desireless state of pure, sensuous discrimination as the proper attitude toward works of art, did not make it the starting point of his system, but a consequence. Why, then, has it been so insistently employed, especially of late, as the chief datum in artistic experience?

Probably under pressure of the psychologistic currents that have tended, for the last fifty years at least, to force all philosophical problems of art into the confines of behaviorism and pragmatism, where they find neither development nor solution, but are assigned to vague realms of "value" and "interest," in which nothing of great value or interest has yet been done. The existence of art is accounted for, its value admitted, and there's an end of it. But the issues that really challenge the aesthetician – e.g., the exact nature and degree of interrelation among the arts, the meaning of "essential" and "unessential," the problem of translatability, or transposability, of artistic ideas – either cannot arise in a psychologistic context, or are answered, without real investigation, on the strength of some general premise that seems to cover them. The whole tenor of modern philosophy, especially in America, is uncongenial to serious speculation on the meaning and difficulty and seriousness of art works. Yet the pragmatic outlook, linked as it is with natural science, holds such sway over us that no academic discussion can resist its magnetic, orienting concepts; its basic psychologism underlies every doctrine that really looks respectable.

Now, the watchword of this established doctrine is "experience." If the leading philosophers publish assorted essays under such titles as *Freedom and Experience*,[7] or center their systematic discourse around *Experience and Natune*,[8] so that in their aesthetics, too, we are presented with *The Aesthetic Experience*[9] and *Art as Experience*,[10] it is natural enough that artists, who are amateurs in philosophy, try to treat their subject in the same vein, and write: *Experiencing American Pictures*,[11] or: *Dance – A Creative Art Experience*.[12] As far as possible, these writers who grope more or less for principles of intellectual analysis adopt the current terminology, and therewith they are committed to the prevailing fashion of thought.

Since this fashion has grown up under the mentorship of natural science, it brings with it not only the great ideals of empiricism, namely observation, analysis and verification, but also certain cherished hypotheses, primarily from the least perfect and successful of the sciences, psychology and sociology. The chief assumption that determines the entire procedure of pragmatic philosophy is that all human interests are direct or oblique manifestations of "drives" motivated by animal needs. This premise limits the class of admitted human interests to such as can, by one device or another, be interpreted in terms of animal psychology. An astonishingly great part of human behavior really does bear such interpretation without strain; and pragmatists, so far, do not admit that there is any point where the principle definitely fails, and its use falsifies our empirical findings.

The effect of the genetic premise on art theory is that aesthetic values must be treated either as direct satisfactions, i.e. pleasures, or as instrumental values, that is to say, means to fulfillment of biological needs. It is either a leisure interest, like sports and hobbies, or it is valuable for getting on with the world's work – strengthening morale, integrating social groups, or venting dangerous repressed feelings in a harmless emotional catharsis. But in either case, artistic experience is not essentially different from ordinary physical, practical, and social experience.[13]

The true connoisseurs of art, however, feel at once that to treat great art as a source of experiences not essentially different from the experiences of daily life – a stimulus to one's active feelings, and perhaps a means of communication between persons or groups, promoting mutual appreciation – is to miss the very essence of it, the thing that makes art as important as science or even religion, yet sets it apart as an autonomous, creative function of a typically human mind. If, then, they feel constrained by the prevailing academic tradition to analyze their experience, attitude, response, or enjoyment, they can only begin by saving that aesthetic experience is different from any other, the attitude toward works of art is a highly special one, the characteristic response is an entirely separate emotion, something more than common enjoyment – not related to the pleasures or displeasures furnished by one's actual surroundings, and therefore disturbed by them rather than integrated with the contemporary scene.

This conviction does not spring from a sentimental concern for the glamor and dignity of the arts, as Mr. Dewey suggests;[14] it arises from the fact that when people in whom appreciation for some art – be it painting, music, drama, or what not – is spontaneous and pronounced, are induced by a psychologistic fashion to reflect on their attitude toward the works they appreciate, they find it not at all comparable with the attitude they have toward a new automobile, a beloved creature, or a glorious morning. They feel a different emotion, and in a different way. Since art is viewed as a special kind of "experience," inaccessible to those who cannot enter into the proper spirit, a veritable cult of the "aesthetic attitude" has grown up among patrons of the art gallery and the concert hall.

But the aesthetic attitude, which is supposed to beget the art experience in the presence of suitable objects (what makes them suitable seems to be a minor question, relegated to a time when "science" shall be ready to answer it), is hard to achieve, harder to maintain, and rarely complete. H. S. Langfeld, who wrote a whole book about it, described it as an attitude "that for most individuals has to be cultivated if it is to exist at all in midst of the opposing and therefore disturbing influences which are always present."[15] And David Prall, in his excellent *Aesthetic Analysis*, observes: "Even a young musical fanatic at a concert of his favorite music has some slight attention left for the comfort of his body and his posture, some vague sense of the direction of exits, a degree of attention most easily raised into prominence by any interference with his comfort by his neighbor's movements, or accidental noises coming from elsewhere, whether these indicate the danger of fire or some milder reason for taking action. Complete aesthetic absorption, strictly relevant to one object, is at least rare; the world as exclusively aesthetic surface is seldom if ever the sole object of our attention."[16]

Few listeners or spectators, in fact, ever quite attain the state which Roger Fry described, in *Vision and Design*, as "disinterested intensity of contemplation"[17] – the only state in which one may really perceive a work of art, and experience the aesthetic emotion. Most people are too busy or too lazy to uncouple their minds from all their usual interests before looking at a picture or a vase. That explains, presumably, what he remarked somewhat earlier in the same essay: "In proportion as art becomes purer the number of people to whom it appeals gets less. It cuts out all the romantic overtones which are the usual bait by which men are induced to accept a work of art. It appeals only to the aesthetic sensibility, and that in most men is comparatively weak."[18]

If the groundwork of all genuine art experience is really such a sophisticated, rare, and artificial attitude, it is something of a miracle that the world recognizes works of art as public treasures at all. And that primitive peoples, from the cave dwellers of Altamira to the early Greeks, should quite unmistakably have known what was beautiful, becomes a sheer absurdity.

There is that, at least, to be said for the pragmatists: they recognize the art interest as something natural and robust, not a precarious hot-house flower reserved for the very cultured and initiate. But the small compass of possible human interests permitted by their biological premises blinds them to the fact that a very spontaneous, even primitive activity may none the less be peculiarly human, and may require long study in its own terms before its relations to the rest of our behavior become clear. To say, as I. A. Richards does, that if we knew more about the nervous system and its responses to "certain stimuli" (note that "certain," when applied to hypothetical data, means "uncertain," since the data cannot be exactly designated) we would find that "the unpredictable and miraculous differences . . . in the total responses which slight changes in the arrangement of stimuli produce, can be fully accounted for in terms of the sensitiveness of the nervous system; and the mysteries of 'forms' are merely a consequence of our present ignorance of the detail of its action,"[19] is not only an absurd pretension (for how do we know what facts we would find and what their implications would prove to be, before we have found them?), but an empty hypothesis, because there is no elementary success that indicates the direction in which neurological aesthetics could develop. If a theoretical beginning existed, one could imagine an extension of the same procedure to describe artistic experience in terms of conditioned reflexes, rudimentary impulses, or perhaps cerebral vibrations; but so far the data furnished by galvanometers and encephalographs have not borne on artistic problems, even to the extent of explaining the simple, obvious difference of effect between a major scale and its parallel minor. The proposition that if we knew the facts we would find them to be thus and thus is merely an article of innocent, pseudo-scientific faith.

The psychological approach, dictated by the general empiricist trend in philosophy, has not brought us within range of any genuine problems of art. So, instead of studying the "slight changes of stimuli" which cause "unpredictable and miraculous changes" in our nervous responses, we might do better to look upon the art object as something in its own right, with properties independent of our prepared reactions – properties which command our reactions, and make art the autonomous and essential factor that it is in every human culture.

The concept of significant form as an articulate expression of feeling, reflecting the verbally ineffable and therefore unknown forms of sentience, offers at least a starting point for such inquiries. All articulation is difficult, exacting, and ingenious; the making of a symbol requires craftsmanship as truly as the making of a convenient bowl or an efficient paddle, and the techniques of expression are even more important social traditions than the skills of self-preservation, which an intelligent being can evolve by himself, at least in rudimentary ways, to meet a given situation. The fundamental technique of expression – language – is something we all have to learn by example and practice, i.e. by conscious or unconscious training.[20] People whose speech training has been very casual are less sensitive to what is exact and fitting for the expression of an idea than those of cultivated habit; not only with regard to arbitrary rules of usage, but in respect of logical *rightness and necessity* of expression, i.e. saying what they mean and not something else. Similarly, I believe, all making of expressive form is a craft. Therefore the normal evolution of art is in close association with practical skills – building, ceramics, weaving, carving, and magical practices of which the average civilized person no longer knows the importance;[21] and therefore, also, sensitivity to the rightness and necessity of visual or musical forms is apt to be more pronounced and sure in persons of some artistic training than in those who have only a bowing acquaintance with the arts. Technique is the means to the creation of expressive form, the symbol of sentience; the art process is the application of some human skill to this essential purpose.

At this point I will make bold to offer a definition of art, which serves to distinguish a "work of art" from anything else in the world, and at the same time to show why, and how, a utilitarian object may be *also* a work of art; and how a work of so-called "pure" art may fail of its purpose and be simply bad, just as a shoe that cannot be worn is simply bad by failing of its purpose. It serves, moreover, to establish the relation of art to physical skill, or making, on the one hand, and to feeling and expression on the other. Here is the tentative definition, on which the following chapters are built: Art is the creation of forms symbolic of human feeling.

The word "creation" is introduced here with full awareness of its problematical character. There is a definite reason to say a craftsman *produces* goods, but *creates* a thing of beauty; a builder *erects* a house, but *creates* an edifice if the house is a real work of architecture, however modest. An artifact as such is merely a combination of material parts, or a modification of a natural object to suit human purposes. It is not a creation, but an arrangement of given factors. A work of art, on the other hand, is more than an "arrangement" of given things – even qualitative things. Something emerges from the arrangement of tones or colors, which was not there before, and this, rather than the arranged material, is the symbol of sentience.

The making of this expressive form is the creative process that enlists a man's utmost technical skill in the service of his utmost conceptual power, imagination. Not the invention of new original turns, nor the adoption of novel themes, merits the word "creative," but the making of any work symbolic of feeling, even in the most canonical context and manner. A thousand people may have used every device and convention of it before. A Greek vase was almost always a creation, although its form was traditional and its decoration deviated but little from that of its numberless forerunners. The creative principle, nonetheless, was probably active in it from the first throw of the clay.

To expound that principle, and develop it in each autonomous realm of art, is the only way to justify the definition, which really is a philosophical theory of art in miniature.

Notes

1 In *Philosophy in a* New *Key* (cited hereafter as *New Key*) the major distinction was drawn between "signs" and "symbols"; Charles W. Morris, in *Signs, Language and Behavior,* distinguishes between "signals" and "symbols." This seems to me a better use of words, since it leaves "sign" to cover both "signal" and "symbol," whereas my former usage left me without any generic term. I have, therefore, adopted his practice, despite the fact that it makes for a discrepancy in the terminology of two books that really belong together.
2 Harvard University Press edition, p. 240; New American Library (Mentor) edition, p. 195.
3 Ibid., p. 8.
4 Ibid., p. 10.
5 Ibid., p. 26.
6 Ibid., p. 10.
7 *Essays in Honor of Horace M. Kallen* (1947).
8 John Dewey (1925).
9 Laurence Buermeyer (1924).
10 John Dewey (1934).
11 Ralph M. Pearson (1943).
12 Margaret H'Doubler (1940).
13 Cf. John Dewey, *Art as Experience*, p. 10: ". . . the forces that create the gulf between producer and consumer in modern society operate to create also a chasm between ordinary and esthetic experience. Finally we have, as a record of this chasm, accepted as if it were normal, the philosophies of art that locate it in a region inhabited by no other

creature, and that emphasize beyond all reason the merely contemplative character of the esthetic."

Also I. A. Richards, *Principles of Literary Criticism*, pp. 16–17: "When we look at a picture, read a poem, or listen to music, we are not doing something quite unlike what we were doing on our way to the Gallery or when we dressed in the morning. The fashion in which the experience is caused in us is different, and as a rule the experience is more complex and, if we are successful, more unified. But our activity is not of a fundamentally different type."

Laurence Buermeyer, in *The Aesthetic Experience*, p. 79, follows his account of artistic expression with the statement: "This does not mean, once more, that what the artist has to say is different in kind from what is to be said in actual life, or that the realm of art is in any essential respect divorced from the realm of reality."

14 Speaking of the separation of art from life "that many theorists and critics pride themselves upon holding and even elaborating," he attributes it to the desire to keep art "spiritual," and says in explanation: "For many persons an aura of mingled awe and unreality encompasses the 'spiritual' and the 'ideal' while 'matter' has become . . . something to be explained away or apologized for." John Dewey, *op. cit.*, p. 6.

15 *The Aesthetic Attitude*, p. 65.

16 *Aesthetic Analysis*, pp. 7–8.

17 *Vision and Design*, p. 29.

18 Ibid., p. 15.

19 *Op. cit.*, p. 172.

20 Cf. *New Key*, Chap. v, "Language."

21 Yet a pervasive magical interest has probably been the natural tie between practical fitness and expressiveness in primitive artifacts. See *New Key*, Chap. ix, "The Genesis of Artistic Import."

29

The Work of Art in the Age of Mechanical Reproduction

Walter Benjamin

Walter Benjamin (1892–1940) was a German literary critic, who, when the Nazis took power, fled to Paris and, seven years later, took his own life to avoid capture when France fell. He viewed art not as an autonomous realm but as reflecting historical, political, and economic conditions.

Our fine arts were developed, their types and uses were established, in times very different from the present, by men whose power of action upon things was insignificant in comparison with ours. But the amazing growth of our techniques, the adaptability and precision they have attained, the ideas and habits they are creating, make it a certainty that profound changes are impending in the ancient craft of the Beautiful. In all the arts there is a physical component which can no longer be considered or treated as it used to be, which cannot remain unaffected by our modern knowledge and power. For the last twenty years neither matter nor space nor time has been what it was from time immemorial. We must expect great innovations to transform the entire technique of the arts, thereby affecting artistic invention itself and perhaps even bringing about an amazing change in our very notion of art.[1]

—*Paul Valéry*, Pièces sur l'art, *"La Conquète de l'ubiquité," Paris.*

Preface

When Marx undertook his critique of the capitalistic mode of production, this mode was in its infancy. Marx directed his efforts in such a way as to give them prognostic value. He went back to the basic conditions underlying capitalistic production and through his presentation showed what could be expected of capitalism in the future.

Walter Benjamin, "The Work of Art in the Age of Mechanical Reproduction," in *Continental Aesthetics: Romanticism to Postmodernism, An Anthology*, ed. Richard Kearney and David Rasmussen (Oxford: Blackwell Publishing, 2001), pp. 166–81.

The result was that one could expect it not only to exploit the proletariat with increasing intensity, but ultimately to create conditions which would make it possible to abolish capitalism itself.

The transformation of the superstructure, which takes place far more slowly than that of the substructure, has taken more than half a century to manifest in all areas of culture the change in the conditions of production. Only today can it be indicated what form this has taken. Certain prognostic requirements should be met by these statements. However, theses about the art of the proletariat after its assumption of power or about the art of a classless society would have less bearing on these demands than theses about the developmental tendencies of art under present conditions of production. Their dialectic is no less noticeable in the superstructure than in the economy. It would therefore be wrong to underestimate the value of such theses as a weapon. They brush aside a number of outmoded concepts, such as creativity and genius, eternal value and mystery – concepts whose uncontrolled (and at present almost uncontrollable) application would lead to a processing of data in the Fascist sense. The concepts which are introduced into the theory of art in what follows differ from the more familiar terms in that they are completely useless for the purposes of Fascism. They are, on the other hand, useful for the formulation of revolutionary demands in the politics of art.

I

In principle a work of art has always been reproducible. Manmade artifacts could always be imitated by men. Replicas were made by pupils in practice of their craft, by masters for diffusing their works, and, finally, by third parties in the pursuit of gain. Mechanical reproduction of a work of art, however, represents something new. Historically, it advanced intermittently and in leaps at long intervals, but with accelerated intensity. The Greek knew only two procedures of technically reproducing works of art: founding and stamping. Bronzes, terra cottas, and coins were the only art works which they could produce in quantity. All others were unique and could not be mechanically reproduced. With the woodcut graphic art became mechanically reproducible for the first time, long before script became reproducible by print. The enormous changes which printing, the mechanical reproduction of writing, has brought about in literature are a familiar story. However, within the phenomenon which we are here examining from the perspective of world history, print is merely a special, though particularly important, case. During the Middle Ages engraving and etching were added to the woodcut; at the beginning of the nineteenth century lithography made its appearance.

With lithography the technique of reproduction reached an essentially new stage. This much more direct process was distinguished by the tracing of the design on a stone rather than its incision on a block of wood or its etching on a copperplate and permitted graphic art for the first time to put its products on the market, not only in large numbers as hitherto, but also in daily changing forms. Lithography enabled graphic art to illustrate everyday life, and it began to keep pace with printing. But only a few decades after its invention, lithography was surpassed by photography. For the first time in the process of pictorial reproduction, photography freed the hand of the most important artistic functions which henceforth devolved only upon the eye looking into a lens. Since the eye perceives more swiftly than the hand can draw, the process of pictorial reproduction was accelerated so enormously that it could keep pace with speech. A film operator shooting a scene in the studio captures the images at the speed of an actor's speech. Just as lithography virtually implied the illustrated newspaper, so did photography foreshadow the sound film. The technical reproduction of sound was tackled at the end of the last century. These convergent endeavors made predictable a situation which Paul Valéry pointed up in this sentence: "Just as water, gas, and electricity are brought into our houses from far off to satisfy our needs in response to a minimal effort, so we shall be supplied with visual or auditory images, which will appear and disappear at a simple movement of the hand, hardly more than a sign" (["The Conquest of Ubiquity,"] p. 226). Around 1900 technical reproduction had reached a standard that not only permitted it to reproduce all transmitted works of art and thus to cause the most profound change in their impact upon the public; it also had captured a place of its own among the artistic processes. For the study of this standard nothing is more revealing than the nature of the repercussions that these two different manifestations – the reproduction of works of art and the art of the film – have had on art in its traditional form.

II

Even the most perfect reproduction of a work of art is lacking in one element: its presence in time and space, its unique existence at the place where it happens to be. This unique existence of the work of art determined the history to which it was subject throughout the time of its existence. This includes the changes which it may have suffered in physical condition over the years as well as the various changes in its ownership.[2] The traces of the first can be revealed only by chemical or physical analyses which it is impossible to perform on a reproduction; changes of ownership are subject to a tradition which must be traced from the situation of the original.

The presence of the original is the prerequisite to the concept of authenticity. Chemical analyses of the patina of a bronze can help to establish this, as does the proof that a given manuscript of the Middle Ages stems from an archive of the fifteenth century. The whole sphere of authenticity is outside technical – and, of course, not only technical – reproducibility.[3] Confronted with its manual reproduction, which was usually branded as a forgery, the original preserved all its authority; not so *vis à vis* technical reproduction. The reason is twofold. First, process reproduction is more independent of the original than manual reproduction. For example, in photography, process reproduction can bring out those aspects of the original that are unattainable to the naked eye yet accessible to the lens, which is adjustable and chooses its angle at will. And photographic reproduction, with the aid of certain processes, such as enlargement or slow motion, can capture images which escape natural vision. Secondly, technical reproduction can put the copy of the original into situations which would be out of reach for the original itself. Above all, it enables the original to meet the beholder halfway, be it in the form of a photograph or a phonograph record. The cathedral leaves its locale to be received in the studio of a lover of art; the choral production, performed in an auditorium or in the open air, resounds in the drawing room.

The situations into which the product of mechanical reproduction can be brought may not touch the actual work of art, yet the quality of its presence is always depreciated. This holds not only for the art work but also, for instance, for a landscape which passes in review before the spectator in a movie. In the case of the art object, a most sensitive nucleus – namely, its authenticity – is interfered with whereas no natural object is vulnerable on that score. The authenticity of a thing is the essence of all that is transmissible from its beginning, ranging from its substantive duration to its testimony to the history which it has experienced. Since the historical testimony rests on the authenticity, the former, too, is jeopardized by reproduction when substantive duration ceases to matter. And what is really jeopardized when the historical testimony is affected is the authority of the object.[4]

One might subsume the eliminated element in the term "aura" and go on to say: that which withers in the age of mechanical reproduction is the aura of the work of art. This is a symptomatic process whose significance points beyond the realm of art. One might generalize by saying: the technique of reproduction detaches the reproduced object from the domain of tradition. By making many reproductions it substitutes a plurality of copies for a unique existence. And in permitting the reproduction to meet the beholder or listener in his own particular situation, it reactivates the object reproduced. These two processes lead to a tremendous shattering of tradition which is the obverse of the contemporary crisis and renewal of mankind. Both processes are intimately connected with the contemporary mass movements. Their most powerful agent is the film. Its social significance, particularly in its most positive form, is inconceivable without its destructive, cathartic aspect, that is, the liquidation of the traditional value of the cultural heritage. This phenomenon is most palpable in the great historical films. It extends to ever new positions. In 1927 Abel Gance exclaimed enthusiastically: "Shakespeare, Rembrandt, Beethoven will make films . . . all legends, all mythologies and all myths, all founders of religion, and the very religions . . . await their exposed resurrection, and the heroes crowd each other at the gate."[5] Presumably without intending it, he issued an invitation to a far-reaching liquidation.

III

During long periods of history, the mode of human sense perception changes with humanity's entire mode of existence. The manner in which human sense perception is organized, the medium in which it is accomplished, is determined not only by nature but by historical circumstances as well. The fifth century, with its great shifts of population, saw the birth of the late Roman art industry and the Vienna Genesis, and there developed not only an art different from that of antiquity but also a new kind of perception. The scholars of the Viennese school, Riegl and Wickhoff, who resisted the weight of classical tradition under which these later art forms had been buried, were the first to draw conclusions from them concerning the organization of perception at the time. However far-reaching their insight, these scholars limited themselves to showing the significant, formal hallmark which characterized perception in late Roman times. They did not attempt – and, perhaps, saw no way – to show the social transformations expressed by these changes of perception. The conditions for an analogous insight are more favorable in the present. And if changes in the medium of contemporary perception can be comprehended as decay of the aura, it is possible to show its social causes.

The concept of aura which was proposed above with reference to historical objects may usefully be illustrated with reference to the aura of natural ones. We define the aura of the latter as the unique phenomenon of a distance, however close it may be. If, while resting on a summer afternoon, you follow with your eyes a mountain range on the horizon or a branch which casts its shadow over you, you experience that aura of those mountains, of that branch. This image makes it easy to comprehend the social bases of the contemporary decay of the aura. It rests on two circumstances, both of which are related to the increasing significance of the masses in contemporary life. Namely, the desire of contemporary masses to bring things "closer" spatially and humanly, which is just as ardent as their bent toward overcoming the uniqueness of every reality by accepting its reproduction.[6] Every day the urge grows stronger to get hold of an object at very close range by way of its likeness, its reproduction. Unmistakably, reproduction as offered by picture magazines and newsreels differs from the image seen by the unarmed eye. Uniqueness and permanence are as closely linked in the latter as are transitoriness and reproducibility in the former. To pry an object from its shell, to destroy its aura, is the mark of a perception whose "sense of the universal equality of things" has increased to such a degree that it extracts it even from a unique object by means of reproduction. Thus is manifested in the field of perception what in the theoretical sphere is noticeable in the increasing importance of statistics. The adjustment of reality to the masses and of the masses to reality is a process of unlimited scope, as much for thinking as for perception.

IV

The uniqueness of a work of art is inseparable from its being imbedded in the fabric of tradition. This tradition itself is thoroughly alive and extremely changeable. An ancient statue of Venus, for example, stood in a different traditional context with the Greeks, who made it an object of veneration, than with the clerics of the Middle Ages, who viewed it as an ominous idol. Both of them, however, were equally confronted with its uniqueness, that is, its aura. Originally the contextual integration of art in tradition found its expression in the cult. We know that the earliest art works originated in the service of a ritual – first the magical, then the religious kind. It is significant that the existence of the work of art with reference to its aura is never entirely separated from its ritual function.[7] In other words, the unique value of the "authentic" work of art has its basis in ritual, the location of its original use value. This ritualistic basis, however remote, is still recognizable as secularized ritual even in the most profane forms of the cult of beauty.[8] The secular cult of beauty, developed during the Renaissance and prevailing for three centuries, clearly showed that ritualistic basis in its decline and the first deep crisis which befell it. With the advent of the first truly revolutionary means of reproduction, photography, simultaneously with the rise of socialism, art sensed the approaching crisis which has become evident a century later.

At the time, art reacted with the doctrine of *L'art pour L'art*, that is, with a theology of art. This gave rise to what might be called a negative theology in the form of the idea of "pure" art, which not only denied any social function of art but also any categorizing by subject matter. (In poetry, Mallarmé was the first to take this position.)

An analysis of art in the age of mechanical reproduction must do justice to these relationships, for they lead us to an all-important insight: for the first time in world history, mechanical reproduction emancipates the work of art from its parasitical dependence on ritual. To an ever greater degree the work of art reproduced becomes the work of art designed for reproducibility.[9] From a photographic negative, for example, one can make any number of prints; to ask for the "authentic" print makes no sense. But the instant the criterion of authenticity ceases to be applicable to artistic production, the total function of art is reversed. Instead of being based on ritual, it begins to be based on another practice – politics.

V

Works of art are received and valued on different planes. Two polar types stand out: with one, the accent is on the cult value; with the other, on the exhibition value of the work.[10] Artistic production begins with ceremonial objects destined to serve in a cult. One may assume that what mattered was their existence, not their being on view. The elk portrayed by the man of the Stone Age on the walls of his cave was an instrument of magic. He did expose it to his fellow men, but in the main it was meant for the spirits. Today the cult value would seem to demand that the work of art remain hidden. Certain statues of gods are accessible only to the priest in the cella; certain Madonnas remain covered nearly all year round; certain sculptures on medieval cathedrals are invisible to the spectator on ground level. With the emancipation of the various art practices from ritual go increasing opportunities for the exhibition of their products. It is easier to exhibit a portrait bust that can be sent here and there than to exhibit the statue of a divinity that has its fixed place in the interior of a temple. The same holds for the painting as against the mosaic or fresco that preceded it. And even though the public presentability of a mass originally may have been just as great as that of a symphony, the latter originated at the moment when its public presentability promised to surpass that of the mass.

With the different methods of technical reproduction of a work of art, its fitness for exhibition increased to such an extent that the quantitative shift between its two poles turned into a qualitative transformation of its nature. This is comparable to the situation of the work of art in prehistoric times when, by the absolute emphasis on its cult value, it was, first and foremost, an instrument of magic. Only later did it come to be recognized as a work of art. In the same way today, by the absolute emphasis on its exhibition value the work of art becomes a creation with entirely new functions, among which the one we are conscious of, the artistic function, later may be recognized as incidental.[11] This much is certain: today photography and the film are the most serviceable exemplifications of this new function.

VI

In photography, exhibition value begins to displace cult value all along the line. But cult value does not give way without resistance. It retires into an ultimate retrenchment: the human countenance. It is no accident that the portrait was the focal point of early photography. The cult of remembrance of loved ones, absent or dead, offers a last refuge for the cult value of the picture. For the last time the aura emanates from the early photographs in the fleeting expression of a human face. This is what constitutes their melancholy, incomparable beauty. But as man withdraws from the photographic image, the exhibition value for the first time shows its superiority to the ritual valuc. To have pinpointed this new stage constitutes the incomparable significance of Atget, who, around 1900, took photographs of deserted Paris streets. It has quite justly been said of him that he photographed them like scenes of crime. The scene of a crime, too, is deserted; it is photographed for the purpose of establishing evidence. With Atget, photographs become standard evidence for historical occurrences, and acquire a hidden political significance. They demand a specific kind of approach; free-floating contemplation is not appropriate to them. They stir the viewer; he feels challenged by them in a new way. At the same time picture magazines begin to put up signposts for him, right ones or wrong ones, no matter. For the first time, captions have become obligatory. And it is clear that they have an altogether different character than the title of a painting. The directives which the captions give to those looking at pictures in illustrated magazines soon become even more explicit and more imperative in the film where the meaning of each single picture appears to be prescribed by the sequence of all preceding ones.

VII

The nineteenth-century dispute as to the artistic value of painting versus photography today seems devious and confused. This does not diminish its importance, however; if anything, it underlines it. The dispute was in fact the symptom of a historical transformation the universal impact of which was not realized by either of the rivals. When the age of mechanical reproduction separated art from its basis in cult, the semblance of its autonomy disappeared forever. The resulting change in the function of art transcended the perspective of the century; for a long time it even escaped that of the twentieth century, which experienced the development of the film.

Earlier much futile thought had been devoted to the question of whether photography is an art. The primary question – whether the very invention of photography had not transformed the entire nature of art – was not raised. Soon the film theoreticians asked the same ill-considered question with regard to the film. But the difficulties which photography caused traditional aesthetics were mere child's play as compared to those raised by the film. Whence the insensitive and forced character of early theories of the film. Abel Gance, for instance, compares the film with hieroglyphs: "Here, by a remarkable regression, we have come hack to the level of expression of the Egyptians. . . . Pictorial language has not yet matured because our eyes have not yet adjusted to it. There is as yet insufficient respect for, insufficient cult of, what it expresses."[12] Or, in the words of Séverin-Mars: "What art has been granted a dream more poetical and more real at the same time! Approached in this fashion the film might represent an incomparable means of expression. Only the most high-minded persons, in the most perfect and mysterious moments of their lives, should be allowed to enter its ambience."[13] Alexandre Arnoux concludes his fantasy about the silent film with the question: "Do not all the bold descriptions we have given amount to the definition of prayer?"[14] It is instructive to note how their desire to class the film among the "arts" forces these theoreticians to read ritual elements into it – with a striking lack of discretion. Yet when these speculations were published, films like *L'Opinion publique* and *The Gold Rush* had already appeared. This, however, did not keep Abel Gance from adducing hieroglyphs for purposes of comparison, nor Séverin-Mars from speaking of the film as one might speak of paintings by Fra Angelico. Characteristically, even today ultrareactionary authors give the film a similar contextual significance – if not an outright sacred one, then at least a supernatural one. Commenting on Max Reinhardt's film version of *A Midsummer Night's Dream,* Werfel states that undoubtedly it was the sterile copying of the exterior world with its streets, interiors, railroad stations, restaurants, motorcars, and beaches which until now had obstructed the elevation of the film to the realm of art. "The film has not yet realized its true meaning, its real possibilities . . . these consist in its unique faculty to express by natural means and with incomparable persuasiveness all that is fairylike, marvelous, supernatural."[15]

VIII

The artistic performance of a stage actor is definitely presented to the public by the actor in person; that of the screen actor, however, is presented by a camera, with a twofold consequence. The camera that presents the performance of the film actor to the public need not respect the performance as an integral whole. Guided by the cameraman, the camera continually changes its position with respect to the performance. The sequence of positional views which the editor composes from the material supplied him constitutes the completed film. It comprises certain factors of movement which are in reality those of the camera, not to mention special camera angles, close-ups, etc. Hence, the performance of the actor is subjected to a series of optical tests. This is the first consequence of the fact that the actor's performance is presented by means of camera. Also, the film actor lacks the opportunity of the stage actor to adjust to the audience during his performance, since he does not present his performance to the audience in person. This permits the audience to take the position of a critic, without experiencing any personal contact with the actor. The audience's identification with the actor is really an identification with the camera. Consequently the audience takes the position of the camera; its approach is that of testing.[16] This is not the approach to which cult values may be exposed.

IX

For the film, what matters primarily is that the actor represents himself to the public before the camera, rather than representing someone else. One of the first to sense the actor's metamorphosis by this form of testing was Pirandello. Though his remarks on the subject in his novel *Si Gira* were limited to the negative aspects of the question and to the silent film only, this hardly impairs their validity. For in this respect, the sound film did not change anything essential. What matters is that the part is acted not for an audience but for a mechanical contrivance – in the case of the sound film, for two of them. "The film actor," wrote Pirandello, "feels as if in exile – exiled not only from the stage but also from himself. With a vague sense of discomfort he feels inexplicable emptiness: his body loses its corporeality, it evaporates, it is deprived of reality, life, voice, and the noises caused by his moving about, in order to be changed into a mute image, flickering an instant on the screen, then vanishing into silence. . . . The projector will play with his shadow before the public, and he himself must be content to play before the camera."[17] This situation might also be characterized as follows: for the first time – and this is the effect of the film – man has to operate with his whole living person, yet forgoing its aura. For aura is tied to his presence; there can be no replica of it. The aura which, on the stage, emanates from Macbeth, cannot be separated for the spectators from that of the actor. However, the singularity of the shot in the studio is that the camera is substituted for the public. Consequently, the aura that envelops the actor vanishes, and with it the aura of the figure he portrays.

It is not surprising that it should be a dramatist such as Pirandello who, in characterizing the film, inadvertently touches on the very crisis in which we see the theater. Any thorough study proves that there is indeed no greater contrast than that of the stage play to a work of art that is completely subject to or, like the film, founded in, mechanical reproduction. Experts have long recognized that in the film "the greatest effects are almost always obtained by 'acting' as little as possible. . . ." In 1932 Rudolf Arnheim saw "the latest trend . . . in treating the actor as a stage prop chosen for its characteristics and . . . inserted at the proper place."[18] With this idea something else is closely connected. The stage actor identifies himself with the character of his role. The film actor very often is denied this opportunity. His creation is by no means all of a piece; it is composed of many separate performances. Besides certain fortuitous considerations, such as cost of studio, availability of fellow players, décor, etc., there are elementary necessities of equipment that split the actor's work into a series of mountable episodes. In particular, lighting and its installation require the presentation of an event that, on the screen, unfolds as a rapid and unified scene, in a sequence of separate shootings which may take hours at the studio; not to mention more obvious montage. Thus a jump from the window can be shot in the studio as a jump from a scaffold, and the ensuing flight, if need be, can be shot weeks later when outdoor scenes are taken. Far more paradoxical cases can easily be construed. Let us assume that an actor is supposed to be startled by a knock at the door. If his reaction is not satisfactory, the director can resort to an expedient: when the actor happens to be at the studio again he has a shot fired behind him without his being forewarned of it. The frightened reaction can be shot now and be cut into the screen version. Nothing more strikingly shows that art has left the realm of the "beautiful semblance" which, so far, had been taken to be the only sphere where art could thrive.

X

The feeling of strangeness that overcomes the actor before the camera, as Pirandello describes it, is basically of the same kind as the estrangement felt before one's own image in the mirror. But now the reflected image has become separable, transportable. And where is it transported? Before the public.[19] Never for a moment does the screen actor cease to be conscious of this fact. While facing the camera he knows that ultimately he will face the public, the consumers who constitute the market. This market, where he offers not only his labor but also his whole self, his heart and soul, is beyond his reach. During the shooting he has as little contact with it as any article made in a factory. This may contribute to that oppression, that new anxiety which, according to Pirandello, grips the actor before the camera. The film responds to the shrivelling of the aura with an artificial build-up of the "personality" outside the studio. The cult of the movie star, fostered by the money of the film industry, preserves not the unique aura of the person but the "spell of the personality," the phony spell of a commodity. So long as the movie-makers' capital sets the fashion, as a rule no other revolutionary merit can be accredited to today's film than the promotion of a revolutionary criticism of traditional concepts of art. We do not deny that in some cases today's films can also promote revolutionary criticism of social conditions, even of the distribution of property. However, our present study is no more specifically concerned with this than is the film production of Western Europe.

It is inherent in the technique of the film as well as that of sports that everybody who witnesses its accomplishments is somewhat of an expert. This is obvious to anyone listening to a group of newspaper boys leaning on their bicycles and discussing the outcome of a bicycle race. It is not for nothing that newspaper publishers arrange races for their delivery boys. These arouse great interest among the participants, for the victor has an opportunity to rise from delivery boy to professional racer. Similarly, the newsreel offers everyone the opportunity to rise from passer-by to movie extra. In this way any man might even find himself part of a work of art, as witness Vertoff's *Three Songs About Lenin* or Ivens' *Borinage*. Any man today can lay claim to being filmed. This claim can best be elucidated by a comparative look at the historical situation of contemporary literature.

For centuries a small number of writers were confronted by many thousands of readers. This changed toward the end of the last century. With the increasing extension of the press, which kept placing new political, religious, scientific, professional, and local organs before the readers, an increasing number of readers became writers – at first, occasional ones. It began with the daily press opening to its readers space for "letters to the editor." And today there is hardly a gainfully employed European who could not, in principle, find an opportunity to publish somewhere or other comments on his work, grievances, documentary reports, or that sort of thing. Thus, the distinction between author and public is about to lose its basic character. The difference becomes merely functional; it may vary from case to case. At any moment the reader is ready to turn into a writer. As expert, which he had to become willy-nilly in an extremely specialized work process, even if only in some minor respect, the reader gains access to authorship. In the Soviet Union work itself is given a voice. To present it verbally is part of a man's ability to perform the work. Literary license is now founded on polytechnic rather than specialized training and thus becomes common property.[20]

All this can easily be applied to the film, where transitions that in literature took centuries have come about in a decade. In cinematic practice, particularly in Russia, this change-over has partially become established reality. Some of the players whom we meet in Russian films are not actors in our sense but people who portray *themselves* – and primarily in their own work process. In Western Europe the capitalistic exploitation of the film denies consideration to modern man's legitimate claim to being reproduced. Under these circumstances the film industry is trying hard to spur the interest of the masses through illusion-promoting spectacles and dubious speculations.

XI

The shooting of a film, especially of a sound film, affords a spectacle unimaginable anywhere at any time before this. It presents a process in which it is impossible to assign to a spectator a viewpoint which would exclude from the actual scene such extraneous accessories as camera equipment, lighting machinery, staff assistants, etc. – unless his eye were on a line parallel with the lens. This circumstance, more than any other, renders superficial and insignificant any possible similarity between a scene in the studio and one on the stage. In the theater one is well aware of the place from which the play cannot immediately be detected as illusionary. There is no such place for the movie scene that is being shot. Its illusionary nature is that of the second degree, the result of cutting. That is to say, in the studio the mechanical equipment has penetrated so deeply into reality that its pure aspect freed from the foreign substance of equipment is the result of a special procedure, namely, the shooting by the specially adjusted camera and the mounting of the shot together with other similar ones. The equipment-free aspect of reality here has become the height of artifice; the sight of immediate reality has become an orchid in the land of technology.

Even more revealing is the comparison of these circumstances, which differ so much from those of the theater, with the situation in painting. Here the question is: How does the cameraman compare with the painter? To answer this we take recourse to an analogy with a surgical operation. The surgeon represents the polar opposite of the magician. The magician heals a sick person by the laying on of hands; the surgeon cuts into the patient's body. The magician maintains the natural distance between the patient and himself; though he reduces it very slightly by the laying on of hands, he greatly increases it by virtue of his authority. The surgeon does exactly the reverse, he greatly diminishes the distance between himself and the patient by penetrating into the patient's body, and increases it but little by the caution with which his hand moves among the organs. In short, in contrast to the magician – who is still hidden in the medical practitioner – the surgeon at the decisive moment abstains from facing the patient man to man; rather, it is though the operation that he penetrates into him.

Magician and surgeon compare to painter and cameraman. The painter maintains in his work a natural distance from reality, the cameraman penetrates deeply into its web.[21] There is a tremendous difference between the pictures they obtain. That of the painter is a total one, that of the cameraman consists of multiple fragments which are assembled under a new law. Thus, for contemporary man the representation of reality by the film is incomparably more significant than that of the painter, since it offers, precisely because of the thoroughgoing permeation of reality with mechanical equipment, an aspect of reality which is free of all equipment. And that is what one is entitled to ask from a work of art.

XII

Mechanical reproduction of art changes the reaction of the masses toward art. The reactionary attitude toward a Picasso painting changes into the progressive reaction toward a Chaplin movie. The progressive reaction is characterized by the direct, intimate fusion of visual and emotional enjoyment with the orientation of the expert. Such fusion is of great social significance. The greater the decrease in the social significance of an art form, the sharper the distinction between criticism and enjoyment by the public. The conventional is uncritically enjoyed, and the truly new is criticized with aversion. With regard to the screen, the critical and the receptive attitudes of the public coincide. The decisive reason for this is that individual reactions are predetermined by the mass audience response they are about to produce, and this is nowhere more pronounced than in the film. The moment these responses become manifest they control each other. Again, the comparison with painting is fruitful. A painting has always had an excellent chance to be viewed by one person or by a few. The simultaneous contemplation of paintings by a large public, such as developed in the nineteenth century, is an early symptom of the crisis of painting, a crisis which was by no means occasioned exclusively by photography but rather in a relatively independent manner by the appeal of art works to the masses.

Painting simply is in no position to present an object for simultaneous collective experience, as it was possible for architecture at all times, for the epic poem in the past, and for the movie today. Although this circumstance in itself should not lead one to conclusions about the social role of painting, it does constitute a serious threat as soon as painting, under special conditions and, as it were, against its nature, is confronted directly by the masses. In the churches and monasteries of the Middle Ages and at the princely courts up to the end of the eighteenth century, a collective reception of paintings did not occur simultaneously, but by graduated and hierarchized mediation. The change that has come about is an expression of the particular conflict in which painting was implicated by the mechanical reproducibility of paintings. Although paintings began to be publicly exhibited in galleries and salons, there was no way for the masses to organize and control themselves in their reception.[22] Thus the same public which responds in a progressive manner toward a grotesque film is bound to respond in a reactionary manner to surrealism.

XIII

The characteristics of the film lie not only in the manner in which man presents himself to mechanical equipment but also in the manner in which, by means of this apparatus, man can represent his environment. A glance at occupational psychology illustrates the testing capacity of the equipment. Psychoanalysis illustrates it in a different perspective. The film has enriched our field of perception with methods which can be illustrated by those of Freudian theory. Fifty years ago, a slip of the tongue passed more or less unnoticed. Only exceptionally may such a slip have revealed dimensions of depth in a conversation which had seemed to be taking its course on the surface. Since the *Psychopathology of Everyday Life* things have changed. This book isolated and made analyzable things which had heretofore floated along unnoticed in the broad stream of perception. For the entire spectrum of optical, and now also acoustical, perception the film has brought about a similar deepening of apperception. It is only an obverse of this fact that behavior items shown in a movie can be analyzed much more precisely and from more points of view than those presented on paintings or on the stage. As compared with painting, filmed behavior lends itself more readily to analysis because of its incomparably more precise statements of the situation. In comparison with the stage scene, the filmed behavior item lends itself more readily to analysis because it can be isolated more easily. This circumstance derives its chief importance from its tendency to promote the mutual penetration of art and science. Actually, of a screened behavior item which is neatly brought out in a certain situation, like a muscle of a body, it is difficult to say which is more fascinating, its artistic value or its value for science. To demonstrate the identity of the artistic and scientific uses of photography which heretofore usually were separated will be one of the revolutionary functions of the film.[23]

By close-ups of the things around us, by focusing on hidden details of familiar objects, by exploring commonplace milieus under the ingenious guidance of the camera, the film, on the one hand, extends our comprehension of the necessities which rule our lives; on the other hand, it manages to assure us of an immense and unexpected field of action. Our taverns and our metropolitan streets, our offices and furnished rooms, our railroad stations and our factories appeared to have us locked up hopelessly. Then came the film and burst this prison-world asunder by the dynamite of the tenth of a second, so that now, in the midst of its far-flung ruins and debris, we calmly and adventurously go traveling. With the close-up, space expands; with slow motion, movement is extended. The enlargement of a snapshot does not simply render more precise what in any case was visible, though unclear: it reveals entirely new structural formations of the subject. So, too, slow motion not only presents familiar qualities of movement but reveals in them entirely unknown ones "which, far from looking like retarded rapid movements, give the effect of singularly gliding, floating, supernatural motions."[24] Evidently a different nature opens itself to the camera than opens to the naked eye – if only because an unconsciously penetrated space is substituted for a space consciously explored by man. Even if one has a general knowledge of the way people walk, one knows nothing of a person's posture during the fractional second of a stride. The act of reaching for a lighter or a spoon is familiar routine, yet we hardly know what really goes on between hand and metal, not to mention how this fluctuates with our moods. Here the camera intervenes with the resources of its lowerings and liftings, its interruptions and isolations, its extensions and accelerations, its enlargements and reductions. The camera introduces us to unconscious optics as does psychoanalysis to unconscious impulses.

XIV

One of the foremost tasks of art has always been the creation of a demand which could be fully satisfied only later.[25] The history of every art form shows critical epochs in which a certain art form aspires to effects which could be fully obtained only with a changed technical standard, that is to say, in a new art form. The extravagances and crudities of art which thus appear, particularly in the so-called decadent epochs, actually arise from the nucleus of its richest historical energies. In recent years, such barbarisms were abundant in Dadaism. It is only now that its impulse becomes discernible: Dadaism attempted to create by pictorial – and literary – means the effects which the public today seeks in the film.

Every fundamentally new, pioneering creation of demands will carry beyond its goal. Dadaism did so to the extent that it sacrificed the market values which are so characteristic of the film in favor of higher ambitions – though of course it was not conscious of such intentions as here described. The Dadaists attached much less importance to the sales value of their work than to its uselessness for contemplative immersion. The studied degradation of their material was not the least of their means to achieve this uselessness. Their poems are "word salad" containing obscenities and every imaginable waste product of language. The same is true of their paintings, on which they mounted buttons and tickets. What they intended and achieved was a relentless destruction of the aura of their creations, which they branded as reproductions with the very means of production. Before a painting of Arp's or a poem by August Stramm it is impossible to take time for contemplation and evaluation as one would before a canvas of Derain's or a poem by Rilke. In the decline of middle-class society, contemplation became a school for asocial behavior; it was countered by distraction as a variant of social conduct.[26] Dadaistic activities actually assured a rather vehement distraction by making works of art the center of scandal. One requirement was foremost: to outrage the public.

From an alluring appearance or persuasive structure of sound the work of art of the Dadaists became an instrument of ballistics. It hit the spectator like a bullet, it happened to him, thus acquiring a tactile quality. It promoted a demand for the film, the distracting element of which is also primarily tactile, being based on changes of place and focus which periodically assail the spectator. Let us compare the screen on which a film unfolds with the canvas of a painting. The painting invites the spectator to contemplation; before it the spectator can abandon himself to his associations. Before the movie frame he cannot do so. No sooner has his eye grasped a scene than it is already changed. It cannot be arrested. Duhamel, who detests the film and knows nothing of its significance, though something of its structure, notes this circumstance as follows: "I can no longer think what I want to think. My thoughts have been replaced by moving images."[27] The spectator's process of association in view of these images is indeed interrupted by their constant, sudden change. This constitutes the shock effect of the film, which, like all shocks, should be cushioned by heightened presence of mind.[28] By means of its technical structure, the film has taken the physical shock effect out of the wrappers in which Dadaism had, as it were, kept it inside the moral shock effect.[29]

XV

The mass is a matrix from which all traditional behavior toward works of art issues today in a new form. Quantity has been transmuted into quality. The greatly increased mass of participants has produced a change in the mode of participation. The fact that the new mode of participation first appeared in a disreputable form must not confuse the spectator. Yet some people have launched spirited attacks against precisely this superficial aspect. Among these,

Duhamel has expressed himself in the most radical manner. What he objects to most is the kind of participation which the movie elicits from the masses. Duhamel calls the movie "a pastime for helots, a diversion for uneducated, wretched, worn-out creatures who are consumed by their worries . . . , a spectacle which requires no concentration and presupposes no intelligence . . . , which kindles no light in the heart and awakens no hope other than the ridiculous one of someday becoming a 'star' in Los Angeles."[30] Clearly, this is at bottom the same ancient lament that the masses seek distraction whereas art demands concentration from the spectator. That is a commonplace. The question remains whether it provides a platform for the analysis of the film. A closer look is needed here. Distraction and concentration form polar opposites which may be stated as follows: A man who concentrates before a work of art is absorbed by it. He enters into this work of art the way legend tells of the Chinese painter when he viewed his finished painting. In contrast, the distracted mass absorbs the work of art. This is most obvious with regard to buildings. Architecture has always represented the prototype of a work of art the reception of which is consummated by a collectivity in a state of distraction. The laws of its reception are most instructive.

Buildings have been man's companions since primeval times. Many art forms have developed and perished. Tragedy begins with the Greeks, is extinguished with them, and after centuries its "rules" only are revived. The epic poem, which had its origin in the youth of nations, expires in Europe at the end of the Renaissance. Panel painting is a creation of the Middle Ages, and nothing guarantees its uninterrupted existence. But the human need for shelter is lasting. Architecture has never been idle. Its history is more ancient than that of any other art, and its claim to being a living force has significance in every attempt to comprehend the relationship of the masses to art. Buildings are appropriated in a twofold manner: by use and by perception – or rather, by touch and sight. Such appropriation cannot be understood in terms of the attentive concentration of a tourist before a famous building. On the tactile side there is no counterpart to contemplation on the optical side. Tactile appropriation is accomplished not so much by attention as by habit. As regards architecture, habit determines to a large extent even optical reception. The latter, too, occurs much less through rapt attention than by noticing the object in incidental fashion. This mode of appropriation, developed with reference to architecture, in certain circumstances acquires canonical value. For the tasks which face the human apparatus of perception at the turning points of history cannot be solved by optical means, that is, by contemplation, alone. They are mastered gradually by habit, under the guidance of tactile appropriation.

The distracted person, too, can form habits. More, the ability to master certain tasks in a state of distraction proves that their solution has become a matter of habit. Distraction as provided by art presents a covert control of the extent to which new tasks have become soluble by apperception. Since, moreover, individuals are tempted to avoid such tasks, art will tackle the most difficult and most important one where it is able to mobilize the masses. Today it does so in the film. Reception in a state of distraction, which is increasing noticeably in all fields of art and is symptomatic of profound changes in apperception, finds in the film its true means of exercise. The film with its shock effect meets this mode of reception halfway. The film makes the cult value recede into the background not only by putting the public in the position of the critic, but also by the fact that at the movies this position requires no attention. The public is an examiner, but an absent-minded one.

Epilogue

The growing proletarianization of modern man and the increasing formation of masses are two aspects of the same process. Fascism attempts to organize the newly created proletarian masses without affecting the property structure which the masses strive to eliminate. Fascism sees its salvation in giving these masses not their right, but instead a chance to express themselves.[31] The masses have a right to change property relations; Fascism seeks to give them an expression while preserving property. The logical result of Fascism is the introduction of aesthetics into political life. The violation of the masses, whom Fascism, with its *Führer* cult, forces to their knees, has its counterpart in the violation of an apparatus which pressed into the production of ritual values.

All efforts to render politics aesthetic culminate in one thing: war. War and war only can set a goal for mass movements on the largest scale while respecting the traditional property system. This is the political formula for the situation. The technological formula may be stated as follows: Only war makes it possible to mobilize all of today's technical resources while maintaining the property system. It goes without saying that the Fascist apotheosis of war does not employ such arguments. Still, Marinetti says in his manifesto on the Ethiopian colonial war: "For twenty-seven years we Futurists have rebelled against the branding of war as antiaesthetic . . . Accordingly we state: . . . War is beautiful because it establishes man's dominion over the subjugated machinery by means of gas masks, terrifying megaphones, flame throwers, and small tanks. War is beautiful because it initiates the dreamt-of metalization of the human body. War is beautiful because it enriches a flowering meadow with the fiery orchids of machine guns. War is beautiful because it combines the gunfire, the cannonades, the cease-fire, the scents, and the stench of putrefaction into a symphony. War is beautiful because it creates new architecture, like that of the big tanks, the geometrical formation flights, the smoke spirals from burning villages, and many others . . . Poets and artists of Futurism! . . . remember these principles of an aesthetics of war so that your struggle for a new literature and a new graphic art . . . may be illumined by them!"

This manifesto has the virtue of clarity. Its formulations deserve to be accepted by dialecticians. To the latter, the aesthetics of today's war appears as follows: If the natural utilization of productive forces is impeded by the property system, the increase in technical devices, in speed, and in the sources of energy will press for an unnatural utilization, and this is found in war. The destructiveness of war furnishes proof that society has not been mature enough to incorporate technology as its organ, that technology has not been sufficiently developed to cope with the elemental forces of society. The horrible features of imperialistic warfare are attributable to the discrepancy between the tremendous means of production and their inadequate utilization in the process of production – in other words, to unemployment and the lack of markets. Imperialistic war is a rebellion of technology which collects, in the form of "human material," the claims to which society has denied its natural material. Instead of draining rivers, society directs a human stream into a bed of trenches; instead of dropping seeds from airplanes, it drops incendiary bombs over cities; and through gas warfare the aura is abolished in a new way.

"*Fiat ars – pereat mundus,*" says Fascism, and, as Marinetti admits, expects war to supply the artistic gratification of a sense perception that has been changed by technology. This is evidently the consummation of "*l'art pour l'art.*" Mankind, which in Homer's time was an object of contemplation for the Olympian gods, now is one for itself. Its self-alienation has reached such a degree that it can experience its own destruction as an aesthetic pleasure of the first order. This is the situation of politics which Fascism is rendering aesthetic. Communism responds by politicizing art.

Notes

1 Quoted from Paul Valéry, *Aesthetics*, "The Conquest of Ubiquity," translated by Ralph Manheim, p. 225. Pantheon Books, Bollingen Series, New York, 1964.

2 Of course, the history of a work of art encompasses more than this. The history of the "Mona Lisa," for instance, encompasses the kind and number of its copies made in the 17th, 18th, and 19th centuries.

3 Precisely because authenticity is not reproducible, the intensive penetration of certain (mechanical) processes of reproduction was instrumental in differentiating and grading authenticity. To develop such differentiations was an important function of the trade in works of art. The invention of the woodcut may be said to have struck at the root of the quality of authenticity even before its late flowering. To be sure, at the time of its origin a medieval picture of the Madonna could not yet be said to be "authentic." It became "authentic" only during the succeeding centuries and perhaps most strikingly so during the last one.

4 The poorest provincial staging of *Faust* is superior to a Faust film in that, ideally, it competes with the first performance at Weimar. Before the screen it is unprofitable to remember traditional contents which might come to mind before the stage – for instance, that Goethe's friend Johann Heinrich Merck is hidden in Mephisto, and the like.

5 Abel Gance, "Le Temps de l'image est venu," *L'Art cinématographique*, Vol. 2, pp. 94f., Paris, 1927.

6 To satisfy the human interest of the masses may mean to have one's social function removed from

the field of vision. Nothing guarantees that a portraitist of today, when painting a famous surgeon at the breakfast table in the midst of his family, depicts his social function more precisely than a painter of the 17th century who portrayed his medical doctors as representing this profession, like Rembrandt in his "Anatomy Lesson."

7 The definition of the aura as a "unique phenomenon of a distance however close it may be" represents nothing but the formulation of the cult value of the work of art in categories of space and time perception. Distance is the opposite of closeness. The essentially distant object is the unapproachable one. Unapproachability is indeed a major quality of the cult image. True to its nature, it remains "distant, however close it may be." The closeness which one may gain from its subject matter does not impair the distance which it retains in its appearance.

8 To the extent to which the cult value of the painting is secularized the ideas of its fundamental uniqueness lose distinctness. In the imagination of the beholder the uniqueness of the phenomena which hold sway in the cult image is more and more displaced by the empirical uniqueness of the creator or of his creative achievement. To be sure, never completely so; the concept of authenticity always transcends mere genuineness. (This is particularly apparent in the collector who always retains some traces of the fetishist and who, by owning the work of art, shares in its ritual power.) Nevertheless, the function of the concept of authenticity remains determinate in the evaluation of art; with the secularization of art, authenticity displaces the cult value of the work.

9 In the case of films, mechanical reproduction is not, as with literature and painting, an external condition for mass distribution. Mechanical reproduction is inherent in the very technique of film production. This technique not only permits in the most direct way but virtually causes mass distribution. It enforces distribution because the production of a film is so expensive that an individual who, for instance, might afford to buy a painting no longer can afford to buy a film. In 1927 it was calculated that a major film, in order to pay its way, had to reach an audience of nine million. With the sound film, to be sure, a setback in its international distribution occurred at first: audiences became limited by language barriers. This coincided with the Fascist emphasis on national interests. It is more important to focus on this connection with Fascism than on this setback, which was soon minimized by synchronization. The simultaneity of both phenomena is attributable to the depression. The same disturbances which, on a larger scale, led to an attempt to maintain the existing property structure by sheer force led the endangered film capital to speed up the development of the sound film. The introduction of the sound film brought about a temporary relief, not only because it again brought the masses into the theaters but also because it merged new capital from the electrical industry with that of the film industry. Thus, viewed from the outside, the sound film promoted national interests, but seen from the inside it helped to internationalize film production even more than previously.

10 This polarity cannot come into its own in the aesthetics of Idealism. Its idea of beauty comprises these polar opposites without differentiating between them and consequently excludes their polarity. Yet in Hegel this polarity announces itself as clearly as possible within the limits of Idealism. We quote from his *Philosophy of History*:

> Images were known of old. Piety at an early time required them for worship, but it could do without *beautiful* images. These might even be disturbing. In every beautiful painting there is also something nonspiritual, merely external, but its spirit speaks to man through its beauty. Worshipping, conversely, is concerned with the work as an object, for it is but a spiritless stupor of the soul.... Fine art has arisen ... in the church ..., although it has already gone beyond its principle as art.

Likewise, the following passage from *The Philosophy of Fine Art* indicates that Hegel sensed a problem here.

> We are beyond the stage of reverence for works of art as divine and objects deserving our worship. The impression they produce is one of a more reflective kind, and the emotions they arouse require a higher test ..." – G. W. F. Hegel, *The Philosophy of Fine Art*, trans., with notes, by F. P. B. Osmaston, Vol. I, p. 12, London, 1920.

The transition from the first kind of artistic reception to the second characterizes the history of artistic reception in general. Apart from that, a certain oscillation between these two polar modes of reception can be demonstrated for each work of art. Take the Sistine Madonna. Since Hubert Grimme's research it has been known that the Madonna originally was painted for the purpose of exhibition. Grimme's research was inspired by the question: What is the purpose of the molding in the foreground of the painting which the two cupids lean upon? How, Grimme asked further, did Raphael come to furnish the sky with two draperies? Research proved that the Madonna had been commissioned for the public lying-in-state of Pope Sixtus. The Popes lay in state in a certain side chapel of St. Peter's. On that occasion Raphael's picture had been fastened in a nichelike background of the chapel, supported by the coffin. In this picture Raphael portrays the Madonna approaching the papal coffin in clouds from the background of the niche, which was demarcated by green drapes. At the obsequies of Sixtus a preeminent exhibition value of Raphael's picture was taken advantage of. Some time later it was placed on the high altar in the church of the Black Friars at Piacenza. The reason for this exile is to be found in the Roman rites which forbid the use of paintings exhibited at obsequies as cult objects on the high altar. This regulation devalued Raphael's picture to some degree. In order to obtain an adequate price nevertheless, the Papal See resolved to add to the bargain the tacit toleration of the picture above the high altar. To avoid attention the picture was given to the monks of the far-off provincial town.

11 Bertolt Brecht, on a different level, engaged in analogous reflections: "If the concept of 'work of art' can no longer be applied to the thing that emerges once the work is transformed into a commodity, we have to eliminate this concept with cautious care but without fear, lest we liquidate the function of the very thing as well. For it has to go through this phase without mental reservation, and not as noncommittal deviation from the straight path; rather, what happens here with the work of art will change it fundamentally and erase its past to such an extent that should the old concept be taken up again – and it will, why not? – it will no longer stir any memory of the thing it once designated."

12 Abel Gance, ["Le Temps de l'image,"] pp. 100–1.

13 Séverin-Mars, quoted by Abel Gance, ["Le Temps de l'image,"] p. 100.

14 Alexandre Arnoux, *Cinéma pris*, 1929, p. 28.

15 Franz Werfel, "Ein Sommernachtstraum, Ein Film von Shakespeare und Reinhardt," *Neues Wiener Journal*, cited in *Lu* 15, November, 1935.

16 "The film . . . provides – or could provide – useful insight into the details of human actions . . . Character is never used as a source of motivation; the inner life of the persons never supplies the principal cause of the plot and seldom is its main result." (Bertolt Brecht, *Versuche*, "Der Dreigroschenprozess," p. 268.) The expansion of the field of the testable which mechanical equipment brings about for the actor corresponds to the extraordinary expansion of the field of the testable brought about for the individual through economic conditions. Thus, vocational aptitude tests become constantly more important. What matters in these tests are segmental performances of the individual. The film shot and the vocational aptitude test are taken before a committee of experts. The camera director in the studio occupies a place identical with that of the examiner during aptitude tests.

17 Luigi Pirandello, *Si Gira*, quoted by Léon Pierre-Quint, "Signification du cinéma," *L'Art cinématographique*, Vol. 2, pp. 14–15.

18 Rudolf Arnheim, *Film als Kunst*, Berlin, 1932, pp. 176f. In this context certain seemingly unimportant details in which the film director deviates from stage practices gain in interest. Such is the attempt to let the actor play without make-up, as made among others by Dreyer in his *Jeanne d'Arc*. Dreyer spent months seeking the forty actors who constitute the Inquisitors' tribunal. The search for these actors resembled that for stage properties that are hard to come by. Dreyer made every effort to avoid resemblances of age, build, and physiognomy. If the actor thus becomes a stage property, this latter, on the other hand, frequently functions as actor. At least it is not unusual for the film to assign a role to the stage property. Instead of choosing at random from a great wealth of examples, let us concentrate on a particularly convincing one. A clock that is working will always be a disturbance on the stage. There it cannot be permitted its function of measuring time. Even in a naturalistic play, astronomical time would clash with theatrical time. Under these circumstances it is highly revealing that the film can, whenever appropriate, use time as measured by a clock. From this more than from many other touches it may clearly be recognized that under certain circumstances each and every prop in a film may assume important functions. From here it is but one step to Pudovkin's statement that "the playing of an actor which is connected with an object and is built around it . . . is always one of the strongest methods of cinematic construction." (W. Pudovkin, *Filmregie und Filmmanuskript*, Berlin, 1928, p. 126.) The film is the first art form capable of demonstrating how matter plays tricks on man. Hence, films can be an excellent means of materialistic representation.

19 The change noted here in the method of exhibition caused by mechanical reproduction applies to politics as well. The present crisis of the bourgeois democracies comprises a crisis of the conditions which determine the public presentation of the rulers. Democracies exhibit a member of government directly and personally before the nation's

representatives. Parliament is his public. Since the innovations of camera and recording equipment make it possible for the orator to become audible and visible to an unlimited number of persons, the presentation of the man of politics before camera and recording equipment becomes paramount. Parliaments, as much as theaters, are deserted. Radio and film not only affect the function of the professional actor but likewise the function of those who also exhibit themselves before this mechanical equipment, those who govern. Though their tasks may be different, the change affects equally the actor and the ruler. The trend is toward establishing controllable and transferrable skills under certain social conditions. This results in a new selection, a selection before the equipment from which the star and the dictator emerge victorious.

20 The privileged character of the respective techniques is lost. Aldous Huxley writes:

> Advances in technology have led . . . to vulgarity. . . . Process reproduction and the rotary press have made possible the indefinite multiplication of writing and pictures. Universal education and relatively high wages have created an enormous public who know how to read and can afford to buy reading and pictorial matter. A great industry has been called into existence in order to supply these commodities. Now, artistic talent is a very rare phenomenon; whence it follows . . . that, at every epoch and in all countries, most art has been bad. But the proportion of trash in the total artistic output is greater now than at any other period. That it must be so is a matter of simple arithmetic. The population of Western Europe has a little more than doubled during the last century. But the amount of reading – and seeing – matter has increased, I should imagine, at least twenty and possibly fifty or even a hundred times. If there were n men of talent in a population of x millions, there will presumably be 2n men of talent among 2x millions. The situation may be summed up thus. For every page of print and pictures published a century ago, twenty or perhaps even a hundred pages are published today. But for every man of talent then living, there are now only two men of talent. It may be of course that, thanks to universal education, many potential talents which in the past would have been still-born are now enabled to realize themselves. Let us assume, then, that there are now three or even four men of talent to every one of earlier times. It still remains true to say that the consumption of reading – and seeing – matter has far outstripped the natural production of gifted writers and draughtsmen. It is the same with hearing-matter. Prosperity, the gramophone and the radio have created an audience of hearers who consume an amount of hearing-matter that has increased out of all proportion to the increase of population and the consequent natural increase of talented musicians. It follows from all this that in all the arts the output of trash is both absolutely and relatively greater than it was in the past; and that it must remain greater for just so long as the world continues to consume the present inordinate quantities of reading-matter, seeing-matter, and hearing-matter." – Aldous Huxley, *Beyond the Mexique Bay. A Traveller's Journal*, London, 1949, pp. 274ff. First published in 1934.

This mode of observation is obviously not progressive.

21 The boldness of the cameraman is indeed comparable to that of the surgeon. Luc Durtain lists among specific technical sleights of hand those "which are required in surgery in the case of certain difficult operations. I choose as an example a case from oto-rhino-laryngology; . . . the so-called endonasal perspective procedure; or I refer to the acrobatic tricks of larynx surgery which have to be performed following the reversed picture in the laryngoscope. I might also speak of ear surgery which suggests the precision work of watchmakers. What range of the most subtle muscular acrobatics is required from the man who wants to repair or save the human body! We have only to think of the couching of a cataract where there is virtually a debate of steel with nearly fluid tissue, or of the major abdominal operations (laparotomy)." – Luc Durtain [. . .].

22 This mode of observation may seem crude, but as the great theoretician Leonardo has shown, crude modes of observation may at times be usefully adduced. Leonardo compares painting and music as follows: "Painting is superior to music because, unlike unfortunate music, it does not have to die as soon as it is born . . . Music which is consumed in the very act of its birth is inferior to painting which the use of varnish has rendered eternal." (Trattato I, 29.)

23 Renaissance painting offers a revealing analogy to this situation. The incomparable development of this art and its significance rested not least on the integration of a number of new sciences, or at least of new scientific data. Renaissance painting made use of anatomy and perspective, of mathematics, meteorology, and chromatology. Valéry writes:

"What could be further from us than the strange claim of a Leonardo to whom painting was a supreme goal and the ultimate demonstration of knowledge? Leonardo was convinced that painting demanded universal knowledge, and he did not even shrink from a theoretical analysis which to us is stunning because of its very depth and precision . . ." – Paul Valéry, *Pièces sur l'art*, "Autour de Corot," Paris, p. 191.

24 Rudolf Arnheim, *Film als Kunst*, p. 138.

25 "The work of art," says André Breton, "is valuable only in so far as it is vibrated by the reflexes of the future." Indeed, every developed art form intersects three lines of development. Technology works toward a certain form of art. Before the advent of the film there were photo booklets with pictures which flitted by the onlooker upon pressure of the thumb, thus portraying a boxing bout or a tennis match. Then there were the slot machines in bazaars; their picture sequences were produced by the turning of a crank.

Secondly, the traditional art forms in certain phases of their development strenuously work toward effects which later are effortlessly attained by the new ones. Before the rise of the movie the Dadaists' performances tried to create an audience reaction which Chaplin later evoked in a more natural way.

Thirdly, unspectacular social changes often promote a change in receptivity which will benefit the new art form. Before the movie had begun to create its public, pictures that were no longer immobile captivated an assembled audience in the so-called *Kaiserpanorama*. Here the public assembled before a screen into which stereoscopes were mounted, one to each beholder. By a mechanical process individual pictures appeared briefly before the stereoscopes, then made way for others. Edison still had to use similar devices in presenting the first movie strip before the film screen and projection were known. This strip was presented to a small public which stared into the apparatus in which the succession of pictures was reeling off. Incidentally, the institution of the *Kaiserpanorama* shows very clearly a dialectic of the development. Shortly before the movie turned the reception of pictures into a collective one, the individual viewing of pictures in these swiftly outmoded establishments came into play once more with an intensity comparable to that of the ancient priest beholding the statue of a divinity in the cella.

26 The theological archetype of this contemplation is the awareness of being alone with one's God. Such awareness, in the heyday of the bourgeoisie, went to strengthen the freedom to shake off clerical tutelage. During the decline of the bourgeoisie this awareness had to take into account the hidden tendency to withdraw from public affairs those forces which the individual draws upon in his communion with God.

27 Georges Duhamel, *Scènes de la vie future*, Paris, 1930, p. 52.

28 The film is the art form that is in keeping with the increased threat to his life which modern man has to face. Man's need to expose himself to shock effects is his adjustment to the dangers threatening him. The film corresponds to profound changes in the apperceptive apparatus – changes that are experienced on an individual scale by the man in the street in big-city traffic, on a historical scale by every present-day citizen.

29 As for Dadaism, insights important for Cubism and Futurism are to be gained from the movie. Both appear as deficient attempts of art to accommodate the pervasion of reality by the apparatus. In contrast to the film, these schools did not try to use the apparatus as such for the artistic presentation of reality, but aimed at some sort of alloy in the joint presentation of reality and apparatus. In Cubism, the premonition that this apparatus will be structurally based on optics plays a dominant part; in Futurism, it is the premonition of the effects of this apparatus which are brought out by the rapid sequence of the film strip.

30 Duhamel, *Scènes de la vie future*, p. 58.

31 One technical feature is significant here, especially with regard to newsreels, the propagandist importance of which can hardly he overestimated. Mass reproduction is aided especially by the reproduction of masses. In big parades and monster rallies, in sports events, and in war, all of which nowadays are captured by camera and sound recording, the masses are brought face to face with themselves. This process, whose significance need not be stressed, is intimately connected with the development of the techniques of reproduction and photography. Mass movements are usually discerned more clearly by a camera than by the naked eye. A bird's-eye view best captures gatherings of hundreds of thousands. And even though such a view may be as accessible to the human eye as it is to the camera, the image received by the eye cannot be enlarged the way a negative is enlarged. This means that mass movements, including war, constitute a form of human behavior which particularly favors mechanical equipment.

30

The Origin of the Work of Art

Martin Heidegger

Martin Heidegger (1889–1976) was a German philosopher who was a professor at the University of Freiburg. His political relationships have been much discussed, but his philosophical influence remains unquestionable.

Origin here means that from and by which something is what it is and as it is. What something is, as it is, we call its essence or nature. The origin of something is the source of its nature. The question concerning the origin of the work of art asks about the source of its nature. On the usual view, the work arises out of and by means of the activity of the artist. But by what and whence is the artist what he is? By the work; for to say that the work does credit to the master means that it is the work that first lets the artist emerge as a master of his art. The artist is the origin of the work. The work is the origin of the artist. Neither is without the other. Nevertheless, neither is the sole support of the other. In themselves and in their interrelations artist and work *are* each of them by virtue of a third thing which is prior to both, namely that which also gives artist and work of art their names – art. [. . .]

[. . .] [T]he question of the origin of the work of art becomes a question about the nature of art.

Martin Heidegger, "The Origin of the Work of Art," in *Poetry, Language, Thought* (New York: HarperCollins Publishers, 1971), pp. 17–36, 38–9, 41–6, 48–52, 55–9, 64–6, 69–71, 77–8.

Since the question whether and how art in general exists must still remain open, we shall attempt to discover the nature of art in the place where art undoubtedly prevails in a real way. Art is present in the art work. But what and how is a work of art? [. . .]

Works of art are familiar to everyone. Architectural and sculptural works can be seen installed in public places, in churches, and in dwellings. Art works of the most diverse periods and peoples are housed in collections and exhibitions. If we consider the works in their untouched actuality and do not deceive ourselves, the result is that the works are as naturally present as are things. The picture hangs on the wall like a rifle or a hat. A painting, e.g., the one by Van Gogh that represents a pair of peasant shoes, travels from one exhibition to another. Works of art are shipped like coal from the Ruhr and logs from the Black Forest. During the First World War Hölderlin's hymns were packed in the soldier's knapsack together with cleaning gear. Beethoven's quartets lie in the storerooms of the publishing house like potatoes in a cellar.

All works have this thingly character. What would they be without it? But perhaps this rather crude and external view of the work is objectionable to us. Shippers or charwomen in museums may operate with such conceptions of the work of art. We, however, have to take works as they are encountered by those who experience and enjoy them. But even the much-vaunted aesthetic experience cannot get around the thingly aspect of the art work. There is something stony in a work of architecture, wooden in a carving, colored in a painting, spoken in a linguistic work, sonorous in a musical composition. The thingly element is so irremovably present in the art work that we are compelled rather to say conversely that the architectural work is in stone, the carving is in wood, the painting in color, the linguistic work in speech, the musical composition in sound. "Obviously," it will be replied. No doubt. But what is this self-evident thingly element in the work of art? [. . .]

Our aim is to arrive at the immediate and full reality of the work of art, for only in this way shall we discover real art also within it. Hence we must first bring to view the thingly element of the work. To this end it is necessary that we should know with sufficient clarity what a thing is. Only then can we say whether the art work is a thing, but a thing to which something else adheres; only then can we decide whether the work is at bottom something else and not a thing at all.

Thing and Work

What in truth is the thing, so far as it is a thing? When we inquire in this way, our aim is to come to know the thing-being (thingness) of the thing. The point is to discover the thingly character of the thing. To this end we have to be acquainted with the sphere to which all those entities belong which we have long called by the name of thing.

The stone in the road is a thing, as is the clod in the field. A jug is a thing, as is the well beside the road. But what about the milk in the jug and the water in the well? These too are things if the cloud in the sky and the thistle in the field, the leaf in the autumn breeze and the hawk over the wood, are rightly called by the name of thing. All these must indeed be called things, if the name is applied even to that which does not, like those just enumerated, show itself, i.e., that which does not appear. According to Kant, the whole of the world, for example, and even God himself, is a thing of this sort, a thing that does not itself appear, namely, a "thing-in-itself." In the language of philosophy both things-in-themselves and things that appear, all beings that in any way are, are called things.

Airplanes and radio sets are nowadays among the things closest to us, but when we have ultimate things in mind we think of something altogether different. Death and judgment – these are ultimate things. On the whole the word "thing" here designates whatever is not simply nothing. In this sense the work of art is also a thing, so far as it is not simply nothing. Yet this concept is of no use to us, at least immediately, in our attempt to delimit entities that have the mode of being of a thing, as against those having the mode of being of a work. And besides, we hesitate to call God a thing. In the same way we hesitate to consider the peasant in the field, the stoker at the boiler, the teacher in the school as things. A man is not a thing. It is true that we speak of a young girl who is faced with a task too difficult for her as being a young thing, still too young for it, but only because we feel that being human is in a certain way missing here and think that instead we have to do here with the factor that constitutes the thingly character of things. We hesitate even to call the deer in the forest clearing, the beetle in the grass, the blade of grass a thing. We would sooner think of a hammer as a thing, or a shoe, or an ax, or a clock. But even these are not mere things. Only a stone, a clod of earth, a piece of wood are for us such mere things. Lifeless beings of nature and objects of use. Natural things and utensils are the things commonly so called.

We thus see ourselves brought back from the widest domain, within which everything is a thing (thing = *res* = *ens* = an entity), including even the highest and last things, to the narrow precinct of mere things. "Mere" here means, first, the pure thing, which is simply a thing and nothing more; but then, at the same time, it means that which is only a thing, in an almost pejorative sense. It is mere things, excluding even use-objects, that count as things in the strict sense. What does the thingly character of these thins, then, consist in? It is in reference to these that the thingness of things must be determinable. This determination enables us to characterize what it is that is thingly as such. Thus prepared, we are able to characterize the almost palpable reality of works, in which something else inheres. [...]

The interpretations of the thingness of the thing which, predominant in the course of Western thought, have long become self-evident and are now in everyday use, may be reduced to three.

This block of granite, for example, is a mere thing. It is hard, heavy, extended, bulky, shapeless, rough, colored, partly dull, partly shiny. We can take note of all these features in the stone. Thus we acknowledge its characteristics. But still, the traits signify something proper to the stone itself. They are its properties. The thing has them. The thing? What are we thinking of when we now have the thing in mind? Obviously a thing is not merely an aggregate of traits, nor an accumulation of properties by which that aggregate arises. A thing, as everyone thinks he knows, is that around which the properties have assembled. We speak in this connection of the core of things. [...]

Our reliance on the current interpretation of the thing is only seemingly well founded. But in addition this thing-concept (the thing as bearer of its characteristics) holds not only of the mere thing in its strict sense, but also of any being whatsoever. Hence it cannot be used to set apart thingly beings from non-thingly beings. Yet even before all reflection, attentive dwelling within the sphere of things already tells us that this thing-concept does not hit upon the thingly element of the thing, its independent and self-contained character. Occasionally we still have the feeling that violence has long been done to the thingly element of things and that thought has played a part in this violence, for which reason people disavow thought instead of taking pains to make it more thoughtful. But in defining the nature of the thing, what is the use of a feeling, however certain, if thought alone has the right to speak here? Perhaps however what we call feeling or mood, here and in similar instances, is more reasonable – that is, more intelligently perceptive – because more open to Being than all that reason which, having meanwhile become *ratio*, was misinterpreted as being rational. The hankering after the irrational, as abortive offspring of the unthought rational, therewith performed a curious service. To be sure, the current thing-concept always fits each thing. Nevertheless it does not lay hold of the thing as it is in its own being, but makes an assault upon it.

Can such an assault perhaps be avoided – and how? Only, certainly, by granting the thing, as it were, a free field to display its thingly character directly. Everything that might interpose itself between the thing and us in apprehending and talking about it must first be set aside. Only then do we yield ourselves to the undisguised presence of the thing. But we do not need first to call or arrange for this situation in which we let things encounter us without mediation. The situation always prevails. In what the senses of sight, hearing, and touch convey, in the sensations of color, sound, roughness, hardness, things move us bodily, in the literal meaning of the word. The thing is the *aistheton*, that which is perceptible by sensations in the senses belonging to sensibility. Hence the concept later becomes a commonplace according to which a thing is nothing but the unity of a manifold of what is given in the senses. Whether this unity is conceived as sum or as totality or as form alters nothing in the standard character of this thing-concept.

Now this interpretation of the thingness of the thing is as correct and demonstrable in every case as the previous one. This already suffices to cast doubt on its truth. If we consider moreover what we are searching for, the thingly character of the thing, then this thing-concept again leaves us at a loss. We never really first perceive a throng of sensations, e.g., tones and noises, in the appearance of things – as this thing-concept alleges; rather we hear the storm whistling in the chimney, we hear the three-motored plane, we hear the Mercedes in immediate distinction from the Volkswagen. Much closer to us than all sensations are the things themselves. We hear the door shut in the house and never hear acoustical sensations or even mere sounds. In order to hear a bare sound we have to listen away from things, divert our ear from them, i.e., listen abstractly.

In the thing-concept just mentioned there is not so much an assault upon the thing as rather an inordinate attempt to bring it into the greatest possible proximity to us. But a thing never reaches that position as long as we assign as its thingly feature what is perceived by the senses. Whereas the first interpretation keeps the thing at arm's length from us, as it were, and sets it too far off, the second makes it press too hard upon us. In both interpretations the thing vanishes. It is therefore necessary to avoid the exaggerations of both. The thing itself must be allowed to remain in its self-containment. It must be accepted in its own constancy. This the third interpretation seems to do, which is just as old as the first two.

That which gives things their constancy and pith but is also at the same time the source of their particular mode of sensuous pressure – colored, resonant, hard, massive – is the matter in things. In this analysis of the thing as matter (*hule*), form (*morphe*) is already coposited. What is constant in a thing, its consistency, lies in the fact that matter stands together with a form. The thing is formed matter. This interpretation appeals to the immediate view with which the thing solicits us by its looks (*eidos*). In this synthesis of matter and form a thing-concept has finally been found which applies equally to things of nature and to use-objects.

This concept puts us in a position to answer the question concerning the thingly element in the work of art. The thingly element is manifestly the matter of which it consists. Matter is the substrate and field for the artist's formative action. But we could have advanced this obvious and well-known definition of the thingly element at the very outset. Why do we make a detour through other current thing-concepts? Because we also mistrust this concept of the thing, which represents it as formed matter.

But is not precisely this pair of concepts, matter–form, usually employed in the domain in which we are supposed to be moving? To be sure. The distinction of matter and form is *the conceptual schema which is used, in the greatest variety of ways, quite generally for all art theory and aesthetics.* This incontestable fact, however, proves neither that the distinction of matter and form is adequately founded, nor that it belongs originally to the domain of art and the art work. Moreover, the range of application of this pair of concepts has long extended far beyond the field of aesthetics. Form and content are the most hackneyed concepts under which anything and everything may be subsumed. And if form is correlated with the rational and matter with the irrational; if the rational is taken to be the logical and the irrational the alogical; if in addition the subject–object relation is coupled with the conceptual pair form–matter; then representation has at its command a conceptual machinery that nothing is capable of withstanding.

If, however, it is thus with the distinction between matter and form, how then shall we make use of it to lay hold of the particular domain of mere things by contrast with all other entities? But perhaps this characterization in terms of matter and form would recover its defining power if only we reversed the process of expanding and emptying these concepts. Certainly, but this presupposes that we know in what sphere of beings they realize their true defining power. That this is the domain of mere things is so far only an assumption. Reference to the copious use made of this conceptual framework in aesthetics might sooner lead to the idea that matter and form are specifications stemming from the nature of the art work and were in the first place transferred from it back to the thing. Where does the matter–form structure have its origin – in the thingly character of the thing or in the workly character of the art work?

The self-contained block of granite is something material in a definite if unshapely form. Form means here the distribution and arrangement of the material parts in spatial locations, resulting in a particular shape, namely that of a block. But a jug, an ax, a shoe are also matter occurring in a form. Form as shape is not the consequence here of a prior distribution of the matter. The form, on the contrary, determines the arrangement of the matter. Even more, it prescribes in each case the kind and selection of the matter – impermeable for a jug, sufficiently hard for an ax, firm yet flexible for shoes. The interfusion of form and matter prevailing here is, moreover, controlled beforehand by the purposes served by jug, ax, shoes. Such usefulness is never assigned or added on afterward to a being of the type of a jug, ax, or pair of shoes. But neither is it something that floats somewhere above it as an end.

Usefulness is the basic feature from which this entity regards us, that is, flashes at us and thereby is present and thus is this entity. Both the formative act and the choice of material – a choice given with the act – and therewith the dominance of the conjunction of matter and form, are all grounded in such usefulness. A being that falls under usefulness is always the product of a process of making. It is made as a piece of equipment for something. As determination of beings, accordingly, matter and form have their proper place in the essential nature of equipment. This name designates what is produced expressly for employment and use. Matter and form are in no case original determinations of the thingness of the mere thing.

A piece of equipment, a pair of shoes for instance, when finished, is also self-contained like the mere thing, but it does not have the character of having taken shape by itself like the granite boulder. On the other hand, equipment displays an affinity with the art work insofar as it is something produced by the human hand. However, by its self-sufficient presence the work of art is similar rather to the mere thing which has taken shape by itself and is self-contained. Nevertheless we do not count such works among mere things. As a rule it is the use-objects around us that are the nearest and authentic things. Thus the piece of equipment is half thing, because characterized by thingliness, and yet it is something more; at the same time it is half art work and yet something less, because lacking the self-sufficiency of the art work. Equipment has a peculiar position intermediate between thing and work, assuming that such a calculated ordering of them is permissible. [...]

The situation stands revealed as soon as we speak of things in the strict sense as mere things. The "mere," after all, means the removal of the character of usefulness and of being made. The mere thing is a sort of equipment, albeit equipment denuded of its equipmental being. Thing-being consists in what is then left over. But this remnant is not actually defined in its ontological character. It remains doubtful whether the thingly character comes to view at all in the process of stripping off everything equipmental. Thus the third mode of interpretation of the thing, that which follows the lead of the matter–form structure, also turns out to be an assault upon the thing.

These three modes of defining thingness conceive of the thing as a bearer of traits, as the unity of a manifold of sensations, as formed matter. [...] [W]e risk the attempt to bring to view and express in words the thingly character of the thing, the equipmental character of equipment, and the workly character of the work. To this end, however, only one element is needful: to keep at a distance all the preconceptions and assaults of the above modes of thought, to leave the thing to rest in its own self, for instance, in its thing-being. What seems easier than to let a being be just the being that it is? Or does this turn out to be the most difficult of tasks, particularly if such an intention – to let a being be as it is – represents the opposite of the indifference that simply turns its back upon the being itself in favor of an unexamined concept of being? We ought to turn toward the being, think about it in regard to its being, but by means of this thinking at the same time let it rest upon itself in its very own being.

This exertion of thought seems to meet with its greatest resistance in defining the thingness of the thing; for where else could the cause lie of the failure of the efforts mentioned? The unpretentious thing evades thought most stubbornly. Or can it be that this self-refusal of the mere thing, this self-contained independence, belongs precisely to the nature of the thing? Must not this strange and uncommunicative feature of the nature of the thing become intimately familiar to thought that tries to think the thing? If so, then we should not force our way to its thingly character.

That the thingness of the thing is particularly difficult to express and only seldom expressible is infallibly documented by the history of its interpretation indicated above. This history coincides with the destiny in accordance with which Western thought has hitherto thought the Being of beings. However, not only do we now establish this point; at the same time we discover a clue in this history. Is it an accident that in the interpretation of the thing the view that takes matter and form as guide attains to special dominance? This definition of the thing derives from an interpretation of the equipmental being of equipment. And equipment, having come into being through human making, is particularly familiar to human thinking. At the same time, this familiar being has a peculiar intermediate position between thing and work. We shall follow this clue and search first for the equipmental character of equipment. [...]

We choose as example a common sort of equipment – a pair of peasant shoes. We do not even need to exhibit actual pieces of this sort of useful article in order to describe them. Everyone is acquainted with them. But since it is a matter here of direct description, it may be well to facilitate the visual realization of them. For this purpose a pictorial representation suffices. We shall choose a well-known painting by Van Gogh, who painted such shoes several times. But what is there to see here? Everyone knows what shoes consist of. If they are not wooden or bast shoes, there will be leather soles and uppers, joined together by thread and nails. Such gear serves to clothe the feet. Depending on the use to which the shoes are to be put, whether for work in the field or for dancing, matter and form will differ.

Such statements, no doubt correct, only explicate what we already know. The equipmental quality of equipment consists in its usefulness. But what about this usefulness itself? In conceiving it, do we already conceive along with it the equipmental character of equipment? In order to succeed in doing this, must we not look out for useful equipment in its use? The peasant woman wears her shoes in the field. Only here are they what they are. They are all the more genuinely so, the less the peasant woman thinks about the shoes while she is at work, or looks at them at all, or is even aware of them. She stands and walks in them. That is how shoes actually serve. It is in this process of the use of equipment that we must actually encounter the character of equipment.

As long as we only imagine a pair of shoes in general, or simply look at the empty, unused shoes as they merely stand there in the picture, we shall never discover what the equipmental being of the equipment in truth is. From Van Gogh's painting we cannot even tell where these shoes stand. There is nothing surrounding this pair of peasant shoes in or to which they might belong – only an undefined space. There are not even clods of soil from the field or the field-path sticking to them, which would at least hint at their use. A pair of peasant shoes and nothing more. And yet –

From the dark opening of the worn insides of the shoes the toilsome tread of the worker stares forth. In the stiffly rugged heaviness of the shoes there is the accumulated tenacity of her slow trudge through the far-spreading and ever-uniform furrows of the field swept by a raw wind. On the leather lie the dampness and richness of the soil. Under the soles slides the loneliness of the field-path as evening falls. In the shoes vibrates the silent call of the earth, its quiet gift of the ripening grain and its unexplained self-refusal in the fallow desolation of the wintry field. This equipment is pervaded by uncomplaining anxiety as to the certainty of bread, the wordless joy of having once more withstood want, the trembling before the impending childbed and shivering at the surrounding menace of death. This equipment belongs to the *earth*, and it is protected in the *world* of the peasant woman. From out of this protected belonging the equipment itself rises to its resting-within-itself.

But perhaps it is only in the picture that we notice all this about the shoes. The peasant woman, on the other hand, simply wears them. If only this simple wearing were so simple. When she takes off her shoes late in the evening in deep but healthy fatigue, and reaches out for them again in the still dim dawn, or passes them by on the day of rest, she knows all this without noticing or reflecting. The equipmental quality of the equipment consists indeed in its usefulness. But this usefulness itself rests in the abundance of an essential being of the equipment. We call it reliability. By virtue of this reliability the peasant woman is made privy to the silent call of the earth; by virtue of the reliability of the equipment she is sure of her world. World and earth exist for her, and for those who are with her in her mode of being, only thus – in the equipment. We say "only" and therewith fall into error; for the reliability of the equipment first gives to the simple world its security and assures to the earth the freedom of its steady thrust.

The equipmental being of equipment, reliability, keeps gathered within itself all things according to their manner and extent. The usefulness of equipment is nevertheless only the essential consequence of reliability. The former vibrates in the latter and would be nothing without it. A single piece of equipment is worn out and used up; but at the same time the use itself also falls into disuse, wears away, and becomes usual. Thus equipmentality wastes away, sinks into mere stuff. In such wasting, reliability vanishes. This dwindling, however, to which use-things owe their boringly obtrusive usualness, is only one more testimony to the original nature of equipmental being. The worn-out usualness of the equipment then obtrudes itself as the sole mode of being, apparently peculiar to it exclusively. Only blank usefulness now remains visible. It awakens the impression that the origin of equipment lies in a mere fabricating that impresses a form upon some matter. Nevertheless in its genuinely equipmental being, equipment stems from a more distant source. Matter and form and their distinction have a deeper origin.

The repose of equipment resting within itself consists in its reliability. Only in this reliability do we discern what equipment in truth is. But we still know nothing of what we first sought: the thing's thingly character. And we know nothing at all of what we really and solely seek: the workly character of the work in the sense of the work of art.

Or have we already learned something unwittingly, in passing so to speak, about the work-being of the work?

The equipmental quality of equipment was discovered. But how? Not by a description and explanation of a pair shoes actually present; not by a report about the process of making shoes; and also not by the observation of the actual use of shoes occurring here and there; but only by bringing ourselves before Van Gogh's painting. This painting spoke. In the vicinity of the work we were suddenly somewhere else than we usually tend to be.

The art work let us know what shoes are in truth. It would be the worst self-deception to think that our description, as a subjective action, had first depicted everything thus and then projected it into the painting. If anything is questionable here, it is rather that we experienced too little in the neighborhood of the work and that we expressed the experience too crudely and too literally. But above all, the work did not, as it might seem at first, serve merely for a better visualizing of what a piece of equipment is. Rather, the equipmentality of equipment first genuinely arrives at its appearance through the work and only in the work.

What happens here? What is at work in the work? Van Gogh's painting is the disclosure of what the equipment, the pair of peasant shoes, *is* in truth. This entity emerges into the unconcealedness of its being. The Greeks called the unconcealediness of beings *aletheia.* We say "truth" and think little enough in using this word. If there occurs in the work a disclosure of a particular being, disclosing what and how it is, then there is here an occurring, a happening of truth at work.

In the work of art the truth of an entity has set itself to work "To set" means here: to bring to a stand. Some particular entity, a pair of peasant shoes, comes in the work to stand in the light of its being. The being of the being comes into the steadiness of its shining.

The nature of art would then be this: the truth of beings setting itself to work. [. . .]

We seek the reality of the art work in order to find there the art prevailing within it. The thingly substructure is what proved to be the most immediate reality in the work. But to comprehend this thingly feature the traditional thing-concepts are not adequate; for they themselves fail to grasp the nature of the thing. The currently predominant thing-concept, thing as formed matter, is not even derived from the nature of the thing but from the nature of equipment. It also turned out that equipmental being generally has long since occupied a peculiar preeminence in the interpretation of beings. This preeminence of equipmentality, which however did not actually come to mind, suggested that we pose the question of equipment anew while avoiding the current interpretations.

We allowed a work to tell us what equipment is. By this means, almost clandestinely, it came to light what is at work in the work: the disclosure of the particular being in its being, the happening of truth. If, however, the reality of the work can be defined solely by means of what is at work in the work, then what about our intention to seek out the real art work in its reality? As long as we supposed that the reality of the work lay primarily in its thingly substructure we were going astray. We are now confronted by a remarkable result of our considerations – if it still deserves to be called a result at all. Two points become clear:

First: the dominant thing-concepts are inadequate as means of grasping the thingly aspect of the work.

Second: what we tried to treat as the most immediate reality of the work, its thingly substructure, does not belong to the work in that way at all.

As soon as we look for such a thingly substructure in the work, we have unwittingly taken the work as equipment, to which we then also ascribe a superstructure supposed to contain its artistic quality. But the work is not a piece of equipment that is fitted out in addition with an aesthetic value that adheres to it. The work is no more anything of the kind than the bare thing is a piece of equipment that merely lacks the specific equipmental characteristics of usefulness and being made.

Our formulation of the question of the work has been shaken because we asked, not about the work but half about a thing and half about equipment. Still, this formulation of the question was not first developed by us. It is the formulation native to aesthetics. The way in which aesthetics views the art work from the outset is dominated by the traditional interpretation of all beings. But the shaking of this accustomed formulation is not the essential point. What matters is a first opening of our vision to the fact that what is workly in the work, equipmental in equipment, and thingly in the thing comes closer to us only when we think the Being of beings. To this end it is necessary beforehand that the barriers of our preconceptions fall away and that the current pseudo concepts be set aside. That is why we had to take this detour. But it brings us directly to a road that may lead to a determination of the thingly feature in the work. The thingly feature in the work should not be denied; but if it belongs admittedly to the work-being of the work, it must be conceived by way of the work's workly nature. If this is so, then the road toward the determination of the thingly reality of the work leads not from thing to work but from work to thing.

The art work opens up in its own way the Being of beings. This opening up, i.e., this deconcealing, i.e., the truth of beings, happens in the work. In the art work, the truth of what is has set itself to work. Art is truth setting itself to work. What is truth itself, that it sometimes comes to pass as art? What is this setting-itself-to-work?

The Work and Truth

[...] Where does a work belong? The work belongs, as work, uniquely within the realm that is opened up by itself. For the work-being of the work is present in, and only in, such opening up. We said that in the work there was a happening of truth at work. The reference to Van Gogh's picture tried to point to this happening. With regard to it there arose the question as to what truth is and how truth can happen.

We now ask the question of truth with a view to the work. But in order to become more familiar with what the question involves, it is necessary to make visible once more the happening of truth in the work. For this attempt let us deliberately select a work that cannot be ranked as representational art.

A building, a Greek temple, portrays nothing. It simply stands there in the middle of the rock-cleft valley. The building encloses the figure of the god, and in this concealment lets it stand out into the holy precinct through the open portico. By means of the temple, the god is present in the temple. This presence of the god is in itself the extension and delimitation of the precinct as a holy precinct. The temple and its precinct, however, do not fade away into the indefinite. It is the temple-work that first fits together and at the same time gathers around itself the unity of those paths and relations in which birth and death, disaster and blessing, victory and disgrace, endurance and decline acquire the shape of destiny for human being. The all-governing expanse of this open relational context is the world of this historical people. Only from and in this expanse does the nation first return to itself for the fulfillment of its vocation.

Standing there, the building rests on the rocky ground. This resting of the work draws up out of the rock the mystery of that rock's clumsy yet spontaneous support. Standing there, the building holds its ground against the storm raging above it and so first makes the storm itself manifest in its violence. The luster and gleam of the stone, though itself apparently glowing only by the grace of the sun, yet first brings to light the light of the day, the breadth of the sky, the darkness of the night. The temple's firm towering makes visible the invisible space of air. The steadfastness of the work contrasts with the surge of the surf, and its own repose brings out the raging of the sea. Tree and grass, eagle and bull, snake and cricket first enter into their distinctive shapes and thus come to appear as what they are. The Greeks early called this emerging and rising in itself and in all things *phusis*. It clears and illuminates, also, that on which and in which man bases his dwelling. We call this ground the *earth*. What this word says is not to be associated with the idea of a mass of matter deposited somewhere, or with the merely astronomical idea of a planet. Earth is that whence the arising brings back and shelters everything that arises without violation. In the things that arise, earth is present as the sheltering agent.

The temple-work, standing there, opens up a world and at the same time sets this world back again on earth, which itself only thus emerges as native ground. But men and animals, plants and things, are never present and familiar as unchangeable objects, only to represent incidentally also a fitting environment for the temple, which one fine day is added to what is already there. We shall get closer to what *is*, rather, if we think of all this in reverse order, assuming of course that we have, to begin with, an eye for how differently everything then faces us. Mere reversing, done for its own sake, reveals nothing.

The temple, in its standing there, first gives to things their look and to men their outlook on themselves. This view remains open as long as the work is a work, as long as the god has not fled from it. It is the same with the sculpture of the god, votive offering of the victor in the athletic games. It is not a portrait whose purpose is to make it easier to realize how the god looks; rather, it is a work that lets the god himself be present and thus *is* the god himself. The same holds for the linguistic work. In the tragedy nothing is staged or displayed theatrically, but the battle of the new gods against the old is being fought. The linguistic work, originating in the speech of the people, does not refer to this battle; it transforms the people's saying so that now every living word fights the battle and puts up for decision what is holy and what unholy, what great and what small, what brave and what cowardly, what lofty and what flighty, what master and what slave (cf. Heraclitus, Fragment 53).

In what, then, does the work-being of the work consist? Keeping steadily in view the points just crudely enough indicated, two essential features of the work may for the moment be brought out more distinctly. We set out here, from the long familiar foreground of the work's being, the thingly character which gives support to our customary attitude toward the work.

When a work is brought into a collection or placed in an exhibition we say also that it is "set up." But this setting up differs essentially from setting up in the sense of erecting a building, raising a statue, presenting a tragedy at a holy festival. Such setting up is erecting in the sense of dedication and praise. Here "setting up" no longer means a bare placing. To dedicate means to consecrate, in the sense that in setting up the work the holy is opened up as holy and the god is invoked into the openness of his presence. Praise belongs to dedication as doing honor to the dignity and splendor of the god. Dignity and splendor are not properties beside and behind which the god, too, stands as something distinct, but it is rather in the dignity, in the splendor that the god is present. In the reflected glory of this splendor there glows, i.e., there lightens itself, what we called the word. To e-rect means: to open the right in the sense of a guiding measure, a form in which what belongs to the nature of being gives guidance. But why is the setting up of a work an erecting that consecrates and praises? Because the work, in its work-being, demands it. How is it that the work comes to demand such a setting up? Because it itself, in its own work-being, is something that sets up. What does the work, as work, set up? Towering up within itself, the work opens up a *world* and keeps it abidingly in force.

To be a work means to set up a world. But what is it to be a world? The answer was hinted at when we referred to the temple. On the path we must follow here, the nature of world can only be indicated. What is more, this indication limits itself to warding off anything that might at first distort our view of the world's nature.

The world is not the mere collection of the countable or uncountable, familiar and unfamiliar things that are just there. But neither is it a merely imagined framework added by our representation to the sum of such given things. The *world worlds*, and is more fully in being than the tangible and perceptible realm in which we believe ourselves to be at home. World is never an object that stands before us and can be seen. World is the ever-nonobjective to which we are subject as long as the paths of birth and death, blessing and curse keep us transported into Being. Wherever those decisions of our history that relate to our very being are made, are taken up and abandoned by us, go unrecognized and are rediscovered by new inquiry, there the world worlds. A stone is worldless. Plant and animal likewise have no world; but they belong to the covert throng of a surrounding into which they are linked. The peasant woman, on the other hand, has a world because she dwells in the overtness of beings, of the things that are. Her equipment, in its reliability, gives to this world a necessity and nearness of its own. By the opening up of a world, all things gain their lingering and hastening, their remoteness and nearness, their scope and limits. In a world's worlding is gathered that spaciousness out of which the protective grace of the gods is granted or withheld. Even this doom of the god remaining absent is a way in which world worlds.

A work, by being a work, makes space for that spaciousness. "To make space for" means here especially to liberate the Open and to establish it in its structure. This in-stalling occurs through the erecting mentioned earlier. The work as work sets up a world. The work holds open the Open of the world. But the setting up of a world is only the first essential feature in the work-being of a work to be referred to here. Starting again from the foreground of the work, we shall attempt to make clear in the same way the second essential feature that belongs with the first.

When a work is created, brought forth out of this or that work-material – stone, wood, metal, color, language, tone – we say also that it is made, set forth out of it. But just as the work requires a setting up in the sense of a consecrating-praising erection, because the work's work-being consists in the setting up of a world, so a setting forth is needed because the work-being of the work itself has the character of setting forth. The work as work, in its presencing, is a setting forth, a making. But what does the work set forth? We come to know about this only when we explore what comes to the fore and is customarily spoken of as the making or production of works.

To work-being there belongs the setting up of a world. Thinking of it within this perspective, what is the nature of that in the work which is usually called the work material? Because it is determined by usefulness and serviceability, equipment takes into its service that of which it consists: the matter. In fabricating equipment – e.g., an ax – stone is used, and used up. It disappears into usefulness. The material is all the better and more suitable the less it resists perishing in the equipment being of the equipment. By contrast the temple-work, in setting up a world, does not cause the material to disappear, but rather causes it to come forth for the very first time and to come into the Open of the work's world. The rock comes to bear and rest and so first becomes rock; metals come to glitter and shimmer, colors to glow, tones to sing, the word to speak. All this comes forth as the work sets itself back into the massiveness and heaviness of stone, into the firmness and pliancy of wood, into the hardness and luster of metal, into the lighting and darkening of color, into the clang of tone, and into the naming power of the word.

That into which the work sets itself back and which it causes to come forth in this setting back of itself we called the earth. Earth is that which comes forth and shelters. Earth, self-dependent, is effortless and untiring. Upon the earth and in it, historical man grounds his dwelling in the world. In setting up a world, the work sets forth the earth. This setting forth must be thought here in the strict sense of the word. The work moves the earth itself into the Open of a world and keeps it there. *The work lets the earth be an earth.* [. . .]

The setting up of a world and the setting forth of earth are two essential features in the work-being of the work. They belong together, however, in the unity of work-being. This is the unity we seek when we ponder the self-subsistence of the work and try to express in words this closed, unitary repose of self-support. [. . .]

The world is the self-disclosing openness of the broad paths of the simple and essential decisions in the destiny of an historical people. The earth is the spontaneous forthcoming of that which is continually self-secluding and to that extent sheltering and concealing. World and earth are essentially different from one another and yet are never separated. The world grounds itself on the earth, and earth juts through world. But the relation between world and earth does not wither away into the empty unity of opposites unconcerned with one another. The world, in resting upon the earth, strives to surmount it. As self-opening it cannot endure anything closed. The earth, however, as sheltering and concealing, tends always to draw the world into itself and keep it there.

The opposition of world and earth is a striving. But we would surely all too easily falsify its nature if we were to confound striving with discord and dispute, and thus see it only as disorder and destruction. In essential striving, rather, the opponents raise each other into the self-assertion of their natures. Self-assertion of nature, however, is never a rigid insistence upon some contingent state, but surrender to the concealed originality of the source of one's own being. In the struggle, each opponent carries the other beyond itself. Thus the striving becomes ever more intense as striving, and more authentically what it is. The more the struggle overdoes itself on its own part, the more inflexibly do the opponents let themselves go into the intimacy of simple belonging to one another. The earth cannot dispense with the Open of the world if it itself is to appear as earth in the liberated surge of its self-seclusion. The world, again, cannot soar out of the earth's sight if, as the governing breadth and path of all essential destiny, it is to ground itself on a resolute foundation.

In setting up a world and setting forth the earth, the work is an instigating of this striving. This does not happen so that the work should at the same time settle and put an end to the conflict in an insipid agreement, but so that the strife may remain a strife. Setting up a world and setting forth the earth, the work accomplishes this striving. The work-being of the work consists in the fighting of the battle between world and earth. It is because the struggle arrives at its high point in the simplicity of intimacy that the unity of the work comes about in the fighting of the battle. The fighting of the battle is the continually self-over-reaching gathering of the work's agitation. The repose of the work that rests in itself thus has its presencing in the intimacy of striving.

From this repose of the work we can now first see what is at work in the work. Until now it was a merely provisional assertion that in an art work the truth is set to work. In what way does truth happen in the work-being of the work, i.e., now, how does truth happen in the fighting of the battle between world and earth? What is truth?

How slight and stunted our knowledge of the nature of truth is, is shown by the laxity we permit ourselves in using this basic word. By truth is usually meant this or that particular truth. That means: something true. A cognition articulated in a proposition can be of this sort. However, we call not only a proposition true, but also a thing, true gold in contrast with sham gold. True here means genuine, real gold. What does the expression "real" mean here? To us it is what is in truth. The true is what corresponds to the real, and the real is what is in truth. The circle has closed again.

What does "in truth" mean? [. . .]

Truth means the nature of the true. We think this nature in recollecting the Greek word *aletheia*, the unconcealedness of beings. [. . .]

If here and elsewhere we conceive of truth as unconcealedness, we are not merely taking refuge in a more literal translation of a Greek word. We are reminding ourselves of what, unexperienced and unthought, underlies our familiar and therefore outworn nature of truth in the sense of correctness. [. . .]

But it is not we who presuppose the unconcealedness of beings; rather, the unconcealedness of beings (Being) puts us into such a condition of being that in our representation we always remain installed within and in attendance upon unconcealedness. Not only must that in *conformity* with which a cognition orders itself be already in some way unconcealed. The entire *realm* in which this "conforming to something" goes on must already occur as a whole in the unconcealed; and this holds equally of that *for* which the conformity of a proposition to fact becomes manifest. With all our correct representations we would get nowhere, we could not even presuppose that there already is manifest something to which we can conform ourselves, unless the unconcealedness of beings had already exposed us to, placed us in that lighted realm in which every being stands for us and from which it withdraws. [. . .]

This Open happens in the midst of beings. It exhibits an essential feature which we have already mentioned. To the Open there belong a world and the earth. But the world is not simply the Open that corresponds to clearing, and the earth is not simply the Closed that corresponds to concealment. Rather, the world is the clearing of the paths of the essential guiding directions with which all decision complies. Every decision, however, bases itself on something not mastered, something concealed, confusing; else it would never be a decision. The earth is not simply the Closed but rather that which rises up as self-closing. World and earth are always intrinsically and essentially in conflict, belligerent by nature.

Only as such do they enter into the conflict of clearing and concealing.

Earth juts through the world and world grounds itself on the earth only so far as truth happens as the primal conflict between clearing and concealing. But how does truth happen? We answer: it happens in a few essential ways. One of these ways in which truth happens is the work-being of the work. Setting up a world and setting forth the earth, the work is the fighting of the battle in which the unconcealedness of beings as a whole, or truth, is won.

Truth happens in the temple's standing where it is. This does not mean that something is correctly represented and rendered here, but that what is as a whole is brought into unconcealedness and held therein. To hold (*halten*) originally means to tend, keep, take care (*hüten*). Truth happens in Van Gogh's painting. This does not mean that something is correctly portrayed, but rather that in the revelation of the equipmental being of the shoes, that which is as a whole – world and earth in their counterplay – attains to unconcealedness.

Thus in the work it is truth, not only something true, that is at work. The picture that shows the peasant shoes, the poem that says the Roman fountain, do not just make manifest what this isolated being as such is – if indeed they manifest anything at all; rather, they make unconcealedness as such happen in regard to what is as a whole. The more simply and authentically the shoes are engrossed in their nature, the more plainly and purely the fountain is engrossed in its nature – the more directly and engagingly do all beings attain to a greater degree of being along with them. That is how self-concealing being is illuminated. Light of this kind joins its shining to and into the work. This shining, joined in the work, is the beautiful. *Beauty is one way in which truth occurs as unconcealedness.*

We now, indeed, grasp the nature of truth more clearly in certain respects. What is at work in the work may accordingly have become more clear. [. . .]

Truth and Art

Art is the origin of the art work and of the artist. Origin is the source of the nature in which the being of an entity is present. What is art? We seek its nature in the actual work. The actual reality of the work has been defined by that which is at work in the work, by the happening of truth. This happening we think of as the fighting of the conflict between world and earth. Repose occurs in the concentrated agitation of this conflict. The independence or self-composure of the work is grounded here. [. . .]

The work's createdness, however, can obviously be grasped only in terms of the process of creation. Thus, constrained by the facts, we must consent after all to go into the activity of the artist in order to arrive at the origin of the work of art. The attempt to define the work-being of the work purely in terms of the work itself proves to be unfeasible.

In turning away now from the work to examine the nature of the creative process, we should like nevertheless to keep in mind what was said first of the picture of the peasant shoes and later of the Greek temple.

We think of creation as a bringing forth. But the making of equipment, too, is a bringing forth. Handicraft – a remarkable play of language – does not, to be sure, create works, not even when we contrast, as we must, the handmade with the factory product. But what is it that distinguishes bringing forth as creation from bringing forth in the mode of making? It is as difficult to track down the essential features of the creation of works and the making of equipment as it is easy to distinguish verbally between the two modes of bringing forth. Going along with first appearances we find the same procedure in the activity of potter and sculptor, of joiner and painter. The creation of a work requires craftsmanship. Great artists prize craftsmanship most highly. They are the first to call for its painstaking cultivation, based on complete mastery. They above all others constantly strive to educate themselves ever anew in thorough craftsmanship. [. . .]

The readiness of equipment and the createdness of the work agree in this, that in each case something is produced. But in contrast to all other modes of production, the work is distinguished by being created so that its createdness is part of the created work. But does not this hold true for everything brought forth, indeed for anything that has in any way come to be? Everything brought forth surely has this endowment of having been brought forth, if it has any endowment at all. Certainly. But in the work, createdness is expressly created into the created being, so that it stands out from it, from the being thus brought forth, in an expressly particular way. If this is how matters stand, then we must also be able to discover and experience the createdness explicitly in the work.

The emergence of createdness from the work does not mean that the work is to give the impression of having been made by a great artist. The point is not that the created being be certified as the performance of a capable person, so that the producer is thereby brought to public notice. It is not the "N. N. fecit" that is to be made known. Rather, the simple "factum est" is to be held forth into the Open by the work: namely this, that unconcealedness of what is has happened here, and that as this happening it happens here for the first time; or, that such a work *is* at all rather than is not. The thrust that the work as this work is, and the uninterruptedness of this plain thrust, constitute the steadfastness of the work's self-subsistence. Precisely where the artist and the process and the circumstances of the genesis of the work remain unknown, this thrust, this "*that* it is" of createdness, emerges into view most purely from the work.

To be sure, "that" it is made is a property also of all equipment that is available and in use. But this "that" does not become prominent in the equipment; it disappears in usefulness. The more handy a piece of equipment is, the more inconspicuous it remains that, for example, such a hammer is and the more exclusively does the equipment keep itself in its equipmentality. In general, of everything present to us, we can note that it *is*; but this also, if it is noted at all, is noted only soon to fall into oblivion, as is the wont of everything commonplace. And what is more commonplace than this, that a being is? In a work, by contrast, this fact, that it *is* as a work, is just what is unusual. The event of its being created does not simply reverberate through the work; rather, the work casts before itself the eventful fact that the work is as this work, and it has constantly this fact about itself. The more essentially the work opens itself, the more luminous becomes the uniqueness of the fact that it is rather than is not. The more essentially this thrust comes into the Open, the stronger and more solitary the work becomes. In the bringing forth of the work there lies this offering "that it be." [. . .]

The more solitarily the work, fixed in the figure, stands on its own and the more cleanly it seems to cut all ties to human beings, the more simply does the thrust come into the Open that such a work *is*, and the more essentially is the extraordinary thrust to the surface and the long-familiar thrust down. But this multiple thrusting is nothing violent, for the more purely the work is itself transported into the openness of beings – an openness opened by itself – the more simply does it transport us into this openness and thus at the same time transport us out of the realm of the ordinary. To submit to this displacement means: to transform our accustomed ties to world and to earth and henceforth to restrain all usual doing and prizing, knowing and looking, in order to stay within the truth that is happening in the work. Only the restraint of this staying lets what is created be the work that it is. This letting the work be a work we call the preserving of the work. It is only for such preserving that the work yields itself in its createdness as actual, i.e., now: present in the manner of a work.

Just as a work cannot be without being created but is essentially in need of creators, so what is created cannot itself come into being without those who preserve it. [. . .]

To determine the thing's thingness neither consideration of the bearer of properties is adequate, nor that of the manifold of sense data in their unity, and least of all that of the matter – form structure regarded by itself, which is derived from equipment. Anticipating a meaningful and weighty interpretation of the thingly character of things, we must aim at the thing's belonging to the earth. The nature of the earth, in its free and unhurried bearing and self-closure, reveals itself, however, only in the earth's jutting into a world, in the opposition of the two. This conflict is fixed in place in the figure of the work and becomes manifest by it. What holds true of equipment – namely that we come to know its equipmental character specifically only through the work itself – also holds of the thingly character of the thing. The fact that we never know thingness directly, and if we know it at all, then only vaguely and thus require the work – this fact proves indirectly that in the work's work-being the happening of truth, the opening up or disclosure of what is, is at work. [. . .]

In the work, the happening of truth is at work and, indeed, at work according to the manner of a work. Accordingly the nature of art was defined to begin with as the setting-into-work of truth. Yet this definition is intentionally ambiguous. It says on the one hand: art is the fixing in place of a self-establishing truth in the figure. This happens in creation as the bringing forth of the unconcealedness of what is. Setting-into-work, however, also means: the bringing of work-being into movement and happening. This happens as preservation. Thus art is: the creative preserving of truth in the work. *Art then is the becoming and happening of truth.* Does truth, then, arise out of nothing? It does indeed if by nothing is meant the mere not of that which is, and if we here think of that which is as an object present in the ordinary way, which thereafter comes to light and is challenged by the existence of the work as only presumptively a true being. Truth is never gathered from objects that are present and ordinary. Rather, the opening up of the Open, and the clearing of what is, happens only as the openness is projected, sketched out, that makes its advent in thrownness. [. . .]

Art is the setting-into-work of truth. In this proposition an essential ambiguity is hidden, in which truth is at once the subject and the object of the setting. But subject and object are unsuitable names here. They keep us from thinking precisely this ambiguous nature, a task that no longer belongs to this consideration. Art is historical, and as historical it is the creative preserving of truth in the work. Art happens as poetry. Poetry is founding in the triple sense of bestowing, grounding, and beginning. Art, as founding, is essentially historical. This means not only that art has a history in the external sense that in the course of time it, too, appears along with many other things, and in the process changes and passes away and offers changing aspects for historiology. Art is history in the essential sense that it grounds history.

Art lets truth originate. Art, founding preserving, is the spring that leaps to the truth of what is, in the work. To originate something by a leap, to bring something into being from out of the source of its nature in a founding leap – this is what the word origin (German *Ursprung*, literally, primal leap) means.

The origin of the work of art – that is, the origin of both the creators and the preservers, which is to say of a people's historical existence, is art. This is so because art is by nature an origin: a distinctive way in which truth comes into being, that is, becomes historical.

We inquire into the nature of art. Why do we inquire in this way? We inquire in this way in order to be able to ask more truly whether art is or is not an origin in our historical existence, whether and under what conditions it can and must be an origin.

Such reflection cannot force art and its coming-to-be. But this reflective knowledge is the preliminary and therefore indispensable preparation for the becoming of art. Only such knowledge prepares its space for art, their way for the creators, their location for the preservers.

In such knowledge, which can only grow slowly, the question is decided whether art can be an origin and then must be a head start, or whether it is to remain a mere appendix and then can only be carried along as a routine cultural phenomenon.

Are we in our existence historically at the origin? Do we know, which means do we give heed to, the nature of the origin? Or, in our relation to art, do we still merely make appeal to a cultivated acquaintance with the past?

For this either-or and its decision there is an infallible sign. Hölderlin, the poet – whose work still confronts the Germans as a test to be stood – named it in saying:

> Schwer verlässt
> was nahe dem Ursprung wohnet, den Ort.

> Reluctantly
> that which dwells near its origin departs.
> – "The Journey," verses 18–19

31

Aesthetic Theory

Theodor Adorno

Theodor Adorno (1903–69) was a German social theorist who viewed capitalism as usurping freedom and art as a domain in which freedom can be attained.

Art, Society, Aesthetics

1 Loss of certainty

Today it goes without saying that nothing concerning art goes without saying, much less without thinking. Everything about art has become problematic: its inner life, its relation to society, even its right to exist. One would have thought that the loss of an intuitive and naive approach to art would be offset by a tendency to increased reflection which seizes upon the chance to fill the void of infinite possibilities. This has not happened. What looked at first like an expansion of art turned out to be its contraction. The great expanse of the unforeseen which revolutionary artistic movements began to explore around 1910 did not live up to the promise of happiness and adventure it had held out. What has happened instead is that the process begun at that time came to corrode the very same categories which were its own reason for being. An ever-increasing number of things artistic were drawn into an eddy of new taboos, and rather than enjoy their newly won freedom, artists everywhere were quick to look for some presumed foundation for what they were doing. This flight into a new order, however flimsy, is a reflection of the fact that absolute freedom in art – which is a particular – contradicts the abiding unfreedom of the social whole. That is why the place and function of art in society have become uncertain. To put it another way, the autonomy art gained after having freed itself from its earlier cult function and its derivatives depended on the idea of humanity. As society grew less humane, art became less autonomous. Those constituent elements of art that were suffused with the ideal of humanity have lost their force.

All the same, autonomy is an irrevocable aspect of art. There is no point in trying to allay the self-doubts of art – doubts, incidentally, which find expression in art itself – by restoring to her a social role. Such attempts are in vain. Today, however, autonomous art shows signs of being blind. A trait of art from time immemorial, blindness in the age of emancipation has become the dominant characteristic despite, and because of; the fact that, as Hegel realized, art can no longer afford to be naive art. Nowadays artistic

Theodor Adorno, *Aesthetic Theory*, ed. Gretel Adorno and Rolf Tiedemann, trans. Robert Hullot-Kentor (Minneapolis: University of Minnesota Press, 1977), pp. 242–53.

sophistication amalgamates itself with a *naïveté* of a different and stronger kind, which is the uncertainty about the purpose of art and the conditions for its continued existence. Did art not lose its foundation when it gained complete freedom from external purposes? Questions like this touch on the intrinsically historical nature of aesthetics.

Works of art, it is said, leave the real empirical world behind, producing a counter-realm of their own, a realm which is an existent like the empirical world. This claim is false; it implies an *a priori* affirmation of that which is, no matter how 'tragic' the content of the work of art may be. Those clichés about art casting a glow of happiness and harmony over an unhappy and divided real world are loathsome because they make a mockery of any emphatic concept of art by looking only at perverse bourgeois practices such as the employment of art as a dispenser of solace. These clichés also point to the wound of art itself. Having dissociated itself from religion and its redemptive truths, art was able to flourish. Once secularized, however, art was condemned, for lack of any hope for a real alternative, to offer to the existing world a kind of solace that reinforced the fetters autonomous art had wanted to shake off. There is a sense in which the principle of autonomy is itself solace of this kind, for in claiming to be able to posit a well-rounded totality entirely on its own, the principle of artistic autonomy willy-nilly creates the false impression that the world outside is such a rounded whole, too. By rejecting reality – and this is not a form of escapism but an inherent quality of art – art vindicated reality.

Helmut Kuhn's thesis[1] that every work of art is a paean would be true if it were critical in spirit, which it is not. Given the abnormities of real life today, the affirmative essence of art, while an integral part of art, has become insufferable. True art challenges its own essence, thereby heightening the sense of uncertainty that dwells in the artist.

It would be wrong, too, to try to dispose of art through abstract negation. Art undergoes qualitative change when it attacks its traditional foundations. Thus art becomes a qualitatively different entity by virtue of its opposition, at the level of artistic form, to the existing world and also by virtue of its readiness to aid and shape that world. Neither the concept of solace nor its opposite, refusal, captures the meaning of art.

2 Origins – a false question

The concept of art balks at being defined, for it is a historically changing constellation of moments. Nor can the nature of art be ascertained by going back to the origin of art in order to find some fundamental and primary layer that supports everything else. The late romantics believed in the supremacy and purity of archaic art. This view is no more persuasive than the opposite argument, put forth by classicists, that the earliest works of art are impure and muddy, inasmuch as they were inseparable from magic, from historical records and from practical aims, like wanting to communicate over long distances by means of calling and blowing sounds. There is no way of deciding the issue because historical facts are hard to come by.

Similarly, any attempt to subsume the historical genesis of art ontologically under some supreme principle would necessarily get lost in a mass of detail. The only theoretically relevant insight that might be obtained is the negative one that, for the plurality of what are called 'the arts', there does not even seem to exist a universal concept of art able to accommodate them all.[2] Studies devoted to prehistoric art tend to present raw empirical material side by side with wild speculation. Johann Jakob Bachofen is the best-known example here.

Philosophers are used to distinguishing conceptually between two types of problems of origin, one belonging to metaphysics, the other to primal history. Upholding this distinction too rigidly leads however to a distortion of the literal meaning of the concept of origin.[3] The definition of art does indeed depend on what art once was, but it must also take into account what has become of art and what might possibly become of it in the future. Art, we said, is different from empirical reality. Now this difference itself does not stay the same; it changes because art changes. History, for example, has transformed certain cult objects into art long after they were first produced. Or, to give another example, at a certain moment in time particular art objects have ceased to be viewed as art. In this connection, the abstractly posed question of whether a phenomenon like the film is art or something else is instructive, although it leads nowhere. As we saw, art has a changing scope and it may be just as well not to try to define sharply what's inside and what's outside of it.

What are called questions of aesthetic constitution are demarcated by the tension between the motive force of art and art as past history. It is through its dynamic laws, not through some invariable principle, that art can be understood. It is defined by its relation to what is different from art. This other makes it possible for us to arrive at a substantive understanding of the specifically artistic in art. It is this approach to art that alone meets the criteria of a materialist and dialectical aesthetic, which evolves by segregating itself from its own matrix. Its law of motion and its law of form are one and the same.

Central to contemporary aesthetics is the assumption that even a product of historical becoming may be true. It was Nietzsche who developed this notion in reference to traditional philosophy. Rephrasing and putting a point to Nietzsche's insight, I think truth exists only as a product of historical becoming. As far as art is concerned, this is true throughout: works of art became what they are by negating their origin. It was only fairly recently, namely after art had become thoroughly secular and subject to a process of technological evolution and after secularization had firmly taken hold, that art acquired another important feature: an inner logic of development. Art should not be blamed for its one-time ignominious relation to magical abracadabra, human servitude and entertainment, for it has after all annihilated these dependencies along with the memory of its fall from grace. Moreover, it is an over-simplification to think that dinner music, for example, could never achieve the heights of autonomous music just because it was dinner music. Conversely, it is also fallacious to argue that dinner music, because it represented a service to mankind, has the edge on autonomous music with its haughty refusal to be serviceable to anything or to anybody. Let us remember, too, that the greatest part of what passes for musical art today is an echo of the contemptuous clatter of dinner music. Unfortunately, this fact does nothing to make the quality of early eighteenth-century dinner music any better.

3 Truth, life and death of art

The Hegelian notion of a possible withering away of art is consistent with the historical essence of art as a product of becoming. This seemingly paradoxical fact, that Hegel conceived of art as something mortal while at the same time treating it as a moment of absolute spirit, is fully in line with the dual character of his system. His view however implies a conclusion he would never have drawn himself, namely that the content of art – its absolute aspect, according to Hegel – is not identical with the dimension of life and death. It is conceivable that that content might precisely be art's mortality. Music is a case in point. A latecomer among the arts, great music may well turn out to be an art form that was possible only during a limited period of human history. The revolt of art which programmatically defined itself in terms of a new stance towards the objective, historical world has become a revolt against art. Whether art will survive these developments is anybody's guess. Nobody however should ignore the fact that for once reactionary cultural pessimism and a critical theory of culture see eye to eye on the following proposition: art may, as Hegel speculated it would, soon enter the age of its demise. A century ago Rimbaud's dictum intuitively anticipated the history of modern art; later his silence and his being co-opted on becoming an employee anticipated the decline of art.

Aesthetics today is powerless to avert its becoming a necrologue of art. What it can and must avoid is making graveside speeches, soothsaying the end of everything, savouring past achievements and jumping on the bandwagon of barbarism – which barbarism is no better and no worse than the culture that rallies to its side, with the two fully deserving each other. Assuming art is abolished, abolishes itself; vanishes or barely hangs on to a precarious existence – all this does not mean that the content of past art will necessarily go down the drain, too. Art could well be survived by its past content in a new and different society, rid of its barbarous culture.

What [have] already died are not only aesthetic forms but also many substantive motifs. To mention only one example, the literature about adultery, which had its efflorescence during the Victorian period and into the early twentieth century, is difficult to appreciate today, what with the dissolution of the bourgeois nuclear family and the loosening up of monogamy. A popular version of that kind of literature today has found a new but miserable home: illustrated magazines. The authentic element in *Madame Bovary*, at one time an integral part of the subject matter of the novel, has long since outlived both that content and its demise – a statement that is not at all meant to lure anybody into the optimistic belief in the invincibility of the spirit. There are of course many instances where the death of the content of a work of art has in fact entailed the perdition of the higher authentic moment as well. What makes art and its products mortal – and this includes heteronomous and autonomous art, with the latter vindicating the social division of labour and the special position held therein by the intellect – what makes art mortal is the fact that it is not only art but something other than, and opposed to, art. Admixed to the concept of art is the germ that will dialectically supersede art.

4 *On the relation between art and society*

Aesthetic refraction is as incomplete without the refracted object as imagination is without the imagined object. This has special significance for the problem of the inherent functionality of art. Tied to the real world, art adopts the principle of self-preservation of that world, turning it into the ideal of self-identical art, the essence of which Schönberg once summed up in the statement that the painter paints a picture rather than what it represents. Implied here is the idea that every work of art spontaneously aims at being identical with itself, just as in the world outside a fake identity is everywhere forcibly imposed on objects by the insatiable subject. Aesthetic identity is different, however, in one important respect: it is meant to assist the non-identical in its struggle against the repressive identification compulsion that rules the outside world. It is by virtue of its separation from empirical reality that the work of art can become a being of a higher order, fashioning the relation between the whole and its parts in accordance with its own needs. Works of art are after images or replicas of empirical life, inasmuch as they proffer to the latter what in the outside world is being denied them. In the process they slough off a repressive, external–empirical mode of experiencing the world. Whereas the line separating art from real life should not be fudged, least of all by glorifying the artist, it must be kept in mind that works of art are alive, have a life *sui generis*. Their life is more than just an outward fate. Over time, great works reveal new faces of themselves, they age, they become rigid, and they die. Being human artefacts, they do not 'live' in the same sense as human beings. Of course not. To put the accent on the artefactual aspect in works of art seems to imply that the way in which they came to be is important. It is not. The emphasis must be on their inner constitution. They have life because they speak in ways nature and man cannot. They talk because there is communication between their individual constituents, which cannot be said of things that exist in a state of mere diffusion.

As artefacts, works of art communicate not only internally but also with the external reality which they try to get away from and which none the less is the substratum of their content. Art negates the conceptualization foisted on the real world and yet harbours in its own substance elements of the empirically existent. Assuming that one has to differentiate form and content before grasping their mediation, we can say that art's opposition to the real world is in the realm of form; but this occurs, generally speaking, in a mediated way such that aesthetic form is a sedimentation of content. What seem like pure forms in art, namely those of traditional music, do in all respects, and all the way down to details of musical idiom, derive from external content such as dance. Similarly, ornaments in the visual arts originally tended to be cult symbols. Members of the Warburg Institute were following this lead, studying the derivability of aesthetic forms from contents in the context of classical antiquity and its influence on later periods. This kind of work needs to be undertaken on a larger scale.

The manner in which art communicates with the outside world is in fact also a lack of communication, because art seeks, blissfully or unhappily, to seclude itself from the world. This non-communication points to the fractured nature of art. It is natural to think that art's autonomous domain has no mere in common with the outside world than a few borrowed elements undergoing radical change in the context of art. But there is more to it than that. There is some truth to the historical cliché which states that the developments of artistic methods, usually lumped together under the term 'style', correspond to social development. Even the most sublime work of art takes up a definite position *vis-à-vis* reality by stepping out-side of reality's spell, not abstractly once and for all, but occasionally and in concrete ways, when it unconsciously and tacitly polemicizes against the condition of society at a particular point in time.

How can works of art be like windowless monads, representing something which is other than they? There is only one way to explain this, which is to view them as being subject to a dynamic or immanent historicity and a dialectical tension between nature and domination of nature, a dialectic that seems to be of the same kind as the dialectic of society. Or to put it more cautiously, the dialectic of art resembles the social dialectic without consciously imitating it. The productive force of useful labour and that of art are the same. They both have the same teleology. And what might be termed aesthetic relations of production – defined as everything that provides an outlet for the productive forces of art or everything in which these forces become embedded – are sedimentations of social relations of production bearing the imprint of the latter. Thus in all dimensions of its productive process art has a twofold essence, being both an autonomous entity and a social fact in the Durkheimian sense of the term.

It is through this relationship to the empirical that works of art salvage, albeit in neutralized fashion, something that once upon a time was literally a shared experience of all mankind and which enlightenment has since expelled. Art, too, partakes of enlightenment, but in a different way: works of art do not lie; what they say is literally true. Their reality however lies in the fact that they are answers to questions brought before them from outside. The tension in art therefore has meaning only in relation to the tension outside. The fundamental layers of artistic experience are akin to the objective world from which art recoils.

The unresolved antagonisms of reality reappear in art in the guise of immanent problems of artistic form. This, and not the deliberate injection of objective moments or social content, defines art's relation to society. The aesthetic tensions manifesting themselves in works of art express the essence of reality in and through their emancipation from the factual façade of exteriority. Art's simultaneous dissociation from and secret connection with empirical being confirms the strength of Hegel's analysis of the nature of a conceptual barrier (*Schranke*): the intellect, argues Hegel against Kant, no sooner posits a barrier than it has to go beyond it, absorbing into itself that against which the barrier was set up.[4] We have here, among other things, a basis for a non-moralistic critique of the idea of *l'art pour l'art* with its abstract negation of the empirical and with its monomaniac separatism in aesthetic theory.

Freedom, the presupposition of art and the self-glorifying conception art has of itself, is the cunning of art's reason. Blissfully soaring above the real world, art is still chained by each of its elements to the empirical other, into which it may even sink back altogether at every instant. In their relation to empirical reality works of art recall the theologumenon that in a state of redemption everything will be just as it is and yet wholly different. There is an unmistakable similarity in all this with the development of the profane. The profane secularizes the sacred realm to the point where the latter is the only secular thing left. The sacred realm is thus objectified, staked out as it were, because its moment of untruth awaits secularization as much as it tries to avert it through incantation.

It follows that art is not defined once and for all by the scope of an immutable concept. Rather, the concept of art is a fragile balance attained now and then, quite similar to the psychological equilibrium between id and ego. Disturbances continually upset the balance, keeping the process in motion. Every work of art is an instant; every great work of art is a stoppage of the process, a momentary standing still, whereas a persistent eye sees only the process. While it is true that works of art provide answers to their own questions, it is equally true that in so doing they become questions for themselves. Take a look at the widespread inclination (which to this day has not been mitigated by education) to perceive art in terms of extra-aesthetic or pre-aesthetic criteria. This tendency is, on the one hand, a mark of atrocious backwardness or of the regressive consciousness of many people. On the other hand, there is no denying that that tendency is promoted by something in art itself. If art is perceived strictly in aesthetic terms, then it cannot be properly perceived in aesthetic terms. The artist must feel the presence of the empirical other in the foreground of his own experience in order to be able to sublimate that experience, thus freeing himself from his confinement to content while at the same time saving the being-for-itself of art from slipping into outright indifference toward the world.

Art is and is not being-for-itself. Without a heterogeneous moment, art cannot achieve autonomy. Great epics that survive their own oblivion were originally shot through with historical and geographical reporting. Valéry, for one, was aware of the degree to which the Homeric, pagan-germanic and Christian epics contained raw materials that had never been melted down and recast by the laws of form, noting that this did not diminish their rank in comparison with 'pure' works of art. Similarly, tragedy, the likely origin of the abstract idea of aesthetic autonomy, was also an after-image of pragmatically oriented cult acts. At no point in its history of progressive emancipation was art able to stamp out that moment. And the reason is not that the bonds were simply too strong. Long before socialist realism rationally planned its debasement, the realistic novel, which was at its height as a literary form in the nineteenth century, bears the marks of reportage, anticipating what was later to become the task of social science surveys. Conversely, the fanatic thoroughness of linguistic integration that characterizes *Madame Bovary*, for instance, is probably the result of the contrary moment. The continued relevance of this work is due to the unity of both.

In art, the criterion of success is twofold: first, works of art must be able to integrate materials and details into their immanent law of form; and, second, they must not try to erase the fractures left by the process of integration, preserving instead in the aesthetic whole the traces of those elements which resisted integration. Integration as such does not guarantee quality. There is no privileged single category, not even the aesthetically central one of form, that defines the essence of art and suffices to judge its product. In short, art has defining characteristics that go against the grain of what philosophy of art ordinarily conceives as art. Hegel is the exception. His aesthetics of content recognized the moment of otherness inherent in art, thus superseding the old aesthetic of form. The latter seems to be operating with too pure a concept of art, even though it has at least one advantage, which is that it does not, unlike Hegel's (and Kierkegaard's) substantive aesthetics, place obstacles in the way of certain historical developments such as abstract painting. This is one weakness of Hegel's aesthetic. The other is that, by conceiving form in terms of content, Hegel's theory of art regresses to a position that can only be called 'pre-aesthetic' and crude. Hegel mistakes the replicatory (*abbildende*) or discursive treatment of content for the kind of otherness that is constitutive of art. He sins, as it were, against his own dialectical concept of aesthetics, with results that he could not foresee. He in effect helped prepare the way for the banausic tendency to transform art into an ideology of repression.

The moment of unreality and non-existence in art is not independent of the existent, as though it were posited or invented by some arbitrary will. Rather, that moment of unreality is a structure resulting from quantitative relations between elements of being, relations which are in turn a response to, and an echo of, the imperfections of real conditions, their constraints, their contradictions, and their potentialities. Art is related to its other like a magnet to a field of iron filings. The elements of art as well as their constellation, or what is commonly thought to be the spiritual essence of art, point back to the real other. The identity of the works of art with existent reality also accounts for the centripetal force that enables them to gather unto themselves the traces and *membra disiecta*[5] of real life. Their affinity with the world lies in a principle that is conceived to be a contrast to that world but is in fact no different from the principle whereby spirit has dominated the world. Synthesis is not some process of imposing order on the elements of a work of art. It is important, rather, that the elements interact with each other; hence there is a sense in which synthesis is a mere repetition of the pre-established interdependence among elements, which interdependence is a product of otherness, of non-art. Synthesis, therefore, is firmly grounded in the material aspects of works of art.

There is a link between the aesthetic moment of form and non-violence. In its difference from the existent, art of necessity constitutes itself in terms of that which is not a work of art yet is indispensable for its being. The emphasis on non-intentionality in art, noticeable first in the sympathy for popular art in Apollinaire, early Cubism and Wedekind (who derided what he called 'art-artists'), indicates that art became aware, however dimly, that it interacted with its opposite. This new self-conception of art gave rise to a critical turn signalling an end to the illusory equation of art with pure spirituality.

5 *Critique of the psychoanalytic theory of art*

Art is the social antithesis of society. The constitution of the domain of art resembles the constitution of an inner space of ideas in the individual. Both areas intersect in the concept of sublimation. Hence it is natural and promising to attempt to conceptualize art in terms of some theory of psychic life.

A comparison between an anthropological theory of human constants and a psychoanalytic one would seem to favour the latter. But caution is in order: psychoanalysis is better suited to explain purely psychic phenomena than aesthetic ones. According to psychoanalytic theory, works of art are essentially projections of the unconscious. Psychoanalysis thus puts the emphasis on the individual producer of art and the interpretation of aesthetic content as psychic content, to the detriment of the categories of form. What psychoanalysis does when it turns to the analysis of art is to transfer the banausic sensitivity of the therapist to such unlikely objects as Leonardo and Baudelaire. It is important to debunk such studies, which are frequently offshoots of the biographical genre, in no uncertain terms; for despite their stress on sex they are hopelessly philistine in conception, dismissing as neurotics men of art who in fact merely objectified in their work the negativity of life. The book by Laforgue, for instance, seriously accuses Baudelaire of having suffered from a mother complex.[6] The author does not even touch on the problem of whether Baudelaire could have written the *Fleurs du mal* had he been healthy, let alone whether, because of the neurosis, the poems turned out worse than they might otherwise have been. Psychic normalcy is raised to a criterion of judgment even in the case of someone like Baudelaire, whose greatness was so unequivocally tied up with the absence of a *mens sana*. The tenor of psychoanalytic monographs on artists conveys the sense of an implicit ought: that art should deal affirmatively with the negativity of experience. To the psychoanalytic authors, the negative moment is just a mark of the process of repression finding its way into the work of art.

From the point of view of psychoanalysis, art is day-dreaming. It is a view that, on the one hand, mistakes works of art for documents, lodged in the dreaming person's head. On the other hand, as a kind of trade-off for having first excised the extra-mental sphere, it reduces art to content, in strange opposition incidentally to Freud, who after all had already emphasized the importance of dream *work*, With their assumption of an analogy between dreaming and artistic creation, psychoanalysts, like all positivists, vastly overrate the moment of fiction in art. The projection that occurs in the creative process is not at all the decisive moment in works of art; equally important are idiom, material and, above all, the product itself, the latter being virtually ignored by psychoanalysts. For example, the psychoanalytic thesis that music is a defence mechanism against impending paranoia, while it may well be clinically correct, is useless for an appreciation of the quality and substance of a single musical composition.

Compared with the idealist theory of art, the psychoanalytic one has the advantage of bringing to light those elements in art that are not art-like. In so doing, psychoanalysis helps to free art from its enthralment to absolute spirit. Its opposition against vulgar idealism, which gives to art a sanctuary in some allegedly higher sphere and avidly protects it against all insights into its own essence and above all into the connection it has with instinct – this opposition is part of the spirit of enlightenment. To the extent to which psychoanalysis decodes the social character of a work and its author, it is able to furnish concrete, mediating links between the structure of works of art and that of society. On the other hand, psychoanalysis, not unlike idealism, is spreading its own kind of enthralment by reducing art to an absolutely subjective system of signs denoting drive states of the subject. Given this tendency, psychoanalysis is able to decipher phenomena but not the phenomenon of art itself. To psychoanalysis works of art are factual. It neglects to consider their real objectivity, their inner consistency, the level of form, their critical impulses, their relation to non-psychic reality and, last but not least, their truth content.

A woman painter, in the spirit of sincerity that governs a pact between analyst and patient, once complained in the doctor's office that she was appalled at the poor quality of the engravings he had hung up to decorate his walls, whereupon he explained to her that she was merely showing her aggression . . . Works of art are much less replicas and properties of the artist than a physician likes to think who knows artists only as persons lying on a couch. Only a dilettante will even try to reduce everything about art to the unconscious, reiterating one hackneyed psychoanalytic cliché after another. In the process of artistic production, unconscious drives are one impetus among many. They become integrated with the work of art through the law of form. The real human being who created the work is no more a part of that work than a real horse is a part of a painted one.

Works of art are not some kind of thematic apperception tests, either. In so far as psychoanalysis implies that they are, it reveals another seamy side of its anti-aestheticism. Part of the blame for this ignorance of what art is all about lies, incidentally, in the pre-eminence psychoanalysis gives to the reality principle. Adaptation to reality has the status of a *summum bonum*, whereas any deviation from the reality principle is immediately branded as an escape. The experience of reality is such that it provides all kinds of legitimate grounds for wanting to escape. This exposes the harmonistic ideology behind the psychoanalytic indignation about people's escape mechanisms. Even at the level of psychology, the need for art can be given a better justification than it has so far got from psychoanalysis. It is true, there is an element of escape in imagination, but the two are not synonymous.

Art transcends the reality principle in the direction both of something higher and of something even more mundane. There is no reason to point a taunting finger at that. The image of the artist as a neurotic, tolerated by and integrated into the social division of labour, is a distortion. In artists of the highest calibre like Beethoven and Rembrandt, the keenest awareness of reality was joined to an equally acute sense of alienation from reality. It is phenomena like this which would be truly appropriate subjects for a psychology of art. Its task would be to decode the work of art as something that is identical with the artist and yet different from him, inasmuch as it represents labour spent upon a resistant other. And if art has one psychoanalytically relevant root, it has got to be that of omnipotence fantasy. But again, what shines forth in these fantasies beneath the raw psychological need for power is the desire to bring about a better world. This sets free the entire dialectic of art and society. By contrast, the psychological view of the art work in terms of a purely subjective language of the unconscious does not even come close to a dialectical understanding.

6 *Kant and Freud on art*

Freud's theory of art as wish-fulfilment has its antithesis in the theory of Kant. Kant states at the start of the 'Analytic of the Beautiful' that the first moment of a judgment of taste is disinterested satisfaction,[7] where interest is defined as 'the satisfaction which we combine with the representation of the existence of an object'.[8] Right away there is an ambiguity. It is impossible to tell whether Kant means, by representation of the existence of an object, the empirical object dealt with in a work of art, in other words its subject matter or content, or whether he means the work of art itself. Is he referring to the pretty nude model or to the sweetly pleasing sound of a piece of music (which, incidentally, can be pure artistic trash or an integral part of artistic quality)? Kant's stress on representation flows directly from his subjectivist approach, which locates the aesthetic quality in the effect a work of art has upon the viewer. This is in accord with the rationalist tradition, notably Moses Mendelsohn. While staying in the old tradition of an aesthetic that emphasizes effect (*Wirkungsaesthetik*), the *Critique of Judgment* is none the less a radical immanent critique of then contemporary rationalist aesthetics. Let us remember that the significance of Kantian subjectivism as a whole lies in its objective intention, its attempt to salvage objectivity by means of an analysis of subjective moments.

It is through the concept of disinterestedness that Kant breaks up the supremacy of pleasure in aesthetics. Satisfaction is meant to preserve effect but disinterestedness draws away from it. Bereft of what Kant calls interest, satisfaction and pleasure become wholly indeterminate, losing the capacity to define the beautiful. All the same, the doctrine of disinterested satisfaction is impoverished in view of the richness of aesthetic phenomena. It reduces them either to the formally beautiful – a questionable entity when viewed in isolation – or in the case of natural objects to the sublime. The reduction of art to absolute form misses the point about the why and wherefore of art. Kant's murky footnote,[9] which says that a judgment about an object of satisfaction is disinterested, i.e. not based on interest, even though it may be 'interesting', i.e. capable of evoking an interest, testifies honestly, if indirectly, to the fact that he was aware of a difficulty. Kant separates aesthetic feeling – and therefore, according to his own understanding, virtually the whole of art – from the faculty of desire at which the 'representation of the existence of an object' is aimed. Or, as he puts it, satisfaction in such a representation 'always has reference to the faculty of desire'.[10] Kant was the first to have gained an insight that was never to be forgotten since: namely, that aesthetic conduct is free of immediate desire. Thus he rescued art from the greedy clutches of a kind of insensitivity that forever wants to touch and savour it.

Comparing Kant and Freud, it is interesting to note that the Kantian motif is not entirely foreign to the Freudian theory. Even for Freud, works of art, far from being direct wish-fulfilment, transform repressed libido into socially productive accomplishments. What is, of course, uncritically presupposed in this theory is the social value of art, whose quality as art simply rests on public reputation. By putting the difference between art, on the one hand, and the faculty of desire and empirical reality, on the other, into much sharper relief than Freud, Kant does more than simply idealize art. Isolating the aesthetic from the empirical sphere, he constitutes art. He then, however, proceeds to arrest this process of constitution in the framework of his transcendental philosophy, simplistically equating constitution with the essence of art and ignoring the fact that the subjective instinctual components of art crop up, in different form, even in the most mature manifestations of art.

In his theory of sublimation, on the other hand, Freud was more clearly aware of the dynamic nature of art, The price he paid was no smaller than Kant's. For Freud, the spiritual essence of art remains hidden. For Kant, it does emerge from the distinctions between aesthetic, practical and appetitive behaviour, Kant's preference for sensuous intuition notwithstanding. In the Freudian view works of art, although pro-ducts of sublimation, are little more than plenipotentiaries of sensuous impulses made unrecognizable to some degree by a kind of dream-work.

A comparison between two thinkers as different as Kant and Freud – Kant, for example, not only rejected philosophical psychologism but with age also became hostile to psychology as such – is justified by the presence of a common denominator that outweighs the differences between the Kantian construction of the transcendental subject and the Freudian focus on the empirical subject. Where they differ is in their positive and negative approaches, respectively, to the faculty of desire. What they have in common, however, is the underlying subjective orientation. For both, the work of art exists only in relation to the individual who contemplates or produces it. There is a mechanism in Kant's thought that forces him, both in moral and in aesthetic philosophy, to consider the ontic, empirical individual to a larger extent than seems warranted by the notion of the transcendental subject. In aesthetics this implies that there can be no pleasure without a living being to whom an object is pleasing. Without explicit recognition, Kant devotes the entire *Critique of Judgment* to an analysis of *constituta*. Therefore, despite the programmatic idea of building a bridge between theoretical and practical pure reason, the faculty of judgment turns out to be *sui generis* in relation to both forms of reason.

Perhaps the most important taboo in art is the one that prohibits an animal-like attitude toward the object, say, a desire to devour it or otherwise to subjugate it to one's body. Now, the strength of such a taboo is matched by the strength of the repressed urge. Hence, all art contains in itself a negative moment from which it tries to get away. If Kant's disinterestedness is to be more than a synonym for indifference, it has to have a trace of untamed interest somewhere. Indeed, there is much to be said for the thesis that the dignity of works of art depends on the magnitude of the interest from which they were wrested. Kant denies this in order to protect his concept of freedom from spurious heteronomies that he saw lurking everywhere. In this regard, his theory of art is tainted by an insufficiency of his theory of practical reason. In the context of Kant's philosophy, the idea of a beautiful object possessing a kind of independence from the sovereign ego must seem like a digression into intelligible worlds. The source from which art antithetically originates, as well as the content of art, are of no concern to Kant, who instead posits something as formal as aesthetic satisfaction as the defining characteristic of art. His aesthetics presents the paradox of a castrated hedonism, of a theory of pleasure without pleasure. This position fails to do justice either to artistic experience wherein satisfaction is a subordinate moment in a larger whole, or to the material–corporeal interest, i.e. repressed and unsatisfied needs that resonate in their aesthetic negations – the works of art – turning them into something more than empty patterns.

Aesthetic disinterestedness has moved interest beyond particularity. Objectively, the interest in constituting an aesthetic totality entailed an interest in the proper arrangement of the social whole. In the last analysis aesthetic interest aimed not at some particular fulfilment, but at the fulfilment of infinite possibilities, which in turn cannot be thought without fulfilment of the particular.

A corresponding weakness can be noticed in Freud's theory of art, which is a good deal more idealistic than Freud had thought it was. By placing works of art squarely into a realm of psychic immanence, Freud's theory loses sight of their antithetical relation to the non-subjective, which thus remains unmolested, as it were, by the thorns pointed toward it by works of art. As a result, psychic processes like instinctual denial and adaptation are left as the only relevant aspects of art. Psychologistic interpretations of art are in league with the philistine view that art is a conciliatory force capable of smoothing over differences, or that it is the dream of a better life, never mind the fact that such dreams should recall the negativity from which they were forcibly extracted. Psychoanalysis in conformist fashion simply takes over the prevalent view of art as some sort of beneficent cultural heritage. To this corresponds the aesthetic hedonism which has psychoanalysis banish all negativity from art *qua* result, pushing the analysis of that negativity back to the level of instinctual conflict. Once successful sublimation and integration become the be-all and end-all of a work of art, it loses the power to transcend mere existence. However, as soon as we conceive of the work of art in terms of its ability to keep a hold on the negativity of the real and to enter into a definite relation to it, we have to change the concept of disinterestedness as well. In contrast to the Kantian and Freudian views on the matter, works of art necessarily evolve in a dialectic of interests and disinterestedness.

There is a grain of validity even in a contemplative attitude towards art, inasmuch as it underscores the important posture of art's turning away from immediate praxis and refusing to play the worldly game. This has long been a component of artistic behaviour. We see here, incidentally, that works of art are tied up with specific modes of behaviour; indeed, that they *are* modes of behaviour. Now it is only those works of art that manifest themselves as modes of behaviour which have a reason for being. Art is like a plenipotentiary of a type of praxis that is better than the prevailing praxis of society, dominated as it is by brutal self-interest. This is what art criticizes. It gives the lie to the notion that production for production's sake is necessary, by opting for a mode of praxis beyond labour. Art's *promesse du bonheur*, then, has an even more emphatically critical meaning: it not only expresses the idea that current praxis denies happiness, but also carries the connotation that happiness is something beyond praxis. The chasm between praxis and happiness is surveyed and measured by the power of negativity of the work of art.

Surely a writer like Kafka does anything but appeal to our faculty of desire. Prose writings such as *Metamorphosis* and *Penal Colony*, on the contrary, seem to call forth in us responses like real anxiety, a violent drawing back, an almost physical revulsion. They seem to be the opposite of desire. Yet these phenomena of psychic defence and rejection have more in common with desire than with the old Kantian disinterestedness. Kafka and the literature that followed his example have swept away the notion of disinterestedness. In relation to Kafka's works, disinterestedness is a completely inadequate concept of interpretation. In the last analysis the postulate of disinterestedness debases all art, turning it into a pleasant or useful plaything, in accord with Horace's *ars poetica*. Idealist aesthetics and its contemporaneous art products have emancipated themselves from this misconception. The precondition for the autonomy of artistic experience is the abandonment of the attitude of tasting and savouring. The trajectory leading to aesthetic autonomy passes through the stage of disinterestedness; and well it should, for it was during this stage that art emancipated itself from cuisine and pornography, an emancipation that has become irrevocable. However, art does not come to rest in disinterestedness. It moves on. And in so doing it reproduces, in different form, the interest inherent in disinterestedness. In a false world all *hedone* is false. This goes for artistic pleasure, too. Art renounces happiness for the sake of happiness, thus enabling desire to survive in art.

7 Enjoyment of art

In Kant, we saw that enjoyment comes in the guise of disinterestedness, a guise that makes enjoyment unrecognizable. What ordinary language and conformist aesthetics have termed enjoyment of art, on analogy with real enjoyment, has probably never existed and will probably never exist. The individual has a limited share in artistic experience as such. This share varies with the quality of a work of art: the better the work, the smaller the subjective component in it. To fetishize the enjoyment of art is to be a crude and insensitive person, who tends to give himself away by describing something as a 'feast for the eye',

Let us acknowledge a limitation of this critique, though: if the last trace of enjoyment were expunged from art, we would face the embarrassing question of what works of art are for. Still, it remains a fact that people enjoy works of art the less, the more they know about them, and vice versa. If we must discuss attitudes to art works at all, it is probably correct to say that the traditional attitude was one not of enjoyment but of admiration – admiration for what those works are in themselves, regardless of their relation to the viewer. What the viewer noticed in them and what enraptured him was their truth (again, Kafka is a good example of art as truth). They were not some kind of higher type of means of enjoyment. The relation between the viewer and work had nothing to do with the incorporation of art by the viewer. On the contrary the viewer seemed to vanish in the work of art. This holds *a fortiori* for the products of modern art that come at the viewer sometimes like train engines in a film.

If you ask a musician if he enjoys playing his instrument, he will probably reply: 'I hate it', just like the grimacing cellist in the American joke. People who have a genuine relation to art would rather immerse themselves in art than reduce art to an object. They cannot live without art, but its individual manifestations are not so many sources of pleasure for them. It goes without saying that nobody would concern himself with art if he did not get something out of it. But this does not mean that people should actually draw up balance sheets, entering such items as 'Heard Ninth Symphony tonight, enjoyed myself so and so much'. Unfortunately, such feeble-minded thinking has by now almost become the commonsensical rule. The bourgeois wants his art luxurious, his life ascetic. It would make more sense if it were the other way around.

Having deprived people of real gratification in the sphere of immediate sense experience, reified consciousness is feeding them a substitute in the form of sensuously dressed-up art, assigning to art a place that is beneath its dignity. On the surface, the strategy seems to move the works of art closer to the consumer by stressing their sensuous attraction. At a deeper level, what happens is that he becomes alienated from them, as he begins to treat them like a commodity belonging to him and yet expropriable at any moment. This raises fears in him. In short, the false attitude towards art is intimately related to anxieties about loss of property; for the fetishistic notion of art as a good which can be owned and, through reflection, destroyed corresponds neatly with the idea of a piece of property in the psychic household.

Like art as a whole, the classification of art as one among the means of enjoyment is a product of historical development. Granted, the magical and animistic predecessors of works of art were components of ritual practices and hence devoid of aesthetic autonomy. But they were certainly not to be enjoyed, for they were sacred. It was only after art had become thoroughly spiritualized that those who did not understand it began to clamour resentfully for a new species of consumer art that would be able to give them something to enjoy. Conversely, the artists, full of aversion against these demands, were forced to find ever more ingenious ways to spiritualize art even further, No nude Greek sculpture was a pin-up. This explains in part why there is such a friendly attitude in modernism towards the distant past and towards primitive exotic places: modern artists are pleased to find examples there of an art that abstracts from natural objects and their desirability. Hegel, too, in his analysis of what he called symbolic art saw the non-sensuous moment in archaic art. Protesting against the universal mediation of life through commodities, the element of pleasure in art is mediable in its own way, in that he who vanished in a work of art is *ipso facto* exempted from the penury of life. Such pleasure can take on inebriating proportions. At this point one cannot help realizing just how meagre the concept of aesthetic enjoyment really is when we compare it with drunkenness – so meagre, in fact, that what it stands for does not even seem worth going after. Strangely enough, the aesthetic theory that has singled out subjective feeling as the ground of the beautiful has never seriously analysed that feeling. What descriptions there are of it appear, all and sundry, to be lacking in depth. The subjectivist approach to art simply fails to understand that the subjective experience of art in itself is meaningless, and that in order to grasp the importance of art one has to zero in on the artistic object rather than on the fun of the art lover.

The concept of aesthetic enjoyment was a bad compromise between the social essence of art and the critical tendencies inherent in it. Underlying this compromise is a bourgeois mentality which, after sternly noting how useless art is for the business of self-preservation, grudgingly concedes to art a place in society, provided it offers at least a kind of use-value modelled on the phenomenon of sensuous pleasure. This expectation perverts the nature of art as well as the nature of real sensuous pleasure, for art is unable to provide it. There is no denying that an individual who cannot differentiate sensually between a beautiful sound and a dissonant one, between brilliant colours and dull ones, lacks the ability for artistic experience. But this ability ought not to be hypostatized. To be sure, artistic experience requires a considerable capacity for sensual differentiation as a medium of creativity, but in true art the pleasure component is not given free rein; depending on the time, it is more or less narrowly circumscribed. In periods following an age of asceticism, pleasure became an emancipatory force. This is true of the Renaissance in its relation to the Middle Ages. It is also true of impressionism in its relation to the Victorian age. At other times, the metaphysical content of human sadness manifested itself in art when erotic stimuli were allowed to permeate artistic form. However strong historically the tendency towards a recurrence of pleasure may be, pleasure remains infantile when it asserts itself directly and without mediation. Art absorbs pleasure as remembrance and longing; it does not copy it, does not seek to produce pleasure as an immediate effect. Aversion against the crudely sensuous in art may have been the undoing of impressionism, which had gone too far in the hedonistic direction.

Notes

1 H. Kuhn, *Schriften zur Ästhetik* (Munich 1966), pp. 236ff.
2 Cf. T. W. Adorno, *Ohne Leitbild. Parva Aesthetica*, 2nd ed. (Frankfurt 1968), pp. 168ff.
3 [Presumably Adorno is alluding here to the dynamic connotation of *Ursprung* (origin) as a 'primal leap'.]
4 [Cf G. W. F. Hegel, *Science of Logic*, 1, section 1, ch. 2.]
5 [Scattered parts.]
6 [René Laforgue, *The Defeat of Baudelaire: a Psychoanalytical Study of the Neurosis of Charles Baudelaire* (London 1932).]
7 I. Kant, *Critique of Judgment*, trans. J. H. Bernard (New York 1951), p. 39.
8 Ibid., p. 38.
9 Ibid., p. 39.
10 Ibid., p. 38.

32

Truth and Method

Hans-Georg Gadamer

Hans-Georg Gadamer (1900–2002), an important German philosopher who studied with Heidegger, is well known for his work on the theory of interpretation.

The Ontology of the Work of Art and its Hermeneutical Significance

1 Play as the Clue to Ontological Explanation

(A) The concept of play

I select as my starting-point a notion that has played a major role in aesthetics: the concept of play. I wish to free this concept from the subjective meaning which it has in Kant and Schiller and which dominates the whole of modern aesthetics and philosophy of man. If, in connection with the experience of art, we speak of play, this refers neither to the attitude nor even to the state of mind of the creator or of those enjoying the work of art, nor to the freedom of a subjectivity expressed in play, but to the mode of being of the work of art itself. In analysing aesthetic consciousness we recognised that the concept of aesthetic consciousness confronted with an object does not correspond to the real situation. This is why the concept of play is important in my exposition.

Hans-Georg Gadamer, *Truth and Method*, 2nd edition, trans. Joel Weinsheimer and Donald G. Marshall. (London: Continuum International Publishing, 2005).

We can certainly distinguish between play and the attitude of the player, which, as such, belongs with the other attitudes of subjectivity. Thus it can be said that for the player play is not serious: that is why he plays. We can try to define the concept of play from this point of view. What is merely play is not serious. Play has its own relation to what is serious. It is not only that the latter gives it its 'purpose': we play 'for the sake of recreation', as Aristotle says.[1] It is more important that play itself contains its own, even sacred, seriousness. Yet, in the attitude of play, all those purposive relations which determine active and caring existence have not simply disappeared, but in a curious way acquire a different quality. The player himself knows that play is only play and exists in a world which is determined by the seriousness of purposes. But he does not know this in such a way that, as a player, he actually intends this relation to seriousness. Play fulfils its purpose only if the player loses himself in his play. It is not that relation to seriousness which directs us away from play, but only seriousness in playing makes the play wholly play. One who doesn't take the game seriously is a spoilsport. The mode of being of play does not allow the player to behave towards play as if it were an object. The player knows very well what play is, and that what he is doing is 'only a game'; but he does not know what exactly he 'knows' in knowing that.

Our question concerning the nature of play itself cannot, therefore, find an answer if we look to the subjective reflection of the player to provide it.[2] Instead, we are enquiring into the mode of being of play as such. We have seen that it is not the aesthetic consciousness, but the experience of art and thus the question of the mode of being of the work of art that must form the object of our examination. But this was precisely the experience of the work of art which I maintained in opposition to the levelling process of the aesthetic consciousness: namely, that the work of art is not an object that stands over against a subject for itself. Instead the work of art has its true being in the fact that it becomes an experience changing the person experiencing it. The 'subject' of the experience of art, that which remains and endures, is not the subjectivity of the person who experiences it, but the work itself. This is the point at which the mode of being of play becomes significant. For play has its own essence, independent of the consciousness of those who play. Play also exists – indeed, exists properly – when the thematic horizon is not limited by any being-for-itself of subjectivity, and where there are no subjects who are behaving 'playfully'.

The players are not the subjects of play; instead play merely reaches presentation through the players. We can see this first from the use of the word, especially from its multiple metaphorical applications, which Buytendijk in particular has noted.[3]

The metaphorical usage has here, as always, a methodological priority. If a word is applied to a sphere to which it did not originally belong, the actual 'original' meaning emerges quite clearly. Language has performed in advance a work of abstraction which is, as such, the task of conceptual analysis. Now thinking needs only to make use of this advance achievement.

The same is also true of etymologies. They are far less reliable because they are abstractions which are not performed by language, but by linguistic science, which can never be wholly verified by language itself: that is, by their actual usage. Hence even when they are right, they are not proofs, but advance achievements of conceptual analysis, and only in this obtain a firm foundation.[4]

If we examine how the word 'play' is used and concentrate on its so-called transferred meanings we find talk of the play of light, the play of the waves, the play of a component in a bearing-case, the inter-play of limbs, the play of forces, the play of gnats, even a play on words. In each case what is intended is the to-and-fro movement which is not tied to any goal which would bring it to an end. This accords with the original meaning of the word spiel as 'dance', which is still found in many word forms (e.g. in Spielmann, jongleur).[5] The movement which is play has no goal which brings it to an end; rather it renews itself in constant repetition. The movement backwards and forwards is obviously so central for the definition of a game that it is not important who or what performs this movement. The movement of play as such has, as it were, no substrate. It is the game that is played – it is irrelevant whether or not there is a subject who plays. The play is the performance of the movement as such. Thus we speak of the play of colours and do not mean only that there is one colour, that plays against another, but that there is one process or sight, in which one can see a changing variety of colours.

Hence the mode of being of play is not such that there must be a subject who takes up a playing attitude in order that the game may be played. Rather, the most original sense of playing is the medial one. Thus we say that something is 'playing' somewhere or at some time, that something is going on (sich abspielt, im Spiele ist).[6]

This linguistic observation seems to me to be an indirect indication that play is not to be understood as a kind of activity. As far as language is concerned, the actual subject of play is obviously not the subjectivity of an individual who among other activities also plays, but instead the play itself. Only we are so used to relating a phenomenon such as playing to the sphere of subjectivity and its attitudes that we remain closed to these indications from the spirit of language.

However, modern research has conceived the nature of play so widely that it is led more or less to the verge of that attitude to it that is based on subjectivity. Huizinga has investigated the element of play in all cultures and above all worked out the connection of children's and animal play with the 'sacred plays of the religious cult'. That led him to recognise the curious lack of decisiveness in the playing consciousness, which makes it absolutely impossible to decide between belief and non-belief. 'The savage himself knows no conceptional distinction between being and playing; he knows of no identity, image or symbol. And that is why it may be asked whether one does not get closest to the mental condition of the savage in his sacred actions by holding on to the primary idea of play. In our idea of play the difference between faith and pretence is dissolved'.[7]

Here the primacy of play over the consciousness of the player is fundamentally acknowledged and, in fact, even the experiences of play that the psychologist and anthropologist have to describe are illuminated afresh if one starts from the medial sense of the word spielen. Play obviously represents an order in which the to-and-fro motion of play follows of itself. It is part of play that the movement is not only without goal or purpose but also without effort. It happens, as it were, by itself. The ease of play, which naturally does not mean that there is any real absence of effort, but phenomenologically refers only to the absence of strain,[8] is experienced subjectively as relaxation. The structure of play absorbs the player into itself, and thus takes from him the burden of the initiative, which constitutes the actual strain of existence. This is seen also in the spontaneous tendency to repetition that emerges in the player and in the constant self-renewal of play, which influences its form (e.g. the refrain).

The fact that the mode of being of play is so close to the mobile form of nature permits us to make an important methodological conclusion. It is obviously not correct to say that animals too play and that we can even say metaphorically that water and light play. Rather, on the contrary, we can say that man too plays. His playing is a natural process. The meaning of his play, precisely because – and insofar as – he is part of nature, is a pure self-presentation. Thus it becomes finally meaningless to distinguish in this sphere between literal and metaphorical usage.

But above all there comes from this medial sense of play the connection with the being of the work of art. Nature, inasmuch as it is without purpose or intention, as it is, without exertion, a constantly self-renewing play, can appear as a model for art. Thus Friedrich Schlegel writes: 'All the sacred games of art are only remote imitations of the infinite play of the world, the eternally self-creating work of art'.[9]

Another question that Huizinga discusses is also clarified as a result of the fundamental role of the to-and-fro movement of play, namely the playful character of the contest. It is true that it does not appear to the contestant that he is playing. But there arises through the contest the tense movement to-and-fro from which the victor emerges, thus showing the whole to be a game. The movement to-and-fro obviously belongs so essentially to the game that there is an ultimate sense in which you cannot have a game by yourself. In order for there to be a game, there always has to be, not necessarily literally another player, but something else with which the player plays and which automatically responds to his move with a countermove. Thus the cat at play chooses the ball of wool because it responds to play, and ball games will be with us forever because the ball is freely mobile in every direction, appearing to do surprising things of its own accord.

The primacy of the game over the players engaged in it is experienced by the players themselves in a special way, where it is a question of human subjectivity that adopts an attitude of play. Once more it is the improper uses of the word that offer the most information about its proper essence. Thus we say of someone that he plays with possibilities or with plans. What we mean is clear. He still has not committed himself to the possibilities as to serious aims. He still has the freedom to decide one way or the other, for one or the other possibility. On the other hand this freedom is not without danger. Rather the game itself is a risk for the player. One can only play with serious possibilities. This means obviously that one may become so engrossed in them that they, as it were, outplay one and prevail over one. The attraction of the game, which it exercises on the player, lies in this risk. One enjoys a freedom of decision, which at the same time is endangered and irrevocably limited. One has only to think of jig-saw puzzles, games of patience etc. But the same is true in serious matters. If someone, for the sake of enjoying his own freedom of decision, avoids making pressing decisions or plays with possibilities that he is not seriously envisaging and which, therefore, offer no risk that he will choose them and thereby limit himself, we say he is only 'playing with life' (verspielt).

This suggests a general characteristic of the way in which the nature of play is reflected in an attitude of play: all playing is a being-played. The attraction of a game, the fascination it exerts, consists precisely in the fact that the game tends to master the players. Even when it is a case of games in which one seeks to accomplish tasks that one has set oneself, there is a risk whether or not it will 'work', 'succeed', and 'succeed again', which is the attraction of the game. Whoever 'tries' is in fact the one who is tried. The real subject of the game (this is shown in precisely those experiences in which there is only a single player) is not the player, but instead the game itself. The game is what holds the player in its spell, draws him into play, and keeps him there.

This is shown also by the fact that games have their own proper spirit.[10] But even this does not refer to the mood or the mental state of those who play the game. Rather, this difference of mental attitude in the playing of different games and in the desire to play them is a result and not the cause of the difference of the games themselves. Games themselves differ from one another by their spirit. The reason for this is that the to-and-fro movement, which is what constitutes the game, is differently arranged. The particular nature of a game lies in the rules and structures which prescribe the way that the area of the game is filled. This is true universally, whenever there is a game. It is true, for example, of the play of fountains and of playing animals. The area in which the game is played is, as it were, set by the nature of the game itself and is defined far more by the structure that determines the movement of the game than by what it comes up against, i.e. the boundaries of the free area, which limits movement from outside.

Apart from these general determining factors, it seems to me characteristic of human play that it plays something. That means that the structure of movement to which it submits has a definite quality which the player 'chooses'. He first of all expressly separates off his playing behaviour from his other behaviour by wanting to play. But even within his readiness to play he makes a choice. He chooses this game and not that. It accords with this that the movement of the game is not simply the free area in which one 'plays oneself out', but is one that is specially marked out and reserved for the movement of the game. The human game requires its playing field. The setting apart of the playing field – just like that of sacred precincts, as Huizinga rightly points out[11] – sets the sphere of play as a closed world without transition and mediation over against the world of aims. That all play is a playing of something is true here, where the ordered to-and-fro movement of the game is determined as an attitude and marks itself off from other attitudes. The playing man is, even in his play, still someone who takes up an attitude, even if the proper essence of the game consists in his getting rid of the tension which he feels in his attitude to his aims. This determines more exactly why playing is always a playing of something. Every game presents the man who plays it with a task. He cannot enjoy the freedom of playing himself out except by transforming the aims of his behaviour into mere tasks of the game. Thus the child gives itself a task in playing with the ball, and such tasks are playful ones, because the purpose of the game is not really the solution of the task, but the ordering and shaping of the movement of the game itself.

Obviously the characteristic lightness and sense of relief which we find in the attitude of play depends on the particular character of the task set by the game, and comes from solving it.

One can say that to perform a task successfully 'represents it'. One can say this all the more when it is a question of a game, for here the fulfilment of the task does not point to any purposive context. Play is really limited to representing itself. Thus its mode of being is self-representation. But self-representation is a universal aspect of the being of nature. We know today how inadequate biological conceptions of purpose are when it comes to understanding the form of living things.[12] It is likewise true of play that to ask what its life-function is and its biological purpose is is an inadequate approach. It is, pre-eminently, self-representation.

The self-representation of human play depends, as we have seen, on behaviour which is tied to the make-believe goals of the game, but the 'meaning' of the latter does not in fact depend on achieving these goals. Rather, in spending oneself on the task of the game, one is, in fact, playing oneself out. The self-representation of the game involves the player's achieving, as it were, his own self-representation by playing, i.e. representing something. Only because play is always representation is human play able to find the task of the game in representation itself. Thus there are games which must be called representation games, either in that, by the use of meaningful allusion, they have something about them of representation (say 'Tinker, Tailor, Soldier, Sailor') or in that the game itself consists in representing something (e.g. when children play motor-cars).

All representation is potentially representative for someone. That this possibility is intended is the characteristic feature of the playful nature of art. The closed world of play lets down as it were, one of its walls.[13] A religious rite and a play in a theatre obviously do not represent in the same sense as the playing child. Their being is not exhausted by the fact that they represent; at the same time they point beyond themselves to the audience which is sharing in them. Play here is no longer the mere self-representation of an ordered movement, nor mere representation, in which the playing child is totally absorbed, but it is 'representing for someone'. This assignment in all representation comes to the fore here and is constitutive of the being of art.

In general, games, however much they are in essence representations and however much the players represent themselves in them, are not represented for anyone, i.e. they are not aimed at an audience. Children play for themselves, even when they represent. And not even those games, e.g. sports, which are played before spectators are aimed at them. Indeed, they threaten to lose their real play character as a contest precisely by becoming a show. A procession as part of a religious rite is more than a demonstration, since its real meaning is to embrace the whole religious community. And yet the religious act is a genuine representation for the community, and equally a theatrical drama is a playful act that, of its nature, calls for an audience. The representation of a god in a religious rite, the representation of a myth in a play, are play not only in the sense that the participating players are wholly absorbed in the representative play and find in it their heightened self-representation, but also in that the players represent a meaningful whole for an audience. Thus it is not really the absence of a fourth wall that turned the play into a show. Rather, openness towards the spectator is part of the closedness of the play. The audience only completes what the play as such is.[14]

This is the point which shows the importance of the medial nature of the play process. We have seen that play does not have its being in the consciousness or the attitude of the player, but on the contrary draws the latter into its area and fills him with its spirit. The player experiences the game as a reality that surpasses him. This is more than ever the case where it itself is 'intended' as such a reality – for instance the play which appears as representation for an audience.

Even a theatrical drama remains a game, i.e. it has the structure of a game, which is that of a closed world. But the religious or profane drama, however much it represents a world that is wholly closed within itself, is as if open toward the side of the spectator, in whom it achieves its whole significance. The players play their roles as in any game, and thus the play is represented, but the play itself is the whole, comprising players and spectators. In fact, it is experienced properly by, and presents itself as what is 'meant' to, one who is not acting in the play, but is watching. In him the game is raised, as it were, to its perfection.

For the players this means that they do not simply fulfil their roles as in any game – rather, they play their roles, they represent them for the audience. Their mode of participation in the game is no longer determined by the fact that they are completely absorbed in it, but by their playing their role in relation and regard to the whole of the play, in which not they, but the audience is to become absorbed. When a play activity becomes a play in the theatre a total switch takes place. It puts the spectator in the place of the player. He – and not the player – is the person for and in whom the play takes place. Of course this does not mean that the player is not able to experience the significance of the whole, in which he plays his representing role. The spectator has only methodological precedence. In that the play is presented for him, it becomes apparent that it bears within itself a meaning that must be understood and that can therefore be detached from the behaviour of the player. Basically the difference between the player and the spectator is removed here. The requirement that the play itself be intended in its meaningfulness is the same for both.

This is still the case even when the play community is sealed off against all spectators, either because it opposes the social institutionalisation of artistic life, as in so-called chamber music, which seeks to be music-making in a fuller sense, because it is performed for the players themselves and not for an audience. If someone performs music in this way, he is also in fact trying to make the music 'sound well', but that means that it would be properly there for any listener. Artistic presentation, by its nature, exists for someone, even if there is no one there who listens or watches only.

(B) Transformation into structure and total mediation

I call this development, in which human play finds its true perfection in being art, 'the transformation into structure'. Only through this development does play acquire its ideality, so that it can be intended and understood as play. Only now does it emerge as detached from the representing activity of the players and consist in the pure appearance of what they are playing. As such the play – even the unforeseen elements of improvisation – is fundamentally repeatable and hence permanent. It has the character of a work, of an ergon and not only of energeia.[15] In this sense I call it a structure.

What can be separated in this way from the representing activity of the player still remains dependent on representation. This dependence does not mean that it is only through the particular persons representing it that the play acquires its definite meaning, not even through him who as the originator of the work is its real creator, the artist. Rather, the play has, in relation to them all, an absolute autonomy, and that is what is suggested by the idea of transformation.

The implications for the definition of the nature of art emerge when one takes the sense of transformation seriously. Transformation is not change, even a change that is especially far-reaching. A change always means that what is changed also remains the same and is held on to. However totally it may change, something changes in it. In terms of categories, all change (alloiosis) belongs in the sphere of quality, i.e. of an accident of substance. But transformation means that something is suddenly and as a whole something else, that this other transformed thing that it has become is its true being, in comparison with which its earlier being is nothing. When we find someone transformed we mean precisely this, that he has become, as it were, another person. There cannot here be any transition of gradual change leading from one to the other, since the one is the denial of the other. Thus the transformation into a structure means that what existed previously no longer exists. But also that what now exists, what represents itself in the play of art, is what is lasting and true.

It is clear here that to start from subjectivity is to miss the point. What no longer exists is the players – with the poet or the composer being considered as one of the players. None of them has his own existence for himself, which he retains so that his acting would mean that he 'only acts'. If we describe from the point of view of the actor what his acting is, then obviously it is not transformation, but disguise. A man who is disguised does not want to be recognised, but instead to appear as someone else and be taken for him. In the eyes of others he no longer wants to be himself, but to be taken for someone else. Thus he does not want to be discovered or recognised. He plays another person, but in the way that we play something in our daily intercourse with other people, i.e. that we merely pretend, act a part and create an impression. A person who plays such a game denies, to all appearances, continuity with himself. But in truth that means that he holds on to this continuity with himself for himself and only keeps it from those before whom he is acting.

According to all that we have observed concerning the nature of play, this subjective distinction between oneself and the play, which is what acting a part is, is not the true nature of play. Play itself is, rather, transformation of such a kind that the identity of the player does not continue to exist for anybody. Everybody asks instead what it is supposed to be, what is 'meant'. The players (or poets) no longer exist, but only what of theirs is played.

But, above all, what no longer exists is the world, in which we live as our own. Transformation into a structure is not simply transposition into another world. Certainly it is another, closed world in which play takes place. But inasmuch as it is a structure, it has, so to speak, found its measure in itself and measures itself by nothing outside it. Thus the action of a drama – in this it still entirely resembles the religious act – exists absolutely as something that rests within itself. It no longer permits of any comparison with reality as the secret measure of all copied similarity. It is raised above all such comparisons – and hence also above the question whether it is all real – because a superior truth speaks from it. Even Plato, the most radical critic of the high estimation of art in the history of philosophy, speaks sometimes, without differentiating between them, of the comedy and tragedy of life and of the stage.[16] For this difference disappears if one knows how to see the meaning of the game that unfolds before one. The pleasure offered in the spectacle is the same in both cases: it is the joy of knowledge.

This gives the full meaning to what we called transformation into a structure. The transformation is a transformation into the true. It is not enchantment in the sense of a bewitchment that waits for the redeeming word that will transform things to what they were, but it is itself redemption and transformation back into true being. In the representation of play, what is emerges. In it is produced and brought to the light what otherwise is constantly hidden and withdrawn. If someone knows how to perceive the comedy and tragedy of life, he is able to resist the suggestiveness of purposes which conceal the game that is played with us.

'Reality' always stands in a horizon of the future of observed and feared or, at any rate, still undecided possibilities. Hence it is always the case that mutually exclusive expectations are aroused, not all of which can be fulfilled. The undecidedness of the future is what permits such a superfluity of expectations that reality necessarily falls behind them. If, now, in a particular case, a meaningful whole completes and fulfils itself in reality, such that no lines of meaning scatter in the void, then this reality is itself like a drama. Equally, someone who is able to see the whole of reality as a closed circle of meaning, in which everything is fulfilled, will speak of the comedy and tragedy of life. In these cases, in which reality is understood as a play, there emerges what the reality of play is, which we call the play of art. The being of all play is always realisation, sheer fulfilment, energeia which has its telos within itself. The world of the work of art, in which play expresses itself fully in the unity of its course, is in fact a wholly transformed world. By means of it everyone recognises that that is how things are.

Thus the concept of transformation characterises the independent and superior mode of being of what we called structures. From this viewpoint 'reality' is defined as what is untransformed, and art as the raising up of this reality into its truth. Also the classical theory of art, which bases all art on the idea of mimesis, imitation, has obviously started from play which, in the form of dancing, is the representation of the divine.[17]

But the concept of imitation can only describe the play of art if one retains the element of knowledge contained in imitation. What is represented is there – this is the original imitative situation. If a person imitates something, he produces what he knows and in the way that he knows it. A child begins to play by imitation, doing what he knows and affirming his own being in the process. Also, children's delight in dressing-up, to which Aristotle refers, does not seek to be a hiding of themselves, a pretence, in order to be discovered and recognised behind it but, on the contrary, a representation of such a kind that only what is represented exists. The child does not want at any cost to be discovered behind his disguise. He intends that what he represents should exist, and if something is to be guessed, then this is it. What it 'is' should be recognised.[18]

We have established that the element of knowledge in imitation is recognition. But what is recognition? A more exact analysis of the phenomenon will make quite clear to us the nature of representation, which is what we are concerned with. As we know, Aristotle emphasises that artistic representation even makes the unpleasant appear as pleasant,[19] and Kant for this reason defined art as the beautiful representation of something, because it is even able to make the ugly appear beautiful.[20] But this obviously does not refer to artificiality and artistic technique. One does not, as with a circus performer, admire the art with which something is done. This has only secondary interest. What one experiences in a work of art and what one is directed towards is rather how true it is, i.e. to what extent one knows and recognises something and oneself.

But we do not understand what recognition is in its profoundest nature, if we only see that something that we know already is known again, i.e. that what is familiar is recognised again. The joy of recognition is rather that more becomes known than is already known. In recognition what we know emerges, as if through an illumination, from all the chance and variable circumstances that condition it and is grasped in its essence. It is known as something.

This is the central motif of Platonism. In his theory of anamnesis Plato combined the mythical idea of remembrance with his dialectic, which sought in the logos, i.e. the ideality of language, the truth of being.[21] In fact this kind of idealism of being is already suggested in the phenomenon of recognition. The 'known' enters into its true being and manifests itself as what it is only when it is recognised. As recognised it is grasped in its essence, detached from its accidental aspects. This is wholly true of the kind of recognition that takes place in relation to what is represented in a play. This kind of representation leaves behind it everything that is accidental and unessential, e.g. the private particular being of the actor. He disappears entirely in the recognition of what he is representing. But even that which is represented, a well-known event of mythological tradition, is raised by its representation, as it were, to its own validity and truth. With regard to the recognition of the true, the being of representation is superior to the being of the material represented, the Achilles of Homer more than the original Achilles.

Thus the basic mimic situation that we are discussing not only involves what is represented being there, but also that it has in this way come to exist more fully. Imitation and representation are not merely a second version, a copy, but a recognition of the essence. Because they are not merely repetition, but a 'bringing forth', the spectator is also involved in them. They contain the essential relation to everyone for whom the representation exists.

Indeed, one can say even more: the presentation of the essence, far from being a mere imitation, is necessarily revelatory. When someone makes an imitation, he has to leave out and to heighten. Because he is pointing to something, he has to exaggerate, whether he likes it or not. Hence there exists an unbridgeable gulf between the one thing, that is a likeness, and the other that it seeks to resemble. As we know, Plato insisted on this ontological gulf, on the greater or lesser distance between the copy and the original, and for this reason considered imitation and representation in the play of art, as an imitation of an imitation, in the third rank.[22] Nevertheless, in the representation of art, recognition is operative, which has the character of genuine knowledge of essence, and since Plato considers all knowledge of being to be recognition, this is the ground of Aristotle's remark that poetry is more philosophical than history.[23]

Thus imitation, as representation, has a clear cognitive function. Therefore the idea of imitation was able to continue in the theory of art for as long as the significance of art as knowledge was unquestioned. But that is valid only while it is held that knowledge of the true is knowledge of the essence,[24] for art supports this kind of knowledge in a convincing way. For the nominalism of modern science, however, and its idea of reality, from which Kant drew the conclusion that aesthetics has nothing to do with knowledge, the concept of mimesis has lost its aesthetic force.

Having seen the difficulties of this subjective development in aesthetics, we are forced to return to the older tradition. If art is not the variety of changing experiences whose object is each time filled subjectively with meaning like an empty mould, representation must be recognised as the mode of being of the work of art. This was prepared for by the idea of representation being derived from the idea of play, in that self-representation is the true nature of play – and hence of the work of art also. The playing of the play is what speaks to the spectator, through its representation, and this in such a way that the spectator, despite the distance between it and himself, still belongs to it.

This is seen most clearly in the type of representation that is a religious rite. Here the relation to the community is obvious. An aesthetic consciousness, however reflective, can no longer consider that only the aesthetic differentiation, which sees the aesthetic object in its own right, discovers the true meaning of the religious picture or the religious rite. No one will be able to hold that the performance of the ritual act is unessential to religious truth.

This is equally true for drama, and what it is as a piece of literature. The performance of a play, likewise, cannot be simply detached from the play itself, as if it were something that is not part of its essential being, but is as subjective and fluid as the aesthetic experiences in which it is experienced. Rather, in the performance, and only in it – as we see most clearly in the case of music – do we encounter the work itself, as the divine is encountered in the religious rite. Here the methodological advantage of starting from the idea of play becomes clear. The work of art cannot be simply isolated from the 'contingency' of the chance conditions in which it appears, and where there is this kind of isolation, the result is an abstraction which reduces the actual being of the work. It itself belongs to the world to which it represents itself. A drama exists really only when it is played, and certainly music must resound.

My thesis, then, is that the being of art cannot be determined as an object of an aesthetic awareness because, on the contrary, the aesthetic attitude is more than it knows of itself. It is a part of the essential process of representation and is an essential part of play as play.

What are the ontological consequences of this? If we start in this way from the play character of play, what emerges for the closer definition of the nature of aesthetic being? This much is clear: drama and the work of art understood in its own terms is not a mere schema of rules or prescriptions of attitudes, within which play can freely realise itself. The playing of the drama does not ask to be understood as the satisfying of a need to play, but as the coming into existence of the work of literature itself. And so there arises the question of the being proper to a poetic work that comes to be only in performance and in theatrical representation, although it is still its own proper being that is there represented.

Let us recall the phrase used above of the 'transformation into a structure'. Play is structure – this means that despite its dependence on being played it is a meaningful whole which can be repeatedly represented as such and the significance of which can be understood. But the structure is also play, because – despite this theoretical unity – it achieves its full being only each time it is played. It is the complementary nature of the two sides of the one thing that we seek to underline, as against the abstraction of aesthetic differentiation.

We may now formulate this by opposing to aesthetic differentiation, the properly constitutive element of aesthetic consciousness, 'aesthetic non-differentiation'. It has become clear that what is imitated in imitation, what is formed by the poet, represented by the actor, recognised by the spectator is to such an extent what is meant – that in which the significance of the representation lies – that the poetic formation or the achievement involved in the representation are not distinguished from it. When a distinction is made, it is between the material and the forming, between the poem and the 'conception'. But these distinctions are of a secondary nature. What the actor plays and the spectator recognises are the forms and the action itself, as they are intended by the poet. Thus we have here a double mimesis: the writer represents and the actor represents. But even this double mimesis is one: it is the same thing that comes to existence in each case.

More exactly, one can say that the mimic representation of the performance brings 'into being-there what the written play actually requires. The double distinction between a drama and its subject matter and a drama and performance corresponds to a double non-distinction as the unity of the truth which one recognises in the play of art. It is to move out of the actual experience of a piece of literature if one investigates the origin of the plot on which it is based, and equally it is to move out of the actual experience of the drama if the spectator reflects about the conception behind a performance or about the proficiency of the actors. This kind of reflection already contains the aesthetic differentiation of the work itself from its representation. But for the meaningfulness of the experience as such it is, as we have seen, not even important whether the tragic or comic scene which is played before one takes place on the stage or in life – if one is only a spectator. What we have called a structure is one insofar as it presents itself as a meaningful whole. It does not exist in itself, nor is it experienced in a communication accidental to it, but it gains, through being communicated, its proper being.

No matter how much the variety of the performances or realisations of such a structure goes back to the conception of the players – it also does not remain enclosed in the subjectivity of what they think, but it is embodied there. Thus it is not at all a question of a mere subjective variety of conceptions, but of the possibilities of being that the work itself possesses, which lays itself out in the variety of its aspects.

This is not to deny that here there is a possible starting-point for aesthetic reflection. In different performances of the same play, say, one can distinguish between one kind of mediation and another, just as one can conceive the conditions of access to works of art of a different kind in various ways, e.g. when one looks at a building from the point of view of how it would look on its own or how its surroundings ought to look. Or when one is faced with the question of the restoration of a painting. In all these cases the work itself is distinguished from its 'representation'.[25] But one fails to appreciate the compelling quality of the work of art if one regards the variations possible in the representation as free and optional. In fact they are all subject to the supreme criterion of the 'right' representation.[26]

We know this in the modern theatre as the tradition that stems from a production, the creation of a role, or the practice of a musical performance. Here there is no random succession, a mere variety of conceptions, but rather from the constant following of models and from a productive and changing development there is cultivated a tradition with which every new attempt must come to terms. The interpretative artist too has a sure consciousness of this. The way that he approaches a work or a role is always related in some way to models which did the same. But it has nothing to do with blind imitation. Although the tradition that is created by a great actor, producer or musician remains effective as a model, it is not a brake on free creation, but has become so one with the work that the concern with this model stimulates the creative interpretative powers of an artist no less than the concern with the work itself. The reproductive arts have this special quality that the works with which they are concerned are explicitly left open to this kind of re-creation and thus have visibly, opened the identity and continuity of the work of art towards its future.[27]

Perhaps the criterion that determines here whether something is 'a correct representation' is a highly mobile and relative one. But the compelling quality of the representation is not lessened by the fact that it cannot have any fixed criterion. Thus we do not allow the interpretation of a piece of music or a drama the freedom to take the fixed 'text' as a basis for a lot of ad-lib effects, and yet we would regard the canonisation of a particular interpretation, e.g. in a gramophone recording conducted by the composer, or the detailed notes on performance which come from the canonised first performance, as a failure to understand the actual task of interpretation. A 'correctness', striven for in this way, would not do justice to the true binding nature of the work, which imposes itself on every interpreter in a special and immediate way and does not allow him to make things easy for himself by simply imitating a model.

It is also, as we know, wrong to limit the 'freedom' of interpretative choice to externals or marginal phenomena and not rather to think of the whole of an interpretation in a way that is both bound and free. Interpretation is probably, in a certain sense, re-creation, but this re-creation does not follow the process of the creative act, but the lines of the created work which has to be brought to representation in accord with the meaning the interpreter finds in it. Thus, for example, performances of music played on old instruments are not as faithful as they seem. Rather, they are an imitation of an imitation and in danger 'of standing at a third remove from the truth' (Plato).

In view of the finite nature of our historical existence there is, it would seem, something absurd about the whole idea of a uniquely correct interpretation. We shall come back to this in another context. Here the obvious fact, that every interpretation seeks to be correct, serves only to confirm that the non-differentiation of the interpretation from the work itself is the actual experience of the work. This accords with the fact that the aesthetic consciousness is generally able to make the aesthetic distinction between the work and its interpretation only in a critical way, i.e. where the interpretation breaks down. The communication of the work is, in principle, a total one.

Total communication means that the communicating element cancels itself out. In other words, reproduction (in the case of drama and music, but also with the recitation of stories or poetry) does not become, as such, thematic, but the work presents itself through it and in it. We shall see that the same is true of the character of approach and encounter in which buildings and statues present themselves. Here also the approach is not, as such, thematic, but neither is it true that one would have to abstract from life-references in order to grasp the work itself. Rather, it exists within them. The fact that works come out of a past from which they stretch into the present as permanent monuments, still does not make their being into an object of aesthetic or historical consciousness. As long as they still fulfil their function, they are contemporaneous with every age. Even if their place is only in museums as works of art, they are not entirely alienated from themselves. Not only does a work of art never completely lose the trace of its original function which enables an expert to reconstruct it, but the work of art that has its place next to others in a gallery is still its own origin. It affirms itself, and the way in which it does that – by 'killing' other things or using them profitably to complement itself – is still part of itself.

We ask what this identity is that presents itself so differently in the changing course of ages and circumstances. It does not disintegrate into the changing aspects of itself so that it would lose all identity, but it is there in them all. They all belong to it. They are all contemporaneous with it. Thus we have the task of giving an interpretation of the work of art in terms of time.

(C) The temporality of the aesthetic

What kind of contemporaneity is this? What kind of temporality belongs to aesthetic being? This contemporaneity and presentness of aesthetic being is called, in general, its timelessness. But this timelessness has to be thought of together with the temporality to which it essentially belongs. Timelessness is primarily only a dialectical feature which arises out of temporality and in contrast with it. Even if one speaks of two kinds of temporality, a historical and a supra-historical one, as does Sedlmayr, for example, following Batader and with reference to Bollnow, in an effort to determine the temporality of the work of art,[28] one cannot move beyond a dialectical tension between the two. The supra-historical 'sacred' time, in which the 'present' is not the fleeting movement but the fullness of time, is described from the point of view of existential temporality. The inadequacy of this kind of antithesis emerges when one inevitably discovers that 'true time' projects into historical–existential 'appearance time'. This kind of projection would obviously have the character of an epiphany, but this means that for the experiencing consciousness it is without continuity.

This involves again all the difficulties of the aesthetic awareness, which we pointed out above. For it is precisely continuity that every understanding of time has to achieve, even when it is a question of the temporality of a work of art. Here the misunderstanding of Heidegger's ontological exposition of the time horizon avenges itself. Instead of holding on to the methodological significance of the existential analytic of There-being, people treat this existential, historical temporality of There-being, determined by care and the movement towards death, i.e. radical finiteness, as one among many possible ways of understanding existence, and it is forgotten that it is the mode of being of understanding itself which is here revealed as temporality. The withdrawal of the proper temporality of the work of art as 'sacred time' from transient historical time remains, in fact, a mere mirroring of the human and finite experience of art. Only a biblical theology of time, starting not from the standpoint of human self-understanding, but from divine revelation, would be able to speak of a 'sacred time' and theologically justify the analogy between the timelessness of the work of art and this 'sacred time'. Without this kind of theological justification, to speak of 'sacred time' obscures the real problem, which does not lie in the atemporality of the work of art but in its temporality. Thus we take up our question again: what kind of temporality is this?[29]

We started from the position that the work of art is play, i.e. that its actual being cannot be detached from its representation and that in the representation the unity and identity of a structure emerge. To be dependent on self-representation is part of its nature. This means that however much it may be changed and distorted in the representation, it still remains itself. This constitutes the validity of every representation, that it contains a relation to the structure itself and submits itself to the criterion of its correctness. Even the extreme of a wholly distorting representation confirms this. It becomes known as a distortion inasmuch as the representation is intended and appreciated as the representation of the structure. The representation has, in an indissoluble, indelible way the character of the repetition. Repetition does not mean here that something is repeated in the literal sense, i.e. can be reduced to something original. Rather, every repetition is equally an original of the work.

We know this kind of highly puzzling time structure from festivals.[30] It is in the nature, at least of periodic festivals, to be repeated. We call that the return of the festival. But the returning festival is neither another, nor the mere remembrance of the one that was originally celebrated. The originally sacral character of all festivals obviously excludes the kind of distinction that we know in the time-experience of the present; memory and expectation. The time-experience of the festival is rather its celebration, a present time sui generis.

The temporal character of celebration is difficult to grasp on the basis of the customary chronological experience of succession. If the return of the festival is related to the usual experience of time and its dimensions, it appears as historical temporality. The festival changes from one time to the next. For there are always other things going on at the same time. Nevertheless it would still remain, under this historical aspect, one and the same festival that undergoes this kind of change. It was originally of a certain nature and was celebrated in this way, then different, and then different again.

However, this aspect does not cover the time character of the festival that comes from its being celebrated. For the essence of the festival its historical connections are secondary. As a festival it is not an identity, in the manner of an historical event, but neither is it determined by its origin so that there was once the 'real' festival – as distinct from the way in which it came later to be celebrated. From the start it belonged to it that it should be regularly celebrated. Thus it is its own original essence always to be something different (even when celebrated in exactly the same way). An entity that exists only by always being something different is temporal in a more radical sense than everything that belongs to history. It has its being only in becoming and in return.[31]

A festival exists only in being celebrated. This is not to say that it is of a subjective character and has its being only in the subjectivity of those celebrating it. Rather the festival is celebrated because it is there. The same is true of drama – it must be represented for the spectator, and yet its being is by no means just the point of intersection of the experiences that the spectators have. Rather the contrary is true, that the being of the spectator is determined by his being there present. To be present does not mean simply to be in the presence of something else that is there at the same time. To be present means to share. If someone was present at something, he knows all about how it really was. It is only in a derived sense that presence at something means also a kind of subjective attitude, that of attention to something. Thus to watch something is a genuine mode of sharing. Perhaps we may remind the reader of the idea of sacral communion which lies behind the original Greek idea of theoria. Theoros means someone who takes part in a mission to a festival. Such a person has no other qualification and function than to be there. Thus the theoros is a spectator in the literal sense of the word, who shares in the solemn act through his presence at it and in this way acquires his sacred quality: for example, of inviolability.

In the same way, Greek metaphysics still conceives the nature of theoria and of nous as pure presence to what is truly real,[32] and also the capacity to be able to act theoretically is defined for us by the fact that in attending to something it is possible to forget one's own purposes.[33] But theoria is not to be conceived primarily as an attitude of subjectivity, as a self-determination of the subjective consciousness, but in terms of what it is contemplating. Theoria is a true sharing, not something active, but something passive (pathos), namely being totally involved in and carried away by what one sees. It is from this point that people have tried recently to explain the religious background of the Greek idea of reason.[34]

We started by saying that the true being of the spectator, who is part of the play of art, cannot be adequately understood in terms of subjectivity, as an attitude of the aesthetic consciousness. But this does not mean that the nature of the spectator cannot be described in terms of being present at something, in the way that we pointed out. To be present, as a subjective act of a human attitude, has the character of being outside oneself. Even Plato, in his *Phaedrus*, makes the mistake of judging the ecstasy of being outside oneself from the point of view of rational reasonableness and of seeing it as the mere negation of being within oneself, i.e. as a kind of madness. In fact, being outside oneself is the positive possibility of being wholly with something else. This kind of being present is a self-forgetfulness, and it is the nature of the spectator to give himself in self-forgetfulness to what he is watching. Self-forgetfulness here is anything but a primitive condition, for it arises from the attention to the object, which is the positive act of the spectator.[35]

Obviously there is an important difference between a spectator who gives himself entirely to the play of art, and someone who merely gapes at something out of curiosity. It is also characteristic of curiosity that it is as if drawn away by what it looks at, that it forgets itself entirely in it, and cannot tear itself away from it. But the important thing about an object of curiosity is that it is basically of no concern to the spectator, it has no meaning for him. There is nothing in it which he would really be able to come back to and which would focus his attention. For it is the formal quality of novelty, i.e. abstract difference, which makes up the charm of what one looks at. This is seen in the fact that its dialectical complement is becoming bored and jaded. Whereas that which presents itself to the spectator as the play of art does not simply exhaust itself in the ecstatic emotion of the moment, but has a claim to permanence and the permanence of a claim.

The word 'claim' does not occur here by accident. In the type of theological reflection which started with Kierkegaard and which we call 'dialectical theology' this idea has made possible a theological explanation of what is meant by Kierkegaard's notion of simultaneity. A claim is something lasting. Its justification (or pretended justification) is the first thing. Because a claim continues, it can be affirmed at any time. A claim exists against someone and must therefore be asserted against him; but the concept of a claim also contains the idea that it is not itself a fixed demand, the fulfilment of which is agreed by both sides, but is, rather, the ground for such. A claim is the legal basis for an unspecified demand. If it is to be answered in such a way as to be settled, then it must first take the form of a demand when it is made. It belongs to the permanence of a claim that it is concretised into a demand.

The application to lutheran theology is that the claim of the call to faith persists since the proclamation of the gospel and is made afresh in preaching. The words of the sermon perform this total mediation which otherwise is the work of the religious rite, say, of the mass. We shall see that the word is called also in other ways to mediate contemporaneity, and that therefore in the problem of hermeneutics it has the chief place.

At any rate 'contemporaneity' forms part of the being of the work of art. It constitutes the nature of 'being present'. It is not the simultaneity of the aesthetic consciousness, for that simultaneity refers to the coexistence and the equal validity of different aesthetic objects of experience in the one consciousness. Contemporaneity, however, here means that a single thing that presents itself to us achieves in its presentation full presentness, however remote its origin may be. Thus contemporaneity is not a mode of givenness in consciousness, but a task for consciousness and an achievement that is required of it. It consists in holding on to the object in such a way that it becomes contemporaneous, but this means that all mediation is dissolved in total presentness.

This idea of contemporaneity comes, as we know, from Kierkegaard, who gave to it a particular theological emphasis.[36] Contemporaneity, for Kierkegaard, does not mean existing at the same time, but is a formulation of the believer's task of so totally combining one's town presence and the redeeming act of Christ, that the latter is experienced as something present (not as something in the past) and is taken seriously as such. Against this the simultaneity of the aesthetic consciousness depends on the concealment of the task that contemporaneity sets.

Hence contemporaneity is something that is found especially in the religious act, and in the sermon. The sense of being present is here the genuine sharing in the redemptive action itself. No one can doubt that the aesthetic differentiation, e.g. of a 'beautiful' ceremony or of a 'good' sermon is, in view of the appeal that is made to us, misplaced. Now I maintain that the same thing is basically true for the experience of art.

Here also mediation must be conceived as total. Neither the separate life of the creating artist – his biography – nor that of the performer who acts a work, nor that of the spectator who is watching the play, has any separate legitimacy in the face of the being of the work of art.

What unfolds before one is for every one so lifted out of the continuing progression of the world and so self-enclosed as to make an independent circle of meaning that no one is motivated to go beyond it to another future and reality. The spectator is set at an absolute distance which makes any practical, purposive share in it impossible. But the distance is, in the literal sense, aesthetic distance, for it is the distance from seeing that makes possible the proper and comprehensive sharing in what is represented before one. Thus to the ecstatic self-forgetfulness of the spectator there corresponds his continuity with himself. Precisely that in which he loses himself as a spectator requires his own continuity. It is the truth of his own world, the religious and moral world in which he lives, which presents itself to him and in which he recognises himself. Just as the parousia, absolute presence, describes the ontological mode of aesthetic being, and a work of art is the same wherever it becomes such a presence, so the absolute moment in which a spectator stands is at once self-forgetfulness and reconciliation with self. That which detaches him from everything also gives him back the whole of his being.

The dependence of aesthetic being on representation does not mean any deficiency, any lack of autonomous determination of meaning. It belongs to its essence. The spectator is an essential element of the kind of play that we call aesthetic. Let us remember here the famous definition of tragedy which we find in Aristotle's *Poetics*. There the attitude of the spectator is expressly included in the definition.

(D) *The example of the tragic*

The Aristotelian theory of tragedy may serve as an example for the structure of aesthetic being as a whole. It exists in the content of a poetics and seems to be valid only for dramatic poetry. However, the tragic is a basic phenomenon, a meaningful structure which does not exist only in tragedy, the tragic work of art in the narrower sense, but can have its place also in other artistic genres, especially epic. Indeed, it is not even a specifically artistic phenomenon, inasmuch as it is found also in life. For this reason, the tragic is seen by modern scholars (Richard Hamann, Max Scheler[37]) as something extra-aesthetic. It is an ethical and metaphysical phenomenon that enters into the sphere of aesthetic problems only from outside. But after we have seen how questionable the idea of the aesthetic is, we must now raise the contrary issue, namely, whether the tragic is not, rather, a basic aesthetic phenomenon. The nature of the aesthetic has emerged for us as play and representation. Thus we may also consult the theory of the tragic play, the poetics of tragedy, as to the essence of the tragic.

What we find reflected in thought about the tragic, from Aristotle down to the present, is by no means of an unchangeable nature. There is no doubt that the essence of tragedy is presented in Attic tragedy in a unique way; and differently for Aristotle, for whom Euripides was the 'most tragic',[38] differently again for someone to whom Aeschylus reveals the truth of the tragic phenomenon, and very differently for someone who thinks of Shakespeare. But this change does not simply mean that the question of the unified nature of the tragic would be without an object, but rather, on the contrary, that the phenomenon presents itself in an outline given by a historical unity. The reflection of classical tragedy in modern tragedy of which Kierkegaard speaks is constantly present in all modern thinking on the tragic. If we start with Aristotle, we shall see the whole scope of the tragic phenomenon. In his famous definition of tragedy Aristotle made a point that had a great influence on the problem of the aesthetic: he included in the definition of tragedy the effect on the spectator.

I cannot hope to treat his famous and much discussed definition fully here. But the mere fact that the spectator is taken into the definition makes clear what was said above concerning the essential part that the spectator plays in a drama. The way in which the spectator is part of it makes apparent the meaningfulness of the figure of play. Thus the distance that the spectator retains from the drama is not an optional attitude, but the essential relation whose ground lies in the meaningful unity of the play. Tragedy is the unity of a tragic succession of events that is experienced as such. But what is experienced as a tragic succession of events, even if it is not a play that is shown on the stage, but a tragedy in 'life', is a closed circle of meaning that resists, of itself, all penetration and influence. What is understood as tragic must simply be accepted. Hence it is, in fact, a basic 'aesthetic' phenomenon.

We learn from Aristotle that the representation of the tragic action has a specific effect on the spectator. The representation works through eleos and phobos. The traditional translation of these emotions by 'pity' and 'terror' gives them a far too subjective tinge. Aristotle is not at all concerned with pity or with the evaluation of pity as it has changed through the centuries,[39] and fear is similarly not to be understood as an inner emotion. Rather both are events that overwhelm man and sweep him away. Eleos is the distress that comes over us in the face of what we call distressing. Thus the fate of Oedipus is distressing (the example that Aristotle always returns to). The English word 'distress' is a good equivalent because it too refers not merely to an inner state, but likewise to its manifestation. Accordingly, phobos is not just a state of mind but, as Aristotle says, a cold shudder[40] that makes one's blood run cold, that makes one shiver. In the particular sense in which, in this definition of tragedy, phobos is combined with eleos, phobos means the shivers of apprehension which come over us for someone whom we see rushing to his destruction and for whom we fear. Distress and apprehension are modes of ecstasis, being outside oneself, which testify to the power of what is taking place before us.

Now Aristotle says of these emotions that they are what the play uses in order to purify us of them. As is well-known, this translation is doubtful, especially the sense of the genitive.[41] But what Aristotle means seems to me to be quite independent of this, and this must ultimately show why two conceptions so different grammatically can continue to be held so firmly. It seems clear to me that Aristotle is thinking of the tragic pensiveness that comes over the spectator at a tragedy. But pensiveness is a kind of relief and resolution, in which pain and pleasure are variously mixed. How can Aristotle call this condition a purification? What is the impure element in feeling, and how is this removed in the tragic emotion? The answer seems to me the following: being overcome by distress and horror involves a painful division. There is a disjunction with what is happening, a refusal to accept, that rebels against the agonising events. But it is precisely the effect of the tragic catastrophe that this disjunction with what exists is removed. The heart is freed from constraint. We are freed not only from the spell in which the painful and horrifying nature of the tragic destiny had held us, but at the same time we are free from everything that divides us from what is.

Thus tragic pensiveness reflects a kind of affirmation, a return to ourselves, and if, as is often the case in modern tragedy, the hero is affected in his own consciousness by the emotion, he himself shares a little in this affirmation, in that he accepts his fate.

But what is the real object of this affirmation? What is affirmed? Certainly not the justice of a moral world order. The notorious tragic theory of guilt that scarcely retains any importance for Aristotle is not a suitable explanation for modern tragedy. For tragedy does not exist where guilt and expiation correspond to each other in the right measure, where a moral bill of guilt is paid in full. Nor in modern tragedy can and must there be a full subjectivisation of guilt and of fate. Rather the excess of tragic consequences is typical of the nature of the tragic. Despite all the subjectivisation of guilt in modern tragedy it still retains an element of that classical sense of the power of destiny that, in the very disproportion between guilt and fate, reveals itself as the same for all. Hebbel seems to stand on the borderline of what can still be called tragedy, so exactly is subjective guilt fitted into the course of the tragic action. For the same reason the idea of christian tragedy presents a special problem, since in the light of divine salvation history the values of happiness and misfortune that are constitutive of the tragic action no longer determine human destiny. Even Kierkegaard's[42] brilliant contrast of the classical suffering that followed from a curse laid on a family, with the suffering that rends the consciousness that is not at one with itself, but involved in conflict, only reaches the bounds of the tragic. His rewritten *Antigone*[43] would no longer be a tragedy.

So we must repeat the question: what is affirmed here of the spectator? Obviously it is the disproportionate, terrible immensity of the consequences that flow from a guilty deed which is the real claim made on the spectator. The tragic affirmation is the fulfilment of this claim. It has the character of a genuine communion. It is something truly common which is experienced in such an excess of tragic suffering. The spectator recognises himself and his own finiteness in the face of the power of fate. What happens to the great ones of the earth has an exemplary significance. The tragic emotion is not a response to the tragic course of events as such or to the justice of the fate that overtakes the hero, but to the metaphysical order of being that is true for all. To see that 'this is how it is' is a kind of self-knowledge for the spectator, who emerges with new insight from the illusions in which he lives. The tragic affirmation is an insight which the spectator has by virtue of the continuity of significance in which he places himself.

It follows from this analysis of the tragic not only that it is a basic aesthetic idea, inasmuch as the distance of the spectator is part of the essence of the tragic but, more importantly, that the distance of the spectator, which determines the nature of the aesthetic, does not include the 'aesthetic differentiation' which we recognised as a feature of 'aesthetic consciousness'. The spectator does not hold himself aloof at a distance of aesthetic consciousness enjoying the art of representation,[44] but in the communion of being present. The real emphasis of the tragic phenomenon lies ultimately on what is represented and recognised and to share in it is not a question of choice. However much the tragic play that is performed solemnly in the theatre represents an exceptional situation in the life of everyone, it is not an experience of an adventure producing a temporary intoxication from which one re-awakens to one's true being, but the emotion that seizes the spectator deepens in fact his continuity with himself. The tragic emotion flows from the self-knowledge that the spectator acquires. He finds himself in the tragic action, because it is his own world, familiar to him from religious or historical tradition, that he encounters, and even if this tradition is no longer binding for a later consciousness – as was already the case with Aristotle, and was certainly true of Seneca or Corneille – there is more in the continuing effect of such tragic works and themes than merely the continuing validity of a literary model. It is not only assumed that the spectator is still familiar with the legend, but it is also necessary that its language still really reaches him. Only then can the encounter with the tragic theme and tragic work become an encounter with self.

What is true here of the tragic, however, is true in a far wider context. For the writer, free invention is always only one side of a communication which is conditioned by what is pre-given as valid. He does not freely invent his plot, however much he imagines that he does. Rather there remains up to the present day some of the old basis of the mimesis theory. The free invention of the writer is the presentation of a common truth that is binding on the writer also.

It is the same with the other arts, especially the plastic arts. The aesthetic myth of freely creative imagination that transforms experience into literature proves only that in the nineteenth century the store of mythical and historical tradition was no longer a self-evident possession. But even then the aesthetic myth of imagination and of the invention of genius is an exaggeration that does not stand up to reality. The choice of material and the formation of it still does not proceed from the free discretion of the artist and is not the mere expression of his inner life. Rather does the artist address people whose minds are prepared and chooses what he expects will have an effect on them. He himself stands in the same tradition as the public that he is aiming at and which he gathers around him. In this sense it is true that he does not need to know explicitly as an individual, a thinking consciousness, what he is doing and what his work says. It is never simply a strange world of magic, of intoxication, of dream to which the play, sculptor or viewer is swept away, but it is always his own world to which he comes to belong more fully by recognising himself more profoundly in it. There remains a continuity of meaning which links the work of art with the world of real existence and from which even the alienated consciousness of a cultured society never quite detaches itself.

Let us sum up. What is aesthetic being? We have sought to show something general in the idea of play and of the transformation into a structure, which is characteristic of the play of art: namely, that the presentation or performance of a work of literature or of music is something essential, and not incidental, for in this is merely completed what the works of art already are: the being there of what is represented in them. The specific temporality of aesthetic being, of having its being in the process of being represented, becomes existent in reproduction as a separate, independent phenomenon.

Notes

1 Aristotle, *Pol.* VIII, 3 1337 b 39 and elsewhere. Cf. *Eth. Nic. x*, 6, 1176 b 33: *paizein hopos spoudaze kat' anacharsin orthos echein dokei.*

2 Kurt Riezler, in his brilliant *Traktat vom Schönen*, has started with the subjectivity of the player and hence preserved the antithesis of play and seriousness, so that the idea of play becomes too restricted for him and he has to say: 'We doubt whether the play of children is only play' and 'The play of art is not only piay'.

3 F. J. J. Buytendijk, *Wesen und Sinn des Spiels*, l933.

4 This obvious point must be made against those who seek to criticise the truth of Heidegger's statements on the basis of his etymological practice.

5 Cf J. Trier, *Beiträge zur Geschichte der deutschen Sprache und Literatur* 67, 1947.

6 J. Huizinga *(Homo ludens, Vom Ursprung der Kultur im Spiel*, p. 43) points out the following linguistic facts: 'One can certainly say in German *ein Spiel treiben* ("to play a game") and in Dutch *een spelltje doen* (the same), but the appropriate verb is really *spielen* ("to play") itself. *Man spielt ein Spiel* ("one plays a game"). In other words, in order to express the kind of activity, the idea contained in the noun must be repeated in the verb. That means, it seems that the action is of such a particular and independent kind that it is different from the usual kinds of activity. Playing is not an activity in the usual sense'. Similarly, the phrase *ein spielchen macken* (to take a hand) describes a use of one's time that is by no means play.

7 Huizinga, loc. cit., p. 32.

8 Rilke writes in the fifth Duino Elegy: 'wo sich das reine Zuwenig unbegreiflich verwandelt – umspringt in jenes leere Zuviel' ('where the sheer dearth is incomprehensibly transformed – switches into that void excess').

9 Friedrich Schlegel, *Cespräch über die Poesie* (*Friedrich Schlegels* Jugendschriften, ed. J. Minor, 1882, II, p. 364).

10 F. G. Junger, *Die Spiele.*

11 Huizinga, loc. cit., p. 17.

12 In numerous writings Adolf Portmann has made this criticism and given a new basis to the legitimacy of the morphological approach.

13 Cf. Rudolf Kassner, *Zahl und Gesicht*, p. 161f. Kassner states that 'the extraordinary unity and duality of child and doll' is connected with the fact that the fourth 'open wall of the audience' (as in a religious rite) is missing. I am arguing the other way round that it is precisely this fourth wall of the audience that closes the play world of the *world of art.*

14 Cf. note 13.

15 I am making use here of the classical distinction in which Aristotle (*Eth. Eud.* Bl; *Eth. Nic.* VI, 5, 1140 a 20) separates the *poesis* from the *praxis.*

16 Plato, *Phileb.*, 50b.

17 Cf. the recent research by Koller, *Mimesis*, 1954, which proves the original connection between *mimesis* and dance.

18 Aristotle, *Poet.* 4 esp. 1448 b 16: 'inferring what class each object belongs to; for example that this individual is a so-and-so' (Else trans.).

19 Loc. cit. 1448 b 10.

20 Kant, *Critique of Judgcment*, § 48.

21 Plato, *Phaed.* 73ff.

22 Plato, *Republic* x.

23 Aristotle, *Poet.*, 9, 1451 b 6.

24 Anna Tumarkin has been able to show very clearly in the aesthetics of the eighteenth century the transition from 'imitation' to 'expression' (*Festschrift für Samuel Singer*, 1930).

25 It is a problem of a particular kind whether the formative process itself should not be seen also as an aesthetic reflection on the work. It is undeniable that when he considers the idea of his work the creator can ponder and critically compare and judge various possibilities of carrying it out. But this sober awareness which is part of creation itself seems to me to be something very different from aesthetic reflection and aesthetic criticism, which is able to be stimulated by the work itself. It may be that what was the object of the creator's reflection, i.e. the possibilities of form, can also be the occasion of aesthetic criticism. But even in the case of this kind of agreement in content between creative and critical reflection the criterion is different. Aesthetic criticism is based on the disturbance of unified understanding, whereas the aesthetic reflection of the creator is directed towards establishment of the unity of the work itself. We shall see later the hermeneutical consequences of this point. It still seems to me a remnant of the false psychologism that stems from taste and genius aesthetics if one makes the processes of production and of reproduction coincide in the

idea. This is to fail to appreciate the event of the success of a work, which goes beyond the subjectivity both of the creator and of the spectator or listener.

26 Although I think his analyses on the 'schematism' of the literary work of art have been too little noted, I can not agree when R. Ingarden (in his 'Bemerkungen zum Problem des ästhetischen Werturteils', *Rivista di Estetica*, 1959) sees in the process of the concretisation of an 'aesthetic object' the area of the aesthetic evaluation of the work of art. The aesthetic object is not constituted in the aesthetic experience of grasping it, but the work of art itself is experienced in its aesthetic quality through the process of its concretisation and creation. In this I agree fully with L. Pareyson's aesthetics of *formativita*.

27 This is not limited to the interpretative arts, but includes any work of art, in fact any meaningful structure, that is raised to a new understanding, as we shall see later.

28 Hans Sedlmayr, *Kunst und Wahrheit*, 1958, p. 140ff.

29 For the following, compare the fine analyses by R. and G. Koebner, *Vom Schönen und seiner Wahrheit*, 1957, which I came across only when my own work was completed. Cf. the review in the *Philosophische Rundschau* 7, p. 79.

30 Walter F. Otto and Karl Kerényi have noted the importance of the festival for the history of religions and anthropology (cf. Karl Kerényi, *Vom Wesen des Festes*, Paideuma, 1938).

31 Aristotle refers to the characteristic mode of being of the *apeiron*; for instance in his discussion of the mode of being of the day, the games, and hence the festival – a discussion that does not forget Anaximander. (*Physics* III, 6, 206 a 20). Had Anaximander already sought to define the fact that the *apeiron* never came to an end in relation to such pure time phenomena? Did he perhaps intend more than can be conceived in the Aristotelian ideas of becoming and being? For the image of the day recurs in another connection with a special function: in Plato's *Parmenides* (131b) Socrates seeks to demonstrate the relation of the idea to things in terms of the presence of the day, which exists for all. Here by means of the nature of the day, there is demonstrated not what exists only as it passes away, but the unsharable presence and *parousia* of something that remains the same, despite the fact that the day is everywhere different. When the early thinkers thought of being, i.e. presence, did that which was presence for them appear in the light of a sacral communion in which the divine shows itself? The *parousia* of the divine is still for Aristotle the most real being, *energeia* (Met. XIII, 7) which is limited by no *dunamei*. The character of this time cannot be grasped in terms of the usual experience of succession. The dimensions of time and the experience of these dimensions cause us to see the return of the festival only as something historical: the one and the same thing changes from time to time. But in fact a festival is not one and the same thing; it exists by being always something different. An entity that exists only in always being something else is temporal in a radical sense: it has its being in becoming. Cf. on the ontological character of the 'while' (*Weile*) M. Heidegger, *Holzwege*, p. 322ff.

32 Cf. my essay 'Zur Vorgeschichte der Metaphysik' on the relationship between '*Zein*' and '*Denken*' in Parmenides (*Anteile*, 1949).

33 Cf. what was said above [*not reproduced here*] about culture, formation (*Bildung*).

34 Cf. Gerhard Krüger, *Einsicht und Leidenschaft. Das Wesen des platonischen Denkens*, first edition (1940). The Introduction in Particular contains important insights. Since then a published lecture by Krüger (*Grundfragen der Philosophie*, 1958) has made his systematic intentions even clearer. Perhaps we may make a few observations on what he says. His criticism of modern thinking and its emancipation from all connections with 'ontic truth' seems to me without foundation. That modern science, however constructively it may proceed, has never abandoned and never can abandon its fundamental connection with experiment, modern philosophy has never been able to forget. One only has to think of Kant's question of how a pure natural science is possible. But one is also very unfair to speculative idealism if one understands it in the onesided way that Krüger does. Its construction of the totality of all determinants of thought is by no means the thinking out of some random view of the world, but desires to bring into thinking the absolute *a posteriori* character of experiment. This is the exact sense of transcendental reflection. The example of Hegel can teach us that even the renewal of classical conceptual realism can be attempted by its aid. Krüger's view of modern thought is based entirely on the desperate extremism of Nietzsche. However, the perspectivism of the latter's 'will-to-power' is not in agreement with idealistic philosophy but, on the contrary, has grown up on the soil which nineteenth-century historicism had prepared after the collapse of idealist philosophy. Hence I am not able to give the same value as Krüger to Dilthey's theory of knowledge in the human sciences.

Rather, the important thing, in my view, is to correct the philosophical interpretation of the modern human sciences, which even in Dilthey proves to be too dominated by the onesided methodological thinking of the exact natural sciences. I certainly agree with Krüger when he appeals to the experience of life and the experience of the artist. But the continuing validity of these for our thinking seems to me to show that the contrast between classical thought and modern thought, in Krüger's oversimplified formulation, is itself a modern construction.

If we are reflecting on the experience of art – as opposed to the subjectivisation of philosophical aesthetics – we are not concerned simply with a question of aesthetics, but with an adequate self-interpretation of modern thought in general, which has more in it than the modern concept of method recognises.

35 E. Fink has tried to clarify the meaning of man's being outside himself in enthusiasm by making a distinction which is obviously inspired by Plato's *Phaedrus*. But whereas there the counter-ideal of pure rationality makes the distinction that between good and bad madness, Fink lacks a corresponding criterion when he contrasts 'purely human rapture' with that enthusiasm by which man is in God. For ultimately 'purely human rapture' is also a being away from oneself and an involvement with something else which man is not able to achieve of himself, but which comes over him, and thus seems indistinguishable from enthusiasm. That there is a kind of rapture which it is in man's power to induce and that enthusiasm is the experience of a superior power which simply overwhelms us: these distinctions of control over oneself and of being overwhelmed are themselves conceived in terms of power and therefore do not do justice to the interrelation of being outside oneself and being involved with something, which is the case in every form of rapture and enthusiasm. The forms of 'purely human rapture' described by Fink are themselves, if only they are not narcissistically and psychologically misinterpreted, modes of 'finite self-transcendence of finiteness' (cf. Eugen Fink, *Vom Wesen des Enthusiasmus*, esp. pp. 22–5).

36 Kierkegaard, *Philosophical Fragments*, ch. 4, and elsewhere.

37 Richard Hamann, *Asthetik*, p. 97: 'Hence the tragic has nothing to do with aesthetics', Max Scheler, *Vom Umsturz der Werte*, 'Zum Phänomen des Tragischen': 'It is even doubtful whether the tragic is an essentially "aesthetic" phenomenon'. For the meaning of the word 'tragedy' see E. Staiger, *Die Kunst der Interpretation*, p. 132ff.

38 Aristotle, *Poetics*, 13, 1453 a 29. Kierkegaard, *Either–Or* I.

39 Max Kommerell (*Lessing und Aristoteles*) has described this history of pity, but not distinguished sufficiently from it the original sense of *eleos*. Cf. also W. Schadewaldt, "Furcht und Mitleid?", *Hermes* 83, 1955, p. 129ff. and the supplementary article by H. Flashar, *Hermes* 1956, pp. 12–48.

40 Aristotle, *Rhet.*, II, 13, 1389 b 32.

41 Cf. M. Kommerell, who gives an account of the older interpretations: loc. cit., pp. 262–72. There have also been those who defend the objective genitive, e.g. K. H. Volkmann-Schluck in 'Varia Variorum' (*Festschrift für Karl Reinhardt*, 1952).

42 Kierkegaard, *Either–Or*, I.

43 Ibid.

44 Aristotle, *Poetics*, 4, 1448 b 18: '. . . but by virtue of its workmanship or its finish or some other cause of that kind'. (Else trans.).

Part III

Contemporary Aesthetics and Philosophy of Art

33

Introduction

Susan L. Feagin and Aaron Meskin

Susan L. Feagin is Visiting Research Professor of Philosophy at Temple University and editor of the *Journal of Aesthetics and Art Criticism.*

Ever since Plato, philosophers have asked *ti esti* questions – "What is it?" questions – which ask for definitions in terms of necessary and sufficient conditions. In aesthetics, the most central question of all has been "What is art?," though definitions of related phenomena, such as beauty, creativity, imagination, and the aesthetic, have also been sought. In the mid-twentieth century, under the influence of Ludwig Wittgenstein and ordinary language philosophy in general, it could no longer be assumed that such questions were most pressing. In "Aesthetic Problems of Modern Philosophy," Stanley Cavell exploits some of the strategies of ordinary language philosophy to examine some philosophical claims about art, meaning, and value. Cavell argues, for example, that the so-called "heresy of paraphrase," the view that the meaning of a metaphor or a poem cannot be paraphrased, is no heresy at all. As ordinarily used, paraphrases are not only possible but necessary for understanding a metaphor or poem, though providing it certainly does not exhaust the responsibilities of a critic. Cavell also explores the extent to which criticism should be thought of as offering proofs of a critic's claims about meaning and value, and to what extent critics have more authority than general readers. Comparing art criticism with philosophers' appeals to ordinary language, he proposes that in both cases the goal should not be proof, but to get readers "to prove something, test something," against themselves.

Susan L. Feagin and Aaron Meskin, "Introduction to Contemporary Aesthetics." New in this volume.

Morris Weitz was also deeply influenced by the ordinary language philosophy that was popular in England at the time. In "The Role of Theory in Aesthetics," he claims that if we follow the methodology proposed by Wittgenstein, to "look and see what it is that we call 'art,'" we will not find any features that are shared by all and only works of art. Indeed, he proposes that it is easier to tell whether something is an artwork than to tell whether it satisfies any of the various definitions that have been offered through the years, such as whether something possesses significant form or is a vehicle for the communication of the artist's emotions. Thus, even if it were possible to define art, there would be no point to it, since we can already tell what is art and what isn't. Furthermore, it is *not* possible to define art, he claims, because a definition would necessarily "foreclose on" the very creativity that we take to be central to the arts. Weitz concludes that aesthetic theory, by which he means a definition of art in terms of necessary and sufficient conditions, is "never forthcoming in aesthetics," while pointing out that we can still learn something by looking at the definitions that philosophers have proposed, since each one identifies something that we take to be valuable about at least some works of art.

The impact of Weitz's paper cannot be overestimated – as Noël Carroll puts it, "nothing taunts a philosopher so well as the claim that something is impossible"[1] – and no topic has been more central to contemporary philosophical aesthetics than how to define art. Weitz's argument about creativity, for example, far from showing that art cannot be defined, instead seems to identify creativity as a necessary condition for it. Equally troubling is his claim that it is easy to tell whether something is an artwork or not, especially in light of numerous developments in the arts during the twentieth century, when many artists strove to make art that could not be distinguished from non-art just by looking at or listening to it. These developments include the visual avant-garde in the early twentieth century; conceptual art in the third quarter of the century; the explosion of new art media, especially technologies of visual and auditory reproduction, around the turn of the century; and cultural traditions around the globe that challenge long-held notions of the nature of art and the aesthetic.

For Arthur Danto, the central task in the philosophy of art is to account for the difference between a work of art and something that is not art when they are perceptually indistinguishable from each other. Danto agrees with Weitz that, if we "look and see what it is that we call 'art,'" we shall discover no features that all and only artworks have in common. He concludes, contra Weitz, not that art cannot be defined, but that its defining features cannot lie in the way something looks. Art will be definable, if at all, in terms of relational properties that are not themselves perceivable, but knowledge of which can alter the way one sees a work. On Danto's view, to "see something as art requires something the eye cannot de[s]cry – an atmosphere of artistic theory, a knowledge of the history of art: an artworld." It is noteworthy that, on this account, not all art is valuable: what is impressive about Andy Warhol's *Brillo Boxes*, he maintains, is not that it is great art, or even good art, but that it is art at all.

Inspired by Danto's claims about the importance of the artworld, and similarly convinced that what distinguishes art from non-art is not perceivable in the object itself, George Dickie proposes that something is a work of art in virtue of, roughly, its relationship to an institutional framework and a set of practices. Within such a framework, an object can have the status of being a work of art – of being a *candidate* for appreciation – conferred upon it. In line with Weitz, Dickie criticizes traditional theorizing about art that aims at isolating a *single* valuable property found in art (imitation or skillful likeness, representational content, expressive power, formal unity, and so on) that could serve as its defining feature. In line with Danto, Dickie separates the theory of what art is from the theory of why art is *valuable*, and locates the former in non-exhibited and relational features of a work.

Over decades, Danto, Dickie, and a host of philosophers have attempted to prove Weitz wrong by providing definitions of art, but others have questioned whether aesthetics or the philosophy of art rests on defining art at all. Nelson Goodman, for example, rejects the very terms of the debate, charging that "If attempts to answer the question 'What is art?' characteristically end in frustration and confusion, perhaps – as so often in philosophy – the question is the wrong one." Goodman proposes that the right question is "When is art?," and instead of offering necessary and sufficient conditions, he identifies various "symptoms of the aesthetic" that have to do with the ways objects may function symbolically. An alternative suggestion, put forth by Noël Carroll in "Identifying Art," is that the motivation to define art can be dealt with by a non-definitional approach to identifying art.

Such general metaphysical questions about the possibility of defining art are joined by questions about the ontological status of particular works. Paintings and sculptures may seem to be physical objects, for example, but poems and pieces of music certainly do not – at least not in any ordinary sense of "physical object." Further, what determines whether two inscriptions are copies of the same poem, or two performances are performances of the same musical work? If all scores of a piece of music are destroyed, it does not follow that the work is destroyed; but if no one remembers it, does it still exist? The situation is different with respect to paintings: if the painted canvas is destroyed, the painting is destroyed, even if someone has an eidetic memory of the way the painting looks. If a person produces a painting from such a memory, that painting is not the original painting, but if a person performs a musical work based on such a memory, that person performs the original piece of music.

Danto is concerned with some of these questions in "The Artworld," specifically, how one object could be an artwork but a perceptual replica of it might not be, and how artworks may incorporate "mere real things" as part of them. Another key figure in debates over the ontological status of individual works is Richard Wollheim. In *Art and Its Objects*, borrowing from notions originally developed by the philosopher Charles Sanders Peirce, Wollheim defends the view that poems and plays are types whose instances are tokens of a type. But there are many kinds of types. For example, it is tempting to identify musical and literary works, conceived as types, with purely abstract structures – somewhat akin to mathematical entities such as numbers or formulae or idealized geometric figures such as circles and squares. There are no "real squares" in nature; the type "square" is an ideal towards which, let us say, drawn squares aspire. Jerrold Levinson argues against the view, often attributed to Peter Kivy, that musical works are purely abstract structures, and instead advances the position that musical works are "indicated structures, in which a particular person and time figure ineliminably." Musical works, thus identified, can be created and destroyed, unlike abstract structures, such as numbers and squares, whose existence is not dependent on there being physical tokens of them. One can then also explain how a piece of music might be audibly indistinguishable from a "merely real" set of sounds, and from another piece whose performance involves the production of an indistinguishable set of sounds.

Frank Sibley is another important twentieth-century philosopher who was profoundly influenced by post-war, "ordinary language" philosophy in England, especially as practiced by John Austin, H. P. Grice, and Gilbert Ryle. In his 1959 essay, "Aesthetic Concepts," Sibley calls attention to a group of terms whose application is not rule-governed; rather, "taste or perceptiveness" is required to apply them. He calls these terms 'aesthetic terms' and examples include 'unified,' 'lifeless,' 'graceful,' and 'elegant.' He distinguishes them from words that are rarely used as aesthetic terms, such as 'red,' 'noisy,' and 'brackish.' The application of some of these non-aesthetic terms, such as color terms like 'red,' are also not rule-governed, but their application still does not require taste. Sibley is interested in the acquisition and deployment of taste by individuals, and in the use of such terms in criticism, including whether critics can rationally defend their critical judgments and how they assist others to see what they see, or hear what they hear.

Mary Mothersill's Kantian-inspired book *Beauty Restored* is concerned with beauty and with aesthetic judgments in general with respect to reconciling the allegedly non-rule-governed nature of aesthetic judgments with their apparent claim to objectivity. Others have attempted to show that objectivity can be assured through appeal to the notion of the aesthetic itself, construed as a specific type of attitude. George Dickie critiques two versions of an aesthetic attitude theory: as a particular type of action that one may take towards a work of art, and as an ordinary action performed in a special way. He argues that most of what is referred to as taking an aesthetic attitude is simply a matter of attending closely to a work. Further, he claims that aesthetic attitude theories are misleading for aesthetic theory in three important ways: they mischaracterize what is of aesthetic relevance, they misdescribe a critic's relation to a work of art, and they fail to correctly capture the relationship between moral and aesthetic value.

Abetted by Dickie's critiques, the generally deflationist attitude towards the aesthetic in general during the latter part of the twentieth century elevated issues concerning specific art forms into prominence, with special attention to how the various arts differ from one another. Kendall Walton's 1970 "Categories of Art" is a key paper in this shift. Like Sibley, Walton is largely interested in aesthetic characterizations of artworks (such as 'tense,' 'mysterious,' 'energetic,' 'coherent'), and also like Sibley he assumes that a work's aesthetic features depend in some way on its non-aesthetic features. Foundational to his view is the point that one perceives a work differently when one perceives it in different categories. Jonathan Swift's "A Modest Proposal," for example, is experienced differently when read as a serious proposal and when read as a satire. "Springtime for Hitler," the play within the Broadway play *The Producers*, is successful if perceived as a comedy, but unsuccessful if perceived as a drama. According to Walton, several factors are relevant to determining which categories a work is *correctly* perceived in, and they include contextual features such as an artist's intentions and the categories generally recognized by the society at the time, but also non-contextual features such as the category in which a work turns out to be a better work. Nevertheless, he concludes that "certain facts about he origins of works of art have an *essential* role in criticism, that aesthetic judgments rest on them in an absolutely fundamental way."

One of the more interesting applications of Walton's work is in the field of environmental aesthetics, where Allen Carlson developed the view about what it is to appreciate nature, as such, that is sometimes referred to as "scientific cognitivism." Carlson proposes that *scientific* knowledge of nature substitutes for artists' intentions and socially recognized categories or types as a way to establish a *correct* context for appreciation. In this way, scientific knowledge enables us to "appreciate nature for what it is and for the qualities it has."

Not everyone has wanted to appeal to artists' intentions, even when talking about art. In 1946, William Wimsatt and Monroe Beardsley argued in "The Intentional Fallacy" that an artist's intentions are "neither available nor desirable as a standard for judging the success of a work of literary art." They pointedly reject some of the excesses of nineteenth-century romanticism, especially the tendency to idolize the artist, and advise that one can tell if a work is successful or not by examining the work, rather than by, as they pithily put it, "consulting the oracle." They also reject the excessively biographical literary criticism of their own day, which tended to be more biography than criticism – "higher gossip," as it is sometimes called – and unconnected to anything of interest in the work itself.

The title of Wimsatt and Beardsley's paper has provided what is perhaps the most well-known catchphrase in philosophy of art in the twentieth century, unfortunately fostering the assumption that it has the same unquestionable status as well-known logical fallacies such as affirming the consequent and appeals to pity. We have already noted the turn towards contextualism in Danto with respect to identifying something as art. Walton's contextualism – which has implications for perception, interpretation, and value – is clearly incompatible with Wimsatt and Beardsley's anti-intentionalism in holding that the artist's intentions are always relevant, even if not a decisive factor in determining a work's type or category and hence for how it is to be perceived. Evaluating an artist's work depends of course on interpreting it correctly. In "Art, Intention, and Conversation," Noël Carroll provides an important contemporary defense of the centrality of intentions to artistic interpretation, arguing that the centrality of broadly conversational interests in art make authorial intentions crucial to interpretation.

Alexander Nehamas agrees with Carroll that the role of the author is central to our interpretive engagement with art, but disagrees with Carroll in suggesting that it is not the actual author who should concern us, but rather the "postulated author," a hypothesized, "historically plausible" entity based on the qualities displayed in the work along with what we know of its context of production. Nehamas thus responds to Wimsatt and Beardsley's charge that artists' intentions are not available: we seek to understand what the author has done as a "regulative ideal," even if a complete understanding of the actual author is not attainable. A similar view, commonly known as hypothetical intentionalism, is advocated by Jenefer Robinson in her work on literary style. Robinson argues that individual literary style is understood as a matter of the expression of an author's "qualities of mind, attitudes, personality traits" and so on. Like Nehamas, she resists attributing these traits to the actual author as opposed to an "implied author," that is, "the author as she seems to be from the evidence of the work." Note that this can work in the author's favor, as Walton also saw, insofar as a work may succeed in ways the artist did not contemplate, intend, or possibly even understand.

Another legacy of romanticism, with a typical twentieth-century twist, is the idea that art is expression. Tolstoy and Collingwood attempted to *define* art as expression, and hence as necessarily involved in communicating emotion, whereas in the latter half of the twentieth century the focus shifts towards a puzzle that arises when we are inclined to say of *some* works of art that they express emotions or possess an emotional quality. *People* have and express emotions, but how could an artwork, an inanimate object, do so? Some simple options can be eliminated. Neither the emotional state of the artist when making the work, nor the emotion experienced by perceivers of the work, captures what it is for *the work* to express that emotion. A composer may write a joyous piece of music even when feeling grumpy; some sad music might make a listener feel happily content or simply unmoved. Addressing how an emotion can be in the work, Guy Sircello focuses on the importance of "artistic acts," the way in which artists do certain things, whereas Peter Kivy's account is rooted in perceived resemblances between musical works and human physiognomy.

It seems undeniable that many artworks also evoke emotional responses in their appreciators, and that the power to do so is one of the things that people value about them. It is a widespread view among psychologists and philosophers who work on emotion that having an emotion requires (among other things) having certain beliefs, with different beliefs for different emotions. For example, to be proud one must believe that one accomplished something worthwhile; to pity someone requires believing that that person has suffered undeserved misfortune; to be afraid one must believe that one is in danger, and so on. But when reading fiction, it seems that one typically lacks the relevant beliefs: one may pity Anna Karenina without believing that there is someone, Anna Karenina, who actually suffers misfortune. So one is left with a dilemma: either what one experiences is not, contrary to appearances, an emotion; or, if it is an emotion, it is irrational, since the relevant belief would be irrational. The dilemma arises from the fact that we *value* the emotive power of art, so one should be reluctant to grant that one's emotional response is either not real or irrational. In "Fearing Fictions," Kendall Walton argues that we have genuine feelings that are similar to the corresponding emotions, though not the emotions themselves. He calls them "quasi-emotions," not because they lack affect, but, to the contrary, because one lacks the belief components that emotions require. He also accounts for our tendency to refer to responses to fiction as if they were real emotions: they arise with games of "make-believe" in which our imaginings play roles in responding to fiction that beliefs play in real life.

Our sympathies with fictional characters often depend on our having certain sorts of values – indeed, moral and political values – which raises questions about the relationship between aesthetic value and other types of values. Plato and Aristotle did not take the value of drama and poetry to be independent of their moral value; neither did Hume, who comments briefly on the subject at the end of his essay on the standard of taste. Nevertheless, the exact relationship between them is hard to pin down. Berys Gaut argues that many works of art "manifest . . . ethical or moral attitudes" and that such attitudes are relevant to an overall artistic evaluation of them. More broadly, feminist philosophers, such as Mary Devereaux, reject what they see as the autonomy granted to art in Anglo-American aesthetics (crystallized, for some, in the idea of the aesthetic attitude) in favor of an aesthetics that is more socially and politically informed and engaged.

For over two millennia, philosophers such as Plato, Aristotle, Hume, Kant, and Hegel have been interested in art and beauty, creativity, meaning, imagination, emotions expressed in and evoked by the arts, and the value that any or all of these phenomena might have. As in other eras, developments within the contemporary scene make aesthetics a rich and exciting field within philosophy. There continues to be a lively debate about puzzles that arise in the arts in general, and this work is increasingly informed by methods and results from other areas of philosophy and related disciplines. At the same time, more attention is being paid to problems that arise in specific media, problems whose resolution may be aided by information about the production and history of works of that type.

Note

1 Noël Carroll, *Introduction to Theories of Art Today* (Madison; WI: University of Wisconsin Press, 2000), p. 5.

34

Aesthetic Problems of Modern Philosophy

Stanley Cavell

Stanley Cavell is Professor Emeritus of Philosophy at Harvard University.

The Spirit of the Age is not easy to place, ontologically or empirically; and it is idle to suggest that creative effort must express its age, either because that cannot fail to happen, or because a new effort can create a new age. Still, one knows what it means when an art historian says, thinking of the succession of plastic styles, 'not everything is possible in every period'.[1] And that is equally true for every person and every philosophy. But then one is never sure what is possible until it happens; and when it happens it may produce a sense of revolution, of the past escaped and our problems solved – even when we also know that one man's solution is another man's problem.

Wittgenstein expressed his sense both of the revolutionary break his later methods descry in philosophy, and of their relation to methods in aesthetics and ethics.[2] I have tried, in what follows, to suggest ways in which such feelings or claims can be understood, believing them to be essential in understanding Wittgenstein's later philosophy as a whole. The opening section outlines two problems in aesthetics each of which seems to yield to the possibilities of Wittgensteinian procedures, and in turn to illuminate them. The concluding section suggests resemblances between one kind of judgment recognizable as aesthetic and the characteristic claim of Wittgenstein – and of ordinary language philosophers generally – to voice 'what we should ordinarily say'.

What I have written, and I suppose the way I have written, grows from a sense that philosophy is in one of its periodic crises of method, heightened by a worry I am sure is not mine alone, that method dictates to content; that, for example, an intellectual commitment to analytical philosophy trains concern away from the wider, traditional problems of human culture which may have brought one to philosophy in the first place. Yet one can find oneself unable to relinquish either the method or the alien concern.

A free eclecticism of method is one obvious solution to such a problem. Another solution may be to discover further freedoms or possibilities within the method one finds closest to oneself. I lean here towards the latter of these alternatives, hoping to make philosophy yet another kind of problem for itself; in particular, to make the medium of philosophy – that is, of Wittgensteinian and, more generally, of ordinary language philosophy – a significant problem for aesthetics.

Stanley Cavell, "Aesthetic Problems of Modern Philosophy," in *Philosophy in America*, ed. Max Black (Ithaca, NY: Cornell University Press, 1965), pp. 74–97. © 1965. Reprinted by permission of Taylor & Francis Books UK.

Two Problems of Aesthetics[3]

Let us begin with a sheer matter of words – the controversy about whether a poem, or more modestly, a metaphor, can be paraphrased. Cleanth Brooks, in his *Well Wrought Urn*,[4] provided a convenient title for it in the expression 'The Heresy of Paraphrase', the heresy, namely, of supposing that a 'poem constitutes a "statement" of some sort' (p. 179); a heresy in which 'most of our difficulties in criticism are rooted'. (p. 184)

> The truth of the matter is that all such formulations [of what a poem says] lead away from the centre of the poem – not toward it; that the 'prose sense' of the poem is not a rack on which the stuff of the poem is hung; that it does not represent the 'inner' structure or the 'essential' structure or the 'real' structure of the poem. (p. 182) We can very properly use paraphrases as pointers and as short-hand references provided that we know what we are doing. But it is highly important that we know what we are doing and that we see plainly that the paraphrase is not the real core of meaning which constitutes the essence of the poem. (p. 180)

We may have some trouble in seeing plainly that the paraphrase is *not* the real core, or essence, or essential structure or inner or real structure of a poem; the same trouble we should have in understanding what *is* any or all of these things, since it takes so much philosophy just to state them. It is hard to imagine that someone has just flatly given it out that the essence, core, structure, and the rest, of a poem is its paraphrase. Probably somebody has been saying that poetry uses ornaments of style, or requires special poetic words; or has been saying what a poem means, or what it ought to mean – doing something that makes someone else, in a fit of philosophy, say that this is distorting a poem's essence. Now the person who is accused in Brooks' writ is probably going to deny guilt, feel that words are being put into his mouth, and answer that he knows perfectly well that a 'paraphrase, of course, is not the equivalent of a poem; a poem is more than its paraphrasable content'. Those are the words of Yvor Winters, whose work Professor Brooks uses as '[furnishing] perhaps the most respectable example of the paraphrastic heresy' (p. 183).[5] And so the argument goes, and goes. It has the gait of a false issue – by which I do not mean that it will be easy to straighten out.

One clear symptom of this is Brooks' recurrent concessions that, of course, a paraphrase is all right – if you know what you're doing. Which is about like saying that of course criticism is all right, in its place; which is true enough. But how, in particular, are we to assess a critic's reading the opening stanza of Wordsworth's 'Intimations' Ode and writing: '. . . the poet begins by saying that he has lost something' (Brooks, p. 116). We can ransack that stanza and never find the expression 'lost something' in it. Then the critic will be offended – rightly – and he may reply: Well, it does not actually say this, but it means it, it implies it; do you suggest that it does not mean that? And of course we do not. But then the critic has a *theory* about what he is doing when he says what a poem means, and so he will have to add some appendices to his readings of the poetry explaining that when he says what a poem means he does not say exactly quite just what the poem means; that is, he only points to its meaning, or rather 'points to the area in which the meaning lies'. But even this last does not seem to him humility enough, and he may be moved to a footnote in which he says that his own analyses are 'at best crude approximations of the poem'. (p. 189) By this time someone is likely to burst out with: But *of course* a paraphrase says what the poem says, and an *approximate* paraphrase is merely a bad paraphrase; with greater effort or sensibility you could have got it exactly right. To which one response would be: 'Oh, I can tell you exactly what the Ode means', and then read the Ode aloud.

Is there no real way out of this air of self-defeat, no way to get *satisfying* answers? Can we discover what, in such an exchange, is causing that uneasy sense that the speakers are talking past one another? Surely each knows exactly what the other means; neither is pointing to the smallest fact that the other fails to see.

For one suggestion, look again at Brooks' temptation to say that his readings *approximate* to (the meaning of) the poem. He is not there confessing his personal ineptitude; he means that any paraphrase, the best, will be only an approximation. So he is not saying, what he was accused of saying, that his own paraphrase was, in some more or less definite way, inexact or faulty: he denies the ordinary contrast between 'approximate' and 'exact'. And can he not do that if he wants to? Well, if I am right, he *did* do it. Although it is not clear that he *wanted* to. Perhaps he was *led* to it; and did he realize that, and would his realizing it make any difference? It may help to say: In speaking of the paraphrase as approximating to the poem (the meaning of the poem?) he himself furthers the suggestion that paraphrase and poem operate, as it were, at the same level, are the same kind of thing. (One shade of colour approximates to another shade, it does not approximate, nor does it fail to approximate, to the object of which it is the colour. An arrow pointing approximately north is exactly pointing somewhere. One paraphrase may be approximately the same, have approximately the same meaning, as another paraphrase.) And then he has to do everything at his philosophical disposal to keep paraphrase and poem from coinciding; in particular, speak of cores and essences and structures of the poem that are not reached by the paraphrase. It is as if someone got it into his head that really pointing to an object would require actually touching it, and then, realizing that this would make life very inconvenient, reconciled himself to common sense by saying: of course we *can* point to objects, but we must realize what we are doing, and that most of the time this is only approximately pointing to them.

This is the sort of thing that happens with astonishing frequency in philosophy. We impose a demand for absoluteness (typically of some simple physical kind) upon a concept, and then, finding that our ordinary use of this concept does not meet our demand, we accommodate this discrepancy as nearly as possible. Take these familiar patterns: we do not really see material objects, but only see them indirectly; we cannot be certain of any empirical proposition, but only practically certain; we cannot really know what another person is feeling, but only infer it. One of Wittgenstein's greatest services, to my mind, is to show how constant a feature of philosophy this pattern is: this is something that his diagnoses are meant to explain ('We have a certain picture of how something must be'; 'Language is idling; not doing work; being used apart from its ordinary language games'). Whether his diagnoses are themselves satisfying is another question. It is not very likely, because if the phenomenon is as common as he seems to have shown, its explanation will evidently have to be very much clearer and more complete than his sketches provide.

This much, however, is true: If you put such phrases as 'giving the meaning', 'giving a paraphrase', 'saying exactly what something means (or what somebody said)', and so on, into the ordinary contexts (the 'language games') in which they are used, you will not find that you are worried that you have not really *done* these things. We could say: *That* is what doing them really is. Only that serenity will last just so long as someone does not start philosophizing about it. Not that I want to stop him; only I want to know what it is he is then doing, and why he follows just those particular tracks.

We owe it to Winters to make it clear that he does not say any of the philosophical things Brooks attributes to him. His thesis, having expressed his total acquiescence to the fact that paraphrases are not poems, is that *some* poems cannot be paraphrased – in particular, poems of the chief poetic talent of the United States during the second and third decades of the twentieth century; that poems which are unparaphrasable are, in that specific way, defective; and that therefore this poetic talent was led in regrettable directions. The merit of this argument for us, whether we agree with its animus or not, and trying to keep special theories about poetic discourse at arm's length, is its recognition that paraphrasability is one definite characteristic of uses of language, a characteristic that some expressions have and some do not have. It suggests itself that uses of language can be distinguished according to whether or not they possess this characteristic, and further distinguished by the kind of paraphrase they demand. Let us pursue this suggestion with a few examples, following Wittgenstein's idea that we can find out what kind of object anything (grammatically) is (for example, a meaning) by investigating expressions which show the kind of thing said about it (for example, 'explaining the meaning').

It is worth saying that the clearest case of a use of language having no paraphrase is its literal use. If I tell you, 'Juliet [the girl next door] is not yet fourteen years old' and you ask me what I mean, I might do many things – ask you what *you* mean, or perhaps try to teach you the meaning of some expression you cannot yet use (which, as Wittgenstein goes to extraordinary lengths to show, is not the same thing as *telling* you what it means). Or again, if I say, 'Sufficient unto the day is the evil thereof', which I take to be the literal truth, then if I need to explain my meaning to you I shall need to do other things: I shall perhaps not be surprised that you do not get my meaning and so I shall hardly ask you, in my former spirit, what you mean in asking me for it; nor shall I, unless my disappointment pricks me into offense, offer to teach you the meaning of an English expression. What I might do is to try to *put my thought another way*, and perhaps refer you, depending upon who you are, to a range of similar or identical thoughts expressed by others. What I cannot (logically) do in either the first or the second case is to *paraphrase* what I said.

Now suppose I am asked what someone means who says 'Juliet is the sun'. Again my options are different, and specific. Again I am not, not in the same way, surprised that you ask; but I shall *not* try to put the thought another way – which seems to be the whole truth in the view that metaphors are unparaphrasable, that their meaning is bound up in the very words they employ. (The addition adds nothing: where else is it imagined, in that context, that meanings are bound, or found?) I may say something like: Romeo means that Juliet is the warmth of his world; that his day begins with her; that only in her nourishment can he grow. And his declaration suggests that the moon, which other lovers use as emblems of their love, is merely her reflected light, and dead in comparison; and so on. In a word, I paraphrase it. Moreover, if I could not provide an explanation of this form, then that is a very good reason, a perfect reason, for supposing that I do not know what it means. Metaphors are paraphrasable. (And if that is true, it is tautologous.) When, Croce denied the possibility of paraphrase, he at least had the grace to assert that there were no metaphors.

Two points now emerge: (1) The 'and so on' which ends my example of paraphrase is significant. It registers what William Empson calls the 'pregnancy' of metaphors, the burgeoning of meaning in them. Call it what you like; in this feature metaphors differ from some, but perhaps not all, literal discourse. And differ from the similar device of simile: the inclusion of 'like' in an expression changes the rhetoric. If you say 'Juliet is like the sun', two alterations at least seem obvious: the drive of it leads me to expect you to continue by saying in what definite respects they are like (similes are just a little bit pregnant); and, in complement, I *wait* for you to tell me what you mean, to deliver your meaning, so to speak. It is not up to me to find as much as I can in your words. The over-reading of metaphors so often complained of, no doubt justly, is a hazard they must run for their high interest. (2) To give the paraphrase, to understand the metaphor, I must understand the ordinary or dictionary meaning of the words it contains, *and* understand that they are not there being used in their ordinary way, that the meanings they invite are not to be found opposite them in a dictionary. In this respect the words in metaphors function as they do in idioms. But idioms are, again, specifically different. 'I fell flat on my face' seems an appropriate case. To explain its meaning is simply to *tell* it – one might say you don't *explain* it at all; either you know what it means or you don't; there is no richer and poorer among its explanations; you need imagine nothing special in the mind of the person using it. And you will find it in a dictionary, though in special locations; which suggests that, unlike metaphors, the number of idioms in a language is finite.[6]

One final remark about the difference between idioms and metaphors. Any theory concerned to account for peculiarities of metaphor of the sort I have listed will wonder over the literal meaning its words, in that combination, have. This is a response, I take it, to the fact that a metaphorical expression (in the '*A* is *B*' form at least) sounds like an ordinary assertion, though perhaps not made by an ordinary mind. Theory aside, I want to look at the suggestion, often made, that what metaphors literally say is *false*. (This is a response to the well-marked characteristic of 'psychic tension' set up in metaphors. The mark is used by Empson; I do not know the patent.) But to say that Juliet is the sun is not to say something false; it is, at best, wildly false, and that is not being just false. This is part of the fact that if we are to suggest that what the metaphor says is true, we shall have to say it is wildly true – mythically or magically or primitively true. (Romeo just may be young enough, or crazed or heretic enough, to have meant his words literally.) About some idioms, however, it is fair to say that their words literally say something that is quite false; something, that is, which could easily, though maybe comically, imagined to be true. Someone might actually fall flat on his face, have a thorn in his side, a bee in his bonnet, a bug in his ear, or a fly in his ointment – even all at once, Then what are we to say about the literal meaning of a metaphor? That it has none? And that what it literally says is not false, *and* not true? And that it is not an assertion? But it sounds like one: and people do think it is true and people do think it is false. I am suggesting that it is such facts that will need investigating if we are to satisfy ourselves about metaphors; that we are going to keep getting philosophical theories about metaphor until such facts are investigated; and that this is not an occasion for adjudication, for the only thing we could offer now in that line would be: all the theories are right in what they say. And that seems to imply that all are wrong as well.

At this point we might be able to give more content to the idea that some modes of figurative language are such that in them what an expression means cannot be said at all, at least not in any of the more or less familiar, conventionalized ways so far noticed. Not because these modes are flatly literal – there is, as it were, room for an explanation, but we cannot enter it. About such an expression it may be right to say: I know what it means but I can't say what it means. And this would no longer suggest, as it would if said about a metaphor, that you really do not know what it means – or: it might suggest it, but you couldn't be sure.

Examples of such uses of language would, I think, characteristically occur in specific kinds of poetry, for example Symbolist, Surrealist or Imagist. Such a use seems to me present in a line like Hart Crane's 'The mind is brushed by sparrow wings' [cited, among others, in the Winters essay], and in Wallace Stevens' 'as a calm darkens among water-lights', from *Sunday Morning*. Paraphrasing the lines, or explaining their meaning, or telling it, or putting the thought another way – all these are out of the question. One may be able to say nothing except that a feeling has been voiced by a kindred spirit and that if someone does not get it he is not in one's world, or not of one's flesh. The lines may, that is, be left as touchstones of intimacy. Or one might try *describing* more or less elaborately a particular day or evening, a certain place and mood and gesture, in whose presence the line in question comes to seem a natural expression, the only expression.

This seems to be what Winters, who profitably distinguishes several varieties of such uses of languages, distrusts and dislikes in his defence of reason, as he also seems prepared for the reply that this is not a *failing* of language but a feature of a specific approach of language. At least I think it is a reply of this sort, which I believe to be right, that he wishes to repudiate by appealing to 'the fallacy of expressive (or imitative) form', instanced by him at one point as 'Whitman trying to express a loose America by writing loose poetry', or 'Mr. Joyce [endeavouring] to express disintegration by breaking down his form'. It is useful to have a name for this fallacy, which no doubt some people commit. But his remarks seem a bit quick in their notation of what Whitman and Joyce were trying to express, and in their explanation of why they had to express themselves as they did; too sure that a break with the past of the order represented in modern art was not itself necessary in order to defend reason; too sure that convention can still be attacked in conventional ways. And they suggest scorn for the position that a high task of art has become, in our bombardment of sound, to create silence. (*Being* silent for that purpose might be a good example of the fallacy of imitative form. But that would depend on the context.) The fact is that I feel I would have to forgo too much of modern art were I to take his view of it.

Before we leave him, we owe it to Brooks to acknowledge a feature of Winters' position which may be causing his antipathy to it. Having wished to save Winters from a misconstruction of paraphrase, we gave back to that notion a specificity which, it now emerges, opens him to further objection. For his claim that poems that cannot be paraphrased – or, as he also puts it, do not 'rest on a formulable logic' – are therefore defective now means or implies that all poems not made essentially of metaphorical language (and/or similes, idioms, literal statements) are defective. It is certainly to be hoped that all *criticism* be rational, to be demanded that it form coherent propositions about its art. But to suppose that this requires all poetry to be 'formulable', in the sense that it must, whatever its form and pressure, yield to paraphrase, the way single metaphors specifically do, is not only unreasonable past defence but incurs what we might call the fallacy of expressive criticism.

In summary: Brooks is wrong to say that poems cannot in principle be fully paraphrased, but right to be worried about the relation between paraphrase and poem; Winters is right in his perception that some poetry is 'formulable' and some not, but wrong in the assurance he draws from that fact; both respond to, but fail to follow, the relation between criticism and its object. And now, I think, we can be brought more unprotectedly to face the whole question that motivates such a conflict, namely what it is we are doing when we describe or explain a work of art; what function criticism serves; whether different arts, or forms of art, require different forms of criticism; what we may expect to learn from criticism, both about a particular piece of art and about the nature of art generally.

The second problem in aesthetics must be sketched even more swiftly and crudely.

Is such music as is called 'atonal' (not distinguishing that, for our purposes now, from the term 'twelve-tone') really without tonality? (The little I will say could be paralleled, I think, in discussing the nature of the painting or sculpture called abstract or non-objective.) The arguments are bitter and, to my knowledge, without issue; and many musicians have felt within themselves both an affirmative and a negative answer.[7] Against the idea that this music lacks tonality are (1) the theory that we are so trained to our perception of musical organization that we cannot help hearing it in a tonal frame of reference; and (2) the fact that one *can*, often, *say* what key a so-called 'atonal' piece is in. In favour of the idea that it lacks tonality are (1) a theory of composition which says that it does, and whose point was just to escape that limitation, while yet maintaining coherence; and (2) the fact that it simply sounds so different. Without our now even glancing at the theories, let us look at the fact we recorded as 'being able to say, often, what key a piece is in'. Does that have the weight it seems to have? An instance which once convinced me of its decisiveness was this: in listening to a song of Schoenberg's, I had a clear sense that I could, at three points; hear it cadence (I almost said, try to resolve) in F# minor. Then surely it is *in* F# minor? Well, the Chopin *Barcarolle* is in the key of F# major. How do I know that? Because I can hear it try to cadence in F# major? Three or more times? And after that I am convinced it is, feel slightly relieved and even triumphant that I have been able to hear some F# major? But that is absurd. I *know* the key; everyone knows it; everyone knows it from the opening measure – well, at least before the bass figure that begins on the pitch of F#: it does not take a brick wall to fall on us. I would not even know how to go about doubting its key or *trying* to hear it in its key. And I know it because I know that now it has moved to the sub-dominant of the key, and now the dominant of the key is being extended, and now it is modulating, and now it is modulating to a more distant key. And to know all this is to know the grammar of the expression 'musical key'. Sometimes, to be sure, a solidly tonal composer will, especially in 'development sections', obliterate the sense of placement in a key; but this is here a special effect, and depends upon an undoubted establishment of key. So if I insist upon saying that atonal music is really tonal (and to be said it has to be insisted upon) I have, so far as my ear goes, to forgo the grammar of the expression 'tonality' or 'musical key' – or almost all of it: I can retain 'almost cadences in' and 'sounds like the dominant of' but not 'related key', 'distant key', 'modulation' etc. And then I am in danger of not knowing what I am saying. Wittgenstein says that 'the speaking of language is part of an activity, or of a form of life' (*Investigations*, par. 23), and also 'To imagine a language means to imagine a form of life' (ibid., par. 19). The language of tonality is part of a particular form of life, one containing the music we are most familiar with; associated with, or consisting of, particular ways of being trained to perform it and to listen to it; involving particular ways of being corrected, particular ways of responding to mistakes, to nuance, above all to recurrence and to variation and modification. No wonder we want to preserve the idea of tonality: to give all *that* up seems like giving up the idea of music altogether. I think it *is* – *like* it.

I shall not try to say why it is not fully that. I shall only mention that it cannot be enough to point to the obvious fact that musical instruments, with their familiar or unfamiliar powers, are employed – because *that* fact does not prevent us from asking, But is it music? Nor enough to appeal to the fact that we can point to pitches, intervals, lines and rhythm – because we probably do not for the most part know what we are pointing to with these terms. I mean we do not know *which* lines are significant (try to play the 'melody' or 'bass' of a piece of Webern's) and which intervals to hear as organizing. More important, I think, is the fact that we may see an undoubted musician speak about such things and behave toward them in ways similar (not, I think, more than similar) to the ways he behaves toward, say, Beethoven, and then we may sense that, though similar, it is a new world and that to understand a new world it is imperative to concentrate upon its inhabitants. (Of course there will be the usual consequences of mimicry and pretension.) Moreover, but still perhaps even more rarely, we may find ourselves *within* the experience of such compositions, following them; and then the question whether this is music and the problem of its tonal sense, will be . . . not answered or solved, but rather they will disappear, seem irrelevant.

That is, of course, Wittgenstein's sense of the way philosophical problems end. It is true that for him, in the *Investigations* at any rate, this happens when we have gone through a process of bringing ourselves back into our natural forms of life, putting our souls back into our bodies; whereas I had to describe the accommodation of the new music as one of naturalizing ourselves to a new form of life, a new world. That a resolution of this sort is described as the solution of a philosophical problem, and as the goal of its particular mode of criticism, represents for me the most original contribution Wittgenstein offers philosophy. I can think of no closer title for it, in an established philosophical vocabulary, than Hegel's use of the term *Aufhebung.* We cannot translate the term: 'cancelling', 'negating', 'fulfilling' etc. are all partial, and 'sublate' transfers the problem. It seems to me to capture that sense of *satisfaction* in our representation of rival positions which I was asking for when I rehearsed the problems of Brooks and Winters. Of course we are no longer very apt to suppose, with Hegel, that History will make us a present of it: we are too aware of its brilliant ironies and its aborted revolutions for that. But as an ideal of (one kind of) philosophical criticism – a criticism in which it is pointless for one side to refute the other, because its cause and topic is the self getting in its own way – it seems about right.

In the *Tractatus* Wittgenstein says: 'The solution of the problem of life is seen in the vanishing of the problem' (6.521); and in the *Investigations* he says: '. . . the clarity that we are aiming at is indeed *complete* clarity. But this simply means that the philosophical problems should *completely* disappear' (par. 133), Yet he calls these problems *solved* (*Investigations*, ibid.); and he says that when 'there are . . . no questions left . . . this itself is the *answer*' (*Tractatus*; 6.25, my emphasis). In the central concept of his later work, this would seem to mean that the problems of life and the problems of philosophy have related grammars, because solutions to them both have the same form: their problems are solved only when they disappear, and answers are arrived at only when there are no longer questions – when, as it were, our accounts have cancelled them.

But in the *Investigations* this turns out to be more of an answer than, left this way, it seems to be; for it more explicitly dictates and displays the ways philosophy is to proceed in investigating problems, ways leading to what he calls 'perspicuous representation' (*übersichtliche Darstellung*). It is my impression that many philosophers do not like Wittgenstein's comparing what he calls his 'methods' to therapies (par. 133); but for me part of what he means by this comparison is brought out in thinking of the progress of psychoanalytic therapy. The more one learns, so to speak, the hang of oneself, and mounts one's problems, the less one is able to *say* what one has learned; not because you have *forgotten* what it was, but because nothing you said would seem like an answer or a solution: there is no longer any question or problem which your words would match. You have reached conviction, but not about a proposition; and consistency, but not in a theory. You are different, what you recognize as problems are different, your world is different. ('The world of the happy man is a different one from that of the unhappy man' (*Tractatus*, 6.43).) And this is the sense, the only sense, in which what a work of art means cannot be *said.* Believing it is seeing it.

When Wittgenstein says that 'the concept of a perspicuous representation . . . earmarks the form of account we give' (par. 122), I take him to be making a grammatical remark about what he calls a 'grammatical investigation', which is what his *Investigations* consist in (par. 90): no other form of resolution will count as philosophical. He says of his 'form of account' that it is 'the way we look at things'; and he then asks, parenthetically, 'Is this a "Weltanschauung"?' (par. 122). The answer to that question is, I take it, not No. Not, perhaps, Yes; because it is not a *special*, or competing, way of looking at things. But not No; because its mark of success is that the world seem – be – different. As usual, the claim to severe philosophical advance entails a reconception of the subject, a specific sense of revolution.

Aesthetic Judgment and a Philosophical Claim

Another good cause for stumbling over the procedures of ordinary language philosophy lies in its characteristic appeal to what 'we' say and mean, or cannot or must say or mean. A good cause, since it is a very particular, not to say peculiar appeal, and one would expect philosophers dependent upon it themselves to be concerned for its investigation. I will suggest that the aesthetic judgment models the sort of claim entered by these philosophers, and that the familiar lack of conclusiveness in aesthetic argument, rather than showing up an irrationality, shows the kind of rationality it has, and needs.

Hume is always a respectable place to begin. Near the middle of his essay 'Of the Standard of Taste', he has recourse to a story from *Don Quixote* which is to illustrate that 'delicacy' of taste said to be essential to those critics who are to form our standard of it.

> It is with good reason, says Sancho to the squire with the great nose, that I pretend to have a judgment in wine: This is a quality hereditary in our family. Two of my kinsmen were once called in to give their opinion of a hogshead, which was supposed to be excellent, being old and of a good vintage. One of them tastes it; considers it; and after mature reflection pronounces the wine to be good, were it not for a small taste of leather, which he perceived in it. The other, after using the same precautions, gives also his verdict in favour of the wine; but with the reserve of a taste of iron, which he could easily distinguish. You cannot imagine how much they were both ridiculed for their judgment. But who laughed in the end? On emptying the hogshead, there was found at the bottom, an old key with a leathern thong tied to it.

First of all, the fine drama of this gesture is greater than its factual decisiveness – a bit quixotic, so to say: for the taste may have been present and the object not, or the object present and the taste not. Second, and more important, the gesture misrepresents the efforts of the critic and the sort of vindication to which he aspires. It dissociates the exercise of taste from the discipline of accounting for it: but *all* that makes the critic's expression of taste worth more than another man's is his ability to produce for himself the thong and key of his response; and his vindication comes not from his pointing out that it is, or was, in the barrel, but in getting us to taste it there. Sancho's ancestors, he tells us, in each case after the precautions of reflection, both pronounced in favour of the wine; but he does not tell us what those reflections were, nor whether they were vindicated in their favourable verdict. Hume's essay, I take it, undertakes to explore just such questions, but in his understandable difficulty in directing us to the genuine critic and distinguishing him from the pretender, he says about him just what he, or anyone, says about art itself: that he is valuable, that we may disagree about his merits in a particular case, and that some, in the long run, 'will be acknowledged by universal sentiment to have a preference above others'. But this seems to put the critic's worth at the mercy of the history of taste; whereas his value to us is that he is able to make that history a part of his data, knowing that in itself, as it stands, it proves nothing – except popularity. His value to art and culture is not that he agrees with its taste – which would make him useful for guiding one's investments in the art market – but that he sets the terms in which our tastes, whatever they happen to be, may be protected, or overcome. Sancho's descendants would, by the eighteenth century, have risen to gentlemen, exercising distinction in a world which knew what was right, and not needing to make their tastes their own. But it is Quixote who is the patron saint of the critic, desperate to preserve the best of his culture against itself, and surviving any failure but that of his honesty and his expression of it.

The idea of the agreement or 'reconciliation' of taste controls Hume's argument; it is agreement that the standard of taste is to provide, so far as that is attainable. Hume's descendants, catching the assumption that agreement provides the vindication of judgment, but no longer able to hope for either, have found that aesthetic (and moral and political) judgments, lack something: the arguments that support them are not conclusive the way arguments in logic are, nor rational the way arguments in science are. Indeed they are not, and if they were there would be no such subject as art (or morality) and no such art as criticism. It does not follow, however, that such judgments are not conclusive and rational.

Let us turn to Kant on the subject, who is, here as elsewhere, deeper and obscurer. Universal agreement, or as he also calls it, the 'harmony of sentiment' or 'a common sense of mankind', makes its appearance in the *Critique of Judgment* not as an empirical problem – which is scarcely surprising about Kant's procedure – but as an *a priori* requirement setting the (transcendental) conditions under which such judgments as we call aesthetic could be made *überhaupt.* Kant begins by saying that aesthetic judgment is not 'theoretical', not 'logical', not 'objective', but one 'whose determining ground can be *no other than subjective*'.[8] Today, or anyway the day before yesterday, and largely under his influence, we would have said it is not cognitive; which says so little that it *might* have been harmless enough. Kant goes on immediately to distinguish two kinds of 'aesthetical judgments', or, as he also calls them, judgments of taste; and here, unfortunately, his influence trickled out. The first kind he calls the taste of sense, the second the taste of reflection; the former concerns merely what we find pleasant, the latter must – logically must, some of us would say – concern and claim more than that. And it is only the second whose topic is the beautiful, whose role, that is, would be aesthetic in its more familiar sense. The something more these judgments must do is to 'demand' or 'impute' or 'claim' general validity, universal agreement with it; and when we make such judgments we go on claiming this agreement even though we know from experience that they will not receive it. (Are we, then, just wilful or stupid in going on making them?) Kant also describes our feeling or belief when we make such judgments – judgments in which we demand 'the assent of everyone', although we cannot 'postulate' this assent as we could in making an ordinary empirical judgment – as one of '[speaking] with a universal voice'. That is the sort of thing that we are likely nowadays to call a piece of psychology, which is no doubt right enough. But we would take that to mean that it marks an accidental accompaniment of such judgments; whereas Kant says about this claim to universal validity, this voice, that it 'so essentially belongs to a judgment by which we describe anything as *beautiful* that, if this were not thought in it, it would never come into our thoughts to use the expression at all, but everything which pleases without a concept would be counted as pleasant'.[9] The possibility of stupidity here is not one of continuing to demand agreement in the face of the fact that we won't attain it; but the stupidity of going on making aesthetic judgments at all (or moral or political ones) in the face of what they cost us, the difficulties of finding them for ourselves and the risk of explicit isolation.

Kant seems to be saying that apart from a certain spirit in which we make judgments we could have no concepts of the sort we think of as aesthetic.[10] What can the basis for such a claim be? Let us look at the examples he gives of his two kinds of aesthetic judgments.

> . . . [someone] is quite contented that if he says, "Canary wine is pleasant," another man may correct his expression and remind him that he ought to say, "It is pleasant *to me.*" And this is the case not only as regards the taste of the tongue, the palate, and the throat, but for whatever is pleasant to anyone's eyes and ears. . . . To strive here with the design of reproving as incorrect another man's judgment which is different from our own, as if the judgments were logically opposed, would be folly. . . .
>
> The case is quite different with the beautiful. It would (on the contrary) be laughable if a man who imagined anything to his own taste thought to justify himself by saying: "This object (the house we see, the coat that person wears, the concert we hear, the poem submitted to our judgment) is beautiful *for me.*" For he must not call it *beautiful* if it merely pleases him. . . .

What are these examples supposed to show? That using a form of expression in one context is all right, and using it in another is not all right. But what I wish to focus upon is the kind of rightness and wrongness invoked: it is not a matter of factual rectitude, nor of formal indiscretion but of saying something laughable, or which would be folly. It is such consequences that are taken to display a difference in the kind of judgment in question, in the nature of the concepts employed, and even in the nature of the reality the concepts capture. One hardly knows whether to call this a metaphysical or a logical difference. Kant called it a transcendental difference; Wittgenstein would call it a grammatical difference. And how can psychological differences like finding something laughable or foolish (which perhaps not *every* person would) be thought to betray such potent, or anyway different, differences?

Here we hit upon what is, to my mind, the most sensitive index of misunderstanding and bitterness between the positivist and the post-positivist components of analytical philosophy: the positivist grits his teeth when he hears an analysis given out as a logical one which is so painfully remote from formality, so obviously a question of how you happen to feel at the moment, so psychological; the philosopher who proceeds from everyday language stares back helplessly, asking, 'Don't you feel the difference? Listen: you *must* see it.' Surely, both know what the other knows, and each thinks the other is perverse, or irrelevant, or worse. (Here I must appeal to the experience of anyone who has been engaged in such encounters.) Any explanation of this is going to be hard to acquire. I offer the following guess, not because it can command much attention in itself, but as a way of suggesting the level I would expect a satisfying explanation to reach, a way of indicating why we lack as yet the concepts, even the facts, which must form a serious accommodation.

We know of the efforts of such philosophers as Frege and Husserl to undo the 'psychologizing' of logic (like Kant's undoing Hume's psychologizing of knowledge): now, the shortest way I might describe such a book as the *Philosophical Investigations* is to say that it attempts to undo the psychologizing of psychology, to show the necessity controlling our application of psychological and behavioural categories; even, one could say, show the necessities in human action and passion themselves.[11] And at the same time it seems to turn all of philosophy into psychology – matters of what we call things, how we treat them, what their role is in our lives.

For one last glance, let us adapt Kant's examples to a form which is more fashionable, and think of the sort of reasons we offer for such judgments:

1. *A*: Canary wine is pleasant.
   B: How can you say that? It tastes like canary droppings.
   A: Well, I like it.
2. *A*: He plays beautifully doesn't he?
   B1: Yes; too beautifully. Beethoven is not Chopin.

Or he may answer:

B2: How can you say that? There was no line, no structure, no idea what the music was about. He's simply an impressive colourist.

Now, how will *A* reply? Can he now say: 'Well, I liked it'? Of course he *can;* but don't we feel that here that would be a feeble rejoinder, a *retreat* to personal taste? Because *B*'s reasons are obviously relevant to the evaluation of performance, and because they are *arguable*, in ways that anyone who knows about such things will know how to pursue. *A doesn't have* to pursue them; but if he doesn't, there is a price he will have to pay in our estimate of him. Is that enough to show it is a different kind of judgment? We are still in the realm of the psychological. But I wish to say that the price is necessary, and specific to the sorts of judgments we call aesthetic.

Go back to my saying 'he doesn't have to pursue' the discussion, and compare the following case:

A: There is a goldfinch in the garden.
B: How do you know?
A: From the colour of its head.
B: But goldcrests also have heads that colour.
A: Well, *I* think it's a goldfinch (it's a goldfinch to me).

This is no longer a feeble rejoinder, a retreat to personal opinion: and the price that would be paid here is not, as it would be in the former case, that he is not very articulate, or not discriminating, or has perverse tastes: the price here is that he is either mad, or doesn't know what the word 'know' means, or is in some other way unintelligible to us. That is, *we rule him out* as a competent interlocutor in matters of knowledge (about birds?): whatever is going on, he *doesn't* know there is a goldfinch in the garden, whatever (else) he thinks he 'knows'. But we do not, at least not with the same flatness and good conscience, and not with the same consequences, rule out the person who liked the performance of the Beethoven: he still has a claim upon us, however attenuated; he *may* even have reasons for his judgment, or counters to your objections, which for some reason he can't give (perhaps because you've brow-beaten him into amnesia).

Leaving these descriptions so cruelly incomplete, I think one can now imagine the familiar response: 'But you admit that arguments in the aesthetic case may go on, may perhaps never end, and that they needn't go on, perhaps can't go on in some cases, and that they may have different "prices" (whatever they may mean), presumably depending on where they stop. How do you get logic out of that? What you cannot claim is that either party to the dispute, whether in the case Kant calls the taste of sense or the case he calls the taste of reflection, can *prove* his judgment. And would he want to even if he could? Isn't that, indeed, what all your talk about criticism was about: The person accounts for his own feelings, and then, at best "proves" them *to* another, shows them to whomever he wants to know them, the best way he can, the most effective way. That's scarcely logic; and how can you deny that it is psychology?'

It may help to reply to this: You call it psychology just because it so obviously is not logic, and it must be one or the other.[12] Contrariwise, I should admit that I call it 'logic' mostly because it so obviously is not 'psychology' in the way I think you mean it. I do not really think it is either of those activities, in the senses we attach to them now; but I cannot describe to anyone's satisfaction *what* it is. Wittgenstein called it 'grammar'; others might call it 'phenomenology'.

Those of us who keep finding ourselves wanting to call such differences 'logical' are, I think, responding to a sense of necessity we feel in them, together with a sense that necessity is, partly, a matter of the *ways* a judgment is supported, the ways in which conviction in it is produced: it is only by virtue of these recurrent patterns of support that a remark will count as – will be – aesthetic, or a mere matter of taste, or moral, propagandistic, religious, magical, scientific, philosophical. [. . .] It is essential to making an aesthetic judgment that at some point we be prepared to say in its support: don't you see, don't you hear, don't you dig? The best critic will know the best points. Because if you do not see *something*, without explanation, then there is nothing further to discuss. Which does not mean that the critic has no recourse: he can start training and instructing you and preaching at you – a direction in which criticism invariably will start to veer. (A critic like Ruskin may be a calamity, but he is no accident.) At some point, the critic will have to say: this is what I see. Reasons – at definite points, for definite reasons, in different circumstances – come to an end. (*Cf. Investigations*, par. 217.)

Those who refuse the term 'logic' are responding to a sense of arbitrariness in these differences, together with a sense that 'logic' is a matter of arriving at conviction in such a way that anyone who can follow the argument must, unless he finds something definitely wrong with it, *accept the conclusion*, agree with it. I do not know what the gains or disadvantages would be of unfastening the term 'logic' from that constant pattern of support or justification whose peculiarity is that it leads those competent at it to this kind of agreement, and extending it to patterns of justification having other purposes and peculiarities. All I am arguing for is that *pattern* and *agreement* are distinct features of the notion of logic.

If we say that the *hope* of agreement motivates our engaging in these various patterns of support, then we must also say, what I take Kant to have seen, that even were agreement in fact to emerge, our judgments, so far as aesthetic, would remain as essentially subjective, in his sense, as they ever were. Otherwise, art and the criticism of art would not have their special importance nor elicit their own forms of distrust and of gratitude. The problem of the critic, as of the artist, is not to discount his subjectivity, but to include it; not to overcome it in agreement, but to master it in exemplary ways. Then his work outlasts the fashions and arguments of a particular age. That is the beauty of it.

Kant's 'universal voice' is, with perhaps a slight shift of accent, what we hear recorded in the philosopher's claims about 'what we say': such claims are at least as close to what Kant calls aesthetical judgments as they are to ordinary empirical hypotheses. Though the philosopher seems to claim, or depend upon, severer agreement than is carried by the aesthetic analogue, I wish to suggest that it is a claim or dependence of the same kind.

We should immediately notice an obvious failure in the analogy between aesthetic judgments and the philosophical claim to voice what we say. The philosophical claim seems clearly open to refutation by an empirical collection of data about what people in fact say, whereas it makes no obvious sense to confirm or disconfirm such a judgment as 'The Hammerklavier Sonata is a perverse work' by collecting data to find out whether the Sonata is in fact perverse. It is out of the question to enter into this difficult range of problems now. But I cannot forbear mentioning several points which I have tried elsewhere to suggest, with, to judge from results, evident unsuccess.[13]

(1) I take it to be a phenomenological fact about philosophizing from everyday language that one feels empirical evidence about one's language to be irrelevant to one's claims. If such philosophizing is to be understood, then that fact about it must be understood. I am not saying that evidence about how (other) people speak can never make an ordinary language philosopher withdraw his typical claims; but I find it important that the most characteristic pressure against him is applied by producing or deepening an example which shows him that *he* would not say what he says 'we' say.

(2) The appeal to 'what we should say if . . .' requires that we imagine an example or story, sometimes one more or less similar to events which may happen any day, sometimes one unlike anything we have known. Whatever the difficulties will be in trying to characterize this procedure fully and clearly, this much can be said at once: if we find we disagree about what we should say, it would make no obvious sense to attempt to confirm or disconfirm one or other of our responses by collecting data to show which of us is in fact right. What we should do is either (*a*) to try to determine why we disagree (perhaps we are imagining the story differently) – just as, if we agree in response we will, when we start philosophizing about this fact, want to know why we agree, what it shows about our concepts; or (*b*) we will, if the disagreement cannot be explained, either find some explanation for *that*, or else discard the example. Disagreement is not disconfirming: it is as much a datum for philosophizing as agreement is. At this stage philosophizing has, hopefully, not yet begun.

(3) Such facts perhaps only amount to saying that the philosophy of ordinary language is not about language, anyway not in any sense in which it is not also about the world. Ordinary language philosophy is about whatever ordinary language is about.

The philosopher appealing to everyday language turns to the reader not to convince him without proof but to get him to prove something, test something, against himself. He is saying: look and find out whether you can see what I see, wish to say what I wish to say. Of course he often seems to answer or beg his own question by posing it in plural form: 'We say . . . ; We want to say . . . ; we can imagine . . . ; We feel as if we had to penetrate phenomena, repair a spider's web; We are under the illusion . . . ; We are dazzled . . . the idea now absorbs us . . . ; we are dissatisfied. . . .' But this plural is still first person: it does not, to use Kant's word, 'postulate' that 'we', you and I and he, say and want and imagine and feel and suffer together. If we do not, then the philosopher's remarks are irrelevant to us. Of course he doesn't think they are irrelevant, but the implication is that philosophy, like art, is, and should be, powerless to *prove* its relevance; and that says something about the kind of relevance it wishes to have. All the philosopher, this kind of philosopher, can do is to express, as fully as he can, his world, and attract our undivided attention to our own.

Kant's attention to the 'universal voice' expressed in aesthetic judgment seems to me, finally, to afford some explanation of that air of dogmatism which claims about what 'we' say seem to carry for critics of ordinary language procedures, and which they find repugnant and intolerant. I think that air of dogmatism is indeed present in such claims; but if that is intolerant, that is because tolerance could only mean, as in liberals it often does, that the kind of claim in question is not taken seriously. It is, after all, a claim about *our lives;* it is differences, or oppositions, of these that tolerance, if it is to be achieved, must be directed toward. About what we should say when, we do not expect to have to tolerate much difference, believing that if we could articulate it fully we would have spoken for all men, found the necessities common to us all. Philosophy has always hoped for that; so, perhaps, has science. But philosophy concerns those necessities we cannot, being human, fail to know. Except that nothing is more human than to deny them.

Notes

1 Heinrich Wolfflin, *Principles of Art History*, foreword to the 7th German edition. Quoted by E. H. Gombrich, *Art and Illusion*, New York 1960, p. 4.

2 Reported by G. E. Moore, 'Wittgenstein's Lectures in 1930–33', reprinted in Moore's *Philosophical Papers*, London 1959, p. 315.

3 Most of the material in this section was presented to a meeting of the American Society for Aesthetics at Harvard University in October 1962.

4 *The Well Wrought Urn*, New York 1947. All page references to Brooks are to this edition. 'The Heresy of Paraphrase' is the title of the concluding chapter.

5 For Winters' position, I have relied solely on his central essay, 'The Experimental School in American Poetry' from *Primitivism and Decadence*, itself republished, together with earlier of his critical works, under the title *In Defense of Reason.*

6 In some, though not all, of these respects the procedure of 'giving the meaning' of an idiom is like that in translating: one might think of it as translating from a given language into itself. Then how is it different from defining, or giving a synonym?

7 I am told, by Professor David Lewin, that this was true of Anton Webern, who was in doubt about his own music in this regard.

8 All quotations from Kant are from sections 7 and 8 of the *Critique of Judgment.*

9 One might compare with this Wittgenstein's question: 'What gives us *so much as the idea* that living beings, things, can feel?' *Investigations*, par. 283.

10 Another way of describing this assumption or demand, this thing of speaking with a universal voice, of judging 'not merely for himself, but for all men', Kant also describes as '(speaking) of beauty as if it were a property of things'. Only 'as if' because it cannot be an ordinary property of things: its presence or absence cannot be established in the way ordinary properties are; that is, they cannot be established publicly, and we don't know (there aren't any) causal conditions, or usable rules, for producing, or altering, or erasing, or increasing this 'property'. Then why not just say it *isn't* a property of an object? I suppose there would be no reason not to say this, if we could find another way of recording our conviction that it is one, anyway that what we are pointing to is *there,* in the object; and our knowledge that men make objects that create this response in us, and make them exactly with the idea that they will create it; and the fact that, while we know not everyone will agree with us when we say it is present, we think they are *missing something* if they don't.

11 Consider, for example, the question: 'Could someone have a feeling of ardent love or hope for the space of one second – *no matter what* preceded or followed this second?'; *Investigations,* par. 583. We shall not wish to say that this is logically impossible, or that it can in no way be imagined. But we might say: given our world this cannot happen; it is not, in our language, what 'love' or 'hope' mean; necessary in our world that this is not what love and hope are. I take it that our most common philosophical understanding of such notions as necessity, contingency, synthetic and analytic statements will not know what to make of our saying such things.

12 I do think that is the *entire* content of 'psychology' in such objections. Such a person knows what he means by logic: how to do it, how to recognize it when he sees it done, what he can expect from it, etc. But who knows any of this about the 'psychology' in question?

13 See J. Fodor and J. Katz, 'The Availability of What We Say', in the *Philosophical Review,* January 1963, an attack, primarily, on my paper 'Must We Mean What We Say?' which appeared in *Inquiry* in 1958 (vol. I, no. 3).

35

The Role of Theory in Aesthetics

Morris Weitz

Morris Weitz (1916–81) was Professor of Philosophy at Brandeis University and Ohio State University.

Theory has been central in aesthetics and is still the preoccupation of the philosophy of art. Its main avowed concern remains the determination of the nature of art which can be formulated into a definition of it. It construes definition as the statement of the necessary and sufficient properties of what is being defined, where the statement purports to be a true or false claim about the essence of art, what characterizes and distinguishes it from everything else. Each of the great theories of art – Formalism, Voluntarism, Emotionalism, Intellectualism, Intuitionism, Organicism – converges on the attempt to state the defining properties of art. Each claims that it is the true theory because it has formulated correctly into a real definition the nature of art; and that the others are false because they have left out some necessary or sufficient property. Many theorists contend that their enterprise is no mere intellectual exercise but an absolute necessity for any understanding of art and our proper evaluation of it. Unless we know what art is, they say, what are its necessary and sufficient properties, we cannot begin to respond to it adequately or to say why one work is good or better than another. Aesthetic theory, thus, is important not only in itself but for the foundations of both appreciation and criticism. Philosophers, critics, and even artists who have written on art, agree that what is primary in aesthetics is a theory about the nature of art.

Is aesthetic theory, in the sense of a true definition or set of necessary and sufficient properties of art, possible? If nothing else does, the history of aesthetics itself should give one enormous pause here. For, in spite of the many theories, we seem no nearer our goal today than we were in Plato's time. Each age, each art-movement, each philosophy of art, tries over and over again to establish the stated ideal only to be succeeded by a new or revised theory, rooted, at least in part, in the repudiation of preceding ones. Even today, almost everyone interested in aesthetic matters is still deeply wedded to the hope that the correct theory of art is forthcoming. We need only examine the numerous new books on art in which new definitions are proffered; or, in our own country especially, the basic textbooks and anthologies to recognize how strong the priority of a theory of art is.

In this essay I want to plead for the rejection of this problem. I want to show that theory – in the requisite classical sense – is *never* forthcoming in aesthetics, and that we would do much better

Morris Weitz, "The Role of Theory in Aesthetics," *Journal of Aesthetics and Art Criticism*, 15/1 (1956): 27–35.

as philosophers to supplant the question, "What is the nature of art?," by other questions, the answers to which will provide us with all the understanding of the arts there can be. I want to show that the inadequacies of the theories are not primarily occasioned by any legitimate difficulty such e.g., as the vast complexity of art, which might be corrected by further probing and research. Their basic inadequacies reside instead in a fundamental misconception of art. Aesthetic theory – all of it – is wrong in principle in thinking that a correct theory is possible because it radically misconstrues the logic of the concept of art. Its main contention that "art" is amenable to real or any kind of true definition is false. Its attempt to discover the necessary and sufficient properties of art is logically misbegotten for the very simple reason that such a set and, consequently, such a formula about it, is never forthcoming. Art, as the logic of the concept shows, has no set of necessary and sufficient properties, hence a theory of it is logically impossible and not merely factually difficult. Aesthetic theory tries to define what cannot be defined in its requisite sense. But in recommending the repudiation of aesthetic theory I shall not argue from this, as too many others have done, that its logical confusions render it meaningless or worthless. On the contrary, I wish to reassess its role and its contribution primarily in order to show that it is of the greatest importance to our understanding of the arts.

Let us now survey briefly some of the more famous extant aesthetic theories in order to see if they do incorporate correct and adequate statements about the nature of art. In each of these there is the assumption that it is the true enumeration of the defining properties of art, with the implication that previous theories have stressed wrong definitions. Thus, to begin with, consider a famous version of Formalist theory, that propounded by Bell and Fry. It is true that they speak mostly of painting in their writings but both assert that what they find in that art can be generalized for what is "art" in the others as well. The essence of painting, they maintain, are the plastic elements in relation. Its defining property is significant form, i.e., certain combinations of lines, colors, shapes, volumes – everything on the canvas except the representational elements – which evoke a unique response to such combinations. Painting is definable as plastic organization. The nature of art, what it *really* is, so their theory goes, is a unique combination of certain elements (the specifiable plastic ones) in their relations. Anything which is art is an instance of significant form; and anything which is not art has no such form.

To this the Emotionalist replies that the truly essential property of art has been left out. Tolstoy, Ducasse, or any of the advocates of this theory, find that the requisite defining property is not significant form but rather the expression of emotion in some sensuous public medium. Without projection of emotion into some piece of stone or words or sounds, etc., there can be no art. Art is really such embodiment. It is this that uniquely characterizes art, and any true, real definition of it, contained in some adequate theory of art, must so state it.

The Intuitionist disclaims both emotion and form as defining properties. In Croce's version, for example, art is identified not with some physical, public object but with a specific creative, cognitive and spiritual act. Art is really a first stage of knowledge in which certain human beings (artists) bring their images and intuitions into lyrical clarification or expression. As such, it is an awareness, non-conceptual in character, of the unique individuality of things; and since it exists below the level of conceptualization or action, it is without scientific or moral content. Croce singles out as the defining essence of art this first stage of spiritual life and advances its identification with art as a philosophically true theory or definition.

The Organicist says to all of this that art is really a class of organic wholes consisting of distinguishable, albeit inseparable, elements in their causally efficacious relations which are presented in some sensuous medium. In A. C. Bradley, in piece-meal versions of it in literary criticism, or in my own generalized adaptation of it in my *Philosophy of the Arts*, what is claimed is that anything which is a work of art is in its nature a unique complex of interrelated parts – in painting, for example, lines, colors, volumes, subjects, etc., all interacting upon one another on a paint surface of some sort. Certainly, at one time at least it seemed to me that this organic theory constituted the one true and real definition of art.

My final example is the most interesting of all, logically speaking. This is the Voluntarist theory of Parker. In his writings on art, Parker persistently calls into question the traditional simple-minded definitions of aesthetics. "The assumption underlying every philosophy of art is the existence of some common nature present in all the arts."[1] "All the so popular brief definitions of art – 'significant form,' 'expression,' 'intuition,' 'objectified pleasure' – are fallacious, either because, while true of art, they are also true of much that is not art, and hence fail to differentiate art from other things; or else because they neglect some essential aspect of art."[2] But instead of inveighing against the attempt at definition of art itself, Parker insists that what is needed is a complex definition rather than a simple one. "The definition of art must therefore be in terms of a complex of characteristics. Failure to recognize this has been the fault of all the well-known definitions."[3] His own version of Voluntarism is the theory that art is essentially three things: embodiment of wishes and desires imaginatively satisfied, language, which characterizes the public medium of art, and harmony, which unifies the language with the layers of imaginative projections. Thus, for Parker, it is a true definition to say of art that it is ". . . the provision of satisfaction through the imagination, social significance, and harmony. I am claiming that nothing except works of art possesses all three of these marks."[4]

Now, all of these sample theories are inadequate in many different ways. Each purports to be a complete statement about the defining features of all works of art and yet each of them leaves out something which the others take to be central. Some are circular, e.g., the Bell-Fry theory of art as significant form which is defined in part in terms of our response to significant form. Some of them, in their search for necessary and sufficient properties, emphasize too few properties, like (again) the Bell-Fry definition which leaves out subject-representation in painting, or the Croce theory which omits inclusion of the very important feature of the public, physical character, say, of architecture. Others are too general and cover objects that are not art as well as works of art. Organicism is surely such a view since it can be applied to *any* causal unity in the natural world as well as to art.[5] Still others rest on dubious principles, e.g., Parker's claim that art embodies imaginative satisfactions, rather than real ones; or Croce's assertion that there is non-conceptual knowledge. Consequently, even if art has one set of necessary and sufficient properties, none of the theories we have noted or, for that matter, no aesthetic theory yet proposed, has enumerated that set to the satisfaction of all concerned.

Then there is a different sort of difficulty. As real definitions, these theories are supposed to be factual reports on art. If they are, may we not ask, Are they empirical and open to verification or falsification? For example, what would confirm or disconfirm the theory that art is significant form or embodiment of emotion or creative synthesis of images? There does not even seem to be a hint of the kind of evidence which might be forthcoming to test these theories; and indeed one wonders if they are perhaps honorific definitions of "art," that is, proposed redefinitions in terms of some *chosen* conditions for applying the concept of art, and not true or false reports on the essential properties of art at all.

But all these criticisms of traditional aesthetic theories – that they are circular, incomplete, untestable, pseudo-factual, disguised proposals to change the meaning of concepts – have been made before. My intention is to go beyond these to make a much more fundamental criticism, namely, that aesthetic theory is a logically vain attempt to define what cannot be defined, to state the necessary and sufficient properties of that which has no necessary and sufficient properties, to conceive the concept of art as closed when its very use reveals and demands its openness.

The problem with which we must begin is not "What is art?," but "What sort of concept is 'art'?" Indeed, the root problem of philosophy itself is to explain the relation between the employment of certain kinds of concepts and the conditions under which they can be correctly applied. If I may paraphrase Wittgenstein, we must not ask, What is the nature of any philosophical x?, or even, according to the semanticist, What does "x" mean?, a transformation that leads to the disastrous interpretation of "art" as a name for some specifiable class of objects; but rather, What is the use or employment of "x"? What does "x" do in the language? This, I take it, is the initial question, the begin-all if not the end-all of any philosophical problem and solution. Thus, in aesthetics, our first problem is the elucidation of the actual employment of the concept of art, to give a logical description of the actual functioning of the concept, including a description of the conditions under which we correctly use it or its correlates.

My model in this type of logical description or philosophy derives from Wittgenstein. It is also he who, in his refutation of philosophical theorizing in the sense of constructing definitions of philosophical entities, has furnished contemporary aesthetics with a starting point for any future progress. In his new work, *Philosophical Investigations*,[6] Wittgenstein raises as an illustrative question, What is a game? The traditional philosophical, theoretical answer would be in terms of some exhaustive set of properties common to all games. To this Wittgenstein says, let us consider what we call "games": "I mean board-games, card-games, ball-games, Olympic games, and so on. What is common to them all? – Don't say: 'there *must* be something common, or they would not be called "games"' but *look and see* whether there is anything common to all. – For if you look at them you will not see something that is common to *all*, but similarities, relationships, and a whole series of them at that . . ."

Card games are like board games in some respects but not in others. Not all games are amusing, nor is there always winning or losing or competition. Some games resemble others in some respects – that is all. What we find are no necessary and sufficient properties, only "a complicated network of similarities overlapping and crisscrossing," such that we can say of games that they form a family with family resemblances and no common trait. If one asks what a game is, we pick out sample games, describe these, and add, "This and *similar things* are called 'games'." This is all we need to say and indeed all any of us knows about games. Knowing what a game is is not knowing some real definition or theory but being able to recognize and explain games and to decide which among imaginary and new examples would or would not be called "games."

The problem of the nature of art is like that of the nature of games, at least in these respects: If we actually look and see what it is that we call "art," we will also find no common properties – only strands of similarities. Knowing what art is is not apprehending some manifest or latent essence but being able to recognize, describe, and explain those things we call "art" in virtue of these similarities.

But the basic resemblance between these concepts is their open texture. In elucidating them, certain (paradigm) cases can be given, about which there can be no question as to their being correctly described as "art" or "game," but no exhaustive set of cases can be given. I can list some cases and some conditions under which I can apply correctly the concept of art but I cannot list all of them, for the all-important reason that unforeseeable or novel conditions are always forthcoming or envisageable.

A concept is open if its conditions of application are emendable and corrigible; i.e., if a situation or case can be imagined or secured which would call for some sort of *decision* on our part to extend the use of the concept to cover this, or to close the concept and invent a new one to deal with the new case and its new property. If necessary and sufficient conditions for the application of a concept can be stated, the concept is a closed one. But this can happen only in logic or mathematics where concepts are constructed and completely defined. It cannot occur with empirically-descriptive and normative concepts unless we arbitrarily close them by stipulating the ranges of their uses.

I can illustrate this open character of "art" best by examples drawn from its sub-concepts. Consider questions like "Is Dos Passos' *U. S. A.* a novel?," "Is V. Woolf's *To the Lighthouse* a novel?," "Is Joyce's *Finnegan's Wake* a novel?" On the traditional view, these are construed as factual problems to be answered yes or no in accordance with the presence or absence of defining properties. But certainly this is not how any of these questions is answered. Once it arises, as it has many times in the development of the novel from Richardson to Joyce (e.g., "Is Gide's *The School for Wives* a novel or a diary?"), what is at stake is no factual analysis concerning necessary and sufficient properties but a decision as to whether the work under examination is similar in certain respects to other works, already called "novels," and consequently warrants the extension of the concept to cover the new case. The new work is narrative, fictional, contains character delineation and dialogue but (say) it has no regular time-sequence in the plot or is interspersed with actual newspaper reports. It is like recognized novels, A, B, C . . . , in some respects but not like them in others. But then neither were B and C like A in some respects when it was decided to extend the concept applied to A to B and C. Because work N + 1 (the brand new work) is like A, B, C . . . N in certain respects – has strands of similarity to them – the concept is extended and a new phase of the novel engendered. "Is N 1 a novel?," then, is no factual, but rather a decision problem, where the verdict turns on whether or not we enlarge our set of conditions for applying the concept.

What is true of the novel is, I think, true of every sub-concept of art: "tragedy," "comedy," "painting," "opera," etc., of "art" itself. No "Is X a novel, painting, opera, work of art, etc.?" question allows of a definitive answer in the sense of a factual yes or no report. "Is this *collage* a painting or not?" does not rest on any set of necessary and sufficient properties of painting but on whether we decide – as we did! – to extend "painting" to cover this case.

"Art," itself, is an open concept. New conditions (cases) have constantly arisen and will undoubtedly constantly arise; new art forms, new movements will emerge, which will demand decisions on the part of those interested, usually professional critics, as to whether the concept should be extended or not. Aestheticians may lay down similarity conditions but never necessary and sufficient ones for the correct application of the concept. With "art" its conditions of application can never be exhaustively enumerated since new cases can always be envisaged or created by artists, or even nature, which would call for a decision on someone's part to extend or to close the old or to invent a new concept. (E.g., "It's not a sculpture, it's a mobile.")

What I am arguing, then, is that the very expansive, adventurous character of art, its ever-present changes and novel creations, makes it logically impossible to ensure any set of defining properties. We can, of course, choose to close the concept. But to do this with "art" or "tragedy" or "portraiture," etc., is ludicrous since it forecloses on the very conditions of creativity in the arts.

Of course there are legitimate and serviceable closed concepts in art. But these are always those whose boundaries of conditions have been drawn for a *special* purpose. Consider the difference, for example, between "tragedy" and "(extant) Greek tragedy." The first is open and must remain so to allow for the possibility of new conditions, e.g., a play in which the hero is not noble or fallen or in which there is no hero but other elements that are like those of plays we already call "tragedy." The second is closed. The plays it can be applied to, the conditions under which it can be correctly used are all in, once the boundary, "Greek," is drawn. Here the critic can work out a theory or real definition in which he lists the common properties at least of the extant Greek tragedies. Aristotle's definition, false as it is as a theory of all the plays of Aeschylus, Sophocles, and Euripides, since it does not cover some of them,[7] properly called "tragedies," can be interpreted as a real (albeit incorrect) definition of this closed concept; although it can also be, as it unfortunately has been, conceived as a purported real definition of "tragedy," in which case it suffers from the logical mistake of trying to define what cannot be defined – of trying to squeeze what is an open concept into an honorific formula for a closed concept.

What is supremely important, if the critic is not to become muddled, is to get absolutely clear about the way in which he conceives his concepts; otherwise he goes from the problem of trying to define "tragedy," etc., to an arbitrary closing of the concept in terms of certain preferred conditions or characteristics which he sums up in some linguistic recommendation that he mistakenly thinks is a real definition of the open concept. Thus, many critics and aestheticians ask, "What is tragedy?," choose a class of samples for which they may give a true account of its common properties, and then go on to construe this account of the chosen closed class as a true definition or theory of the whole open class of tragedy. This, I think, is the logical mechanism of most of the so-called theories of the sub-concepts of art: "tragedy," "comedy," "novel," etc. In effect, this whole procedure, subtly deceptive as it is, amounts to a transformation of correct criteria for *recognizing* members of certain legitimately closed classes of works of art into recommended criteria for *evaluating* any putative member of the class.

The primary task of aesthetics is not to seek a theory but to elucidate the concept of art.

Specifically, it is to describe the conditions under which we employ the concept correctly. Definition, reconstruction, patterns of analysis are out of place here since they distort and add nothing to our understanding of art. What, then, is the logic of "X is a work of art"?

As we actually use the concept, "Art" is both descriptive (like "chair") and evaluative (like "good"); i.e., we sometimes say, "This is a work of art," to describe something and we sometimes say it to evaluate something. Neither use surprises anyone.

What, first, is the logic of "X is a work of art," when it is a descriptive utterance? What are the conditions under which we would be making such an utterance correctly? There are no necessary and sufficient conditions but there are the strands of similarity conditions, i.e., bundles of properties, none of which need be present but most of which are, when we describe things as works of art. I shall call these the "criteria of recognition" of works of art. All of these have served as the defining criteria of the individual traditional theories of art; so we are already familiar with them. Thus, mostly, when we describe something as a work of art, we do so under the conditions of there being present some sort of artifact, made by human skill, ingenuity, and imagination, which embodies in its sensuous, public medium – stone, wood, sounds, words, etc. – certain distinguishable elements and relations. Special theorists would add conditions like satisfaction of wishes, objectification or expression of emotion, some act of empathy, and so on; but these latter conditions seem to be quite adventitious, present to some but not to other spectators when things are described as works of art. "X is a work of art and contains *no* emotion, expression, act of empathy, satisfaction, etc.," is perfectly good sense and may frequently be true. "X is a work of art and . . . was made by no one," or . . . "exists only in the mind and not in any publicly observable thing," or . . . "was made by accident when he spilled the paint on the canvas," in each case of which a normal condition is denied, are also sensible and capable of being true in certain circumstances. None of the criteria of recognition is a defining one, either necessary or sufficient, because we can sometimes assert of something that it is a work of art and go on to deny any one of these conditions, even the one which has traditionally been taken to be basic, namely, that of being an artifact: Consider, "This piece of driftwood is a lovely piece of sculpture." Thus, to say of anything that it is a work of art is to commit oneself to the presence of *some* of these conditions. One would scarcely describe X as a work of art if X were not an artifact, or a collection of elements sensuously presented in a medium, or a product of human skill, and so on. If none of the conditions were present, if there were no criteria present for recognizing something as a work of art, we would not describe it as one. But, even so, no one of these or any collection of them is either necessary or sufficient.

The elucidation of the descriptive use of "Art" creates little difficulty. But the elucidation of the evaluative use does. For many, especially theorists, "This is a work of art" does more than describe; it also praises. Its conditions of utterance, therefore, include certain preferred properties or characteristics of art. I shall call these "criteria of evaluation." Consider a typical example of this evaluative use, the view according to which to say of something that it is a work of art is to imply that it is a *successful* harmonization of elements. Many of the honorific definitions of art and its sub-concepts are of this form. What is at stake here is that "Art" is construed as an evaluative term which is either identified with its criterion or justified in terms of it. "Art" is defined in terms of its evaluative property, e.g., successful harmonization. On such a view, to say "X is a work of art" is (1) to say something which is taken *to mean* "X is a successful harmonization" (e.g., "Art *is* significant form") or (2) to say something praiseworthy *on the basis* of its successful harmonization. Theorists are never clear whether it is (1) or (2) which is being put forward. Most of them, concerned as they are with this evaluative use, formulate (2), i.e., that feature of art that *makes* it art in the praise-sense, and then go on to state (1), i.e., the definition of "Art" in terms of its art-making feature. And this is clearly to confuse the conditions under which we say something evaluatively with the meaning of what we say. "This is a work of art," said evaluatively, cannot mean "This is a successful harmonization of elements" – except by stipulation – but at most is said in virtue of the art-making property, which is taken as a (the) criterion of "Art," when "Art" is employed to assess. "This is a work of art," used evaluatively, serves to praise and not to affirm the reason why it is said.

The evaluative use of "Art," although distinct from the conditions of its use, relates in a very intimate way to these conditions. For, in every instance of "This is a work of art" (used to praise), what happens is that the criterion of evaluation (e.g., successful harmonization) for the employment of the concept of art is converted into a criterion of recognition. This is why, on its evaluative use, "This is a work of art" implies "This has P," where "P" is some chosen art-making property. Thus, if one chooses to employ "Art" evaluatively, as many do, so that "This is a work of art and not (aesthetically) good" makes no sense, he uses "Art" in such a way that he refuses to *call* anything a work of art unless it embodies his criterion of excellence.

There is nothing wrong with the evaluative use; in fact, there is good reason for using "Art" to praise. But what cannot be maintained is that theories of the evaluative use of "Art" are true and real definitions of the necessary and sufficient properties of art. Instead they are honorific definitions, pure and simple, in which "Art" has been redefined in terms of chosen criteria.

But what makes them – these honorific definitions – so supremely valuable is not their disguised linguistic recommendations; rather it is the *debates* over the reasons for changing the criteria of the concept of art which are built into the definitions. In each of the great theories of art, whether correctly understood as honorific definitions or incorrectly accepted as real definitions, what is of the utmost importance are the reasons profferred in the argument for the respective theory, that is, the reasons given for the chosen or preferred criterion of excellence and evaluation. It is this perennial debate over these criteria of evaluation which makes the history of aesthetic theory the important study it is. The value of each of the theories resides in its attempt to state and to justify certain criteria which are either neglected or distorted by previous theories. Look at the Bell-Fry theory again. Of course, "Art is significant form" cannot be accepted as a true, real definition of art; and most certainly it actually functions in their aesthetics as a redefinition of art in terms of the chosen condition of significant form. But what gives it its aesthetic importance is what lies behind the formula: In an age in which literary and representational elements have become paramount in painting, *return* to the plastic ones since these are indigenous to painting. Thus, the role of the theory is not to define anything but to use the definitional form, almost epigrammatically, to pin-point a crucial recommendation to turn our attention once again to the plastic elements in painting.

Once we, as philosophers, understand this distinction between the formula and what lies behind it, it behooves us to deal generously with the traditional theories of art; because incorporated in every one of them is a debate over and argument for emphasizing or centering upon some particular feature of art which has been neglected or perverted. If we take the aesthetic theories literally, as we have seen, they all fail; but if we reconstrue them, in terms of their function and point, as serious and argued-for recommendations to concentrate on certain criteria of excellence in art, we shall see that aesthetic theory is far from worthless. Indeed, it becomes as central as anything in aesthetics, in our understanding of art, for it teaches us what to look for and how to look at it in art. What is central and must be articulated in all the theories are their debates over the reasons for excellence in art – debates over emotional depth, profound truths, natural beauty, exactitude, freshness of treatment, and so on, as criteria of evaluation – the whole of which converges on the perennial problem of what makes a work of art good. To understand the role of aesthetic theory is not to conceive it as definition, logically doomed to failure, but to read it as summaries of seriously made recommendations to attend in certain ways to certain features of art.

Notes

1 D. Parker, "The Nature of Art," reprinted in E. Vivas and M. Krieger, *The Problems of Aesthetics* (N.Y., 1953), p. 90.
2 Ibid., pp. 93–4.
3 Ibid., p. 94.
4 Ibid., p. 104.
5 See M. Macdonald's review of my *Philosophy of the Arts, Mind*, Oct., 1951, pp. 561–4, for a brilliant

discussion of this objection to the Organic theory.

6 L. Wittgenstein, *Philosophical Investigations* (Oxford, 1953), tr. by K. Anscombe; see esp. Part I, Sections 65–75. All quotations are from these sections.

7 See H. D. F. Kitto, *Greek Tragedy* (London, 1939), on this point.

36

The Artworld

Arthur Danto

Arthur Danto is Emeritus Johnsonian Professor of Philosophy at Columbia University.

Hamlet:
Do you see nothing there!
The Queen:
Nothing at all; yet all that is I see.
Shakespeare: *Hamlet*, Act III, Scene IV

Hamlet and Socrates, though in praise and deprecation respectively, spoke of art as a mirror held up to nature. As with many disagreements in attitude, this one has a factual basis. Socrates saw mirrors as but reflecting what we can already see; so art, insofar as mirrorlike, yields idle accurate duplications of the appearances of things, and is of no cognitive benefit whatever. Hamlet, more acutely, recognized a remarkable feature of reflecting surfaces, namely that they show us what we could not otherwise perceive – our own face and form – and so art, insofar as it is mirrorlike, reveals us to ourselves, and is, even by socratic criteria, of some cognitive utility after all. As a philosopher, however, I find Socrates' discussion defective on other, perhaps less profound grounds than these. If a mirror-image of *o* is indeed an imitation of *o*, then, if art is imitation, mirror-images are art. But in fact mirroring objects no more is art than returning weapons to a madman is justice; and reference to mirrorings would be just the sly sort of counterinstance we would expect Socrates to bring forward in rebuttal of the theory he instead uses them to illustrate. If that theory requires us to class *these* as art, it thereby shows its inadequacy: "is an imitation" will not do as a sufficient condition for "is art." Yet, perhaps because artists *were* engaged in imitation, in Socrates' time and after, the insufficiency of the theory was not noticed until the invention of photography. Once rejected as a sufficient condition, mimesis was quickly discarded as even a necessary one; and since the achievement of Kandinsky, mimetic features have been relegated to the periphery of critical concern, so much so that some works survive in spite of possessing those virtues, excellence in which was once celebrated as the essence of art, narrowly escaping demotion to mere illustrations.

It is, of course, indispensable in socratic discussion that all participants be masters of the concept up for analysis, since the aim is to match

Arthur Danto, "The Artworld," *Journal of Philosophy*, 61/19 (1964): 571–84.

a real defining expression to a term in active use, and the test for adequacy presumably consists in showing that the former analyzes and applies to all and only those things of which the latter is true, The popular disclaimer notwithstanding, then, Socrates' auditors purportedly knew what art was as well as what they liked; and a theory of art, regarded here as a real definition of 'Art', is accordingly not to be of great use in helping men to recognize instances of its application. Their antecedent ability to do this is precisely what the adequacy of the theory is to be tested against, the problem being only to make explicit what they already know. It is *our* use of the term that the theory allegedly means to capture, but we are supposed able, in the words of a recent writer, "to separate those objects which are works of art from those which are not, because . . . we know how correctly to use the word 'art' and to apply the phrase 'work of art'." Theories, on this account, are somewhat like mirror-images on Socrates' account, showing forth what we already know, wordy reflections of the actual linguistic practice we are masters in.

But telling artworks from other things is not so simple a matter, even for native speakers, and these days one might not be aware he was on artistic terrain without an artistic theory to tell him so. And part of the reason for this lies in the fact that terrain is constituted artistic in virtue of artistic theories, so that one use of theories, in addition to helping us discriminate art from the rest, consists in making art possible. Glaucon and the others could hardly have known what was art and what not: otherwise they would never have been taken in by mirror-images.

I

Suppose one thinks of the discovery of a whole new class of artworks as something analogous to the discovery of a whole new class of facts anywhere, viz., as something for theoreticians to explain. In science, as elsewhere, we often accommodate new facts to old theories via auxiliary hypotheses, a pardonable enough conservatism when the theory in question is deemed too valuable to be jettisoned all at once. Now the Imitation Theory of Art (IT) is, if one but thinks it through, an exceedingly powerful theory, explaining a great many phenomena connected with the causation and evaluation of artworks, bringing a surprising unity into a complex domain. Moreover, it is a simple matter to shore it up against many purported counterinstances by such auxiliary hypotheses as that the artist who deviates from mimeticity is perverse, inept, or mad. Ineptitude, chicanery, or folly are, in fact, testable predications. Suppose, then, tests reveal that these hypotheses fail to hold, that the theory, now beyond repair, must be replaced. And a new theory is worked out, capturing what it can of the old theory's competence, together with the heretofore recalcitrant facts. One might, thinking along these lines, represent certain episodes in the history of art as not dissimilar to certain episodes in the history of science, where a conceptual revolution is being effected and where refusal to countenance certain facts, while in part due to prejudice, inertia, and self-interest, is due also to the fact that a well-established, or at least widely credited theory is being threatened in such a way that all coherence goes.

Some such episode transpired with the advent of post-impressionist paintings. In terms of the prevailing artistic theory (IT), it was impossible to accept these as art unless inept art: otherwise they could be discounted as hoaxes, self-advertisements, or the visual counterparts of madmen's ravings. So to get them accepted *as* art, on a footing with the *Transfiguration* (not to speak of a Landseer stag), required not so much a revolution in taste as a theoretical revision of rather considerable proportions, involving not only the artistic enfranchisement of these objects, but an emphasis upon newly significant features of accepted artworks, so that quite different accounts of their status as artworks would now have to be given. As a result of the new theory's acceptance, not only were post-impressionist paintings taken up as art, but numbers of objects (masks, weapons, etc.) were transferred from anthropological museums (and heterogeneous other places) to *musées des beaux arts*, though, as we would expect from the fact that a criterion for the acceptance of a new theory is that it account for whatever the older one did, nothing had to be transferred out of the *musée des beaux arts* – even if there were internal rearrangements as between storage rooms and exhibition space. Countless native speakers hung upon suburban mantelpieces innumerable replicas of paradigm cases for teaching the expression 'work of art' that would have sent their Edwardian forebears into linguistic apoplexy.

To be sure, I distort by speaking of a theory: historically, there were several, all, interestingly enough, more or less defined in terms of the IT. Art-historical complexities must yield before the exigencies of logical exposition, and I shall speak as though there were one replacing theory, partially compensating for historical falsity by choosing one which was actually enunciated. According to it, the artists in question were to be understood not as unsuccessfully imitating real forms but as successfully creating new ones, quite as real as the forms which the older art had been thought, in its best examples, to be creditably imitating. Art, after all, had long since been thought of as creative (Vasari says that God was the first artist), and the post-impressionists were to be explained as genuinely creative, aiming, in Roger Fry's words, "not at illusion but reality." This theory (RT) furnished a whole new mode of looking at painting, old and new. Indeed, one might almost interpret the crude drawing in Van Gogh and Cézanne, the dislocation of form from contour in Rouault and Dufy, the arbitrary use of color planes in Gauguin and the Fauves, as so many ways of drawing attention to the fact that these were *non-imitations*, specifically intended not to deceive. Logically, this would be roughly like printing "Not Legal Tender" across a brilliantly counterfeited dollar bill, the resulting object (counterfeit *cum* inscription) rendered incapable of deceiving anyone. It is not an illusory dollar bill, but then, just because it is non-illusory it does not automatically become a real dollar bill either. It rather occupies a freshly opened area between real objects and real facsimiles of real objects: it is a non-facsimile, if one requires a word, and a new contribution to the world. Thus, Van Gogh's *Potato Eaters*, as a consequence of certain unmistakable distortions, turns out to be a non-facsimile of real-life potato eaters; and inasmuch as these are not facsimiles of potato eaters, Van Gogh's picture, as a non-imitation, had as much right to be called a real object as did its putative subjects. By means of this theory (RT), artworks re-entered the thick of things from which socratic theory (IT) had sought to evict them: if no *more* real than what carpenters wrought, they were at least no *less* real. The Post-Impressionist won a victory in ontology.

It is in terms of RT that we must understand the artworks around us today. Thus Roy Lichtenstein paints comic-strip panels, though ten or twelve feet high. These are reasonably faithful projections onto a gigantesque scale of the homely frames from the daily tabloid, but it is precisely the scale that counts. A skilled engraver might incise *The Virgin and the Chancellor Rollin* on a pinhead, and it would be recognizable as such to the keen of sight, but an engraving of a Barnett Newman on a similar scale would be a blob, disappearing in the reduction. A *photograph* of a Lichtenstein is indiscernible from a photograph of a counterpart panel from *Steve Canyon*; but the photograph fails to capture the scale, and hence is as inaccurate a reproduction as a black-and-white engraving of Botticelli, scale being essential here as color there. Lichtensteins, then, are not imitations but *new entities*, as giant whelks would be. Jasper Johns, by contrast, paints objects with respect to which questions of scale are irrelevant. Yet his objects cannot be imitations, for they have the remarkable property that any intended copy of a member of this class of objects is automatically a member of the class itself, so that these objects are logically inimitable. Thus, a copy of a numeral just *is* that numeral: a painting of 3 is a 3 made of paint. Johns, in addition, paints targets, flags, and maps. Finally, in what I hope are not unwitting footnotes to Plato, two of our pioneers – Robert Rauschenberg and Claes Oldenburg – have made genuine beds.

Rauschenberg's bed hangs on a wall, and is streaked with some desultory housepaint. Oldenburg's bed is a rhomboid, narrower at one end than the other, with what one might speak of as a built-in perspective: ideal for small bedrooms. As beds, these sell at singularly inflated prices, but one *could* sleep in either of them: Rauschenberg has expressed the fear that someone might just climb into his bed and fall asleep. Imagine, now, a certain Testadura – a plain speaker and noted philistine – who is not aware that these are art, and who takes them to be reality simple and pure. He attributes the paintstreaks on Rauschenberg's bed to the slovenliness of the owner, and the bias in the Oldenburg bed to the ineptitude of the builder or the whimsy, perhaps, of whoever had it "custom-made." These would be mistakes, but mistakes of rather an odd kind, and not terribly different from that made by the stunned birds who pecked the sham grapes of Zeuxis. They mistook art for reality, and so has Testadura. But it was meant to *be* reality, according to RT. Can one have mistaken reality for reality? How shall we describe Testadura's error? What, after all, prevents Oldenburg's creation from being a misshapen bed? This is equivalent to asking what makes it art, and with this query we enter a domain of conceptual inquiry where native speakers are poor guides: *they* are lost themselves.

II

To mistake an artwork for a real object is no great feat when an artwork is the real object one mistakes it for. The problem is how to avoid such errors, or to remove them once they are made. The artwork is a bed, and not a bed-illusion; so there is nothing like the traumatic encounter against a flat surface that brought it home to the birds of Zeuxis that they had been duped. Except for the guard cautioning Testadura not to sleep on the artworks, he might never have discovered that this was an artwork and not a bed; and since, after all, one cannot discover that a bed is not a bed, how is Testadura to realize that he has made an error? A certain sort of explanation is required, for the error here is a curiously philosophical one, rather like, if we may assume as correct some well-known views of P. F. Strawson, mistaking a person for a material body when the truth is that a person *is* a material body in the sense that a whole class of predicates, sensibly applicable to material bodies, are sensibly, and by appeal to no different criteria, applicable to persons. So you cannot *discover* that a person is not a material body.

We begin by explaining, perhaps, that the paintstreaks are not to be explained away, that they are *part* of the object, so the object is not a mere bed with – as it happens – streaks of paint spilled over it, but a complex object fabricated out of a bed and some paintstreaks: a paint-bed. Similarly, a person is not a material body with – as it happens – some thoughts superadded, but is a complex entity made up of a body and some conscious states: a conscious-body. Persons, like artworks, must then be taken as irreducible to *parts* of themselves, and are in that sense primitive. Or, more accurately, the paintstreaks are not part of the real object – the bed – which happens to be part of the artwork, but are, *like* the bed, part of the artwork as such. And this might be generalized into a rough characterization of artworks that happen to contain real objects as parts of themselves: not every part of an artwork *A* is part of a real object *R* when *R* is part of *A* and can, moreover, be detached from *A* and seen *merely* as *R*. The mistake thus far will have been to mistake *A* for *part* of itself, namely *R*, even though it would not be incorrect to say that *A* is *R*, that the artwork is a bed. It is the 'is' which requires clarification here.

There is an *is* that figures prominently in statements concerning artworks which is not the *is* of either identity or predication; nor is it the *is* of existence, of identification, or some special *is* made up to serve a philosophic end. Nevertheless, it is in common usage, and is readily mastered by children. It is the sense of *is* in accordance with which a child, shown a circle and a triangle and asked which is him and which his sister, will point to the triangle saying "That is me"; or, in response to my question, the person next to me points to the man in purple and says "That one is Lear"; or in the gallery I point, for my companion's benefit, to a spot in the painting before us and say "That white dab is Icarus," We do not mean, in these instances, that whatever is pointed to stands for, or represents, what it is said to be, for the *word* 'Icarus' stands for or represents Icarus: yet I would not in the same sense of *is* point to the word and say "That is Icarus." The sentence "That *a* is *b* "is perfectly compatible with "That *a* is not *b*" when the first employs this sense of *is* and the second employs some other, though *a* and *b* are used nonambiguously throughout. Often, indeed, the truth of the first *requires* the truth of the second. The first, in fact, is incompatible with "That *a* is not *b*" only when the *is* is used nonambiguously throughout. For want of a word I shall designate this the *is of artistic identification*; in each case in which it is used, the *a* stands for some specific physical property of, or physical part of, an object; and, finally, it is a necessary condition for something to be an artwork that some part or property of it be designable by the subject of a sentence that employs this special *is*. It is an *is*, incidentally, which has near-relatives in marginal and mythical pronouncements. (Thus, one *is* Quetzalcoatl; those *are* the Pillars of Hercules.)

Let me illustrate. Two painters are asked to decorate the east and west walls of a science library with frescoes to be respectively called *Newton's First Law* and *Newton's Third Law*. These paintings, when finally unveiled, look, scale apart, as follows:

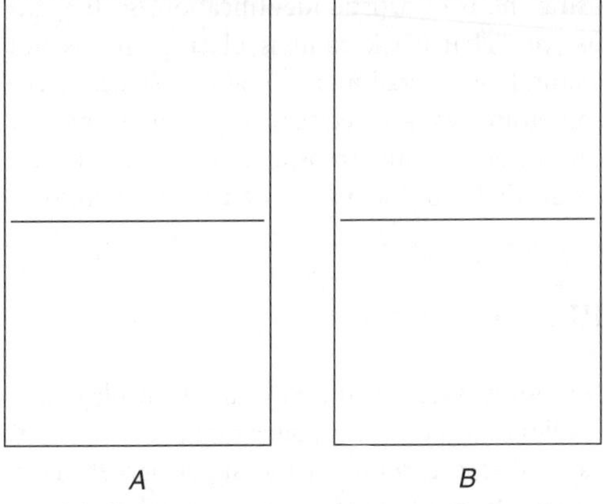

As objects I shall suppose the works to be indiscernible: a black, horizontal line on a white ground, equally large in each dimension and element. *B* explains his work as follows: a mass, pressing downward, is met by a mass pressing upward: the lower mass reacts equally and oppositely to the upper one. *A* explains his work as follows: the line through the space is the path of an isolated particle. The path goes from edge to edge, to give the sense of its *going beyond*. If it ended or began within the space, the line would be curved: and it is parallel to the top and bottom edges, for if it were closer to one than to another, there would have to be a force accounting for it, and this is inconsistent with its being the path of an *isolated* particle.

Much follows from these artistic identifications. To regard the middle line as an edge (mass meeting mass) imposes the need to identify the top and bottom half of the picture as rectangles, and as two distinct parts (not necessarily as two masses, for the line could be the edge of *one* mass jutting up – or down – into empty space). If it is an edge, we cannot thus take the entire area of the painting as a single space: it is rather composed of two forms, or one form and a non-form. We could take the entire area as a single space only by taking the middle horizontal as a *line* which is not an edge. But this almost requires a three-dimensional identification of the whole picture: the area can be a flat surface which the line is *above* (*Jet-flight*), or *below* (*Submarine-path*), or *on* (*Line*), or *in* (*Fissure*), or *through* (*Newton's First Law*) – though in this last case the area is not a flat surface but a transparent cross section of absolute space. We could make all these prepositional qualifications clear by imagining perpendicular cross sections to the picture plane. Then, depending upon the applicable prepositional clause, the area is (artistically) interrupted or not by the horizontal element. If we take the line as *through* space, the edges of the picture are not really the edges of the space: the space goes beyond the picture if the line itself does; and we are in the same space as the line is. As *B*, the edges of the picture can be *part* of the picture in case the masses go right to the edges, so that the edges of the picture are *their* edges. In that case, the vertices of the picture would be the vertices of the masses, except that the masses have four vertices more than the picture itself does: here four vertices would be part of the art work which were not part of the real object. Again, the faces of the masses could be the face of the picture, and in looking at the picture, we are looking at these faces: but *space* has no face, and on the reading of *A* the work has to be read as faceless, and the face of the physical object would not be part of the artwork. Notice here how one artistic identification engenders another artistic identification, and how, consistently with a given identification, we are *required* to give others and *precluded* from still others: indeed, a given identification determines how many elements the work is to contain. These different identifications are incompatible with one another, or generally so, and each might be said to make a different artwork, even though each artwork contains the identical real object as part of itself – or at least parts of the identical real object as parts of itself. There are, of course, senseless identifications: no one could, I think, sensibly read the middle horizontal as *Love's Labour's Lost* or *The Ascendency of St. Erasmus*. Finally, notice how acceptance of one identification rather than another is in effect to exchange one *world* for another. We could, indeed, enter a quiet poetic world by identifying the upper area with a clear and cloudless sky, reflected in the still surface of the water below, whiteness kept from whiteness only by the unreal boundary of the horizon.

And now Testadura, having hovered in the wings throughout this discussion, protests that *all he sees is paint*: a white painted oblong with a black line painted across it. And how right he really is: that is all he sees or that anybody can, we aesthetes included. So, if he asks us to show him what there is further to see, to demonstrate through pointing that this is an artwork (*Sea and Sky*), we cannot comply, for he has overlooked nothing (and it would be absurd to suppose he had, that there was something tiny we could point to and he, peering closely, say "So it is! A work of art after all!"). We cannot help him until he has mastered the *is of artistic identification* and so *constitutes* it a work of art. If he cannot achieve this, he will never look upon artworks: he will be like a child who sees sticks as sticks.

But what about pure abstractions, say something that looks just like *A* but is entitled No. 7? The 10th Street abstractionist blankly insists that there is nothing here but white paint and black, and none of our literary identifications need apply. What then distinguishes him from Testadura, whose philistine utterances are indiscernible from his? And how can it be an artwork for him and not for Testadura, when they agree that there is nothing that does not meet the eye? The answer, unpopular as it is likely to be to purists of every variety, lies in the fact that this artist has returned to the physicality of paint through an atmosphere compounded of artistic theories and the history of recent and remote painting, elements of which he is trying to refine out of his own work; and as a consequence of this his work belongs in this atmosphere and is part of this history. He has achieved abstraction through rejection of artistic identifications, returning to the real world from which such identifications remove us (he thinks), somewhat in the mode of Ch'ing Yuan, who wrote:

> Before I had studied Zen for thirty years, I saw mountains as mountains and waters as waters. When I arrived at a more intimate knowledge, I came to the point where I saw that mountains are not mountains, and waters are not waters. But now that I have got the very substance I am at rest. For it is just that I see mountains once again as mountains, and waters once again as waters.

His identification of what he has made is logically dependent upon the theories and history he rejects. The difference between his utterance and Testadura's "This is black paint and white paint and nothing more" lies in the fact that he is still using the *is* of artistic identification, so that his use of "That black paint is black paint" is not a tautology. Testadura is not at that stage. To see something as art requires something the eye cannot decry – an atmosphere of artistic theory, a knowledge of the history of art: an artworld.

III

Mr. Andy Warhol, the Pop artist, displays facsimiles of Brillo cartons, piled high, in neat stacks, as in the stockroom of the supermarket. They happen to be of wood, painted to look like cardboard, and why not? To paraphrase the critic of the *Times*, if one may make the facsimile of a human being out of bronze, why not the facsimile of a Brillo carton out of plywood? The cost of these boxes happens to be 2×10^3 that of their homely counterparts in real life – a differential hardly ascribable to their advantage in durability. In fact the Brillo people might, at some slight increase in cost, make their boxes out of plywood without these becoming artworks, and Warhol might make *his* out of cardboard without their ceasing to be art. So we may forget questions of intrinsic value, and ask why the Brillo people cannot manufacture art and why Warhol cannot *but* make artworks. Well, his are made by hand, to be sure. Which is like an insane reversal of Picasso's strategy in pasting the label from a bottle of Suze onto a drawing, saying as it were that the academic artist, concerned with exact imitation, must always fall short of the real thing: so why not just *use* the real thing? The Pop artist laboriously reproduces machine-made objects by hand, e.g., painting the labels on coffee cans (one can hear the familiar commendation "Entirely made by hand" falling painfully out of the guide's vocabulary when confronted by these objects). But the difference cannot consist in craft: a man who carved pebbles out of stones and carefully constructed a work called *Gravel Pile* might invoke the labor theory of value to account for the price he demands; but the question is, What makes it art? And why need Warhol *make* these things anyway? Why not just scrawl his signature across one? Or crush one up and display it as *Crushed Brillo Box* ("A protest against mechanization . . .") or simply display a Brillo carton as *Uncrushed Brillo Box* ("A bold affirmation of the plastic authenticity of industrial . . .")? Is this man a kind of Midas, turning whatever he touches into the gold of pure art? And the whole world consisting of latent artworks waiting, like the bread and wine of reality, to be transfigured, through some dark mystery, into the indiscernible flesh and blood of the sacrament? Never mind that the Brillo box may not be good, much less great art. The impressive thing is that it is art at all. But if it is, why are not the indiscernible Brillo boxes that are in the stockroom? Or *has* the whole distinction between art and reality broken down?

Suppose a man collects objects (ready-mades), including a Brillo carton; we praise the exhibit for variety, ingenuity, what you will. Next he exhibits nothing but Brillo cartons, and we criticize it as dull, repetitive, self-plagiarizing – or (more profoundly) claim that he is obsessed by regularity and repetition, as in *Marienbad*. Or he piles them high, leaving a narrow path; we tread our way through the smooth opaque stacks and find it an unsettling experience, and write it up as the closing in of consumer products, confining us as prisoners: or we say he is a modern pyramid builder. True, we don't say these things about the stockboy. But then a stockroom is not an art gallery, and we cannot readily separate the Brillo cartons from the gallery they are in, any more than we can separate the Rauschenberg bed from the paint upon it. Outside the gallery, they are pasteboard cartons. But then, scoured clean of paint, Rauschenberg's bed is a bed, just what it was before it was transformed into art. But then if we think this matter through, we discover that the artist has failed, really and of necessity, to produce a mere real object. He has produced an artwork, his use of real Brillo cartons being but an expansion of the resources available to artists, a contribution to *artists' materials*, as oil paint was, or *tuche*.

What in the end makes the difference between a Brillo box and a work of art consisting of a Brillo Box is a certain theory of art. It is the theory that takes it up into the world of art, and keeps it from collapsing into the real object which it is (in a sense of *is* other than that of artistic identification). Of course, without the theory, one is unlikely to see it as art, and in order to see it as part of the artworld, one must have mastered a good deal of artistic theory as well as a considerable amount of the history of recent New York painting. It could not have been art fifty years ago. But then there could not have been, everything being equal, flight insurance in the Middle Ages, or Etruscan typewriter erasers. The world has to be ready for certain things, the artworld no less than the real one. It is the role of artistic theories, these days as always, to make the artworld, and art, possible. It would, I should think, never have occurred to the painters of Lascaux that they were producing *art* on those walls. Not unless there were neolithic aestheticians.

IV

The artworld stands to the real world in something like the relationship in which the City of God stands to the Earthly City. Certain objects, like certain individuals, enjoy a double citizenship, but there remains, the RT notwithstanding, a fundamental contrast between artworks and real objects. Perhaps this was already dimly sensed by the early framers of the IT who, inchoately realizing the nonreality of art, were perhaps limited only in supposing that the sole way objects had of being other than real is to be sham, so that artworks necessarily had to be imitations of real objects. This was too narrow. So Yeats saw in writing "Once out of nature I shall never take / My bodily form from any natural thing." It is but a matter of choice: and the Brillo box of the artworld may be just the Brillo box of the real one, separated and united by the *is* of artistic identification. But I should like to say some final words about the theories that make artworks possible, and their relationship to one another. In so doing, I shall beg some of the hardest philosophical questions I know.

I shall now think of pairs of predicates related to each other as "opposites," conceding straight off the vagueness of this *démodé* term. Contradictory predicates are not opposites, since one of each of them must apply to every object in the universe, and neither of a pair of opposites need apply to some objects in the universe. An object must first be of a certain kind before either of a pair of opposites applies to it, and then at most and at least one of the opposites must apply to it. So opposites are not contraries, for contraries may both be false of some objects in the universe, but opposites cannot both be false; for of some objects, neither of a pair of opposites *sensibly* applies, unless the object is of the right sort. Then, if the object is of the required kind, the opposites behave as contradictories. If *F* and non-*F* are opposites, an object *o* must be of a certain kind *K* before either of these sensibly applies; but if *o* is a member of *K*, then *o* either is *F* or non-*F*, to the exclusion of the other. The class of pairs of opposites that sensibly apply to the $(\hat{o})Ko$ I shall designate as the class of *K-relevant predicates*. And a necessary condition for an object to be of a kind *K* is that at least one pair of *K*-relevant opposites be sensibly applicable to it. But, in fact, if an object is of kind *K*, at least and at most one of each *K*-relevant pair of opposites applies to it.

I am now interested in the *K*-relevant predicates for the class *K* of artworks. And let *F* and non-*F* be an opposite pair of such predicates. Now it might happen that, throughout an entire period of time, every artwork is non-*F*. But since nothing thus far is both an artwork and *F*, it might never occur to anyone that non-*F* is an artistically relevant predicate. The non-*F*-ness of artworks goes unmarked. By contrast, all works up to a given time might be *G*, it never occurring to anyone until that time that something might both be an artwork and non-*G*; indeed, it might have been thought that *G* was a *defining trait* of artworks when in fact something might first have to be an artwork before *G* is sensibly predicable of it – in which case non-*G* might also be predicable of artworks, and *G* itself then could not have been a defining trait of this class.

Let *G* be 'is representational' and let *F* be 'is expressionist'. At a given time, these and their opposites are perhaps the only art-relevant predicates in critical use. Now letting '+' stand for a given predicate *P* and '–' for its opposite non-*P*, we may construct a style matrix more or less as follows:

F	*G*
+	+
+	–
–	+
–	–

The rows determine available styles, given the active critical vocabulary: representational expressionistic (e.g., Fauvism); representational nonexpressionistic (Ingres); nonrepresentational expressionistic (Abstract Expressionism); nonrepresentational nonexpressionist (hard-edge abstraction). Plainly, as we add art-relevant predicates, we increase the number of available styles at the rate of 2^n. It is, of course, not easy to see in advance which predicates are going to be added or replaced by their opposites, but suppose an artist determines that *H* shall henceforth be artistically relevant for his paintings. Then, in fact, both *H* and non-*H* become artistically relevant for *all* painting, and if his is the first and only painting that is *H*, every other painting in existence becomes non-*H*, and the entire community of paintings is enriched, together with a doubling of the available style opportunities. It is this retroactive enrichment of the entities in the artworld that makes it possible to discuss Raphael and De Kooning together, or Lichtenstein and Michelangelo. The greater the variety of artistically relevant predicates, the more complex the individual members of the artworld become; and the more one knows of the entire population of the artworld, the richer one's experience with any of its members.

In this regard, notice that, if there are *m* artistically relevant predicates, there is always a bottom row with *m* minuses. This row is apt to be occupied by purists. Having scoured their canvasses clear of what they regard as inessential, they credit themselves with having distilled out the essence of art. But this is just their fallacy: exactly as many artistically relevant predicates stand true of their square monochromes as stand true of any member of the Artworld, and they can *exist* as artworks only insofar as "impure" paintings exist. Strictly speaking, a black square by Reinhardt is artistically as rich as Titian's

Sacred and Profane Love. This explains how less is more.

Fashion, as it happens, favors certain rows of the style matrix: museums, connoisseurs, and others are makeweights in the Artworld. To insist, or seek to, that all artists become representational, perhaps to gain entry into a specially prestigious exhibition, cuts the available style matrix in half: there are then $2^n/2$ ways of satisfying the requirement, and museums then can exhibit all these "approaches" to the topic they have set. But this is a matter of almost purely sociological interest: one row in the matrix is as legitimate as another. An artistic breakthrough consists, I suppose, in adding the possibility of a column to the matrix. Artists then, with greater or less alacrity, occupy the positions thus opened up: this is a remarkable feature of contemporary art, and for those unfamiliar with the matrix, it is hard, and perhaps impossible, to recognize certain positions as occupied by artworks. Nor would these things be artworks without the theories and the histories of the Artworld.

Brillo boxes enter the artworld with that same tonic incongruity the *commedia dell'arte* characters bring into *Ariadne auf Naxos*. Whatever is the artistically relevant predicate in virtue of which they gain their entry, the rest of the Artworld becomes that much the richer in having the opposite predicate available and applicable to its members. And, to return to the views of Hamlet with which we began this discussion, Brillo boxes may reveal us to ourselves as well as anything might: as a mirror held up to nature, they might serve to catch the conscience of our kings.

37

What is Art? An Institutional Analysis

George Dickie

George Dickie is Professor Emeritus of Philosophy at the University of Chicago at Illinois.

The attempt to define "art" by specifying its necessary and sufficient conditions is an old endeavor. The first definition – the imitation theory – despite what now seem like obvious difficulties, more or less satisfied everyone until some time in the nineteenth century. After the expression theory of art broke the domination of the imitation theory, many definitions purporting to reveal the necessary and sufficient conditions of art appeared. In the mid-1950s, several philosophers, inspired by Wittgenstein's talk about concepts, began arguing that there are no necessary and sufficient conditions for art. Until recently, this argument had persuaded so many philosophers of the futility of trying to define art that the flow of definitions had all but ceased. Although I will ultimately try to show that "art" can be defined, the denial of that possibility has had the very great value of forcing us to look deeper into the concept of "art." The parade of dreary and superficial definitions that had been presented was, for a variety of reasons, eminently rejectable. The traditional attempts to define "art," from the imitation theory on, may be thought of as Phase I and the contention that "art" cannot be defined as Phase II. I want to supply Phase III by defining "art" in such a way as to avoid the difficulties of the traditional definitions and to incorporate the insights of the later analysis. I should note that the imitation theory of the fine arts seems to have been adopted by those who held it without much serious thought and perhaps cannot be considered as a self-conscious theory of art in the way that the later theories can be.

The traditional attempts at definition have sometimes failed to see beyond prominent but accidental features of works of art, features that have characterized art at a particular stage in its historical development. For example, until quite recently the works of art clearly recognizable as such were either obviously representational or assumed to be representational. Paintings and sculptures were obviously so, and music was widely assumed in some sense also to be representational. Literature was representational in that it described familiar scenes of life. It was, then, easy enough to think that imitation must be the essence of art. The imitation theory focused on a readily evident relational property of works of art, namely, art's relation to subject matter. The development of nonobjective art showed that imitation is not even an always-accompanying property of art, much less an essential one.

The theory of art as the expression of emotion has focused on another relational property of

George Dickie, "What is Art? An Institutional Analysis," in *Art and the Aesthetic: An Institutional Analysis* (Ithaca, NY: Cornell University Press, 1974), pp. 19–52.

works of art, the relation of a work to its creator. The expression theory also has proved inadequate, and no other subsequent definition has been satisfactory. Although not fully satisfying as definitions, the imitation and expression theories do provide a clue: both singled out *relational* properties of art as essential. As I shall try to show, the two defining characteristics of art are indeed relational properties, and one of them turns out to be exceedingly complex.

I

The best-known denial that "art" can be defined occurs in Morris Weitz's article "The Role of Theory in Aesthetics."[1] Weitz's conclusion depends upon two arguments which may be called his "generalization argument" and his "classification argument." In stating the "generalization argument" Weitz distinguishes, quite correctly, between the generic conception of "art" and the various subconcepts of art such as tragedy, the novel, painting, and the like. He then goes on to give an argument purporting to show that the subconcept "novel" is open, that is, that the members of the class of novels do not share any essential or defining characteristics. He then asserts without further argument that what is true of novels is true of all other subconcepts of art. The generalization from one subconcept to all subconcepts may or may not be justified, but I am not questioning it here. I do question, however, Weitz's additional contention, also asserted without argument, that the generic conception of "art" is open. The best that can be said of his conclusion about the generic sense is that it is unsupported. All or some of the subconcepts of art may be open and the generic conception of art still be closed. That is, it is possible that all or some of the subconcepts of art, such as novel, tragedy, sculpture, and painting, may lack necessary and sufficient conditions and at the same time that "work of art," which is the genus of all the subconcepts, can be defined in terms of necessary and sufficient conditions. Tragedies may not have any characteristics in common which would distinguish them from, say, comedies *within the domain of art*, but it may be that there are common characteristics that works of art have which distinguish them from nonart. Nothing prevents a "closed genus/open species" relationship. Weitz himself has recently cited what he takes to be a similar (although reversed) example of genus-species relationship. He argues that "game" (the genus) is open but that "major league baseball" (a species) is closed.[2]

His second argument, "the classification argument," claims to show that not even the characteristic of artifactuality is a necessary feature of art. Weitz's conclusion here is something of a surprise, because it has been widely assumed by philosophers and nonphilosophers alike that a work of art is necessarily an artifact. His argument is simply that we sometimes utter such statements as "This piece of driftwood is a lovely piece of sculpture," and since such utterances are perfectly intelligible, it follows that some nonartifacts such as certain pieces of driftwood are works of art (sculptures). In other words, something need not be an artifact in order to be correctly classified as a work of art. I will try to rebut this argument shortly.

Recently, Maurice Mandelbaum has raised a question about Wittgenstein's famous contention that "game" cannot be defined and Weitz's thesis about "art."[3] His challenge to both is based on the charge that they have been concerned only with what Mandelbaum calls "exhibited" characteristics and that consequently each has failed to take account of the nonexhibited, relational aspects of games and art. By "exhibited" characteristics Mandelbaum means easily perceived properties such as the fact that a ball is used in a certain kind of game, that a painting has a triangular composition, that an area in a painting is red, or that the plot of a tragedy contains a reversal of fortune. Mandelbaum concludes that when we consider the nonexhibited properties of games, we see that they have in common "the potentiality of . . . [an] . . . absorbing non-practical interest to either participants or spectators."[4] Mandelbaum may or may not be right about "game," but what interests me is the application of his suggestion about nonexhibited properties to the discussion of the definition of art. Although he does not attempt a definition of "art," Mandelbaum does suggest that feature(s) common to all works of art may perhaps be discovered that will be a basis for the definition of "art," if the nonexhibited features of art are attended to.

Having noted Mandelbaum's invaluable suggestion about definition, I now return to Weitz's argument concerning artifactuality. In an earlier attempt to show Weitz wrong, I thought it sufficient to point out that there are two senses of "work of art," an evaluative sense and a classificatory one; Weitz himself distinguishes these in his article as the evaluative and the descriptive senses of art. My earlier argument was that if there is more than one sense of "work of art," then the fact that "This piece of driftwood is a lovely piece of sculpture" is intelligible does not prove what Weitz wants it to prove. Weitz would have to show that "sculpture" is being used in the sentence in question in the classificatory sense, and this he makes no attempt to do. My argument assumed that once the distinction is made, it is obvious that "sculpture" is here being used in the evaluative sense. Richard Sclafani has subsequently noted that my argument shows only that Weitz's argument is inconclusive and that Weitz might still be right, even though his argument does not prove his conclusion. Sclafani, however, has constructed a stronger argument against Weitz on this point.[5]

Sclafani shows that there is a third sense of "work of art" and that "driftwood cases" (the nonartifact cases) fall under it. He begins by comparing a paradigm work of art, Brancusi's *Bird in Space*, with a piece of driftwood which looks very much like it. Sclafani says that it seems natural to say of the piece of driftwood that it is a work of art and that we do so because it has so many properties in common with the Brancusi piece. He then asks us to reflect on our characterization of the driftwood and the *direction* it has taken. We say the driftwood is art because of its resemblance to some paradigm work of art or because the driftwood shares properties with several paradigm works of art. The paradigm work or works are of course always artifacts; the direction of our move is from paradigmatic (artifactual) works of art to nonartifactual "art." Sclafani quite correctly takes this to indicate that there is a primary, paradigmatic sense of "work of art" (my classificatory sense) and a derivative or secondary sense into which the "driftwood cases" fall. Weitz is right in a way in saying that the driftwood is art, but wrong in concluding that artifactuality is unnecessary for (the primary sense of) art.

There are then at least three distinct senses of "work of art": the primary or classificatory sense, the secondary or derivative, and the evaluative. Perhaps in most uses of Weitz's driftwood sentence example, both the derivative and the evaluative senses would be involved: the derivative sense if the driftwood shared a number of properties with some paradigm work of art and the evaluative sense if the shared properties were found to be valuable by the speaker. Sclafani gives a case in which only the evaluative sense functions, when someone says, "Sally's cake is a work of art." In most uses of such a sentence "work of art" would simply mean that its referent has valuable qualities. Admittedly, one can imagine contexts in which the derivative sense would apply to cakes. (Given the situation in art today, one can easily imagine cakes to which the primary sense of art could be applied.) If, however, someone were to say, "This Rembrandt is a work of art," both the classificatory and the evaluative senses would be functioning. The expression "this Rembrandt" would convey the information that its referent is a work of art in the classificatory sense, and "is a work of art" could then only reasonably be understood in the evaluative sense. Finally, someone might say of a sea shell or other natural object which resembles a man's face but is otherwise uninteresting, "This shell (or other natural object) is a work of art." In this case, only the derivative sense would be used.

We utter sentences in which the expression "work of art" has the evaluative sense with considerable frequency, applying it to both natural objects and artifacts. We speak of works of art in the derived sense with somewhat less frequency. The classificatory sense of "work of art," which indicates simply that a thing belongs to a certain category of artifacts, occurs, however, very infrequently in our discourse. We rarely utter sentences in which we use the classificatory sense, because it is such a basic notion: we generally know immediately whether an object is a work of art, so that generally no one needs to say, by way of classification, "That is a work of art," although recent developments in art such as junk sculpture and found art may occasionally force such remarks. Even if we do not often talk about art in this classificatory sense, however, it is a basic concept that structures and guides our thinking about our world and its contents.

II

It is now clear that artifactuality is a necessary condition (call it the genus) of the primary sense of art. This fact, however, does not seem very surprising and would not even be very interesting except that Weitz and others have denied it. Artifactuality alone, however, is not the whole story and another necessary condition (the differentia) has to be specified in order to have a satisfactory definition of "art." Like artifactuality, the second condition is a nonexhibited property, which turns out to be as complicated as artifactuality is simple. The attempt to discover and specify the second condition of art will involve an examination of the intricate complexities of the "artworld." W. E. Kennick, defending a view similar to Weitz's, contends that the kind of approach to be employed here, following Mandelbaum's lead, is futile. He concludes that "the attempt to define Art in terms of what we do with certain objects is as doomed as any other."[6] He tries to support this conclusion by referring to such things as the fact that the ancient Egyptians sealed up paintings and sculptures in tombs. There are two difficulties with Kennick's argument. First, that the Egyptians sealed up paintings and sculptures in tombs does not show that they regarded them differently from the way in which we regard them. They might have put them there for the dead to appreciate or simply because they belonged to the dead person. The Egyptian practice does not establish so radical a difference between their conception of art and ours that a definition subsuming both is impossible. Second, one need not assume that we and the ancient Egyptians share a common conception of art. It would be enough to be able to specify the necessary and sufficient conditions for the concept of art which we have (we present-day Americans, we present-day Westerners, we Westerners since the organization of the system of the arts in or about the eighteenth century – I am not sure of the exact limits of the "we"). Kennick notwithstanding, we are most likely to discover the differentia of art by considering "what we do with certain objects." Of course, no thing guarantees that any given thing we might do or an ancient Egyptian might have done with a work of art will throw light on the concept of art. Not every "doing" will reveal what is required.

Although he does not attempt to formulate a definition, Arthur Danto in his provocative article, "The Artworld," has suggested the direction that must be taken by an attempt to define "art,"[7] In reflecting on art and its history together with such present-day developments as Warhol's *Brillo Carton* and Rauschenberg's *Bed*, Danto writes, "To see something as art requires something the eye cannot descry – an atmosphere of artistic theory, a knowledge of history of art: an artworld."[8] Admittedly, this stimulating comment is in need of elucidation, but it is clear that in speaking of "something the eye cannot descry" Danto is agreeing with Mandelbaum that nonexhibited properties are of great importance in constituting something as art. In speaking of atmosphere and history, however, Danto's remark carries us a step further than Mandelbaum's analysis. Danto points to the rich structure in which particular works of art are embedded: he indicates *the institutional nature of art.*[9]

I shall use Danto's term "artworld" to refer to the broad social institution in which works of art have their place.[10] But is there such an institution? George Bernard Shaw speaks somewhere of the apostolic line of succession stretching from Aeschylus to himself. Shaw was no doubt speaking for effect and to draw attention to himself, as he often did, but there is an important truth implied by his remark. There is a long tradition or continuing institution of the theater having its origins in ancient Greek religion and other Greek institutions. That tradition has run very thin at times and perhaps even ceased to exist altogether during some periods, only to be reborn out of its memory and the need for art. The institutions associated with the theater have varied from time to time: in the beginning it was Greek religion and the Greek state; in medieval times, the church; more recently, private business and the state (national theater). What has remained constant with its own identity throughout its history is the theater itself as an established way of doing and behaving, what I shall call in Chapter 7 the primary convention of the theater. This institutionalized behavior occurs on both sides of the "footlights": both the players and the audience are involved and go to make up the institution of the theater. The roles of the actors and the audience are defined by the traditions of the theater.

What the author, management, and players present is art, and it is art because it is presented within the theater-world framework. Plays are written to have a place in the theater system and they exist as plays, that is, as art, within that system. Of course, I do not wish to deny that plays also exist as literary works, that is, as art within the literary system: the theater system and the literary system overlap. Let me make clear what I mean by speaking of the artworld as an institution. Among the meanings of "institution" in *Webster's New Collegiate Dictionary* are the following: "3. That which is instituted as: a. An established practice, law, custom, etc. b. An established society or corporation." When I call the artworld an institution I am saying that it is an established practice. Some persons have thought that an institution must be an established society or corporation and, consequently, have misunderstood my claim about the artworld.

Theater is only one of the systems within the artworld. Each of the systems has had its own origins and historical development. We have some information about the later stages of these developments, but we have to guess about the origins of the basic art systems. I suppose that we have complete knowledge of certain recently developed subsystems or genres such as Dada and happenings. Even if our knowledge is not as complete as we wish it were, however, we do have substantial information about the systems of the artworld as they currently exist and as they have existed for some time. One central feature all of the systems have in common is that each is a framework for the *presenting* of particular works of art. Given the great variety of the systems of the artworld it is not surprising that works of art have no exhibited properties in common. If, however, we step back and view the works in their institutional setting, we will be able to see the essential properties they share.

Theater is a rich and instructive illustration of the institutional nature of art. But it is a development within the domain of painting and sculpture – Dadaism – that most easily reveals the institutional essence of art. Duchamp and friends conferred the status of art on "ready-mades" (urinals, hatracks, snow shovels, and the like), and when we reflect on their deeds we can take note of a kind of human action which has until now gone unnoticed and unappreciated – the action of conferring the status of art. Painters and sculptors, of course, have been engaging all along in the action of conferring this status on the objects they create. As long, however, as the created objects were conventional, given the paradigms of the times, the objects themselves and their fascinating exhibited properties were the focus of the attention of not only spectators and critics but of philosophers of art as well. When an artist of an earlier era painted a picture, he did some or all of a number of things: depicted a human being, portrayed a certain man, fulfilled a commission, worked at his livelihood, and so on. In addition he also acted as an agent of the artworld and conferred the status of art on his creation. Philosophers of art attended to only some of the properties the created object acquired from these various actions, for example, to the representational or to the expressive features of the objects. They entirely ignored the nonexhibited property of status. When however, the objects are bizarre, as those of the Dadaists are, our attention is forced away from the objects' obvious properties to a consideration of the objects in their social context. As works of art Duchamp's "ready-mades" may not be worth much, but as examples of art they are very valuable for art theory. I am not claiming that Duchamp and friends invented the conferring of the status of art; they simply used an existing institutional device in an unusual way. Duchamp did not invent the artworld, because it was there all along.

The artworld consists of a bundle of systems: theater, painting, sculpture, literature, music, and so on, each of which furnishes an institutional background for the conferring of the status on objects within its domain. No limit can be placed on the number of systems that can be brought under the generic conception of art, and each of the major systems contains further subsystems. These features of the artworld provide the elasticity whereby creativity of even the most radical sort can be accommodated. A whole new system comparable to the theater, for example, could be added in one fell swoop. What is more likely is that a new subsystem would be added within a system. For example, junk sculpture added within sculpture, happenings added within theater. Such additions might in time develop into full-blown systems. Thus, the radical creativity, adventuresomeness, and exuberance of art of which Weitz speaks is possible within the concept of art, even though it is closed by the necessary and sufficient conditions of artifactuality and conferred status.

Having now briefly described the artworld, I am in a position to specify a definition of "work of art." The definition will be given in terms of artifactuality and the conferred status of art or, more strictly speaking, the conferred status of candidate for appreciation. Once the definition has been stated, a great deal will still remain to be said by way of clarification: A work of art in the classificatory sense is (1) an artifact (2) a set of the aspects of which has had conferred upon it the status of candidate for appreciation by some person or persons acting on behalf of a certain social institution (the artworld).

The second condition of the definition makes use of four variously interconnected notions: (1) acting on behalf of an institution, (2) conferring of status, (3) being a candidate, and (4) appreciation. The first two of these are so closely related that they must be discussed together. I shall first describe paradigm cases of conferring status outside the artworld and then show how similar actions take place within the artworld. The most clear-cut examples of the conferring of status are certain legal actions of the state. A king's conferring of knighthood, a grand jury's indicting someone, the chairman of the election board certifying that someone is qualified to run for office, or a minister's pronouncing a couple man and wife are examples in which a person or persons acting on behalf of a social institution (the state) confer(s) *legal* status on persons. The congress or a legally constituted commission may confer the status of national park or monument on an area or thing. The examples given suggest that pomp and ceremony are required to establish legal status, but this is not so, although of course a legal system is presupposed. For example, in some jurisdictions common-law marriage is possible – a legal status acquired without ceremony. The conferring of a PhD degree on someone by a university, the election of someone as president of the Rotary, and the declaring of an object as a relic of the church are examples in which a person or persons confer(s) nonlegal status on persons or things. In such cases some social system or other must exist as the framework within which the conferring takes place, but, as before, ceremony is not required to establish status: for example, a person can acquire the status of wise man or village idiot within a community without ceremony.

Some may feel that the notion of conferring status within the artworld is excessively vague. Certainly this notion is not as clear-cut as the conferring of status within the legal system, where procedures and lines of authority are explicitly defined and incorporated into law. The counterparts in the artworld to specified procedures and lines of authority are nowhere codified, and the artworld carries on its business at the level of customary practice. Still there *is* a practice and this defines a social institution. A social institution need not have a formally established constitution, officers, and bylaws in order to exist and have the capacity to confer status – some social institutions are formal and some are informal. The artworld could become formalized, and perhaps has been to some extent in certain political contexts, but most people who are interested in art would probably consider this a bad thing. Such formality would threaten the freshness and exuberance of art. The core personnel of the artworld is a loosely organized, but nevertheless related, set of persons including artists (understood to refer to painters, writers, composers), producers, museum directors, museum-goers, theater-goers, reporters for newspapers, critics for publications of all sorts, art historians, art theorists, philosophers of art, and others. These are the people who keep the machinery of the artworld working and thereby provide for its continuing existence. In addition, every person who sees himself as a member of the artworld is thereby a member. Although I have called the persons just listed the core personnel of the artworld, there is a minimum core within that core without which the artworld would not exist. This essential core consists of artists who create the works, "presenters" to present the works, and "goers" who appreciate the works. This minimum core might be called "the presentation group," for it consists of artists whose activity is necessary if anything is to be presented, the presenters (actors, stage managers, and so on), and the goers whose presence and cooperation is necessary in order for anything to be presented. A given person might play more than one of these essential roles in the case of the presentation of a particular work. Critics, historians, and philosophers of art become members of the artworld at some time after the minimum core personnel of a particular art system get that system into operation. All of these roles are institutionalized and must be learned in one way or another by the participants. For example, a theater-goer is not just someone who happens to enter a theater; he is a person who enters with certain expectations and knowledge about what he will experience and an understanding of how he should behave in the face of what he will experience.

Assuming that the existence of the artworld has been established or at least made plausible, the problem is now to see how status is conferred by this institution. My thesis is that, in a way analogous to the way in which a person is certified as qualified for office, or two persons acquire the status of common-law marriage within a legal system, or a person is elected president of the Rotary, or a person acquires the status of wise man within a community, so an artifact can acquire the status of candidate for appreciation within the social system called "the artworld." How can one tell when the status has been conferred? An artifact's hanging in an art museum as part of a show and a performance at a theater are sure signs. There is, of course, no guarantee that one can always know whether something is a candidate for appreciation, just as one cannot always tell whether a given person is a knight or is married. When an object's status depends upon nonexhibited characteristics, a simple look at the object will not necessarily reveal that status. The nonexhibited relation *may* be symbolized by some badge, for example, by a wedding ring, in which case a simple look will reveal the status.

The more important question is that of how the status of candidate for appreciation is conferred. The examples just mentioned, display in a museum and a performance in a theater, seem to suggest that a number of persons are required for the actual conferring of the status. In one sense a number of persons are required but in another sense only one person is required: a number of persons are required to make up the social institution of the artworld, but only one person is required to act on behalf of the artworld and to confer the status of candidate for appreciation. In fact, many works of art are seen only by one person – the one who creates them – but they are still art. The status in question may be acquired by a single person's acting on behalf of the artworld and *treating an artifact as a candidate for appreciation*. Of course, nothing prevents a group of persons from conferring the status, but it is usually conferred by a single person, the artist who creates the artifact. It may be helpful to compare and contrast the notion of conferring the status of candidate for appreciation with a case in which something is simply presented for appreciation: hopefully this will throw light on the notion of status of candidate. Consider the case of a salesman of plumbing supplies who spreads his wares before us. "Placing before" and "conferring the status of candidate for appreciation" are very different notions, and this difference can be brought out by comparing the salesman's action with the superficially similar act of Duchamp in entering a urinal which he christened *Fountain* in that now-famous art show. The difference is that Duchamp's action took place within the institutional setting of the artworld and the plumbing salesman's action took place outside of it. The salesman could do what Duchamp did, that is, convert a urinal into a work of art, but such a thing probably would not occur to him. Please remember that *Fountain's* being a work of art does not mean that it is a good one, nor does this qualification insinuate that it is a bad one either. The antics of a particular present-day artist serve to reinforce the point of the Duchamp case and also to emphasize a significance of the practice of naming works of art. Walter de Maria has in the case of one of his works even gone through the motions, no doubt as a burlesque, of using a procedure used by many legal and some nonlegal institutions – the procedure of licensing. His *High Energy Bar* (a stainless-steel bar) is accompanied by a certificate bearing the name of the work and stating that the bar is a work of art only when the certificate is present. In addition to highlighting the status of art by "certifying" it on a document, this example serves to suggest a significance of the act of naming works of art. An object may acquire the status of art without ever being named but giving it a title makes clear to whomever is interested that an object is a work of art. Specific titles function in a variety of ways – as aids to understanding a work or as a convenient way of identifying it, for example – but any title at all (even *Untitled*) is a badge of status.[11]

The third notion involved in the second condition of the definition is candidacy: a member of the artworld confers the status of candidate for appreciation. The definition does not require that a work of art actually be appreciated, even by one person. The fact is that many, perhaps most, works of art go unappreciated. It is important not to build into the definition of the classificatory sense of "work of art" value properties such as actual appreciation: to do so would make it impossible to speak of unappreciated works of art. Building in value properties might even make it awkward to speak of bad works of art. A theory of art must preserve certain central features of the way in which we talk about art, and we do find it necessary sometimes to speak of unappreciated art and of bad art. Also, not every aspect of a work is included in the candidacy for appreciation; for example, the color of the back of a painting is not ordinarily considered to be something which someone might think it appropriate to appreciate. The problem of which aspects of a work of art are to be included within the candidacy for appreciation is a question I shall pursue later in Chapter 7 in trying to give an analysis of the notion of aesthetic object. The definition of "work of art" should not, therefore, be understood as asserting that every aspect of a work is included within the candidacy for appreciation.

The fourth notion involved in the second condition of the definition is appreciation itself. Some may assume that the definition is referring to a special kind of *aesthetic* appreciation. I shall argue later in Chapters 4, 5, and 6 that there is no reason to think that there is a special kind of aesthetic consciousness, attention, or perception. Similarly, I do not think there is any reason to think that there is a special kind of aesthetic appreciation. All that is meant by "appreciation" in the definition is something like "in experiencing the qualities of a thing one finds them worthy or valuable," and this meaning applies quite generally both inside and outside the domain of art. Several persons have felt that my account of the institutional theory of art is incomplete because of what they see as my insufficient analysis of "appreciation." They have, I believe, thought that there are different kinds of appreciation and that the appreciation in the appreciation of art is somehow typically different from the appreciation in the appreciation of nonart. But the only sense in which there is a difference between the appreciation of art and the appreciation of nonart is that the appreciations have different *objects*. The institutional structure in which the art object is embedded, not different kinds of appreciation, makes the difference between the appreciation of art and the appreciation of nonart.

In a recent article[12] Ted Cohen has raised a question concerning (1) candidacy for appreciation and (2) appreciation as these two were treated in my original attempt to define "art."[13] He claims that in order for it to be possible for candidacy for appreciation to be conferred on something it must be possible for that thing to be appreciated. Perhaps he is right about this; in any event, I cannot think of any reason to disagree with him on this point. The possibility of appreciation is one constraint on the definition: if something cannot be appreciated, it cannot become art. The question that now arises is: is there anything which it is impossible to appreciate? Cohen claims many things cannot be appreciated; for example, "ordinary thumbtacks, cheap white envelopes, the plastic forks given at some drive-in restaurants."[14] But more importantly, he claims that *Fountain* cannot be appreciated. He says that *Fountain* has a point which can be appreciated, but that it is Duchamp's gesture that has significance (can be appreciated) and not *Fountain* itself. I agree that *Fountain* has the significance Cohen attributes to it, namely, that it was a protest against the art of its day. But why cannot the ordinary qualities of *Fountain* – its gleaming white surface, the depth revealed when it reflects images of surrounding objects, its pleasing oval shape – be appreciated. It has qualities similar to those of works by Brancusi and Moore which many do not balk at saying they appreciate. Similarly, thumbtacks, envelopes, and plastic forks have qualities that can be appreciated if one makes the effort to focus attention on them. One of the values of photography is its ability to focus on and bring out the qualities of quite ordinary objects. And the same sort of thing can be done without the benefit of photography by just looking. In short, it seems unlikely to me that any object would not have some quality which is appreciatable and thus likely that the constraint Cohen suggests may well be vacuous. But even if there are some objects that cannot be appreciated, *Fountain* and the other Dadaist creations are not among them.

I should note that in accepting Cohen's claim I am saying that every work of art must have some minimal *potential* value or worthiness. This fact, however, does not collapse the distinction between the evaluative sense and the classificatory sense of "work of art." The evaluative sense is used when the object it is predicated of is deemed *to be* of substantial, actual value, and that object may be a natural object. I will further note that the appreciatability of a work of art in the classificatory sense is *potential* value which in a given case may never be realized.[15]

The definition I have given contains a reference to the artworld. Consequently, some may have the uncomfortable feeling that my definition is viciously circular. Admittedly, in a sense the definition is circular, but it is not viciously so. If I had said something like "A work of art is an artifact on which a status has been conferred by the artworld" and then said of the artworld only that it confers the status of candidacy for appreciation, then the definition would be viciously circular because the circle would be so small and *uninformative.* I have, however, devoted a considerable amount of space in this chapter to describing and analyzing the historical, organizational, and functional intricacies of the artworld, and if this account is accurate the reader has received a considerable amount of *information* about the artworld. The circle I have run is not small and it is not uninformative. If, in the end, the artworld cannot be described independently of art, that is, if the description contains references to art historians, art reporters, plays, theaters, and so on, then the definition strictly speaking is circular. It is not, however, viciously so, because the whole account in which the definition is embedded contains a great deal of information about the artworld. One must not focus narrowly on the definition alone: for what is important to see is that art is an institutional concept and this requires seeing the definition in the context of the whole account. I suspect that the "problem" of circularity will arise frequently, perhaps always, when institutional concepts are dealt with.

III

The instances of Dadaist art and similar present-day developments which have served to bring the institutional nature of art to our attention suggest several questions. First, if Duchamp can convert such artifacts as a urinal, a snow shovel, and a hatrack into works of art, why can't natural objects such as driftwood also become works of art in the classificatory sense? Perhaps they can if any one of a number of things is done to them. One way in which this might happen would be for someone to pick up a natural object, take it home, and hang it on the wall. Another way would be to pick up a natural object and enter it in an exhibition. I was assuming earlier, by the way, that the piece of driftwood referred to in Weitz's sentence was in place on a beach and untouched by human hand or at least untouched by any human intention and therefore was art in the evaluative or derivative sense. Natural objects which become works of art in the classificatory sense are artifactualized without the use of tools – artifactuality is conferred on the object rather than worked on it. This means that natural objects which become works of art acquire their artifactuality at the same time that the status of candidate for appreciation is conferred on them, although the act that confers artifactuality is not the same act that confers the status of candidate for appreciation. But perhaps a similar thing ordinarily happens with paintings and poems; they come to exist as artifacts at the same time that they have the status of candidate for appreciation conferred on them. Of course, being an artifact and being a candidate for appreciation are not the same thing – they are two properties which may be acquired at the same time. Many may find the notion of artifactuality being conferred rather than "worked" on an object too strange to accept and admittedly it is an unusual conception. It may be that a special account will have to be worked out for exhibited driftwood and similar cases.

Another question arising with some frequency in connection with discussions of the concept of art and seeming especially relevant in the context of the institutional theory is "How are we to conceive of paintings done by individuals such as Betsy the chimpanzee from the Baltimore Zoo?"

Calling Betsy's products paintings is not meant to prejudge that they are works of art, it is just that some word is needed to refer to them. The question of whether Betsy's paintings are art depends upon what is done with them. For example, a year or two ago the Field Museum of Natural History in Chicago exhibited some chimpanzee and gorilla paintings. We must say that these paintings are not works of art. If, however, they had been exhibited a few miles away at the Chicago Art Institute they would have been works of art – the paintings would have been art if the director of the Art Institute had been willing to go out on a limb for his fellow primates. A great deal depends upon the institutional setting: one institutional setting is congenial to conferring the status of art and the other is not. Please note that although paintings such as Betsy's would remain her paintings even if exhibited at an art museum, they would be the *art* of the person responsible for their being exhibited. Betsy would not (I assume) be able to conceive of herself in such a way as to be a member of the artworld and, hence, would not be able to confer the relevant status. Art is a concept which necessarily involves human intentionality. These last remarks are not intended to denigrate the value (including beauty) of the paintings of chimpanzees shown at natural history museums or the creations of bower birds, but as remarks about what falls under a particular concept.

Danto in "Art Works and Real Things" discusses defeating conditions of the ascriptivity of art.[16] He considers fake paintings, that is, copies of original paintings which are attributed to the creators of the original paintings. He argues that a painting's being a fake prevents it from being a work of art, maintaining that originality is an analytical requirement of being a work of art. That a work is derivative or imitative does not, however, he thinks, prevent it from being a work of art. I think Danto is right about fake paintings, and I can express this in terms of my own account by saying that originality in paintings is an antecedent requirement for the conferring of the candidacy for appreciation. Similar sorts of things would have to be said for similar cases in the arts other than painting. One consequence of this requirement is that there are many works of nonart which people take to be works of art, namely, those fake paintings which are not known to be fakes. When fakes are discovered to be fakes, they do not lose that status of art because they never had the status in the first place, despite what almost everyone had thought. There is some analogy here with patent law. Once an invention has been patented, one exactly like it cannot be patented – the patent for just that invention has been "used up." In the case of patenting, of course, whether the second device is a copy or independently derived is unimportant, but the copying aspect is crucial in the artistic case. The Van Meegeren painting that was not a copy of an actual Vermeer but a painting done in the manner of Vermeer with a forged signature is a somewhat more complicated case. The painting with the forged signature is not a work of art, but if Van Meegeren had signed his own name the painting would have been.

Strictly speaking, since originality is an analytic requirement for a painting to be a work of art, an originality clause should be incorporated into my definition of "work of art." But since I have not given any analysis of the originality requirement with respect to works other than paintings, I am not in a position to supplement the definition in this way. All I can say at this time is what I said just above, namely, that originality in paintings is an antecedent requirement for the conferring of the candidacy for appreciation and that considerations of a similar sort probably apply in the other arts.

Weitz charges that the defining of "art" or its subconcepts forecloses on creativity. Some of the traditional definitions of "art" *may* have and some of the traditional definitions of its subconcepts probably *did* foreclose on creativity, but this danger is now past. At one time a playwright, for example, may have conceived of and wished to write a play with tragic features but lacking a defining characteristic as specified by, say, Aristotle's definition of "tragedy." Faced with this dilemma the playwright might have been intimidated into abandoning his project. With the present-day disregard for established genres, however, and the clamor for novelty in art, this obstacle to creativity no longer exists. Today, if a new and unusual work is created and it is similar to some members of an established type of art, it will usually be accommodated within that type, or if the new work is very unlike any existing works then a new subconcept will probably be created. Artists today are not easily intimidated, and they regard art genres as loose guidelines rather than rigid specifications. Even if a philosopher's remarks were to have an effect on what artists do today, the institutional conception of art would certainly not foreclose on creativity. The requirement of artifactuality cannot prevent creativity, since artifactuality is a necessary condition of creativity. There cannot be an instance of creativity without an artifact of some kind being produced. The second requirement involving the conferring of status could not inhibit creativity; in fact, it encourages it. Since under the definition anything whatever may become art, the definition imposes no restraints on creativity.

The institutional theory of art may sound like saying, "A work of art is an object of which someone has said, 'I christen this object a work of art.'" And it is rather like that, although this does not mean that the conferring of the status of art is a simple matter. Just as the christening of a child has as its background the history and structure of the church, conferring the status of art has as its background the Byzantine complexity of the artworld. Some may find it strange that in the nonart cases discussed, there are ways in which the conferring can go wrong, while that does not appear to be true in art. For example, an indictment might be improperly drawn up and the person charged would not actually be indicted, but nothing parallel seems possible in the case of art. This fact just reflects the differences between the artworld and legal institutions: the legal system deals with matters of grave personal consequences and its procedures must reflect this; the artworld deals with important matters also but they are of a different sort entirely. The artworld does not require rigid procedures; it admits and even encourages frivolity and caprice without losing its serious purpose. Please note that not all legal procedures are as rigid as court procedures and that mistakes made in conferring certain kinds of legal status are not fatal to that status. A minister may make mistakes in reading the marriage ceremony, but the couple that stands before him will still acquire the status of being married. If, however, a mistake cannot be made *in* conferring the status of art, a mistake can be made *by* conferring it. In conferring the status of art on an object one assumes a certain kind of responsibility for the object in its new status – presenting a candidate for appreciation always allows the possibility that no one will appreciate it and that the person who did the conferring will thereby lose face. One *can* make a work of art out of a sow's ear, but that does not necessarily make it a silk purse.

IV

Once the institutional nature of art is noted, the roles that such "theories of art" as the imitation and expression theories played in thinking about art can be seen in an interesting perspective. For example, as long as all art was imitative or thought to be imitative, imitation was thought to be a universal property of art. Not surprisingly, what was thought to be the only universal property of art was taken to be the defining property of art. What happened was that an assumed always-accompanying property was mistaken for an essential property, and this mistake led to a mistaken theory of art. Once the imitation theory was formulated, it tended to work in a normative way to encourage artists to be imitative. Of course, philosophical theories do not generally have much effect on the practices of men. The imitation theory in the past may, however, have had more than the usual slight impact, because it was based on a widespread feature of art and therefore reinforced an emphasis on an easily perceived characteristic and because the class of artists was relatively small and contained lines of communication.

The role played by the expression theory was quite different from that of the imitation theory. It was seen as a replacement for the imitation theory and served as its correction. Developments in art had shown that the imitation theory was incorrect and it was quite natural to seek a substitute that focused on another exhibited property of art, in this case its expressive qualities, interpreting them as expressions of the artists. I suspect that the expression theory had a normative role in a way that the imitation theory did not. That is, the expression theory was on the part of many of its proponents an attempt to "reform" art. Whether the expression theorists saw themselves as attempting to influence the creation of art with a certain kind of content or to separate art from something which pretended to be art, they aimed at reform.

From the point of view of the institutional theory, both the imitation theory and the expression theory are mistaken as theories of art. If, however, they are approached as attempts to focus attention on aspects of art (its representative and expressive qualities) which have been and continue to be of great importance, then they have served and continue to serve a valuable function. The institutional definition of "art" does not reveal everything that art can do. A great deal remains to be said about the kinds of thing that art can do, and the imitation and expression theories indicate what *some* of these things are, although not in a perfectly straightforward way.

Notes

1 *Journal of Aesthetics and Art Criticism*, September 1956, pp. 27–35. See also Paul Ziff's "The Task of Defining a Work of Art," *Philosophical Review*, January 1953, pp. 58–78; and W. E. Kennick's "Does Traditional Aesthetics Rest on a Mistake?" *Mind*, July 1958, pp. 317–34.

2 "Wittgenstein's Aesthetics," in *Language and Aesthetics*, Benjamin R. Tilghman, ed. (Lawrence, Kans., 1973), p. 14. This paper was read at a symposium at Kansas State University in April 1970. Monroe Beardsley has pointed out to me that the relationship between "game" and "major league baseball" is one of class and member rather than of genus and species.

3 "Family Resemblances and Generalizations Concerning the Arts," *American Philosophical Quarterly*, July 1965, pp. 219–28; reprinted in *Problems in Aesthetics*, Morris Weitz, ed., 2d ed. (London, 1970), pp. 181–97.

4 Ibid., p. 185 in the Weitz anthology.

5 "'Art' and Artifactuality," *Southwestern Journal of Philosophy*, Fall 1970, pp. 105–8.

6 "Does Traditional Aesthetics Rest on a Mistake?" p. 330.

7 *Journal of Philosophy*, October 15, 1964, pp. 571–84.

8 Ibid., p. 580.

9 Danto does not develop an institutional account of art in his article nor in a subsequent related article entitled "Art Works and Real Things," *Theoria*, Parts 1–3, 1973, pp. 1–17. In both articles Danto's primary concern is to discuss what he calls the Imitation Theory and the Real Theory of Art. Many of the things he says in these two articles are consistent with and can be incorporated into an institutional account, and his brief remarks in the later article about the ascriptivity of art are similar to the institutional theory. The institutional theory is one possible version of the ascriptivity theory.

10 This remark is not intended as a definition of the term "artworld," I am merely indicating what the expression is used to *refer* to. "Artworld" is nowhere defined in this book, although the referent of the expression is described in some detail.

11 Recently in an article entitled "The Republic of Art" in *British Journal of Aesthetics*, April 1969, pp. 145–56, T. J. Diffey has talked about the status of art being conferred. He, however, is attempting to give an account of something like an evaluative sense of "work of art" rather than the classificatory sense, and consequently the scope of his theory is much narrower than mine.

12 "The Possibility of Art: Remarks on a Proposal by Dickie," *Philosophical Review*, January 1973, pp. 69–82.

13 "Defining Art," *American Philosophical Quarterly*, July 1969, pp. 253–6.

14 "The Possibility of Art," p. 78.

15 I realized that I must make the two points noted in this paragraph as the result of a conversation with Mark Venezia. I wish to thank him for the stimulation of his remarks.

16 Pages 12–14.

38

When is Art?

Nelson Goodman

Nelson Goodman (1906–98) was Professor of Philosophy at Harvard University.

1. The Pure in Art

If attempts to answer the question "What is art?" characteristically end in frustration and confusion, perhaps – as so often in philosophy – the question is the wrong one. A reconception of the problem, together with application of some results of a study of the theory of symbols, may help to clarify such moot matters as the role of symbolism in art and the status as art of the 'found object' and so-called 'conceptual art'.

One remarkable view of the relation of symbols to works of art is illustrated in an incident bitingly reported by Mary McCarthy:[1]

> Seven years ago, when I taught in a progressive college, I had a pretty girl student in one of my classes who wanted to be a short-story writer. She was not studying with me, but she knew that I sometimes wrote short stories, and one day, breathless and glowing, she came up to me in the hall, to tell me that she had just written a story that her writing teacher, a Mr. Converse, was terribly excited about. "He thinks it's wonderful" she said, "and he's going to help me fix it up for publication."
>
> I asked what the story was about; the girl was a rather simple being who loved clothes and dates. Her answer had a deprecating tone. It was about a girl (herself) and some sailors she had met on the train. But then her face, which had looked perturbed for a moment, gladdened.
>
> "Mr. Converse is going over it with me and we're going to put in the symbols."

Nelson Goodman, "When is Art?," in *Ways of Worldmaking* (Indianapolis, IN: Hackett Publishing, 1978), pp. 57–70.

Today the bright-eyed art student will more likely be told, with equal subtlety, to keep out the symbols; but the underlying assumption is the same: that symbols, whether enhancements or distractions, are extrinsic to the work itself. A kindred notion seems to be reflected in what we take to be symbolic art. We think first of such works as Bosch's *Garden of Delight* or Goya's *Caprichos* or the Unicorn tapestries or Dali's drooping watches, and then perhaps of religious paintings, the more mystical the better. What is remarkable here is less the association of the symbolic with the esoteric or unearthly than the classification of works as symbolic upon the basis of their having symbols as their subject matter – that is, upon the basis of their depicting rather than of being symbols. This leaves as nonsymbolic art not only works that depict nothing but also portraits, still-lifes, and landscapes where the subjects are rendered in a straightforward way without arcane allusions and do not themselves stand as symbols.

On the other hand, when we choose works for classification as nonsymbolic, as art without symbols, we confine ourselves to works without subjects; for example, to purely abstract or decorative or formal paintings or buildings or musical compositions. Works that represent anything, no matter what and no matter how prosaically, are excluded; for to represent is surely to refer, to stand for, to symbolize. Every representational work is a symbol; and art without symbols is restricted to art without subject.

That representational works are symbolic according to one usage and nonsymbolic according to another matters little so long as we do not confuse the two usages. What matters very much, though, according to many contemporary artists and critics, is to isolate the work of art as such from whatever it symbolizes or refers to in any way. Let me set forth in quotation marks, since I am offering it for consideration without now expressing any opinion of it, a composite statement of a currently much advocated program or policy or point of view:

> "What a picture symbolizes is external to it, and extraneous to the picture as a work of art. Its subject if it has one, its references – subtle or obvious – by means of symbols from some more or less well-recognized vocabulary, have nothing to do with its aesthetic or artistic significance or character. Whatever a picture refers to or stands for in any way, overt or occult, lies outside it. What really counts is not any such relationship to something else, not what the picture symbolizes, but what it is in itself – what its own intrinsic qualities are. Moreover, the more a picture focuses attention on what it symbolizes, the more we are distracted from its own properties. Accordingly, any symbolization by a picture is not only irrelevant but disturbing. Really pure art shuns all symbolization, refers to nothing, and is to be taken for just what it is, for its inherent character, not for anything it is associated with by some such remote relation as symbolization."

Such a manifesto packs punch. The counsel to concentrate on the intrinsic rather than the extrinsic, the insistence that a work of art is what it is rather than what it symbolizes, and the conclusion that pure art dispenses with external reference of all kinds have the solid sound of straight thinking, and promise to extricate art from smothering thickets of interpretation and commentary.

2. A Dilemma

But a dilemma confronts us here, If we accept this doctrine of the formalist or purist, we seem to be saying that the content of such works as the *Garden of Delight* and the *Caprichos* doesn't really matter and might better be left out. If we reject the doctrine, we seem to be holding that what counts is not just what a work is but lots of things it isn't. In the one case we seem to be advocating lobotomy on many great works; in the other we seem to be condoning impurity in art, emphasizing the extraneous.

The best course, I think, is to recognize the purist position as all right and all wrong. But how can that be? Let's begin by agreeing that what is extraneous is extraneous. But is what a symbol symbolizes always external to it? Certainly not for symbols of all kinds. Consider the symbols:

(*a*) "this string of words", which stands for itself;
(*b*) "word", which applies to itself among other words;
(*c*) "short", which applies to itself and some other words and many other things; and
(*d*) "having seven syllables", which has seven syllables.

Obviously what some symbols symbolize does not lie entirely outside the symbols. The cases cited are, of course, quite special ones, and the analogues among pictures – that is, pictures that are pictures of themselves or include themselves in what they depict – can perhaps be set aside as too rare and idiosyncratic to carry any weight. Let's agree for the present that what a work represents, except in a few cases like these, is external to it and extraneous.

Does this mean that any work that represents nothing meets the purist's demands? Not at all. In the first place, some surely symbolic works such as Bosch's paintings of weird monsters, or the tapestry of a unicorn, represent nothing; for there are no such monsters or demons or unicorns anywhere but in such pictures or in verbal descriptions. To say that the tapestry 'represents a unicorn' amounts only to saying that it is a unicorn-picture, not that there is any animal, or anything at all that it portrays.[2] These works, even though there is nothing they represent, hardly satisfy the purist. Perhaps, though, this is just another philosopher's quibble; and I won't press the point. Let's agree that such pictures, though they represent nothing, are representational in character, hence symbolic and so not 'pure'. All the same, we must note in passing that their being representational involves no representation of anything outside them, so that the purist's objection to them cannot be on that ground. His case will have to be modified in one way or another, with some sacrifice of simplicity and force.

In the second place, not only representational works are symbolic. An abstract painting that represents nothing and is not representational at all may express, and so symbolize, a feeling or other quality, or an emotion or idea.[3] Just because expression is a way of symbolizing something outside the painting – which does not itself sense, feel or think – the purist rejects abstract expressionist as well as representational works.

For a work to be an instance of 'pure' art, of art without symbols, it must on this view neither represent nor express nor even be representational or expressive. But is that enough? Granted, such a work does not stand for anything outside it; all it has are its own properties. But of course if we put it that way, all the properties any picture or anything else has – even such a property as that of representing a given person – are properties of the picture, not properties outside it.

The predictable response is that the important distinction among the several properties a work may have lies between its internal or intrinsic and its external or extrinsic properties; that while all are indeed its own properties, some of them obviously relate the picture to other things; and that a nonrepresentational, nonexpressive work has only internal properties.

This plainly doesn't work; for under any even faintly plausible classification of properties into internal and external, any picture or anything else has properties of both kinds. That a picture is in the Metropolitan Museum, that it was painted in Duluth, that it is younger than Methuselah, would hardly be called internal properties. Getting rid of representation and expression does not give us something free of such external or extraneous properties.

Furthermore, the very distinction between internal and external properties is a notoriously muddled one. Presumably the colors and shapes in a picture must be considered internal; but if an external property is one that relates the picture or object to something else, then colors and shapes obviously must be counted as external; for the color or shape of an object not only may be shared by other objects but also relates the object to others having the same or different colors or shapes.

Sometimes, the terms "internal" and "intrinsic" are dropped in favor of "formal". But the formal in this context cannot be a matter of shape alone. It must include color, and if color, what else? Texture? Size? Material? Of course, we may at will enumerate properties that are to be called formal; but the 'at will' gives the case away. The rationale, the justification, evaporates. The properties left out as nonformal can no longer be characterized as all and only those that relate the picture to something outside it. So we are still faced with the question what if any *principle* is involved – the question how the properties that matter in a nonrepresentational, nonexpressive painting are distinguished from the rest.

I think there is an answer to the question; but to approach it, we'll have to drop all this high-sounding talk of art and philosophy, and come down to earth with a thud.

3. Samples

Consider again an ordinary swatch of textile in a tailor's or upholsterer's sample book. It is unlikely to be a work of art or to picture or express anything. It's simply a sample – a simple sample. But what is it a sample of? Texture, color, weave, thickness, fiber content. . . . ; the whole point of this sample, we are tempted to say, is that it was cut from a bolt and has all the same properties as the rest of the material. But that would be too hasty.

Let me tell you two stories – or one story with two parts. Mrs. Mary Tricias studied such a sample book, made her selection, and ordered from her favorite textile shop enough material for her overstuffed chair and sofa – insisting that it be exactly like the sample. When the bundle came she opened it eagerly and was dismayed when several hundred 2″ × 3″ pieces with zigzag edges exactly like the sample fluttered to the floor. When she called the shop, protesting loudly, the proprietor replied, injured and weary, "But Mrs. Tricias, you said the material must be exactly like the sample. When it arrived from the factory yesterday, I kept my assistants here half the night cutting it up to match the sample."

This incident was nearly forgotten some months later, when Mrs. Tricias, having sewed the pieces together and covered her furniture, decided to have a party. She went to the local bakery, selected a chocolate cupcake from those on display and ordered enough for fifty guests, to be delivered two weeks later. Just as the guests were beginning to arrive, a truck drove up with a single huge cake. The lady running the bake-shop was utterly discouraged by the complaint. "But Mrs. Tricias, you have no idea how much trouble we went to. My husband runs the textile shop and he warned me that your order would have to be in one piece."

The moral of this story is not simply that you can't win, but that a sample is a sample of some of its properties but not others. The swatch is a sample of texture, color, etc. but not of size or shape. The cupcake is a sample of color, texture, size, and shape, but still not of all its properties. Mrs. Tricias would have complained even more loudly if what was delivered to her was like the sample in having been baked on that same day two weeks earlier.

Now in general which of its properties is a sample a sample of? Not all its properties; for then the sample would be a sample of nothing but itself. And not its 'formal' or 'internal' or, indeed, any one specifiable set of properties. The kind of property sampled differs from case to case: the cupcake but not the swatch is a sample of size and shape; a specimen of ore may be a sample of what was mined at a given time and place. Moreover, the sampled properties vary widely with context and circumstance. Although the swatch is normally a sample of its texture, etc. but not of its shape or size, if I show it to you in answer to the question "What is an upholsterer's sample?" it then functions not as a sample of the material but as a sample of an upholsterer's sample, so that its size and shape are now among the properties it is a sample of.

In sum, the point is that a sample is a sample of – or *exemplifies* – only some of its properties, and that the properties to which it bears this relationship of exemplification[4] vary with circumstances and can only be distinguished as those properties that it serves, under the given circumstances, as a sample of. Being a sample of or exemplifying is a relationship something like that of being a friend; my friends are not distinguished by any single identifiable property or cluster of properties, but only by standing, for a period of time, in the relationship of friendship with me.

The implications for our problem concerning works of art may now be apparent. The properties that count in a purist painting are those that the picture makes manifest, selects, focuses upon, exhibits, heightens in our consciousness – those that it shows forth – in short, those properties that it does not merely possess but *exemplifies*, stands as a sample of.

If I am right about this, then even the purist's purest painting symbolizes. It exemplifies certain of its properties. But to exemplify is surely to symbolize – exemplification no less than representation or expression is a form of reference. A work of art, however free of representation and expression, is still a symbol even though what it symbolizes be not things or people or feelings but certain patterns of shape, color, texture that it shows forth.

What, then, of the purist's initial pronouncement that I said facetiously is all right and all wrong? It is all right in saying that what is extraneous is extraneous, in pointing out that what a picture represents often matters very little, in arguing that neither representation nor expression is required of a work, and in stressing the importance of so-called intrinsic or internal or 'formal' properties. But the statement is all wrong in assuming that representation and expression are the only symbolic functions that paintings may perform, in supposing that what a symbol symbolizes is always outside it, and in insisting that what counts in a painting is the mere possession rather than the exemplification of certain properties.

Whoever looks for art without symbols, then, will find none – if all the ways that works symbolize are taken into account. Art without representation or expression or exemplification – yes; art without all three – *no*.

To point out that purist art consists simply in the avoidance of certain kinds of symbolization is not to condemn it but only to uncover the fallacy in the usual manifestos advocating purist art to the exclusion of all other kinds. I am not debating the relative virtues of different schools or types or ways of painting. What seems to me more important is that recognition of the symbolic function of even purist painting gives us a clue to the perennial problem of when we do and when we don't have a work of art.

The literature of aesthetics is littered with desperate attempts to answer the question "What is art?" This question, often hopelessly confused with the question "What is good art?", is acute in the case of found art – the stone picked out of the driveway and exhibited in a museum – and is further aggravated by the promotion of so-called environmental and conceptual art. Is a smashed automobile fender in an art gallery a work of art? What of something that is not even an object, and not exhibited in any gallery or museum – for example, the digging and filling-in of a hole in Central Park as prescribed by Oldenburg? If these are works of art, then are all stones in the driveway and all objects and occurrences works of art? If not, what distinguishes what is from what is not a work of art? That an artist calls it a work of art? That it is exhibited in a museum or gallery? No such answer carries any conviction.

As I remarked at the outset, part of the trouble lies in asking the wrong question – in failing to recognize that a thing may function as a work of art at some times and not at others. In crucial cases, the real question is not "What objects are (permanently) works of art?" but "When is an object a work of art?" – or more briefly, as in my title, "When is art?"

My answer is that just as an object may be a symbol – for instance, a sample – at certain times and under certain circumstances and not at others, so an object may be a work of art at some times and not at others. Indeed, just by virtue of functioning as a symbol in a certain way does an object become, while so functioning, a work of art. The stone is normally no work of art while in the driveway, but may be so when on display in an art museum. In the driveway, it usually performs no symbolic function. In the art museum, it exemplifies certain of its properties – e.g., properties of shape, color, texture. The hole-digging and filling functions as a work insofar as our attention is directed to it as an exemplifying symbol. On the other hand, a Rembrandt painting may cease to function as a work of art when used to replace a broken window or as a blanket.

Now, of course, to function as a symbol in some way or other is not in itself to function as a work of art. Our swatch, when serving as a sample, does not then and thereby become a work of art. Things function as works of art only when their symbolic functioning has certain characteristics. Our stone in a museum of geology takes on symbolic functions as a sample of the stones of a given period, origin, or composition, but it is not then functioning as a work of art.

The question just what characteristics distinguish or are indicative of the symbolizing that constitutes functioning as a work of art calls for careful study in the light of a general theory of symbols. That is more than I can undertake here, but I venture the tentative thought that there are five symptoms of the aesthetic:[5] (1) syntactic density, where the finest differences in certain respects constitute a difference between symbols – for example, an ungraduated mercury thermometer as contrasted with an electronic digital-read-out instrument; (2) semantic density, where symbols are provided for things distinguished by the finest differences in certain respects – for example, not only the ungraduated thermometer again but also ordinary English, though it is not syntactically dense; (3) relative repleteness, where comparatively many aspects of a symbol are significant – for example, a single-line drawing of a mountain by Hokusai where every feature of shape, line, thickness, etc. counts, in contrast with perhaps the same line as a chart of daily stockmarket averages, where all that counts is the height of the line above the base; (4) exemplification, where a symbol, whether or not it denotes, symbolizes by serving as a sample of properties it literally or metaphorically possesses; and finally (5) multiple and complex reference, where a symbol performs several integrated and interacting referential functions,[6] some direct and some mediated through other symbols.

These symptoms provide no definition, much less a full-blooded description or a celebration.

Presence or absence of one or more of them does not qualify or disqualify anything as aesthetic; nor does the extent to which these features are present measure the extent to which an object or experience is aesthetic.[7] Symptoms, after all, are but clues; the patient may have the symptoms without the disease, or the disease without the symptoms. And even for these five symptoms to come somewhere near being disjunctively necessary and conjunctively (as a syndrome) sufficient might well call for some redrawing of the vague and vagrant borderlines of the aesthetic. Still, notice that these properties tend to focus attention on the symbol rather than, or at least along with, what it refers to. Where we can never determine precisely just which symbol of a system we have or whether we have the same one on a second occasion, where the referent is so elusive that properly fitting a symbol to it requires endless care, where more rather than fewer features of the symbol count, where the symbol is an instance of properties it symbolizes and may perform many interrelated simple and complex referential functions, we cannot merely look through the symbol to what it refers to as we do in obeying traffic lights or reading scientific texts, but must attend constantly to the symbol itself as in seeing paintings or reading poetry. This emphasis upon the nontransparency of a work of art, upon the primacy of the work over what it refers to, far from involving denial or disregard of symbolic functions, derives from certain characteristics of a work as a symbol.[8]

Quite apart from specifying the particular characteristics differentiating aesthetic from other symbolization, the answer to the question "When is art?" thus seems to me clearly to be in terms of symbolic function. Perhaps to say that an object is art when and only when it so functions is to overstate the case or to speak elliptically. The Rembrandt painting remains a work of art, as it remains a painting, while functioning only as a blanket; and the stone from the driveway may not strictly become art by functioning as art.[9] Similarly, a chair remains a chair even if never sat on, and a packing case remains a packing case even if never used except for sitting on. To say what art does is not to say what art is; but I submit that the former is the matter of primary and peculiar concern. The further question of defining stable property in terms of ephemeral function – the what in terms of the when – is not confined to the arts but is quite general, and is the same for defining chairs as for defining objects of art. The parade of instant and inadequate answers is also much the same: that whether an object is art – or a chair – depends upon intent or upon whether it sometimes or usually or always or exclusively functions as such. Because all this tends to obscure more special and significant questions concerning art, I have turned my attention from what art is to what art does.

A salient feature of symbolization, I have urged, is that it may come and go. An object may symbolize different things at different times, and nothing at other times. An inert or purely utilitarian object may come to function as art, and a work of art may come to function as an inert or purely utilitarian object. Perhaps, rather than art being long and life short, both are transient.

The bearing that this inquiry into the nature of works of art has upon the overall undertaking of this book should by now have become quite clear. How an object or event functions as a work explains how, through certain modes of reference, what so functions may contribute to a vision of – and to the making of – a world.

Notes

1 "Settling the Colonel's Hash", *Harper's Magazine*, 1954; reprinted in *On the Contrary* (Farrar, Straus and Cudahy, 1961), p. 225.

2 See further "On Likeness of Meaning" (1949) and "On Some Differences about Meaning" (1953), *PP*, pp. 221–38; also *LA*, pp. 21–6.

3 Motion, for instance, as well as emotion may be expressed in a black and white picture; for example, see [...] the discussion of expression in *LA*, pp. 85–95.

4 For further discussion of exemplification, see *LA*, pp. 52–67.

5 See *LA*, pp. 252–5 and the earlier passages there alluded to. The fifth symptom has been added above as the result of conversations with Professors Paul Hernadi and Alan Nagel of the University of Iowa.

6 This excludes ordinary ambiguity, where a term has two or more quite independent denotations at quite different times and in quite different contexts.

7 That poetry, for example, which is not syntactically dense, is less art or less likely to be art than painting that exhibits all four symptoms thus does not at all follow. Some aesthetic symbols may have fewer of the symptoms than some nonaesthetic symbols. This is sometimes misunderstood.

8 This is another version of the dictum that the purist is all right and all wrong.

9 Just as what is not red may look or be said to be red at *certain times*, so what is not art may function as or be said to be art at certain times. That an object functions as art at a given time, that it has the status of art at that time, and that it is art at that time may all be taken as saying the same thing – so long as we take none of these as ascribing to the object any stable status.

39

Identifying Art

Noël Carroll

Noël Carroll is Andrew W. Mellon Professor of Humanities and Professor of Philosophy at Temple University.

Definition and Identification

Recent attempts to define art, such as the Institutional Theory of Art and the Historical Definition of Art, have proven thus far to be inconclusive. Both supply useful clues to how we go about identifying art. But neither is a satisfactory reconstruction of the way in which we go about identifying art. And yet we *are* able to identify art – to classify candidates as artworks – with a very high degree of consensus. Thus the question of how we manage to do it remains pressing.

Moreover, this is not merely an academic question. Classifying artifacts as artworks is central to our practice of art. Classifying a candidate as an artwork – subsuming it under the category of art – is integral to determining how we should respond to it. Should a scattering of dirt and grease on the floor be interpreted or cleaned up? Should we attend to the expressive properties of an amalgam of crushed and mangled automobile chassis or consign them to the junkyard? If art, these objects bear scrutiny and interpretation. If not, we call the Department of Sanitation.

Noël Carroll, "Identifying Art," in *Philosophy of Art: A Contemporary Introduction* (New York: Routledge, 1999), pp. 249–64.

Furthermore, the concept of art is an important one for the characterization of social reality. It supports many significant generalizations, such as: that every known culture has artistic practices; that there is more art today than there was in the fifteenth century; that the production of art is a major social activity in Bali; that art is an important factor in the creation of cultural identity; and so on. The concept of art also figures in certain counterfactual generalizations, e.g., that any society without art would be humanly diminished. And, as we have seen, the concept of art can also play an explanatory role: Why are they writing so much about that urinal? Because it is an artwork.

The concept of art is indispensable for social life as we know it. But how do we go about applying it? How do we identify objects as artworks; how do we classify artifacts under this concept? Throughout this book we have encountered a number of attempts to treat this as a matter of applying an essential definition. The representational theory of art, neorepresentationalism, the expression theory, formalism, neoformalism, aesthetic definitions, institutional theories, and the Historical Definition of Art have all, in turn, tried to articulate necessary and sufficient conditions for art status.

In this, there is an underlying assumption that we identify candidates by subsuming them under a definition. That definition is one that many philosophers have supposed we possess, if only implicitly, and that we apply to candidates tacitly. Successive theories have attempted to recover it and to make it explicit.

Clearly, a certain view of the nature of concepts underwrites all these attempts. Concepts are regarded as essential definitions. That is, concepts are taken to be definitions that supply necessary and sufficient conditions for membership in the category they designate. Art is a concept; so, the story goes, the concept of art must have necessary and sufficient conditions for application to particular instances.

But, as the Neo-Wittgensteinians suggested, it may not be the case that all of our concepts are to be understood on the model of definitions with necessary and sufficient conditions. Indeed, quite a few of our concepts go undefined, and yet we are able to apply them successfully. Might not art be such a concept?

The Neo-Wittgensteinian claims that it is. On behalf of this conclusion, she offers an argument that it must be, since defining art is not consistent with the expansionary nature of art, *and* she further hypothesizes that we apply the concept of art in virtue of the family resemblance method, not in virtue of definitions replete with necessary and sufficient conditions. Unfortunately, neither of these claims is ultimately successful, for reasons that were explored in the first part of this chapter [*not reproduced here*].

But despite the failure of these specific arguments, the possibility remains that neither is art the sort of concept that is structured by necessary and sufficient conditions nor that we do classify artifacts as artworks by means of definitions. Evidently, we do not identify artworks in accordance with the family resemblance method. But the defeat of that hypothesis does not entail that there is not some other nondefinitional method upon which we rely to sort artworks from other sorts of things.

We cannot presume on the basis of the past failure of definitional theories of art that art cannot be defined. Perhaps one day someone will construct a perfectly noncontroversial, comprehensive definition of all art. But, at the same time, it should also be apparent that we do not go about determining what is art and what isn't on the basis of such a definition. If we do possess such a definition, albeit implicitly, why is it so damnably hard to excavate?

On the other hand, it is widely acknowledged that many of the concepts that we use with admirable effectiveness are not governed by essential definitions. This supplies us with at least a *prima facie* reason for exploring the possibility that we apply the concept of art, as we do so many other concepts, without relying – explicitly or implicitly – on definitions.

Undoubtedly, there is a great tradition in philosophy that presupposes that concepts must be understood in terms of necessary and sufficient conditions. But that tradition has been presented with serious challenges on many fronts, including not only Neo-Wittgensteinianism, but what is called prototype theory in psychology and the causal theory of reference in the analysis of natural kinds. It is not important, at this juncture, to examine each of these challenges. It is enough to note that the authority of the definitional approach to concepts is not unqualified. That at least warrants inquiry into alternative models of the concept of art. And once such a model is set forth, it remains to be seen whether it does a better job of explaining how we identify artifacts as artworks – how we classify candidates as art – than competing approaches do, including not only definitional approaches, but the family resemblance method as well.

Identification and Historical Narration

One way to approach the question of how we classify artifacts as artworks is to consider how we proceed in problem situations. That is, what do we do when the question of whether or not a candidate is art arises? How do we establish that a proposed artwork is an artwork in cases where the suspicion is abroad that it is not art – or even, perhaps, that it is a hoax? Such situations should reveal something about the way in which we identify candidates as artworks because, in circumstances like these, our thinking about what makes something art comes to the fore. A challenge to the art status of a work forces us to become explicit about the grounds upon which we generally classify something as art.

Notably, throughout the twentieth century, given the continuous activity of the avant-garde, accusations have abounded that this or that candidate is not art. Some examples include:

Duchamp's readymades, Jackson Pollock's drip paintings, Merce Cunningham's choreography, Robert Mapplethorpe's photography, and, more recently, pieces by Damien Hirst and Janine Antoni. Frequently such misgivings are voiced not only by bewildered and sometimes disgruntled members of the viewing public, but also by their critical representatives in the fourth estate, Declaring that something is not art – or worse, that it is a confidence trick – is always good for an indignant, spirited newspaper editorial.

How are such challenges, when they occur, met? If we look at the course of such debates, we find that generally the proponent of the work in question responds by telling a story that links the contested work to preceding art – and to art-making practices and contexts – in such a way that the work under fire can be seen to be the intelligible outcome of recognizable modes of thinking and making of a sort already commonly adjudged to be artistic.

This mode of proceeding, like the Historical Definition of Art, of course, presupposes that we already know that some objects are art, that we understand what is important about these objects, and that there is agreement about this. Then, using this antecedent knowledge as a baseline, we attempt to show how the new work at issue evolves from work already acknowledged to be artistic, guided by concerns regarded by all as central to the practice. Thus, the figural distortion of German expressionist painters is not dismissed as an inept attempt at verisimilitude and, therefore, as defective or pseudo art, but as an intelligible and well-precedented artistic response – a revolt – against realism (a revolt undertaken for the sake of securing a widely and antecedently acknowledged artistic value, namely expressivity).

Typically, the question of whether or not x is an artwork arises in a context in which some skeptic fails to see how the object under dispute could have been produced within the network of practices with which she is familiar – that is, if those practices are to remain the same practices. There is a perceived gap, so to speak, between the anomalous, usually avant-garde, production x and an already existing body of work with an antecedently acknowledged tradition of making and thinking. In order to establish the status of x as an artwork, the proponent of x must fill in that gap. And the standard way of filling in that gap is to produce a certain type of historical narrative, one that supplies the sequence of activities of thinking and making required to, in a manner of speaking, fill in the distance between a Rembrandt and a readymade.

To counter the suspicion that x is not a work of art, the friend of x has to show how x emerged intelligibly from acknowledged practices via the same sort of thinking, acting, decision-making and so forth that is already familiar in the practice. This involves telling a certain kind of story about the work in question: namely, a historical narrative of how x came to be produced as an intelligible response to an antecedently acknowledged art-historical situation about whose art status a consensus already exists. With a contested work what we try to do is place it within a tradition where it becomes more and more intelligible. And the standard way of doing this is to produce an historical narrative.

For example, when Andy Warhol's *Brillo Box* appeared in 1963, questions about its status as art were raised. After all, it looked just like the cartons of Brillo in the grocery storeroom. Those weren't artworks. Why regard Warhol's, which looked just like them, as artworks? Wasn't the whole thing just a prank, or, worse, a scam?

In order to meet this objection, the defender of *Brillo Box* begins by pointing out something about the art-historical context in which the work appeared. For much of the twentieth century, a great deal of art had been dedicated to addressing the question of the nature of art. Much modern painting has been overtly flat precisely for the purpose of asserting the idea that, in reality, paintings are flat, two-dimensional things, not the illusions of three-dimensional objects they were often said to be. Painters in this tradition – which would include Braque, Picasso, Pollock, Klein, and so on – were thought to be involved in a philosophical venture, the project of defining the nature of their artform. This was a reflexive enterprise – a matter of artworks reflecting on their own nature as artworks.

In this historical context, Warhol's *Brillo Box* can be seen as a contribution to an ongoing dialogue or conversation in the artworld. That is, Warhol's *Brillo Box* poses the question "What is art?" in a particularly penetrating way, asking of itself what makes this object an artwork when its indiscernible counterparts – everyday Brillo Boxes – are not artworks? Warhol's *Brillo Box* thus addressed an antecedently acknowledged, ongoing artworld concern in a creative way by focussing the reflexive artworld question "What is art?" in a canny and strikingly perspicuous manner, reframing and redirecting it as the question: "What makes art-works different from real things?"

Seen in its historical context, Warhol's *Brillo Box* is an intelligible contribution to an evolving artworld project. Once one is made aware of the historical context of the work, Warhol's *Brillo Box* can be placed as a rational, if not ingenious, expansion upon antecedently acknowledged artworld modes of making and thinking. If those antecedent modes of thinking and making – from Cubism forwards – resulted in artworks, then *Brillo Box*, as an extension of acknowledged artworld practices, is art as well. That is, if one can construct an accurate historical narrative that renders intelligible the emergence of *Brillo Box*, as the result of rational decision-making from accepted artworld practices, then that establishes the art status of *Brillo Box*, or, at least, it shifts the burden of proof entirely onto the skeptics.

Of course, in some cases, skeptics may not accept the starting point of the historical narrative that we wish to recite. Perhaps some skeptics will query whether Cubism is art, and, therefore, will not – until Cubism's credentials are established – accept developments from it, like Warhol's *Brillo Box*, as artworks.

However, here, the friend of Warhol merely needs to start her historical narrative earlier, at some point in art history that the skeptic accepts as an exemplary moment. Suppose, in the case at hand, that the skeptic accepts impressionism as art. Then, our narrative defense of *Brillo Box* will begin with impressionism and its consequences, such as neo-impressionism, illuminating the way in which the relevant reflexive preoccupations were evident even in the nineteenth century. Then we shall go on to show the intelligible maturation of this concern through Cubism to Warhol. That is, our response to the skeptic will still be a historical narrative, though a historical narrative that starts a bit earlier than the first one we told.

So far the situations to which we have been alluding are ones where an artwork is put forward and is then challenged. That challenge, it seems, is generally met by telling an historical narrative, an historical narrative that *explains* why the artifact in question is an artwork. However, it is also frequently the case that such historical narratives are told *before* skeptics raise their objections. These narratives – which may be recounted in manifestos, gallery handouts, interviews, lecture-demonstrations, critical reviews, docents' talks, and so on – are not advanced simply to forestall criticism, but to enable viewers to understand where the artist is coming from, to see why her choices make sense given the logic of the artworld situation in which she finds herself.

When an artwork is challenged or likely to be challenged, our response is not a definition, but an explanation. That is, we do not produce a definition and apply it to the case at hand, since, as we've seen, it is exceedingly difficult to find any noncontroversial definition. Instead, we try to explain why the candidate is an artwork. We point to acknowledged artworld precedents, practices, and aims, including the antecedents of the work in question, the artworld problematic that the new work addresses, and the rationale for the choices the artist made given the options available to her. This explanation takes the form of a historical narrative. If the narrative is an accurate and reasonable one, this generally suffices to establish that the candidate is an artwork.

If this is how we generally establish that a candidate is art in cases where there is some dispute, it also reveals something about how we incorporate objects in the category of art in the ordinary course of affairs. Where we can weave the candidate into the ongoing history of art as we know it, we are disposed to classify an artifact as an artwork. We classify a candidate as an artwork by placing it in a tradition. We use our knowledge of the tradition – including our knowledge of its genres, its history, and its aims – to determine whether a new work belongs to the tradition.

Where a candidate can be shown to be a continuation of an antecedently acknowledged artistic tradition – where we are able to understand it as an intelligible development or outcome from standing artistic practices (and not from other well-known practices) – then we are satisfied that it is art in the classificatory sense. A historical narrative may not establish that a candidate is good of its kind; but it is typically enough to establish that it is art.

It is an important feature of art that it develops; even in relatively static traditions, there is development. As we have seen throughout this book, developments in art history have been a problem for the philosophy of art. Attempts to define art have often failed because they do not anticipate the future developments in the history of art. Representational theories of art scarcely anticipated the rise of abstract art; expression theories hardly forsaw the revolt against expression; and so forth. One advantage of the narrative approach is that it is sensitive to the tendency of art to evolve along often unpredictable pathways, since narrative itself is a tool for rendering change intelligible.

The narrative approach attempts to handle the developmental aspect of art – including its local developments – by treating it as a conversation. As in a conversation, so in artistic practice there is an expectation of artists that they be concerned to make original contributions to the tradition in which they work. These contributions can range along the creative scale from slight variations in established genres to wholesale revolutions. Art history is analogous to a conversation, in certain respects, in that each artist-discussant makes, or, at least, is expected to make a contribution.

However, as in a conversation, the contribution must have some relevance to what has gone before. Otherwise, there simply is no conversation. In relation to their predecessors, artists must be posing or answering some relevant question, amplifying what someone else has proposed, or disagreeing or even repudiating it – demonstrating that some neglected option is possible – and the like. In such ways as this, the artist's contribution should be pertinent to the already existing practices of the artworld – to its abiding concerns, procedures and interests. What the narratives we have been discussing do is to make salient the relevance of new works to the evolving conversation of art history. For, of course, if such works are completely irrelevant to art history, there is no reason to suppose that they are artworks.

The problem frequently presented by avant-garde art is that some of the artist's interlocutors – the general public and its representatives among the critical estate – often fail to catch the relevance of the artist's "remark" to the ongoing context. The audience may, so to say, discern the "originality" of the work, but not its relevance. There is, in other words, a glitch in the conversation.

But if this is the problem, there is an obvious way to repair it. Reconstruct the conversation in such a way that the relevance of the artist's contribution is made evident. Bring perhaps unremarked or unnoticed presuppositions into the open. Point to overlooked features of the context. Make the intentions of the artist explicit, and show that said intentions are intelligible in terms of the conversation and its context, and so on.

Of course, reconstructing the conversation in this way amounts to a historical narrative. Where something is missing from the conversation – some connection – it is supplied by retelling the conversation in a way that historically reconstructs it, while simultaneously filling it in. Where we can produce a genuine, historical narrative of this sort, we have, generally, sufficient grounds for categorizing a candidate as an artwork. Historical narration is a reliable method for identifying art – for explaining why a candidate is an artwork – and, moreover, it has a solid claim for being the method that we generally employ.

The narrative approach to classifying artworks establishes the art status of a candidate by connecting the work in question to previously acknowledged artworks and practices. In this regard, it may appear to recall the family resemblance approach. However, the narrative approach is not merely an affair of similarities between past and present art. The pertinent correspondences must be shown to be part of a narrative development. Such historical narratives track processes of cause and effect, decision and action, and lines of influence.

Unlike the Neo-Wittgensteinian method for identifying artworks, the narrative approach links present art to past art not in terms of some unspecified notion of resemblance, but in terms of its descent – its genetic (or causal) linkage to earlier acknowledged artworks and artistic practices. Thus, according to the narrative approach, contemporary avant-garde works are classified as artworks in virtue of their ancestry, where that ancestry is explained by means of a narrative or genealogy. Thus, with its emphasis on genetic links between new art and past paradigms, the narrative approach not only differs from Neo-Wittgensteinianism, but avoids the problems of the family resemblance method.

Of course, many works do not require such elaborate genealogical briefs on their behalf. That is probably due to the fact that in most cases we already understand how to place them in the tradition. But where there is some question about the art status of a work *vis à vis* the tradition, as there often is with new and avant-garde art, the canonical method for negotiating the issue is historical narration. Historical narratives, whether implicitly understood or explicitly constructed, are the means we employ to identify candidates as members of the category art.

Undoubtedly, the suggestion that we sort objects into a kind (such as art) by means of a historical narrative will strike some readers as bizarre. This is because we often derive our models of kindhood from physics and chemistry, where elements are grouped in virtue of some intrinsic, micro-physical property that explains its other projectible properties. But not all kinds, even in the sciences, are like this. For example, species are historical entities – they are groups of organisms that are sorted together by virtue of their common history rather than by virtue of intrinsic resemblances that they bear to each other.

The reason for this is that species, by their nature, evolve, typically showing variations not merely in some of their peripheral characteristics, but, in principle, in all of their features. No particular feature, no matter how central to our stereotype of the species – to its genotype or morphology – is essential for an organism to be a member of the species in question. What is crucial, as Darwin claimed, is descent.

Indeed, within the branch of biology called systematics, one important debate was between pheneticists – who proposed to sort species in terms of allegedly essential similarities between organisms – versus cladists – who argued that taxa are unified historically by the mechanism of common descent. In certain respects, this debate in biology repeats themes rehearsed in the philosophy of art, including not only the problem of fixing the essential properties of a kind that is essentially evolving, but also the problem of the slackness of similarity as an organizing concept.

Of course, there are also important differences between questions of art classification and speciation. We are now only speaking of selected analogies between the two. However, the fact that cladism is regarded as a respectable solution to the problem of speciation at least indicates that in certain cases history can supply the grounds for membership in a kind. And if descent is a viable condition for classifying an organism as a member of a biological species, there need be no problem, at least in principle, with supposing that candidates are also classified under the concept of art in virtue of descent as explicated by the appropriate types of historical narratives.

We have already noted that it is not the case generally that we classify objects by means of definitions. There are alternative means. For example, biologists determine species membership in terms of descent. Moreover, when we look at how problem cases go in debates about art, it seems persuasive that such debates are canonically joined by advancing historical narratives on behalf of contested works. Membership in the category of art, like species membership, also appears to be a matter of descent. Similarly, the way to identify artifacts as artworks is to explain their genealogy, where this is a matter of telling a historical narrative.

Historical Narratives: Their Strengths and Weaknesses

The claim before us is that identifying art is more plausibly understood as a matter of narration rather than definition. To weigh this claim effectively, a little more has to be said about the nature of the narratives in question. Only then can we go on to assess the strengths and weaknesses of this approach relative to competing approaches.

Though the relevant sort of narrative understanding is often merely implicit in the great many instances where we identify rather conventional candidates as art, it comes into the foreground in disputed cases, such as the more radical examples of avant-garde art. On such occasions, the way in which we defend the art status of an avant-garde candidate is to connect it to practices that are already acknowledged to be artistic. Since this kind of narrative is an *historical* narrative, it is committed to being accurate. It is by accurately narrating the descent of the new work from the tradition that we explain why the new work should be counted as art.

This way of proceeding also tells us something important about the relevant sort of identifying narratives; it tells us where they begin. They begin at some historical juncture where everyone agrees we know that artistic practices are involved. Identifying narratives must begin at such a juncture, since it is the point of this type of narrative to explain the art status of some present, disputed candidate, like *Brillo Box*, by showing that it emerged from and is connected to such an acknowledged artworld context, through a perfectly intelligible sequence of choices of a sort based on existing artistic aims that are themselves acknowledged to be alive and accepted in the artworld under discussion.

We also know where identifying narratives end; they end with the production or presentation of the artifact in question. An identifying narrative of this sort gets us from an acknowledged artworld and its practices to the prospective entry into that artworld of a new work by a sequence of intervening steps. What do those steps involve?

To simplify matters, let us consider a case where the new work is a revolutionary avant-garde production, an abstract film in which none of the images are recognizable figures. There is no story, just a disjunctive flow of shapes, as in some of the work of Stan Brakhage. Some viewers might be tempted to dismiss work like this as nothing but incoherent footage – certainly, they might say, it is not art. In its defense, however, we can offer the following narrative.

Most film-making is dominated by stories, told through moving pictures. At the same time, everyone acknowledges that film-making is a visual art. But storytelling by means of pictures designed to advance the narrative often causes viewers to forget about the visual dimension of films – to fail to attend to how films look, so wrapped up are we in following the story.

Confronted with a situation like this one, an artist like Brakhage wants to reclaim the visual attention of the audience. So, he makes films that virtually command audiences to pay attention to the look of his films. He does this by the almost willful subtraction of every other sort of source of attention – such as narrative and pictorial content – from his films. This is a coherent move for an artist like Brakhage to make – one in keeping with an acknowledged aim of film-making – given the artistic context in which he found himself.

That is, operating in an acknowledged artworld context, Brakhage assesses that context as one where insufficient attention is paid to the visual structure of films. This is an ironic state of affairs, since film is a visual art. On the grounds of such an unquestionably artistically intelligible assessment, Brakhage resolved to change the situation by making films that compelled audiences to attend to visual form, an altogether acceptable artistic aim, as all would agree, for a film-maker to have. Though the results were works that disposed some to challenge the status of Brakhage's works as films as well as their status as art, Brakhage's choices – to work without narrative, to explore radical abstraction – were eminently reasonable choices, given his options in the existing context and his resolve to change that context.

Such an account explains why Brakhage's films are art. They are art because they originate in an incontestable artistic context as the result of motivations that informed persons already agree are genuinely artistic ones – such as the reclamation of the visual. Brakhage's films can be explained in terms of the adoption of a series of actions and alternatives that are appropriate means to an end for a person like himself, who has arrived at an intelligible assessment of his artworld context in such a way that his resolve to change it is in accordance with recognizable and live purposes of the practice.

Putting this into narrative form, then, we can say: Given the artistic practices of the dominant cinema, Brakhage worried that the relentless emphasis on narrative and pictorial content repressed rather than enhanced the attentiveness of the audience to things visual – an anomalous state of affairs for an avowedly visual art. Because of his assessment, he resolved to change the situation. He searched for artistic strategies that would promote audience attention to the purely visual. He excised narrative and pictorial elements from his films so that they would not draw attention away from our concentration on the look of the film. The results are films that appear to be very different from standard filmworld fare, but which nevertheless reclaim the sheer visual potential of the medium.

If this narrative is historically accurate, and if it provides us with the best explanation of Brakhage's films, then there is little alternative but to regard his films as artworks. If there are no better explanations – no more comprehensive and accurate accounts of why they are as they are – then this explanation recommends that we classify Brakhage's films as art-works. Given the historical accuracy of this account, what other classification would make as much sense? Thus, from an explanatory point of view, a historical narrative, when accurate, provides us with a compelling argument for classifying something like a Brakhage film as an artwork. Indeed, given the details of such a narrative – supposing them to be historically accurate – it is difficult to imagine how else we might classify such an artifact.

Identifying narratives, then, are historical narratives that, like all historical narratives, are committed to accuracy. They have a beginning, a middle, and an end. The beginning of the story involves the description of some acknowledged art-historical context. The end of the story is a description of the production and/or presentation of the candidate for art status. The middle of the story connects the beginning to the end. The middle of such narratives, moreover, connects the beginning to the end by tracing the adoption of a series of actions and alternatives that supply the appropriate kinds of means for a person who has arrived at an intelligible assessment of the art-historical context, described in the beginning, such that she is resolved to change it in some way in accordance with recognizable and live purposes of the practice.

According to the historical approach, artworks are identified in virtue of their descent. Unlike the Institutional Theory of Art, tracing the ancestry of an artwork, rather than applying a definition, accounts for how we classify candidates as artworks. One strong point of the Institutional Theory is the stress it places on the importance of the reciprocal understanding shared by artists and audiences. But this insight is readily incorporated into the historical approach, because the historical approach too supposes that artists and audiences must share certain understandings, namely, an understanding of art history, its practices, and the aims and purposes that underpin those practices.

At the same time, the historical approach avoids the most frequently cited pitfall of the Institutional Theory – specifically, the charge of circularity. The reason for this is simple: circularity is a defect in definitions, not narratives. It is a requirement of definitions that they not be circular, but the identifying narratives advocated by the historical approach are not definitions. Consequently, they are not susceptible to charges of circularity. Such narratives do presuppose that we do know something about antecedent artistic practices, as does any theory of art. But since the concept of art is not being invoked to define the concept of art, the issue of circularity disappears for the historical method of identifying artworks.

The historical approach also differs from the Historical Definition of Art insofar as the former is not a definition. A major virtue of the Historical Definition of Art is that it calls attention to the importance of the artistic intention to promote acknowledged art regards. The method of historical narration is also sensitive to this constitutive element of the practice of art, since it counts the intended facilitation of accepted art regards as among the aims of art that may govern artistic choices. Brakhage intended to abet attention to the visual; Warhol intended his work to be regarded reflexively. These were both accepted art regards, and they figure importantly in the relevant identifying narratives.

However, unlike the Historical Definition, the method of historical narration does not restrict the aims that motivate genuine artistic choice to art regards. Any live purpose of acknowledged practices of artmaking – not merely the promotion of art regards – may play an enfranchising role in identifying narratives. Earlier, given the emphasis of the Historical Definition on art regards, we worried that sculptures of demons designed to send viewers running away in terror could not be art, since the intended effect of the work, if successful, appeared to preclude any acknowledged art regard. But this is not a problem for the method of historical narration, since, if causing flight is an acknowledged purpose of art in the relevant artworld, identifying narratives will track objects made under its aegis.

Moreover, that the method of historical narration stresses that the artistic aims referred to by identifying narratives be "*recognized and live*" purposes of the practice avoids another problem of the Historical Definition of Art. The proponent of the Historical Definition seemed compelled to accept home videos as art, since they are intended to support a historically, well-precedented art regard – the mere appreciation of verisimilitude. However, since the method of historical narration only endorses consideration of purposes that are alive in the prevailing practice, it does not have similar unfortunate consequences, since in today's artworld, as a matter of historical fact, the intention *simply* to promote the appreciation of perceptual verisimilitude is no longer a recognized and/or live artistic aim.

The method of historical narration avoids some of the shortcomings of its predecessors, which certainly counts in its favor. However, it is also open to some of the criticisms that beset the Institutional Theory and the Historical Definition. Like the Historical Definition, it will not count as artworks objects that we abstract from their nonartistic historical context and merely use as art, such as Eskimo fish hooks displayed by museum curators because of their beauty. But perhaps cases like this are not really so clear-cut. That we use certain things as art – like traffic signs as wall decoration – does not clearly make artworks of those things. So maybe examples like this present problems neither for Historical Definitions nor for the method of historical narration.

Like the Institutional Theory, the method of historical narration is inhospitable to the notion of the solitary artist. It regards art as a practice in which newcomers are granted entry to the artworld in virtue of their social ancestry – their relation to their precedessors, their history, customs and acknowledged purposes. Thus, artworks produced in an artworld of one are beyond the reach of identifying narratives. Is this a liability of the historical approach?

Here the proponent of the historical approach can make several replies. The first is to say that all that she claims is that an identifying narrative provides a sufficient condition for classifying artworks. Thus, there may be other grounds for identifying a candidate as an artwork, even if historical narration is the standard way. If the work of a truly solitary artist is art, then there may be some exceptional grounds for calling it such. However, that would not call into question the central claim that identifying narration, with its emphasis on art as a social practice, is by far our most typical means for establishing art status.

This is a fairly conciliatory response. Of course, the proponent of the historical method might also make a stronger reply. Like the Institutional Theorist, she might argue that, given the social nature of human beings, the possibility of a truly solitary artist is at best a logical fiction. From an anthropological point of view, the prospect of utterly asocial art has the probability of zero. Thus, if we are concerned with modeling how we go about classifying art with respect to the real world, then neglecting hypothetical cases of so-called solitary artists is not a pressing problem. After all, if we ever encountered anything approaching the case of our imagined Neolithic tribesman, his stone edifice would probably strike us as enigmatic rather than artistic. At best, we might call it proto-art, but if we are completely unable to situate it in the context of any ongoing social practices, we will remain nervous about regarding it as an instance of art proper.

Whether either of these attempted defenses of the historical approach is creditable is a matter for readers to debate. However, there is another possible problem with the historical approach that deserves airing. We began this chapter by pointing out that the issue of identifying art has been a particularly urgent one for twentieth-century philosophy because of the cascade of new and different kinds of art – avant-garde art, on the one hand, and art from other cultures, such as tribal art, on the other hand. The method of historical narration is, we have seen, well suited to handle cases of avant-garde innovation. But what about tribal art?

At first blush, there does not appear to be a problem here. Tribal arts will have their own traditions and identifying a candidate for inclusion in that tradition will proceed, as in more familiar cases, by way of historical narration. But this answer, it might be suggested, ignores a deeper question – namely, how does someone outside the tradition in question establish that the aforesaid tradition is an artistic practice? If it is an artistic tradition, the narrative model is applicable. But how do we know with alien traditions that the narrative model is available?

In such cases, one needs to look for reasons other than narrative reasons for regarding the alien tradition as artistic. The likeliest place to look is at the earliest known stages of the alien tradition. If in its earliest stages the practices of the alien tradition (what are sometimes called protosystems) are intended to perform the same functions – such as representation, decoration, and signification – in the relevant societies that the earliest stages of our own tradition performed in our culture, then we have grounds to regard the alien tradition as an artistic practice. And once we regard the earlier stages of the alien tradition as an artistic practice, then we may go on to identify subsequent contributions to the tradition as artworks by tracing their lineage from their artistic forebears.

But this solution to the problem requires that the historical method of identifying artworks needs to be supplemented, on some occasions, by a functional analysis of the role of certain practices in alien cultures. And this entails that we have not provided a single answer to the question of how we go about identifying artworks. Is this a problem?

The proponent of the historical method is apt to say "no." The admission that sometimes, but only sometimes, we resort to functional analysis only shows that historical narration is not the only strategy we use for classifying art, but this is consistent with the claim that it is our primary means of identifying art. Historical narration does not collapse into functional analysis, since functional analysis only makes sense with respect to protosystems. We do not look for functional analogies between aboriginal art and postmodernism; we only make comparisons at the level of the earliest stages of the traditions under consideration. The fact that we employ more than one method for identifying art merely reflects the complexity of the phenomenon. It would be nice to have a single answer to the question of how we identify art, but if the data are too complex, we should not let our desire for a single answer obscure the truth.

On the other hand, the advocates of rival viewpoints, like the Institutional Theory and the Historical Definition of Art, may say that it is a notable virtue of their approaches respectively that they provide a more economical account of how we identify artworks. They will assert that, all things being equal, a single answer to the question is better than a mixed answer. But are all things equal? If the method of historical narration is not as economical as some of its competitors, does this apparent liability outweigh the advantages it offers?

Those advantages include providing an account of how we identify art-works without embracing a controversial definition of art. Arriving at a satisfactory definition of art has proven arrestingly elusive. This does not show that art cannot be defined. But inasmuch as no one has been able to do it successfully, it seems unlikely that all along we have been classifying art by means of an essential definition. We must be using some other method. The method of historical narration, sometimes supplemented by the functional analysis of protosystems, seems like the most plausible one on offer. It is certainly superior to alternative nondefinitional methods, like the family resemblance approach.

Also, as already noted, the avant-garde has been a continuing problem for philosophies of art. Many of the most famous theories of art – including the representational theory of art, the expression theory, formalism, and aesthetic theories of art – have been wrecked by the appearance of avant-garde innovations. Compared to these approaches, the method of historical narration has nothing to fear from the avant-garde; as a procedure for identifying art it is well tailored to incorporating the mutations of the avant-garde into the continuous evolution of art. Of course, there are other approaches to identifying art that are also receptive to avant-garde experimentation, including the Institutional Theory, but the historical method of narration, to its comparative advantage, avoids many of the most troubling criticisms leveled at competing approaches.

This is not to say that the method of historical narration is obviously the only choice for solving the problem of identifying art. [. . .] Its strengths and weaknesses must be assessed against the advantages and disadvantages of a wide variety of rival approaches. It is up to the reader to ponder these alternatives critically, or to discover her own solution to the problem with a full appreciation of the complexity of the issues.

40

The Myth of the Aesthetic Attitude

George Dickie

Some recent articles[1] have suggested the unsatisfactoriness of the notion of the aesthetic attitude and it is now time for a fresh look at that encrusted article of faith. This conception has been valuable to aesthetics and criticism in helping wean them from a sole concern with beauty and related notions.[2] However, I shall argue that the aesthetic attitude is a myth and while, as G. Ryle has said, "Myths often do a lot of theoretical good while they are still new,"[3] this particular one is no longer useful and in fact misleads aesthetic theory.

There is a range of theories which differ according to how strongly the aesthetic attitude is characterized. This variation is reflected in the language the theories employ. The strongest variety is Edward Bullough's theory of psychical distance, recently defended by Sheila Dawson.[4] The central technical term of this theory is "distance" used as a verb to denote an action which either constitutes or is necessary for the aesthetic attitude. These theorists use such sentences as "He distanced (or failed to distance) the play." The second variety is widely held but has been defended most vigorously in recent years by Jerome Stolnitz and Eliseo Vivas. The *central* technical term of this variety is "disinterested"[5] used either as an adverb or as an adjective. This weaker theory speaks not of a special kind of action (distancing) but of an ordinary kind of action (attending) done in a certain way (disinterestedly). These first two versions are perhaps not as different as my classification suggests. However, the language of the two is different enough to justify separate discussions. My discussion of this second variety will for the most part make use of Jerome Stolnitz' book[6] which is a thorough, consistent, and large-scale version of the attitude theory. The weakest version of the attitude theory can be found in Vincent Tomas' statement "If looking at a picture and attending closely to how it looks is not really to be in the aesthetic attitude, then what on earth is?"[7] In the following I shall be concerned with the notion of *aesthetic* attitude and this notion may have little or no connection with the ordinary notion of an *attitude.*

I

Psychical distance, according to Bullough, is a psychological process by virtue of which a person *puts* some object (be it a painting, a play, or a dangerous fog at sea) "out of gear" with the practical interests of the self. Miss Dawson maintains

George Dickie, "The Myth of the Aesthetic Attitude," *American Philosophical Quarterly*, 1/1 (1964): 56–65.

that it is "the beauty of the phenomenon, which captures our attention, puts us out of gear with practical life, and forces us, if we are receptive, to view it on the level of aesthetic consciousness."[8]

Later she maintains that some persons (critics, actors, members of an orchestra, and the like) "distance deliberately."[9] Miss Dawson, following Bullough, discusses cases in which people are unable to bring off an act of distancing or are incapable of being induced into a state of being distanced. She uses Bullough's example of the jealous ("under-distanced") husband at a performance of *Othello* who is unable to keep his attention on the play because he keeps thinking of his own wife's suspicious behavior. On the other hand, if "we are mainly concerned with the technical details of its [the play's] presentation, then we are said to be over-distanced."[10] There is, then, a species of action – distancing – which may be deliberately done and which initiates a state of consciousness – being distanced.

The question is: Are there actions denoted by "to distance" or states of consciousness denoted by "being distanced"? When the curtain goes up, when we walk up to a painting, or when we look at a sunset are we ever induced into a state of being distanced either by being struck by the beauty of the object or by pulling off an act of distancing? I do not recall committing any such special actions or of being induced into any special state, and I have no reason to suspect that I am atypical in this respect. The distance-theorist may perhaps ask, "But are you not usually oblivious to noises and sights other than those of the play or to the marks on the wall around the painting?" The answer is of course – "Yes." But if "to distance" and "being distanced" simply mean that one's attention is focused, what is the point of introducing new technical terms and speaking as if these terms refer to special kinds of acts and states of consciousness? The distance-theorist might argue further, "But surely you put the play (painting, sunset) 'out of gear' with your practical interests?" This question seems to me to be a very odd way of asking (by employing the technical metaphor "out of gear") if I attended to the play rather than thought about my wife or wondered how they managed to move the scenery about. Why not ask me straight out if I paid attention? Thus, when Miss Dawson says that the jealous husband under-distanced *Othello* and that the person with a consuming interest in techniques of stagecraft over-distanced the play, these are just technical and misleading ways of describing two different cases of inattention. In both cases something is being attended to, but in neither case is it the action of the play. To introduce the technical terms "distance," "under-distance," and "over-distance" does nothing but send us chasing after phantom acts and states of consciousness.

Miss Dawson's commitment to the theory of distance (as a kind of mental insulation material necessary for a work of art if it is to be enjoyed aesthetically) leads her to draw a conclusion so curious as to throw suspicion on the theory.

> One remembers the horrible loss of distance in *Peter Pan* – the moment when Peter says "Do you believe in fairies? . . . If you believe, clap your hands!" the moment when most children would like to slink out of the theatre and not a few cry – not because Tinkerbell may die, but because the magic is gone. What, after all, should we feel like if Lear were to leave Cordelia, come to the front of the stage and say, "All the grown-ups who think that she loves me, shout 'Yes'."[11]

It is hard to believe that the responses of any children could be as theory-bound as those Miss Dawson describes. In fact, Peter Pan's request for applause is a dramatic high point to which children respond enthusiastically. The playwright gives the children a momentary chance to become actors in the play. The children do not at that moment lose or snap out of a state of being distanced because they never had or were in any such thing to begin with. The comparison of Peter Pan's appeal to the hypothetical one by Lear is pointless. *Peter Pan* is a magical play in which almost anything can happen, but *King Lear* is a play of a different kind. There are, by the way, many plays in which an actor directly addresses the audience (*Our Town, The Marriage Broker, A Taste of Honey,* for example) without causing the play to be less valuable. Such plays are unusual, but what is unusual is not necessarily bad; there is no point in trying to lay down rules to which every play must conform independently of the kind of play it is.

It is perhaps worth noting that Susanne Langer reports the reaction she had as a child to this scene in *Peter Pan*.[12] As she remembers it, Peter Pan's appeal shattered the illusion and caused her acute misery. However, she reports that all the other children clapped and laughed and enjoyed themselves.

II

The second way of conceiving of the aesthetic attitude – as the ordinary action of attending done in a certain way (disinterestedly) – is illustrated by the work of Jerome Stolnitz and Eliseo Vivas. Stolnitz defines "aesthetic attitude" as "disinterested and sympathetic attention to and contemplation of any object of awareness whatever, for its own sake alone."[13] Stolnitz defines the main terms of his definition: "disinterested" means "no concern for any ulterior purpose";[14] "sympathetic" means "accept the object on its own terms to appreciate it";[15] and "contemplation" means "perception directed toward the object in its own right and the spectator is not concerned to analyze it or ask questions about it."[16]

The notion of disinterestedness, which Stolnitz has elsewhere shown[17] to be seminal for modern aesthetic theory, is the key term here. Thus, it is necessary to be clear about the nature of disinterested attention to the various arts. It can make sense to speak, for example, of listening disinterestedly to music only if it makes sense to speak of listening interestedly to music. It would make no sense to speak of walking *fast* unless walking could be done *slowly*. Using Stolnitz' definition of "disinterestedness," the two situations would have to be described as "listening with no ulterior purpose" (disinterestedly) and "listening with an ulterior purpose" (interestedly). Note that what initially appears to be a perceptual distinction – listening in a certain way (interestedly or disinterestedly) – turns out to be a motivational or an intentional distinction – listening for or with a certain purpose. Suppose Jones listens to a piece of music for the purpose of being able to analyze and describe it on an examination the next day and Smith listens to the same music with no such ulterior purpose. There is certainly a difference between the motives and intentions of the two men: Jones has an ulterior purpose and Smith does not, but this does not mean Jones's *listening* differs from Smith's. It is possible that both men enjoy the music or that both be bored. The attention of either or both may flag and so on. It is important to note that a person's motive or intention is different from his action (Jones's listening to the music, for example). There is only one way to *listen* to (to attend to) music, although the listening may be more or less attentive and there may be a variety of motives, intentions, and reasons for doing so and a variety of ways of being distracted from the music.

In order to avoid a common mistake of aestheticians – drawing a conclusion about one kind of art and assuming it holds for all the arts – the question of disinterested attention must be considered for arts other than music. How would one look at a painting disinterestedly or interestedly? An example of alleged interested viewing might be the case in which a painting reminds Jones of his grandfather and Jones proceeds to muse about or to regale a companion with tales of his grandfather's pioneer exploits. Such incidents would be characterized by attitude-theorists as examples of using a work of art as a vehicle for associations and so on, i.e., cases of interested attention. But Jones is not looking at (attending to) the painting at all, although he may be facing it with his eyes open. Jones is now musing or attending to the story he is telling, although he had to look at the painting at first to notice that it resembled his grandfather. Jones is not now looking at the painting interestedly, since he is not now looking at (attending to) the painting. Jones's thinking or telling a story about his grandfather is no more a part of the painting than his speculating about the artist's intentions is and, hence, his musing, telling, speculating, and so on cannot properly be described as attending to the painting interestedly. What attitude-aestheticians are calling attention to is the occurrence of irrelevant associations which distract the viewer from the painting or whatever. But distraction is not a special kind of attention, it is a kind of inattention.

Consider now disinterestedness and plays. I shall make use of some interesting examples offered by J. O. Urmson,[18] but I am not claiming that Urmson is an attitude-theorist. Urmson never speaks in his article of aesthetic attitude but rather of aesthetic satisfaction. In addition to aesthetic satisfaction, Urmson mentions economic, moral, personal, and intellectual satisfactions. I think the attitude-theorist would consider these last four kinds of satisfaction as "ulterior purposes" and, hence, cases of interested attention. Urmson considers the case of a man in the audience of a play who is delighted.[19] It is discovered that his delight is *solely* the result of the fact that there is a full house – the man is the impresario of the production. Urmson is right in calling *this* impresario's satisfaction economic rather than aesthetic, although there is a certain oddness about the example as it finds the impresario sitting *in the audience.* However, my concern is not with Urmson's examples as such but with the attitude theory. This impresario is certainly an interested party in the fullest sense of the word, but is his behavior an instance of interested attention as distinct from the supposed disinterested attention of the average citizen who sits beside him? In the situation as described by Urmson it would not make any sense to say that the impresario is attending to the play at all, since his *sole* concern at the moment is the till. If he can be said to be attending to anything (rather than just thinking about it) it is the size of the house. I do not mean to suggest that an impresario could not attend to his play if he found himself taking up a seat in a full house; I am challenging the sense of disinterested attention. As an example of personal satisfaction Urmson mentions the spectator whose daughter is in the play. Intellectual satisfaction involves the solution of technical problems of plays and moral satisfaction the consideration of the effects of the play on the viewer's conduct. All three of these candidates which the attitude-theorist would propose as cases of interested attention turn out to be just different ways of being distracted from the play and, hence, not cases of interested attention to the play. Of course, there is no reason to think that in any of these cases the distraction or inattention must be total, although it could be. In fact, such inattentions often occur but are so fleeting that nothing of the play, music, or whatever is missed or lost.

The example of a playwright watching a rehearsal or an out-of-town performance with a view to rewriting the script has been suggested to me as a case in which a spectator is certainly attending to the play (unlike our impresario) and attending in an interested manner. This case is unlike those just discussed but is similar to the earlier case of Jones (not Smith) listening to a particular piece of music. Our playwright – like Jones, who was to be examined on the music – has ulterior motives. Furthermore, the playwright, unlike an ordinary spectator, can change the script after the performance or during a rehearsal. But how is our playwright's *attention* (as distinguished from his motives and intentions) different from that of an ordinary viewer? The playwright might enjoy or be bored by the performance as any spectator might be. The playwright's attention might even flag. In short, the kinds of things which may happen to the playwright's attention are no different from those that may happen to an ordinary spectator, although the two may have quite different motives and intentions.

For the discussion of disinterested-interested reading of literature it is appropriate to turn to the arguments of Eliseo Vivas whose work is largely concerned with literature. Vivas remarks that "By approaching a poem in a nonaesthetic mode it may function as history, as social criticism, as diagnostic evidence of the author's neuroses, and in an indefinite number of other ways."[20] Vivas further notes that according to Plato "the Greeks used Homer as an authority on war and almost anything under the sun," and that a certain poem "can be read as erotic poetry or as an account of a mystical experience."[21] The difference between reading a poem *as* history or whatever (reading it nonaesthetically) and reading it aesthetically depends on how *we* approach or read it. A poem "does not come self-labelled,"[22] but presumably is a poem only when it is read in a certain way – when it is an object of aesthetic experience. For Vivas, being an aesthetic object means being the object of the aesthetic attitude. He defines the aesthetic experience as "an experience of rapt attention which involves the intransitive apprehension of an object's immanent meanings and values in their full presentational immediacy."[23] Vivas maintains that his definition "helps me understand better what I can and what I cannot do when I read *The Brothers* [*Karamazov*]" and his definition "forces us to acknowledge that *The Brothers Karamazov* can hardly be read as art. . . ."[24] This acknowledgment means that we probably cannot intransitively apprehend *The Brothers* because of its size and complexity.

"Intransitive" is the key term here and Vivas' meaning must be made clear. A number of passages reveal his meaning but perhaps the following is the best. "Having once seen a hockey game in slow motion, I am prepared to testify that it was an object of pure intransitive experience [attention] – for I was not *interested* in which team won the game and no external factors mingled with my interest in the beautiful rhythmic flow of the slow-moving men."[25] It appears that Vivas' "intransitive attention" has the same meaning as Stolnitz' "disinterested attention," namely, "attending with no ulterior purpose."[26] Thus, the question to ask is "How does one attend to (read) a poem or any literary work transitively?" One can certainly attend to (read) a poem for a variety of different purposes and because of a variety of different reasons, but can one attend to a poem transitively? I do not think so, but let us consider the examples Vivas offers. He mentions "a type of reader" who uses a poem or parts of a poem as a spring-board for "loose, uncontrolled, relaxed day-dreaming, wool-gathering rambles, free from the contextual control" of the poem.[27] But surely it would be wrong to say such musing is a case of transitively attending to a poem, since it is clearly a case of not attending to a poem. Another supposed way of attending to a poem transitively is by approaching it "as diagnostic evidence of the author's neuroses." Vivas is right if he means that there is no critical point in doing this since it does not throw light on the poem. But this is a case of *using* information gleaned from a poem to make inferences about its author rather than attending to a poem. If anything can be said to be attended to here it is the author's neuroses (at least they are being thought about). This kind of case is perhaps best thought of as a rather special way of getting distracted from a poem. Of course, such "biographical" distractions might be insignificant and momentary enough so as scarcely to distract attention from the poem (a flash of insight or understanding about the poet). On the other hand, such distractions may turn into dissertations and whole careers. Such an interest may lead a reader to concentrate his attention (when he does read a poem) on certain "informational" aspects of a poem and to ignore the remaining aspects. As deplorable as such a sustained practice may be, it is at best a case of attending to certain features of a poem and ignoring others.

Another way that poetry may allegedly be read transitively is by reading it as history. This case is different from the two preceding ones since poetry often *contains* history (makes historical statements or at least references) but does not (usually) contain statements about the author's neuroses and so on nor does it contain statements about what a reader's free associations are about (otherwise we would not call them "*free* associations"). Reading a poem as history suggests that we are attending to (thinking about) historical events by way of attending to a poem – the poem is a time-telescope. Consider the following two sets of lines:

> In fourteen hundred and ninety-two
> Columbus sailed the ocean blue.
> Or like stout Cortez when with eagle eyes
> He star'd at the Pacific – and all his men
> Look'd at each other with a wild surmise –
> Silent, upon a peak in Darien.

Someone might read both of these raptly and not know that they make historical references (inaccurately in one case) – might this be a case of intransitive attention? How would the above reading differ – so far as attention is concerned – from the case of a reader who recognized the historical content of the poetic lines? The two readings do not differ as far as attention is concerned. History in a part of these sets of poetic lines and the two readings differ in that the first fails to take account of an aspect of the poetic lines (its historical content) and the second does not fail to do so. Perhaps by "reading as history" Vivas means "reading *simply* as history." But even this meaning does not mark out a special kind of attention but rather means that only a single aspect of a poem is being noticed and that its rhyme, meter, and so on are ignored. Reading a poem as social criticism can be analyzed in a fashion similar to reading as history. Some poems simply are or contain social criticism, and a complete reading must not fail to notice this fact.

The above cases of alleged interested attending can be sorted out in the following way. Jones listening to the music and our playwright watching the rehearsal are both attending with ulterior motives to a work of art, but there is no reason to suppose that the attention of either is different in kind from that of an ordinary spectator. The reader who reads a poem as history is simply attending to an aspect of a poem. On the other hand, the remaining cases – Jones beside the painting telling of his grandfather, the gloating impresario, daydreaming while "reading" a poem, and so on – are simply cases of not attending to the work of art.

In general, I conclude that "disinterestedness" or "intransitiveness" cannot properly be used to refer to a special kind of attention. "Disinterestedness" is a term which is used to make clear that an action has certain kinds of motives. Hence, we speak of disinterested findings (of boards of inquiry), disinterested verdicts (of judges and juries), and so on. Attending to an object, of course, has its motives but the attending itself is not interested or disinterested according to whether its motives are of the kind which motivate interested or disinterested action (as findings and verdicts might), although the attending may be more or less close.

I have argued that the second way of conceiving the aesthetic attitude is also a myth, or at least that its main content – disinterested attention – is; but I must now try to establish that the view misleads aesthetic theory. I shall argue that the attitude-theorist is incorrect about (1) the way in which he wishes to set the limits of aesthetic relevance; (2) the relation of the critic to a work of art; and (3) the relation of morality to aesthetic value.

Since I shall make use of the treatment of aesthetic relevance in Jerome Stolnitz' book, let me make clear that I am not necessarily denying the relevance of the specific items he cites but disagreeing with his criterion of relevance. His criterion of relevance is derived from his definition of "aesthetic attitude" and is set forth at the very beginning of his book. This procedure leads Monroe Beardsley in his review of the book to remark that Stolnitz' discussion is premature.[28] Beardsley suggests "that relevance cannot be satisfactorily discussed until after a careful treatment of the several arts, their dimensions and capacities."[29]

First, what is meant by "aesthetic relevance"? Stolnitz defines the problem by asking the question: "Is it ever 'relevant' to the aesthetic experience to have thoughts or images or bits of knowledge which are not present within the object itself?"[30] Stolnitz begins by summarizing Bullough's experiment and discussion of single colors and associations.[31] Some associations absorb the spectator's attention and distract him from the color and some associations "fuse" with the color. Associations of the latter kind are aesthetic and the former are not. Stolnitz draws the following conclusion about associations:

> If the aesthetic experience is as we have described it, then whether an association is aesthetic depends on whether it is compatible with the attitude of "disinterested attention." If the association re-enforces the focusing of attention upon the object, by "fusing" with the object and thereby giving it added "life and significance," it is genuinely aesthetic. If, however, it arrogates attention to itself and away from the object, it undermines the aesthetic attitude.[32]

It is not clear how something could *fuse* with a single color, but "fusion" is one of those words in aesthetics which is rarely defined. Stolnitz then makes use of a more fruitful example, one from I. A. Richards' *Practical Criticism*.[33] He cites the responses of students to the poem which begins:

> Between the erect and solemn trees
> I will go down upon my knees;
> I shall not find this day
> So meet a place to pray.

The image of a rugby forward running arose in the mind of one student-reader on reading the third verse of this poem. A cathedral was suggested to a second reader of the poem. The cathedral image "is congruous with both the verbal meaning of the poem and the emotions and mood which it expresses. It does not divert attention away from the poem."[34] The rugby image is presumably incongruous and diverts attention from the poem.

It is a confusion to take compatibility with disinterested attention as a criterion of relevance. If, as I have tried to show, *disinterested attention* is a confused notion, then it will not do as a satisfactory criterion. Also, when Stolnitz comes to show why the cathedral image is, and the rugby image is not relevant, the criterion he actually uses is *congruousness with the meaning of the poem*, which is quite independent of the notion of disinterestedness. The problem is perhaps best described as the problem of relevance to a poem, or more generally, to a work of art, rather than aesthetic relevance.

A second way in which the attitude theory misleads aesthetics is its contention that a critic's relationship to a work of art is different in kind from the relationship of other persons to the work. H. S. Langfeld in an early statement of this view wrote that we may "slip from the attitude of aesthetic enjoyment to the attitude of the critic." He characterizes the critical attitude as "intellectually occupied in coldly estimating . . . merits" and the aesthetic attitude as responding "emotionally to" a work of art.[35] At the beginning of his book in the discussion of the aesthetic attitude, Stolnitz declares that if a percipient of a work of art "has the purpose of passing judgment upon it, his attitude is not aesthetic."[36] He develops this line at a later stage of his book, arguing that appreciation (perceiving with the aesthetic attitude) and criticism (seeking for reasons to support an evaluation of a work) are (1) distinct and (2) "psychologically opposed to each other."[37] The critical attitude is questioning, analytical, probing for strengths and weakness, and so on. The aesthetic attitude is just the opposite: "It commits our allegiance to the object freely and unquestioningly"; "the spectator 'surrenders' himself to the work of art."[38] "Just because the two attitudes are inimical, whenever criticism obtrudes, it reduces aesthetic interest."[39] Stolnitz does not, of course, argue that criticism is unimportant for appreciation. He maintains criticism plays an important and necessary role in preparing a person to appreciate the nuances, detail, form, and so on of works of art. We are quite right, he says, thus to read and listen perceptively and acutely, but he questions, "Does this mean that we must analyze, measure in terms of value-criteria, etc., *during* the supposedly aesthetic experience?"[40] His answer is "No" and he maintains that criticism must occur "*prior* to the aesthetic encounter,"[41] or it will interfere with appreciation.

How does Stolnitz know that criticism will always interfere with appreciation? His conclusion sounds like one based upon the observations of actual cases, but I do not think it is. I believe it is a logical consequence of his definition of aesthetic attitude in terms of disinterested attention (no ulterior purpose). According to his view, to appreciate an object aesthetically one has to perceive it with no ulterior purpose. But the critic has an ulterior purpose – to analyze and evaluate the object he perceives – hence, in so far as a person functions as a critic he cannot function as an appreciator. But here, as previously, Stolnitz confuses a perceptual distinction with a motivational one. If it were possible to *attend* disinterestedly or interestedly, then perhaps the critic (as percipient) would differ from other percipients. But if my earlier argument about attending is correct, the critic differs from other percipients only in his motives and intentions and not in the way in which he attends to a work of art.

Of course, it might just be a fact that the search for reasons is incompatible with the appreciation of art, but I do not think it is. Several years ago I participated in a series of panel discussions of films. During the showing of each film we were to discuss, I had to take note of various aspects of the film (actor's performance, dramatic development, organization of the screen-plane and screen-space at given moments, and so on) in order later to discuss the films. I believe that this practice not only helped educate me to appreciate subsequent films but that it enhanced the appreciation of the films I was analyzing. I noticed and was able to appreciate things about the films I was watching which ordinarily out of laziness I would not have noticed. I see no reason why the same should not be the case with the professional critic or any critical percipient. If many professional critics seem to appreciate so few works, it is not because they are critics, but perhaps because the percentage of good works of art is fairly small and they suffer from a kind of combat fatigue.

I am unable to see any significant difference between "perceptively and acutely" attending to a work of art (which Stolnitz holds enhances appreciation) and searching for reasons, so far as the experience of a work of art is concerned. If I attend perceptively and acutely, I will have certain standards and/or paradigms in mind (not necessarily consciously) and will be keenly aware of the elements and relations in the work and will evaluate them to some degree. Stolnitz writes as if criticism takes place and then is over and done with, but the search for and finding of reasons (noticing this fits in with that, and so on) is continuous in practiced appreciators. A practiced viewer does not even have to be looking for a reason, he may just notice a line or an area in a painting, for example, and the line or area becomes a reason why he thinks the painting better or worse. A person may be a critic (not necessarily a good one) without meaning to be or without even realizing it.

There is one final line worth pursuing. Stolnitz' remarks suggest that one reason he thinks criticism and appreciation incompatible is that they compete with one another for time (this would be especially bad in the cases of performed works). But seeking and finding reasons (criticism) does not compete for time with appreciation. First, to seek for a reason means to be ready and able to notice something and to be thus ready and able as one attends does not compete for time with the attending. In fact, I should suppose that seeking for reasons would tend to focus attention more securely on the work of art. Second, finding a reason is an achievement, like winning a race. (It takes time to run a race but not to win it.) Consider the finding of the following reasons. How much time does it take to "see" that a note is off key (or on key)? How long does it take to notice that an actor mispronounces a word (or does it right)? How much time does it take to realize that a character's action does not fit his already established personality? (One is struck by it.) How long does it take to apprehend that a happy ending is out of place? It does not take time to find any of these reasons or reasons in general. Finding a reason is like coming to understand – it is done in a flash. I do not mean to suggest that one cannot be mistaken in finding a reason. What may appear to be a fault or a merit (a found reason) in the middle of a performance (or during one look at a painting and so forth) may turn out to be just the opposite when seen from the perspective of the whole performance (or other looks at the painting).

A third way in which the attitude theory misleads aesthetic theory is its contention that aesthetic value is always independent of morality. This view is perhaps not peculiar to the attitude theory, but it is a logical consequence of the attitude approach. Two quotations from attitude-theorists will establish the drift of their view of morality and aesthetic value.

> We are either concerned with the beauty of the object or with some other value of the same. Just as soon, for example, as ethical considerations occur to our mind, our attitude shifts.[42]
>
> Any of us might reject a novel because it seems to conflict with our moral beliefs . . . When we do so . . . We have *not* read the book aesthetically, for we have interposed moral . . . responses of our own which are alien to it. This disrupts the aesthetic attitude. We cannot then say that the novel is *aesthetically* bad, for we have not permitted ourselves to consider it aesthetically. To maintain the aesthetic attitude, we must follow the lead of the object and respond in concert with it.[43]

This conception of the aesthetic attitude functions to hold the moral aspects and the *aesthetic* aspects of the work of art firmly apart. Presumably, although it is difficult to see one's way clearly here, the moral aspects of a work of art cannot be an object of aesthetic attention because aesthetic attention is by definition disinterested and the moral aspects are somehow practical (interested). I suspect that there are a number of confusions involved in the assumption of the incompatibility of aesthetic attention and the moral aspects of art, but I shall not attempt to make these clear, since the root of the assumption – disinterested attention – is a confused notion. Some way other than in terms of the aesthetic attitude, then, is needed to discuss the relation of morality and aesthetic value.

David Pole in a recent article[44] has argued that the moral vision which a work of art may embody is *aesthetically* significant. It should perhaps be remarked at this point that not all works of art embody a moral vision and perhaps some kinds of art (music, for example) cannot embody a moral vision, but certainly some novels, some poems, and some films and plays do. I assume it is unnecessary to show how novels and so on have this moral aspect. Pole notes the curious fact that while so many critics approach works of art in "overtly moralistic terms," it is a "philosophical commonplace . . . that the ethical and the aesthetic modes . . . form different categories."[45] I suspect that many philosophers would simply say that these critics are confused about their roles. But Pole assumes that philosophical theory "should take notice of practice"[46] and surely he is right. In agreeing with Pole's assumption I should like to reserve the right to argue in specific cases that a critic may be misguided. This right is especially necessary in a field such as aesthetics because the language and practice of critics is so often burdened with ancient theory. Perhaps *all* moralistic criticism is wrong but philosophers should not rule it out of order at the very beginning by use of a definition.

Pole thinks that the moral vision presented by a particular work of art will be either true or false (perhaps a mixture of true and false might occur). If a work has a false moral vision, then something "is lacking within the work itself. But to say that is to say that the [work] is internally incoherent; some particular aspect must jar with what – on the strength of the rest – we claim a right to demand. And here the moral fault that we have found will count as an aesthetic fault too."[47] Pole is trying to show that the assessment of the moral vision of a work of art is just a special case of coherence or incoherence, and since everyone would agree that coherence is an aesthetic category, the assessment of the moral vision is an aesthetic assessment.

I think Pole's conclusion is correct but take exception to some of his arguments. First, I am uncertain whether it is proper to speak of a moral vision being true or false, and would want to make a more modest claim – that a moral vision can be judged to be acceptable or unacceptable. (I am not claiming Pole is wrong and my claim is not inconsistent with his.) Second, I do not see that a false (or unacceptable) moral vision makes a work incoherent. I should suppose that to say a work is coherent or incoherent is to speak about how its parts fit together and this involves no reference to something outside the work as the work's truth or falsity does.

In any event, it seems to me that a faulty moral vision can be shown to be an aesthetic fault independently of Pole's consideration of truth and coherence. As Pole's argument implies, a work's moral vision is a *part* of the work. Thus, any statement – descriptive or evaluative – about the work's moral vision is a statement about the *work*; and any statement about a *work* is a critical statement and, hence, falls within the aesthetic domain. To judge a moral vision to be morally unacceptable is to judge it defective and this amounts to saying that the work of art has a defective part. (Of course, a judgment of the acceptability of a moral vision may be wrong, as a judgment of an action sometimes is, but this fallibility does not make any difference.) Thus, a work's moral vision may be an aesthetic merit or defect just as a work's degree of unity is a merit or defect. But what justifies saying that a moral vision is a part of a work of art? Perhaps "part" is not quite the right word but it serves to make the point clear enough. A novel's moral vision is an essential part of the novel and if it were removed (I am not sure how such surgery could be carried out) the novel would be greatly changed. Anyway, a novel's moral vision is not like its covers or binding. However, someone might still argue that even though a work's moral vision is defective and the moral vision is part of the work, that this defect is not an *aesthetic* defect. How is "aesthetic" being used here? It is being used to segregate certain aspects or parts of works of art such as formal and stylistic aspects from such aspects as a work's moral vision. But it seems to me that the separation is only nominal. "Aesthetic" has been selected as a name for a certain sub-set of characteristics of works of art. I certainly cannot object to such a stipulation, since an underlying aim of this essay is to suggest the vacuousness of the term "aesthetic." My concern at this point is simply to insist that a work's moral vision is a part of the work and that, therefore, a critic can legitimately describe and evaluate it. I would *call* any defect or merit which a critic can legitimately point out an aesthetic defect or merit, but what we call it does not matter.

It would, of course, be a mistake to judge a work solely on the basis of its moral vision (it is only one part). The fact that some critics have judged works of art in this way is perhaps as much responsible as the theory of aesthetic attitude for the attempts to separate morality from the aesthetic. In fact, such criticism is no doubt at least partly responsible for the rise of the notion of the aesthetic attitude.

If the foregoing arguments are correct, the second way of conceiving the aesthetic attitude misleads aesthetic theory in at least three ways.

III

In answer to a hypothetical question about what is seen in viewing a portrait with the aesthetic attitude, Tomas in part responds "If looking at a picture and attending closely to how it looks is not really to be in the aesthetic attitude, then what on earth is?"[48] I shall take this sentence as formulating the weakest version of the aesthetic attitude. (I am ignoring Tomas' distinction between appearance and reality. See note 7. My remarks, thus, are not a critique of Tomas' argument; I am simply using one of his sentences.) First, this sentence speaks only of "looking at a picture," but "listening to a piece of music," "watching and listening to a play," and so on could be added easily enough. After thus expanding the sentence, it can be contracted into the general form: "Being in the aesthetic attitude is attending closely to a work of art (or a natural object)."

But the aesthetic attitude ("the hallmark of modern aesthetics") in this formulation is a great letdown – it no longer seems to say anything significant. Nevertheless, this does seem to be all that is left after the aesthetic attitude has been purged of *distancing* and *disinterestedness.* The only thing which prevents the aesthetic attitude from collapsing into simple attention is the qualification *closely*. One may, I suppose, attend to a work of art more or less closely, but this fact does not seem to signify anything very important. When "being in the aesthetic attitude" is equated with "attending (closely)," the equation neither involves any mythical element nor could it possibly mislead aesthetic theory. But if the definition has no vices, it seems to have no virtues either. When the aesthetic attitude finally turns out to be simply attending (closely), the final version should perhaps not be called "the weakest" but rather "the vacuous version" of the aesthetic attitude.

Stolnitz is no doubt historically correct that the notion of the aesthetic attitude has played an important role in the freeing of aesthetic theory from an overweening concern with beauty. It is easy to see how the slogan, "Anything can become an object of the aesthetic attitude," could help accomplish this liberation. It is worth noting, however, that the same goal could have been (and perhaps to some extent was) realized by simply noting that works of art are often ugly or contain ugliness, or have features which are difficult to include within beauty. No doubt, in more recent times people have been encouraged *to take an aesthetic attitude toward a painting* as a way of lowering their prejudices, say, against abstract and non-objective art. So if the notion of aesthetic attitude has turned out to have no theoretical value for aesthetics, it has had practical value for the appreciation of art in a way similar to that of Clive Bell's suspect notion of significant form.

Notes

1 See Marshall Cohen, "Appearance and the Aesthetic Attitude," *Journal of Philosophy,* vol. 56 (1959), p. 926; and Joseph Margolis, "Aesthetic Perception," *Journal of Aesthetics and Art Criticism,* vol. 19 (1960), p. 211. Margolis gives an argument, but it is so compact as to be at best only suggestive.

2 Jerome Stolnitz, "Some Questions Concerning Aesthetic Perception," *Philosophy and Phenomenological Research,* vol. 22 (1961), p. 69.

3 *The Concept of Mind* (London, 1949), p. 23.

4 "'Distancing' as an Aesthetic Principle," *Australasian Journal of Philosophy,* vol. 39 (1961), pp. 155–74.

5 "Disinterested" is Stolnitz' term. Vivas uses "intransitive."

6 *Aesthetics and Philosophy of Art Criticism* (Boston, 1960), p. 510.

7 "Aesthetic Vision," *The Philosophical Review,* vol. 68 (1959), p. 63. I shall ignore Tomas' attempt to distinguish between appearance and reality since it seems to confuse rather than clarify aesthetic theory. See F. Sibley, "Aesthetics and the Looks of Things," *Journal of Philosophy,* vol. 56 (1959), pp. 905–15; M. Cohen, op. cit., pp. 915–26; and J. Stolnitz, "Some Questions Concerning Aesthetic Perception," op. cit., pp. 69–87. Tomas discusses only visual art and the aesthetic attitude, but his remarks could be generalized into a comprehensive theory.

8 Dawson, op. cit., p. 158.

9 Ibid., pp. 159–60.

10 Ibid., p. 159.

11 Ibid., p. 168.

12 *Feeling and Form* (New York, 1953), p. 318.

13 *Aesthetics and Philosophy of Art Criticism*, pp. 34–5.

14 Ibid., p. 35.

15 Ibid., p. 36.

16 Ibid., p. 38.

17 "On the Origins of 'Aesthetic Disinterestedness'," *The Journal of Aesthetics and Art Criticism,* vol. 20 (1961), pp. 131–43.

18 "What Makes a Situation Aesthetic?" in *Philosophy Looks at the Arts,* Joseph Margolis (ed.) (New York, 1962). Reprinted from *Proceedings of the Aristotelian Society, Supplementary Volume* 31 (1957), pp. 75–92.
19 Ibid., p. 15.
20 Contextualism Reconsidered," *The Journal of Aesthetics and Art Criticism,* vol. 18 (1959), pp. 224–5.
21 Ibid., p. 225.
22 Loc. cit.
23 Ibid., p. 227.
24 Ibid., p. 237.
25 Ibid., p. 228. (Italics mine.)
26 Vivas' remark about the improbability of being able to read *The Brothers Karamazov* as art suggests that "intransitive attention" may sometimes mean for him "that which can be attended to at one time" or "that which can be held before the mind at one time." However, this second possible meaning is not one which is relevant here.
27 Vivas. op. cit., p. 231.
28 *The Journal of Philosophy,* vol. 57 (1960), p. 624.
29 Loc. cit.
30 Op. cit., p. 53.
31 Ibid., p. 54.
32 Ibid., pp. 54–5.
33 Ibid., pp. 55–6.
34 Ibid., p. 56.
35 *The Aesthetic Attitude* (New York, 1920), p. 79.
36 Op. cit., p. 35.
37 Ibid., p. 377.
38 Ibid., pp. 377–8.
39 Ibid., p. 379.
40 Ibid., p. 380.
41 Loc. cit.
42 H. S. Langfeld, op. cit., p. 73.
43 J. Stolnitz, op. cit., p. 36.
44 "Morality and the Assessment of Literature," *Philosophy,* vol. 37 (1962), pp. 193–207.
45 Ibid., p. 193.
46 Loc. cit.
47 Ibid., p. 206.
48 Tomas, op. cit., p. 63.

41

Art and Its Objects

Richard Wollheim

Richard Wollheim (1923–2003) was Professor of Philosophy at the University of California, Berkeley.

4

Let us begin with the hypothesis that works of art are physical objects. I shall call this for the sake of brevity the "physical-object hypothesis." Such a hypothesis is a natural starting point: if only for the reason that it is plausible to assume that things are physical objects unless they very obviously aren't. Certain things very obviously aren't physical objects. Now though it may not be obvious that works of art are physical objects, they don't seem to belong among these other things. They don't, that is, immediately group themselves along with thoughts, or periods of history, or numbers, or mirages. Furthermore, and more substantively, this hypothesis accords with many traditional conceptions of Art and its objects and what they are.

5

Nevertheless the hypothesis that all works of art are physical objects can be challenged. For our purposes it will be useful, and instructive, to divide this challenge into two parts: the division conveniently corresponding to a division within the arts themselves. For in the case of certain arts the argument is that there is no physical object that can with any plausibility be identified as the work of art: there is no object existing in space and time (as physical objects must) that can be picked out and thought of as a piece of music or a novel. In the case of other arts – most notably painting and sculpture – the argument is that, though there are physical objects of a standard and acceptable kind that could be, indeed generally are, identified as works of art, such identifications are wrong.

The first part of this challenge is, as we shall see, by far the harder to meet. However it is, fortunately, not it, but the second part of the challenge, that potentially raises such difficulties for aesthetics.

Richard Wollheim, *Art and Its Objects* (Cambridge: Cambridge University Press, 1980), sections 4–10, 15–16, 18–20, 35–8 (pp. 3–10; 20–4; 26–30; 64–76)

6

That there is a physical object that can be identified as *Ulysses* or *Der Rosenkavalier* is not a view that can long survive the demand that we should pick out or point to that object. There is, of course, the copy of *Ulysses* that is on my table before me now, there is the performance of *Der*

Rosenkavalier that I will go to tonight, and both these two things may (with some latitude, it is true, in the case of the performance) be regarded as physical objects. Furthermore, a common way of referring to these objects is by saying things like "*Ulysses* is on my table," "I shall see *Rosenkavalier* tonight": from which it would be tempting (but erroneous) to conclude that *Ulysses* just is my copy of it, *Rosenkavalier* just is tonight's performance.

Tempting, but erroneous; and there are a number of very succinct ways of bringing out the error involved. For instance, it would follow that if I lost my copy of *Ulysses*, *Ulysses* would become a lost work. Again, it would follow that if the critics disliked tonight's performance of *Rosenkavalier*, then they dislike *Rosenkavalier*. Clearly neither of these inferences is acceptable.

We have here two locutions or ways of describing the facts: one in terms of works of art, the other in terms of copies, performances, etc. of works of art. Just because there are contexts in which these two locutions are interchangeable, this does not mean that there are no contexts, moreover no contexts of a substantive kind, in which they are not interchangeable. There very evidently are such contexts, and the physical-object hypothesis would seem to overlook them to its utter detriment.

7

But, it might now be maintained, of course it is absurd to identify *Ulysses* with my copy of it or *Der Bosenkavalier* with tonight's performance, but nothing follows from this of a general character about the wrongness of identifying works of art with physical objects. For what was wrong in these two cases was the actual physical object that was picked out and with which the identification was then made. The validity of the physical-object hypothesis, like that of any other hypothesis, is quite unaffected by the consequences of misapplying it.

For instance, it is obviously wrong to say that *Ulysses* is my copy of it. Nevertheless, there is a physical object, of precisely the same order of being as my copy, though significantly not called a "copy," with which such an identification would be quite correct. This object is the author's manuscript: that, in other words, which Joyce wrote when he wrote *Ulysses*.

On the intimate connection, which undoubtedly does exist, between a novel or a poem on the one hand and the author's manuscript on the other, I shall have something to add later. But the connection does not justify us in asserting that one just is the other. Indeed, to do so seems open to objections not all that dissimilar from those we have just been considering. The critic, for instance, who admires *Ulysses* does not necessarily admire the manuscript. Nor is the critic who has seen or handled the manuscript in a privileged position as such when it comes to judgment on the novel. And – here we have come to an objection directly parallel to that which seemed fatal to identifying *Ulysses* with my copy of it – it would be possible for the manuscript to be lost and *Ulysses* to survive. None of this can be admitted by the person who thinks that *Ulysses* and the manuscript are one and the same thing.

To this last objection someone might retort that there are cases (e.g., *Love's Labour Won*, Kleist's *Robert Guiscard*) where the manuscript is lost and the work is lost, and moreover the work is lost because the manuscript is lost. Of course there is no real argument here, since nothing more is claimed than that there are *some* cases like this. Nevertheless the retort is worth pursuing, for the significance of such cases is precisely the opposite of that intended. Instead of reinforcing, they actually diminish, the status of the manuscript. For if we now ask, When is the work lost when the manuscript is lost?, the answer is, When and only when the manuscript is unique: but then this would be true for any copy of the work were it unique.

Moreover, it is significant that in the case of *Rosenkavalier* it is not even possible to construct an argument corresponding to the one about *Ulysses*. To identify an opera or any other piece of music with the composer's holograph, which looks the corresponding thing to do, is implausible because (for instance), whereas an opera can be heard, a holograph cannot be. In consequence it is common at this stage of the argument, when music is considered, to introduce a new notion, that of the ideal performance, and then to identify the piece of music with this. There are many difficulties here: in the present context it is enough to point out that this step could not conceivably satisfy the purpose for which it was intended; that is, that of saving the physical-object hypothesis. For an ideal performance cannot be, even in the attenuated sense in which we have extended the term to ordinary performances, a physical object.

8

A final and desperate expedient to save the physical-object hypothesis is to suggest that all those works of art which cannot plausibly be identified with physical objects are identical with classes of such objects. A novel, of which there are copies, is not my or your copy but is the class of all its copies. An opera, of which there are performances, is not tonight's or last night's performance, nor even the ideal performance, but is the class of all its performances. (Of course, strictly speaking, this suggestion doesn't save the hypothesis at all: since a class of physical objects isn't necessarily, indeed is most unlikely to be, a physical object itself. But it saves something like the spirit of the hypothesis.)

However, it is not difficult to think of objections to this suggestion. Ordinarily we conceive of a novelist as writing a novel, or a composer as finishing an opera. But both these ideas imply some moment in time at which the work is complete. Now suppose (which is not unlikely) that the copies of a novel or the performances of an opera go on being produced for an indefinite period: then, on the present suggestion, there is no such moment, let alone one in their creator's lifetime. So we cannot say that *Ulysses* was written by Joyce, or that Strauss composed *Der Rosenkavalier*. Or, again, there is the problem of the unperformed symphony, or the poem of which there is not even a manuscript: in what sense can we now say that these things even *exist?*

But perhaps a more serious, certainly a more interesting, objection is that in this suggestion what is totally unexplained is why the various copies of *Ulysses* are all said to be copies of *Ulysses* and nothing else, why all the performances of *Der Rosenkavalier* are reckoned performances of that one opera. For the ordinary explanation of how we come to group copies or performances as being of this book or of that opera is by reference to something else, something other than themselves, to which they stand in some special relation. (Exactly what this other thing is, or what is the special relation in which they stand to it is, of course, something we are as yet totally unable to say.) But the effect, indeed precisely the point, of the present suggestion is to eliminate the possibility of any such reference: if a novel or opera just is its copies or its performances, then we cannot, for purposes of identification, refer from the latter to the former.

The possibility that remains is that the various particular objects, the copies or performances, are grouped as they are, not by reference to some other thing to which they are related, but in virtue of some relation that holds between them: more specifically, in virtue of resemblance.

But, in the first place, all copies of *Ulysses*, and certainly all performances of *Der Rosenkavalier*, are not perfect matches. And if it is now said that the differences do not matter, either because the various copies or performance resemble each other in all relevant respects, or because they resemble each other more than they resemble the copies or performances of any other novel or opera, neither answer is adequate. The first answer begs the issue, in that to talk of relevant respects presupposes that we know how, say, copies of *Ulysses* are grouped together: the second answer evades the issue, in that though it may tell us why we do not, say, reckon any of the performances of *Der Rosenkavalier* as performances of *Arabella*, it gives us no indication why we do not set some of them up separately, as performances of some third opera.

Secondly, it seems strange to refer to the resemblance between the copies of *Ulysses* or the performances of *Rosenkavalier* as though this were a brute fact: a fact, moreover, which could be used to explain why they were copies or performances of what they are. It would be more natural to think of this so-called "fact" as something that itself stood in need of explanation: and, moreover, as finding its explanation in just that which it is here invoked to explain. In other words, to say that certain copies or performances are of *Ulysses* or *Rosenkavalier* because they resemble one another seems precisely to reverse the natural order of thought: the resemblance, we would think, follows from, or is to be understood in terms of, the fact that they are of the same novel or opera.

9

However, those who are ready to concede that some kinds of work of art are not physical objects will yet insist that others are. *Ulysses* and *Der Rosenkavalier* may not be physical objects, but the *Donna Velata* and Donatello's *St. George* most certainly are.

I have already suggested (section 5) that the challenge to the physical-object hypothesis can be divided into two parts. It will be clear that I am now about to embark on the second part of the challenge: namely, that which allows that there are (some) physical objects that could conceivably be identified as works of art, but insists that it would be quite erroneous to make the identification.

(To some, such a course of action may seem superfluous. For enough has been said to disprove the physical-object hypothesis. That is true; but the argument that is to come has its intrinsic interest, and for that reason is worth developing. Those for whom the interest of all philosophical argument is essentially polemical, and who have been convinced by the preceding argument, may choose to think of that which is to follow as bearing upon a revised or weakened version of the physical-object hypothesis: namely, that some works of art are physical objects.)

10

In the Pitti there is a canvas (No. 245) 85 cm × 64 cm: in the Museo Nazionale, Florence, there is a piece of marble 209 cm high. It is with these physical objects that those who claim that the *Donna Velata* and the *St. George* are physical objects would naturally identify them.

This identification can be disputed in (roughly) one or other of two ways. It can be argued that the work of art has properties which are incompatible with certain properties that the physical object has, alternatively it can be argued that the work of art has properties which no physical object could have: in neither case could the work of art be the physical object.

An argument of the first kind would run: We say of the *St. George* that it moves with life (Vasari). Yet the block of marble is inanimate. Therefore the *St. George* cannot be that block of marble. An argument of the second kind would run: We say of the *Donna Velata* that it is exalted and dignified (Wölfflin). Yet a piece of canvas in the Pitti cannot conceivably have these qualities. Therefore the *Donna Velata* cannot be that piece of canvas.

These two arguments, I suggest, are not merely instances of these two ways of arguing, they are characteristic instances. For the argument that there is an incompatibility of property between works of art and physical objects characteristically concentrates on the representational properties of works of art. The argument that works of art have properties that physical objects could not have characteristically concentrates on the expressive properties of works of art. The terms "representational" and "expressive" are used here in a very wide fashion, which, is it hoped, will become clear as the discussion proceeds.

[. . .]

15

We might begin by considering two false views of how works of art acquire their expressiveness: not simply so as to put them behind us, but because each is in its way a pointer to the truth. Neither view requires us to suppose that works of art are anything other than physical objects.

The first view is that works of art are expressive because they have been produced in a certain state of mind or feeling on the part of the artist: and to this the rider is often attached, that it is this mental or emotional condition that they express. But if we take the view first of all with the rider attached, its falsehood is apparent. For it is a common happening that a painter or sculptor modifies or even rejects a work of his because he finds that it fails to correspond to what he experienced at the time. If, however, we drop the rider, the view now seems arbitrary or perhaps incomplete. For there seems to be no reason why a work should be expressive simply because it was produced in some heightened condition if it is also admitted that the work and the condition need not have the same character. (It would be like trying to explain why a man who has measles is ill by citing the fact that he was in contact with someone else who was also ill when that other person was not ill with measles or anything related to measles.) It must be understood that I am not criticising the view because it allows an artist to express in his work a condition other than that which he was in at the time: my case is rather that the view does wrong both to allow this fact and to insist that the expressiveness of the work can be accounted for exclusively in terms of the artist's condition.

However, what is probably the more fundamental objection to this view, and is the point that has been emphasised by many recent philosophers, is that the work's expressiveness now becomes a purely external feature of it. It is no longer something that we can or might observe, it is something that we infer from what we observe: it has been detached from the object as it manifests itself to us, and placed in its history, so that it now belongs more to the biography of the artist than to criticism of the work. And this seems wrong. For the qualities of gravity, sweetness, fear, that we invoke in describing works of art seem essential to our understanding of them; and if they are, they cannot be extrinsic to the works themselves. They cannot be, that is, mere attributes of the experiences or activities of Masaccio, of Raphael, of Grünewald – they inhere rather in the Brancacci frescoes, in the Granduca Madonna, in the Isenheim Altarpiece.

The second view is that works of art are expressive because they produce or are able to produce a certain state of mind or feeling in the spectator: moreover (and in the case of this view it is difficult to imagine the rider ever detached), it is this mental or emotional condition that they express. This view is open to objections that closely parallel those we have just considered.

For, in the first place, it seems clearly false. Before works even of the most extreme emotional intensity, like Bernini's St. Teresa or the black paintings of Goya, it is possible to remain more or less unexcited to the emotion that it would be agreed they express. Indeed, there are many theories that make it a distinguishing or defining feature of art that it should be viewed with detachment, that there should be a distancing on the part of the spectator between what the work expresses and what he experiences: although it is worth noting, in passing, that those theorists who have been most certain that works of art do not arouse emotion, have also been uncertain, in some cases confused, as to how this comes about: sometimes attributing it to the artist, sometimes to the spectator; sometimes, that is, saying that the artist refrains from giving the work the necessary causal power, sometimes saying that the spectator holds himself back from reacting to this power.

However, the main objection to this view, as to the previous one, is that it removes what we ordinarily think of as one of the essential characteristics of the work of art from among its manifest properties, locating it this time not in its past but in its hidden or dispositional endowment. And if it is now argued that this is a very pertinent difference, in that the latter is, in principle at least, susceptible to our personal verification in a way in which the former never could be, this misses the point. Certainly we can actualize the disposition, by bringing it about that the work produces in us the condition it is supposed to express: and there is clearly no corresponding way in which we can actualize the past. But though this is so, this still does not make the disposition itself – and it is with this, after all, that the work's expressiveness is equated – any the more a property that we can observe.

16

And yet there seems to be something to both these views: as an examination of some hypothetical cases might bring out.

For let us imagine that we are presented with a physical object – we shall not for the moment assume that it either is or is supposed to be a work of art – and the claim is made on its behalf, in a way that commands our serious attention, that it is expressive of a certain emotion: say, grief. We then learn that it had been produced quite casually, as a diversion or as part of a game: and we must further suppose that it arouses neither in us nor in anyone else anything more than mild pleasure. Can we, in the light of these facts, accept the claim? It is conceivable that we might; having certain special reasons.

But now let us imagine that the claim is made on behalf not of a single or isolated object, but of a whole class of objects of which our original example would be a fair specimen, and it turns out that what was true of it is true of all of them both as to how they were produced and as to what they produce in us. Surely it is impossible to imagine any circumstances in which we would allow *this* claim.

But what are we to conclude from this? Are we to say that the two views are true in a general way, and that error arises only when we think of them as applying in each and every case? The argument appears to point in this direction, but at the same time it seems an unsatisfactory state in which to leave the matter. (Certain contemporary moral philosophers, it is true, seem to find a parallel situation in their own area perfectly congenial, when they say that an individual action can be right even though it does not satisfy the utilitarian criterion, provided that that sort of action, or that that action in general, satisfies the criterion: the utilitarian criterion, in other words, applies on the whole, though not in each and every case.)

The difficulty here is this: Suppose we relax the necessary condition in the particular case because it is satisfied in general, with what right do we continue to regard the condition that is satisfied in general as necessary? Ordinarily the argument for regarding a condition as necessary is that there could not be, or at any rate is not, anything of the requisite kind that does not satisfy it. But this argument is not open to us here. Accordingly, at the lowest, we must be prepared to give some account of how the exceptions arise: or, alternatively, why we are so insistent on the condition in general. To return to the example: it seems unacceptable to say that a single object can express grief though it was not produced in, nor is it productive of, that emotion, but that a class of objects cannot express grief unless most of them, or some of them, or a fair sample of them, satisfy these conditions – unless we can explain why we discriminate in this way.

At this point what we might do is to turn back and look at the special reasons, as I called them, which we might have for allowing an individual object to be expressive of grief though it did not satisfy the conditions that hold generally. There seem to be roughly two lines of thought which if followed might allow us to concede expressiveness. We might think, "Though the person who made this object didn't feel grief when he made it, yet this is the sort of thing I would make if I felt grief. . . ." Alternatively we might think, "Though I don't feel grief when I look at this here and now, yet I am sure that in other circumstances I would. . . ." Now, if I am right in thinking that these are the relevant considerations, we can begin to see some reason for our discrimination between the particular and the general case. For there is an evident difficulty in seeing how these considerations could apply to a whole class of objects: given, that is, that the class is reasonably large. For our confidence that a certain kind of object was what we would produce if we experienced grief would be shaken by the fact that not one (or very few) had actually been produced in grief: equally, our confidence that in other circumstances we should feel grief in looking at them could hardly survive the fact that no one (or scarcely anyone) ever had. The special reasons no longer operating, the necessary conditions reassert themselves.

[. . .]

18

The question, however, might now be raised. Suppose the two criteria, which hitherto have been taken so closely together, should diverge: for they might: how could we settle the issue? And the difficulty here is not just that there is no simple answer to the question, but that it looks as though any answer given to it would be arbitrary. Does this, therefore, mean that the two criteria are quite independent, and that the whole concept of expression, if, that is, it is constituted as I have suggested, is a contingent conjunction of two elements, which could as easily fall apart as together?

I shall argue that the concept of expression, at any rate as this applies to the arts, is indeed complex, in that it lies at the intersection of two constituent notions of expression. We can gain some guidance as to these notions from the two views of expression we have been considering, for they are both reflected in, though also distorted by, these views. But, whereas the two views seem quite contingently connected, and have no clear point of union, once we understand what these notions are we can see how and why they interact. Through them we can gain a better insight into the concept of expression as a whole.

In the first place, and perhaps most primitively, we think of a work of art as expressive in the sense in which a gesture or a cry would be expressive: that is to say, we conceive of it as coming so directly and immediately out of some particular emotional or mental state that it bears unmistakeable marks of that state upon it. In this sense the word remains very close to its etymology: *ex-primere*, to squeeze out or press out. An expression is a secretion of an inner state. I shall refer to this as "natural expression." Alongside this notion is another, which we apply when we think of an object as expressive of a certain condition because, when we are in that condition, it seems to us to match, or correspond with, what we experience inwardly: and perhaps when the condition passes, the object is also good for reminding us of it in some special poignant way, or for reviving it for us. For an object to be expressive in this sense, there is no requirement that it should originate in the condition that it expresses, nor indeed is there any stipulation about its genesis: for these purposes it is simply a piece of the environment which we appropriate on account of the way it seems to reiterate something in us. Expression in this sense I shall (following a famous nineteenth-century usage) call "correspondence."

We may now link this with the preceding discussion by saying that the preoccupation with what the artist felt, or might have felt, reflects a concern with the work of art as a piece of natural expression: whereas the preoccupation with what the spectator feels, or might feel, reflects a concern with the work of art as an example of correspondence.

But though these two notions are logically distinct, in practice they are bound to interact: indeed, it is arguable that it goes beyond the limit of legitimate abstraction to imagine one without the other. We can see this by considering the notion of appropriateness, or fittingness, conceived as a relation holding between expression and expressed. We might think that such a relation has a place only in connection with correspondences. For in the case of natural expression, the link between inner and outer is surely too powerful or too intimate to allow its mediation. It is not because tears seem like grief that we regard them as an expression of grief: nor does a man when he resorts to tears do so because they match his condition. So we might think. But in reality, at any level above the most primitive, natural expression will always be coloured or influenced by some sense of what is appropriate; there will be a feedback from judgment, however inchoate or unconscious this may be, to gesture or exclamation. Again, when we turn to correspondence, it might seem that here we are guided entirely by appropriateness or the fit: that is to say, we appeal uniquely to the appearances or characteristics of objects, which hold for us, in some quite unanalyzed way, an emotional significance. We do not (we might think) check these reactions against observed correlations. But once again this is a simplification. Apart from a few primitive cases, no physiognomic perception will be independent of what is for us the supreme example of the relationship between inner and outer: that is, the human body as the expression of the psyche. When we endow a natural object or an artifact with expressive meaning, we tend to see it corporeally: that is, we tend to credit it with a particular look which bears a marked analogy to some look that the human body wears and that is constantly conjoined with an inner state.

19

To the question, Can a work of art be a physical object if it is also expressive?, it now looks as though we can, on the basis of the preceding account of expression, give an affirmative answer. For that account was elaborated with specifically in mind those arts where it is most plausible to think of a work of art as a physical object. But it may seem that with both the two notions of expression that I have tried to formulate, there remains an unexamined or problematic residue. And in the two cases the problem is much the same.

It may be stated like this: Granted that in each case the process I have described is perfectly comprehensible, how do we come at the end of it to attribute a human emotion to an object? In both cases the object has certain characteristics. In one case these characteristics mirror, in the other case they are caused by, certain inner states of ours. Why, on the basis of this, do the names of the inner states get transposed to the objects?

The difficulty with this objection might be put by saying that it treats a philosophical reconstruction of a part of our language as though it were a historical account. For it is not at all clear that, in the cases where we attribute emotions to objects in the ways that I have tried to describe, we have any other way of talking about the objects themselves. There is not necessarily a prior description in nonemotive terms, on which we superimpose the emotive description. Or, to put the same point in nonlinguistic terms, it is not always the case that things that we see as expressive, we can or could see in any other way. In such cases what we need is not a justification, but an explanation, of our language. That I hope to have given.

20

We have now completed our discussion of the physical-object hypothesis, and this would be a good moment at which to pause and review the situation.

The hypothesis, taken literally, has been clearly shown to be false: in that there are arts where it is impossible to find physical objects that are even candidates for being identified with works of art (sections 6–8). However, as far as those other arts are concerned where such physical objects can be found, the arguments against the identification – namely, those based on the fact that works of art have properties not predicable of physical objects – seemed less cogent (sections 9–19). I have now to justify the assertion that I made at the very beginning of the discussion (section 5), that it was only in so far as it related to these latter arts that the challenge to this hypothesis had any fundamental significance for aesthetics.

The general issue raised, whether works of art are physical objects, seems to compress two questions: the difference between which can be brought out by accenting first one, then the other, constituent word in the operative phrase. Are works of art *physical* objects? Are works of art physical *objects*? The first question would be a question about the stuff or constitution of works of art, what in the broadest sense they are made of: more specifically, Are they mental? or physical? are they constructs of the mind? The second question would be a question about the category to which works of art belong, about the criteria of identity and individuation applicable to them: more specifically, Are they universals, of which there are instances?, or classes, of which there are members?, are they particulars? Roughly speaking, the first question might be regarded as metaphysical, the second as logical. And, confusingly enough, both can be put in the form of a question about what kind of thing a work of art is.

Applying this distinction to the preceding discussion, we can now see that the method of falsifying the hypothesis that all works of art are physical objects has been to establish that there are some works of art that are not objects (or particulars) at all: whereas the further part of the case, which depends upon establishing that those works of art which are objects are nevertheless not physical, has not been made good. If my original assertion is to be vindicated, I am now required to show that what is of moment in aesthetics is the physicality of works of art rather than their particularity.

[. . .]

35

Before, however, pursuing this last point, the consequences of which will occupy us more or less for the rest of this essay, I want to break off the present discussion (which began with section 20) and go back and take up an undischarged commitment: which is that of considering the consequences of rejecting the hypothesis that works of art are physical objects, in so far as those arts are concerned where there is no physical object with which the work of art could be plausibly identified. This will, of course, be in pursuance of my general aim – which has also directed the preceding discussion – of establishing that the rejection of the hypothesis has serious consequences for the philosophy of art only in so far as those arts are concerned where there *is* such an object.

I have already stated (sections 5, 20) that, once it is conceded that certain works of art are not physical *objects*, the subsequent problem that arises, which can be put by asking, What sort of thing are they?, is essentially a logical problem. It is that of determining the criteria of identity and individuation appropriate to, say, a piece of music or a novel. I shall characterise the status of such things by saying that they are (to employ a term introduced by Peirce) *types*. Correlative to the term "type" is the term "token." Those physical objects which (as we have seen) can out of desperation be thought to be works of art in cases where there are no physical objects that can plausibly be thought of in this way, are *tokens*. In other words, *Ulysses* and *Der Rosenkavalier* are types; my copy of *Ulysses* and tonight's performance of *Rosenkavalier* are tokens of those types. The question now arises, What is a type?

The question is very difficult, and, unfortunately, to treat it with the care and attention to detail that it deserves is beyond the scope of this essay.

We might begin by contrasting a type with other sorts of thing that it is not. Most obviously we could contrast a type with a *particular*: this I shall take as done. Then we could contrast it with other various kinds of nonparticulars: with a *class* (of which we say that it has *members*), and a *universal* (of which we say that it has *instances*). An example of a class would be the class of red things: an example of a universal would be redness: and examples of a type would be the word "red" and the Red Flag – where this latter phrase is taken to mean not this or that piece of material, kept in a chest or taken out and flown at a masthead, but the flag of revolution, raised for the first time in 1830 and that which many would willingly follow to their death.

Let us introduce as a blanket expression for types, classes, universals, the term *generic entity*, and, as a blanket expression for those things which fall under them, the term *element*. Now we can say that the various generic entities can be distinguished according to the different ways or relationships in which they stand to their elements. These relationships can be arranged on a scale of intimacy or intrinsicality. At one end of the scale we find classes, where the relationship is at its most external or extrinsic: for a class is merely made of, or constituted by, its members which are extensionally conjoined to form it. The class of red things is simply a construct out of all those things which are (timelessly) red. In the case of universals the relation is more intimate: in that a universal is present in all its instances. Redness is in all red things. With types we find the relationship between the generic entity and its elements at its most intimate: for not merely is the type present in all its tokens like the universal in all its instances, but for much of the time we think and talk of the type as though it were itself a kind of token, though a peculiarly important or pre-eminent one. In many ways we treat the Red Flag as though it were a red flag (cf. "We'll keep the Red Flag flying high").

These varying relations in which the different generic entities stand to their elements are also reflected (if, that is, this is *another* fact) in the degree to which both the generic entities and their elements can satisfy the same predicates. Here we need to make a distinction between sharing properties and properties being transmitted. I shall say that when A and B are both *f*, *f* is shared by A and B. I shall further say that when A is *f* because B is *f*, or B is *f* because A is *f*, *f* is transmitted between A and B. (I shall ignore the sense or direction of the transmission, i.e. I shall not trouble, even where it is possible, to discriminate between the two sorts of situation I have mentioned as instances of transmission.)

First, we must obviously exclude from consideration properties that can pertain only to tokens (e.g. properties of location in space and time) and equally those which pertain only to types (e.g. "was invented by"). When we have done this, the situation looks roughly as follows: Classes can share properties with their members (e.g. the class of big things is big), but this is very rare: moreover, where it occurs it will be a purely contingent or fortuitous affair, i.e. there will be no transmitted properties. In the cases of both universals and types, there will be shared properties. Red things may be said to be exhilarating, and so also redness. Every red flag is rectangular, and so is the Red Flag itself. Moreover, many, if not all, the shared properties will be transmitted.

Let us now confine our attention to transmitted properties because it is only they which are relevant to the difference in relationship between, on the one hand, universals and types and, on the other hand, their elements. Now there would seem to be two differences in respect of transmitted properties which distinguish universals from types. In the first place, there is likely to be a far larger range of transmitted properties in the case of types than there is with universals. The second difference is this: that in the case of universals no property that an instance of a certain universal has necessarily, i.e. that it has in virtue of being an instance of that universal, can be transmitted to the universal. In the case of types, on the other hand, all and only those properties that a token of a certain type has necessarily, i.e. that it has in virtue of being a token of that type, will be transmitted to the type. Examples would be: Redness, as we have seen, may be exhilarating, and, if it is, it is so for the same reason that its instances are, i.e. the property is transmitted. But redness cannot be red or coloured, which its instances are necessarily. On the other hand, the Union Jack is coloured and rectangular, properties which all its tokens have necessarily: but even if all its tokens happened to be made of linen, this would not mean that the Union Jack itself was made of linen.

To this somewhat negative account of a type – concentrated largely on what a type is not – we now need to append something of a more positive kind, which would say what it is for various particulars to be gathered together as tokens of the same type. For it will be appreciated that there corresponds to every universal and to every type a class: to redness the class of red things, to the Red Flag the class of red flags. But the converse it not true. The question therefore arises, What are the characteristic circumstances in which we postulate a type? The question, we must appreciate, is entirely conceptual: it is a question about the structure of our language.

A very important set of circumstances in which we postulate types – perhaps a central set, in the sense that it may be possible to explain the remaining circumstances by reference to them – is where we can correlate a class of particulars with a piece of human invention: these particulars may then be regarded as tokens of a certain type. This characterization is vague, and deliberately so: for it is intended to comprehend a considerable spectrum of cases. At one end we have the case where a particular is produced, and is then copied: at the other end, we have the case where a set of instructions is drawn up which, if followed, give rise to an indefinite number of particulars. An example of the former would be the Brigitte Bardot looks: an example of the latter would be the Minuet. Intervening cases are constituted by the production of a particular which was made in order to be copied, e.g. the Boeing 707, or the construction of a mould or matrix which generates further particulars, e.g. the Penny Black. There are many ways of arranging the cases – according, say, to the degree of human intention that enters into the proliferation of the type, or according to the degree of match that exists between the original piece of invention and the tokens that flow from it. But there are certain resemblances between all the cases: and with ingenuity one can see a natural extension of the original characterization to cover cases where the invention is more classificatory than constructive in nature, e.g. the Red Admiral.

36

It will be clear that the preceding characterization of a type and its tokens offers us a framework within which we can (at any rate roughly) understand the logical status of things like operas, ballets, poems, etchings, etc.: that is to say, account for their principles of identity and individuation. To show exactly where these various kinds of things lie within this framework would involve a great deal of detailed analysis, more than can be attempted here, and probably of little intrinsic interest. I shall touch very briefly upon two general sets of problems, both of which concern the feasibility of the project. In this section I shall deal with the question of how the type is identified or (what is much the same thing) how the tokens of a given type are generated. In the next section I shall deal with the question of what properties we are entitled to ascribe to a type. These two sets of questions are not entirely distinct: as we can see from the fact that there is a third set of questions intermediate between the other two, concerning how we determine whether two particulars are or are not tokens of the same type. These latter questions, which arise for instance sharply in connection with translation, I shall pass over. I mention them solely to place those which I shall deal with in perspective.

First, then, as to how the type is identified. In the case of any work of art that it is plausible to think of as a type, there is what I have called a piece of human invention: and these pieces of invention fall along the whole spectrum of cases as I characterized it. At one end of the scale, there is the case of a poem, which comes into being when certain words are set down on paper or perhaps, earlier still, when they are said over in the poet's head (cf. the Croce-Collingwood theory). At the other end of the scale is an opera which comes into being when a certain set of instructions, i.e. the score, is written down, in accordance with which performances can be produced. As an intervening case we might note a film, of which different copies are made: or an etching or engraving, where different sheets are pulled from the same matrix, i.e. the plate.

There is little difficulty in all this, so long as we bear in mind from the beginning the variety of ways in which the different types can be identified, or (to put it another way) in which the tokens can be generated from the initial piece of invention. It is if we begin with too limited a range of examples that distortions can occur. For instance, it might be argued that, if the tokens of a certain poem are the many different inscriptions that occur in books reproducing the word order of the poet's manuscript, then "strictly speaking" the tokens of an opera must be the various pieces of sheet music or printed scores that reproduce the marks on the composer's holograph. Alternatively, if we insist that it is the performances of the opera that are the tokens, then, it is argued, it must be the many readings or "voicings" of the poem that are *its* tokens.

Such arguments might seem to be unduly barren or pedantic, if it were not that they revealed something about the divergent media of art: moreover, if they did not bear upon the issues to be discussed in the next section.

37

It is, we have seen, a feature of types and their tokens, not merely that they may share properties, but that when they do, these properties may be transmitted. The question we have now to ask is whether a limit can be set upon the properties that may be transmitted: more specifically, since it is the type that is the work of art and therefore that with which we are expressly concerned, whether there are any properties – always of course excluding those properties which can be predicated only of particulars – that belong to tokens and cannot be said *ipso facto* to belong to their types.

It might be thought that we have an answer, or at least a partial answer, to this question in the suggestion already made, that the properties transmitted between token and type are only those which the tokens possess necessarily. But a moment's reflection will show that any answer along these lines is bound to be trivial. For there is no way of determining the properties that a token of a given type has necessarily, independently of determining the properties of that type: accordingly, we cannot use the former in order to ascertain the latter. We cannot hope to discover what the properties of the Red Flag are by finding out what properties the various red flags have necessarily: for how can we come to know that e.g. this red flag is necessarily red, prior to knowing that the Red Flag itself is red?

There are, however, three observations that can be made here on the basis of our most general intuitions. The first is that there are no properties or sets of properties that cannot pass from token to type. With the usual reservations, there is nothing that can be predicated of a performance of a piece of music that could not also be predicated of that piece of music itself. This point is vital. For it is this that ensures what I have called the harmlessness of denying the physical-object hypothesis in the domain of those arts where the denial consists in saying that works of art are not physical *objects*. For though they may not be objects but types, this does not prevent them from having physical properties. There is nothing that prevents us from saying that Donne's *Satires* are harsh on the ear, or that Dürer's engraving of St. Anthony has a very differentiated texture, or that the conclusion of "Celeste Aida" is pianissimo.

The second observation is that, though any single property may be transmitted from token to type, it does not follow that all will be: or to put it another way, a token will have some of its properties necessarily, but it need not have all of them necessarily. The full significance of this point will emerge later.

Thirdly, in the case of *some* arts it is necessary that not all properties should be transmitted from token to type: though it remains true that for any single property it might be transmitted. The reference here is, of course, to the performing arts – to operas, plays, symphonies, ballet. It follows from what was said above that anything that can be predicated of a performance of a piece of music can also be predicated of the piece of music itself: to this we must now add that not every property that can be predicated of the former *ipso facto* belongs to the latter. This point is generally covered by saying that in such cases there is essentially an element of *interpretation*, where for these purposes interpretation may be regarded as the production of a token that has properties in excess of those of the type.

"Essentially" is a word that needs to be taken very seriously here. For, in the first place, there are certain factors that might disguise from us the fact that every performance of a work of art involves, or is, an interpretation. One such factor would be antiquarianism. We could – certainly if the evidence were available – imagine a *Richard III* produced just as Burbage played it, or *Das Klagende Lied* performed just as Mahler conducted it. But though it would be possible to bring about in this way a replica of Burbage's playing or Mahler's conducting, we should none the less have interpretations of *Richard III* and *Das Klagende Lied*, for this is what Burbage's playing and Mahler's conducting were, though admittedly the first, Secondly, it would be wrong to think of the element of interpretation – assuming that this is now conceded to be present in the case of all performances – as showing something defective. Suzanne Langer, for instance, has characterized the situation in the performing arts by saying that e.g. the piece of music the composer writes is "an incomplete work": "the performance" she says "is the completion of a musical work." But this suggests that the point to which the composer carries the work is one which he could, or even should, have gone beyond. To see how radical a reconstruction this involves of the ways in which we conceive the performing arts, we need to envisage what would be involved if it were to be even possible to eliminate interpretation. For instance, one requirement would be that we should have for each performing art what might be called, in some very strong sense, a universal notation: such that we could designate in it every characteristic that now originates at the point of performance. Can we imagine across the full range of the arts what such a notation would be like? With such a notation there would no longer be any executant arts: the whole of the execution would have been anticipated in the notation. What assurance can we have that the reduction of these arts to mere mechanical skills would not in turn have crucial repercussions upon the way in which we regard or assess the performing arts?

38

However, if we no longer regard it as a defect in certain arts that they require interpretation, it might still seem unsatisfactory that there should be this discrepancy within the arts: that, for instance, the composer or the dramatist should be denied the kind of control over his work that the poet or the painter enjoys.

In part, there just *is* a discrepancy within the arts. And this discrepancy is grounded in very simple facts of very high generality, which anyhow lie outside art: such as that words are different from pigments; or that it is human beings we employ to act and human beings are not all exactly alike, If this is the source of dissatisfaction, the only remedy would be to limit art very strictly to a set of processes or stuffs that were absolutely homogeneous in kind.

In part, however, the dissatisfaction comes from exaggerating the discrepancy, and from overlooking the fact that in the nonperforming arts there is a range of ways in which the spectator or audience can take the work of art. It is, I suggest, no coincidence that *this* activity, of taking the poem or painting or novel in one way rather than another, is also called "interpretation." For the effect in the two cases is the same, in that the control of the artist over his work is relaxed.

Against this parallelism between the two kinds of interpretation, two objections can be raised. The first is that the two kinds of interpretation differ in order or level. For whereas performative interpretation occurs only within certain arts, critical interpretation pertains to all: more specifically a critical interpretation can be placed upon any given performative interpretation – so the point of the parallelism vanishes, in that the performing arts still remain in a peculiar or discrepant situation. Now I do not want to deny that any performance of a piece of music or a play can give rise to a critical interpretation: the question, however, is, When this happens, is this on the same level as a performative interpretation? I want to maintain that we can fruitfully regard it as being so. For in so far as we remain concerned with the play or the piece of music, what we are doing is in the nature of suggesting or arguing for alternative performances, which would have presented the original work differently: we are not suggesting or arguing for alternative ways in which the actual performance might be taken. Our interpretation is on the occasion of a performance, not about it. The situation is, of course, complicated to a degree that cannot be unravelled here by the fact that acting and playing music are also arts, and in criticising individual performances we are sometimes conversant about those arts: which is why I qualified my remark by saying "in so far as we remain concerned with the play or piece of music."

The second and more serious objection to the parallelism between the two kinds of interpretation is that they differ as to necessity. For whereas a tragedy or a string quartet have to be interpreted, a poem or a painting need not be. At any given moment it may be necessary to interpret them, but that will be only because of the historical incompleteness of our comprehension of the work. Once we have really grasped it, further interpretation will no longer be called for. In other words, critical interpretation ultimately eliminates itself: whereas a piece of music or a play cannot be performed once and for all.

On this last argument I wish to make two preliminary observations: First, the argument must not draw any support (as the formulation here would seem to) from the indubitable but irrelevant fact that a performance is a transient not an enduring phenomenon. The relevant fact is not that a piece of music or a play must always be performed anew but that it can always be performed afresh, i.e. that every new performance can involve a new interpretation. The question then is, Is there not in the case of the non-performing arts the same permanent possibility of new interpretation? Secondly, the argument seems to be ambiguous between two formulations, which are not clearly, though in fact they may be, equivalent: the ostensibly stronger one, that in the case of a poem or painting all interpretations can ultimately be eliminated; and the ostensibly weaker one, that in these cases all interpretations save one can ultimately be eliminated.

Against the eliminability of interpretation, the only decisive argument is one drawn from our actual experience of art. There are, however, supplementary considerations, the full force of which can be assessed only as this essay progresses, which relate to the value of art. Allusions to both can be found in a brilliant and suggestive work, Valéry's "Réflexions sur l'Art."

In the first place the value of art, as has been traditionally recognized, does not exist exclusively, or even primarily, for the artist. It is shared equally between the artist and his audience. One view of how this sharing is effected, which is prevalent but implausible, is that the artist makes something of value, which he then hands on to the audience, which is thereby enriched. Another view is that in art there is a characteristic ambiguity, or perhaps better plasticity, introduced into the roles of activity and passivity: the artist is active, but so also is the spectator, and the spectator's activity consists in interpretation. "A creator" Valéry puts it "is one who makes others create."

Secondly – and this point too has received some recognition – the value of art is not exhausted by what the artist, or even by what the artist and the spectator, gain from it: it is not contained by the transaction between them. The work of art itself has a residual value. In certain "subjectivist" views – as e.g. in the critical theory of I. A. Richards – the value of art is made to seem contingent: contingent, that is, upon there being found no better or more effective way in which certain experiences assessed to be valuable can be aroused in, or transmitted between, the minds of the artist and his audience. Now it is difficult to see how such a conclusion can be avoided if the work of art is held to be inherently exhaustible in interpretation. In section 29 the view was considered that works of art are translucent; the view we are now asked to consider would seem to suggest that they are transparent, and as such ultimately expendable or "throw-away." It is against such a view that Valéry argued that we should regard works of art as constituting "a new and impenetrable element" which is interposed between the artist and the spectator. The ineliminability of interpretation he characterises, provocatively, as "the creative misunderstanding."

42

What a Musical Work Is

Jerrold Levinson

Jerrold Levinson is Distinguished University Professor of Philosophy at the University of Maryland, College Park.

What *exactly* did Beethoven compose? That is the question I will begin with. Well, for one, Beethoven composed a quintet for piano and winds (flute, oboe, clarinet, horn) in E-flat, Opus 16, in 1797. But what sort of thing is it, this quintet which was the outcome of Beethoven's creative activity? What does it consist in or of? Shall we say that Beethoven composed actual *sounds*? No, for sounds die out, but the quintet has endured. Did Beethoven compose a *score?* No, since many are familiar with Beethoven's composition who have had no contact with its score.[1]

Philosophers have long been puzzled about the identity or nature of the art object in non-physical arts, e.g., music and literature. In these arts – unlike painting and sculpture – there is no particular physical "thing" that one can plausibly take to be the artwork itself. This puzzlement has sometimes led philosophers (e.g., Croce) to maintain that musical and literary works are purely mental – that they are in fact private intuitive experiences in the minds of composers and poets. But this does not seem likely, since experiences can be neither played nor read nor heard. More generally, the Crocean view puts the objectivity of musical and literary works in dire peril – they become inaccessible and unsharable. Fortunately, however, there is a way of accepting the nonphysicality of such works without undermining their objectivity.

Those familiar with recent reflection on the ontological question for works of art will know of the widespread consensus that a musical work is in fact a variety of abstract object – to wit, a structural type or kind.[2] Instances of this type are to be found in the individual performances of the work. The type can be heard through its instances, and yet exists independently of its instances. I believe this to be basically correct. A piece of music is *some* sort of structural type, and as such is both nonphysical and publicly available. But *what* sort of type is it? I aim in this paper to say as precisely as I can what structural type it is that a musical work should be identified with.

The most natural and common proposal on this question is that a musical work is a *sound* structure – a structure, sequence, or pattern of sounds, pure and simple.[3] My first objective will be to show that this proposal is deeply unsatisfactory, that a musical work is more than just a sound structure *per se.* I will do this by developing three different objections to the sound-structure view. In the course of developing these

Jerrold Levinson, "What a Musical Work Is," *Journal of Philosophy*, 77/1 (1980): 5–28.

objections, three requirements or desiderata for a more adequate view will emerge. The rightness – or at least plausibility – of those requirements will, I think, be apparent at that point. My second objective will then be to suggest a structural type that does satisfy the requirements, and thus can be identified with a musical work.[4]

At the outset, however, I should make clear that I am confining my inquiry to that paradigm of a musical work, the fully notated "classical" composition of Western culture, for example, Beethoven's Quintet for piano and winds in E-flat, Opus 16. So when I speak of a "musical work" in this paper it should be understood that I am speaking only of these paradigm musical works, and thus that all claims herein regarding musical works are to be construed with this implicit restriction.

I

The first objection to the view that musical works are sound structures is this. If musical works were sound structures, then musical works could not, properly speaking, be created by their composers. For sound structures are types of a pure sort which exist at all times. This is apparent from the fact that they – and the individual component sound types[5] that they comprise – can always have had instances.[6] A sound event conforming to the sound structure of Beethoven's Quintet, Opus 16 logically could have occurred in the Paleozoic era.[7] Less contentiously, perhaps, such an event surely could have taken place in 1760 – ten years before Beethoven was born. But if that sound structure was capable of being *instantiated* then, it clearly must have *existed* at that time. Beethoven's compositional activity was not necessary in order for a certain sound-structure type to exist. It was not necessary to the possibility of certain sound events occurring which would be instances of that structure. Sound structures *per se* are not created by being scored – they exist before any compositional activity. Sound structures predate their first instantiation or conception because they are possible of exemplification *before* that point.[8] So, if composers truly create their works – i.e., bring them into existence – then musical works cannot be sound structures.

We can also defend the pre-existence of pure sound structures (i.e., existence prior to any instantiation or conception) in a somewhat different manner. We need only remind ourselves that purely sound structures are in effect mathematical objects – they are *sequences* of sets of sonic elements. (Sonic elements are such as pitches, timbres, durations, etc.) Now if the pre-existence of simple sonic element types be granted – and I think it must be – it follows automatically that all sets and all sequences of sets of these elements also pre-exist. Therefore pure sound structures are pre-existent. But if pure sound structures pre-exist, then it is not open for them to be objects of creational activity. So again, if composers are truly creators, their works cannot be pure sound structures.[9]

But why should we insist that composers truly create their compositions? Why is this a reasonable requirement? This question needs to be answered. A defense of the desideratum of true creation follows.

The main reason for holding to it is that it is one of the most firmly entrenched of our beliefs concerning art. There is probably no idea more central to thought about art than that it is an activity in which participants create things – these things being artworks. The whole tradition of art assumes art is creative in the strict sense, that it is a godlike activity in which the artist brings into being what did not exist beforehand – much as a demiurge forms a world out of inchoate matter. The notion that artists truly *add* to the world, in company with cake-bakers, house-builders, lawmakers, and theory-constructers, is surely a deep-rooted idea that merits preservation if at all possible. The suggestion that some artists, composers in particular, instead merely *discover* or *select* for attention entities they have no hand in creating is so contrary to this basic intuition regarding artists and their works that we have a strong prima facie reason to reject it if we can. If it is possible to align musical works with indisputably creatable artworks such as paintings and sculptures, then it seems we should do so.

A second, closely related reason to preserve true creation vis-à-vis musical works is that some of the status, significance, and value we attach to musical composition derives from our belief in this. If we conceive of Beethoven's Fifth Symphony as existing sempiternally, before

Beethoven's compositional act, a small part of the glory that surrounds Beethoven's composition of the piece seems to be removed. There is a special glow that envelops composers, as well as other artists, because we think of them as true creators. We marvel at a great piece of music *in part* because we marvel that, had its composer not engaged in a certain activity, the piece would (almost surely) not now exist; but it does exist, and we are grateful to the composer for precisely that. Ecclesiastes was wrong – there *are* ever some things new under the sun, musical compositions being among the most splendid of them – and splendid, at least in part, in virtue of this absolute newness.

Shall we then accept the creatability requirement as suggested? Before we do so a last qualm should be addressed. It is open for someone to admit the importance of musical composition being characterized by true creation and yet waive the creatability of works themselves. Such a person will point to entities associated with the compositional process which composers unequivocally bring into existence – e.g., thoughts, scores, performances – and claim that true creation need be extended no further. Now it is certainly true that these entities are strictly created, and we may also accord composers some recognition of their creativity in regard to these things. But the fact of the matter remains that *works* are the main items, the center and aim of the whole enterprise, and that since musical works are not identical with scores, performances, or thoughts,[10] if those are the only things actually created, then much is lost. "Composers are true creators" acquires a hollow ring. Creation in music shrinks to an outer veneer with no inner core.

I propose then that a most adequate account of the musical work should satisfy the following requirement, that of *creatability*[11]:

(Cre) Musical works must be such that they do *not* exist prior to the composer's compositional activity, but are *brought into* existence *by* that activity.

II

The second objection to the view that musical works are sound structures is this. (1) If musical works were just sound structures, then, if two distinct composers determine the same sound structure, they necessarily compose the same musical work. (2) But distinct composers determining the same sound structure in fact inevitably produce different musical works.[12] Therefore, musical works cannot be sound structures *simpliciter*. The rest of this section is devoted to supporting and elucidating the second premise of this argument.

Composers who produce identical scores in the same notational system with the same conventions of interpretation will determine the same sound structure. But the musical works they thereby compose will generally not be the same. The reason for this is that certain attributes of musical works are dependent on more than the sound structures contained. In particular, the aesthetic and artistic attributes of a piece of music are partly a function of, and must be gauged with reference to, the total musico-historical context in which the composer is situated while composing his piece. Since the musico-historical contexts of composing individuals are invariably different, then even if their works are identical in sound structure, they will differ widely in aesthetic and artistic attributes. But then, by Leibniz's law, the musical works themselves must be non-identical; if W_1 has any attribute that W_2 lacks, or *vice versa*, then $W_1 \neq W_2$.

I will not attempt to give a strict definition of musico-historical context, but will confine myself to pointing out a large part of what is involved in it. The total musico-historical context of a composer *P* at a time *t* can be said to include at least the following: (a) the whole of cultural, social, and political history prior to *t*,[13] (b) the whole of musical development up to *t*, (c) musical styles prevalent at *t*, (d) dominant musical influences at *t*, (e) musical activities of *P*'s contemporaries at *t*, (f) *P*'s apparent style at *t*, (g) *P*'s musical repertoire[14] at *t*, (h) *P*'s oeuvre at *t*, (i) musical influences operating on *P* at *t*. These factors contributing to the total musico-historical context might be conveniently divided into two groups, a–d and e–i. The former, which we could call the *general* musico-historical context, consists of factors relevant to anyone's composing at *t*; the latter, which we could call the *individual* musico-historical context, consists of factors relevant specifically to *P*'s composing at *t*. In any event, all these factors operate to differentiate aesthetically or artistically musical works identical in sound structure, thus making it impossible to identify those works with their sound structures. I now provide several illustrations of this.[15]

(1) A work identical in sound structure with Schoenberg's *Pierrot Lunaire* (1912), but composed by Richard Strauss in 1897 would be aesthetically different from Schoenberg's work. Call it 'Pierrot Lunaire*'. As a Straussian work, *Pierrot Lunaire** would follow hard upon Brahms's *German Requiem,* would be contemporaneous with Debussy's *Nocturnes*, and would be taken as the next step in Strauss's development after *Also Sprach Zarathustra.* As such it would be more *bizarre,* more *upsetting,* more *anguished,* more *eerie* even than Shoenberg's work, since perceived against a musical tradition, a field of current styles, and an oeuvre with respect to which the musical characteristics of the sound structure involved in *Pierrot Lunaire* appear doubly extreme.[16]

(2) Mendelssohn's *Midsummer's Night Dream Overture* (1826) is admitted by all to be a highly *original* piece of music. Music of such elfin delicacy and feel for tone color had never before been written. But a score written in 1900 detailing the very same sound structure as is found in Mendelssohn's piece would clearly result in a work that was surpassingly *unoriginal.*

(3) Brahms's Piano Sonata Opus 2 (1852), an early work, is strongly *Liszt-influenced*, as any perceptive listener can discern. However, a work identical with it in sound structure, but written by Beethoven, could hardly have had the property of being Liszt-influenced. And it would have had a visionary quality that Brahms's piece does not have.

(4) The symphonies of Johann Stamitz (1717–57) are generally regarded as seminal works in the development of orchestral music. They employ many attention-getting devices novel for their time, one of which is known as the "Mannheim rocket" – essentially a loud ascending scale figure for unison strings. A symphony of Stamitz containing Mannheim rockets and the like is an *exciting* piece of music. But a piece written today which was identical in sound structure with one of Stamitz's symphonies, Mannheim rockets and all, would not be so much exciting as it would be exceedingly *funny.* Stamitz's symphony is to be heard in the context of Stamitz's earlier works, the persistence of late Baroque style, the contemporary activities of the young Mozart, and the Napoleonic wars. "Modern Stamitz"'s symphony would be heard in the context of "Modern Stamitz"'s earlier works (which are probably dodecaphonic), the existence of aleatory and electronic music, the musical enterprises both of Pierre Boulez and of Elton John, and the threat of nuclear annihilation.

(5) One of the passages in Bartok's *Concerto for Orchestra* (1943) satirizes Shostakovitch's *Seventh Symphony* ("Leningrad") of 1941, whose bombast was apparently not to Bartok's liking. A theme from that symphony is quoted and commented on musically in an unmistakable manner. But notice that if Bartok had written the very same score in *1939,* the work he would then have composed could not have had the same property of satirizing Shostakovitch's *Seventh Symphony.* Nor would the work that would have resulted from *Shostakovitch's* penning that score in 1943.

These examples should serve to convince the reader that there is always some aesthetic or artistic difference between structurally identical compositions in the offing in virtue of differing musico-historical contexts. Even small differences in musico-historical context – e.g., an extra work in *P*'s oeuvre, a slight change in style dominant in *P*'s milieu, some musical influence deleted from *P*'s development as a composer – seem certain to induce some change in kind or degree in some aesthetic or artistic quality, however difficult it might be in such cases to pinpoint this change verbally.

For example, suppose there had been a composer (call him "Toenburg") in 1912 identical with Schoenberg in all musico-historical respects – e.g., birthdate, country, style, musical development, artistic intentions, etc., except that Toenburg had never written anything like *Verklarte Nacht* though he had in his oeuvre works structurally identical with everything else Schoenberg wrote before 1912. Now suppose simultaneously with Schoenberg he sketches the sound structure of *Pierrot Lunaire.* Toenburg has not produced the same musical work as Schoenberg, I maintain, if only because his work has a slightly different aesthetic/artistic content owing to the absence of a Verklarte-Nacht-ish piece in Toenburg's oeuvre. Schoenberg's *Pierrot Lunaire* is properly heard with reference to Schoenberg's oeuvre in 1912, and Toenberg's *Pierrot Lunaire* with reference to Toenburg's oeuvre in 1912. One thus hears something in Schoenberg's piece by virtue of resonance with *Verklarte Nacht* that is not present in Toenberg's piece – perhaps a stronger reminiscence of Expressionist sighs?

Before formulating a second requirement of adequacy, as suggested by the fatal problem that contextual differentiation poses for the equation of musical works with pure sound structures, I must confront an objection that may be lurking in the wings. The objection in short is that the aesthetic and artistic differences I have been discussing are not really an obstacle to equating works and sound structures, because these supposed differences between *works* due to compositional context really just boil down to facts about their *composers*, and are not attributes of works at all. The objection is understandable, but I find it rather unconvincing for several reasons which I will briefly detail.

(1) Artistic and aesthetic attributions made of musical works are as direct and undisguised as attributions typically made of composers. It seems to be as straightforwardly true that the Eroica symphony is noble, bold, original, revolutionary, influenced by Haydn, and reflective of Beethoven's thoughts about Napoleon, as it is that Beethoven had certain personal qualities, was a genius, changed the course of Western music, studied with Haydn, and at one point idolized Napoleon. (2) Whereas we may admit some plausibility to reducing artistic attributions (e.g., 'original', 'influenced by Haydn') to attributes of persons, there is no plausibility in so reducing aesthetic attributions; it is absurd to maintain that "*W* is scintillating," for example, is just a way of saying "*W*'s composer is scintillating." (3) Finally, in the case of artistic attributions, not only do they appear as entrenched and legitimate as parallel attributions to composers, but, if anything, they often seem to be primary. Consider originality, for example, and imagine a composer and oeuvre that possess it. Surely the composer is original because *his works* are original; his works are not original because *he is*.

I thus propose a second requirement – that of *fine individuation* – to which any acceptable theory of the musical work should conform:

(Ind) Musical works must be such that composers composing in different musico-historical contexts[17] who determine identical sound structures invariably compose distinct musical works.

III

The third objection to the view that musical works are sound structures is this. If musical works were simply sound structures, then they would not essentially involve any particular means of performance. But the paradigm musical works that we are investigating in this paper, e.g., Beethoven's Quintet Opus 16, clearly *do* involve quite specific means of performance, i.e., particular instruments, in an essential way. The instrumentation of musical works is an integral part of those works. So musical works cannot be simply sound structures *per se*. Arguments in defense of the claim that performance means are an essential component of musical works now follow.

(1) Composers do not describe pure sound patterns in qualitative terms, leaving their means of production undiscussed. Rather, what they directly specify are means of production, through which a pure sound pattern is indirectly indicated. The score of Beethoven's Quintet, Opus 16, is not a recipe for providing an instance of a sound pattern *per se*, in whatever way you might like. Rather, it instructs one to produce an instance of a certain sound pattern through carrying out certain operations on certain instruments. When Beethoven writes a middle C for the oboe, he has done more than require an oboe-like sound at a certain pitch – he has called for such a sound as emanating from that quaint reed we call an "oboe." The idea that composers of the last 300 years were generally engaged in composing pure sound patterns, to which they were usually kind enough to append suggestions as to how they might be realized, is highly implausible. Composers are familiar with tone colors only insofar as they are familiar with instruments that possess them. We do not find composers creating pure combinations of tone color, and then later searching about for instruments that can realize or approximate these aural canvases; it would obviously be pointless or at least frustrating to do

so. Composers often call for complex sounds that they have never heard before and can scarcely imagine – e.g., the sound of two trombones and three piccolos intoning middle C while four saxophones and five xylophones intone the C-sharp a half-step above; it is obvious here that what is primarily composed is not a pure untethered sound but an instrumental combination.[18]

(2) Scores are generally taken to be definitive of musical works, at least in conjunction with the conventions of notational interpretation assumed to be operative at the time of composition. It is hard to miss the fact that scores of musical works call for specific instruments in no uncertain terms. When we read in Beethoven's score the demand 'clarinet' (rather, 'Klarinett') we may wonder whether a clarinet of 1970 vintage and construction will do as well as one of 1800, but we have still been given a fairly definite idea of what sort of instrument is required. There is nothing in scores themselves that suggests that instrumental specifications are to be regarded as optional – any more than specifications of pitch, rhythm, or dynamics. Nor does the surrounding musical practice of the time encourage such a way of regarding them.[19] If we are not to abandon the principle that properly understood scores have a central role in determining the identity of musical works, then we must insist that the Quintet, Op. 16, without a clarinet is not the same piece – even if all sound-structural characteristics (including timbre) are preserved. To feel free to disregard as prominent an aspect of scores as performing means is to leave it open for someone to disregard any aspect of a score he does not wish to conform to – e.g., tempo, accidentals, accents, articulation, harmony – and claim that one nevertheless has the same work.[20] The only way it seems one could justify regarding performing-means specifications as just optional features of scores is to simply *assume* that musical works are nothing but sound structures *per se*.

Consider a sound event aurally indistinguishable from a typical performance of Beethoven's Quintet Opus 16, but issuing from a versatile synthesizer, or perhaps a piano plus a set of newly designed wind instruments, two hundred in number, each capable of just two or three notes. If performance means were not an integral aspect of a musical work, then there would be no question that this sound event constitutes a performance of Beethoven's Quintet Opus 16. But there is indeed such a question. It makes perfect sense to deny that it is such a performance on the grounds that the sounds heard did not derive from a piano and four standard woodwinds. We can count something as a performance of Beethoven's Quintet Opus 16 only if it involves the participation of the instruments for which the piece was written – or better – of the instruments that were written into the piece.

(3) To regard performing means as essential to musical works is to maintain that the sound structure of a work cannot be divorced from the instruments and voices through which that structure is fixed, and regarded as the work itself. The strongest reason why it cannot be so divorced is that the aesthetic content of a musical work is determined not only by its sound structure, and not only by its musico-historical context, but also in part by the actual means of production chosen for making that structure audible. The character of a musical composition, e.g., Beethoven's Quintet Opus 16 for piano and winds, is partly a function of how its sound structure relates to the potentialities of a certain instrument or set of instruments designated to produce that structure for audition. To assess that character correctly one must take cognizance not only of the qualitative nature of sounds heard but also of their source of origin. Musical compositions, by and large, have reasonably definite characters; that is to say, we can and do ascribe to them many fairly specific aesthetic qualities. But if prescribed performing forces were not intrinsic to musical compositions, then those compositions would not have the reasonably definite characters we clearly believe them to have. The determinateness of a work's aesthetic qualities is in peril if performing means are viewed as inessential so long as exact sound structure is preserved.

Consider a musical work *W* with specified performing means *M* which has some fairly specific aesthetic quality ø. The sound structure of *W* as produced by different performing means *N*, however, will invariably strike us either as not ø at all, or else as ø to a greater or lesser degree than before. Therefore, if means of sound production are not regarded as an integral part of musical works, then *W* cannot be said determinately to have the attribute ø. So if we wish to preserve a wide range of determinate aesthetic attributions, we must recognize performing means to be an essential component of musical works. I now provide two illustrations of this point.[21]

(a) Beethoven's Hammerklavier Sonata is a sublime, craggy, and heaven-storming piece of music. The closing passages (marked by ascending chordal trills) are surely among the most imposing and awesome in all music. However, if we understand the very sounds of the Hammerklavier Sonata to originate from a full-range synthesizer, as opposed to a mere 88-key piano of metal, wood, and felt, it no longer seems so sublime, so craggy, so awesome. The aesthetic qualities of the Hammerklavier Sonata depend in part on the strain that its sound structure imposes on the sonic capabilities of the piano; if we are not hearing its sound structure *as* produced by a piano then we are not sensing this strain, and thus our assessment of aesthetic content is altered. The closing passages of the Hammerklavier are awesome in part because we seem to hear the piano bursting at the seams and its keyboard on the verge of exhaustion. On a 10-octave electronic synthesizer those passages do not have quite that quality, and a hearing of them with knowledge of source is an aesthetically different experience. The lesson here applies, I believe, to all musical works (of the paradigm sort). Their aesthetic attributes always depend, if not so dramatically, in part on the performing forces understood to belong to them.

(b) Consider a baroque concerto for two violins, such as Bach's Concerto in D minor, BWV1043. In such pieces one often finds a phrase (A) assigned to one violin, which is immediately followed by the *very same* phrase (B) assigned to the other violin. Now when one hears such passages *as* issuing from *two* violins (even if in a given performance there are no discernible differences between A and B in timbre or phrasing), a sense of question-and-answer, of relaxation and unhurriedness is communicated. But if one were to construe such passages as issuing from a *single* violin, that quality would be absent, and in its place the passages would assume a more emphatic, insistent, and repetitive cast.

(4) The dependence of aesthetic attributes on assumed or understood performing forces should now be apparent. The dependence of artistic attributes is even more plain. (a) Consider Paganini's Caprice Opus 1, No. 17. This piece surely deserves and receives the attribution 'virtuosic'. But if we did not conceive of the Caprice No. 17 as essentially for the violin, as inherently a *violin piece* (and not just a *violin-sounding piece*), then it would not merit that attribution. For, as executed by a computer or by some novel string instrument using nonviolinistic technique, its sound structure might not be particularly difficult to get through. (b) Imagine a piece written for violin to be played in such a way that certain passages sound more like a flute than they do like a violin. Such a piece would surely be accounted *unusual*, and to some degree, *original* as well. Understood as a piece for violin and occasional flute, however, it might have nothing unusual or original about it at all. Retaining the sound structure while setting actual performance means adrift completely dissolves part of the piece's artistic import. (c) According to one respected critic, Beethoven in the Quintet Opus 16 was interested in solving problems of balance between piano and winds – a nominally incompatible array of instruments – and succeeded in his own individual way.[22] It is not hard to agree with this assessment; thus, 'solves the problem of balance between piano and winds' is an attribution true of Beethoven's Quintet. It is difficult to see how this would be so if the Quintet is purely a sound structure, if piano and winds are not strictly part of the piece at all.[23]

I thus propose a third requirement for any account of the musical work: *inclusion of performance means*:

(Per) Musical works must be such that specific means of performance or sound production are integral to them.

IV

If musical works are not sound structures *simpliciter*, then what are they? The type that is a musical work must be capable of being created, must be individuated by context of composition, and must be inclusive of means of performance. The third desideratum is most easily met, and will be addressed first.

I propose that a musical work be taken to involve not only a pure sound structure, but also a structure of performing means. If the sound structure of a piece is basically a sequence of sounds qualitatively defined, then the performing-means structure is a parallel sequence of performing means specified for realizing the sounds at each point. Thus a musical work consists of at least two structures. It is a compound or conjunction of a sound structure and a performing-means structure. This compound is itself just a more complex structure; call it an "S/PM" structure, for short.[24] Beethoven's Opus 16 Quintet is at base an S/PM structure; the means of producing the sounds belonging to it are no more dispensable to its identity as a composition than the nature and order of those sounds themselves. This satisfies requirement (Per).

To satisfy the first and second requirements of adequacy we arrived at, it is necessary to realize that a musical work is not a structure of the *pure* sort at all, and thus not even a S/PM structure *simpliciter*. A S/PM structure is no more creatable or context-individuated than a sound structure is. I propose that we recognize a musical work to be a more complicated entity, namely this:

(MW) S/PM structure-as-indicated-by-*X*-at-*t*

where *X* is a particular person – the composer – and *t* is the time of composition. For the paradigmatic pieces we are concerned with, the composer typically indicates (fixes, determines, selects) an S/PM structure by creating a score. The *piece* he thereby composes is the S/PM structure-as-indicated by him on that occasion.

An S/PM structure-as-indicated-by-*X*-at-*t*, unlike an S/PM structure *simpliciter*, does not pre-exist the activity of composition and is thus capable of being created. When a composer θ composes a piece of music, he indicates an S/PM structure ψ, but he does not bring ψ into being. However, through the act of indicating ψ, he does bring into being something that did not previously exist – namely, ψ-as-indicated-by-θ-at-t_1. Before the compositional act at t_1, no relation obtains between θ and ψ. Composition establishes the relation of indication between θ and ψ. As a result of the compositional act, I suggest, the world contains a new entity, ψ-as-indicated-by-θ-at-t_1. Let me call such entities *indicated structures*. And let me represent indicated structures by expressions of form "S/PM*x*t." It is important to realize that indicated structures are entities distinct from the pure structures *per se* from which they are derived. Thus, in particular, $\psi^*\theta^*t_1$ is *not* just the structure ψ with the accidental property of having been indicated by θ at t_1 – $\psi^*\theta^*t_1$ and ψ are strictly non-identical, though of course related. $\psi^*\theta^*t_1$, unlike ψ, can be and is created through θ's composing. Thus requirement (Cre) is satisfied.

Indicated structures also serve to satisfy our second requirement (Ind). If musical works are indicated structures of the sort we have suggested, then two such works, $\psi^*\theta^*t_1$ and $\alpha^*\phi^*t_2$ are identical iff (i) $\psi = \alpha$, (ii) $\theta = \phi$, and (iii) $t_1 = t_2$. But if musical works are necessarily distinct if composed either by different people or at different times, then it certainly follows that works composed in different musico-historical contexts will be distinct, since any difference of musico-historical context from one work to another can be traced to a difference of composer or time or both. Put otherwise, musico-historical context (as explained in section II) is a function of time and person; given a time and person, musico-historical context is fixed. So requirement (Ind) is satisfied. That it is satisfied by our proposal with something to spare is a matter I will return to in section V. I now endeavor to increase the reader's grasp of what indicated structures are.

Indicated structures are a different class of type from pure structures. Types of the latter class we may call *implicit* types, and those of the former class *initiated* types. *Implicit* types include all purely abstract structures that are not inconsistent, e.g., geometrical figures, family relationships, strings of words, series of moves in chess, ways of placing five balls in three bins, etc. By calling them "implicit types" I mean to suggest that their existence is implicitly granted when a general framework of possibilities is given. For example, given that there is space, there are all the possible configurations in space; given there is the game of chess, there are all the possible combinations of allowed moves. Sound structures *simpliciter* are clearly implicit types. Given that there are sounds of various kinds, then all possible patterns and sequences of those sounds must be granted existence immediately as well. For a sound structure, in company with all pure structures, is always capable of instantiation before the point at which it is noticed, recognized, mentioned, or singled out. And thus its existence must predate that point. The same goes for a performance-means structure *simpliciter*. Given performing means (i.e., instruments) of various kinds, then all possible combinations and sequences of such means exist as well. The compound of these two, a sound/performance–means structure, thus of course also counts as an implicit type.

The other class of types, *initiated* types, are so called because they begin to exist only when they are initiated by an intentional human act of some kind. All those of interest can, I think, be construed as arising from an operation, like indication, performed upon a pure structure. Typically, this indication is effected by producing an exemplar of the structure involved, or a blueprint of it. In so indicating (or determining) the structure, the exemplar or blueprint inaugurates the type which is the *indicated* structure, the structure-as-indicated-by-*x*-at-*t*. All indicated structures are, perforce, initiated types.

Initiated types include such types as the Ford Thunderbird, the Lincoln penny, the hedgehog. The Ford Thunderbird is not simply a pure structure of metal, glass, and plastic. The pure structure that is embodied in the Thunderbird has existed *at least* since the invention of plastic (1870); there could certainly have been instances of it in 1900. But the Ford Thunderbird was created in 1957; so there could not have been instances of the Thunderbird in 1900. The Ford Thunderbird is an *initiated* type; it is a metal/glass/plastic structure-as-indicated (or determined) by the Ford Motor Company on such and such a date. It begins to exist as a result of an act of human indication or determination. The instances of this type are more than just instances of a pure structure – they are instances of an indicated structure. The Lincoln penny is similarly not a pure structure, an abstract pattern *tout court*, but a structure-as-indicated, a pattern-as-denominated-by-the-U.S. Government. Objects conforming to the pattern *tout court* but existing in 100 AD in Imperial Rome would not be instances of the Lincoln penny. Even the hedgehog is probably best understood, not as a pure biological structure, but rather as a biological structure-as-determined-or-fixed by natural terrestrial evolution at a particular point in history. The creatures we call "hedgehogs" possess a certain structure and stand in certain causal relations to some particular creatures which came into existence at a given past date. The biological structure of the hedgehog might have been instantiated in the Mesozoic era, or on Uranus, but nothing existing at that time, or at that place, could be an instance of the hedgehog as we understand it. Musical works, as I have suggested, are indicated structures too, and thus types that do not already exist but must instead be initiated. The same is true of poems, plays, and novels – each of these is an entity more individual and temporally bound than the pure verbal structure embodied in it.

The distinction between indicated structure and pure structure can perhaps be made clearer by analogy with the distinction between sentence and statement long enshrined in the philosophy of language.[25] These distinctions are motivated in similar ways. Statements were recognized partly in response to the need for entities individuated in some respects more finely than sentences, in order to provide bearers for the varying truth values that turned up in connection with a given sentence on different occasions.[26] Just so, indicated structures are recognized in response to the need for entities more finely individuated than pure structures, in order to provide bearers for various incompatible sets of aesthetic, artistic, cultural, semantic, and genetic properties. We allow that a given sentence can make different statements when uttered in different circumstances. Similarly, we realize that a given sound/performance–means structure yields different indicated structures, or musical works, when indicated in different musico-historical contexts.[27]

V

I have proposed that musical works be identified with rather specific indicated structures, in which a particular person and time figure ineliminably. The proposal MW was made, recall, in order to satisfy the creatability and individuation requirements. However, as I noted at that point, MW satisfies the individuation requirement with logical room to spare. Perhaps both requirements can be satisfied without invoking types that are quite so particularized? The obvious alternative is that a musical work is this sort of type:

(MW') S/PM structure-as-indicated-in-musico-historical-context-C

Such types would be both creatable and sufficiently individuated. A type of this sort, like an MW type, comes into existence through some *actual* indication of an S/PM structure by a person at a time – a person who at that certain time is situated in a particular context. But the type's identity is not inherently tied to that of any individual as such. Thus, two composers composing simultaneously but independently in the same musico-historical context who determine the same S/PM structure create *distinct* MW types, but the *same* MW' type.

Given these two proposals, then, which satisfy all our desiderata, do we have reason to prefer one or the other? I will discuss one consideration in favor of MW', and three considerations in favor of MW.

(1) On the MW' proposal, it is at least logically possible for a musical work to have been composed by a person other than the person who actually composed it. If A is the actual composer of a musical work, ψ-as-indicated-in-C_1, then all we need imagine is that someone other than A was the person to first indicate the S/PM structure ψ in musico-historical context C_1. On the MW proposal, however, it becomes *logically impossible* for a work to have been composed by other than its actual composer. Could someone else have composed Beethoven's Quintet Opus 16, according to MW? For example, could Hummel have done so? No, because if ψ is the S/PM structure of the Quintet Opus 16, then all that Hummel might have composed is ψ-as-indicated-by-Hummel-in-1797, and not ψ-as-indicated-by-Beethoven-in-1797.[28] It must be admitted to be somewhat counterintuitive for a theory to make the composer of a work essential to that work.

(2) We can turn this consequence upside-down, however. One might cite as a virtue of the MW proposal that it gives a composer *logical insurance* that his works are his very own, that no one else has or ever could compose a work identical to any of his. If A's musical work is an MW type, then even a fellow composer situated in an identical musico-historical context determining the same S/PM structure composes a distinct musical work. It seems to me this is a desirable consequence, from the point of view of preserving the uniqueness of compositional activity. Why should a composer have to fear, however abstractly, that his work is not exclusively his, any more than a painter painting a painting or a sculptor sculpting a sculpture need be troubled about whether his work is at least numerically distinct from anyone else's? Why not adopt a construal of 'musical work' (and of 'poem', 'novel', 'dance', etc.) which, while maintaining musical works as abstract types, guarantees this individuation by artist for them as well? Considerations (1) and (2) thus appear to fairly well cancel each other out.

(3) A more decisive reason, however, for ensuring by proposal MW that composers A and B who determine the same S/PM structure in the same musico-historical context yet compose distinct works W_1 and W_2, is that, although W_1 and W_2 do not, it seems, differ structurally or aesthetically or artistically at the time of composition t, differences of an artistic sort are almost certain to develop after t. So, unless we wish to embrace the awkwardness of saying that two musical works can be identical when composed, but non-identical at some later point, we have a strong incentive to adopt MW. W_1 and W_2 will almost certainly diverge artistically because of the gross improbability that A and B will continue to be subject to the exact same influences to the same degree and that A's and B's oeuvres will continue to appear identical after the composition of W_1 and W_2. If A's and B's artistic careers do exhibit these differences after t, then W_1 and W_2 will acquire somewhat different artistic significance, since W_1 will eventually be seen properly against A's total development, and W_2 against B's total development. W_1 may turn out to be *a seminal work*, whereas W_2 turns out to be *a false start*. Or W_1 may turn out to be *much more influential* than W_2, owing to the fact that A comes to be much better known than B. In any case, there will be *some* divergence in artistic attributions, if not always so marked, unless A and B remain artistic duplicates of one another throughout their lives (and thereafter). Since circumstances subsequent to a work's composition are not comprised in musico-historical context of composition, proposal MW' leaves us open for the awkwardness mentioned above, MW forestalls this problem completely.[29]

(4) A last consideration inclining us to MW comprises certain intuitions concerning what would count as a performance of what. It seems that, in order for a performance to be a performance *of W*, not only must it fit and be intended to fit the S/PM structure of *A*'s work *W*; there must also be some *connection*, more or less direct, between the sound event produced and *A*'s creative activity. Whether this is primarily an intentional or causal connection is a difficult question,[30] but, unless it is present, I think we are loath to say that *A*'s work has been performed. Consider two composers, Sterngrab and Grotesteen, who compose quartets with identical S/PM structures; suppose even that they share the same musico-historical context. Now imagine that the Aloysious Ensemble, who are great friends of Sterngrab, give the ill-attended première of Sterngrab's Quartet Opus 21. Clearly, the Aloysious have performed Sterngrab's Quartet Opus 21 – but have they also performed Grotesteen's Quartet Opus 21? I think not. Why? For several reasons: they don't know Grotesteen; they weren't using Grotesteen's scores; they didn't believe themselves to be presenting Grotesteen's work – in short, there was no connection between their performance and Grotesteen the creator. Grotesteen's creating his Opus 21 Quartet had nothing whatever to do with the sound event produced by the Aloysious Ensemble on the aforementioned occasion. Now, if Sterngrab's Quartet has performances that Grotesteen's does not, and *vice versa*, then, again by Leibniz's law, Sterngrab's and Grotesteen's quartets cannot be identical. On proposal MW', Sterngrab and Grotesteen have composed the same musical work; on proposal MW, their works are distinct. That MW squares with this intuition regarding identification of performances is thus one more point in its favor.

I therefore rest with the account of musical works represented by MW. In the next section I offer some remarks on performances and transcriptions in light of this account.

VI

(1) On my view, the following must all be distinguished: (a) instances of *W*; (b) instances of the sound structure of *W*; (c) instances of the S/PM structure of *W*; (d) performances of *W*. An *instance* of a musical work *W* is a sound event which conforms *completely* to the sound/performance–means structure of *W* and which exhibits the required connection[31] to the indicative activity wherein *W*'s composer *A* creates *W*. An instance of *W* is typically produced, either directly or indirectly, from a score that can be causally traced and is intentionally related by the performer, to the act of creation of *W* by *A*. Thus, all instances of *W* are instances of *W*'s sound structure, and instances of *W*'s S/PM structure – but the reverse is not the case.

Instances are a subclass of the set of performances of a work. A *performance* of a musical work *W* is a sound event which is *intended* to instantiate *W* – i.e., represents an attempt to exemplify *W*'s S/PM structure in accordance with *A*'s indication of it[32] – and which *succeeds to a reasonable degree.*[33] Since one cannot instantiate a musical work – an S/PM structure-as-indicated-by-*X*-at-*t* – without intending to, because instantiating *that* demands conscious guidance by instructions, memories, or the like which one regards as deriving from *A*'s indicative act at *t*, it follows that the instances of *W* are all to be found among the performances of *W*. However, not all performances of *W* count as instances of *W*; many if not most attempts to exemplify S/PM structures fail by some margin. So these cannot count as instances of *W*, but they *are* performances – namely *incorrect* performances. (Of course, that they are strictly incorrect by no means entails that they are bad.) There are not, however, any incorrect *instances* of *W*; the *correct* performances of *W* are its instances, and no others.[34]

Finally, let me note that musical works as I understand them *can* be heard in or through their performances. One *hears* an S/PM structure-as-indicated-by-*X*-at-*t* whenever one hears an instance of that S/PM structure produced by performers who, roughly speaking, are guided by *X*'s indication of the S/PM structure in question. And one *knows* precisely what musical work, i.e., structure-as-indicated, one is hearing if one knows what creative act is in effect the guiding source of the sound event being produced.

(2) On my view of what a musical work (of the paradigm sort) is, it follows immediately that a transcription of a musical work is a distinct

musical work, whether it involves alteration of the sound structure (the normal case), or *even* of just the performance-means structure. It is a virtue of my view that it gives a clear answer to this question, which is often thought to be only arbitrarily decidable. If we want such pieces to have the definite aesthetic qualities we take them to have, instrumentation must be considered inseparable from them. Thus, we need not rely, in endorsing the distinctness position on transcriptions vis-à-vis original works, merely on the principle of fidelity to the composer's intended instrumentation. Rather we are also constrained by higher-order considerations of preserving the aesthetic integrity of such pieces.

In conclusion, let me stress some obvious consequences of accepting the theory of the musical work that I have proposed. First, composers would retain the status of creator in the strictest sense. Second, musical composition would be revealed as necessarily personalized. Third, musical composition could not fail to be seen as a historically rooted activity whose products must be understood with reference to their points of origin. Fourth, it would be recognized that the pure sound structure of a musical work, while graspable in isolation, does not exhaust the work structurally, and thus that the underlying means of performance must be taken into account as well if the work is to be correctly assessed.[35]

Notes

1 There are of course several other objections to these proposals, and to the Crocean proposal mentioned below. I do not mean to suggest that those I recall are clearly decisive by themselves.

2 See, for example, C. L. Stevenson, "On 'What Is a Poem?'," *Philosophical Review*, LXVI, 3 (July 1957): 329–62; J. Margolis, *The Language of Art and Art Criticism* (Detroit: Wayne State UP, 1965); R. Wollheim, *Art and Its Objects* (New York: Harper & Row, 1968).

3 It should be understood at the outset that sound structure includes not only pitches and rhythms, but also timbres, dynamics, accents – that is, all "purely aural" properties of sound.

4 The present paper owes a debt to two recent theories of the musical work: N. Wolterstorff, "Toward an Ontology of Artworks," *Noûs*, IX, 2 (May 1975): 115–42; and K. Walton, "The Presentation and Portrayal of Sound Patterns," *In Theory Only* (February 1977): 3–16. These writers are aware of some of the considerations that I adduce pointing to the complexity of a musical type. However, I believe they do not take them seriously enough, and thus are inclined to acquiesce in the view that musical works *are* or *may be* just sound structures. The present paper aims squarely to reject that view and to formulate one more adequate.

5 E.g., F# minor triad, three-note French-dotted rhythmic figure, middle C of bassoon timbre, etc.

6 This point is made by Wolterstorff, op. cit., p. 138.

7 Though of course lack of suitable production facilities made this impossible in some nonlogical sense.

8 I am aware that someone might hold that in saying that a certain novel sound instance is possible at *t*, all we are committed to is that the sound structure of which it *would be* an instance might possibly *come into existence* at *t*, simultaneously with its first instance. But I do not think this a plausible view; in saying that a certain sound event could occur at *t* we are saying something stronger than that the structure it would exemplify might come into existence – we are saying that that structure is right then available.

9 Some who yet resist the idea that pure sound structures pre-exist compositional activity are possibly failing to distinguish between *structure* and *construction*. It is true that constructions need to have been constructed in order to exist; it does not follow that structures need to have been constructed – i.e., actually put together from parts – in order to exist. The Brooklyn Bridge is a construction, and embodies a structure. The Brooklyn Bridge did not exist before its construction. But the geometrical structure it embodies, which required and received no construction, has always existed.

Given that there will still be some who are attracted to the view that pure sound structures are in some way created by composers, presumably through mental activity, and that these are their works, I will take this occasion to point out briefly two untoward consequences of such a view. The first is that instances of pure sound structures can always have been sounded accidentally before any composer thinks them into existence by directing his attention on the realm of sounds. In which case we would then be countenancing compositions that have instances before those compositions begin to exist. The second is that a person who conceives or sketches a sound structure new to him has no (logical) assurance that he has in fact composed *anything*. For if composing is bringing sound structures into existence, one may fail to do so in writing a score, provided someone else has conceived the same structure earlier. Notice that this is not a matter of the latecomer having composed the *same* work as his predecessor, but rather – what he and we would surely find incredible – a matter of his having composed *no* work at all.

10 Though composers compose their works *by* writing scores, having thoughts, or, less typically, producing performances.

11 It would be well to note here that, even if one rejects the requirement of creatability, abandonment of the sound-structure view in favor of something like the view I eventually propose will be demanded by the second and third requirements developed. And those requirements strike me as being nonnegotiable.

12 Notice that if we assume that composing musical works is strictly creating them, it follows immediately that two composers cannot compose the very same musical work (no matter what sound structures they determine) unless they are either composing jointly or composing independently but simultaneously. This is just a consequence of the fact that the same thing cannot be created both at t and at a later time t'. (The same goes for a single composer on temporally separate occasions; if composing is creating, a composer cannot compose the same work twice.) I will not, however, in this section assume that composing is strict creation.

13 Cf. J. L. Borges, "Pierre Menard, Author of the Quixote" [in *Labyrinths* (New York: New Directions, 1962)] for a fictional demonstration of the dependence of artistic meaning on the historical context of creation.

14 Cf. Wollheim, op. cit., pp. 48–54, for a discussion of the dependence of a work's expression on the artistic repertoire of the artist. The notion of "repertoire" is roughly that of a set of alternative decisions or choices within which an artist appears to be operating in creating his works. Wollheim extracts this idea from E. K. Gombrich's discussions of artistic expression in *Art and Illusion* and *Meditations on a Hobby-Horse*.

15 The convincingness of these examples depends crucially on accepting something like the following principle: "Works of art *truly have* those attributes which they *appear* to have when *correctly* perceived or regarded." I cannot provide a defense of this principle here, but it has been well argued for by C. Stevenson, "Interpretation and Evaluation in Aesthetics" [in W. E. Kennick, *Art and Philosophy* (New York: St. Martin's, 1964)], and Walton, "Categories of Art," *Philosophical Review*, LXVI, 3 (July 1970): 334–67, among others.

16 It is a mistake to regard this illustration as concerned with what *Pierrot Lunaire* would have been like if *it* had been composed by Strauss. (I am not even sure what *that* supposition amounts to.) The illustration rather concerns a possible musical work that possesses the same sound structure as *Pierrot Lunaire*, but is composed by Strauss in 1897. This work would be distinct from *Pierrot Lunaire*, because aesthetically divergent. But if musical works were identified with sound structures it could *not* be distinct.

Another way of casting the argument using this example would be as follows. Consider a possible world Q in which both Schoenberg's *Pierrot Lunaire* and Strauss's *Pierrot Lunaire** exist, and call the sound structure they have in common "K." In Q, the works diverge aesthetically and hence are non-identical. Clearly, the works cannot both be identified with their common sound structure, but to so identify only one of them would be perfectly arbitrary. So in Q, *Pierrot Lunaire* $\neq K$. But then in the actual world as well, *Pierrot Lunaire* $\neq K$. Why? Owing to the necessity that attaches to identity and difference. If two things are non-identical in any possible world, they are non-identical in every possible world in which they exist. Put otherwise, statements of identity and difference involving rigid designators are necessary. 'Pierrot Lunaire' and 'K' designate rigidly; they are proper names, not definite descriptions. Thus 'Pierrot Lunaire $\neq K$' is necessarily true, since true in Q. Therefore, in the actual world, *Pierrot Lunaire* $\neq K$. [The argument can be recast in this way, *mutatis mutandis*, for illustrations (2)–(5) as well.]

17 This includes a single composer on separate occasions.

18 It is inevitable that someone will object at this point that certain composers, in certain periods, did not compose with definite instruments in mind and did not make specific instrumentation integral to their works. This may be true to some extent. But two points must be noted. First, I have set out to define the nature of the *paradigmatic* musical composition in Western culture, of which Beethoven's Quintet, Opus 16 is an example. It is enough for my purpose that most "classical" compositions, and effectively all from 1750 to the present, integrally involve quite definite means of performance. Second, even in a case such as J. S. Bach, where controversy has long existed as to

exactly what performing forces Bach intended, called for, or would have allowed in such compositions as *The Well-Tempered Clavier* or the Brandenburg Concerto No. 2, it is clear there are still more restrictions as to performing forces which must be considered part of those compositions. Thus, *The Well-Tempered Clavier* may not be a work belonging solely to the harpsichord (as opposed to the clavichord or fortepiano), but it is clearly a work for *keyboard*, and a performance of its sound structure on five violins would just for that reason not be a performance of *it*. And although the performance component of the Brandenburg Concerto No. 2 may be indeterminate between a trumpet and a natural horn in that prominent instrumental part, it certainly excludes the alto saxophone. Finally, a composition such as Bach's *Art of the Fugue*, for which perhaps no means of sound production are either prescribed or proscribed, is in this context merely the exception that proves the rule.

19 This should not be confounded with the fact that many composers were ready and willing to adapt their works in response to exigencies – in short, to license transcriptions.

20 This is not to say that *everything* found in scores is constitutive of musical works. Some markings do not fix the identity of a work hut are instead of the nature of advice, inspiration, helpful instruction, etc. However, the suggestion that instrumental specifications are of this sort is totally insupportable.

21 Cf. Walton, "Categories of Art," op. cit., pp. 349/50, for related examples.

22 James Lyons, liner notes, phonograph record *Nonesuch* 71054.

23 The best one could say would be that the Quintet achieved a satisfactory blending of piano-ish sounds and woodwind-ish sounds.

24 One could alternatively speak of a single structure which, construed rightly, entails both the required sounds and the required means of sound production. This would be a structure of *performed sounds*, as opposed to "pure" sounds. For example, one such *performed sound* would correspond to the following specification: "Middle C of half-note duration played on oboe." Clearly this implies both a certain sound qualitatively defined and a means of producing it.

The main reason I favor the S/PM formulation is that it is more transparent. It preserves some continuity with the sound-structure view which it supersedes, and displays more clearly than the performed-sound formulation that, although a musical work is *more* than a sound structure, it most definitely *includes* a sound structure.

25 This analogy was brought to my attention by Warren Ingber.

26 See, for example, J. L. Austin's "Truth," *Proceedings of the Aristotelian Society*, supp. vol. XXIV (1950): 111–28.

27 The analogy might even be reversed, so as to illuminate the nature of statements. If musical works are structures-as-indicated . . . , then possibly statements just are: sentences-as-uttered . . .

28 I am assuming, of course, that Hummel could not possibly have *been* Beethoven. If he *could* have, then I suppose that, even on MW, Hummel might have composed Beethoven's Quintet.

29 I will take this opportunity to point out that although aesthetic and artistic attributes have played a large role in this paper, I have not insisted on them as *essential* to musical works, but only as relevant – in common with all other attributes – to *individuating* them. The argument has nowhere required as a premise that such attributes are essential attributes. It has assumed only that aesthetic/artistic attributes *truly belong* to works in a *reasonably determinate* fashion. As for what attributes *are* essential to musical works, given MW, it seems that certain structural and genetic attributes would have to be admitted: S/PM structure, composer, date of composition. But it is not obvious that aesthetic/artistic attributes will turn out to be essential, i.e., possessed by a work in all possible worlds it inhabits. Consider a possible world in which Schoenberg determines the S/PM structure of *Verklarte Nacht* during 1899 but in which Wagner had never existed. The resultant work might still be *Verklarte Nacht*, though some of its aesthetic/artistic attributes would be subtly different.

30 Quandaries arise when these considerations conflict, which I will not attempt to deal with here. For example, suppose the Aloysious Ensemble are actually reading copies of Grotesteen's score while believing themselves to be playing Sterngrab's score. Do they perform Sterngrab's Quartet, Grotesteen's Quartet, or both?

31 I will assume here that the required connection is primarily, if not wholly, intentional.

32 And thus an attempt to exemplify an S/PM-as-indicated-by-*X*-at-*t*.

33 What constitutes a "reasonable degree," and thus what differentiates poor or marginal performance from nonperformance, is for many compositions perhaps marked by the ability of an informed and sensitive listener to grasp, at least roughly, what S/PM structure is struggling to be presented. For example, even an especially informed and sensitive listener would grasp approximately nothing of the Hammerklavier Sonata from *my* attempt to

present its structure, since my facility at the piano is next to nil – no performance (much less an instance) of the Hammerklavier Sonata can issue from me or my ilk.

34 Thus I am in opposition to Wolterstorff's suggestion, in "Toward an Ontology of Artworks," op. cit., that musical works be construed as norm-kinds, i.e., as having correct and incorrect, or proper and improper, or standard and defective instances. What we say about musical works can, I think, be more perspicuously interpreted in terms of the distinction between instance and performance. Further, construing instance as requiring full conformity to score (i.e., as an all-or-none proposition) has the virtue, as Nelson Goodman pointed out in *Languages of Art* (Indianapolis: Bobbs-Merrill, 1968), of assuring preservation of a work's identity from work to instance and from instance to work. But by also distinguishing between instance and performance (which Goodman does not do) one can sweeten the judgment, say, that Rubinstein's playing of the Chopin Ballade No. 3 with two mistakes is not an *instance* of the work, with the willing admission that it is surely a *performance* of it (and possibly a great one).

35 It is worth observing that, if the position developed in this paper is correct, it may have interesting implications not only for the identity of other sorts of art work (this I take to be obvious), but for the identity of abstract cultural objects of various sorts – e.g., scientific theories, speeches, laws, games. A physical theory, for example, can't be *simply* a set of sentences, propositions, or equations *if* it is in fact the possessor of properties such as brilliance, revolutionariness, derivativeness, immediate acceptance. For that very set of sentences, propositions, or equations might be found in another theory occurring fifty years earlier or later which lacked those properties.

43

Aesthetic Concepts

Frank Sibley

Frank Sibley (1923–96) was Professor of Philosophy at Lancaster University.

The remarks we make about works of art are of many kinds. In this paper I wish to distinguish between two broad groups. We say that a novel has a great number of characters and deals with life in a manufacturing town; that a painting uses pale colors, predominantly blues and greens, and has kneeling figures in the foreground; that the theme in a fugue is inverted at such a point and that there is a stretto at the close; that the action of a play takes place in the span of one day and that there is a reconciliation scene in the fifth act. Such remarks may be made by, and such features pointed out to, anyone with normal eyes, ears, and intelligence. On the other hand, we also say that a poem is tightly-knit or deeply moving; that a picture lacks balance, or has a certain serenity and repose, or that the grouping of the figures sets up an exciting tension; that the characters in a novel never really come to life, or that a certain episode strikes a false note. The making of such remarks as these requires the exercise of taste, perceptiveness, or sensitivity, of aesthetic discrimination or appreciation. Accordingly, when a word or expression is such that taste or perceptiveness is required in order to apply it, I shall call it an *aesthetic* term or expression, and I shall, correspondingly, speak of *aesthetic* concepts or taste concepts.[1]

Frank Sibley, "Aesthetic Concepts," *Philosophical Review*, 68/4 (1959): 421–50.

Aesthetic terms span a great range of types and could be grouped into various kinds and sub-species. But it is not my present purpose to attempt any such grouping; I am interested in what they all have in common. Their almost endless variety is adequately displayed in the following list: *unified, balanced, integrated, lifeless, serene, somber, dynamic, powerful, vivid, delicate, moving, trite, sentimental, tragic.* The list of course is not limited to adjectives; expressions in artistic contexts like "telling contrast," "sets up a tension," "conveys a sense of," or "holds it together" are equally good illustrations. It includes terms used by both layman and critic alike, as well as some which are mainly the property of professional critics and specialists.

I have gone for my examples of aesthetic expressions in the first place to critical and evaluative discourse about works of art because it is there particularly that they abound. But now I wish to widen the topic; we employ terms the use of which requires an exercise of taste not only when discussing the arts but quite liberally throughout discourse in everyday life. The examples given above are expressions which, appearing in critical contexts, most usually, if not invariably, have an aesthetic use; outside critical discourse the majority of them more frequently have some other use unconnected with taste. But many expressions do double duty even in everyday discourse, sometimes being used as aesthetic expressions and sometimes not. Other words again, whether in artistic or daily discourse, function only or predominantly as aesthetic terms; of this kind are *graceful, delicate, dainty, handsome, comely, elegant, garish.* Finally, to make the contrast with all the preceding examples, there are many words which are seldom used as aesthetic terms at all: *red, noisy, brackish, clammy, square, docile, curved, evanescent, intelligent, faithful, derelict, tardy, freakish.*

Clearly, when we employ words as aesthetic terms we are often making and using metaphors, pressing into service words which do not primarily function in this manner. Certainly also, many words *have come* to be aesthetic terms by some kind of metaphorical transference. This is so with those like "dynamic," "melancholy," "balanced," "tightly-knit" which, except in artistic and critical writings, are not normally aesthetic terms. But the aesthetic vocabulary must not be thought wholly metaphorical. Many words, including the most common (*lovely, pretty, beautiful, dainty, graceful, elegant*), are certainly not being used metaphorically when employed as aesthetic terms, the very good reason being that this is their primary or only use, some of them having no current non-aesthetic uses. And though expressions like "dynamic," "balanced," and so forth *have come* by a metaphorical shift to be aesthetic terms, their employment in criticism can scarcely be said to be more than quasi-metaphorical. Having entered the language of art description and criticism as metaphors they are now standard vocabulary in that language.[2]

The expressions I am calling aesthetic terms form no small segment of our discourse. Often, it is true, people with normal intelligence and good eyesight and hearing lack, at least in some measure, the sensitivity required to apply them; a man need not be stupid or have poor eyesight to fail to see that something is graceful. Thus taste or sensitivity is somewhat more rare than certain other human capacities; people who exhibit a sensitivity both wide-ranging and refined are a minority. It is over the application of aesthetic terms too that, notoriously, disputes and differences sometimes go helplessly unsettled. But almost everybody is able to exercise taste to some degree and in some matters. It is surprising therefore that aesthetic terms have been so largely neglected. They have received glancing treatment in the course of other aesthetic discussions; but as a broad category they have not received the direct attention they merit.

The foregoing has marked out the area I wish to discuss. One warning should perhaps be given. When I speak of taste in this paper, I shall not be dealing with questions which center upon expressions like "a matter of taste" (meaning, roughly, a matter of personal preference or liking). It is with an ability to *notice* or *discern* things that I am concerned.

I

In order to support our application of an aesthetic term, we often refer to features the mention of which involves other aesthetic terms: "it has an extraordinary vitality because of its free and vigorous style of drawing," "graceful in the smooth flow of its lines," "dainty because of the delicacy and harmony of its coloring." It is as normal to do this as it is to justify one mental epithet by other epithets of the same general type, *intelligent* by *ingenious, inventive, acute,* and so on. But often when we apply aesthetic terms, we explain why by referring to features which do *not* depend for their recognition upon an exercise of taste: "delicate because of its pastel shades and curving lines," or "it lacks balance because one group of figures is so far off to the left and is so brightly illuminated." When no explanation of this kind is offered, it is legitimate to ask or search for one. Finding a satisfactory answer may sometimes be difficult, but one cannot ordinarily reject the question. When we cannot ourselves quite say what non-aesthetic features make something delicate or unbalanced or powerful or moving, the good critic often puts his finger on something which strikes us as the right explanation. In short, aesthetic words apply ultimately because of, and aesthetic qualities ultimately depend upon, the presence of features which, like curving or angular lines, color contrasts, placing of masses, or speed of movement, are visible, audible, or otherwise discernible without any exercise of taste or sensibility. Whatever kind of dependence this is, and there are various relationships between aesthetic qualities and non-aesthetic features, what I want to make clear in this section is that there are no non-aesthetic features which serve as *conditions* for applying aesthetic terms. Aesthetic or taste concepts are not in this respect condition-governed at all.

There is little temptation to suppose that aesthetic terms resemble words which, like "square," are applied in accordance with a set of necessary and sufficient conditions. For whereas each square is square in virtue of the *same* set of conditions, four equal sides and four right angles, aesthetic terms apply to widely varied objects; one thing is graceful because of these features, another because of those, and so on almost endlessly. In recent times philosophers have broken the spell of the strict necessary-and-sufficient model by showing that many everyday concepts are not of that type. Instead, they have described various other types of concepts which are governed only in a much looser way by conditions. However, since these newer models provide satisfactory accounts of many familiar concepts, it might plausibly be thought that aesthetic concepts are of some such kind and that they similarly are governed in some looser way by conditions. I want to argue that aesthetic concepts differ radically from any of these other concepts.

Amongst these concepts to which attention has recently been paid are those for which no *necessary* conditions can be provided, but for which there are a number of relevant features, A, B, C, D, E, such that the presence of some groups or combinations of these features is *sufficient* for the application of the concept. The list of relevant features may be an open one; that is, given A, B, C, D, E, we may not wish to close off the possible relevance of other unlisted features beyond E. Examples of such concepts might be "dilatory," "discourteous," "possessive," "capricious," "prosperous," "intelligent" [. . .]. If we begin a list of features relevant to "intelligent" with, for example, ability to grasp and follow various kinds of instructions, ability to master facts and marshall evidence, ability to solve mathematical or chess problems, we might go on adding to this list almost indefinitely.

However, with concepts of this sort, although decisions may have to be made and judgment exercised, it is always possible to extract and state, from cases which have *already* clearly been decided, the sets of features or conditions which were regarded as sufficient in those cases. These relevant features which I am calling conditions are, it should be noted, features which, though not sufficient *alone* and needing to be combined with other similar features, always carry some weight and can count only in one direction. Being a good chess player can count only *towards* and not *against* intelligence. Whereas mention of it may enter sensibly along with other remarks in expressions like "I say he is intelligent because . . ." or "the reason I call him intelligent is that . . . ," it cannot be used to complete such negative expressions as "I say he is *un*intelligent because . . ." But what I want particularly to emphasize about features which function as conditions for a term is that *some* group or set of them *is* sufficient fully to ensure or warrant the application of that term. An individual characterized by some of these features may not yet qualify to be called lazy or intelligent, and so on, beyond all question, but all that is needed is to add some further (indefinite) number of such characterizations and the point is reached where we have enough. There are individuals possessing a number of such features of whom one cannot deny, cannot but admit, that they are intelligent. We have left necessary-and-sufficient conditions behind, but we are still in the realm of conditions.

But aesthetic concepts are not condition-governed even in this way. There are no sufficient conditions, no non-aesthetic features such that the presence of some set or number of them will beyond question justify or warrant the application of an aesthetic term. It is impossible (barring certain limited exceptions [. . .] to make any statements corresponding to those we can make for condition-governed words. We are able to say "If it is true he can do this, and that, and the other, then one just cannot deny that he is intelligent," or "if he does A, B, and C, I don't see how it can be denied that he is lazy," but we cannot make *any* general statement of the form "If the vase is pale pink, somewhat curving, lightly mottled, and so forth, it will be delicate, cannot but be delicate." Nor again can one say *any* such things here as "Being tall and thin is not enough *alone* to ensure that a vase is delicate, but if it is, for example, slightly curving and pale colored (and so forth) as well, it cannot be denied that it is." Things may be described to us in non-aesthetic terms as fully as we please but we are not thereby put in the position of having to admit (or being unable to deny) that they are delicate or graceful or garish or exquisitely balanced.[3]

No doubt there are some respects in which aesthetic terms *are* governed by conditions or rules. For instance, it may be impossible that a thing should be garish if all its colors are pale pastels, or flamboyant if all its lines are straight. There may be, that is, descriptions using only non-aesthetic terms which are incompatible with descriptions employing certain aesthetic terms. If I am told that a painting in the next room consists solely of one or two bars of very pale blue and very pale grey set at right angles on a pale fawn ground, I can be sure that it cannot be fiery or garish or gaudy or flamboyant. A description of this sort may make certain aesthetic terms *in*applicable or *in*appropriate; and if from this description I inferred that the picture was, or even might be, fiery or gaudy or flamboyant, this might be taken as showing a failure to understand these words. I do not wish to deny therefore that taste concepts may be governed *negatively* by conditions.[4] What I am emphasizing is that they quite lack governing conditions of a sort many other concepts possess. Though on *seeing* the picture we might say, and rightly, that it is delicate or serene or restful or sickly or insipid, no *description* in non-aesthetic words permits us to claim that these or any other aesthetic terms must undeniably apply to it.

I have said that if an object is characterized *solely* by certain sorts of features this may count decisively against the possibility of applying to it certain aesthetic words. But of course the presence of just *a few* such features need not count decisively; other features may be enough to outweigh those which, on their own, would render the aesthetic term inapplicable. A painting might be garish even though much of its color is pale. These facts call attention to a further feature of taste concepts. One *can* find general features or descriptions which in some sense count in one direction only, only *for* or only *against* the application of certain aesthetic terms. Angularity, fatness, brightness, or intensity of color are typically not associated with delicacy or grace. Slimness, lightness, gentle curves, lack of intensity of color are associated with delicacy, but not with flamboyance, majesty, grandeur, splendor or garishness. This is shown by the naturalness of saying, for example, that someone is graceful *because* she's so light, but i*n spite of* being quite angular or heavily built; and by the corresponding oddity of saying that something is graceful *because* it is so heavy or angular, or delicate *because* of its bright and intense coloring. This may therefore sound quite similar to what I have said already about conditions. There are nevertheless very significant differences. Although there is this sense in which slimness, lightness, lack of intensity of color, and so on, count only towards, not against, delicacy, these features can be said, at best, to count only *typically* or *characteristically* towards delicacy; they do not count towards in the same sense as condition-features count towards laziness or intelligence.

One way of reinforcing this is to notice how features which are characteristically associated with one aesthetic term may also be similarly associated with other and rather different aesthetic terms. "Graceful" and "delicate" may be on the one hand sharply contrasted with terms like "violent," "grand," "fiery," "garish," or "massive" which have characteristic non-aesthetic features quite unlike those for "delicate" and "graceful." But on the other hand they may also be contrasted with aesthetic terms which stand much closer to them, like "flaccid," "weakly," "washed out," "lanky," "anaemic," "wan," "insipid"; and the range of features characteristic of *these* qualities, pale color, slimness, lightness, lack of angularity and sharp contrast, is virtually identical with the range for "delicate" and "graceful." Similarly many of the features typically associated with 'joyous," "fiery," "robust," or "dynamic" are identical with those associated with "garish," "strident," "turbulent," "gaudy," or "chaotic." Thus an object which is described very fully, but exclusively in terms of qualities characteristic of delicacy, may turn out on inspection to be not delicate at all, but anaemic or insipid. The failures of novices and the artistically inept prove that quite close similarity in point of line, color, or technique gives no assurance of gracefulness or delicacy. A failure and a success in the manner of Degas may be generally more alike, so far as their non-aesthetic features go, than either is like a successful Fragonard. But it is not necessary to go even this far to make my main point. A painting which has only the kind of features one would associate with vigor and energy but which even so fails to be vigorous and energetic *need* not have some other character, need not be instead, say, strident or chaotic. It may fail to have any particular character whatever. It may employ bright colors, and the like, without being particularly lively and vigorous at all; but one may feel unable to describe it as chaotic or strident or garish either. It is, rather, simply lacking in character (though of course this too is an aesthetic judgment; taste is exercised also in seeing that the painting has no character).

There are of course many features which do not in these ways characteristically count for (or against) particular aesthetic qualities. One poem has strength and power because of the regularity of its meter and rhyme; another is monotonous and lacks drive and strength because of its regular meter and rhyme. We do not feel the need to switch from "because of" to "in spite of." However, I have concentrated upon features which are characteristically associated with aesthetic qualities because, if a case could be made for the view that taste concepts are condition-governed, these would seem to be the most promising candidates for governing conditions. But to say that features are associated only *characteristically* with an aesthetic term *is* to say that they are not conditions; no description however full, even in terms characteristic of gracefulness, puts it beyond question that something is graceful in the way a description may put it beyond question that someone is lazy or intelligent.

It is important to observe that I have not merely been claiming that no sufficient conditions can be stated for taste concepts. For if this were all, taste concepts might not be after all really different from one kind of concept recently discussed. They could be accommodated perhaps with those concepts which Professor H. L. A. Hart has called "defeasible"; it is a characteristic of defeasible concepts that we cannot state sufficient conditions for them because, for any sets we offer, there is always an (open) list of defeating conditions any of which might rule out the application of the concept. The most we can say schematically for a defeasible concept is that, for example, A, B, and C together are sufficient for the concept to apply *unless* some feature is present which overrides or voids them. But, I want to emphasize, the very fact that we *can* say this sort of thing shows that we are still to that extent in the realm of conditions.[5] The features governing defeasible concepts can ordinarily count only one way, *either* for *or* against. To take Hart's example, "offer" and "acceptance" can count only towards the existence of a valid contract, and fraudulent misrepresentation, duress, and lunacy can count only against. And even with defeasible concepts, if we are told that there are no voiding features present, we can know that some set of conditions or features, A, B, C, . . . , is enough, in this absence of voiding features, to ensure, for example, that there is a contract. The very notion of a defeasible concept seems to require that some group of features *would* be sufficient in the absence of overriding or voiding features. Defeasible concepts lack *sufficient* conditions then, but they are still, in the sense described, condition-governed. My claim about taste concepts is stronger; that they are not, except negatively, governed by conditions at all. We could not conclude, even if we were told of the absence of all "voiding" or uncharacteristic features (no angularities, and the like), that an object must certainly be graceful, however fully it was described to us as possessing features characteristic of gracefulness.

My arguments and illustrations so far have been rather simply schematic. Many concepts, including most of the examples I have used (*intelligent*, and so on [. . .]), are much more thoroughly open and complex than my illustrations suggest. Not only may there be an open list of relevant conditions; it may be impossible to give rules telling how many features from the list are needed for a sufficient set or in which combinations; impossible similarly to give rules covering the extent or degree to which such features need to be present in those combinations. Indeed, we may have to abandon as futile any attempt to describe conditions or formulate rules, and content ourselves with giving only some very general account of the concept, making reference to samples or cases or precedents. We cannot master or employ these concepts therefore simply by being equipped with lists of conditions, readily applicable procedures or sets of rules, however complex. For to exhibit a mastery of one of these concepts we must be able to go ahead and apply the word correctly to new individual cases, at least to central ones; and each new case may be a uniquely different object, just as each intelligent child or student may differ from others in relevant features and exhibit a unique combination of kinds and degrees of achievement and ability. In dealing with these new cases mechanical rules and procedures would be useless; we have to exercise our judgment, guided by a complex set of examples and precedents. Here then there is a marked superficial similarity to aesthetic concepts. For in using aesthetic terms we learn from samples and examples, not rules, and we have to apply them, likewise, without guidance by rules or readily applicable procedures, to new and unique instances. Neither kind of concept admits of a "mechanical" employment.

Nevertheless it is at least noteworthy that in applying words like "lazy" or "intelligent" to new and unique instances we say that we are required to exercise *judgment*; it would be indeed odd to say that we are exercising *taste.* In exercising judgment we are called upon to weigh the pros and cons against each other, and perhaps sometimes to decide whether a quite new feature is to be counted as weighing on one side or on the other. But this goes to show that, though we may learn from and rely upon samples and precedents rather than a set of stated conditions, we are not out of the realm of general conditions and guiding principles. Samples and precedents necessarily embody, and are used by us to illustrate, the complex web of governing and relevant conditions. To profit by precedents we have to understand them; and we must argue consistently from case to case. This is the very function of precedents. Thus it is possible, even with these very loosely condition-governed concepts, to take clear or paradigm cases, to say "this is X because . . . ," and follow it up with an account of features which clinch the matter.

Nothing like this is possible with aesthetic terms. Examples undoubtedly play a crucial role in giving us a grasp of these concepts; but we do not and cannot derive from these examples conditions and principles, however complex, which will guide us consistently and intelligibly in applying the terms to new cases. When, with a clear case of something which is in fact graceful or balanced or tightly-knit but which I have not seen, someone tells me why it is, what features make it so, it is always possible for me to wonder whether, in spite of these features, it really is graceful, balanced, and so on.

The point I have argued may be reinforced in the following way. A man who failed to realize the nature of taste concepts, or someone who, knowing he lacked sensitivity in aesthetic matters, did not want to reveal this lack might by assiduous application and shrewd observation provide himself with some rules and generalizations; and by inductive procedures and intelligent guessing, he might frequently say the right things. But he could have no great confidence or certainty; a slight change in an object might at any time unpredictably ruin his calculations, and he might as easily have been wrong as right. No matter how careful he has been about working out a set of consistent principles and conditions, he is only in a position to think that the object is very possibly delicate. With concepts like *lazy, intelligent,* or *contract,* someone who intelligently formulated rules that led him aright appreciably often *would* thereby show the beginning of a grasp of those concepts; but the person we are considering is not even beginning to show an awareness of what delicacy is. Though he sometimes says the right thing, he has not seen, but guessed, that the object is delicate. However intelligent he might be, we could easily tell him wrongly that something was delicate and "explain" why without his being able to detect the deception. (I am ignoring complications now about negative conditions.) But if we did the same with, say, "intelligent" he could at least often uncover some incompatibility or other which would need explaining. In a world of beings like himself he would have no use for concepts like delicacy. As it is, these concepts would play a quite different role in his life. He would, for himself, have no more reason to choose tasteful objects, pictures, and so on, than a deaf man would to avoid noisy places. He could not be praised for exercising taste; at best his ingenuity and intelligence might come in for mention. In "appraising" pictures, statuettes, poems, he would be doing something quite different from what other people do when they exercise taste.

At this point I want to notice in passing that there are times when it may look as if an aesthetic word could be applied according to a rule. These cases vary in type; I shall mention only one. One might say, in using "delicate" of glassware perhaps, that the thinner the glass, other things being equal, the more delicate it is. Similarly, with fabrics, furniture, and so on, there are perhaps times when the thinner or more smoothly finished or more highly polished something is, the more certainly some aesthetic term or other applies. On such occasions someone could formulate a rule and follow it in applying the word to a given range of articles. Now it may be that sometimes when this is so, the word being used is not really an aesthetic term at all; "delicate" applied to glass in this way may at times really mean no more than "thin" or "fragile." But this is certainly not always the case; people often *are* exercising taste even when they say that glass is very delicate because it is so thin, and know that it would be less so if thicker and more so if thinner, These instances where there appear to be rules are peripheral cases of the use of aesthetic terms. If someone did merely follow a rule we should not say he was exercising taste, and we should hesitate to admit that he had any real notion of delicacy until he satisfied us that he could discern it in other instances where no rule was available. In any event, these occasions when aesthetic words can be applied by rule are exceptional, not central or typical.[6]

It must not be thought that the impossibility of stating any conditions (other than negative) for the application of aesthetic terms results from an accidental poverty or lack of precision in language, or that it is simply a question of extreme complexity. It is true that words like "pink," "bluish," "curving," "mottled" do not permit of anything like a specific naming of each and every varied shade, curve, mottling, and blending. But if we were to give special names much more liberally than either we or even the specialists do (and no doubt there are limits beyond which we could not go), or even if, instead of names, we were to use vast numbers of specimens and samples of particular shades, shapes, mottlings, lines, and configurations, it would still be impossible, and for the same reasons, to supply any conditions.

We do indeed, in talking about a work of art, concern ourselves with its individual and specific features. We say that it is delicate not simply because it is in pale colors but because of *those* pale colors, that it is graceful not because its outline curves slightly but because of *that* particular curve. We use expressions like "because of *its* pale coloring," "because of *the* flecks of bright blue," "because of *the* way the lines converge" where it is clear we are referring not to the presence of general features but to very specific and particular ones. But it is obvious that even with the help of precise names, or even samples and illustrations, of particular shades of color, contours and lines, any attempt to state conditions would be futile. After all, the very same feature, say a color or shape or line of a particular sort, which helps make one work may quite spoil another. "It would be quite delicate if it were not for that pale color there" may be said about the very color which is singled out in another picture as being largely responsible for its delicate quality. No doubt one way of putting this is to say that the features which make something delicate or graceful, and so on, are combined in a peculiar and unique way; that the aesthetic quality depends upon exactly this individual or unique combination of just these specific colors and shapes so that even a slight change might make all the difference. Nothing is to be achieved by trying to single out or separate features and generalizing about them.

I have now argued that taste concepts are not and cannot be condition- or rule-governed.[7] Not to be so governed is one of their essential characteristics. In arguing this I first claimed in a general way that no non-aesthetic features are possible candidates for conditions, and then considered more particularly both the "characteristic" general features associated with aesthetic terms and the individual or specific features found in particular objects. I have not attempted to examine what relationship these individual features do bear to aesthetic qualities. An examination of the locutions we use when we refer to them in the course of explaining or supporting our application of an aesthetic term reinforces with linguistic evidence the fact that we are certainly not offering them as explanatory or justifying *conditions*. When we are asked why we say a certain person is lazy or intelligent or courageous, we are being asked in virtue of what we *call* him this; we reply with "because of the way he regularly leaves his work unfinished," or "because of the ease with which he handles such and such problems," and so on. But when we are asked to say why, in our opinion, a picture lacks balance or is somber in tone, or why a poem is moving or tightly organized, we are doing a different kind of thing. We may use similar locutions: "his verse has strength and variety *because of the way* he handles the meter and employs the caesura," or "it is nobly austere *because* of the lack of detail and the restricted palette." But we can also express what we want to by using quite other expressions: "it is the handling of meter and caesura which is *responsible for* its strength and variety," "its nobly austere quality is *due to* the lack of detail and the use of a restricted palette," "its lack of balance *results from* the highlighting of the figures on the left," "those minor chords *make it* extremely moving," "those converging lines *give it* an extraordinary unity." These are locutions we cannot switch to with "lazy" or "intelligent"; to say what *makes* him lazy, what is *responsible for* his laziness, what it is *due to*, is to broach another question entirely.

One after another, in recent discussions, writers have insisted that aesthetic judgments are not "mechanical": "Critics do not formulate general standards and apply these mechanically to all, or to classes of, works of art." "Technical points can be settled rapidly, by the application of rules," but aesthetic questions "cannot be settled by any mechanical method." Instead, these writers on aesthetics have emphasized that there is no substitute for individual judgment" with its "spontaneity and speculation" and that "The final standard . . . [is] the judgment of personal taste."[8] What is surprising is that, though such things have been repeated again and again, no one seems to have said what is meant by "taste" or by the word "mechanical." There are many judgments besides those requiring taste which demand "spontaneity" and "individual judgment" and are not "mechanical." Without a detailed comparison we cannot see in what particular way *aesthetic* judgments are not "mechanical," or how they differ from those other judgments, nor can we begin to specify what taste is. This I have attempted. It is a characteristic and essential feature of judgments which employ an aesthetic term that they cannot be made by appealing, in the sense explained, to conditions.[9] This, I believe, is a logical feature of aesthetic or taste judgments in general, though I have argued it here only as regards the more restricted range of judgments which employ aesthetic terms. It is part of what "taste" means.

II

A great deal of work remains to be done on taste concepts. In the remainder of this paper I shall offer some further suggestions which may help towards an understanding of them.

The realization that aesthetic concepts are not governed by conditions is likely to give rise to puzzlement over how we manage to apply the words in our aesthetic vocabulary. If we are not following rules and there are no conditions to appeal to, how are we to know when they are applicable? One very natural way to counter this question is to point out that some other sorts of concepts also are not condition-governed. We do not apply simple color words by following rules or in accordance with principles. We see that the book is red by looking, just as we tell that the tea is sweet by tasting it. So too, it might be said, we just see (or fail to see) that things are delicate, balanced, and the like. This kind of comparison between the exercise of taste and the use of the five senses is indeed familiar; our use of the word "taste" itself shows that the comparison is age-old and very natural. Yet whatever the similarities, there are great dissimilarities too. A careful comparison cannot be attempted here though it would be valuable; but certain differences stand out, and writers who have emphasized that aesthetic judgments are not "mechanical" have sometimes dwelt on and been puzzled by them.

In the first place, while our ability to discern aesthetic features is dependent upon our possession of good eyesight, hearing, and so on, people normally endowed with senses and understanding may nevertheless fail to discern them. "Those who listen to a concert, walk round a gallery, read a poem may have roughly similar sense perceptions, but some get a great deal more than others," Miss Macdonald says; but she adds that she is "puzzled by this feature 'in the object' which can be seen only by a specially qualified observer" and asks, "What is this 'something more'?"[10]

It is this difference between aesthetic and perceptual qualities which in part leads to the view that "works of art are esoteric objects . . . not simple objects of sense perception."[11] But there is no good reason for calling an object esoteric simply because we discern aesthetic qualities in it. The *objects* to which we apply aesthetic words are of the most diverse kinds and by no means esoteric: people and buildings, flowers and gardens, vases and furniture, as well as poems and music. Nor does there seem any good reason for calling the *qualities* themselves esoteric. It is true that someone with perfect eyes or ears might miss them, but we do after all say we *observe* or *notice* them ("Did you notice how very graceful she was?," "Did you observe the exquisite balance in all his pictures?"). In fact, they are very familiar indeed. We learn while quite young to use many aesthetic words, though they are, as one might expect from their dependence upon our ability to see, hear, distinguish colors, and the like, not the earliest words we learn; and our mastery and sophistication in using them develop along with the rest of our vocabulary. They are not rarities; some ranges of them are in regular use in everyday discourse.

The second notable difference between the exercise of taste and the use of the five senses lies in the way we support those judgments in which aesthetic concepts are employed. Although we use these concepts without rules or conditions, we do defend or support our judgments, and convince others of their rightness, by talking; "disputation about art is not futile," as Miss Macdonald says, for critics do "attempt a certain kind of explanation of works of art with the object of establishing correct judgments."[12] Thus even though this disputation does not consist in "deductive or inductive inference" or "reasoning," its occurrence is enough to show how very different these judgments are from those of a simple perceptual sort.

Now the critic's talk, it is clear, frequently consists in mentioning or pointing out the features, including easily discernible non-aesthetic ones, upon which the aesthetic qualities depend. But the puzzling question remains how, by mentioning these features, the critic is thereby justifying or supporting his judgments. To this question a number of recent writers have given an answer. Stuart Hampshire, for example, says that "One engages in aesthetic discussion for the sake of what one might see on the way . . . if one has been brought to see what there is to be seen in the object, the purpose of discussion is achieved . . . The point is to bring people to see these features."[13] The critic's talk, that is, often serves to support his judgments in a special way; it gets us to *see* what he has seen, namely, the aesthetic qualities of the object. But even when it is agreed that this is one of the main things that critics do, puzzlement tends to break out again over *how* they do it. How is it that by talking about features of the work (largely non-aesthetic ones) we can manage to bring others to see what they had not seen? "What sort of endowment is this which *talking* can modify? . . . Discussion does not improve eyesight and hearing" (my italics).[14]

Yet of course we do succeed in applying aesthetic terms, and we frequently do succeed by talking (and pointing and gesturing in certain ways) in bringing others to see what we see. One begins to suspect that puzzlement over how we can possibly do this, and puzzlement over the "esoteric" character of aesthetic qualities too, arises from bearing in mind inappropriate philosophical models. When someone is unable to see that the book on the table is brown, we cannot get him to see that it is by talking; consequently it seems puzzling that we might get someone to see that the vase is graceful by talking. If we are to dispel this puzzlement and recognize aesthetic concepts and qualities for what they are, we must abandon unsuitable models and investigate how we actually employ these concepts. With so much interest in and agreement about *what* the critic does, one might expect descriptions of *how* he does it to have been given. But little has been said about this, and what has been said is unsatisfactory.

Miss Macdonald,[15] for example, subscribes to this view of the critic's task as presenting "what is not obvious to casual or uninstructed inspection," and she does ask the question "What sort of considerations are involved, *and how*, to justify a critical verdict?" (my italics). But she does not in fact go on to answer it. She addresses herself instead to the different, though related, question of the interpretation of art works. In complex works different critics claim, often justifiably, to discern different features; hence Miss Macdonald suggests that in critical discourse the critic is bringing us to see what he sees by offering new interpretations. But if the question is "what (the critic) does and how he does it," he cannot be represented either wholly or even mainly as providing new interpretations. His task quite as often is simply to help us appreciate qualities which other critics have regularly found in the works he discusses. To put the stress upon new interpretations is to leave untouched the question how, by talking, he can help us to see *either* the newly appreciated aesthetic qualities *or* the old. In any case, besides complex poems or plays which may bear many interpretations, there are also relatively simple ones. There are also vases, buildings, and furniture, not to mention faces, sunsets, and scenery, about which no questions of "interpretation" arise but of which we talk in similar ways and make similar judgments. So the "puzzling" questions remain: how do we support these judgments and how do we bring others to see what we see?

Hampshire,[16] who likewise believes that the critic brings us "to see what there is to be seen in the object," does give some account of how the critic does this. "The greatest service of the critic" is to point out, isolate, and place in a frame of attention the "particular features of the particular object which *make* it ugly or beautiful"; for it is "difficult to see and hear all that there is to see and hear," and simply a prejudice to suppose that while "things really do have colours and shapes . . . there do not exist literally and objectively, concordances of colours and perceived rhythms and balances of shapes." However, these "extraordinary qualities" which the critic "may have seen (in the wider sense of 'see')" are "qualities which are of no direct practical interest." Consequently, to bring us to see them the critic employs "an unnatural use of words in description"; "the common vocabulary, being created for practical purposes, obstructs any disinterested perception of things"; and so these qualities "are normally described metaphorically by some transference of terms from the common vocabulary."

Much of what Hampshire says is right. But there is also something quite wrong in the view that the "common" vocabulary "obstructs" our aesthetic purposes, that it is "unnatural" to take it over and use it metaphorically, and that the critic "is under the necessity of building . . . a vocabulary *in opposition to the main tendency of his language*" (my italics). First, while we do often coin new metaphors in order to describe aesthetic qualities, we are by no means always under the necessity of wresting the "common vocabulary" from its "natural" uses to serve our purposes. There does exist, as I observed earlier, a large and accepted vocabulary of aesthetic terms some of which, whatever their metaphorical origins, are now not metaphors at all, others of which are at most quasi-metaphorical. Second, this view that our use of metaphor and quasi-metaphor for aesthetic purposes is unnatural or a makeshift into which we are forced by a language designed for other purposes misrepresents fundamentally the character of aesthetic qualities and aesthetic language. There is nothing unnatural about using words like "forceful," "dynamic," or "tightly-knit" in criticism; they do their work perfectly and are exactly the words needed for the purposes they serve. We do not want or need to replace them by words which lack the metaphorical element. In using them to describe works of art, the very point is that we are noticing aesthetic qualities related to their literal or common meanings. If we possessed a quite different word from "dynamic," one we could use to point out an aesthetic quality unrelated to the common meaning of "dynamic," it could not be used to describe that quality which "dynamic" does serve to point out. Hampshire pictures "a colony of aesthetes, disengaged from practical needs and manipulations" and says that "descriptions of aesthetic qualities, which for us are metaphorical, might seem to them to have an altogether literal and familiar sense"; they might use "a more directly descriptive vocabulary." But if they had a new and "directly descriptive" vocabulary lacking the links with non-aesthetic properties and interests which our vocabulary possesses, they would have to remain silent about many of the aesthetic qualities we can describe; further, if they were more completely "disengaged from practical needs" and other non-aesthetic awarenesses and interests, they would perforce be blind to many aesthetic qualities we can appreciate. The links between aesthetic qualities and non-aesthetic ones are both obvious and vital. Aesthetic concepts, all of them, carry with them attachments and in one way or another are tethered to or parasitic upon non-aesthetic features. The fact that many aesthetic terms are metaphorical or quasi-metaphorical in no way means that common language is an ill-adapted tool with which we have to struggle. When someone writes as Hampshire does, one suspects again that critical language is being judged against other models. To use language which is frequently metaphorical might be strange for some *other* purpose or from the standpoint of doing something else, but for the purpose and from the standpoint of making aesthetic observations it is not. To say it is an unnatural use of language for doing *this* is to imply there is or could be for this purpose some other and "natural" use. But these *are* natural ways of talking about aesthetic matters.

To help understand what the critic does, then, how he supports his judgments and gets his audience to see what he sees, I shall attempt a brief description of the methods we use as critics.[17]

(1) We may simply mention or point out non-aesthetic features: "Notice these flecks of color, that dark mass there, those lines." By merely drawing attention to those easily discernible features which make the painting luminous or warm or dynamic, we often succeed in bringing someone to see these aesthetic qualities. We get him to see B by mentioning something different, A. Sometimes in doing this we are drawing attention to features which may have gone unnoticed by an untrained or insufficiently attentive eye or ear: "Just listen for the repeated figure in the left hand," "Did you notice the figure of Icarus in the Breughel? It is very small." Sometimes they are features which have been seen or heard but of which the significance or purpose has been missed in any of a variety of ways: "Notice how much darker he has made the central figure, how much brighter these colors are than the adjacent ones," "Of course, you've observed the ploughman in the foreground; but had you considered how he, like everyone else in the picture, is going about his business without noticing the fall of Icarus?" In mentioning features which may be discerned by anyone with normal eyes, ears, and intelligence, we are singling out what may serve as a kind of key to grasping or seeing something else (and the key may not be the same for each person).

(2) On the other hand we often simply mention the very qualities we want people to see, We point to a painting and say, "Notice how nervous and delicate the drawing is," or "See what energy and vitality it has." The use of the aesthetic term itself may do the trick; we say what the quality or character is, and people who had not seen it before see it.

(3) Most often, there is a linking, of remarks about aesthetic and non-aesthetic features: "Have you noticed this line and that, and the points of bright color here and there . . . don't they give it vitality, energy?"

(4) We do, in addition, often make extensive and helpful use of similes and genuine metaphors: "It's as if there are small points of light burning," "as though he had thrown on the paint violently and in anger," "the light shimmers, the lines dance, everything is air, lightness and gaiety," "his canvasses are fires, they crackle, burn, and blaze, even at their most subdued always restlessly flickering, but often bursting into flame, great pyrotechnic displays," and so on.

(5) We make use of contrasts, comparisons, and reminiscences: "Suppose he had made that a lighter yellow, moved it to the right, how flat it would have fallen," "Don't you think it has something of the quality of a Rembrandt?," "Hasn't it the same serenity, peace, and quality of light of those summer evenings in Norfolk?" We use what keys we have to the known sensitivity, susceptibilities, and experience of our audience.

Critics and commentators may range, in their methods, from one extreme to the other, from painstaking concentration on points of detail, line and color, vowels and rhymes, to more or less flowery and luxuriant metaphor. Even the enthusiastic biographical sketch decorated with suitable epithet and metaphor may serve. What is best depends on both the audience and the work under discussion. But this would not be a complete sketch unless certain other notes were added.

(6) Repetition and reiteration often play an important role. When we are in front of a canvas we may come back time and again to the same points, drawing attention to the same lines and shapes, repeating the same words, "swirling," "balance," "luminosity," or the same similes and metaphors, as if time and familiarity, looking harder, listening more carefully, paying closer attention may help. So again with variation; it often helps to talk round what we have said, to build up, supplement with more talk *of the same kind*. When someone misses the swirling quality, when one epithet or one metaphor does not

work, we throw in related ones; we speak of its wild movement, how it twists and turns, writhes and whirls, as though, failing to score a direct hit, we may succeed with a barrage of near-synonyms.

(7) Finally, besides our verbal performances, the rest of our behavior is important. We accompany our talk with appropriate tones of voice, expression, nods, looks, and gestures. A critic may sometimes do more with a sweep of the arm than by talking. An appropriate gesture may make us see the violence in a painting or the character of a melodic line.

These ways of acting and talking are not significantly different whether we are dealing with a particular work, paragraph, or line, or speaking of an artist's work as a whole, or even drawing attention to a sunset or scenery. But even with the speaker doing all this, we may fail to see what he sees. There may be a point, though there need be no limit except that imposed by time and patience, at which he gives up and sets us (or himself) down as lacking in some way, defective in sensitivity. He may tell us to look or read again, or to read or look at other things and then come back again to this; he may suspect there are experiences in life we have missed. But these are the things he does. This is what succeeds if anything does; indeed it is all that can be done.

By realizing clearly that, whether we are dealing with art or scenery or people or natural objects, this is how we operate with aesthetic concepts, we may recognize this sphere of human activity for what it is. We operate with different kinds of concepts in different ways. If we want someone to agree that a color is red we may take it into a good light and ask him to look; if it is viridian we may fetch a color chart and make him compare; if we want him to agree that a figure is fourteen-sided we get him to count; and to bring him to agree that something is dilapidated or that someone is lazy we may do other things, citing features, reasoning and arguing about them, weighing and balancing. These are the methods appropriate to these various concepts. But the ways we get someone to see aesthetic qualities are different; they are of the kind I have described. With each kind of concept we can describe what we do and how we do it. But the methods suited to these other concepts will not do for aesthetic ones, or vice versa. We cannot prove by argument that something is graceful; but this is no more puzzling than our inability to prove, by using the methods, metaphors, and gestures of the art critic, that it will be mate in ten moves. The questions raised admit of no answer beyond the sort of description I have given. To go on to ask, with puzzlement, how it is that *when* we do these things people come to see, is like asking how is it that, when we take the book into a good light, our companion agrees with us that it is red. There is no place for this kind of question or puzzlement. Aesthetic concepts are as natural, as little esoteric, as any others. It is against the background of different and philosophically more familiar models that they seem queer or puzzling.

I have described how people justify aesthetic judgments and bring others to see aesthetic qualities in things. I shall end by showing that the methods I have outlined are the ones natural for and characteristic of taste concepts from the start. When someone tries to convince me that a painting is delicate or balanced, I have some understanding of these terms already and know in a sense what I am looking for. But if there is puzzlement over how, by talking, he can bring me to see these qualities in this picture, there should be a corresponding puzzlement over how I learned to use aesthetic terms and discern aesthetic qualities in the first place. We may ask, therefore, how we learn to do these things; and this is to inquire (1) what natural potentialities and tendencies people have and (2) how we develop and take advantage of these capacities in training and teaching. Now for the second of these, there is no doubt that our ability to notice and respond to aesthetic qualities is cultivated and developed by our contacts with parents and teachers from quite an early age. What is interesting for my present purpose is that, while we are being taught in the presence of examples what grace, delicacy, and so on are, the methods used, the language and behavior, are of a piece with those of the critic.

To pursue these two questions, consider first those words like "dynamic," "melancholy," "balanced," "taut," or "gay" the aesthetic use of which is quasi-metaphorical. It has already been emphasized that we could not use them thus without some experience of situations where they are used literally. The present inquiry is how we shift from literal to aesthetic uses of them. For this it is required that there be certain abilities and tendencies to link experiences, to regard certain things as similar, and to see, explore, and be interested in these similarities. It is a feature of human intelligence and sensitivity that we do spontaneously do these things and that the tendency can be encouraged and developed. It is no more baffling that we should employ aesthetic terms of this sort than that we should make metaphors at all. Easy and smooth transitions by which we shift to the use of these aesthetic terms are not hard to find. We suggest to children that simple pieces of music are hurrying or running or skipping or dawdling, from there we move to lively, gay, jolly, happy, smiling, or sad, and, as their experiences and vocabulary broaden, to solemn, dynamic, or melancholy. But the child also discovers for himself many of these parallels and takes interest or delight in them. He is likely on his own to skip, march, clap, or laugh with the music, and without this natural tendency our training would get nowhere. Insofar, however, as we do take advantage of this tendency and help him by training, *we do just what the critic does.* We may merely need to persuade the child to pay attention, to look or listen; or we may simply *call* the music jolly. But we are also likely to use, as the critic does, reiteration, synonyms, parallels, contrasts, similes, metaphors, gestures, and other expressive behavior.

Of course the recognition of similarities and simple metaphorical extensions are not the only transitions to the aesthetic use of language. Others are made in different ways; for instance, by the kind of peripheral cases I mentioned earlier. When our admiration is for something as simple as the thinness of a glass or the smoothness of a fabric, it is not difficult to call attention to such things, evoke a similar delight, and introduce suitable aesthetic terms. These transitions are only the beginnings; it may often be questionable whether a term is yet being used aesthetically or not. Many of the terms I have mentioned may be used in ways which are not straightforwardly literal but of which we should hesitate to say that they demanded much yet by way of aesthetic sensitivity. We speak of warm and cool colors, and we may say of a brightly colored picture that at least it is gay and lively. When we have brought someone to make this sort of metaphorical extension of terms, he has made one of the transitional steps from which he may move on to uses which more obviously deserve to be called aesthetic and demand more aesthetic appreciation. When I said at the outset that aesthetic sensitivity was rarer than some other natural endowments, I was not denying that it varies in degree from the rudimentary to the refined. Most people learn easily to make the kinds of remarks I am now considering. But when someone can call bright canvasses gay and lively without being able to spot the one which is really vibrant, or can recognize the obvious outward vigor and energy of a student composition played *con fuoco* while failing to see that it lacks inner fire and drive, we do not regard his aesthetic sensitivity in these areas as particularly developed. However, once these transitions from common to aesthetic uses are begun in the more obvious cases, the domain of aesthetic concepts may broaden out, become more subtle, and even partly autonomous. The initial steps, however varied the metaphorical shifts and however varied the experiences upon which they are parasitic, are natural and easy.

Much the same is true when we turn to those words which have no standard non-aesthetic use, "lovely," "pretty," "dainty," "graceful," "elegant." We cannot say that these are learned by a metaphorical shift. But they still are linked to non-aesthetic features in many ways and the learning of them also is made possible by certain kinds of natural response, reaction, and ability. We learn them not so much by noticing similarities, but by our attention being caught and focussed in other ways. Certain phenomena which are outstanding or remarkable or unusual catch the eye or ear, seize our attention and interest, and move us to surprise, admiration, delight, fear, or distaste. Children begin by reacting in these ways to spectacular sunsets, woods in autumn, roses, dandelions, and other striking and colorful objects, and it is in these circumstances that we find ourselves introducing general aesthetic words like "lovely," "pretty," and "ugly." It is not an accident that the first lessons in aesthetic appreciation consist in drawing the child's attention to roses rather than to grass; nor is it surprising that we remark to him on the autumn colors rather than on the subdued tints of winter, We all of us, not only children, pay aesthetic attention more readily and easily to such outstanding and easily noticeable things. We notice with pleasure early spring grass or the first snow, hills of notably marked and varied contours, scenery flecked with a great variety of color or dappled variously with sun and shadow. We are struck and impressed by great size or mass, as with mountains or cathedrals. We are similarly responsive to unusual precision or minuteness or remarkable feats of skill, as with complex and elaborate filigree, or intricate wood carving and fan-vaulting. It is at these times, taking advantage of these natural interests and admirations, that we first teach the simpler aesthetic words. People of moderate aesthetic sensitivity and sophistication continue to exhibit aesthetic interest mainly on such occasions and to use only the more general words ("pretty," "lovely," and the like). But these situations may serve as a beginning from which we extend our aesthetic interests to wider and less obvious fields, mastering as we go the more subtle and specific vocabulary of taste. The principles do not change; the basis for learning more specific terms like "graceful," "delicate," and "elegant" is also our interest in and admiration for various natural properties ("She seems to move effortlessly, as if floating," "So very thin and fragile, as if a breeze might destroy it," "So small and yet so intricate," "So economical and perfectly adapted").[18] And even with these terms which are not metaphorical themselves, we rely in the same way upon the critic's methods, including comparison, illustration, and metaphor, to teach or make clear what they mean.

I have wished to emphasize in the latter part of this paper the natural basis of responses of various kinds without which aesthetic terms could not be learned. I have also outlined what some of the features are to which we naturally respond: similarities of various sorts, notable colors, shapes, scents, size, intricacy, and much else besides. Even the non-metaphorical aesthetic terms have significant links with all kinds of natural features by which our interest, wonder, admiration, delight, or distaste is aroused. But in particular I have wanted to urge that it should not strike us as puzzling that the critic supports his judgments and brings us to see aesthetic qualities by pointing out key features and talking about them in the way he does. It is by the very same methods that people helped us develop our aesthetic sense and master its vocabulary from the beginning. If we responded to those methods then, it is not surprising that we respond to the critic's discourse now. It would be surprising if, by using this language and behavior, people could *not* sometimes bring us to see the aesthetic qualities of things; for this would prove us lacking in one characteristically human kind of awareness and activity.

Notes

1 I shall speak loosely of an "aesthetic term," even when, because the word sometimes has other uses, it would be more correct to speak of its *use* as an aesthetic term. I shall also speak of "non-aesthetic" words, concepts, features, and so on. None of the terms other writers use, "natural," "observable," "perceptual," "physical," "objective" (qualities), "neutral," "descriptive" (language), when they approach the distinction I am making, is really apt for my purpose.

2 A contrast will reinforce this. If a critic were to describe a passage of music as chattering, carbonated, or gritty, a painter's coloring as vitreous, farinaceous, or effervescent, or a writer's style as glutinous, or abrasive, he *would* be using live metaphors rather than drawing on the more normal language of criticism. Words like "athletic," "vertiginous," "silken" may fall somewhere between.

3 In a paper reprinted in *Aesthetics and Language*, ed. by W. Elton (Oxford, 1954), pp. 131–46, Arnold Isenberg discusses certain problems about aesthetic concepts and qualities. Like others who approach these problems, he does not isolate them, as I do, from questions about verdicts on the *merits* of works of art, or from questions about *likings* and *preferences*. He says something parallel to my remarks above: "There is not in all the world's criticism a single purely descriptive statement concerning which one is prepared to say beforehand, 'if it is true, I shall *like* that work so much the better'" (p. 139, my italics). I should think *this* is highly questionable.

4 Isenberg (op. cit., p. 132) makes a similar point: "If we had been told that the colours of a certain painting are garish, it would be *astonishing* to find that they are *all* very pale and unsaturated" (my italics). But if we say "all" rather than "predominantly," then "astonishing" is the wrong word. What I call "negative conditions" must be distinguished from what I call below features "characteristically" associated or not associated with a taste concept.

5 H. L. A. Hart, "The Ascription of Responsibility and Rights" in *Logic and Language*, First Series, ed. by A. G. N. Flew (Oxford, 1951). Hart indeed speaks of "conditions" throughout, see p. 148.

6 I cannot in the compass of this paper discuss the other types of apparent exceptions to my thesis. Cases where a man *lacking* in sensitivity might learn and follow a rule, as above, ought to be distinguished from cases where someone who *possesses* sensitivity might know, from a non-aesthetic description, that an aesthetic term applies. I have stated my thesis as though this latter kind of case never occurs because I have had my eye on the logical features of *typical* aesthetic judgments and have preferred to over- rather than understate my view. But with certain aesthetic terms, especially negative ones, there may be some rare genuine exceptions when a description enables us to visualize very fully, and when what is described belongs to certain restricted classes of things, say human faces or animal forms. Perhaps a description like "One eye red and rheumy, the other missing, a wart-covered nose, a twisted mouth, a greenish pallor" may justify in a strong sense ("must be," "cannot but be") the judgments "ugly" or "hideous." If so, such cases are marginal, form a very small minority, and are uncharacteristic or atypical of aesthetic judgments in general. Usually when, on hearing a description, we say "it *must* be very beautiful (graceful, or the like)," we mean no more than "it surely must be, it's only remotely possible that it isn't." Different again are situations, and these are very numerous, where we can move quite simply from "bright colors" to "gay," or from "reds and yellows" to "warm," but where we are as yet only on the borderline of anything that could be called an expression of taste or aesthetic sensibility. I have stressed the importance of this transitional and border area between non-aesthetic and obviously aesthetic judgments below.

7 Helen Knight says (Elton, op. cit., p. 152) that "piquant" (one of my "aesthetic" terms) "depends on" various features (a *retroussé* nose, a pointed chin, and the like) and that these features are *criteria* for it; this is what I am denying. She also maintains that "good," when applied to works of art, depends on *criteria* like balance, solidity, depth, profundity (my aesthetic terms again; I should place piquancy in this list). I would deny this too, though I regard it as a different question and do not consider it in this paper. The two questions need separating: the relation of non-aesthetic features (*retroussé*, pointed) to aesthetic qualities, and the relation of aesthetic qualities to "aesthetically good" (verdicts). Most writings which touch on the nature of aesthetic concepts have this other (verdict) question mainly in mind. Mrs. Knight blurs this difference when she says, for example, "'piquant' is the same kind of word as 'good'."

8 See articles by Margaret Macdonald and J. A. Passmore in Elton, op. cit., pp. 118, 41, 40, 119.

9 As I indicated above, I have dealt only with the relation of *non-aesthetic* to aesthetic features. Perhaps a description in aesthetic terms may occasionally suffice for applying another aesthetic term. Johnson's Dictionary gives "handsome" as "beautiful with dignity"; Shorter O. E. D. gives "pretty" as "beautiful in a slight, dainty, or diminutive way."

10 Macdonald in Elton, op. cit., pp. 114, 119. See also pp. 120, 122.

11 Macdonald, ibid., pp. 114, 120–3. She speaks of non-aesthetic properties here as "physical" or "observable" qualities, and distinguishes between "physical object" and "work of art."

12 Ibid., pp. 115–16; cf. also John Holloway, *Proceedings of the Aristotelian Society*, Supplementary Vol. XXIII (1949), pp. 175–6.

13 Stuart Hampshire in Elton, op. cit., p. 165. Cf. also remarks in Elton by Isenberg (pp. 142, 145), Passmore (p. 38), in *Philosophy and Psycho-analysis* by John Wisdom (Oxford, 1953), pp. 223–4, and in Holloway, op. cit., p. 175.

14 Macdonald, op. cit., pp. 119–20.

15 Ibid, see pp. 127, 122, 125, 115. Other writers also place the stress on interpretation, cf. Holloway, op. cit., p. 173ff.

16 Op. cit., pp. 165–8.

17 Holloway, op. cit., pp. 173–4, lists some of these very briefly.

18 It is worth noticing that most of the words which in current usage are primarily or exclusively aesthetic terms had earlier non-aesthetic uses and gained their present use by some kind of metaphorical shift. Without reposing too great weight on these etymological facts, it can be seen that their history reflects connections with the responses, interests, and natural features I have mentioned as underlying the learning and use of aesthetic terms. These transitions suggest both the dependence of aesthetic upon other interests, and what some of these interests are. Connected with liking, delight, affection, regard, estimation, or choice – *beautiful, graceful, delicate, lovely, exquisite, elegant, dainty*; with fear or repulsion – *ugly*; with what notably catches the eye or attention – *garish, splendid, gaudy*; with what attracts by notable rarity, precision, skill, ingenuity, elaboration – *dainty, nice, pretty, exquisite*; with adaptation to function, suitability to ease of handling – *handsome*.

44

Beauty Restored

Mary Mothersill

Mary Mothersill is Professor Emerita of Philosophy at Barnard College, Columbia University.

11. Under the titles respectively of 'criteria' and 'good-making characteristics', principles of taste and laws of taste coexist in an uneasy symbiosis: if one were scotched the other could not long survive. The truth, as it seems to me, is that there are not and never will be any laws of taste. Since principles of taste are, by hypothesis, normative principles, it does not follow that there are no principles of taste. But once belief in principles of taste is deprived of the support provided by imagined laws, its force is weakened, It has nothing to sustain it except the unexamined modal argument that forces a choice between principles of taste and skepticism (or subjectivism).

Nothing that would count as a strict proof of my negative thesis could be immune to the charge of question-begging. What is needed is a hypothesis that has disconfirmation-conditions, and the one I shall defend is that nobody believes in laws of taste. Of course, to make my case persuasive, I must in the first place show how one might be led to acquiesce in what one did not believe and, second, explain why the mere *possibility* of laws of taste, of truths yet to be discovered, seems attractive. Let me try, by expanding on the account offered earlier, to make the conception as plausible as possible by imposing some restrictions. In contrast with, say, the patellar reflex, aesthetic response is conditioned by such factors as the education, background, and sensibilities of the subject. This means that there will have to be two universal quantifiers, and though it doesn't matter which comes first, let us begin by defining the population for which a law might hold, and let us assume that we have agreed on a non-circular specification of requirements for being a 'qualified subject'. Let us further take it as given that an item can become a cause of pleasure to S only in the context of some appropriate activity: novels must be read, music listened to, and so forth. Let us, out of deference to convention, assume that the objects in question are works of art or works of art in a specified medium or genre. These, after all, are at the center of the controversy; the 'good-making characteristics' of cloud formations, seashells, or sunsets are not often in dispute, and someone who was willing to agree that preferences among natural phenomena are not governed by law might feel that the important question had not been broached.

A law of taste, then, would have the form: 'For all S (S being a qualified subject), any x (where x is a work of art, a poem, a sonata, etc.) that has property ϕ will be *pro tanto* a cause of pleasure to

Mary Mothersill, "The First Thesis," in *Beauty Restored* (Oxford: Oxford University Press, 1986), pp. 100–22.

S.' The *'pro tanto'* qualification is important because it recognizes the fact that one and the same work of art may please in some respect and displease in another; it allows room for critical deliberation, the weighing of virtues against defects which precedes the all-things-considered verdict. Let us assume that I (MM) am a qualified subject in the areas of, say, music and literature: a law of taste with the appropriate scope would then predict my likes and dislikes. The hypothesis 'Work *O*, since it has property ϕ, will be liked by MM' is confirmed or disconfirmed on the occasion of the presentation of *O* to me. Although my smiles, applause, yawns, or fidgeting may be noted by my companions, I am in a privileged position with respect to confirmation and so well situated to discover the laws that determine my preferences and (by extension) the preferences of others who satisfy the 'qualified subject' requirement. It need not be assumed that I have insight into the *basis* of my disposition to be pleased by works of art that are ϕ: half-forgotten influences, childhood conditioning, or unconscious wishes may be involved. It is my own pleasure that is accessible to introspection: the psychogenesis of my susceptibility is a different story. But this poses no special problem: a law may be well established even though (as Hume keeps insisting) its 'secret springs' remain hidden. The question I need to consider is whether my tastes in music and in literature can be generalized in a way that would qualify them as law-governed.

There is certainly *something* that I learn from past experiences – something that I use in making the predictions that guide my present choice. Flipping a coin is not the usual way of deciding what novel to buy or what concert to attend. I seem to draw on the knowledge that is characterized by C. I. Lewis as 'knowing what one likes.'

> The wise man is he who knows where good lies, and knows how to act so that it may be attained. Even to know what one likes is a form of knowledge. Whether knowing what one likes is veridical knowledge of objective values or not, is a matter calling for further consideration. But without prejudice to that question, it may be observed that one who knows what he likes possesses that kind of knowledge which consists in the ability to predict the accrual or non-accrual, under given conditions, of value-quality in his own experience. One who knows, for example, that he likes Bach and dislikes Stravinsky, may be as great a musical ignoramus as anyone chooses to allege, but when he looks at the concert program, he knows what to expect. His value-prediction has verifiable content and possesses genuine cognitive significance.[1]

Let me imagine myself in the situation that Lewis describes and ask whether what I know in 'knowing what I like' gives me 'the ability to predict the accrual or non-accrual, under given conditions, of value-quality in my own experience'. In what sense is it true that when I look at the concert program, I 'know what to expect'? Suppose that all the program says is 'Music by Bach'. I might say to myself, 'In that case, I'll like it since it will comprise some or others of the following: the Two Part Inventions, the Three Part Inventions, the Mass in B Minor, the Italian Concerto . . .' (I know the entire corpus.) But whatever its reliability as a basis for prediction, the generalization here is not a law because it is not lawlike. It does not warrant an inference to unfamiliar pieces since by hypothesis there are none. Nor does it support counterfactuals on the order of 'If *Le Sacre du Printemps* had been written by Bach, I would have liked it'. Let us assume, then, that my generalization is based on samples: I have heard and enjoyed some but not all of Bach's music. Then there is a problem with the antecedent: the music I enjoyed in the past was described as having been composed by Bach, but typographer's errors are possible and there are (so I am told) genuine disputes over attribution. (Let's say that some pieces credited to Bach are really by Telemann.) Ought I in that case revise the antecedent to 'If I *believe* that a piece of music was composed by Bach, then I'm sure I'll like it?' (Someone else might make that claim about me, but it would be understood as a sort of Pavlovian joke: 'She salivates every time she hears the phrase "by Bach".') There is a further difficulty: accurate, first-personal prediction is not the only function imagined for laws of taste. Those who talk of 'good-making characteristics' envisage situations in which I can *account* for my pleasure in speaking to a neophyte, someone who is in the process of becoming a qualified subject. Imagine that other person to be Colette; she listens to Bach, and the phrase that comes to her mind is 'a musical sewing-machine'. I want to explain to her why I like that music and 'because I have every reason to believe that it was written by Bach' is not going to help. For one thing, she already knows that: her interest (if it exists) is in knowing what there is in the music that anyone could find to like. By the same token, she will not be impressed by a purely autobiographical explanation, like 'It was the first piece I ever learned to play. I adored my piano teacher, etc.'

Any statement, including any generalization, that purports to relate an affect to its cause is, in an obvious sense, a 'psychological' claim, but although works of art may be made to serve a diagnostic function (the 'subject' may be an individual or, as for archaeologists, a vanished culture), in less special circumstances the focus of attention and the center of interest are in the work of art as distinct from the mental idiosyncrasies of a particular perceiver or of the artist who created it.

And yet (to go back to 'knowing what one likes') it does seem that, provided I have relatively stable tastes, a consistent pattern of successful prediction suggests that there is lawlike generalization in the offing. Imagine that, acting on the belief that it was written by Bach, I listen to a piece of music and, as I predicted, it pleases me. I subsequently discover that experts are divided: some say Telemann was the composer and others say Pachelbel. Since, in any event, I *did* like it, perhaps I should revise my hypothesis to read, 'If it is by Bach or Telemann or Pachelbel, then I'm sure it will please me.' This suggests a way around the previous difficulty, since there are features that are common to the music of these three composers – harmonic, contrapuntal, and structural similarities that define baroque music. Perhaps it is among these features that I should look for a value for ϕ. They have been identified and analyzed by musicologists and might simply be listed in the antecedent of my conditional, which will now promise that any work in the baroque 'style' is a work that I will like. But though my generalization is now lawlike, it begins to look unpromising as a basis for prediction. The characteristics of baroque music are easy to reproduce: composition students learn early on how to write polyphony, and computers can be programmed to turn out an unlimited and indefinitely various number of 'compositions' that meet the requirements. Do my recollected experiences of Bach (or Telemann or Pachelbel) give me any reason at *all* to think that I will enjoy whatever the computer offers me? Lewis is right on one point: I do know 'what to expect'; what I don't know is whether the expected, once it arrives, will please me. That is to say that my powers fail at the crucial point, namely 'the ability to predict the accrual or non-accrual of value-quality' in my own experience.

But mightn't there be persons who just *do* like *any* music as long as it is in the baroque style? It is not impossible, but I have never met such a person. What is true is that getting to know music of a particular period takes time and patience. As a novice, I may find a certain style congenial and yet be unable to tell one composer – even one piece – from another, unable to distinguish Bach from 'Bach-type' computer music. We learn from experience. (It once seemed to me that Elizabethan drama was marvelous; but then after a certain amount of time spent on Webster, Marlowe, Peele, *et al.*, it came to me that what I had thought was Elizabethan was really Shakespearean, and later still that it was clearly identifiable only in three plays.) But suppose that my musical or literary education had been, for one reason or another, arrested and that I had never gone beyond the stage of liking anything in the baroque style or any tale of violence projected with flamboyant imagery in iambic pentameter. Wouldn't I then be entitled to affirm on the basis of evidence a lawlike generalization concerning my own taste?

The question is complicated: let us change the example and suppose (since Bach and Shakespeare cloud the picture) that what I like is detective stories. At the airport newstand I morosely survey the paperbacks, and it is borne in on me that Agatha Christie is dead. I note, however, that P. D. James is touted as one who has 'inherited the crown' and this moves me to buy two of her books. They turn out to be pretty good – lead to an 'accrual of value-quality' in experience – but nonetheless disappointing. My expectations with respect to the genre are fulfilled; there is the murder, the detective, the suspects, the false clues, and so forth, and yet something vital is missing. Hard to pin down: perhaps it is James's rather heavy forays into depth psychology or maybe a tendency to dwell in a non-Agatha-

Christie manner on the grislier of the grisly details. Not, in any event, what I had hoped for, but how shall I word the prediction that led to my choice? 'If *Death of a Nightingale* is a detective story and has that specially pleasing Agatha-Christie quality, then I will like it.' But here the generalization, although lawlike, is uninteresting: what it amounts to is that if a detective story resembles detective stories I have enjoyed in respect of my enjoying it, then I will enjoy it. How about, 'If it's a detective story, I'm bound to like it'? But that is something I do not believe, nor will it help to add a *pro tanto* modifier. (I have read *bona fide* detective stories that were irredeemably boring and awful.) The only way to save the *pro tanto* version is to make *it* uninteresting: 'If there is even one quality that pleases me, then the work will please me to some extent.'

The test for my general hypothesis is as follows: try to come up with a lawlike generalization about your own preferences and ask yourself (a) whether it is interesting, and (b) if it is, whether you actually believe it. My own findings are entirely negative. That the test be in the first person is important: a curious snobbery persuades us that while we ourselves are sensitive and complex creatures, other people's likes and dislikes are thoroughly routine and easily predictable. There are laws of taste, in other words, but they don't apply to me. This odd belief may owe something to the fact that in the art world and the world of entertainment, there are discernable fashions and trends. Movie makers and clothes designers hire market-research experts to study opinion samples and make projections which enable the producers to anticipate and cater to what the public appears to want. The resulting generalizations, whether or not they are dignified by the title 'laws', are not adapted to serving the purposes that Lewis had in mind. Suppose it is established that in a certain month a significant percentage of movie-goers describe *Jaws II* as 'highly enjoyable'. One *might* reason, 'Since I'm an average sort of person, I'll probably enjoy it too,' but such an inference, shaky at best, is not based on 'knowing what I like', in the sense that Lewis intends the phrase.

The temptation to believe that other people can make successful predictions based on laws of taste may originate in a second way: suppose that you and I are adventurous eclectics: we like to submit ourselves to what is novel, 'experimental', *avant-garde.* We perceive that there are many who have no such urge and whose tastes are restricted in range. A man, say, may read nothing but detective stories or, having heard part of a piece by Stravinsky, decide not to listen to any more Stravinsky. Both may make choices in accord with a policy, but the policy is not a law of taste. The detective-story addict does not say, 'As long as it's a detective story, I'll enjoy it,' but rather, 'Unless it's a detective story, I won't read it.' Since *we* can predict his choices, we imagine that *he* is making successful predictions about the 'accrual of value-quality' in his experience. But, of course, that need not be true; he might enjoy some much more than others or perhaps not really 'enjoy' any of them. (Reading can serve as an analgesic.) The snobbishness comes in thinking of persons who have a narrow range of preference in the way that Descartes thought of animals, namely as if they were machines.

One last try at explaining 'knowing what one likes' in a way that would make it plausible to think of first-personal predictions as based on laws of taste. Instead of considering particular composers whose work I have liked in the past or definable *kinds* of music, imagine that, checking the concert program, I say, 'Since it's the *B Minor Mass,* I know that I'll like it.' People say such things, and what could be a better reason for going to a concert? But what is the law that I here appeal to? Is it that *anything* that qualifies as a performance of the *B Minor Mass* will please me? No one could seriously hold such a belief. In the passage I have been trying to interpret, Lewis speaks of predicting the 'accrual of value-quality' under 'given conditions'. What he means is 'optimal conditions'; and, as far as I can see, there is no way of spelling out, or even sketching, the optimal conditions which will not result in an uninteresting law. Think of the things that could go wrong: the conductor is drunk; my feet hurt; the intonation of the strings is off; the person beside me snores; a fire breaks out . . . I will enjoy it *Deo volente,* if 'all goes well', which is to say that I will enjoy it unless some one or another of indefinitely numerous contingencies prevents me from enjoying it. But then how to account for the grain of truth in what Lewis says? Although it is true that my knowledge (in the sense of acquaintance) of the *B Minor Mass* is grounded in remembered performances, the lawlike generalization that quantifies over performances is, as I have suggested, either an uninteresting law or one that no sane person would believe. It would be better to think of my reasoning as based, not on any law, but on projection of a particular judgment of taste under its avowal aspect. 'The *B Minor Mass* is beautiful (has artistic merit, etc.) implicates (tenselessly) 'It gives me pleasure.' Remembered pleasure fosters hope, and it is hope, in contrast with prediction on the basis of law, that guides my choice. 'It's the *B Minor Mass*' articulates one plausible *kind* of reason for attending a concert. (It can't be the *only* kind: otherwise none of us would have got any further than '*Twinkle, Twinkle, Little Star*'.) The education of taste is possible because there are reasons for choice other than 'knowing what one likes'. There are many such reasons: simple curiosity about another time or culture, boredom with the familiar – through overexposure Bach does begin to *sound* to me like a 'musical sewing-machine'. Then there are the enthusiasms of my friends or my heroes. (Young men on the Grand Tour would make a point of following in the footsteps of Goethe, to stand at the very spots from which he had admired the view.) We might be inclined to think that anticipation of pleasure based on hearsay (or superstition) is a less reliable guide than anticipation based on recollected pleasure. The truth is that both are so unreliable that comparisons are pointless. Stanley Cavell speaks of the element of risk involved in 'submitting ourselves' to modernist art,[2] but the risk is endemic: how important disappointment seems depends on the level of our expectation and the extent of our investment. Sometimes it may be no more than a wasted afternoon. But it could be significant; I might spend five years learning Greek in order to read the *Iliad* only to find it, in the end, a bore. (In his travel diary, Herbert Spencer wrote: 'Visited Niagara Falls; exactly as anticipated.' Why does this strike us as funny?)

12. In 'Psychology as Philosophy' (1974) Donald Davidson draws a distinction which can be extended to the present context. He argues that although a particular action can be displayed as intentional by citing the beliefs and desires that were its cause, it is not possible to specify in general the conditions that are necessary and sufficient for an action's being intentional. As a consequence, there can be, as he puts it, no 'serious' laws connecting reasons and actions.

> By a serious law, I mean more than a statistical generalization (the statistical laws of physics are serious because they give sharply fixed probabilities, which spring from the nature of the theory); it must be a law that, while it may have provisos limiting its application, allows us to determine in advance whether or not the conditions of application are satisfied. It is an error to compare a truism like 'If a man wants to eat an acorn omlette, then he generally will if the opportunity exists and no other desire overrides' with a law that says how fast a body will fall in a vacuum. It is an error, because in the latter case but not in the former, we can tell in advance whether the condition holds, and we know what allowance to make if it doesn't.[3]

My suggestion is that there are no laws of taste that are serious: some people are partial to baroque music (or to Bach), some to detective stories (or to Agatha Christie). Such a bias will express itself naturally in choosing what we listen to or what we read, and the choice will involve the anticipation or the hope of pleasure. But nothing I have learned from past experience gives me grounds for saying in advance of a work by Bach or of a detective story that provided it manifests a particular feature, I will be pleased by it. In the recent literature, Arnold Isenberg was the first to state this point clearly. In 1949 he wrote:

> There is not in all the world's criticism a single purely descriptive statement concerning which one is prepared to say beforehand, 'If it is true, I shall like that work so much the better.'[4]

But perhaps, as pro-theorists like to argue, it is just a matter of time, and once the data are more thoroughly analyzed, what Lewis calls 'the positive science of aesthetics' will emerge.

> [I]t is an obvious fact – and no criticism of anybody need be read into the observation of it – that the science of aesthetics remains largely undeveloped. Subsidiary principles – 'principles of composition' in one or another of the fine arts – are available in considerable number and are fairly well attested. But these are about the only

> positive content of it which is presently assured. As has been observed, there is not even as yet any general agreement amongst aestheticians as to the categories in terms of which such positive 'laws should be formulated.[5]

In a footnote Lewis adds the comment:

> It is of course true that particular aesthetic judgments do not necessarily wait upon the development of the positive science, nor presume command of it. In any field, the development of the positive science requires an antecedently determined body of particular truths. There were correct logical judgments before Aristotle, geometrical determinations before Euclid, and attested physical facts before Galileo and Newton. Had there not been, these positive sciences could never have arisen.[6]

But the analogy here is not quite right: Socrates knew (and sometimes exploited) the difference between a good argument and a bad one; Aristotle abstracted from rules observed in practice, gave them names and developed their consequences in a systematic way. No subsequent argument has satisfied the Aristotelian conditions for being a valid argument, without being valid. Aristotle also recognized that *Oedipus Rex* had great dramatic merit, and in seeking to analyze the sources of its power was led to formulate precepts for the aspiring dramatist. The results, although they improve our understanding of Sophocles and of Greek tragedy in general, do not have anything analogous to the status that belongs to the rules for valid argument. In speaking of 'subsidiary principles', Lewis may have had Aristotle's suggestions in mind. But Lewis is mistaken in saying that such 'principles of composition' are 'fairly well attested': it is a truism of literary history that Aristotelian 'correctness' is compatible with artistic failure and that there are dramatic masterworks, such as *Antony and Cleopatra*, that flatly contravene the 'rules'.

'But of course', someone might say, 'a work of genius transcends the rules', thus invoking a picture credited to the Romantics – its actual origins are neo-classical or earlier – in which conformity to 'principles of composition' will guarantee a modicum of success (measured in terms of the 'accrual of value-quality' in experience) while allowing for the occasional prodigy, the artist whose extraordinary and inexplicable powers enable (and entitle) him to 'snatch a grace beyond the reach of art'. Every 'positive science', it might be argued, has to live with phenomena that 'defy explanation'; pharmacology thrives despite the fact that it cannot explain the benign effects of salicylic acid. (The ancients chewed on willow-leaves; we ingest aspirin by the megaton.) But the picture is false to the facts: audiences derive pleasure from, say *Jaws II*; audiences (not necessarily an exclusive disjunction) derive pleasure from *Oedipus Rex*. The former phenomenon is not less but *more* mysterious than the latter. (*Jaws* itself if a puzzle; why should anyone want more of the same? And why do we take it for granted that appeal to a low taste is transparent?) In *Oedipus*, by contrast, there is, as far as causes of pleasure are concerned, an embarrassment of riches: there is the poetry – in itself it could redeem a weak plot – and then, what might have survived less exhilarating poetry, the plot, and the 'character' – in short those elements which Aristotle found worth noting. And here is a second way in which the Lewis analogy is off target: not only are there 'antecedently determined' truths in the history of the arts, there are (without benefit of 'positive science') accepted accounts of what, in particular cases, does the determining; take Aristotle's analysis of *Oedipus*. Isenberg, in the paper cited above, puts the point well:

> Most of us believe that the idea of progress applies to science, does not apply to art, applies in some unusual and not very clear sense, to philosophy. What about criticism? Are there 'discoveries' and 'contributions' in this field? Is it reasonable to expect better evaluations of art after a thousand years of investigation than before? The question is not a simple one: it admits of different answers on different interpretations. But I do think that some critical judgments have been and are every day being 'proved' as well as in the nature of the case they can be proved. I think we have already numerous passages which are not to be corrected or improved upon. And if this opinion is right, then it could not be the case that the validation of critical judgments waits upon the discovery of aesthetic laws.[7]

In summary, the idea that there are laws of taste yet to be discovered encounters two obstacles: (i) candidate laws prove to be either uninteresting or readily disconfirmed; (ii) the claims of particular judgments of taste have been 'validated' in the sense that particular critical passages are acknowledged to offer insight into what, in a particular work, causes our pleasure.

Isenberg thinks it is at least possible to *imagine* a law of taste and to see that if there were one, it would be of no critical use:

> Let us suppose even that we *had* some law which stated that a certain color combination, a certain melodic sequence, a certain type of dramatic hero has everywhere and always a positive emotional effect. To the extent that this law holds, there is, of course, that much less disagreement in criticism; but there is no better method for resolving disagreement. We are not more fully convinced in our own judgment because we know its explanation; and we cannot hope to convince an imaginary opponent by appealing to this explanation, which by hypothesis does not hold for him.[8]

I am not so sure that the supposition can be made intelligible: suppose that the preferred color combination is red and green and that it can be represented by reference to the color cone as RG. If it has 'always and everywhere a positive emotional effect', then its power must be independent of say, belief contexts; perception of RG causes pleasure in the way that taking drugs causes pleasure, and this seems remote from the conception of a law of *taste*. But suppose it came to pass? How would we respond? Would all houses and cars be painted RG? Would we never get tired, or cease to notice it? Would timid artists eschew a wider palette? (Perhaps RG would be used to redeem weak painting as depictions of kittens and sad-eyed waifs are used.) In any event, Isenberg is right about the consequences for criticism: we would be no better off than we are. If of two RG paintings one causes more pleasure than the other, then the explanation must lie in differences of composition, form, execution, and the like. If even a tiny little RG area was a 'good-making characteristic' then some increment of pleasure needs no explanation and calls for no comment.

Principles of taste have been supposed to provide logical support for the judgment of taste under its normative aspect, that is, considered as a verdict. If there are no (serious) laws of taste, then Beardsley's account in which by specifying a 'good-making characteristic' one provides *ipso facto* a 'criterion' or a 'good reason', cannot be correct. On the other hand, the elision of the causal and the criterial which Beardsley leaves unexplained, invites the Humean question about deriving an 'ought' from an 'is'. If, as I have been supposing, laws of taste are imagined to be causal laws, straightforwardly descriptive, then, even if there were such laws, the question of principles or 'criteria' would remain open. Conversely, from the fact (as it seems) that there are no laws of taste it does not follow that there are no principles of taste. (In parallel: that there are no laws of motivation does not entail that no moral principles are valid.) Nonetheless, once the distinction between laws and principles is sharpened, the question of how alleged principles of taste acquire their authority becomes a pressing question. If property ø is randomly distributed over works of art that please me and fail to please me, why should I allow a principle to the effect that ø is a virtue in works of art to figure as a premise in my critical reasoning?

Notice that the statistical generalizations mentioned in the preceding section are of no help: that works with property ø are liked by 70 per cent of a given population provides at best grounds for a chancy forecast. It does not provide what Lewis has in mind when he speaks of a principle by reference to which we may 'recognize the aesthetically valuable in cases of doubt'.

One instant (but drastic) remedy is available: one might, following Santayana, discount the term 'verdict' as a courtesy title and claim that the substance of the judgment of taste is exhausted in the avowal that, on our present assumptions, it implicates. Independent of whether there are or are not laws of taste, principles of taste are then displayed as pure sham; to enunciate a 'principle' is simply to project one's own spontaneous and 'ultimately irrational' impulse.[9] But Santayana, as has been noted, offers neither arguments nor evidence in support of a thesis which, as he himself acknowledges, runs counter to everyday beliefs. If we take the normative aspects of the judgment of taste at face value and allow the term 'verdict' to stand – if, further, we assume with the pro-theorists that all 'good reasons' must have the deductive backing of principles of taste, then we will have to sever the link between verdicts and avowals. I may reason my way to a favorable verdict of *O* by showing that *O* exhibits 'criterial feature' ø and leave completely open the question of whether *O* is a cause of pleasure to me. There are indeed philosophers who are prepared to accept this consequence. Joseph Margolis writes:

> If I judge a particular work of art to be good, I am bound, on demand, to supply the justifying reasons; I have not yet supplied them in issuing the judgment. But if the justifying reasons are admitted to be true, and to be the proper sort of reasons sufficient for the finding, one cannot withhold the finding on presentation of the reasons.[10]

However:

> The finding or judgment (or verdict) is not an expression of taste and is only contingently related to our actual taste . . . It is altogether conceivable that one likes what one judges to be artistically poor or fails to appreciate what one knows to be excellent.[11]

What Margolis says is not exactly false but, so to speak, out of touch. I am *not* obligated to produce a justification, still less a 'proof' for every judgment that I make; how *could* I be? I do, on occasion, try to show what it is about a particular work that leads me to think it a good work of art, but unless I *liked* the work in question, this exercise would be bizarre. Much that is nonstandard is no doubt 'conceivable', but the question opens complicated issues that extend beyond aesthetics, and jauntiness is out of place. A plain truth may be dismaying to a degree that blocks acceptance: an obligation may be genuine and yet perceived in context as one that ought not to be discharged. Our affective life, no less than our cognitive and practical, is full of hesitation, missteps and obliquities: a complex work of art judged good on the whole may have its defective, disturbing aspects. Our taste in general is apt to be in various degrees corrupt; we have, and may know that we have, certain blind spots; age may impair capacity so that, like Wordsworth, we recollect a beauty in what no longer has the power to please.

> It is not now as it hath been of yore; –
> Turn wheresoe'er I may,
> By night or day,
> The things which I have seen I now can see no more.[12]

But to speak of confusion, mistake or loss is to presume a norm, and the norm surely is to judge beautiful what one finds beautiful, and to find something beautiful is to find it a source of pleasure. (Consider Kant's wild rose or the simple melodic line of Schubert's *Lindenbaum*: ask yourself whether you can make sense of the notion of judging beautiful what you yourself find boring or repellent.)

Like other pro-theorists, Margolis cannot think of any examples of 'good reasons'. Thus, although he claims that such reasons provide 'fairly clear-cut criteria that are decisive',[13] yet

> the central difficulty in evaluation, even in evaluation by professionals, seems to be that, apart from applying academic canons, evaluating works of art is characteristically informal, in the sense that one cannot say in advance what the appropriate *set* of criteria is for evaluating this or that object.[14]

Criteria that cannot be specified 'in advance' are, one might think, no criteria. Nonetheless the incoherence is instructive and suggests a possibility which I shall explore at the beginning of the following section.

In summary: Kant thought that the *First Thesis* [*FT*], namely that there are no principles of taste, could be established on grounds that are completely *a priori*, as perhaps it can. I have been trying to show that by following an indirect route one can arrive at Kant's destination with a minimum of theoretical apparatus. I argue that there are no serious laws of taste and that, without laws, the conception of principles (or criteria) assumes an unattractively arbitrary aspect. There is the added fact that those who believe there *must* be principles have not been able to say what they are, even though we are given to understand that they are in continual use. Finally, I would say, as of laws of taste, that no one believes (really believes) in principles of taste. In his informal moments, Kant himself appeals to experience and observation. Thus:

> If anyone reads me his poem, or brings me to a play, which, all said and done, fails to commend itself to my taste, then let him adduce Batteux or Lessing, or still older and more famous critics of taste, with all the host of rules laid down by them, as a proof of the beauty of his poem; let certain passages particularly displeasing to me accord completely with the rules of beauty (as set out by these critics and universally recognized): I stop my ears: I do not want to hear any reasons or any arguments about the matter. I would prefer to suppose that those rules of the critics were at fault, or at least have no application, than to allow my judgment to be determined by *a priori* proofs.[15]

Again:

> There can . . . be no rule according to which anyone is able to be compelled to recognize anything as beautiful. Whether a dress, a house, or a flower is beautiful is a matter upon which one declines to allow one's judgment to be swayed by any reasons or principles. We want to get a look at the Object with our own eyes, just as if our delight depended on sensation.[16]

Kant presents *FT* as an *a priori* truth, as obvious to the layman as to the philosopher. The layman simply rejects appeal to principles; the philosopher sees that the very idea of a principle of taste involves contradiction. What responses on the part of the layman are typical is a matter of observation, and in my opinion Kant's finding is correct. But the second, stronger claim needs reasoned support. From one point of view the whole of the 'First Part' of the *Third Critique* provides what is called for: once you realize how it is that the domain of taste is an autonomous domain and you see why the claims of the judgment of taste need a transcendental deduction – in short, once you have grasped Kant's aesthetic theory, the *FT* will be recognized as a necessary truth, one that someone who accepts the theory cannot consistently deny. The trouble is that Kant's theory, as even the most sympathetic reader must admit, is not *self-evidently* adequate: there are real problems of interpretation and a number of unresolved ambiguities. (Paul Guyer has argued persuasively that Kant is addressing two different questions, one logical, the other psychological, and that some of the obscurities of his argument come from his attempt to deal with them simultaneously.) Moreover, it was only rather late in his career that Kant himself realized that the perplexities of aesthetics call for formal philosophical treatment. His earlier view had been that there are *no* interesting *a priori* truths, that empirical generalizations are all that is possible and all that is required. (Whether Kant entertained the possibility of actual 'laws of taste' in the sense in which I understand the term is not clear to me.) However that may be, to claim that *FT* is not merely true but *necessarily* true is to assume a burden of proof – one that I would just as soon decline. In support of *FT* I want to argue that attempts to deny it have an unmistakably hollow ring: nobody believes – really believes – either in principles or in laws of taste. The reader may think that my claim is no less high-handed than Kant's. What about the philosophers who appear to be committed, either explicitly or (like the anti-theorists) through inadvertence, to laws and principles of taste? I grant the powerful impression that no good will ever come of a proposal that leans on the distinction between 'believes' and 'really believes' and will try not to lean on it. I have no clear view of the limits of 'possible' belief or of epistemic logic in general. All I can do is cast a shadow of doubt.

13. Let us consider Kant's modal version of *FT* according to which a principle of taste that supports an inference to a judgment of taste is 'absolutely impossible'. Two kinds of counterclaim might count as denials, one the contrary, the other, the contradictory of *FT*. The contrary would be the claim that inference-supporting principles, far from being impossible, are necessary. The contradictory would be the claim that since there are in fact principles of taste in use, sanctioning inferences acknowledged as valid, it cannot be that principles of taste are 'impossible'. The parallel counterclaims with respect to laws of taste would be (i) there *must* be laws of taste (although perhaps yet to be discovered), and (ii) there *is* a law of taste, namely *L*, which is widely acknowledged, which explains (or predicts) affective response.

The reasons adduced in support of the contrary of *FT* can be briefly summarized: (i) There must be principles of taste since otherwise every verdict would have equal status and every work of art equal value – an unacceptable consequence. To reject subjectivism is *ipso facto* to acknowledge principles of taste. (ii) Critical description of a work of art is selective, for example, mentions 'complex formal structure' but not 'weight or insurable value'. Where there is selection there must be a reason for selection, and the reason must be that the features mentioned are taken to be *prima facie* 'criterial features', that is, principles of taste. Thus every remark about a work of art 'presupposes' principles of taste (and hence 'presupposes' a theory) even if the critic in question does not acknowledge or does not know what the principles are.[17] The argument for laws of taste follows the same pattern: if there are no laws, then every positive affective response, for example, every case of someone's being pleased by a work of art, would be inexplicable – an unacceptable consequence which runs counter to the assumption that every event has a cause. And further, critics do offer explanations of the powers of works of art to affect the viewer or hearer, and hence laws of taste, even if undiscovered, are 'presupposed'. The first argument for principles and laws depends on the assumption that in each case there is one and only one alternative and that that alternative is unacceptable. But none of the authors I have mentioned gives any reason at all for the assumption; in the case of principles it is supposed to be *evident* that either aesthetics is the exact counterpart of ethics or it is nothing. Therefore the argument is unconvincing. The second line – what might be called the 'M. Jourdain argument' – is sophistic in the way in which Hampshire's appeal to the unavoidability of choice is sophistic, and cannot but strike us as somewhat silly. It does not, of course, follow from the fact that an argument is defective that its conclusion is false, still less that its conclusion is not believed.

But let us consider what it *is* to believe that there must be principles and laws of taste. What is most striking, as has been noted, is the reluctance on the part of those who hold the view to cite any examples. In the case of laws, there is at least a surface plausibility to the notion that laws of taste, when finally formulated, will be the consequences of very sophisticated neurophysiological theories which are still in the making. But that won't work for principles: some critical verdicts, we are told, are in fact justified; no justification is possible save by reference to principle, but no single example of a justifying principle can be given. (Imagine, by way of analogy, someone who held that moral decisions are familiar occurrences, that no decision is possible except by reference to moral principles, but who claimed that because of the 'complexity of the subject matter' it is not possible to cite any moral principle.)

It seems to me, in short, that what is presented as the contrary to *FT* is a belief that lacks content. One can conjecture that in the background lurk some true and sensible thoughts, such as that an aesthetic theory, as a theory, must provide principles of some sort and that part of the task of a theory would be to give an account of the procedures by which judgments of taste are justified or validated (or imagined to be justified or validated). But such sensible reflections are not inconsistent with *FT* and so cannot count as contraries.

As for the alleged contradictory of *FT*, we can turn to Beardsley, the most candid and forthcoming of the pro-theorists. A critic, he observes, might say that 'grandeur of imagery' is a 'good-making feature' of Wordsworth's *Ode: Intimations of Immortality*, and that 'vagueness of theme' is one of its defects.[18] Beardsley asks us to consider whether, supposing we accept the critic's claim, we are not committed to the generalizations 'Grand imagery is always a merit in poetry' and 'Vague themes are always a defect in poetry'. Drawing on the distinction – one that he might be persuaded to admit – examples are to be thought of as candidate laws, laying down conditions with respect to the 'accrual of value-quality in experience'. As laws, they are uninteresting: there is no procedure that could confirm the truth of 'The imagery is grand' that would not simultaneously confirm 'There is at least something in this poem that pleases me.' Were the imagery, though large-scale, displeasing, it would be characterized not as 'grand', but as 'overblown' or 'grandiose'. Now to every uninteresting law of taste there corresponds what I shall call an 'innocuous' principle of taste. Thus if Beardsley's generalizations are construed as principles, what is proposed is that if the imagery of a poem has the merit of grandeur, then the poem as a whole has some merit. Such a criterion can never lead us astray; what satisfies the antecedent satisfies the consequent. There are various conceptions of belief, and perhaps some would allow a place in my catalogue of beliefs for uninteresting laws and innocuous principles. (If the principle of identity is included, why not?) On the other hand, 'believes *p*' is contrasted with 'disbelieves *p*' or 'believes *not-p*', and it isn't clear that those expressions have any application in this case – which is to say that we don't know what belief in an innocuous principle of taste *amounts to* and hence we may doubt whether such a belief should be described as a belief in the contradictory of *FT*.

Of course, one may not *see* that a principle of taste is innocuous. (On first inspection, 'Where there is no property, there is no theft,' might be taken as a summary of anturopological findings.) How could something that seems so obvious be overlooked? I believe that the explanation is as follows: in contrast with the generalizations to which they are supposed to commit us, the two claims about the Wordsworth *Ode*, namely that grandeur of imagery is one of its merits and vagueness of theme one of its defects, are *not* uninteresting. Indeed, I would argue that both are false: vagueness of theme is not a defect in the *Ode,* for the theme is not vague; it is in clear and poignant focus. The imagery, on the other hand, strikes me as unimpressive. 'Grandeur', a term that fits the imagery of, say, *Samson Agonistes* or *Antony and Cleopatra,* seems entirely out of place in application to Wordsworth. I disagree with Beardsley, but our disagreement is surely closer to a disagreement on a point of fact than on a matter of principle. (It is not as if he believed in truth-telling while I believed nothing more virtuous than a successful lie, we do not live in different worlds.) Indeed, we agree that the *Ode* is a successful poem: it is just that what he sees as a redeeming feature I see as in need of redemption. There is no reason to think the difference irresolvable; if he were interested, I think I could persuade him that my view is correct.

Critical debate allows for significant differences, and it is only when these are misrepresented as oppositions of principle that triviality ensues. What masks the triviality is the proviso – a point on which all concerned are most emphatic – that a feature becomes 'good-making' only in context and the 'reason' that cites the feature a 'good reason' only *pro tanto.* Thus Beardsley writes:

> It does not seem that the contribution of each feature of an aesthetic object can be considered in an atomistic fashion . . . We might hold that to claim brilliant imagery as a merit in one poem is to commit yourself to some general principle about the capacity of grand imagery to help along poems, at least poems in which certain other features are present.[19]

He continues (disconcertingly):

> But to commit yourself to the existence of such a principle is, of course, not to be able to state it . . .
>
> The critic may have a hunch that in the *Ode* the grandeur of imagery is a good-making feature, but then it would become a critical question whether it is always such or whether its being such depends upon being associated with other features.[20]

Notice that 'Grandeur of imagery is always a poetic merit', understood as an innocuous principle, is independent of context, true no matter what, even if, for example, I am right and Beardsley is wrong about the imagery of the *Ode.* So *that* cannot be what he has in mind. Suppose that in defense of his particular claim, he cites the lines:

> Not in entire forgetfulness,
> And not in utter nakedness,
> But trailing clouds of glory do we come
> From God who is our home:[21]

and focuses on the phrase 'trailing clouds of glory' as an instance of 'grandeur of imagery'. Considered 'in an atomistic fashion', the phrase has perhaps some slight merit but certainly does not tempt us to suppose that some mediocre poem would be 'helped along' if 'trailing clouds of glory' could somehow be worked into it. As Beardsley says, it is a merit only when 'certain other features are present'. Let us call the requisite additional features the 'supportive context' of the phrase in question. Let ø be the feature or features that comprise the supportive context. Then the putative principle will be to the effect that '*x* is ø and contains the phrase "trailing clouds of glory"' picks out a good-making feature for poems and qualifies as a 'good reason' in favor of a positive verdict. But what value can we assign to ø? If it is spelled out in innocuous principles then 'trailing clouds of glory' will not be supported by ø: indeed it will be dispensable, since any phrase at all, conjoined with poetic merit, will establish a modicum of over-all poetic merit. What is the alternative? Suppose ø is 'being in the form of an ode'. Then the resulting principle is unbelievable: 'trailing clouds of glory' will not add luster to just any old ode. No, the only plausible value for ø is the complex feature, '*x* is a poem that goes as follows: "There was a time when meadow, grove and stream . . ."' And this is to say that 'trailing clouds of glory' is an image that contributes to the merit of Wordsworth's *Ode*. I agree, though it takes more than one good image to justify 'grandeur of imagery'.

In summary: by way of defending my claim, namely that no one believes the denial of *FT*, I distinguished the contrary, 'There must be principles (or laws) of taste' from the contradictory, 'There is at least one law of taste which is as follows . . .' Philosophers who affirm one or the other counterclaim may be confused but they are not dolts. It is true that some coherent account of critical reasoning is called for; it is also true that particular works of art have particular merits and particular defects. What I have suggested is that neither claim in itself counts as a denial of *FT* and that unless one wants to allow uninteresting laws and correlative innocuous principles as objects of belief, nothing much remains.

Notes

1 C. I. Lewis, *An Analysis of Knowledge and Valuation* (La Salle: Open Court, 1946), p. 372.

2 Stanley Cavell, 'Music Discomposed', in *Art, Mind, and Religion*, ed. W. H. Capitan and D. D. Merrill (Pittsburgh: University of Pittsburgh Press, 1967), p. 188 (Reprinted in Stanley Cavell, *Must We Mean What We Say?* New York: Scribner's, 1969.)

3 Donald Davidson, 'Psychology as Philosophy', in *Philosophy of Psychology*, ed. S. C. Brown (London: Macmillan and New York: Barnes and Noble, 1975), p. 233. (Reprinted in Donald Davidson, *Essays on Actions and Events*. Oxford: Clarendon Press, 1980.)

4 Arnold Isenberg, 'Critical Communication', *Philosophical Review*, 54, 4(1949), p. 164.

5 Lewis, p. 469.

6 Ibid.

7 Isenberg, p. 160.

8 Ibid.

9 George Santayana, *The Sense of Beauty* (New York: Scribner's, 1896), p. 17.

10 Joseph Margolis, *The Language of Art and Art Criticism* (Detroit: Wayne State University Press, 1965), p. 138.

11 Ibid.

12 Wordsworth, *Ode: Intimations of Immortality from Recollections of Early Childhood.*

13 Margolis, p. 140.

14 Ibid., p. 143.

15 Immanuel Kant, *Critique of Judgment*, trans. J. C. Meredith (Oxford: Clarendon Press, 1964), p. 140.

16 Ibid., p. 56.

17 F. E. Sparohott, *The Structure of Aesthetics* (London: Routledge and Kegan Paul, 1963), p. 12.

18 Monroe Beardsley, *Aesthetics: Problems in the Philosophy of Criticism* (New York: Harcourt, Brace, 1958), p. 464.

19 Ibid.

20 Ibid.

21 Wordsworth, *Ode*.

45

Categories of Art

Kendall Walton

Kendall Walton is Charles L. Stevenson Collegiate Professor of Philosophy and Professor, School of Art and Design at the University of Michigan.

I. Introduction

> *False judgments enter art history if we judge from the impression which pictures of different epochs, placed side by side, make on us. . . . They speak a different language.*[1]

Paintings and sculptures are to be looked at; sonatas and songs are to be heard. What is important about these works of art, as works of art, is what can be seen or heard in them.[2] Inspired partly by apparent commonplaces such as these, many recent aesthetic theorists have attempted to purge from criticism of works of art supposedly extraneous excursions into matters not (or not "directly") available to inspection of the works, and to focus attention on the works themselves. Circumstances connected with a work's origin, in particular, are frequently held to have no essential bearing on an assessment of its aesthetic nature – for example, who created the work, how, and when; the artist's intentions and expectations concerning it, his philosophical views, psychological state, and love life; the artistic traditions and intellectual atmosphere of his society. Once produced (it is argued) the work must stand or fall on its own; it must be judged for what it is, regardless of how it came to be as it is.

Arguments for the irrelevance of such historical circumstances to aesthetic judgments about works of art may, but need not, involve the claim that these circumstances are not of "aesthetic" interest or importance, though obviously they are often important in biographical, historical, psychological, or sociological researches. One might consider an artist's action in producing a work to be aesthetically interesting, an "aesthetic object" in its own right, while vehemently maintaining its irrelevance to an aesthetic investigation of the work. Robert Rauschenberg once carefully obliterated a drawing by de Kooning, titled the bare canvas "Erased De Kooning Drawing," framed it, and exhibited it.[3] His doing this might be taken as symbolic or expressive (of an attitude toward art, or toward life in general, or whatever) in an "aesthetically" significant manner, perhaps somewhat as an action of a character in a play might be, and yet thought to have no bearing whatever on the aesthetic nature of the finished product. The issue I am here concerned with is how far critical questions about works of art can be *separated* from questions about their histories.[4]

Kendall Walton, "Categories of Art," *Philosophical Review*, 79/3 (1970): 334–67.

One who wants to make this separation quite sharp may regard the basic facts of art along the following lines. Works of art are simply objects with various properties, of which we are primarily interested in perceptual ones – visual properties of paintings, audible properties of music, and so forth.[5] A work's perceptual properties include "aesthetic" as well as "nonaesthetic" ones – the sense of mystery and tension of a painting as well as its dark coloring and diagonal composition; the energy, exuberance, and coherence of a sonata, as well as its meters, rhythms, pitches, timbres, and so forth; the balance and serenity of a Gothic cathedral as well as its dimensions, lines, and symmetries.[6] Aesthetic properties are features or characteristics of works of art just as much as nonaesthetic ones are.[7] They are *in* the works, to be seen, heard, or otherwise perceived there. Seeing a painting's sense of mystery or hearing a sonata's coherence might require looking or listening longer or harder than does perceiving colors and shapes, rhythms and pitches; it may even require special training or a special kind of sensitivity. But these qualities must be discoverable simply by examining the works themselves if they are discoverable at all. It is never even partly *in virtue of* the circumstances of a work's origin that it has a sense of mystery or is coherent or serene. Such circumstances sometimes provide hints concerning what to look for in a work, what we might reasonably expect to find by examining it. But these hints are always theoretically dispensable; a work's aesthetic properties must "in principle" be ascertainable without their help. Surely (it seems) a Rembrandt portrait does not have (or lack) a sense of mystery in virtue of the fact that Rembrandt intended it to have (or to lack) that quality, any more than a contractor's intention to make a roof leakproof makes it so; nor is the portrait mysterious in virtue of any other facts about what Rembrandt thought or how he went about painting the portrait or what his society happened to be like. Such circumstances are important to the result only in so far as they had an effect on the pattern of paint splotches that became attached to the canvas, and the canvas can be examined without in any way considering how the splotches got there. It would not matter in the least to the aesthetic properties of the portrait if the paint had been applied to the canvas not by Rembrandt at all, but by a chimpanzee or a cyclone in a paint shop.

The view sketched above can easily seem very persuasive. But the tendency of critics to discuss the histories of works of art in the course of justifying aesthetic judgments about them has been remarkably persistent. This is partly because hints derived from facts about a work's history, however dispensable they may be "in principle," are often crucially important in practice. (One might simply not think to listen for a recurring series of intervals in a piece of music, until he learns that the composer meant the work to be structured around it.) No doubt it is partly due also to genuine confusions on the part of critics. But I will argue that (some) facts about the origins of works of art have an *essential* role in criticism, that aesthetic judgments rest on them in an absolutely fundamental way. For this reason, and for another as well, the view that works of art should be judged simply by what can be perceived in them is seriously misleading, though there is something right in the idea that what matters aesthetically about a painting or a sonata is just how it looks or sounds.

II. Standard, Variable, and Contra-Standard Properties

I will continue to call tension, mystery, energy, coherence, balance, serenity, sentimentality, pallidness, disunity, grotesqueness, and so forth, as well as colors and shapes, pitches and timbres *properties* of works of art, though "property" is to be construed broadly enough not to beg any important questions. I will also, following Sibley, call properties of the former sort "aesthetic" properties, but purely for reasons of convenience I will include in this category "representational" and "resemblance" properties, which Sibley excludes – for example, the property of representing or being a picture of Napoleon, that of depicting an old man (as) stooping over a fire, that of resembling, or merely suggesting, a human face, claws (the petals of Van Gogh's sunflowers), or (in music) footsteps or conversation. It is not essential for my purposes to delimit with any exactness the class of aesthetic properties (if indeed any such delimitation is possible), for I am more interested in discussing particular examples of such properties than in making generalizations about the class as a whole. It will be obvious, however, that what I say about the examples I deal with is also applicable to a great many other properties we would want to call aesthetic.

Sibley points out that a work's aesthetic properties depend on its nonaesthetic properties; the former are "emergent" or "*Gestalt*" properties based on the latter.[8] I take this to be true of all the examples of aesthetic properties we will be dealing with, including representational and resemblance ones. It is because of the configuration of colors and shapes on a painting, perhaps in particular its dark colors and diagonal composition, that it has a sense of mystery and tension, if it does. The colors and shapes of a portrait are responsible for its resembling an old man and (perhaps with its title) its depicting an old man. The coherence or unity of a piece of music (for example, Beethoven's *Fifth Symphony*) may be largely due to the frequent recurrence of a rhythmic motive, and the regular meter of a song plus the absence of harmonic modulation and of large intervals in the voice part may make it serene or peaceful.

Moreover, a work *seems* or *appears* to us to have certain aesthetic properties because we observe in it, or it appears to us to have, certain nonaesthetic features (though it may not be necessary to notice consciously all the relevant nonaesthetic features). A painting depicting an old man may not look like an old man to someone who is color-blind, or when it is seen from an extreme angle or in bad lighting conditions so that its colors or shapes are distorted or obscured. Beethoven's *Fifth Symphony* performed in such a sloppy manner that many occurrences of the four-note rhythmic motive do not sound similar may seem incoherent or disunified.

I will argue, however, that a work's aesthetic properties depend not only on its nonaesthetic ones, but also on which of its nonaesthetic properties are "standard," which "variable," and which "contra-standard," in senses to be explained. I will approach this thesis by way of the psychological point that what aesthetic properties a work seems to us to have depends not only on what nonaesthetic features we perceive in it, but also on which of them are standard, which variable, and which contra-standard *for us* (in a sense also to be explained).

It is necessary to introduce first a distinction between standard, variable, and contra-standard properties relative to perceptually distinguishable categories of works of art. Such categories include media, genre, styles, forms, and so forth – for example, the categories of paintings, cubist paintings, Gothic architecture, classical sonatas, paintings in the style of Cézanne, and music in the style of late Beethoven – if they are interpreted in such a way that membership is determined solely by features that can be perceived in a work when it is experienced in the normal manner. Thus whether or not a piece of music was written in the eighteenth century is irrelevant to whether it belongs to the category of classical sonatas (interpreted in this way), and whether a work was produced by Cézanne or Beethoven has nothing essential to do with whether it is in the style of Cézanne or late Beethoven. The category of etchings as normally construed is not perceptually distinguishable in the requisite sense, for to be an etching is, I take it, simply to have been produced in a particular manner. But the category of *apparent* etchings, works which *look* like etchings from the quality of their lines, whether they are etchings or not, is perceptually distinguishable. A category will not count as "perceptually distinguishable" in my sense if in order to determine perceptually whether something belongs to it, it is necessary (in some or all cases) to determine which categories it is correctly perceived in partly or wholly on the basis of nonperceptual considerations. (See Section IV below.) This prevents, for example, the category of serene things from being perceptually distinguishable in this sense.

A feature of a work of art is *standard* with respect to a (perceptually distinguishable) category just in case it is among those in virtue of which works in that category belong to that category – that is, just in case the lack of that feature would disqualify, or tend to disqualify, a work from that category. A feature is *variable* with respect to a category just in case it has nothing to do with works' belonging to that category; the possession or lack of the feature is irrelevant to whether a work qualifies for the category. Finally, a *contra-standard* feature with respect to a category is the absence of a standard feature with respect to that category – that is, a feature whose presence tends to *disqualify* works as members of the category. Needless to say, it will not be clear in *all* cases whether a feature of a work is standard, variable, or contra-standard relative to a given category, since the criteria for classifying works of art are far from precise. But clear examples are abundant. The flatness of a painting and the motionlessness of its markings are standard, and its particular shapes and colors are variable, relative to the category of painting. A protruding three-dimensional object or an electrically driven twitching of the canvas would be contra-standard relative to this category. The straight lines in stick-figure drawings and squarish shapes in cubist paintings are standard with respect to those categories respectively, though they are variable with respect to the categories of drawing and painting. The exposition-development-recapitulation form of a classical sonata is standard, and its thematic material is variable, relative to the category of sonatas.

In order to explain what I mean by features being standard, variable, or contra-standard *for a person on a particular occasion*, I must introduce the notion of perceiving a work in, or as belonging to, a certain (perceptually distinguishable) category.[9] To perceive a work in a certain category is to perceive the "*Gestalt*" of that category in the work. This needs some explanation. People familiar with Brahmsian music – that is, music in the style of Brahms (notably, works of Johannes Brahms) – or impressionist paintings can frequently recognize members of these categories by recognizing the Brahmsian or impressionist *Gestalt* qualities. Such recognition is dependent on perception of particular features that are standard relative to these categories, but it is not a matter of *inferring* from the presence of such features that a work is Brahmsian or impressionist. One may not notice many of the relevant features, and he may be very vague about which ones are relevant. If I recognize a work as Brahmsian by first noting its lush textures, its basically traditional harmonic and formal structure, its superimposition and alternation of duple and triple meters, and so forth, and recalling that these characteristics are typical of Brahmsian works, I have not recognized it by hearing the Brahmsian *Gestalt.* To do that is simply to recognize it by its Brahmsian *sound*, without necessarily paying attention to the features ("cues") responsible for it. Similarly, recognizing an impressionist painting by its impressionist *Gestalt,* is recognizing the impressionist *look* about it, which we are familiar with from other impressionist paintings; not applying a rule we have learned for recognizing it from its features.

To *perceive* a *Gestalt* quality in a work – that is, to perceive it in a certain category – is not, or not merely, to *recognize* that *Gestalt* quality. Recognition is a momentary occurrence, whereas perceiving a quality is a continuous state which may last for a short or long time. (For the same reason, seeing the ambiguous duck-rabbit figure as a duck is not, or not merely, recognizing a property of it.) We perceive the Brahmsian or impressionist *Gestalt* in a work when, and as long as, it *sounds* (*looks*) Brahmsian or impressionist to us. This involves perceiving (not necessarily being aware of) features standard relative to that category. But it is not *just* this, nor this plus the intellectual realization that these features make the work Brahmsian, or impressionist. These features are perceived combined into a single *Gestalt* quality.

We can of course perceive a work in several or many different categories at once. A Brahms sonata might be heard simultaneously as a piece of music, a sonata, a romantic work, and a Brahmsian work. Some pairs of categories, however, seem to be such that one cannot perceive a work as belonging to both at once, much as one cannot see the duck-rabbit both as a duck and as a rabbit simultaneously. One cannot see a photographic image simultaneously as a still photograph and as (part of) a film, nor can one see something both in the category of paintings and at the same time in the category (to be explained shortly) of *guernicas*.

It will be useful to point out some of the *causes* of our perceiving works in certain categories. (*a*) In which categories we perceive a work depends in part, of course, on what other works we are familiar with. The more works of a certain sort we have experienced, the more likely it is that we will perceive a particular work in that category. (*b*) What we have heard critics and others say about works we have experienced, how they have categorized them, and what resemblances they have pointed out to us is also important. If no one has ever explained to me what is distinctive about Schubert's style (as opposed to the styles of, say, Schumann, Mendelssohn, Beethoven, Brahms, Hugo Wolf), or even pointed out that there is such a distinctive style, I may never have learned to hear the Schubertian *Gestalt* quality, even if I have heard many of Schubert's works, and so I may not hear his works as Schubertian. (*c*) How we are introduced to the particular work in question may be involved. If a Cézanne painting is exhibited in a collection of French Impressionist works, or if before seeing it we are told that it is French Impressionist, we are more likely to see it as French Impressionist than if it is exhibited in a random collection and we are not told anything about it beforehand.

I will say that a feature of a work is standard for a particular person on a particular occasion when, and only when, it is standard relative to some category in which he perceives it, and is not contra-standard relative to any category in which he perceives it. A feature is variable for a person on an occasion just when it is variable relative to *all* of the categories in which he perceives it. And a feature is contra-standard for a person on an occasion just when it is contra-standard relative to *any* of the categories in which he perceives it.[10]

III. A Point about Perception

I turn now to my psychological thesis that what aesthetic properties a work seems to have, what aesthetic effect it has on us, how it strikes us aesthetically often depends (in part) on which of its features are standard, which variable, and which contra-standard for us. I offer a series of examples in support of this thesis.

(*a*) Representational and resemblance properties provide perhaps the most obvious illustration of this thesis. Many works of art look like or resemble other objects – people, buildings, mountains, bowls of fruit, and so forth. Rembrandt's "Titus Reading" looks like a boy, and in particular like Rembrandt's son; Picasso's "Les Demoiselles d'Avignon" looks like five women, four standing and one sitting (though not *especially* like any particular women). A portrait may even be said to be a *perfect* likeness of the sitter, or to capture his image *exactly*.

An important consideration in determining whether a work *depicts* or *represents* a particular object, or an object of a certain sort (for example, Rembrandt's son, or simply *a* boy), in the sense of being a picture, sculpture, or whatever of it[11] is whether the work resembles that object, or objects of that kind. A significant degree of resemblance is, I suggest, a necessary condition in most contexts for such representation or depiction,[12] though the resemblance need not be obvious at first glance. If we are unable to see a similarity between a painting purportedly of a woman and women, I think we would have to suppose either that there is such a similarity which we have not yet discovered (as one might fail to see a face in a maze of lines), or that it simply is not a picture of a woman. Resemblance is of course not a *sufficient* condition for representation, since a portrait (containing only one figure) might resemble both the sitter and his twin brother equally but is not a portrait of both of them. (The title might determine which of them it depicts.)[13]

It takes only a touch of perversity, however, to find much of our talk about resemblances between works of art and other things preposterous. Paintings and people are *very* different sorts of things. Paintings are pieces of canvas supporting splotches of paint, while people are live, three-dimensional, flesh-and-blood animals. Moreover, except rarely and under special conditions of observation (probably including bad lighting) paintings and people *look* very different. Paintings look like pieces of canvas (or anyway flat surfaces) covered with paint and people look like flesh-and-blood animals. There is practically no danger of confusing them. How, then, can anyone seriously hold that a portrait resembles the sitter to any significant extent, let alone that it is a perfect likeness of him? Yet it remains true that many paintings strike us as resembling people, sometimes very much or even exactly – despite the fact that they look so very different!

To resolve this paradox we must recognize that the resemblances we perceive between, for example, portraits and people, those that are relevant in determining what works of art depict or represent, are resemblances of a somewhat special sort, tied up with the categories in which we perceive such works. The properties of a work which are standard for us are ordinarily irrelevant to what we take it to look like or resemble in the relevant sense, and hence to what we take it to depict or represent. The properties of a portrait which make it *so* different from, so easily distinguishable from, a person – such as its flatness and its *painted* look – are standard for us. Hence these properties just do not count with regard to what (or whom) it looks like. It is only the properties which are variable for us, the colors and shapes on the work's surface, that make it look to us like what it does. And these are the ones which are taken as relevant in determining what (if anything) the work represents.[14]

Other examples will reinforce this point. A marble bust of a Roman emperor seems to us to resemble a man with, say, an aquiline nose, a wrinkled brow, and an expression of grim determination, and we take it to represent a man with, or as having, those characteristics. But why don't we say that it resembles and represents a perpetually motionless man, of uniform (marble) color, who is severed at the chest? It is similar to such a man, it seems, and much more so than to a normally colored, mobile, and whole man. But we are not struck by the former similarity when we see the bust, obvious though it is on reflection. The bust's uniform color, motionlessness, and abrupt ending at the chest are standard properties relative to the category of busts, and since we see it as a bust they are standard for us. Similarly, black-and-white drawings do not look to us like colorless scenes and we do not take them to depict things as being colorless, nor do we regard stick-figure drawings as resembling and depicting only very thin people. A cubist work might look like a person with a cubical head to someone not familiar with the cubist style. But the standardness of such cubical shapes for people who see it as a cubist work prevents them from making that comparison.

The shapes of a painting or a still photograph of a high jumper in action are motionless, but these pictures do not look to us like a high jumper frozen in midair. Indeed, depending on features of the pictures which are variable for us (for example, the exact positions of the figures, swirling brush strokes in the painting, slight blurrings of the photographic image) the athlete may seem in a frenzy of activity; the pictures may convey a vivid sense of movement. But if static images exactly like those of the two pictures occur in a motion picture, and we see it as a motion picture, they probably would strike us as resembling a static athlete. This is because the immobility of the images is standard relative to the category of still pictures and variable relative to that of motion pictures. (Since we are so familiar with still pictures it might be difficult to see the static images as motion pictures for very long, rather than as [filmed] still pictures. But we could not help seeing them that way if we had no acquaintance at all with the medium of still pictures.) My point here is brought out by the tremendous aesthetic difference we are likely to experience between a film of a dancer moving *very* slowly and a still picture of him, even if "objectively" the two images are very nearly identical. We might well find the former studied, calm, deliberate, laborious, and the latter dynamic, energetic, flowing, or frenzied.

In general, then, what we regard a work as resembling, and as representing, depends on the properties of the work which are variable, and not on those which are standard for us.[15] The latter properties serve to determine what *kind* of a representation the work is, rather than what it represents or resembles. We take them for granted, as it were, in representations of that kind. This principle helps to explain also how clouds can look like elephants, how diatonic orchestral music can suggest a conversation or a person crying or laughing, and how a twelve-year-old boy can look like his middle-aged father.

We can now see how a portrait can be an *exact* likeness of the sitter, despite the huge differences between the two. The differences, in so far as they involve properties standard for us, simply do not count against likeness, and hence not against exact likeness. Similarly, a boy not only can resemble his father but can be his "spitting image," despite the boy's relative youthfulness. It is clear that the notions of resemblance and exact resemblance that we are concerned with are not even cousins of the notion of perceptual indistinguishability.

(*b*) The importance of the distinction between standard and variable properties is by no means limited to cases involving representation or resemblance. Imagine a society which does not have an established medium of painting, but does produce a kind of work of art called *guernicas*. *Guernicas* are like versions of Picasso's "Guernica" done in various bas-relief dimensions. All of them are surfaces with the colors and shapes of Picasso's "Guernica," but the surfaces are molded to protrude from the wall like relief maps of different kinds of terrain. Some *guernicas* have rolling surfaces, others are sharp and jagged, still others contain several relatively flat planes at various angles to each other, and so forth. Picasso's "Guernica" would be counted as a *guernica* in this society – a perfectly flat one – rather than as a painting. Its flatness is variable and the figures on its surface are standard relative to the category of *guernicas*. Thus the flatness, which is standard for us, would be variable for members of the other society (if they should come across "Guernica") and the figures on the surface, which are variable for us, would be standard for them. This would make for a profound difference between our aesthetic reaction to "Guernica" and theirs. It seems violent, dynamic, vital, disturbing to us. But I imagine it would strike them as cold, stark, lifeless, or serene and restful, or perhaps bland, dull, boring – but in any case *not* violent, dynamic, and vital. We do not pay attention to or take note of "Guernica"'s flatness; this is a feature we take for granted in paintings, as it were. But for the other society this is "Guernica"'s most striking and noteworthy characteristic – what is *expressive* about it. Conversely, "Guernica"'s color patches, which we find noteworthy and expressive, are insignificant to them.

It is important to notice that this difference in aesthetic response is not due *solely* to the fact that we are much more familiar with flat works of art than they are, and they are more familiar with "Guernica"'s colors and shapes. Someone equally familiar with paintings and *guernicas* might, I think, see Picasso's "Guernica" as a painting on some occasions, and as a *guernica* on others. On the former occasions it will probably look dynamic, violent, and so forth to him, and on the latter cold, serene, bland, or lifeless. Whether he sees the work in a museum of paintings or a museum of *guernicas*, or whether he has been told that it is a painting or a *guernica*, may influence how he sees it. But I think he might be able to shift at will from one way of seeing it to the other, somewhat as one shifts between seeing the duck-rabbit as a duck and seeing it as a rabbit.

This example and the previous ones might give the impression that in general only features of a work that are variable for us are aesthetically important – that these are the expressive, aesthetically active properties, as far as we are concerned, whereas features standard for us are aesthetically inert, But this notion is quite mistaken, as the following examples will demonstrate. Properties standard for us are not aesthetically lifeless, though the life that they have, the aesthetic effect they have on us, is typically very different from what it would be if they were variable for us.

(*c*) Because of the very fact that features standard for us do not seem striking or noteworthy, that they are somehow expected or taken for granted, they can contribute to a work a sense of order, inevitability, stability, correctness. This is perhaps most notably true of large-scale structural properties in the time arts. The exposition-development-recapitulation form (including the typical key and thematic relationships) of the first movements of classical sonatas, symphonies, and string quartets is standard with respect to the category of works in sonata-allegro form, and standard for listeners, including most of us, who hear them as belonging to that category. So proceeding along the lines of sonata-allegro form seems *right* to us; to our ears that is how sonatas are *supposed* to behave. We feel that we know where we are and where we are going throughout the work – more so, I suggest, than we would if we were not familiar with sonata-allegro form, if following the strictures of that form were variable rather than standard for us.[16] Properties standard for us do not always have this sort of unifying effect, however. The fact that a piano sonata contains only piano sounds, or uses the Western system of harmony throughout, does not make it seem unified to us. The reason, I think, is that these properties are *too* standard for us in a sense that needs explicating (cf. note 10). Nevertheless, sonata form is unifying partly because it is standard rather than variable for us.

(*d*) That a work (or part of it) has a certain determinate characteristic (for example, of size, speed, length, volume) is often variable relative to a particular category, when it is nevertheless standard for that category that the variable characteristic falls within a certain range. In such cases the aesthetic effect of the determinate variable property may be colored by the standard limits of the range. Hence these limits function as an aesthetic catalyst, even if not as an active ingredient.

Piano music is frequently marked *sostenuto*, *cantabile*, *legato*, or *lyrical*. But how can the pianist possibly carry out such instructions? Piano tones diminish in volume drastically immediately after the key is struck, becoming inaudible relatively promptly, and there is no way the player can prevent this. If a singer or violinist should produce sounds even approaching a piano's in suddenness of demise, they would be nerve-wrackingly sharp and percussive – anything but *cantabile* or lyrical! Yet piano music *can* be *cantabile*, *legato*, or lyrical nevertheless; sometimes it is extraordinarily so (for example, a good performance of the *Adagio Cantabile* movement of Beethoven's *Pathétique* sonata). What makes this possible is the very fact that the drastic diminution of piano tones cannot be prevented, and hence never is. It is a standard feature for piano music. A pianist can, however, by a variety of devices, control a tone's rate of diminution and length within the limits dictated by the nature of the instrument.[17] Piano tones may thus be *more or less* sustained within these limits, and *how* sustained they are, how quickly or slowly they diminish and how long they last, within the range of possibilities, is variable for piano music. A piano passage that sounds lyrical or *cantabile* to us is one in which the individual tones are *relatively* sustained, given the capabilities of the instrument. Such a passage sounds lyrical only because piano music is limited as it is, and we hear it as piano music; that is, the limitations are standard properties for us. The character of the passage is determined not merely by the "absolute" nature of the sounds, but by that in relation to the standard property of what piano tones can be like.[18]

This principle helps to explain the lack of energy and brilliance that we sometimes find even in very fast passages of electronic music. The energy and brilliance of a fast violin or piano passage derives not merely from the absolute speed of the music (together with accents, rhythmic characteristics, and so forth), but from the fact that it is fast *for that particular medium*. In electronic music different pitches can succeed one another at any frequency up to and including that at which they are no longer separately distinguishable. Because of this it is difficult to make electronic music *sound* fast (energetic, violent). For when we have heard enough electronic music to be aware of the possibilities we do not feel that the speed of a passage approaches a limit, no matter how fast it is.[19]

There are also visual correlates of these musical examples. A small elephant, one which is smaller than most elephants with which we are familiar, might impress us as charming, cute, delicate, or puny. This is not simply because of its (absolute) size, but because it is small *for an elephant*. To people who are familiar not with our elephants but with a race of mini-elephants, the same animal may look massive, strong, dominant, threatening, lumbering, if it is large for a mini-elephant. The size of elephants is variable relative to the class of elephants, but it varies only within a certain (not precisely specifiable) range. It is a standard property of elephants that they do fall within this range. How an elephant's size affects us aesthetically depends, since we see it as an elephant, on whether it falls in the upper, middle, or lower part of the range.

(*e*) Properties standard for a certain category which do not derive from physical limitations of the medium can be regarded as results of more or less conventional "rules" for producing works in the given category (for example, the "rules" of sixteenth-century counterpoint, or those for twelve-tone music). These rules may combine to create a dilemma for the artist which, if he is talented, he may resolve ingeniously and gracefully. The result may be a work with an aesthetic character very different from what it would have had if it had not been for those rules. Suppose that the first movement of a sonata in G major modulates to C-sharp major by the end of the development section. A rule of sonata form decrees that it must return to G for the recapitulation. But the keys of G and C-sharp are as unrelated as any two keys can be; it is difficult to modulate smoothly and quickly from one to the other. Suppose also that while the sonata is in C-sharp there are signs that, given other rules of sonata form, indicate that the recapitulation is imminent (for example, motivic hints of the return, an emotional climax, or a cadenza). Listeners who hear it as a work in sonata form are likely to have a distinct feeling of unease, tension, uncertainty, as the time for the recapitulation approaches. If the composer with a stroke of ingenuity accomplishes the necessary modulation quickly, efficiently, and naturally, this will give them a feeling of relief – one might say of deliverance. The movement to C-sharp (which may have seemed alien and brashly adventurous) will have proven to be quite appropriate, and the entire sequence will in retrospect have a sense of correctness and perfection about it. Our impression of it is likely, I think, to be very much like our impression of a "beautiful" or "elegant" proof in mathematics. (Indeed the composer's task in this example is not unlike that of producing such a proof.)

But suppose that the rule for sonatas were that the recapitulation must be *either* in the original key *or* in the key one half-step below it. Thus in the example above the recapitulation could have been in F-sharp major rather than G major. This possibility removes the sense of tension from the occurrence of C-sharp major in the development section, for a modulation from C-sharp to F-sharp is as easy as any modulation is (since C-sharp is the dominant of F-sharp). Of course, there would also be no special *release* of tension when the modulation to G is effected, there being no tension to be released. In fact, that modulation probably would be rather surprising, since the permissible modulation to F-sharp would be much more natural.

Thus the effect that the sonata has on us depends on which of its properties are dictated by "rules," which ones are standard relative to the category of sonatas and hence standard for us.

(*f*) I turn now to features which are contra-standard for us – that is, ones which have a tendency to disqualify a work from a category in which we nevertheless perceive it. We are likely to find such features shocking, or disconcerting, or startling, or upsetting, just because they are contra-standard for us. Their presence may be so obtrusive that they obscure the work's variable properties. Three-dimensional objects protruding from a canvas and movement in a sculpture are contra-standard relative to the categories of painting and (traditional) sculpture respectively. These features are contra-standard for us, and probably shocking, if despite them we perceive the works possessing them in the mentioned categories. The monochromatic paintings of Yves Klein are disturbing to us (at least at first) for this reason: we see them as paintings, though they contain the feature contra-standard for paintings of being one solid color. Notice that we find other similarly monochromatic surfaces – for example, walls of living rooms – not in the least disturbing, and indeed quite unnoteworthy.

If we are exposed frequently to works containing a certain kind of feature which is contra-standard for us, we ordinarily adjust our categories to accommodate it, making it contra-standard for us no longer. The first painting with a three-dimensional object glued to it was no doubt shocking. But now that the technique has become commonplace we are not shocked. This is because we no longer see these works as *paintings*, but rather as members of either (*a*) a new category – *collages* – in which case the offending feature has become standard rather than contra-standard for us, or (*b*) an expanded category which includes paintings both with and without attached objects, in which case that feature is variable for us.

But it is not just the rarity, unusualness, or unexpectedness of a feature that makes it shocking. If a work differs *too* significantly from the norms of a certain category we do not perceive it in that category and hence the difference is not contra-standard for us, even if we have not previously experienced works differing from that category in that way. A sculpture which is constantly and vigorously in motion would be so obviously and radically different from traditional sculptures that we probably would not perceive it as one even if it is the first moving sculpture we have come across. We would either perceive it as a *kinetic* sculpture, or simply remain confused. In contrast, a sculptured bust which is traditional in every respect except that one ear twitches slightly every thirty seconds would be perceived as an ordinary sculpture. So the twitching ear would be contra-standard for us and would be considerably more unsettling than the much greater movement of the other kinetic sculpture. Similarly, a very small colored area of an otherwise entirely black-and-white drawing would be very disconcerting. But if enough additional color is added to it we will see it as a colored rather than a black-and-white drawing, and the shock will vanish.

This point helps to explain a difference between the harmonic aberrations of Wagner's *Tristan and Isolde* on the one hand and on the other Debussy's *Pelléas et Mélisande* and *Jeux* and Schoenberg's *Pierrot Lunaire* as well as his later twelve-tone works. The latter are not merely *more* aberrant, *less* tonal, than *Tristan*. They differ from traditional tonal music in such respects and to such an extent that they are not heard as tonal at all. *Tristan*, however, retains enough of the apparatus of tonality, despite its deviations, to be heard as a tonal work. For this reason its lesser deviations are often the more shocking.[20] *Tristan* plays on harmonic traditions by selectively following and flaunting them, while *Pierrot Lunaire* and the others simply ignore them.

Shock then arises from features that are not just rare or unique, but ones that are contra-standard relative to categories in which objects possessing them are perceived. But it must be emphasized that to be contra-standard relative to a certain category is not merely to be rare or unique *among things of that category*. The melodic line of Schubert's song, "*Im Walde*," is probably unique; it probably does not occur in any other songs, or other works of any sort. But it is not contra-standard relative to the category of songs, because it does not tend to disqualify the work from that category. Nor is it contra-standard relative to any other category to which we hear the work as belonging. And clearly we do not find this melodic line at all upsetting. What is important is not the rarity of a feature, but its connection with the classification of the work. Features contra-standard for us are perceived as being misfits in a category which the work strikes us as belonging to, as doing *violence* to such a category, and being rare in a category is not the same thing as being a misfit in it.

It should be clear from the above examples that how a work affects us aesthetically – what aesthetic properties it seems to us to have and what ones we are inclined to attribute to it – depends in a variety of important ways on which of its features are standard, which variable, and which contra-standard for us. Moreover, this is obviously not an isolated or exceptional phenomenon, but a pervasive characteristic of aesthetic perception. I should emphasize that my purpose has not been to establish general principles about how each of the three sorts of properties affects us. How any particular feature affects us depends also on many variables I have not discussed. The important point is that in many cases whether a feature is standard, variable, or contra-standard for us has a great deal to do with what effect it has on us. We must now begin to assess the theoretical consequences of this.

IV. Truth and Falsity

The fact that what aesthetic properties a thing seems to have may depend on what categories it is perceived in raises a question about how to determine what aesthetic properties it really does have. If "Guernica" appears dynamic when seen as a painting, and not dynamic when seen as a *guernica*, is it dynamic or not? Can one way of seeing it be ruled correct, and the other incorrect? One way of approaching this problem is to deny that the apparently conflicting aesthetic judgments of people who perceive a work in different categories actually do conflict.[21]

Judgments that works of art have certain aesthetic properties, it might be suggested, implicitly involve reference to some particular set of categories. Thus our claim that "Guernica" is dynamic really amounts to the claim that it is (as we might say) dynamic *as a painting*, or for people who see it as a painting. The judgment that it is not dynamic made by people who see it as a *guernica* amounts simply to the judgment that it is not dynamic *as a guernica*. Interpreted in these ways, the two judgments are of course quite compatible. Terms like "large" and "small" provide a convenient model for this interpretation. An elephant might be both small as an elephant and large as a mini-elephant, and hence it might be called truly either "large" or "small," depending on which category is implicitly referred to.

I think that aesthetic judgments are in *some* contexts amenable to such category-relative interpretations, especially aesthetic judgments about natural objects (clouds, mountains, sunsets) rather than works of art. (It will be evident that the alternative account suggested below is not readily applicable to most judgments about natural objects.) But most of our aesthetic judgments can be forced into this mold only at the cost of distorting them beyond recognition.

My main objection is that category-relative interpretations do not allow aesthetic judgments to be mistaken often enough. It would certainly be natural to consider a person who calls "Guernica" stark, cold, or dull, because he sees it as a *guernica*, to be *mistaken*: he misunderstands the work because he is looking at it in the wrong way. Similarly, one who asserts that a good performance of the *Adagio Cantabile* of Beethoven's *Pathétique* is percussive, or that a Roman bust looks like a unicolored, immobile man severed at the chest and depicts him as such, is simply wrong, even if his judgment is a result of his perceiving the work in different categories from those in which we perceive it. Moreover, we do not accord a status any more privileged to our own aesthetic judgments. We are likely to regard, for example, cubist paintings, serial music, or Chinese music as formless, incoherent, or disturbing on our first contact with these forms largely because, I suggest, we would not be perceiving the works as cubist paintings, serial music, or Chinese music. But after becoming familiar with these kinds of art we would probably *retract* our previous judgments, admit that they were mistaken. It would be quite inappropriate to protest that what we meant previously was merely that the works were formless or disturbing for the categories in which we then perceived them, while admitting that they are not for the categories of cubist paintings, or serial, or Chinese music. The conflict between apparently incompatible aesthetic judgments made while perceiving a work in different categories does not simply evaporate when the difference of categories is pointed out, as does the conflict between the claims that an animal is large and that it is small, when it is made clear that the person making the first claim regarded it as a mini-elephant and the one making the second regarded it as an elephant. The latter judgments do not (necessarily) reflect a real disagreement about the size of the animal, but the former do reflect a real disagreement about the aesthetic nature of the work.

Thus it seems that, at least in some cases, it is *correct* to perceive a work in certain categories, and *incorrect* to perceive it in certain others; that is, our judgments of it when we perceive it in the former are likely to be true, and those we make when perceiving it in the latter false. This provides us with absolute senses of "standard," "variable," and "contra-standard": features of a work are standard, variable, or contra-standard absolutely just in case they are standard, variable, or contra-standard (respectively) for people who perceive the work correctly. (Thus an absolutely standard feature is standard relative to some category in which the work is correctly perceived and contra-standard relative to none, an absolutely variable feature is variable relative to all such categories, and an absolutely contra-standard feature is contra-standard relative to at least one such category.)

How is it to be determined in which categories a work is correctly perceived? There is certainly no very precise or well-defined procedure to be followed. Different criteria are emphasized by different people and in different situations. But there are several fairly definite considerations which typically figure in critical discussions and fit our intuitions reasonably well. I suggest that the following circumstances count toward its being correct to perceive a work, *W*, in a given category, *C*:

(*i*) The presence in *W* of a relatively large number of features standard with respect to *C*. The correct way of perceiving a work is likely to be that in which it has a minimum of contra-standard features for us. I take the relevance of this consideration to be obvious. It cannot be correct to perceive Rembrandt's "Titus Reading" as a kinetic sculpture, if this is possible, just because that work has too few of the features which make kinetic sculptures kinetic sculptures. But of course this does not get us very far, for "Guernica," for example, qualifies equally well on this count for being perceived as a painting and as a *guernica*.

(*ii*) The fact, if it is one, that *W* is better, or more interesting or pleasing aesthetically, or more worth experiencing when perceived in *C* than it is when perceived in alternative ways. The correct way of perceiving a work is likely to be the way in which it comes off best.

(*iii*) The fact, if it is one, that the artist who produced *W* intended or expected it to be perceived in *C*, or thought of it as a *C*.

(*iv*) The fact, if it is one, that *C* is well established in and recognized by the society in which *W* was produced. A category is well established in and recognized by a society if the members of the society are familiar with works in that category, consider a work's membership in it a fact worth mentioning, exhibit works of that category together, and so forth – that is, roughly if that category figures importantly in their way of classifying works of art. The categories of impressionist painting and Brahmsian music are well established and recognized in our society; those of *guernicas*, paintings with diagonal composition containing green crosses, and pieces of music containing between four and eight F-sharps and at least seventeen quarter notes every eight bars are not. The categories in which a work is correctly perceived, according to this condition, are generally the ones in which the artist's contemporaries did perceive or would have perceived it.

In certain cases I think the mechanical process by which a work was produced, or (for example, in architecture) the non-perceptible physical characteristics or internal structure of a work, is relevant. A work is probably correctly perceived as an apparent etching rather than, say, an apparent woodcut or line drawing, if it was produced by the etching process. The strength of materials in a building, or the presence of steel girders inside wooden or plaster columns counts toward (not necessarily conclusively) the correctness of perceiving it in the category of buildings with visual characteristics typical of buildings constructed in that manner. Because of their limited applicability I will not discuss these considerations further here.

What can be said in support of the relevance of conditions (*ii*), (*iii*), and (*iv*)? In the examples mentioned above, the categories in which we consider a work correctly perceived seem to meet (to the best of our knowledge) each of these three conditions. I would suppose that "Guernica" is better seen as a painting than it would be seen as a *guernica* (though this would be hard to prove). In any case, Picasso certainly intended it to be seen as a painting rather than a *guernica*, and the category of paintings is, and that of *guernicas* is not, well established in his (that is, our) society. But this of course does not show that (*ii*), (*iii*), and (*iv*) *each* is relevant. It tends to indicate only that one or other of them, or some combination, is relevant. The difficulty of assessing each of the three conditions individually is complicated by the fact that by and large they can be expected to coincide, to yield identical conclusions. Since an artist usually intends his works for his contemporaries he is likely to intend them to be perceived in categories established in and recognized by his society. Moreover, it is reasonable to expect works to come off better when perceived in the intended categories than when perceived in others. An artist tries to produce works which are well worth experiencing when perceived in the intended way and, unless we have reason to think he is totally incompetent, there is some presumption that he succeeded at least to some extent. But it is more or less a matter of chance whether the work comes off well when perceived in some unintended way. The convergence of the three conditions, however, at the same time diminishes the *practical* importance of justifying them individually, since in most cases we can decide how to judge particular works of art without doing so. But the theoretical question remains.

I will begin with (*ii*). If we are faced with a choice between two ways of perceiving a work, and the work is very much better perceived in one way than it is perceived in the other, I think that, at least in the absence of contrary considerations, we would be strongly inclined to settle on the former way of perceiving it as the *correct* way. The process of trying to determine what is in a work consists partly in casting around among otherwise plausible ways of perceiving it for one in which the work is good. We feel we are coming to a correct understanding of a work when we begin to like or enjoy it; we are finding what is really there when it seems to be worth experiencing.

But if (*ii*) is relevant, it is quite clearly not the *only* relevant consideration. Take any work of art we can agree is of fourth- or fifth- or tenth-rate quality. It is quite possible that if this work were perceived in some far-fetched set of categories that someone might dream up, it would appear to be first-rate, a masterpiece. Finding such *ad hoc* categories obviously would require talent and ingenuity on the order of that necessary to produce a masterpiece in the first place. But we can sketch how one might begin searching for them. (*a*) If the mediocre work suffers from some disturbingly prominent feature that distracts from whatever merits the work has, this feature might be toned down by choosing categories with respect to which it is standard, rather than variable or contra-standard. When the work is perceived in the new way the offending feature may be no more distracting than the flatness of a painting is to us. (*b*) If the work suffers from an overabundance of clichés it might be livened up by choosing categories with respect to which the clichés are variable or contra-standard rather than standard. (*c*) If it needs ingenuity we might devise a set of rules in terms of which the work finds itself in a dilemma and then ingeniously escapes from it, and build these rules into a set of categories. Surely, however, if there are categories waiting to be discovered which would transform a mediocre work into a masterpiece, it does not follow that the work really is a hitherto unrecognized masterpiece. The fact that when perceived in such categories it would appear exciting, ingenious, and so forth, rather than grating, cliché-ridden, pedestrian, does not make it so. It *cannot* be correct, I suggest, to perceive a work in categories which are totally foreign to the artist and his society, even if it comes across as a masterpiece in them.[22]

This brings us to the historical conditions (*iii*) and (*iv*). I see no way of avoiding the conclusion that one or the other of them at least is relevant in determining in what categories a work is correctly perceived. I consider both relevant, but will not argue here for the independent relevance of (*iv*). (*iii*) merits special attention in light of the recent prevalence of disputes about the importance of artists' intentions. To test the relevance of (*iii*) we must consider a case in which (*iii*) and (*iv*) diverge. One such instance occurred during the early days of the twelve-tone movement in music. Schoenberg no doubt intended even his earliest twelve-tone works to be heard as such. But this category was certainly not then well established or recognized in his society: virtually none of his contemporaries (except close associates such as Berg and Webern), even musically sophisticated ones, would have (or could have) heard these works in that category. But it seems to me that even the very first twelve-tone compositions are correctly heard as such, that the judgments one who hears them otherwise would make of them (for example, that they are chaotic, formless) are mistaken. I think this would be so even if Schoenberg had been working entirely alone, if *none* of his contemporaries had any inkling of the twelve-tone system. No doubt the first twelve-tone compositions are much better when heard in the category of twelve-tone works than when they are heard in any other way people might be likely to hear them. But as we have seen this cannot *by itself* account for the correctness of hearing them in the former way. The only other feature of the situation which could be relevant, so far as I can see, is Schoenberg's intention.

The above example is unusual in that Schoenberg was extraordinarily self-conscious about what he was doing, having explicitly formulated rules – that is, specified standard properties – for twelve-tone composition. Artists are of course not often so self-conscious, even when producing revolutionary works of art. Their intentions as to which categories their works are to be perceived in are not nearly as clear as Schoenberg's were, and often they change their minds considerably during the process of creation. In such cases (as well as ones in which the artists' intentions are unknown) the question of what categories a work is correctly perceived in is, I think, left by default to condition (*iv*), together with (*i*) and (*ii*). But it seems to me that in almost all cases at least one of the historical conditions, (*iii*) and (*iv*), is of crucial importance.

My account of the rules governing decisions about what categories works are correctly perceived in leaves a lot undone. There are bound to be a large number of undecidable cases on my criteria. Artists' intentions are frequently unclear, variable, or undiscoverable. Many works belong to categories which are borderline cases of being well established in the artists' societies (perhaps, for example, the categories of rococo music – for instance, C. P. E. Bach – of music in the style of early Mozart, and of very thin metal sculptured figures of the kind that Giacometti made). Many works fall between well-established categories (for example, between impressionist and cubist paintings), possessing *some* of the standard features relative to each, and so neither clearly qualify nor clearly fail to qualify on the basis of condition (*i*) to be perceived in either. There is, in addition, the question of what relative weights to accord the various conditions when they conflict.

It would be a mistake, however, to try to tighten up much further the rules for deciding how works are correctly perceived. To do so would be simply to legislate gratuitously, since the intuitions and precedents we have to go on are highly variable and often confused. But it is important to notice just where these intuitions and precedents are inconclusive, for doing so will expose the sources of many critical disputes. One such dispute might well arise concerning Giacometti's thin metal sculptures. To a critic who sees them simply as sculptures, or sculptures of people, they look frail, emaciated, wispy, or wiry. But that is not how they would strike a critic who sees them in the category of thin metal sculptures of that sort (just as stick figures do not strike us as wispy or emaciated). He would be impressed not by the thinness of the sculptures, but by the expressive nature of the positions of their limbs, and so forth, and so no doubt would attribute very different aesthetic properties to them. Which of the two ways of seeing these works is correct is, I suspect, undecidable. It is not clear whether enough such works have been made and have been regarded sufficiently often as constituting a category for that category to be deemed well established in Giacometti's society. And I doubt whether any of the other conditions settle the issue conclusively. So perhaps the dispute between the two critics is essentially unresolvable. The most that we can do is to point out just what sort of a difference of perception underlies the dispute, and why it is unresolvable.

The occurrence of such impasses is by no means something to be regretted. Works may be fascinating precisely because of shifts between equally permissible ways of perceiving them. And the enormous richness of some works is due in part to the variety of permissible, and worthwhile, ways of perceiving them. But it should be emphasized that even when my criteria do not clearly specify a *single* set of categories in which a work is correctly perceived, there are bound to be possible ways of perceiving it (which we may or may not have thought of) that they definitely rule out.

The question posed at the outset of this section was how to determine what aesthetic properties a work has, given that which ones it seems to have depends on what categories it is perceived in, on which of its properties are standard, which variable, and which contra-standard for us. I have sketched in rough outline rules for deciding in what categories a work is *correctly* perceived (and hence which of its features are absolutely standard, variable, and contra-standard). The aesthetic properties it actually possesses are those that are to be found in it when it is perceived correctly.[23]

V. Conclusion

I return now to the issues raised in Section I. (I will adopt for the remainder of this paper the simplifying assumption that there is only one correct way of perceiving any work. Nothing important depends on this.) If a work's aesthetic properties are those that are to be found in it when it is perceived correctly, and the correct way to perceive it is determined partly by historical facts about the artist's intention and/or his society, no examination of the work itself, however thorough, will by itself reveal those properties.[24] If we are confronted by a work about whose origins we know absolutely nothing (for example, one lifted from the dust at an as yet unexcavated archaeological site on Mars), we would simply not be in a position to judge it aesthetically. We could not possibly tell by staring at it, no matter how intently and intelligently, whether it is coherent, or serene, or dynamic, for by staring we cannot tell whether it is to be seen as a sculpture, a *guernica*, or some other exotic or mundane kind of work of art. (We could attribute aesthetic properties to it in the way we do to natural objects, which of course does not involve consideration of historical facts about artists or their societies. But to do this would not be to treat the object as a *work* of art.)

It should be emphasized that the relevant historical facts are not merely useful aids to aesthetic judgment; they do not simply provide hints concerning what might be found in the work. Rather they help to *determine* what aesthetic properties a work has; they, together with the work's nonaesthetic features, *make* it coherent, serene, or whatever. If the origin of a work which is coherent and serene had been different in crucial respects, the work would not have had these qualities; we would not merely have lacked a means for *discovering* them. And of two works which differ *only* in respect of their origins – that is, which are perceptually indistinguishable – one might be coherent or serene, and the other not. Thus, since artists' intentions are among the relevant historical considerations, the "intentional fallacy" is not a fallacy at all. I have of course made no claims about the relevance of artists' intentions as to the aesthetic properties that their works should have, and these intentions are among those most discussed in writings on aesthetics. I am willing to agree that whether an artist intended his work to be coherent or serene has nothing essential to do with whether it is coherent or serene. But this must not be allowed to seduce us into thinking that *no* intentions are relevant.

Aesthetic properties, then, are not to be found in works themselves in the straightforward way that colors and shapes or pitches and rhythms are. But I do not mean to deny that we perceive aesthetic properties in works of art. I see the serenity of a painting, and hear the coherence of a sonata, despite the fact that the presence of these qualities in the works depends partly on circumstances of their origin, which I cannot (now) perceive. Jones's marital status is part of what makes him a bachelor, if he is one, and we cannot tell his marital status just by looking at him, though we can thus ascertain his sex. Hence, I suppose, his bachelorhood is not a property we can be said to perceive in him. But the aesthetic properties of a work do not depend on historical facts about it in anything like the way Jones's bachelorhood depends on his marital status. The point is not that the historical facts (or in what categories the work is correctly perceived, or which of its properties are absolutely standard, variable, and contra-standard) function as *grounds* in any ordinary sense for aesthetic judgments. By themselves they do not, in general, count either for or against the presence of any particular aesthetic property. And they are not part of a larger body of information (also including data about the work derived from an examination of it) from which conclusions about the work's aesthetic properties are to be deduced or inferred. We must learn to *perceive* the work in the correct categories, as determined in part by the historical facts, and judge it by what we then perceive in it. The historical facts help to determine whether a painting is, for example, serene *only* (as far as my arguments go) by affecting what way of perceiving the painting must reveal this quality if it is truly attributable to the work.

We must not, however, expect to judge a work simply by setting ourselves to perceive it correctly, once it is determined what the correct way of perceiving it is. For one cannot, in general, perceive a work in a given set of categories simply by setting himself to do it. I could not possibly, merely by an act of will, see "Guernica" as a *guernica* rather than a painting, or hear a succession of street sounds in any arbitrary category one might dream up, even if the category has been explained to me in detail. (Nor can I imagine except in a rather vague way what it would be like, for example, to see "Guernica" as a *guernica*.) One cannot merely decide to respond appropriately to a work – to be shocked or unnerved or surprised by its (absolutely) contra-standard features, to find its standard features familiar or mundane, and to react to its variable features in other ways – once he knows the correct categories. Perceiving a work in a certain category or set of categories is a skill that must be acquired by training, and exposure to a great many other works of the category or categories in question is ordinarily, I believe, an essential part of this training. (But an effort of will may facilitate the training, and once the skill is acquired one may be able to decide at will whether or not to perceive it in that or those categories.) This has important consequences concerning how best to approach works of art of kinds that are new to us – contemporary works in new idioms, works from foreign cultures, or newly resurrected works from the ancient past. It is no use just immersing ourselves in a particular work, even with the knowledge of what categories it is correctly perceived in, for that alone will not enable us to perceive it in those categories. We must become familiar with a considerable variety of works of similar sorts.

When dealing with works of more familiar kinds it is not generally necessary to undertake deliberately the task of training ourselves to be able to perceive them in the correct categories (expect perhaps when those categories include relatively subtle ones). But this is almost always, I think, only because we have been trained unwittingly. Even the ability to see paintings as paintings had to be acquired, it seems to me, by repeated exposure to a great many paintings. The critic must thus go beyond the work before him in order to judge it aesthetically, not only to discover what the correct categories are, but also to be able to perceive it in them. The latter does not require consideration of historical facts, or consideration of facts at all, but it requires directing one's attention nonetheless to things other than the work in question.

Probably no one would deny that *some* sort of perceptual training is necessary, in many if not all instances, for apprehending a work's serenity or coherence, or other aesthetic properties. And of course it is not only *aesthetic* properties whose apprehension by the senses requires training. But the kind of training required in the aesthetic cases (and perhaps some others as well) has not been properly appreciated. In order to learn how to recognize gulls of various kinds, or the sex of chicks, or a certain person's handwriting, one must usually have gulls of those kinds, or chicks of the two sexes, or examples of that person's handwriting pointed out to him, practice recognizing them himself, and be corrected when he makes mistakes. But the training important for discovering the serenity or coherence of a work of art that I have been discussing is not of this sort (though this sort of training might be important as well). Acquiring the ability to perceive a serene or coherent work in the correct categories is not a matter of having had serene or coherent things pointed out to one, or having practiced recognizing them. What is important is not (or not merely) experience with other serene and coherent things, but experience with other things of the appropriate categories.

Much of the argument in this paper has been directed against the seemingly common-sense notion that aesthetic judgments about works of art are to be based solely on what can be perceived in them, how they look or sound. That notion is seriously misleading, I claim, on two quite different counts. I do not deny that paintings and sonatas are to be judged solely on what can be seen or heard in them – when they are perceived correctly. But examining a work with the senses can by itself reveal neither how it is correct to perceive it, nor how to perceive it that way.

Notes

1 Heinrich Wölfflin, *Principles of Art History*, trans. by M. D. Hottinger (7th ed.; New York, 1929), p. 228.

2 "[W]e should all agree, I think, ... that any quality that cannot even in principle be heard in it [a musical composition] does not belong to it as music." Monroe Beardsley, *Aesthetics: Problems in the Philosophy of Criticism* (New York, 1958), pp. 31–2.

3 Cf. Calvin Tompkins, *The Bride and the Bachelors* (New York, 1965), pp. 210–11.

4 Monroe Beardsley argues for a relatively strict separation (op. cit., pp. 17–34). Some of the strongest recent attempts to enforce this separation are to be found in discussions of the so-called "intentional fallacy," beginning with William Wimsatt and Beardsley, "The Intentional Fallacy," *Sewanee Review*, LIV (1946), which has been widely cited and reprinted. Despite the name of the "fallacy" these discussions are not limited to consideration of the relevance of artists' *intentions*.

5 The aesthetic properties of works of literature are not happily called "perceptual." For reasons connected with this it is sometimes awkward to treat literature together with the visual arts and music. (The notion of perceiving a work in a category, to be introduced shortly, is not straightforwardly applicable to literary works.) Hence in this paper I will concentrate on visual and musical works, though I believe that the central points I make concerning them hold, with suitable modifications, for novels, plays, and poems as well.

6 Frank Sibley distinguishes between "aesthetic" and "nonaesthetic" terms and concepts in "Aesthetic Concepts," *Philosophical Review*, LXVIII (1959).

7 Cf. Paul Ziff, "Art and the 'Object of Art,'" in Ziff, *Philosophic Turnings* (Ithaca, NY, 1966), pp. 12–16 (originally published in *Mind*, N. S. LX [1951]).

8 "Aesthetic and Nonaesthetic," *Philosophical Review*, LXXII (1965).

9 This is a very difficult notion to make precise, and I do not claim to have succeeded entirely. But the following comments seem to me to go in the right direction, and, together with the examples in the next section, they should clarify it sufficiently for my present purposes.

10 In order to avoid excessive complexity and length, I am ignoring some considerations that might be important at a later stage of investigation. In particular, I think it would be important at some point to distinguish between different *degrees* or *levels* of standardness, variableness, and contra-standardness for a person; to speak, e.g., of features being *more* or *less* standard for him. At least two distinct sorts of grounds for such differences of degree should be recognized. (*a*) Distinctions between perceiving a work in a certain category to a greater and lesser extent should be allowed for, with corresponding differences of degree in the standardness for the perceiver of properties relative to that category. (*b*) A feature which is standard relative to more, and/or more specific, categories in which a person perceives the work should thereby count as more standard for him. Thus, if we see something as a painting and also as a French Impressionist painting, features standard relative to both categories are more standard for us than features standard relative only to the latter.

11 This excludes, e.g., the sense of "represent" in which a picture might represent justice or courage, and probably other senses as well.

12 This does not hold for the special case of photography. A photograph is a photograph of a woman no matter what it looks like, I take it, if a woman was in front of the lens when it was produced.

13 Nelson Goodman denies that resemblance is necessary for representation – and obviously not merely because of isolated or marginal examples of non-resembling representations (p. 5). I cannot treat his arguments here, but rather than reject *en masse* the common-sense beliefs that pictures do resemble significantly what they depict and that they depict what they do partly because of such resemblances, if Goodman advocates rejecting them, I prefer to recognize a sense of "resemblance" in which these beliefs are true. My disagreement with him is perhaps less sharp than it appears since, as will be evident, I am quite willing to grant that the relevant resemblances are "conventional." Cf. Goodman, *Languages of Art* (Indianapolis, 1968), p. 39, n. 31.

14 The connection between features variable for us and what the work looks like is by no means a straightforward or simple one, however. It may involve "rules" which are more or less "conventional" (e.g., the "laws" of perspective). Cf. E. H. Gombrich, *Art and Illusion* (New York, 1960) and Nelson Goodman, op cit.

15 There is at least one group of exceptions to this. Obviously features of a work which are standard for us because they are standard relative to some *representational* category which we see it in – e.g., the category of nudes, still lifes, or landscapes – do help determine what the work looks like to us and what we take it to depict.

16 The presence of clichés in a work sometimes allows it to contain drastically disorderly elements without becoming chaotic or incoherent. Cf. Anton Ehrenzweig, *The Hidden Order of Art* (London, 1967), pp. 114–16.

17 The timing of the release of the key affects the tone's length. Use of the sustaining pedal can lessen slightly a tone's diminuendo by reinforcing its overtones with sympathetic vibrations from other strings. The rate of diminuendo is affected somewhat more drastically by the force with which the key is struck. The more forcefully it is struck the greater is the tone's relative diminuendo. (Obviously the rate of diminuendo cannot be controlled in this way independently of the tone's initial volume.) The successive tones of a melody can be made to overlap so that each tone's sharp attack is partially obscured by the lingering end of the preceding tone. A melodic tone may also be reinforced after it begins by sympathetic vibrations from harmonically related accompanying figures, contributed by the composer.

18 "[T]he musical media we know thus far derive their whole character and their usefulness as musical media precisely from their limitations." Roger Sessions, "Problems and Issues Facing the Composer Today," in Paul Henry Lang, *Problems of Modern Music* (New York, 1960), p. 31.

19 One way to make electronic music sound fast would be to make it sound like some traditional instrument, thereby trading on the limitations of that instrument.

20 Cf. William W. Austin, *Music in the 20th Century* (New York, 1966), pp. 205–6; and Eric Salzman, *Twentieth-Century Music: An Introduction* (Englewood Cliffs, NJ, 1967), pp. 5, 8, 19.

21 I am ruling out the view that the notions of truth and falsity are not applicable to aesthetic judgments, on the ground that it would force us to reject so much of our normal discourse and common-sense intuitions about art that theoretical aesthetics, conceived as attempting to understand the institution of art, would hardly have left a recognizable subject matter to investigate. (Cf. the quotation from Wölfflin, above.)

22 To say that it is incorrect (in my sense) to perceive a work in certain categories is not necessarily to claim that one *ought not* to perceive it that way. I heartily recommend perceiving mediocre works in categories that make perceiving them worthwhile whenever possible. The point is that one is not likely to *judge* the work correctly when he perceives it incorrectly.

23 This is a considerable oversimplification. If there are two equally correct ways of perceiving a work, and it appears to have a certain aesthetic property perceived in one but not the other of them, does it actually possess this property or not? There is no easy general answer. Probably in some such cases the question is undecidable. But I think we would sometimes be willing to say that a work is, e.g., touching or serene if it seems so when perceived in one correct way (or, more hesitantly, that there is "something very touching, or serene, about it"), while allowing that it does not seem so when perceived in another way which we do not want to rule incorrect. In some cases works have aesthetic properties (e.g., intriguing, subtle, alive, interesting, deep) which are not apparent on perceiving it in any single acceptable way, but which depend on the multiplicity of acceptable ways of perceiving it and relations between them. None of these complications relieves the critic of the responsibility for determining in what way or ways it is correct to perceive a work.

24 But this, plus a general knowledge of what sorts of works were produced when and by whom, might.

46

Appreciation and the Natural Environment

Allen Carlson

Allen Carlson is Professor of Philosophy at the University of Alberta.

I

With art objects there is a straightforward sense in which we know both what and how to aesthetically appreciate. We know *what* to appreciate in that, first, we can distinguish a work and its parts from that which is not it nor a part of it. And, second, we can distinguish its aesthetically relevant aspects from its aspects without such relevance. We know that we are to appreciate the sound of the piano in the concert hall and not the coughing which interrupts it; we know that we are to appreciate that a painting is graceful, but not that it happens to hang in the Louvre. In a similar vein, we know *how* to appreciate in that we know what "acts of aspection" to perform in regard to different works. Ziff says:

> ... to contemplate a painting is to perform one act of aspection; to scan it is to perform another; to study, observe, survey, inspect, examine, scrutinise, etc., are still other acts of aspection.
>
> ... I survey a Tintoretto, while I scan an H. Bosch. Thus I step back to look at the Tintoretto, up to look at the Bosch. Different actions are involved. Do you drink brandy in the way you drink beer?[1]

It is clear that we have such knowledge of what and how to aesthetically appreciate. It is, I believe, also clear what the grounds are for this knowledge. Works of art are our own creations; it is for this reason that we know what is and what is not a part of a work, which of its aspects are of aesthetic significance, and how to appreciate them. We have made them for the purpose of aesthetic appreciation; in order for them to fulfill this purpose this knowledge must be accessible. In making an object we know what we make and thus its parts and its purpose. Hence in knowing what we make we know what to do with that which we make. In the more general cases the point is clear enough: In creating a painting, we know that what we make is a painting. In knowing this we know that it ends at its frame, that its colors are aesthetically important, but where it hangs is not, and that we are to look at it rather than, say, listen to it. All this is involved in what it is to be a painting. Moreover, this point holds for more particular cases as well. Works of different particular types have different kinds of boundaries, have different foci of aesthetic significance, and perhaps most important demand different acts of aspection. In knowing the type we know what and how to appreciate. Ziff again:

Allen Carlson, "Appreciation and the Natural Environment," *Journal of Aesthetics and Art Criticism*, 37/3 (1979): 267–75.

> Generally speaking, a different act of aspection is performed in connection with works belonging to different schools of art, which is why the classification of style is of the essence. Venetian paintings lend themselves to an act of aspection involving attention to balanced masses: contours are of no importance, for they are scarcely to be found. The Florentine school demands attention to contours, the linear style predominates. Look for light in a Claude, for color in a Bonnard, for contoured volume in a Signorelli.[2]

I take the above to be essentially beyond serious dispute, except as to the details of the complete account. If it were not the case, our complementary institutions of art and of the aesthetic appreciation of art would not be as they are. We would not have the artworld which we do. But the subject of this paper is not art nor the artworld. Rather: it is the aesthetic appreciation of nature. The question I wish to investigate is the question of what and how to aesthetically appreciate in respect to natural environment. It is of interest since the account which is implicit in the above remarks and which I believe to be the correct account for art cannot be applied to the natural environment without at least some modification. Thus initially the questions of what and how to appreciate in respect to nature appear to be open questions.

II

In this section I consider some paradigms of aesthetic appreciation which *prima facie* seem applicable as models for the appreciation of the natural environment. In this I follow tradition to some extent in that these paradigms are ones which have been offered as or assumed to be appropriate models for the appreciation of nature. However, I think we will discover that these models are not as promising as they may initially appear to be.

The first such paradigm I call the object model. In the artworld non-representational sculpture best fits this model of appreciation. When we appreciate such sculpture we appreciate it as the actual physical object which it is. The qualities to be aesthetically appreciated are the sensuous and design qualities of the actual object and perhaps certain abstract expressive qualities. The sculpture need not represent anything external to itself; it need not lead the appreciator beyond itself: it may be a self-contained aesthetic unit. Consider a Brancusi sculpture, for example, the famous *Bird In Space* (1919). It has no representational connections with the rest of reality and no relational connections with its immediate surroundings and yet it has significant aesthetic qualities. It glistens, has balance and grace, and expresses flight itself.

Clearly it is possible to aesthetically appreciate an object of nature in the way indicated by this model. For example, we may appreciate a rock or a piece of driftwood in the same way as we appreciate a Brancusi sculpture: we actually or contemplatively remove the object from its surroundings and dwell on its sensuous and design qualities and its possible expressive qualities. Moreover, there are considerations which support the plausibility of this model for appreciation of the natural environment. First, natural objects are in fact often appreciated in precisely this way: mantel pieces are littered with pieces of rock and driftwood. Second, the model fits well with one feature of natural objects: such objects, like the Brancusi sculpture, do not have representational ties to the rest of reality. Third and most important, the model involves an accepted, traditional aesthetic approach. As Sparshott notes, "When one talks of the aesthetic this or that, one is usually thinking of it as entering into a subject/object relation."[3]

In spite of these considerations, however, I think there are aspects of the object model which make it inappropriate for nature. Santayana, in discussing the aesthetic appreciation of nature (which he calls the love of nature) notes that certain problems arise because the natural landscape has "indeterminate form." He then observes that although the landscape contains many objects which have determinate forms, "if the attention is directed specifically to them, we have no longer what, by a curious limitation of the word, is called the love of nature."[4] I think this limitation is not as curious as Santayana seems to think it is. The limitation marks the distinction between appreciating nature and appreciating the objects of nature. The importance of this distinction is seen by realizing the difficulty of appreciating nature by means of the object model. For example, on one understanding of the object model, the objects of nature when so appreciated become "ready-mades" or "found art." The artworld grants "artistic enfranchisement" to a piece of driftwood just as it has to Duchamp's urinal or to the real Brillo cartons discussed by Danto.[5] If this magic is successful the result is art. Questions of what and how to aesthetically appreciate are answered, of course, but in respect to art rather than nature; the appreciation of nature is lost in the shuffle. Appreciating sculpture which was once driftwood is no closer to appreciating nature than is appreciating a totem pole which was once a tree or a purse which was once a sow's ear. In all such cases the conversion from nature to art (or artifact) is complete; only the means of conversion are different.

There is, however, another understanding of how the object model applies to the objects of nature. On this understanding natural objects are simply (actually or contemplatively) removed from their surroundings, but they do not become art, they remain natural objects. Here we do not appreciate the objects *qua* art objects, but rather *qua* natural objects. We do not consider the rock on our mantel a ready-made sculpture, we consider it only an aesthetically pleasing rock. In such a case, as the example of non-representational sculpture suggests, our appreciation is limited to the sensuous and design qualities of the natural object and perhaps a few abstract expressive qualities: Our rock has a wonderfully smooth and gracefully curved surface and expresses solidity.

The above suggests that, even when it does not require natural objects to be seen as art objects, the object model imposes a certain limitation on our appreciation of natural objects. The limitation is the result of the removal of the object from its surroundings which the object model requires in order even to begin to provide answers to questions of what and how to appreciate. But in requiring such a removal the object model becomes problematic. The object model is most appropriate for those art objects which are self-contained aesthetic units. These objects are such that neither the environment of their creation nor the environment of their display are aesthetically relevant: the removal of a self-contained art object from its environment of creation will not vary its aesthetic qualities and the environment of display of such an object should not affect its aesthetic qualities. However, natural objects possess what we might call an organic unity with their environment of creation: such objects are a part of and have developed out of the elements of their environments by means of the forces at work within those environments. Thus the environments of creation are aesthetically relevant to natural objects. And for this reason the environments of display are equally relevant in virtue of the fact that these environments will be either the same as or different from the environments of creation. In either case the aesthetic qualities of natural objects will be affected. Consider again our rock: on the mantel it may seem wonderfully smooth and gracefully curved and expressive of solidity, but in its environment of creation it will have more and different aesthetic qualities – qualities which are the product of the relationship between it and its environment. It is here expressive of the particular forces which shaped and continue to shape it and displays for aesthetic appreciation its place in and its relation to its environment. Moreover, depending upon its place in that environment it may not express many of those qualities, for example, solidity, which it appears to express when on the mantle.

I conclude that the object model, even without changing nature into art, faces a problem as a paradigm for the aesthetic appreciation of nature. The problem is a dilemma: either we remove the object from its environment or we leave it where it is. If the object is removed, the model applies to the object and suggests answers to the questions of what and how to appreciate. But the result is the appreciation of a comparatively limited set of aesthetic qualities. On the other hand if the object is not removed, the model seemingly does not constitute an adequate model for a very large part of the appreciation which is possible. Thus it makes little headway with the what and how questions. In either case the object model does not provide a successful paradigm for the aesthetic appreciation of nature. It appears after all not a very "curious limitation" that when our attention is directed specifically toward the objects in the environment it is not called the love of nature.

The second paradigm for the aesthetic appreciation of nature I call the scenery or landscape model. In the artworld this model of appreciation is illustrated by landscape painting; in fact the model probably owes its existence to this art form. In one of its favored senses "landscape" means a prospect – usually a grandiose prospect – seen from a specific standpoint and distance; a landscape painting is traditionally a representation of such a prospect.[6] When aesthetically appreciating landscape paintings (or any representative paintings, for that matter) the emphasis is not on the actual object (the painting) nor on the object represented (the actual prospect); rather it is on the representation of the object and its represented features. Thus in landscape painting the appreciative emphasis is on those qualities which play an essential role in representing a prospect: visual qualities related to coloration and overall design. These are the qualities which are traditionally significant in landscape painting and which are the focus of the landscape model of appreciation. We thus have a model of appreciation which encourages perceiving and appreciating nature as if it were a landscape painting, as a grandiose prospect seen from a specific standpoint and distance. It is a model which centers attention on those aesthetic qualities of color and design which are seen and seen at a distance.

It is quite evident that the scenery or landscape model has been historically significant in our aesthetic appreciation of nature.[7] For example, this model was evident in the eighteenth and nineteenth centuries in the use of the "Claude-glass," a small, tinted, convex mirror with which tourists viewed the landscape. Thomas West's popular guidebook to the Lake District (first published in 1778) says of the glass:

> . . . where the objects are great and near, it removes them to a due distance, and shews them in the soft colours of nature, and most regular perspective the eye can perceive, art teach, or science demonstrate . . . to the glass is reserved the finished picture, in highest colouring, and just perspective.[8]

In a somewhat similar fashion, the modern tourist reveals his preference for this model of appreciation by frequenting "scenic viewpoints" where the actual space between the tourist and the prescribed "view" often constitutes "a due distance" which aids the impression of "soft colours of nature, and the most regular perspective the eye can perceive, art teach, or science demonstrate." And the "regularity" of the perspective is often enhanced by the positioning of the viewpoint itself. Moreover, the modern tourist also desires "the finished picture, in highest colouring, and just perspective"; whether this be the "scene" framed and balanced in his camera's viewfinder, the result of this in the form of a kodachrome slide, and/or the "artistically" composed postcard and calendar reproductions of the "scene" which often attract more appreciation than that which they "reproduce." R. Rees has described the situation as follows:

> . . . the taste has been for a view, for scenery, not for landscape in the original Dutch – and present geographical – meaning of [the] term, which denotes our ordinary, everyday surroundings. The average modern sightseer, unlike many of the Romantic poets and painters who were accomplished naturalists, is interested *not* in natural forms and processes, but in a prospect.[9]

It is clear that in addition to being historically important, the landscape model, like the object model, gives us at least initial guidelines as to what and how to appreciate in regard to nature. We appreciate the natural environment as if it were a landscape painting. The model requires dividing the environment into scenes or blocks of scenery, each of which is to be viewed from a particular point by a viewer who is separated by the appropriate spatial (and emotional?) distance. A drive through the country is not unlike a walk through a gallery of landscape paintings. When seen in this light, this model of appreciation causes a certain uneasiness in a number of thinkers. Some, such as ecologist Paul Shepard, seemingly believe this kind of appreciation of the natural environment so misguided that they entertain doubts about the wisdom of *any* aesthetic approach to nature.[10] Others find the model to be ethically suspect. For example, after pointing out that the modern sightseer is interested only in a prospect, Rees concludes:

> In this respect the Romantic Movement was a mixed blessing. In certain phases of its development it stimulated the movement for the protection of nature, but in its picturesque phase it

> simply confirmed our anthropocentrism by suggesting that nature exists to please as well as to serve us. Our ethics, if the word can be used to describe our attitudes and behaviour toward the environment, have lagged behind our aesthetics. It is an unfortunate lapse which allows us to abuse our local environments and venerate the Alps and the Rockies.[11]

What has not been as generally noted, however, is that this model of appreciation is suspect not only on ethical grounds, but also on aesthetic grounds. The model requires us to view the environment as if it were a static representation which is essentially "two dimensional." It requires the reduction of the environment to a scene or view. But what must be kept in mind is that the environment is not a scene, not a representation, not static, and not two dimensional. The point is that the model requires the appreciation of the environment not as what it is and with the qualities it has, but rather as something which it is not and with qualities it does not have. The model is in fact inappropriate to the actual nature of the object of appreciation. Consequently it not only, as the object model, unduly limits our appreciation – in this case to visual qualities related to coloration and overall design, it also misleads it. Hepburn puts this point in a general way:

> Supposing that a person's aesthetic education . . . instills in him the attitudes, the tactics of approach, the expectations proper to the appreciation of art works only, such a person will either pay very little aesthetic heed to natural objects or else heed them in the wrong way. He will look – and of course look in vain – for what can be found and enjoyed only in art.[12]

III

I conclude that the landscape model, as the object model, is inadequate as a paradigm for the aesthetic appreciation of nature. However, the reason for its inadequacy is instructive. The landscape model is made inadequate because it is inappropriate to the nature of the natural environment. Perhaps to see what and how to appreciate in respect to the natural environment, we must consider the nature of that environment more carefully. In this regard there are two rather obvious points which I wish to emphasize. The first is that the natural environment is an environment; the second is that it is natural.

When we conceptualize the natural environment as "nature" I think we are tempted to think of it as an object. When we conceptualize it as "landscape" we are certainly led to thinking of it as scenery. Consequently perhaps the concept of the "natural environment" is somewhat preferable. At least it makes explicit that it is an environment which is under consideration. The object model and the landscape model each in its own way fail to take account of this. But what is involved in taking this into account? Here I wish initially to follow up some remarks made by Sparshott. He suggests that to consider something environmentally is primarily to consider it in regard to the relation of "self to setting," rather than "subject to object" or "traveler to scene."[13] An environment is the setting in which we exist as a "sentient part"; it is our surroundings. Sparshott points out that as our surroundings, our setting, the environment is that which we take for granted, that which we hardly notice – it is necessarily unobtrusive. If any one part of it becomes obtrusive, it is in danger of being seen as an object or a scene, not as our environment. As Sparshott says, "When a man starts talking about 'environmental values' we usually take him to be talking about aesthetic values of a background sort."[14]

The aesthetic values of the environment being primarily background values has obvious ramifications for the questions of what and how to appreciate. In regard to what to appreciate this suggests the answer "everything," for in an essentially unobtrusive setting there seems little basis for including and excluding. I will return to this shortly. In regard to how to appreciate, the answer suggested is in terms of all those ways in which we normally are aware of and experience our surroundings. Sparshott notes that "if environmental aspects are background aspects, eye and ear lose part of their privilege" and goes on to mention smell, touch, and taste, and even warmth and coolness, barometric pressure and humidity as possibly relevant.[15] This points in the right direction, but as Sparshott also notes, it seems to involve a difficulty: that "the concept of the aesthetic tugs in a different direction" – the direction of the subject/object relation involving primarily the visual scrutiny of an aesthetic object.[16]

However, I do not think this difficulty need be as serious as Sparshott seems to think. I suspect the apparent tension here is not due to the concept of the aesthetic being necessarily tied to the subject/object relation or to the visual, but rather is due to its being antithetical to the appreciation of anything only as unobtrusive background. To confirm this we need to consider the concept of the aesthetic as it is elaborated by John Dewey in *Art as Experience.*[17] Dewey's concept is such that anything which is aesthetically appreciated must be obtrusive, it must be foreground, but it need not be an object and it need not be seen (or only seen). Moreover, to assume that that which is aesthetically appreciated need be an object or only seen is to confine aesthetic appreciation to either the object model or the landscape model, which, as we have noted, impose unacceptable limitations on the aesthetic appreciation of the natural environment.

I suggest then that the beginning of an answer to the question of *how* to aesthetically appreciate an environment is something like the following: We must experience our background setting in all those ways in which we normally experience it, by sight, smell, touch, and whatever. However, we must experience it not as unobtrusive background, but as obtrusive foreground! What is involved in such an "act of aspection" is not completely clear. Dewey gives us an idea in remarks such as:

> To grasp the sources of esthetic experience it is . . . necessary to have recourse to animal life below the human scale. . . . The live animal is fully present, all there, in all of its actions: in its wary glances, its sharp sniffing, its abrupt cocking of ears. All senses are equally on the *qui vive.*[18]

And perhaps the following description by Yi-Fu Tuan gives some further indication:

> An adult must learn to be yielding and careless like a child if he were to enjoy nature polymorphously. He needs to slip into old clothes so that he could feel free to stretch out on the hay beside the brook and bathe in a meld of physical sensations: the smell of the hay and of horse dung; the warmth of the ground, its hard and soft contours; the warmth of the sun tempered by breeze; the tickling of an ant making its way up the calf of his leg; the play of shifting leaf shadows on his face; the sound of water over the pebbles and boulders, the sound of cicadas and distant traffic. Such an environment might break all the formal rules of euphony and aesthetics, substituting confusion for order, and yet be wholly satisfying.[19]

Tuan's account as to how to appreciate fits well with our earlier answer to the question of what to appreciate, *viz.* everything. This answer, of course, will not do. We cannot appreciate everything; there must be limits and emphasis in our aesthetic appreciation of nature as there are in our appreciation of art. Without such limits and emphases our experience of the natural environment would be *only* "a meld of physical sensations" without any meaning or significance. It would be a Jamesian "blooming, buzzing confusion" which truly substitited "confusion for order" and which, I suspect contra to Tuan, would not be wholly satisfying. Such experience would be too far removed from our aesthetic appreciation of art to merit the label "aesthetic" or even the label "appreciation." Consider again the case of art. In this case, as noted in Section I, the boundaries and foci of aesthetic significance of works of art are a function of the type of art in question, e.g., paintings end at their frames and their colors are significant. Moreover, I suggested that our knowledge of such matters is due to art works being our creations. Here it is relevant to note the second point which I wish to emphasize about natural environments: they are natural. The natural environment is not a work of art. As such it has no boundaries or foci of aesthetic significance which are given as a result of our creation nor of which we have knowledge because of our involvement in such creation.

The fact that nature is natural – not our creation – does not mean, however, that we must be without knowledge of it. Natural objects are such that we can discover things about them which are independent of any involvement by us in their creation. Thus although we have not created nature, we yet know a great deal about it. This knowledge, essentially common sense/ scientific knowledge, seems to me the only viable candidate for playing the role in regard to the appreciation of nature which our knowledge of types of art, artistic traditions, and the like plays in regard to the appreciation of art. Consider the aesthetic appreciation of an environment such as that described by Tuan. We experience the environment as obtrusive foreground – the smell of the hay and of the horse dung, the feel of the ant, the sound of the cicadas and of the distant traffic all force themselves upon us. We experience a "meld of sensations" but, as noted, if our state is to be aesthetic appreciation rather than just the having of raw experience, the meld cannot be simply a "blooming, buzzing confusion." Rather it must be what Dewey called a consummatory experience: one in which knowledge and intelligence transform raw experience by making it determinate, harmonious, and meaningful. For example, in order for there to be aesthetic appreciation we must recognize the smell of the hay and that of the horse dung and perhaps distinguish between them; we must feel the ant at least as an insect rather than as, say, a twitch. Such recognizing and distinguishing results in certain aspects of the obtrusive foreground becoming foci of aesthetic significance. Moreover, they are natural foci appropriate to the particular natural environment we are appreciating. Likewise our knowledge of the environment may yield certain appropriate boundaries or limits to the experience. For example, since we are aesthetically appreciating a certain kind of environment, the sound of cicadas may be appreciated as a proper part of the setting, while the sound of the distant traffic is excluded much as we ignore the coughing in the concert hall.

What I am suggesting is that the question of *what* to aesthetically appreciate in the natural environment is to be answered in a way analogous to the similar question about art. The difference is that in the case of the natural environment the relevant knowledge is the common sense/scientific knowledge which we have discovered about the environment in question. This knowledge gives us the appropriate foci of aesthetic significance and the appropriate boundaries of the setting so that our experience becomes one of aesthetic appreciation. If to aesthetically appreciate art we must have knowledge of artistic traditions and styles within those traditions, to aesthetically appreciate nature we must have knowledge of the different environments of nature and of the systems and elements within those environments. In the way in which the art critic and the art historian are well equipped to aesthetically appreciate art, the naturalist and the ecologist are well equipped to aesthetically appreciate nature.[20]

The point I have now made about what to appreciate in nature also has ramifications for how to appreciate nature. When discussing the nature of an environment, I suggested that Tuan's description seems to indicate a general act of aspection appropriate for any environment. However, since natural environments differ in type it seems that within this general act of aspection there might be differences which should be noted. To aesthetically appreciate an environment we experience our surroundings as obtrusive foreground allowing our knowledge of that environment to select certain foci of aesthetic significance and perhaps exclude others, thereby limiting the experience. But certainly there are also different kinds of appropriate acts of aspection which can likewise be selected by our knowledge of environments. Ziff tells us to look for contours in the Florentine school and for color in a Bonnard, to survey a Tintoretto and to scan a Bosch. Consider different natural environments. It seems that we must survey a prairie environment, looking at the subtle contours of the land, feeling the wind blowing across the open space, and smelling the mix of prairie grasses and flowers. But such an act of aspection has little place in a dense forest environment. Here we must examine and scrutinize, inspecting the detail of the forest floor, listening carefully for the sounds of birds and smelling carefully for the scent of spruce and pine. Likewise, the description of environmental appreciation given by Tuan, in addition to being a model for environmental acts of aspection in general, is also a description of the act of aspection appropriate for a particular kind of environment – one perhaps best described as pastoral. Different natural environments require different acts of aspection; and as in the case of what to appreciate, our knowledge of the environment in question indicates how to appreciate, that is, indicates the appropriate act of aspection.

The model I am thus presenting for the aesthetic appreciation of nature might be termed the environmental model. It involves recognizing that nature is an environment and thus a setting within which we exist and which we normally experience with our complete range of senses as our unobtrusive background. But our experience being aesthetic requires unobtrusive background to be experienced as obtrusive foreground. The result is the experience of a "blooming, buzzing confusion" which in order to be appreciated must be tempered by the knowledge which we have discovered about the natural environment so experienced. Our knowledge of the nature of the particular environments yields the appropriate boundaries of appreciation, the particular foci of aesthetic significance, and the relevant act or acts of aspection for that type of environment. We thus have a model which begins to give answers to the questions of what and how to appreciate in respect to the natural environment and which seems to do so with due regard for the nature of that environment. And this is important not only for aesthetic but also for moral and ecological reasons.

IV

In this paper I have attempted to open discussion on the questions of what and how to aesthetically appreciate in regard to nature. In doing so I have argued that two traditional approaches, each of which more or less assimilates the appreciation of nature to the appreciation of certain art forms, leave much to be desired. However, the approach which I have suggested, the environmental model, yet follows closely the general structure of our aesthetic appreciation of art. This approach does not depend on an assimilation of natural objects to art objects or of landscapes to scenery, but rather on an application of the general structure of aesthetic appreciation of art to something which is not art. What is important is to recognize that nature is an environment and is natural, and to make that recognition central to our aesthetic appreciation. Thereby we will aesthetically appreciate nature for what it is and for the qualities it has. And we will avoid being the person described by Hepburn who "will either pay very little aesthetic heed to natural objects or else heed them in the wrong way," who "will look – and of course look in vain – for what can be found and enjoyed only in art."[21]

Notes

1 Paul Ziff, "Reasons in Art Criticism," *Philosophy and Education*, ed. I. Scheffler (Boston, 1958). Reprinted in *Art and Philosophy*, ed. W. E. Kennick (New York, 1964), p. 620.

2 Ibid. Ziff is mainly concerned with the way in which knowledge of types yields different acts of aspection. For an elaboration of this point and its ramifications concerning what is and is not aesthetically significant in a work, see K. Walton, "Categories of Art," *Philosophical Review* (1970), 334–67. How our knowledge of art (and the artworld) yields the boundaries between art and the rest of reality is interestingly discussed in A. Danto, "The Artistic Enfranchisement of Real Objects: The Artworld," *Journal of Philosophy* (1964), 571–84.

3 F. E. Sparshott, "Figuring the Ground: Notes on Some Theoretical Problems of the Aesthetic Environment," *Journal of Aesthetic Education* (1972), 13.

4 George Santayana, *The Sense of Beauty* (New York, 1961), p. 100.

5 Danto, op. cit., p. 579.

6 This favored sense of "landscape" is brought out by Yi-Fu Tuan. See *Topophilia: A Study of Environmental Perception, Attitudes, and Values* (Englewood Cliffs, 1974), pp. 132–3, or "Man and Nature: An Eclectic Reading," *Landscape*, Vol. 15 (1966), 30.

7 For a good, brief discussion of this point, see R. Rees, "The Scenery Cult: Changing Landscape Tastes over Three Centuries," *Landscape*, Vol. 19 (1975). Note the following remarks by E. H. Gombrich in "The Renaissance Theory of Art and the Rise of Landscape," *Norm and Form: Studies in the Art of the Renaissance* (London, 1971), pp. 117–18: ". . . I believe that the idea of natural beauty as an inspiration of art . . . is, to say the least, a very dangerous oversimplification. Perhaps it even reverses the actual process by which man discovers the beauty of nature. We call a scenery 'picturesque' . . . if it reminds us of paintings we have seen. . . . Similarly, so it seems, the discovery of Alpine scenery does not precede but follows the spread of prints and paintings with mountain panoramas."

8 Thomas West, *Guide to the Lakes* (London: 1778) as quoted in J. T. Ogden, "From Spatial to Aesthetic Distance in the Eighteenth Century," *Journal of the History of Ideas*, Vol. XXXV (1974), 66–7.

9 R. Rees, "The Taste for Mountain Scenery," *History Today*, Vol. XXV (1975), 312.

10 Paul Shepard, *The Tender Carnivore and the Sacred Game* (New York, 1973), pp. 147–8. Shepard made this position more explicit at a lecture at Athabasca University, Edmonton, Alberta, November 16, 1974.

11 Rees, "Mountain Scenery," op. cit., p. 312. Ethical worries are also expressed by Tuan, *Topophilia*, op. cit., Chapter 8, and R. A. Smith and C. M. Smith, "Aesthetics and Environmental Education," *Journal of Aesthetic Education* (1970), 131–2. Smith and Smith put the point as follows: "Perhaps there is a special form of arrogance in experiencing nature strictly in the categories of art, for the attitude involved here implies an acceptance, though perhaps only momentarily, of the notion that natural elements have been arranged for the sake of the man's aesthetic pleasure. It is possible that this is what Kant had in mind when he said that in the appreciation of natural beauty one ought not assume that nature has fashioned its forms for our delight and that, instead, 'it is we who receive nature with favour, and not nature that does us a favour.'"

12 R. W. Hepburn, "Aesthetic Appreciation of Nature," *Aesthetics and the Modern World*, ed. H. Osborne (London, 1968), p. 53. Hepburn implicitly argues that our aesthetic appreciation of nature is enhanced by our "realizing" that an object is what it is and has the qualities which it has. See pp. 60–5.

13 Sparshott, op. cit., pp. 12–13. Sparshott also considers other possible relations which are not directly relevant here. Moreover, I suspect he considers the "traveler to scene" relation to be more significant than I do.

14 Ibid., pp. 17–18.

15 Ibid., p. 21.

16 Ibid., pp. 13–14, p. 21.

17 John Dewey, *Art as Experience* (New York, 1958), especially Chapters I–III.

18 Ibid., pp. 18–19.

19 Tuan, *Topophilia*, op. cit., p. 96.

20 I have in mind here individuals such as John Muir and Aldo Leopold. See, for example, Leopold's *A Sand County Almanac*.

21 Hepburn, op. cit., p. 53.

47

The Intentional Fallacy

W. K. Wimsatt, Jr. and Monroe Beardsley

W. K. Wimsatt, Jr. (1907–75) was Professor of English at Yale University. Monroe Beardsley (1915–85) was Professor of Philosophy at Temple University.

"He owns with toil he wrote the following scenes;
But, if they're naught, ne'er spare him for his pains:
Damn him the more; have no commiseration
For dullness on mature deliberation."

William Congreve
Prologue to The Way of the World

I

The claim of the author's "intention" upon the critic's judgment has been challenged in a number of recent discussions, notably in the debate entitled *The Personal Heresy*, between Professors Lewis and Tillyard. But it seems doubtful if this claim and most of its romantic corollaries are as yet subject to any widespread questioning. The present writers, in a short article entitled "Intention" for a *Dictionary*[1] of literary criticism, raised the issue but were unable to pursue its implications at any length. We argued that the design or intention of the author is neither available nor desirable as a standard for judging the success of a work of literary art, and it seems to us that this is a principle which goes deep into some differences in the history of critical attitudes. It is a principle which accepted or rejected points to the polar opposites of classical "imitation" and romantic expression. It entails many specific truths about inspiration, authenticity, biography, literary history and scholarship, and about some trends of contemporary poetry, especially its allusiveness. There is hardly a problem of literary criticism in which the critic's approach will not be qualified by his view of "intention."

"Intention," as we shall use the term, corresponds to *what he intended* in a formula which more or less explicitly has had wide acceptance. "In order to judge the poet's performance, we must know *what he intended*." Intention is design

W. K. Wimsatt, Jr. and Monroe Beardsley, "The Intentional Fallacy," in *The Verbal Icon: Studies in the Meaning of Poetry*, ed. W. K. Wimsatt, Jr. (Lexington: University of Kentucky Press, 1954), pp. 3–18.

or plan in the author's mind. Intention has obvious affinities for the author's attitude toward his work, the way he felt, what made him write.

We begin our discussion with a series of propositions summarized and abstracted to a degree where they seem to us axiomatic.

1. A poem does not come into existence by accident. The words of a poem, as Professor Stoll has remarked, come out of a head, not out of a hat. Yet to insist on the designing intellect as a *cause* of a poem is not to grant the design or intention as a *standard* by which the critic is to judge the worth of the poet's performance.

2. One must ask how a critic expects to get an answer to the question about intention. How is he to find out what the poet tried to do? If the poet succeeded in doing it, then the poem itself shows what he was trying to do. And if the poet did not succeed, then the poem is not adequate evidence, and the critic must go outside the poem – for evidence of an intention that did not become effective in the poem. "Only one *caveat* must be borne in mind," says an eminent intentionalist[2] in a moment when his theory repudiates itself; "the poet's aim must be judged at the moment of the creative act, that is to say, by the art of the poem itself."

3. Judging a poem is like judging a pudding or a machine. One demands that it work. It is only because an artifact works that we infer the intention of an artificer. "A poem should not mean but be." A poem can *be* only through its *meaning* – since its medium is words – yet it *is*, simply *is*, in the sense that we have no excuse for inquiring what part is intended or meant. Poetry is a feat of style by which a complex of meaning is handled all at once. Poetry succeeds because all or most of what is said or implied is relevant; what is irrelevant has been excluded, like lumps from pudding and "bugs" from machinery. In this respect poetry differs from practical messages, which are successful if and only if we correctly infer the intention. They are more abstract than poetry.

4. The meaning of a poem may certainly be a personal one, in the sense that a poem expresses a personality or state of soul rather than a physical object like an apple. But even a short lyric poem is dramatic, the response of a speaker (no matter how abstractly conceived) to a situation (no matter how universalized). We ought to impute the thoughts and attitudes of the poem immediately to the dramatic *speaker*, and if to the author at all, only by an act of biographical inference.

5. There is a sense in which an author, by revision, may better achieve his original intention. But it is a very abstract sense. He intended to write a better work, or a better work of a certain kind, and now has done it. But it follows that his former concrete intention was not his intention. "He's the man we were in search of, that's true," says Hardy's rustic constable, "and yet he's not the man we were in search of. For the man we were in search of was not the man we wanted."

"Is not a critic," asks Professor Stoll, "a judge, who does not explore his own consciousness, but determines the author's meaning or intention, as if the poem were a will, a contract, or the constitution? The poem is not the critic's own." He has accurately diagnosed two forms of irresponsibility, one of which he prefers. Our view is yet different. The poem is not the critic's own and not the author's (it is detached from the author at birth and goes about the world beyond his power to intend about it or control it). The poem belongs to the public. It is embodied in language, the peculiar possession of the public, and it is about the human being, an object of public knowledge. What is said about the poem is subject to the same scrutiny as any statement in linguistics or in the general science of psychology.

A critic of our *Dictionary* article, Ananda K. Coomaraswamy, has argued[3] that there are two kinds of inquiry about a work of art: (1) whether the artist achieved his intentions; (2) whether the work of art "ought ever to have been undertaken at all" and so "whether it is worth preserving." Number (2), Coomaraswamy maintains, is not "criticism of any work of art *qua* work of art," but is rather moral criticism; number (1) is artistic criticism. But we maintain that (2) need not be moral criticism: that there is another way of deciding whether works of art are worth preserving and whether, in a sense, they "ought" to have been undertaken, and this is the way of objective criticism of works of art as such, the way which enables us to distinguish between a skillful murder and a skillful poem. A skillful murder is an example which Coomaraswamy uses, and in his system the difference between the murder and the poem is simply a "moral" one, not an "artistic" one, since each if carried out according to plan is "artistically" successful. We maintain that (2) is an inquiry of more worth than (1), and since (2) and not (1) is capable of distinguishing poetry from murder, the name "artistic criticism" is properly given to (2).

II

It is not so much a historical statement as a definition to say that the intentional fallacy is a romantic one. When a rhetorician of the first century AD writes: "Sublimity is the echo of a great soul," or when he tells us that "Homer enters into the sublime actions of his heroes" and "shares the full inspiration of the combat," we shall not be surprised to find this rhetorician considered as a distant harbinger of romanticism and greeted in the warmest terms by Saintsbury. One may wish to argue whether Longinus should be called romantic, but there can hardly be a doubt that in one important way he is.

Goethe's three questions for "constructive criticism" are "What did the author set out to do? Was his plan reasonable and sensible, and how far did he succeed in carrying it out?" If one leaves out the middle question, one has in effect the system of Croce – the culmination and crowning philosophic expression of romanticism. The beautiful is the successful intuition-expression, and the ugly is the unsuccessful; the intuition or private part of art is *the* aesthetic fact, and the medium or public part is not the subject of aesthetic at all.

> The Madonna of Cimabue is still in the Church of Santa Maria Novella; but does she speak to the visitor of to-day as to the Florentines of the thirteenth century?
>
> *Historical interpretation* labors . . . to reintegrate in us the psychological conditions which have changed in the course of history. It . . . enables us to see a work of art (a physical object) as its *author saw* it in the moment of production.[4]

The first italics are Croce's, the second ours. The upshot of Croce's system is an ambiguous emphasis on history. With such passages as a point of departure a critic may write a nice analysis of the meaning or "spirit" of a play by Shakespeare or Corneille – a process that involves close historical study but remains aesthetic criticism – or he may, with equal plausibility, produce an essay in sociology, biography, or other kinds of non-aesthetic history.

III

> *I went to the poets; tragic, dithyrambic, and all sorts. . . . I took them some of the most elaborate passages in their own writings, and asked what was the meaning of them. . . . Will you believe me? . . . there is hardly a person present who would not have talked better about their poetry than they did themselves. Then I knew that not by wisdom do poets write poetry, but by a sort of genius and inspiration.*

That reiterated mistrust of the poets which we hear from Socrates may have been part of a rigorously ascetic view in which we hardly wish to participate, yet Plato's Socrates saw a truth about the poetic mind which the world no longer commonly sees – so much criticism, and that the most inspirational and most affectionately remembered, has proceeded from the poets themselves.

Certainly the poets have had something to say that the critic and professor could not say; their message has been more exciting: that poetry should come as naturally as leaves to a tree, that poetry is the lava of the imagination; or that it is emotion recollected in tranquillity. But it is necessary that we realize the character and authority of such testimony. There is only a fine shade of difference between such expressions and a kind of earnest advice that authors often give. Thus Edward Young, Carlyle, Walter Pater:

> I know two golden rules from *ethics*, which are no less golden in *Composition*, than in life, 1. *Know thyself*; 2dly, *Reverence thyself*.

> This is the grand secret for finding readers and retaining them: let him who would move and convince others, be first moved and convinced himself. Horace's rule, *Si vis me fiere*, is applicable in a wider sense than the literal one. To every poet, to every writer, we might say: Be true, if you would be believed.

> Truth! there can be no merit, no craft at all, without that. And further, all beauty is in the long run only *fineness* of truth, or what we call expression, the finer accommodation of speech to that vision within.

And Housman's little handbook to the poetic mind yields this illustration:

> Having drunk a pint of beer at luncheon – beer is a sedative to the brain, and my afternoons are the least intellectual portion of my life – I would go out for a walk of two or three hours. As I went along, thinking of nothing in particular, only looking at things around me and following the progress of the seasons, there would flow into my mind, with sudden and unaccountable emotion, sometimes a line or two of verse, sometimes a whole stanza at once.

This is the logical terminus of the series already quoted. Here is a confession of how poems were written which would do as a definition of poetry just as well as "emotion recollected in tranquillity" – and which the young poet might equally well take to heart as a practical rule. Drink a pint of beer, relax, go walking, think on nothing in particular, look at things, surrender yourself to yourself, search for the truth in your own soul, listen to the sound of your own inside voice, discover and express the *vraie vérité*.

It is probably true that all this is excellent advice for poets. The young imagination fired by Wordsworth and Carlyle is probably closer to the verge of producing a poem than the mind of the student who has been sobered by Aristotle or Richards. The art of inspiring poets, or at least of inciting something like poetry in young persons, has probably gone further in our day than ever before. Books of creative writing such as those issued from the Lincoln School are interesting evidence of what a child can do.[5] All this, however, would appear to belong to an art separate from criticism – to a psychological discipline, a system of self-development, a yoga, which the young poet perhaps does well to notice, but which is something different from the public art of evaluating poems.

Coleridge and Arnold were better critics than most poets have been, and if the critical tendency dried up the poetry in Arnold and perhaps in Coleridge, it is not inconsistent with our argument, which is that judgment of poems is different from the art of producing them. Coleridge has given us the classic "anodyne" story, and tells what he can about the genesis of a poem which he calls a "psychological curiosity," but his definitions of poetry and of the poetic quality "imagination" are to be found elsewhere and in quite other terms.

It would be convenient if the passwords of the intentional school, "sincerity," "fidelity," "spontaneity," "authenticity," "genuineness," "originality," could be equated with terms such as "integrity," "relevance," "unity," "function," "maturity," "subtlety," "adequacy," and other more precise terms of evaluation – in short, if "expression" always meant aesthetic achievement. But this is not so.

"Aesthetic" art, says Professor Curt Ducasse, an ingenious theorist of expression, is the conscious objectification of feelings, in which an intrinsic part is the critical moment. The artist corrects the objectification when it is not adequate. But this may mean that the earlier attempt was not successful in objectifying the self, or "it may also mean that it was a successful objectification of a self which, when it confronted us clearly, we disowned and repudiated in favor of another."[6] What is the standard by which we disown or accept the self? Professor Ducasse does not say. Whatever it may be, however, this standard is an element in the definition of art which will not reduce to terms of objectification. The evaluation of the work of art remains public; the work is measured against something outside the author.

IV

There is criticism of poetry and there is author psychology, which when applied to the present or future takes the form of inspirational promotion; but author psychology can be historical too, and then we have literary biography, a legitimate and attractive study in itself, one approach, as Professor Tillyard would argue, to personality, the poem being only a parallel approach. Certainly it need not be with a derogatory purpose that one points out personal studies, as distinct from poetic studies, in the realm of literary scholarship. Yet there is danger of confusing personal and poetic studies; and there is the fault of writing the personal as if it were poetic.

There is a difference between internal and external evidence for the meaning of a poem. And the paradox is only verbal and superficial that what is (1) internal is also public: it is discovered through the semantics and syntax of a poem, through our habitual knowledge of the language, through grammars, dictionaries, and all the literature which is the source of dictionaries, in general through all that makes a language and culture; while what is (2) external is private or idiosyncratic; not a part of the work as a linguistic fact: it consists of revelations (in journals, for example, or letters or reported conversations) about how or why the poet wrote the poem – to what lady, while sitting on what lawn, or at the death of what friend or brother. There is (3) an intermediate kind of evidence about the character of the author or about private or semiprivate meanings attached to words or topics by the author or by a coterie of which he is a member. The meaning of words is the history of words, and the biography of an author, his use of a word, and the associations which the word had for *him*, are part of the word's history and meaning.[7] But the three types of evidence, especially (2) and (3), shade into one another so subtly that it is not always easy to draw a line between examples, and hence arises the difficulty for criticism. The use of biographical evidence need not involve intentionalism, because while it may be evidence of what the author intended, it may also be evidence of the meaning of his words and the dramatic character of his utterance. On the other hand, it may not be all this. And a critic who is concerned with evidence of type (1) and moderately with that of type (3) will in the long run produce a different sort of comment from that of the critic who is concerned with (2) and with (3) where it shades into (2).

The whole glittering parade of Professor Lowes' *Road to Xanadu*, for instance, runs along the border between types (2) and (3) or boldly traverses the romantic region of (2). "'Kubla Khan'" says Professor Lowes, "is the fabric of a vision, but every image that rose up in its weaving had passed that way before. And it would seem that there is nothing haphazard or fortuitious in their return." This is not quite clear – not even when Professor Lowes explains that there were clusters of associations, like hooked atoms, which were drawn into complex relation with other clusters in the deep well of Coleridge's memory, and which then coalesced and issued forth as poems. If there was nothing "haphazard or fortuitous" in the way the images returned to the surface, that may mean (1) that Coleridge could not produce what he did not have, that he was limited in his creation by what he had read or otherwise experienced, or (2) that having received certain clusters of associations, he was bound to return them in just the way he did, and that the value of the poem may be described in terms of the experiences on which he had to draw. The latter pair of propositions (a sort of Hartleyan associationism which Coleridge himself repudiated in the *Biographia)* may not be assented to. There were certainly other combinations, other poems, worse or better, that might have been written by men who had read Bartram and Purchas and Bruce and Milton. And this will be true no matter how many times we are able to add to the brilliant complex of Coleridge's reading. In certain flourishes (such as the sentence we have quoted) and in chapter headings like "The Shaping Spirit," "The Magical Synthesis," "Imagination Creatrix," it may be that Professor Lowes pretends to say more about the actual poems than he does. There is a certain deceptive variation in these fancy chapter titles; one expects to pass on to a new stage in the argument, and one finds – more and more sources, more and more about "the streamy nature of association."[8]

"Wohin der Weg?" quotes Professor Lowes for the motto of his book. "Kein Weg! Ins Unbretretene." Precisely because the way is *unbetreten*, we should say, it leads away from the poem. Bartram's *Travels* contains a good deal of the history of certain words and of certain romantic Floridian conceptions that appear in "Kubla Khan." And a good deal of that history has passed and was then passing into the very stuff of our language. Perhaps a person who has read Bartram appreciates the poem more than one who has not. Or, by looking up the vocabulary of "Kubla Khan" in the *Oxford English Dictionary*, or by reading some of the other books there quoted, a person may know the poem better. But it would seem to pertain little to the poem to know that

Coleridge had read Bartram. There is a gross body of life, of sensory and mental experience, which lies behind and in some sense causes every poem, but can never be and need not be known in the verbal and hence intellectual composition which is the poem. For all the objects of our manifold experience, for every unity, there is an action of the mind which cuts off roots, melts away context – or indeed we should never have objects or ideas or anything to talk about.

It is probable that there is nothing in Professor Lowes' vast book which could detract from anyone's appreciation of either *The Ancient Mariner* or Kubla Khan." We next present a case where preoccupation with evidence of type (3) has gone so far as to distort a critic's view of a poem (yet a case not so obvious as those that abound in our critical journals).

In a well-known poem by John Donne appears this quatrain:

> Moving of th'earth brings harmes and feares,
>   Men reckon what it did and meant,
> But trepidation of the spheares,
>   Though greater farre, is innocent.

A recent critic in an elaborate treatment of Donne's learning has written of this quatrain as follows:

> He touches the emotional pulse of the situation by a skillful allusion to the new and the old astronomy.... Of the new astronomy, the "moving of the earth" is the most radical principle; of the old, the "trepidation of the spheares" is the motion of the greatest complexity.... The poet must exhort his love to quietness and calm upon his departure; and for this purpose the figure based upon the latter motion (trepidation), long absorbed into the traditional astronomy, fittingly suggests the tension of the moment without arousing the "harmes and feares" implicit in the figure of the moving earth.[9]

The argument is plausible and rests on a well substantiated thesis that Donne was deeply interested in the new astronomy and its repercussions in the theological realm. In various works Donne shows his familiarity with Kepler's *De Stella Nova*, with Galileo's *Siderius Nuncius*, with William Gilbert's *De Magnete*, and with Clavius' commentary on the *De Sphaera* of Sacrobosco. He refers to the new science in his Sermon at Paul's Cross and in a letter to Sir Henry Goodyer. In *The First Anniversary* he says the "new philosophy calls all in doubt." In the *Elegy* on *Prince Henry* he says that the "least moving of the center" makes "the world to shake."

It is difficult to answer argument like this, and impossible to answer it with evidence of like nature. There is no reason why Donne might not have written a stanza in which the two kinds of celestial motion stood for two sorts of emotion at parting. And if we become full of astronomical ideas and see Donne only against the background of the new science, we may believe that he did. But the text itself remains to be dealt with, the analyzable vehicle of a complicated metaphor. And one may observe: (1) that the movement of the earth according to the Copernician theory is a celestial motion, smooth and regular, and while it might cause religious or philosophic fears, it could not be associated with the crudity and earthiness of the kind of commotion which the speaker in the poem wishes to discourage; (2) that there is another moving of the earth, an earthquake, which has just these qualities and is to be associated with the tear-floods and sigh-tempests of the second stanza of the poem; (3) that "trepidation" is an appropriate opposite of earthquake, because each is a shaking or vibratory motion; and "trepidation of the spheares" is "greater farre" than an earthquake, but not much greater (if two such motions can be compared as to greatness) than the annual motion of the earth; (4) that reckoning what it "did and meant" shows that the event has passed, like an earthquake, not like the incessant celestial movement of the earth. Perhaps a knowledge of Donne's interest in the new science may add another shade of meaning, an overtone to the stanza in question, though to say even this runs against the words. To make the geocentric and heliocentric antithesis the core of the metaphor is to disregard the English language, to prefer private evidence to public, external to internal.

V

If the distinction between kinds of evidence has implications for the historical critic, it has them no less for the contemporary poet and his critic. Or, since every rule for a poet is but another side of a judgment by a critic, and since the past is the realm of the scholar and critic, and the future and present that of the poet and the critical leaders of taste, we may say that the problems arising in literary scholarship from the intentional fallacy are matched by others which arise in the world of progressive experiment.

The question of "allusiveness," for example, as acutely posed by the poetry of Eliot, is certainly one where a false judgment is likely to involve the intentional fallacy. The frequency and depth of literary allusion in the poetry of Eliot and others has driven so many in pursuit of full meanings to the *Golden Bough* and the Elizabethan drama that it has become a kind of commonplace to suppose that we do not know what a poet means unless we have traced him in his reading – a supposition redolent with intentional implications. The stand taken by F. O. Matthiessen is a sound one and partially forestalls the difficulty.

> If one reads these lines with an attentive ear and is sensitive to their sudden shifts in movement, the contrast between the actual Thames and the idealized vision of it during an age before it flowed through a megalopolis is sharply conveyed by that movement itself, whether or not one recognizes the refrain to be from Spenser.

Eliot's allusions work when we know them – and to a great extent when we do not know them – through their suggestive power.

But sometimes we find allusions supported by notes, and it is a nice question whether the notes function more as guides to send us where we may be educated, or more as indications in themselves about the character of the allusions. "Nearly everything of importance . . . that is apposite to an appreciation of 'The Waste Land,'"writes Matthiessen of Miss Weston's book, "has been incorporated into the structure of the poem itself, or into Eliot's Notes." And with such an admission it may begin to appear that it would not much matter if Eliot invented his sources (as Sir Walter Scott invented chapter epigraphs from "old plays" and "anonymous" authors, or as Coleridge wrote marginal glosses for *The Ancient Mariner*). Allusions to Dante, Webster, Marvell, or Baudelaire doubtless gain something because these writers existed, but it is doubtful whether the same can be said for an allusion to an obscure Elizabethan:

> The sound of horns and motors, which shall
> bring Sweeney to Mrs. Porter in the spring.

"Cf. Day, *Parliament of Bees*": says Eliot,

> When of a sudden, listening, you shall hear,
> A noise of horns and hunting, which shall
> bring
> Actaeon to Diana in the spring,
> Where all shall see her naked skin.

The irony is completed by the quotation itself; had Eliot, as is quite conceivable, composed these lines to furnish his own background, there would be no loss of validity. The conviction may grow as one reads Eliot's next note: "I do not know the origin of the ballad from which these lines are taken: it was reported to me from Sydney, Australia." The important word in this note – on Mrs. Porter and her daughter who washed their feet in soda water – is "ballad." And if one should feel from the lines themselves their "ballad" quality, there would be little need for the note. Ultimately, the inquiry must focus on the integrity of such notes as parts of the poem, for where they constitute special information about the meaning of phrases in the poem, they ought to be subject to the same scrutiny as any of the other words in which it is written. Matthiessen believes the notes were the price Eliot "had to pay in order to avoid what he would have considered muffling the energy of his poem by extended connecting links in the text itself." But it may be questioned whether the notes and the need for them are not equally muffling. F. W. Bateson has plausibly argued that Tennyson's "The Sailor Boy" would be better if half the stanzas were omitted, and the best versions of ballads like "Sir Patrick Spens" owe their power to the very audacity with which the minstrel has taken for granted the story upon which he comments. What then if a poet finds he cannot take so much for granted in a more recondite context and rather than write informatively, supplies notes? It can be said in favor of this plan that at least the notes do not pretend to be dramatic, as they would if written in verse. On the other hand, the notes may look like unassimilated material lying loose beside the poem, necessary for the meaning of the verbal symbol, but not integrated, so that the symbol stands incomplete.

We mean to suggest by the above analysis that whereas notes tend to seem to justify themselves as external indexes to the author's *intention*, yet they ought to be judged like any other parts of a composition (verbal arrangement special to a particular context), and when so judged their reality as parts of the poem, or their imaginative integration with the rest of the poem, may come into question. Matthiessen, for instance, sees that Eliot's titles for poems and his epigraphs are informative apparatus, like the notes. But while he is worried by some of the notes and thinks that Eliot "appears to be mocking himself for writing the note at the same time that he wants to convey something by it," Matthiessen believes that the "device" of epigraphs "is not at all open to the objection of not being sufficiently structural." "The *intention*," he says, "is to enable the poet to secure a condensed expression in the poem itself." "In each case the epigraph *is designed* to form an integral part of the effect of the poem." And Eliot himself, in his notes, has justified his poetic practice in terms of intention.

> The Hanged Man, a member of the traditional pack, fits my purpose in two ways: because he is associated in my mind with the Hanged God of Frazer, and because I associate him with the hooded figure in the passage of the disciples to Emmaus in Part V . . . The man with Three Staves (an authentic member of the Tarot pack) I associate, quite arbitrarily, with the Fisher King himself.

And perhaps he is to be taken more seriously here, when off guard in a note, than when in his Norton Lectures he comments on the difficulty of saying what a poem means and adds playfully that he thinks of prefixing to a second edition of *Ash Wednesday* some lines from *Don Juan*:

> I don't pretend that I quite understand
> My own meaning when I would be *very* fine;
> But the fact is that I have nothing planned
> Unless it were to be a moment merry.

If Eliot and other contemporary poets have any characteristic fault, it may be in *planning* too much.

Allusiveness in poetry is one of several critical issues by which we have illustrated the more abstract issue of intentionalism, but it may be for today the most important illustration. As a poetic practice allusiveness would appear to be in some recent poems an extreme corollary of the romantic intentionalist assumption, and as a critical issue it challenges and brings to light in a special way the basic premise of intentionalism. The following instance from the poetry of Eliot may serve to epitomize the practical implications of what we have been saying. In Eliot's "Love Song of J. Alfred Prufrock," toward the end, occurs the line: "I have heard the mermaids singing, each to each," and this bears a certain resemblance to a line in a Song by John Donne, "Teach me to heare Mermaides singing," so that for the reader acquainted to a certain degree with Donne's poetry, the critical question arises: Is Eliot's line an allusion to Donne's? Is Prufrock thinking about Donne? Is Eliot thinking about Donne? We suggest that there are two radically different ways of looking for an answer to this question. There is (1) the way of poetic analysis and exegesis, which inquires whether it makes any sense if Eliot-Prufrock *is* thinking about Donne. In an earlier part of the poem, when Prufrock asks, "Would it have been worth while, . . . To have squeezed the universe into a ball," his words take half their sadness and irony from certain energetic and passionate lines of Marvell's "To His Coy Mistress." But the exegetical inquirer may wonder whether mermaids considered as "strange sights" (to hear them is in Donne's poem analogous to getting with child a mandrake root) have much to do with Prufrock's mermaids, which seem to be symbols of romance and dynamism, and which incidentally have literary authentication, if they need it, in a line of a sonnet by Gérard de Nerval. This method of inquiry may lead to the conclusion that the given resemblance between Eliot and Donne is without significance and is better not thought of, or the method may have the disadvantage of providing no certain conclusion. Nevertheless, we submit that this is the true and objective way of criticism, as contrasted to what the very uncertainty of exegesis might tempt a second kind of critic to undertake: (2) the way of biographical or genetic inquiry, in which, taking advantage of the fact that Eliot is still alive, and in the spirit of a man who would settle a bet, the critic writes to Eliot and asks him what he meant, or if he had Donne in mind. We shall not here weigh the probabilities – whether Eliot would answer that he meant nothing at all, had nothing at all in mind – a sufficiently good answer to such a question – or in an unguarded moment might furnish a clear and, within its limit, irrefutable answer. Our point is that such an answer to such an inquiry would have nothing to do with the poem "Prufrock"; it would not be a critical inquiry. Critical inquiries, unlike bets, are not settled in this way. Critical inquiries are not settled by consulting the oracle.

Notes

1 *Dictionary of World Literature*, Joseph T. Shipley, ed. (New York, 1942), 326–9.
2 J. E. Spingarn, "The New Criticism," in *Criticism in America* (New York, 1924), pp. 24–5.
3 Ananda K. Coomaraswamy, "Intention," in *American Bookman*, I(1944), 41–8.
4 It is true that Croce himself in his *Ariosto, Shakespeare and Corneille* (London, 1920), Ch. 7, "The Practical Personality and the Poetical Personality," and in his *Defence of Poetry* (Oxford, 1934), p. 24, and elsewhere, early and late, has delivered telling attacks on emotive geneticism, but the main drive of the *Aesthetic* is surely toward a kind of cognitive intentionalism.
5 See Hughes Mearns, *Creative Youth* (Garden City, 1925), esp. pp. 27–9. The technique of inspiring poems has apparently been outdone more recently by the study of inspiration in successful poets and other artists. See, for instance, Rosamond E. M. Harding, *An Anatomy of Inspiration* (Cambridge, 1940); Julius Portnoy, *A Psychology of Art Creation* (Philadelphia, 1942); Rudolf Arnheim and others, *Poets at Work* (New York, 1947); Phyllis Bartlett, *Poems in Process* (New York, 1951); Brewer Ghiselin, ed., *The Creative Process: A Symposium* (Berkeley and Los Angeles, 1952).
6 Curt Ducasse, *The Philosophy of Art* (New York, 1929), p. 116.
7 And the history of words *after* a poem is written may contribute meanings which if relevant to the original pattern should not be ruled out by a scruple about intention.
8 Chs. 8, "The Pattern," and 16, "The Known and Familiar Landscape," will be found of most help to the student of the poem.
9 Charles M. Coffin, *John Donne and the New Philosophy* (New York, 1927), 97–8.

48

The Postulated Author: Critical Monism as a Regulative Ideal

Alexander Nehamas

Alexander Nehamas is Edmund N. Carpenter II Class of 1943 Professor in the Humanities, Professor of Philosophy, and Professor of Comparative Literature at Princeton University.

Il n'y a pas une parole qu'on puisse comprendre, si l'on va au fond.
—Paul Valéry

Critical pluralism, broadly stated, is the view that literary texts, unlike natural phenomena, for which there is only one correct explanation, can be given many equally acceptable, even though incompatible, interpretations. But the thesis that, in contrast to science, "the use . . . of diverse but complementary vantages [is] not only rationally justifiable, but necessary to the understanding of art, and indeed of any subject of humanistic inquiry" seems to me to make a virtue out of necessity and a necessity out of fact.[1]

Such a fact is that within sixty years of its publication, a fiction like Kafka's *Metamorphosis* had already provoked 148 studies, of an astonishing variety.[2] This fact has been transformed into a virtue by Stanley Corngold, who accounts for this flood of criticism by attributing it to the very point of the story and, ultimately, to the very nature of literature. Corngold interprets Samsa's change into what is an essentially vague, incomplete, and indescribable monster as an allegory for writing itself – an activity which, according to many recent literary theorists, is bound to result in imperfect communication, unavoidable misunderstanding, and inevitable misreading: "The negativity of the vermin has to be seen as rooted . . . in the literary enterprise itself . . . The creature . . . is . . . language itself (*parole*) – a word broken loose from the context of language (*langage*), fallen into a void of meaning which it cannot signify, near others who cannot understand it" (*Commentator' Despair*, pp. 26, 27). If this is so, why should we be surprised that the story, like all literature, will not yield itself to a definitive interpretation?

But of course Corngold's view is reached through an interpretation which must be itself correct if it is to explain why there cannot be a correct interpretation of the story. And this

Alexander Nehamas, "The Postulated Author: Critical Monism as a Regulative Ideal," *Critical Inquiry*, 8/1 (1981): 133–49. © 1981. Reprinted by permission of the author and University of Chicago Press.

paradox of method is parallel to a paradox of content. *The Metamorphosis*, on this view, concerns the inability of literature to achieve perfect communication and so to receive final interpretation. This is what the story communicates. But if it succeeds in communicating it, it communicates that it fails to communicate; and if it fails, since this failure is what it communicates, it succeeds!

The claim that literature can ultimately communicate only that it cannot ultimately communicate is not uncommon in recent literary theory.[3] I suspect that it is reached by illegitimately extending the thesis that words are polysemous or radically ambiguous. The extension is made by assuming that if a text has a property (if, in particular, a word is ambiguous), then it refers to that property (the word signifies ambiguity). Thus, for example, given the fact that the sentence "The green is either" is ungrammatical, Jacques Derrida infers that "it signifies an example of ungrammaticality."[4] To offer another example, J. Hillis Miller assumes that the history of words is essential to their meaning and writes:

> The effect of etymological retracing is not to ground the word solidly but to render it unstable, equivocal, wavering, abysmal. All etymology is false etymology, both in the sense that there is always some bend or discontinuity in the etymological line, and in the sense that etymology always fails to find an *etymon*, a true literal meaning at the origin.[5]

If texts indeed consist of words so construed, it may seem to follow that "a text never has a single meaning, but is the crossroads of multiple ambiguous meanings"[6] and that therefore every text "is 'unreadable', if by 'readable' one means open to a single, definitive, univocal interpretation."[7] This raises two questions. The first, which I shall not try to answer here, is why we must assume that a word must have had an original literal use in order to be univocal now and why we need to accept the "Rousseauistic or Condillacian law that all words were originally metaphors."[8] The second, to which I shall pay close attention, is why we must agree that to be "readable," a text must have a definitive interpretation – if by "definitive" we mean "unrevisable." For though the absence of an unrevisable interpretation implies that we can change our mind about what a text means, it does not imply that what a text means changes along with our mind.

Deconstructive critics begin with the realization that written texts are enormously independent of their writers and then proceed to sever altogether, at least in theory, the connection between author and text. Since writing remains "when the author of the writing no longer answers for what he has written," Derrida argues, "the text is cut off from all absolute responsibility, from *consciousness* as the ultimate authority, orphaned and separated at birth."[9] Geoffrey Hartman traces the idea of recovering authors' intentions to the Renaissance, with its concern for establishing original texts, and argues that "the more learning and scholarship we bring to an author, with the aim of defining his difference or individual contribution, the less certainty there seems to be of succeeding in this." Hartman concludes that "the notion of unique works of art, certified by the personal name of the author, fades away into nostalgia."[10] Michel Foucault goes even further and claims that the author is a fiction created, more or less, by Saint Jerome, now moribund and an object of indifference: "What matter who's talking?"[11] In a work otherwise unsympathetic to post-structuralisrm, Jonathan Culler accepts this view when he writes, "The meaning of a sentence, one might say, is not a form or an essence, present at the moment of its production and lying behind it as a truth to be recovered, but the series of developments to which it gives rise, as determined by past and future relations between words and the conventions of semiotic systems."[12] The object of criticism cannot therefore be what the author meant by a text but what a text means in itself. Since in itself a text means what its constituents have ever meant, and since (according to deconstruction) no constituent is univocal, the text turns out to be the "crossroads" of all of its constituents' incompatible senses.

This radical pluralism is thus grounded on a view about the nature of texts, some of the many meanings of which are exhibited, with equal plausibility, by different interpretations. But interpretations, too, are written texts, and they also need to but cannot be read. Just as every reading is a misreading, so it will be in turn misread. As Miller says,

> The new turn in criticism involves an interrogation of the notion of the self-enclosed literary work and of the idea that any work has a fixed, identifiable meaning. The literary work is seen in various ways as open and unpredictably productive. The reading of a poem is part of the poem. This reading is productive in its turn. It produces multiple interpretations, further language about the poem's language, in an interminable activity without necessary closure.[13]

But we, at least, have now been brought to the closure of the exposition which opened with our paradoxical reading of *The Metamorphosis.* According to this reading, writing cannot communicate; every text is misread since a reading is just an effort to impose a single coherent meaning on the text and thus presupposes that communication has succeeded. Itself an instance of this law, *The Metamorphosis* has generated a large number of readings; yet, "any reading can be shown to be a misreading on evidence drawn from the text itself."[14] Every reading will thus be replaced, and every new reading will be in turn misread, all circling continually around a nonexistent center, each an effort to isolate an imaginary "literal meaning at the origin," each a falcon without a falconer.

Appalled by the anarchy he takes this view to lead into, E. D. Hirsch has insisted that one of each text's many interpretations, the author's own, must be taken as canonical: "If the meaning of the text is not the author's, then no interpretation can possibly correspond to *the* meaning of a text, since the text can have no determinate or determinable meaning."[15] Behind this view lies a theory of meaning which is ultimately derived from the work of I. A. Richards, who wrote that

> [the] logical use of words with constant senses that are the same for each occurrence . . . is an extremely artificial sort of behavior. . . . And the fluidity, the incessant delicate variation of the meaning of our words . . . is the virtue of language for our other purposes. [It is not true] that if a passage means one thing it cannot mean another and an incompatible thing.[16]

Hirsch maintains his monism in the light of, or perhaps despite, his theory about the meaning of texts: "The nature of the text is to have no meaning except that which an interpreter wills into existence. . . . A text [is] only an occasion for meaning, in itself an ambiguous form devoid of the consciousness where meaning abides."[17]

To this view, which bears important similarities to the approach of Hirsch's opponents, one can make, with the King in *Alice in Wonderland*, an easy reply: "If there's no meaning in it . . . that saves a lot of trouble, you know, as we needn't try to find any." But the witticism and its wording only serve to raise the crucial question: Is a text's meaning found, or is it made? Both sides initially agree that meaning is made, that a text means just what it is taken to mean by its interpreters.[18] Deconstruction infers that critics should therefore do self-consciously what they do in any case, which is to make their own meaning out of every text. Hirsch, by contrast, claims that critics ought now to go on to discover the meaning which a text was made to have by its author.

There is a large gap between the monism advocated by Hirsch and the radical pluralism which follows from the writing of some deconstructive critics. Within this gap are located some recent writers who argue that the meaning of a text is partly found and partly made. This argument is the basis for the limited pluralism of M. H. Abrams, Peter Jones, and Jack Meiland, according to which the "rules of the language" to which a text belongs determine a fundamental level of meaning, independent of all points of view, given to and found by the interpreter.[19] But just as the locutionary content of a sentence does not by itself determine what illocution that sentence is being used to perform in a particular case, so this "central core," though it limits the legitimate overall interpretations of a text, does not exhaust its meaning. Meiland, for example, calls this fundamental level the "textual meaning" and distinguishes it from the "literary meaning," over which critical disagreement occurs. He writes that "the agreed-upon textual meaning can serve as a criterion of validity for interpretations at the level of literary meaning. . . . Any literary interpretation which does not cohere with basic agreed-upon textual meaning can be ruled out as an invalid interpretation" ("Interpretation," p. 36).

The central difficulty with this view is that, in my opinion, it simply tends to reify whatever it is that a text's interpreters do and do not, at some particular time, agree about. Textually, Meiland writes, "*Romeo and Juliet* is about a man and a woman who are in love with one another, whose families prevent their marrying, and who die due to a tragic misunderstanding" ("Interpretation," p. 35). But is this obvious because it is determined solely by the rules of English, or is it because it constitutes such a minimal interpretation, chosen just because the critics of the text are likely to agree about it?[20]

The existence of a well-defined notion of literal or dictionary meaning which can be of use to this view is itself problematic. Do dictionaries give us what words must essentially mean in all their uses, or do they simply supply us with a rough guess, a coarse grid against which, but not necessarily within which, to locate individual words and phrases? Whatever the answer to this question, even if we assume that the notion of a word's literal meaning is well defined, the difficulties of this theory are far from over. The main problem is that it is not possible to identify "textual meaning" with the literal meaning of the words of which a text consists. The words' literal meaning is specified through a set of roughly synonymous words supplied by the dictionary. But the textual meaning is a summary or paraphrase, that is, an interpretation (however minimal) of what these words, *given their literal meaning*, are being used to do on this particular occasion.

If textual meaning is a minimal interpretation of a text, then it is not surprising that it is compatible with a number of "literary" meanings, since these now turn out to be more specific interpretations of the text. For it is clear that a number of more particular specifications of any object are compatible with a more general specification of that object, even if they conflict with one another. Something can be an item of furniture and also a chair, a chaise, or a sofa; it can be any of these and also Louis XVI, Empire, or Directory style. None of this shows that it *is* all of these things. Similarly, though the textual meaning of *Romeo and Juliet* fails to determine a single overall reading of the play, this does not show that the play does have the many literary meanings that have been attributed to it. Compatibility with textual meaning is at best a necessary condition for validity, but this trivial fact offers no support for any sort of pluralism.

Such compatibility is *at best* necessary for validity because in fact we can both disagree about and revise our views of textual meaning. The object we were just imagining may turn out not to be an item of furniture at all but a strange machine; just so, we may revise our minimal interpretation of *Romeo and Juliet.* Though we are likely to agree about textual meaning, we cannot take this agreement for granted; textual meaning depends on substantive as well as on linguistic considerations. Are Romeo and Juliet, for example, a man and a woman or a boy and a girl? But more importantly, in many cases where our minimal and more specific interpretations are in conflict, we may choose to modify the former rather than to reject the latter. Our construal of Romeo's scream, "The time and my intent is savage-wild/More fierce and inexorable far/Than empty tigers and the roaring sea" has serious consequences for the nature of the misunderstanding which leads to his death.

But if textual meaning is not given, if it is also, like literary meaning, the product of revisable interpretation, have we not granted deconstruction all that it wanted in the first place?[21] Derrida is describing a view not unlike Meiland's when he writes that "the concept of a centered structure is in fact the concept of a free-play based on a fundamental ground, a free-play which is constituted upon a fundamental immobility and a reassuring certitude, which is itself beyond the reach of the free-play."[22] The "center" is for Derrida the obvious or intuitive reading of a text, Meiland's textual meaning. Derrida argues that even the most obvious reading is the result of interpretation and can therefore be questioned, revised, or displaced.[23]

This is, I think, correct. Just as in scientific explanation there are no data immune to revision, so in literary criticism there are no readings impervious to question. But the fact about science does not show that apparently competing scientific theories are incommensurable and that therefore we cannot judge between them or that each such theory concerns its own distinct world.[24] Similarly, the point about criticism does not show that different interpretations of a text are, even if apparently incompatible, equally acceptable or that a text has as many meanings as there are interpretations of it. Readings are neither arbitrary nor self-validating simply because they are all subject to revision. Newer readings are always guided by the strengths and weaknesses of those which already exist; and though this process may never stop, it is not for that very reason blind.

Jones has tried to supply stronger support for the pluralist thesis. He claims that interpretation, "the business of making sense of the text, of rendering it coherent," is necessarily "aspectival"; he understands aspect as both "the point of view from which something is seen, and the appearance or face of the object perused" (*Philosophy and the Novel,* pp. 182, 181). His conclusion is that since every interpretation involves a viewpoint, and since no viewpoint (biographical, Marxist, psychoanalytical, etc.) is privileged, different readings of a text, even if apparently incompatible, can be equally acceptable.

Now consider the following case. In *The Metamorphosis*, there is a picture of a woman on the wall of Samsa's bedroom. A number of widely diverse readings of the story all take the picture as an object of Samsa's sexual interest. This unexciting fact is sufficient to show that though the activity of interpretation can proceed from different viewpoints, its results need not therefore be themselves different. Nor is it easy to show that if the results of different approaches are indeed different, then they are equally plausible. For we can, I think, produce a better (not simply a different) interpretation of the role this picture plays in Kafka's story. The text speaks of a glossy-magazine picture of "a lady done up in a fur hat and a fur boa, sitting upright and raising against the viewer a heavy fur muff in which her whole forearm has disappeared." Now Heinz Politzer describes this picture as "vulgar . . . animallike"; Robert Adams thinks that it is of an "impudent salacity"; Hellmuth Kaiser claims that it portrays an "erotically active, aggressive woman"; and Peter Dow Webster takes this woman as an "earth-mother."[25] These descriptions do not correspond to anything in the text, but once they are casually introduced, they tend to become, for some, parts of the story itself, and the picture thus acquires an erotic content. It is a short step from this to finding sexual significance in the insect's covering the picture with his body in order to protect it from being taken from his room along with the rest of his furniture. But what we do know about the picture is that it comes from a magazine and that it is of no one in particular (which accounts, incidentally, for its sketchy description). It is an object of no character and no individuality. If anything about it is interesting, it is that while it seems to be a picture of no interest, Gregor has made a frame for it himself: this is the only productive work we know him to have done, the only thing he has actually made. What he is protecting from being taken away, by assuming a position dictated to him more by his anatomy than by his desires, is his only real creation, his only real possession. That his most expressive action has been devoted to framing and bringing into prominence an object which is not so vulgar as it is banal underscores the shallowness of Gregor's relationship to the world and the depth of his attachment to that shallowness.

Interpretation is therefore in one sense aspectival, but criticism is not for this reason less than "objective." Different *ways* of trying to understand a text may well be equally legitimate: there probably isn't a general argument to the effect that psychoanalytic criticism, for example, should not be practiced. But simply because an activity can be pursued in different ways, it does not follow that different results must be reached; nor that if they are, then they must be equally plausible.

Jones draws this stronger conclusion when he slips into considering interpretation no longer as an activity but as that activity's very product: "The background against which, or the viewpoint from which, we interpret a text generally provides the most interesting differences between interpretations, between the patterns of coherence different critics determine" (*Philosophy and the Novel,* p. 186). Just as "aspect" covered both viewpoints and what is seen from them, so "interpretation" covers both the "business" of finding a pattern of coherence in a text and that pattern itself. Yet though it is necessarily true that to peruse an object we must (geometrically, so to speak) do so through one of its appearances, faces, or aspects, what we peruse is not the appearance but the object. We cannot simply appeal to the different methods critics use in order to justify their different readings, though we sometimes think we can because we take what is true of the process of interpretation to be true of its product.

We are concerned with a pluralism of contents, not of modes or methods, with the view that the results of different approaches to a text, even if apparently incompatible, can be equally plausible parts or aspects of what the text means.[26] This would be, for example, the view that Gregor's metamorphosis stands as much for his alienation from a world of unproductive labor as for his regression to the anal stage because of an unresolved Oedipal conflict. Both views, so stated, seem plausible, and so does the pluralist position which tries to account for this appearance. But if we look at the texture of these interpretations, their plausibility ceases to be striking. The psychoanalytic reading, for example, must construe Gregor's father's kicking the vermin when it is stuck in a doorway as an act of pure aggression; Gregor, by contrast, and quite correctly, sees it as his "salvation." The Marxist reading fails to account for the effect his sister's music has on Gregor just before his death. Interesting difficulties facing interpretation are usually found on this specific level; we often grant a particular reading plausibility by not looking enough at its details.[27]

Actually, the proliferation of difficulties on this specific level may make it seem again as though the deconstructive view that every reading is a misreading is correct. And, in a way, it is, since every reading can be confronted with contrary evidence. But the absence of a reading which cannot be improved, which accounts for every feature, does not make a text "unreadable": it only indicates that there is more to understand. There is no definite description, explanation, or theory of anything. And though replacement may not proceed from worse to better in every individual case, it tends on the whole to preserve good readings in order to supplant them with others that are better.

This implies that we understand *The Metamorphosis* better today than it was understood in the past and that we will come to understand it better in the future. And though no aspect of our understanding of the story is given, we can on each occasion agree on the significance of some of its elements in a way which allows us to compare and evaluate, even if only tentatively, alternative readings.[28] This is not obvious as long as we try to compare in general terms a Marxist, say, and a psychoanalytic reading of *The Metamorphosis*: on this level, to ask "Which is better?" is to ask a silly question. But the point begins to appear if we turn to the specific, if less exciting, issues which we have been discussing here.

Miller writes, correctly, that "the 'obvious or univocal reading' of a [text] is not identical to the [text] itself"[29] – no reading ever is. Readings, interpretations, do not re-create or duplicate a text's meaning, they describe it.[30] To understand a text at all is to have an interpretation of it, and it is only in the light of one interpretation that we come to see, if and when we do, that a text can be read differently, that another interpretation is better. Thus from the point of view of a particular reading, the meaning which a later interpretation will attribute to a text does not exist. Nevertheless, the later interpretation does not, in absolute terms, create that meaning: it finds a meaning which, from its own point of view, had always been there. This is so, of course, only from its own point of view. But we cannot coherently describe this as "only a point of view" unless we produce yet another interpretation attributing to the text yet another meaning from yet another point of view (to be specified as such only by means of a further interpretation).

Meaning does not therefore reside in texts independently of all interpretation, there to be discovered once and for all or, if we are not lucky, to be forever lost; but this is not to say that it is fabricated. The critical monism which I advocate is a regulative ideal and identifies the meaning of a text with whatever is specified by that text's ideal interpretation. Such an interpretation would account for all of the text's features, though we can never reach it since it is unlikely that we can even understand what it is to speak of "all the features" of anything. What we do have (and that is what we need) is the notion of one interpretation answering more questions about a text than another and thus being closer to that hypothetical ideal which would answer all questions. The direction in which this ideal lies may change as new interpretations reveal features of a text previously unnoticed, rearrange the significance of those already accounted for, or even cause us to change some of our general critical canons. And though, in this way, there may not be a single ideal interpretation of a text toward which all of our actual interpretations in fact lead, the transition from one interpretation to another can still be rational and justified. To interpret a text is to place it in a context which accounts for as many of its features as possible; but which features to account for, which are more significant than others, is itself a question conditioned by those interpretations of the text which already exist.[31]

To interpret a text is to place it in a context, and this is to construe it as someone's production, directed at certain purposes. A purpose is neither the end toward which motives aim, nor a text's "perlocutionary" effects, nor again a message lying behind the surface.[32] Meaning is a symbolic relation; and what an object symbolizes depends partly on which of many systems it can be construed as an element of.[33] At least the choice of symbol system is an intentional act, and to appeal to intention is to appeal to a particular explanation of why a text, or one of its features, is as it is. The picture of the woman is used in *The Metamorphosis* to show the banality of Gregor's life. This account is intentional in that it is teleological. But it is not thereby vulnerable to those sound arguments against appealing to intention construed as "design or plan in the author's mind" or as the efficient cause of that feature.[34]

To interpret a text is to consider it as its author's production.[35] Literary texts are produced by agents and must be understood as such. This seems to me self-evident; even deconstructive criticism generally accepts it, though it insists that the choice of agent is conventional and arbitrary. And since texts are products of expressive actions, understanding them is inseparably tied to understanding their agents. But just as the author is not identical with a text's fictional narrator, so he is also distinct from its historical writer. The author is postulated as the agent whose actions account for the text's features; he is a character, a hypothesis which is accepted provisionally, guides interpretation, and is in turn modified in its light. The author, unlike the writer, is not a text's efficient cause but, so to speak, its formal cause, manifested in thought not identical with it.[36]

A methodological constraint on this view is that the postulated author be historically plausible; the principle is that a text does not mean what its writer could not, historically, have meant by it. For example, we cannot attribute to particular words meanings which they came to have only after the writer's death.[37] What a writer could mean can be determined by linguistic or biographical considerations but also by facts about the history of literature and the world, psychology, anthropology, and much else besides, a change in our understanding of any of which can cause us to change our understanding of the text.

Meaning therefore depends on an author's intentions even if a writer is not aware of it. Since the author's intentions depend on what the writer could have meant, a text's meaning is to that extent a thing of the past, though its understanding is itself a thing of the future. Without Freud we would not have seen the sexual elements which are now part and parcel of *Oedipus Rex*. But if the Oedipal conflict is as basic to behavior as Freud thought, then the historical Sophocles, unaware of it as he may have been, could have considered it an issue. And we can argue from this that the character Sophocles, the play's author, did consider it an issue; it is then part of the play's meaning even if we could not have realized it until this century.

We must not, by contrast, accept a view of *The Metamorphosis* which holds that hours on the clock correspond to years in Gregor's life and that he

> should have caught the five o'clock train for work, that is, a psychic change should have occurred at the normal age of five, . . . [that is,] the formation of the superego. . . . But here it is, already six-thirty (Gregor is six and a half years old); he has missed the train or psychic energy necessary for progression.[38]

Kafka could not have known this highly technical, and highly doubtful, theory of development. Even if the theory were true, it simply lacks the power and generality of the Oedipal conflict which might convince us that Kafka could have come by it on his own and that it therefore belongs to the story.

The principle of the postulated author is not sheer invention. We can find it reflected in the practice of a critic like Quentin Skinner, who refuses to read some seventeenth-century legal texts as concerned with the doctrine of the judicial review of statute because the concept of judicial review did not arise until the next century.[39] Adams, to cite a clearly literary case, interprets the number three in *The Metamorphosis* as a symbol for masculinity, on the grounds that "Kafka might have learned of the association through any of several channels" though there is no evidence that he did.[40] Finally, Miller supports his view that Stevens' rock, in the poem of that title, stands for literal language partly because "Stevens might even have known (why should he not have known?) the world 'curiologic' . . . [from the] Greek *kuriologia*, the use of literal expressions."[41]

Now in one sense there is something arbitrary about constructing a historically plausible figure as a text's author. In principle we could always construct a different context and a different author and so give an unhistorical reading. This is not unlike the arbitrariness of our interpreting representational paintings as projections of familiar Euclidean space, since any two-dimensional figure can be construed as the projection of indefinitely many alternative worlds. Just as the effort to construct such worlds could be worth making, we could always try to read a text differently, postulating a different author and progressively refining our conception as new readings come to affect those from which they emerged. Progress in this direction would show a text to be, in a genuine and valuable sense, polysemous. But what we actually find in criticism is a number of self-consciously partial alternatives, directed only at some of the text's features in the expectation that many more partial, non-competing readings will emerge. This can no more support the view that each text, as a whole, has many meanings than can the claim that, given any interpretation of a text, a different one could always be constructed. What we need in both cases is an actual reading at least as general and powerful as the reading whose uniqueness is being questioned and with which it is incompatible.[42]

The monism I have presented is not threatened by the existence of many partial readings of a text since it can exploit discoveries made through such readings in pursuing a more complete understanding of the text. Methodological pluralism is compatible with a monism of content. The regulative end is to construct, for each text, a complete historically plausible author – a character who may not coincide with the actual writer's self-understanding, fragmentary and incomplete as it probably is. What a writer takes a text to mean is relevant but not telling evidence in literary criticism. Further, our construction will never be complete: in constructing the author of *The Metamorphosis*, we shall have to consider his close relation, perhaps his identity, with the author of *The Castle*, whose precursor is Kierkegaard (another character who may appear different through this connection) and who is in turn the precursor of Jorge Luis Borges and other future authors. Changes in literature and in everything that is relevant to it (in everything, that is) will change the constraints imposed upon the postulated author. And there is no reason to think that we shall ever abandon this construction, except perhaps that our interest may one day be exhausted.

Critical pluralists sometimes argue as Jones does that all interpretations are necessarily partial, that criticism "is always . . . of a selection of properties" (*Philosophy and the Novel*, p. 193). If different critics were in fact necessarily concerned with different textual features, it might follow that different readings, being nonoverlapping, were equally acceptable.[43] But this is no more true than the claim, often made in this connection, that to see a feature differently is to see a different feature.[44] Like all theorizing, interpretation is based on some features of a text but is of the text as a whole. It is therefore partial only in the trivial sense that no reading can ever account for all of a text's features, not because distinct readings are directed at distinct features. Being partial in this sense means simply that there is no final, unrevisable interpretation of any text; but then why should we want such a reading?

The aim of interpretation is to capture the past in the future: to capture – not to recapture – first, because the iterative prefix suggests that meaning, which was once manifest, must now be found again. But the postulated author dispenses with this assumption. Literary texts are produced by very complicated actions, while the significance of even our simplest acts is often far from clear. Parts of the meaning of a text may become clear only because of developments occurring long after its composition. And though the fact that an author means something may be equivalent to the fact that a writer could have meant it, this is not to say that the writer did, on whatever level, actually mean it.

Second, the notion of recapturing the past suggests the repetition of an earlier act of consciousness and generates the hermeneutic problem of how we can put ourselves in the position of another epoch or culture, how we can see the world as they saw it, "from within."[45] Skirting most of the issues, I will simply deny that the aim of criticism is to recreate the original understanding of a text – particularly if by this we mean the experience of an original audience. It is quite true that we can never recreate the experience of the original audience of, say, *The Clouds*. It is not even clear whose experience we should pursue: the common experience of all the spectators of the comedy's first performance? that of an "average" member? the experience of Socrates or of Anytus? It is equally true that we cannot hope to recreate even our contemporaries' experience of a text. And if it is claimed that my experience of *The Clouds* is more similar to yours than it is to Anytus', I will agree only if you can show that our interpretations are more similar. But if this is how we construe "understanding," then capturing the Athenians' understanding of *The Clouds* presents no theoretical difficulties. We must find what they thought, said, and wrote about it. This is in principle public information whose loss, even if it is final, poses no logical or hermeneutical problems.[46]

Still, criticism does not aim to capture what a text's original audience actually took it to mean but to find what the text means. We want to develop an interpretation which will be consistent with what we know about a text's language, its writer, its original audience, its genre, the possibilities of writing, history, psychology, anthropology, and much else. What a text means is what it could mean to its writer. But this is not what it did mean to the writer and to the text's original audience, nor need they have been able to understand it given only the articulated knowledge of human affairs which they then had. The meaning of a text, like the significance of an action, may take forever to become manifest.

Some critics believe that many texts, or parts of texts, have been correctly interpreted once and for all.[47] This, I have tried to suggest, is unlikely. Others, fearing perhaps that a final interpretation will make the text itself dispensable, deny this possibility on the grounds that all texts are essentially ambiguous and thus always open to new readings.[48] I have tried to show that we do not need to accept this latter view in order to justify what is, after all, the most basic consequence of the openendedness of all knowledge.

As I stated earlier, though texts belong to the past, their understanding belongs to the future. To do just what I have said we shouldn't, let me quote, quite out of context, Sidney's "The poet . . . doth grow in effect another nature." Consider this nature not as the world the text represents but as the text itself. Each text is to our many interpretations what nature is to our many theories, and each is inexhaustible. Understanding a text is, in two ways, a historical enterprise: not only does it employ history but it also unfolds in time and depends on everything we now do and will come to know about the world, which includes ourselves. Understanding a text is as easy, or as difficult, as that. In interpreting a text we must come to understand an action, and so we must understand an agent and therefore other actions and other agents as well and what they took for granted, what they meant, believed, and what they wanted. For this reason, each text is inexhaustible: its context is the world.

Notes

1 M. H. Abrams, "A Note on Wittgenstein and Literary Criticism," *English Literary History* 41 (Winter 1974): 552.

2 These studies are listed and discussed in Stanley Corngold, *The Commentator's Despair: The Interpretation of Kafka's "Metamorphosis"* (Port Washington, NY, and London, 1973); all further references to this work will be included in the text. Many more interpretations of the story have, of course, been offered since.

3 Jacques Derrida, for example, forcefully defends this view in *Speech and Phenomena* (Evanston, III., 1973); *Of Grammatology* (Baltimore, 1974); and *Writing and Difference* (Chicago, 1976). See also *La Dissémination* (Paris, 1972).

4 Derrida, "Signature Event Context," *Glyph* 1 (1977): 185. See also J. Hillis Miller, "The Critic as Host," in *Deconstruction and Criticism*, ed. Harold Bloom et al. (New York, 1979), p. 225. In another, brilliant essay, Miller relies heavily on the principle that if an artwork employs certain conventions, then it is also about those conventions ("The Fiction of Realism: *Sketches by Boz, Oliver Twist*, and Cruickshank's Illustrations," in *Dickens Centennial Essays*, ed. Ada Nisbet and Blake Nevius [Berkeley, 1971], pp. 85–153).

5 Miller, "Ariadne's Thread: Repetition and the Narrative Line," *Critical Inquiry* 3 (Autumn 1976): 70. See also "Critic as Host," pp. 218–20.

6 Miller, "Tradition and Difference," *Diacritics* 2 (1972): 12.

7 Miller, "Critic as Host," p. 226. See also Paul de Man, "Nietzsche's Theory of Rhetoric," *Symposium* 28 (Spring 1974): 44, and Geoffrey Hartman, "Literary Criticism and Its Discontents," *Critical Inquiry* 3 (Winter 1976): 205.

8 Miller, "Ariadne's Thread," p. 70; cf. "Tradition and Difference," p. 11. The same claim has been made at length by Derrida, "White Mythology: Metaphor in the Text of Philosophy," *New Literary History* 6 (Autumn 1974): 5–74. For a criticism of this view, as exhibited in the early work of Nietzsche, see Arthur Danto, *Nietzsche as Philosopher* (New York, 1965), pp. 37–47.

9 Derrida, "Signature Event Context," p. 181.

10 Hartman, "Criticism and Its Discontents," pp. 204–5; all further references to this essay will be included in the text.

11 Michel Foucault, "What Is an Author?" *Language, Counter-Memory, Practice,* ed. Donald F. Bouchard, trans. Bouchard and Sherry Simon (Ithaca, NY, 1977), pp. 113–38.

12 Jonathan Culler, *Structuralist Poetics* (Ithaca, NY, 1975), p. 132. This view, as I suggest below, ultimately derives from New Criticism; see n. 16 below.

13 Miller, "Stevens' Rock and Criticism as Cure, II," *Georgia Review* 30 (Summer 1976): 333.

14 Ibid.

15 E. D. Hirsch, *Validity in Interpretation* (New Haven, Conn., 1967), p. 5. On the prescriptive nature of Hirsch's view, see Jack Meiland, "Interpretation as a Cognitive Discipline," *Philosophy and Literature* 2 (Spring 1978): 24–8.

16 I. A. Richards, *Interpretation in Teaching* (New York, 1938), p. 256. New Criticism assumed that "words . . . include at least potentially, within their appearance in a given setting, (all) the meanings they have had . . . in previous contexts" (Richard Strier, "The Poetics of Surrender: An Exposition and Critique of New Critical Poetics," *Critical Inquiry* 2 [Autumn 1975]: 173–4). Monroe Beardsley accepts this principle in *The Possibility of Criticism* (Detroit, 1970), pp. 19–20. If so, however, what reason is there to think that the changing meanings of the words of a text will be subject to a single univocal interpretation, as Beardsley believes? It is this monism which deconstruction has abandoned in its claim that words actually possess, in every appearance, all the meanings they have ever had, that every passage does mean "another and an incompatible thing."

17 Hirsch, "Three Dimensions of Hermeneutics," *New Literary History* 3 (Winter 1972): 246. Despite some evidence to the contrary (e.g., p. 256), Hirsch generally seems to accept this radical thesis of textual indeterminacy. For considerations weighing against this thesis, see Meiland, "Interpretation" (n. 15 above), pp. 32–3, and Beardsley, *Possibility of Criticism*, pp. 24–6.

18 See Hirsch, "Three Dimensions of Hermeneutics," p. 247: "If an ancient text has been interpreted as a Christian allegory, that is unanswerable proof that it can be so interpreted." But is this proof that the text has been *legitimately* so interpreted? Hirsch seems to presuppose that *in some sense* such a reading is accurate to the text; but this seems to beg the question at issue.

19 See Abrams, "Note on Wittgenstein"; "Rationality and Imagination in Cultural History: A Reply to Wayne Booth," *Critical Inquiry* 2 (Spring 1976): 447–64, esp. 457; "What's the Use of Theorizing about the Arts?" in *In Search of Literary History*, ed. Morton Bloomfield (Ithaca, NY, 1972), pp. 3–54; and "The Deconstructive Angel," *Critical Inquiry* 3 (Spring 1977): 425–38; Peter Jones, *Philosophy and the Novel* (Oxford, 1975), ch. 5, esp. pp. 182–3; all further references to this book will be included in the text; Meiland, "Interpretation," esp. pp. 29–31 and 35–7; all further references to this essay will be included in the text. See also Quentin Skinner, "Motives, Intentions, and the Interpretation of Texts," *New Literary History* 3 (Winter 1972): 393–408.

20 Meiland is, in any case, correct that such agreement as does exist is a sufficient objection to Hirsch's thesis of the radical indeterminacy of textual meaning.

21 Meiland is clear on the dependence of textual meaning upon interpretation (see "Interpretation," p. 36), but he thinks that it results simply from the interpretation of physical marks as words and thus attributes to it a privileged status.

22 Derrida, "Structure, Sign, and Play in the Discourse of the Human Sciences," in *The Structuralist Controversy*, ed. Richard Macksey and Eugenio Donato (Baltimore, 1970), p. 248; rpt. in *Writing and Difference*, pp. 278–93. Cf. Miller, "Critic as Host," p. 218: "Is the 'obvious' reading, though, so 'obvious' or even so 'univocal'? . . . Is not the obvious reading perhaps equivocal rather than univocal, most equivocal in its intimate familiarity and in its ability to have got itself taken for granted as 'obvious' and single-voiced?"

23 See Culler, *Structuralist Poetics*, pp. 244–5, for an elaboration of Derrida's position. The view that no part of the meaning of a text is given, which I have been supporting, bears close affinities to the

approach of Stanley Fish. See, for example, "Interpreting the *Variorum*" (*Critical Inquiry* 2 [Spring 1976]: 473), where Fish attacks "the assumption that there *is* a sense, that is embedded or encoded in the text, and that can be taken in at a single glance." I diverge from Fish in his inferring that meaning cannot be located in the text but in its readers' experiences. See also his "Literature in the Reader: Affective Stylistics," *Self-Consuming Artifacts: The Experience of Seventeenth-Century Literature* (Berkeley, 1972), pp. 382–427.

24 On this point, see Hilary Putnam, "Meaning and Reference," in *Naming, Necessity, and Natural Kinds*, ed. Stephen Schwartz (Ithaca, NY, 1977), pp. 119–32, and "The Meaning of 'Meaning,'" *Mind, Language, and Reality* (Cambridge, 1975), pp. 215–72. For a different argument to this conclusion, see Larry Laudan, *Progress and Its Problems* (Berkeley, 1977), p. 141ff.

25 Heinz Politzer, *Franz Kafka: Parable and Paradox* (Ithaca, NY, 1966), p. 72; Robert M. Adams, *Strains of Discord: Studies in Literary Openness* (Ithaca, NY, 1958), p. 152; Hellmuth Kaiser, "Kafka's Fantasy of Punishment," Peter Dow Webster, "Franz Kafka's 'Metamorphosis' as Death and Resurrection Fantasy," and Corngold, "Metamorphosis of the Metaphor," in *The Metamorphosis*, trans. and ed. Corngold (New York, 1972), pp. 153, 158, and 11, respectively. I quote from Corngold's translation.

26 Wayne Booth deals with issues generated by methodological pluralism in *Critical Understanding* (Chicago, 1979), but his discussion, especially pp. 284–301, extends to pluralism of contents.

27 For the Marxist argument, see Bluma Goldstein, "Bachelors and Work: Social and Economic Conditions in 'The Judgment,' 'The Metamorphosis' and *The Trial*," in *The Kafka Debate*, ed. Angel Flores (New York, 1977), pp. 147–75 and 3–5. For the Freudian view, see Kaiser, "Kafka's Fantasy of Punishment," esp. p. 152.

28 Monroe Beardsley makes a similar point in his review of Booth's *Critical Understanding* in *Philosophy and Literature* 4 (Fall 1980): 257–65.

29 Miller, "Critic as Host," p. 224.

30 Stanley Cavell provides an excellent discussion of this issue in "Aesthetic Problems of Modern Philosophy," *Must We Mean What We Say?* (New York, 1969), p. 74ff.

31 Putnam discusses such a view in relation to the philosophy of science and epistemology in "Realism and Reason," *Meaning and the Moral Sciences* (London, 1978), pp. 123–40.

32 The first view is held by Skinner, "Motives," pp. 401–2. For the perlocution view, see Meiland, "Interpretation," p. 39ff, and Skinner, "Motives," p. 403. For the meaning-as-message view, see, e.g., Richard Kuhns, "Criticism and the Problem of Intention," *Journal of Philosophy* 57 (January 1960): for Kuhns, interpretation is the activity of "getting at the message which may go beyond the plain literal sense" (p. 7). The notion of meaning as message has recently been criticized by Wolfgang Iser in *The Act of Reading* (Baltimore, 1978), though he seems to me to conclude too quickly that meaning is "imagistic in character" (p. 8).

33 This is one of the central theses in Nelson Goodman's *Languages of Art* (Indianapolis, 1968), though Goodman avoids any discussion of intention.

34 See W. K. Wimsatt, Jr., and Beardsley, "The Intentional Fallacy," in Wimsatt, *The Verbal Icon* (Lexington, Ky., 1954), for the source of most of those arguments. Cavell ("A Matter of Meaning It," *Must We Mean What We Say?*, pp. 234–7) disagrees with Beardsley but offers a different account of intention.

35 This position may seem to transgress against the original New Criticism, structuralism (e.g., Roland Barthes, *Sur Racine* [Paris, 1963]), more recent theory sympathetic to the New Critics (e.g., John Ellis, *The Theory of Literary Criticism: A Logical Analysis* [Berkeley, 1974]), deconstruction, and approaches to interpretation via the activity of reading (e.g., Iser, *The Act of Reading*, and Fish, "Literature in the Reader" [n. 23 above]).

36 My postulated author is not unrelated to Booth's "implied author," to whom he appeals both in *Critical Understanding* and in *The Rhetoric of Fiction* (Chicago, 1961), and to Kendall Walton's "apparent artist," discussed in his "Style and the Products and Processes of Art," in *The Concept of Style*, ed. Berel Lang (Philadelphia, 1979), pp. 45–66. I discuss this issue in more detail in another paper, "What an Author Is" (to be presented at the MLA convention, December 1981).

37 Beardsley argues that we can attribute such meanings to texts; see *Possibility of Criticism*, p. 19.

38 Webster, "'Metamorphosis' as Death and Resurrection Fantasy" (n. 25 above), pp. 161–2.

39 Skinner, "Motives," pp. 406–7 and n. 41.

40 Adams, *Strains of Discord* (n. 25 above), p. 173.

41 Miller, "Stevens' Rock and Criticism as Cure," *Georgia Review* 30 (Spring 1976): 10.

42 Booth makes a similar point in more detail in *Critical Understanding*, pp. 168–9.

43 Though, strictly speaking, what would follow is that distinct parts of a text have distinct meanings, not that the text *as a whole* has more than one meaning.

44 Jones sometimes suggests this with his notion of the "interpreted-text"; see *Philosophy and the Novel*, p. 193.

45 For a discussion of problems connected with the hermeneutic circle, see Anthony Savile, "Historicity and the Hermeneutic Circle," *New Literary History* 10 (Autumn 1978): 49–70, and "Tradition and Interpretation," *Journal of Aesthetics and Art Criticism* 36 (Spring 1978): 303 and 315.

46 If it is now argued that even if we had the Athenians' interpretation, we could never really understand it, we can again apply the previous dilemma. We cannot understand their views because we cannot experience things as they did (which applies to any communication whatever) or because we lack background knowledge which they possessed (and which raises no problems in principle).

47 See Savile, "Tradition and Interpretation," p. 307; Abrams, "Rationality and Imagination" (n. 19 above), p. 457; and Hirsch, *Validity in Interpretation*, p. 171.

48 Iser, for example, seems to think that the dispensability of the text is a danger which taking meaning as "imagistic" avoids; see *The Act of Reading*, p. 4ff. But this fear is widespread; see Cavell's discussion of Cleanth Brooks and Yvor Winters on paraphrase in "Aesthetic Problems." Claims to the effect that what is important about literary texts is not what they mean but their "emotional impact" are prompted by such a fear.

49

Art, Intention, and Conversation

Noël Carroll

I

In the normal course of affairs, when confronted with an utterance, our standard cognitive goal is to figure out what the speaker intends to say. And, on one very plausible theory of language, the meaning of an utterance is explicated in terms of the speaker's intention to reveal to an auditor that the speaker intends the auditor to respond in a certain way.[1] That is, the meaning of a particular language token is explained by means of certain of a speaker's intentions.

Likewise, in interpreting or explaining nonverbal behavior, we typically advert to the agent's intentions. This is not to say that we may not be concerned with the unintended consequences of an action; but even in order to explain unintended consequences, one will need a conception of the agent's intentions. Nor is this reliance on intention something that is relevant only to living people; historians spend a great deal of their professional activity attempting to establish what historical agents intended by their words and their deeds, with the aim of rendering the past intelligible. Furthermore, we generally presume that they can succeed in their attempts even with respect to authors and agents who lived long ago and about whom the documentary record is scant.

Nevertheless, though it seems natural to interpret words and actions in terms of authorial intention, arguments of many sorts have been advanced for nearly fifty years to deny the relevance of authorial intention to the interpretation of works of art in general and to works of literature in particular. Call this anti-intentionalism. Whereas ordinarily we interpret for intentions, anti-intentionalism maintains that art and literature either cannot or should not be treated in this way, Likewise, where characteristically we may use what we know of a person – her biography, if you will – to supply clues to, or, at least, constraints on our hypotheses about her meanings,[2] many theorists of art and literature regard reference to an author's biography as either illegitimate or superfluous.

The realm of art and literature, on the anti-intentionalist view, is or should be sufficiently different from other domains of human intercourse so that the difference mandates a different form of interpretation, one in which authorial intent is irrelevant. In this essay, I scrutinize some of the grounds for drawing distinctions between

Noël Carroll, "Art, Intention, and Conversation," in *Intention and Interpretation*, ed. Gary Iseminger (Philadelphia: Temple University Press, 1992), pp. 97–131.

art and life that advance the thought that authorial intent is irrelevant; and, in contrast, I also try to suggest some hitherto neglected continuities between art and life that might motivate a concern for authorial intention in the interpretation of art and literature.

II

Historically speaking, anti-intentionalism, under the title of "the intentional fallacy,"[3] arose in a context in which biographical criticism flourished – that is, the interpretation of such things as novels as allegories of their authors' lives. Authors were geniuses whose remarkable personalities we came to know and appreciate all the more by treating their fictions as oblique biographies.[4] Undoubtedly, this sort of criticism promoted distorted interpretations – as any intentionalist would agree, insofar as it is not likely that Kafka intended to speak of his father in writing *The Metamorphosis*. But in banishing all reference to authorial intention, to authorial reports of intention, and to the author's biography,[5] anti-intentionalism was an exercise in overkill. That is, in performing the useful service of disposing of what might be better called "the biographer's fallacy," anti-intentionalists embraced a number of philosophical commitments that went far beyond their own purposes, as well as beyond plausibility.

Indeed, anti-intentionalism is often promoted as a means for rejecting critical practices that most of us would agree are misguided. It is generally unclear, however, whether one has to go all the way to anti-intentionalism in order to avoid the errors in question.

For example, anti-intentionalism was advocated as a principle that could dispense with taking outlandish authorial pronouncements seriously. Monroe Beardsley writes "if a sculptor tells us that his statue was intended to be smooth and blue, but our senses tell us it is rough and pink, we go by our senses."[6] This example is meant to serve as an "intuition-pump";[7] if we agree that a sculptor cannot make a pink statue blue by reporting that it was his intention to make a blue sculpture, then it must be the case that we regard such intentions – and such reports of intention – as irrelevant.

This solution to the case is too hasty, however, and the example need not force the intentionalist into anti-intentionalism. For with cases in which the authorial pronouncement is so arbitrary, we may discount it, not because we think that authorial intentions are irrelevant, but because we think that the report is insincere. That is, we do not believe that the sculptor in Beardsley's example really had the intention of making a blue statue by painting it pink.

Intentions are constituted, in part, of beliefs, on Beardsley's own view,[8] and we can resist attributing the belief to an artist that one makes something blue by painting it pink. We need not resort to the hypothesis of anti-intentionalism in such a case, but can instead suspect that the artist was putting us on, perhaps for the purpose of notoriety. That is, competent language users, especially trained artists, are presumed to know the difference between blue and pink. Flouting this distinction leads to the suspicion of irony.

For an actual literary example of the sort of problem that Beardsley has in mind, we could consider Andrew Greeley's sensational novel *Ascent into Hell*. Like many of Greeley's works, this story is a titillating tale of Catholic priests and sex, a kind of soft-core pornography, spiced with religious taboos. Greeley, however, has a note preceding the text of the novel entitled "Passover," in which he offers a symbolic reading of that ceremony, thereby perhaps insinuating that we should take the text of *Ascent into Hell* as an allegory of Passover.

Needless to say, it is difficult to regard the sexual escapades in the book as a serious Passover allegory. But the intentionalist is not forced to accept Greeley's implied intention at face value. One can simply, on the basis of the novel, note that Greeley could not genuinely have the belief that it could be read as that allegory, nor would he have written the text as he did if he had the desire – another component of intentions on Beardsley's view[9] – to render a modern-day Passover theme. In fact, one may hypothesize that Greeley included the red herring about Passover in order to reassure his Catholic readership that his book was not irreligious.

But, in any event, the intentionalist can reject the "Passover" interpretation of *Ascent into Hell* in the face of Greeley's implied intentions by denying that it is plausible to accept the authenticity of Greeley's ostensible intent. Thus, the problem of aberrant authorial pronouncements need not drive us toward anti-intentionalism.[10]

Another frequent intuition-pump, employed in early arguments against intentionalism, argues that commending poems insofar as they realize authorial intentions is usually circular. For in many (most?) instances, including those of Shakespeare and Homer, we have no evidence of authorial intention other than their poems. Consequently, if we commend such a poem on the basis of its realization of intentions, and our sole evidence for that intention is the poem itself, then our commendation is tantamount to the assertion that the poem succeeds because it is the way it is because it is the way it is.

We cannot, in these instances, have grounds for discerning failed authorial intentions because the way the artwork is provides our only access to the intention. If it appears muddled, then that is evidence that the artist intended it to be muddled and, therefore, that it succeeded in realizing his intention. That is, commending works of art for realizing authorial intentions when the way work is is our only evidence of intentions threatens to force us to the counterintuitive conclusion that all works of art are commendable.[11]

The unwarranted presupposition here, of course, is that the artwork cannot provide evidence of failed intentions. In the introduction to his *The Structure of Scientific Revolutions*, Thomas Kuhn writes at one point that "having been weaned on these distinctions [the "context of discovery" versus "context of justification"] and others like them, I could scarcely be more aware of their import and force."[12] Clearly, any alert reader will note that Kuhn has said the opposite of what he meant to say. He intended to communicate that he had been *nurtured* on these distinctions, and not that he had been *weaned* on them.[13]

The text itself, in terms of the entire direction of what is being said, makes evident what Kuhn has in mind. Also, we know that the confusion over the dictionary meaning of *weaned*, like the meanings of such words as *fulsome* and *sleek*, is quite common among contemporary English speakers; so it is easy to recognize that Kuhn should not have written what he, in fact, wrote, given his intentions. From the text itself and our knowledge of language usage, we can infer that the sentence failed to realize Kuhn's intentions and that, from his own viewpoint, it is not a great sentence. And, similarly, with artworks – given their genre, their style, their historical context, and their overall aesthetic direction – one can say by looking at a given work that the author's intention has misfired, whether or not we go on to commend or criticize it.

Undoubtedly, as the preceding discussion indicates, one of the deepest commitments of early anti-intentionalism was the notion that authorial intention is somehow *outside* the artwork and that attempts to invoke it on the basis of the artwork itself are epistemologically suspect. Underlying this view is a conception of authorial intentions as private, episodic mental events that are logically independent of the artworks they give rise to in the way that Humean causes are logically independent of effects. What we have access to, in general, for purposes of evaluation and interpretation is the work itself. The authorial intention is an external cause of the artwork of dubious availability.

However, this view of authorial intention gradually came to be challenged by another view – call it the neo-Wittgensteinian view[14] – according to which an intention is thought to be a purpose, manifest in the artwork, that regulates the way the artwork is. Authorial intention, then, is discoverable by the inspection and contemplation of the work itself.[15] Indeed, the artwork is criterial to attributions of intention.

Searching for authorial intention is, consequently, not a matter of going outside the artwork, looking for some independent, private, mental episode or cause that is logically remote from the meaning or value of the work. The intention is evident in the work itself, and, insofar as the intention is identified as the purposive structure of the work, the intention is the focus of our interest in and attention to the artwork. On the external-episode view, authorial intention is a dispensable, if not distracting, adjunct to the artwork, which adjunct is best ignored. But on the neo-Wittgensteinian approach, tracking the intention – the purposive structure of the work – is the very point of appreciation.

Given the conception of authorial intention as external to and independent of the artwork, the anti-intentionalist claim of its irrelevance to the meaning of the work is eminently comprehensible. But with developments in the philosophies of action, mind, and language, the neo-Wittgensteinian picture of authorial intention seems more attractive. The persuasiveness of anti-intentionalism comes to hinge on which view of intention in general theorists find more plausible. And to the extent that early anti-intentionalism was based upon a crude view of intention, its conclusions are questionable.[16] Moreover, the more attractive, neo-Wittgensteinian view of intention not only makes authorial intention relevant to the interpretation of artworks but implies that in interpreting an artwork, we are attempting to determine the author's intentions. Thus, at this point in the debate, if anti-intentionalism is to remain persuasive, it must do so not only without presupposing a crude view of intention but also must accommodate the neo-Wittgensteinian picture of intention.

With these dialectical constraints in mind, it seems that two anti-intentionalist strategies have become popular recently. The first relies on adducing ontological reasons based on the nature of artworks to deny the relevance of authorial intention to interpretation. The second argues for the irrelevance of intention by exploring the aesthetic interests that audiences have in art. That is, the first sort of argument – the ontological argument – advances anti-intentionalism on the grounds of the nature of the artwork, while the second sort of argument – the aesthetic argument – is grounded on what might be thought of as policy considerations about the best way to regard artworks for aesthetic purposes. Both kinds of arguments presuppose that artworks, for one reason or another, are to be or should be interpreted differently from ordinary words and actions.

III

As noted earlier, we ordinarily interpret words and deeds with the cognitive goal of ascertaining the intentions of authors and agents. As the investigations of historians reveals, there seems to be no principled difficulty in such practices even when the agents in question are long dead and the record fragmentary. Thus, the question arises, Why should matters stand differently when it comes to art? Should not artworks be interpreted in the way in which we customarily interpret other words and actions? At this point, the anti-intentionalist may attempt to argue that artworks are ontologically different from ordinary words and deeds, and therefore different interpretive practices are appropriate to them; specifically, given the nature of artworks in general and literature in particular, authorial intent is irrelevant to interpretation.

This conviction of ontological difference can be found in different and indeed widely disparate literary theorists. It is, for example, an article of faith of contemporary literary critics who endorse Roland Barthes's notion of "the death of the author."[17] And it is, at the same time, a view that underpins the more traditional approaches of the New Criticism, as that approach was defended by the late Monroe Beardsley.[18] Perhaps this convergence of theorists of different stripes on anti-intentionalism should be less surprising than it seems, for both Barthes and Beardsley arrived at their positions – albeit in different decades and in different countries – while in the process of reacting to what was earlier called biographical criticism.

Though Roland Barthes does not explicitly speak of the issue of intention, he clearly believes that, with a literary text, the reader's activity should not be constrained by the "myth" that the author is confiding in us. One reason advanced in support of this view is that

> writing is the destruction of every voice, of every point of origin. Writing is that neutral, composite, oblique space where our subject slips away, the negative where all identity is lost, starting with the very identity of the body of writing.
>
> No doubt it has always been that way. As soon as a fact is *narrated* no longer with a view to acting directly on reality but intransitively, that is to say, finally outside of any function other than that of the very practice of the symbol itself, this disconnection occurs, the voice loses its origin, the author enters into his own death, writing begins.[19]

What Barthes seems to be getting at here is that once writing is divorced from ordinary usage – that is, when language does not serve the purpose of acting on reality – the relevance of an author's intention in writing drops out, and the word sequence is attended to in terms of its play of potential meaning ("the very practice of the symbol itself") .This is a feature of poetry explicitly recognized in modernist writing following Mallarmé, but it implicitly has been a feature of literature all along ("No doubt it has always been that way.")[20]

Ordinary language is tied to acting on reality, and that is the grounds for our preoccupation with authorial intent. But when language is detached from that purpose – when language is aesthetized? – the cognitive goal of fixing authorial intent becomes feckless. That literary language is not practical severs its conceptual connection to authorial intention. As soon as language is employed ("narrated . . .") in what theorists of a more traditional bent than Barthes would call an *aesthetic* way, the conceptual pressure to make sense of it in the light of authorial intent dissolves, and the reader can explore it for all its potential meanings and associations.

In his "Intentions and Interpretations: A Fallacy Revived," Monroe Beardsley, deploying the machinery of speech-act theory, independently evolves an argument that, though different from Barthes's, also parallels it in pertinent respects. The argument begins by drawing a distinction between performing an illocutionary action and representing one. When a pickpocket takes my wallet and I say, "You stole my wallet," I perform the illocutionary act of accusation. An illocutionary action is generated (according to Beardsley, following Alvin Goldman) by the production of a text under certain conditions, and according to certain language conventions.[21] In contrast, when a stage actor, playing a character, says, "You stole my wallet," to another actor, playing another character, she is not performing an illocutionary action; she is representing one.

The relation between performing illocutionary actions and representing them is to be understood on the model of pictorial representation. Just as Beardsley argues that the relation of a pictorial depiction to its referent is that of selective similarity, he maintains that the representation of an illocutionary action resembles the performance of illocutionary action in certain, selected respects (i.e., reproduces certain, but not all, of the conditions requisite for the performance of the illocutionary action). For example, when I accuse a culprit of filching my wallet, I believe that he has taken my wallet; an actor, though repeating much of the formula for accusation, does not believe her fellow actor has stolen anything. Thus, a representation of accusation resembles it in many respects, but not in every respect – for instance, it fails to fulfill the condition of conviction in the culprit's guilt.

Most ordinary discourse is preoccupied with the performance of a multitude of illocutionary actions. Literature, in contrast, specializes in the representation of illocutionary actions. In this respect, once the author's intent to represent illocutionary actions is recognized, thereby acknowledging the neo-Wittgensteinian claim of a conceptual relation between an act and its animating intention, the representation of the illocutionary action is regarded as a selective imitation of the performance of a fictional character – either the literal characters in the text or what has sometimes been called an implied narrator or an implied speaker or dramatis persona.

So when Wordsworth writes about England that "she is a fen," this is not Wordsworth directly performing an illocutionary act of accusation. Wordsworth, in writing poetry, signals his intent to represent the illocutionary act of accusation, which, in this case, is the imitation of an implied speaker's disparaging of England.

The language in the poem is not a performance of an illocutionary act of accusation by Wordsworth. It is a representation of such an action by an implied speaker. Thus, the meaning of the language token is not tied to Wordsworth's intention, nor need it be understood in the context of Wordsworth's biography. It is a representation that can be comprehended solely in terms of the conventions of language.

The author of the performance in the text, so to speak, is the implied speaker; since all we know of the implied speaker are the words in the text – since the implied speaker, a fictional entity, has no existence outside the text – there can be no question of his extratextual intentions. There is no extratextual author, so there are no governing, extratextual intentions. Just as the issue of the number of children Lady Macbeth has is underdetermined by the fiction, so there is no access to implied authorial intent beyond the page.

Beardsley agrees that in ordinary language the cognitive goal of interpretation is the discernment of the speaker's intentions. But the language in literature is not a matter of the author's performance of an illocutionary act. It is a representation of the illocutionary acts of characters and implied speakers. And such fictional speakers have no intentions beyond the words on the page, which must, in consequence, be understood solely in terms of the conventions of language (and without recourse to the intentions of actual authors). It is as if in creating fictional characters, through illocutionary-act representation, actual authors' intentions are ontologically detached from the language sequence in favor of the meanings of characters, both literal and implied, which in turn can, for metaphysical reasons,[22] only be a matter of grasping of linguistic conventions (the literal sense of the words, and the conventions or established strategies for comprehending the sense of verbal contexts and metaphors).

The language in a literary text in being represented language – perhaps, this is what Barthes intends by "narrated . . . intransitively" – becomes the linguistic "performance" of the characters – implied and literal – and thereby is disconnected from the intentions of actual authors by means of a fictional frame (Barthes's notion that language is detached from acting on reality). Moreover, the "intentions" of characters have no existence beyond the page and are available solely in terms of linguistic conventions. Stated formally, Beardsley's argument seems to be as follows:

1. If *x* is a literary work, then *x* is only a representation of an illocutionary act.
2. Though actual authorial intentions are relevant to whether *x* is a representation of an illocutionary act, what *x* is a representation of (its meaning) is solely a matter of the relevant linguistic conventions (the literal sense of words and the conventions or established strategies for grasping the sense of a verbal context and metaphors) *and not* a matter of fixing authorial intent.
3. Therefore, if *x* is a literary work, then what *x* is a representation of is solely a matter of the relevant conventions.

Thus, in interpreting the language in a literary text, we will be concerned with the meanings of characters – literal ones, implied authors, or dramatis personae. And since these characters have no existence outside the words in the text, interpreting their meanings is exclusively a matter of convention. The actual author, metaphorically speaking, banishes himself from the text in the process of representing illocutionary actions. This argument grants some role to authorial intention as an ingredient in identifying the author's act as one of representing. But once the representational frame is in place, so to speak, the author's intentions are outside it. And given the ontological status of the representational frame, it is a category mistake to be preoccupied with authorial intent; it is metaphysically irrelevant.

(Moreover, though this argument is stated in terms of literature, one supposes that it can be extended to other art forms, given, for example, Beardsley's analogies between pictorial representation and illocutionary representation – perhaps landscapes are to be understood as vistas seen by implied observers.)

It is absolutely central in this argument that literary language and ordinary language be ontologically distinct. Literary language is a special zone, so, even if in ordinary language authorial intent is a guide to meaning, it is not relevant in literature because literature is not a performance but a representation. In ordinary language, we are prone to say that when a speaker disambiguates her earlier utterance, she has told us the meaning of the utterance. With literature, however, there is no comparable resort to the author's intent, for the relevant speaker is not the living author but various dramatis personae who are ontologically unavailable for comment. If their words are ambiguous, one suspects that Beardsley would be prone to say that the dramatic speaker is being represented as ambiguous.

The crux of Beardsley's argument is, given the distinction between performing and representing, the claim that literature is by definition a matter of representing illocutionary acts.[23] This effectively boils down to the assertion that all literature is essentially fictional. For even if a literary text does not deploy imaginary characters and places, it is involved in presenting its persons, places, and events through the fictional medium of an implied speaker or narrator. Such claims are not unfamiliar.[24] If anti-intentionalism depends on this generalization, however, it is surely in trouble.[25]

Pretheoretically, many works of what we classify as literature fall into the category of nonfiction. Lucretius's *Concerning the Nature of Things* is one example; *The Mahabharata* is another. Both appear to be illocutionary acts of assertion, even if what they assert turns out to be false. It does not seem correct to attribute to Lucretius the intention of representing the illocutionary acts of an Epicurean philosopher – he was an Epicurean philosopher philosophizing. Similarly, the authors of *The Mahabharata* were not imitating the telling of the history of their race; they were telling it. Nor do we need, I think, to travel to the distant past for our counterexamples. When in "Howl," Allen Ginsberg wrote "I saw the best minds of my generation destroyed by madness," there is every indication that, however hyperbolically, he is speaking in his own voice and not representing the illocutionary act of accusation of some "angel-headed hipster." The notion of implied narrators and dramatic speakers, no matter how useful in explicating a great deal of literature, does not afford a necessary condition for being a literary text.[26]

Thus, a literary text is not necessarily a representation of an illocutionary act; it may be a performance of an illocutionary act of assertion, accusation, and so forth. Therefore, the fact that many literary texts involve representations of illocutionary acts does not entail that every literary text must be interpreted without concern for authorial intent in contradistinction to ordinary language.

Of course, it would be a mistake to conflate the representations of illocutionary acts presented through fictional characters with the performance of illocutionary acts by actual authors. It would be an error to identify Emily Brontë with the narrator of *Wuthering Heights.* But that distinction can be readily marked without resorting to the extreme theoretical concession that the literary speaker is always fictional.

Not only are there entire literary works that it seems ill advised to regard as representations of illocutionary acts. There are also many parts of literary works that do not appear to be representations of illocutionary acts: the discourse on whales in Melville's *Moby Dick*, the history of symbols in Hugo's *Hunchback of Notre Dame*, and the philosophy of history in Tolstoy's *War and Peace*. Though housed in fiction, where they undeniably perform a literary function, they are also essays whose authors produced them in order to make assertions. In interpreting these interludes, one needs to approach them as one would any other form of cognitive discourse. Some may be tempted to prefer to read them as representations of illocutionary acts when one finds a particular author's ideas rather hare-brained. But such considerations – however cosmetically well intended – are, in fact, irrelevant to the issue of whether the passages in question are performances of illocutionary acts rather than representations thereof. Furthermore, if, as I argue, these are performances of illocutionary acts of assertion, then in such instances, it will be appropriate, as Beardsley would appear compelled to admit, to interpret them with the cognitive goal of discerning what the authors intended.

So far, we have been whittling away at the first premise of Beardsley's arguments by finding poems and passages to which the generalization does not apply and by arguing that in these instances, given Beardsley's own views, interpreting with respect to authorial intention is as appropriate as it is in the case of ordinary illocutionary acts of assertion. But the million-dollar question is: How extensive a problem does this pose for the anti-intentionalist?

My own hunch is that the problem will be very extensive. For once we admit that there can be explicit nonfictional passages (which may range in scale from clauses and sentences to chapters and beyond) housed in fiction – and which are best construed as performances of illocutionary actions – the door is opened to the recognition that there are many implicit or implied propositions in literary works as well, which are also best conceived in terms of performances. *Brave New World* expresses a point of view about what Huxley sees as the prospect of utilitarian social control. I see no particular advantage in rephrasing this observation in terms of the point of view of a fictional dramatic speaker. And, of course, if it is suggested that we must advert to talk of implied speakers in order to deflect the worries of anti-intentionalism, that begs the question at issue.

Authors, in fact, often make political (Gorky's *Mother*), philosophical (Sartre's *Nausea*), and moral (James's *The Ambassadors*) points through their literary writings. This is a commonly known, openly recognized, and frequently discussed practice in our literary culture. These points are very often secured through oblique techniques – implication, allegory, presupposition, illustration (unaccompanied with explicative commentary), and so on. That is, such points need not be and often are not directly stated. For this very reason, they are one of the most common objects of literary interpretation. And there is no reason to believe that in every case the implicit points found in literary works are merely the notions of a fictional speaker or an implied author rather than the actual author.

This is not to deny that there may be literary works in which the moral, philosophical, religious, political, and other views are only constituents of dramatic speakers or implied authors. It is only to reject the position that all the implicit points made in literary works are the representations of the implied commitments of fictional speakers.

There may be no general epistemological principle that we can apply to tell whether, in a given instance, the implied point belongs to the actual author or to an implied author. We may have to proceed in this matter on a case-by-case basis, relying on the results of practical criticism (of a sort that at least countenances the applicability of intentionalist hypotheses). But given the practices of our literary culture, that seems a better procedure than negotiating our lack of an epistemological principle by jettisoning the idea that actual authors communicate their commitments to us through literary works[27] – or, to return the issue to Beardsley's idiom, that actual authors do not ever perform illocutionary acts, even in fiction, rather than merely, only, always representing them.

Often it seems that arguments about the relevance of authorial intent to interpretation become so preoccupied with the issue at the level of word sequences that sight is lost of the fact that much of our interpretive activity is spent in trying to ascertain the point, often the implicit or implied point, of large segments of discourse and entire works. For example, we may be concerned with what a whole novel is getting at – its thesis, as Beardsley once called it.[28] And it seems to me natural, in many instances, to regard the theses we encounter in literary works as that which the author intends, through the production of the text, that the reader recognizes as the intended point. If we can regard implicit thesis projection with nonfictional import as a form of illocutionary action, there is no reason to think that it cannot be performed by actual authors. Implicit thesis projection may be a device employed in the construction of an implied author. But I see no reason to agree that it is always so employed.

For example, in Donald Barthelme's story "Alice," there is a recurring strategy of surreal and disorienting lists. In interpreting this strategy, we are not primarily concerned with elucidating the meaning of words or word sequences, but, and this is more important, in ascertaining Barthelme's point in employing these lists – that is, we are concerned with why he made the story this way. A likely hypothesis is that he intended this mode of organization to suggest the currently fashionable antihumanist notion that the subject is decentered.[29] Here the object of interpretation is what Barthelme has *done*, and even though what he has said in the narrow sense is material to what he has done, the intentionalist idiom of *action* seems central to the way in which we characterize thesis projection through artistic strategies.

Not all literature is fictional, and not even all the assertions in fictions are representations of illocutionary actions. Pretheoretically, literary works, including parts of some fiction, can involve performances of illocutionary acts. Thus, if it is an appropriate cognitive goal with respect to performances of illocutionary acts to read for intentions, then, in certain circumstances, reading literature for authorial intention is plausible. There indeed may be times when reading representations of illocutionary acts for authorial intent is misguided for the reasons Beardsley advances. Nevertheless, those reasons cannot provide the grounds for a comprehensive anti-intentionalism with respect to literature (not to mention art in general).

Moreover, if there is implicit thesis projection of nonfictional import – whereby actual authors express their views about life, society, morality, and so forth – and a great deal of literary (indeed, artistic) interpretation concerns the identification of such theses, then intentionalist criticism has a wide arena of legitimate activity.

So far, I have been concerned to undermine the first premise of my reconstruction of

Beardsley's argument. Literary works need not only be representations of illocutionary actions. But Beardsley's second premise also bears scrutiny. Its purpose is to exclude intentionalist interpretive activity on the grounds that its meaning can only be a matter of conventions because its speakers (fictional characters and implied authors) do not exist and therefore have no intentions. And, in any event, even if in some sense "intentions" could be imputed to them, they are not the intentions of the actual author, since he or she is not the speaker.

This premise may have some plausibility if it is narrowly construed to pertain only to the meaning of word sequences. But literary meaning – that is, the object of literary interpretation – need not be concerned solely with the meaning of word sequences even when it comes to the representation of illocutionary acts. Literary interpretation may ask questions about the point of constructing a character in this or that way and thus may investigate the representation of illocutionary acts in a text in terms of the contribution it makes to the point of the character as an element in the overall design of the work.

That is, in representing a character or an implied author and his or her fictional illocutions in a certain way, a theme may be adumbrated. We may ask, why did so-and-so say that in that way at that point in the text – how does it fit into the larger argument of the story or poem? And such questions about the point of character construction and the representation of the illocutionary acts that constitute them seem to me referable to the intentions of the actual author, without risking the kind of ontological gaff Beardsley feels must arise when actual authors are introduced into the interpretation of the meaning of representations of illocutionary acts. Thus, even if it were true that all literary works are only representations of illocutionary acts, that would not preclude intentionalist interpretation of literary meaning in the broad sense.

Of course, we might also wonder whether the actual author is as remote from representations of illocutionary acts as Beardsley supposes. As a historian of philosophy, Beardsley himself, along with an entire profession, appears to find little problem in deriving Plato's doctrine from Socratic dialogues. Surely these are no less representations of illocutionary acts, in Beardsley's terminology, than is the experiential proof of God's existence offered at the end of *The Brothers Karamazov*. But if we can, at least sometimes, feel justified in treating Plato/Socrates intentionalistically, with respect to illocutionary representations, why should we hesitate treating Dostoyevsky/Alyosha similarly?

Problems arise, then, with both of Beardsley's premises. I have spent more time with Beardsley's formulation than with Barthes's, since I think that it is obviously more developed. Nevertheless, though Barthes does not mobilize speech-act theory, I think that his notion of the death of the author is susceptible to a number of the points made against Beardsley. Barthes apparently maintains that when language is divorced from the goal of acting on reality ("narrated . . . intransitively"), the relevance of the author disappears, and a space is opened for the reader to explore the text in terms of all its intertextual associations. The reader, in a manner of speaking, becomes a writer and the critic, a creator.

I am not sure that once language is used "intransitively," the author becomes irrelevant, since identifying such a use would appear to depend on fixing the author's intention to work in certain genres or forms, namely, those that function intransitively. That is, how will the interpreter know that the writing in question is of the right sort to be read in a writerly fashion without adverting to authorial intentions?

Barthes claims that when writing is divorced from the purpose of acting directly on reality, the author becomes irrelevant. Whether this is persuasive depends on what this divorce from reality amounts to. Does the notion of no longer operating directly on reality reduce to Beardsley-type claims about representations of illocutionary acts or to the notion that literature is essentially fictional? If so, Barthes must deal with the kinds of objections rehearsed already.[30] But if the notion does not dissolve into the view that all writing (literature?) is fiction, then one wonders how often writing is divorced from the purpose of acting on reality. That is, supposing Barthes is correct and once writing is detached from the purpose of acting on reality, the author becomes irrelevant, the crucial question concerns the frequency of this phenomenon.

Barthes clearly thinks it happens a great deal. But, generously construed, the idea of writing acting on reality seems to me to apply quite uncontroversially to much literature that is used to criticize society, to champion moral views, to afford insight into social behavior, to reinforce values, to encourage our sympathies, to elicit our hatred, to give voice to our experience, and so on. If this is said not to be a matter of *directly* acting on reality, we need an account of what Barthes means here. If he has the issue of fiction in mind, we have already provided the counterexamples. Moreover, if narrating intransitively means just any writing where the author is not in the presence of her or his audience – writing detached from the physical context of utterance – that, counterintuitively, implies that such things as book orders do not operate directly on reality.[31]

If Barthes has something else in mind, the burden of proof is on him (or his followers) to produce it. For insofar as it is common practice for authors to strive to affect reality by means of their writing and insofar as they appear in some sense to succeed, then it would seem, given Barthes's own argument, that in certain instances (many?), the author is not dead, and there is no conceptual pressure to treat him or her as such.

Undoubtedly, there may be poems – one thinks of the Exquisite Corpses of the Surrealists – in which the writer opens the text to the free play of the reader (though even here the author's intent to enable readers to see the world differently cannot be forgotten). Nevertheless, artistic attempts to secure the death of the author by, so to say, authorial suicide, no matter how interesting and legitimate experimentally, do not force us to concede that, in general the author is, in every respect, irrelevant to the interpretation of the text – even if we accept Barthes's criterion of acting or not acting on reality as the mark of authorial life and death.

Both Barthes and Beardsley frame their arguments in terms of literature, though I think that it is fair to say that both would advocate anti-intentionalism across the interpretation of the arts.[32] But their anti-intentionalism seems to me to be most persuasive when it is applied to such things as word sequences, whose meanings are extremely conventionalized. In other art forms, where there are not such highly articulated codes of meaning, our interpretations of artistic performances are more akin to discerning the sense of an action than to reading.

If a choreographer mounts a dance in a theater in the round rather than on a proscenium stage, we attempt to figure out the significance of this *choice* by thinking about what he or she is trying to do with respect to historical and contemporary theatrical practices relative to the work in question. The *meaning* of "theater in the round" is neither fixed nor semiotically bound to other theatrical "signs" in a way that can be read the way a text may be (either determinately, à la Beardsley, or intertextually, à la Barthes). Instead, its interpretation depends on locating the purpose that the strategy in question serves for what the author is attempting to do.[33] And it is hard to see how such artistic *doings* – which describe most activity outside literature[34] – can be explicated without reference to the *intentional* activity of authors.

IV

So far, we have explored anti-intentionalist arguments that preclude reference to authorial intent on the grounds of the putatively special ontological nature of art in general and literature in particular. Our own position has been that these considerations do not require us in general to treat literature differently from ordinary discourse, except perhaps in certain limited instances – for example, where the meaning of a character's or an implied narrator's literal utterance token, per se, is underdetermined due to the constraints of fiction. But even in the face of these limitations, there are many other cases and aspects of literary and fictional discourse where there is no ontological barrier to the cognitive goal of attempting to discern authorial intention as an object of interpretation. Thus, anti-intentionalism does not, on ontological grounds, afford grounds for believing that authorial intent is irrelevant in every instance of interpretation.

The ontological considerations of the anti-intentionalists, which were canvassed earlier, might be called "reasons of art" in that they declare reference to authorial intent out-of-bounds because of the special nature of art. With respect to discourse, such reasons of art presume that literary discourse is metaphysically different from ordinary discourse in a way that makes reading literature for authorial intent a kind of category error. We have challenged the generality and applicability of this position and concluded that there is no reason why, across the board, reading literary works with the cognitive goal of identifying authorial intentions is inadmissible; indeed, at times – for example, with respect to authorial *doings* – it seems the most plausible way to proceed.

There are other "reasons of art" that we have not yet considered. The idea behind the ontological arguments is that it is in some sense impossible to fix authorial intent and that the aim should be abandoned as any other impossible goal should be abandoned. Nevertheless, an anti-intentionalist might admit that the ontological arguments are not generally conclusive, yet adduce reasons of art that show that reading for authorial intent *should not* be pursued, even though it could be pursued. These reasons of art might be called aesthetic. That is, whereas ontological arguments advance reasons of art that maintain that intentionalism is, strictly speaking, impossible, aesthetic arguments admit that intentionalist criticism is possible, but *recommend* that it not be embraced for what might be called aesthetic policy reasons.

Isolating pure aesthetic arguments for anti-intentionalism is a bit difficult, since most anti-intentionalists believe in the ontological distinction between literary language and ordinary language, and as a result they weave their ontological and aesthetic arguments together in ways that are hard to disentangle. The supposed aesthetic advantages of anti-intentionalism are often introduced only to be ultimately backed up by ontological considerations. But it is possible to construct an aesthetic argument without reference to ontological claims about the nature of art in general or of literature in particular.

For example, Monroe Beardsley writes:

> What is the primary purpose of literary interpretation? It is, I would say, to help readers approach literary works from the aesthetic point of view, that is, with an interest in actualizing their (artistic) goodness. The work is an object, capable (presumably) of affording aesthetic satisfaction. The problem is to know what is there to be responded to; and the literary interpreter helps us to discern what is there so that we can enjoy it more fully.[35]

Here, the underlying idea is that an artistic object has a purpose: affording aesthetic satisfaction. This is why we attend to artworks. Our object is to derive as much aesthetic satisfaction as is possible from the object. The role of the interpreter is to show us what there is in the object that promotes aesthetic experience. Nevertheless, one can readily imagine that what an author intended to say by means of an artwork is less aesthetically provocative than alternative "readings" of the work. For Beardsley, these readings, with respect to literature, have to be constrained by what the words of the text mean conventionally. Even with this caveat, it is easy to imagine instances in which what the author intended is less aesthetically exciting than an alternate, conventionally admissible reading.

Moreover, since the point of consuming art, and of interpretation as an adjunct to artistic consumption, is to maximize aesthetic satisfaction, we should always favor those interpretations that afford the best aesthetic experience that is compatible with established textual meaning conventions. Furthermore, since aesthetic richness is our overriding concern, we need only interpret with an eye to that which is most aesthetically satisfying and linguistically plausible. Whether or not the meanings we attribute to the text were authorially intended is irrelevant. The proof of the pudding is in the tasting.

Of course, the best reading of the text – the one that is most aesthetically satisfying and also at least linguistically plausible – may coincide with the author's intended meaning, but that is of accidental importance. What is essential for the purposes of aesthetic consumption is that it be the best interpretation – the one that points to the maximum available aesthetic enjoyment – conceivable within the constraints of linguistic plausibility. Thus, for aesthetic purposes, we may always forgo concern for authorial intent in favor of the best aesthetic interpretation.

Where authorial intention and the best interpretation coincide, the reason we accept the interpretation has to do with aesthetic richness rather than authorial intention. Where there may be divergences between authorial intentions and textual meanings (that are richer than the putative authorial ones), we go with the latter because maximizing aesthetic satisfaction is our goal. As a matter of aesthetic policy, the best procedure is always to regard authorial intention as irrelevant because it either adds nothing to our aesthetic satisfaction or it may even stand in the way of arriving at the most enjoyable experience of the work.

On Beardsley's view, there is generally a determinate best interpretation. However, the aesthetic argument can also be mobilized by theorists who eschew determinate meanings, preferring the "play of signification of the text." Here, the argument might begin by recalling that a text can be interpreted either as the utterance of an author or as a word sequence.[36] Read as a word sequence, the text may have multiple meanings compatible with the conventions of language. Given this, the question becomes, What is the best way to read the text – authorially or, so to speak, textually?

In defense of reading the text as a word sequence, one can invoke the Kantian notion that aesthetic experience involves the play of understanding and imagination. That is, taking the text as a word sequence allows us to contemplate it for multiple, diverse meanings and their possible connections. It provides the best way for us to maximize our aesthetic experience of the text, permitting us to track the text for its play of meaning and alternative import. Reading for authorial intent, where the author intends a determinate meaning rather than an "open text,"[37] may obstruct the delectation of the various shifts in meaning that would otherwise be available to the reader who takes the text as a word sequence. Thus, for the purpose of maximizing our aesthetic experience – construed here to be a matter of cognitive play with meanings – the best policy is to attend to the work as a word sequence rather than as an authorial utterance.

The conservative version of this aesthetic argument might hold that texts could be read as word sequences or as authorial utterances and that there is no reason why the intentionalist preference for authorial utterance must be given priority over the possibility of reading the text as a word sequence. Both readings are possible, and neither recommendation is binding.[38] So, if a good reason – like the Kantian aesthetic invoked earlier – can be advanced for anti-intentionalist interpretive practices, then the claims of intentionalism can be suspended. This does not preclude intentionalist interpretation, but only denies that interpretation must always be constrained by intentionalist considerations.

A more radical version of the aesthetic argument would advocate that intentionalist considerations are *always* best bracketed because they stand in the way of, or are irrelevant to, maximizing interpretive play.[39] Concern for authorial intent "closes" down the text; it limits the artwork as a source of interpretive enjoyment; it restrains the imagination (of the audience) unduly. This recommendation may be accompanied by the vague and perhaps confusing cliché that artworks are inexhaustible, insofar as word sequences, ex hypothesi, will tend to have more meanings than authorial utterances. But the argument can proceed without claiming that art-works are literally inexhaustible; only to urge that, for the purpose of making literary experience more exciting, we should treat artworks that way, rather as Morris Zapp in David Lodge's *Changing Places* keeps reinterpreting Jane Austen in the light of every literary theory that comes down the pike. That is, keeping artworks interpretively open – for example, by reading for word sequence meaning rather than authorial meaning – makes for more zestful encounters with art.

The radical version of the aesthetic argument seems to me to underwrite a great deal of contemporary literary criticism. Ironically, where someone like Beardsley supports anti-intentionalism because of his convictions about the autonomy of the artwork and the literary text,[40] contemporary literary critics advocate anti-intentionalism for the sake of the freedom and autonomy of the reader. In Barthes, for example, the "death of the author" corresponds to the birth of the reader.

Admittedly, for Barthes, this is grounded in ontological arguments about the nature of writing. Yet one feels that, with Barthes and his followers, the ontological argument itself is attractive because its conclusion suits their preference for an autonomous reader, one who creatively participates in making the meaning of the text by tracing the multiple and not necessarily converging linguistic trajectories that reading divorced from a concern with authorial utterance allows.[41]

Aesthetic arguments for anti-intentionalism are a subclass of the general view that interpretations are purpose-relative.[42] One could advance anti-intentionalism, then, for purposes other than aesthetic gratification under the banner of purpose-relative interpretation; one could, for example, maintain that anti-intentionalism best realizes some moral or ideological goal, which outweighs whatever aims intentionalism supports.[43] Since I believe that the purpose that critics most often presuppose anti-intentionalism serves best is aesthetic enrichment, however, I focus the discussion on this issue.

With aesthetic arguments, the anti-intentionalist admits, in my reconstruction of the debate, that one could read for authorial intent, but maintains that we have certain aims in pursuing artworks that, so to speak, trump our concerns with authorial meaning. These aims center on the maximization of aesthetic satisfaction. Aesthetic satisfaction is the overriding interest that we have in consuming artworks. So in order to secure said satisfaction, we are best advised to take it that the aesthetically most satisfying interpretation outranks all others, most notably where a competing view is an intentionalist interpretation.

In order to develop this argument fully, the anti-intentionalist needs to say something about aesthetic satisfaction. This may cause difficulties in several registers. The first is the long-standing problem of defining the way in which we are to understand "the aesthetic" in *aesthetic satisfaction*. Moreover, there may be rival views of what constitutes aesthetic satisfaction – Beardsleyan determinate meaning of a certain sort, or the inexhaustible play of meaning in the text. Which of these views must the anti-intentionalist endorse? But even supposing these technical difficulties with characterizing aesthetic satisfaction can be met, I remain unconvinced by aesthetic arguments for anti-intentionalism.

The heart of my disagreement is that it seems unproven that we have overriding interests in maximizing aesthetic satisfaction with respect to artworks. My reason for reservations here have to do with my suspicion that in dealing with artworks we have more interests than aesthetic interests – as "aesthetic interests" are usually construed within the philosophical tradition – and that there is no reason to think that these interests are always trumped by aesthetic ones. Indeed, as I argue, these other-than-aesthetic interests may in fact mandate constraints on the pursuit of aesthetic interest in ways that count against anti-intentionalism and for intentionalism. I would not wish to deny that we have interests in securing aesthetic satisfaction from artworks. But that interest needs to be reconciled with other, potentially conflictive interests that we also bring to artworks.

What are these other interests or purposes? Broadly speaking, I would call them "conversational." When we read a literary text or contemplate a painting, we enter a relationship with its creator that is roughly analogous to a conversation. Obviously, it is not as interactive as an ordinary conversation, for we are not receiving spontaneous feedback concerning our own responses. But just as an ordinary conversation gives us a stake in understanding our interlocutor, so does interaction with an artwork.

We would not think that we had had a genuine conversation with someone whom we were not satisfied we understood. Conversations, rewarding ones at least, involve a sense of community or communion that itself rests on communication. A fulfilling conversation requires that we have the conviction of having grasped what our interlocutor meant or intended to say. This is evinced by the extent to which we struggle to clarify their meanings. A conversation that left us with only our own clever construals or educated guesses, no matter how aesthetically rich, would leave us with the sense that something was missing. That we had neither communed nor communicated.

Not all conversations involve both communion and communication. Probably many firings do not. But what, for want of a better term, we might call serious conversations do have, as a constitutive value, the prospect of community. Likewise, I want to maintain, this prospect of community supplies a major impetus motivating our interest in engaging literary texts and artworks. We may read to be entertained, to learn, and to be moved, but we also seek out artworks in order to converse or commune with their makers. We want to understand the author, even if that will lead to rejecting his or her point of view.

An important part of why we are interested in art is that it affords not only an opportunity to reap aesthetic satisfaction but is an opportunity to exercise our interpretive abilities in the context of a genuine conversation. Clever construals, even if aesthetically dazzling, do not necessarily serve our desire to commune or communicate with another person. Insofar as our pursuit of art is underwritten by, and is an exemplary occasion for, a generic human interest in communicating with others, it is not clear that a concern with aesthetics alone serves our purposes best.

Moreover, in stressing our conversational interest in artworks in terms of understanding the artist, I am not reverting to the notion that we pursue art in order to commune with remarkable personalities. Instead, I am making the more modest claim that art is obviously in part a matter of communication and that we bring to it our ordinary human disposition to understand what another human being is saying to us.

The idea of the maximization of aesthetic satisfaction has a very "consumerist" ring to it. In Buberesque lingo, it reduces our relation to the text to an I/It relationship. What I am trying to defend is the idea that, with artworks, we are also interested in an I/Thou relation to the author of the text. This interest in communicating with others is perhaps so deeply a part of our motive in, for example, reading that we may not have it in the forefront of our attention. But when we pick up Tom Wolfe's *Bonfire of the Vanities*, surely one of our abiding interests is to learn what someone else, namely Tom Wolfe, thinks about contemporary New York. And, the extent to which we have this conversational interest in the text limits the range of aesthetically enhancing interpretations we can countenance. That is, the purpose of aesthetic maximization will have to be brought into line with our conversational interests, which interests are patently concerned with authorial intent.

Furthermore, if I am right about the conversational interests that we have in artworks and literary texts, then our concern with authorial intention will not simply issue from the mutual respect we have for our interlocutor; it will also be based on an interest in protecting our sense of self-respect in the process of conversation. In order to clarify this point, a somewhat extended example may be useful.

In contemporary film criticism, films are often commended because they *transgress* what are called the codes of Hollywood filmmaking, thereby striking this or that blow for emancipation. Within the context of recent film criticism, it is appropriate to regard disturbances of continuity editing, disorienting narrative ellipses, or disruptions of eyeline matches as subversions of a dominant and ideologically suspect form of filmmaking, and given the historical evolution of the language game in which avant-garde filmmaking is practiced, the attribution of such meanings to contemporary films is warranted, especially on intentionalist grounds.

Once interpretations of narrative incoherences in recent films as subversions or transgressions of Hollywood International were in place, however, film critics, such as J. Hoberman of the *Village Voice*, began to attempt to project those readings backward. That is, if a narrative incoherence or an editing discontinuity in a film in 1988 counts as a transgression, why not count a similar disturbance in a film of 1959 as equally transgressive? Thus, a hack film by Edward Wood, *Plan 9 from Outer Space*, is celebrated as transgressive as if it were a postmodernist exercise in collage.[44]

Plan 9 from Outer Space is a cheap, slapdash attempt to make a feature film for very little, and in cutting corners to save money it violates – in outlandish ways – many of the decorums of Hollywood filmmaking that later avant-gardists also seek to affront. So insofar as the work of contemporary avant-gardists is aesthetically valued for its transgressiveness, why not appreciate *Plan 9 from Outer Space* under an analogous interpretation? Call it "unintentional modernism," but it is modernism nonetheless and appreciable as such.[45]

One reason to withhold such an interpretation from *Plan 9*, of course, is that transgression is an intentional concept, and all the evidence indicates that Edward Wood did not have the same intentions to subvert the Hollywood style of filmmaking that contemporary avant-gardists have. Indeed, given the venue Wood trafficked in, it seems that the best hypothesis about his intentions is that he was attempting to imitate the Hollywood style of filmmaking in the cheapest way possible. Given what we know of Edward Wood and the B-film world in which he practiced his trade, it is implausible to attribute to him the intention of attempting to subvert the Hollywood codes of filmmaking for the kinds of purposes endorsed by contemporary avant-gardists.

An intention is made up of beliefs and desires. It is incredible to attribute to Edward Wood the kinds of beliefs that contemporary avant-garde filmmakers have about the techniques, purposes, and effects of subverting Hollywood cinema. Those beliefs (and avant-garde desires) were not available in the film world Edward Wood inhabited, nor can we surmise that even if Wood could have formulated such beliefs, it would be plausible to attribute to him the intention to implement them. For it is at the least uncharitable to assign to Wood the belief that his audiences could have interpreted his narrative discontinuities and editing howlers as blows struck against a Hollywood aesthetic.[46] That is, it is virtually impossible that Wood could have had the intentions – the beliefs and the desires – that contemporary avant-gardists have about the meanings of disjunctive exposition or the effects of such exposition on audiences.

Historically, it is undoubtedly most accurate to regard Edward Wood's narrative non sequiturs and nonstandard editing as mistakes within the norms of Hollywood filmmaking. One would think that the critic interested in transgression would want to have a way to distinguish between mistakes and transgressions. And the most obvious way to make such a distinction is to require that transgressions be intentional, which requires that the filmmaker in question have the knowledge and the will to violate Hollywood norms of filmmaking as a form of artistic protest. Insofar as it is anachronistic to impute the requisite knowledge (of the discourse of avant-garde theory) or the desire to subvert Hollywood codes to Wood, it is better to regard his violations of certain norms as mistakes. And, in general, it would seem that connoisseurs of artistic transgression would have an interest in being able to distinguish mistakes from subversions – interests that should drive them toward intentionalism.

Nevertheless, it is at this point that an aesthetic argument for anti-intentionalism may be brought to bear. To wit: if a transgression interpretation of *Plan 9 from Outer Space* yields a more aesthetically satisfying encounter with the film, and our primary purpose in interpretation is in promoting maximum aesthetic satisfaction, why not suspend qualms about intention and take *Plan 9 from Outer Space* as a masterpiece of postmodernist disjunction *à la lettre*? Here, the anti-intentionalist might agree that such an interpretation cannot be squared with what it is plausible to say of the film, given the possible intentions of the historical director. But why not sacrifice the distinction between mistakes and transgressions if in the long run it supplies us with more aesthetically satisfying experiences?

That is, the argument against taking *Plan 9* as a transgression rests on the supposition that it is not a reasonable hypothesis of what Wood could have meant in producing the film. But so what? If we drop a commitment to discerning authorial intent, and regard any norm violation as a transgression, would not that make *Plan 9* more aesthetically interesting, and if our premium is on aesthetic interest, would not anti-intentionalist criticism be our best bet?

But I submit that insofar as we have a conversational interest in artworks, we will want to reject this sort of aesthetic argument. For if we take ourselves to be aiming at a genuine conversation, ignoring Wood's palpable intentions, it seems to me, can only undermine our sense of ourselves as authentic participants in the conversation. For, from the point of view of genuine conversation, we are being willfully silly in regarding *Plan 9* as a transgression of Hollywood codes of filmmaking. We are behaving as if we believed that a randomly collected series of phrases, derived from turning the dial of our car radio at one-second intervals, harbored the message of an oracle, while simultaneously we agree that all forms of divination are preposterous.

In his *Concluding Unscientific Postscript*, Kierkegaard notes that a comic moment arises when "a sober man engages in sympathetic and confidential conversation with one whom he does not know is intoxicated, while the observer knows of the condition. The contradiction lies in the mutuality presupposed by the conversation, that it is not there, and that the sober man has not noticed its absence."[47] By analogy, in supposing that Wood is a kind of Godard, we are acting as if a stream of drunken incoherencies constitute[s] an enigmatic code. Indeed, we are placing ourselves in an even more ridiculous position than the butt of Kierkegaard's mishap, for we have voluntarily entered this situation.

In Kosinski's *Being There*, the naïf Chance utters all sorts of remarks about his garden, which other characters take to be of great gnomic significance. Since they are unaware that Chance is a simpleton, they are, in effect, applying something like Culler's anti-intentionalist rule of significance[48] to the sayings of a fool. The result, as with Kierkegaard's imagined conversation with the drunk, is comic. Taking something like *Plan 9* to be a radical transgression of Hollywood International seems to me to be a matter of willingly adopting the ludicrous position that those characters suffer inadvertently. It undermines any self-respecting view we could have of ourselves as participants in a conversation. Whatever aesthetic satisfaction we could claim of such an exchange would have to be bought at the conversational cost of making ourselves rather obtuse.

Aesthetic arguments for anti-intentionalism proceed as if aesthetic satisfaction were the only important interest we could have with respect to artworks. Thus, wherever other putative interests impede aesthetic interests, they must give way. But aesthetic satisfaction is not the only major source of value that we have in interacting with artworks; the interaction is also a matter of a conversation between the artist and us – a human encounter – in which we have a desire to know what the artist intends, not only out of respect for the artist, but also because we have a personal interest in being a capable respondent. In endorsing the anti-intentionalist view that aesthetic satisfaction trumps all other interests, we seem to be willing to go for aesthetic pleasure at all costs, including, most notably, any value we might place on having a genuine conversational exchange with another human being. For, as the *Plan 9* example suggests, we are willing to act as if we had encountered a profound, reflexive meditation on the dominant cinema, when, in fact, it is readily apparent that we are dealing with a botched and virtually incoherent atrocity.

Aesthetic arguments in favor of anti-intentionalism presume a species of aesthetic hedonism. They presuppose that aesthetic pleasure or satisfaction is our only legitimate interest with regard to artworks. Here it is useful to recall Robert Nozick's very provocative, antihedonistic thought experiment – the experience machine.

> Suppose there were an experience machine that would give you any experience you desired. Super-duper neuropsychologists could stimulate your brain so that you would think and feel you were writing a great novel, or making a friend, or reading an interesting book. All the time you would be floating in a tank, with electrodes attached to your brain. Should you plug into the machine for life, preprogramming your life's experiences?[49]

Nozick thinks that our answer here will be obviously no, and part of the reason is that we wish to be a certain kind of person and do various things and not just have experiences as if we were such a person and as if we were doing those things. In other words, the pleasure of these simulated experiences is not enough; we have a stake in actually having the experiences in question. Applied to the aesthetic case, what I am trying to defend in the name of conversational interests is the claim that we have an investment in really encountering interesting and brilliant authors, not simply in counterfeiting such encounters. Knowing that *Plan 9* is a schlock quickie, but responding to it as if it were superbly transgressive, is akin to knowingly taking the heroics performed in Nozick's experience machine as if they were actual adventures. It is a matter of sacrificing genuine conversational experiences for aesthetic pleasures. And in doing so, one is willing to lower one's self-esteem for the sake of an aesthetic high.[50]

Of course, the problem I have raised with the use and abuse of the concept of transgression by contemporary film critics brings up general problems with aesthetic arguments in favor of anti-intentionalism. For example, the pervasive problems of allusion and irony are strictly analogous to the problems that we have sketched with respect to transgression. One could render both Richard Bach's *Jonathan Livingston Seagull*[51] and Heinrich Anacker's anti-Semitic, pro-Nazi "Exodus of the Parasites"[52] more aesthetically satisfying by regarding them as ironic. Yet I suspect that we resist this kind of interpretive temptation. And this resistance, I think, can be explained by our conversational interests in artworks. We have every justification for believing that these works are tawdry but sincere, and behaving as though they were ironic – whatever aesthetic satisfaction that might promote – would place us in what we recognize to be an ersatz conversation. We would be, respectively, laughing *with* what we know we should be laughing *at*, and appalled *along* with what we know we should be appalled *at*. Our conversation would not be authentic in either event, and whatever aesthetic satisfaction we secured would be purchased by making ourselves conversationally incompetent. Insofar as one of the abiding values we pursue in encounters with artworks is conversational, we are not willing to turn these particular pig's ears into silver purses.

Stanley Cavell has argued that one of the audience's major preoccupations with modern art is whether it is sincere. Given the dadaist tendencies of contemporary art, the spectator cares whether he or she is being fooled by the artist.[53] The encounter with the artwork is a human situation in which our self-esteem may be felt to be at risk. Likewise, I want to stress that insofar as the artistic context is a kind of conversation, we also may be concerned not only that the artist is given his or her due but that we carry through our end of the conversation. In terms of self-esteem, we have an interest not only in not being gulled by the artist but also in not fooling ourselves. And this interest gives us reason to reject interpretations of artworks that, however aesthetically satisfying they may be, cannot sensibly be connected to the intentions of their authors. The simulacrum of a brilliant conversation cannot be willfully substituted for a brilliant conversation and be a genuinely rewarding experience.

If these thoughts about our conversational interests in works of art are convincing, then they indicate that it is not true that the prospect of aesthetic satisfaction trumps every other desideratum when it comes to interpretation. Aesthetic satisfaction does not obviate our conversational interests in artworks. Moreover, our conversational interest in artworks is best served by intentionalism. Thus, in order to coordinate our aesthetic interests and our conversational interests, the best policy would not appear to be anti-intentionalism but the pursuit of aesthetic satisfaction constrained by our best hypotheses about authorial intent.

These hypotheses, moreover, will often depend on facts available to us about the biography of the artist. That the artist lived in fifteenth-century Italy, for example, will constrain attribution of his supposed intent to explore the themes of Greenbergian modernism in his canvases. Biographical data, in other words, can play a role in hypothesizing the artist's intention, while the recognition of the artist's intention, in turn, constrains the kinds of satisfactions, and, correspondingly, the kinds of interpretations we may advance with respect to artworks.[54] Not only is authorial intention derivable from artworks, *pace* the ontological arguments reviewed in the previous section; authorial intention – and biographical information – are relevant to the realization of the aims, particularly the conversational aims, we bring to artworks. Aesthetic arguments do not show that anti-intentionalism is the best interpretive policy to endorse given our purposes with respect to artworks. For we are interested in art as an occasion for communication with others as well as a source of aesthetic pleasure. And to the extent that communication or communion is among the leading purposes of art, authorial intention must always figure in interpretation, at least as a constraint on whatever other purposes we seek.

Notes

1 H. P. Grice, "Meaning," *Philosophical Review* 66 (1957). See also Grice's *Studies in the Way of Words* (Cambridge, Mass.: Harvard University Press, 1989).

2 The idea of interpretations as *hypotheses* about authorial intentions is derived from William Tolhurst, "On What a Text Is and How It Means," *British Journal of Aesthetics* 19 (1979).

3 See W. K. Wimsatt, Jr., and Monroe C. Beardsley, "The Intentional Fallacy," *Swanee Review* 54 (1946). This is an expansion of their "Intention," in *Dictionary of World Literature*, ed. J. T. Shipley (New York: Philosophical Library, 1943).

4 See, for example, E. M. W. Tillyard and C. S. Lewis, *The Personal Heresy: A Controversy* (London: Oxford University Press, 1939). Stein Haugom Olsen makes the very interesting claim that the intentional fallacy evolved from the personal heresy but that the shift to intention talk also changed the debate in fateful ways. See Stein Haugom Olsen, *The End of Literary Theory* (Cambridge: Cambridge University Press, 1987), pp. 27–8.

5 Anti-intentionalists have not always been careful to keep the issues of authorial intention, reports of authorial intention, and biography apart. But one should. For example, one may believe that authorial intent is relevant to interpretation and at the same time maintain strong reservations about the authority of authorial pronouncements

about the meaning of their artworks. On the distinction between intention and biography, see Colin Lyas, "Personal Qualities and the Intentional Fallacy," *Philosophy and the Arts: Royal Institute of Philosophy Lectures*, vol. 6 (New York: St. Martin's Press, 1973).

6 Monroe C. Beardsley, *Aesthetics* (New York: Harcourt, Brace, and World, 1958), p. 20.

7 For a discussion of the notion of "intuition-pumps," see Daniel Dennett, *Elbow Room* (Cambridge, Mass.: MIT Press, 1984).

8 Monroe C. Beardsley, "An Aesthetic Definition of Art," in *What Is Art*? ed. Hugh Curtler (New York: Haven, 1984); and Monroe C. Beardsley, "Intending," in *Values and Morals*, ed. Alvin I. Goldman and Jaegwon Kim (Dordrecht: Reidel, 1978).

9 Beardsley, "Intending."

10 For related arguments dealing with the problem of arbitrary authorial pronouncements, see P. D. Juhl, *Interpretation: An Essay in the Philosophy of Literary Criticism* (Princeton: Princeton University Press, 1980), esp. chap. 7, sec. 4.

11 Beardsley, *Aesthetics*, p. 458.

12 Thomas Kuhn, *The Structure of Scientific Revolutions* (Chicago: University of Chicago Press, 1970), p. 9.

13 If Kuhn had really meant "weaned" here, he should have written "weaned from," not "weaned on."

14 The *locus classicus* of this view of intention is G. E. M. Anscombe's *Intention* (Oxford: Blackwell, 1959). Mary Mothersill provides a brief but useful sketch of the history of these countervailing views of intention in her *Beauty Restored* (Oxford: Oxford University Press, 1984),pp. 15–21.

15 See, for example, Stanley Cavell, "Music Discomposed," in his *Must We Mean What We Say*? (Cambridge: Cambridge University Press, 1976), p. 181. Also see "A Matter of Meaning It" in the same volume. These originally appeared in *Art, Mind and Religion*, ed W. H. Capitan and D. D. Merrill (Pittsburgh: University of Pittsburgh Press, 1967). Also relevant is Richard Kuhns, "Criticism and the Problem of Intention," *Journal of Philosophy* 57 (1960). Other arguments in the neo-Wittgensteinian vein include Frank Cioffi, "Intention and Interpretation in Criticism," *Proceedings of the Aristotelian Society* 64 (1963–4); and A. J. Close, "Don Quixote and the 'Intentionalist Fallacy,'" in *On Literary Intention: Critical Essays*, ed. David Newton-de Molina (Edinburgh: Edinburgh University Press, 1976).

16 Monroe Beardsley himself seems to have agreed that the earlier view of intention upon which his arguments were based [is] inadequate – which is one reason why he developed what I call the ontological argument for anti-intentionalism that is examined later in this essay. See Monroe C. Beardsley, "Intentions and Interpretations: A Fallacy Revived," in *The Aesthetic Point of View*, ed. Michael J. Wreen and Donald M. Callen (Ithaca, NY: Cornell University Press, 1982), p. 189.

17 Roland Barthes, "The Death of the Author," in his *Image-Music-Text* (New York: Hill and Wang, 1977). See also Roland Barthes, "From Work to Text," in *Textual Strategies: Perspectives in Post-Structuralist Criticism*, ed. Josue V. Harari (Ithaca, NY: Cornell University Press, 1979).

18 In his *American Formalism and the Problem of Interpretation* (Houston: Rice University Press, 1986), J. Timothy Bagwell argues that the notion of a difference between literary and ordinary language underlies the early anti-intentionalism of Wimsatt and Beardsley. In this essay, I want to extend that insight to Beardsley's later arguments in his "Intentions and Interpretations."

19 Barthes, "Death of the Author," p. 143.

20 There may be an interesting parallel with the New Criticism and even Beardsley's defense of it here. Not only may Barthes's infatuation with polysemy correlate to the New Critical valorization of ambiguity, but also the New Criticism, it can be argued, arose as a critical practice allied with modernism – namely, that of Eliot. Indeed, even Beardsley's treatment of allusion fits nicely with Eliot's willingness to ascribe interpretations retrospectively. Moreover, both the New Criticism and Barthes may be involved in generalizing the critical position appropriate to the works of art they champion to all works of art.

Of course, the analogy I wish to draw is limited. There are also immense differences between Barthes and Beardsley. Barthes moves from the irrelevance of the author to fairly wide-ranging intertextuality, whereas Beardsley, given a commitment to the autonomy of the artwork, advances a constrained form of objective interpretation. That is, Barthes's position elicits a great deal of free play on the part of the reader, whereas Beardsley remains committed to the possibility of true interpretations.

On Eliot's retrospective anti-intentionalist interpretations, see T. S. Eliot, "Tradition and the Individual Talent," in *Twentieth-Century Literary Theory*, ed. Vassilis Lambropoulos and David Neal Miller (Albany: State University of New York Press, 1987).

21 Beardsley, "Intentions and Interpretations," p. 190.

22 Characters, implied on otherwise, do not exist *de re*.

23 This view is also advanced by Graham Hough, who traces it to Austin. See Graham Hough, "An Eighth Type of Ambiguity," in Newton-de Molina, *On Literary Intention*.

24 See Richard Ohmann, "Speech Acts and the Definition of Literature," *Philosophy and Rhetoric* 4 (1971); Richard Ohmann, "Speech, Action and Style," in *Literary Style: A Symposium*, ed. Seymour Chatman (London: Oxford University Press, 1971); Barbara Herrnstein Smith, "Poetry as Fiction," in *New Directions in Literary History*, ed. Ralph Cohen (Baltimore: Johns Hopkins University Press, 1974); see also chap. 2 of Barbara Herrnstein Smith, *On the Margins of Discourse: The Relation of Literature to Language* (Chicago: University of Chicago Press, 1978). Indeed, Smith suggests an argument that somewhat parallels Beardsley's in her "The Ethics of interpretation," in *On the Margins of Discourse*. For Beardsley's defense of the notion that lyric poems are representations, see his "Fiction as Representation," *Synthese* 46 (1981).

25 To be fair to Beardsley, it is important to note that in his "Philosophy of Literature," he appears to admit that there are literary works that are not fictional; this leads him to develop an aesthetic definition of literature – that is, one based on aesthetic intentions rather than on fiction. But it is hard to see that that admission will not undercut the argument in "Intentions and Interpretations." See Monroe C. Beardsley, "The Philosophy of Literature," in *Aesthetics: A Critical Anthology*, ed. George Dickie and Richard J. Sclafani (New York: St. Martin's Press, 1977), p. 325.

26 See John R. Searle, "The Logical Status of Fictional Discourse," *New Literary History* 6 (1974).

27 I suspect that one reason for adopting the notion of an implied author as a general hypothesis applying to all literary works by critical theorists may be an attempt – parallel to phenomenalism – to fend off skeptical, epistemological anxieties. That is, lacking a general principle for telling when one is confronted by the views of an actual author versus an implied author, one opts for a kind of reductionism – there are only, always implied authors. But this sort of reductionism hardly explains the behavior of our literary practices in general – we argue not only about but with Mailer's views on sex, death, and manliness.

In regard to my last point, one might respond in the spirit of Boris Tomasevkij, the Russian Formalist critic. He thinks of the public character of an author as a fictional creation – a fabrication existing in newspapers, published journals, and correspondence. Extrapolating from his position, one might try to say that we are arguing, not really with Mailer, but with the character of Mailer as he exists in our literary culture. But, as intriguing as this idea might be, I think we are often arguing with the real Norman Mailer, not a publicity fabrication or an implied author. See Boris Tomasevskij, "Literature and Biography," in Lambropoulos and Miller, *Twentieth-Century Literary Theory*.

Perhaps another motive for commitment to the generalized application of the notion of the implied author is that it is a means of adjusting to and accepting the intentional fallacy. But in this case, the claim that all literary expression is mediated by implied speakers cannot be used in an argument with intentionalism without begging the question.

28 Beardsley, *Aesthetics*, pp. 409–11.

29 This interpretation is derived from Christopher Butler, "Saving the Reader," in *Future Literary Theory*, ed. Ralph Cohen (New York: Routlegde, 1989).

30 Jonathan Culler, a literary theorist in the Barthesian tradition, seems to take it that the literary work is divorced from reality because it is fictional, and therefore not a speech act. It functions differently, as a result, than ordinary language. This view sits strangely with his view that in reading literary texts with their consequent, wide-ranging semiosis we learn about the processes of the production of meaning in general. That is, how can the literary texts be essentially different than ordinary discourse, yet shed light on the processes of ordinary discourse? See Jonathan Culler, *Structuralist Poetics* (Ithaca, NY: Cornell University Press, 1975), pp. 139 and 264–5.

31 Furthermore, if the mark of whether language is acting on reality is the presence of the speaker to the listener, then this would seem to make theatrical utterances a case of acting directly on reality, which is a consequence that I infer Barthes would reject.

32 One wonders, of course, whether Beardsley could extend the distinction between performances of illocutionary acts and representations of illocutionary acts across all the arts, since it is not clear that speech-act theory can be made to fit the cases of pictures, statues, and so on.

33 For a more extended account of this, see Noël Carroll, "Trois propositions pour une critique de la danse contemporaine," in *La Danse au défi*, ed. Michele Febvre (Montreal: Editions Parachute, 1987).

34 As well, a great deal of literature will have to be understood in terms of choices and doings rather

than solely in terms of manipulations of linguistic conventions. The way in which an author modulates a suspense structure, for example, will have to be explained in terms of what he is trying to do; there are no fixed conventions to fall back on. Instead, the author will adopt a certain strategy that we will have to interpret intentionalistically. Similarly, the remarks about Barthelme's "Alice" indicate that with what I call strategies, the intentionalistic idiom of action is best suited for much of what we think of as the object of literary interpretation.

35 Monroe C. Beardsley, *The Possibility of Criticism* (Detroit: Wayne State University Press, 1970), p. 34.

36 For elaborations of this distinction, see Tolhurst, "On What a Text Is," and Jack W. Meiland, "The Meanings of a Text," *British Journal of Aesthetics* 21 (1981).

37 This notion is elaborated on by Umberto Eco in his *The Open Work* (Cambridge, Mass.: Harvard University Press, 1989).

38 I take this to be the point of Jack Meiland's "The Meanings of a Text.'

39 It stands in the way of maximizing interpretive play if the authorial intent is determinate; it is irrelevant because if we adopt anti-intentionalist interpretive practices, then whether or not the author intended an "open text," we will read it in that like anyway.

40 For a diagnosis of this, see Mary Sirridge, "Artistic Intention and Critical Prerogative," *British Journal of Aesthetics* 18 (1978).

41 See, for example, the high premium Barthes assigns to "writerly reading" in his *The Pleasure of the Text* (New York: Hill and Wang, 1975).

42 This position has been defended by Laurent Stern in his "On Interpreting," *Journal of Aesthetics and Art Criticism* 39 (1980); and Laurent Stern's "Facts and Interpretations," address to the Pacific Division meetings of time American Philosophical Association, Spring 1988.

43 A moral purpose that anti-intentionalism might be thought to advance is the emancipation of the spectator, a view with respect to interpretation that parallels the aspiration of many modern artists. But one wonders here whether the freedom of the reader here is genuinely moral or whether it is merely a strained moralization of the *free* play of cognition enjoined by Kantian aestheticism.

Or it might be felt that opening the artwork to interpretive play affords some kind of consciousness-raising heuristic; Jonathan Culler seems to have this view at the end of *Structuralist Poetics* where engaging the nonauthorially constrained play of textual signs teaches the reader something about the process of semiosis in general (p. 264). This claim would depend on a very controversial view of how language, in general, functions.

One could also imagine a literary theorist defending anti-intentionalism as securing an institutional purpose. That is, since the literary-critical institution is predicated on the production of interpretations, anti-intentionalism is facilitating because it keeps more interpretive options open. Nevertheless, the job security of literary critics hardly seems like the kind of overriding purpose that would move the rest of us.

Interestingly, intentionalism has also been defended for what might be thought of as institutional purposes. E. D. Hirsch, for example, wants to defend literary criticism as a cognitive discipline, and he believes that this requires determinate meaning, a commitment best served, on his account, by authorial intention. In this respect, Hirsch, unlike P. D. Juhl, is advancing intentionalism as a means to secure an end of the literary institution rather than as a thesis about the nature of meaning. See E. D. Hirsch, Jr., *Validity in Interpretation* (New Haven: Yale University Press, 1967); and E. D. Hirsch, Jr., *The Aims of Interpretation* (Chicago: University of Chicago Press, 1976).

44 This is not an invented example. See J. Hoberman, "Bad Movies," *Film Comment*, July–August 1980. Similar arguments appear in Hoberman's "Vulgar Modernism," *Artforum*, February 1982.

Moreover, I should stress that the issue raised by Hoberman's critical practice is not isolated. For it is often the case that the developments of avant-garde art are projected or read backward with respect to earlier works in the tradition. Thus, previously we saw Barthes's tendency to regard Mallarmé's modernist aspiration to efface authorship as a feature of all antecedent writing.

45 Hoberman, "Bad Movies."

46 Intentionalist criticism is guided by what a given text or artwork could have meant to the work's contemporary informed audience. Reference to what the audience could have understood is not to be taken as an alternative to intentionalist criticism, however, but as a means of identifying authorial intent. For, ex hypothesi, we begin by attributing to the author the intention of communicating – of getting her audience to recognize her intention. Thus, what we conjecture as the intention of the author charitably is something that the author could reasonably believe the audience – that is, the informed audience – could recognize. It should also be noted that included

under the rubric of intentionalist criticism is the elucidation of the author's presuppositions, especially the elucidation of the stylistic choice structure through which the author's intentional activity takes place. And again, what an informed audience could perceive as a stylistic option guides our hypotheses about the author's intentions for the reasons already given.

47 Søren Kierkegaard, *Concluding Unscientific Postscript* (Princeton: Princeton University Press, 1941), p. 466.

48 Culler, *Structuralist Poetics*, p. 115.

49 Robert Nozick, *Anarchy, State, and Utopia* (New York: Basic Books, 1974), p. 42.

50 Why, it might be asked, if this analysis is correct, do so many critics seem willing to indulge anti-intentionalist criticism? One hypothesis is that by means of theoretical devices like unconscious or ideological motivation, they believe that they are getting at the author's actual intentions.

51 This example comes from Denis Dutton, "Why Intentionalism Won't Go Away,' in *Literature and the Question of Philosophy*, ed. Anthony Cascardi (Baltimore: Johns Hopkins University Press, 1987).

52 Juhl, *Interpretation*, pp. 121–4.

53 Cavell, "Music Discomposed."

54 Daniel Nathan has argued that intentionalist arguments often depend on having access to contextual information about the text – rather than biographical evidence – and that the anti-intentionalist also may, in principle, have access to contextual information. I think, however, that an example like Edward Wood indicates than biographical information may also be required. For Wood was a contemporary of the Surrealist filmmaker Buñuel, someone who had the intellectual resources and the will to make a transgressive film. Thus, knowing that the filmmaker was Wood, and knowing something about Wood, and that the filmmaker was not Buñuel, is crucial to our dismissal of *Plan 9* as a mistake. See Daniel O. Nathan, "Irony and the Artist's Intentions," *British Journal of Aesthetics* 23 (1982).

50

The Ethical Criticism of Art

Berys Gaut

Berys Gaut is Senior Lecturer in Moral Philosophy at the University of St. Andrews.

Ethicism

This essay argues that the ethical criticism of art is a proper and legitimate aesthetic activity. More precisely, it defends a view I term *ethicism*. Ethicism is the thesis that the ethical assessment of attitudes manifested by works of art is a legitimate aspect of the aesthetic evaluation of those works, such that, if a work manifests ethically reprehensible attitudes, it is to that extent aesthetically defective, and if a work manifests ethically commendable attitudes, it is to that extent aesthetically meritorious.

This thesis needs elucidation. The ethicist principle is a pro tanto one: it holds that a work is aesthetically meritorious (or defective) *insofar as* it manifests ethically admirable (or reprehensible) attitudes. (The claim could also be put like this: manifesting ethically admirable attitudes *counts toward* the aesthetic merit of a work, and manifesting ethically reprehensible attitudes *counts against* its aesthetic merit.) The ethicist does not hold that manifesting ethically commendable attitudes is a necessary condition for a work to be aesthetically good: there can be good, even great, works of art that are ethically flawed. Examples include Wagner's Ring Cycle, which is marred by the anti-Semitism displayed in the portrayal of the *Nibelungen*; some of T. S. Eliot's poems, such as *Sweeney among the Nightingales*, which are similarly tainted by anti-Semitism; and Leni Riefenstahl's striking propaganda film, *The Triumph of the Will*, deeply flawed by its craven adulation of Hitler. Nor does the ethicist thesis hold that manifesting ethically good attitudes is a sufficient condition for a work to be aesthetically good: there are works such as Harriet Beecher Stowe's *Uncle Tom's Cabin* which, though the ethical attitudes they display are admirable, are in many ways uninspired and disappointing. The ethicist can deny these necessity and sufficiency claims, because she holds that there are a plurality of aesthetic values, of which the ethical values of artworks are but a single kind.[1] So, for instance, a work of art may be judged to be aesthetically good *insofar as* it is beautiful, is formally unified and strongly expressive, but aesthetically bad *insofar as* it trivializes the issues with which it deals and manifests ethically reprehensible attitudes. We then need to make an *all-things-considered* judgment, balancing these aesthetic merits and demerits one against another to determine whether the work is, all things considered, good. And we should not suppose that

Berys Gaut, "The Ethical Criticism of Art," in *Aesthetics and Ethics: Essays at the Intersection*, ed. Jerrold Levinson (Cambridge: Cambridge University Press, 1998), pp. 182–203.

there is any mechanically applicable weighing method that could determine the truth of such a judgment: overall judgments are plausibly ones that resist any form of codification in terms of mechanically applicable principles. These kinds of pro tanto and all-things-considered judgments are common in other evaluative domains, notably the moral domain.[2]

The notion of the aesthetic adopted here should be construed broadly. In the narrow sense of the term, aesthetic value properties are those that ground a certain kind of sensory or contemplative pleasure or displeasure. In this sense, beauty, elegance, gracefulness, and their contraries are aesthetic value properties. However, the sense adopted here is broader: I mean by "aesthetic value" the value of an object *qua* work of art, that is, its artistic value. This broader sense is required, since not all of the values of an object *qua* work of art are narrowly aesthetic. Besides a work's beauty, we may, for instance, aesthetically admire it for its cognitive insight (subject, as we shall see, to certain conditions), its articulated expression of joy, the fact that it is deeply moving, and so on. However, this broader sense of "aesthetic" does not mean that just any property of a work of art counts as aesthetic. Works of art have many other sorts of value properties that are not values of them *qua* works of art: they can have investment value, value as status symbols, and so forth.[3]

The notion of manifesting an attitude should be construed in terms of a work's displaying pro or con attitudes toward some state of affairs or things, which the work may do in many ways besides explicitly stating an opinion about them.[4] (Such attitudes can run the gamut from unmixed approval through neutrality to unmixed disapproval, and also include various complex and nuanced attitudes that display both approbatory and disapprobatory aspects, such as those revealed in jealous or conflicted attitudes.) What is relevant for ethicism are the attitudes *really* possessed by a work, not those it merely claims to possess; so the attitudes manifested may be correctly attributable only by subtle and informed critical judgment. A novel may state that it condemns the sexual activities it describes, but from the subtly lubricious and prying manner in which it dwells on them, it may be correct to attribute to it an attitude of titillation, not of moralistic disgust. Just as we can distinguish between the attitudes people really have and those they merely claim to have by looking at their behavior, so we can distinguish between real and claimed attitudes of works by looking at the detailed manner in which events are presented.

Ethicism does not entail the causal thesis that good art ethically improves people.[5] Since the ethicist principle is a pro tanto one, it allows for the existence of great but ethically flawed works; and even if all aesthetically good works were ethically sound, it would not follow that they improve people, any more than it follows that earnest ethical advice improves people, for they may be unmoved by even the most heartfelt exhortation. Much of the ethical discussion about art, particularly concerning the supposedly pernicious effects of some popular films and music genres, has been concerned with the question of whether such art morally corrupts. This is a version of the causal thesis and should be kept distinct from ethicism. Further, ethicism has nothing to say about the issue of censorship, nor does it give any grounds of support to either the friends or foes of artistic censorship. All that follows from ethicism is that if a work manifests morally bad attitudes it is to that extent aesthetically flawed, flawed as a work of art. The fact that a work of art is aesthetically flawed is not grounds for its censorship: if it were, the art museums of the world would suffer serious depletion.

Objections to Ethicism

1. Ethicism fails to distinguish sharply enough between ethical and aesthetic evaluation. There is an aesthetic attitude in terms of which we aesthetically evaluate works; this aesthetic attitude is distinct from the ethical attitude we may adopt toward works; and ethical assessment is never a concern of the aesthetic attitude. So the ethical criticism of works is irrelevant to their aesthetic value.

The existence of the aesthetic attitude has, of course, been much disputed.[6] But, even if we accept its existence, its adoption is compatible with ethicism. To see why, we need to specify in more detail what the aesthetic attitude is. There are two basic ways of doing this: the aesthetic attitude may be individuated by some feature intrinsic to it or by its formal objects.

Consider the case in which the attitude is individuated by its formal objects: these may be understood in narrow aesthetic fashion, as beauty and its subspecies, such as grace and elegance, or characterized more broadly by the criteria to which formalists appeal, such as Beardsley's unity, complexity, and intensity.[7] Since the presence of these properties arguably does not require, or suffice for, the presence of ethical properties, it may be held that ethical assessment is irrelevant to aesthetic evaluation.[8] Yet this objection is unconvincing, for the list of properties deployed is too narrow to embrace all those of aesthetic relevance. In the assessment of art, appeal is made to such properties as raw expressive power and deep cognitive insight as well as to beauty, elegance, and grace; and the relevance of these expressive and cognitive values explains how there can be great works, such as *Les Desmoiselles d'Avignon*, that are militantly ugly. So the narrow aesthetic view fails. In more sophisticated fashion, the formalist appeals to purely intrinsic properties of works as aesthetically relevant, an appeal motivated by a conception of the work of art as autonomous from its context. But that conception is flawed, for a work can be fully interpreted only by situating it within its generative context.[9] There is reason, then, to spurn the restricted diet of aesthetically relevant properties offered by the narrow aesthetic and formalist views, and as yet no reason to exclude ethical properties from a heartier menu.

The alternative is to individuate the aesthetic attitude by some feature intrinsic to it, and for the opponent of ethicism the most promising feature is the detachment or disengagement we purportedly display toward fictional events. Since it is logically impossible to intervene in such events, the will is detached, practical concerns are quiescent, an attitude of contemplation is adopted. Given the practical character of morality, it follows that ethical assessment plays no role in aesthetic attitude and therefore no role in aesthetic evaluation. But the step from the claim that the will is disengaged and therefore that ethical assessment has no role to play does not follow: there is similarly no possibility of altering historical events, and we are in this sense forced to have a detached or contemplative attitude toward them, but we still ethically assess historical characters and actions. If it is objected that we are ethically engaged in history because we hope to draw from it lessons for our current practice, the same may be said of the lessons we can draw from fiction, such as the psychological insights that Freud discovered there.

The point about ethics and the will deserves elaboration, for it will be relevant to the position defended later. On what might be termed the *purely practical* conception of ethics, the ethical assessment of a person's character is determined only by what he does and by the motives that determine his actions. Any feelings or thoughts that play no role in motivating actions are ethically irrelevant: thoughts, fantasies, and desires, however gruesome, inappropriate, or corrupt we would judge the actions they motivate to be, are not themselves ethically bad, unless they issue in actions that express these feelings and thoughts. So a person may be ethically good while having these feelings and thoughts, and his goodness may consist partly in his capacity to resist their influence on the will, for these feelings and thoughts may have arisen purely passively in him, and he is not to be held responsible for their occurrence.[10] This view, as has just been noted, speedily runs into problems in historical cases where the will cannot be engaged, yet where ethical assessment is still appropriate. But it can be shown to be flawed on other grounds too. Much of our ethical assessment is directed at what people feel, even though these feelings do not motivate their actions. Suppose that Joe is praised for some deserved achievement by his friends, but he later discovers that they are secretly deeply jealous and resentful of him. Their feelings have not motivated their actions, yet we would properly regard these people as less ethically good were we to discover this about them. They are flawed because of what they feel, not because of what they did or their motives for doing it. Also, that people feel deep sympathy for us, even though they are completely unable to help us in our distress, is something that we care about and that properly makes us think better of them. In fact, much of our vocabulary of ethical assessment is directed wholly or in part at the assessment of feelings: we criticize people for being crude, insensitive, callous, or uncaring; we praise them for being warm, friendly, and sensitive. So for the ethical assessment of character an *affective-practical* conception of assessment is correct, a conception which holds that not just actions and motives, but also feelings that do not motivate, are ethically significant. Virtue of character is "concerned with feelings and actions," as Aristotle correctly observes.[11] Such an affective-practical conception of ethical assessment allows the ethical assessment of the feelings that people have when they respond to fictions, even though they cannot act toward the fictional events described.

2. A more radical objection holds that ethical assessment has no place in the assessment of art. Works of art can at best manifest attitudes toward those fictional characters and situations they describe, and such attitudes are not ethically assessable, since they are directed toward merely imagined objects – such objects cannot be harmed or hurt in reality, for they do not exist. What is ethically assessable, in contrast, are attitudes directed toward real characters and situations, but works of art do not manifest attitudes toward such things, for they do not describe them. Hence, there is no place left for the ethical assessment of art.

Even at first blush, the objection is hyperbolic, since not all works of art are fictions: Riefenstahl's film is a documentary of the 1934 Nuremberg rally, and Hitler was not a fictional character. So, at best, the argument would apply only to a subclass of works of art. Second, attitudes directed toward only imagined states of affairs can in fact properly be ethically assessed. Consider a man whose sexual life consists entirely of rape fantasies, fantasies he has not about women he sees in real life, but about women he only imagines. Would we say that there is nothing to be said from an ethical point of view about the attitude he manifests in his imaginings about these fictional women? Clearly, what a person imagines and how he responds to those imaginings play an important part in the ethical assessment of his character. The mere fact that the women he imagines cannot be harmed does not bracket his inner life from ethical assessment, since what is at issue are the attitudes he manifests in his fantasy life. And nothing in our judgment about him requires us to assume that what is bad about his fantasies is that he may act on them – perhaps he is confined to prison for life. He stands ethically condemned for what and how he imagines, independently of how he acts or may act. (Here again, we return to the ethical importance of feelings, but see now that feelings toward merely imagined people can be ethically relevant too.) Further, the attitudes people (and works) manifest toward imagined scenarios have implications for their attitudes toward their real-life counterparts, for the attitudes are partly directed toward kinds, not just individuals.[12] When the rape fantasist imagines his fictional women, he is imagining them *as women*, that is, as beings of a kind that also has instances in the real world; and that he imagines them as women is, of course, essential to his imaginative project. Thus, by virtue of adopting such an attitude toward his imagined women, he implicitly adopts that attitude toward their real-life counterparts – and so reveals something of his attitude toward real-life women. Indeed, it is inevitable that, however apparently exotic the fictional world, the kinds shared between it and the real world will be vast, given the limits on the human imagination, the interests we have in fiction (which include exploring possibilities that reorder the actual world), and interpretive constraints, which involve drawing on background information about the real world in the interpretation of fictions. So the attitudes manifested toward fictional entities will have many implications for attitudes manifested toward real entities.

3. Ethical assessment is relevant to a work's aesthetic merit, but ethicism gives the connection the wrong valence: works can be good precisely *because* they violate our sense of moral rectitude. Often the most fascinating characters in works are the evil ones, such as Satan in *Paradise Lost*. And recall the passage in *King Lear* in which blind Gloucester asks Lear, "Dost thou know me?" and Lear replies, "I remember thine eyes well enough. Dost thou squiny at me? / No, do thy worst, blind Cupid, I'll not love." As Lawrence Hyman writes, "The dramatic effect requires our moral disapproval," but Shakespeare manages to "transfigure that moral shock into aesthetic pleasure."[13]

It is important to distinguish between the evil or insensitive characters represented by a work and the attitude the work displays toward those characters. Only the latter is relevant to the ethicist thesis. Satan is indeed fascinating because evil, but the work represents him as such, showing the seductive power of evil, and does not approve of his actions. Milton was not a Satanist. And while the power of Lear's bad joke does rest on its hearty heartlessness, it is part of the point of *Lear* that the flamboyant insensitivity displayed by Lear in his derangement is of a piece with the gross egoism that leads to disaster, an egoism overcome only by grief and loss, and transmuted into a finer moral wisdom. Lear's attitude toward Gloucester is represented by the play, but not shared by it. It is true that some works, such as de Sade's *Juliette*, not merely represent evil, but also manifest approval toward that evil. If this work has indeed any serious aesthetic merit, it can in part be traced to the literary skill with which it represents the attitude of finding sexual torture erotically attractive; yet the ethicist can consistently and plausibly maintain that the novel's own espousal of this attitude is an aesthetic defect in it.

It may be objected that the novel's approbatory attitude toward evil is a reason why it is aesthetically good: evil arouses our curiosity, for the evil person may do and experience things we can scarcely imagine, let alone understand; and the novel's ability to satisfy this curiosity, to show us what it is like to engage in such actions, is a prime source of its aesthetic merit. Yet from the fact that we are fascinated by the attitudes manifested, we cannot conclude that our interest in them is aesthetic: our fascination with Adolf Hitler or Jeffrey Dahmer is not an aesthetic one, and our interest in de Sade's work may similarly stem from a curiosity about psychopathic states of mind. Suppose, however, that our interest in *Juliette* is aesthetic, perhaps because of the way that interest is inflected by a concern with the work's stylistic and rhetorical system. This still does not undermine ethicism. For our interest here is in being able to imagine what it is like to have evil attitudes, and so in coming to understand them, and this is satisfied by the vivid *representation* of an evil attitude. But, again, representation of an attitude by a work does not require the work itself to share that attitude: works may manifest disapproval toward characters or narrators who are represented as evil. Moreover, if, as the objection holds, it is our curiosity that is aroused, we have a cognitive interest in not seeing evil approved of, for such approval implies that there is something good about an attitude we know to be bad.

Some Arguments for Ethicism

There are, of course, further objections and elaborations open to the opponent of ethicism, some of which will be touched on later, but enough has been said to give rational hope that they may be laid to rest. The question remains as to why ethicism should be endorsed. Part of the answer is to be sought in its congruence with our considered aesthetic judgments; we do decry works for their insensitivity, their moral crudity, their lack of integrity, their celebration of cruelty, their slimy salaciousness. But it is the mark of an interesting philosophical thesis that, while some find it obviously true, others find it obviously false; and ethicism is, fortunately and unfortunately, an interesting philosophical thesis. So it would be good to have an argument for its truth.

1. George Dickie has advanced a simple argument for the truth of ethicism. A work of art's moral vision is an (essential) part of that work; any statement about an (essential) part of a work of art is an aesthetic statement about that work; so a statement about a work of art's moral vision is an aesthetic statement about the work.[14]

However, it is not true that any statement about an essential part of a work is an aesthetic statement about it. For instance, it is essential to a poem that it be composed of the particular words that comprise it. So it is essential to it that it have in it the particular letters that it has. So, if it is true of a particular poem that it has in it exactly as many letter *e*'s as it has letter *c*'s, then that is an essential feature of the poem. But that is not an *aesthetic* statement about the work, since it standardly plays no role in our appreciation of it.[15] Likewise, consider a statue carved in limestone. It is essential to its being the particular statue which it is that it be composed of the crushed shells of ancient sea creatures. But whereas the statue's texture and color are generally relevant to its aesthetic merits, the mere fact that it is composed of crushed shells is not. For, again, this fact standardly plays no role in our appreciation of it as a work of art. So a premise on which Dickie's argument rests is false.

2. Perhaps the most influential opponents of ethicism have been formalists.[16] However, David Pole not only has argued that ethicism is

compatible with formalism, but has tried to derive ethicism from it. He holds that the immorality of a work is a formal defect in it, since it is a type of internal incoherence. For if a work of art presents a morally bad view, it will do so by distorting or glossing over something it presents. But then something is lacking within the work itself and so "some particular aspect [of the work] must jar with what – on the strength of the rest – we claim a right to demand." This jarring is an internal incoherence in the work and thus a defect that the formalist would acknowledge as such.[17]

If a work is morally corrupt, it follows that it distorts something and so jars with a truth about the world, but it does not follow that it has to jar with anything else in the work, for the work may be systematically immoral. *The Triumph of the Will*, for instance, is held together thematically by its offensive celebration of Nazism. So Pole's formalist derivation of ethicism fails.[18]

3. An approach glanced at by Hume and elaborated by Wayne Booth holds that literary assessment is akin to an act of befriending, for one assesses the implied author of a work as a suitable friend. A good friend may possess a variety of merits (being intelligent, good company, lively, etc.), and some of these are ethical: she is trustworthy, sensitive, kind, and so on. So assessing someone as a friend involves among other things assessing her ethical character, a character displayed in the case of the implied author in the literary work in which she is manifested.[19]

The approach has its merits, and captures the pro tanto structure of ethicism well, but it is ill-equipped to cope with some Hollywood films whose impersonality and industrial-style production may give the audience little sense of an implied author or authors, but whose ethical stance may elicit their aesthetic condemnation. And the approach also runs afoul of one of the objections considered earlier; for the implied author is a fictional construct, albeit one implicit in, rather than described by, the text. If fictional characters, such as Satan and Lear, can be interesting because of their moral failings, the corrupt fictional character of an author can similarly be interesting, and the aesthetic merit of her work be accordingly enhanced. Appeal to the characters of fictional beings will not ground ethicism.

4. More promising is an argument that may be extrapolated from views defended by Richard Eldridge and Martha Nussbaum. For Eldridge a person's moral self-understanding cannot completely be captured by general theories, but must be developed and sustained by an awareness of the relation of her story to the stories of others, an awareness that literature is peculiarly well placed to articulate and extend: "all we can do is to attempt to find ourselves in cases, in narratives of the development of persons."[20] For Nussbaum, too, morality is a matter of the appreciation of particular cases, and literature can refine our awareness of moral particularities in a way that eludes the flailing grasp of philosophy: "To show forth the force and truth of the Aristotelian claim that 'the decision rests with perception,' we need, then – either side by side with a philosophical 'outline' or inside it – texts which display to us the complexity, the indeterminacy, the sheer *difficulty* of moral choice."[21] This conception of literature as moral philosophy naturally suggests a cognitivist argument for ethicism: it is an aesthetic merit in a work that it gives insight into some state of affairs, and literature can yield insights into moral reality of a depth and precision that no other cultural form is well placed to match; so the moral insights delivered by literary works enhance their aesthetic worth.

There is much here that should be retained and accounted for in any successful defense of ethicism, and an attempt will be made to do so in what follows. Yet the argument rests on a radically particularist account of morality, which denies the existence of any general and informative moral principles. If that view be denied, as I believe it should,[22] the idea of literature as the culmination of moral philosophy is rendered less compelling. And even if the claims of literature were rendered more modest, we would still require an explanation of why the insights literature can provide are aesthetically relevant. Works of art can be interesting and informative as social documents, but the fact that much can be learned from them about the attitudes and circumstances of their time does not ipso facto make them aesthetically better: one can learn much about Victorian agricultural politics from *Tess*, and on the subject of nineteenth-century whaling practices *Moby-Dick* is excruciatingly informative. Likewise, old photographs and films can have great value as documentary sources of their times, but these cognitive merits do not thereby improve these objects *qua* works of art. So the cognitivist approach must be supplemented in order to give an account of the conditions under which cognitive merits are aesthetically relevant.[23]

The Merited-Response Argument

Ethicism is a thesis about a work's manifestation of certain attitudes, but in what does this manifestation of attitudes consist? It is obvious that works prescribe the imagining of certain events: a horror film may prescribe imagining teenagers being assaulted by a monster; *Juliette* prescribes imagining that acts of sexual torture occur. Perhaps less obviously, works also prescribe certain responses to these fictional events: the loud, atonal music of the horror film prescribes us to react to the represented events with fear, *Juliette* invites the reader to find sexual torture erotically attractive, to be aroused by it, to be amused by the contortions described, to admire the intricacy of their implementation, and so forth.[24] The approbatory attitude that *Juliette* exhibits toward sexual torture, then, is manifested in the responses it prescribes its readers to have toward such torture. The attitudes of works are manifested in the responses they prescribe to their audiences.

It is important to construe this claim correctly to avoid an objection. Consider a novel that prescribes its readers to be amused at a character's undeserved suffering but that does so in order to show up the ease with which the reader can be seduced into callous responses. Then one response (amusement) is prescribed, but a very different attitude is manifested by the work (disapproval of the ease with which we can be morally seduced); hence, the manifestation of attitudes is wholly distinct from and independent of the prescription of responses. What this objection reveals is that prescriptions, like attitudes, come in a hierarchy, with higher-order prescriptions taking lower-order ones as their objects. Thus, my amusement at the character's suffering is prescribed, but there is a higher-order prescription that this amusement itself be regarded as callous and therefore as unmerited. So the complete set of prescriptions that a work makes must be examined in order to discover what attitudes it manifests: taking individual prescriptions out of context may mislead us about the work's attitudes. Here, as elsewhere, the application of the ethicist principle requires a grasp of interpretive subtleties and contextual factors. Talk of prescriptions from now on should be construed as involving the complete set of relevant prescriptions that a work makes toward fictional events.

The claim that works prescribe certain responses to the events described is widely applicable. *Jane Eyre*, for instance, prescribes the imagining of the course of a love affair between Jane and Rochester, and also prescribes us to admire Jane's fortitude, to want things to turn out well for her, to be moved by her plight, to be attracted to this relationship as an ideal of love, and so forth. Similar remarks apply to paintings, films, and other representational arts. Music without a text is also subject to ethical criticism if we can properly ascribe to the music a presented situation and a prescribed response to it. If Shostakovich's symphonies are a musical protest against the Stalinist regime, we can ethically assess them.

The notion of a response is to be understood broadly, covering a wide range of states directed at represented events and characters, including being pleased at something, feeling an emotion toward it, being amused about it, and desiring something with respect to it – wanting it to continue or stop, wanting to know what happens next. Such states are characteristically affective, some essentially so, such as pleasure and the emotions, while in the case of others, such as desires, there is no necessity that they be felt, although they generally are.

The responses are not simply imagined: we are prescribed by *Juliette* actually to find erotically attractive the fictional events, to be amused by them, to enjoy them, to admire this kind of activity. So the novel does not just present imagined events, it also presents a point of view on them, a perspective constituted in part by actual feelings, emotions, and desires that the reader is prescribed to have toward the merely imagined events. Given that the notion of a response covers such things as enjoyment and amusement, it is evident that some kinds of response are actual, not just imagined. Some philosophers have denied that we feel actual emotions toward fictional events, but there are, I believe, good reasons for holding this to be possible.[25]

Though a work may prescribe a response, it does not follow that it succeeds in making this response merited: horror fictions may be unfrightening, comedies unamusing, thrillers unthrilling. This is not just to say that fear, amusement, and thrills are not produced in the audience; for people may respond in a way that is inappropriate. Rather, the question is whether the prescribed response is merited, whether it is appropriate or inappropriate to respond in the way the work prescribes. If I am afraid of a harmless victim in a horror movie because of her passing resemblance to an old tormentor of mine, my fear is inappropriate. And my admiration for a character in a novel can be criticized for being based on a misunderstanding of what he did in the story. So prescribed responses are subject to evaluative criteria.

Some of these criteria are ethical ones. As noted earlier, responses outside the context of art are subject to ethical evaluation. I can criticize someone for taking pleasure in others' pain, for being amused by sadistic cruelty, for being angry at someone when she has done no wrong, for desiring the bad. The same is true when responses are directed at fictional events, for these responses are actual, not just imagined ones. If we actually enjoy or are amused by some exhibition of sadistic cruelty in a novel, that shows us in a bad light, reflects ill on our ethical character, and we can properly be criticized for responding in this fashion.

If a work prescribes a response that is unmerited, it has failed in an aim internal to it, and that is a defect. But not all defects in works of art are aesthetic ones. From the point of view of shipping them to art exhibitions, many of Tintoretto's paintings are very bad, since they are so large and fragile that they can be moved only at great risk. But that is not an aesthetic defect. Is the failure of a prescribed response to be merited an *aesthetic* defect (i.e., is it a defect in the work *qua* work of art)? That this is so is evidently true of many artistic genres: thrillers that do not merit the audience being thrilled, tragedies that do not merit fear and pity for their protagonists, comedies that are not amusing, melodramas that do not merit sadness and pity are all aesthetic failures in these respects. Works outside these genres, which similarly prescribe a range of responses, are likewise aesthetic failures if the responses are unmerited. And in general it is a bad work of art that leaves us bored and offers no enjoyment at all. We are also concerned not just with whether a response occurs, but with the quality of that response: humor may be crude, unimaginative, or flat, or may be revelatory, profound, or inspiring. And the aesthetic criticism of a work as being manipulative, sentimental, insensible, or crude is founded on a mismatch between the response the work prescribes the reader to feel and the response actually merited by the work's presentation of the fictional situation.

The aesthetic relevance of prescribed responses wins further support from noting that much of the value of art derives from its deployment of an affective mode of cognition – derives from the way works teach us, not by giving us merely intellectual knowledge, but by bringing that knowledge home to us. This teaching is not just about how the world is, but can reveal new conceptions of the world in the light of which we can experience our situation, can teach us new ideals, can impart new concepts and discriminatory skills – having read Dickens, we can recognize the Micawbers of the world. And the way knowledge is brought home to us is by making it vividly present, so disposing us to reorder our thoughts, feelings, and motivations in the light of it. We all know we will die, but it may take a great work of art to drive that point fully home, to make it vividly present. We may think of the universe as devoid of transcendent meaning, but it may take *Waiting for Godot* to make that thought concrete and real. We may believe in the value of love, but it may take *Jane Eyre* to render that ideal unforgettably alluring. On the cognitive-affective view of the value of art, whether prescribed responses are merited will be of aesthetic significance, since such responses constitute a cognitive-affective perspective on the events recounted. For such responses not merely are affective, but include a cognitive component, being directed toward some state of affairs or thing, and bringing it under evaluative concepts.[26] By prescribing us to be amused, to enjoy, to be aroused by scenes of sexual torture, *Juliette* aims to get us to approve of the imagined events, to think of them as in some way desirable, and so to endorse an evaluation about events of that kind.

These observations can be assembled into an argument for ethicism. A work's manifestation of an attitude is a matter of the work's prescribing certain responses toward the events described. If these responses are unmerited, because unethical, we have reason not to respond in the way prescribed. Our having reason not to respond in the way prescribed is a failure of the work. What responses the work prescribes is of aesthetic relevance. So the fact that we have reason not to respond in the way prescribed is an *aesthetic* failure of the work, that is to say, is an aesthetic defect. So a work's manifestation of ethically bad attitudes is an aesthetic defect in it. Mutatis mutandis, a parallel argument shows that a work's manifestation of ethically commendable attitudes is an aesthetic merit in it, since we have reason to adopt a prescribed response that is ethically commendable. So ethicism is true.

To illustrate: a comedy presents certain events as funny (prescribes a humorous response to them), but if this involves being amused at heartless cruelty, we have reason not to be amused. Hence, the work's humor is flawed, and that is an aesthetic defect in it. If a work prescribes our enjoyment (as almost all art does to some extent), but if we are supposed to enjoy, say, gratuitous suffering, then we can properly refuse to enjoy it, and hence the work fails aesthetically. If a work seeks to get us to pity some characters, but they are unworthy of pity because of their vicious actions, we have reason not to pity them, and hence the work is aesthetically flawed. Conversely, if the comedy's humor is revelatory, emancipating us from the narrow bonds of prejudice, getting us to see a situation in a different and better moral light and respond accordingly, we have reason to adopt the response, and the work succeeds aesthetically in this respect. If the enjoyment it offers derives from this kind of revelatory humor, we have reason to enjoy the work. And if a work prescribes pity toward characters who suffer unfairly and through no fault of their own, we have reason to pity them, and the work succeeds aesthetically in this way. Similar remarks apply to the range of other responses prescribed by works, such as admiring characters, being angry on their behalf, wanting things for them, and so forth.

The merited-response argument for ethicism captures what is plausible in the last two of the arguments surveyed earlier, but sidesteps the pitfalls into which they stumble. If a work prescribes certain attitudes, these may be sufficiently patterned to justify crediting an implied author to it, and this explains why the befriending argument looks plausible. But the merited-response argument has the advantage of avoiding the problems that stem from taking the implied author as foundational in an argument for ethicism. And the cognitive argument is not so much rejected as incorporated into the current argument, which makes use of a cognitive-affective view of art. Art can teach us about what is ethically correct, but the aesthetic relevance of this teaching is guaranteed only when the work displays it in the responses it prescribes to story events. While tacking on to a novel a claim that a certain type of committed love is an ideal will not do much for its aesthetic worth, getting us to *feel* the attraction of that ideal as embodied in a particular relationship is the central and animating excellence of several novels, including *Jane Eyre*.

Objections to the Argument

1. The argument does not support ethicism. To say that a prescribed response is unmerited is to say that the work is emotionally unengaging; but then the work's failure is a result of the failure to engage, and not of its ethical corruption. Indeed, if, despite its ethical corruption, the work does emotionally engage, then its ethical badness is not an aesthetic defect.

The objection misconstrues the argument, even in respect of responses that are emotions. A work may engage an emotion even when it does not merit it (it may, for instance, manipulate us into feeling a sort of pity we know is merely sentimental), and only merited emotions are relevant to the argument. It is whether the emotion is merited that is important, and ethical merits are partly constitutive of whether the emotion is merited; hence, ethical values play a direct role in determining whether the work is aesthetically defective.

2. The argument is structurally unsound. Starting from a claim about ethical merit, ethicism ends up with a claim about aesthetic merit, so the argument commits a fallacy of equivocation in moving from an ethical reason to an aesthetic one, for there are no other resources available for making the transition.

There is no equivocation: the claim used to make the transition is that whether prescribed responses are merited is aesthetically relevant, and among the criteria that are relevant to determining whether they are merited are ethical ones. This is a substantive claim, and one that has been argued for by appeal to the language of art criticism and a supporting claim that art deploys an affective mode of cognition.

3. The aesthetic defects of a work cannot be reduced to a failure of prescribed responses: while some works clearly prescribe responses, other works need not, or may fail in respects in which no particular response is prescribed.

The point is correct, but the ethicist defense does not require that all aesthetic defects be failures of prescribed responses, for it is enough to establish its truth that some aesthetic defects are of this kind.

4. Works may prescribe responses that are not aesthetically relevant: a royal portrait may be designed to impart a sense of awe and respect toward the king depicted, and a religious work may aim at enhancing the viewer's sense of religious reverence, but such responses are aesthetically irrelevant. So ethicism rests on a false premise.

This is not so. A painting is not just (or even) a beautiful object: it aims to convey complex thoughts and feelings about its subject, providing an individual perspective on the object represented. Thus it is that a painting not only can be a representation, but can also embody a way of thinking in an affectively charged way about its subject, and this perspective on its subject is an important object of our aesthetic interest in the work. So if a painting does not succeed in meriting the responses prescribed, it fails on a dimension of aesthetic excellence.

5. Finally, the argument rests on a claim that real responses, not merely imagined ones, can be had toward fictions. Yet that claim has in respect of emotional responses been powerfully contested: some philosophers have argued that certain emotions cannot be really directed at fictional entities.[27] Thus, ethicism rests on a contentious claim, and its truth is hostage to the fortunes of this thesis.

The merited-response argument has indeed been framed by appeal to real emotions directed at fictions, both because I hold that such emotions can be had toward fictions and because the argument proceeds smoothly with this claim. But it is not in fact essential to the argument to appeal to fiction-directed real emotions. (The thesis that fiction-directed real emotions are possible I shall refer to as *emotional realism*, as opposed to *emotional irrealism*, which denies the possibility of such emotions.) There is a class of responses toward fictions – responses of pleasure and displeasure – that both sides to the dispute can agree to be real. It is evident that one can actually enjoy or be displeased by fictional events: one can actually enjoy Jane Eyre's (fictional) happiness at the end of the novel. Scarcely more contentious is the thought that there are many other fiction-directed responses that are real: I don't have to check to see whether a story is fictional or not in order to know whether I am really amused by it or only imagining that I am so. I don't have to know whether described events really occurred to know whether I am disgusted by them.[28] The battle between realists and irrealists is over the reality of those specific kinds of responses that are emotions, and indeed chiefly over the reality of pity and fear directed at fictions.

Ethicism can be fully defended by appeal to those responses the reality of which is relatively uncontentious. For these include pleasure and displeasure, which are pervasive in our responses to fictions, and, as we noted, a person can be ethically criticized for what she takes pleasure or displeasure in. Someone who actually enjoys imagined suffering can properly be condemned for this response. Hence, pleasure and displeasure felt toward fictions are the only kinds of responses the reality of which one needs to appeal to in order to defend ethicism successfully.

Further, the appeal to actual responses was made in order to avoid a possible objection that the audience's responses are only imagined, and the audience is not ethically at fault if it only imagines a response, as opposed to actually possessing it. But the claim that imagined responses are not ethically assessable can be denied in its full generality. Certain imagined responses, particularly when they are compulsive, vivid, or ones that in various ways fully engage their imaginers, may ground ethical criticism, for they too may be deeply expressive of the imaginer's moral character (for instance, the rape fantasist discussed earlier may be ethically criticized, even if he only imagines being aroused by the imagined scenarios). Hence, emotional irrealists can support ethicism on the grounds that people can be ethically condemned for some of their merely imagined responses.[29] Further, as we noted earlier, works that manifest certain attitudes toward fictional entities implicitly manifest the same attitudes toward real entities of that kind. Reading this in terms of prescribed imagined responses, the irrealist can hold that works prescribing an imagined response toward fictional entities implicitly prescribe the counterpart real response to real entities of that kind. Since no one denies that real emotional responses can be directed at real entities, the irrealist can hold that artworks are aesthetically flawed by virtue of the moral reprehensibility of the implied emotions directed at real states of affairs.[30] Thus, it is not essential to the success of the merited-response argument that emotional realism be true: emotional irrealists can and should sign up to it as well.

So the merited-response argument stands. And the truth of ethicism shows that the aesthetic and the ethical are intertwined. While those who have supposed them to form a unity have overstated their closeness, the two evaluative domains have proved to be more tightly and surprisingly interconnected than many had thought possible.

Notes

1 The view that the *only* aesthetic merits of works are ethical ones is known as *moralism* and is elegantly dispatched by R. W. Beardsmore, *Art and Morality* (London: Macmillan Press, 1971), chap. 2.

2 For a defense of this claim see my "Moral Pluralism," *Philosophical Papers* 22 (1993): 17–40, and my "Rag Bags, Disputes and Moral Pluralism," *Utilitas* [11 (1999): 37–48].

3 For my account of what a work of art is, see my "'Art' as a Cluster Concept," *Theories of Art,* ed. Noël Carroll (Madison: University of Wisconsin Press, [2000]). It may be objected to this broader sense of "aesthetic" that it does not encompass the aesthetic properties of nature. Since we are here concerned only with artworks, this restriction would not matter for present purposes; but also note that the notion naturally extends to include aesthetic properties of nature, since nature may share some of the value properties that objects have *qua* artworks. These include narrow aesthetic properties and also various formal and metaphorically ascribed properties. (For a discussion of the latter and their significance, see my "Metaphor and the Understanding of Art," *Proceedings of the Aristotelian Society* 97 [1996–7]: 223–41.)

4 Evidently, talk of works manifesting attitudes is quite in order – we can, for instance, properly talk of *Small World* manifesting an attitude of wry amusement toward academic conferences. Talk of works manifesting attitudes is, I would argue, equivalent to talk of artists manifesting attitudes in works, though the sense of the terms needs careful specification, and the artist here is not to be understood as a mere fictional construct. (See Guy Sircello, "Expressive Properties of Art," in *Philosophy Looks at the Arts*, ed. Joseph Margolis, 3d ed. [Philadelphia: Temple University Press, 1987], for a suggestive discussion of the relation between what artists do and the properties their works possess.) However, given the fact that we can properly talk of works manifesting attitudes, investigation of this equivalence need not be pursued here.

5 Those who evince sympathy with this distinct causal claim include Kant, Matthew Arnold, Anthony Savile, and Anne Sheppard. Kant claims that the harmonious accord between cognitive faculties that beauty produces in the man of good taste "at the same time promotes the sensibility of the mind for moral feeling." *Critique of Aesthetic Judgement,* trans. J. C. Meredith (Oxford: Oxford University Press, 1952), 39. See also Matthew Arnold, *Culture and Anarchy: An Essay in Political and Social Criticism,* 3d ed. (London: Smith, Elder, 1882), passim; Anthony Savile, *The Test of Time* (Oxford: Oxford University Press, 1982), chap. 5, sect. II; and Anne Sheppard, *Aesthetics* (Oxford: Oxford University Press, 1987), 151.

6 For the locus classicus of skepticism about the aesthetic attitude, see George Dickie, "The Myth of the Aesthetic Attitude," in *Philosophy Looks at the Arts*, ed. Margolis. As noted later, Dickie also uses an attack on the aesthetic attitude to argue for a variant of ethicism.

7 Monroe Beardsley, *Aesthetics,* 2d ed. (Indianapolis: Hackett, 1981), 462ff.

8 However, as will be seen later, some formalists, including David Pole, would deny this claim, and argue for the validity of ethical criticism.

9 See my "Interpreting the Arts: The Patchwork Theory," *Journal of Aesthetics and Art Criticism* 51 (1993): 597–609. For an extended critique of autonomism in reference to its implications for the ethical assessment of art, see Noël Carroll,

"Moderate Moralism," *British Journal of Aesthetics* 36 (1996): 223–38.

10 This conception is Kantian in spirit, though Kant's own view differs from it in salient ways. His view is in one way narrower: it is only duty (not feelings) that can motivate actions that have genuine moral worth (or, on one reading of his position, feelings can operate only as primary motives of morally good action, while the secondary motive must be duty; see Marcia W. Baron, *Kantian Ethics Almost Without Apology* [Ithaca, NY: Cornell University Press, 1996], chap. 4). In addition, Kant holds that actions are not directly assessable; only their maxims are.

11 Aristotle, *Nicomachean Ethics* 2.6 1106b16, trans. Terence Irwin (Indianapolis: Hackett, 1985).

12 Interpretive skill is needed, of course, to establish what the relevant properties of fictional characters are toward which attitudes are manifested. This can be a subtle matter; for instance, in some jokes a character being Irish is merely a conventional way of indicating stupidity and need not imply any derogatory attitudes toward Irish people. For a discussion of humor that is closely related to the issues discussed in this essay, see my "Just Joking: The Ethics and Aesthetics of Humor," *Philosophy and Literature* [22.1 (1998): 51–68].

13 Lawrence Hyman, "Morality and Literature: The Necessary Conflict," *British Journal of Aesthetics* 24 (1984): 149–55, at 154–5.

14 George Dickie, "The Myth of the Aesthetic Attitude," in *Philosophy Looks at the Arts*, ed. Margolis, 113. In his *Evaluating Art* (Philadelphia: Temple University Press, 1988), chap. 7, Dickie also endorses the cognitivist derivation of ethicism that I discuss later. I place 'essential' in parentheses, since Dickie makes the argument without explicitly using it, but appeals to it when giving the example of a novel; his argument is strengthened by appeal to the notion.

15 I do not mean to deny, of course, that in the case of certain poems this fact might play a role in the appreciation of the work. For instance, if a poet wished to demonstrate his skill by writing a poem containing exactly the same number of every letter of the alphabet, yet the resulting poem did not have this feature, this would reflect badly on his artistry. So in some unusual cases facts about the number of different letters in a poem might be aesthetically relevant. But Dickie's argument requires it to be *always* true that such facts are aesthetically relevant.

16 E.g., Monroe Beardsley, *Aesthetics,* 2d ed. (Indianapolis: Hackett, 1981). Though he attacks only moralism directly (564–7), it is clear from his remarks on page 457 that moral criteria play no part in the objective reasons that, he believes, exhaustively specify aesthetic evaluation.

17 David Pole, "Morality and the Assessment of Literature," in his *Aesthetics, Form and Emotion* (London: Duckworth, 1983), 49–50.

18 A parallel criticism is made by Dickie, "The Myth of the Aesthetic Attitude," 113.

19 Hume remarks, "We choose our favourite author as we do our friend" in his "Of the Standard of Taste," in *Critical Theory Since Plato*, ed. Hazard Adams (San Diego, Calif.: Harcourt Brace Jovanovich, 1971), 321. See also Wayne Booth, *The Company We Keep: An Ethics of Fiction* (Berkeley: University of California Press, 1988), esp. chaps. 7 and 8.

20 Richard Eldridge, *On Moral Personhood: Philosophy, Literature, Criticism and Self-Knowledge* (Chicago: University of Chicago Press, 1989), 20.

21 Martha Nussbaum, "Flawed Crystals: James's *The Golden Bowl* and Literature as Moral Philosophy," *New Literary History 15* (1983): 43.

22 See my "Moral Pluralism."

23 Richard W. Miller, "Truth in Beauty," *American Philosophical Quarterly* 16 (1979): 317–25, argues that truth is sometimes aesthetically relevant, since the "aesthetic goals of some works include the combination, in appropriate ways, of the true depiction of certain aspects of reality with other, exclusively and uncontroversially aesthetic virtues" (319). If there are ethical truths, this would yield a cognitivist defense of the relevance in certain conditions of the depiction of ethical truths to aesthetic worth. Miller's piece is important, since it seeks explicitly to meet the relevance problem, and his strategy shares some features with that advanced in the present essay though it differs in an important respect in appealing directly to truth rather than to merited responses. But given his stress on the fact that it is not the truth of ideas per se that is aesthetically relevant, but their cognitive manner of expression, his approach appears to yield the result that if immoral views (such as Baudelaire's sexism) are well expressed in his poems, then their immorality does not constitute an aesthetic defect in the poems (322). Thus, the position yielded by Miller's argument is incompatible with ethicism and, given the argument for ethicism advanced later, is to be rejected as it stands.

24 The notion of prescribing imagined feelings is to be found in Kendall Walton, *Mimesis as Make-Believe: On the Foundations of the Representational Arts* (Cambridge, Mass.: Harvard University Press, 1990), chap. 7.2. The claim that actual feelings can be prescribed is defended by Richard Moran in "The Expression of Feeling in Imagination,"

Philosophical Review 103 (1994): 75–106. I am indebted at several points in this section to Moran's discussion.

25 For defenses of the view that real emotions can be felt toward events known to be merely imagined, see Noël Carroll, *The Philosophy of Horror or Paradoxes of the Heart* (New York: Routledge, 1990), 60–88, and Patricia Greenspan, *Emotions and Reasons: An Inquiry into Emotional Justification* (New York: Routledge, 1988), esp. part I.

26 For cognitive-evaluative views of responses, see Greenspan, *Emotions and Reasons*; Robert C. Roberts, "What an Emotion Is: A Sketch," *Philosophical Review* 97 (1988): 183–209; and Elijah Millgram, "Pleasure in Practical Reasoning," *Monist* 76 (1993): 394–415.

27 See, e.g., Walton, *Mimesis as Make-Believe*, 241–55; and Gregory Currie *The Nature of Fiction* (Cambridge University Press, 1990), chap. 5.

28 Compare Carroll, *The Philosophy of Horror*.

29 A point I owe to Kendall Walton. See his "Morals in Fiction and Fictional Morality," *Proceedings of the Aristotelian Society* suppl. vol. 68 (1994): 27–50, for an irrealist discussion of the ethical criticism of art.

30 I owe this point to Jerrold Levinson.

51

Expressive Properties of Art

Guy Sircello

Guy Sircello (1936–92) was Professor of Philosophy at the University of California, Irvine.

Romantic ideas about mind and its relation to art did not receive their clearest expression until the twentieth century. Then philosophers like Croce, Collingwood, Cassirer, Dewey, and Langer tried to spell out exactly how it is that art can be expressive. But to many other twentieth-century philosophers, especially to those working in the various "analytical" styles whose intellectual ancestry was anything but Romantic, those philosophical discussions of expression in art were puzzling. This puzzlement can best be seen in the work of Monroe Beardsley and O. K. Bouwsma, philosophers who represent two distinct strains in recent analytical philosophy.

I think it is fair to understand the puzzlement of both Beardsley and Bouwsma in the following way. We understand relatively well what it is for a *person* to express such things as feelings, emotions, attitudes, moods, etc. But if we say that sonatas, poems, or paintings also express those sorts of things either we are saying something patently false or we are saying something true in an uninformative, misleading, and therefore pointless way. For to say of works of art that they express those sorts of things seems to imply that they are very much like persons. Therefore, unless we believe that philosophers who think of art as expression believe the unbelievable, that is, that art has feelings, attitudes, and moods and can express them, we must believe that such philosophers are trying, however inadequately, to come to grips with genuine truths about art.

Furthermore, there is such an obvious disparity between the nature of art and the thesis that art can express the same sorts of things that people do that we cannot understand that thesis as simply a clumsy and inept way of stating some truths about art. We must understand it, rather, as a kind of *theoretical* statement, that is, as a deliberately contrived and elaborated way of construing some simple facts about art. Both Beardsley and Bouwsma thus speak of the "Expression *Theory*" of art.

What are the facts which the Expression Theory is meant to interpret? Although Beardsley and Bouwsma differ slightly in the way they put the point, they agree that works of art have "anthropomorphic" properties. That is, we may often properly characterize works of art as, for example, gay, sad, witty, pompous, austere, aloof, impersonal, sentimental, etc. A "theory" of art as expression, therefore, can say no more than that art works have properties designated by the same words which designate feelings, emotions,

Guy Sircello, "Expressive Properties of Art," in *Mind and Art: An Essay on the Varieties of Expression*, ed. Guy Sircello (Princeton: Princeton University Press, 1972), pp. 16–46.

attitudes, moods, and personal characteristics of human beings.

The nature of these properties has not been probed very deeply by analytical critics of the Expression Theory. Beardsley calls them "qualities." Bouwsma prefers to call them "characters," pointing out their affinity with the "characters" of a number of things like sounds, words, numerals, and faces. In case this suggestion is unhelpful, Bouwsma further invites us to conceive the relation of the "character" to the art work in terms of the relation of redness to the apple in a red apple. At this point he is exactly in line with Beardsley, who mentions a red rose instead of a red apple.[1]

The Bouwsma-Beardsley position on the question of expression in art is currently rather widely accepted. Indeed, John Hospers, writing in the *Encyclopedia of Philosophy*, has, in effect, canonized the view.[2] Accordingly, I shall refer to it henceforth as the Canonical Position. Now despite the fact that it has illuminated the concept of expression in art, the Canonical Position is false in some respects and inadequate in others. In this chapter [. . .] I shall argue (1) that attributions of "characters," or "anthropomorphic qualities," to works of art come in a number of different varieties, (2) that the simple thing-property relation is not an adequate model for understanding any of those varieties, (3) that there are far better reasons for calling art "expressive" than are allowed by the Canonical interpretation of Expression Theory, (4) that the presence of "anthropomorphic qualities" in works of art is not the only fact about art which makes it expressive, and (5) that the features of art which make it expressive have precise parallels in non-artistic areas of culture such as philosophy, historiography and science.

The Canonical Position has two incorrect presuppositions. The first is that works of art are very much like such natural objects as roses and apples as well as, I suppose, such natural quasi- and non-objects as hills, brooks, winds, and skies. The second is that the anthropomorphic predicates of art are not essentially different from simple color terms like "red" and "yellow." No one has seriously argued, as far as I know, that any art work is *just* like some natural "object." Everyone admits that there are basic differences between art and nature, most of them related to the fact that art is made by human beings and natural things are not. What the first presupposition of the Canonical Position amounts to, therefore, is that as far as the anthropomorphic predicates are concerned works of art are not different from natural objects.[3]

It is fairly easy to show that this presupposition is false by the following strategy. Anthropomorphic predicates are applied to natural things in virtue of certain non-anthropomorphic properties of those things. Of course these properties vary, depending on the particular predicate as well as on the thing to which it applied. Hills, for example, may be austere in virtue of their color, their vegetation (or lack of it), or their contours; an ocean may be angry in virtue of its sound and the force and size of its waves; a tree may be sad in virtue of the droop and shape of its branches. With respect to a number of art works to which anthropomorphic predicates are applied, I shall inquire what it is about those works in virtue of which the predicates are applicable. This strategy will yield categorial features of art which do not belong to natural things.

(1) Like most of Raphael's Madonna paintings, the one called *La Belle Jardinière* can be described as calm and serene. It is fairly clear what there is about this painting which makes it calm and serene: the regular composition based on an equilateral triangle, the gentle and loving expressions on the faces of the Mother, the Child, and the infant John the Baptist, the placid landscape, the delicate trees, the soft blue of the sky, the gentle ripples in the Mother's garments blown by a slight breeze, and, finally, the equanimity and quiet with which the artist views his subject and records the details of the scene.

(2) We might reasonably describe Hans Hofmann's *The Golden Wall* as an aggressive abstract painting. But in this painting there is no representational content in the usual sense and therefore nothing aggressive is depicted. What is aggressive is the color scheme, which is predominantly red and yellow. Blue and green are also used as contrasting colors, but even these colors, especially the blue, are made to look aggressive because of their intensity. Furthermore, by the way they are juxtaposed, the patches of color are made to appear as though they were rushing out towards the observer and even as though they

were competing with one another in this rush towards the observer.

(3) We might say of Poussin's *The Rape of the Sabine Women* (either version, but especially the one in the Metropolitan Museum of Art in New York City) that it is calm and aloof. Yet it is quite clear that the depicted scene is *not* calm and that no one in it, with the possible exception of Romulus, who is directing the attack, is aloof. It is rather, as we say, that Poussin calmly observes the scene and paints it in an aloof, detached way.

(4) Breughel's painting called *Wedding Dance in the Open Air* can be aptly if superficially described as gay and happy. In this case however it is surely the occasion and the activities of the depicted peasants which are happy. Perhaps the prominent red used throughout the painting can be called "gay." The faces of the peasants however are neither happy nor gay. They are bland, stupid, and even brutal. It is this fact which makes the painting ironic rather than gay or happy. Yet there is certainly nothing about a peasant wedding, the dull peasants, or their heavy dance which is ironic. The irony lies in the fact that the painter "views," "observes," or depicts the happy scene ironically.

(5) John Milton's "L'Allegro" is not only "about" high spirits, but it is surely a high-spirited, i.e. gay and joyful, poem. The gaiety and joy are evident in several ways. First, the scenes and images are gay and joyful: Zephir playing with Aurora, maids and youths dancing and dallying, the poet himself living a life of "unreproved" pleasure with Mirth. Second, the diction and rhythms are light-hearted: "Haste thee nymphs and bring with thee / Jest and youthful Jollity, / Quips and Cranks, and wanton Wiles, / Nods, and Becks and Wreathed Smiles."

(6) Another sort of example entirely is William Wordsworth's sentimental poem "We Are Seven." This poem is quite obviously not *about* sentimentality. It purports simply to record the conversation between the poet and a child. Neither the child nor the poet (that is, the "character" in the poem), moreover, is sentimental. The child matter-of-factly reports her firm conviction there are still seven members of her family despite the fact that two of them are dead. The poet is trying, in a rather obtuse and hard-headed sort of way, to get her to admit that there are only five. But the little girl is made to win the point by having the last word in the poem. She is thus made to seem "right" even though no explicit authorization is given to her point of view. By presenting the little girl's case so sympathetically, Wordsworth (the poet who wrote the poem, not the "character" in the poem) treats the attitude of the little girl, as well as the death of her siblings, sentimentally.

(7) The case of "The Dungeon" by Coleridge is different again. At least the first half of this poem is angry. But it is not about anger or angry persons. It is a diatribe in verse (and certainly not a poor poem on that account) against the cruelty, injustice, and wasteful ineffectiveness of prisons.

(8) T. S. Eliot's "The Lovesong of J. Alfred Prufrock" can, with considerable justice, be called a compassionate poem. In this case it is quite clear that the compassion exists in the way in which the character Prufrock is portrayed as a gentle and sensitive, if weak, victim of ugly and sordid surroundings.

(9) Suppose that we say that the second movement of Beethoven's "Eroica" symphony is sad with a dignified and noble sadness characteristic of Beethoven. In this case the sadness is in the slowness of the tempo, and the special quality of the sadness comes from the stateliness of the march rhythm, from the use of "heavy" instruments like horns and tympani and from the sheer length of the movement.

(10) A somewhat different case is presented by Mozart's music for Papageno, which is gay, carefree, light-headed and lighthearted like Papageno himself. What differentiates this case from (9), of course, is that the Mozart music is intended to suit a certain kind of character, whereas the Beethoven has no clear and explicit "representational" content. Despite this difference, however, the "anthropomorphic qualities" of the Mozart music are, like those of the Beethoven, audible in properties of the sound: in the simple harmonies, tripping rhythms, and lilting melodies of Papageno songs.

(11) A slightly different case from either (9) or (10) is that presented by the first movement of Vivaldi's "Spring" Concerto. The first lilting, happy theme represents the joyful advent of spring. This is followed by the gentle music of the winds and waters of spring. Next, this pleasantness is interrupted by the angry music

representing a thunder shower, after which the happy, gentle music returns. In this music the "programmatic" content is clear and explicit because we know the poetry from which Vivaldi composed the music.

(12) Quite different from the three cases immediately preceding is the witty Grandfather theme from Prokoviev's *Peter and the Wolf.* Grandfather's music, played by a bassoon, is large, lumbering, and pompous like Grandfather himself. But what makes it witty is that it portrays a dignified old man as just a bit ridiculous. Through the music Prokoviev pokes gentle fun at the old man, fun which is well-motivated by the story itself. For in the end Peter turns out to be more than equal to the danger which Grandfather has ordered him to avoid.

(13) Finally, there is music like the utterly impersonal and detached music of John Cage, exemplified in *Variations II* played by David Tudor on (with) the piano. But where can we locate the "qualities" of impersonality and detachment in Cage's music? They do not seem to be "properties" of the sounds and sound-sequences in the way that gaiety is a property of Papageno's music or sadness is a property of Beethoven's. Indeed, we feel that these "anthropomorphic qualities" of Cage's music depend on the very fact that the sounds themselves are completely lacking in "human" properties. They are as characterless as any of a thousand random noises we hear every day. In fact, *Variations II* does have the apparent randomness and disorganization of mere noise. But we would not be inclined to call *any* random sequences of noises "impersonal" and "detached," even if they sounded very much like the sounds of *Variations II.* The predicates "impersonal" and "detached" are not applied to Cage's music simply in virtue of some features of its sounds. These "qualities" of *Variations II* arise rather from the fact that the composer presents what sounds like mere noise as music. Cage offers this "noise" for us to attend to and concentrate upon. Moreover, he offers it to us without "comment," and with no intention that it evoke, represent, or suggest anything beyond itself. That is to say, Cage offers these noise-like sounds in a totally uninvolved, detached, impersonal way, seeking in no way to touch our emotional life.

From the preceding examples we can see that there are some respects in which anthropomorphic predicates are applied to works of art in virtue of features of those works which they share or could share with some natural things. In the Raphael it is the composition of the painting which accounts in part for the "calm" of the painting. But "composition" here refers simply to the configuration of lines and shapes, which sorts of features can of course be shared by natural objects. Similarly, the aggressiveness of Hofmann's painting is due to its colors and their arrangement. In the Beethoven and Mozart examples the anthropomorphic qualities are traceable to features of sound which can be present in natural phenomena. The ocean crashing on the shore, a twig tapping against a windowpane, the gurgle of a stream – all of these can have "tempi," "rhythms," and even "tone color." Natural "melodies" are present in the rustle of trees and the howl of winds as well as in the songs of birds. Even the anthropomorphic qualities of verbal art can be like properties of natural things. For, as the example of "L'Allegro" shows, such qualities can be attributed to poetry at least partly in virtue of the tempo and rhythm of its verses.

Some of the above examples of anthropomorphic qualities applied to art, however, show that such qualities sometimes belong to works of art in virtue of what those works represent, describe, depict, or portray. Thus the calm and serenity of the Raphael is due in part to the countryside, the sky, the garments, and the faces depicted; the gaiety of the Breughel comes from the gaiety of the depicted scene, and the high spirits of Milton's poem are due to the gay, happy scenes and images described and presented. In cases of this sort, neither paintings nor poems are comparable to natural things with respect to the way they bear their anthropomorphic qualities. And the situation is similar with respect to all other forms of representational art, whether prose fiction, drama, ballet, opera, or sculpture. Only architecture and music are generally incapable of bearing anthropomorphic qualities in this way. This is true, moreover, even for music with a sort of representational content such as the Mozart music mentioned in (10) above. For it is not due to the fact that Mozart's songs are written for a gay, lighthearted character that they are properly described as gay and lighthearted. It is rather that the songs suit Papageno precisely in virtue of the gaiety and lightheartedness of their "sound" and are thereby capable of portraying him musically.

There is a second way in which anthropomorphic predicates may be applied to art works which is unlike the ways in which such predicates apply to natural things. In the discussion of (1) through (13) above we discovered the following:

(*a*) *La Belle Jardinière* is calm and serene partly because Raphael *views* his subject calmly and quietly.
(*b*) *The Rape of the Sabine Women* is aloof and detached because Poussin calmly *observes* the violent scene and *paints* it in an aloof, detached way.
(*c*) *Wedding Dance in the Open Air* is an ironic painting because Breughel *treats* the gaiety of the wedding scene ironically.
(*d*) "We Are Seven" is a sentimental poem because Wordsworth *treats* his subject matter sentimentally.
(*e*) "The Dungeon" is an angry poem because in it the poet angrily *inveighs* against the institution of imprisonment.
(*f*) "The Lovesong of J. Alfred Prufrock" is a compassionate poem because the poet compassionately *portrays* the plight of his "hero."
(*g*) Prokoviev's Grandfather theme is witty because the composer wittily *comments* on the character in his ballet.
(*h*) Cage's *Variations II* is impersonal because the composer *presents* his noise-like sounds in an impersonal, uninvolved way.

I have italicized the verbs in the above in order to point up the fact that the respective anthropomorphic predicate is applied to the work of art in virtue of what the artist *does* in that work. In order to have a convenient way of referring to this class of anthropomorphic predicates, I shall henceforth refer to what verbs of the sort italicized above designate as "artistic acts." I do not intend this bit of nomenclature to have any metaphysical import. That is, I do not mean that the viewings, observings, paintings, presentings, portrayings, and treatings covered by the term "artistic acts" all belong to a category properly called "acts." Nor do I mean that all activities properly called "artistic" are covered by my term "artistic act." As shall come out later, many artistic activities are neither identical with, constituents of, nor constituted by "artistic acts." Furthermore, I do not want to suggest that "artistic acts" have anything more in common than what I have already pointed out and what I shall go on to specify. To do a complete metaphysics of artistic acts might be an interesting philosophical job but one which would distract me from my main purpose [here].

What the preceding discussion has shown is that the view of art presupposed by the Canonical Position ignores complexities in works of art which are essential in understanding how they can bear anthropomorphic predicates. Even more significant is the discovery that anthropomorphic predicates apply to art works in virtue of "artistic acts" in these works. For, as I shall argue presently at length, it is precisely this feature of art works which enables them to be *expressions* and which thereby shows that the Canonical Position has missed a great deal of truth in classical Expression Theory.

As far as I know, no adherent of the Canonical Position, with one exception to be noted below, has recognized the existence of what I call "artistic acts," much less seen their relevance to expression in art. But it is not difficult to anticipate the first defensive move a proponent of the Canonical Position would likely make against the threat posed by "artistic acts." It would go somewhat as follows. What the "discovery" of "artistic acts" shows is merely that not all applications of anthropomorphic predicates to art works attribute qualities to those works. They merely *seem* to do so because of their grammatical form. But in fact statements of this sort say nothing at all about the art work; they describe the artist. After all, "artistic acts" are acts of the artists, and they cannot possibly be acts of (i.e. performed by) the art works themselves.

However superficially plausible this objection is, it can be shown to have little force. First, the objection presupposes a false dichotomy: a statement must be descriptive either of a work of art *or* of its artist. On the contrary, there seems to be no reason why when we talk in the above examples of the painting's aloofness, the poem's sentimentality, etc., we cannot be talking *both* about the painting or poem and about how Poussin painted or how Wordsworth treated his subject. And it is in fact the case that we are talking about both. The best proof of this is that the *grounds* for the truth of the descriptions of artistic acts in (*a*) through (*g*) above can come from the art work in question. One knows by looking at Poussin's painting that he has painted the scene in an aloof, detached way. The cold light, the statuesque poses, the painstaking linearity are all visible in the work. Similarly, we recognize by reading Wordsworth's poem that he treats his subject sentimentally. That is just what it is to give the child, who believes that the dead are present among the living, the advantage over the matter-of-fact adult. We can also recognize the impersonality of *Variations II* by listening to its neutral, noise-like sounds. A test for statements describing art in anthropomorphic terms is always and quite naturally a scrutiny of the art, even when the terms are applied in virtue of "artistic acts."

Moreover it is not as if this sort of attention to the work of art were merely a second-best way of testing such statements. One does not look, listen, or read in order to *infer* something about the aloof way Poussin painted, the compassionate way Eliot portrayed his hero, etc. We must not imagine that had we actually been with the artist at work, we could *really*, i.e. immediately and indubitably, have seen his aloofness, compassion, sentimentality, etc. How absurd to think that when Poussin's way of painting is described as aloof, what is meant is that Poussin arched his eyebrows slightly, maintained an impassive expression on his face, and moved his arms slowly and deliberately while he painted the picture. Or that because Eliot portrays Prufrock compassionately, he penned the manuscript of his poem with tears in his eyes. Not only would such facts not be needed to support statements about Poussin's aloofness or Eliot's compassion, but they are totally irrelevant to such statements. For even if we knew the way Poussin looked and moved when he was painting the Sabine picture or the way Eliot's face looked when he penned "Prufrock," we could not infer that the painting and poem were, respectively, aloof and compassionate in the ways we are discussing.

The foregoing considerations do not mean that the "artistic acts" in question are not truly acts of the artists, that is, are not truly something which the artists have done. Nor do they imply that these artistic acts are phantom acts, airy nothings existing mysteriously in works of art and disembodied from any agents.[4] They simply mean that these acts are not identifiable or describable independently of the works "in" which they are done. Probably nothing makes this point clearer than the fact that descriptions of artistic acts of this sort can be known to be true even when little or nothing is known about the author, much less what he looked like and what his behavior was like at the precise time that he was making his art. It can be truly said, for example, that Homer describes with some sentimentality the meeting of the returned Odysseus and aged dog Argos. And yet it would be absurd to say that the truth of that statement waits upon some detailed knowledge about Homer, even the existence of whom is a matter of considerable dispute.

Artistic acts are peculiar in that descriptions of them are at once and necessarily descriptions of art works. They are in this way distinguishable from other sorts of acts of artists which contribute to the production of works of art, e.g. looking at the canvas, chiseling marble, penning words, applying paint, revising a manuscript, thinking to oneself, etc. But artistic acts, for all their peculiarity, are not entirely alone in the universe; there are other sorts of things which people do which are analogous to artistic acts in significant ways. Note the following: A person may scowl angrily, and thereby have an angry scowl on his face; he may smile sadly and thereby have a sad smile on his face; he may gesture impatiently and thus make an impatient gesture; he may shout defiantly and produce thereby a defiant shout; he may pout sullenly and a sullen pout will appear on his face; his eyes may gleam happily and there will be a happy gleam in his eyes; he may tug at his forelock shyly or give a shy tug at his forelock. What is interesting about these clauses is that they show how an anthropomorphic term can be applied either adverbially to "acts" or adjectivally to "things" without a difference in the sense of the term or of the sentences in which it is used. This sort of shift in the grammatical category of a term is clearly analogous to what is possible with respect to those anthropomorphic predicates applied to works of art in virtue of their artistic acts. Thus one may, without change of meaning, say either that Eliot's "Prufrock" is a compassionate poem or that Eliot portrays Prufrock compassionately in his poem; that Poussin paints his violent scene in an aloof, detached way or that the Sabine picture is an aloof, detached painting.[5]

This grammatical shift is possible in both sorts of cases because of the inseparability of the "act" and the "thing." One does not *infer* from a smile on a person's face that he is smiling any more than one *infers* that Eliot portrayed Prufrock compassionately from his compassionate poem, and for analogous reasons. The "acts" of smiling, pouting, shouting, tugging are not even describable without also and at once describing the smile, pout, shout, or tug. Smiling, after all, is not an act which produces or results in a smile so that something could interfere to prevent the smiling from bringing off the smile. "Smiling" and "smile," we are inclined to say, are simply two grammatically different ways of referring to the same "thing."[6]

Now the parallel I want to point out is not between smile-smiling, pout-pouting, tug-tugging, on the one hand; and poem-portraying, picture-(act of) painting, music-presenting, on the other. For clearly Poussin's Sabine painting is more than (is not simply identical with) Poussin's aloof way of painting the violent scene; Eliot's poem is more than his compassionate way of portraying its title character; Cage's music is more than his impersonal presentation of noise-like sounds. When we have described these artistic acts we have not by any means completely described the respective art works. The analogy rather is between smile-smiling and portrayal-portraying, presentation-presenting, treatment-treating, view-viewing, etc. Therefore, when we designate artistic acts by a noun term, those acts seem to be "parts" or "moments" of the works of art to which they pertain. We may then more properly understand the way in which an anthropomorphic adjective applies to an art work in virtue of such a "part" in something like the way in which a person's whole face is called sad in virtue merely of his sad smile or his sad gaze, or in which a person's behavior is generally angry in virtue (merely) of his quick movements and angry tone of voice. In these cases, too, it is not as if the terms "sad" and "angry" *completely* described the face or the behavior or even all parts and aspects of the face and behavior even though they can *generally* characterize the face and the behavior.

The foregoing comparison points out that not only is it the case that anthropomorphic predicates do not always apply to art works the way predicates, anthropomorphic or not, apply to natural objects, but that sometimes anthropomorphic predicates apply to works of art rather like the way that they apply to verbal, gestural, and facial *expressions*. For sad smiles are characteristic expressions of sadness in a person; angry scowls, of anger; shy tugs at forelocks, of diffidence; sullen pouts, of petulance. And this is an all-important point which the Canonical Position has missed in its interpretation of the Expression Theory of Art. Had proponents of the Canonical Position pursued their inquiry into anthropomorphic predicates further, they would have been forced to question whether such predicates apply to art in the way they apply to objects or in the way they apply to common human expressions.

Instead of pursuing this line of questioning, however, they were misled by the noun-adjective form of their favorite example – sad music – into their object-quality interpretation of Expression Theory, an interpretation which of course makes that "theory" seem very far removed indeed from the "facts" which were alleged to have motivated it. Small wonder that Beardsley's final judgment on Expression Theory is that it "renders itself obsolete" after it has reminded us that anthropomorphic predicates may reasonably be applied to art works. Even O. K. Bouwsma, who of all the proponents of the Canonical Position comes closest to the point I am maintaining, was not able to see quite where his comparison between sad music and sad faces leads. For instead of making a transition from sad faces to sad *expressions* on faces, he takes the (rather longer) way from sad faces to red apples.

There is more to the comparison between artistic acts and facial, vocal, and gestural expressions than the formal or grammatical similarities just noted. Even more important are the parallels between the "significance" of things like sad smiles and angry scowls and the "significance" of aloofness or irony in paintings, sentimentality or compassion in poems, and impersonality or wittiness in music. For there are parallels between what facial, gestural and vocal expressions, on the one hand, and artistic acts, on the other, can tell us about the persons responsible for them. In order to draw out these parallels explicitly I shall use the cases of an angry scowl and a compassionate portrayal in the mode of Eliot's "Prufrock."

First, it is obvious that an angry scowl on a person's face might well mean that the person is angry. It might be more than simply an expression of anger; it might be an expression of *his* anger. Now it should need very little argument to show that a compassionate poem like "Prufrock" might be an expression of the poet's own compassion. He might be a person with a generally sympathetic and pitying attitude towards modern man and his situation. In that case, a poem like "Prufrock," at least a poem with "Prufrock's" kind of compassion, is precisely what one could expect from the poet, just as one could expect an angry man to scowl angrily. But just as we cannot reasonably expect that *every* time a person is angry he scowls angrily, we cannot expect that every man who is a poet and who has compassion towards his fellows will produce poetry with the compassion of "Prufrock," If a man can keep his anger from showing in his face, a poet can, with whatever greater difficulties and whatever more interesting implications for himself and his poetry, keep his compassion from showing in his poetry.

Moreover, just as there is no necessity that a man's anger show in his face, there is no necessity that an angry scowl betoken anger in the scowler. There is a looseness of connection between anger and angry expressions which is matched by a looseness between compassion and compassionate poems. One reason that a man might have an angry scowl on his face is that he is *affecting* anger, for any of a number of reasons. Now although the range of reasons for affecting compassion in his poetry might be different from the range of reasons for affecting anger in his face, it is nevertheless possible that a corpus of poetry with "Prufrock's" sort of compassion might betoken nothing more than an affectation of compassion. This might be the case if, for example, the poet is extremely "hard" and sarcastic but thinks of these traits as defects. He might then quite deliberately write "compassionate" poetry in order to mask his true self and present himself to the world as the man he believes he should be.

On the other hand, both angry scowls and compassionate poetry might be the result simply of a desire to imitate, Children especially will often imitate expressions on people's faces, but even adults sometimes have occasion to imitate such expressions, e.g. in relating an anecdote. A poet might write poems with Eliot's sort of compassion in them in imitation of Eliot's early attitude. This imitation might be executed by a clever teacher in order to show more vividly than by merely pointing them out the means Eliot used to convey his special sympathy in "Prufrock." Or Eliot might be imitated because his techniques and style, together with the attitudes they imply, have become fashionable among serious poets or because these attitudes strike a responsive chord among serious poets. The latter sorts of imitation are rather like the imitations which a child might make of a person whom he regards as a model. It is not unusual for a girl who admires a female teacher, say, to practice smiling in that teacher's kind, gentle way or for a very young boy at play to "get angry" in the same way he has seen his father get angry.

A poet might write poems with the compassion of "Prufrock," not because he is either affecting or imitating the attitude of that poem, but because he is *practicing* writing poetry in different styles and different "moods." This may be just something like a technical exercise for him, or it may be part of a search for a characteristic attitude or stance which seems to be truly "his own." He thus "tries on" a number of different poetic "masks," so to speak, to see how they fit him. In a similar way, an adolescent girl grimacing before her mirror might "try on" various facial expressions to see how they "look on her" and to discover which is her "best," or perhaps her most characteristic face: innocent, sullen, sultry, haughty, or even angry.

Finally, an angry scowl on a face might be there when the person is portraying an angry person on the stage. There is a similar sort of situation in which compassionate poetry might be written not as betokening a characteristic of the poem's real author but as betokening the traits of a *character* in a play or novel who is *represented* as having written the poem. No actual examples of such a character come immediately to mind; but we surely have no trouble imagining a master of stylistic imitation writing a novelized account of modern literature in which he exhibits examples of the "Prufrock"-like poetry of an Eliot-like figure.

What I have argued so far is not that all art is expression, nor even that all art works with artistic acts anthropomorphically qualified are expressions. My argument shows only that artistic acts in works of art are remarkably like common facial, vocal, and gestural expressions. It also demonstrates that precisely in virtue of their artistic acts and of the similarity they bear to common kinds of expressions, works of art may serve as expressions of those feelings, emotions, attitudes, moods, and/or personal characteristics of their creators which are designated by the anthropomorphic predicates applicable to the art works themselves. And it thereby demonstrates that one presupposition of the Canonical Position is clearly wrong: namely, that art works, insofar as they allow of anthropomorphic predicates, are essentially like natural things untouched by man.

But the second presupposition of the Canonical Position, to wit, that anthropomorphic predicates of art are like simple color words, is also false. It is false with respect to all of the three ways, distinguished earlier, that anthropomorphic predicates can be applied to works of art. And it is *a fortiori* false with respect to those predicates which are applied to art in two or three ways at once, as most of them are. The falsity of the presupposition can be brought out in an interesting way by showing how the three ways of applying anthropomorphic predicates to art bear a certain resemblance to color attributions which are rather unlike simply calling a (clearly) red rose red or an (indubitably) green hill green.

Suppose that a sign painter is painting a sign in three colors: yellow, red, and blue. Since the sign is large, he is required to move his equipment several times during the job. Suppose that he employs an assistant to attend to this business. Now we can imagine that the painter will have occasion to give directions to his assistant. He might say, "Bring me the red bucket, but leave the blue and yellow ones there, since I'll need them on that side later." Now if we suppose that the color of all the paint containers is black, when the painter calls for the "red bucket," he must mean "the bucket of red paint," and would surely be so understood by his assistant. In the context the phrase "red bucket" only *appears* to have the same grammatical form as "red rose." I suggest that to the extent that a painting or other representational work of art is called "gay" or "sad" solely in virtue of its subject matter or parts thereof, the latter terms function *more* like "red" in "red bucket" than in "red rose."

It is a common opinion that "sad" in "sad smile" and "gay" in "gay laughter" function metaphorically.[7] There may well be a use of "metaphor" such that the opinion is true. Whether there is such a use will not be determined until there exists a thorough philosophical study of metaphor; and I do not intend to offer one here. But even if it turns out to be true that such uses of anthropomorphic words are metaphorical, it cannot be very useful simply to say it. For such uses *appear* not to be metaphorical at all. After all, it is not as if calling a smile sad were representing the smile as, as it were, feeling sad, acting sad, weeping and dragging its feet. To see a smile's sadness is not to discern the tenuous and subtle "likeness" between the smile and a sad person. It is much more straightforward to think that a smile is sad because it is a smile *characteristic* of a sad person who smiles; that laughter is gay because such laughter is *characteristic* laughter of persons who are gay. In this respect "sad smile" is rather like "six-year-old behavior" or "Slavic cheekbones." These phrases do not indirectly point to unexpected similarities between a sort of behavior and six-year-old children or between cheekbones and persons. They designate, respectively, behavior which is *characteristic* of six-year-old children and cheekbones *characteristic* of Slavs. And there is no inclination at all to call these phrases "metaphorical."

Yet to say that a sad smile is a smile characteristic of sad people is not to deny what the Canonical Position affirms, namely, that "sad" designates a "property" or "character" of the smile. Surely there is something about the smile which marks it as sad: its droopiness, its weakness, its wanness. But the term "sad" still has a different import from "droopy," "weak," or "wan" when applied to smiles, even though all the latter terms are also characteristic smiles of sad persons. The difference is that the term "sad" *explicitly* relates the character of the smile to sadness of persons. A comparable sort of color term might be "cherry red." "Cherry red" is like the term "bright red with bluish undertones" in that they both designate roughly the same shade of red, which is characteristic of cherries. But the former term is unlike the latter in that it *explicitly* relates the color to cherries.

It might seem that the Canonical Position would be correct in its interpretation of anthropomorphic terms as they apply to those features of works of art which they can share with natural things. For the term "sad" applied to the second movement of the "Eroica" and to a weeping willow must surely denote some properties of the music and of the tree. And they do: drooping branches in the tree; slow rhythm and "heavy" sound in the Beethoven. But "sad" differs from "drooping," "slow," and "heavy" as in the preceding case; it immediately relates the properties of the sounds and the branches to properties of other things which are sad. In these cases "sad" does function metaphorically, harboring, as it were, a comparison within itself. To find an analogy among color words, this use of "sad" is like "reddish." Like "reddish," which quite self-consciously does not denote true redness, "sad" in "sad tree" does not denote true sadness but only a kind of likeness of it. This use of "sad" is also arguably analogous to the use of "red" in "His face turned red with shame," But whether "sad tree" and "sad rhythm" are closer to "reddish clay" or to "red face" is, if determinable at all, unimportant for my point. For "reddish clay" and "red face" are equally unlike "red rose" and "red apple" when the latter refer to a full-blown American Beauty and a ripe Washington Delicious.

In this section I have argued that anthropomorphic terms, when applied to art, are *more* like "red" in "red bucket (of paint)," "cherry red" in "cherry red silk," or "reddish" in "reddish clay" than like "red" in "red rose." But, in truth, anthropomorphic predicates of art are not *very* much like any of these. The reason is that what all anthropomorphic predicates ultimately relate to are human emotions, feelings, attitudes, moods, and personal traits, none of which are very much at all like colors. But there is point in drawing out the comparison between anthropomorphic predicates and color-terms more complicated than "red" in "red rose." The point is that "red" as applied to bucket, "cherry red," and "reddish" are all in some way relational terms in ways that "red" said of a rose is not. "Red bucket" means "bucket *of* red paint"; "cherry red" means "the red *characteristic of* cherries"; and "reddish" means "of a color *rather like* red." Had proponents of the Canonical Position troubled to refine their comparison between anthropomorphic predicates and color predicates, they might have been forced to recognize the relational aspects of the former. Eventually they might have been led to see that anthropomorphic terms finally relate to various forms of the "inner lives" of human beings. And *that* is where Expression Theory begins. The Canonical model of the red rose (or apple) ultimately fails to help us understand how anthropomorphic predicates apply to art because such predicates are not very much like simple quality-words and what they apply to are not very much like natural objects.

In spite of all the above arguments, the Canonical Position is not left utterly defenseless. Although it is the notion of "artistic acts" which is most threatening to the Canonical Position, proponents of that position have been almost totally unaware of this threat. Not totally unaware, however. There is a brief passage in Monroe Beardsley's book *Aesthetics: Problems in the Philosophy of Criticism* in which he mentions an artist's "treatment" and "handling," two examples of what I have called "artistic acts." Beardsley does not relate them, however, to the analysis of anthropomorphic terms. He discusses them under the rubric "misleading idioms," and he suggests that all talk about art concerning "handling" and "treatment" not only can be but should be translated into talk which makes no mention of these sorts of acts.[8]

These are meager clues, but from them it is possible to excogitate an objection to my notion of "artistic arts" which a defender of the Canonical Position might raise. We should first note a remark which Beardsley makes elsewhere in his book when he is concluding his interpretation of Expression Theory. He states that all remarks about the expressiveness of an art work can be "translated" into statements about the anthropomorphic qualities either of the subject matter or of the "design," i.e., roughly the properties which the work could share with natural things.[9] A defense against the notion of "artistic acts" might thus run as follows: Any statement which describes an artistic act anthropomorphically can be "translated" into a statement which describes features of the work of art other than its artistic acts. So stated, however, the defense is ambiguous; it has two plausible and interesting interpretations. First, it might mean that any anthropomorphic description of an artistic act in a work can be replaced, without loss of meaning, by a description of the subject matter and/or design of the work in terms of the same anthropomorphic predicate. Or it might mean that there are descriptions, of whatever sort, of the subject matter and/or design of a work which, given any true anthropomorphic description of an artistic act in that work, entail that description.

The first interpretation of the objection is easily shown to be false. All that is required is that some examples of art be adduced in which anthropomorphic predicates are applicable with some plausibility to an "artistic act" but which are in no other way plausibly attributable to the work. Let us look again at the works of Poussin, Eliot, and Prokoviev discussed earlier in this chapter.

In the Poussin painting of the rape of the Sabines there is nothing about the violent subject matter which could be called "aloof." Certainly the attackers and the attacked are not aloof. Romulus, the general in charge, is a relatively *calm* surveyor of the melee, but he cannot be called aloof, partly because we cannot see him well enough to tell what his attitude is. "Aloof" does not apply with regard to the formal elements of the Poussin painting either. It is difficult even to imagine what "aloof" lines, masses, colors, or an "aloof" arrangement thereof might be. The light in the painting is rather cold, and that feature does indeed contribute to the aloofness of the work. "Cold light" is not, however, the same as "aloof light," which does not even appear to be a sensible combination of words.

A similar analysis is possible with respect to Eliot's "Prufrock." If we consider first the "material" elements of the poem – its rhythm, meter, sound qualities, etc. – we realize that "compassionate" simply cannot apply to those features meaningfully. Moreover, there is nothing about the subject matter of "Prufrock" which is compassionate. Certainly Prufrock himself is not compassionate; he is simply confused, a victim of his own fears and anxieties, and of the meanness and triviality of his routinized life and soulless companions.

Finally, the wittiness of Prokoviev's Grandfather theme cannot be supposed to be a "property" of the music the way its comic qualities are. The music is amusing, or comic, because the wheeziness of the bassoon is funny and because the melody imitates the "structure" of a funny movement (one *must* move in an amusing way to that melody). Moreover, although Grandfather himself is funny, he is definitely not witty. What is comical, amusing, or funny is not always witty. To be witty is generally to make, say, or do something comical, amusing, or funny "on purpose." That is why Prokoviev's musical *portrayal* of a comical grandfather is witty. Similar analyses of the Breughel painting, the Wordsworth poem and the Cage music mentioned previously could obviously be carried out. But the point, I take it, is already sufficiently well made.

The second interpretation of the hypothetical attack on the importance of artistic acts borrows any initial plausibility it possesses from the fact that anthropomorphic descriptions of artistic acts can be "explained" or "justified" in terms which neither mention artistic acts nor use any of the terms which describe them. For example, one might point out the irony in the Breughel painting discussed above by noting the combination of the gay scene and the dull faces of its participants. Or one might justify the "aloofness" he sees in the Poussin by remarking on the cold light, clear lines, and statuesque poses in a scene of violence and turmoil. And in discussing the impersonality of *Variations II* it is necessary to mention that the Cage work sounds like accidentally produced noise, which is senseless and emotionally neutral, but that this noise-like sound is to all *other* appearances music, i.e. it is scored, it is performed on a musical instrument, it is even reproduced on recordings. From these facts about the way in which anthropomorphic descriptions are justified, it might seem plausible that the statements which figure in the justification *entail* the original description. But such is not the case, as the following will show.

It has been suggested that the reason that Breughel's peasant faces are dull and stupid-looking is that the painter was simply unable to paint faces which were happy. Whether the suggestion is true or well supported by the evidence is not an issue here. What is important is that were there any reason for believing Breughel to have been incompetent in that way, then there might be (not necessarily "would be") that much less reason for believing that there is irony in Breughel's *Wedding Dance*. That is because Breughel's incompetence and Breughel's irony *can* in this case function as mutually exclusive ways of accounting for a "discrepancy" in the picture. Of course, there are ways of admitting both the incompetence and the irony. It is possible to suppose, for example, that Breughel used his particular incompetence in making an ironic "statement" about peasant existence. Such a supposition would imply that Breughel was aware of his limitation and made use of it in his work. However, were it *known* that the *only* reason for the discrepancy in the painting was Breughel's incompetence, the "irony" would disappear. It makes no difference, incidentally, that such a thing could probably *never* be known. I am making a logical point regarding the way an attribution of a certain sort to an "artistic act" relates to other aspects of a painting like the Breughel. In short, certain facts about the painting's subject matter do indeed "ground" the attribution but by no means logically entail that attribution. And that is so for the good reason that the same facts about the subject matter are consistent with a supposition about Breughel which might be incompatible with the description of the painting as ironic.

A similar point can be illustrated in Poussin's Sabine painting. In that work there is a discrepancy between the violent scene, on the one hand, and the "still," clear figures, on the other. Two persons might agree about the character of the figures and the character of the depicted scene, however, and yet disagree whether these facts entail that Poussin painted the rape of the Sabines in an aloof, reserved way. One viewer might think simply that the work is incoherent, that Poussin's coldly classical means are not suited to the end he had in mind, namely, to depict the violence of the event. In this quite reasonable view, the discrepancy makes the painting "fall apart" rather than "add up" to an aloof and reserved point of view. Here then are two incompatible descriptions of a work which are equally well grounded on facts which allegedly "entail" one of the descriptions. I am mindful that it might be objected that there are other features of the Sabine painting than the ones mentioned which preclude the judgment of "incoherence" and necessitate the judgment of "aloofness." The best I can say is that there seem to me to be no such additional features contributing to the "aloofness" of the painting and that the burden of proof is upon those who disagree.[10]

Finally, let us suppose that a devoted listener of traditional Western music scoffs at the description of Cage's *Variations II* as "impersonal music." He insists that it is nothing but what it sounds like – meaningless noise. He charges that Cage is a fraud whose "music" is a gigantic hoax, a put-on, and that Cage is laughing up his sleeve at those who take him seriously, perform his "scores," record the performances, and listen gravely to his nonsense. He has, the traditional listener says, read some of Cage's "ideological" material relating, to his "music" but he has noted how laden with irony it is. To him that shows that Cage is not to be taken seriously because he does not take himself seriously. Now such a doubter does not disagree with the description of *Variations II* which is used to justify calling it "impersonal." The disagreement concerns rather the way we are to assess John Cage. Are we to judge him to be a responsible and serious, albeit radically innovative, composer of music or not? It is only when Cage's seriousness is assumed that the term "impersonality" applies to his music. Otherwise, the aforementioned justification for calling it impersonal is equally justification for calling it nonsense.

What the above three cases demonstrate is that a true anthropomorphic description of an artistic act might presuppose conditions having nothing necessarily to do with the way the formal elements and/or subject matter are describable. The conditions mentioned are (1) the competence of the artist, (2) the coherence of the work, (3) the seriousness of the artist. But there are surely other examples which would bring light to other conditions of this sort. With sufficient ingenuity one could likely discover and/or construct examples of art in which anthropomorphic descriptions of artistic acts would or would not be applicable depending upon how one assessed the artist with respect to, say, his maturity, his sanity, his self-consciousness, his sensitivity, or his intelligence.

Now it is probably too rigid to regard "competence," "coherence," "seriousness," "maturity," "sanity," and the rest as denoting necessary *conditions* for the legitimate description of all artistic arts. It is probably not true that the artist *must* be serious, competent, sane, etc., and that the work *must* be coherent in order for any anthropomorphic description (of an artistic act) to apply to any work. What these terms should be taken as denoting are "parameters" according to which an artist or a work can be measured in whatever respect is relevant in a particular case. To do so would be to admit that there is probably not a single set of particular conditions of these sorts presupposed in *all* descriptions of artistic acts. Naming these parameters simply points out the *sorts* of considerations which *might* be relevant in particular descriptions of artistic acts, leaving it an open question which of these parameters are relevant, and to what degree, in particular cases.

In any event, what the recognition of such parameters means is that any attempt to save the Canonical Position by "eliminating" descriptions of artistic acts in favor of "logically equivalent" descriptions of formal elements and/or represented subject matter is doomed to fail. For the description of artistic acts in anthropomorphic terms does presuppose something about the artist which cannot be known *simply* by attending to his art. A similar point holds with respect to common expressions. The look of a sullen pout on a person's face does not mean that the person is pouting sullenly if we discover that the look results from the natural lay of his face. And thus it is that no description simply of the configuration of the person's face can *entail* the statement that the person is pouting sullenly.

But it is equally true that the assertion that a person is pouting sullenly is incompatible with the claim that the person's face has the same configuration as it does when he is not pouting sullenly. The sullen pout *must* make a difference visible on the face. Analogously, for an anthropomorphic predicate of an artistic act to be applicable to a work of art there *must* be *some* features of the material elements and/or the subject of the work which *justify* the attribution of the term, even though they do not *entail* that attribution. One thing, however, is never presupposed or implied when an anthropomorphic predicate is truly applied to a work, namely, that the predicate is truly applicable to the *artist*. In this, too, works of art are like expressions.

Notes

1 Cf. Monroe Beardsley, *Aesthetics: Problems in the Philosophy of Criticism* (New York: Harcourt, Brace, 1958), pp. 321–32; and O. K. Bouwsma, "The Expression Theory of Art," in *Philosophical Analysis*, ed. Max Black (Ithaca: Cornell University Press, 1950), pp. 75–101.

2 *The Encyclopedia of Philosophy*, ed. Paul Edwards (New York: Macmillan and The Free Press, 1967), I, 47.

3 I hope it is clear that throughout this discussion the emphasis is on "natural," not on "object." But I will, for convenience, use the terms "object" and "thing" to cover non-objects and non-things as well.

4 Nor are they "virtual," i.e. unreal, acts, as I have maintained in another place. Cf. my "Perceptual Acts and Pictorial Art: A Defense of Expression Theory," *Journal of Philosophy*. LXII (1965), 669–77. Giving these acts a separate and unusual metaphysical status not only complicates the universe needlessly, it is unfaithful to the commonsense facts of the situation. There are no good reasons to deny what our ways of talking implicitly affirm, namely, that "artistic acts," perceptual and otherwise, are "acts" of the artist.

5 Of course it is true that sometimes when anthropomorphic terms are predicated of art works, they apply to subject matters and to "material" aspects of the work such as lines, colors, sounds, masses, etc., as well as to "artistic acts." My point above is only that anthropomorphic adjectives may be applied to a work only in virtue of an artistic act, in which case it is, without change of meaning, immediately applicable in adverbial form to that act.

6 It is no objection to this assertion that in virtue of the natural lay of their faces some people have perpetual "smiles," "smirks," "pouts," etc., on their faces even when they do not smile, smirk, or pout. Of course, a "smile" of this sort is different from a smile; that is what the scare quotes signify. But even though a person with such a "smile" on his face is not thereby smiling, he is, significantly, "smiling."

7 Nelson Goodman's recent theory of expression seems to depend rather heavily on the opinion

that such uses of anthropomorphic predicates are metaphorical. As far as I can tell, however, Goodman merely asserts and does not argue for this opinion. Nor does he offer anything more than the briefest sketch of a theory of metaphor, which could be used to support his assertion. See his *Languages of Art: An Approach to a Theory of Symbols* (Indianapolis: Bobbs-Merrill, 1968), pp. 50–1, 80–95.

8 Beardsley, *Aesthetics*, pp. 80ff.

9 Ibid. p. 332.

10 These statements commit me to the position that a positive judgment about the Poussin cannot be deduced from any descriptions of the painting of the sort which "ground" its aloofness. For arguments in favor of this general position see my "Subjectivity and Justification in Aesthetic Judgments," *Journal of Aesthetics and Art Criticism*, XXVII (1968), 3–12.

52

Style and Personality in the Literary Work

Jenefer Robinson

Jenefer Robinson is Professor of Philosophy at the University of Cincinnati.

Introduction

In this paper I want to describe and defend a certain conception of literary style. If we look at literary style in the way I shall suggest, it will explain many of the problems that surround this elusive concept such as why something can be an element of style in the work of one author and not in another, what the difference is between individual style and general style, and how style differs from "signature." The ordinary conception of style is that it consists of nothing but a set of verbal elements such as a certain kind of vocabulary, imagery, sentence structure and so on. On my conception, however, a literary style is rather a way of *doing* certain things, such as describing characters, commenting on the action and manipulating the plot. I shall claim that an author's way of doing these things is an expression of her personality, or, more accurately, of the personality she seems to have. The verbal elements of style gain their stylistic significance by contributing to the expression of this personality, and they cannot be identified as *stylistic* elements independently of the personality they help to express.

Jenefer Robinson, "Style and Personality in the Literary Work," *Philosophical Review*, 94/2 (1985): 227–47.

Many theorists and critics have written as if style were an expression of personality. A good recent example is an essay on the first paragraph of Henry James' novel *The Ambassadors*, in which the writer, Ian Watt, claims that

> the most obvious and demonstrable features of James' prose style, its vocabulary and syntax, are direct reflections of his attitude to life and his conception of the novel . . .[1]

Watt lists some of the most notable elements in James' style: the preference for "non-transitive" verbs, the widespread use of abstract nouns, the prevalence of the word "that," the presence of "elegant yariation" in the way in which something is referred to, and the predominance of negatives and near-negatives. Then Watt proceeds to show how these stylistic elements are expressive of James' *interest* in the abstract, his *preoccupation* with what is going on in the consciousness of his characters and his *attitude* of humorous compassion for them.

This essay is an attempt to explain and justify the assumption of Watt and others like him that style is essentially an expression of qualities of mind, attitudes, interests and personality traits which appear to be the author's own. My thesis is a thesis about what Richard Wollheim calls "individual style" and not about the style of periods or of groups of writers within a period.[2] I do not want to suggest that the unity of period or group styles, such as the Augustan style, can be explained in terms of the "personality" of a group or period. One other point should be mentioned. I believe that my remarks apply equally well to the non-literary arts, but for reasons of space I shall not attempt to justify this claim here.

I Style as the Expression of Personality

In this first section I shall argue that style is essentially a way of doing something and that it is expressive of personality. Further, I shall suggest that what count as the verbal elements of style are precisely those elements which contribute to the expression of personality.

Intuitively, my style of dress, work, speech, decision-making and so on is the mode or manner or way in which I dress, work, speak and make decisions. In short it is the way I *do* these things. In ordinary contexts, then, a style is always a way of *doing* something. No less intuitively, my style of dressing, working, speaking and making decisions is typically an *expression* of (some features of) my personality, character, mind or sensibility. Thus my vulgar way of dressing is likely to be an expression of my vulgar sensibility, my witty, intellectual way of speaking an expression of my witty, intellectual mind, and my uncompromisingly courageous way of making decisions an expression of my uncompromisingly courageous character.

In saying that a person's way of doing things is an *expression* of that person's traits of mind, character or personality, I am saying (1) that the person's way of doing things exhibits or manifests these traits, and (2) that it is these traits which cause the person to do things in the way they do. Thus these traits leave a matching imprint or trace upon the actions which express them. If my timid way of behaving at parties is an expression of my timid character, then (1) my behavior exhibits or manifests timidity – I behave in a manifestly timid fashion, blushing, refusing to talk to strangers, hiding in the washrooms, etc. – and (2) my timid behavior is caused by my timid character, i.e., it is not due to the fact that (say) I am pretending to be timid, imitating a timid person or acting the part of a timid person in a play, nor is it the result of secret arrogance and contempt for parties. In general, if a person's actions are an expression of her personality, then those actions have the character that they have – compassionate, timid, courageous or whatever – in virtue of the fact that they are caused by the corresponding trait of mind or character in that person, compassion, timidity or courage. In expression, as the word itself suggests, an "inner" state is expressed or forced out into "outer" behavior. An "inner" quality of mind, character or personality causes the "outer" behavior to be the way it is, and also leaves its "trace" upon that behavior. A timid or compassionate character leaves a "trace" of timidity or compassion upon the actions which express it.[3]

Just as a person's style of dressing, working and speaking is the mode or manner or way in which she dresses, works and speaks, so an author's style of description, character delineation and treatment of a theme is the mode or manner or way in which she describes things, delineates character and treats her theme. In other words, it is her way of *doing* certain things, such as describing or characterizing a setting, delineating character, treating or presenting a theme, and commenting on the action. Moreover, the writer's way of describing, delineating, commenting and so on is typically an *expression* of (some features of) her personality, character, mind or sensibility. Thus James' humorous yet compassionate way of describing Strether's bewilderment expresses the writer's own humorous yet compassionate attitude. Jane Austen's ironic way of describing social pretension expresses her ironic attitude to social pretension.

Now, a style is not simply a way of doing something. We do not say that a person has a *style* of doing so-and-so unless that person does so-and-so in a relatively consistent fashion. Thus we say I have a vulgar and flamboyant *style* of dressing only if I consistently dress in a vulgar and flamboyant way. It may be, of course, that my way of dressing differs considerably from one day to the next: yesterday I wore a purple silk pyjama suit, today I am wearing a frilly scarlet mini-dress and tomorrow it will be leather dungarees and a transparent blouse. Despite these differences, however, we still say that I have a consistent way of dressing, because all my outfits are consistently vulgar and flamboyant. Moreover, my style of dressing is expressive of a particular feature of my personality, namely vulgarity and flamboyance. In an exactly similar way, we say that Jane Austen has a *style* of describing social pretension, because she consistently describes social pretension in an *ironic* way and the way she describes social pretension is expressive of a particular feature of her outlook, namely her irony.

So far I have talked only about a person's style of doing a particular thing, such as dressing. By contrast, when we say that a person has "a style," we normally mean that he or she has the same style of doing a number of different things. Thus when we accuse John of having a vulgar and flamboyant style, we may be referring to the vulgar and flamboyant way in which John not only dresses but also talks and entertains his dinner guests. Again, in characterizing Mary's style as generous, open, casual and easy-going, we may mean that Mary is generous, open, casual and easy-going in almost everything that she does. In this case Mary's style is expressive not of a single trait but of a number of traits which together 'sum up' Mary's personality.

In just the same way, a person's literary style is their style of performing a wide range of (literary) activities. Thus, clearly, Jane Austen's style is not simply her style of doing any one thing, such as describing social pretention, but rather her style of doing a number of things, such as *describing, portraying* and *treating* her characters, theme and social setting, *commenting* on the action, *presenting* various points of view, and so on. In short, to borrow a concept from Guy Sircello, it is the way in which she performs the various "artistic acts"[4] which constitute the writing of a literary work. Now, a style of doing a wide range of things is just like a style of doing a particular thing in that it consistently expresses certain features of the mind, personality, etc., of the agent. We say that Mary has "a style" in virtue of the consistently generous, open, casual and easy-going way in which she does a number of different things. Similarly, a writer has a literary style in virtue of the fact that her style of performing a wide variety of artistic acts expresses the same qualities of (her) mind and temperament. For example, James' style of *treating* Strether, of *portraying* the difference between what Strether thinks of Waymarsh and what he thinks he thinks, of *emphasizing* the abstract and the timeless, of *commenting* on Strether's bewilderment and so on together constitute what we call "James' style." And this style owes its coherence to the fact that all these artistic acts express the same set of attitudes, interests and qualities of mind.

Of course, not every artistic act of a writer in a particular work expresses exactly the same qualities of mind, character or personality. In *Emma*, for example, Jane Austen portrays Mrs. Elton in a quite different way from Jane Fairfax. This is because Jane Austen's attitude to Mrs. Elton is quite different from her attitude to Jane Fairfax. In the one portrayal she expresses (among other things) her love of the ridiculous, and in the other she expresses (among other things) her compassion for suffering sensibility. But Jane Austen's way of portraying Mrs. Elton and her way of portraying Jane Fairfax, as well as her way of portraying the other characters in the novel, her way of describing their personal relationships, her way of developing the plot, and all the other innumerable artistic acts which go into writing the novel *Emma* together add up to the style in which *Emma* is written, a style which expresses all those attitudes that together form the personality of the author of *Emma*.

If a writer has an individual style, then the way she writes has a certain consistency: the same traits of mind, character and personality are expressed throughout her work. Now, at a particular point in a novel, the writer may seem to express anxiety about, anger at or contempt towards a particular character, event or idea, although the writer does not seem to be a chronically anxious, angry or contemptuous sort of person. However, such "occasional" properties should not be thought of as properties of style. Only those properties which are "standing" or long-term properties can be considered stylistic. Thus stylistic qualities are likely to be qualities of mind, moral qualities and deep-seated character traits, rather than mood or emotional qualities such as "angry," "joyful," and "afraid." In the same way, we do not treat every angry, joyful or fearful action performed in real life as an expression of basic character or personality; it is only when someone consistently acts in a choleric or a cheerful way, that we infer to her essentially choleric or cheerful nature.

I have argued that a literary style is a way of performing "artistic acts," describing a setting, portraying character, manipulating plot and so on, and it is the writer's way of performing these acts which is expressive of all those standing traits, attitudes, qualities of mind and so on that together form her personality. What, then, is the relation between the performance of these acts and what have traditionally been thought of as the verbal elements of style, such as a certain vocabulary, imagery and sentence structure? When a writer describes a setting and portrays character, she uses words, and the kind of word she uses, the sort of sentence structure she forms and so on together constitute the elements of verbal style. If a writer manipulates his theme from the point of view of one whose main interest is in thought and the development of consciousness (James) or if she portrays her characters with a judicious mixture of irony and compassion (Austen), then he or she does so by using language in certain ways.

Obviously the presence of certain verbal elements does not *entail* that a particular personality is being expressed.[5] If, however, (on a reasonable interpretation) those verbal elements are being used by a writer to perform artistic acts in a particular way, then we can infer from the way the acts are performed to characteristics of the writer's mind, character and personality. For example, Henry James uses negatives, abstract nouns, etc., in order to describe Strether's state of consciousness, to comment on Strether's bewilderment and to characterize Strether's attitude to Waymarsh, and he thereby expresses qualities of his own mind and personality.

Moreover, negatives, abstract nouns, non-transitive verbs, elegant variation and so on are verbal elements which at first sight seem to have nothing in common. What links them all together, however, as elements of "James' style" is their use in the artistic acts James performs: they are all elements of his style because they all contribute to the expression of his personality and attitudes. For example, using these particular verbal elements, James thereby describes Strether's state of consciousness in a particular judicious, abstractive, expository way and thereby expresses his own "subjective and abstractive tendency,"[6] his interest in the relations between minds (Strether's, the narrator's, the reader's), his moral sensitivity and his cool and judicious intellect.

II The Personality of the Implied Author

So far in this essay I have written as if the personality expressed by the style of a work were that of the writer herself. I have suggested that we infer from the way in which the writer performs the artistic acts in a work to the presence of personality traits and so on *in the writer* which cause her to perform those acts in the way that she does. But this is an oversimplification. What is more typically expressed by the style of a work is not the personality of the actual author, but of what, following Wayne Booth, we might call the "implied author,"[7] that is, the author as she seems to be from the evidence of the work. Thus however querulous and intolerant the actual Tolstoy may have been in real life, the implied author of *Anna Karenina* is full of compassionate understanding.

Because the way in which people act typically expresses features of their minds, attitudes and personalities, we are justified in making inferences from the way in which people perform actions to the presence in them of certain character or personality traits. If we see Mary constantly acting in a generous and compassionate way, then, barring any evidence to the contrary, it is reasonable to infer that Mary has a generous and compassionate nature which is responsible for her generous and compassionate actions.[8] The situation is more complicated, however, when we are considering acts performed by an author in the composition of a literary work. Although it may sometimes be legitimate to infer from the way these acts are performed to personality traits in the actual author, it is normally the case that the personality expressed by the style of a literary work is not that of the actual author but that of the implied author.

This might sound as if the author were trying to mislead us. After all if in real life it turns out that Mary's generous and compassionate actions are entirely due to her desire to impress John, then we might well accuse her of deceiving us – or at least John – about her true nature. She seems to be a generous and compassionate person but in fact is not. However, the situation is significantly different in the literary case. It is, after all, a commonplace convention of fiction-writing that the author more or less consciously "puts on" or "adopts" a persona to tell "her" story, but normally at any rate the author is not thereby trying to deceive us into believing that this assumed persona or personality is her own.[9] When we make inferences from the way the artistic acts in a work are performed to the personality of this implied author, the "person" who seems to be performing these acts, we are aware that the personality which leaves its "trace" on the way those acts are performed is a personality created and adopted by the author and which may be different from that of the author herself.[10] Thus, as Booth points out, even the implied author of *Emma* does not have all her qualities in common with the real Jane Austen. Both are wise, witty, unsentimental and so on, but the implied author of *Emma* has a moral perfection beyond the scope of the real Jane Austen.[11]

Some literary works deliberately exploit a number of different styles. A good example is James Joyce's *Ulysses*. In this case the style of at least some of the different episodes of the book should be identified with the style not of the implied author "James Joyce" but of the narrator of that episode. The personality expressed by the style of the Cyclops episode, for example, is not the personality which the author seems to have; the coarse and unpleasant personality expressed belongs only to the nameless narrator of the episode. Notice, however, that this kind of case is parasitic upon the normal case: it is because a style is normally an expression of the personality of the writer that we infer from the style of the Cyclops episode to the presence of a coarse and unpleasant person writing or narrating it.[12]

Does it make sense to talk about "the style" of *Ulysses*? In a way it does not, because *Ulysses* contains so many different styles (some of which are not even "individual" styles).[13] Nevertheless, we can identify an implied author of *Ulysses* and detect the way in which he appears to *manipulate* the narrative point of view, *treat* the *Ulysses* theme, *characterize* Molly Bloom, etc. The way these artistic acts are performed is part of *the style of Ulysses*. For example, the presence of many different narrators with different styles is itself a feature of *Joyce's* style and it is expressive of certain traits that Joyce seems to have, such as a boisterous creativity, a delight in the expressive capacities of language and an interest in the way reality can be viewed and reported from so many different points of view.[14]

One of the ways in which we identify "Joyce's style" is by looking at Joyce's oeuvre as a whole. Thus we may be inclined to see the style of the early Stephen episodes in *Ulysses* (as opposed to, say, the Cyclops episode) as in "Joyce's style" partly because they are in somewhat the same style as other works by Joyce, notably *A Portrait of the Artist*. The style of an oeuvre, just like the style of an individual work, is an expression of the personality of the implied author of that oeuvre. Just as we sometimes find a variety of styles in a single work (like *Ulysses*), so it is possible to find in a single oeuvre a variety of styles corresponding to radically different implied authors. But in the normal case the implied author of different works in a single oeuvre is recognizably the "same person." Of course no two works do or even can express exactly the same personality, but there will normally be striking similarities. Typically, the personality expressed by an author's style matures over time. Thus the implied author of Jane Austen's books becomes less acerbic in her wit, more compassionate and tender;[15] the implied author of Henry James' works becomes ever more complex, subtle and abstract in his thinking and moralizing. A style grows and matures with the personality it expresses.

III An Objection Considered

My thesis has been that the defining feature of a literary work which has an individual style is that the work is an expression of the personality of the implied author,[16] and that what links the diverse verbal elements of style together into a coherent whole is that they all contribute to the expression of this particular personality. One objection to this thesis is that there are many qualities of a work which *prima facie* are qualities of its style but which do not seem to express any qualities of mind or personality in the implied author. In particular, there are formal qualities (euphonious, Latinate, colloquial, ornate) and expressive qualities (dramatic, heroic, violent) which may be attributed to the style of a work but which are not (or need not be) qualities of the implied author's mind or personality.

In this section of the paper I shall argue that such formal and expressive qualities are not always qualities of the individual style of a work, and that when they are it is only because they contribute to the expression of qualities of mind, personality, etc. in the implied author. Among works which possess striking formal or expressive qualities (euphony, violence, etc.), I distinguish three sorts of case: (1) works which have such properties but lack style altogether, (2) works which have such properties and also belong to a general style category but which lack individual style, and (3) works which have such properties and which also possess individual style.

(1) Intuitively, there could be a piece of characterless prose which nevertheless happens to be *euphonious*, i.e., the words it contains make a pleasing musical sound. Imagine, for example, an incompetent Freshman English paper in which the ideas are unclearly expressed, the sentence structure confused and the choice of words unimaginative. No one reading the paper would attribute to it an individual style. Yet, quite by chance, the ill-chosen words are euphonious: l's, m's and n's predominate, there are only a few plosives or fricatives, and the vowel sounds fit together in a melodious way. To say that this work is in a "euphonious style," however, is at best misleading, since intuitively it is not in a style at all. The possession of just one striking formal quality, such as euphony, is not normally sufficient to endow a work with style. Indeed even a string of nonsense syllables may be euphonious, although presumably they cannot be in a style. Hence euphony does not always contribute to individual style, just because it may be a quality of a work that lacks style altogether. On my view, of course, a euphonious work that lacks individual style is a euphonious work which fails to express any individual personality in the implied author.

(2) A more interesting situation arises when a work is in a "euphonious style" in the sense that it belongs to what Wollheim calls a "general" style category, although it does not possess *individual* style. General style categories, such as period or school styles, group together writers, painters or other artists who seem to the critic and historian to have important characteristics in common, for example, the Elizabethan pastoral lyric style or the style of the school of Donne (the Metaphysical style). To belong to a general category of literary style often involves obeying certain conventions and using certain techniques. Thus the style of Elizabethan pastoral love lyrics demands a certain stylized way of referring to the lover and the beloved, of describing their surroundings and so on. The imagery and the poetic forms employed all fall within a fairly narrow and predictable range. More importantly for my present argument, membership in a particular general style category often requires a work to have certain formal and expressive qualities. Thus the style of an Elizabethan pastoral love lyric is supposed to be charming and euphonious, the Metaphysical style colloquial and dramatic, and the Miltonic epic style (i.e., the style of works which imitate *Paradise Lost*) Latinate and heroic.

Now, intuitively, there is a distinction between merely belonging to a general style category and having a formed individual style. For example, although a poem must be (somewhat) colloquial and (somewhat) dramatic in order to count as a Metaphysical poem at all, it does not follow that every minor lyric by Carew or Suckling has an individual style. Indeed we may often be hard-pressed to distinguish between the lesser works of Carew and Suckling, just because they do lack "individuality." Similarly, many of the poems in the collection *England's Helicon* obey all the requirements of the Elizabethan pastoral lyric style and yet remain "characterless." They are charming and euphonious but they have an anonymous air about them: they do not seem to have been written by anyone in particular. In short, a work which belongs to a general style category may have certain striking formal or expressive qualities even though it lacks individual style. An Elizabethan love lyric may be euphonious, a Metaphysical poem dramatic, a Miltonic epic Latinate without necessarily being in an individual style.

One of the merits of my theory of style is that it allows us to define and explain this intuitive distinction between individual and general style. On my view, the crucial difference is that whereas having an individual style necessarily involves the expression of personality in the implied author, belonging to a general style category has no such implications. Elsewhere[17] I have argued for this position in much greater detail than is either possible or appropriate here. If I am right, however, it follows that there can be works belonging to a general style category which possess the formal and expressive qualities characteristic of that style but which do not express any individual personality in the implied author. Hence these formal and expressive qualities, although qualities of general style, do not contribute to any individual style in the work just because they do not contribute to the expression of an individual personality in the implied author of the work.

(3) Finally, formal and expressive qualities such as "Latinate," "euphonious" and "dramatic" may be qualities that are present in works of individual style and which do contribute to the expression of personality in those works. It does not follow, however, that the implied author is a Latinate, euphonious or dramatic sort of fellow. These qualities in themselves do not express any particular trait in the implied author. Rather they can help to express many diverse traits, depending upon the artistic acts to which they contribute. In a similar way, Henry James' fondness for negatives does not in itself express any feature of "his" personality; it is the way the negatives are used in the performance of artistic acts, such as describing Strether's state of mind, which gives this feature of James' work its stylistic significance.

The quality of euphony, for example, may indeed contribute to individual style, but it does so by contributing to the expression of individual personality in a work. Consequently the contribution it makes is very different in different works. Both Swinburne's "Garden of Proserpine" and large passages of Milton's "Paradise Lost" can be described as euphonious, but the personalities expressed in the individual style of these two works are very different. In the Swinburne poem the gentle, musical sounds help to express the implied author's sense of world-weariness, melancholy and resignation,[18] whereas the famous Miltonic melody generally serves to help express the implied author's sense of the dignity and grandeur of his theme. To say that both works are in a "euphonious style" means simply that euphony is a formal quality of both works, which in both cases contributes to individual style. The way it contributes, however, is quite different in the two cases. Similarly it could be argued that both Jane Austen and Donne have *dramatic* styles, but clearly the dramatic qualities in each help to express quite different personalities and hence contribute quite differently to the styles of each.[19]

In summary then, the formal and expressive qualities I have been discussing are not always qualities of the individual style of a work: they may be present in works lacking any style at all or in works which belong to a general style category but do not have individual style. Moreover, even when such qualities contribute to the individual style of a work, they do so in very different ways. The 'same' quality in two different works may contribute to the expression of quite different traits of mind and personality in the implied authors of those works.

There are two interesting corollaries of my discussion. First, it would seem to follow that no verbal element or formal or expressive quality in a work is always and inevitably an element or quality of individual style. Even such qualities as "euphonious" and "Latinate" do not contribute to individual style wherever they appear, and even when they do contribute to individual style, they do so in virtue of how they are used in the artistic acts in the work. Secondly, it would also seem to follow that *any* verbal element or formal or expressive quality in a work *can* be an element or quality of individual style, provided it contributes in the appropriate way to the expression of personality in the implied author.

In short, if my thesis is correct, then there is no "taxonomy" or checklist of style elements, that is, elements which contribute to individual style wherever they appear.[20] Euphony, Latinate diction, and the presence of many negatives are elements of individual style only if they are used in such a way as to contribute to the expression of traits of mind and personality in the implied author.

We cannot, therefore, identify the elements of individual style merely as the most striking or salient features of a work. On the one hand there are striking features which do not invariably contribute to individual style. I have argued that euphony, for example, may be a striking feature of works which lack individual style. Again, it would be a striking feature of a work if all the proper names in it began with the letter

'X', yet intuitively this would not be a feature of its *style* (although it could be if, for example, it were used to express the implied author's sense of fun).

On the other hand, moreover, there are many elements which are not particularly salient but which contribute to individual style. Thus a certain writer who has a formed individual style may have a preference for the indefinite article over the definite which contributes in a small way to the expression of her generalizing imagination and tendency to abstraction. Again, any careful, sensitive reader of *The Ambassadors* can tell that James tends to "interpolate" elements in his sentences, but we may not notice that the interpolations typically occur between verb or adjective and complement, or between auxiliary and main verb, and that they cluster towards the center of a sentence.[21] Yet it is non-salient elements such as these which contribute significantly to James' style, because they all help to express "James'" characteristic attitudes, interests and qualities of mind and personality.

IV Some Problems Resolved

I have argued that if a literary work has an individual style, the artistic acts in the work are performed in such a way as to express qualities of mind, attitudes, personality traits, etc., which make up the individual personality of the implied author of the work. The verbal elements of (individual) style are those elements which contribute to the expression of this personality. There is no "checklist" of elements or qualities which inherently or intrinsically contribute to individual style, no matter where they appear.

So far I have merely tried to make my thesis seem reasonable and to forestall some possible objections to it. In this final section I should like to make some more positive remarks in its favor. The best reason for accepting my theory is that it answers an array of difficult questions surrounding the concept of style.

(1) First, my theory explains why a correct description of a writer's style mentions some of its verbal characteristics but not others. On my view, what count as the elements of a style are precisely those verbal elements which contribute to the expression of the implied author's personality. In Henry James, for example, the relevant verbal elements include the recurrent use of non-transitive verbs, abstract nouns, negatives and the word 'that'. These all help to contribute to the expression of "James'" personality. But we could, no doubt, if we searched for them, discover many recurrent elements in James' work which are not stylistically significant. Thus perhaps it would turn out that James had a penchant for nouns beginning with the letter 'f' or that his sentences invariably had an even number of words in them. A description of James' style would not mention these elements, however, precisely because they do not contribute to the expression of the personality of the implied author. In short, many quite diverse and seemingly unrelated verbal elements belong to the same style in virtue of the fact that they all contribute to the expression of the same personality. It is only if the frequent use of nouns beginning with the letter 'f' can be shown to contribute to this personality that this particular verbal characteristic would be an element of style.

(2) For similar reasons, my theory explains why it is that the same verbal element may have stylistic significance in one work or author and no stylistic significance, or a different significance, in another work or author. For the same stylistic element may play no expressive role in the one case and an important role in the other. Alternatively, it may simply play different expressive roles in the two cases. Suppose, for example, that two writers tend to use the indefinite article rather than the definite. In one writer, who has a formed individual style, this may contribute to the expression of her generalizing imagination and tendency to abstraction. In the other writer, it may be an accident and it may have no expressive effect in the work, or perhaps it indicates a lack of strength and precision in the style. In the first writer we have located the presence of a stylistic element; in the second writer the same element has no stylistic significance or a different one. If we were to view a person's style as consisting of a set of elements which we can check off on a checklist, then it would make no sense to say that a particular element is sometimes stylistic and sometimes not. But if we view style as a function of the literary personality expressed by a work in the way I have suggested, then the problem dissolves.

(3) It is commonly believed that if a writer or a work has an individual style, this implies that the various stylistic elements have a certain unity. Yet there are no intrinsic connections among the features of James' style, for example: why should negatives, abstract nouns and 'elegant variation' go together to form a unified style? My theory explains in a clear way what stylistic unity amounts to: a style has a unity because it is the expression of the personality of the implied author. Just as we see the way a person performs the various actions of daily life as expressive of different facets of her personality, so we see the way in which a writer seems to perform the various artistic acts in a literary work as expressive of different facets of "her" personality. The many disparate elements of verbal style fit together only because they are being used to express the "same" personality: the writer uses the elements of verbal style to describe her characters, treat her theme, etc., thereby seeming to reveal a set of personality traits, qualities of mind, attitudes and so forth which "makes sense" out of (unifies) this multitude of artistic acts.

The question arises as to whether this set of "standing" traits forms a coherent personality. The concept of a "unified" or coherent personality is admittedly somewhat vague, since the most disparate and apparently inconsistent psychological traits seem capable of coexisting in normal, rational people.[22] All I need to insist on, however, is that if a work has an individual style then the different traits expressed by the various artistic acts in the work (portraying Jane Fairfax, characterizing Emma's treatment of her father, etc.) coexist in a way which is consistent with our knowledge of persons and human nature. Moreover, the same traits must be consistently expressed throughout a work. Thus the implied author of *Le Rouge et le Noir* both admires and despises the aristocratic world to which Julien Sorel aspires, but because he does so consistently and because the conflict in his attitudes is one which we recognize as possible in a basically rational person, his admiration and scorn are both part of the personality expressed by the style of the work.[23] If however, a work expresses no individual personality at all or if the personality expressed is a confusion of different traits which do not fit together in an intelligible way, then it follows from my thesis that the work in question lacks individual style.[24]

(4) It used to be a commonplace of literary theory that the subject-matter of a text is *what* the writer writes about, whereas the style is *how* she writes about it. This distinction has recently been questioned by several writers, including Nelson Goodman who argues that

> some differences in style consist entirely of differences in what is said. Suppose one historian writes in terms of military conflicts, another in terms of social changes; or suppose one biographer stresses public careers, another personalities.[25]

The theory of style which I have outlined in this essay accounts for the intuition that sometimes features of subject-matter may be stylistic features and explains which features of subject-matter will count as stylistic and why. Briefly, a feature of subject-matter is of stylistic relevance just in case it is expressive of the implied author's personality. Thus it is reasonable to construe the subject-matter of *The Ambassadors* as the development of Strether's consciousness. In this case the choice of subject-matter is clearly of stylistic relevance. Again the differences in the histories and biographies envisioned by Goodman are clearly differences in the personalities of the implied authors of these works.

(5) My theory also has a satisfying explanation for the difference between what Goodman calls "style" and "signature." A "signature" is anything which identifies a work as being by a particular author, school, or whatever, such as an actual signiture. A "signature," however, may have no stylistic significance. Goodman says:

> Although a style is metaphorically a signature, a literal signature is no feature of style.[26]

It is true that a style, like a "signature," may *identify* a work or an author, but the way it performs the identification is quite different. A "signature" may have nothing to do with the qualities of the implied author expressed by a work. Perhaps it is an actual signature or perhaps some other convention is used: a writer might be uniquely identifiable by the particular Latin tag which appears at the head of all her books, regardless of their subject-matter or style (if any). A style, on the other hand, identifies a work or an author because it is an expression of a set of attitudes, qualities of mind, character traits and so on which are unique to the implied author of that work or oeuvre.

(6) Finally, as I have already remarked, one of the virtues of my theory is that it allows me to clarify the distinction between general and individual style.[27] If a work belongs to a general style category, then, although it may have formal and expressive qualities that are distinctive of that style, it may nevertheless remain "characterless": no personality "informs" the work. Alternatively, there may be personality traits expressed but they do not seem to belong to any particular individual. The work has an "anonymous" air about it, because the artistic acts are performed in a way which is common to a large number of different writers.[28] By contrast, as I have argued throughout this paper, the defining quality of an individual style is that it expresses a coherent set of attitudes, qualities of mind and so on which seem to belong to the individual writer of the work: a work which has an individual style expresses the personality of the implied author of that work.

Notes

1 Ian Watt, "The First Paragraph of *The Ambassadors*: An Explication," reprinted in *Henry James*, ed. Tony Tanner (London: Macmillan, 1968), p. 301.

2 See Richard Wollheim, "Pictorial Style: Two Views," in *The Concept of Style*, ed. Berel Lang (Philadelphia: University of Pennsylvania Press, 1979), pp. 129–45. My chief debt in this paper is to Wollheim, whose remark that style has "psychological reality" provided its initial stimulus.

3 See especially Richard Wollheim, "Expression," in Royal Institute of Philosophy Lectures, Vol. I, 1966–7, *The Human Agent* (New York: St. Martin's Press, 1968), and *Art and its Objects* (2nd edition; Cambridge: Cambridge University Press, 1980), sections 15–19. See also Guy Sircello, *Mind and Art* (Princeton: Princeton University Press, 1972).

4 Guy Sircello, *Mind and Art*, Chapter 1. I am not sure whether Sircello would approve of the use to which I put the concept of artistic acts.

5 See Frank Sibley, "Aesthetic Concepts," in *Philosophy Looks at the Arts*, ed. Joseph Margolis (New York: Scribner, 1962), and a large subsequent literature.

6 Watt, "The First Paragraph of *The Ambassadors*," p. 291.

7 Wayne Booth, *The Rhetoric of Fiction* (Chicago: University of Chicago Press, 1961), especially pp. 70–7. Kendall Walton has developed the related, but more general notion of an "apparent artist" in his paper "Points of View in Narrative and Depictive Representation", *Noûs* 10 (1976), pp. 49–61, and elsewhere. Walton's own theory of style, in which the idea of the "apparent artist" plays an important role, is to be found in "Style and the Products and Processes of Art," in *The Concept of Style*, ed. Berel Lang (Philadelphia: University of Pennsylvania Press, 1979).

8 What "having a compassionate nature" means is a large question: presumably at the least it involves having certain beliefs and desires and being prone to certain kinds of behavior. For a discussion of compassion, see Lawrence Blum, "Compassion," in *Explaining Emotions*, ed. Amelie Rorty (Berkeley: University of California Press, 1980).

9 It is not appropriate for me to argue here for any general thesis about the correct way to interpret literary texts, but it is interesting to notice that my view that style is the expression of personality fits very nicely with a plausible theory of critical interpretation recently defended by Alexander Nehamas ("The Postulated Author: Critical Monism as a Regulative Ideal," *Critical Inquiry* 8 (Autumn, 1981), pp. 133–49). In his words,

> To interpret a text is to consider it as its author's production. Literary texts are produced by agents and must be understood as such. . . . And since texts are products of expressive actions, understanding them is inseparably tied to understanding their agents.

Here Nehamas uses the word "author" to mean "implied author." His claim is that a text must be read as an expression of the attitudes and so on of the implied author. Of course it could turn out that Nehamas is wrong and the correct way to read literary texts is as the expression of attitudes in the actual author. My thesis can accommodate either view.

10 Compare the way in which actors "adopt" the personality which they express.

11 See Booth, *The Rhetoric of Fiction*, p. 265.

12 Compare *Tristram Shandy* which is written in Tristram's (the narrator's) style. The implied author seems to have a personality much like that

of Tristram, but he is distinct from Tristram and appears from time to time to correct Tristram's opinions in helpful footnotes.

13 See, for example, *The Oxen of the Sun* episode.

14 Notice that plays can have individual style despite the fact that they contain many different "voices."

15 However, the implied author of the late fragment *The Watsons* may seem less mature than the implied author of *Persuasion.*

16 From now on I shall write as if the personality expressed by the style of a work were that of the implied author, because typically this is the case. However the implied author may sometimes have all his or her properties in common with the actual author. Moreover, as I have already noticed, in some cases the personality expressed is that of the narrator.

17 "General and Individual Style in Literature," *The Journal of Aesthetics and Art Criticism*, 43 (1984), I argue there that if a work belongs to a general style category, such as a school or period style, then it obeys certain rules and observes certain conventions, some of which undoubtedly foster certain kinds of formal and expressive properties. However, it is possible to write works which belong to a general style category and succeed to some extent in achieving the formal and expressive goals of that category without thereby expressing an individual personality in the implied author.

18

There go the loves that wither,
  The old loves with wearier wings;
And all dead years draw thither,
  And all disastrous things; . . .

19 Sometimes a writer performs the artistic act of "expressing" some quality, in the external world, as when she, for example, "expresses" the violence of a battle or the fragility of an elf. Again, however, it is not the violence or fragility themselves which contribute to style, but the way in which violence or fragility is "expressed" (in this sense) by the writer. Thus one woman may "express" the violence of a battle with gusto, thereby expressing "her" enjoyment of fast-moving action and enthusiasm for heroic exploits, whereas another may "express" the violence with cool detachment, thereby expressing "her" ironic awareness of human folly. For further discussion of this issue, see Guy Sircello, *Mind and Art,* Chapter 4, and my "Expressing the Way the World Is," *Journal of Aesthetic Education* 13 (1979), pp. 29–44.

20 Cf. Richard Wollheim, "Pictorial Style: Two Views." It is possible that there are taxonomies for *general* style categories, unlike individual style.

21 See Seymour Chatman, *The Later Style of Henry James* (Oxford: Blackwell, 1972), pp. 126–7. Chatman's book contains many more examples of non-salient (as well as salient) verbal features that are important to James' style. In his comparison between a successful parody of James' style (by Max Beerbohm) and a rather unsuccessful one (by W. H. D. Rouse), Chatman shows how Beerbohm incorporates into his parody many features of James' style which were obviously not salient to Rouse.

22 See the work on emotions by Amelie Rorty, "Explaining Emotions," and Patricia Greenspan, "A Case of Mixed Feelings: Ambivalence and the Logic of Emotion," both in Rorty, ed., *Explaining Emotions.*

23 Lee Brown brought this example to my attention.

24 If for example, *for no apparent reason*, an author describes a certain character with unqualified approval in chapters 1, 3 and 5 and with a certain kind of qualified disapproval in chapters 2, 4 and 6, then it might be that the implied author is schizophrenic or, more likely, simply a confused creation.

25 Nelson Goodman, "The Status of Style," *Critical Inquiry* 1 (1975), p. 801. Goodman's explanation for this fact is different from mine, however.

26 Goodman, "The Status of Style," p. 807.

27 See also my "General and Individual Style in Literature."

28 There are some general style categories such as the heroic epic, in which individual style is rarely found and might even be deemed inappropriate. The Homeric epics, however, do seem to contain passages that have individual style. It is interesting to note that the argument over the authorship of the *Iliad* is partly an argument about style and personality in the work. Those parts of the *Iliad* which have individual style provide a strong argument for scholars who wish to argue that there was one central author of the *Iliad* (call him "Homer") even though parts of it had been handed down by an oral tradition. By contrast, scholars who argue that there were a number of bards who contributed importantly to the creation of the *Iliad* point to the fact that there is no individual style to the *Iliad* as a whole. Interestingly, both sets of experts seem implicitly to grant the connection between individual style and an individual personality

which is expressed in the style. For an introduction to the problem of multiple authorship in the *Iliad*, see E. R. Dodds, "Homer," in *The Language and Background of Homer*, ed. G. S. Kirk (Cambridge: Cambridge University Press, 1964), pp. 1–21.

53

Emotions in the Music

Peter Kivy

Peter Kivy is Board of Governors Professor of Philosophy at Rutgers, the State University of New Jersey.

There has been a growing consensus among philosophers of music that, contrary to the skeptical claims of Hanslick, it makes perfect sense to describe music in expressive terms, and that, again contrary to Hanslick's skeptical claims, there is more or less general agreement, among qualified listeners, as to what the music is expressive of, in any given instance, if, that is, it is expressive of anything (which need not necessarily be the case). More specifically, there has been a growing consensus that music can be, and often is, expressive of the garden-variety emotions, such as sorrow, joy, fear, hope, and a few other basic emotions like these.

As well, the consensus generally is that, when we say a passage of music is sorrowful, or fearful, or the like, we are not describing a disposition of the music to arouse such an emotion in us, but ascribing such an emotion, as a perceived property to the music itself. This way in which the musical emotions are perceived, as, rather, in the music, than in us, with the music as their cause, was well captured by the late American philosopher O. K. Bouwsma, when he quipped that the emotion is more like the redness to the apple than like the burp to the cider.

But this view, though initially appealing, is not without its problems, the most discussed of which is *how* the emotion can be *in* the music. We all understand how an emotion can be 'in' something as a 'disposition.' Sad news is news that makes people sad: the sadness is in the news merely in the sense of a tendency of such news to sadden people. There is no 'metaphysical' problem there: that is, no problem about the nature of the property we are ascribing to the news.

Likewise, we all understand quite well what we are saying when we assert that a person is sad: the sadness is a conscious state of that person; that feeling of depression and lassitude one experiences upon losing a loved one or suffering a great disappointment. Again, there is no 'metaphysical' problem about how a person can possess the 'property' of sadness; what its mode of existence is. Sadness is a conscious state and persons are capable of having conscious states.

But music is not capable of being in conscious states (needless to say), so it can't possess sadness in *that* way. And, since it is the consensus that it doesn't possess the thing as a disposition to make us sad, or, as we have seen, as a representational

Peter Kivy, "Emotions in the Music," in *Introduction to a Philosophy of Music* (Oxford: Oxford University Press, 2002), pp. 31–48.

property that is, as a representation of sadness, how exactly *does* it – the music – possess the sadness? It is all very well to say, with Bouwsma, that it is as the redness to the apple rather than the burp to the cider. However, that does not really answer our question. For, although we have a pretty good idea of how redness 'inheres' in apples and other red things, what we *don't* have is a pretty good idea of how the emotions 'inhere' in the music. Indeed, some people think we don't have any idea at all.

One of the traditional ways philosophers have of dealing with such cases is to try to make an analogy between the problematic case and an unproblematic one that it relevantly resembles. In the present instance, what might make us less uncomfortable with the notion of emotions 'inhering' in music as perceptual properties would be to discover cases in our ordinary experience where we commonly accept as a matter of course the notion of perceptual emotive properties belonging to non-sentient 'objects.'

Such a general argument was advanced by the remarkable American philosopher Charles Hartshorne in his highly original book *The Philosophy and Psychology of Sensation* (1934), many years before the problem emerged decisively for contemporary philosophy of music. Hartshorne adduced the common phenomenon of the emotive tone of colors to illustrate the point that emotions can be part of our perceptual field in perfectly ordinary circumstances well known to us all. Thus, he pointed out, yellow is a 'cheerful' color, not because it makes us cheerful but because its cheerfulness just *is* a part of its perceived quality, inseparable from its yellowness. That's just how we perceive yellow. In the same vein, he instanced other colors, as well as sounds, and other visual aspects of our world. In so doing, Hartshorne drew our attention to the fact that music is not alone in possessing for us emotions as perceived qualities of our sensible experience. The phenomenon is ubiquitous to our perceptual world. It should make us less uncomfortable, then, with the phenomenon in music if we realize that it is not merely a *musical* phenomenon but a phenomenon of human perceptual experience in general.

Nevertheless, the skeptical may reply, the problem of how emotions can be possessed by music, as perceptual qualities, has hardly been solved by discovering that objects other than music possess them. Indeed, it could be argued that the problem has actually been exacerbated. For now we have the problem not only for music, but for the other objects as well. If it is mysterious how music can possess emotive qualities, it is equally mysterious, for example, how colors can possess them. First we had one problem; now we have *two*.

Hartshorne's answer to how emotive properties constitute part of the perceptual world of insentient matter is unlikely to appeal to the contemporary analytic mind. Indeed, his philosophy is a kind of 'panpsychism': the view that so-called. 'insentient' matter has itself at least a degree of sentience. In other words, Hartshorne does *not* explain how insentient matter can come to possess emotive properties, but, rather, blurs the distinction between sentient and insentient; which is to say, to a degree, it's sentience all the way down.

As I say, few will be willing to take such a drastic step with Hartshorne, although, I hasten to add, he is not some wild-eyed fanatic, in touch with astral forces, but a cool-headed philosopher of the first rank whose works abound in useful and penetrating insights. So for those of us who are not attracted to anything as beyond human experience as what Hartshorne offers, a more mundane answer must be sought for the question of how music can possess perceptual emotive properties. It is a comfort, indeed, to know that music shares this expressive aspect with such everyday objects as simple colors, and helps to assure us that there is nothing bizarre or seemingly outside the realm of the human to call a passage of music mournful or jolly or anguished. However, that does not replace the need for an explanation of *how* music can possess such emotions as perceived properties.

One thing to notice, straightaway, about the comparison of the cheerfulness of a musical passage and, say, the cheerfulness of the color yellow is that the cheerfulness of yellow, as yellow itself; is a 'simple' property whereas the cheerfulness of music is a 'complex' one. What this means is that, if I say, 'This kerchief is yellow,' and you say, 'No, it's orange,' there is nothing else I can point to in the kerchief to show or convince you that the kerchief really is yellow and not orange. I cannot respond to your denial by saying something like: 'But don't you see it is such-and-such and so-and-so, so it *must* be yellow.' This, of course, does not mean that there is *no* way I can try to show you that the kerchief is yellow, not orange. The usual procedure would be for us to view it in sunlight rather than artificial light, or make sure one of us is not sight-impaired in some way, and so on. What I *cannot* do, because yellow is a simple property is to point to something *else* in the kerchief and say: 'It's yellow because of *that*.' Yellow is not a complex property, so there is no 'that' to point to.

The same seems to be true of the cheerfulness of yellow. Like the yellowness itself; it is a simple quality. The cheerfulness just is a quality of the yellowness. Yellowness is not cheerful in virtue of some other perceived quality or qualities that it has beyond the yellowness (which is simply what it is).

But when we go from the cheerfulness of the color yellow to the cheerfulness of a musical passage, the situation is radically altered. When I say that a passage of music is cheerful or melancholy, I can *defend* my claim by pointing to other features of the music in virtue of which the music is cheerful or melancholy (or whatever). I can say: 'Notice the rapid, skipping tempo, the bright major tonalities, the generally loud level of sound, the leaping, galloping themes. That's what makes it so cheerful.' Or: 'Notice the slow, dragging tempo, the dark minor tonalities, the subdued, quiet dynamics, the faltering, drooping themes. *That's* what makes it so mournful.' In this sense, the cheerfulness, mournfulness, and other emotive qualities of music are 'complex' qualities, not simple ones like the cheerfulness of the color yellow. They are also the kinds of quality that are sometimes called 'emergent,' because they perceptually 'emerge' from the other qualities that make them up. The cheerfulness of the music is a new quality, so to speak, that is produced by the combined force of the bright major tonality, the rapid skipping tempo, the loud dynamics, the leaping, galloping themes.

Calling the emotive qualities of music 'complex' qualities emphasizes the fact that a passage of music is cheerful, or melancholy, or whatever in virtue of *other* musical features that make it so. Calling them 'emergent' qualities emphasizes the fact that they are perceived as distinct qualities in their own right, separate from the qualities that may 'produce' them.

That the emotive qualities of music are *complex* qualities should not be thought to imply that when someone is hearing, say, the melancholy quality of a musical passage, he or she is necessarily aware of the other qualities productive of the melancholy. A person may be hearing the melancholic quality of the music without being aware *that* the music is melancholy in virtue of its slow, halting tempo, subdued dynamics, dark minor tonalities, faltering, drooping themes. He or she may not even know that it is those kinds of musical features that are generally responsible for making music melancholy. But if someone *fails* to hear the melancholy in the music, he or she can, often, be helped to hear it by having attention drawn to those features: 'Listen to its slow, halting tempo, those dark minor tonalities, the subdued dynamics, the faltering, drooping themes. Now don't you hear the melancholy?' Frequently the answer will be 'yes.'

Among those who think that the garden-variety emotions belong to music as perceptual, heard qualities, there is little dissension from the belief that these qualities are complex, emergent qualities in the sense explained just now. Furthermore, there is general agreement about what features of music are associated with what emotive qualities. Indeed, this is not just a 'theoretical' agreement among philosophers but a 'practical' agreement among composers and ordinary listeners as well. We know the latter because for well over 300 years composers have consistently utilized just those musical features to set melancholy and cheerful and fearful texts that we, as listeners, perceive to be the features responsible for the melancholy, cheerful, fearful emotive qualities we hear in textless music, as well as the features that make the music appropriate to the emotive tone of the texts the composers set. This is not a philosopher's pipe dream but a basic fact of musical listening, and of the musical craft in the West for centuries.

However, because there is general agreement that this piece of music is melancholy in virtue of its dark, minor tonalities, subdued dynamics, slow, halting tempo, drooping, halting melody, that piece cheerful in virtue of its light, major harmonies, loud dynamics, fast, skipping tempo, leaping, galloping melodies, does not solve the problem of how or why the music is in the first case melancholy, and in the second cheerful. Why, after all, don't I just hear the dark, minor harmonies, the subdued dynamics, the slow, halting tempo, the dropping, halting melodies? Why do I *also* hear the *melancholy*? This is the problem.

The most tempting approach to the problem of how emotions get 'into' the music is one that I am intimately familiar with, as I have been tempted by it myself. This approach begins with the thought that sad music being in slow, halting tempo, subdued in dynamics, with drooping, faltering melodies, and sad people walking in slow halting gait, with drooping bodies, speaking in subdued halting voice, cannot be altogether coincidental. Nor can it be altogether coincidental that cheerful musical works and cheerful people move rapidly, speak loudly, and even leap about, melodically in the music, bodily in people. In other words, there seems to be a direct analogy between how people look and sound when they *express* the garden-variety emotions (at least *some* of them) and how music sounds or is described when it is perceived as *expressive* of those same emotions. The intuition is that there must be some causal explanation lurking in this analogy: that the way we customarily express the garden-variety emotions must somehow explain why we hear those emotions in the music.

In my 1980 book *The Corded Shell*, later reprinted, with major additions, as *Sound Sentiment*, I attempted to give an account of musical expressiveness based, in large part, on the analogy between musical expressiveness and human *expression*. To facilitate that project I substituted for Hartshorne's example of the cheerfulness of yellow my own example of a St Bernard's sad face.

The St Bernard's face is not *expressing* sadness. The face of the St Bernard is sad even when the creature is happy, it being at the other end that she *expresses* her emotions. The face, rather, is *expressive* of sadness: the sadness is a quality of the face as the cheerfulness is a quality of the yellow color. But, unlike the color yellow, the face of the St Bernard is a *complex* perceptual object and, hence, makes a far better analogue to the expressive musical object, which is also *a complex* one. What does the analogy have to teach us.

It seems fairly clear that the sadness of the St Bernard's face is there in virtue of our seeing it as a kind of caricature – but a recognizable resemblance – of the human visage when expressing sadness. Furthermore, we can point to individual aspects of the canine face – the sad eyes, the wrinkled brow, the drooping mouth and ears, the dewlap – that are exaggerated reflections of just such sadness-expressing features of a human face. The theory of musical expressiveness now under discussion is that expressive music is to human expressive features, overall, as the St Bernard's face is to the 'expressing' human countenance. Can this claim be substantiated?

We might usefully distinguish among the following three kinds of expressive features of music that the theory under discussion must deal with. First, there are the features of music that might be claimed to 'sound like' the sounds human beings make in expressing their emotions: the most obvious being speech. Second, there are the features of music that are said to resemble, in their sound, visible aspects of human expression behavior: for example, human gesture and bodily movement. Third, there are certain musical features, notably the major, minor, and diminished chords (to be explained in a moment), that have, for most people, the emotive tones of cheerfulness, melancholy and anguish, respectively, but that, because they are, like yellow and its cheerfulness, simple perceptual qualities, do not seem to resemble either the sound of human expression, or its visible aspect. The chords by themselves, in other words, do not have a linear (but only a vertical) structure, and so do not seem to be able to be construed as resembling human expression behavior, which *does* exhibit complex structure: there is no structure in the chords to resemble the structure of human utterance and behavior.

The resemblance of the sounds of music to the sounds of human beings expressing their emotions is something that, as we have seen, has been claimed ever since antiquity, and was the motivating force behind the endeavors of the Florentine *Camerata*, in the sixteenth century, to revive, as they saw it, ancient sung drama. But whereas Plato and the *Camerata* utilized the supposed resemblance to explain how they thought, music can arouse the emotions, the present project is to utilize it to explain how music can embody them as heard qualities.

The first question for such a theory would appear to be whether there really is a perceived resemblance between the sounds of music and the sounds of human expression. Let us take, for example, music that is heard as melancholy, and music that is heard as cheerful.

Certainly this much can be said. Melancholy music and melancholy speech and utterance have some obvious sound qualities in common. Melancholy people tend to express themselves in soft, subdued tones of voice; and melancholy music tends to be soft and subdued. Melancholy people tend to speak slowly and haltingly; and melancholy music tends to be in slow tempi and halting rhythm. Melancholy people's voices tend to 'sink,' and tend to remain in the low vocal register; and melancholy music too exhibits the same characteristics.

In contrast, cheerful people express themselves in bright, loud, sometimes even raucous – certainly not subdued – tones; and cheerful music tends to be bright, loud, and in the high register. Cheerful people are not slow or halting in speech and utterance but bright and sprightly; and cheerful music, likewise, is quick and sprightly. Cheerful people's voices rise energetically into the high register; and so too do the melodies of cheerful music.

In all of this particular attention should be paid to melody. For there is no aspect of Western music that is more amenable to analogy with the rise and fall in pitch of the human speaking voice than the rise and fall in pitch of music's melodic line. Furthermore, melody is that aspect of music that, historically, has been singled out most frequently as the primary *expressive* aspect. This perceived analogy between melody and speech is a leitmotif in writings about music's expressiveness from Plato to the *Camerata* to the eighteenth-century philosophers to the present day. The cheerful melodic line, like the cheerful speaking voice, is high, loud, fast, 'running' and 'leaping.' The anguished melody, like the anguished speaking voice, shrieks and cries, leaps in dissonant intervals, and proceeds in jerks,' with irregular pauses.

But beyond the phenomenon of music's 'sounding like' the vocal expressions of melancholy or cheerful people, many listeners perceive an analogy between the heard properties of music and visible human behavior as well. Music is customarily described in terms very similar to those we use to describe the motion of the human body under the influence of such emotions as melancholy and cheerfulness. Thus a musical phrase may leap joyously or droop, or falter, like a person in motion. To put it more generally, music is customarily described in terms of motion; and so the same descriptions we use to characterize it are frequently the ones we use to describe the visible motions of the human body in the expression of the garden-variety emotions.

I called this theory of musical expressiveness, in *The Corded Shell*, the 'contour theory,' because, to put it somewhat figuratively, the contour' of music, its sonic 'shape,' bears a structural analogy to the heard and seen manifestations of human emotive expression. One thing to be noticed straightaway about the contour theory is that it is going to have trouble with our third kind of expressive musical feature, the major, minor, and diminished chords; for *they* do not have any contour at all, so find no analogue, apparently, in the contours of human expression behavior. I shall deal with these seemingly anomalous expressive features in a moment. But before I do I want to complete this account of the contour theory.

The contour theory of musical expressiveness faces immediate problems. To begin with, it must not become a representational theory: it must not, that is to say, be construed as the theory that music 'represents' the voice and gesture of human expression, the way paint on canvas represents the visible features of the world. For representation does not capture the way we experience the emotive qualities of music. We do not, that is to say, hear sounds as representations of melancholy and cheerful behavior, the way we see paint on canvas as a representation of melancholy and cheerful men and women, and *then* hear the music, in virtue of these representations, as melancholy and cheerful. We hear the melancholy and cheerfulness of the music immediately, in the music, and can be quite unaware of the features of the music in virtue of which it is melancholy or cheerful. And even if we are consciously aware of the expressive-making features of the music, which we may frequently be, we do not perceive them as representations of anything.

Furthermore, there must be some explanation produced, in defense of the contour theory, for why it is the similarity in structure between music and *expression behavior* that plays so important a role in the listening experience. After all, the contour of music is probably similar in structure to inanimate sounds and natural objects, as well as to human expression behavior. What's so special about expression behavior that *it* should be singled out for mention above those other things?

Finally, does the contour theory do any better a job of capturing our experience of music's expressive qualities than a representational theory would do? Can it capture the way we experience the emotions in music, namely as directly perceived perceptual qualities?

In order for the analogy between musical contour and the contour of human expression behavior to work non-representationally, it must work subliminally: that is to say, we must not be fully aware of what is going on; we must not be aware of the analogy. Let us, for the moment, assume that this is what is happening. But why should we hear *emotions* in the music because of this subliminal perception, and not something else?

I believe one possible answer to this question can be found in a well-known perceptual phenomenon. When presented with ambiguous figures, we tend to see them as animate rather than inanimate forms: as living rather than non-living entities. We tend to see living forms in clouds, in stains on walls, in the shadowy things lurking in the woods. We see the stick as a snake. Why? Because, perhaps, we are hard-wired by evolution – by natural selection – to do so. Evolution says: 'Better safe than sorry. Better wrong than eaten.' Living things can be dangers to you. It is better to see the stick, immediately, incorrectly, as a snake, than to be snake bit, in pondering the question, if it turns out to be a snake after all.

Now, if this be true of sights, might it not be true of sounds as well? Might it not be the case that we are hard-wired by natural selection to hear sounds, where possible, as animate: where possible, as in music, as utterance and 'behavior'? I advance that as a possible, perhaps plausible, hypothesis. If it is true, it tells us why we hear the analogue of musical contour to human behavior and not to the other things it might resemble.

But if we hear sound as animate, why do we hear it as *expressively* animate? Well, if you want to carry through the 'survival' idea, it is to our advantage to know what emotive attitude is being evinced towards us by the living creature we may be encountering. If it is anger, we must prepare for fight or flight to be safe. If it is a benign emotion, other behavior is appropriate.

One might also add to these 'evolutionary' considerations the fact that just those 'simple' emotions we tend to hear in music are emotions whose expression behavior in human beings has direct analogues in the expression behavior of the higher primates and other mammals. In other words, their modes of expression seem hard-wired and deep in the inherited nature not only of us, but of other animals as well. This can be seen as corroborating evidence for the evolutionary story already told.

But now a further question presses itself upon us. In the case of ambiguous visual phenomena, we are conscious of what we are seeing (or think we are seeing). I take the stick for a snake and *run.* However, that does not seem to be what is happening in music. We are conscious of the expressive property, the emotion; we are not conscious of taking the musical contour for human utterance or behavior. Is there any plausible reason for this to be the case? We can't just *assume* it to make our theory work.

Well, consider this. The sense of sight is the primary 'survival' sense for human beings (and other of the higher primates). The sense of hearing is *not*, although it may very well have been for our ancestors way down the evolutionary chain. Thus there is no need for us *consciously* to hear things as threatening the way we consciously see things that way. So it is not completely unreasonable to suppose that what may very well have been a propensity consciously to hear ambiguous sounds as animate and (potentially) threatening has atrophied in us, like the appendix, and remains a vestigial relic of a more sound-oriented past. To put it another way, it is not completely unreasonable, on evolutionary grounds, to think that, while the seeing of ambiguous forms as animate remains a conscious phenomenon of human perception, the hearing of sounds that way has sunk back into semi-consciousness as a kind of 'background noise.'

Here, then, is *one* theory of how music comes to embody expressive qualities like melancholy and cheerfulness. It is agreed on all hands that music is melancholy, and cheerful, and so on, in virtue of certain standardly accepted features. It is perennially remarked on that these features bear analogy to the expression behavior, bodily, gestural, vocal, linguistic, of human beings. One can construct an evolutionary story of how and why we might be subconsciously, subliminally aware of this analogy and that this should cause us to perceive the music as melancholy or cheerful or the like as we perceive the sadness of the St Bernard's face. I have named this theory the contour theory of musical expressiveness.

But we have yet to work one further element into the contour theory: that is the expressive chords, major, minor, and diminished. These chords are generally perceived as cheerful, melancholy, and anguished, respectively; and you can hear this for yourself by playing the three notes together on the piano: first, C–E–G (major); then C–E flat–G (minor); finally, C–E flat–G flat (diminished). The problem is that these individual chords, not having a contour, being experienced as simple qualities, do not seem to bear any analogy at all to human behavior – hence must be expressive of cheerfulness, melancholy, and anguish in some *other* way than that allowed for by the contour theory of musical expressiveness. So the contour theory cannot be the whole story.

At least this much can be said for the contour theory straightaway. It is no worse off than any other theory in this regard. There is *no* generally accepted explanation for the difference in emotive quality between the major and minor chords, over which much ink has been spilled in the last 300 years. So, that the contour theory cannot provide one is no great deficit. But there is no harm, anyhow, in trying. Here are two suggestions.

The first suggestion is that we hear the vertical structure of the chords as a kind of contour. Compared to the major triad – that is, the major three-note chord, C–E–G – the minor triad has a lowered third: that is, the E is the third of the C-major chord, the E flat is the third lowered a half step, the smallest interval in the Western harmonic system. (The E is called the 'third' because it is the third note up from the C: that is, C (1), D (2), E (3). The G is called the 'fifth' because it is the fifth note up.) Now think of the lowered third, E flat as kind of sagging, or sinking, depressingly from E to E flat. Might that give a depressing, melancholy cast to the C-minor triad? There is a downward tending contour of the C-minor triad, as compared to the C-major one, like the downcast contour of the melancholy speaking voice or posture. And the diminished triad, C–E flat–G flat, is even more depressed: it has both a sinking third *and* a sinking fifth. Pretty far-fetched? Perhaps so.

Well, then, let's try this. Perhaps the chords should not be considered as isolated elements but in context: that is to say, functioning *in* musical structure. Perhaps it is from their function within musical compositions that they gain their emotive color.

If you go to the piano again, and play the major triad, C–E–G, the minor triad, C–E flat–G, and the diminished triad, C–E flat–G flat, in succession, I think you will perceive a big difference between the first two and the third. The diminished triad is an 'active' chord: that is to say, it sounds as if it must go somewhere; it must, as a musician would say, be 'resolved.' It can't stay at rest where it is. Or, another way of putting it: you couldn't hear it as the final chord of a musical composition. To hear what I mean, now lower the G flat to D flat, and raise the C to D flat. You have, in doing that, 'resolved' the diminished chord, and you can hear for yourself that things are now 'at rest.'

Might one suggest, then, that what gives the diminished chord its dark, anguished quality it its function, in musical structure, as an active, unconsummated, unresolved chord? It is restless, so to say, in its musical function; when it occurs in a compositional structure, at least until fairly recently in the history of the Western harmonic system, it imparts that restlessness to the contour of the melody it accompanies. From its 'syntactic' or 'grammatical' role in music it gains, by association, as it were, even when alone, its restless, 'anxious' emotive tone.

Furthermore, might this not be true, to a lesser degree, of the minor triad as well? It is, indeed, a matter of historical fact that the minor chord, until well into the nineteenth century, was considered more active than the major, which is why compositions in the minor mode for a long time almost invariably ended on a major rather than a minor chord. And, although ending on a minor chord is now no big deal, I think we still feel the minor ending as more restless than the major. You can hear this for yourself by resolving the diminished triad, C–E flat–G flat, two different ways: first, by lowering the G flat one whole step to E (F flat) and raising the C one half step to D flat; and then doing what you did before, lowering the G flat to F and raising the C to D flat. Do this a few times in succession. Which resolution sounds more 'restful' to you? I would venture to predict that it is going to be the latter: the major resolution. For what you did first was to resolve the diminished chord to D flat minor, and then to resolve it to D flat major. I think you, like your musical ancestors for over three centuries, found the major resolution grammatically and emotionally the more fulfilling one: the one that sounds the most stationary; the one that sounds the most completely *final*.

I don't know if this attempt to accommodate the major, minor, and diminished chords to the contour theory of musical expressiveness is any more plausible than the first. In any event, even where the contour theory does best, with the larger structural elements of music, particularly melody, it is not without serious problems and many detractors.

In the version of the contour theory that I have given, *my own version*, there are numerous difficulties that even I find daunting. Here are some.

To begin with, how convincing *is* the claim that there are recognizable analogies or similarities between music and the 'shape' of human expression? Do melodies *really* much resemble human speech in any significant way? Many people think the similarities adduced pretty far-fetched. And when one goes to supposed analogies between how music sounds and how human expression *looks*, there is bound to be more skepticism still. Does it make any sense at all to say that a passage of music is melancholy in virtue of sounding the way a human being gestures or moves when he or she is melancholy? Can music *sound* like a gesture or bodily posture? Can sense modalities be crossed that way? There is certainly plenty of room for doubt about it.

Furthermore, the whole psychological apparatus that the contour theory requires is highly conjectural, to say the least. What evidence, if any, is there for the claim that listeners subliminally hear the analogy, if indeed it exists, between the contour of music and human expression? And even if they do hear it, does that adequately explain our experience of hearing emotions *in* the music as perceptual qualities? As well, does the phenomenon of seeing things in ambiguous figures – seeing the stick as a snake, or the faces and figures in clouds – transfer to sounds and what we hear (if anything) in them?

Finally, what of the evolutionary explanation offered for, first, the tendency to 'animate' ambiguous figures and, second, the difference between this tendency, as evinced in visual perception, and as evinced in hearing? Are they plausible? Is there evidence for *either*?

The biologist Stephen J. Gould scorns such armchair evolutionary explanations as I have given, labeling them, contemptuously, 'just-so stories,' the point being that a natural selection story, just like Kipling's fanciful 'explanations' for how the leopard got its spots, or the elephant its trunk, can be made up by almost anyone, including an amateur like myself, for any trait you like. So it is probably wise not to place much faith in these exercises. The skeptical, therefore, will be wary of the evolutionary support I have adduced for the claims that, all things being equal, we will see living forms rather than nonliving ones in ambiguous perceptual arrays, and, second, that, because of the primacy of sight over hearing as a 'survival sense,' in human beings, our perception of 'animate' forms in sounds, as opposed to sights, will be dim or subliminal, as the contour theory requires.

Add all of these difficulties together and the contour theory begins to look pretty shaky. Indeed, it looks shaky not only to its detractors but to at least one of its supporters as well: *me*. Having vigorously defended the contour theory on two separate occasions, I can no longer say that I am not without serious qualms.

But the funny thing about the contour theory, or, in general, the theory that music is expressive of the garden-variety emotions by virtue of analogy to human expression behavior, both vocal and bodily, 'is its perennial attraction. It simply refuses to die, in spite of its numerous difficulties. There doesn't seem to be another, more plausible alternative.

That there isn't another game in town, of course, does not constitute much of an argument for the contour theory or its relations. Tomorrow is another day, and may well bring another, more convincing account.

What, then, should we do here and now? When a problem remains unsolved, one obvious strategy is to work at it until it gives up its secret, and only *then* go on to the problem that logically follows next. But that is not the strategy I think will have the best results. I think it a mistake for us to remain bogged down with the question of *how* music comes to embody the garden-variety emotions as perceptual qualities. Rather, since there is a consensus, more or less, that music does exhibit the expressive qualities in this way, let us now go on to examine what role, as so understood, they play in musical structure and the musical experience.

Let us, then, treat music, in this regard, as what the scientists call a 'black box': that is to say, a machine whose inner workings are unknown to us. We know what goes in, and what comes out, but what causes what goes in to produce what comes out – of that we are ignorant. With regard to how music comes to exhibit the garden-variety emotions as perceptual qualities, it is to us a black box. We know what goes in: the musical features that, for three centuries, have been associated with the particular emotions music is expressive of. And we know what goes out: the expressive qualities the music is heard to be expressive of. And rather than becoming obsessed with penetrating this black box, we should, or at least *some* of us should, go on to see what implications this new way of looking at music's expressive qualities (for it *is* a new way) has for our understanding of music as a whole.

54

Fearing Fictions

Kendall Walton

[T]he plot [of a tragedy] must be structured . . . that the one who is hearing the events unroll shudders with fear and feels pity at what happens: which is what one would experience on hearing the plot of the Oedipus.

Aristotle, Poetics[1]

I

Charles is watching a horror movie about a terrible green slime. He cringes in his seat as the slime oozes slowly but relentlessly over the earth destroying everything in its path. Soon a greasy head emerges from the undulating mass, and two beady eyes roll around, finally fixing on the camera. The slime, picking up speed, oozes on a new course straight toward the viewers. Charles emits a shriek and clutches desperately at his chair. Afterwards, still shaken, Charles confesses that he was "terrified" of the slime. *Was* he?

This question is part of the larger issue of how "remote" fictional worlds are from the real world. There is a definite barrier against *physical* interactions between fictional worlds and the real world. Spectators at a play are prevented from rendering aid to a heroine in distress. There is no way that Charles can dam up the slime, or take a sample for laboratory analysis.[2] But, as Charles's case dramatically illustrates, this barrier appears to be psychologically transparent. It would seem that real people can, and frequently do, have psychological attitudes toward merely fictional entities, despite the impossibility of physical intervention. Readers or spectators detest Iago, worry about Tom Sawyer and Becky lost in the cave, pity Willy Loman, envy Superman – and Charles fears the slime.

But I am skeptical. We do indeed get "caught up" in stories; we often become "emotionally involved" when we read novels or watch plays or films. But to construe this involvement as consisting of our having psychological attitudes toward fictional entities is, I think, to tolerate mystery and court confusion. I shall offer a different and, in my opinion, a much more illuminating account of it.

This issue is of fundamental importance. It is crucially related to the basic question of why and how fiction is important, why we find it valuable, why we do not dismiss novels, films, and plays as "mere fiction" and hence unworthy of serious

Kendall Walton, "Fearing Fictions," *Journal of Philosophy*, 75/1 (1978): 5–27.

attention. My conclusions in this paper will lead to some tentative suggestions about this basic question.

II

Physical interaction is possible only with what actually exists. That is why Charles cannot dam up the slime, and why in general real people cannot have physical contact with mere fictions. But the nonexistence of the slime does not prevent Charles from fearing it. One may fear a ghost or a burglar even if there is none; one may be afraid of an earthquake that is destined never to occur.

But a person who fears a nonexistent burglar *believes* that there is, or at least might be, one. He believes that he is in danger, that there is a possibility of his being harmed by a burglar. It is *conceivable* that Charles should believe himself to be endangered by the green slime. He might take the film to be a live documentary, a news flash. If he does, naturally he is afraid.

But the situation I have in mind is the more usual and more interesting one in which Charles is not deceived in this straightforward way. Charles knows perfectly well that the slime is not real and that he is in no danger. Is he afraid even so? He says that he is afraid, and he is in a state which is undeniably similar, in some respects, to that of a person who is frightened of a pending real-world disaster. His muscles are tensed, he clutches his chair, his pulse quickens, his adrenalin flows. Let us call this physiological/psychological state "quasi-fear." Whether it is actual fear (or a component of actual fear) is the question at issue.

Charles's state is crucially different from that of a person with an ordinary case of fear. The fact that Charles is fully aware that the slime is fictional is, I think, good reason to deny that what he feels is fear. It seems a principle of common sense, one which ought not to be abandoned if there is any reasonable alternative, that fear[3] must be accompanied by, or must involve, a belief that one is in danger, Charles does not believe that he is in danger; so he is not afraid.

Charles might try to convince us that he was afraid by shuddering and declaring dramatically that he was "*really terrified.*" This emphasizes the intensity of his experience. But we need not deny that he had an intense experience. The question is whether his experience, however intense, was one of fear of the slime. The fact that Charles, and others, call it "fear" is not conclusive, even if we grant that in doing so they express a truth. For we need to know whether the statement that Charles was afraid is to be taken literally or not.

More sophisticated defenders of the claim that Charles is afraid may argue that Charles *does* believe that the green slime is real and is a real threat to him. There are, to be sure, strong reasons for allowing that Charles realizes that the slime is only fictional and poses no danger. If he didn't we should expect him to flee the theater, call the police, warn his family. But perhaps it is *also* true that Charles believes, in some way or "on some level," that the slime is real and really threatens him. It has been said that in cases like this one "suspends one's disbelief," or that "part" of a person believes something which another part of him disbelieves, or that one finds oneself (almost?) believing something one nevertheless knows to be false. We must see what can be made of these notions.

One possibility is that Charles *half* believes that there is a real danger, and that he is, literally, at least half afraid. To half believe something is to be not quite sure that it is true, but also not quite sure that it is not true. But Charles has *no* doubts about whether he is in the presence of an actual slime. If he half believed, and were half afraid, we would expect him to have *some* inclination to act on his fear in the normal ways. Even a hesitant belief, a mere suspicion, that the slime is real would induce any normal person seriously to consider calling the police and warning his family. Charles gives no thought whatever to such courses of action. He is not *uncertain* whether the slime is real; he is perfectly sure that it is not.

Moreover, the fear symptoms that Charles does exhibit are not symptoms of a mere suspicion that the slime is real and a queasy feeling of half fear. They are symptoms of the certainty of grave and immediate danger, and sheer terror. Charles's heart pounds violently, he gasps for breath, he grasps the chair until his knuckles are white. This is not the behavior of a man who realizes basically that he is safe but suffers flickers of doubt. If it indicates fear at all, it indicates acute and overwhelming terror. Thus, to compromise on this issue, to say that Charles half believes he is in danger and is half afraid, is not a reasonable alternative.

One might claim that Charles believes he is in danger, but that this is not a hesitant or weak or half belief, but rather a belief of a special kind – a "gut" belief as opposed to an "intellectual" one. Compare a person who hates flying. He realizes, in one sense, that airplanes are (relatively) safe. He says, honestly, that they are, and can quote statistics to prove it. Nevertheless, he avoids traveling by air whenever possible. He is brilliant at devising excuses. And if he must board a plane he becomes nervous and upset. I grant that this person believes at a "gut" level that flying is dangerous, despite his "intellectual" belief to the contrary. I grant also that he is really afraid of flying.

But Charles is different. The air traveler performs *deliberate* actions that one would expect of someone who thinks flying is dangerous, or at least he is strongly inclined to perform such actions. If he does not actually decide against traveling by air he has a strong inclination to do so. But Charles does not have even an inclination to leave the theater or call the police. The only signs that he might really believe he is endangered are his more or less automatic, nondeliberate, reactions: his pulse rate, his sweaty palms, his knotted stomach, his spontaneous shriek.[4] This justifies us in treating the two cases differently.

Deliberate actions are done for reasons; they are done because of what the agent wants and what he thinks will bring about what he wants. There is a presumption that such actions are reasonable in light of the agent's beliefs and desires (however unreasonable the beliefs and desires may be). So we postulate beliefs or desires to make sense of them. People also have reasons for doing things that they are inclined to do but, for other reasons, refrain from doing. If the air traveler thinks that flying is dangerous, then, assuming that he wants to live, his actions or tendencies thereto are reasonable. Otherwise, they probably are not. So we legitimately infer that he does believe, at least on a "gut" level, that flying is dangerous. But we don't have to make the same kind of sense of Charles's automatic responses. One doesn't have reasons for things one doesn't *do*, like sweating, increasing one's pulse rate, knotting one's stomach (involuntarily). So there is no need to attribute beliefs (or desires) to Charles which will render these responses reasonable.[5] Thus, we can justifiably infer the air passenger's ("gut") belief in the danger of flying from his deliberate behavior or inclinations, and yet refuse to infer from Charles's automatic responses that he thinks he is in danger.

Someone might reply that at moments of special crisis during the movie – e.g., when the slime first spots Charles – Charles "loses hold of reality" and, *momentarily*, takes the slime to be real and really fears it. These moments are too short for Charles to think about doing anything; so (one might claim) it isn't surprising that his belief and fear are not accompanied by the normal inclinations to act.

This move is unconvincing. In the first place, Charles's quasi-fear responses are not merely momentary; he may have his heart in his throat throughout most of the movie, yet without experiencing the slightest inclination to flee or call the police. These long-term responses, and Charles's propensity to describe them afterwards in terms of "fear," need to be understood even if it is allowed that there are moments of real fear interspersed among them. Furthermore, however tempting the momentary-fear idea might be, comparable views of other psychological states are much less appealing. When we say that someone "pitied" Willy Loman or "admired" Superman, it is unlikely that we have in mind special moments during his experience of the work when he forgot, momentarily, that he was dealing with fiction and felt flashes of actual pity or admiration. The person's "sense of reality" may well have been robust and healthy throughout his experience of the work, uninterrupted by anything like the special moments of crisis Charles experiences during the horror movie. Moreover, it may be appropriate to say that someone "pities" Willy or "admires" Superman even when he is not watching the play or reading the cartoon. The momentary-*fear* theory, even if it were plausible, would not throw much light on cases in which we apparently have other psychological attitudes toward fictions.

Although Charles is not really afraid of the fictional slime depicted in the movie, the movie might nevertheless produce real fear in him. It might cause him to be afraid of something other than the slime it depicts. If Charles is a child, the movie may make him wonder whether there might not be real slimes or other exotic horrors *like* the one depicted in the movie, even if he fully realizes that the movie-slime itself is not real. Charles may well fear these suspected actual dangers; he might have nightmares about them for days afterwards. (*Jaws* caused a lot of people to fear sharks which they thought might really exist. But whether they were afraid of the fictional sharks in the movie is another question.)

If Charles is an older movie-goer with a heart condition, he may be afraid of the movie itself. Perhaps he knows that any excitement could trigger a heart attack, and fears that the movie will cause excitement, e.g., by depicting the slime as being especially aggressive or threatening. This is real fear. But it is fear of the depiction of the slime, not fear of the slime that is depicted.

Why is it so natural to describe Charles as afraid of the slime, if he is not, and how *is* his experience to be characterized? In what follows I shall develop a theory to answer these questions.

III

Propositions that are, as we say, "true in (the world of)" a novel or painting or film are *fictional.* Thus it is fictional that there is a society of tiny people called "Lilliputians." And in the example discussed above it is fictional that a terrible green slime is on the loose. Other fictional propositions are associated not with works of art but with games of make-believe, dreams, and imaginings. If it is "true in a game of make-believe" that Johnnie is a pirate, then fictionally Johnnie is a pirate. If someone dreams or imagines that he is a hero, then it is fictional that he is a hero.

Fictional truths[6] come in groups, and each of these groups constitutes a "fictional world." The fact that fictionally there was a society of tiny people and the fact that fictionally a man named "Gulliver" was a ship's physician belong to the same fictional world. The fact that fictionally a green slime is on the loose belongs to a different one. There is, roughly, a distinct fictional world corresponding to each novel, painting, film, game of make-believe, dream, or daydream.

All fictional truths are in one way or another man-made. But there are two importantly different ways of making them, and two corresponding kinds of fictional truths. One way to make a proposition fictional is simply to imagine that it is true. If it is fictional that a person is a hero because he imagines himself to be a hero, then this fictional truth is an *imaginary* one. Imagining is not always a deliberate, self-conscious act. We sometimes find ourselves imagining things more or less spontaneously, without having decided to do so. Thoughts pop into our heads unbidden. Dreams can be understood as simply very spontaneous imaginings.

Fictional truths of the second kind are established in a less direct manner. Participants in a game of mud pies may decide to recognize a principle to the effect that whenever there is a glob of mud in a certain orange crate, it is "true in the game of make-believe," i.e., it is fictional, that there is a pie in the oven. This fictional truth is a *make-believe* one. The principles in force in a given game of make-believe are, of course, just those principles which participants in the game recognize or accept, or understand to be in force.

It can be make-believe that there is a pie in the oven without anyone's imagining that there is. This will be so if there is a glob in the crate which no one knows about. (Later, after discovering the glob, a child might say, "There was a pie in the oven all along, but we didn't know it.") But propositions that are known to be make-believe are usually imaginary as well. When kids playing mud pies do know about a glob in the crate by virtue of which it is make-believe that a pie is in the oven, they imagine that there is a pie in the oven.

Principles of make-believe that are in force in a game need not have been formulated explicitly or deliberately adopted. When children agree to let globs of mud "be" pies they are in effect establishing a great many unstated principles linking make-believe properties of pies to properties of globs. It is implicitly understood that the size and shape of globs determine the make-believe size and shape of pies; it is understood, for example, that make-believedly a pie is one handspan across just in case that is the size of the appropriate glob. It is understood also that if Johnnie throws a glob at Mary then make-believedly Johnnie throws a pie at Mary. (It is *not* understood that if a glob is 40 per cent clay then make-believedly a pie is 40 per cent clay.)

It is not always easy to say whether or not someone does accept, implicitly, a given principle of make-believe. But we should notice that much of the plausibility of attributing to children implicit acceptance of a principle linking the make-believe size and shape of pies to the size and shape of globs rests on the dispositional fact that if the children should discover a glob to have a certain size or shape they would imagine, more or less automatically, that a pie has that size or shape. The children are disposed to imagine pies as having whatever size and shape properties they think the relevant globs have. In general, nondeliberate, spontaneous imagining, prompted in a systematic way by beliefs about the real world, is an important indication of implicit acceptance of principles of make-believe. I do not claim that a person disposed to imagine, nondeliberately, that *p* when he believes that *q necessarily* recognizes a principle of make-believe whereby if *q* then it is make-believe that *p*. It must be his understanding that whenever it is true that *q*, *whether he knows it or not*, it will be fictional that *p*. It may be difficult to ascertain whether this is his understanding, especially since his understanding may be entirely implicit. But the spontaneity of a person's imagining that *p* on learning that *q* strongly suggests that he thinks of *p* as having been fictional even before he realized that *q*.

A game of make-believe and its constituent principles need not be shared publicly. One might set up one's own personal game, adopting principles that no one else recognizes. And at least some of the principles constituting a personal game of make-believe may be implicit, principles which the person simply takes for granted.

Representational works of art generate make-believe truths. *Gulliver's Travels* generates the truth that make-believedly there is a society of six-inch-tall people. It is make-believe that a green slime is on the loose in virtue of the images on the screen of Charles's horror movie. These make-believe truths are generated because the relevant principles of make-believe are understood to be in force. But few such principles are ever formulated, and our recognition of most of them is implicit. Some probably seem so natural that we assume them to be in force almost automatically. Others we pick up easily through unreflective experience with the arts.[7]

IV

> *[The actor] on a stage plays at being another before a gathering of people who play at taking him for that other person.*
>
> Jorge Luis Borges[8]

Compare Charles with a child playing an ordinary game of make-believe with his father. The father, pretending to be a ferocious monster, cunningly stalks the child and, at a crucial moment, lunges viciously at him. The child flees, screaming, to the next room. The scream is more or less involuntary, and so is the flight. But the child has a delighted grin on his face even while he runs, and he unhesitatingly comes back for more. He is perfectly aware that his father is only "playing," that the whole thing is "just a game," and that only make-believedly is there a vicious monster after him. He is not really afraid.

The child obviously belongs to the fictional world of the game of make-believe. It is make-believe that the monster lunges, not into thin air, but at the child. Make-believedly the child is in grave and mortal danger. And when the child screams and runs, make-believedly he knows he is in danger and is afraid. The game is a sort of theatrical event in which the father is an actor portraying a monster and the child is an actor playing himself.

I propose to regard Charles similarly. When the slime raises its head, spies the camera, and begins oozing toward it, it is make-believe that Charles is threatened. And when as a result Charles gasps and grips his chair, make-believedly he is afraid. Charles is playing a game of make-believe in which he uses the images on the screen as props. He too is an actor impersonating himself. In this section I shall explain this proposal in detail. My main arguments for it will come later.

Charles differs in some important respects from an ordinary on-stage, self-portraying actor. One difference has to do with what makes it make-believe that Charles is afraid. Facts about Charles generate (*de re*) make-believe truths about him; in this respect he is like an actor portraying himself on stage. But the sorts of facts about Charles which do the generating are different. Make-believe truths about Charles are generated at least partly by what he thinks and feels, not just by how he acts. It is partly the fact that Charles is in a state of quasi-fear, the fact that he feels his heart pounding, his muscles tensed, etc., which makes it make-believe that he is afraid. It would not be appropriate to describe him as "afraid" if he were not in some such state.[9]

Charles's quasi-fear is not responsible, by itself, for the fact that make-believedly it is the *slime* he fears, nor even for the fact that make-believedly he is afraid rather than angry or excited or merely upset. Here Charles's (actual) beliefs come into play. Charles believes (he knows) that make-believedly the green slime is bearing down on him and he is in danger of being destroyed by it. His quasi-fear results from this belief.[10] What makes it make-believe that Charles is afraid rather than angry or excited or upset is the fact that his quasi-fear is caused by the belief that make-believedly he is in danger. And his belief that make-believedly it is the slime that endangers him is what makes it make-believe that the slime is the object of his fear. In short, my suggestion is this: the fact that Charles is quasi-afraid as a result of realizing that make-believedly the slime threatens him generates the truth that make-believedly he is afraid of the slime.[11]

An on-stage actor, by contrast, generates make-believe truths solely by his acting, by his behavior. Whether it is make-believe that the character portrayed is afraid or not depends just on what the actor says and does and how he contorts his face, regardless of what he actually thinks or feels. It makes no difference whether his actual emotional state is anything like fear. This is just as true when the actor is playing himself as it is when he is portraying some other character. The actor may find that putting himself into a certain frame of mind makes it easier to act in the appropriate ways. Nevertheless, it is how he acts, not his state of mind, that determines whether make-believedly he is afraid.

This is how our conventions for theater work, and it is entirely reasonable that they should work this way. Audiences cannot be expected to have a clear idea of an actor's personal thoughts and feelings while he is performing. That would require knowledge of his off-stage personality and of recent events that may have affected his mood (e.g., an argument with his director or his wife). Moreover, acting involves a certain amount of dissembling; actors hide some aspects of their mental states from the audience. If make-believe truths depended on actors' private thoughts and feelings, it would be awkward and unreasonably difficult for spectators to ascertain what is going on in the fictional world. It is not surprising that the make-believe truths for which actors on stage are responsible are understood to be generated by just what is visible from the galleries.

But Charles is not performing for an audience. It is not his job to get across to anyone else what make-believedly is true of himself. Probably no one but him much cares whether or not make-believedly he is afraid. So there is no reason why his actual state of mind should not have a role in generating make-believe truths about himself.

It is not so clear in the monster game what makes it make-believe that the child is afraid of a monster. The child *might* be performing for the benefit of an audience; he might be *showing* someone, an onlooker, or just his father, that make-believedly he is afraid. If so, perhaps he is like an on-stage actor. Perhaps we should regard his observable behavior as responsible for the fact that make-believedly he is afraid. But there is room for doubt here. The child experiences quasi-fear sensations as Charles does. And his audience probably has much surer access to his mental state than theater audiences have to those of actors. The audience may know him well, and the child does not try so hard or so skillfully to hide his actual mental state as actors do. It may be perfectly evident to the audience that the child has a case of quasi-fear, and also that this is a result of his realization that make-believedly a monster is after him. So it is not unreasonable to regard the child's mental state as helping to generate make-believe truths.

A more definite account of the situation is possible if the child is participating in the game solely for his own amusement, with no thought of an audience. In this case the child himself, at least, almost certainly understands his make-believe fear to depend on his mental state rather than (just) his behavior.[12] In fact, let us suppose that the child is an undemonstrative sort who does not scream or run or betray his "fear" in any other especially overt way. His participation in the game is purely passive. Nevertheless the child does experience quasi-fear when make-believedly the monster attacks him, and he still would describe himself as being "afraid" (although he knows that there is no danger and that his "fear" isn't real). Certainly in this case it is (partly) his quasi-fear that generates the make-believe truth he expresses when he says he is "afraid."

My proposal is to construe Charles on the model of this undemonstrative child. Charles may, of course, exhibit his "fear" in certain observable ways. But his observable behavior is not meant to show anyone else that make-believedly he is afraid. It is likely to go unnoticed by others, and even Charles himself may be unaware of it. No one, least of all Charles, regards his observable behavior as generating the truth that make-believedly he is afraid.

V

It is clear enough now what makes it make-believe that Charles fears the slime, assuming that make-believedly he does fear the slime. But more needs to be said in support of my claim that this is a make-believe truth. What needs to be established is that the relevant principle of make-believe is accepted or recognized by someone, that someone understands it to be in force. I contend that Charles, at least, does so understand it.

It is clear that Charles imagines himself to be afraid of the slime (though he knows he is not). He thinks of himself as being afraid of it; he readily describes his experience as one of "fear" – once he has a chance to catch his breath. So it is at least imaginary (and hence fictional) that he fears the slime.

Charles's act of imagining himself afraid of the slime is hardly a deliberate or reflective act. It is triggered more or less automatically by his awareness of his quasi-fear sensations. He is simply disposed to think of himself as fearing the slime, without deciding to do so, when during the movie he feels his heart racing, his muscles tensed, and so forth. It is just such a disposition as this, we recall [. . .], that goes with implicit recognition of a principle of make-believe. If a child is disposed to imagine a pie to be six inches across when he discovers that that is the size of a glob of mud, this makes it reasonable to regard him as recognizing a principle whereby the glob's being that size makes it make-believe that the pie is also. Similarly, Charles's tendency to imagine himself afraid of the slime when he finds himself in the relevant mental state constitutes persuasive grounds for attributing to him acceptance of a principle whereby his experience makes it make-believe that he is afraid.[13]

Several further considerations will increase the plausibility of this conclusion. First, I have claimed only that Charles recognizes the principle of make-believe. There is no particular reason why anyone else should recognize it, since ordinarily only Charles is in a position to apply it and only he is interested in the make-believe truth that results. Others might know about it and realize how important it is to Charles. But even so the principle clearly is in important respects a personal one. It differs in this regard from the principles whereby an on-stage actor's behavior generates make-believe truths, and also from those whereby images on the movie screen generate make-believe truths about the activities of the green slime. *These* principles are fully public; they are clearly (even if implicitly) recognized by everyone watching the play or movie. Everyone in the audience applies them and is interested in the resulting make-believe truths.

This makes it reasonable to recognize two distinct games of make-believe connected with the horror movie – a public game and Charles's personal game – and two corresponding fictional worlds. The situation is analogous to that of an illustrated edition of a novel. Consider an edition of Dostoyevsky's *Crime and Punishment* which includes a drawing of Raskolnikov. The text of the novel, considered alone, establishes a fictional world comprising the make-believe truths that it generates, e.g., the truth that make-believedly a man named "Raskolnikov" killed an old lady. The illustration is normally understood not as establishing its own separate fictional world, but as combining with the novel to form a "larger" world. This larger world contains the make-believe truths generated by the text alone, plus those generated by the illustration (e.g., that make-believedly Raskolnikov has wavy hair and a receding chin), and also those generated by both together (e.g., that make-believedly a man with wavy hair killed an old lady). So we have two fictional worlds, one included within the other: the world of the novel and the world of the novel-plus-illustration.

Charles's state of mind supplements the movie he is watching in the way an illustration supplements what it illustrates. The movie considered alone establishes a fictional world consisting only of the make-believe truths that it generates (e.g., that make-believedly there is a green slime on the loose). But Charles recognizes, in addition, a larger world in which these make-believe truths are joined by truths generated by Charles's experience as he watches the movie, and also by truths generated by the images on the screen and Charles's experience together. It is only in this more inclusive world that make-believedly Charles fears the slime. (And it is the larger world that occupies Charles's attention when he is caught up in the movie.)

The analogy between Charles's case and the illustrated novel is not perfect. The novel-plus-illustration world is publicly recognized, whereas the fictional world established by the movie plus Charles's experience of it probably is not. Dolls provide an analogy which is better in this respect. Anyone who sees a doll of a certain sort will recognize that it generates the truth that make-believedly there is a blonde baby girl. The doll, regarded simply as a sculpture to be observed from a distance, generates, make-believe truths such as this. But a child playing with the doll is playing a more personal game of make-believe, one in which she herself is a self-portraying actor and the doll serves as a prop. What she does with the doll generates make-believe truths, e.g., the truth that make-believedly she is dressing the baby for a trip to town. Similarly, Charles uses the screen images as props in a personal game of make-believe in which he himself is a character. He plays his own game with the images. The screen images, of course, do not lend themselves to bring "dressed" or manipulated in all the ways that dolls do, and this limits the extent of Charles's participation in the game. But the relations and interactions between Charles and the images do generate a number of important make-believe truths: that make-believedly Charles notices the slime and stares apprehensively at it, that make-believedly it turns toward him and attacks, and that make-believedly he is scared out of his wits.[14]

One source of uneasiness about my claim that make-believedly Charles fears the slime may have been the impression that this can be so only if Charles belongs to the fictional world of the *movie.* (The movie itself doesn't depict Charles, nor does it make any reference to him, so he doesn't belong to the movie-world.) My two-worlds theory shows that this impression is mistaken and hence that the uneasiness based on it is out of place.

I have portrayed Charles so far as participating rather automatically in his game of make-believe. But he might easily slip into participating deliberately. The naturalness of his doing so gives added support to my claim that Charles does recognize a make-believe world that he and the slime share, even when his participation is not deliberate. Suppose that during the movie Charles exclaims, deliberately, to a companion or to himself, "Yikes, here it comes! Watch out!" How are we to understand this verbal action? Certainly Charles is not seriously asserting that a slime is coming and warning himself or his companion of it. Presumably he is asserting that it is *make-believe* that a slime is coming. But the indexical, 'here', carries an implicit reference to the speaker. So Charles's exclamation shows that he takes it to be make-believe that the slime is headed toward *him*; it shows that he regards himself as coexisting with the slime in a make-believe world.

But this does not take us to the bottom of the matter. "Yikes!" and "Watch out!" are not assertions, and so not assertions of what make-believedly is the case. Moreover, if in saying, "Here it comes," Charles were merely making an assertion about what make-believedly is the case, he could well have made this explicit and exclaimed instead, "Make-believedly the slime is coming!" or "The slime is coming, in the fictional world!" But these variants lack the flavor of the original. Charles's exclamatory tone is absurdly out of place when the make-believe status of the danger is made explicit. Compare how ridiculous it would be for an actor playing Horatio in a performance of *Hamlet* to exclaim, when the ghost appears, "Look, my lord, it comes, in the fictional world of the play!"

The comparison is apt. For Charles is doing just what actors do, *pretending* to make an assertion. He is pretending to assert (seriously) that the slime is headed his way. (Pretending to assert this is not incompatible with actually asserting that make-behievedly the slime is coming. Charles might be doing both at once.) In my terms,

Charles understands his utterance of 'Here it comes!' to generate the truth that make-believedly he asserts (seriously) that the slime is coming. He is playing along with the fiction of the movie, incorporating it into a game of make-believe of his own. This makes it obvious why it would not do to say, "Here it comes, in the fictional world!" Saying that is simply not (normally) how one would pretend to assert that a slime is (really) coming. The rest of Charles's verbal behavior is now easily explainable as well. In saying "Yikes!" and "Watch out!" he is pretending to express amazement or terror and pretending to issue a (serious) warning; make-believedly he is doing these things.

We have now arrived at the solution to a pair of puzzles. Why is it that in everyday conversation we regularly omit phrases like 'in the fictional world' and 'in the novel', whereas we rarely omit other intentional operators such as 'It is believed that', 'Jones wished that', 'Jones denies that'? Why do we so naturally say just "Tom and Becky were lost in a cave" rather than "In the novel Tom and Becky were lost in a cave," whereas it would be almost unheard of to shorten "Jones wishes that a golden mountain would appear on the horizon" to simply "A golden mountain will appear on the horizon" (even if the context makes it clear that Jones's wishes are the subject of conversation)?

The explanation lies in our habit of playing along with fictions, of make-believedly asserting, pretending to assert, what we know to be only make-believedly the case. We mustn't be too quick to assume that an utterance of '*p*' is merely an ellipsis for 'Make-believedly *p*' (or for 'In the novel *p*'). This assumption is wrong if the speaker make-believedly is asserting that *p*, rather than (or in addition to) asserting that make-believedly *p*, Charles's frantic, "Yikes, here it comes!" is an obvious case in point. A case only slightly less obvious is that of a person reading *The Adventures of Tom Sawyer* who remarks, gravely and with an expression of deep concern, that Tom and Becky are lost in a cave.

I do not suggest that the omission of 'in the novel' is *never* a mere ellipsis. "Tom and Becky were lost in a cave" uttered by a critic analyzing the novel could easily have been expanded to "In the novel Tom and Becky were lost in a cave" without altering the character of the remark. The critic probably is not pretending to assert that Tom and Becky were (actually) lost in a cave. But our habit of dropping fictional operators persists even in sober criticism, and testifies to the ease with which we can be induced to play along, deliberately, with a work of fiction.

In German the indicative mood is used ordinarily only when the speaker is committed to the truth of the sentence or clause in question. But fictional statements constitute a striking exception to this generalization; the indicative is used in fictional statements even though the speaker is *not* committed to their truth. (One says, for example, "*Robinson Crusoe hat einen Schiffbruch überlebt*," which is indicative, even though one is not claiming that there actually was a person named "Robinson Crusoe" who survived a shipwreck.)

The explanation is that speakers are often pretending to express their commitment to the truth of sentences or clauses in fictional contexts. So naturally they use the indicative mood in these cases; they speak as they would if they were not pretending. And the habit of using the indicative persists even when there is little or no such pretense.

VI

The treatment of Charles's "fear of the slime" suggested above can serve as a model for understanding other psychological attitudes ostensibly directed toward fictional things. When it is said that someone pities Willy Loman, or worries about Tom and Becky, or detests Iago, or envies Superman, what is said is probably not literally true.[15] But the person is, actually, in a distinctive psychological (emotional?) state, even if that state is not pity or worry or hate or envy. And his being in this state is a result of his awareness of certain make-believe truths: that make-believedly Willy is an innocent victim of cruel circumstances, that make-believedly Tom and Becky might perish in the cave, that make-believedly Iago deceived Othello about Desdemona, that make-believedly Superman can do almost anything. The fact that the person's psychological state is as it is, and is caused by such beliefs, makes it make-believe that he pities Willy, worries about Tom and Becky, hates Iago, or envies Superman.

We have here a particularly intimate relation between the real world and fictional worlds. Insofar as make-believe truths are generated by a spectator's or reader's state of mind, he is no mere "external observer" of the fictional world. Ascertaining what make-believedly is true of himself is to a large extent a matter of introspection (or of whatever sort of "privileged access" one has to one's own beliefs and sensations). In fact, when Charles watches the horror movie, for example, introspection is involved in ascertaining not merely that make-believedly he is afraid of the slime, but also make-believe truths about the nature and progress of his fear. If it is make-believe that his fear is overwhelming, or that it is only momentary, this is so because his quasi-fear sensations are overwhelming, or are only momentary. Make-believedly his fear grows more or less intense, or becomes almost unbearable, or finally subsides, etc., as his quasi-fear feelings change in these ways. So it is by attention to the nature of his own actual experience that Charles is aware of make-believe truths about the nature of his fear. He follows the progress of his make-believe fear by introspection, much as one who is literally afraid follows the progress of his actual fear.

It would not be too far wrong to say that Charles actually experiences his make-believe fear. I don't mean that there is a special kind of fear, make-believe fear, which Charles experiences. What he actually experiences, his quasi-fear feelings, are not feelings of fear. But it is true *of them* that *make-believedly* they are feelings of fear. They generate *de re* make-believe truths about themselves, and so belong to the fictional world just as Charles himself does. What Charles actually experiences is such that make-believedly it is (an experience of) fear.

Cases like that of Charles contrast strikingly with others in which an actual person belongs to a fictional world. Consider a performance of William Luce's play about Emily Dickinson, *The Belle of Amherst*, in which Julie Harris plays Emily Dickinson. Suppose that Emily Dickinson herself, with the help of a time machine or a fortuitous reincarnation, is in the audience. In order to discover make-believe truths about herself, including what make-believedly she thinks and feels, Dickinson must observe Julie Harris's actions, just as any spectator must. It is as though she is watching another person, despite the fact that that "person," the character, is herself. Dickinson has no special intimacy with make-believe truths about her own mental state.[16] The situation is basically the same if Dickinson should replace Julie Harris in the lead role and act the part herself. She still must judge from her external behavior, from what spectators could observe, whether or not it is make-believe that she is afraid or worried or whatever – and she might easily be mistaken about how she looks to spectators. It is still as though she considers herself "from the outside," from the perspective of another person.

This is clearly not true of Charles. It is not as though Charles were confronting another person, a fictional version of himself, but rather as though he himself actually fears the slime. (Nevertheless, he does not.) Make-believe facts about his fear, especially the fact that make-believedly it is his, are portrayed to Charles in an extraordinarily realistic manner. And make-believe facts about our pity for Willy, our dislike of Iago, and so forth, are similarly vivid to us. We and Charles feel ourselves to be part of fictional worlds, to be intimately involved with the slime, or Willy, or with whatever constituents of fictional worlds are, make-believedly, objects of our feelings and attitudes.

We see, now, how fictional worlds can seem to us almost as "real" as the real world is, even though we know perfectly well that they are not. We have begun to understand what happens when we get emotionally "involved" in a novel or play or film, when we are "caught up in the story."

The theory I have presented is designed to capture intuitions lying behind the traditional ideas that the normal or desired attitude toward fiction involves a "*suspension of disbelief*," or a "*decrease of distance*." These phrases are unfortunate. They strongly suggest that people do not (completely) disbelieve what they read in novels and see on the stage or screen, that, e.g., we somehow accept it as fact that a boy named "Huckleberry Finn" floated down the Mississippi River – at least while we are engrossed in the novel. The normal reader does not accept this as fact, nor should he. Our disbelief is "suspended" only in the sense that it is, in some ways, set aside or ignored. We don't believe that there was a Huck Finn, but what interests us is the fact that *make-believedly* there was one, and that make-believedly he floated down the Mississippi and did various other things. But this hardly accounts for the sense of "decreased distance" between us and fictions. It still has us peering down on fictional worlds from reality above, however fascinated we might be, for some mysterious reason, by what we see.

On my theory we accomplish the "decrease of distance" not by promoting fictions to our level but by descending to theirs. (More accurately, we *extend* ourselves to their level, since we do not stop actually existing when it becomes fictional that we exist.) *Make-believedly* we do believe, we know, that Huck Finn floated down the Mississippi. And make-believedly we have various feelings and attitudes about him and his adventures. Rather than somehow fooling ourselves into thinking fictions are real, we become fictional. So we end up "on the same level" with fictions. And our presence there is accomplished in the extraordinarily realistic manner that I described. This enables us to comprehend our sense of closeness to fictions, without attributing to ourselves patently false beliefs.

We are now in a position to expect progress on the fundamental question of why and how fiction is important. Why don't we dismiss novels, plays, and films as "mere fiction" and hence unworthy of serious attention?

Much has been said about the value and importance of dreams, fantasy, and children's games of make-believe.[17] It has been suggested, variously, that such activities serve to clarify one's feelings, help one to work out conflicts, provide an outlet for the expression of repressed or socially unacceptable feelings, prepare one emotionally for possible future crises by providing "practice" in facing imaginary crises. It is natural to presume that our experience of representational works of art is valuable for similar reasons. But this presumption is not very plausible, I think, unless something like the theory I have presented is correct.

It is my impression that people are usually, perhaps always, characters in their own dreams and daydreams. We dream and fantasize about ourselves. Sometimes one's role in one's dream-world or fantasy-world is limited to that of observing other goings-on. But to have even this role *is* to belong to the fictional world. (We must distinguish between being, in one's dream, an observer of certain events, and merely "observing," having, a dream about those events.) Similarly, children are nearly always characters in their games of make-believe. To play dolls or school, hobby horses or mud pies, is to be an actor portraying oneself.

I suggest that much of the value of dreaming, fantasizing, and making-believe depends crucially on one's thinking of oneself as belonging to a fictional world. It is chiefly by fictionally facing certain situations, engaging in certain activities, and having or expressing certain feelings, I think, that a dreamer, fantasizer, or game player comes to terms with his actual feelings – that he discovers them, learns to accept them, purges himself of them, or whatever exactly it is that he does.

If I am right about this, people can be expected to derive similar benefits from novels, plays, and films only if it is fictional that they themselves exist and participate (if only as observers) in the events portrayed in the works, i.e., only if my theory is on the right track.

I find encouragement for these speculations in the deliberate use of role-playing in educational simulation games, and as a therapeutic technique in certain kinds of psychotherapy (e.g., Gestalt therapy). A therapist may ask his patient to pretend that his mother is present, or that some inanimate object is his mother, and to "talk to her." He may then be asked to "be" the mother, and to say how he feels (when he "is" the mother), how he acts, what he looks like, etc. I will not venture an explanation of how such therapeutic techniques are effective, nor of why simulation games work. But whatever explanation is appropriate will, I suspect, go a long way toward explaining why we are as interested in works of fiction as we are, and clarifying what we get from them. The important place that novels, plays, and films have in our lives appears mysterious only on the supposition that we merely stand outside fictional worlds and look in, pressing our noses against an inviolable barrier. Once our presence within fictional worlds is recognized, suitable explanations seem within reach.

VII

A more immediate benefit of my theory is its capacity to handle puzzles. I conclude with the resolution of two more. First, consider a playgoer who finds happy endings asinine or dull, and hopes that the play he is watching will end tragically. He "wants the heroine to suffer a cruel fate," for only if she does, he thinks, will the play be worth watching. But at the same time he is caught up in the story and "sympathizes with the heroine"; he "wants her to escape." It is obvious that these two apparent desires may perfectly well coexist. Are we to say that the spectator is *torn* between opposite interests, that he wants the heroine to survive and also wants her not to? This does not ring true. Both of the playgoer's "conflicting desires" may be wholehearted. He may hope unreservedly that the work will end with disaster for the heroine, and he may, with equal singlemindedness, "want her to escape such an undeserved fate." Moreover, he may be entirely aware of both "desires," and yet feel no particular conflict between them.

My theory provides a neat explanation. It is merely make-believe that the spectator sympathizes with the heroine and wants her to escape. And he (really) wants it to be make-believe that she suffers a cruel end. He does not have conflicting desires. Nor, for that matter, is it make-believe that he does.

The second puzzle concerns why it is that works last as well as they do, how they can survive multiple readings or viewings without losing their effectiveness.[18]

Suspense of one kind or another is an important ingredient in our experience of most works: Will Jack, of *Jack and the Beanstalk*, succeed in ripping off the giant without being caught? Will Tom and Becky find their way out of the cave? Will Hamlet ever get around to avenging the murder of his father? What is in store for Julius Caesar on the Ides of March? Will Godot come?

But how can there be suspense if we already know how things will turn out? Why, for example, should Tom and Becky's plight concern or even interest a reader who knows, from reading the novel previously, that eventually they will escape from the cave? One might have supposed that, once we have experienced a work often enough to learn thoroughly the relevant features of the plot, it would lose its capacity to create suspense, and that future readings or viewings of it would lack the excitement of the first one. But this frequently is not what happens. *Some* works, to be sure, fade quickly from exposure, and familiarity does alter our experience in certain ways. But the power of many works is remarkably permanent, and the nature of their effectiveness remarkably consistent. In particular, suspense may remain a crucial element in our response to a work almost no matter how familiar we are with it. One may "worry" just as intensely about Tom and Becky while rereading *The Adventures of Tom Sawyer*, despite one's knowledge of the outcome, as would a person reading it for the first time. A child listening to *Jack and the Beanstalk* for the umpteenth time, long after she has memorized it word for word, may feel much the same excitement when the giant discovers Jack and goes after him, the same gripping suspense, that she felt when she first heard the story. Children, far from being bored by familiar stories, often beg to hear the same ones over and over again.

None of this is surprising on my theory. The child hearing *Jack and the Beanstalk* knows that make-believedly Jack will escape, but make-believedly she does *not* know that he will – until the reading of the passage describing his escape. She is engaged in her own game of make-believe during the reading, a game in which make-believedly she learns for the first time about Jack and the giant as she hears about them.[19] It is her make-believe uncertainty (the fact that make-believedly she is uncertain), not any actual uncertainty, that is responsible for the excitement and suspense that she feels. The point of hearing the story is not, or not merely, to learn about Jack's confrontation with the giant, but to play a game of make-believe. One cannot learn, each time one hears the story, what make-believedly Jack and the giant do, unless one always forgets in between times. But one can and does participate each time in a game of make-believe. The point of hearing *Jack and the Beanstalk* is to have the experience of being such that, *make-believedly*, one realizes with trepidation the danger Jack faces, waits breathlessly to see whether the giant will awake, feels sudden terror when he does awake, and finally learns with admiration and relief how Jack chops down the beanstalk, killing the giant.

Why play the same game over and over? In the first place, the game may not be exactly the same each time, even if the readings are the same. On one occasion it may be make-believe that the child is paralyzed by fear for Jack, overwhelmed by the gravity of the situation, and emotionally drained when Jack finally bests the giant. On another occasion it may be make-believe that the child is not very seriously concerned about Jack's safety and that her dominant feelings are admiration for Jack's exploits, the thrill of adventure, and a sense of exhilaration at the final outcome. But even if the game is much the same from reading to reading, one's emotional needs may require the therapy of several or many repetitions.

Notes

1 Chapter 14. Translated by Gerald F. Else (Ann Arbor: The University of Michigan Press, 1967).

2 I examine this barrier in a companion piece to the present paper, "How Remote Are Fictional Worlds from the Real World?," *Journal of Aesthetics and Art Criticism* [37, 1 (1978): 11–23].

3 By 'fear' I mean fear for oneself. Obviously a person can be afraid for someone else without believing that he himself is in danger. One must believe that the person for whom one fears is in danger.

4 Charles *might* scream *deliberately*. But insofar as he does, it is probably clear that he is only pretending to take the slime seriously. (See section V.)

5 Charles's responses are *caused* partly by a belief, though not the belief that he is in danger. (See section IV.) This belief is not a *reason* for responding as he does, and it doesn't make it "reasonable," in the relevant sense, to respond in those ways.

6 A "fictional truth" is the fact that a certain proposition is fictional.

7 I have developed the notion of make-believe truths and other ideas presented in this section more fully elsewhere, especially in "Pictures and Make-believe," *Philosophical Review*, LXXXI, 3 (July 1973): 283–319. Cf. also "Are Representations Symbols?," *The Monist*, LVIII, 2 (April 1974): 236–54. I should indicate that, in my view, there are no propositions "about" mere fictions, and hence none that are make-believe. It is make-believe not that Gulliver visited Lilliput, but that a man named "Gulliver" visited a place called "Lilliput." I shall occasionally ignore this point in the interest of simplicity, for example, when I write in section V as though the same slime resides in two different fictional worlds. Compare "How Remote Are Fictional Worlds from the Real World?," op. cit., note 22.

8 From "Everything and Nothing," Borges, *Labyrinths: Selected Stories and Other Writings*, Donald A. Yates and James E. Irby, eds. (New York: New Directions, 1962), p. 248.

9 It is arguable that the purely physiological aspects of quasi-fear, such as the increase of adrenalin in the blood, which Charles could ascertain only by clinical tests, are not part of what makes it make-believe that he is afraid. Thus one might want to understand 'quasi-fear' as referring only to the more psychological aspects of Charles's condition: the feelings or sensations that go with increased adrenalin, faster pulse rate, muscular tension, etc.

10 One can't help wondering why Charles's realization that make-believedly he is in danger produces quasi-fear in him, why it brings about a state similar to real fear, even though he knows he is not really in danger. This question is important, but we need not speculate about it here. For now we need only note that Charles's belief does result in quasi-fear, however this fact is to be explained.

11 This, I think, is at least approximately right. It is perhaps equally plausible, however, to say that the fact that Charles *believes* his quasi-fear to be caused by his realization that the slime endangers him is what makes it make-believe that his state is one of fear of the slime. There is no need to choose now between my suggestion and this variant.

12 Observers might, at the same time, understand his behavior alone to be responsible for his make-believe fear. The child and the observers might recognize somewhat different principles of make-believe,

13 These grounds are not conclusive. But the question of whether Charles accepts this principle is especially tricky, and there is reason to doubt that it can be settled conclusively. One would have to determine whether it is Charles's understanding that, if he were to have the quasi-fear sensations, etc., without realizing that he does and hence without imagining that he is afraid, it would still be fictional that he is afraid. If so, the fictional truth depends not on his imagining but on his quasi-fear, etc. It is hard to decide whether this is Charles's understanding, mainly because it is hard to conceive of his being ignorant of his quasi-fear sensations, etc. But insofar as I can get a grip on the question I think that the answer is affirmative.

14 One important difference between dolls and the screen images is that the dolls generate *de re* make-believe truths about themselves and the images do not. The doll is such that make-believedly *it* is a baby that is being dressed for a trip to town. But

a screen image is not such that make-believedly it (the image itself) is a green slime.

15 Assuming of course that the person realizes that he is dealing with a work of fiction. Even so, arguments are needed to show that such statements are not literally true, and I shall not provide them here. But it is plausible that pity, worry about, hate, and envy are such that one cannot have them without believing that their objects exist, just as one cannot fear something without believing that it threatens one. Yet even if one can, and does, envy a character, for example, it may *also* be make-believe that one does so, and this make-believe truth may be generated by facts of the sort my theory indicates.

16 I have in mind those make-believe truths about her mental state which are generated by what happens on stage. Dickinson is not only a character in the play, but also a spectator. In the latter capacity she is like Charles; her actual mental state generates make-believe truths about herself. Dickinson is in a curiously ambiguous position. But it is not an uncommon one; people frequently have dreams in which they watch themselves ("from the outside") doing things.

17 A good source concerning make-believe games is Jerome L. Singer, et al., *The Child's World of Make-Believe* (New York: Academic Press, 1973).

18 David Lewis pointed out to me the relevance of my theory to this puzzle.

19 It is probably make-believe that someone (the narrator), whose word the child can trust, is giving her a serious report about a confrontation between a boy named "Jack" and a giant. Cf. my "Points of View in Narrative and Depictive Representation," *Noûs*, x, 1 (March 1976): 49–61.

55

Oppressive Texts, Resisting Readers, and the Gendered Spectator: The "New" Aesthetics

Mary Devereaux

Mary Devereaux is a member of the faculty in the Research Ethics Program at the University of California, San Diego.

I

At the heart of recent feminist theorizing about art is the claim that various forms of representation – painting, photography, film – assume a "male gaze." The notion of the gaze has both a literal and a figurative component. Narrowly construed, it refers to actual looking. Broadly, or more metaphorically, it refers to a way of thinking about, and acting in, the world.

In literal terms, the gaze is male when men do the looking. Men look both as spectators and as characters within works. In figurative terms, to say that the gaze is male refers to a way of seeing which takes women as its object. In this broad sense, the gaze is male whenever it directs itself at, and takes pleasure in, women, where women function as erotic objects. Many feminists claim that most art, most of the time, places women in this position. In Laura Mulvey's words, man is the bearer of the gaze, woman its object.[1]

Mary Devereaux, "Oppressive Texts, Resisting Readers, and the Gendered Spectator: The 'New' Aesthetics," *Journal of Aesthetics and Art Criticism*, 48/4 (1990): 337–47.

Feminist theorists, like many other theorists, take as basic the tenet that no vision, not even artistic vision, is neutral vision. All vision is colored by the "spectacles" through which we see the world. The notion that all seeing is "a way of seeing" contrasts sharply with the traditional realist assumption that observation can be cleanly separated from interpretation, at least under certain ideally specified conditions. In part, feminist theorists can be understood as reiterating a familiar, but still important, objection to the naive notion of the innocent eye. As E. H. Gombrich convincingly argues, observation is never innocent. In his words, "Whenever we receive a visual impression, we react by docketing it, filing it, grouping it in one way or another, even if the impression is only that of an inkblot or a fingerprint. . . . [T]he postulate of an unbiased eye demands the impossible."[2] Observation is always conditioned by perspective and expectation.

Yet, feminist claims that our representations inscribe a male gaze involve more than a denial of the eye's innocence. They involve asserting the central role that gender plays in formulating those expectations. Feminist theorists insist, moreover, that these expectations are disproportionately affected by male needs, beliefs and desires. Both men and women have learned to see the world through male eyes. So, for example, women throughout their lives expend enormous amounts of time and energy and money making themselves "beautiful." In undertaking this costly process, women judge themselves according to internalized standards of what is pleasing to men. As Sandra Bartky observes, adolescent girls "learn to appraise themselves as they are shortly to be appraised."[3] In this sense, the eyes are female, but the gaze is male.

Feminist theorists object to seeing the world "through male eyes." They equate the male gaze with patriarchy. The notion of patriarchy is key here. Defined as a social system structured upon the supremacy of the father and the legal dependence of wives and children, patriarchy makes women depend upon men not only for status and privilege, but for their very identity. The assumption is that this arrangement oppresses women. It also, as both feminists and non-feminists have argued, oppresses men, although not necessarily in the same way as it oppresses women.

This oppression occurs at the symbolic as well as the material level. Women, as the first editorial of the film journal, *Camera Obscura*, announced, "are oppressed not only economically and politically, but also in the very forms of reasoning, signifying and symbolical exchange of our culture."[4] Thus, to take a familiar but powerful example, in English "he" functions as the unmarked term, "she" as the marked term. "His" attributes define all humanity (i.e., "mankind"); "hers" define only women. The higher priority assigned to male attributes passes unnoticed because our language, like our thinking, equates "male" gender with "gender neutral."

Art, as another form of symbolical exchange, also participates in this oppression. In both its high and low forms, feminist theorists argue, art inscribes "a masculinist discourse" which we learn to reproduce in our everyday lives. Feminist theorists here draw on the insight that art both reflects the conditions of life and helps to establish and maintain them. The male gaze inscribed in art triggers what Elizabeth Flynn and Patrocinio Schweickart describe as a deep-seated impulse for women to adapt themselves to the male viewpoint.[5] Griselda Pollock goes further, arguing that the history of art itself is a series of representational practices which actively encourage definitions of sexual difference that contribute to the present configuration of sexual politics and power relations.[6]

For this reason, much of feminist theorizing about art is critical in tone. From its perspective, the artistic canon is androcentric, and hence, politically repressive. In Schweickart's words, "For a woman, then, books do not necessarily spell salvation."[7] Briefly summarized, the feminist critique of representation rests on the equation: the medium = male = patriarchal = oppressive.

Some will greet this equation as exaggerated, even absurd. The idea that art is political or ideologically charged contradicts the deeply held belief that art speaks to and for all human beings. Socrates' charges against the poets notwithstanding, the Western European tradition characterizes art as liberating, enlightening, uplifting. Art's effects are positive; the experiences it offers intrinsically valuable, In categorizing art with other forms of patriarchal oppression, feminist theorists reject the division of art and politics basic to Anglo-American aesthetics.

The implications of this rejection are important and far-reaching. In dividing the artworld into male and female, feminist theorists irrevocably link the production and consumption of art with issues of power and control. Outside the Anglo-American paradigm, this linkage is not new. The Marxist tradition in aesthetics has long placed the concept of power at the center of the discussion of art. Marxism's emphasis on how class and other social forces and practices enter into the reading of any text lays the groundwork for feminist investigations of how gender enters the exchange with the text.

What is original to feminism is the linkage of art with sexual politics. Issues of sexual politics lie at the center of current academic debate in English Departments, Film Studies programs and feminist theory groups. Aesthetics, at least in America, has been slower to notice or respond to this debate. Although an occasional feminist paper has appeared on the program at the annual American Society for Aesthetics meetings, *The Journal of Aesthetics and Art Criticism* has prior to this writing never published a work of feminist theory. This omission is even more surprising given that philosophers from Plato to Nelson Goodman have been preoccupied with issues of representation – an issue that feminism, from another direction, centrally addresses.

This lack of attention to issues transforming the discussion of art in other disciplines is frequently attributed to a difference in vocabulary. Feminist theory has its roots in Foucault and Lacan, not in Plato, Aristotle and Kant. Confronted with talk of "mirror stages," "voyeurism," and "difference," practitioners of traditional aesthetics may feel trapped by the jargon of a foreign discourse, one not bound by rules their own training insists upon. Stanley Cavell describes the experience of reading these works as involving a different set of satisfactions.[8] Whatever the promise of these satisfactions, some will maintain, it is difficult not to lose patience with contemporary writers whose texts demand the exegetical labors normally reserved for the dead and the "truly great."

On this account, feminist theories remain marginalized due both to their difficulty and unfamiliarity. But this explanation does not, I think, tell the whole story. Regular readers of the *Journal* have no doubt noticed the growing number of articles dealing with the latest developments in literary theory (the work of Stanley Fish, Jacques Derrida, Mikhail Bakhtin), hermeneutics (Hans-Georg Gadamer) and the philosophy of language (Donald Davidson). In each of these cases, vocabulary and methodology pose formidable challenges. Not every reader will find such challenges worth the time or effort. But clearly, in aesthetics, as in philosophy generally, difficulty alone never warrants exclusion.

The reason feminist theories of art and aesthetics have so long remained unmentioned lies deeper, I think. At stake in the debate over feminism are deeply entrenched assumptions about the universal value of art and aesthetic experience. The overthrow of these assumptions – linchpins of aesthetic theory since Kant – constitutes what art historian, Linda Nochlin, describes as a Kuhnian paradigm shift.[9] The new paradigm is a feminist paradigm and what we face is a conceptual revolution. If I am right, then the deeper explanation for the lack of attention to feminist theories lies in the natural resistance of those suddenly faced with the overthrow of an entrenched way of thinking.

As recent developments in the philosophy of science and ethics highlight, aesthetics cannot simply "add on" feminist theories as it might add new works by Goodman, Arthur Danto or George Dickie. To take feminism seriously involves rethinking our basic concepts and recasting the history of the discipline. And that requires more than adding women's names to the canonical list of great philosophers.

The requirement that we engage in such radical rethinking may seem burdensome and unnecessary. It is helpful to the self-esteem of women or to women who are feminists. But what of those who do not fit into either of these two categories? What, they may wonder, do they have to gain from feminist aesthetics?

In part to answer such questions, I want in the next section to return to the notion of the male gaze. In examining this key feminist notion more carefully, I hope to make clear the intrinsic interest of this approach to aesthetics and to suggest why its concerns merit serious consideration.

To this end, I want to investigate how gendered vision works in one specific representational practice, namely film. Film is a natural choice for such a study because it is a medium so fundamentally built around the activity of looking. It is also, not surprisingly, the medium where the male gaze has been most extensively discussed.

The relationship of gender and cinematic vision is extremely complicated. A complete analysis of this topic would require several hundred pages. In what follows, I focus on two key claims, namely, that in cinema the gaze is male and that the cinematic text is a male text. I seek to make clear how these claims should be understood and then to situate them philosophically. In confining myself to what I take to be the core claims of this debate, I will of necessity leave aside many important, but internal, issues in film theory.

II

Despite the extensive literature which refers to and relies upon it, the concept of the male gaze remains difficult to understand. It is so in part because, as noted above, the male gaze refers both to literal and metaphorical vision. A further difficulty in understanding the male gaze arises from the failure to distinguish three different gazes: that of film-maker, the characters within the film and the spectator. With each of these gazes, literal and figurative seeing interact in a variety of ways.

In the first case, that of the film-maker, someone looks through the viewfinder of a camera, someone (often the same person) looks at the rushes after the day's shooting and someone looks at the film's final cut. This person may be male, but need not be. Women, too, make movies and have done so since the early days of the medium (e.g., Maya Deren, Dorothy Artner, Leni Riefenstahl).

What does it mean then to say that at this level the gaze is male? It means that despite the presence of women directors and screenwriters, the institutions of film-making remain largely populated by men. Not all films have male authors, but whoever makes movies must work nonetheless within a system owned and operated by men. At the level of the film-maker, then, men do not always do the looking, but they generally control who does. The male gaze is not always male, but *it is always male-dominated.*

By male-dominated, feminist theorists mean male-gendered, not simply possessed of male anatomy. A key move distinguishes sex from gender. A child is born sexed; through education and experience, it acquires gender. On this account, education and experience create the particular way of seeing which the term, "the male gaze," describes. Male institutional control thus refers not to the anatomy of film world personnel, which includes both men and women, but to the way film, however authored, contributes to the hegemony of men over women.

From a feminist point of view, this control matters because it "builds in" a preference for a particular type of film, i.e., one which positions women in ways consistent with patriarchal assumptions. Movies promote a way of seeing which takes man as subject, women as object. Simone de Beauvoir's *The Second Sex* puts the point succinctly. "Representation of the world, like the world itself, is the work of men; they describe it from their own point of view, which they confuse with absolute truth."[10]

As de Beauvoir explains, women, unlike men, do not learn to describe the world from their own point of view. As the "other," woman learns to submerge or renounce her subjectivity. She finds her identity in the subjectivity of the men to whom she is attached (father, husband, lover). In the eyes of men, she finds her identity as the object of men's desire.

In arguing that cinema, too, assigns woman this position, feminist theorists link male control of film institutions with a patriarchal way of seeing. At this point it should be clear that in attempting to describe the literal gaze of the film-maker, the question of whether men or women do the looking is not at root the issue. The real issue centers on whether, whoever stands behind the camera, a patriarchal way of seeing the world prevails. The discussion of the literal gaze thus very quickly becomes a discussion of the figurative gaze.

I do not want to deny the heuristic usefulness of talking about "literal" looking in film. Someone does look through the lens of the camera, and film-going is irrefutably a visual experience. Moreover, the medium itself offers a range of devices for representing what characters on screen themselves see, e.g., the long sequences in Alfred Hitchcock's *Vertigo* in which we see what the protagonist, Scottie, sees as he follows Madeleine.

A deeper and more damaging objection to the literal/figurative distinction emerges from the claim that literal seeing is always already figurative. Men – like women – do not simply look. Their looking – where and when they do it and at what – mimics a particular way of thinking about and acting in the world. So understood, seeing never escapes *a way* of seeing.

How then does the figurative way of seeing deemed "male" translate to the screen? How *are* women represented from the male point of view? And, with what effect on the spectator? To answer these questions requires shifting our attention from the film-maker's gaze to the manipulation of the gaze within film. At the textual level, feminist theorists have focused most directly on the story films of Hollywood as opposed to the international art cinema, experimental film or documentary film. Attention to the Hollywood film arose naturally from the broad popularity and profound influence which this tradition exercised on American cultural life.

Feminist theorists initially attacked the Hollywood film for its patriarchal content. Early feminist works such as Molly Haskell's *From Reverence to Rape*[11] examined how the portraits of the Good Girl, the Vamp and the Dutiful Wife presented so forcefully in westerns, detective films and melodramas reinforced a cultural mythology. In film after film, that mythology defined the value of women as their value to men. The good girl was a dutiful daughter who preserved herself (i.e., her virginity) for the right man "to take" from her. The bad girl, in contrast, flaunts her sexuality indiscriminately, "losing" her virginity or "giving it away."

Haskell's broadly sociological approach understood movies to tell the same stories we heard outside the theatre. In the movies, as in life, good girls were rewarded, bad girls punished. Any alternative point of view, one which might tell a different tale or the same tale differently, was effectively excluded. Put in the strongest terms, the charge was that the Hollywood film "belonged to patriarchy."[12] This commitment need not be intentional. Nor need it be confined to the works of male directors. Yet, as an institution, cinema, like television, was held to participate in and help to perpetuate a system of social organization which assigns power and privilege by gender.

Admittedly, not all films perpetuate patriarchy. Individual films may resist this arrangement. The strong-headed heroines typically played by Katharine Hepburn, Lauren Bacall and Bette Davis do not conform to this stereotype, nor do films such as Howard Hawks' *His Girl Friday.* As feminist critics themselves have demonstrated, the films of Hollywood evidence more variation and internal tension than a charge of monolithic patriarchy allows.

In speaking of Hollywood film as "belonging to patriarchy," something more subtle is at work than overt stereotyping. At the simplest level, Haskell and others had maintained, film reinforced women's dependence on men. As noted above, women on screen regularly won their happiness in the service of others (Griffith's Dear One, Marion as the amiable spouse in *Shane*). When they depart from societal norms, as Hepburn's high-level diplomat does in *Woman of the Year,* they are revealed to be cold-hearted and in need of "re-education." Tess learns from her husband Sam to place work second to companionate time with spouse and the duties of parenting. Those who refuse this role, find themselves alone and lonely (e.g., Tess' Aunt Ellen). Those who opt for illicit instead of married love, end up dead (e.g., Marion in *Psycho,* Alex in *Fatal Attraction*).

Thus, as Mary Ann Doane convincingly argues, at a more complex level, the Hollywood film functions as "a recuperative strategy" designed to return the wayward woman to the fold.[13] This return operates both within the narrative and externally, in the narrative's effect on its female audience. Internally, the Hollywood narrative typically charts the course by which a woman in a non-normative role cedes her control to a man.[14] The happy ending in which Tess returns to Sam serves externally to "recuperate" wayward members of the female audience as well. The message is that for a woman, unlike for a man, the satisfactions of solitude, work, or adventure cannot compare to those of caring for husband and children.

The classic Hollywood film reinforces this message stylistically by confining the spectator to the point of view of the narrative hero. In Tania Modleski's words, "the film spectator apparently has no choice but to identify with the male protagonist, who exerts an active, controlling gaze over a passive female object." By consistently stressing the man's point of view, the Hollywood film thus negates the female character's view.[15]

Stressing the male protagonist's point of view need not involve confining us consistently to his visual field. The one well-known experiment which confined us consistently to the first-person visual field of a character, Robert Montgomery's *The Lady in the Lake*, failed miserably to convey that character's figurative point of view. We saw what he saw, but we didn't feel what he felt. More typical narrative films, such as *The Big Sleep*, alternate between what the protagonist sees and what other characters see. Hawks gives us not only Marlowe looking at Vivian but Vivian looking at Marlowe. The gaze is thus not directly that of the protagonist.

Nevertheless, within the Hollywood film there is a long tradition of women performing for the camera. Women sing, dance, dress and undress, all before the steady, often adoring, gaze of an implied spectator. Frequently, female performance plays a role in the plot, as when Vivian sings for Marlowe and the audience at Eddie Mars' nightclub. But whether playing fictional characters who sing and dance before an audience or not, Marlene Dietrich, Marilyn Monroe, Ingrid Bergman and other female "stars," perform *for* the camera. As Stanley Cavell has pointed out, in photographing beautiful women, the cinema has found one of the subjects most congenial to it. But "congenial" here means the congeniality of men making films for men.

The male controlled institutions of film-making thus place women on screen in a particular position. As eroticized objects, women are doubly victimized. As Ann Kaplan argues, the male gaze involves more than simply looking; it carries with it the threat of action and possession. This power to act and possess is not reciprocal. Women can receive and return a gaze, but they cannot act upon it.[16]

To be fully operative as a mechanism of oppression, the male gaze depends upon a second condition. Not only must looking come with some "back-up" – physical, economic, social – but "being looked at" must also activate some level of female narcissism. Women themselves must not be indifferent to the gaze turned upon them; they must have internalized a certain assignment of positions.[17]

It is this disequilibrium in power both inside and outside the arena of looking which makes the male gaze different from what some have called a female or gender-neutral gaze. Consider the oft-cited cases where men serve as the object of the gaze, as in the recent spate of Richard Gere movies (*Breathless, American Gigolo*). Despite the "role reversal," the degradation which women suffer in occupying the role of "looked at" is not matched by their male counterparts.

It would be useful at this point to make a distinction, one between objectification, aestheticization and degradation.[18] "Objectification," as I am using the term, means no more than to make someone or something the object of my gaze. There is nothing inherently oppressive about objectification understood in this way. Nor is the filmic male gaze any more objectifying than any other gaze. Aestheticization, defined here, means simply treating people or things as objects of aesthetic contemplation. There is nothing inherently oppressive about aestheticization. Both objectification and aestheticization may be degrading, but they need not be. "Degradation" is a complex notion, associated with such concepts as respect, human dignity and worth, To degrade is to demean or debase someone, where this involves not only failing to respect, but also, in some sense, actively diminishing the value or dignity of the person. Rape, slavery and torture provide three obvious examples of degradation.[19]

Given these distinctions, it is easy to see that male characters, like their female counterparts, may be objectified or even, as in the case of Richard Gere, aestheticized (or eroticized). And they, like women, may also be portrayed in degraded or less than fully human ways. It is with respect to actual degradation that the asymmetry between men and women reappears. For in the case of women, unlike that of men, real life degradation often runs parallel to portrayals of degradation. Because women frequently lack power off screen, they are more likely to be degraded by their portrayals on screen. Even if men are portrayed in degrading ways, their real life power shields them from actual degradation.

As I've said above, objectification and aestheticization are not in themselves degrading. Nevertheless, feminist theorists are correct that Hollywood films reflect and encourage a cultural proclivity to treat the female body and the female self *only* as objects of aesthetic contemplation. And they are also correct in suggesting that this way of treating women *is* degrading. While, as I have argued, movie-making and movie-watching cannot be held solely responsible for the oppression of women, feminist theorists rightly emphasize the connection between how we represent our lives and lived experience itself.

In turning, finally, to the effect of the film text on its spectators, I want first to consider the means by which the gender bias of many Hollywood films remains hidden. The Hollywood film conventionally presents its telling as, to quote de Beauvoir again, "absolute truth." It depends for its effect upon creating a narrative illusion. The film story must unfold transparently, as though happening before our very eyes. It is crucial to such film-making that it proceed without calling attention to itself as a story. In this, the stylistic conventions of Hollywood follow those of the 19th century realist novel. For a film to acknowledge its status as a story or fiction admits a point of view, a place from which its story gets told. Devices such as Godard's use of stop-action and words written across the screen aim to resist narrative illusionism. They announce the film as a film, as a fiction, a construct.[20]

For many feminists, as for many Marxists, the narrative illusion central to the classic Hollywood film is politically compromised. Hollywood films are said to foster strong character identification and full absorption in the action. This absorption in turn is believed to encourage viewer passivity. At its worst, warned Max Horkheimer and Theodor Adorno, such film-making undermines individual autonomy. It renders its audience a "mass" easily manipulated in the interests of the status quo.

In an effort to encourage active, critically engaged spectatorship, feminist theorists often exaggerate the connection between conventional Hollywood techniques of storytelling and passive spectatorship. Passive spectatorship is not, however, restricted to Hollywood narratives, nor do all such films aim for, or achieve, such an effect, e.g., Spike Lee's *Do the Right Thing*. To the extent that the average Hollywood product *does* encourage passivity, it renders *both* male and female spectators passive. Unfortunately, feminist critics often lose sight of this point.

In calling for active reading to replace this passivity, feminist critiques of the Hollywood film here parallel Brecht's critique of Aristotelian drama. Both denounce what they see as efforts to elicit the passive empathy of the spectator; both ask for art to break the narrative illusion. However, feminist theorists go beyond Brecht's analysis to examine how identification differs in male and female spectators. Gender, they rightly assert, plays a key role in eliciting the empathy and identification typical of narrative film.

The analysis of film's effects on the spectator brings us to the third and, I would argue, most important site at which the male gaze operates. In developing a theory of spectatorship, feminist theorists move beyond an initial concern with film content and style to explore the mechanisms of viewing. To the question "how does film represent women?" is added the question "what sources of satisfaction do these representations of women offer the spectator?" At what many now call its second stage, feminist film theory shifts attention from the literary critical and sociological reading of individual films to the more broadly theoretical project of describing the unconscious mechanisms involved in watching movies.[21]

Primary among these mechanisms is voyeuristic pleasure. In this view, enormously influential among film theorists, spectators derive erotic pleasure through the opportunities for looking which the cinema affords. As Christian Metz argues in *The Imaginary Signifier* (1975), the darkened theatre, the absence of the object viewed, and its inability to return the gaze all contribute to the idea that film viewing constitutes unauthorized looking.[22] From its early association with the Nickelodeon, the motion picture has come to function as a metaphor for the illicit activity of the voyeur, as Alfred Hitchcock's 1954 film, *Rear Window*, illustrates. Lest one miss the point, Hitchcock makes L. B. Jeffries – an inveterate voyeur – a photographer.[23]

The question of how film plays to our already existing desires, fantasies, and fears received one of its most influential treatments in Laura Mulvey's now classic, "Visual Pleasure and Narrative Cinema." Mulvey begins from the premise that film reflects the psychical obsessions of the society which produces it. In making this assumption, Mulvey, like most other second wave theorists, draws heavily on psychoanalysis, particularly Freud and Lacan. She sets out to analyze the characteristic sources of pleasure and unpleasure offered by the cinema.

Narrative cinema, by which she means narrative in the unself-conscious mode described above, provides the spectator with two sources of pleasure. First, it provides what Freud calls "scopophilic" pleasure, the pleasure of viewing another as an erotic object. As we saw above, this pleasure characteristically takes the form of looking at women. In film after film, women function both as erotic objects for characters within the movie, as Vivian does for Marlowe, and as erotic objects for the spectator in the movie-house, as Lauren Bacall does for us. Thus, women's presence on screen presupposes the appreciative glance of a male spectator.

Men, in contrast, only rarely function as eroticized objects for female (or male) spectators. Men, Mulvey points out, feel uncomfortable in such a role. Neither the ruling assumptions of patriarchy "nor the psychical structures that back it up" encourage the male "to gaze at his exhibitionist like."[24] Instead, man's role is to function as the locus of narrative action. His role, on screen as off, involves shooting the bad guys and blazing the trails. The male movie star attracts our admiration and respect by his deeds. We are encouraged to *identify with* him, to imagine ourselves doing what he does.

In Freudian terms, the male functions as an "ego-ideal," not as an object of erotic desire. The possibility of identifying with this ego-ideal offers the spectator a second, contrasting source of pleasure, i.e., the pleasure of identifying with the characters projected on screen. Since, on Mulvey's analysis, it is the male hero who makes things happen and controls them, we typically identify with him. Thus, the spectator's gaze is male in two senses, both in its direction at women as objects of erotic fascination and in its identification with the male protagonist. The division of male and female roles on screen mimics traditional gender roles: women functioning as the passive objects of the viewer's gaze; men functioning as the active subjects of the viewer's imagination.

In playing to our existing desires, fantasies and fears, film also offers what Mulvey calls unpleasure. In the patriarchal unconscious, woman represents the threat of castration. This threat the Hollywood film typically meets in one of two ways. It may contain the threat posed by the mystery and fearsomeness of women by domesticating them, typically through marriage (e.g., *Notorious*), or, more drastically, by killing them off, as in *Fatal Attraction.* Alternatively, the threat may be denied altogether by elevating the woman to the status of a fetish. In the latter case, the woman becomes reassuring instead of dangerous.[25]

To summarize, then, the male gaze refers to three interlocking forms of control. With respect to the film-maker, it refers to male control of the practices of film-making. This control leads, at the level of the film text, to a product whose content and style inscribe the patriarchal unconscious of the culture at large. Lastly, these devices position the male or female audience member to find in film a way of seeing which calms our fears and satisfies our desires.

This is a provocative account of film spectatorship. To ask who is doing the looking assumes all spectators are not similarly positioned, i.e., that factors such as gender have a role to play in structuring – maybe even in constituting – what we see. Mulvey's original analysis, however, leaves the *female* spectator with no active viewing position except to identify with the male protagonist. In identifying with the women on screen, the female spectator is assumed to align herself with the female-as-object.[26] More recent feminist theory rightly inquires how Mulvey's account explains the pleasure which women derive from going to the movies. As Ann Kaplan has asked, is the female spectator's pleasure, like the man's, the pleasure of looking at women, the masochistic pleasure of enjoying objectification, or the sadistic pleasure of identifying with the men who oppress her?[27]

In "Afterthoughts on Visual Pleasure and Narrative Cinema," Mulvey herself proposes, more positively, that identification with the male allows the female spectator to revert, at least imaginatively, to the active independence of what Freud termed the female child's "early masculine period." In this "tomboy" phase, she takes pleasure in a freedom that correct femininity will later repress.[28]

In moving beyond the static model of active male/passive female, current theories of spectatorship acknowledge women's resistance to the position assigned to them in patriarchal culture. There remains, however, a tendency to speak of *the* female spectator as if all women shared the same aims and aspirations and came to film texts similarly equipped. To make these assumptions overlooks important differences between women of color and white women, rich and poor, women and feminists and different varieties of feminists.

Similarly, feminist theories of spectatorship tend to speak of *the* male spectator as though all men's gazes are male. This assertion assumes, unjustifiably, that all men are equally powerful and that they stand equally to gain from the arrangements of patriarchy. Such assumptions contradict feminism's own insistence on the relationship between power and variables such as economic standing, education, ethnic identity, sexual orientation and so on. Thus, for example, in feminist terms, the male gaze is not only sexist but also heterosexist. Should not then an adequate theory of spectatorship also include an account of how the male gaze operates when the spectator is not heterosexual?

As these objections suggest, a more fine-grained analysis of spectatorship undermines the easy identification of male viewer with "the male gaze." The characterization of the male gaze as "totally active" is, I suggest, difficult to sustain once we move beyond the assumption that all men occupy the same position in a patriarchal social system. Moreover, the assumed activity and control of the male spectator is at odds with the widespread notion that the Hollywood film monolithically encourages a form of passive spectatorship. Equating the male gaze with the active gaze ignores the passive element involved in looking at movies. The male spectator, whatever his real political and social power, cannot interact with the on-screen woman. She appears, but is physically absent.

As I hope to have made clear, the notion of the male gaze cannot simply be identified with the way men see the world. The gaze, properly understood, has undergone certain refinements. It describes a way of seeing the world which is typically male. But it is not a way of seeing confined to men nor is it the province of all men.

Part of what makes feminist theories interesting and powerful is their attention to factors which affect how we see and respond to texts. Gender is one of these factors. As they evolve, feminist film theories, like feminist theories more generally have, however, increasingly recognized the necessity to move beyond a simple binary analysis of gender. In articulating the interconnections between gender and other variables, such as sexual orientation, race, and class, a feminist orientation serves to fine-tune our understanding of art and its effects upon us.

III

What general conclusions can we draw from this analysis of the male gaze? That film works to reinforce societal norms? That it is male? That film, like art generally, may be harmful to women? Such conclusions are now common in film studies. As noted earlier, we find similar arguments in older, more entrenched, fields such as literature and art history. As a body of theory, feminism has succeeded in placing the question of gender at the center of contemporary literary and artistic theory. As I suggested earlier, this new agenda has unsettling consequences for traditional aesthetics. The new agenda seeks not only to have us surrender certain longstanding assumptions, but to replace them with whole new ways of thinking about art and our relationship to it. I want to conclude therefore by sketching briefly some of these changes and raising several questions for us to consider.

First, feminist theorists ask us to replace the conception of the artwork as an autonomous object – a thing of beauty and a joy forever – with a messier conception of art. Seen in these terms, the artwork moves from an autonomous realm of value to the everyday realm of social and political praxis. It gains a history which overflows the former bounds of "art history." Who makes art and what type of art gets made depend, we learn, on the interaction of the artworld with other worlds.

In drawing our attention to culture in the broadest sense, feminist theorists rely on an alternative, European view of art. In this, feminist aesthetics constitutes part of a larger movement away from "autonomous" aesthetics. Even within Anglo-American aesthetics, the old paradigm no longer holds the place it once did. Our understanding of representation, of the pleasures and powers of art, and of spectatorship have been immeasurably enriched by the expanded context in which we now look at art. Yet, in this enlarged context, how does a concept of the "aesthetic," if by that we mean the *purely* aesthetic, function? Is the discipline of aesthetics possible apart from sociology, cultural studies, identity politics?

Second, feminist theorists propose that we reexamine art's claim to speak for all of us. Does art speak in a gender-neutral voice or does it privilege some experiences and ways of seeing over others? Traditional aesthetics inherits from Aristotle belief in a universal human condition of which art, at least great art, speaks.

Feminist theorists challenge the adequacy of the classic, Aristotelian model not only with respect to the Hollywood film (which some might argue is not great enough to qualify as "great" art), but with respect to all art. The films of Sergei Eisenstein and Jean Renoir, like the plays of Shakespeare, all speak in "particular" voices. On the new view, the artwork, like the generic pronoun, speaks for "mankind," but mankind includes only some of us.[29]

To question art's autonomy and universality need not imply that these artworks are without value – quite the contrary – although their value may differ from what we once supposed. Nothing in feminist theory precludes ranking Henry James a more important novelist than Jane Austen or Alice Walker a greater writer than John Steinbeck.

In making these evaluative rankings, feminist theorists do insist, however, that we acknowledge the criteria used in defining "important" and "great." Does "great" mean the forcefully written or the spare, the heartfelt or the coolly reasoned, the typical or the innovative? When is a text forcefully written and who decides? Feminist theorists offer a framework from within which we may – indeed, should – raise such questions. Only when we explicitly acknowledge the criteria used in making these judgements do we create space for competing criteria.

In denying that artworks or the criteria we use to judge them are value-neutral, feminist theorists also urge a third proposal. We are asked to reconsider our relationship to established artistic traditions. The canon, still heralded by some as a reservoir for the best of human thinking, is accused of excluding and silencing women (among other groups). At the very least, a feminist perspective requires that we rethink our relationship to the artistic tradition in terms which do not assume a monolithic "we." Describing existing artistic traditions as uniformly enlightening and liberating ignores those for whom the authority of those traditions is unquestionably problematic. Thus, we must ask whether the coming of age stories of Holden Caulfield and David Copperfield affect adolescent girls in the same way as adolescent boys, and what significance this difference, if any, makes. Being willing to ask *who* is doing the reading forces us to question whether the pleasures of art are invariant and impervious to factors such as class, race and gender.

Fourthly, feminist theorists alter the characterization of reading or viewing as neutral activities. Like hermeneutics and reader-response theories, they seek to explain how the social and historical placement of the spectator affects the meaning derived from the text. Meaning is no longer determined exclusively by the text. Aside from emphasizing the social and historical context in which interpretation occurs, feminist theorists break new ground in demonstrating how texts themselves "assume" a particular reader through narrative and stylistic devices. The best of feminist theorizing executes this demonstration through a careful analysis of texts.

In advancing new theories of readership, however, what justifies feminist theorists in assigning "the woman reader" a central place in the analysis of texts? If it is meaningful to think in terms of "the woman reader," then why not in terms of "the lesbian reader,"[30] "the adolescent reader," "the ideal reader," "the over-educated reader"? Are all of these categories equally important, and according to what theoretical or political criteria?

Lastly, feminist theorists, like other post-structuralist theorists, endeavor to make the unnoticed noticed. They adopt from the Frankfurt School the belief that the informed spectator is a more critical spectator, and the critical spectator is one less likely to be victimized by the text.

Calls for critical reading are unlikely to meet resistance among aestheticians. But what of claims that art may not be good for us? – At the very least, not all art and not for all of us. In adopting a *politics of art*, feminist theorists confront Anglo-American aesthetics head-on. They replace reverence for art with skepticism. They ask that we be willing to rethink what we value and the reasons we value it.

In suggesting that this challenge deserves serious consideration, I might be understood to claim that all traditional aesthetics is useless, that the accomplishments of the last century are a chimera. This is not my intent. My intent is instead to describe the cognitive dissonance which marks the current situation in aesthetics. If feminism constitutes a new paradigm, then we may wish to ponder how far the old model of aesthetics and the new are commensurable. Is traditional aesthetics contingently or necessarily associated with patriarchy? Can the "gender-neutral" aesthetics of the traditional model be reformed or must it be rejected?

Aside from these theoretical issues, feminist theory raises several practical issues which demand attention. If art contributes to the disequilibrium in power between the sexes, then what should we do? Should we simply quit going to the movies?

Raising such questions returns us to the Socratic tradition which urges caution in the face of art's power. Socrates followed that warning with a call for censorship. With this suggestion, however, many feminists would not agree. Feminist theory confronts the ancient problem of art's potential for harm with two other, far more promising, strategies. Neither appears to have occurred to Socrates. I want therefore to conclude by looking very briefly at these solutions.

IV

The first proposed solution consists in a call for a new type of art. Some feminists, Claire Johnson for example, have proposed the creation of a counter-cinema to compete with the mainstream Hollywood cinema.[31] This strategy, like establishing public radio and television stations, aims to offer an alternative to the usual fare.

The suggestion to create an alternative art might please Socrates. It would allow him to replace Homer's epics with his own, more philosophically informed, tales. This so-called revision of the canon would meet the Socratic objections to art whose content and form encouraged a weakening of the requisite moral virtues.

Creating new artistic traditions provides an alternative to the passive reception of dominant traditions. This strategy is most often described as creating a female voice or female gaze. It allows women to write their own texts, their own history. Achieving such a "female gaze" requires more than simply providing women with access to the means of film-making. As Diane Waldman correctly argues, women don't make better, less "patriarchal" films simply because they are women, as if women automatically had access to resources not available to the male psyche. The required transformation of film depends not upon some female essence, but upon a consciously adopted political perspective.[32]

Adopting such a perspective has resulted in interesting films by Mulvey, Sally Potter, Lizzie Borden, Barbara Hammer and others. These films strive in a variety of ways to disrupt or rework the narrative conventions of the dominant cinema. Sally Potter's *Thriller*, for example, retells the story of *La Bohème*. In Potter's *film noir* version of the doomed love affair, Mimi investigates her own death. Her voice-over and the fragmented narrative through which her story unfolds resist the character identification and narrative closure typical of traditional narrative. Films such as *Thriller* strive to critique the dominant moods of cinematic representation by privileging heterogeneity and multiplicity of meaning. In this, these films aim to free the spectator to engage more actively with the text. Other films, such as those of Barbara Hammer, seek alternatives to the forms of cinematic pleasure provided by the glossy image of the professional photographer. The range and variety of feminist film-making far exceeds what I can survey here. However, these films are shown primarily in film courses and private film societies. Thus, despite their importance in providing an alternative tradition, their influence on mainstream audiences and film-practices is limited.

The second feminist strategy consists in developing methods of dealing with existing texts. This strategy is variously described as re-reading, as reading against the grain, or as "re-vision." It involves active readership, where I mean reading in the broad sense to include both visual and written texts. These strategies have in common the aim of critique and reappropriation. Thus, they do what good criticism always does. But more than this, they involve learning to see through what Kuhn calls a "new pair of spectacles."[33] This new pair of spectacles provides an education not in *what* to think but *how*. Reading against the grain is a strategy designed by out of power groups to counterbalance the dominant textual traditions by offering alternative interpretations of works within those traditions.

Thought of in these terms, feminist theories offer a different critical perspective. They provide a means of resistance, and an alternative to, the male gaze. Admittedly, just as the male gaze involves a distinct political position, so too a feminist perspective is not, nor should it be regarded as, politically neutral.[34] Yet, as a way of seeing, it importantly differs from its male counterpart in acknowledging itself *as* a way of seeing.

The possibility of such textual strategies is politically important not only for feminists but for others concerned with "neutralizing" the effects of certain artworks or forms of art within a cultural setting committed to the protection of free speech. Reading "against the grain" offers an alternative to the passive readership which censorship assumes, and in its paternalism, encourages.

As an interpretative strategy, it opens to all of us – male and female – the possibility of finding our own way through the text. For various historical and cultural reasons, feminist theorists look more optimistically than did Socrates on the capacity of each of us to find that way. Yet, producing new forms of art and reading against the grain of the old will not by themselves topple the existing gender hierarchy. For that, women must also have power off-screen.

Notes

1 Laura Mulvey, "Visual Pleasure and Narrative Cinema," in *Film Theory and Criticism,* 3rd edn, eds Gerald Mast and Marshall Cohen (Oxford University Press, 1985), pp. 803–16.

2 E. H. Gombrich, *Art and Illusion: A Study in the Psychology of Pictorial Representation* (Princeton University Press, 1960), pp. 297–8.

3 Sandra Bartky, "Women, Bodies and Power: A Research Agenda for Philosophy," *APA Newsletter on Philosophy and Feminism* 89 (1989), p. 79.

4 Robert Lapsley and Michael Westlake, *Film Theory: An Introduction* (Manchester University Press, 1988), p. 23.

5 Elizabeth A. Flynn and Patrocinio P. Schweickart, eds, *Gender and Reading: Essays on Readers, Texts, and Contexts* (Johns Hopkins University Press, 1986), p. xix.

6 Griselda Pollock, *Vision and Difference* (New York: Routledge, 1988), p. 11.

7 Patrocinio Schweickart, "Toward a Feminist Theory of Reading," in *Gender and Reading,* p. 41.

8 Stanley Cavell, *In Quest of the Ordinary: Lines of Skepticism and Romanticism* (University of Chicago Press, 1988), p. 131.

9 Linda Nochlin, *Women, Art and Power and Other Essays* (New York: Harper & Row, 1988), p. 146.

10 Simone de Beauvoir, *The Second Sex,* trans. and ed. H. M. Parshley (New York: Vintage Books, 1974), p. 134.

11 Molly Haskell, *From Reverence to Rape: The Treatment of Women in the Movies* (Harmondsworth: Penguin Books, 1974).

12 B. Deidre Pribram, ed., *Female Spectators: Looking at Film and Television* (New York: Verso, 1988), p. 1.

13 See Mary Ann Doane, *The Desire to Desire: The Woman's Film of the 1940s* (Indiana University Press, 1987), chapter 2.

14 Mary Beth Haralovich, cited in Annette Kuhn, *Women's Pictures: Feminism and the Cinema* (London: Routledge & Kegan Paul, 1982), p. 34.

15 Tania Modleski, *The Women Who Knew Too Much: Hitchcock and Feminist Theory* (New York: Methuen, 1988), p. 73.

16 E. Ann Kaplan, "Is the Gaze Male?" in *Women and Values: Readings in Recent Feminist Philosophy,* ed. Marilyn Peargall (Belmont, California: Wadsworth Publishing Co., 1986), p. 231.

17 The idea that women's oppression depends upon the fulfillment of both of these conditions I owe to a conversation with Tim Gould.

18 I base these distinctions on Lydia Goehr's helpful commentary on an earlier version of this paper. Her comments were presented at the American Society for Aesthetics, Eastern Division Meeting, State College, Pa., 16 March 1990.

19 In saying that acts such as rape degrade their victims, I do not mean to endorse the conventional view of women according to which rape is degrading because it destroys or damages a woman's "purity." I do, however, want to maintain that there is a sense in which rape (along with slavery and torture) is truly degrading. The notion of degradation is complicated and we are likely to have conflicting intuitions. Many of us would like to uphold the Kantian idea that human dignity is inviolable. In this view, human dignity is such that no act can diminish it. On the other hand, there is the also compelling view that certain acts are such that they do degrade and diminish persons. In this latter view, it is the potential for real degradation that makes the rapist's acts so horrible.

20 Interestingly, what is termed the "new" Hollywood cinema has adopted some of the techniques and self-conscious strategies of the international art cinema.

21 This division of feminist film theory into first and second stages can be found, for example, in Lapsley and Westlake, *Film Theory*, p. 25. The same division emerges less explicitly in Claire Johnson, "Women's Cinema as Counter-Cinema," in *Movies and Methods,* ed. Bill Nichols (University of California Press, 1976), pp. 209–15.

22 Christian Metz, from *The Imaginary Signifier, Film Theory and Criticism*, 3rd edn, ed. Gerald Mast and Marshall Cohen (Oxford University Press, 1985), pp. 799–801.

23 See Modleski's chapter on *Rear Window* for a discussion of the film's critical reception.

24 Mulvey, "Visual Pleasure and Narrative Cinema," p. 810.
25 Ibid., p. 811.
26 Pribram, *Female Spectators*, pp. 1–2.
27 Kaplan, "Is the Gaze Male?" p. 252.
28 Laura Mulvey, *Visual and Other Pleasures* (Indiana University Press, 1989), p. 37.
29 For a more detailed analysis of the concepts of art's autonomy and universality, see my "The Philosophical and Political Implications of the Feminist Critique of Aesthetic Autonomy," in *Turning the Century: Feminist Criticism in the 1990s*, Glynis Carr, ed., *The Bucknell Review*, xxxvi (2) (Cranbury, NJ: Associated University Presses, 1992).
30 Jean E. Kennard, "Ourself Behind Ourself: A Theory for Lesbian Readers," in *Gender and Reading*, p. 63.
31 Johnson, "Women's Cinema as Counter-Cinema" (work referred to in note 21).
32 Diane Waldman, "Film Theory and the Gendered Spectator: The Female or the Feminist Reader?" *Camera Obscura* 18 (1988), p. 81.
33 Kuhn, *Women's Pictures*, p. 70.
34 Ibid.

Index